VINTAGE
SS
EST. 1990
MUSICAL INSTRUMENT COMPANY
Chicago, IL • 773-472-3333
Reverb.com/shop/ssvintage

Passionately Buying Vintage and Used Musical Instruments
- Entire collections or individual pieces -
At SS Vintage, we are dedicated and devoted to vintage musical instruments.
Confidential, professional and discreet.
Please allow us the opportunity to work with you!
Top $$ Paid.
No collection too large or too small!
Feel free to email us 24/7
Thank you,
Scott Silver George Coutretsis

George Coutretsis
george@ssvintage.com
www.ssvintage.com
Scott Silver
ss@ssvintage.com

VINTAGE GUITARS & MUSICAL INSTRUMENTS

Always Accepting Quality Consignments

1959 Gibson Les Paul Standard Sunburst Solid Body Electric Guitar.
Sold for $350,000

1954 Fender Stratocaster Sunburst Solid Body Electric Guitar.
Sold for $300,000

1955 Fender Stratocaster Metallic Green Solid Body Electric Guitar.
Sold for $143,750

1953 Fender Telecaster Butterscotch Blonde Solid Body Electric Guitar.
Sold for $75,000

1960 Gibson Les Paul Custom Red Solid Body Electric Guitar.
Sold for $112,500

HA.com/Guitars
Inquiries: Aaron Piscopo
214.409.1273 | AaronP@HA.com

HERITAGE AUCTIONS

Paul R. Minshull #16591. BP 25%; see HA.com 88230

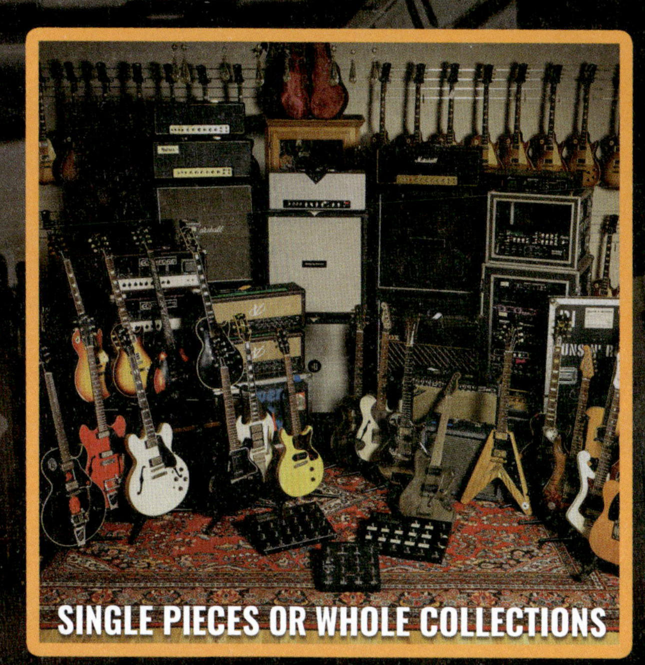

SELL, TRADE, OR CONSIGN!

› MILLIONS $ BOUGHT! MILLIONS $ SOLD!
› **WE PICK UP COLLECTIONS ALL OVER THE COUNTRY!**
› OVER 10,000 ITEMS SOLD THROUGH OUR PLATFORMS!
› **CONSIGNMENTS INCLUDE FULL MARKETING SUPPORT! - SOCIAL MEDIA, VIDEO CONTENT AND MORE!**

INQUIRE AT:
VINTAGEBUYERS@CHICAGOMUSICEXCHANGE.COM
CALL US AT: (773) 525-7773
- LIVE CHAT AVAILABLE EVERY DAY! -

Alan Greenwood launched *Vintage Guitar* magazine in 1986 and in 1990 created *The Official Vintage Guitar Price Guide* (visit www.VintageGuitar.com to see everything *VG* now offers). His collection includes several vintage guitars, amps, effects, and ukuleles from the '20s to the '80s, as well as newer instruments. He lives in Bismarck, North Dakota.

Ram Tuli began collecting guitars as a teenager while he was in the U.S. Navy. He spent most of his professional life working as an engineer and production-plant manager. He has been keeping track of vintage instrument values for more than 40 years, and for the last 20 has been singing and playing lead guitar for the Phoenix-based blues band Psychedelic Mooj. Besides making music, Ram also loves writing detective stories and books about guitars and the Navy.

The Official Vintage Guitar® Price Guide 2026

By Alan Greenwood and Ram W. Tuli

ISBN: 978-1-884883-15-6

Vintage Guitar, PO Box 7301, Bismarck, ND 58507, publishers of Vintage Guitar® magazine and Vintage Guitar® Online at www.VintageGuitar.com. Vintage Guitar is a registered trademark of Vintage Guitar, Inc.

©2025 by Alan Greenwood, all rights reserved under International, Pan American, and Universal Copyright Conventions. No part of this publication may be reproduced or transmitted in any form or by any means, electronic or mechanical, including but not limited to photocopying, recording, or by any information storage and retrieval system, without permission, in writing, from the author.

Cover: 1963 Fender Stratocaster in SeaFoam Green: The Vault at Chicago Music Exchange. 1964 Fender Jaguar and 1965 Jazzmaster in seafoam green: VG Archive.
Back: 2006 Teye Electric Gypsy, 1960s Greco: VG Archive. 1973 Gibson Les Paul Deluxe: Dave Rogers/VG Archive. Kid Ramos: Brad Elligood. Seth Lee Jones: Phil Clarkin. Jedd Hughes: Libby Danforth.

Cover Design: Doug Yellow Bird/Vintage Guitar, Inc.

Printed in the United States of America

In loving memory of Jack David Greenwood, 1990-2020

Dave's
GUITAR SHOP
227 3rd Street South
LaCrosse, WI. 54601
1-608-785-7704
914 South 5th Street
Milwaukee, WI. 53204
1-608-790-9816
110 Market Street
Sun Prairie, WI. 53590
1-608-405-8770
00 South Central Avenue
Marshfield, WI. 54449
1-715-207-0525
Info@davesguitar.com
www.davesguitar.com

CONTROL YOUR LOOK
COMMAND YOUR TONE

BUILD YOURS AT FRALINPICKUPS.COM

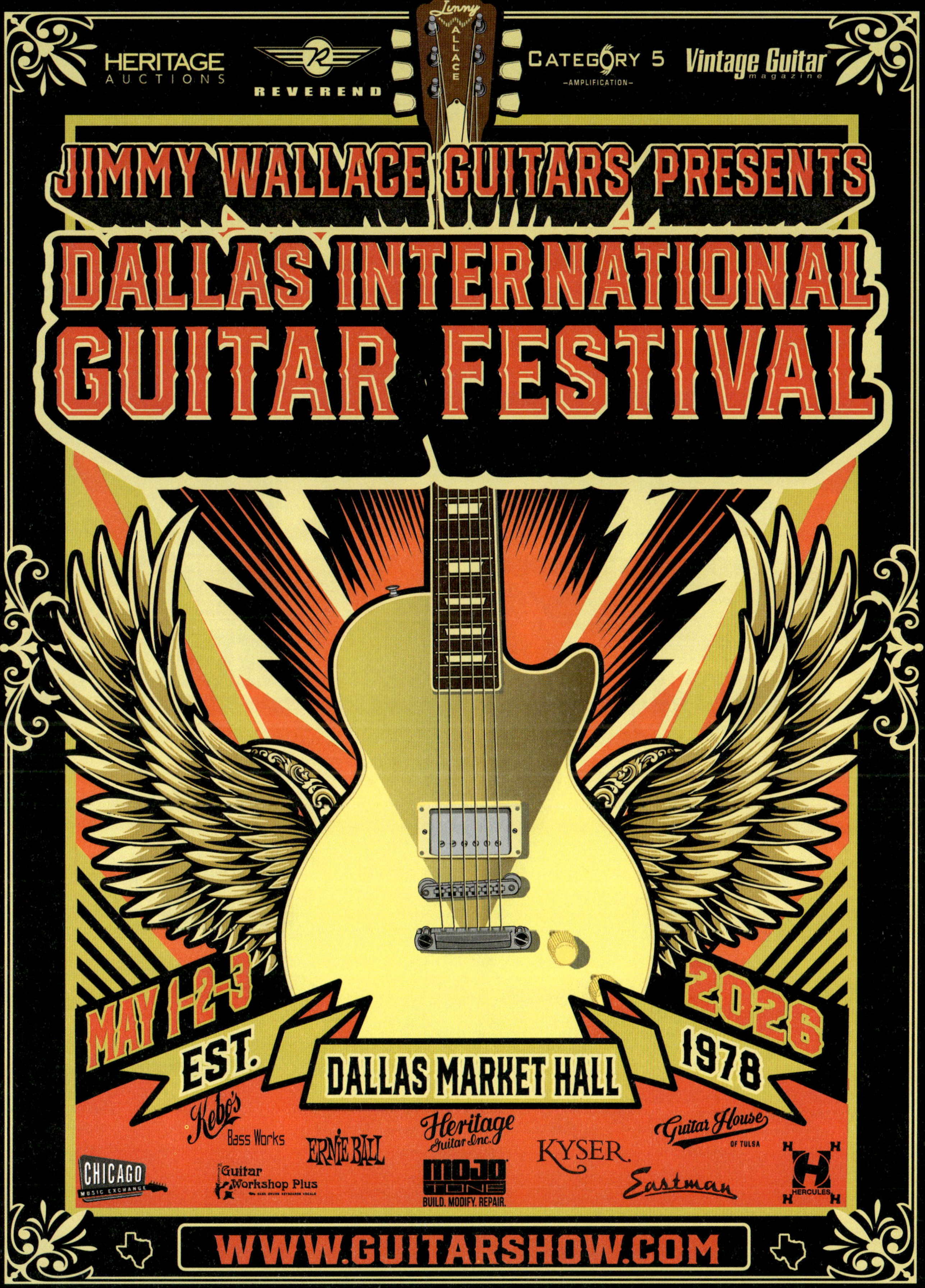

HERITAGE AUCTIONS

REVEREND

Jimmy Wallace

CATEGORY 5 AMPLIFICATION

Vintage Guitar magazine

JIMMY WALLACE GUITARS PRESENTS

DALLAS INTERNATIONAL GUITAR FESTIVAL

MAY 1-2-3 2026

EST. 1978

DALLAS MARKET HALL

Kebo's Bass Works

ERNIE BALL

Heritage Guitar Inc.

KYSER

Guitar House of Tulsa

CHICAGO MUSIC EXCHANGE

Guitar Workshop Plus

MOJO TONE BUILD. MODIFY. REPAIR.

Eastman

HERCULES

WWW.GUITARSHOW.COM

INFO@JIMMYWALLACEGUITARS.COM 469-562-8545

514 MAIN STREET, GARLAND TEXAS 75040

TABLE OF CONTENTS

1973 Gibson Les Paul Deluxe in Red Sparkle and a 1971 sunburst: Dave Rogers/ VG Archives.

Gary's
We Buy, Sell & Trade Fine Vintage Guitars
CLASSIC GUITARS LLC
WE PAY TOP $$$ FOR VINTAGE GUITARS AND BASSES
Serving Investors, Collectors & Professionals worlwide
garysclssc@aol.com 513-891-0555
Call or email for info
Garysguitars.com

Ruth Brinkmann
817-312-7659
ruthmbrinkmann@gmail.com

Dave Crocker
417-850-4751
davelcrocker@gmail.com

Larry Briggs
918-288-2222
amigoshows@stringswest.com

Facebook @ Amigo Guitar Shows
amigoguitarshows.com

Lark Street Music
479 Cedar Lane
Teaneck NJ 07666
201-287-1959
larkstreetmusic.com

SINCE 1968
TOP $$ PAID FOR GUITARS

Vintage Awesome
Rock, Folk, Jazz
Buy, Sell, Trade
8 Minutes from NYC

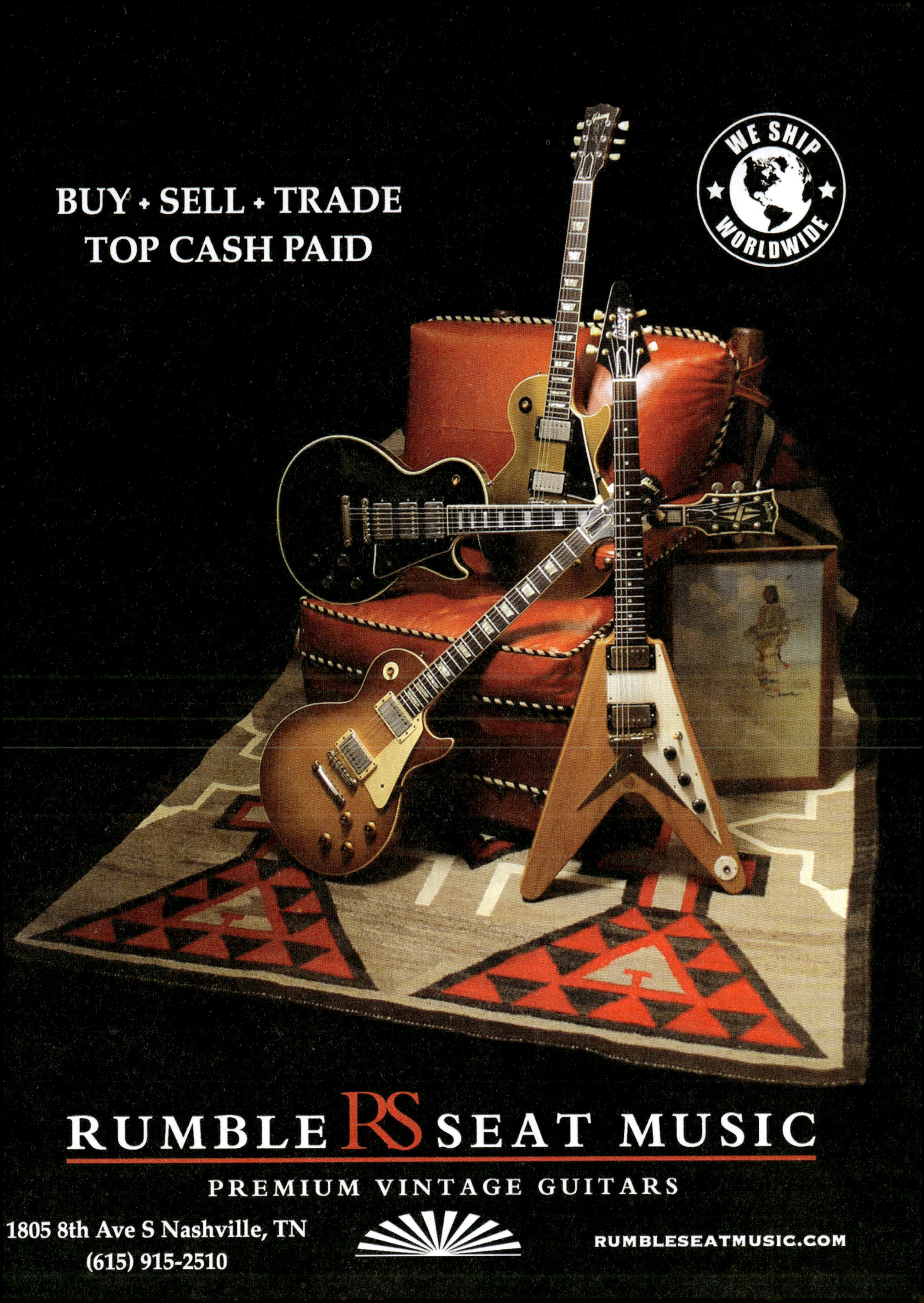

BUY • SELL • TRADE
TOP CASH PAID

WE SHIP WORLDWIDE

RUMBLE RS SEAT MUSIC

PREMIUM VINTAGE GUITARS

1805 8th Ave S Nashville, TN
(615) 915-2510

RUMBLESEATMUSIC.COM

USING THE GUIDE

UNDERSTANDING THE VALUES

Values presented in *The Official Vintage Guitar Price Guide* are for excellent-condition, all-original instruments. Our definition of excellent condition allows for some wear, but the instrument should be well-maintained, with no significant blemishes, wear, repairs, or damage. All-original means the instrument has the parts and finish it had when it left the factory. Replacement parts and refinishes can greatly affect value, as can the appropriate case (or cover) in excellent condition. In many instances, a "wrong" case will not greatly affect value, but with the top-dollar collectibles, it can.

The exception to this is the range on amplifiers, which operate in a high-voltage, high-temperate environment, being manhandled most of their life. Here, the low value is for ones showing wear and tear, but being regularly maintained. They will likely have grounded electrical plugs and non-original electrolytic capacitors. All other passive components in the electrical circuit should be original.

The second price shown is the premium paid for an all-original amp that functions perfectly and is in excellent cosmetic condition.

We use a range of excellent-condition values, as there is seldom agreement on a single price point for vintage and used instruments. A tighter range suggests there is a general consensus, while a wide range means the market isn't in strict agreement. A mint-condition instrument can be worth more than the values listed here.

Repairs affect value differently. Some repair is necessary to keep an instrument in playable condition. The primary concern is the level of expertise displayed in the work and an amateurish repair will lower the value more than one that is obviously professional. A refinished guitar, regardless of the quality of the work, is generally worth 50% or less of the values shown in *The Guide*. A poorly executed neck repair or significant body repair can mean a 50% reduction in a guitar's value. A professional re-fret or minor, nearly invisible body repair will reduce a guitar's value by only 5%.

The values in *The Guide* are for unfaded finishes. Slight color fade reduces value by only 5%, but heavy fading can reduce value by 25% to 50%.

FINDING THE INFORMATION

The table of contents shows the major sections and each is organized in alphabetical order by brand, then by model. In a few instances, there are separate sections for a company's most popular models, especially when there is a large variety of similar instruments. Examples include Fender's Stratocasters, Telecasters, Precision and Jazz basses, and Gibson's Les Pauls. The outer top corner of each page includes a dictionary-type index that tells the models or brands on that page. This provides a quick way to navigate each section.

The Guide has excellent brand histories and in most cases the guitar section has the most detailed information for each brand. When possible, *The Guide* lists each model's years of availability and any design changes that affect values.

More information on many of the brands covered in *The Guide* is available in the pages of *Vintage Guitar* magazine and on our website, www.VintageGuitar.com.

The authors of *The Guide* appreciate your help, so if you find any errors or have additional information on certain brands or models, please drop us a line at Ram@VintageGuitar.com.

NEW RETAIL PRICING INFORMATION

The Guide contains information on individual luthiers and smaller shops. It's difficult to develop values on used instruments produced by these builders because much of their output is custom work, production is low, and/or they haven't been producing for a period of time sufficient to see their instruments enter the used/resale market. To give you an idea about their instruments, we've developed five grades of retail values for new product. These convey only the prices charged by the builder, and are not indicative of the quality of construction.

The five retail-price grades are:
Budget - up to $500,
Intermediate - $501 to $1,500,
Professional - $1,501 to $3,000,
Premium - $3,001 to $10,000,
Presentation - more than $10,000.

The Guide uses the terms "production" and "custom" to differentiate between builders who do true custom work versus those who offer standard production models. "Production" means the company offers specific models, with no variations. "Custom" means they do only custom orders, and "production/custom" indicates they do both. Here's an example:

Bismarck Sound Guitars
2016-present. Premium grade, custom solidbody guitars built by luthier Alan Greenwood in Bismarck, North Dakota.

This tells who the builder is, the type of instruments they build, where they build them, how long they've been operating under that brand, that they do only custom work, and that they ask between $3,000 and $10,000 for their guitars (premium-grade).

Drew Berlin's Vintage Guitars
TRUSTED EXPERIENCE, QUALITY GUITARS

Currently Buying and Consigning Guitar Collections

"For over forty years I have found many of the world's most iconic guitars for the world's greatest players and collectors. Reserve a private showing today."
-Drew Berlin

DUMBLE
Preservation Society®
Tone Chaperone
Authorized Dumble Amps
Sales and Service

"Bursts are my claim to Flame."

'58 Les Paul Standard Sunburst Flame Top
'59 Les Paul Standard Sunburst Flame Top
'60 Les Paul Standard Sunburst Flame Top

213-400-4244 • DrewBerlin.com • Drew@ DrewBerlin.com

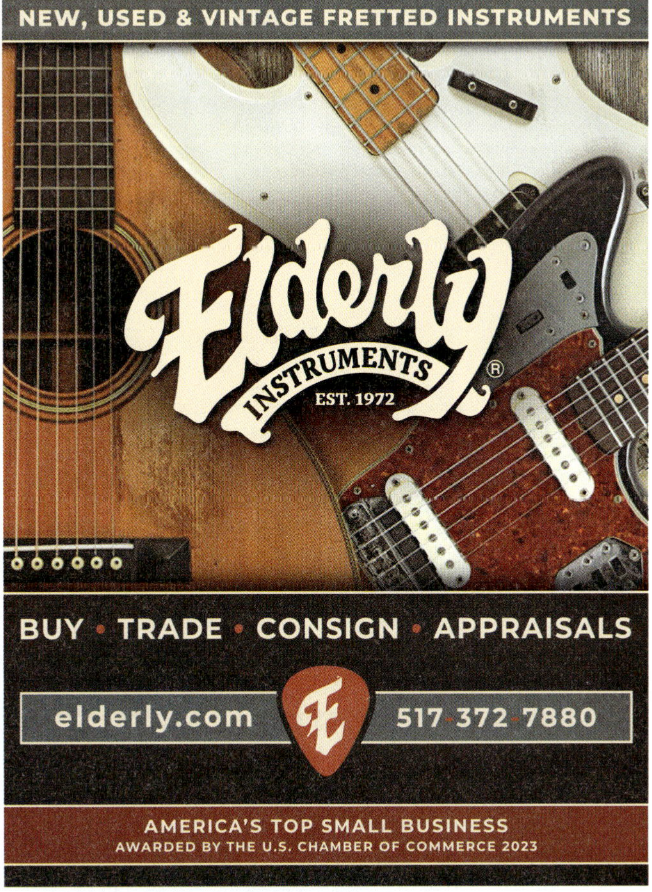

Vintage Fender Stratocaster

More Than 300 Vintage Fender Stratocaster Stocks

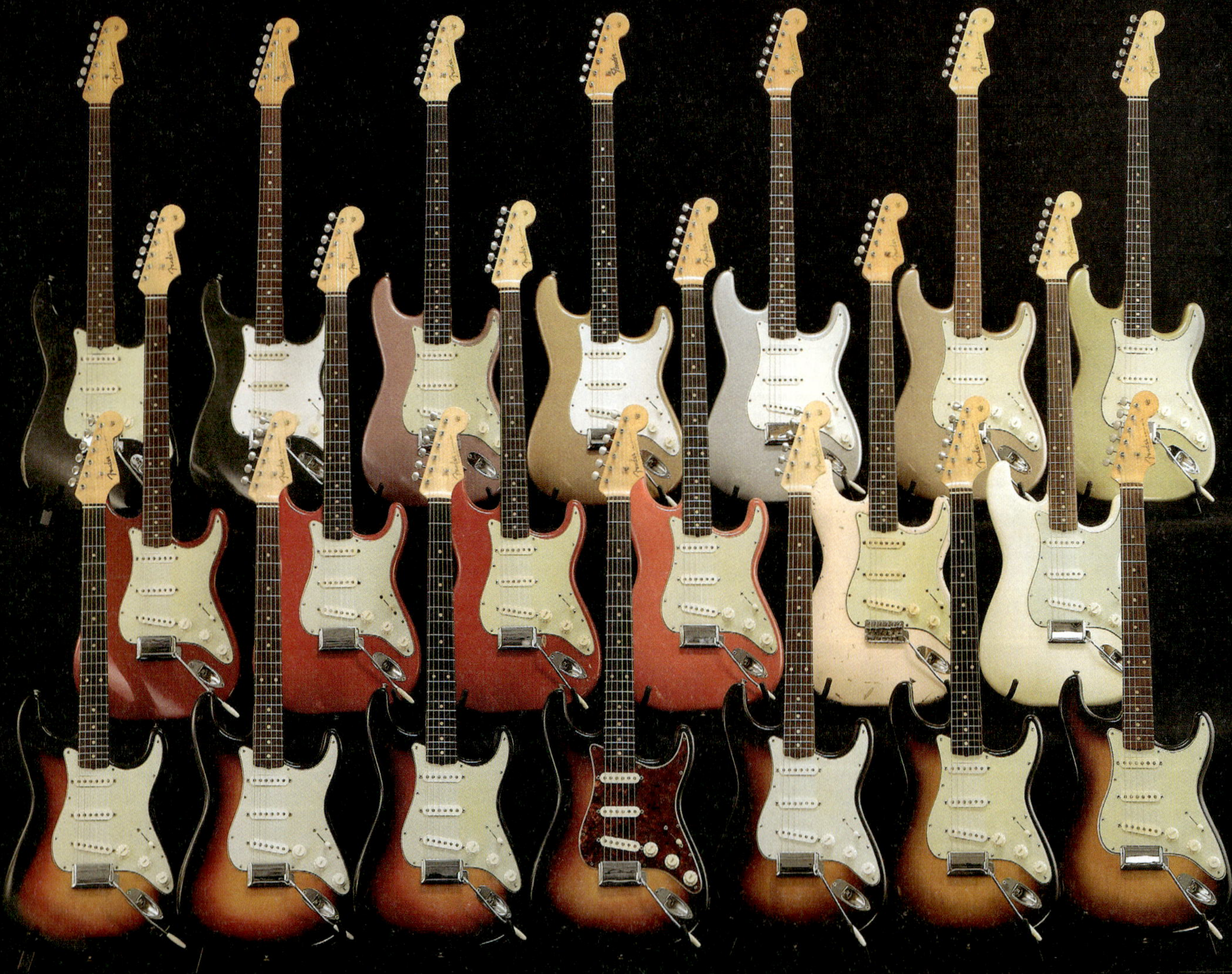

— Wanted —

Vintage Fender Stratocaster,
Vintage Stratocaster Parts, Case & Accessories

Feel free contact us in English any time!!

Top Cash Paid!!

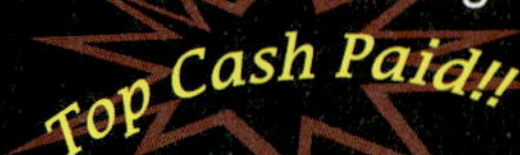

Specialized Shop in Japan

Please Choose your best Vintage Stratocaster!!

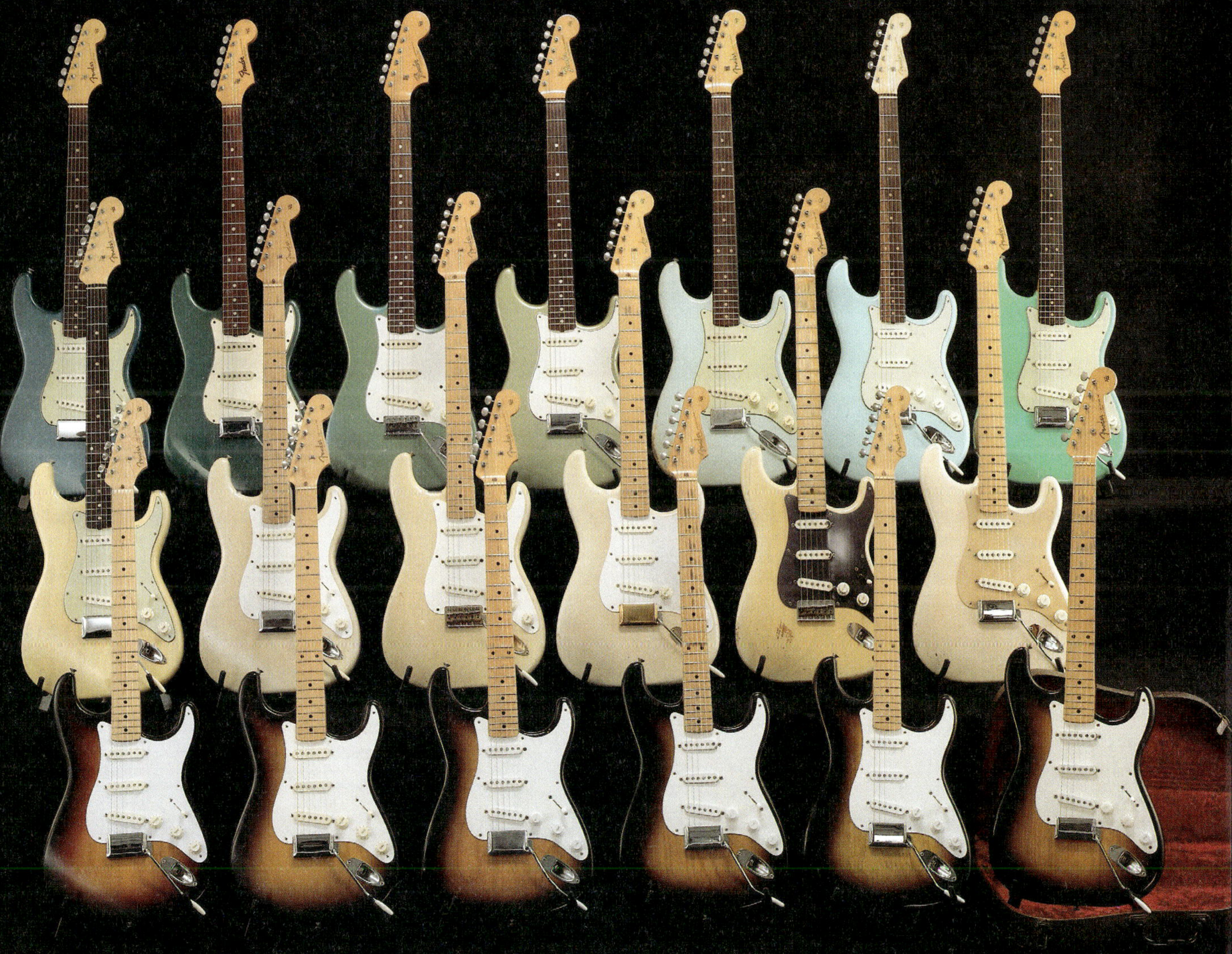

Show Room "Strato-Crazy"
3-8-6-B1, Kanda Kajicho,
Chiyoda-ku, Tokyo, 101-0045, Japan
Phone: +81-3-3257-7117
Business Hours
Wednesday to Friday : 15:00 ~ 19:00
Saturday & Sunday : 13:00 ~ 19:00
Monday & Tuesday : Closed

Vintage Fender Stratocaster specialized shop
H.I.Guitars, Inc. "Strato-Crazy"
E-Mail: higuitars@aol.com
— We Ship Worldwide —
Please Visit Our Websight!!
http://www.hi-guitars.com

INTRODUCTION

After five years of significant growth, the vintage market is contracting. While values for many iconic models in "Excellent High" condition are holding steady, slower sales have driven prices for those in "Excellent Low" down 10-20% from their peak. Unlike certain other collectibles, vintage guitars are not formally graded. In *The Official Vintage Guitar Price Guide*, the highest values shown are for a guitar in immaculate condition, a.k.a. "mint" or essentially uncirculated. These bring a premium because they are exceptionally rare.

Since 1991, *Vintage Guitar*'s 42-Guitar Index has tracked the cumulative value of notable models from the three major brands of the "classic era" - 14 each from Fender, Gibson, and Martin (listed at the end of this introduction). The Index has declined 5% since last year's peak, following an 86% surge over the previous five years.

The 3000-Guitar Index, a broader measure, tracks 34 brands including Fender, Gibson, Gretsch, Martin, Rickenbacker, Travis Bean, Charvel, Hamer, Jackson, Dean, and Ibanez (also listed at the end of this intro). It has declined 3% since its peak, after surging 91% over the previous five years.

A comparison of the two indices along with the S&P 500 is shown in Figure 1.

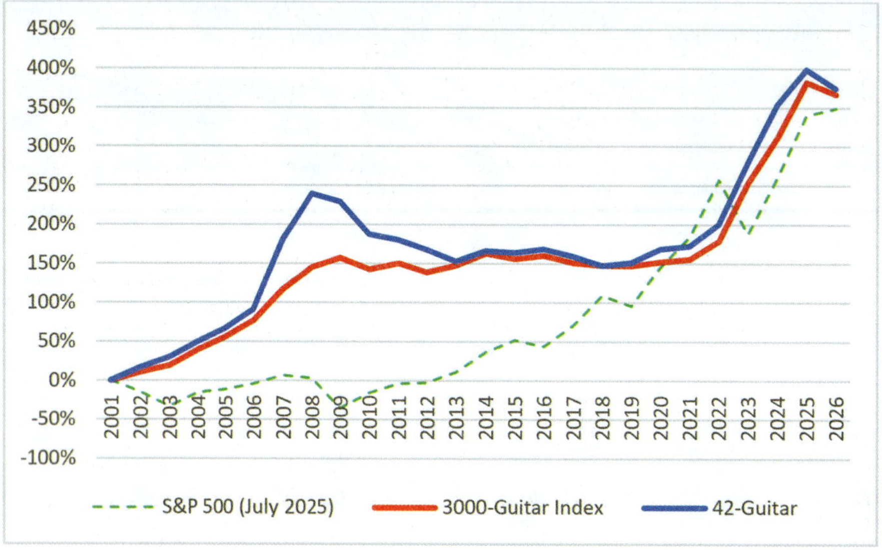

Fig. 1 A Comparison of the 42-Guitar, 3000-Guitar, and S&P 500 Indices Since 2001

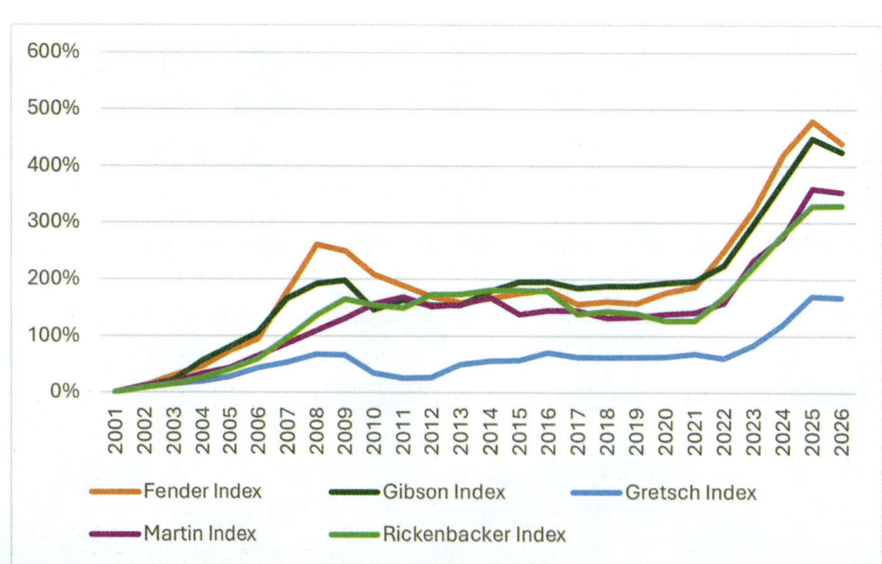

Fig. 2 Big 5 Brand Appreciation since 2001

According to most dealers surveyed by *The Guide*, the market began to decline in fall 2024. Stock market volatility beginning in January '25 (driven by tariffs, trade wars, and other factors) initially spurred the market upward after a brief pause. However, as the S&P 500 regained momentum in spring '25, the market continued its downward trend.

THE VINTAGE MARKET

The 3000-Guitar Index can be broken down by brand, with trends of the "big five" (Fender, Gibson, Gretsch, Martin, and Rickenbacker) summarized in Figure 2. These brands dominate the market. Since publication of the *2024 Guide*, the Fender fell 7%, Gibson dropped 4%, Gretsch and Martin each declined 1%, and Rickenbacker held steady. With the market coming off of its 2024 peak, it's worthwhile to study the long-term trends of the most-collected models. The 10-year annualized return rate for each guitar in the 3000-Guitar Index shows the average yearly gain (or loss) as a percentage. For context, as of July 2025, the S&P 500's 10-year annualized return rate was approximately 13%. To outpace inflation, investments require a nominal return exceeding 3% annually. Here are the guitars with the highest 10-year annualized rates of return.

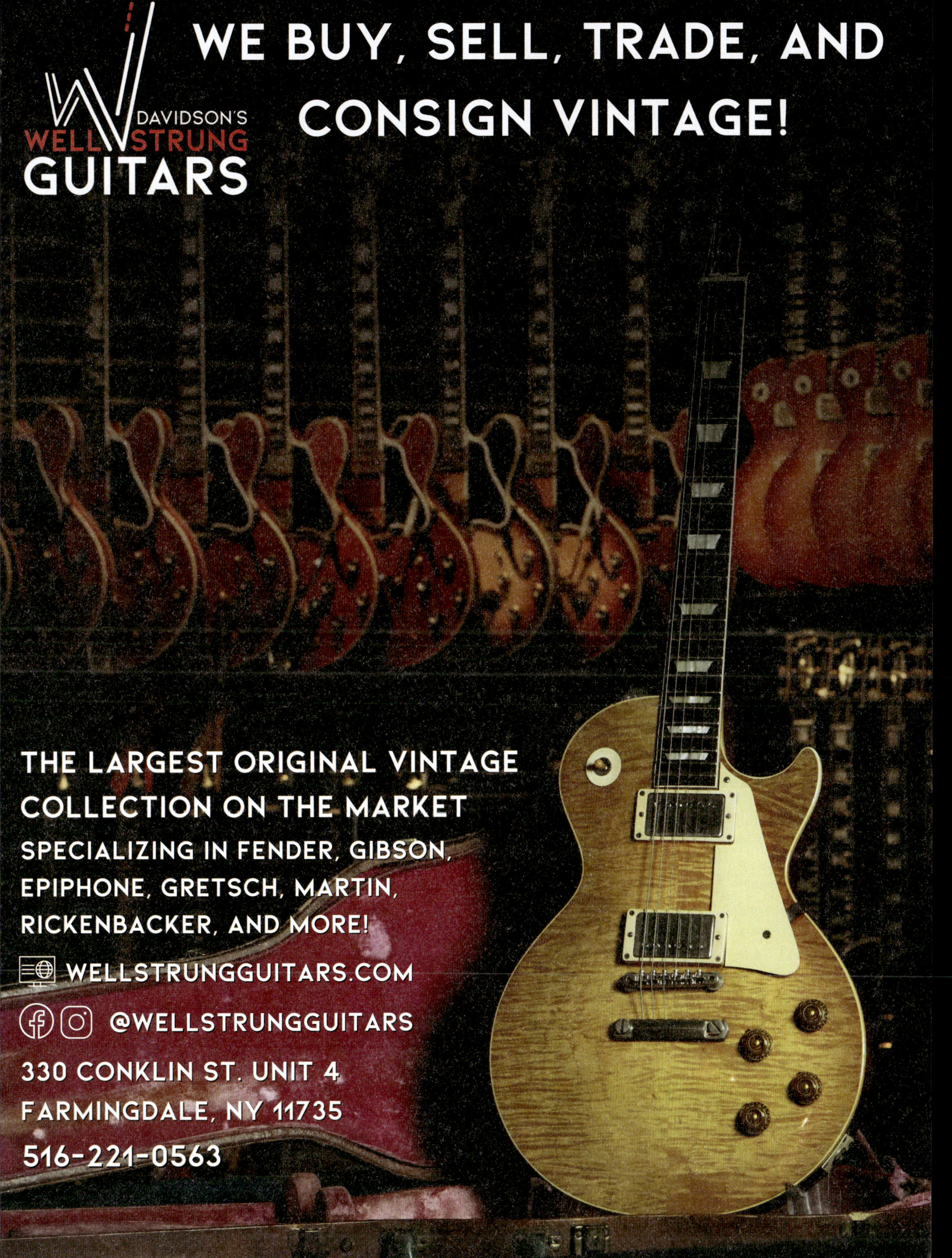
DAVIDSON'S
WELL STRUNG
GUITARS
WE BUY, SELL, TRADE, AND
CONSIGN VINTAGE!
THE LARGEST ORIGINAL VINTAGE
COLLECTION ON THE MARKET
SPECIALIZING IN FENDER, GIBSON,
EPIPHONE, GRETSCH, MARTIN,
RICKENBACKER, AND MORE!
WELLSTRUNGGUITARS.COM
@WELLSTRUNGGUITARS
330 CONKLIN ST. UNIT 4
FARMINGDALE, NY 11735
516-221-0563

GUITARS WITH THE BEST 10-YEAR ANNUALIZED RETURN RATES

Brand	Model	Years	10Y ARR
Gibson	EDS-1275	1958-61 Hollowbody	20.6%
Rickenbacker	Model 1993 RM	1964 Flat Tailpiece	17.5%
Rickenbacker	Model 1993 RM	1964-65 R Tailpiece	16.0%
Fender	Custom Color Jazzmaster	1963-64	14.1%
Gibson	Flying V	1966-69	12.9%
Fender	Broadcaster	1950	12.8%
Bigsby	Handmade Solid Body	1950-56	12.8%
Ibanez	Model 2459 Destroyer	1970s Law Suit Era	12.8%
Burns	Bison	1962	12.6%
Music Man	Edward Van Halen	1991	12.1%
Fender	Rare Color Jazzmaster	1965-68	12.0%
Jackson	Kelly Custom	1986	11.8%
Martin	D-28 E	1959-64	11.6%
Hamer	Standard	1985	11.5%
Fender	Rare Color Stratocaster	1965-68	11.2%
Fender	Duo-Sonic	1956-59	11.1%
Gibson	Les Paul Junior	1954-58 Sunburst Single Cut	11.1%
Martin	D-18	1946-47	11.1%
Hamer	Standard	1975	11.1%
Martin	OO-18	1940-43 Scalloped Braces	11.0%
Fender	Rare Color Jazzmaster	1963-64	10.9%
Martin	O-42	1927-39 Steel	10.9%
Martin	OO-18	1934-39 14-Fret Steel	10.8%
Gretsch	White Falcon	1955	10.8%
Rickenbacker	Model 325	1958 John Lennon Solid Top	10.8%
Gibson	Les Paul Junior Double Cut	1959 Cherry	10.7%
Jackson	Soloist w/Floyd Rose	1984	10.6%
Charvel	EVH Yellow on Black	2004	10.6%
Ibanez	JEM Y2KDNA	2000	10.6%
Fender	Rare Color Jaguar	1963-64	10.5%
Martin	OO-18	1930-33 12-Fret Steel	10.5%
Gibson	Les Paul	1955-56 P-90s Tune-o-matic	10.3%
Fender	Nocaster	1951	10.3%
Rickenbacker	Model 360 12	1965-68 OS Pointed Horns Fireglo	10.2%
Fender	Jazzmaster	1963-64	10.1%
Music Man	Stingray II	1976	10.1%
Gibson	ES-150	1940-42 Metal Cover p/u	10.0%
Gibson	Flying V	1975-81	10.0%

SURVEY ADVISORY BOARD

The information refined on these pages comes from several sources, including the input of many knowledgeable guitar dealers. Without the help of these individuals, it would be very hard for us to provide the information here and in each issue of *Vintage Guitar* magazine. We deeply appreciate the time and effort they provide.

Brian Goff
Bizarre Guitars

Garrett Tung
Boingosaurus Music

Dave Belzer
Burst Brothers

Kim Sherman
Carter Vintage

Daniel Escauriza
Chicago Music Exchange

John Majdalani
Cream City Music

Dave Rogers
Dave's Guitar Shop

David Davidson and Paige Davidson
Davidson's Well Strung Guitars

Drew Berlin
Drew Berlin's Vintage Guitars

Stan Werbin and S.J. "Frog" Forgey
Elderly Instruments

Dewey Bowen
Freedom Guitar

Rick Hogue
Garrett Park Guitars

Gary Dick
Gary's Classic Guitars

Eric Newell
Gruhn Guitars

Richard Johnston
Gryphon Strings

J.D. McDonald
Guitar Maverick

Kennard Machol & Leonard Coulson
Intermountain Guitar & Banjo

Jim Singleton
Jim's Guitars

Kevin Borden
Kebo's BassWorks

Dave Hinson
Killer Vintage

Timm Kummer
Kummer's Vintage Instruments

Buzzy Levine
Lark Street Music

Larry Wexer
Laurence Wexer, Ltd.

Chuck Mahar
Mahar's Vintage Guitars

Artie Leider
McKenzie River Music

Neal Shelton
Neals Music (California)

Lowell Levinger
Players Vintage Instruments

Howie Statland
Rivington Guitars

Eliot Michael
Rumble Seat Music

Eric Schoenberg
Schoenberg Guitars

Richard Gellis
Union Grove Music

Fred Oster
Vintage Instruments

Richard Friedman
We Buy Guitars

Nate Westgor
Willie's American Guitars

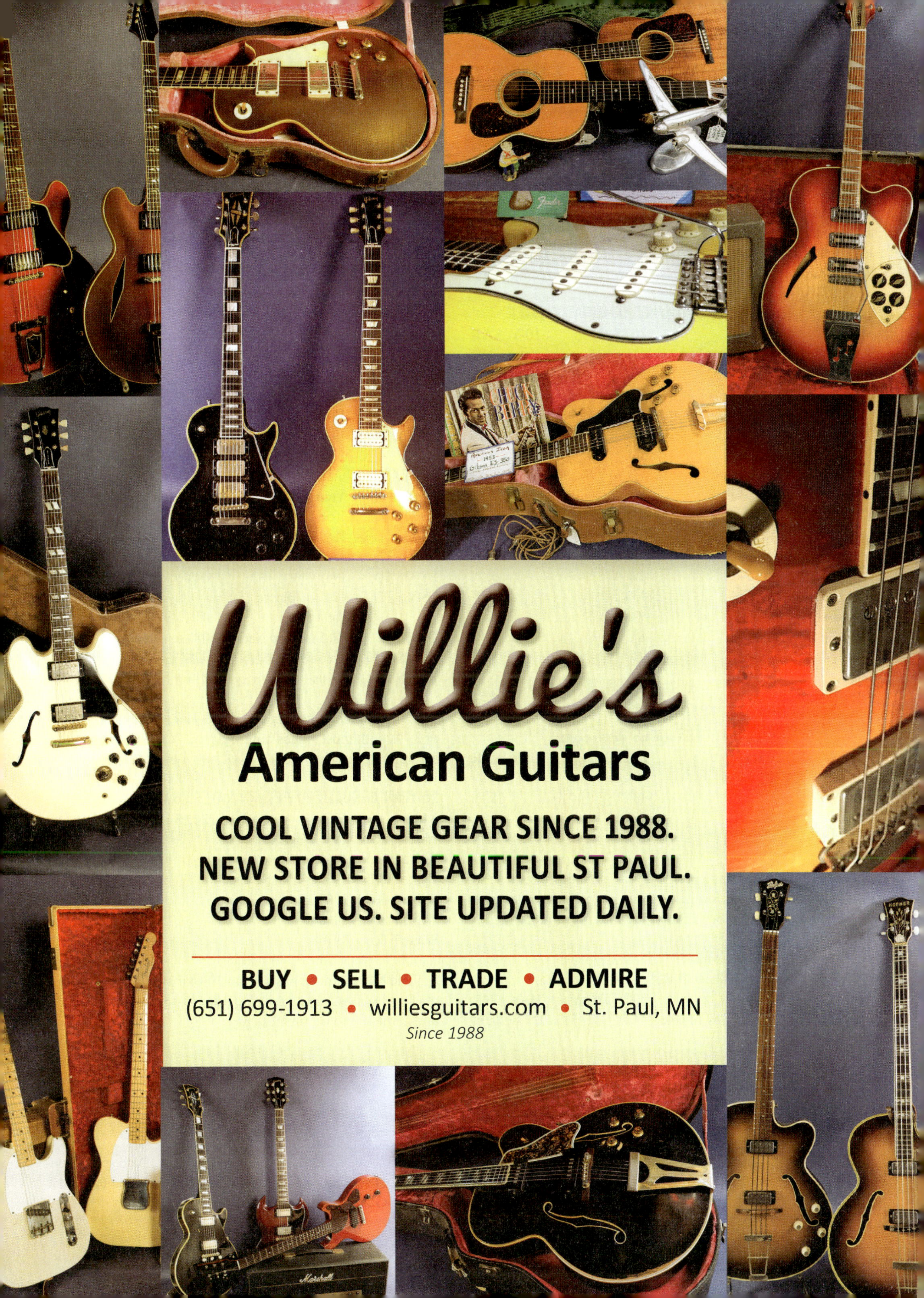
Willie's
American Guitars
COOL VINTAGE GEAR SINCE 1988.
NEW STORE IN BEAUTIFUL ST PAUL.
GOOGLE US. SITE UPDATED DAILY.
BUY • SELL • TRADE • ADMIRE
(651) 699-1913 • williesguitars.com • St. Paul, MN
Since 1988

Gibson	Les Paul	1952-53 P-90s Trapeze	10.0%
Martin	OO-21	1940-43	
		Scalloped Braces	10.0%

The Fender index has a mean 10-year annualized return rate of 6.5%, with most values ranging from 4% to 9%. Values for standard Stratocasters (sunburst), Telecasters (blond), and Jazzmasters (sunburst) are summarized here. The drop in value from their recent 2024 high is also shown.

10-YEAR ANNUALIZED RETURN RATES OF STRATOCASTER

Model	Years	2025 Drop	10-Y AAR
Stratocaster	1954 Earliest Version	-	9.6%
Stratocaster	1955-57	-16%	5.2%
Stratocaster	1958-59	-12%	3.9%
Stratocaster	1960-62	-17%	3.6%
Stratocaster	1963-64	-14%	5.2%
Stratocaster	1965-69	-16%	4.4%
Stratocaster	1970s 4-Bolts	-12%	3.9%
Stratocaster	1970s 3-Bolts	-14%	3.1%

10-YEAR ANNUALIZED RETURN RATES OF TELECASTER

Model	Years	2025 Drop	10-Y ARR
Telecaster	1952-54	-9%	5.6%
Telecaster	1955-57	-13%	5.2%
Telecaster	1958-59	-9%	5.3%
Telecaster	1960-62	-8%	5.4%
Telecaster	1963-64	-9%	5.0%
Telecaster	1965-68	-11%	5.1%
Telecaster	1970s	-6%	4.5%

10-YEAR ANNUALIZED RETURN RATES OF JAZZMASTER

Model	Years	2025 Drop	10-Y ARR
Jazzmaster	1959-62	-13%	7.8%
Jazzmaster	1963-64	-13%	10.1%
Jazzmaster	1965-69	-12%	6.0%
Jazzmaster	1970s	-11%	4.4%

The Gibson index has a mean 10-year annualized return rate of 4.4%, with most values ranging from 1% to 7%. Standard Les Pauls and Cherry Red or sunburst ES-335s are summarized in Tables 5 and 6.

10-YEAR ANNUALIZED RETURN RATES OF LES PAULS

Model	Years	2025 Drop	10-Y ARR
Les Paul	1952-53 P-90s Trapeze	-	10.0%
Les Paul	1953-55 P-90s		
	Stoptail	-11%	8.3%
Les Paul	1955-56 P-90s		
	Tune-o-matic	-6%	10.3%
Les Paul	1957 PAFs		
	White Plastic	-6%	7.9%
Les Paul	1958 'Burst		4.1%
Les Paul	1959 'Burst	-	5.4%
Les Paul	1960 'Burst		
	(blade neck)	-	5.0%
Les Paul	1961 SG Body	-10%	7.2%
Les Paul	1969 Standard		
	Large Headstock	-8%	9.3%
Les Paul	1971 P-90s Goldtop	-11%	8.6%
Les Paul	1972-73 Goldtop	-14%	8.5%
Les Paul	1976-79 Pancake	-11%	4.4%

10-YEAR ANNUALIZED RETURN RATES OF ES-335

Model	Years	2025 Drop	10-Y ARR
ES-335 TD	1958	-17%	7.2%
ES-335 TD	1959	-19%	7.7%
ES-335 TD	1960	-11%	4.0%
ES-335 TD	1961	-14%	3.2%
ES-335 TD	1962-64 Blocks		
	Pat # p/u	-11%	5.0%
ES-335 TD	1965 Narrow Neck	-18%	2.4%
ES-335 TD	1966-69	-17%	2.5%
ES-335 TD	1970s	-11%	-0.1%

The Gretsch index has a mean 10-year annualized return rate of 3.7%, with most values ranging from 1% to 7%. White Falcons are summarized here.

10-YEAR ANNUALIZED RETURN RATES OF WHITE FALCON

Model	Years	2025 Drop	10-Y ARR
White Falcon	1955 Single Cut	-	10.8%
White Falcon	1956-61 Single Cut	-	9.6%
White Falcon	1962-64 Double Cut	-	9.6%
White Falcon	1965-67	-	7.9%
White Falcon	1968-69	-	6.2%
White Falcon	1970s	-3%	5.6%

The Martin index has a mean 10-year annualized return rate of 6%, with most values ranging from 4% to 8%. D-18s and D-28s are summarized on the next page.

UPDATES AND CORRECTIONS

If you spot errors in the information about brands and models, have information on a brand you'd like to see included, or produce instruments for sale and would like to be included in the next edition of *The Guide*, email Wanda at Library@VintageGuitar.com.

If a model is missing from *The Guide*, or if you spot something that needs to be clarified, please drop a line to Ram@VintageGuitar.com.

The Vault Opens: Rare Guitars from a Lifetime of Collecting

When I founded The Guitar Sanctuary, my vision was never just to sell guitars. I wanted to create a home for musicians — a place where artistry, craftsmanship, and community come together. More than a store, it's a place where players find inspiration, whether chasing the perfect tone, searching for a dream instrument, or simply soaking in the energy of a space built by and for musicians.

Photo by Anja Schlein

Over the years, countless extraordinary instruments have passed through our doors, finding their way onto stages, into studios, and into homes. But every so often, I came across a guitar too rare or special to let go, from vintage treasures to master-built one-offs and iconic pieces from the world's best luthiers. Today, that collection stands at 125 guitars, each chosen for its unique voice and soul. As much as I've loved building this collection, guitars aren't meant to sit silent. They're meant to breathe, to vibrate, to inspire. As such, some of the guitars I've personally set aside over the years are now available to the public.

But this release is just one chapter. Every day, our guitar sanctuary showcases some of the finest guitars, amps, and pedals available anywhere — curated for players who value quality, tone, and craftsmanship. Whether you're a pro, a weekend player, or a collector, you'll find something here to spark inspiration. The vault is open, the story continues, and passion is here for all who enter - Geo

Explore these rare pieces — and the rest of our collection at:

www.GuitarSanctuary.com

6633 Virginia Pkwy. McKinney, TX 75071 972.540.6420

10-YEAR ANNUALIZED RETURN RATES OF D-18

Model	Years	2025 Drop	10-Y ARR
D-18	1931-34 12-Fret	-	6.7%
D-18	1935-37 14-Fret	-	7.4%
D-18	1939 Rear X	-	7.7%
D-18	1940-41	-11%	7.2%
D-18	1942-43 Scalloped Braces	-7.6%	
D-18	1944-45 Non-Scalloped Braces	-	-6.1%
D-18	1946-47	-3%	11.1%
D-18	1948-48	-8%	5.7%
D-18	1950-53	-6%	4.7%
D-18	1954-59	-6%	5.8%
D-18	1960-64	-8%	4.4%
D-18	1965	-8%	4.9%
D-18	1966-69	-6%	3.4%
D-18	1970s	-7%	2.0%

10-YEAR ANNUALIZED RETURN RATES OF D-28

Model	Years	2025 Drop	10-Y ARR
D-28	1931-34 12-Fret	-	7.9%
D-28	1935-37 14-Fret	-	7.0%
D-28	1939 Rear X	-	7.6%
D-28	1940-41	-	6.7%
D-28	1942 Scalloped Braces	-	8.7%
D-28	1943 Scalloped Braces	+5%	8.3%
D-28	1944-49 Non-Scalloped, no HB	-7%	4.2%
D-28	1950-53	-7%	2.3%
D-28	1954-59	-7%	3.1%
D-28	1960-64	-4%	3.2%
D-28	1965	-6%	2.7%
D-28	1966-69	-6%	2.3%
D-28	1970s	-5%	5.6%

The Rickenbacker index has a mean 10-year annualized return rate of 3%, with most values ranging from 1% to 7%. The Model 360/12 is summarized here.

10-YEAR ANNUALIZED RETURN RATES OF MODEL 360/12

Model	Years	2025 Drop	10-Y ARR
Model 360/12	1965-68 OSPointed Horns Fireglo	-	10.2%
Model 360/12	1965-69 NS Rounded Horns Mapleglo	-	3.7%
Model 360/12	Early-70s 21 frets	-	1.2%
Model 360/12	1970s 24 frets	-	1.2%

THE EMERGING MARKET

The emerging market is largely dominated by Hamer, Jackson, and B.C. Rich. This table shows notable examples of these brands, ranked high to low.

10-YEAR ANNUALIZED RETURN RATES OF SOME 70s-80s ICONIC MODELS

Brand	Model	Year	2025 Drop	10-Y ARR
Jackson	Kelly Custom	1986	-5%	11.8%
Hamer	Standard	1985	-11%	11.5%
Hamer	Standard	1975	-10%	11.1%
Jackson	Soloist w/Floyd Rose	1984	-8%	10.6%
Jackson	RR USA V-Shaped	1983	-7%	9.6%
BC Rich	Warlock	1986	+20%	9.1%
Hamer	Chaparral	1986	-10%	8.1%
Hamer	Sunburst	1977	-10%	7.9%
BC Rich	Bich-10	1977	+8%	5.0%
BC Rich	Mockingbird	1977	-11%	3.3%
BC Rich	Seagull II	1977	-8%	2.3%

CUSTOM SHOP-MADE ARTIST AND HISTORIC MODELS

Top values have increased for certain ultra-rare/low production models. These are limited-run signature and reissue models from the custom shops at Gibson and Martin. Typically built with a higher degree of attention to detail with premium woods, these command top prices when in mint condition. Gibson artist signature models that are also Murphy Lab aged typically retain their value best.

THE USED-GUITAR MARKET

While many collectors focus on pre-1965 "Golden Era" instruments, nearly 80% of the values listed in *The Guide* are for guitars priced under $5,000. Most are classified as "used," not "vintage," as they were made within the last 30 years. These guitars have declined 10-20% because the market for them remains highly saturated.

VINTAGE BASSES AND AMPS

The Guide also tracks basses and amps (Figure 3). Within the 100-Bass Index (which saw a negligible change from last year), the Fender Precision rose 2%, the Jazz fell 2%, and the Rickenbacker 4001 rose 9%. Instruments in the 100-Bass Index with the highest 10-year annualized return rates are summarized below.

Fender amps within the Vintage Amp Index fell 12%. The Marshall Amp component fell 6%. Now might be a good time to add some tweed or EL34 magic to your collection.

BASSES WITH THE BEST 10-YEAR ANNUALIZED RETURN RATES THIS YEAR

Brand	Model	Years	10Y ARR
Hamer	Standard Bass	1975-1979	19.6%
BC Rich	Bich	1978-1979	15.5%
Fender	Mustang Bass	1966-1967	11.0%
Travis Bean	TB-2000	1974-1979	9.2%
Ibanez	Model 2459B Destroyer	1974-1977	9.1%
Travis Bean	TB-4000 (Wedge)	1974-1979	9.0%
Rickenbacker	Model 4001 Mapleglo	1963-1966	8.0%
Rickenbacker	Model 4001	1970-1972	7.7%
Dean	ML	1977-1983	7.6%
Baldwin	Vibraslim	1965-66	7.5%
Rickenbacker	Model 4001 Fireglo	1961-1963	7.4%
Hofner	Model 500/1 Beatles lefty	1961	7.1%
Alembic	Series II	1970s	7.1%

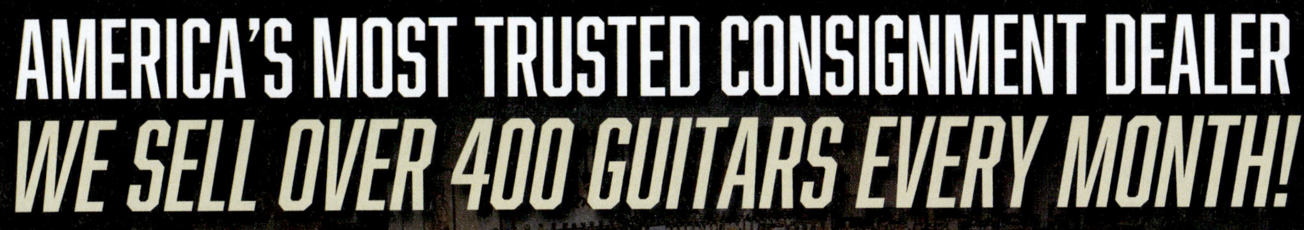

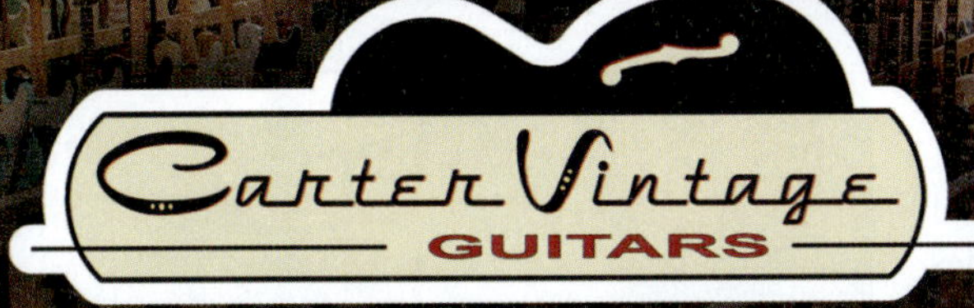

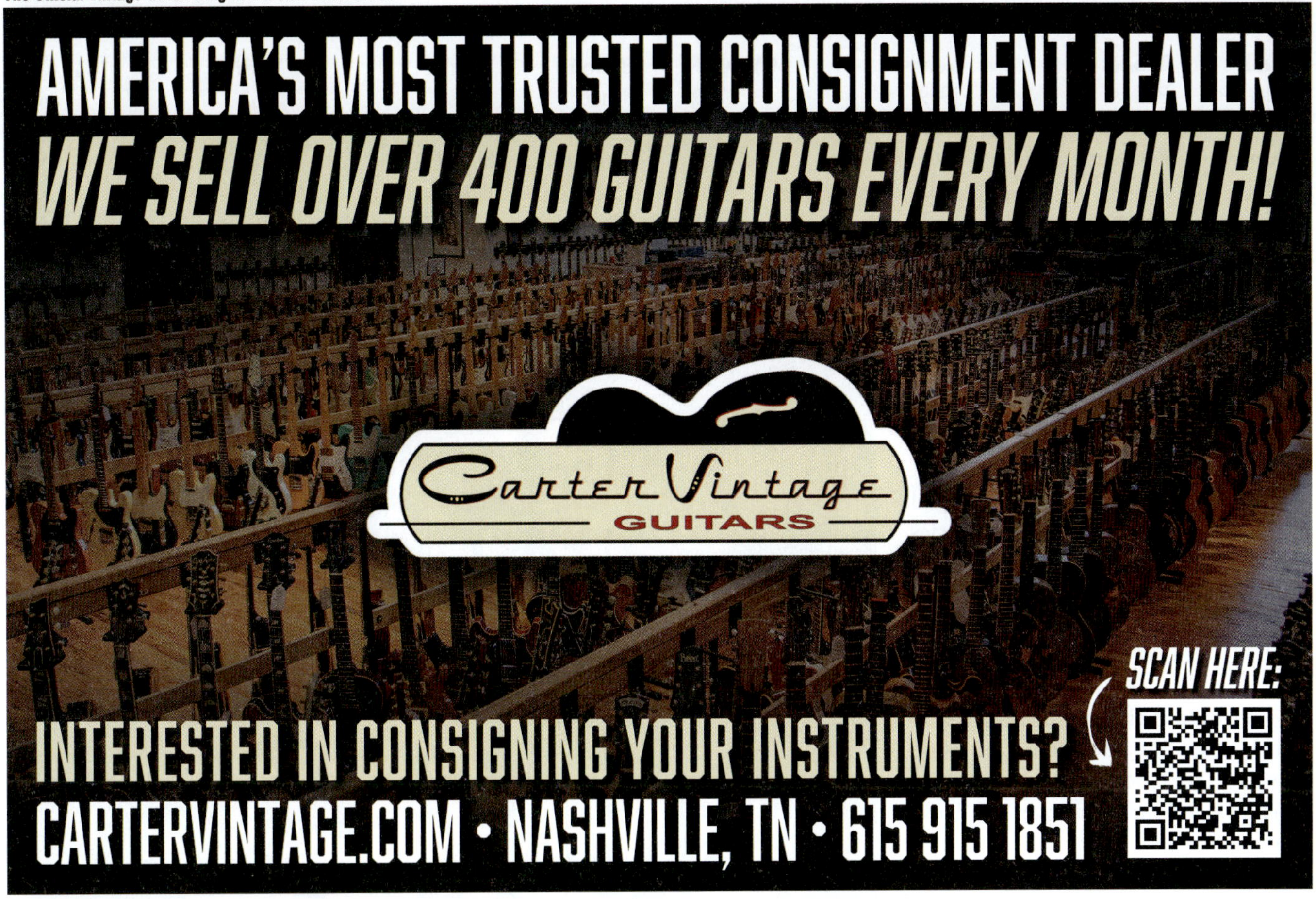
AMERICA'S MOST TRUSTED CONSIGNMENT DEALER
WE SELL OVER 400 GUITARS EVERY MONTH!
Carter Vintage
GUITARS
SCAN HERE:
INTERESTED IN CONSIGNING YOUR INSTRUMENTS?
CARTERVINTAGE.COM • NASHVILLE, TN • 615 915 1851

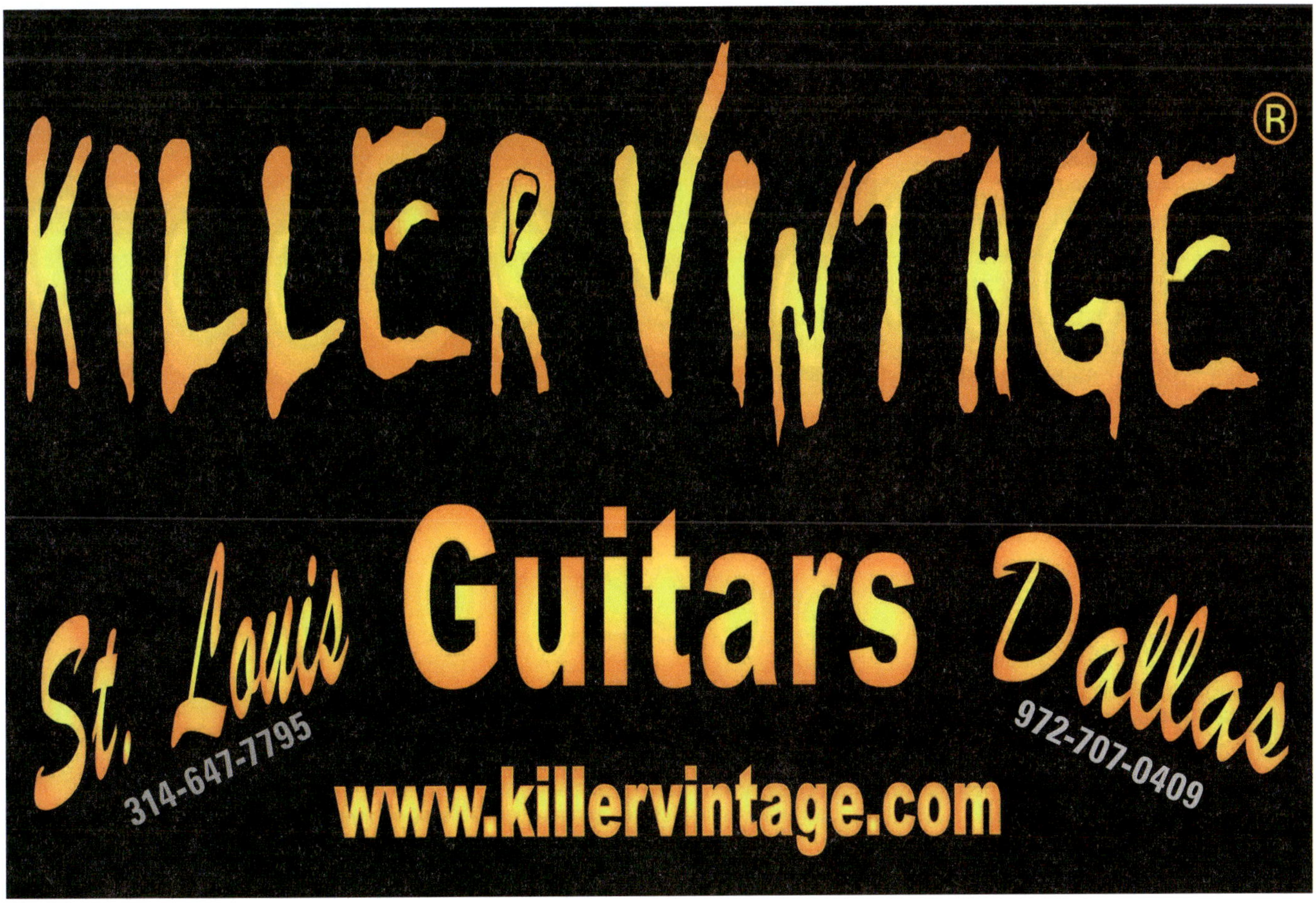
KILLER VINTAGE®
St. Louis Guitars Dallas
314-647-7795
972-707-0409
www.killervintage.com

Brand	Model	Years	10Y ARR
Fender	P-Bass	1969	7.0%
Fender	P-Bass	1963	6.9%
Fender	P-Bass	1961	6.5%
Fender	P-Bass	1962	6.5%
Fender	P-Bass	1971	6.2%
Rickenbacker	Model 4005L (Lightshow)	1972-1975	6.2%
Fender	J-Bass	1962	5.7%
Fender	Telecaster Bass	1969	5.7%
Rickenbacker	Model 4001	1973	5.6%
Fender	P-Bass	1951	5.2%
Fender	J-Bass	1963	5.2%
Fender	J-Bass	1964	5.2%
Ampeg	AEB-1	1966-67	5.2%

MORE INFORMATION

Much of the information in this book comes from *Vintage Guitar magazine*, which is offered in both print and digital formats; you can subscribe at www.VintageGuitar.com. VintageGuitar.com has a trove of feature interviews, instrument histories and profiles, gear and music reviews, along with historical information on the brands and models covered in this book. You'll also find links to exclusive lessons, *VG* podcasts, our online archives of *VG* back issues, the *VG* YouTube channel, and our free e-mail *VG Overdrive* newsletter. Find us on Facebook, YouTube, and Instagram, where we talk guitars and offer prizes. We'd love to have you join us.

The Guide *authors Ram W. Tuli and Alan Greenwood.*

ACKNOWLEDGEMENTS

Guitars beg for personal inspection to inspire a sale, having a large constituency of players nearby will influence the "localized" price. That is why *The Guide* uses dealers from all over the world. Special thanks to the Survey Advisory Board enough for all their help compiling data for *The Guide*. Thanks also to Alex Kiedaisch, Larry Briggs, Joe Spann, Fred Stucky, Collin Whitley, Brett Coleman, Charlie Gelber, Peter Fung, John Dannert, Lee Jackson, James Pittman, Parker Lundgren, Michael Slubowski, Henry Nelson, Tucker Beirne, Kris Blakely, and Jeff Lisec, and to Randy Klimpert for the ukulele section.

Wanda Huether, as Editor of *The Guide*, keeps us all on deadline and makes all this possible. Doug Yellow Bird continues his fine work on the design and layout of the book. Larry Huether and Ward Meeker helped with editing and proofreading, Mike and Donna Naughton handled the advertising and directory listings. We thank all of them for their usual fine work.

Thank you,
Alan Greenwood and Ram Tuli.

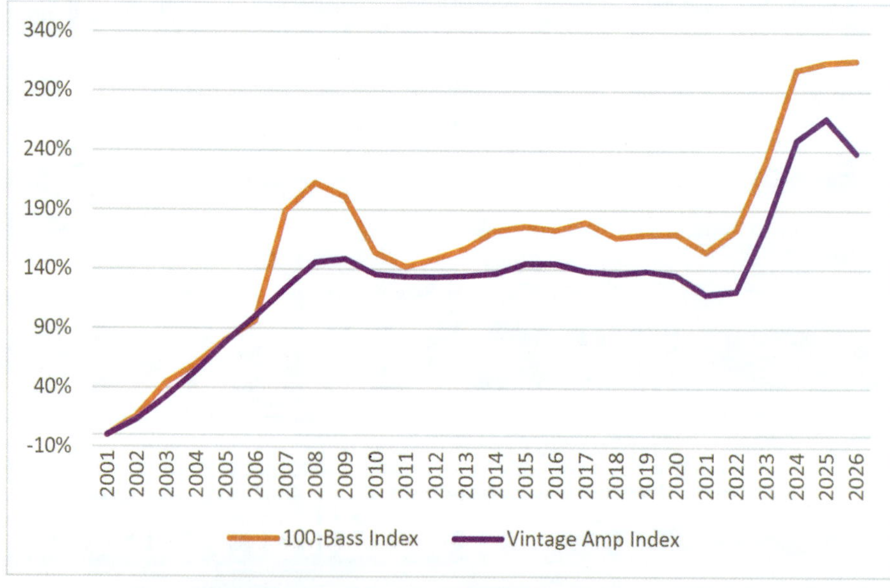

Fig. 3 Comparison of Vintage Bass and Amp Indices

THE 42 GUITAR INDEX

FENDER MODELS

1952 blond Precision Bass
1952 blond Esquire
1953 blond Telecaster
1956 sunburst Stratocaster
1958 sunburst Jazzmaster
1958 blond Telecaster
1960 sunburst Stratocaster
1961 sunburst, stack knob, Jazz Bass
1962 sunburst, 3-knob, Jazz Bass
1963 sunburst Telecaster Custom
1963 sunburst Esquire Custom
1964 Lake Placid Blue Jaguar
1964 sunburst Precision Bass
1966 Candy Apple Red Stratocaster

GIBSON MODELS

1952 sunburst ES-5
1952 Les Paul Model
1954 Les Paul Jr.
1958 sunburst EB-2 Bass
1958 Les Paul Custom
1958 natural ES-335
1958 Super 400CES
1959 Les Paul Jr.
1959 J-160E
1961 ES-355
1961 Les Paul SG
1964 sunburst Thunderbird II Bass
1965 EB-3 Bass
1969 sunburst Citation

MARTIN MODELS

1931 OM-28
1936 00-28
1935 D-18
1944 scalloped-brace 000-28
1944 D-28
1950 D-28
1958 000-18
1959 D-18
1959 D-28E
1962 D-28
1967 GT-75
1968 000-18
1969 N-20
1969 D-45

THE 3,000-GUITAR INDEX

FENDER ELECTRICS

Duo-Sonic ('56 to '69)
Electric XII (All Colors, '65 to '69)
Esquire ('51 to '70)
Jaguar (All Colors, '62 to '75)
Jazzmaster (All Colors, '58 to '81)
Musicmaster ('56 to '81)
Mustang (All Colors, '64 to '81)
Stratocaster (All Colors, '54 to '81)
Telecaster (All Colors, '50 to '81)
Telecaster Custom ('59 to '72)
Telecaster Thinline ('68 to '78)

GIBSON ELECTRICS

Barney Kessel Regular ('61 to '73)
Barney Kessel Custom ('61 to '73)
Byrdland ('56 to '81)
EDS-1275 ('58 to '67; '77 to '81)
ES-120 T ('62 to '70)
ES-125 ('35 to '43; '47 to '70)
ES-125 C ('66 to '70)
ES-125 CD ('65 to '69)
ES-125 T ('56 to '68)
ES-125 TD ('57 to '63)
ES-125 TC ('60 to '70)
ES-125 TDC ('60 to '71)
ES-135 ('54 to '59)
ES-150 ('36 to '42; '46 to '56)
ES-175 ('49 to '71)
ES-175 N ('49 to '59)
ES-175 D ('52 to '81)
ES-175 DN ('52 to '66)
ES-225 T ('55 to '59)
ES-225 TN ('55 to '58)
ES-225 TD ('56 to '59)
ES-225 TDN ('56 to '59)
ES-250 ('39 to '40)
ES-250 N ('39 to '40)
ES-295 ('52 to '58)
ES-300 ('40 to '42; '45 to '53)
ES-300 N ('40 to '42; '45 to '53)
ES-330 T ('59 to '63)
ES-330 TN ('59 to '61)
ES-330 TD ('59 to '72)
ES-330 TDN ('59 to '61)
ES-335 TD ('58 to '81)
ES-335 TDN ('58 to '60)
ES-345 TD ('59 to '81)
ES-345 TDN ('59 to '60)
ES-350 ('47 to '56)
ES-350 N ('47 to '56)
ES-350 T ('56 to '63; '77 to '81)
ES-350 TN ('56 to '63; '77 to '81)
ES-355 TD ('58 to '70)
ES-355 TDSV ('58 to '81)
ES-5 ('49 to '62)
ES-5 N ('49 to '60)
Explorer ('58 to '59; '63 old parts; '75 to '81)
Firebird I ('63 to '69)
Firebird III ('63 to '69)
Firebird V ('63 to '69)
Firebird VII ('63 to '69)
Flying V ('58 to '59; '66 to '70; '75 to '81)
Johnny Smith ('61 to '81)
Johnny Smith D ('61 to '81)
L-4 CES ('58 and '69)
L-4 CESN ('58 and '69)
L-5 CES ('51 to '81)
L-5 CESN ('51 to '81)
L-7 E ('48 to '54)
L-7 CE ('48 to '54)
Les Paul Model ('52 to '57)
Les Paul Standard ('58 to '63; '68 to '69; '71 to '81)
Les Paul Custom ('54 to '63; '68 to '81)
Les Paul Deluxe ('69 to '81)
Les Paul Junior ('54 to '63)
Les Paul Special ('55 to '59)
Les Paul TV ('54 to '59)
Melody Maker ('59 to '70)
Melody Maker D ('60 to '70)
Melody Maker III ('67 to '71)
SG Custom ('63 to '80)
SG Deluxe ('71 to '73)
SG Junior ('63 to '71)
SG Special ('60 to '78)
SG Standard ('63 to '81)
SG TV ('59 to '61)
Super 400 CES ('51 to '81)
Super 400 CESN ('52 to '81)
Tal Fallow ('62 to '71)
Trini Lopez Standard ('64 to '70)
Trini Lopez Deluxe ('64 to '70)

GIBSON ACOUSTICS

Advanced Jumbo ('37)
Country Western ('65)
Everly Brothers ('62)
Hummingbird ('63)
J-45 ('54)
L-5 ('25 to '29)
LG-2 ('58)
SJ-200 ('47)
Southern Jumbo ('43)
Super 400 ('35)

GRETSCH ELECTRICS

Anniversary ('58 to '72)
Atkins Hollowbody 6120 ('54 to '80)
Atkins Solidbody 6121 ('55 to '63)
Astro Jet ('65 to '67)
Country Club ('54 to '81)
Country Gentleman ('57 to '81)
Duo-Jet ('53 to '71)
Jet Firebird ('55 to '71)
Monkees ('66 to '68)
Round Up ('54 to '60)
Silver Jet ('54 to '63)
Tennessean ('58 to '80)
White Falcon ('55 to '81)
White Penguin ('56 to '62)

GRETSCH ACOUSTICS

Rancher ('54)

MARTIN

O-18 (1898 to '81)
O-21 (1889 to '81)
O-28 (1874 to '31)
O-42 (1890 to '42)
O-45 ('04 to '39)
OO-18 (1898 to '81)
OO-21 (1898 to '81)
OO-28 (1898 to '41)

OO-42 (1898 to '43)
OO-45 ('04 to '29)
OOO-18 ('06 to '81)
OOO-28 ('02 to '81)
OOO-42 ('18 to '43)
OOO-45 ('06 to '42)
D-18 ('31 to '81)
D-21 ('55 to '69)
D-28 ('31 to '81)
D-28 E ('59 to '64)
D-45 ('36 to '42)
GT-75 ('65 to '67)
N-20 ('68 to '80)
OM-28 ('29 to '33)
OM-45 ('30 to '33)

RICKENBACKERS

A-22 ('32 to '36)
Combo 400 ('56 to '58)
Combo 420 ('65 to '81)
Combo 425 ('58 to '73)
Combo 450 ('57 to '66)
Combo 600 ('54 to '58)
Combo 650 ('57 to '59)
Combo 800 ('54 to '59)
Combo 850 ('57 to '59)
Combo 900 ('57 to '66)
Combo 950 ('57 to '80)
Electric Spanish ('46 to '49)
ES Ken Roberts ('35 to '39)
Model B Spanish ('35 to '43)
Model 310 ('58 to '70)
Model 315 ('58 to '74)
Model 320 ('58 to '81)
Model 325 ('58 to '75)
Model 330 ('58 to '81)
Model 330 12 ('64 to '81)
Model 331 Light Show ('70 to '75)
Model 335 ('58 to '77)
Model 340 ('58 to '81)
Model 345 ('58 to '74)
Model 360 ('58 to '81)
Model 360 12 ('64 to '81)
Model 365 ('58 to '74)
Model 370 ('58 to '81)
Model 370 12 ('66; '80 to '81)
Model 375 ('58 to '74)
Model 381 ('58 to '74)
Model 420 ('65 to '81)
Model 450 ('70 to '81)
Model 450 12 ('64 to '81)
Model 460 ('61 to '81)
Model 615 ('62 to '77)
Model 625 ('62 to '77)
Model 1000 ('56 to '70)
Model '93 RM ('64 to '67)
Model '96 RM ('64 to '67)
Model '97 RM ('64 to '67)
Model '98 RM ('64 to '67)
S-29 ('40 to '41)

SELECT OTHERS

Ampeg Dan Armstrong Lucite ('69 to '71)
B.C. Rich Bich-10 ('77)
B.C. Rich Bich Supreme ('78 to '79)
B.C. Rich Mockingbird ('76)
B.C. Rich Seagull II ('77)
B.C Rich Warlock ('86)
Bigsby ('48 to '56)
Bourgeois JOM Brazilian ('93)
Burns Bison ('61 to '62)
Burns Marvin ('64)
Charvel Pre-Pro ('80 to '81)
Charvel EVH Art Series (2004 to 2007)
Charvel Model 4 ('87)
Charvel San Dimas ('81 to '86)
Chapman Stick ('70 to '75)
Collings D-2H Brazilian ('94)
Collings SJ ('92)
Coral Sitar 3S19 ('67 to '69)
Danelectro Convertible ('65)
Danelectro Double Neck 3922 ('60)
Danelectro Guitarlin ('63)
Danelectro U2 ('58)
Danelectro Pro-1 ('63)
D'Angelico New Yorker ('38 to '41)
Dean Cadillac ('79)
Dean ML 'Burst ('77 to '86)
Dean V 'Burst ('77 to '81)
Dobro Model 27 Cyclops ('33)
EKO Rocket ('67 to '69)
Epiphone Casino ('61 to '70)
Epiphone Coronet ('60 to '69)
Epiphone Crestwood Custom ('61 to '69)
Epiphone FT-30 Caballero ('59)
Epiphone FT-45 Cortez ('59)
Epiphone FT-79 Texan ('59)
Epiphone Olympic Double ('60 to '63)
Epiphone Rivera ('63)
Epiphone Sheraton ('58)
Epiphone Wilshire ('62 to '66)
Gallagher Doc Watson ('74)
Grammer G-30 ('65)
Guild Aristocrat ('54 to '63)
Guild Bluegrass Special D-50 ('63)
Guild DE-500 ('62 to '65)
Guild Navarre F-50 ('57)
Guild Starfire III ('60 to '66)
Guild Troubadour F-20 ('57)
Hamer Chaparral ('86)
Hamer Standard ('74)
Hamer Standard ('85)
Hamer Sunburst ('77)
Harmony Buck Owens ('69)
Ibanez GB-20 ('81)
Ibanez PS-10 ('78)
Ibanez JEM 77 ('80 to '90)
Ibanez JEMY2KDNA (2000)
Ibanez JEM 10th Anniversary ('96)
Ibanez Joe Satriani 10th Anniversary ('98)
Ibanez 2459 Destroyer ('75 to '79)
Jackson Kelly Custom ('86)
Jackson Randy Rhoads U.S.A. Concorde ('83)
Jackson Soloist w/Floyd Rose ('84 to '86)
Kay K161 Jimmy Reed ('52 to '58)
Kramer Baretta ('84)
Kramer DMZ 3000 ('78)
Larrivee D-70 ('92)
Mosrite Combo Mark I ('66)
Mosrite Joe Maphis Mark XVIII ('64)
Mosrite Ventures ('63 to '68)
Mossman Winter Wheat ('76)
Music Man Edward Van Halen ('91 to '95)
Music Man Sabre II ('78)
Music Man Steve Morse ('87)
Music Man Stingray II ('76)
National Glenwood-99 ('62 to '65)
National Newport 88 ('64)
National Tri-Cone ('29)
National Style-O ('33)
Ovation Adamas 1587 ('80)
Ovation Breadwinner ('75)
PRS Custom 24 "Yellow" ('85)
PRS Custom 24 ('90)
PRS Dragon I ('92)
PRS McCarty Model ('94)
PRS Santana ('96)
Santa Cruz OM ('87)
Santa Cruz Tony Rice ('76)
Stella Flat Top 12 String ('30)
Steinberger GL ('79 to '84)
Taylor 410 ('93)
Taylor 810 ('75)
Travis Bean TB-500 Standard ('75)
Travis Bean TB-1000 Standard ('75)
Travis Bean TB-3000 Wedge ('75)
Tokai Les Paul Reborn ('76 to '82)
Tokai Springy Sound ('76 to '82)
Vox Phantom VI ('62)
Vox Mark VII ('64 to '67)

GUITARS

1966 National Westwood 75 and
1966 Glenwood 99 : VG Archive.

Agile

Airline Archtop
Tom Pfeifer

MODEL YEAR	FEATURES	EXC. COND. LOW	HIGH

17th Street Guitars

2004-2009. Founded by Dave Levine and Colin Liebich. Professional grade, production/custom, solidbody guitars built by luthier John Carruthers in Venice, California.

A Fuller Sound

Luthier Warren Fuller began building professional and premium grade, custom nylon and steel-string flat-tops in '98 in Oakland, California.

Abel

Custom aircraft-grade aluminum body, wood neck, guitars built by twins Jim and Jeff Abel in Evanston, Wyoming. They offered the Abel Axe from '94-'96 and 2000-'01, and still do custom orders. They also made the Rogue Aluminator in the late '90s.

Axe

1994-1996. Offset double-cut aluminum body with dozens of holes in the body, wood neck, various colors by anodizing the aluminum body. Abel Axe logo on the headstock.

1994-1996	Non-trem or trem	$1,000	$1,500

Abilene

Budget and intermediate grade, production, acoustic and electric guitars imported by Samick.

Abyss

See listing under Pederson Custom Guitars.

Acme

1960s. Imported inexpensive copy electric guitar models for the student market.

Acoustic

Ca. 1965-ca. 1987, 2001-2005, 2008-present. Mainly known for solidstate amps, the Acoustic Control Corp. of Los Angeles, California, did offer guitars and basses from around '69 to late '74. The brand has been revived with a new line of amps.

Black Widow

1969-1970, 1972-1974. Double-cut body, 2 pickups, and protective pad on back. The early version (AC500) had 22 frets, ebonite 'board and later one was 24 frets, rosewood 'board. Acoustic outsourced production, possibly to Japan, but final 200 or so guitars produced by Semie Moseley. The AC700 Black Widow 12-string was also available for '69-'70.

1969-1970		$1,800	$2,200
1972-1974		$1,500	$2,000

Agile

1985-present. Budget grade, production, acoustic and electric guitars imported by Rondo Music of Union, New Jersey. They also offer mandolins.

Aims

Ca. 1972-ca. 1976. Aims (American International Music Sales, Inc.) instruments, distributed by Randall Instruments in the mid-'70s, were copies of classic American guitar and bass models. They also offered a line of Aims amps during the same time.

Airline

Ca. 1958-1968, 2004-present. Airline originally was a brand used by Montgomery Ward on acoustic, electric archtop and solidbody guitars and basses, amplifiers, steels, and possibly banjos and mandolins. Instruments manufactured by Kay, Harmony and Valco. In '04, the brand was revived by Eastwood guitars on a line of imported intermediate grade, production, reissue guitars and lap steels.

Acoustic Res-O-Glas Resonator

1964. Res-o-glas, coverplate with M-shaped holes, asymmetrical peghead.

1964		$1,200	$1,800

Amp-In-Case Model

1960s. Double-cut, single pickup, short scale guitar with amplifier built into the case, Airline on grille.

1960s		$900	$1,200

Archtop Acoustic

1950s-1960s. Various models.

1950s-60s	Higher-end	$500	$750
1950s-60s	Lower-end	$250	$400

Electric Hollowbody

1950s-1960s. Various models.

1950s	Kay B Kessel copy	$900	$1,200
1960s	ES-175 copy	$750	$1,200
1960s	Harmony H-54 copy	$500	$800
1960s	Harmony H-75 copy	$800	$1,200
1960s	Harmony H-76 copy	$1,000	$1,500
1960s	Kay B. Kessel Swingmaster copy	$1,000	$1,500
1960s	Kay Swing-master copy	$750	$1,200
1960s	Kay Tuxedo copy	$800	$1,200
1960s	National Town & Country copy	$1,000	$1,500

Electric Res-O-Glas

1960s. Res-o-glas is a form of fiberglass. The bodies and sometimes the necks were made of this material.

1960s	Jack White style	$2,000	$3,000
1960s	JB Hutto style	$2,000	$3,000
1960s	Other styles, 1 pu	$700	$1,200
1960s	Other styles, 2 pus	$1,200	$1,800
1960s	Other styles, 3 pus	$1,300	$2,000

Electric Res-O-Glas Resonator

1960s, 2010-present. Res-o-glas is a form of fiberglass. These models have resonator cones in the body.

1960s		$1,200	$1,800
2010-2024	Folkstar	$800	$1,200

Electric Solidbody (Standard)

1950s-1960s. Various models.

1950s-60s	Lower-end	$600	$900

Electric Solidbody (Deluxe)

1950s-1960s. Appointments may include multiple pickups, block inlays, additional logos, more binding.

1950s-60s	Higher-end	$1,000	$1,500

MODEL YEAR	FEATURES	EXC. COND. LOW	HIGH

Flat-Top Acoustic
1950s-1960s. Various models.

1950s-60s	Higher-end, 14"-15"	$500	$800
1950s-60s	Lower-end, 13"	$300	$500

Alamo
1947-1982. Founded by Charles Eilenberg, Milton Fink, and Southern Music, San Antonio, Texas, and distributed by Bruno & Sons. Alamo started out making radios, phonographs, and instrument cases. In '49 they added amplifiers and lap steels. From '60 to '70, the company produced beginner-grade solidbody and hollow-core body electric Spanish guitars. The amps were all-tube until the '70s. Except for a few Valco-made examples, all instruments were built in San Antonio.

Electric Hollowbody

1950s-70s	Higher-end	$1,000	$1,500
1950s-70s	Lower-end	$700	$1,000

Electric Solidbody

1950s-70s	Higher-end	$1,200	$1,800
1950s-70s	Lower-end	$600	$900

Alamo Guitars
1999-2008. The Alamo brand was revived for a line of handcrafted, professional grade, production/custom, guitars by Alamo Music Products, which also offered Robin and Metropolitan brand guitars and Rio Grande pickups.

Tonemonger
1999-2005. Made by Robin, ash or African Fakimba offset double-cut solidbody, 3 single coils, tremolo.

1999-2005		$1,200	$1,800

Alan Carruth
Professional and premium grade, production/custom, classical and archtop guitars built by luthier Alan Carruth in Newport, New Hampshire. He started building dulcimers in 1970 and added guitars in '74. He also builds violins and harps.

Albanus
Ca. 1954-1977. Luthier Carl Albanus Johnson built around 75 high quality custom archtop guitars in Chicago, Illinois. He died in '77. He also built violins and at least two mandolins.

Alberico, Fabrizio
1998-present. Luthier Fabrizio Alberico builds his premium grade, custom, flat-top and classical guitars in Cheltenham, Ontario.

Alden
2005-present. Budget and intermediate grade, production, acoustic and electric guitars, and basses designed by Alan Entwhistle and imported from China.

Alden (Chicago)
1960s. Chicago's Alden was a department store and mail-order house offering instruments from Chicago builders such as Harmony.

H-45 Stratotone
1960s. Alden's version of the H45 Stratotone Mars model, single plain cover pickup.

1960s		$500	$800

Alembic
1969-present. Premium and presentation grade, production/custom, guitars, baritones, and 12-strings built in Santa Rosa, California. They also build basses. Established in San Francisco by Ron and Susan Wickersham, Alembic started out as a studio working with the Grateful Dead and other bands on a variety of sound gear. By '70 they were building custom basses, later adding guitars and cabinets. By '73, standardized models were being offered.

California Special
1988-2009. Double-cut neck-thru solidbody, six-on-a-side tuners, various colors.

1988-2009		$2,500	$4,500

Darling
2006-present. Exotic woods offered, heart inlay at 12th fret, brass bird tailpiece.

2006-2024		$7,000	$10,000

Distillate
1979-1991. Various wood options.

1979-1991		$2,500	$3,500

Little Darling
2006-present. As the Darling model but slightly smaller.

2006-2024		$6,000	$8,000

Orion
1990-present. Offset double-cut glued neck solidbody, various colors.

1990-2024		$3,000	$4,500

Series I
1972-present. Neck-thru, double-cut solidbody, book matched koa, black walnut core, 3 pickups, optional body styles available, natural.

1970s-2013	12-string	$6,000	$10,000
1970s-2024	6-string	$6,000	$10,000

Alfieri Guitars
1990-2024. Luthier Don Alfieri built his premium and presentation grade, custom/production, acoustic and classical guitars in Long Island, New York. He retired in '24.

Alhambra
1930s. The Alhambra brand was most likely used by a music studio (or distributor) on instruments made by others, including Regal-built resonator instruments.

Allen Guitars
1982-present. Premium grade, production resonators, steel-string flat-tops, and mandolins built by Luthier Randy Allen, Colfax, California.

1960s Alamo Fiesta
Imaged by Heritage Auctions, HA.com

Alembic Little Darling

AlumiSonic Evo-Classic

1976 Alvarez Yairi DY-74

Tom Pfeifer

Alleva-Coppolo Basses and Guitars

1995-present. Professional and premium grade, custom/production, solidbody electric guitars and basses built by luthier Jimmy Coppolo in Dallas, TX for '95-'97, in New York City for '98-2008, Upland, CA for '99-'21 and in Gadsden, AL '21-present.

Aloha

1935-1960s. Private branded by Aloha Publishing and Musical Instruments Company, Chicago, Illinois. Made by others. There was also the Aloha Manufacturing Company of Honolulu which made musical instruments from around 1911 to the late '20s.

Alosa

1947-1958. Luthier Alois Sandner built these acoustic archtop guitars in Germany.

Alpha

1970s-1980s. One of the brand names of guitars built in the Egmond plant in Holland. Sold by Martin for a while in the 1980s.

Alray

1967. Electrics and acoustics built by the Holman-Woodell guitar factory in Neodesha, Kansas, who also marketed similar models under the Holman brand.

Alternative Guitar and Amplifier Company

Intermediate grade, custom/production, solidbody electric guitars and basses made in Piru, California, by luthiers Mal Stich and Sal Gonzales and imported from Korea, beginning in 2006, under the Alternative Guitar and Amplifier Company, and Mal n' Sal brands.

AlumiSonic

2006-present. Luthier Ray Matter builds his production/custom, professional grade, aluminum/wood hybrid electric guitars in Bohemia and West Islip, New York.

Alvarez

1965-present. Intermediate and professional grade, production, acoustic guitars imported by St. Louis Music. They also offer lap steels, banjos and mandolins. Initially high-quality handmade guitars Yairi made by K. (Kazuo) Yairi were exclusively distributed, followed by the lower-priced Alvarez line. In '90 the Westone brand used on electric guitars and basses was replaced with the Alvarez name; these Alvarez electrics were offered until '02. Many Alvarez electric models designed by luthier Dana Sutcliffe; several models designed by Dan Armstrong.

Alvarez Yairi

1966-present. Alvarez Yairi guitars are handcrafted and imported by St. Louis Music.

MODEL YEAR	FEATURES	EXC. COND. LOW	HIGH

Alvarez, Juan

1952-2019. Professional and premium grade, production/custom, classical and flamenco guitars made in Madrid, Spain, originally by luthier Juan Alvarez Gil (died in 2001), then by son Juan Miguel Alvarez.

American Acoustech

1993-2001. Production steel string flat-tops made by Tom Lockwood (former Guild plant manager) and Dave Stutzman (of Stutzman's Guitar Center) as ESVL Inc. in Rochester, New York.

American Archtop Guitars

1995-present. Premium and presentation grade, custom 6- and 7-string archtops by luthier Dale Unger, in Stroudsburg, Pennsylvania.

American Conservatory (Lyon & Healy)

Late-1800s-early-1900s. Guitars, mandolins and harp guitars built by Chicago's Lyon & Healy and sold mainly through various catalog retailers. Mid-level instruments above the quality of Lyon & Healy's Lakeside brand, and generally under their Washburn brand. Generally of negligible value because repair costs often exceed their market value.

Acoustic

1920s	Spanish 6-string	$850	$1,200
1920s	Tenor 4-string	$900	$1,500

G2740 Monster Bass

Early-mid-1900s. Two 6-string neck (one fretless), acoustic flat-top harp guitar, spruce top, birch back and sides with rosewood stain, natural. Their catalog claimed it was "Indispensable to the up-to-date mandolin and guitar club."

1917		$4,000	$6,000

Style G Series Harp Guitar

Early-1900s. Two 6-string necks with standard tuners, 1 neck fretless, rosewood back and sides, spruce top, fancy rope colored wood inlay around soundhole, sides and down the back center seam.

1917	Natural	$4,000	$5,500

American Showster

1986-2004, 2010-2011. Established by Bill Meeker and David Haines, Bayville, New Jersey, building guitars shaped like classic car tailfins or motorcycle gas tanks. The Custom Series was made in the U.S.A., while the Standard Series (introduced in '97) was made in Czechoslovakia. They also made a bass. Bill Meeker started production again around 2010 until his death in late '11.

AS-57 Classic

1987-2004. American-made until 2000, body styled like a '57 Chevy tail fin, basswood body, bolt-on neck, 1 humbucker or 3 single-coils, various colors.

1987-1999	US-made	$3,500	$4,500
2000-2004	Import	$1,200	$1,800

MODEL YEAR	FEATURES	EXC. COND. LOW	HIGH

The Biker/Tank

1987-1989. Alder body shaped like motorcycle gas tank, 3 single-coil or 2 humbucker pickups, maple neck, rosewood 'board.

1987-1989		$1,800	$3,000

Ampeg

1949-present. Founded in '49 by Everett Hull as the Ampeg Bassamp Company in New York and has built amplifiers throughout its history. In '62 the company added instruments with the introduction of their Baby Bass and from '63 to '65, they carried a line of guitars and basses built by Burns of London and imported from England. In '66 the company introduced its own line of basses. In '67, Ampeg was acquired by Unimusic, Inc. From '69-'71 contracted with Dan Armstrong to produce lucite "see-through" guitars and basses with replaceable slide-in pickup design. In '71 the company merged with Magnavox. Beginning around '72 until '75, Ampeg imported the Stud Series copy guitars from Japan. Ampeg shut down production in the spring of '80. MTI bought the company and started importing amps. In '86 St. Louis Music purchased the company. In '97 Ampeg introduced new and reissue American-made guitar and bass models. They discontinued the guitar line in '01 but offered the Dan Armstrong plexi guitar again starting in '05, adding wood-bodied versions in '08. They also offered a bass. In '05 LOUD Technologies acquired SLM and the Ampeg brand. In '18, the brand was sold to Yamaha.

AMG1

1999-2001. Dan Amstrong guitar features, but with mahogany body with quilted maple top, 2 P-90-style or humbucker-style pickups.

1999-2001	Hums, gold hw	$800	$1,200
1999-2001	Kent Armstrong pickups	$600	$900
1999-2001	P-90s, standard hw	$600	$900

Dan Armstrong Lucite

1969-1971. Clear plexiglas solidbody, with interchangeable pickups, Dan Armstrong reports that around 9,000 guitars were produced, introduced in '69, but primary production was in '70-'71, reissued in '98.

1969-1971	Clear	$3,500	$5,000
1969-1971	Smoke	$4,500	$6,000

Dan Armstrong Plexi

1998-2001, 2006-2011. Reissue of Lucite guitar, produced by pickup designer Kent Armstrong (son of Dan Armstrong), offered in smoked (ADAG2) or clear (ADAG1). Latest version is Japanese-made ADA6.

1998-2011	Clear or Smoke	$1,200	$1,800

Heavy Stud (GE-150/GEH-150)

1973-1975. Import from Japan, single-cut body, weight added for sustain, single-coils or humbuckers (GEH).

1973-1975		$700	$1,000

Sonic Six (By Burns)

1964-1965. Solidbody, 2 pickups, tremolo, cherry finish, same as the Burns Nu-Sonic guitar.

1964-1965		$700	$1,000

Stud (GE-100/GET-100)

1973-1975. Import from Japan, double-cut, inexpensive materials, weight added for sustain, GET-100 included tremolo.

1973-1975		$700	$1,000

Super Stud (GE-500)

1973-1975. Double-cut, weight added for sustain, top-of-the-line in Stud Series.

1973-1975		$700	$1,000

Thinline (By Burns)

1963-1964. Semi-hollowbody, 2 f-holes, 2 pickups, double-cut, tremolo, import by Burns of London, same as the Burns TR2 guitar.

1963-1964		$900	$1,300

Wild Dog (By Burns)

1963-1964. Solidbody, 3 pickups, shorter scale, tremolo, sunburst finish, import by Burns of London, same as the Burns Split Sound.

1963-1964		$1,000	$1,500

Wild Dog De Luxe (By Burns)

1963-1964. Solidbody, 3 pickups, bound neck, tremolo, sunburst finish, import by Burns of London, same as the Burns Split Sonic guitar.

1963-1964		$1,000	$1,500

Anderberg

2002-present. Professional and premium grade, production/custom, electric guitars and basses built by luthier Michael Anderberg in Jacksonville, Florida.

Andersen Stringed Instruments

Luthier Steve Andersen builds premium and presentation grade, production/custom flat-tops and archtops in Seattle, Washington, starting in 1978 and he also builds mandolins.

Andreas

1995-2004. Luthier Andreas Pichler built his aluminum-necked, solidbody guitars and basses in Dollach, Austria.

Andrew White Guitars

2000-present. Premium and presentation grade, custom, acoustic flat-top guitars built by luthier Andrew White in Morgantown, West Virginia. He also imports a production line of intermediate and professional grade, acoustic guitars from his factory in Korea.

Andy Powers Musical Instrument Co.

1996-2010. Luthier Andy Powers built his premium and presentation grade, custom, archtop, flat-top, and semi-hollow electric guitars in Oceanside, California. He also built ukes and mandolins.

Angelica

Ca. 1967-ca. 1990s. Entry-level guitars and basses imported from Japan.

American Archtop Standard TD

Ampeg Super Stud GE-500
Imaged by Heritage Auctions, HA.com

GUITARS

1979 Aria Pro II ES-800
Imaged by Heritage Auctions, HA.com

1985 Aria Pro II XR-Series
Rivington Guitars

MODEL YEAR	FEATURES	EXC. COND. LOW	HIGH

Acoustic

1967-1972	Various models	$300	$500

Electric Solidbody

1967-1972	Various models	$400	$800

Angus

Professional and premium grade, custom-made steel and nylon string flat-tops built by Mark Angus in Laguna Beach, California. He started in 1976.

Antares

1980s-1990s. Korean-made budget electric and acoustic guitars imported by Vega Music International of Brea, California.

Acoustic

1980s-90s	Various models	$200	$300

Double Neck 6/4

1990s. Cherry finish double-cut.

1990s		$600	$1,000

Solidbody

1980s-90s	Various models	$250	$400

Antique Acoustics

Luthier Rudolph Blazer builds production/custom flat-tops, 12 strings, and archtops in Tubingen, Germany. He started in the 1970s.

Antonio Hermosa

Imported budget grade, production, acoustic and acoustic/electric classical guitars from The Music Link, starting in 2006.

Antonio Lorca

Intermediate and professional grade, production, classical guitars made in Valencia, Spain.

Apollo

Ca. 1967-1972. Entry-level guitars imported by St. Louis Music. They also offered basses and effects.

Electric

1967-1972. Japanese imports, various models.

1967-1972		$1,000	$1,800

Applause

1976-present. Budget grade, production, acoustic and acoustic/electric guitars, basses, mandolins and ukes and previously solidbody electrics. Originally Kaman Music's entry-level Ovation-styled brand, it is now owned by Drum Workshop, Inc. The instruments were made in the U.S. until around '82 when production was moved to Korea. On the U.S.-made guitars, the back of the neck was molded Urelite, with a cast aluminum neck combining an I-beam neck reinforcement, fingerboard, and frets in one unit. The Korean models have traditional wood necks.

AA Models

1976-1990s. Acoustic, laminate top, plastic or composition body. Specs and features can vary on AA Models.

1976-1981	US-made	$250	$400
1980s-90s	Import	$150	$250

MODEL YEAR	FEATURES	EXC. COND. LOW	HIGH

AE Models

1976-2000s. Acoustic/electric, laminate top, plastic or composition body. Specs and features can vary on AE Models.

1976-1981	US-made	$300	$500
1980-2000s	Import	$200	$400

Applegate

2001-present. Premium grade, production/custom, acoustic and classical guitars built by luthier Brian Applegate in Minneapolis, Minnesota.

APS Custom

2005-present. Luthier Andy Speake builds his production/custom, professional and premium grade, solidbody guitars in Victoria, British Columbia.

Arbor

1983-ca. 2013. Budget and intermediate grade, production, classical, acoustic, and solid and semi-hollow body electric guitars imported by Musicorp (MBT). They also offered basses.

Acoustic

1980s-2013	Various models	$200	$400

Electric

1980s-2013	Various models	$350	$600

Arch Kraft

1933-1934. Full-size acoustic archtop and flat-top guitars. Budget brand produced by the Kay Musical Instrument Company and sold through various distributors.

Aria Diamond

1960s. Brand name used by Aria in the '60s.

Electric

1960s. Various models and appointments in the '60s.

1960s		$500	$1,200

Aria/Aria Pro II

1956-present. Budget, intermediate, and professional grade, production, electric, acoustic, acoustic/electric, and classical guitars. They also make basses, mandolins, and banjos. Aria was established in Japan in '56 and started production of instruments in '60 using the Arai, Aria, Aria Diamond, and Diamond brands. The brand was renamed Aria Pro II in '75. Aria Pro II was used mainly on electric guitars, with Aria used on others. Over the years, they have produced acoustics, banjos, mandolins, electrics, basses, amplifiers, and effects. Around '87 production of cheaper models moved to Korea, reserving Japanese manufacturing for more expensive models. Around '95 some models were made in U.S., though most contemporary guitars sold in U.S. are Korean. In '01, the Pro II part of the name was dropped altogether.

Early Arias don't have serial numbers or pot codes. Serial numbers began to be used in the mid '70s. At least for Aria guitars made by Matsumoku, the serial number contains the year of manufacture in the first

MODEL YEAR	FEATURES	EXC. COND. LOW	HIGH

one or two digits (Y##### or YY####). Thus, a guitar from 1979 might begin with 79####. One from 1981 might begin with 1#####. The scheme becomes less sure after 1987. Some Korean-made guitars use a serial number with year and week indicated in the first four digits (YYWW####). Thus 9628#### would be from the 28th week of 1996. However, this is not the case on all guitars, and some have serial numbers which are not date coded.

Models have been consolidated by sector unless specifically noted.

Acoustic Solid Wood Top

1960s-present. Steel string models, various appointments, generally mid-level imports.

1960s-2024		$600	$1,200

Acoustic Veneer Wood Top

1960s-present. Steel string models, various appointments, generally entry-level imports.

1960s-2024		$300	$600

Classical Solid Wood Top

1960s-present. Various models, various appointments, generally mid-level imports.

1960s-2024		$500	$800

Classical Veneer Wood Top

1960s-present. Various models, various appointments, generally entry-level imports.

1960s-2024		$300	$500

Fullerton Series

1995-2000. Various models with different appointments and configurations based on the classic offset double-cut soldibody.

1995-2000		$700	$1,200

Herb Ellis (PE-175/FA-DLX)

1978-1987 (Model PE-175) and 1988-1993 (Model FA-DLX). Archtop hollowbody, ebony 'board, 2 humbuckers.

1978-1993		$1,200	$1,800

Solidbody

1960s-present. Various models, various appointments, generally mid-level imports.

1960s-2024		$500	$1,200

Titan Artist (TA) Series

1967-2012. Double cut, semi-hollow bodies, 2 pickups, various models.

1967-2012		$900	$1,500

Aristides

2010-present. Dutch engineer Aristides Poort developed the material (arium) used to build production/custom, premium grade, solidbody electric guitars in the Netherlands. They also build basses.

ARK - New Era Guitars

2006-present. Luthier A. R. Klassen builds his professional and premium grade, production/custom, reproductions of vintage Larson Brothers instruments in Chesterton, Indiana.

Armstrong, Rob

Custom steel- and nylon-string flat-tops, 12 strings, and parlor guitars made in Coventry, U.K. by luthier Rob Armstrong, starting in 1971. He also builds mandolins and basses.

Arpeggio Korina

1995-present. Professional, premium and presentation grade, production/custom, korina wood solidbody guitars built by luthier Ron Kayfield in Pennsylvania.

Art & Lutherie

Budget and intermediate grade, production, steel- and nylon-string acoustic and acoustic/electric guitars. Founded by luthier Robert Godin, who also has the Norman, Godin, Seagull, and Patrick & Simon brands of instruments.

Artesano

Intermediate and professional grade, production, classical guitars built in Valencia, Spain, and distributed by Juan Orozco. Orozco also made higher-end classical Orozco Models 8, 10 and 15.

Artinger Custom Guitars

1997-present. Luthier Matt Artinger builds his professional and premium grade, production/custom, hollow, semi-hollow, and chambered solidbody guitars and basses in Emmaus, Pennsylvania.

Artur Lang

1949-1975. German luthier Artur Lang is best known for his archtops but did build classicals early on. His was a small shop and much of his output was custom ordered. The instruments were mostly unbranded, but some had L.A. engraved on the headstock.

Asama

1970s-1980s. Some models of this Japanese line of solidbody guitars featured built-in effects. They also offered basses, effects, drum machines and other music products.

Ashborn

1848-1864. James Ashborn, of Wolcottville, Connecticut, operated one of the largest guitar making factories of the mid-1800s. Models were small parlor-sized instruments with ladder bracing and gut strings. Most of these guitars will need repair. Often of more interest as historical artifacts or museum pieces versus guitar collections.

Model 2

1848-1864. Flat-top, plain appointments, no position markers on the neck, identified by Model number.

1855	Fully repaired	$600	$1,000

Model 5

1848-1864. Flat-top, higher appointments.

1855	Fully repaired	$1,200	$1,500

Asher

1982-present. Luthier Bill Asher builds his professional grade, production/custom, solidbody electric guitars in Venice, California. He also builds lap steels.

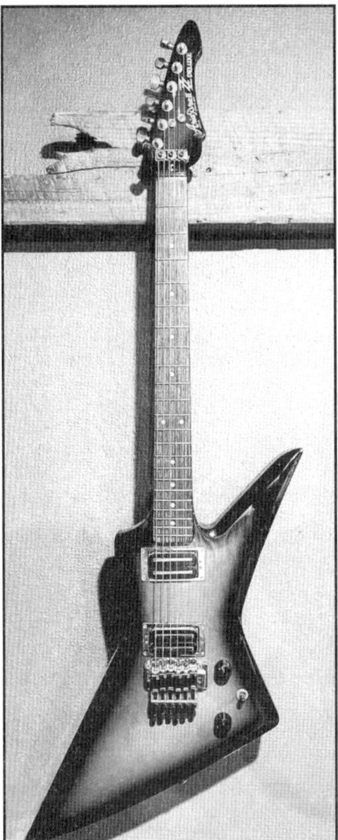

1984 Aria Pro II ZZ Deluxe

Kris Fox

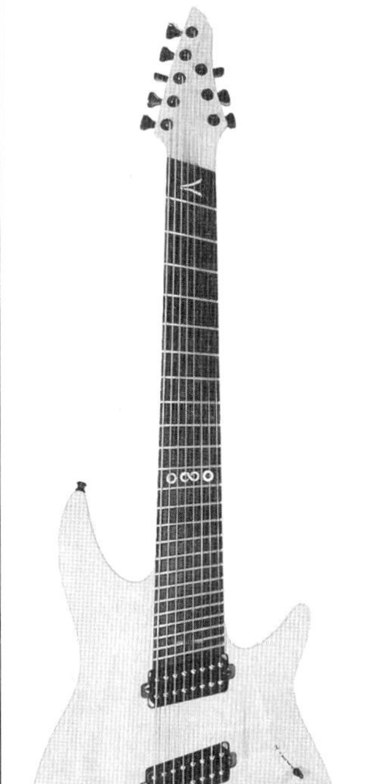

Aristides 080s

GUITARS

Avalon (Ireland)
Auditorium Performer

B.C. Rich Assassin
Imaged by Heritage Auctions, HA.com

MODEL YEAR	FEATURES	EXC. COND. LOW	HIGH

Ashland

Intermediate grade, production, acoustic and acoustic/electric guitars made by Korea's Crafter Guitars.

Astro

1963-1964. The Astro AS-51 was a 1 pickup kit guitar sold by Rickenbacker. German luthier Arthur Strohmer also built archtops bearing this name.

Asturias

Professional and premium grade, production, classical guitars built on Kyushu Island, in Japan.

Atkin Guitars

1995-present. Luthier Alister Atkin builds his production/custom steel and nylon string flat-tops in Canterbury, U.K. He also builds mandolins.

Atlas

Archtop guitars, and possibly other types, built in East Germany and by Zero Sette in Italy.

Atomic

2006-present. Production/custom, intermediate and professional grade, solidbody electric guitars and basses built by luthiers Tim Mulqueeny and Harry Howard in Peoria, Arizona.

Audiovox

Ca. 1935-ca. 1950. Paul Tutmarc's Audiovox Manufacturing, of Seattle, Washington, was a pioneer in electric lap steels, basses, guitars and amps. Tutmarc was a talented Hawaiian steel guitarist and ran a music school and is credited with inventing the electric bass guitar in '35, which his company started selling in the late '30s.

Austin

1999-present. Budget and intermediate grade, production, acoustic, acoustic/electric, resonator, and electric guitars, basses, amps, mandolins, ukes and banjos imported by St. Louis Music.

Acoustic Flat-Top

1999-2024	Various models	$200	$300

Solidbody Electric

1999-2024	Various models	$300	$500

Austin Hatchet

Mid-1970s-mid-1980s. Trademark of distributor Targ and Dinner, Chicago, Illinois.

Hatchet

1981. Travel guitar.

1981		$400	$600

Solidbody Electric

1970s-1980s. Various classic designs.

1970s-80s		$350	$600

Avalon

1920s. Instruments built by the Oscar Schmidt Co. and possibly others. Most likely a brand made for a distributor.

MODEL YEAR	FEATURES	EXC. COND. LOW	HIGH

Avalon (Ireland)

2002-present. Luthiers Stevie Graham, Mark Lyttle, Ernie McMillan, Balazs Prohaszka and Robin Thompson build premium and presentation grade, production/custom, steel-string and classical, acoustic and electro-acoustic guitars in Northern Ireland. In '04-'05 their Silver series was imported from South Korea, and '05 the Gold series from Czech Republic.

Avante

1997-2007. Intermediate grade, production, imported sharp cutaway acoustic baritone guitars designed by Joe Veillette and Michael Tobias and offered by MusicYo. Originally higher priced instruments offered by Alvarez, there was the baritone, a 6-string and a bass.

AV-2 Baritone

1997-2007. Baritone guitar tuned B to B, solid spruce cutaway top, mahogany sides and back.

1997-2007		$500	$800

Avanti

1964-late 1960s. Italian-made guitar brand imported by European Crafts, of Los Angeles. Earlier models were plastic covered; later ones had paint finishes.

Electric Solidbody

1960s. Solidbody, 3 single-coils, dot markers.

1960s		$400	$600

Avar

Late-1960s. Import copy models from Japan, not unlike Teisco, for the U.S. student market.

Solidbody Electric

1969		$400	$600

Aztec

1970s. Japanese-made copy guitars imported into Germany by Hopf.

B.C. Rich

Ca. 1966/67-present. Budget, intermediate, and premium grade, production/custom, import and U.S.-made, electric and acoustic guitars. They also offer basses. Founded by Bernardo Chavez Rico in Los Angeles, California. As a boy he worked for his guitar-maker father Bernardo Mason Rico (Valencian Guitar Shop, Casa Rico, Bernardo's Guitar Shop), building first koa ukes and later, guitars, steel guitars and Martin 12-string conversions. He started using the BC Rich name ca. '66-'67 and made about 300 acoustics until '68, when first solidbody electric made using a Fender neck.

Rich's early models were based on Gibson and Fender designs. The first production instruments were in '69 with 10 fancy Gibson EB-3 bass and 10 matching Les Paul copies, all carved out of single block of mahogany. Early guitars with Gibson humbuckers, then Guild humbuckers, and, from '74-'86, DiMarzio humbuckers. Around 150 BC

MODEL YEAR	FEATURES	EXC. COND. LOW	HIGH

Rich Eagles were imported from Japan in '76. Ca. '76 or '77 some bolt-neck guitars with parts made by Wayne Charvel were offered. Acoustic production ended in '82 (acoustics were again offered in '95).

For '83-'86 the BC Rich N.J. Series (N.J. Nagoya, Japan) was built by Masan Tarada. U.S. Production Series (U.S.-assembled Korean kits) in '84. From '86 on, the N.J. Series was made by Cort in Korea. Korean Rave and Platinum series began around '86. In '87, Rich agreed to let Class Axe of New Jersey market the Korean Rave, Platinum and N.J. Series. Class Axe (with Neal Moser) introduces Virgin in '87 and in '88 Rave and Platinum names are licensed to Class Axe. In '89, Rico licensed the BC Rich name to Class Axe. Both imported and American-made BC Riches are offered during Class Axe management. In 2000, BC Rich became a division of Hanser Music Group.

During '90-'91, Rico begins making his upscale Mason Bernard guitars (approx. 225 made). In '94, Rico resumed making BC Rich guitars in California. He died in 1999.

First 340-360 U.S.-built guitars were numbered sequentially beginning in '72. In '74, serial numbers change to YYZZZ pattern (year plus consecutive production). As production increased in the late-'70s, the year number began getting ahead of itself. By '80 it was 2 years ahead; by '81 as much as 4 years ahead. No serial number codes on imports.

The American B.C. Rich company was first and foremost a custom shop, therefore surprising variants are possible for the models described below, especially in the early years of the company. Many of the first models were offered as either a Standard (also called Deluxe) model or as an upgrade called the Supreme model (technically speaking the Supreme model only applied to the Mockingbird, Eagle, Bich, and Wave).

The prime collector's market for B.C. Rich is the '72-'85 era. The Seagull, Eagle, Mockingbird, Bich, and Wave models are the true vintage models from that '72-'85 epoch. Pre-1985 BC Rich Standard Finishes were Natural, Gloss White, Black, Competition Red, Medium Blue, Metallic Red, and Cherry. Any other finish would be a Custom Color. Most custom colors started appearing in late 1978. Prior to '78, guitars had two tone transparent burst finishes, natural finishes and occasional one-color paint schemes. Custom Color finishes are worth 10% more than standard finish colors.

Assassin

1986-1998, 2000-2010. Double-cut body, 2 humbuckers, maple thru-neck dot markers, various colors.

1986-1989	1st Rico era	$900	$1,300
1989-1993	Class Axe era	$900	$1,300
1994-1998	2nd Rico era USA	$600	$900
2000-2010	Includes QX & PX	$300	$500

B-28 Acoustic

Ca.1967-1982. Acoustic flat-top, hand-built, herringbone trim, pearl R headstock logo.

1967-1982		$1,800	$2,800

B-30 Acoustic

Ca.1967-1982. Acoustic flat-top.

1967-1982		$1,800	$2,800

B-38 Acoustic

Ca.1967-1982. Acoustic flat-top, herringbone trim.

1967-1982		$1,800	$2,800

B-41 Acoustic

1970s. Acoustic flat-top.

1970s		$2,000	$3,000

B-45 Acoustic

1970s. Hand-built, D-style acoustic flat-top.

1970s		$2,500	$3,800

Beast (U.S.A. Custom Shop)

1999-2015. Exaggerated four point cutaway body, flamed or quilted top.

1999-2015		$1,200	$2,000

Bich 6-String (U.S.A. Assembly)

1980-1998. Four-point sleek body, came in Standard top or Supreme with highly figured maple body and active EQ.

1980-1985	Standard/Deluxe	$4,500	$6,000
1986-1988	Standard/Deluxe	$2,000	$2,500
1988	Supreme	$3,500	$4,500
1989-1993	Class Axe era	$2,000	$2,500
1994-1998	2nd Rico era USA	$2,000	$2,500

Bich 10-String

1977-2015. U.S.-made, doubles on 4 low strings.

1977-1982	Koa	$8,500	$12,000
1977-1982	Opaque finish	$7,000	$8,500
1978-1982	Highly flamed	$8,500	$10,000
1985	Highly quilted	$7,000	$9,000
2005-2015	Highly quilted	$6,500	$8,500

Black Hole

1988. Bolt neck, rosewood 'board, integrated pickup design, Floyd Rose.

1988		$600	$900

Body Art Collection

2003-2006. Imports, 'Body Art Collection' headstock logo, different graphics/different models issued each month from January '03 to March '04, 25th Anniversary model available into '06.

2003-2006	Various models	$400	$600

Bronze Series

2001-2007. Made in China. Includes 2 models: Mockingbird and Warlock.

2001-2007		$100	$250

Doubleneck

1980-1988. Doublenecks were sporadically made, specs (and values) may vary.

1980-1988	Bich	$12,000	$15,000
1980-1988	Eagle	$12,000	$15,000
1980-1988	Iron Bird	$10,000	$12,500
1980-1988	Mockingbird	$12,000	$15,000
1980-1988	Seagull	$12,000	$15,000

Eagle

1975-1982, 2000-2004. Made in USA, often called the Eagle model, but also called Eagle Deluxe or Eagle Standard, features include diamond inlays, unbound rosewood fretboard, 3-on-a-side tuners, generally solid mahogany body, some rare examples with maple body or other woods, some with runners or stringers

1982 B.C. Rich Bich

Erik Van Gansen

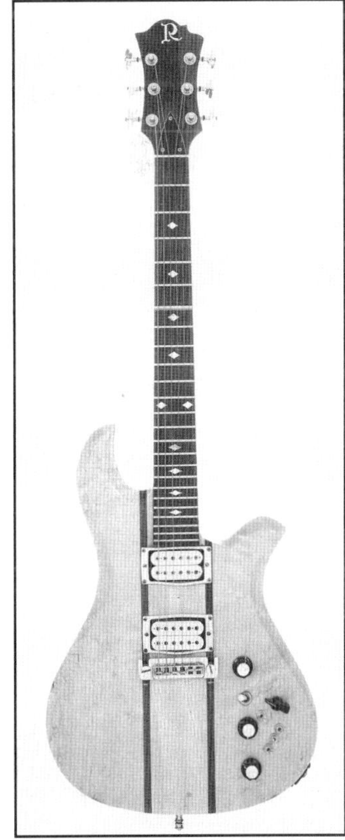

1978 B.C. Rich Eagle

Imaged by Heritage Auctions, HA.com

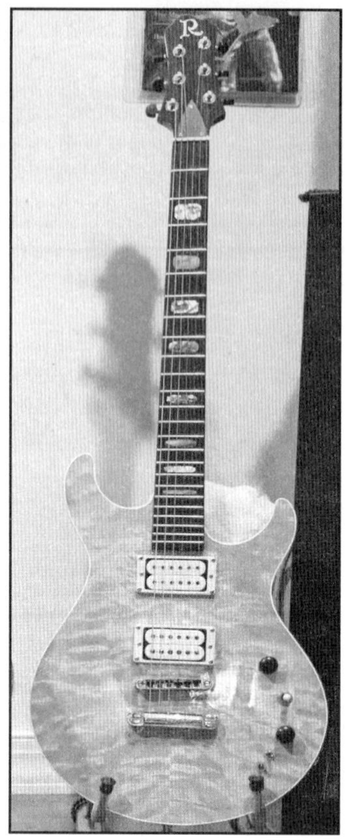

2001 B.C. Rich Exclusive EM I

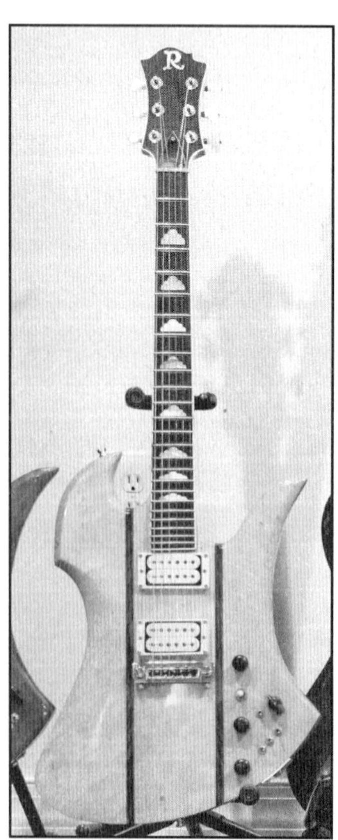

1979 B.C. Rich Mockingbird Supreme

MODEL YEAR	FEATURES	EXC. COND. LOW	HIGH

of alternate exotic wood. (See additional notes in the Eagle Supreme listing.)

1975-1982		$4,000	$6,000

Eagle Special (U.S.A.)

1977-1982. A variant of the Eagle with even more switches and electronic options, the extra options are not particularly considered an advantage in the BC Rich collector community, therefore an Eagle Special is worth less than the Standard or Eagle Supreme.

1977-1982		$4,500	$6,000

Eagle Supreme

1975-1982, 2000-2004. Made in USA, Eagle body style with specific options including cloud inlays, fully bound ebony fretboard, 3-on-a-side headstock, various woods including solid koa, maple, highly-figured maple (birdseye, quilted, curly), other exotic woods offered, most with runners or stringers of alternating wood, also available as single solid wood, mid-'80s with original Kahler tremolo unit option, custom colors and sunburst finishes generally on a custom order basis, certain custom colors are worth more than the values shown, early models ca. '75-'82 had a Leo Quan Badass bridge option and those models are highly favored by collectors, early style control knobs with silver metal inserts, full electronics with Varitone and PreAmp and Grover Imperial bullseye tuners, the earliest models had red head mini-switches (later became silver-chrome switches).

1975-1982		$6,500	$8,500
2000-2004		$4,000	$5,000

Eagle Supreme Condor

1983-1987. Less than 50 made, simplified electronics system based on customer's requests, features can include cloud inlays, fully bound ebony fretboard neck, bound 3-on-a-side headstock, book matched figured maple top over solid mahogany body with slight arch, no runners or stringers, basic electronics with master volume, master tone, and pickup switch, also commonly called Condor Supreme.

1983-1987		$2,500	$3,500

Elvira

2001. Elvira (the witch) photo on black Warlock body, came with Casecore coffin case.

2001		$500	$800

Exclusive EM I

1996-2004. Platinum Series, offset double-cut, bound top, 2 humbuckers.

1996-2004		$250	$400

Gunslinger

1987-1999. Inverted headstock, 1 (Gunslinger I) or 2 (Gunslinger II) humbuckers, recessed cutout behind Floyd Rose allows player to pull notes up 2 full steps.

1987-1989	Graphic designs	$1,000	$1,500
1987-1989	Standard finish	$1,000	$1,500
1989-1993	Class Axe era	$650	$1,000
1994-1999	2nd Rico era, bolt-on	$600	$900
1994-1999	2nd Rico era, neck-thru	$600	$900

MODEL YEAR	FEATURES	EXC. COND. LOW	HIGH

Ironbird

1983-2004. Pointy body and headstock.

1983-1989		$1,500	$2,500
1989-1993	Class Axe era	$1,000	$2,000
1994-1998	2nd Rico era	$1,000	$2,000

Kerry King Wartribe 1 Warlock

2004-2015. Tribal Fire finish, 2 pickups.

2004-2015		$200	$300

Mockingbird

1976-present. Made in USA, also called the Mockingbird Standard or Mockingbird Deluxe, diamond inlays, unbound rosewood 'board, solid mahogany body, rare examples with maple body or other woods, some with runners or stringers of alternate exotic wood. In 2016 'Mk' was added to name (Mk1, Mk3, Mk5, Mk7, Mk9, Mk11). (See additional notes in the Mockingbird Supreme listing.)

1976		$4,000	$5,500
1977-1978	Short horn	$4,000	$5,500
1979-1983	Long horn	$4,000	$5,500
1984		$3,750	$5,000
1985		$3,750	$5,000
1986-1989	Last of 1st Rico era	$2,750	$3,750
1989-1993	Class Axe era	$2,750	$3,750
1994-1999	2nd Rico era, bolt-on	$2,250	$3,250
2000-2024	Custom Shop (COA)	$4,000	$5,000

Mockingbird Ice Acrylic

2004-2006. See-thru acrylic body.

2004-2006		$400	$600

Mockingbird Legacy

2019-present. Mahogany body, koa or quilted maple top, 2 humbucker pickups, Floyd Rose or STQ hardtail, various colors.

2019-2024		$800	$1,200

Mockingbird Supreme

1976-1989. Made in USA, Mockingbird body style with options including cloud inlays, fully bound ebony fretboard, 3-on-a-side headstock, various woods including solid koa, maple, highly-figured maple (birdseye, quilted, curly), other exotic woods offered, most with runners or stringers of alternating wood, also available as single solid wood, mid-'80s with original Kahler trem option, custom colors and sunburst finishes generally on a custom order basis, certain custom colors are worth more than the values shown, early models ca. '76-'82 had a Leo Quan Badass bridge option and those models are highly favored by collectors, early style control knobs with silver metal inserts, full electronics with Varitone and PreAmp and Grover Imperial bullseye tuners, the earliest models had red head mini-switches (later became silver-chrome switches).

1976-1978	Earlier short horn	$5,500	$7,500
1976-1978	Short horn	$5,500	$7,500
1979-1982	Later long horn	$5,500	$7,500
1983-1985		$4,000	$5,500
1986-1989		$4,000	$5,250
1989-1993	Class Axe era	$3,750	$5,000
1994-1999	2nd Rico era	$3,500	$4,500

MODEL YEAR	FEATURES	EXC. COND. LOW	HIGH

Nighthawk

1978-ca.1982. Eagle-shaped body with bolt neck.

1978-1982		$1,000	$1,500

NJ Series/NJC Series

1983-2006. Earlier models made in Japan. Made in Korea '86 forward. All NJ models fall within the same price range. Models include Assassin, Beast, Bich, Ironbird, Eagle, Mockingbird, Outlaw, ST III, Virgin, Warlock. C for Classic added in '06.

1983-1984	Early NJ Japan	$600	$1,000
1985-1986	Later Japan	$500	$900
1987-2006	Made in Korea	$500	$900

Phoenix

1977-ca.1982. Mockingbird-shaped with bolt neck.

1977-1982		$1,000	$2,000

Platinum Series

1986-2006. Lower-priced import versions including Assassin, Beast, Bich, Ironbird, ST, Warlock.

1986-2006		$300	$600

Rave Series

1986-ca. 1990. Korean-made down-market versions of popular models.

1986-1990		$400	$700

Seagull

1972-1975. Single-cut solidbody, neck-thru, 2 humbuckers.

1972-1973	Earliest, 30 made	$4,500	$7,000
1973-1974		$3,500	$5,000
1975		$3,000	$4,500

Seagull II

1974-1977. Double-cut solidbody, neck-thru, 2 humbuckers. Transitional model in '75 between Seagull and Eagle, Seagull Jr. is used interchangable with Seagull II, the company made several variants during this period which some collectors consider to be Seagull Jr. while others consider to be Seagull II. The II/Jr. design was finally changed and called the Eagle.

1974	1st 50, Gibson pus	$4,500	$6,000
1974	Moser, 16 made	$4,500	$8,500
1974	Other from '74	$3,500	$5,000
1976-1977		$3,000	$4,500

Seagull II/Seagull Jr.

1975-1977. Another transitional model starting in '75, the model name Seagull Jr. is used interchangable with Seagull II, the company made several variants during this period which some collectors consider to be Seagull Jr. while others consider to be Seagull II. The design was finally changed and called the Eagle.

1975-1977	II and Jr	$2,800	$4,000

Stealth I Series

1983-1989. Includes Standard (maple body, diamond inlays) and Series II (mahogany body, dot inlays), 2 pickups.

1983-1989	Series II	$2,000	$3,000
1983-1989	Standard	$1,500	$2,500

ST-III (U.S.A.)

1987-1998. Double-cut solidbody, hum/single/single or 2 humbucker pickups, Kahler tremolo.

1987-1989	Bolt-on	$800	$1,200
1987-1989	Neck-thru	$850	$1,300
1989-1993	Class Axe era	$800	$1,200
1994-1998	New Rico era	$800	$1,200

The Mag

2000. U.S. Handcrafted Series Mockingbird Acoustic Supreme, solid spruce top, quilt maple back and sides, pickup with preamp and EQ optional, dark sunburst.

2000		$800	$1,200

Warlock/Warlock Standard

1981-present. Made in the USA, also called Warlock Standard, 4-point sleek body style with widow headstock. In 2016 'Mk' was added to name (Mk1, Mk3, Mk5, Mk7, Mk9, Mk11).

1981-1989	Standard	$3,000	$4,000
1990-1999	2nd Rico era, bolt-on	$1,800	$2,800
1990-1999	2nd Rico era, neck-thru	$2,000	$3,000

Warlock Extreme

2019-present. Mahogany body, spalted maple and quilted maple top, 2 humbucker pickups, Floyd Rose, various colors.

2019-2024		$1,200	$1,800

Warlock Ice Acrylic

2004-2006. See-thru acrylic body.

2004-2006		$400	$600

Wave

1983. U.S.-made, very limited production based upon the Wave bass.

1983		$8,000	$10,000

B.C. Rico

1978-1982. B.C. Rich's first Japan-made guitars were labeled B.C. Rico until they were sued for patent infringement on the Rico name. They made around 200 guitars and basses with the Rico headstock logo. After '82, B.C. Rich offered the NJ Series (Import) models.

Eagle

1978-1982. All mahogany, rosewood 'board, Dimarzio pickups, mother-of-pearl headstock logo.

1978-1982		$2,500	$4,000

Mockingbird

1978-1982. All mahogany, rosewood 'board, Dual DiMarzio humbuckers.

1978-1982		$2,500	$4,000

RW-2A

1978-1982. Acoustic D-style, Brazilian rosewood laminate body, spruce top, herringbone trim, natural finish.

1978-1982		$1,000	$1,500

RW-7

1978-1982. D-style, spruce top, Brazilian rosewood back and sides, abalone markers, natural finish.

1978-1982		$1,000	$1,500

b3 Guitars

2004-present. Premium grade, custom/production, solid, chambered and hollow-body guitars built by luthier Gene Baker in Arroyo Grande, California. He previously made Baker U.S.A. guitars.

1983 BC Rich Warlock

Imaged by Heritage Auctions, HA.com

b3 Phoenix

GUITARS

Babicz Identity Series Dreadnought

1967 Baldwin Model 706 V

Rivington Guitars

MODEL YEAR	FEATURES	EXC. COND. LOW	HIGH

Babicz

2004-present. Started by luthier Jeff Babicz and Jeff Carano, who worked together at Steinberger, the company offers intermediate, professional, and premium grade, production/custom, acoustic and acoustic/electric guitars made in Poughkeepsie, New York, and overseas.

Bacon & Day

Established in 1921 by David Day and Paul Bacon, primarily known for fine quality tenor and plectrum banjos in the '20s and '30s. Purchased by Gretsch ca. '40.

Belmont

1950s. Gretsch era, 2 DeArmond pickups, natural.

1950s		$1,200	$1,800

Flat-Top

1930s-1940s. Large B&D headstock logo, fancy or plain appointments.

1930s	Fancy	$2,500	$3,500
1930s	Plain	$1,500	$2,500
1940s	Fancy	$2,000	$3,000
1940s	Plain	$1,500	$2,500

Ramona Archtop

1938-1940. Sunburst.

1938-1940		$1,200	$1,800

Senorita Archtop

1940. Lower-end, sunburst, mahogany back and sides.

1940		$1,800	$3,000

Silver Bell Style 1 Guitar Banjo (Bacon)

1920s. F-hole flange.

1920s		$3,000	$4,500

Style B Guitar Banjo (Bacon)

1920s. Banjo-resonator body with 6-string guitar neck.

1920s		$1,500	$3,000

Sultana I

1930s. Large 18 1/4" acoustic archtop, Sultana engraved on tailpiece, block markers, bound top and back, sunburst.

1938		$3,500	$5,500

Baden

Founded in 2006, by T.J. Baden, a former vice president of sales and marketing at Taylor guitars, initial production based on six models built in Vietnam, intermediate retail-price grade.

Baker U.S.A.

1997-present. Professional and premium grade, production/custom, solidbody electric guitars. Established by master builder Gene Baker after working at the Custom Shops of Gibson and Fender, Baker produced solid- and hollowbody guitars in Santa Maria, California. They also built basses. Baker also produced the Mean Gene brand of guitars from '88-'90. In September '03, the company was liquidated and the Baker U.S.A. name was sold to Ed Roman. Gene Baker currently builds b3 Guitars.

MODEL YEAR FEATURES EXC. COND. LOW HIGH

Baldwin

1965-1970. Founded in 1862, in Cincinnati, when reed organ and violin teacher Dwight Hamilton Baldwin opened a music store that eventually became one of the largest piano retailers in the Midwest. By 1965, the Baldwin Piano and Organ company was ready to buy into the guitar market but was outbid by CBS for Fender. Baldwin did procure Burns of London in September '65 and sold the guitars in the U.S. under the Baldwin name. Baldwin purchased Gretsch in '67. English production of Baldwin guitars ends in '70, after which Baldwin concentrates on the Gretsch brand.

Baby Bison (Model 560)

1965-1970. Double-cut solidbody, V headstock, 2 pickups, shorter scale, tremolo, black, red or white finishes.

1965-1966		$1,200	$1,800
1966-1970	Model 560	$1,000	$1,500

Bison (Model 511)

1965-1970. Double-cut solidbody, scroll headstock, 3 pickups, tremolo, black or white finishes.

1965-1966		$2,000	$2,500
1966-1970	Model 511	$1,500	$2,000

Double Six (Model 525)

1965-1970. Offset double-cut solidbody, 12 strings, 3 pickups, green or red sunburst.

1965-1966		$2,000	$2,500
1966-1970	Model 525	$2,000	$2,500

G.B. 65

1965-1966. Baldwin's first acoustic/electric, single-cut D-style flat-top, dual bar pickups.

1965-1966		$1,000	$1,500

G.B. 66 De Luxe

1965-1966. Same as Standard with added density control on treble horn, golden sunburst.

1965-1966		$1,200	$1,800

G.B. 66 Standard

1965-1966. Thinline Electric archtop, dual Ultra-Sonic pickups, offset cutaways, red sunburst.

1965-1966		$1,000	$1,500

Jazz Split Sound/Split Sound (Model 503)

1965-1970. Offset double-cut solidbody, scroll headstock, 3 pickups, tremolo, red sunburst or solid colors.

1965-1966		$1,200	$1,800
1966-1970	Model 503	$1,000	$1,500

Marvin (Model 524)

1965-1970. Offset double-cut solidbody, scroll headstock, 3 pickups, tremolo, white or brown finish.

1965-1966		$1,800	$2,200
1966-1970	Model 524	$1,800	$2,200

Model 706

1967-1970. Double-cut semi-hollowbody, scroll headstock, 2 pickups, 2 f-holes, no vibrato, red or golden sunburst.

1967-1970		$1,000	$1,500

Model 706V

1967-1970. Model 706 with vibrato.

1967-1970		$1,000	$1,500

GUITARS

MODEL YEAR | FEATURES | EXC. COND. LOW | HIGH

Model 712R Electric XII

1967-1970. Double-cut semi-hollow body with regular neck, red or gold sunburst.

1967-1970 $800 $1,200

Model 712T Electric XII

1967-1970. Model 712 with thin neck, red or gold sunburst.

1967-1970 $800 $1,200

Model 801CP Electric Classical

1968-1970. Grand concert-sized classical with transducer based pickup system, natural pumpkin finish.

1968-1970 $800 $1,200

Nu-Sonic

1965-1966. Solidbody electric student model, 6-on-a-side tuners, black or cherry finish.

1965-1966 $800 $1,200

Vibraslim (Model 548)

1965-1970. Double-cut semi-hollowbody, 2 pickups, vibrato, 2 f-holes, red or golden sunburst. Notable spec changes with Model 548 in '66.

1965-1966 $1,200 $1,800

1966-1970 Model 548 $1,000 $1,500

Virginian (Model 550)

1965-1970. Single-cut flat-top, 2 pickups (1 on each side of soundhole), scroll headstock, tremolo, natural.

1965-1966 $1,000 $1,500

1966-1970 Model 550 $1,000 $1,500

Ballurio

Luthier Keith Ballurio builds his intermediate, professional, and premium grade, production/custom, solidbody and chambered guitars in Manassas, Virginia, starting in 2000.

Baltimore

2007-2008. Budget grade, production, solidbody electric guitars imported by The Music Link.

Bambu

1970s. Short-lived brand name on a line of guitars built by Japan's Chushin Gakki Co., which also built models for several other manufacturers.

Baranik Guitars

1995-present. Premium grade, production/custom steel-string flat-tops made in Tempe, Arizona by luthier Mike Baranik.

Barclay

1960s. Thinline acoustic/electric archtops, solidbody electric guitars and basses imported from Japan. Generally shorter scale beginner guitars.

Electric Solidbody

1960s. Various models and colors.

1960s $300 $500

Barcus-Berry

Founded by John Berry and Les Barcus, in 1964, introducing the first piezo crystal transducer. Martin guitar/Barcus-Berry products were offered in the mid-'80s. They also offered a line of amps from around '76 to ca. '80.

MODEL YEAR | FEATURES | EXC. COND. LOW | HIGH

Barrington

1988-1991. Imports offered by Barrington Guitar Werks, of Barrington, Illinois. Models included solidbody guitars and basses, archtop electrics, and acoustic flat-tops. Barrington Music Products is still in the music biz, offering LA saxophones and other products.

Acoustic/Electric

1988-1991. Acoustic/electric, flat-top single-cut with typical round soundhole, opaque white.

1988-1991 $200 $300

Solidbody

1988-ca 1991. Barrington's line of pointy headstock, double-cut solidbodies, black.

1988-1991 $200 $300

Bartell of California

1964-1969. Founded by Paul Barth (Magnatone) and Ted Peckles. Mosrite-inspired designs.

Double Neck

1967 $2,000 $5,000

Electric 12

1967. Mosrite-style body.

1967 $1,200 $2,500

Barth

1950s-1960s. Paul Barth was involved with many guitar companies including National, Rickenbacker, Magnatone and others. He also built instruments under his own brand in California, including guitars, lap steels and amps. Most will have either a Barth logo on plastic plate, or decal.

Mark VIII

1959. Double-cut solidbody, 2 pickups, dot markers, Barth headstock logo.

1959 $2,000 $3,000

Bartolini

1960s. European-made (likely Italian) guitars made for the Bartolini Accordion Company. Similar to Gemelli guitars, so most likely from the same manufacturer. Originally plastic covered, they switched to paint finishes by the mid '60s.

Solidbody

1960s $600 $1,200

Bashkin Guitars

1998-present. Luthier Michael Bashkin builds his premium grade, custom, steel-string acoustics in Fort Collins, Colorado.

Basone Guitars

1999-present. Luthier Chris Basaraba builds his custom, professional grade, solid and hollowbody electric guitars and basses in Vancouver, British Columbia.

Bauer, George

1894-1911. Luthier George Bauer built guitars, mandolins, and banjos in Philadelphia, Pennsylvania. He also built instruments with Samuel S. Stewart (S.S. Stewart).

Baranik

Bashkin The SJ

Bazzolo Guitarworks

Benedetto Bambino Elite

Baxendale

1974-present. Luthier Scott Baxendale builds his professional and premium grade, custom, steel-string acoustic and solidbody electric guitars in Athens, Georgia and previously in Colorado, Tennessee, and Texas.

Bay State

Ca.1890-ca.1910. Bay State was a trademark for Boston's John C. Haynes & Co. and offered guitars and banjos.

Parlor

1890-1910. Small parlor size, mahogany body with salt & pepper binding.

MODEL YEAR	FEATURES	EXC. COND. LOW	HIGH
1890-1910		$1,200	$2,000

Bazzolo Guitarworks

1983-2023. Luthier Thomas Bazzolo began building his premium grade, production/custom, classical and flat-top guitars in Lebanon, Connecticut and since 2008 in Sullivan, Maine. He retired in '23.

BC Kingston

1977-present. From 1977 to '96, luthier Brian Kingston built flat-top and semi-hollow acoustic guitars along with a few solidbodies. Presently he builds premium grade, production/custom, archtop jazz and semi-hollow guitars in Prince Edward Island, Canada.

Bear Creek Guitars

Luthier Bill Hardin worked for OMI Dobro and Santa Cruz Guitar before introducing his own line of professional and premium grade, custom-made Weissenborn-style guitars in 1995, made in Kula, Hawaii. He also builds ukes.

Beardsell Guitars

1996-present. Production/custom flat-tops, classical, and electric solidbody guitars built by luthier Allan Beardsell in Toronto, Ontario.

Beaulieu

2006-present. Luthier Hugues Beaulieu builds his production/custom, professional and premium grade, flat-top, flamenco and classical guitars in Pont-Rouge, Quebec.

Beauregard

1992-present. Luthier Mario Beauregard builds his premium and presentation grade, production/custom, flat-top, archtop and jazz guitars in Montreal, Quebec.

Bedell Guitars

1964-present. Intermediate and premium grade, production/custom, flat-top guitars built in Spirit Lake, Iowa and imported from China, designed by luthier Tom Bedell, Dan Mills and Sophia Yang. They also offer Great Divide Guitars and in 2010 acquired Breedlove.

Behringer

1989-present. The German professional audio products company added budget, production, solidbody guitars in '03, sold in amp/guitar packages. They also offer effects and amps.

Beltona

1990-present. Production/custom metal body resonator guitars made in New Zealand by Steve Evans and Bill Johnson. Beltona was originally located in England. They also build mandolins and ukes.

Beltone

1920s-1930s. Acoustic and resonator guitars made by others for New York City distributor Perlberg & Halpin. Martin did make a small number of instruments for Beltone, but most were student-grade models, most likely made by one of the big Chicago builders. They also made mandolins.

Archtop

MODEL YEAR	FEATURES	EXC. COND. LOW	HIGH
1920s-30s		$600	$900

Resonator Copy

1930s. Resonator copy but without a real resonator, rather just an aluminum plate on a wooden top, body mahogany plywood.

MODEL YEAR	FEATURES	EXC. COND. LOW	HIGH
1938		$800	$1,200

Beltone (Import)

1950s-1960s. Japan's Teisco made a variety of brands for others, including the Beltone line of guitars, basses and amps. Carvin sold some of these models in the late 1960s. Italy's Welson guitars also marketed marble and glitter-finished guitars in the U.S. under this brand.

Electric Solidbody

1960s. Japan, 4 pickups.

MODEL YEAR	FEATURES	EXC. COND. LOW	HIGH
1960s		$400	$600

Benedetto

1968-present. Premium and presentation grade, production/custom archtop and chambered solidbody guitars, built by luthier Robert Benedetto. He has also built a few violins and solidbodies. He was in East Stroudsburg, Pennsylvania, up to '99; in Riverview, Florida, for '00-'06; and in Savanah, Georgia, since '07. He is especially known for refining the 7-string guitar. From '99 to '06 he licensed the names of his standard models to Fender (see Benedetto FMIC); during that period, Benedetto only made special order instruments. In '06, Howard Paul joined Benedetto as President of the company to begin manufacturing a broader line of more affordable professional instruments.

Benedetto (FMIC)

1999-2006. Premium and presentation, production/custom, acoustic and electric archtops. From '99 to '06, Bob Benedetto had an agreement with Fender (FMIC) to build Benedetto guitars under his guidance and supervision. The guitars were originally built in the FMIC Guild Custom Shop in Nashville, and later in Fender's Corona, California, facility.

Benedict

1988-present. Founded by Roger Benedict who died unexpectantly in '94. The brand was purchased by luthier Bill Hager in late-'95. He builds professional and premium grade, production/custom, solid and semi-hollow body guitars and basses in Cedar, Minnesota.

Beneteau

1974-present. Custom, premium grade, classical, baritone and steel string acoustic guitars built first in Ottawa, Ontario, and since 1986 in St. Thomas, Ontario by luthier Marc Beneteau. He also builds ukuleles.

Bennett Music Labs

1998-2024. Custom guitars built by luthier Bruce Bennett, who helped design the first Warrior line of instruments with J.D. Lewis. He also built amps and Brown Sound effects and guitars for J. Backlund Designs. Bennett died December, 2024.

Bently

Ca.1985-1998. Student and intermediate grade copy style acoustic and electric guitars imported by St. Louis Music Supply. Includes the Series 10 electrics and the Songwriter acoustics (which have a double reversed B crown logo on the headstock). St. Louis Music replaced the Bently line with the Austin brand.

Berkowitz Guitars

1995-present. Luthier David D. Berkowitz builds his premium grade, custom/production, steel string and baritone guitars and basses in Washington, D.C.

Bernie Rico Jr. Guitars

Professional and premium grade, production/custom, solidbody electrics guitars and basses built by luther Bernie Rico, Jr., the son of B.C. Rich founder, in Hesperia, California.

Bertoncini Stringed Instruments

Luthier Dave Bertoncini began building in 1995, premium grade, custom, flat-top guitars in Olympia, Washington. He has also built solidbody electrics, archtops, mandolins, and ukuleles.

Beyond The Trees

1976-present. Luthier Fred Carlson offers a variety of innovative designs for his professional and presentation grade, production/custom 6- and 12-string flat-tops in Santa Cruz, California. He also produces the Sympitar (a 6-string with added sympathetic strings) and the Dreadnautilus (a unique shaped headless acoustic).

Big Lou Guitar

Mid-2010-present. Located in Perris, California, owner Louis Carroll imports his intermediate grade, production, electric guitars from China.

MODEL YEAR	FEATURES	EXC. COND. LOW	HIGH

Big Tex Guitars

Production/custom, professional grade, vintage-style replica guitars, started in 2000, built for owner Eric Danheim, by luthiers James Love, Mike Simon and Eddie Dale in Houston and Dripping Springs, Texas and Seattle, Washington.

Bigsby

1947-1965, 2002-present. Pedal steel guitars, hollow-chambered electric Spanish guitars, electric mandolins, doublenecks, replacement necks on acoustic guitars, hand vibratos, all handmade by Paul Arthur Bigsby, machinist and motorcycle enthusiast (designer of '30s Crocker motorcycles), in Downey, California. Initially built for special orders.

Bigsby was a pioneer in developing pedal steels. He designed a hand vibrato for Merle Travis. In '48, his neck-through hollow electrics (with Merle Travis) influenced Leo Fender, and Bigsby employed young Semie Moseley. In '56, he designed the Magnatone Mark series guitars and 1 Hawaiian lap steel. He built guitars up to '63.

He built less than 50 Spanish guitars, 6 mandolins, 70 to 150 pedal steels and 12 or so neck replacements. SN was stamped on the end of fingerboard: MMDDYY. In '65, the company was sold to Gibson president Ted McCarty who moved the tremolo/vibrato work to Kalamazoo. Bigsby died in '68. Fred Gretsch purchased the Bigsby company from Ted McCarty in '99 and sold it to Fender in 2019. A solidbody guitar and a pedal steel based upon the original Paul Bigsby designs were introduced in January 2002. These were modeled on the 1963 Bigsby catalog but look very similar to typical Bigsby solidbodys made in the early '50s. Early Bigsby guitars command high value on the collectible market and values here assume authentication by an industry expert.

Standard (Japan)

2007-2008. Various models made in Japan.

2007	Model BY-48N	$1,500	$2,500
2007	Model BY-50	$1,500	$2,500
2007	Model BYS-48	$1,500	$2,500

Standard Solidbody (Spanish)

Late-1940s-1950s, 2002. Standard Guitar, solidbody, natural. Reissue offered in '02.

1948		$250,000	$450,000
1949		$250,000	$450,000
1950-1956		$250,000	$450,000
2002	Reissue	$2,500	$4,000

Bil Mitchell Guitars

1979-present. Luthier Bil Mitchell builds his professional and premium grade, production/custom, flat-top and archtop guitars originally in Wall, New Jersey, and since '02 in Riegelsville, Pennsylvania.

Bill Foley Fine Instruments

2012-present. Luthiers Bill Foley, his son Sam, and Brad Lewis build professional and premium grade, custom electric guitars and basses in Columbus, Ohio.

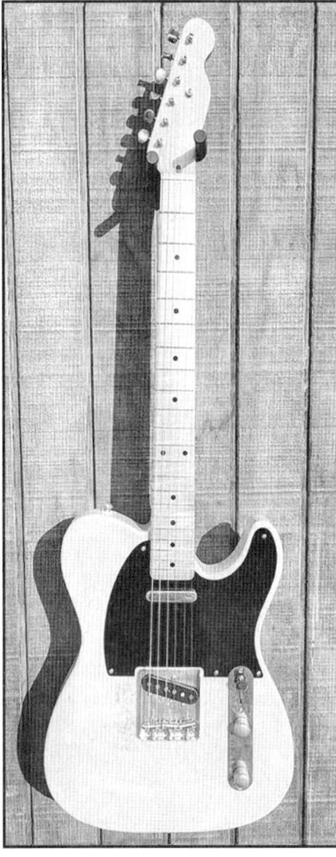

Bennett Music Labs

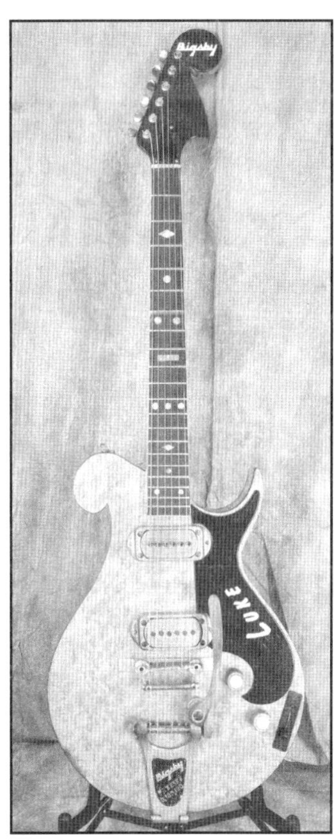

1956 Bigsby Luke Standard

Bilt ESG

Bischoff 9-String

MODEL YEAR	FEATURES	EXC. COND. LOW	HIGH

Bilt Guitars

2010-present. Professional grade, production/custom, solidbody and semi-hollowbody electric guitars built in Des Moines, Iowa by luthiers Bill Henss and Tim Thelen.

Birdsong Guitars

2001-present. Luthiers Scott Beckwith and Jamie Hornbuckle build their professional grade, production/custom, solidbody guitars and basses in Wimberley, Texas.

Bischoff Guitars

1975-present. Professional and premium-grade, custom-made flat-tops built by luthier Gordy Bischoff in Eau Claire, Wisconsin.

Bishline

1985-present. Luthier Robert Bishline, of Tulsa, Oklahoma, mainly builds banjos, but did build flat-tops and resonators in the past, and still does occasionally.

Black Jack

1960s. Violin-body hollowbody electric guitars and basses, possibly others. Imported from Japan by unidentified distributor. Manufacturers unknown, but some may be Arai.

Blackbird

2006-present. Luthier Joe Luttwak builds his professional grade, production/custom, carbon fiber acoustic guitars in San Francisco, California. He also offers a uke.

Blackshear, Tom

1958-2023. Premium and presentation grade, production, classical and flamenco guitars made by luthier Tom Blackshear in San Antonio, Texas, until his death in '23.

Blade

1987-present. Intermediate and professional grade, production, solidbody guitars and basses from luthier Gary Levinson and his Levinson Music Products Ltd. located in Switzerland.

California Custom

1994-2010. California Standard with maple top and high-end appointments.

1994-2010	$1,200	$1,500

California Deluxe/Deluxe

1994-1995. Standard with mahogany body and maple top.

1994-1995	$800	$1,200

California Hybrid

1998-1999. Standard with piezo bridge pickup.

1998-1999	$600	$900

California Standard

1994-2007. Offset double-cut, swamp ash body, bolt neck, 5-way switch.

1994-2007	$600	$900

MODEL YEAR	FEATURES	EXC. COND. LOW	HIGH

R3

1988-1993. Offset double-cut maple solidbody, bolt maple neck, 3 single-coils or single/single/humbucker.

1988-1993	$800	$1,200

R4

1988-1993. R3 with ash body and see-thru color finishes.

1988-1992	$800	$1,200

Texas Series

2003-present. Includes Standard (3 single-coils) and Deluxe (gold hardware, single/single/hum pickups).

2003-2024 Deluxe	$700	$1,000
2003-2010 Special	$600	$900
2003-2023 Standard	$600	$900

Blanchard Guitars

1994-present. Luthier Mark Blanchard builds premium grade, custom steel-string, and classical guitars originally in Mammoth Lakes, California, and since May '03, in northwest Montana.

Blindworm Guitars

2008-present. Luthiers Andrew J. Scott and Steven Sells build premium and presentation grade, production/custom, acoustic, electric and electric-acoustic guitars, basses, mandolins, banjos and others in Colorado Springs, Colorado.

Blount

Professional and premium grade, production/custom, acoustic flat-top guitars built by luthier Kenneth H. Blount Jr. in Sebring, Florida. He started in 1985.

Blue Star

Luthier Bruce Herron began building production/custom guitars in 1984, in Fennville, Michigan. He also builds mandolins, lap steels, dulcimers and ukes.

Bluebird

1920s-1930s. Private brand with Bluebird painted on headstock, built by the Oscar Schmidt Co. and possibly others. Most likely made for distributor.

13" Flat-Top

1930s	$300	$600

Bluebird Guitars

2011-present. Luthiers Rob Bluebird and Gian Maria Camponeschi build premium grade, custom, archtop and solidbody guitars in Rome, Italy. They build production resonator guitars in Bali, Indonesia. They also offer basses and ukuleles.

Blueridge

Early 1980s-present. Intermediate and professional grade, production, solid-top acoustic guitars distributed by Saga. In '00, the product line was redesigned with the input of luthier Greg Rich (Rich and Taylor guitars).

MODEL YEAR	FEATURES	EXC. COND. LOW	HIGH

Bluesouth

1991-ca. 2006. Custom electric guitars built by luthier Ronnie Knight in Muscle Shoals, Alabama. He also built basses.

Boaz Elkayam Guitars

Presentation grade, custom steel, nylon, and flamenco guitars made by luthier Boaz Elkayam, starting in 1985, in Chatsworth, California.

Boedigheimer Instruments

2000-present. Luthier Brian Boedigheimer builds his professional and premium grade, production/custom, semi-hollowbody electric guitars in Red Wing, Minnesota.

Bohmann

1878-ca. 1926. Acoustic flat-top guitars, harp guitars, mandolins, banjos, violins made in Chicago Illinois, by Joseph Bohmann (born 1848, in Czechoslovakia). Bohmann's American Musical Industry founded 1878. Guitar body widths are 12", 13", 14", 15". He had 13 grades of guitars by 1900 (Standard, Concert, Grand Concert sizes). Early American use of plywood. Some painted wood finishes. Special amber-oil varnishes. Tuner bushings. Early ovalled fingerboards. Patented tuner plates and bridge design. Steel engraved label inside. Probably succeeded by son Joseph Frederick Bohmann.

Ca. 1896 12" body faux rosewood, 13", 14" and 15" body faux rosewood birch, 12", 13", 14" and 15" body sunburst maple, 12", 13", 14" and 15" body rosewood. By 1900 Styles 0, 1, 2 and 3 Standard, Concert and Grand Concert maple, Styles 1, 2, 3, 4, 5, 6, 7, 8, 9, 10, 11 and 12 in Standard, Concert, and Grand Concert rosewood.

14 3/4" Flat-Top

Solid spruce top, veneered Brazilian rosewood back and sides, wood marquetry around top and soundhole, natural. Each Bohmann should be valued on a case-by-case basis.

1896-1900	Brazilian	$1,800	$3,000
1896-1900	Other woods	$900	$1,500

Harp Guitar

1896-1899	All styles	$4,000	$8,000

Bolin

1978-present. Professional and premium grade, production/custom, solidbody guitars and basses built by luthier John Bolin in Boise, Idaho. Bolin is well-known for his custom work. His Cobra guitars are promoted and distributed by Sanderson Sales and Marketing as part of the Icons of America Series.

NS

1996-2011. Slot-headstock, bolt-on neck, single-cut solidbody, Seymour Duncan passive pickups or EMG active, from '96 to the fall of 2001 custom-built serial numbers to 0050 then from the fall of '01 to the present production model build starting with SN 0051.

1996-2001	Custom-built	$3,000	$4,500
2001-2011	Standard production	$1,000	$1,500

MODEL YEAR	FEATURES	EXC. COND. LOW	HIGH

Bolt

1988-1991. Founded by luthier Wayne Bolt and Jim Dala Pallu in Schnecksville, Pennsylvania, Bolt's first work was CNC machined OEM necks and bodies made for Kramer and BC Rich. In '90, they started building solidbody Bolt guitars, many with airbrushed graphics. Only about 100 to 125 were built, around 40 with graphics.

Bond

1984-1985. Andrew Bond made around 1,400 Electraglide guitars in Scotland. Logo says 'Bond Guitars, London'.

ElectraGlide

1984-1985. Black carbon graphite 1-piece body and neck, double-cut, 3 single-coils (2 humbuckers were also supposedly available), digital LED controls that required a separate transformer.

1984-1985	With attachments	$2,000	$3,000

Borges Guitars

2000-present. Luthier Julius Borges builds his premium grade, production/custom, acoustic guitars in Groton, Massachusetts.

Boucher

2005-present. Professional and premium grade, acoustic guitars built by luthier Robin Boucher in Quebec.

Boulder Creek Guitars

2007-present. Intermediate and professional grade, production, imported dreadnought, classical, and 12-string guitars, basses and ukes distributed by Morgan Hill Music of Morgan Hill, California.

Bourgeois

1993-1999, 2000-present. Luthier Dana Bourgeois builds his professional and premium grade, production/custom, acoustic and archtop guitars in Lewiston, Maine. Bourgeois co-founded Schoenberg guitars and built Schoenberg models from '86-'90. Bourgeois' 20th Anniversary model was issued in '97. Bourgeois Guitars, per se, went out of business at the end of '99. Patrick Theimer created Pantheon Guitars, which included 7 luthiers (including Bourgeois) working in an old 1840s textile mill in Lewiston, Maine and Bourgeois models continue to be made as part of the Pantheon organization.

A-500

Top-of-the-line acoustic cutaway archtop, natural.

1997		$4,500	$6,500

Blues

1996. D-style, all koa.

1996		$3,500	$4,000

Country Boy

1998-present. Pre-war D-style designed for Ricky Skaggs, Sitka spruce top, mahogany back and sides, Ricky Skaggs label, natural.

1998-2024		$2,500	$4,000

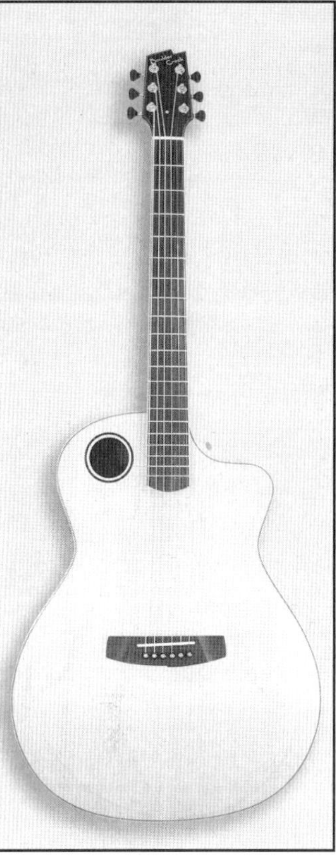

Boulder Creek Grand Auditorium

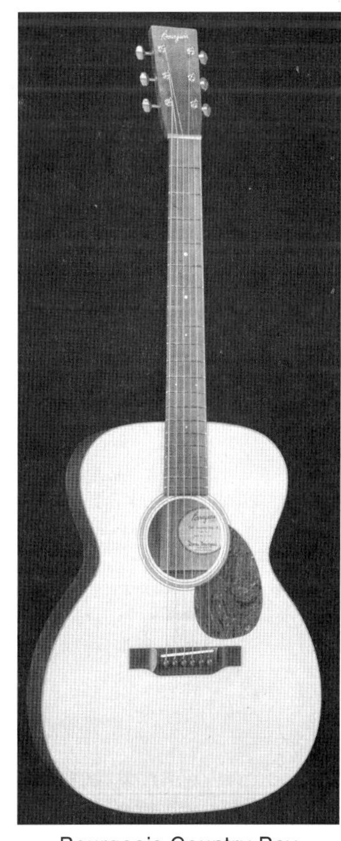

Bourgeois Country Boy

1998 Bourgeois OM
Tom Pfeifer

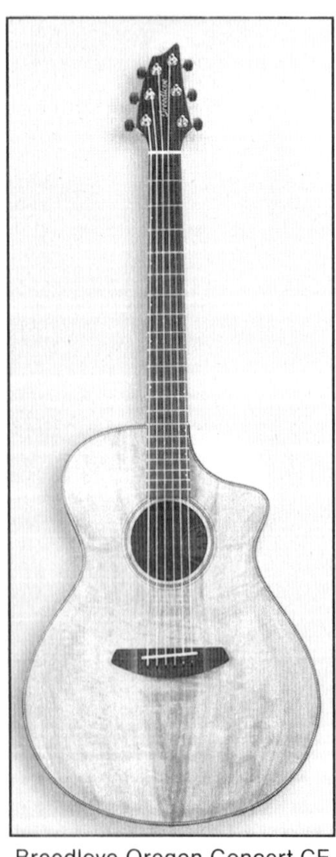
Breedlove Oregon Concert CE

MODEL YEAR	FEATURES	EXC. COND. LOW	HIGH

Country Boy Custom
1999-2016. Adirondack spruce top, figured mahogany back and sides.

1999-2016		$3,500	$4,500

Country Boy Deluxe
2003-2015. Country Boy with Adirondack spruce top, rosewood binding.

2003-2015		$3,500	$5,000

D - 20th Anniversary
1997. 20 made, bear claw spruce top, rosewood back and sides, mother-of-pearl 'board, ornate abalone floral pattern inlay, abalone rosette and border, natural.

1997		$3,500	$4,500

D-150/Style 150/"One-Fifty"
2002-present. Brazilian rosewood, premium Adirondack, abalone rosette. Called Style 150 in '20, then "One-Fifty" in '22.

2002-2024		$6,500	$9,500

DBJC
Jumbo cutaway, Indian rosewood back and sides, redwood top, gloss finish.

2007		$4,000	$5,000

Georgia Dreadnought
2003. Mahogany, Adirondack.

2003		$3,000	$4,000

JOM
1993-2015. Jumbo Orchestra Model flat-top, 15 5/8". Model includes one with cedar top, mahogany back and sides, and one with spruce top, Brazilian rosewood back and sides.

1993	Brazilian rosewood	$6,000	$9,000
1993	Mahogany	$3,000	$4,000
1993-2015	Indian rosewood	$3,500	$5,000

JOMC/OMC
1995-2015. Jumbo Orchestra cutaway, figured mahogany (OMC) and Indian rosewood (JOMC).

1995-2011	OMC, mahogany	$3,500	$5,000
1995-2015	JOMC200, Indian rw	$3,500	$4,500

JR-A
1990s. Artisan Series, 15 5/8", spruce top, rosewood back and sides.

1990s		$2,000	$3,000

LC4 Archtop Limited Edition
2002. Limited edition of 12, signed and numbered, premium Sitka and carved curly maple.

2002		$10,000	$14,000

Martin Simpson
1997-2003. Grand auditorium with unusual cutaway that removes one-half of the upper treble bout, Englemann spruce top, Indian rosewood back and sides, natural.

1997-2003		$3,000	$4,500

OM
1993-1999. Standard size OM, spruce top, rosewood back and sides.

1993-1999		$3,000	$4,000

OM Deluxe Artisan
2002. Indian rosewood, Sitka.

2002		$3,000	$4,500

OM Soloist
1990s-present. Full-sized, soft cutaway flat-top, Adirondack spruce top, figured Brick Red Brazilian rosewood back and sides, natural. Named just Soloist in '22.

1990-2024		$5,500	$7,500

Ricky Skaggs Signature
1998. D-style, rosewood sides and back, spruce top.

1998		$4,000	$6,000

Slope D
1993-2021. D-size, 16", spruce top, mahogany back and sides.

1993-2021		$3,500	$5,000

Vintage D
2000-present. Adirondack spruce (Eastern red spruce) top, optional rosewood back and sides. D dropped from name in '22.

2000-2024	Indian rosewood	$3,500	$5,000
2000s	Brazilian rosewood	$6,500	$9,500

Vintage OM
2005. Madagascar rosewood and Italian spruce top.

2005		$4,000	$5,500

Bown Guitars

Luthier Ralph Bown builds custom steel-string, nylon-string, baritone, and harp guitars, starting 1981, in Walmgate, U.K.

Bozo

1964-present. Bozo (pronounced Bo-zho) Podunavac learned instrument building in his Yugoslavian homeland and arrived in the United States in '59. In '64 he opened his own shop and built a variety of high-end, handmade, acoustic instruments, many being one-of-a-kind. He has built around 570 guitars over the years. There were several thousand Japanese-made (K. Yairi shop) Bell Western models bearing his name made from '79-'80; most of these were sold in Europe. He currently builds premium and presentation grade, custom guitars in Port Charlotte, Florida.

Acoustic
1970s-1980s. US-made, 6- and 12-string, appointments vary.

1970s-80s	Various models	$2,000	$10,000

Bradford

Mid-1960s. Brand name used by the W.T. Grant Company, one of the old Five & Ten style retail stores similar to F.W. Woolworth and Kresge. Many of these guitars and basses were made in Japan by Guyatone.

Acoustic Flat-Top

1960s		$300	$600

Electric Solidbody

1960s	1 or 2 pickups	$300	$500
1960s	3 pickups	$500	$800
1960s	4 pickups	$500	$800

Bradley

1970s. Budget Japanese copy models imported by Veneman's Music Emporium.

MODEL YEAR	FEATURES	EXC. COND. LOW	HIGH

Brawley Basses

Headquartered in Temecula, California, and designed by Keith Brawley, offering solidbody guitars and basses made in Korea.

Brazen

Starting in 2005, owner Steve Tsai, along with luthier Eddie Estrada, offered professional and premium grade, production, electric guitars. Steve also imports a line of intermediate grade guitars from China which are set up in the U.S.

Breedlove

1990-present. Founded by Larry Breedlove and Steve Henderson. Intermediate, professional, premium, and presentation grade, production/custom, steel, and nylon string flat-top built in Bend, Oregon and imported. They also build mandolins, basses, lapsteels and ukes. Several available custom options may add to the values listed here. They offered chambered electric guitars starting in 2008 but in January 2010, Breedlove discontinued all electric guitar production. Also, in '10, they became part of Two Old Hippies.

Brentwood

1970s. Student models built by Kay for store or jobber.

K-100

1970s. 13" student flat-top, K-100 label inside back, K logo on 'guard.

1970s		$75	$120

Brian May Guitar Company

2006-present. Guitarist Brian May teamed up with Barry Moorhouse and Pete Malandrone to offer versions of his Red Special Guitar. They also offered a bass.

Brian May Special

2006-present. Mahogany solidbody, 3 pickups, various colors

2006-2024		$700	$1,000

Brian Moore

1992-present. Founded by Patrick Cummings, Brian Moore and Kevin Kalagher in Brewster, New York; they introduced their first guitars in '94. Initially expensive custom shop guitars with carbon-resin bodies with highly figured wood tops; later went to all wood bodies cut on CNC machines. The intermediate and professional grade, production, iGuitar/i2000series was introduced in 2000 and made in Korea but set up in the U.S. Currently the premium grade, production/custom, Custom Shop Series guitars are handcrafted in La Grange, New York. They also build basses and electric mandolins.

C/DC/MC Series

1994-2011. Various models.

1994-2011		$1,200	$2,500

iGuitar Series

2000-present. Various models.

2000-2024		$1,200	$1,800

Brian Stone Classical Guitars

Luthier Brian Stone builds his classical guitars in Corvallis, Oregon.

Briggs

1999-present. Luthier Jack Briggs builds his professional and premium grade, production/custom, chambered and solidbody guitars in Raleigh, North Carolina.

Broman

1930s. The Broman brand was most likely used by a music studio (or distributor) on instruments made by others, including Regal-built resonator instruments.

Bronson

Ca. 1934-early 1960s. George Bronson was a steel guitar instructor in the Detroit area and his instruments were made by other companies. They were mainly lap steels (usually sold with a matching amp), but some other types were also offered.

Honolulu Master Hawaiian

1938		$2,500	$4,000

Student Hawaiian (Acoustic)

1930s	13" flat-top	$400	$600

Brook Guitars

1993-present. Simon Smidmore and Andy Petherick build their production/custom Brook steel-string, nylon-strings, and archtops in Dartmoor, U.K.

Brown's Guitar Factory

1982-present. Luthier John Brown builds professional and premium grade, production/custom, solidbody guitars, basses and lap steels in Inver Grove Heights, Minnesota.

Bruné, R. E.

1966-present. Luthier Richard Bruné builds his premium and presentation grade, custom, classical and flamenco guitars in Evanston, Illinois. He also offers his professional and premium grade Model 20 and Model 30, which are handmade in a leading guitar workshop in Japan. Bruné's "Guitars with Guts" column appears in Vintage Guitar magazine.

Bruno and Sons

Distributor Bruno and Sons marketed a variety of brands, including their own. Later became part of Kaman Music.

Harp Guitar

1924		$2,500	$4,000

Hollowbody Electric

1960s-1970s. Various imported models.

1960s		$300	$450

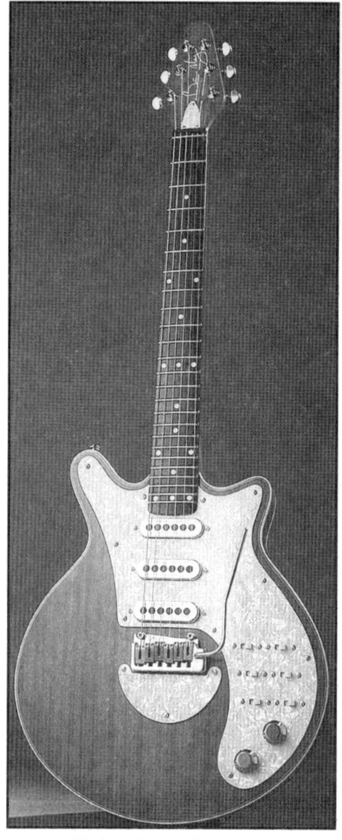

Brian May Special

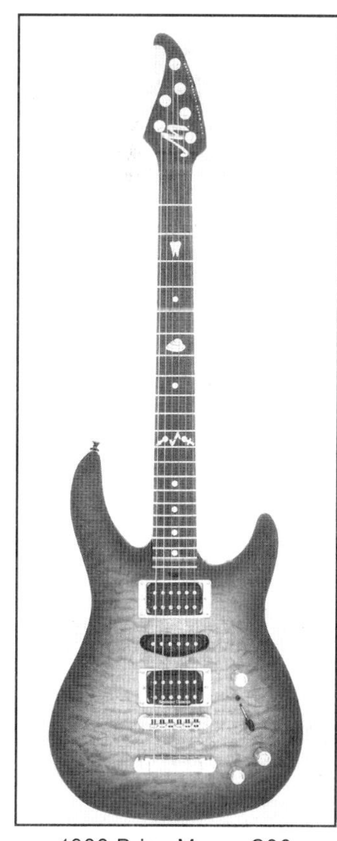

1999 Brian Moore C90

Imaged by Heritage Auctions, HA.com

GUITARS

Buddy Blaze

1965 Burns GB66 Deluxe
Peter Hvidegaard

MODEL YEAR	FEATURES	EXC. COND. LOW	HIGH

Parlor Guitar

1880-1920. Various woods used on back and sides.

1880-1920	Birch	$700	$1,200
1880-1920	Brazilian rosewood	$2,000	$3,000
1880-1920	Mahogany	$1,000	$1,500

Buddy Blaze

1985-2021. Professional and premium grade, custom/production, solidbody electric guitars built by luthier Buddy Blaze from '85 to '87 in Arlington, Texas, then in Kailua Kona, Hawaii. He also designed intermediate grade models which were imported. He died in '21.

Bunker

1961-2021. Founder Dave Bunker built custom guitars and basses while performing in Las Vegas in the '60s and developed a number of innovations. Around '92 Bunker began PBC Guitar Technology with John Pearse and Paul Chernay in Coopersburg, Pennsylvania, building instruments under the PBC brand and, from '94-'96, for Ibanez' USA Custom Series. PBC closed in '97 and Bunker moved back to Washington State to start Bunker Guitar Technology and resumed production of several Bunker models. In early 2002, Bunker Guitars became part of Maple Valley Tone Woods of Port Angeles, Washington and offered intermediate, professional, and premium grade, production/custom, guitars and basses. Most early Bunker guitars were pretty much custom-made in low quantities. Dave Bunker died in '21.

Burke

Ca. 1960-ca. 1966. 6- and 12- string electric guitars built by Glen Burke's Tuning Fork Guitar Company in Eugene and Grants Pass, Oregon and mostly sold in kit form. The guitars featured an aluminum neck-thru design with the body portion of the neck shaped being a rectangular box where the body wings are attached. Being kit guitars finishes, pickups, options and build quality will vary.

Burlesk Guitars

1994-2023. Professional and premium grade, custom, solidbody electric guitars and basses, built by luthier James Burley in Alberta, Canada. Burley died in '23.

Burly Guitars

Luthier Jeff Ayers, starting in 2007, builds professional and premium grade, custom, solid and semi-hollowbody guitars, in Land O' Lakes, Wisconsin.

Burns

1960-1970, 1974-1983, 1992-present. Intermediate and professional grade, production, electric guitars built in the U.K. and Asia. They also build basses. Jim Burns began building guitars in the late-'50s and established Burns London Ltd in '60. Baldwin Organ (see Baldwin listing) purchased the company in '65 and offered the instruments until '70. The Burns name was revived in '91 by Barry Gibson as Burns London, with Jim Burns' involvement, offering reproductions of some of the classic Burns models of the '60s. Jim Burns passed away in August '98. In 2020, it was announced new instruments for '21.

MODEL YEAR	FEATURES	EXC. COND. LOW	HIGH

Baby Bison

1965. Double-cut solidbody, scroll headstock, 2 pickups, shorter scale, tremolo.

1965		$1,200	$1,800

Bison

1964-1965, 2003-2020. Double-cut solidbody, 3 pickups, tremolo, black or white, scroll-headstock, replaced flat headstock Black Bison. Has been reissued with both types of headstocks.

1961-1962	Black, 4 pus, flat hs	$4,000	$6,500
1962-1965	Black, 3 pus, scroll hs	$3,000	$4,000
1962-1965	White, 3 pus, scroll hs	$3,000	$4,000
2003-2020	Reissue	$800	$1,200
2000s	Legend Custom Shop	$1,500	$2,200

Brian May Signature - Red Special

2001-2006. A replica of May's original 'Red Special' but with added whammy-bar, red finish. Korean-made.

2001-2006		$900	$1,500

Cobra

2004-2020. Double-cut solid, 2 pickups.

2004-2020		$200	$300

Double Six

1964-1965, 2003-2020. Solidbody 12-string, double-cut, 3 pickups, greenburst. Reissue made in Korea.

1964-1965		$2,500	$3,000
2003-2020		$400	$600

Flyte

1974-1977. Fighter jet-shaped solidbody, pointed headstock, 2 humbucking pickups, silver, has been reissued.

1974-1977		$1,000	$1,500

GB66 Deluxe

1965. Like 66 Standard, but with bar pickups and add Density control.

1965		$1,200	$1,800

GB66 Deluxe Standard

1965. Offset double-cut, f-holes, 2 Ultra-Sonic pickups.

1965		$1,000	$1,500

Jazz

1962-1965. Offset double-cut solid, shorter scale, 2 pickups.

1962-1965		$1,500	$2,200

Jazz Split Sound

1962-1965. Offset double-cut solid, 3 pickups, tremolo, red sunburst.

1962-1965		$1,800	$2,800

Marquee

2000-2020. Offset double-cut solid, 3 pickups, scroll headstock.

2000-2020		$400	$600

MODEL YEAR	FEATURES	EXC. COND. LOW	HIGH

Marvin

1964-1965, 2000s. Hank Marvin, offset double-cut solidbody, scroll headstock, 3 pickups, tremolo, white.

1964-1965		$2,500	$3,500
2000s	Legend Custom Shop	$1,500	$2,200

Nu-Sonic

1964-1965. Solidbody, 2 pickups, tremolo, white or cherry, has been reissued.

1964-1965		$1,200	$1,800

Sonic

1960-1964. Double shallow cut solid, 2 pickups, cherry.

1960-1964		$1,000	$1,500

Split Sonic

1962-1964. Solidbody, 3 pickups, bound neck, tremolo, red sunburst.

1962-1964		$1,500	$2,200

Steer

2000-2020. Semi-hollowbody, sound-hole, 2 pickups, non-cut and single-cut versions.

2000-2020		$600	$900

TR-2

1963-1964. Semi-hollow, 2 pickups, red sunburst.

1963-1964		$1,200	$1,800

Vibra Artist

1960-1962. Double-cut, mahogany, 3 pickups, 6 knobs.

1960-1962		$1,200	$1,800

Vibraslim

1964-1965. Double-cut, f-holes, 2 pickups, red sunburst.

1964-1965		$1,200	$1,800

Virginian

1964-1965. Burns of London model, later offered as Baldwin Virginian in '65.

1964-1965		$1,500	$2,200

Vista Sonic

1962-1964. Offset double-cut solid, 3 pickups, red sunburst.

1962-1964		$1,500	$2,200

Burnside

1987-1988. Budget solidbody guitars imported by Guild.

Solidbody Electric/Blade

1987-1988. Solidbody, fat pointy headstock.

1987-1988		$200	$250

Burns-Weill

1959. Jim Burns and Henry Weill teamed up to produce three solidbody electric and three solidbody bass models under this English brand. Models included the lower end Fenton, a small single-cutaway, 2 pickups and an elongated headstock and the bizarrely styled RP2G. Henry Weill continued to produce a slightly different RP line under the re-named Fenton-Weill brand.

Burny

1980s-1990s. Solidbody electric guitars from Fernandes and built in Japan, Korea, or China.

Burrell

1984-2010. Luthier Leo Burrell built his professional grade, production/custom, acoustic, semi-hollow, and solidbody guitars and basses in Huntington, West Virginia. Leo retired in '10.

Burton Guitars

1980-present. Custom classical guitars built by luthier Cynthia Burton in Portland, Oregon.

Buscarino Guitars

1981-present. Luthier John Buscarino builds his premium and presentation grade, custom archtops and steel-string and nylon-string flat-tops in Franklin, North Carolina.

Byers, Gregory

1984-present. Premium grade, custom classical and Flamenco guitars built by luthier Gregory Byers in Willits, California.

Byrd

1998-present. Custom/production, professional and premium grade, V-shaped electric guitars, built by luthiers James Byrd and Joe Riggio, in Seattle and several other cities in the state of Washington.

C. Fox

1997-2002. Luthier Charles Fox built his premium grade, production/custom flat-tops in Healdsburg, California. In '02 he closed C. Fox Guitars and moved to Portland, Oregon to build Charles Fox Guitars.

C.F. Mountain

1970s-early 1980s. Japanese copy acoustics made by Hayashi Musical Instrument Ltd with headstock logo that looks very much like that of a certain classic American guitar company.

Acoustic

1970s-80s		$100	$300

CA (Composite Acoustics)

1999-2010, 2011-present. Professional grade, production, carbon fiber composite guitars that were built in Lafayette, Louisiana. The company ceased production in February, '10. At the end of '10 CA was acquired by Peavey, which launched the new Meridian, Mississippi-based line in January, '11.

Califone

1966. Six and 12-string guitars and basses made by Murphy Music Industries (maker of the Murph guitars) for Rheem Califone-Roberts which manufactured tape recorders and related gear. Very few made.

1965 Burns Marvin

Imaged by Heritage Auctions, HA.com

Gregory Byers

2007 Carvin V22OM

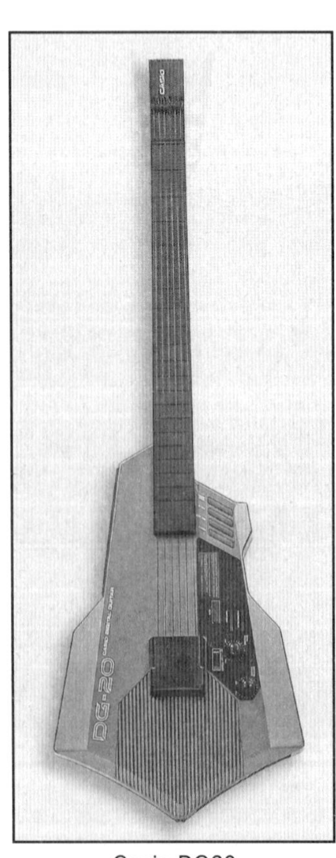

Casio DG20

MODEL YEAR	FEATURES	EXC. COND. LOW	HIGH

Callaham

1989-present. Professional, production/custom, solidbody electric guitars built by luthier Bill Callaham in Winchester, Virginia. They also make tube amp heads.

Camelli

1960s. Line of solidbody electric guitars imported from Italy.

Solidbody Electric

1960s		$500	$1,000

Cameo

1960s-1970s. Japanese- and Korean-made electric and acoustic guitars. They also offered basses.

Electric

1960s-70s	Various models	$500	$800

Campbell American Guitars

2005-2015. Luthier Dean Campbell built his intermediate and professional grade, production/custom, solidbody guitars originally in Pawtucket, Rhode Island, then in Westwood, Massachusetts. From '02 to '05, he built guitars under the Greene & Campbell brand.

Campellone

1978-present. Luthier Mark Campellone builds his premium grade, custom archtops in Greenville, Rhode Island. He also made electrics and basses in the '70s and '80s, switching to archtops around '90.

Deluxe

1990-present. 16" to 18" archtop, middle of the company product line, blond or sunburst.

1990-2024		$5,000	$7,000

Special

1994-present. 16" to 18" archtop, top of the company product line, carved spruce top, carved flamed maple back, flamed maple sides, blond or sunburst.

1994-2024		$4,000	$6,000

Standard

2000-present. 16" to 18" archtop, lower of the 3 model lines offered.

2000-2024		$4,000	$5,500

Canvas

2004-2012. Budget and intermediate grade, production, acoustic and electric guitars, and basses imported from China by America Sejung Corp. until '11, then in South Korea.

Carbonaro

Luthier Robert Carbonaro began building in 1975, premium grade, production/custom, archtop and flat-top guitars in Santa Fe, New Mexico. Relocated his shop to Mexico in 2016, then Vietnam in '19.

Carl Fischer

1920s. Most likely a brand made for a distributor. Instruments built by the Oscar Schmidt Co. and possibly others.

Carlos

Ca.1976-late 1980s. Imported copies of classic American acoustics distributed by Coast Wholesale Music.

Acoustic Flat-Top

1976-1980s	Various models	$300	$500

Carson Robison

1933-1938. Wards sold guitars endorsed by popular country artist Carson Robison. Built by Gibson, the guitars were the same as models sold under the Kalamazoo brand.

Model K

1933-1938. Flat top, ladder, K #926 same as Kalamazoo KG-11, K #1281/#1115 same as Kalamazoo K-14. Becomes the Recording King (Ward's main brand) Model K in '38.

1933-1935	K#926	$1,500	$2,500
1936-1938	K#1281/1115	$1,800	$3,000

Carvin

1946-present. Intermediate and professional grade, production/custom, acoustic and electric guitars, and basses built in San Diego, California. They also offer amps and mandolins. Founded in Los Angeles by Hawaiian guitarist and recording artist Lowell C. Kiesel as the L.C. Kiesel Co. making pickups for guitars. Bakelite Kiesel-brand electric Hawaiian lap steels are introduced in early-'47. Small tube amps introduced ca. '47. By late-'49, the Carvin brand is introduced, combining parts of names of sons Carson and Gavin. Carvin acoustic and electric Spanish archtops are introduced in '54. Instruments are sold by mail-order only. Kiesel brand name revived by Carvin in '15 for use on their guitars.

2,000-4,000 guitars made prior to '70 with no serial number. First serial number appeared in '70, stamped on end of fingerboard, beginning with #5000. All are consecutive. Later SN on neck plates.

Approximate SN ranges include:

1970: First serial number #5000 to 10019 ('79).
'80-'83: 10768 to 15919.
'84-'87: 13666 to 25332.
'88-'90: 22731 to 25683.
'91-'94: 25359 to 42547.
'95-'99: 45879 to 81427.
'00-present: 56162 upward.

Acoustic-Electric AC/AE Series

1990s-2020	Various models	$600	$900

Solidbody B/C/D Series (Mid-Level)

1990s-2020	Various models	$600	$900

Solidbody Carved-Top (Higher-End)

2000s-2020	Various models	$1,200	$1,800

Solidbody DN/DB/DS Series (Doubleneck)

1975-2020	Various models	$2,000	$3,000

Casa Montalvo

1987-present. Intermediate and professional grade, production/custom flamenco and classical guitars made in Mexico for George Katechis of Berkeley Musical Instrument Exchange.

MODEL YEAR	FEATURES	EXC. COND. LOW	HIGH

Casio

In 1987 Casio introduced a line of digital MIDI guitars imported from Japan, sporting plastic bodies and synthesizer features. They offered them for just a few years.

DG1

1980s. Squared plastic body.

1980s		$120	$200

DG10

1987-1989. Self-contained digital guitar.

1987-1989		$300	$500

DG20

1987-1989. Midi-capable digital guitar.

1987-1989		$400	$600

MG-500 Series MIDI Guitar

1987-1989. Cut-off teardrop (MG-500) or Strat-shaped (MG-510), basswood body, maple neck, rosewood 'board, 3 pickups.

1987-1989	500	$800	$1,200
1987-1989	510	$700	$1,000

PG-300

1988-1989. Similar to PG-380, but with less features.

1988-1989		$600	$900

PG-310

1988-1989. Similar to PG-380, but with less features.

1988-1989		$700	$1,000

PG-380

1988-1989. Guitar synth, double-cut, over 80 built-in sounds, midi controller capable.

1988-1989		$900	$1,400

Casper Guitar Technologies

Professional grade, production/custom, solidbody electric guitars and basses built by luthier Stephen Casper in Leisure City, Florida, starting in 2009.

Cat's Eyes

1980s. Made by Tokai, Cat's Eyes headstock logo, see Tokai guitar listings.

Champion

Ca. 1894-1897. Chicago's Robert Maurer built this brand of instruments before switching to the Maurer brand name around 1897.

Champlin Guitars

2006-present. Professional and premium grade, custom, flat-top and archtop guitars, and mandolinettos, built by Devin Champlin in Bellingham, Washington.

Chandler

Intermediate and professional grade, production/custom, solidbody electric guitars built by luthiers Paul and Adrian Chandler in Chico, California. They also build basses, lap steels and pickups. Chandler started making pickguards and accessories in the '70s, adding electric guitars, basses, and effects in '84.

MODEL YEAR	FEATURES	EXC. COND. LOW	HIGH

555 Model

1992-2000s. Sharp double-cut, 3 mini-humbuckers, TV Yellow.

1992-2000s		$1,000	$1,500

Austin Special

1991-1999. Resembles futuristic Danelectro, lipstick pickups, available in 5-string version.

1991-1999		$900	$1,500

Austin Special Baritone

1994-1999. Nicknamed Elvis, gold metalflake finish, mother-of-toilet-seat binding, tremolo, baritone.

1994-1999		$900	$1,500

LectraSlide

2000s. Single-cut, Rezo 'guard, 2 pickups.

2000s		$900	$1,500

Metro

1995-2000. Double-cut slab body, P-90 in neck position and humbucker in the bridge position.

1995-2000		$900	$1,500

Telepathic

1994-2000. Classic single-cut style, 3 models; Basic, Standard, Deluxe.

1994-2000	Basic	$700	$1,000
1994-2000	Deluxe 1122 Model	$900	$1,500
1994-2000	Standard	$800	$1,200

Chantus

Premium grade, production/custom, classical and flamenco guitars built in Austin, Texas, by luthier William King starting in '84. He also builds ukes.

Chapin

Professional and premium grade, production/custom, semi-hollow, solidbody, and acoustic electric guitars built by luthiers Bill Chapin and Fred Campbell in San Jose, California.

Chapman

1970-present. Made by Emmett Chapman, the Stick features 10 strings and is played by tapping both hands. The Grand Stick features 12 strings.

Stick

1970-present. Touch-tap hybrid electric instrument, 10 or 12 strings.

1970-2024	10- or 12-string	$2,500	$4,500

Char

1985-present. Premium grade, custom, classical and steel string acoustic guitars built in Portland, Oregon by luthier Kerry Char. He also builds harp-guitars and ukuleles.

Charis Acoustic

1996-present. Premium grade, custom/production, steel-string guitars built by luthier Bill Wise in Bay City, Michigan.

Charles Fox Guitars

1968-present. Luthier Charles Fox builds his premium and presentation grade, custom, steel and nylon string guitars in Portland, Oregon. He

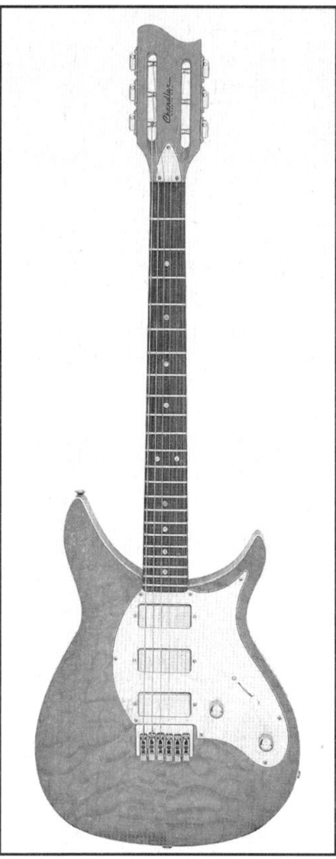

Chandler 555
Imaged by Heritage Auctions, HA.com

Charis Acoustic SJ

GUITARS

EVH Art Series (by Charvel)

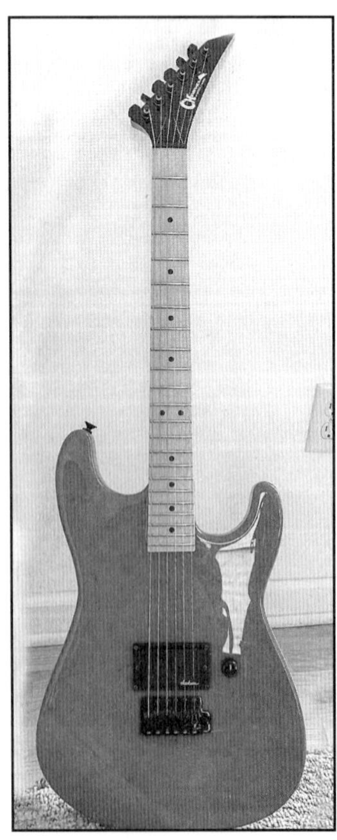

1986 Charvel Model 1

Tritium Guita Worx Randy

also produced GRD acoustic and electric guitars for '78-'82 and C. Fox acoustic guitars for '97-'02. He also operates The American School of Lutherie in Portland.

Charles Shifflett Acoustic Guitars

Premium grade, custom, classical, flamenco, resonator, and harp guitars, basses and banjos built by luthier Charles Shifflett, starting 1990, in High River, Alberta.

Charvel

1976 (1980)-present. Intermediate and professional grade, production, solidbody electric guitars. They also build basses. Founded by Wayne Charvel as Charvel Manufacturing in '76, making guitar parts in Asuza, California. Moved to San Dimas in '78. Also, in '78 Grover Jackson bought out Charvel. In '79 or early '80 Charvel branded guitars are introduced. U.S.-made to '85, a combination of imports and U.S.-made post-'85. Charvel also manufactured the Jackson brand.

Charvel licensed its trademark to IMC (Hondo) in '85. IMC bought Charvel in '86 and moved the factory to Ontario, California. On October 25, 2002, Fender Musical Instruments Corp. (FMIC) took ownership of Jackson/Charvel Manufacturing Inc.

Pre-Pro (Pre-Production) Charvels began in November 1980 and ran until sometime in 1981. These are known as 'non-plated' indicating pre-production versus a production neck plate. Production serialized neck plates are considered to be San Dimas models which have a Charvel logo, serial number, and a PO Box San Dimas notation on the neck plate. These Serialized Plated Charvels came after Pre-Pros. Late '81 and '82 saw the early serialized guitars with 21-fret necks; these are more valuable. During '82 the 22-fret neck was introduced. The so-called Soft Strat-, Tele-, Flying V-, and Explorer-style headstocks are associated with the early San Dimas Charvel models. In late '82 the pointy headstock, called the Jackson style, was introduced. In '82 the Superstrat style with a neck plate was introduced. Superstrats with a Kahler tailpiece have a lower value than the Pre-Pro models (with Fender-style trem tailpiece).

Collectors of vintage Charvels look for the vintage Charvel 3-on-a-side logo. This is a defining feature and a cutoff point for valuations. Bogus builders are replicating early Charvels and attempting to sell them as originals so fakes can be a problem for Charvel collectors, so buyer beware.

Other electric guitar manufacturing info:

1986-1989 Japanese-made Models 1 through 8
1989-1991 Japanese-made 550 XL, 650 XL/ Custom, 750 XL (XL=neck-thru)
1989-1992 Japanese-made Models 275, 375, 475, 575
1990-1991 Korean-made Charvette models
1992-1994 Korean-made Models 325, 425

Early Charvel serial numbers (provided by former Jackson/Charvel associate Tim Wilson):

The first 500 to 750 guitars had no serial number, just marked "Made In U.S.A." on their neckplates. Five digit serial numbers were then used until November '81 when 4-digit numbers were adopted, starting with #1001.

1981: 1001-1095
1982: 1096-1724
1983: 1725-2938
1984: 2939-4261
1985: 4262-5303
1986: 5304-5491

MODEL YEAR	FEATURES	EXC. COND. LOW	HIGH
Pre-Pro			
November 1980-1981. Pre-Pros came in different configurations of body styles, pickups, and finishes. There are five basic Pre-Pro formats: the Standard Body, the Bound Body, the Graphic Body, the Flamed Top, and the Matching Headstock. It is possible to have a combination, such as a Bound Body and Matching Headstock. Line items are based on body style and can feature any one of four neck/headstock-styles used: the so-called Tele-headstock, Strat-headstock, Flying V headstock, and Explorer headstock. Finishes included white, black, red, metallic Lake Placid Blue, and special graphics. All original parts adds considerable value and it is often difficult to determine what is original on these models, so expertise is required. An original Fender brass trem tailpiece, for example, adds considerable value. The Pre-Pro models were prone to modification such as added Kahler and Floyd Rose trems.			
1980-1981	Various options	$9,000	$12,000
275 Deluxe Dinky			
1989-1991. Made in Japan, offset double-cut solidbody, 1 single-coil and 1 humbucker in '89, 2 humbuckers after, tremolo.			
1989-1991		$550	$850
325SL			
1992-1994. Dot inlays.			
1992-1994		$450	$600
325SLX			
1992-1994. Surfcaster-like thinline acoustic/electric, dual cutaways, f-hole, on-board chorus, shark inlays, made in Korea.			
1992-1994		$450	$600
375 Deluxe			
1989-1991. Maple or rosewood 'board, dot inlays, single-single-humbucker.			
1989-1991		$700	$950
475 Deluxe/475 Special			
1989-1991. Introduced as Special, changed to Deluxe in '90, bound rosewood board, shark tooth inlays, 2 oval stacked humbuckers and 1 bridge humbucker. Was also offered as Deluxe Exotic with figured top and back.			
1989-1991		$800	$1,000
525			
1989-1994. Acoustic-electric, single-cut.			
1989-1994		$350	$500

MODEL YEAR	FEATURES	EXC. COND. LOW	HIGH

550XL

1987-1989. Neck-thru (XL), dot markers, 1 single-coil and 1 bridge humbucker.

1987-1989		$800	$1,250

625-C12

1993-2000. Acoustic-electric cutaway 12-string, spruce top.

1993-2000		$350	$500

625F/625ACEL

1993-1995. Acoustic-electric cutaway, figured maple top.

1993-1995		$450	$600

650XL/Custom

1989-1990. Introduced as neck-thru XL and discontinued as Custom, shark fin markers, 2 stacked oval humbuckers and 1 bridge humbucker, custom version of 550XL.

1989-1990		$850	$1,250

750XL Soloist

1989-1990. Shark fin markers, cutaway body, 2 humbuckers, large Charvel logo.

1989-1990		$1,000	$1,500

Avenger

1990-1991. Randy Rhoads-style batwing-shaped solidbody, 1 humbucker, 1 single-coil, tremolo, made in Japan.

1990-1991		$650	$1,000

Charvette

1989-1991. Charvette Series made in Korea, superstrat-style, model number series 100 through 300.

1990-1991		$350	$500

CX Series

1991-1994. Imported solidbodies, body-mounted or pickguard mounted pickups, standard or deluxe tremolo.

1991-1994		$300	$400

EVH Art Series (by Charvel)

2004-2007. Offset double-cut solidbody, 1 humbucker, striped finish.

2004-2007	Black/white	$3,250	$4,500
2004-2007	Black/white on red	$3,250	$4,500
2004-2007	Black/yellow	$4,250	$5,500

Fusion Deluxe

1989-1991. Double-cut solidbody, tremolo, 1 humbucker and 1 single-coil, made in Japan.

1989-1991		$850	$1,125

Fusion Standard/AS FX 1

1993-1996. Double-cut solidbody, tremolo, 1 regular and 2 mini humbuckers, made in Japan, also named AS FX1.

1993-1996		$850	$1,125

Model 1/1A/1C

1986-1988. Offset double-cut solidbody, bolt-on maple neck, dot inlays, 1 humbucker, tremolo, made in Japan. Model 1A has 3 single-coils. Model 1C has 1 humbucker and 2 single-coils.

1986-1988		$850	$1,125

Model 2

1986-1988. As Model 1, but with rosewood 'board.

1986-1988		$850	$1,125

MODEL YEAR	FEATURES	EXC. COND. LOW	HIGH

Model 3/3A/3DR/3L

1986-1989. As Model 2, but with 1 humbucker, 2 single coils. Model 3A has 2 humbuckers. Model 3DR has 1 humbucker and 1 single-coil.

1986-1989		$850	$1,250

Model 4/4A

1986-1988. As Model 2, but with 1 regular humbucker and 2 stacked humbuckers (no pickguard), active electronics, dots in '86, shark-fin inlays after. Model 4A has 2 regular humbuckers and dot markers.

1986-1988		$950	$1,500

Model 5/5A

1986-1988. As Model 4A, but neck-thru, with JE1000TG active electronics. Model 5A is single humbucker and single knob version, limited production, made in Japan.

1986-1988		$950	$1,500

Model 6

1986-1988. As HSS Model 4, but with shark's tooth inlays, standard or various custom finishes.

1986-1988		$950	$1,500

Model 7

1988-1989. Single-cut solidbody, bound top, reversed headstock, 2 single-coils, made in Japan.

1988-1989		$950	$1,500

Model 88 LTD

1988. Double-cut solidbody, 1 slanted humbucker, shark fin inlay, 1000 built, made in Japan.

1988		$950	$1,250

Predator

1989-1991. Offset double-cut, bridge humbucker, single-coil neck, bolt-on.

1989-1991		$600	$850

San Dimas Serialized Plated

1981-1986, 1995-1997. U.S.-made with San Dimas neck plate, bolt neck, rounded headstock early production, pointy headstock later, reissued in mid-'90s.

1981-1982	Soft headstock	$5,500	$8,500
1982-1986	Pointy headstock	$3,000	$5,000
1995-1997	Soft headstock	$1,500	$2,500

San Dimas LTD 25th Anniversary

2006. About 100 made, 25th Anniversary logo on neck plate with production number, highly figured top, high-end appointments.

2006		$1,750	$2,500

San Dimas Reissue (FMIC)

2004-present. USA Select series, alder body, bolt neck.

2004-2011	Custom Shop	$2,000	$2,500
2004-2024	Factory model	$1,000	$1,500

So-Cal Series

2008-2012. Offset double-cut solidbody.

2008-2012	Various options	$850	$1,125

ST Custom

1990-1991. Offset double-cut ash solidbody, 2 single-coils and 1 humbucker, rosewood 'board, tremolo, made in Japan.

1990-1991		$400	$550

ST Deluxe

1990-1991. Same as ST Custom but with maple 'board.

1990-1991		$400	$550

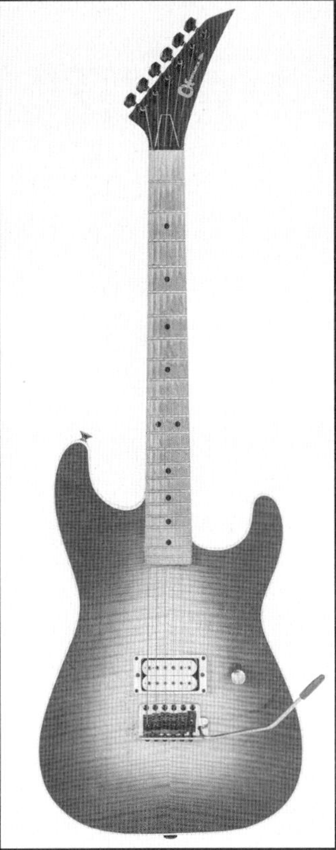

1983 Charvel San Dimas Plated

Imaged by Heritage Auctions, HA.com

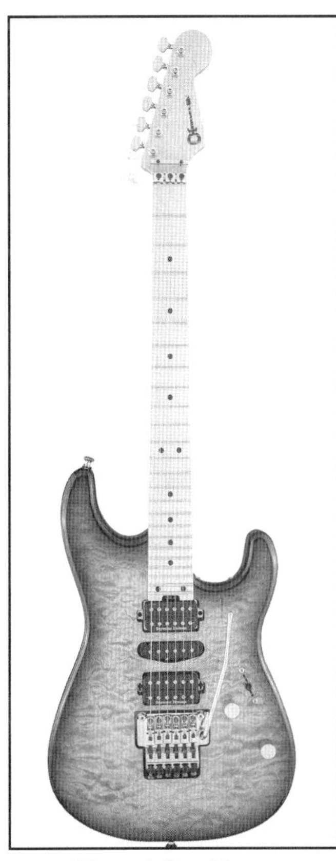

Charvel San Dimas Select Series

GUITARS

Chiquita Travel Guitar

Citron CF1

MODEL YEAR	FEATURES	EXC. COND. LOW	HIGH

Standard

2002-2003. Typical offset double-cut Charvel body, 2 Seymour Duncan humbucker pickups, various opaque colors.

2002-2003		$400	$550

Star

1980-1981. The Star is considered by early-Charvel collectors to be Charvel's only original design with its unique four-point body.

1980-1981		$2,250	$3,000

Surfcaster

1991-1996. Offset double-cut, f-hole, various pickup options, bound body, tremolo, made in Japan.

1991-1996	1 single, 1 hum	$1,250	$1,750
1991-1996	2 singles, hardtail	$1,250	$1,750
1991-1996	2 singles, vibrato	$1,250	$1,750

Surfcaster 12

1991-1996. Made in Japan, 12-string version of Surfcaster, no tremolo.

1991-1996		$1,250	$1,750

Surfcaster Doubleneck

1992. Very limited production, 6/12 double neck, Charvel logo on both necks, black.

1992		$2,000	$3,000

Surfcaster HT (Model SC1)

1996-2000. Made in Japan. Hard Tail (HT) non-tremolo version of Surfcaster, has single-coil and bridge humbucker.

1996-2000		$1,250	$1,750

Chiquita

1979-present. Intermediate grade, production guitars made by Erlewine Guitars in Austin, Texas (see that listing). There was also a mini amp available.

Travel Guitar

1979-present. Developed by Mark Erlewine and ZZ Top's Billy Gibbons, 27" overall length solidbody, 1 or 2 pickups, various colors.

1979-2024		$700	$1,200

Chris George

1966-ca. 2018. Professional and premium grade, custom, archtop, acoustic, electric and resonator guitars built by luthier Chris George, in Tattershall Lincolnshire, U.K. George retired in '18.

Christopher Carrington

1988-present. Production/custom, premium grade, classical and flamenco acoustic guitars built by luthier Chris Carrington in Rockwall, Texas.

Chrysalis Guitars

1998-2015. Luthier Tim White built his premium grade, production/custom Chrysalis Guitar System, which included interchangeable components that can be quickly assembled into a full-size electric/acoustic guitar, in New Boston, New Hampshire. White introduced his new brand, Ridgewing in 2016.

MODEL YEAR	FEATURES	EXC. COND. LOW	HIGH

Cimar/Cimar by Ibanez

Early-1980s. Private brand of Hoshino Musical Instruments, Nagoya, Japan, who also branded Ibanez. Headstock with script Cimar logo or Cimar by Ibanez, copy models and Ibanez near-original models such as the star body.

Cimar

1982	Classical	$200	$300
1982	Double-cut solidbody	$400	$600
1982	Star body style	$400	$600

Cimarron

1978-present. Luthiers John Walsh and Clayton Walsh build their professional grade, production/custom, flat-top acoustic guitars in Ridgway, Colorado. Between '94 and '98 they also produced electric guitars.

Cipher

1960s. Solidbody electric guitars and basses imported from Japan by Inter-Mark. Generally strange-shaped bodies.

Electric Solidbody

1960s. For any student-grade import, a guitar with any missing part, such as a missing control knob or trem arm, is worth much less.

1960s		$400	$600

Citron

1995-present. Luthier Harvey Citron builds his professional and premium grade, production/custom solidbody guitars and basses in Woodstock, New York. He also builds basses. In '75, Citron and Joe Veillette founded Veillette-Citron, which was known for handcrafted, neck-thru guitars and basses. That company closed in '83.

Clark

1985-present. Custom, professional grade, solidbody electric guitars and basses, built by luthier Ed Clark, first in Amityville, New York ('85-'90), then Medford ('91-'99) and presently Lake Ronkonkoma.

Clifford

Clifford was a brand manufactured by Kansas City, Missouri instrument wholesalers J.W. Jenkins & Sons. First introduced in 1895, the brand also offered mandolins.

Clovis

Mid-1960s. Private brand guitars, most likely made by Kay.

Electric Solidbody

Mid-1960s. Kay slab solidbody, 2 pickups.

1965		$500	$750

CMG Guitars

2012-present. Owner Chris Mitchell imports intermediate grade, acoustic and acoustic-electric guitars from China. He also offers professional grade, production/custom, electric guitars built by luthiers Russell Jones and James Horel in Statesboro, Georgia.

MODEL YEAR	FEATURES	EXC. COND. LOW	HIGH

Cole

1890-1919. W.A. Cole, after leaving Fairbanks & Cole, started his own line in 1890. He died in 1909 but the company continued until 1919. He also made mandolins and banjos.

Parlor

1897. Small size, Brazilian rosewood sides and back, spruce top, ebony 'board, slotted headstock, dot markers.

1897		$1,200	$1,800

Coleman Guitars

1976-1983. Custom made presentation grade instruments made in Homosassa, Florida, by luthier Harry Coleman. No headstock logo, Coleman logo on inside center strip.

Collings

1986-present. Professional, premium, and presentation grade, production/custom, flat-top, archtop and electric guitars built in Austin, Texas. They also build mandolins and ukuleles. Bill Collings started guitar repair and began custom building guitars around '73. In '80, he relocated his shop from Houston to Austin and started Collings Guitars in '86. In '06 they moved to a new plant in southwest Austin.

01

2005-present. Mother-of-pearl inlays, Sitka spruce, mahogany neck, back & sides, ebony 'board and bridge, high gloss lacquer finish.

2005-2024		$3,000	$4,000

01A

2010-2017. As 01 with Adirondack spruce top.

2010-2017		$3,200	$4,500

01G

As 01 with German spruce top.

2009		$3,500	$4,800

01SB

Sitka spruce, mahogany.

2006-2015		$3,000	$4,200

02G

German spruce, sunburst.

1996		$4,000	$5,500

02H

Parlor, 12 frets.

2008		$3,500	$5,000

02SB

Parlor, 12 frets, 12-string.

2016		$3,800	$5,200

001G

German spruce.

2009		$3,500	$4,800

001MH

All mahogany body.

2010		$3,000	$4,200

002H

1999-present. Indian rosewood.

1999-2024		$4,000	$5,500

0041

2001. Premium Brazilian rosewood back and sides, Adirondack spruce top, abalone top purfling.

2001		$6,500	$9,500

0001 ICC

0001 with Indian rosewood back and sides.

2003-2013		$4,000	$5,500

0001 Series

1990s-present. 12-fret 000 size, Sitka spruce top (standard) or other top wood options, including mahogany, Adirondack, Honduran mahogany, etc.

1990s-2024	0001 Sitka	$3,500	$5,000
1990s-2024	0001A Adirondack	$3,800	$5,500
2006-2024	0001Mh Mahogany	$3,200	$4,800
2013-2024	0001 Cutaway	$3,800	$5,200

0002H

1994-present. 15" 000-size, 12-fret, Indian rosewood back and sides, spruce top, slotted headstock. AAA Koa back and sides in '96.

1994-1995	Indian rosewood	$4,500	$6,000
1996	AAA Koa	$5,500	$7,000
2007-2024	Indian rosewood	$4,000	$5,500

0002HAC

2009-2024. With cutaway and herringbone trim.

2009-2024		$4,200	$5,800

00041

1999. Indian rosewood sides and back, Sitka spruce top, slotted headstock.

1999		$4,500	$6,000

290 Series

2004-present. Solid Honduran mahogany body, East Indian rosewood 'board, 2 P-90 style pickups, '50s style wiring, high gloss lacquer finish.

2004-2024	Custom/Deluxe	$3,000	$4,800

360 Baritone

2020-present. Solid ash body, doghair finish.

2024		$3,000	$4,500

360 LT

2015-present. Solidbody electric, level top (LT), mahogany, ash or alder body, rosewood 'board, high gloss nitro finish.

2015-2024		$3,000	$4,800

AT 16

2006-present. 16" archtop, limited numbers built, fully carved premium figured maple body and neck, carved solid spruce top, f-holes, high-end appointments, high gloss nitro finish.

2006-2024		$12,000	$18,000

AT 17

2008-present. 17" single-cut archtop, limited numbers built, S-holes, Adirondack or European spruce top, premium flamed maple back and sides, and premium appointments, sunburst or blonde. Options include scale length, pickup and bindings.

2008-2024		$12,000	$18,000

Baby Series

1997-present. Various 3/4 size models, Englemann (E) or German (G) spruce top, rosewood back and sides, Ivoroid with herringbone trim, tortoise 'guard, gloss nitro lacquer finish.

1997-2024	Various models	$3,000	$5,200

C10

1986-present. 000-size, mahogany back and sides, spruce top, sunburst or natural.

1986-2024		$3,000	$4,000

Collings 01

Collings 290 S

Collings DS2H

Collings OM2H T

MODEL YEAR	FEATURES	EXC. COND. LOW	HIGH

C10 Deluxe

1986-present. C10 with Indian rosewood back and sides (mahogany, flamed maple or koa optional), sunburst or natural.

1986-2024	Indian rosewood	$3,500	$4,800
1994-2000s	Flamed maple	$4,000	$5,500
1994-2000s	Koa option	$4,000	$5,800
1994-2000s	Varnish	$3,800	$5,200
1994-2024	Mahogany	$3,200	$4,800

C100

1986-1994, 2019-present. Quadruple 0-size, mahogany back and sides, spruce top, natural, replaced by CJ Jumbo. Reintroduced '19 with Honduran mahogany back, sides and neck.

1986-1994		$3,000	$4,000
2019-2024		$3,000	$4,000

C100 Deluxe

1986-1994, 2019-present. C-100 with rosewood back and sides. Reintroduced in '19 with East Indian rosewood and Honduran mahogany.

1986-1994		$3,500	$4,800

CJ

1995-present. Quadruple 0-size, Sitka spruce top (standard), Indian rosewood back and sides, natural. Various other wood options available.

1995-2024	Sitka, Indian	$4,000	$5,500

CJ A

2019. Adirondack spruce top, Indian rosewood back and sides.

2019		$4,200	$5,800

CJ Koa ASB

2007. Adirondack spruce top, scalloped bracing ASB, flamed koa sides and back.

2007		$4,500	$6,000

CJ Mh

2020-present. Sitka spruce top (standard), Honduran mahogany back, sides and neck, sunburst. Various other wood options available.

2020-2024	Sitka, mahogany	$3,800	$5,200

CJ-35

2014-present. Sitka spruce top (standard), Honduran mahogany back, sides and neck, tigerstripe 'guard. Various other wood options available.

2014-2024	Sitka, mahogany	$3,800	$5,200

CL Series (City Limits)

2004-present. City Limits Jazz series, fully carved flame maple top, solid Honduran mahogany body, East Indian rosewood 'board, high gloss lacquer finish.

2004-2024		$3,000	$4,800

Clarence White

1989-2000. Adirondack top, Brazilian rosewood back and sides (CW-28), or mahogany (CW-18), herringbone trim.

1989-2000	CW-28, Brazilian	$7,000	$10,000
1993-2000	CW-18, Mahogany	$4,000	$5,500

CW Indian A

2019-present. Collings Winfield (CW), named after the Walnut Valley Festival in Winfield, Kansas, modified version of standard dreadnought, Adirondack spruce top, East Indian rosewood back and sides, ivoroid binding with herringbone purfling.

2019-2024		$4,200	$5,800

D1 Gruhn

1989. Short run for Gruhn Guitars, Nashville, Gruhn script headstock logo, signed by Bill Collings, choice of Indian rosewood or curly maple back and sides, Engelman spruce top.

1989		$4,500	$6,000

D1 Series

1992-present. Dreadnought, Sitka spruce top (standard), mahogany back and sides. Various other wood options available.

1992-2018	D1A, Adirondack	$4,000	$5,500
1992-2018	D1H, Herringbone	$4,000	$5,500
1992-2024	D1, Mahogany	$3,800	$5,200
2010	D1VN, Vintage neck	$4,000	$5,500
2016-2024	D1AT, Adirondack, Torrefied	$4,200	$5,800

D2 Series

1986-present. Dreadnought, Sitka spruce top (standard), Indian rosewood back and sides. Various other wood options available.

1986-1995	D2, Sitka, Indian	$4,000	$5,500
1986-2024	D2H, Herringbone	$3,500	$6,000
1994	D2HV, Vintage neck	$4,200	$5,800
1994-2005	D2HB, Brazilian	$7,000	$10,000
2004-2010	D2HAV, Varnish	$4,500	$6,200
2004-2024	D2HA, Adirondack	$4,200	$5,800
2008	D2HGV, German spruce	$4,500	$6,200
2017-2024	D2HT, Traditional	$4,000	$5,800

D3 Series

1990-present. Dreadnought, Sitka spruce top (standard), Brazilian or Indian rosewood back and sides. Various other wood options available.

1990-1999	D3, Brazilian	$7,000	$10,000
2000-2024	D3, Indian	$4,200	$5,800
2004-2024	D3A, Adirondack	$4,500	$6,200

D42

2000s. Brazilian rosewood back and sides, fancy.

2000s		$7,500	$12,000

DS1/DS1A

2004-present. D-size, slope shoulders, 12 fret neck, slotted headstock, mahogany back and sides, A is Adirondack upgrade.

2004-2024		$4,000	$5,800

DS2H/DS2HA

1995-present. D-size, 12-fret, slotted headstock, Sitka spruce top, Indian rosewood back and sides, herringbone purfling. A is Adirondack upgrade.

1995-2024		$4,200	$6,200

DS41

1995-2007. Indian rosewood, fancy, abalone top trim, snowflake markers.

1995-2007		$4,500	$6,000

I-30

2017-present. Flamed maple top, f-holes, mahogany neck, 2 P-90 pickups.

2017-2024		$3,200	$5,200

MODEL YEAR	FEATURES	EXC. COND. LOW	HIGH

I-35 Deluxe

2007-present. Premium flamed maple top (standard), mahogany body, gloss lacquer finish. Various other wood options available.

2007-2024	Various options	$4,500	$6,500

OM1 Series

1994-present. Orchestra model, Sitka spruce top (standard), mahogany back and sides, natural. Various other wood options available.

1994-2024	OM1, Mahogany	$3,500	$4,800
1994-2024	OM1A, Adirondack	$3,800	$5,200
2000-2016	OM1, Koa	$4,000	$5,800
2000-2016	OM1MH, Mahogany	$3,200	$4,800
2007-2016	OM1A, Cutaway, Adirondack	$4,000	$5,500
2016-2024	OM1T, Traditional	$4,000	$5,500
2018-2024	OM1AT, Adirondack	$5,500	$8,500
2020-2024	OM1JL, Julian Lage	$4,500	$6,000

OM2 Series

1990-present. Sitka spruce top (standard), Indian rosewood back and sides. Various other wood options available.

1990-2020	OM2, Sitka, Indian	$4,000	$5,500
1990-2024	OM2H, Herringbone	$4,000	$5,500
1998	OM2HAV, Varnish	$6,500	$10,000
2001	OM2H SSB, Brazilian	$7,000	$10,000
2003-2018	OM2HA, Adirondack	$4,200	$5,800
2008	OM2H GSS, German spruce	$4,500	$6,200
2018-2024	OM2HAT, Traditional, Adirondack	$4,200	$5,800

OM3 Series

1986-present. Sitka spruce top (standard), first Brazilian later Indian rosewood back and sides. Various other wood options available.

1986-1996	OM3HC Cutaway, Indian	$4,200	$5,800
1986-1999	OM3B, Brazilian	$7,000	$10,000
1994-2007	OM3HBA, Adirondack, Brazilian	$7,500	$12,000
2000-2024	OM3, Indian	$4,000	$5,500
2003	OM3, Figured maple	$4,500	$6,000
2004-2024	OM3A, Adirondack	$4,200	$5,800
2008-2024	OM3, Mahogany	$3,800	$5,200

OM41BrzGCut

2007. Brazilian rosewood sides and back, German spruce top, rounded cutaway.

2007		$7,500	$12,000

OM42B

Brazilian rosewood back and sides, Adirondack spruce top, fancy rosette and binding.

2000		$8,000	$12,000

OM42G

German spruce top, Indian rosewood back and sides.

1999		$4,500	$6,000

OMC2H

Adirondack top, Brazilian rosewood back and sides, herringbone trim.

2008		$7,000	$10,000

SJ

1986-present. Spruce top, quilted maple back and sides or Indian rosewood (earlier option), later mahogany.

1986-2024	Various options	$4,000	$5,800

SJ41

1996		$5,500	$8,500

SoCo Deluxe

2007-present. Premium figured maple top over semi-hollow mahogany body, rosewood 'board, f-holes, various finish options.

2007-2024		$3,500	$5,000

Winfield

2004-2006. D-style, Adirondack spruce top, Brazilian or Indian rosewood back and sides, later mahogany.

2004	Indian	$4,500	$6,000
2005-2006	Brazilian	$5,500	$8,500
2006	Mahogany	$4,000	$5,800

Columbia

Late 1800s-early 1900s. The Columbia brand name was used on acoustic guitars by New York's James H. Buckbee Co. until c.1987 and afterwards by Galveston's Thomas Goggan and Brothers.

Comins

1992-present. Premium and presentation grade, custom archtops built by luthier Bill Comins in Willow Grove, Pennsylvania. He also builds mandolins and offers a combo amp built in collaboration with George Alessandro.

Commander

Late 1950s-early 1960s. Archtop acoustic guitars made by Harmony for the Alden catalog company.

Concertone

Ca. 1914-1930s. Concertone was a brand made by Chicago's Slingerland and distributed by Montgomery Ward. The brand was also used on other instruments such as ukuleles.

Conklin

1984-present. Intermediate, professional and premium grade, production/custom, 6-, 7-, 8-, and 12-string solid and hollowbody electrics, by luthier Bill Conklin. He also builds basses. Originally located in Lebanon, Missouri, in '88 the company moved to Springfield, Missouri. Conklin instruments are made in the U.S. and overseas.

Collings OM3

Comins 16 Vintage Burst Concert Model

GUITARS

Conrad Resonator Acoustic
Jack Welch

1968 Coral Hornet
RobbieKeene

MODEL YEAR	FEATURES	EXC. COND. LOW	HIGH

Conn Guitars

Ca.1968-ca.1978. Student to mid-quality classical and acoustic guitars, some with bolt-on necks, also some electrics. Imported from Japan by band instrument manufacturer and distributor Conn/Continental Music Company, Elkhart, Indiana.

Acoustic

1968-1978	Various models	$300	$650

Classical

1968-1978	Student-level	$200	$300

Electric Solidbody

1968-1978	Various models	$350	$600

Connor, Stephan

1995-present. Luthier Stephan Connor builds his premium grade, custom nylon-string guitars in Waltham, Massachusetts.

Conrad Guitars

Ca. 1968-1978. Mid- to better-quality copies of glued-neck Martin and Gibson acoustics and bolt-neck Gibson and Fender solidbodies. They also offered basses, mandolins and banjos. Imported from Japan by David Wexler and Company, Chicago, Illinois.

Acoustic 12-String

1970s. Dreadnought size.

1970s		$300	$500

Acoustical Slimline (40080/40085)

1970s. Rosewood 'board, 2 or 3 DeArmond-style pickups, block markers, sunburst.

1970s		$600	$900

Acoustical Slimline 12-String (40100)

1970s. Rosewood 'board, 2 DeArmond-style pickups, dot markers, sunburst.

1970s		$350	$700

Bison (40035/40030/40065/40005)

1970s. 1 through 4 pickups available, rosewood 'board with dot markers, six-on-side headstock.

1970s		$600	$900

Bumper (40223)

1970s. Clear Lucite solidbody.

1970s		$800	$1,200

Classical Student (40150)

1970s		$200	$300

De Luxe Folk Guitar

1970s. Resonator acoustic, mahogany back, sides and neck, Japanese import.

1970s		$300	$600

Master Size (40178)

1972-1977. Electric archtop, 2 pickups.

1972-1977		$600	$900

Resonator Acoustic

1970s. Flat-top with wood, metal resonator and 8 ports, round neck.

1970s		$700	$1,000

Violin-Shaped 12-String Electric (40176)

1970s. Scroll headstock, 2 pickups, 500/1 control panel, bass side dot markers, sunburst.

1970s		$600	$1,500

Violin-Shaped Electric (40175)

1970s. Scroll headstock, 2 pickups, 500/1 control panel, bass side dot markers, vibrato, sunburst.

1970s		$600	$1,500

White Styrene (1280)

1970s. Solid maple body covered with white styrene, 2 pickups, tremolo, bass side dot markers, white.

1970s		$600	$900

Contessa

1960s. Acoustic, semi-hollow archtop, solidbody and bass guitars made in Italy by Zero Sette and imported by Hohner. They also made banjos.

Acoustic

1960s	Various models	$150	$300

Electric Solidbody

1960s	Various models	$400	$600

Contreras

See listing for Manuel Contreras and Manuel Contreras II.

Coral

1967-1969. In '66 MCA bought Danelectro and in '67 introduced the Coral brand of guitars, basses and amps.

Bellzouki 7021

1967. 12-string electric, modified teardrop shape with body points on treble and bass bouts, 2 pickups.

1967		$1,200	$1,800

Combo/Vincent Bell Combo

1967-1969. Cutaway acoustic/electric, 1 or 2 pickups.

1967-1969	V1N6, 1 pu	$2,200	$3,200
1967-1969	V2N6, 2 pu	$2,800	$3,800

Firefly

1967-1969. Double-cut, f-holes, 2 pickups, vibrato available (2V) and 12-string (2N12), red or sunburst.

1967-1969	F2N, no vibrato	$900	$1,200
1967-1969	F2V, vibrato	$1,000	$1,500
1968-1969	F2N12, 12-string	$1,000	$1,500

Hornet (2 Pickups)

1967-1969. Solidbody, 2 pickups, vibrato available (2V or 3V), sunburst, black or red.

1967-1969	H2N, black or red	$1,000	$1,500
1967-1969	H2N, sunburst	$900	$1,200
1967-1969	H2V, black or red	$1,000	$1,500
1967-1969	H2V, sunburst	$900	$1,200

Hornet (3 Pickups)

1967-1969. As above with 3 pickups, with or without vibrato.

1967-1969	H3N, black or red	$1,200	$1,800
1967-1969	H3N, sunburst	$1,200	$1,800
1967-1969	H3V, black or red	$1,200	$1,800
1967-1969	H3V, sunburst	$1,200	$1,800

Long Horn

1967-1969. Deep double-cut hollowbody, 2 lipstick tube pickups, 6-string (2N6) or 12 (2N12), sunburst.

1967-1969	L2N12	$1,800	$2,500
1967-1969	L2N6	$1,800	$2,500

Scorpion

1967-1969. Offset double-cut solidbody, 12-string, 2 or 3 lipstick tube pickups, vibrato available (2V or 3V).

MODEL YEAR	FEATURES	EXC. COND. LOW	HIGH
1967-1969	S2N12, black or red	$1,000	$1,500
1967-1969	S2N12, sunburst	$1,000	$1,500
1967-1969	S2V12, black or red	$1,000	$1,500
1967-1969	S2V12, sunburst	$1,000	$1,500
1967-1969	S3N12, black or red	$1,000	$1,500
1967-1969	S3N12, sunburst	$1,000	$1,500
1967-1969	S3V12, black or red	$1,200	$1,800
1967-1969	S3V12, sunburst	$1,000	$1,500

Sitar

1967-1969. Six-string guitar with drone strings and 3 pickups (2 under the 6 strings, 1 under the drones), kind of a USA-shaped body.

MODEL YEAR	FEATURES	EXC. COND. LOW	HIGH
1967-1969	3S18, 18-string	$3,200	$4,500
1967-1969	3S19, 19-string	$3,200	$4,500
1967-1969	3S9, 9-string	$3,000	$4,000

Teardrop

1967-1969. Teardrop shaped hollowbody, 2 lipstick tube pickups.

MODEL YEAR	FEATURES	EXC. COND. LOW	HIGH
1967-1969	T2N6	$1,200	$1,800

Córdoba

Line of classical guitars handmade in Portugal and imported by Guitar Salon International. By '13, U.S. production was added.

Classical

MODEL YEAR	FEATURES	EXC. COND. LOW	HIGH
2000s	Higher-end	$1,500	$2,000
2000s	Mid-level	$400	$600
2000s	Student-level	$300	$500

Cordova

1960s. Classical nylon string guitars imported by David Wexler of Chicago.

Grand Concert Model WC-026

1960s. The highest model offered by Cordova, 1-piece rosewood back, laminated rosewood sides, spruce top, natural.

MODEL YEAR	FEATURES	EXC. COND. LOW	HIGH
1960s		$400	$600

Corey James Custom Guitars

2005-present. Luthier Corey James Moilanen builds his professional and premium grade, production/custom solidbody guitars and basses in Howell, Michigan.

Coriani, Paolo

1984-present. Production/custom nylon-string guitars and hurdy-gurdys built by luthier Paolo Coriani in Modeila, Italy.

Cort

1973-present. North Brook, Illinois-based Cort offers budget, intermediate and professional grade, production/custom, acoustic and solidbody, semi-hollow, hollow body electric guitars and basses built in Korea.

Cort was the second significant Korean private label (Hondo brand was the first) to come out of Korea. Jack Westheimer entered into an agreement with Korea's Cort to do Cort-brand, private-label, and Epiphone-brand guitars.

CP Thornton Guitars

1985-present. Luthier Chuck Thornton builds professional and premium grade, production/custom, semi-hollow and solidbody electric guitars in Sumner, Maine. Up to '96 he also built basses.

Crafter

1986-present. Crafter offers budget and intermediate grade, production, classical, acoustic, acoustic/electric, and electric guitars, basses and mandolins made in Korea. They also offer the Cruzer and Ashland brands of instruments. From '72 to '86 they made Sungeum classical guitars.

Cranium

Introduced 1996, professional grade, production/custom, hollow, semi-hollow, and solidbody electrics built by luthier Wayne O'Connor in Peterborough, Ontario.

Crescent Moon

Professional grade, production/custom, solidbody guitars and basses built by luthier Craig Muller in Baltimore, Maryland, starting 1999.

Creston

2004-present. Professional grade, custom, solidbody electric guitars and basses built by luthier Creston Lea in Burlington, Vermont.

Crestwood

1970s. Copies of the popular classical guitars, flat-tops, electric solidbodies and basses of the era, imported by La Playa Distributing Company of Detroit.

Acoustic 12-String

MODEL YEAR	FEATURES	EXC. COND. LOW	HIGH
1970s		$300	$500

Electric

1970s. Various models include near copies of the 335 (Crestwood model 2043, 2045 and 2047), Les Paul Custom (2020), Strat (2073), Jazzmaster (2078), Tele (2082), and the SG Custom (2084).

MODEL YEAR	FEATURES	EXC. COND. LOW	HIGH
1970s		$400	$600

Crimson Guitars

2005-present. Luthiers Benjamin Crowe and Aki Atrill build professional and premium grade, custom, solidbody guitars and basses in Somerset, U.K.

Cromwell

1935-1939. Budget model brand built by Gibson and distributed by mail-order businesses like Grossman, Continental, Richter & Phillips, and Gretsch & Brenner.

1967 Coral Sitar
Izzy Miller

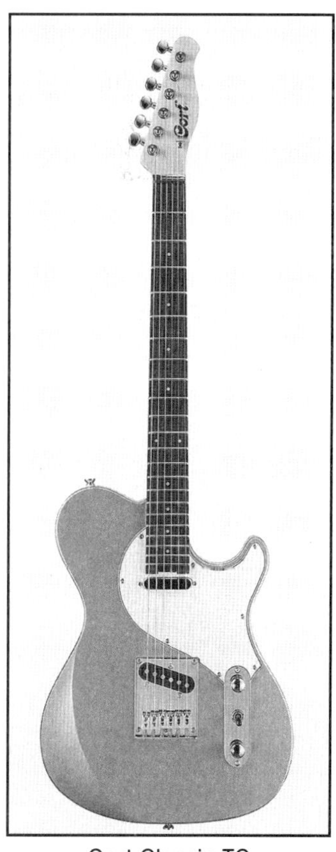

Cort Classic TC

CSR Serenata

1966 Custom Kraft Lexington
Rivington Guitars

MODEL YEAR	FEATURES	EXC. COND. LOW	HIGH

Acoustic Archtop

1935-1939. Archtop acoustic, f-holes, pressed mahogany back and sides, carved and bound top, bound back, 'guard and 'board, no truss rod.

1935-1939	Various models	$1,200	$2,500
1935-1939	With '30s era pu	$1,500	$3,000

Acoustic Flat-Top

1935-1939	G-2 (L-00)	$1,500	$2,500

GT-2 Tenor

1935-1939	1474" flat-top	$1,000	$1,500

GT-4 Tenor

1935-1939	16" archtop	$1,200	$1,800

Cromwell (Guild)

1963-1964. Guild imported these 2- or 3-pickup offset double cut solidbodies from Hagstrom. These were basically part of Hagstrom's Kent line with laminated bodies and birch necks. About 500 were imported into the U.S.

Solidbody

1963-1964		$1,500	$2,200

Crook Custom Guitars

1997-present. Professional grade, custom, solidbody electric guitars and basses built in Moundsville, West Virginia by luthier Bill Crook.

Crossley

2005-present. Professional grade, production/custom, solidbody and chambered electric guitars built in Melbourne, Victoria, Australia by luthier Peter Crossley.

Crown

1960s. Violin-shaped hollowbody electrics, solidbody electric guitars and basses, possibly others. Imported from Japan.

Acoustic Flat-Top

1960s. 6-string and 12-string.

1960s		$200	$300

Electric Archtop

1960s. Double pointed cutaways, 2 humbucking pickups, laminated top, full-depth body.

1960s		$600	$900

Electric Solidbody/Semi-Hollow

1960s. Student-level Japanese import.

1960s	Copy models	$500	$800
1960s	Standard models	$300	$500
1960s	Violin-shaped body	$500	$800

Crucianelli

Early 1960s. Italian guitars imported into the U.S. by Bennett Brothers of New York and Chicago around '63 to '64. Accordion builder Crucianelli also made Imperial, Elite, PANaramic, and Elli-Sound brand guitars.

Cruzer

Intermediate grade, production, solidbody electric guitars, basses, amps, and effects made by Korea's Crafter Guitars.

CSR

1996-present. Father and daughter luthiers Roger and Courtney Kitchens build their premium grade, production/custom, archtop guitars and basses in Byron, Georgia.

Cumpiano

1974-present. Professional and premium grade, custom steel-string and nylon-string guitars, and acoustic basses built by luthier William Cumpiano in Northampton, Massachusetts.

Curbow String Instruments

1994-2007. Premium grade, production/custom, solidbody guitars and basses built by luthier Doug Somervell in Morganton, Georgia. Founded by Greg Curbow who passed away in '05.

Custom

1980s. Line of solidbody guitars and basses introduced in the early '80s by Charles Lawing and Chris Lovell, owners of Strings & Things in Memphis, Tennessee.

Custom Kraft

Late-1950s-1968. A house brand of St. Louis Music Supply, instruments built by Valco and Kay. They also offered basses and amps.

Electric Solidbody

1950s-1960s. U.S.-made or import, entry-level, 1or 2 pickups.

1950s-60s	Import	$300	$500
1950s-60s	USA, Kay, 2 pu	$800	$1,200

Sound Saturator

1960s	12-string	$700	$1,200

Super Zapp

1960s		$800	$1,200

Thin Twin Jimmy Reed (style)

Late-1950s-early-1960s. Single cut, 2 pickups, 4 knobs and toggle, dot markers.

1950s-60s	US-made	$1,200	$1,800

D.J. Hodson

1994-2007. Luthier David J. Hodson built his professional and premium grade, production/custom, acoustic guitars in Loughborough, Leicestershire, U.K. He also built ukes. He passed away in '07.

Daddy Mojo String Instruments Inc.

2005-present. Luthiers Lenny Piroth-Robert and Luca Tripaldi build their intermediate and professional grade, production/custom, solidbody electric, resonator and cigar box guitars in Montreal, Quebec.

Dagmar Custom Guitars

Luthier Pete Swanson builds custom, premium and presentation grade, acoustic and electric archtop guitars in Niagara, Ontario, starting in 2008.

MODEL YEAR	FEATURES	EXC. COND. LOW	HIGH

D'Agostino

1976-early 1990s. Acoustic and electric solidbody guitars and basses imported by PMS Music, founded in New York City by former Maestro executive Pat D'Agostino, his brother Steven D'Agostino, and Mike Confortti. First dreadnought acoustic guitars imported from Japan in '76. First solidbodies manufactured by the EKO custom shop beginning in '77. In '82 solidbody production moved to Japan. Beginning in '84, D'Agostinos were made in Korea. Overall, about 60% of guitars were Japanese, 40% Korean. They also had basses.

Acoustic Flat-Top

1976-1990. Early production in Japan, by mid-'80s, most production in Korea.

1976-1990		$500	$600

Electric Semi-Hollowbody

1981-early 1990s. Early production in Japan, later versions from Korea.

1981-1990		$900	$1,200

Electric Solidbody

1977-early 1990s. Early models made in Italy, later versions from Japan and Korea.

1981-1990		$900	$1,200

Daily Guitars

1976-present. Luthier David Daily builds his premium grade, production/custom classical guitars in Sparks, Nevada.

Daion

1978-1984. Mid- to higher-quality copies imported from Japan. Original designs were introduced in the '80s. Only acoustics were offered at first; in '81 they added acoustic/electric and solid and semi-hollow electrics. They also had basses.

Acoustic

1978-1985. Various flat-top models.

1978-1985	Higher-end	$800	$1,500
1978-1985	Lower-end	$300	$600

Electric

1978-1985. Various solid and semi-hollow body guitars.

1978-1985	Higher-end	$850	$1,500
1978-1985	Lower-end	$300	$600

Daisy Rock

2001-present. Budget and intermediate grade, production, full-scale and 3/4 scale, solidbody, semi-hollow, acoustic, and acoustic/electric guitars and basses. Founded by Tish Ciravolo as a Division of Schecter Guitars, the Daisy line is focused on female customers.

D'Ambrosio

2001-present. Luthier Otto D'Ambrosio builds his premium grade, custom/production, acoustic and electric archtop guitars in Providence, Rhode Island.

Dan Armstrong

Dan Armstrong started playing jazz in Cleveland in the late-'50s. He moved to New York and started doing repairs, eventually opening his own store on 48th Street in '65. By the late-'60s he was designing his Lucite guitars for Ampeg (see Ampeg for those listings). He moved to England in '71, where he developed his line of colored stomp boxes. He returned to the States in '75. Armstrong died in '04.

Wood Body

1973-1975. Sliding pickup, wood body, brown.

1973-1975		$1,500	$3,000

Wood Body AMG 100 (reissue)

Various wood body options, BLD (blond, swamp ash), CH (cherry, mahogany) and BK (black, alder).

2008-2009	BK	$500	$800
2008-2009	BLD	$600	$900
2008-2009	CH	$500	$800

Dan Armstrong Guitars

Introduced 2015, professional grade, production/custom, acrylic solidbody electrics based on the original Dan Armstrong models, built in Everett, Washington.

Dan Kellaway

1976-present. Production/custom, premium grade, classical and steel string guitars built by luthier Dan Kellaway in Singleton NSW, Australia. He also builds mandolins and lutes.

Danelectro

1946-1969, 1996-present. Founded in Red Bank, New Jersey, by Nathan I. (Nate or Nat) Daniel, an electronics enthusiast with amplifier experience. In 1933, Daniel built amps for Thor's Bargain Basement in New York. In '34 he was recruited by Epiphone's Herb Sunshine to build the earliest Electar amps and pickup-making equipment. From '35 to '42, he operated Daniel Electric Laboratories in Manhattan, supplying Epiphone. He started Danelectro in '46 and made his first amps for Montgomery Ward in '47. Over the years, Danelectro made amplifiers, solidbody, semi-hollow and hollowbody electric guitars and basses, electric sitar, and the Bellzouki under the Danelectro, Silvertone, and Coral brands. In '48, began supplying Silvertone amps for Sears (various coverings), with his own brand (brown leatherette) distributed by Targ and Dinner as Danelectro and S.S. Maxwell. He developed an electronic vibrato in '48 on his Vibravox series amps. In '50 he developed a microphone with volume and tone controls and outboard Echo Box reverb unit. In the fall of '54, Danelectro replaced Harmony as provider of Silvertone solidbody guitars for Sears. Also, in '54, the first Danelectro brand guitars appeared with tweed covering, bell headstock, and pickups under the pickguard. The Coke bottle headstock debuts as Silvertone Lightning Bolt in '54 and was used on Danelectros from '56 to '66. The company moved to Red Bank, New Jersey in

D'Ambrosio

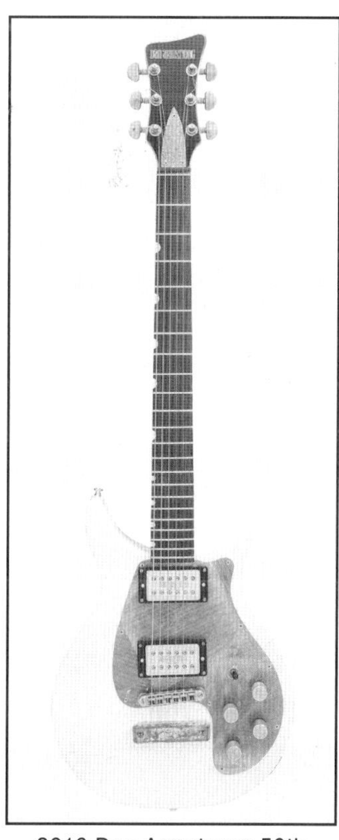

2016 Dan Armstrong 50th Anniversary Custom
Imaged by Heritage Auctions, HA.com

GUITARS

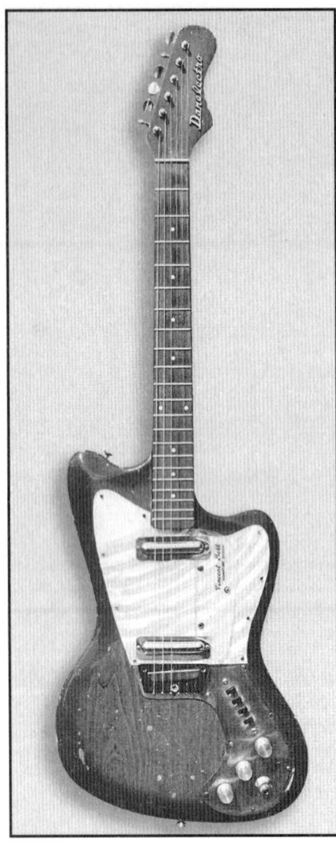
1965 Danelectro Combo/ Vincent Bell

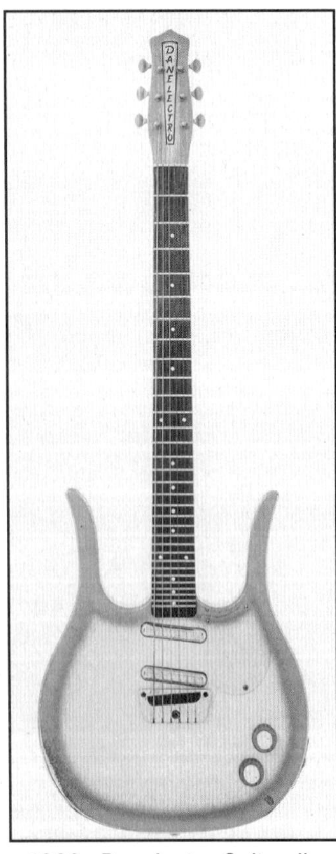
1960s Danelectro Guitaralin
Imaged by Heritage Auctions, HA.com

MODEL YEAR	FEATURES	EXC. COND. LOW	HIGH

'57, and in '58 relocated to Neptune, New Jersey. In '59, Harmony and Kay guitars replaced all but 3 Danelectros in Sears catalog. In '66, MCA buys the company (Daniel remains with company), but by mid-'69, MCA halts production and closes the doors. Some leftover stock is sold to Dan Armstrong, who had a shop in New York at the time. Armstrong assembled several hundred Danelectro guitars as Dan Armstrong Modified with his own pickup design.

Rights to name acquired by Anthony Marc in late-'80s, who assembled several thinline hollowbody guitars, many with Longhorn shape, using Japanese-made bodies and original Danelectro necks and hardware. In '96, the Evets Corporation, of San Clemente, California, introduced a line of effects bearing the Danelectro brand. Amps and guitars, many of which were reissues of the earlier instruments, soon followed. In early 2003, Evets discontinued offering guitar and amps, but revived the guitar and bass line in '05.

MCA-Danelectro-made guitars were called the Dane Series with model numbers starting with an A, B, C, or a D, with A models being the least expensive going up to the D models. All Dane Series instruments came with 1, 2 or 3 pickups and with hand vibrato options. The Dane Series was made from '67 to '69. MCA did carry over the Convertible, Guitarlin 4123, Long Horn Bass-4 and Bass-6 and Doubleneck 3923. MCA also offered the Bellzouki Double Pickup 7021. Each Dane Series includes an electric 12-string. Danelectro also built Coral brand instruments (see Coral).

Prices for pre-MCA Danelectros include the period-correct case. A non-original case can drop the value of the guitar by 10%. In the mid- to late-'50s, these cases were referred to as "coffin cases" because of their unique shape.

Baritone 6-String Reissue

1999-2003, 2008-present. Danelectro has offered several models with 6-string baritone tuning, often with various reissue-year designations, single- or double-cut, 2 or 3 pickups.

1999-2024	Various models	$450	$1,000

Bellzouki

1963-1969. 12-string electric. Teardrop-shaped body, 1 pickup, sunburst (7010) for '63-'66. Vincent Bell model (7020) with modified teardrop shape with 2 body points on both treble and bass bouts and 2 pickups for '63-'66. Same body as Coral Electric Sitar for '67-'69.

1963-1969	1 pu, teardrop body	$900	$1,500
1963-1969	2 pu, pointy body	$1,000	$1,500
1967-1969	2 pu, sitar body	$1,800	$2,500

Companion

1959-1960. Hollowbody double-cut, 2 pickups, concentric TV knobs.

1959-1960		$1,200	$1,800

Convertible

1959-1969. Acoustic/electric, double-cut, guitar was sold with or without the removable single pickup.

1959-1969	Acoustic, no pu, natural	$600	$900
1959-1969	Pickup installed, natural	$1,000	$1,500
1967-1969	Red, white, blue	$1,200	$1,800

Convertible Reissue

1999, 2000-2003. The Convertible Pro was offered '00-'03 with upgraded Gotoh tuners and metalflake and pearl finishes.

1999-2003	Blond or green	$400	$600

Dane A Series

1967-1969. 1or 2 pickups, with or without vibrato (V), solid wood slab body, hard lacquer finish with 4 color options, 12-string also offered.

1967-1969	1N12, 12-string	$1,200	$1,800
1967-1969	2N12, 12-string	$1,300	$2,000
1967-1969	N, 1 pickup	$900	$1,400
1967-1969	N, 2 pickpus	$1,100	$1,600
1967-1969	V, 1 pu, vibrato	$1,100	$1,600
1967-1969	V, 2 pu, vibrato	$1,200	$1,800

Dane B Series

1967-1969. 2 or 3 pickups, with or without vibrato (V), semi-solid Durabody, 6 or 12 strings.

1967-1969	12-string	$1,200	$1,800
1967-1969	6-string, 2 pu	$900	$1,400
1967-1969	6-string, 3 pu	$1,000	$1,500

Dane C Series

1967-1969. 2 or 3 pickups, with or without vibrato (V), semi-solid Durabody with 2-tone Gator finish, 6 or 12 strings.

1967-1969	12-string	$1,600	$2,400
1967-1969	6-string	$1,400	$2,100

Dane D Series

1967-1969. 2 or 3 pickups, with or without vibrato (V), solid wood sculptured thinline body, 'floating adjustable pickguard-fingerguide', master volume with 4 switches, 6 or 12 strings.

1967-1969	12-string	$1,400	$2,100
1967-1969	6-string, 2 pu	$1,000	$1,500
1967-1969	6-string, 3 pu	$1,200	$1,800

Danoblaster Series

2000-2003. Offset double-cuts, 3 pickups, built-in effects - distortion on the Hearsay, distortion, chorus, trem and echo on Innuendo. Also in 12-string and baritone.

2000-2003		$300	$500

DC-2 Model 3021

1959-1966. Jimmy Page model, shorthorn, double pickup.

1959-1966		$1,400	$2,100

DC-3/DDC-3

1999-2003. Shorthorn double-cut, 3 pickups, seal-shaped pickguard, Coke bottle headstock, solid and sparkle finishes.

1999-2003		$500	$800

DC-12/Electric XII

1999-2003. 12-string version of 59-DC.

1999-2003		$500	$800

59-DC/'59 Dano (Reissue)

1998-1999, 2007. Shorthorn double-cut, 2 pickups, seal-shaped pickguard, Coke bottle headstock, '07 version called '59 Dano.

1998-1999		$500	$800

MODEL YEAR	FEATURES	EXC. COND. LOW	HIGH

Deluxe Single Pickup

1959-1966. Double-cut, Coke bottle headstock, 1 pickup, 2 knobs.

1959-1960	Walnut or white	$1,200	$1,800
1961-1966	Walnut, white, honey	$1,100	$1,700

Deluxe Double Pickup

1959-1966. As Single above, but with 2 pickups, and added master volume on later models.

1959-1960	Walnut or white	$1,400	$2,100
1961-1966	Walnut, white, honey	$1,200	$1,800

Deluxe Triple Pickup

1959-1966. As Single above, but with 3 pickups, 3 knobs, and added master volume on later models.

1959-1960	Walnut or white	$1,400	$2,100
1961-1966	Walnut, white, honey	$1,200	$1,800

Doubleneck (3923)

1958-1966. A shorthorn double-cut, bass and 6-string necks, 1 pickup on each neck, Coke bottle headstocks, white sunburst.

1958-1966		$3,200	$4,800

Doubleneck Reissue

1999-2003. Baritone 6-string and standard 6-string double neck, shorthorn body style, or the 6-12 model with a 6-string and 12-string neck. Price includes $75 for a guitar case, but many sales do not seem to include a guitar case because of unusual body size.

1999-2003		$500	$800

Electric Sitar

1968-1969. Traditional looking, oval-bodied sitar, no drone strings as on the Coral Sitar of the same period.

1968-1969		$3,200	$4,500

Guitarlin (4123)

1958-1966. The Longhorn guitar, 2 huge cutaways, 31-fret neck, 2 pickups.

1958-1960		$3,200	$4,800
1961-1966		$2,700	$4,000

Hand Vibrato Single Pickup (4011)

1958-1966. Short horn double-cut, 1 pickup, batwing headstock, simple design vibrato, black w/ white guard.

1958-1966		$1,000	$1,500

Hand Vibrato Double Pickup (4021)

1958-1966. Same as Single Pickup, but with 2 pickups and larger pickguard.

1958-1966		$1,100	$1,700

Hawk

1967-1969. Offered with 1 or 2 pickups, vibrato (V models) or non-vibrato (N models), 12-string model also offered.

1967-1969	1N, 1 pickup	$1,000	$1,500
1967-1969	1N12, 12-string	$1,200	$1,800
1967-1969	1V, vibrato, 1 pu	$1,100	$1,700
1967-1969	2N, 2 pickups	$1,100	$1,700
1967-1969	2N12, 12-string	$1,500	$2,300
1967-1969	2V, vibrato, 2 pu	$1,500	$2,300

Hodad/Hodad 12-String

1999-2003. Unique double-cut with sharp horns, 6 or 12 strings, sparkle finish.

1999-2003		$500	$800

MODEL YEAR	FEATURES	EXC. COND. LOW	HIGH

Model C

1955. Single-cut, 1or 2 pickups, ginger colored vinyl cover.

1955-1958		$700	$1,000

Pro 1

1963-1964. Odd-shaped double-cut electric with squared off corners, 1 pickup.

1963-1964		$900	$1,400

Pro Reissue

2007. Based on '60s Pro 1, but with 2 pickups.

2007		$400	$600

Slimline (SL) Series

1967-1969. Offset waist double-cut, 2 or 3 pickups, with or without vibrato, 6 or 12 string.

1967-1969	12-string	$1,200	$1,800
1967-1969	6-string, 2 pu	$900	$1,400
1967-1969	6-string, 3 pu	$1,100	$1,700

Standard Single Pickup

1958-1966. Nicknamed the Shorthorn, double-cut, 1 pickup, 2 regular control knobs, kidney-shaped pickguard originally, seal-shaped 'guard by ca. 1960, Coke bottle headstock, in black or bronze.

1958-1959	Kidney guard	$900	$1,400
1960-1966	Seal guard	$900	$1,400

Standard Double Pickup

1958-1966. As Single Pickup above but with 2 pickups and 2 stacked, concentric volume/tone controls, in black, bronze and later blond. The black, seal-shaped pickguard version of this guitar is often referred to as the Jimmy Page model because he used one. Reissued in 1998 as 59-DC.

1958-1959	Kidney guard, black	$1,100	$1,700
1960-1966	Bronze	$1,100	$1,700
1960-1966	Jimmy Page, black	$1,400	$2,100
1961-1966	Blond	$1,500	$2,300

Standard Triple Pickup

1958. As Single Pickup above but with 3 pickups and 3 stacked, concentric pointer volume/tone controls, in white to bronze sunburst, very rare.

1958		$1,400	$2,100

Tweed Model

1954-1955. First production models, single-cut, bell-shape headstock, 1 or 2 pickups, tweed vinyl cover.

1954-1955	1 pickup	$4,000	$5,500
1954-1955	2 pickups	$4,500	$6,000

U-1

1955-1958. Single-cut, 1 pickup, 2 regular knobs, bell-shape headstock originally, switching to Coke bottle in late '55. The U Series featured Dano's new 'solid center' block construction.

1955	Enamel, bell hdsk	$900	$1,400
1956-1957	Enamel, Coke hdsk	$900	$1,400
1956-1957	Ivory, Coke hdsk	$1,100	$1,700
1956-1957	Rare color	$3,000	$4,000
1958	Enamel, Coke hdsk	$900	$1,400
1958	Ivory, Coke hdsk	$1,100	$1,700

U-1 '56 Reissue

1998-1999. Reissue of '56 U-1, various colors.

1998-1999		$400	$600

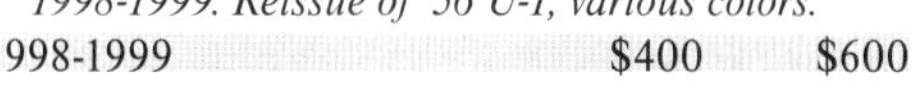

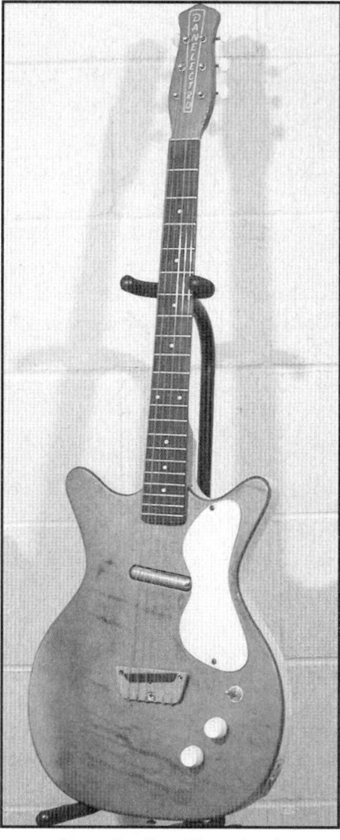

Danelectro Standard Single Pickup

Tom Pfeifer

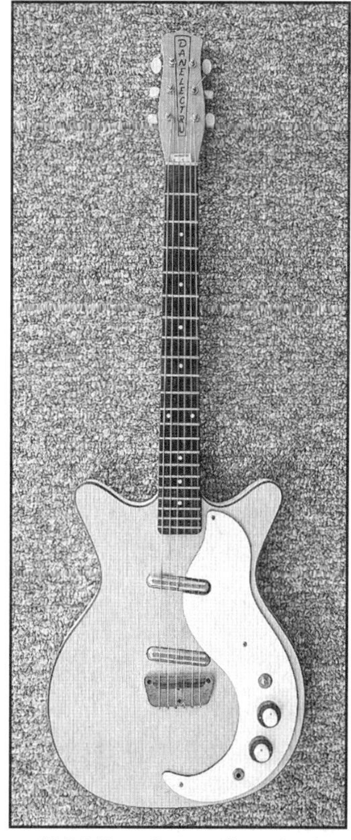

1963 Danelectro Standard Double Pickup

Trey Rabinek

GUITARS

1957 Danelectro U2
Rivington Guitars

Late-'30s D'Angelico Style B
Andy Nelson

MODEL YEAR	FEATURES	EXC. COND. LOW	HIGH

U-2

1955-1958. As U-1, but with 2 pickups and 2 stacked concentric volume/tone controls.

1955	Enamel, bell hdsk	$1,800	$2,500
1956-1957	Enamel, Coke hdsk	$1,800	$2,500
1956-1957	Ivory, Coke hdsk	$2,200	$3,300
1956-1957	Rare color	$5,000	$7,000
1958	Enamel, Coke hdsk	$1,800	$2,700
1958	Ivory, Coke hdsk	$2,300	$3,500

U-2 '56 Reissue

1998-2003. Reissue of '56 U-2, various colors.

1998-2003		$400	$600

U-3

1955-1958. As U-2, but with 3 pickups and 3 stacked concentric volume/tone controls.

1958	Enamel, Coke hdsk	$2,200	$3,500

U-3 '56 Reissue

1999-2003. Reissue of '56 U-3, various colors.

1999-2003		$400	$600

D'Angelico

John D'Angelico built his own line of archtop guitars, mandolins, and violins from 1932 until his death in 1964. His instruments are some of the most sought-after by collectors. The binding on some D'Angelico guitars can become deteriorated and requires replacing.

D'Angelico (L-5 Snakehead)

1932-1935. D'Angelico's L-5-style with snakehead headstock, his first model, sunburst.

1932-1935		$11,500	$14,500

Excel/Exel (Cutaway)

1947-1964. Cutaway, 17" width, 1-and 3-ply bound f-hole.

1947-1949	Natural, original binding	$30,000	$40,000
1947-1949	Sunburst, original binding	$30,000	$40,000
1950-1959	Natural, original binding	$30,000	$40,000
1950-1959	Sunburst, original binding	$30,000	$40,000
1960-1964	Natural	$30,000	$40,000
1960-1964	Sunburst	$30,000	$40,000

Excel/Exel (Non-Cutaway)

1936-1949. Non-cut, 17" width, 1- and 3-ply bound f-hole, natural finishes were typically not offered in the '30s, non-cut Excels were generally not offered after '49 in deference to the Excel cutaway.

1936-1939	Sunburst, straight f-hole	$16,000	$20,000
1938-1939	Sunburst, standard f-hole	$16,000	$20,000
1940-1949	Natural	$17,000	$22,000
1940-1949	Sunburst	$14,000	$18,000

New Yorker (Non-Cutaway)

1936-1949. Non-cut, 18" width, 5-ply-bound f-hole, New Yorker non-cut orders were overshadowed by the cut model orders starting in '47.

1936-1939	Sunburst	$20,000	$28,000
1940-1949	Natural	$22,000	$30,000
1940-1949	Sunburst	$20,000	$28,000

New Yorker Deluxe (Cutaway)

1947-1964. Cutaway, 18" width, 5-ply-bound f-hole, New Yorker non-cut orders were overshadowed by the cut model orders starting in '47.

1947-1949	Natural	$48,000	$62,000
1947-1949	Sunburst	$40,000	$52,000
1950-1959	Natural	$48,000	$62,000
1950-1959	Sunburst	$40,000	$52,000
1960-1964	Natural	$42,000	$55,000
1960-1964	Sunburst	$35,000	$45,000

New Yorker Special

1950-1964. Also called Excel New Yorker or Excel Cutaway New Yorker Cutaway, 17" width, New Yorker styling, not to be confused with D'Angelico Special (A and B style).

1950-1959	Natural	$30,000	$40,000
1950-1959	Sunburst	$25,000	$35,000
1960-1964	Natural	$25,000	$35,000
1960-1964	Sunburst	$24,000	$31,000

Special (Cutaway)

1950-1964. Generally, Style A and B-type instruments made for musicians on a budget, plain specs with little ornamentation, not to be confused with New Yorker Special.

1950-1959	Sunburst	$10,000	$13,000
1960-1964	Sunburst	$9,000	$12,000

Special (Non-Cutaway)

1950-1964. Non-cut Special, not to be confused with New Yorker Special.

1950-1959	Sunburst	$6,000	$7,750
1960-1964	Sunburst	$5,250	$6,750

Style A

1936-1945. Archtop, 17" width, unbound f-holes, block 'board inlays, multi-pointed headstock, nickel-plated metal parts.

1936-1939	Sunburst	$10,000	$13,000
1940-1945	Sunburst	$9,500	$12,000

Style A-1

1936-1945. Unbound f-holes, 17" width, arched headstock, nickel-plated metal parts.

1936-1939	Sunburst	$10,000	$13,000
1940-1945	Sunburst	$9,500	$12,000

Style B

1933-1948. Archtop 17" wide, unbound F-holes, block 'board inlays, gold-plated parts.

1936-1939	Sunburst	$11,000	$15,000
1940-1948	Sunburst	$10,000	$14,000

Style B Special

1933-1948. D'Angelico described variations from standard features with a 'Special' designation, Vintage dealers may also describe these instruments as 'Special'.

1936-1939	Sunburst	$12,000	$15,000
1940-1948	Sunburst	$11,000	$14,000

D'Angelico (D'Angelico Guitars of America)

1988-present. Intermediate and professional grade, production/custom, archtop, flat-top, and solidbody guitars made in South Korea and imported by D'Angelico Guitars of America, of Colts

MODEL YEAR	FEATURES	EXC. COND. LOW	HIGH

Neck, New Jersey. From 1988 to '04, they were premium and presentation grade instruments built in Japan by luthier Hidesato Shino and Vestax. In '12, GTR announced they bought the brand name and are offering premium grade D'Angelicos built in the U.S.

D'Angelico (Lewis)

1994-2011. Luthier Michael Lewis built presentation grade, custom/production, D'Angelico replica guitars in Grass Valley, California, under an agreement with the GHS String Company, which owned the name in the U.S. He also builds guitars and mandolins under the Lewis name.

D'Angelico II

Mid-1990s. Archtops built in the U.S. and distributed by Archtop Enterprises of Merrick, New York. Mainly presentation grade copies of Excel and New Yorker models, but also made lower cost similar models.

Jazz Classic

1990s. Electric archtop, cutaway, carved spruce top, figured maple back and sides, single neck pickup, transparent cherry.

1990s		$2,500	$3,250

Daniel Friederich

1955-2015. Luthier Daniel Friederich built his custom/production, classical guitars in Paris, France.

D'Aquisto

1965-1995. James D'Aquisto apprenticed under D'Angelico until the latter's death, at age 59, in '64. He started making his own brand instruments in '65 and built archtop and flat-top acoustic guitars, solidbody and hollowbody electric guitars. He also designed guitars for Hagstrom and Fender. He died in '95, at age 59.

Avant Garde

1987-1994. 18" wide, non-traditional futuristic model, approximately 5 or 6 instruments were reportedly made, because of low production this pricing is for guidance only.

1990	Blond	$75,000	$95,000

Centura/Centura Deluxe

1993-1994. 17" wide, non-traditional art deco futuristic archtop, approximately 10 made, the last guitars made by this luthier, due to the low production this pricing is for guidance only.

1993-1994	Centura	$90,000	$115,000
1993-1994	Deluxe	$95,000	$125,000

Excel (Cutaway)

1965-1992. Archtop, 17" width, with modern thin-logo started in '81.

1965-1967	Blond	$35,000	$45,000
1965-1967	Sunburst	$30,000	$40,000
1968-1981	Blond	$35,000	$45,000
1968-1981	Sunburst	$30,000	$40,000
1982-1992	Blond	$35,000	$45,000
1982-1992	Sunburst	$33,000	$42,000

MODEL YEAR	FEATURES	EXC. COND. LOW	HIGH

Excel (Flat-Top)

1970s-1980s. Flat-top, 16", flamed maple back and sides, Sitka spruce top, about 15 made, narrow Excel-style headstock, oval soundhole, D'Aquisto script logo on headstock.

1970s-80s		$17,000	$22,000

Hollow Electric

Early model with bar pickup, D'Aquisto headstock, '70s model with humbuckers.

1960s-80s		$14,000	$18,000

Jazz Special

1985	1st version	$15,000	$20,000
1988	2nd version	$21,500	$28,000

New Yorker Classic (Archtop)

1986. Single-cut acoustic archtop with new modern design features such as large S-shaped sound holes.

1986		$51,000	$65,000

New Yorker Classic (Solidbody)

1980s. Only 2 were reported to be made, therefore this pricing is for guidance only.

1980s		$16,000	$20,000

New Yorker Deluxe (Cutaway)

1965-1992. Most are 18" wide.

1965-1981	Blond	$42,000	$55,000
1965-1981	Sunburst	$35,000	$45,000
1982-1992	Blond	$42,000	$55,000
1982-1992	Sunburst	$38,000	$50,000

New Yorker Special (7-String)

1980s. Limited production 7-string, single-cut.

1980s		$30,000	$40,000

New Yorker Special (Cutaway)

1966-1992. Most are 17" wide.

1966-1992	Blond	$26,000	$35,000
1966-1992	Sunburst	$24,000	$30,000

Solo/Solo Deluxe

1992-1993. 18" wide, non-traditional non-cut art deco model, only 2 reported made, because of low production this pricing is for guidance only.

1992-1993		$95,000	$125,000

D'Aquisto (Aria)

May 2002-2013. Premium grade, production, D'Aquisto designs licensed to Aria of Japan by D'Aquisto Strings, Inc., Deer Park, New York.

Various Models

2002-2013		$2,500	$3,500

Dauphin

1970s-late 1990s. Classical and flamenco guitars imported from Spain and Japan by distributor George Dauphinais, located in Springfield, Illinois.

Dave King Acoustics

1980-present. Premium grade, custom/production, acoustic and resonator guitars built by luthier Dave King in Berkshire, U.K.

Dave Maize Acoustic Guitars

1991-present. Luthier Dave Maize builds his professional and premium grade, production/custom, flat-tops and basses in Cave Junction, Oregon.

D'Angelico Guitars of America Deluxe Bobby Weir 3

2002 D'Aquisto (Aria) New Yorker
Mike Thompson

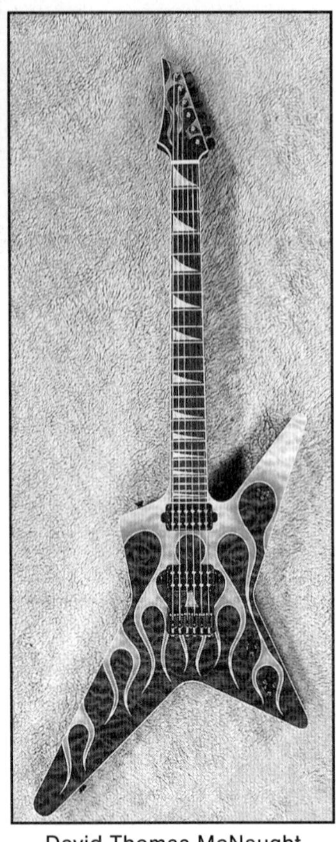

David Thomas McNaught

1981 Dean Cadillac

Imaged by Heritage Auctions, HA.com

David Rubio

1960s-2000. Luthier David Spink built his guitars, lutes, violins, violas, cellos, and harpsichords first in New York, and after '67, in the U.K. While playing in Spain, he acquired the nickname Rubio, after his red beard. He died in '00.

David Thomas McNaught

1989-present. Professional, premium, and presentation grade, custom, solidbody guitars built by luthier David Thomas McNaught and finished by Dave Mansel in Locust, North Carolina. In '97, they added the production/custom DTM line of guitars.

Davis, J. Thomas

1975-present. Premium and presentation grade, custom, steel-string flat-tops, 12-strings, classicals, archtops, Irish citterns and flat-top Irish bouzoukis made by luthier J. Thomas Davis in Columbus, Ohio.

Davoli

See Wandre listing.

DBZ

2008-2012. Solidbody electric guitars from Dean B. Zelinsky, founder of Dean Guitars, and partners Jeff Diamant and Terry Martin. Dean left the partnership February, '12 and established Dean Zelinsky Private Label guitars.

de Jonge, Sergei

1972-present. Premium grade, production/custom classical and steel-string guitars built by luthier Sergei de Jonge originally in Oshawa, Ontario, and since '04 in Chelsea, Quebec.

De Paule Stringed Instruments

1969-1980, 1993-2008. Custom steel-string, nylon-string, archtop, resonator, and Hawaiian guitars built by luthier C. Andrew De Paule in Eugene, Oregon.

Dean

1976-present. Intermediate, professional and premium grade, production/custom, solidbody, hollowbody, acoustic, acoustic/electric, and resonator guitars made in the U.S., Korea, the Czech Republic and China. They also offer basses, banjos, mandolins, and amps. Founded in Evanston, Illinois, by Dean Zelinsky. Original models were upscale versions of Gibson designs with glued necks, fancy tops, DiMarzio pickups and distinctive winged headstocks (V, Z and ML), with production beginning in '77. In '80 the factory was relocated to Chicago. Dean's American manufacturing ends in '86 when all production shifts to Korea. In '91 Zelinsky sold the company to Tropical Music in Miami, Florida. For '93-'94 there was again limited U.S. (California) production of the E'Lite, Cadillac and ML models under the supervision of Zelinsky and Cory Wadley. Korean versions were also produced. In '95, Elliott Rubinson's Armadillo Enterprises, of Clearwater, Florida, bought the Dean brand. In '97 and '98, Dean offered higher-end USA Custom Shop models. In '98, they reintroduced acoustics. From 2000 to '08, Zelinsky was once again involved in the company.

Dating American models: First 2 digits are year of manufacture. Imports have no date codes.

MODEL YEAR	FEATURES	EXC. COND. LOW	HIGH

Baby ML

1982-1986, 2000-2014. Downsized version of ML model.

1982-1986	Import	$400	$900
1982-1986	US-made	$1,000	$1,500

Baby V

1982-1986, 2000-2014. Downsized version of the V model.

1982-1986	Import	$400	$900
1982-1986	US-made	$1,000	$1,500

Baby Z

1982-1986, 2000-2014. Downsized version of the Z model.

1982-1986	Import	$400	$900
1982-1986	US-made	$1,000	$1,500

Bel Aire

1983-1984. Solidbody, possibly the first production guitar with humbucker/single/single pickup layout, U.S.-made, an import model was introduced in '87.

1980s	Import	$450	$700
1983-1984	US-made	$900	$1,500

Budweiser Guitar

Ca.1987. Shaped like Bud logo.

1987		$500	$800

Cadillac (U.S.A.)

1979-1985. Single long treble horn on slab body.

1979-1985		$1,800	$3,000

Cadillac 1980

2006-2018. Block inlays, 2 humbuckers, gold hardware.

2006-2018		$500	$1,200

Cadillac Deluxe (U.S.A.)

1993-1994, 1996-1997. Made in U.S., single longhorn shape, various colors.

1993-1997		$1,800	$3,800

Cadillac Reissue (Import)

1992-1994. Single longhorn shape, 2 humbuckers, various colors.

1992-1994		$400	$900

Cadillac Select

2009-2017. Made in Korea, figured maple top, mahogany, pearl block inlays.

2009-2017		$600	$1,400

Cadillac Standard

1996-1997. Slab body version.

1996-1997		$1,500	$2,500

Del Sol

2008. Import, small double-cut thinline semi-hollow, ES-335 style body, rising sun fretboard markers.

2008		$300	$700

MODEL YEAR	FEATURES	EXC. COND. LOW	HIGH

Dime O Flame (ML)

2005-2018. ML-body, Dimebuckers, burning flames finish, Dime logo on headstock.

2005-2018		$600	$900

Eighty-Eight (Import)

1987-1990. Offset double-cut solidbody, import.

1987-1990		$300	$500

E'Lite

1978-1985, 1994-1996. Single-horn shape.

1978-1985		$1,500	$3,500
1994-1996		$1,000	$2,200

E'Lite Deluxe

1980s. Single-horn shape.

1980s		$1,800	$4,000

EVO XM

2004-present. Single-cut slab body, 2 humbuckers.

2004-2024		$200	$400

Golden E'Lite

1980. Single pointy treble cutaway, fork headstock, gold hardware, ebony 'board, sunburst.

1980		$2,000	$5,000

Hollywood Z (Import)

1985-1986. Bolt-neck Japanese copy of Baby Z, Explorer shape.

1985-1986		$400	$600

Jammer (Import)

1987-1989. Offset double-cut body, bolt-on neck, dot markers, six-on-a-side tuners, various colors offered.

1987-1989		$400	$600

Leslie West Standard

2008-2017. Flame maple top, mahogany body, rosewood 'board.

2008-2017		$600	$1,400

Mach I (Import)

1985-1986. Limited run from Korea, Mach V with six-on-a-side tunes, various colors.

1985-1986		$400	$600

Mach V (Import)

1985-1986. Pointed solidbody, 2 humbucking pickups, maple neck, ebony 'board, locking trem, various colors, limited run from Korea.

1985-1986		$400	$600

Mach VII (U.S.A.)

1985-1986. Mach I styling, made in America, offered in unusual finishes.

1985-1986		$1,500	$2,500

ML (ML Standard/U.S.A.)

1977-1986. There is a flame model and a standard model.

1977-1986	Burst flamed top	$4,000	$5,500
1977-1986	Burst plain top	$3,500	$5,000
1977-1986	Common opaque	$3,000	$4,000

ML (Import)

1983-1990. Korean-made.

1983-1990		$600	$900

ML Dimebag Darrell Rust From Hell

2005. USA Custom Shop, limited run of 120, distressed airbrush finish.

2005		$4,000	$7,500

MODEL YEAR	FEATURES	EXC. COND. LOW	HIGH

Soltero SL

2007-2010. Made in Japan, single-cut solidbody, 2 pickups, flame maple top.

2007-2010		$1,500	$2,200

USA Time Capsule Exotic V

2005-2014. Flying V style, solid mahogany body with exotic spalted and flamed maple top, Dean V neck profile (split V headstock).

2005-2014		$2,000	$4,500

USA Time Capsule Z

2000-2014. Explorer style body, figured maple top.

2000-2014		$1,800	$4,000

V Standard (U.S.A.)

1977-1986. V body, there is a standard and a flame model offered.

1977-1981	Burst flamed top	$4,000	$5,500
1977-1981	Burst plain top	$3,500	$4,500
1977-1981	Common opaque	$2,500	$4,000
1982-1986	Burst flamed top	$3,000	$4,500
1982-1986	Burst plain top	$2,500	$4,000
1982-1986	Common opaque	$2,200	$3,500

Z Standard (U.S.A.)

1977-1986. Long treble cutaway solidbody, 2 humbuckers.

1977-1983	Common finish	$2,500	$4,000
1977-1983	Rare finish	$2,500	$5,500

Z Autograph (Import)

1985-1987. The first Dean import from Korea, offset double-cut, bolt neck, dot markers, offered in several standard colors.

1985-1987		$400	$900

Z Coupe/Z Deluxe

1997-1998. US Custom Shop, mahogany body offered in several standard colors, Z Deluxe with Floyd Rose tremolo.

1997-1998		$1,600	$2,500

Z Korina

1997-1998. US Custom Shop, Z Coupe with korina body, various standard colors.

1997-1998		$2,000	$3,000

Z LTD

1997-1998. US Custom Shop, Z Coupe with bound neck and headstock, offered in several standard colors.

1997-1998		$2,000	$3,000

Dean Markley

The string and pickup manufacturer offered a limited line of guitars and basses for a time in the '80s. They were introduced in '84.

Dean Zelinsky Private Label

2012-present. Premium grade, production/custom, hollow, semi-hollow and solidbody electric guitars built in Chicago, Illinois by luthier Dean Zelinsky, founder of Dean Guitars. He also imports a line of intermediate grade guitars from South Korea and Indonesia.

DeArmond Guitars

1999-2004. Solid, semi-hollow and hollow body guitars based on Guild models and imported from

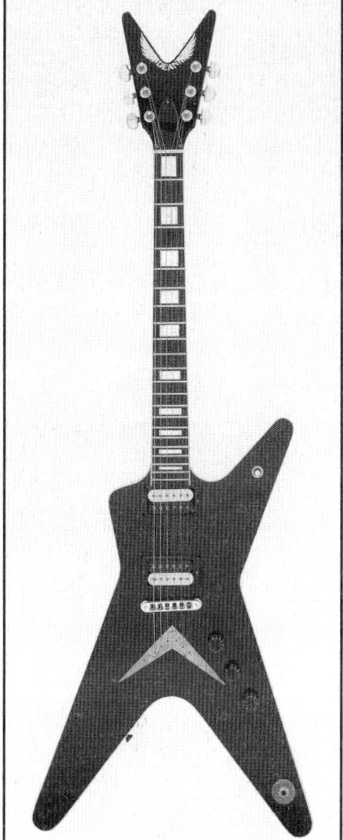

1981 Dean ML

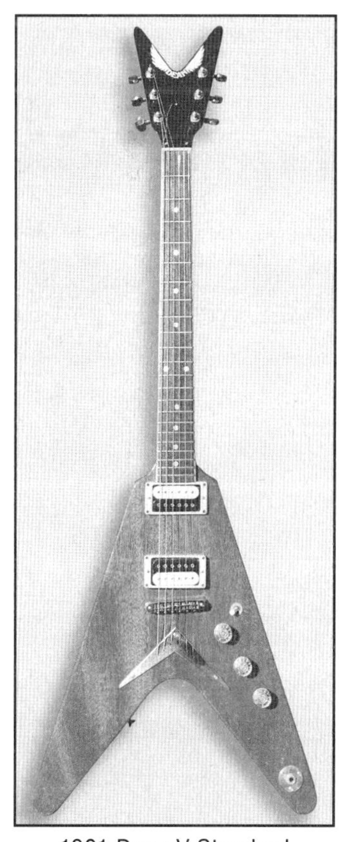

1981 Dean V Standard

Delaney Samantha Fish 512

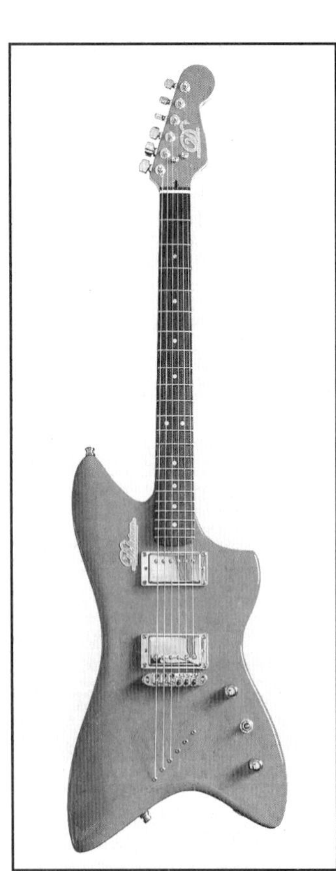
Delirium Bettie Red

MODEL YEAR	FEATURES	EXC. COND. LOW	HIGH

Korea by Fender. They also offered basses. The DeArmond brand was originally used on pickups, effects and amps built by Rowe Industries.

Electric

1999-2004. Various import models, some with USA electronic components.

1999-2004	Various models	$300	$1,200

Dearstone

1993-2017. Luthier Ray Dearstone built his professional and premium grade, custom, archtop and acoustic/electric guitars in Blountville, Tennessee. He also built mandolin family instruments and violins.

Decar

1950s. A private brand sold by Decautur, Illinois music store, Decar headstock logo.

Stratotone H44

1956. Private branded Stratotone with maple neck and fretboard instead of the standard neck/fretboard, 1 pickup and other Harmony H44 Stratotone attributes, bolt-on neck.

1956		$1,200	$1,800

DeCava Guitars

1983-present. Professional and premium grade, production/custom, archtop and classical guitars built by luthier Jim DeCava first in Stratford, then Ansonia, Connecticut. He also builds ukes, banjos, and mandolins.

Decca

Mid-1960s. Acoustic, solid and hollow body guitars, basses and amps made in Japan by Teisco and imported by Decca Records, Decca headstock logo, student-level instruments.

Acoustic Flat-Top

1960s. Decca label on the inside back.

1960s		$200	$600

Electric Solidbody

1960s. Teisco-made in Japan, 3 pickups, sunburst.

1960s		$500	$800

Defil

Based out of Lubin, Poland, Defil made solid and semi-hollowbdy electric guitars at least from the 1970s to the '90s.

DeGennaro

2003-present. Premium grade, custom/production, acoustic, archtop, semi-hollow and solidbody guitars, basses and mandolins built by luthier William DeGennaro in Grand Rapids, Michigan.

Del Oro

1930s-1940s. Flat-top (including cowboy stencil models) and resonator guitars, built by Kay. At least the cowboy stencils were sold by Spiegel.

Small Acoustic

1930s	13" to 14" body	$400	$600

MODEL YEAR	FEATURES	EXC. COND. LOW	HIGH

Del Pilar Guitars

1956-1986. Luthier William Del Pilar made his classical guitars in Brooklyn, New York.

Classical

1950s-1980s. Brazilian rosewood back and sides, cedar top, quilt rosette, 9-ply top binding.

1960-1969		$4,500	$6,000

Del Vecchio

1902-present. Casa Del Vecchio builds a variety of Spanish instruments including acoustic and resonator guitars in São Paulo, Brazil.

Delaney Guitars

2004-present. Luthier Mike Delaney builds his professional grade, production/custom, chambered, solidbody, and semi-hollowbody electric guitars and basses in Atlanta, Georgia. Prior to 2008 he built in Florence, Montana.

Delgado

1928-present. Delgado began in Torreon, Coahuila, Mexico, then moved to Juarez in the '30s with a second location in Tijuana. In '48 they moved to California and opened a shop in Los Angeles. Since 2005, Manuel A. Delgado, a third-generation luthier, builds his premium and presentation grade, production/custom, classical, flamenco and steel string acoustic guitars in Nashville, Tennessee. He also builds basses, mandolins, ukuleles, and banjos.

Delirium Custom Guitars

Luthiers Patrick and Vincent Paul-Victor along with Gael Canonne build their professional and premium grade, production/custom, solidbody electric guitars in Paris and Toulouse, France.

Dell'Arte

1997-present. Production/custom Maccaferri-style guitars from John Kinnard and Alain Cola. In '96, luthier John Kinnard opened a small shop called Finegold Guitars and Mandolins. In '98 he met Alain Cola, a long-time jazz guitarist who was selling Mexican-made copies of Selmer/Maccaferri guitars under the Dell'Arte brand. Cola wanted better workmanship for his guitars, and in October '98, Finegold and Dell'Arte merged. As of May '99, all production is in California.

Delta Guitars

2005-2010. Acoustic, acoustic/electric, and solidbody electric guitars from Musician's Wholesale America, Nashville, Tennessee.

Dennis Hill Guitars

Premium and presentation grade, production/custom, classical and flamenco guitars built by luthier Dennis Hill in Panama City, Florida. He has also built dulcimers, mandolins, and violins.

MODEL YEAR	FEATURES	EXC. COND. LOW	HIGH

Desmond Guitars

1991-present. Luthier Robert B. Desmond builds his premium grade, production/custom classical guitars in Orlando, Florida.

DeTemple

1995-present. Premium grade, production/custom, solidbody electric guitars and basses built by luthier Michael DeTemple in Sherman Oaks, California.

DeVoe Guitars

1975-present. Luthier Lester DeVoe builds his premium grade, production/custom flamenco and classical guitars in Nipomo, California.

Diamond

Ca. 1963-1964. Line of sparkle finish solidbody guitars made in Italy for the Diamond Accordion company.

Ranger

Ca. 1963-1964. Rangers came with 1, 2, 3, or 4 pickups, sparkle finish.

1960s		$600	$1,200

Dick, Edward Victor

1975-present. Luthier Edward Dick currently builds his premium grade, custom, classical guitars in Denver, Colorado (he lived in Peterborough and Ottawa, Ontario until '95). He also operates the Colorado School of Lutherie.

Dickerson

1937-1947. Founded by the Dickerson brothers in '37, primarily for electric lap steels and small amps. Instruments were also private branded for Cleveland's Oahu company, and for the Gourley brand. By '47, the company changed ownership and was renamed Magna Electronics (Magnatone).

Dillion

1996-2021. Dillion, of Cary, North Carolina, offers intermediate grade, production, acoustic, acoustic/electric, hollow-body and solidbody guitars, basses and mandolins made in Korea and Vietnam. Stopped making instruments in '21.

Dillon

1975-2006. Professional and premium grade, custom, flat-tops and basses built by luthier John Dillon in Taos, New Mexico, and in Bloomsburg, Pennsylvania ('81-'01).

Dino's Guitars

Custom, professional grade, electric solidbody guitars built by a social co-op company founded by Alessio Casati and Andy Bagnasco, in Albisola, Italy. They also build effects.

MODEL YEAR	FEATURES	EXC. COND. LOW	HIGH

DiPinto

1995-present. Intermediate and professional grade, production retro-vibe guitars and basses from luthier Chris DiPinto of Philadelphia, Pennsylvania. Until late '99, all instruments built in the U.S., since then all built in Korea.

Ditson

1835-1937. Started in Boston by music publisher Oliver Ditson, by the end of the 1800s the company was one of the East Coast's largest music businesses, operating in several cities and was also involved in distribution and manufacturing of a variety of instruments, including guitars and ukes. From 1916-1930 Ditson guitars were made by Martin. The majority of Martin production was from '16 to '22 with over 500 units sold in '21. Ditson also established Lyon and Healy in Chicago and the John Church Company in Cincinnati.

Values for Ditson Models 111 and 1-45 would be equivalent to those for Martin models from that era with similar specs.

Concert

1916-1922. Similar in size to Martin size 0. Models include Style 1, Style 2 and Style 3.

1916-1922	Style 1	$5,000	$6,500
1916-1922	Style 2	$6,000	$8,000
1916-1922	Style 3	$7,000	$9,000

Standard

1916-1922. Small body similar to Martin size 3, plain styling. Models include Style 1, Style 2 and Style 3.

1916-1922	Style 1	$3,500	$4,500
1916-1922	Style 2	$4,000	$5,000
1916-1922	Style 3	$5,500	$7,000

D'Leco Guitars

1991-2003. Guitarist Maurice Johnson and luthier James W. Dale built premium grade, production/custom archtops in Oklahoma City, Oklahoma.

DM Darling Guitars

Luthier Denis Merrill, began in 2006, builds professional and premium grade, custom, acoustic, classical, resonator and solidbody guitars in Tacoma, Washington. From 1978 to '06 he built under his own name and Merrill Custom Shop. He also builds mandolin family instruments.

Dobro

1929-1942, ca. 1954-2019. Currently, professional, and premium grade, production, wood and metal body resophonic guitars offered by Gibson.

Founded 1929 in Los Angeles by John Dopyera, Rudy Dopyera, Ed Dopyera and Vic Smith (Dobro stands for Dopyera Brothers). Made instruments sold under the Dobro, Regal, Norwood Chimes, Angelus, Rex, Broman, Montgomery Ward, Penetro, Bruno, Alhambra, More Harmony, Orpheum, and Magn-o-tone brands.

Dobro instruments have a single cone facing outward with a spider bridge structure and competed

DeTemple Spirit Series Stellacasta

DiPinto Belvedere Deluxe

1976 Dobro Bicentennial
James Seldin

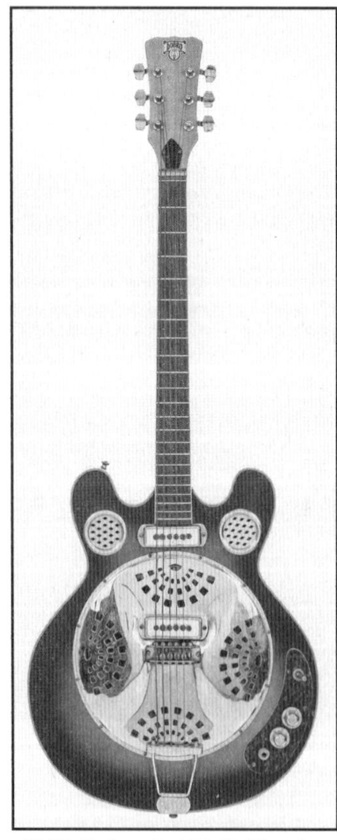
1968 Dobro D-100 Californian
Imaged by Heritage Auctions, HA.com

with National products. Generally, model names are numbers referring to list price and therefore materials and workmanship (e.g., a No. 65 cost $65). Because of this, the same model number may apply to different instruments. However, model numbers are never identified on instruments!

In '30, the company name was changed to Dobro Corporation, Ltd. In '32, Louis Dopyera buys Ted Kleinmeyer's share of National. Louis, Rudy and Ed now hold controlling interest in National, but in '32 John Dopyera left Dobro to pursue the idea of a metal resophonic violin. In December of '34 Ed Dopyera joins National's board of directors (he's also still on Dobro board), and by March of '35 Dobro and National have merged to become the National Dobro Corporation. Dobro moves into National's larger factory but continues to maintain separate production, sales and distribution until relocation to Chicago is complete. Beginning in early-'36 National Dobro starts relocating its offices to Chicago. L.A. production of Dobros continued until '37, after which some guitars continue to be assembled from parts until '39, when the L.A. operations were closed down.

All resonator production ended in '42. Victor Smith, Al Frost and Louis Dopyera bought the company and changed the name to the Valco Manufacturing Company. The Dobro name does not appear when production resumes after World War II.

In mid-'50s - some sources say as early as '54 - Rudy and Ed Dopyera began assembling wood-bodied Dobros from old parts using the name DB Original. In about '59, some 12-fret DB Originals were made for Standel, carrying both DB Original and Standel logos. In around '61, production was moved to Gardena, California, and Louis Dopyera and Valco transferred the Dobro name to Rudy and Ed, who produce the so-called Gardena Dobros. At this time, the modern Dobro logo appeared with a lyre that looks like 2 back-to-back '6s'. Dobro Original debuts ca. '62. In late-'64 the Dobro name was licensed to Ed's son Emil (Ed, Jr.) Dopyera. Ed, Jr. designs a more rounded Dobro (very similar to later Mosrites) and has a falling out with Rudy over it.

In '66 Semi Moseley acquires the rights to the Dobro brand, building some in Gardena, and later moving to Bakersfield, California. Moseley introduced Ed, Jr's design plus a thinline double-cutaway Dobro. He also made MoBros during this time. Moseley Dobros use either Dobro or National cones. In '67 Ed, Sr., Rudy and Gabriella Lazar started the Original Music Instrument Company (OMI) and produced Hound Dog brand Dobros. In '68 Moseley went bankrupt and in '70 OMI obtained the rights to the Dobro brand and begins production of OMI Dobros. In '75 Gabriella's son and daughter, Ron Lazar and Dee Garland, take over OMI. Rudy Dupyera makes and sells Safari brand resonator mandolins. Ed, Sr. dies in '77 and Rudy in '78. In '84 OMI was sold to Chester and Betty Lizak. Both wood and metal-bodied Dobros were produced in Huntington Beach, California. Chester Lizak died in '92. Gibson purchased Dobro in '93 and made Dobros in Nashville, Tennessee.

MODEL YEAR	FEATURES	EXC. COND. LOW	HIGH

Dobros generally feature a serial number which, combined with historical information, provides a clue to dating. For prewar L.A. guitars, see approximation chart below adapted from "Gruhn's Guide to Vintage Guitars." No information exists on DB Originals.

Gardena Dobros had D prefix plus 3 digits beginning with 100 and going into the 500s (reportedly under 500 made). No information is available on Moseley Dobros.

OMI Dobros from '70-'79 have either D prefix for wood bodies or B prefix for metal bodies, plus 3 or 4 numbers for ranking, space, then a single digit for year (D XXXX Y or B XXX Y; e.g., D 172 8 would be wood body #172 from '78). For '80-'87 OMI Dobros, start with first number of year (decade) plus 3 or 4 ranking numbers, space, then year and either D for wood or B for metal bodies (8 XXXX YD or 8 XXX YB; e.g., 8 2006 5B would be metal body #2008 from '85). From '88-'92, at least, a letter and number indicate guitar style, plus 3 or 4 digits for ranking, letter for neck style, 2 digits for year, and letter for body style (AX XXXX NYYD or AX XXX NYYB).

L.A. Guitars (approx. number ranges, not actual production totals):

1929-30	900-2999
1930-31	3000-3999
1931-32	BXXX (Cyclops models only)
1932-33	5000-5599
1934-36	5700-7699
1937-42	8000-9999

Angelus

1933-1937. Wood body, round or square neck, 2-tone walnut finish, continues as Model 19 in Regal-made guitars.

1933-1937	Round neck	$1,200	$2,000
1933-1937	Square neck	$1,500	$2,500

Artist M-16

1934-1935. German silver alloy body, engraved.

1934-1935	H square neck	$3,500	$4,500
1934-1935	M round neck	$6,000	$8,000

Columbia D-12

1967-1968. Acoustic 12-string, typical Dobro resonator with spider style bridge, made during Dobro-Moseley era.

1967-1968		$800	$1,200

Cyclops 45

1932-1933. Bound walnut body, 1 screen hole.

1932-1933	Round neck	$2,500	$3,500
1932-1933	Square neck	$3,000	$4,000

D-40 Texarkana

1965-1967. Mosrite-era (identified by C or D prefix), traditional Dobro style cone and coverplate, dot inlays, Dobro logo on headstock, sunburst wood body. Red and blue finishes available.

1965-1967		$800	$1,200

D-40E Texarkana

1965-1967. D-40 electric with single pickup and 2 knobs.

1965-1967		$1,000	$1,500

MODEL YEAR	FEATURES	EXC. COND. LOW	HIGH

D-100 The Californian

1965-1969. Dobro's version of Mosrite (thus nicknamed the "Mobro") thinline double-cut, resonator, 2 small metal ports, 2 pickups, 2 knobs, sunburst.

1965-1969		$1,200	$2,000

DM-33 California Girl/DM-33H

1996-2006. Chrome-plated bell brass body, biscuit bridge, spider resonator, rosewood 'board. Girl or Hawaiian-scene (H) engraving.

1996-2006		$1,200	$2,000

Dobjo

Dobro body, banjo neck, 5-string.

1989		$1,000	$1,500

Dobro/Regal Model 19

Ca.1934-1938. In the 1930s Dobro licensed Chicago's Regal Company to build Dobro-style guitars. The headstocks on these models can have a Dobro logo, Regal logo, or no logo at all. The 19 is a lower-end model, round holes in coverplate, square neck.

1934-1938		$1,200	$2,000

Dobro/Regal Model 46/47

1935-1942. Dobro/Regal 46, renamed 47 in '39, aluminum body, round neck, 14 frets, slotted headstock, silver finish. Degraded finish was a common problem with the Dobro/Regal 47.

1935-1938	Model 46	$1,500	$2,500
1939-1942	Model 47	$2,000	$2,500

Dobro/Regal Model 62/65

1935-1942. Renamed Model 65 in '39, nickel-plated brass body, Spanish dancer etching, round or square neck. Note: Dobro/Regal 65 should not be confused with Dobro Model 65 which was discontinued earlier.

1935-1942	Model 62	$2,500	$3,200
1935-1942	Model 65	$2,500	$3,200

Dobro/Regal Tenor 27-1/2

1930. Tenor version of Model 27.

1930		$800	$1,200

Dobrolektric

1996-2005. Resonator guitar with single-coil neck pickup, single-cut.

1996-2005		$1,000	$1,500

DS-33/Steel 33

1995-2000. Steel body with light amber sunburst finish, resonator with coverplate, biscuit bridge.

1995-2000		$800	$1,200

DW-90C

2001-2006. Single sharp cutaway, wood body, metal resonator, f-hole upper bass bout.

2001-2006		$800	$1,200

E3 (C, M, W, B)

Late 1970s-1986. Double-cut solidbodies with necks and bodies of laminated select hardwoods, Cinnamon (C), Maple (M), Walnut (W) or plain Black (B) finish, 2 pickups.

1979-1986		$1,000	$1,500

F-60/F-60S

1986-2005. Round neck (60, discontinued '00) or square neck (60S), f-holes, brown sunburst.

1986-2005		$1,000	$1,500

Gardena

1968. Electric Dobro body, 2 knobs, single-coil soap bar pickup.

1968		$800	$1,200

Hound Dog

2002-2019. Laminated wood, 10 1/2" spider-bridge resonator.

2002-2019		$500	$800

Hula Blues

1987-1999. Dark brown wood body (earlier models have much lighter finish), painted Hawaiian scenes, round neck.

1987-1999		$1,000	$1,500

Jerry Douglas

1995-2005. Mahogany body, square neck, limited run of 200 with signature, but also sold without signature.

1995-2005		$1,500	$2,500

Josh Graves

1995-2005. The first 200 made were signed, single bound ample body, spider cone, nickel plated. Includes DW Josh Graves and Uncle Josh Limited models.

1995	Signed	$1,500	$2,500
1996-2005	Unsigned	$1,200	$2,000

Leader 14M/14H

1934-1935. Nickel plated brass body, segmented f-holes.

1934-1935	H square neck	$1,800	$3,000
1934-1935	M round neck	$2,000	$2,500

Model 25

1930-1935. Sunburst wood body, f-holes upper bout, large single metal cone, square neck.

1930-1935		$1,500	$2,500

Model 27 (OMI)

1976-1994. Wood body, square neck.

1976-1994		$1,200	$1,800

Model 27 Cyclops

1932-1933.

1932-1933	Round neck	$1,500	$2,500
1932-1933	Square neck	$1,800	$3,000

Model 27 Deluxe

1995-2005. 27 with figured maple top, nicer appointments.

1996-2005		$1,500	$2,200

Model 27/27G

1933-1937. Regal-made, wooden body.

1933-1937	Round neck	$1,500	$2,500
1933-1937	Square neck	$1,800	$3,000

Model 32

1939-1941. Regal-made, wooden body.

1939-1941		$1,800	$2,700

Model 33 (Duolian)

1972. Only made in '72, becomes Model 90 in '73.

1972		$800	$1,200

Model 33 H

1973-1997 (OMI & Gibson). Same as 33 D, but with etched Hawaiian scenes, available as round or square neck.

1980s-90s	Round neck	$1,300	$2,000
1980s-90s	Square neck	$1,300	$2,000

1932 Dobro Model 27 Cyclops

1935 Dobro Model 27G

Imaged by Heritage Auctions, HA.com

GUITARS

1977 Dobro Model 60
Rivington Guitars

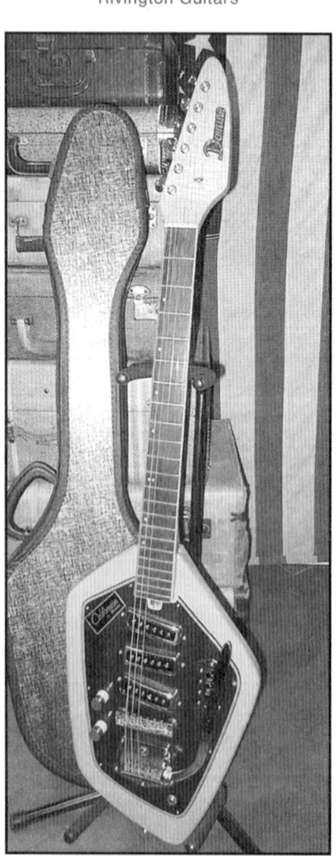
1965 Domino Californian
Rivington Guitars

MODEL YEAR	FEATURES	EXC. COND. LOW	HIGH

Model 35 (32)

1935-1942. Metal body, called Model 32 (not to be confused with wood body 32) for '35-'38.

1935-1942		$1,500	$2,500

Model 36

1932-1937. Wood body with resonator, round or square neck.

1932-1937	Round neck	$1,500	$2,500
1932-1937	Square neck	$1,800	$3,000

Model 36/36S

1970s-1997, 2002-2005. Chrome-plated brass body, round or square (S) neck, dot markers, engraved rose floral art.

1970s-2005		$1,300	$2,000

Model 37

1933-1937. Regal-made wood body, mahogany, bound body and 'board, round or square 12-fret neck.

1933-1937	Round neck	$1,500	$2,500
1933-1937	Square neck	$1,800	$3,000

Model 37 Tenor

1933-1937 (Regal). Tenor version of No. 37.

1933-1937		$1,200	$1,800

Model 45

1934-1939. Regal-made wood body, round or square neck.

1934-1939	Round neck	$1,500	$2,500
1934-1939	Square neck	$1,800	$3,000

Model 55/56 Standard

1929-1934. Model 55 Standard, renamed 56 Standard 1932-1934. Unbound wood body, metal resonator, bound neck, sunburst.

1929-1934	Round neck	$1,500	$2,500
1929-1934	Square neck	$1,800	$3,000

Model 60

1933-1936. Similar to Model 66/66B.

1933-1936	Round neck	$4,000	$5,500
1933-1936	Square neck	$5,000	$6,500

Model 60 Cyclops

1932-1933. Round neck, 12-fret model, black walnut finish.

1932-1933		$3,000	$4,000

Model 60/ 60D (OMI)/ 60DS

1970-1993. Wood body (laminated maple) with Dobro resonator cone, model 60 until '73 when renamed 60 D, and various 60 model features offered, post-'93 was Gibson-owned production.

1970-1993	Model 60 Series	$800	$1,200

Model 63

1973-1996. Wood body, 8-string, square neck.

1973-1996		$800	$1,200

Model 64

1980s-1995. Walnut body, tree-of-life inlay.

1982		$1,200	$1,800

Model 65/66/66B

1929-1933. Wood body with sandblasted ornamental design top and back, metal resonator, sunburst. Model 66 B has bound top.

1929-1931	Model 65	$1,800	$3,500
1932-1933	Model 66	$1,800	$3,000
1932-1933	Model 66B	$2,000	$3,500

Model 66/66 S

1972-1995. Wood body with sandblasted ornamental design top and back, metal resonator, sunburst, round or square (S) neck.

1972-1995		$800	$1,200

Model 75/Lily of the Valley

1972-1997, 2002-2005. Chrome plated bell brass body resonator, round neck, Lily of the Valley engraving.

1972-1997		$1,500	$2,200

Model 85/86

1929-1934. Wood body, triple-bound, round or square neck, renamed 86 in '32.

1929-1934		$2,000	$3,500

Model 90 (Duolian) (OMI)

1972-1995. Chrome-plated, f-holes, etched Hawaiian scene.

1972-1995	Various models	$1,000	$1,500

Model 90 (Woodbody)/WB90G/WB90S

1984-2005. Maple body with upper bout f-holes or sound holes, round neck, metal resonator with spider bridge, sunburst.

1984-2005		$800	$1,200

Model 125 De Luxe

1929-1934. Black walnut body, round or square neck, Dobro De Luxe engraved, triple-bound top, back and 'board, nickel-plated hardware, natural.

1929-1934	Round neck	$4,500	$7,000
1929-1934	Square neck	$8,000	$12,000

Professional 15M/15H

1934-1935. Engraved nickel body, round (M) or square (H) neck, solid peghead.

1934-1935	H square neck	$2,300	$3,500
1934-1935	M round neck	$2,100	$3,200

Dodge

1996-present. Luthier Rick Dodge builds his intermediate and professional grade, production, solidbody guitars with changeable electronic modules in Tallahassee, Florida. He also builds basses.

Doitsch

1930s. Acoustic guitars made by Harmony, most likely for a music store or studio.

Domino

Ca. 1967-1968. Solidbody and hollowbody electric guitars and basses imported from Japan by Maurice Lipsky Music Co. of New York, New York, previously responsible for marketing the Orpheum brand. Models are primarily near-copies of EKO, Vox, and Fender designs, plus some originals. Models were made by Arai or Kawai. Earlier models may have been imported, but this is not yet documented.

Electric

1967-1968. Various models including the Baron, Californian, Californian Rebel, Dawson, and Spartan.

1967-1968		$400	$600

Dommenget

1978-1985, 1988-present. Luthier Boris Dommenget (pronounced dommen-jay) builds his premium

MODEL YEAR	FEATURES	EXC. COND. LOW	HIGH

grade, custom/production, solidbody, flat-top, and archtop guitars in Balje, Germany. From '78 to '85 he was located in Wiesbaden, and from '88-'01 in Hamburg. He and wife Fiona also make pickups.

Don Musser Guitars

Luthier Don Musser, in 1976, began building custom, classical, and flat-top guitars in Silver City, New Mexico. He later moved his shop to Cotopaxi, Colorado.

Doolin Guitars

1997-present. Luthier Mike Doolin builds his premium grade, production/custom acoustics featuring his unique double-cut in Portland, Oregon.

Dorado

Ca. 1972-1973. Six- and 12-string acoustic guitars, solidbody electrics and basses. Brand used briefly by Baldwin/Gretsch on line of Japanese imports.

Acoustic Flat-Top/Acoustic Dobro

1972-1973. Includes folk D, jumbo Western, and grand concert styles (with laminated rosewood back and sides), and Dobro-style.

1972-1973	Higher-end	$500	$800
1972-1973	Lower-end	$300	$500
1972-1973	Mid-level	$400	$600

Solidbody Electric

1972-1973. Includes Model 5985, a double-cut with 2 P-90-style pickups.

1972-1973		$400	$600

Douglas Ching

Luthier Douglas J. Ching builds his premium grade, production/custom, classical, acoustic, and harp guitars currently in Chester, Virginia, and previously in Hawaii ('76-'89) and Michigan ('90-'93). He also builds ukes, lutes and violins.

D'Pergo Custom Guitars

2002-present. Professional, premium, and presentation grade, production/custom, solidbody guitars built in Windham, New Hampshire. Every component of the guitar is built by D'Pergo.

Dragge Guitars

1982-2010. Luthier Peter Dragge builds his custom, steel-string and nylon-string guitars in Ojai, California.

Dragonfly Guitars

1994-present. Professional grade, production/custom, sloped cutaway flat-tops, semi-hollow body electrics, basses and dulcitars built by luthier Dan Richter in Roberts Creek, British Columbia.

Drive

Ca. 2001-ca. 2011. Budget grade, production, import solidbody electric guitars and basses. They also offered solidstate amps.

DTM

See David Thomas McNaught listing.

Dudley Custom Guitars

2005-present. Luthier Peter Dudley builds his custom, premium grade, chambered solidbody electric guitars in Easton, Maryland.

Duelin Guitars

Professional grade, production/custom, 6 ½ string guitars designed by Don Scheib of Simi Valley and built by luthier Mike Lipe in Sun Valley, California.

Duesenberg

1995-present. Professional and premium grade, production/custom, solid and hollow body electric guitars and basses built by luthier Dieter Goelsdorf in Hannover, Germany. Rockinger had a Duesenberg guitar in the 1980s.

Dunwell Guitars

Professional and premium grade, custom, flat-tops built by luthier Alan Dunwell in Nederland, Colorado.

Dupont

Luthier Maurice Dupont builds his classical, archtop, Weissenborn-style and Selmer-style guitars in Cognac, France.

Dwight

See info under Epiphone Dwight guitar.

Dyer

1902-1939. The massive W. J. Dyer & Bro. store in St. Paul, Minnesota, sold a complete line of music related merchandise though they actually built nothing but a few organs. The Larson Brothers of Chicago were commissioned to build harp guitar and harp mandolin pieces for them somewhat following the harp guitar design of Chris Knutsen, until 1912 when the Knutsen patent expired. Although the body design somewhat copied the Knutsen patent the resulting instrument was in a class by itself in comparison. These harp guitars have become the standard by which all others are judged because of their ease of play and the tremendous, beautiful sound they produce. Many modern builders are using the body design and the same structural ideas evidenced in the Larson originals. They were built in Styles 4 (the plainest), 5, 6, 7 and 8. The ornamentation went from the no binding, dot inlay Style 4 to the full treatment, abalone trimmed, tree-of-life fingerboard of the Style 8. All had mahogany back and sides with ebony fingerboard and bridge. There are also a very few Style 3 models found of late that are smaller than the standard and have a lower bout body point. Other Dyer instruments were built by Knutsen. Dyer also carried Stetson brand instruments made by the Larson Brothers.

Dragonfly Guitars

2010 Duesenberg Starplayer TV

Matt Carleson

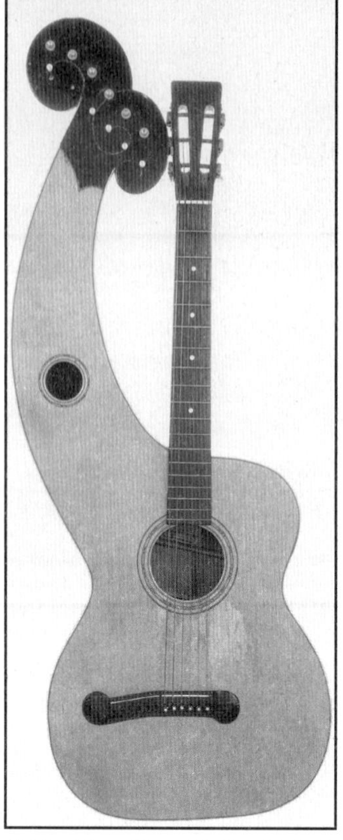

1920s Dyer Harp Guitar Style 5
Imaged by Heritage Auctions, HA.com

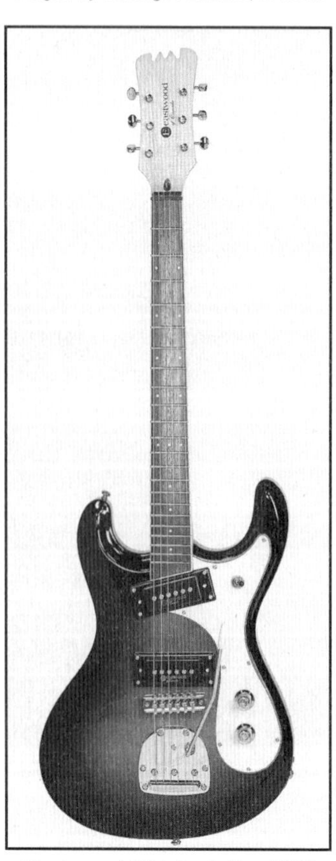

Eastwood Sidejack Pro DLX

MODEL YEAR	FEATURES	EXC. COND. LOW	HIGH

Harp Guitar Style 3

1902-1920s	Small, short scale	$3,000	$4,000

Harp Guitar Style 4

1902-1920s	No binding	$3,500	$5,000

Harp Guitar Style 5

1902-1920s	Bound top	$4,000	$6,000

Harp Guitar Style 6

1902-1920s	Bound top/bottom	$4,500	$7,000

Harp Guitar Style 7

1902-1920s	Fancy inlays	$5,000	$8,000

Harp Guitar Style 8

1902-1920s	Tree-of-life	$7,200	$10,000

Dynacord

1950-present. Dynacord is a German company that makes audio and pro sound amps, as well as other electronic equipment. In 1966-'67 they offered solidbody guitars and basses from the Welson Company of Italy. They also had the Cora guitar and bass which is the center part of a guitar body with a tube frame in a guitar outline. They also offered tape echo machines.

Dynelectron

1960s-late 1970s. This Italian builder offered a variety of guitars and basses but is best known today for their almost exact copies of Danelectro Longhorns of the mid-'60s.

E L Welker

Luthier Eugene L. Welker began building in 1984, premium and presentation grade, production/custom, leather-wrapped archtop guitars in Claremont, New Hampshire.

E.L. Bashore Guitars

2011-2024. Professional grade, custom, steel string and classical acoustic and solidbody electric guitars, basses and banjos built by luthier Eric L. Bashore in Danville, Pennsylvania. He closed his shop in '24.

Earthwood

1972-1985. Acoustic designs by Ernie Ball with input from George Fullerton and made in Newport Beach, California. One of the first to offer acoustic basses.

Eastman

1992-present. Intermediate and professional grade, production, archtop and flat-top guitars and basses, mainly built in China, with some from Germany and Romania. Beijing, China-based Eastman Strings started out building violins and cellos. They added guitars in '02 and mandolins in '04.

Eastwood

1997-present. Mike Robinson's company imports budget and intermediate grade, production, solid and semi-hollowbody guitars, many styled after 1960s models. They also offer basses and mandolins.

MODEL YEAR	FEATURES	EXC. COND. LOW	HIGH

Eaton, William

1976-present. Luthier William Eaton builds custom specialty instruments such as vihuelas, harp guitars, and lyres in Phoenix, Arizona. He is also the Director of the Robetto-Venn School of Luthiery.

Echopark Guitars

2010-present. Premium and presentation grade, production/custom, solidbody electric guitars built by luthier Gabriel Currie in Detroit, Michigan, formerly in Los Angeles, California.

Ed Claxton Guitars

1972-present. Premium grade, custom flat-tops made by luthier Ed Claxton, first in Austin, Texas, and currently in Santa Cruz, California.

Eduardo Duran Ferrer

Luthier Eduardo Duran Ferrer, since 1987, builds premium grade, classical guitars in Granada, Spain.

Edward Klein

1998-present. Premium grade, custom, guitars built by luthier Edward Klein in Mississauga, Ontario.

EER Custom

2005-present. Professional and premium grade, custom, soldibody and semi-hollowbody electric guitars built by luthier Ernest E. Roesler in Forks, Washington.

Egmond

1935-1972. Founded by Ulke Egmond, building acoustic, archtop, semi-hollow and solidbody guitars originally in Eindhoven, later in Best Holland. They also made basses. Egmond also produced instruments under the Orpheum (imported into U.S.), Rosetti (England), Miller, Wilson and Lion brands.

Electric

1960-1972. Solid or semi-hollow bodies.

1960-1972		$500	$1,200

Ehlers

1968-2011. Luthier Rob Ehlers built his premium grade, production/custom, flat-top acoustic guitars, originally in Oregon and from '06 to '11, in Veracruz, Mexico. Rob died in November 2011.

15 CRC

Cutaway, Western red cedar top, Indian rosewood back and sides.

1996		$2,800	$4,200

15 SRC

Cutaway, European spruce top, Indian rosewood back and sides.

1998		$2,800	$4,200

16 BTM

European spruce top, mahogany back and sides, Troubadour peghead, black lacquer finish.

1998		$2,800	$4,200

GUITARS

MODEL YEAR	FEATURES	EXC. COND. LOW	HIGH

16 C

16" lower bout, cutaway, flamed maple sides and back, European spruce top.

1990		$2,800	$4,200

16 SK Concert

16" lower bout, relatively small upper bout, small waist, European spruce top, flamed koa back and sides, diamond markers, natural.

1993		$2,500	$3,800

16 SM

European spruce top, mahogany back and sides.

1999		$2,200	$3,300

16 SSC

Cutaway, European spruce top, English sycamore back and sides.

1996		$2,200	$3,300

25 C

Limited Edition Anniversary Model, European spruce top, Indian rosewood back and sides, abalone top border.

2001		$3,300	$5,000

GJ (Gypsy Jazz)

2000s	D-style	$2,200	$3,300

Eichelbaum Guitars

2006-present. Luthier David Eichelbaum builds his premium grade, custom, flat-tops in Santa Barbara, California.

EKO

1959-present. Originally acoustic, acoustic/electric, electric thinline and full-size archtop hollowbody, solidbody electric guitars and basses built by Oliviero Pigini and Company in Recanati, Italy, and imported by LoDuca Brothers, Milwaukee, Radio and Television Equipment Company in Santa Ana, California, and others. First acoustic guitars followed by sparkle plastic-covered electrics by '62. Sparkle finishes are gone ca. '66. Pigini dies ca. '67. LoDuca Bros. is phased out in early-'70s. By '75 EKO offers some copy guitars and they purchased a custom shop to make other brands by '78. In '85 they ceased production in Italy, continuing the brand for a few years with Asian imports, and continued to distribute other brands. By 2004, the Eko line of guitar was revived with budget and intermediate grade, production, classical, acoustic, acoustic/electric, solidbody, solidbody, and hollowbody guitars made in Asia. They also make basses and amps.

Barracuda VI

1966-ca.1978. Double-cut semi-hollow, 2 pickups, 6-string.

1966-1978		$800	$1,500

Barracuda XII

1966-ca.1978. Double-cut semi-hollow, 2 pickups, 12-string.

1966-1978		$1,000	$1,500

Cobra I/II/III/XII

1966-1978. Double-cut solidbody, 2 knobs. Cobra I has 1 pickup, II 2 pickups and III 3 pickups. 12-string Cobra XII offered '67-'69, has 2 pickups.

1966-1978	Cobra I	$400	$900
1966-1978	Cobra II	$500	$1,000
1966-1978	Cobra III	$700	$1,100
1966-1978	Cobra XII	$800	$1,200

Commander

1965. Single-cut archtop electric, 1 pickup, 2 controls, EKO logo on upper bass bout, maple body in 'dura-glos' finish.

1965		$600	$900

Condor

1966-ca.1969. Double-cut solidbody with 3 or 4 pickups.

1966-1969		$800	$1,200

Dragon

1967-ca.1969. Single-cut archtop, 2 f-holes, 3 pickups, tremolo.

1967-1969		$1,000	$1,500

Flat-Top Acoustic

1960s. Various student-level flat-top acoustic models.

1960s		$300	$500

Florentine

1964-ca.1969. Double-cut archtop, 2 pickups.

1964-1969		$800	$1,200

Kadett/Kadett XII

1967-ca.1978. Double-cut solidbody with point on lower bass side of body, 3 pickups, tremolo. 12- string Kadett XII offered '68-'69.

1967-1978	Kadett	$500	$800
1968-1969	Kadett XII	$500	$1,200

Lancer Stereo

1967-1969. Lancer VI with stereo output (route output to 2 amplifiers requires EKO stereo cable for stereo application).

1967-1969		$600	$900

Lancer VI

1967-ca.1969. Double-cut solidbody, 2 pickups.

1967-1969		$600	$900

Lancer XII

1967-1969. Double-cut solidbody electric, 12-string.

1967-1969		$700	$1,000

Lark I/II

1970. Thin hollow cutaway, sunburst. Lark I has 1 pickup and Lark II 2.

1970	Lark I	$480	$700
1970	Lark II	$500	$800

Model 180

1960s. Cutaway acoustic archtop.

1960s		$500	$800

Model 285 Modello

1960s. Thinline single-cut, 1 pickup.

1962		$600	$900

Model 290/2V

1963-1965. Maple body and neck, ebony 'board, dot markers, 2 pickups, tremolo, renamed Barracuda in '66.

1963-1965		$700	$1,000

Model 300/375

1962. Copy of Hofner Club-style electric, single-cut, 2 pickups, set-neck.

1962		$720	$1,000

Model 400 Ekomaster

1960-1962. Jazzmaster-style, 1, 2 or 4 (2+2) pickups, sparkle finish.

1960-1962	4 pickups	$1,000	$1,500

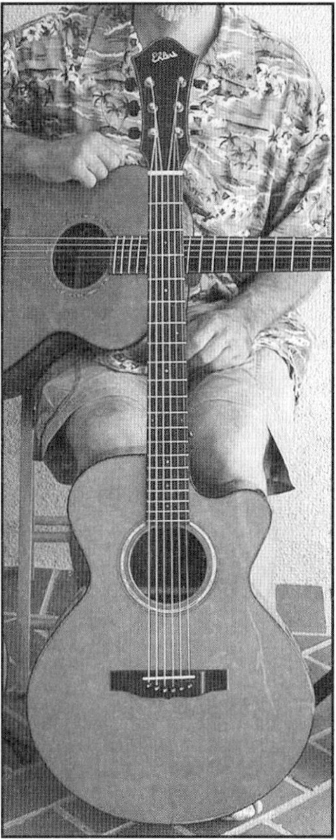

Ehlers 15" SJC
Nort Graham

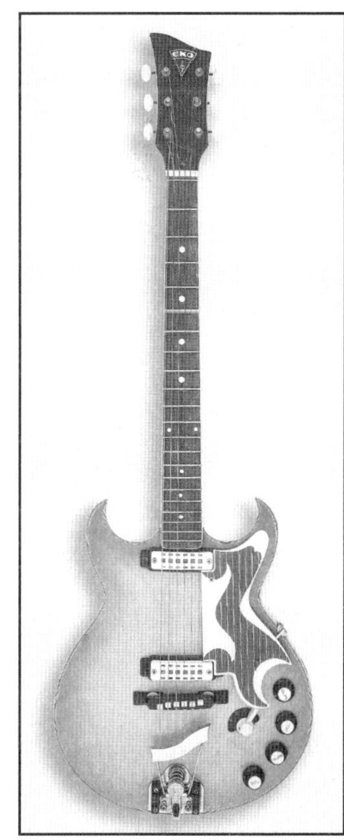

1968 EKO Florentine
Imaged by Heritage Auctions, HA.com

GUITARS

EKO Ranger 12
Seth Andrews

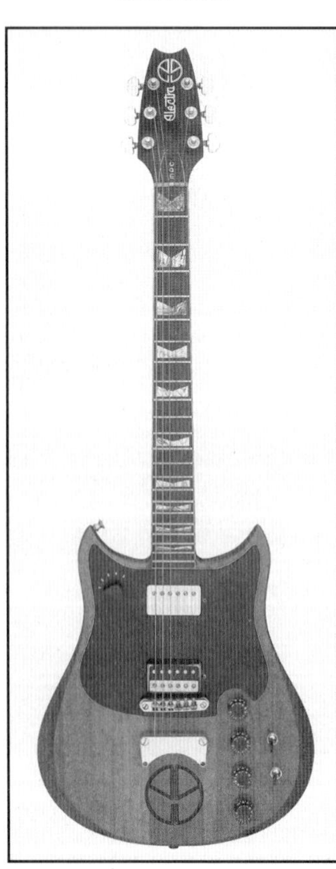

1980 Electra MPC Outlaw
Imaged by Heritage Auctions, HA.com

MODEL YEAR	FEATURES	EXC. COND. LOW	HIGH

Model 500/1 and 500/1V

1961-1965. Plastic covered solidbody, 1 pickup. 500/1 no vibrato, 1V with vibrato.

1961-1965	500/1	$600	$900
1961-1965	500/1V	$800	$1,200

Model 500/2 and 500/3V

1961-1964. Plastic covered solidbody, plastic sparkle finish. 500/2 no vibrato, 2 pickups. 3V with vibrato, 3 pickups.

1961-1965	500/2	$600	$900
1961-1965	500/3V	$800	$1,200

Model 500/4 and 500/4V

1961-1964. Plastic covered solidbody, 4 pickups. 500/4 no vibrato, 4V with vibrato.

1961-1965	500/4	$1,000	$1,500
1961-1965	500/4V	$1,200	$1,800

Model 540 (Classical)

1960s. Nylon-string classical guitar.

1960s		$300	$600

Model 700/3V

1961-1964. Map-shape/tulip-shape body, 3 pickups, vibrato, woodgrain plastic finish.

1961-1964		$1,100	$1,500

Model 700/4V

1961-1967. Map-shape/tulip-shape body, 4 pickups, multiple switches, vibrato.

1961-1967	Red, blue silver sparkle	$1,200	$1,800
1961-1967	Standard finish	$1,100	$1,500

Ranger 6/12

1967-ca.1982. D-size flat-top acoustic, large 3-point 'guard, dot inlays, EKO Ranger label. Ranger 12 is 12-string.

1967-1982	Ranger 12	$500	$1,200
1967-1982	Ranger 6	$400	$900

Ranger 6/12 Electra

1967. Ranger 6/12 with on-board pickup and 2 controls, 6-string with dot markers, 12-string with block markers.

1967	12 Electra	$500	$1,200
1967	6 Electra	$400	$900

Rocket VI/XII (Rokes)

1967-ca.1969. Rocket-shape design, solidbody, 6-string, says Rokes on the headstock, Rokes were a popular English band that endorsed EKO guitars, marketed as the Rocket VI in the U.S.; and as the Rokes in Europe, often called the Rok. Rocket XII is 12-string.

1967-1969	Rocket VI	$1,100	$1,500
1967-1969	Rocket XII	$1,100	$1,500

El Degas

Early 1970s-early '80s. Japanese-made copies of classic America electrics and acoustics, imported by Buegeleisen & Jacobson of New York, New York.

Solidbody

Copies of classic American models, including the Let's Play model.

1970s		$300	$600

El Maya

1970s-1980s. Also labeled Maya. Solidbody, archtop and semi-hollow guitars built by Japan's Chushin Gakki Co., which also built models for several other manufacturers.

MODEL YEAR	FEATURES	EXC. COND. LOW	HIGH

Eleca

2004-present. Student/budget level, production, acoustic and electric guitars, imported by Eleca International. They also offer amps, effects and mandolins.

Electar

See Epiphone listing.

Electra

1970-1984, 2013-present. Imported from Japan by St. Louis Music. Most instruments made by Matsumoku in Japan. The Electra line replaced SLM's Japanese-made Apollo and U.S.-made Custom Kraft lines. The first guitar, simply called The Electra, was a copy of the Ampeg Dan Armstrong lucite guitar and issued in '70, followed quickly by a variety of bolt-neck copies of other brands. In '75 the Tree-of-Life guitars debut and the line is expanded. Open-book headstocks changed to wave or fan shape by '78. Some Korean production began in early-'80s. In the fall of '83, the Electra Brand became Electra Phoenix. By the beginning of '84, the brand became Electra-Westone and by the end of '84 just Westone. In 2013, the brand was revived with guitars built by luthiers Ben Chafin and Mick Donner in Tampa, Florida. Matsumoku-made guitars have serial numbers in which first 1 or 2 digits represent the year of manufacture. Thus, a guitar with a serial number beginning in 0 or 80 would be from 1980.

Concert Professional

Late 1970s. Howard Roberts style, single-cut electric flat-top with oval sound hole, single humbucking pickup, fancy markers.

1977		$900	$1,300

Custom

1970s. Double-cut solidbody, 2 pickups, Custom logo on truss rod, cherry finish.

1970s		$700	$1,000

Elvin Bishop

1976-ca.1980. Double-cut semi-hollow body, tree-of-life inlay.

1976-1980		$800	$1,200

Flying Wedge

1970s. V body, six-on-a-side tuners.

1970s		$800	$1,200

MPC Outlaw

1977-1980. Symmetric horn body, neck-thru, has separate modules (Modular Powered Circuits) that plug in for different effects. Includes X710 (peace sign burned into natural mahogany top), X720 (gray sunburst), X730 (tobacco sunburst) and X 740 (maple top).

1977-1980		$900	$1,300
1977-1980	MPC plug-in module	$150	$200

MPC X310

1976-1980. MPC model, LP solidbody, 2 humbuckers (bridge w/ exposed zebra bobbins), 4 in-line control knobs plus 2 toggles, gold hardware, black finish.

1976-1980		$900	$1,300

MODEL YEAR	FEATURES	EXC. COND. LOW	HIGH

MPC X320

1976-1980. Same as X310, but with transparent cherry red finish over mahogany top.

1976-1980	$900	$1,300

MPC X330

1976-1980. Same as X310, but with cherry sunburst finish on maple top.

1976-1980	$900	$1,300

MPC X340

1976-1980. Same as X310, but with Jacaranda rosewood top.

1976-1980	$900	$1,300

MPC X350

1977-1980. Same as X310, but with tobacco sunburst on a maple top.

1977-1980	$900	$1,300

Phoenix

1980-1984. Classic offset double-cut solidbody, Phoenix logo on headstock.

1980-1984	$400	$600

Rock

1971-1973. Single cut solidbody, becomes the Super Rock in '73.

1971-1973	$550	$800

Super Rock

1973-ca.1978. Renamed from Rock ('71-'73).

1973-1978	$600	$900

X135

1982. Offset double-cut solidbody, 2 humbucker pickups.

1982	$400	$600

X145 60th Anniversary

1982. Classic offset double-cut only made one year, Anniversary plate on back of headstock, single/single/hum pickups.

1982	$400	$600

X150

1975. Offset double-cut, 2 humbucker pickups.

1975	$550	$800

X220 Omega

1976-ca. 1980. Single-cut solidbody, block inlays, Omega logo on truss rod, black with rosewood neck, or natural with figured top and maple neck.

1976-1980	$550	$800

X280/X290 Working Man

1980-1984. Modified double-cut solidbody, 2 exposed-coil humbuckers, dot inlays, natural satin finish (X280) or jet black (X290).

1980-1984	$300	$500

X410

1975. Double-cut thinline acoustic archtop, 2 humbucker pickups, large split triangle markers, open-book style headstock shape.

1975	$900	$1,300

X420

1978. Double-cut thinline acoustic archtop, 2 humbucker pickups, dot markers, wave-shape style headstock.

1978	$600	$900

X935 Endorser

1983-1984. Double-cut solidbody, 2 humbucker pickups, tune-o-matic, dot markers.

1983-1984	$500	$800

X960 Ultima

1981. Hybrid single-cut with additional soft bass bout cutaway, slab solidbody, dot markers, 2 humbucker pickups, wave-shape style headstock.

1981	$550	$800

Electric Gypsy

See listing under Teye.

Electro

1964-1975. The Electro line was manufactured by Electro String Instruments and distributed by Radio-Tel. The Electro logo appeared on the headstock rather than Rickenbacker. Refer to the Rickenbacker section for models.

Electromuse

1940s-1950s. Mainly known for lap steels, Electromuse also offered acoustic and electric hollowbody guitars. They also had tube amps usually sold as a package with a lap steel.

Elferink

1993-present. Production/custom, premium grade, archtop guitars built in the Netherlands by luthier Frans Elferink.

Elijah Jewel

2009-present. Luthier Michael Kerry builds his professional grade, production/custom, acoustic guitars in Mineola, Texas. He also builds mandolins.

Elite

1960s. Guitars made in Italy by the Crucianelli accordion company, which made several other brands.

Elk

Late-1960s. Japanese-made by Elk Gakki Co., Ltd. Many were copies of American designs. They also offered amps and effects.

Elliott Guitars

1966-present. Premium and presentation grade, custom, nylon-string classical and steel-string guitars built by luthier Jeffrey Elliott in Portland, Oregon.

Ellis

2000-present. Luthier Andrew Ellis builds his production/custom, premium grade, steel string acoustic and resophonic guitars in Perth, Western Australia. In 2008 he also added lap steels.

Elli-Sound

1960s. Guitars made in Italy by the Crucianelli accordion company, which made several other brands.

1977 Electra MPC
Rivington Guitars

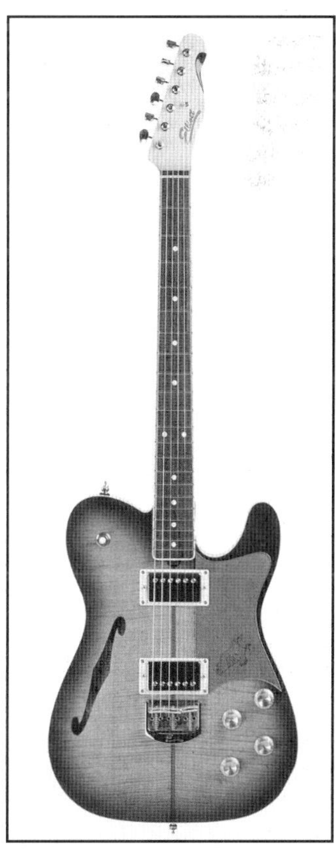

Elliott Raven

GUITARS

Epiphone B.B. King Lucille

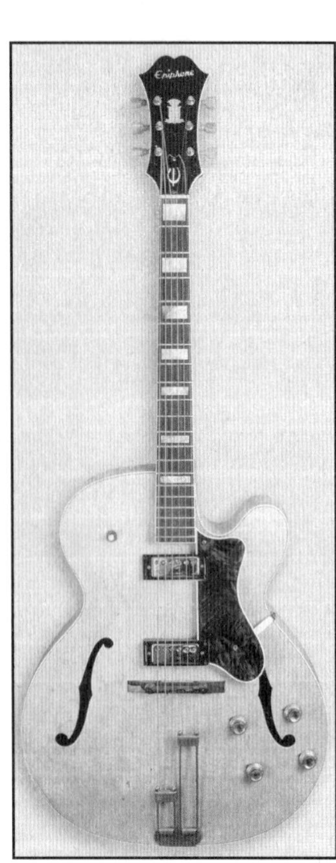
1961 Epiphone Broadway

MODEL YEAR	FEATURES	EXC. COND. LOW	HIGH

Ellsberry Archtop Guitars

2003-2016. Premium and presentation grade, custom/production, acoustic and electric archtops built by luthier James Ellsberry first in Torrance and Harbor City, California, then in Huntington Beach.

Emperador

1966-1992. Guitars and basses imported from Japan by Westheimer Musical Instruments. Early models appear to be made by either Teisco or Kawai; later models were made by Cort.

Acoustic

1960s	Archtop or flat-top	$200	$350

Electric Solidbody

1960s		$300	$500

Empire

1997-present. Professional and premium grade, production/custom, solidbody guitars from Lee Garver's GMW Guitarworks of Glendora, California.

Encore

Mid-1960s-present. Budget grade, production, classical, acoustic, and electric guitars imported from China and Vietnam by John Hornby Skewes & Co. in the U.K. They also offer basses.

Engel Guitars

1990-present. Luthier Robert Engel builds his premium grade, production/custom, hollowbody and solidbody guitars in Stamford, Connecticut.

English Electronics

1960s. Lansing, Michigan, company named after owner, some private branded guitars and amps by Valco (Chicago), many models with large English Electronics vertical logo on headstock.

Tonemaster

1960s. National Val-Pro 84 with neck pickup and bridge mounted pickup, black.

1960s		$750	$1,200

Epcor

1967. Hollowbody electirc guitars and basses built by Joe Hall's Hallmark Guitars in Bakersfield, CA for manufacturer's rep Ed Preager (the EP in the name). Only about 35 were built.

Epi

1970s. Typical Japanese copy-import, Epi logo on headstock with capital letter split-E logo, inside label says "Norlin," probably for Japanese domestic market.

Acoustic Flat-Top

1970s. D-style, mahogany body.

1970s		$300	$500

Epiphone

Ca. 1873-present. Budget, intermediate, professional, and premium grade, production, solidbody, archtop, acoustic, acoustic/electric, resonator, and classical guitars made in the U.S. and overseas. They also offer basses, amps, mandolins, ukes and banjos. Founded in Smyrna, Turkey, by Anastasios Stathopoulos and early instruments had his label. He emigrated to the U.S. in 1903 and changed the name to Stathoupoulo. Anastasios died in '15 and his son, Epaminondas ("Epi") took over. The name changed to House of Stathopoulo in '17 and the company incorporated in '23. In '24 the line of Epiphone Recording banjos debuted and in '28 the company name was changed to the Epiphone Banjo Company. In '43 Epi Stathopoulo died and sons Orphie and Frixo took over. Labor trouble shut down the NYC factory in '51 and the company cut a deal with Conn/Continental and relocated to Philadelphia in '52. Frixo died in '57 and Gibson bought the company. Kalamazoo-made Gibson Epiphones debut in '58. In '69 American production ceased, and Japanese imports began. Some Taiwanese guitars were imported from '79-'81. Limited U.S. production resumed in '82 but sourcing shifted to Korea in '83. In '85 Norlin sold Gibson to Henry Juszkiewicz, Dave Barryman and Gary Zebrowski. In '92 Jim Rosenberg became president of the new Epiphone division.

AJ Masterbilt Series

2004-present. Sloped shoulder D size, solid spruce tops, solid rosewood or mahogany (M) back and sides.

2004-2024	Import	$500	$800

Alleykat

2000-2010. Single cut small body archtop, I humbucker and 1 mini-humbucker.

2000-2010		$400	$700

B.B. King Lucille

1997-2019. Laminated double-cut maple body, 2 humbuckers, Lucille on headstock.

1997-2019		$600	$1,200

Barcelona CE

1999-2000. Classical, solid spruce top, rosewood back and sides, EQ/preamp.

1999-2000		$400	$700

Barcelone (Classical)

1963-1968. Highest model of Epiphone '60s classical guitars, maple back and sides, gold hardware.

1963-1964		$600	$1,000
1965-1968		$500	$900

Bard 12-String

1962-1969. Flat-top, mahogany back and sides, natural or sunburst.

1962-1964		$1,200	$1,800
1965		$1,000	$1,600
1966-1969		$900	$1,500

Beverly

1931-1936. Flat-top, arched back, tenor or Hawaiian versions.

1931-1936	Hawaiian	$900	$1,200
1931-1936	Tenor	$700	$1,000

Biscuit

1997-2000, 2002-2010. Wood body resonator, biscuit bridge, round neck.

1997-2010		$300	$600

MODEL YEAR	FEATURES	EXC. COND. LOW	HIGH

Blackstone

1931-1950. Acoustic archtop, f-holes, sunburst.

1933-1934	Masterbilt	$1,200	$1,800
1935-1937		$1,000	$1,500
1938-1939		$900	$1,300
1940-1941		$800	$1,200
1948-1950		$700	$1,100

Blueshawk Deluxe

2015-2018. Single-cut semi-hollowbody, AAA flamed maple top, mahogany back and sides, 2 P-90s, Midnight Sapphire, Wine red or trans black.

2015-2018		$400	$700

Broadway (Acoustic)

1931-1958. Non-cut acoustic archtop.

1931-1938	Sunburst, walnut body	$3,200	$4,800
1939-1942	Sunburst, maple body	$3,200	$4,800
1946-1958	Natural	$2,800	$4,200
1946-1958	Sunburst	$2,400	$3,600

Broadway Regent (Acoustic Cutaway)

1950-1958. Single-cut acoustic archtop, sunburst.

1950-1958		$2,400	$3,600

Broadway (Electric)

1958-1969. Gibson-made electric archtop, single-cut, 2 New York pickups (mini-humbucking pickups by '61), Frequensator tailpiece, block inlays, sunburst or natural finish with cherry optional in '67 only.

1958-1959	Natural	$3,000	$4,500
1958-1959	Sunburst	$2,500	$3,800
1960-1964	Natural	$2,800	$4,200
1960-1964	Sunburst	$2,500	$3,800
1965	Natural	$2,500	$3,800
1965	Sunburst	$2,200	$3,500
1966-1967	Natural, cherry	$2,200	$3,500
1966-1967	Sunburst	$2,200	$3,500
1968-1969	Natural, cherry	$2,200	$3,500
1968-1969	Sunburst	$2,200	$3,500

Broadway Reissue

1997-2019. Full depth acoustic-electric single cut archtop, 2 humbuckers.

1997-2019		$500	$1,000

Broadway Tenor

1937-1953. Acoustic archtop, sunburst.

1937-1953		$1,200	$1,800

Byron

1949-ca.1955. Acoustic archtop, mahogany back and sides, sunburst.

1949-1955		$700	$1,500

C Series Classical (Import)

1995-2006. Nylon-string classical guitars, including C-25 (mahogany back & sides), C-40 (cedar top, mahogany), C-70-CE (rosewood).

1998-2005	C-40	$150	$300

Caiola Custom

1963-1970. Introduced as Caiola, renamed Caiola Custom in '66, electric thinbody archtop, 2 mini-humbuckers, multi-bound top and back, block inlays, walnut or sunburst finish (walnut only by '68).

1963-1964		$3,000	$5,500
1965		$2,800	$5,000
1966-1970		$2,500	$4,500

Caiola Standard

1966-1970. Electric thinbody archtop, 2 P-90s, single-bound top and back, dot inlays, sunburst or cherry.

1966-1967		$2,200	$4,000
1968-1970		$2,000	$3,800

Casino (1 Pickup)

1961-1969. Thinline hollowbody, double-cut, 1 P-90 pickup, various colors.

1961-1964		$5,000	$7,500
1965		$4,000	$6,000
1966-1969		$3,600	$5,400

Casino (2 Pickups)

1961-1970. Two pickup (P-90) version, various colors. '61-'63 known as Keith Richards model, '64-'65 known as Beatles model.

1961-1962		$7,000	$10,000
1963-1964		$6,000	$9,000
1965		$5,500	$8,500
1966-1970		$5,000	$7,500

Casino (Japan)

1982-1983. Epiphone built a few of its classic models, including the Casino, in Japan from mid-'82 to mid-'83.

1982-1983		$1,200	$1,800

Casino J.L. U.S.A. 1965

2003-2006. 1,965 made.

2003-2006		$2,500	$4,500

Casino Reissue

1995-2019. Import, sunburst.

1995-2019		$500	$1,200

Casino Revolution

1999-2005. Limited production 1965 reissue model, with certificate of authenticity, sanded natural.

1999-2005		$2,800	$4,500

50th Anniversary 1961 Casino

2011. Trapeze (TD) or TremTone vibrato (TDV), limited run of 1,961 built.

2011	TDV	$1,000	$1,500
2011	Trapeze	$1,100	$1,700

70th Anniversary John Lennon Casino

2011. Limited to 70, 35 in sunburst and 35 natural.

2011		$6,500	$8,500

Century

1939-1970. Thinline archtop, non-cut, 1 pickup, trapeze tailpiece, walnut finish, sunburst finish available in '58, Royal Burgundy available '61 and only sunburst finish available by '68.

1939-1948	Oblong shape pu	$2,000	$3,000
1949-1958	NY pickup	$1,800	$2,500
1958-1962	P-90, plate logo	$2,000	$3,000
1963-1964	P-90, no plate logo	$2,000	$3,000
1965-1970	Sunburst, cherry	$1,800	$2,500

Classic (Classical)

1963-1970.

1963-1964		$700	$1,200
1965-1970		$600	$1,100

Collegiate

2004-2005. Les Paul-style body, 1 humbucker, various college graphic decals on body.

2004-2005		$300	$600

2014 Epiphone Casino Reissue

Paul Swanson

1953 Epiphone Century

Rivington Guitars

GUITARS

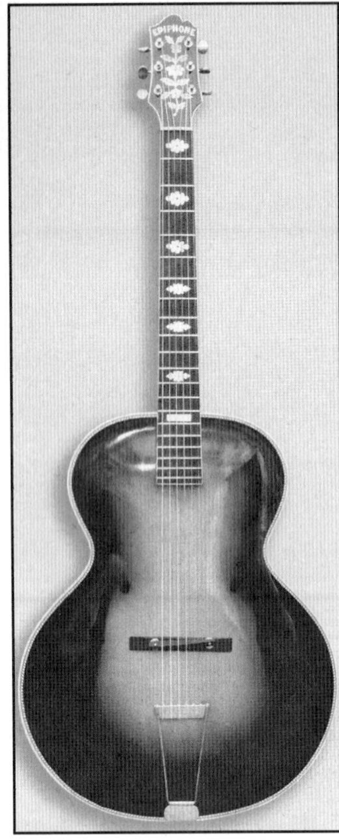

1934 Epiphone De Luxe

1998 Epiphone Del Ray
Rivington Guitars

MODEL YEAR	FEATURES	EXC. COND. LOW	HIGH

Coronet (Electric Archtop)

1939-1949. Electric archtop, laminated mahogany body, 1 pickup, trapeze tailpiece, sunburst, name continued as an electric solidbody in '58.

1939-1949		$1,500	$2,500

Coronet (Solidbody)

1958-1969. Solidbody electric, 1 New York pickup ('58-'59), 1 P-90 ('59-'69), cherry or black finish, Silver Fox finish available by '63, reintroduced as Coronet USA '90-'94, Korean-made '95-'98.

1958-1959	Cherry, NY pu	$5,500	$7,500
1959	Black (rare), NY pu	$9,000	$12,000
1960-1964	Various colors	$4,500	$6,500
1965	Standard color	$3,000	$4,500
1965-1966	Custom color	$6,000	$8,500
1966-1969	Standard color	$3,000	$4,500

Coronet U.S.A.

1990-1994. Made in Nashville, reverse banana headstock, typical Coronet styled body, single-coil and humbucker.

1990-1994		$1,000	$1,500

Coronet (Import)

1995-1998. Import version.

1995-1998		$400	$800

Crestwood Custom

1958-1970. Solidbody, 2 New York pickups ('58-'60), 2 mini-humbuckers ('61-'70), symmetrical body and 3+3 tuners ('58-'62), asymmetrical and 1x6 tuners ('63-'70), slab body with no Gibson equivalent model.

1958-1960	Cherry, NY pus	$5,000	$6,500
1959-1960	Sunburst, NY pus	$5,000	$6,500
1961-1962	Cherry, mini-hums	$4,500	$6,000
1961-1962	White, mini-hums	$5,500	$6,500
1963-1964	Cherry, mini-hums	$3,500	$4,500
1963-1964	Custom color	$6,000	$8,000
1965	Cherry	$3,000	$4,000
1965	Custom color	$6,000	$8,000
1966-1967	Cherry	$3,000	$4,000
1966-1967	Custom color	$4,000	$5,000
1968-1970	Cherry, white	$2,200	$3,000

Crestwood Deluxe

1963-1969. Solidbody with 3 mini-humbuckers, block inlay, cherry, white or Pacific Blue finish, 1x6 tuners.

1963-1964	Cherry, mini-hums	$3,500	$4,500
1963-1964	Custom color	$7,000	$8,500
1965	Cherry	$3,500	$4,500
1965	Custom color	$6,000	$8,000
1966-1967	Cherry	$3,000	$4,000
1966-1967	Custom color	$4,500	$5,500
1968-1969	Cherry, white	$3,000	$4,000

De Luxe

1931-1957. Non-cut acoustic archtop, maple back and sides, trapeze tailpiece ('31-'37), frequensator tailpiece ('37-'57), gold-plated hardware, sunburst or natural finish.

1931-1935	Sunburst, 17 3/8"	$10,000	$15,000
1935-1944	Sunburst, 16 3/8"	$8,000	$12,000
1939-1944	Natural	$8,000	$12,000
1945-1949	Natural	$7,000	$10,500
1945-1949	Sunburst	$6,500	$10,000
1950-1957	Natural	$6,500	$10,000
1950-1957	Sunburst	$6,000	$10,000

De Luxe Regent (Acoustic Archtop)

1948-1952. Acoustic cutaway archtop, high-end appointments, rounded cutaway, natural finish, renamed De Luxe Cutaway in '53.

1948-1952	Natural	$10,500	$16,000
1948-1952	Sunburst	$8,500	$12,500

De Luxe Cutaway/Deluxe Cutaway

1953-1970. Renamed from De Luxe Regent, cataloged Deluxe Cutaway by Gibson in '58, special order by '64 with limited production because acoustic archtops were pretty much replaced by electric archtops. There is also a FT Deluxe Cutaway flat-top (see FT listings).

1953-1957	Natural	$10,000	$15,000
1953-1957	Sunburst	$8,500	$12,500
1958-1959		$9,500	$14,500
1960-1964	Gibson Kalamazoo	$7,500	$11,500
1965-1970	Special order only	$6,500	$10,000

De Luxe Electric (Archtop)

1954-1957. Single-cut electric archtop, 2 pickups, called the Zephyr De Luxe Regent from '48-'54. Produced with a variety of specs, maple or spruce tops, different inlays and pickup combinations.

1954-1957	Natural	$6,000	$9,000
1954-1957	Sunburst	$5,800	$8,800

Del Ray

1995-2000. Offset double-cut body, 2 blade humbuckers, tune-o-matic, flamed maple top.

1995-2000		$500	$800

Devon

1949-1957. Acoustic archtop, non-cut, mahogany back and sides, sunburst finish, optional natural finish by '54.

1950-1957	Sunburst	$2,500	$5,000
1954-1957	Natural	$2,500	$4,000

Don Everly (SQ-180)

1997-2004. Jumbo acoustic reissue, large double 'guard, black gloss finish.

1997-2004		$600	$900

Dot (ES-335 Dot)/Dot Archtop

2000-2020. Dot-neck ES-335.

2000-2020		$400	$600

Dot Studio

2004-2019. Simplified Dot, 2 control knobs, black hardware.

2004-2019		$300	$600

Dove Limited Edition

2008. Dove Limited Edition logo on label, Dove script logo on truss rod cover, classic dove logo art on 'guard and dove inlay on bridge, cherry or ebony.

2008		$400	$600

DR Series/Songmaker Series

2004-present. Dreadnought, spruce top, mahogany back and sides, various models including DR-100 (various colors), DR-200C (single-cut, natural or vintage sunburst), DR-212 (12-string, natural) and DR-500RNS (rosewood, natural satin).

2012-2024	Songmaker DR-212	$300	$500

MODEL YEAR	FEATURES	EXC. COND. LOW	HIGH

Dwight

1963, 1967. Coronet labeled as Dwight and made for Sonny Shields Music of St. Louis, 75 made in '63 and 36 in '67, cherry. National-Supro made Dwight brand lap steels in the '50s.

1963		$4,500	$6,500
1967		$3,500	$4,500

EA/ET/ES Series (Japan)

1970-1979. Production of the Epiphone brand was moved to Japan in '70. Models included the EA (electric thinline) and ET (electric solidbody).

1970-1975	EA-250 Riviera	$600	$780
1970-1975	ET-270	$650	$850
1970-1975	ET-275	$650	$850
1972	ES-255 Casino	$700	$1,000
1975-1979	ET-290 Crestwood	$650	$850

EJ-160E John Lennon

1997-2013. Based on John's Gibson acoustic/electric, sunburst, signature on body.

1997-2013		$500	$800

EJ-200 Series

1994-2020. Solid spruce top, laminate maple body.

1994-2020	Various models	$400	$600

EJ-300

2004-2006. Solid spruce top, laminate rosewood body.

2004-2006		$500	$900

El Diablo

1994-1995. Offset double-cut acoustic/electric, onboard piezo and 3-band EQ, composite back and sides, spruce top, cherry sunburst.

1994-1995		$600	$900

Electar Model M

1935-1939. Epiphone's initial entry into the new electric guitar market of the mid-'30s, 14 3/4" laminate maple archtop, horseshoe pickup, trap door on back for electronics, Electar logo on headstock, oblong pickup replaces horseshoe in late-'37.

1935-1936	2 control knobs	$2,500	$4,500
1937-1939	3 control knobs	$2,500	$4,500

Electar Model M Tenor

1937-1939. Electric tenor 4-string with Electar specs.

1937-1939	3 knobs, natural	$2,000	$4,000

Elitist Series

2003-2019. Made in Japan, higher-grade series, using finer woods and inlays and U.S.-made Gibson pickups.

2003-2004	J-200	$1,200	$1,800
2003-2004	L-00/VS	$1,000	$1,500
2003-2005	'61 SG Standard	$900	$1,400
2003-2005	'65 Texan	$1,200	$1,800
2003-2005	Riviera	$1,400	$2,100
2003-2008	'63 ES-335 Dot	$1,400	$2,100
2003-2008	Byrdland/L5	$1,800	$2,700
2003-2009	Broadway	$1,200	$1,800
2003-2009	LP Custom	$900	$1,400
2003-2009	LP Standard	$900	$1,400
2003-2009	LP Standard '57 Goldtop	$900	$1,400
2003-2009	LP Studio	$760	$1,200
2003-2009	Sheraton	$1,400	$2,100
2003-2019	Casino	$1,200	$1,800
2004-2005	Jim Croce L-00	$900	$1,350
2005	Chet Atkins Country Gent	$1,200	$1,800
2007-2009	LP Plus	$900	$1,400
2012	D Yoakam Trash Casino	$1,200	$1,800

Emperor (Acoustic Archtop)

1935-1954. Acoustic archtop, non-cut, maple back and sides, multi-bound body, gold-plated hardware, sunburst, optional natural finish by '39.

1935-1939	Natural	$10,000	$15,000
1935-1939	Sunburst	$6,700	$10,000
1940-1949	Natural, Sunburst	$7,700	$12,000
1950-1954	Natural	$6,700	$10,000
1950-1954	Sunburst	$6,300	$9,500

Emperor Regent

1948-1953. Acoustic archtop with rounded cutaway, renamed Emperor Cutaway in '53.

1948-1953	Natural	$7,000	$10,000
1948-1953	Sunburst	$6,300	$9,500

Emperor Cutaway

1953-1957. Renamed from Emperor Regent, acoustic archtop, single-cut, maple back and sides, multi-bound body, gold-plated hardware, sunburst or natural.

1953-1957	Natural	$7,700	$11,000
1953-1957	Sunburst	$6,700	$10,000

Emperor Electric

1953-1957. Archtop, single-cut, 3 pickups, multi-bound body, sunburst, called the Zephyr Emperor Regent in '50-'53.

1953-1957		$5,000	$7,000

Emperor (Thinline Electric)

1958-1969. Single-cut, thinline archtop, 3 New York pickups in '58-'60, 3 mini-humbuckers '61 on, multi-bound, gold-plated hardware, sunburst or natural finish until '65 when only sunburst was made.

1958-1959	Natural, 3 NY pus	$9,000	$14,000
1958-1959	Sunburst, 3 NY pus	$7,000	$12,000
1960-1962	Natural	$8,300	$13,000
1960-1962	Sunburst	$6,700	$11,000
1963-1969	Special order	$6,500	$10,000

Emperor/Emperor II

1982-1994. Single-cut archtop jazz guitar, 2 humbuckers, blocks, gold hardware. II was added to name in '93, became Joe Pass Emperor II (see that listing) in '95, although his name was on the guitar as early as '91.

1982-1989	Matsumoku, Japan	$1,500	$2,200
1990-1994		$800	$1,800

Entrada (Classical)

1963-1968. Small classical, 13.25" bout, natural.

1963-1964		$500	$800
1965-1968		$500	$800

ES-175 Premium

2010-2019. Limited Edition, vintage "aged" lacquer finish, various colors.

2010-2019		$700	$1,000

ES-295

1997-2001, 2003-2016. Epiphone's version of classic Gibson goldtop.

1997-2016		$800	$1,200

Epiphone Songmaker DR-212

1967 Epiphone Emperor

RichardSarmento

GUITARS

1958 Epiphone FT 45 Cortez
Jim Dikel

1968 Epiphone FT 79 Texan
Rivington Guitars

MODEL YEAR	FEATURES	EXC. COND. LOW	HIGH

ES-339 PRO/ES-339

2012-present. Maple laminate body, 2 pickups. PRO dropped from name in 2020.

2012-2024		$400	$600

Espana (Classical)

1962-1968. Classical, U.S.-made, maple back and sides, natural, imported in '69 from Japan.

1962-1964		$950	$1,500
1965-1968		$850	$1,300

Exellente

1963-1969, 1994-1995. Flat-top, Brazilian rosewood back and sides (Indian rosewood '68-'69), cloud inlays. Name revived on Gibson Montana insturment in '90s.

1963-1964	Brazilian	$8,000	$12,000
1965	Brazilian	$7,500	$11,000
1966-1967	Brazilian	$7,000	$10,000
1968-1969	Indian	$5,500	$8,000

1958 Korina Explorer

1998-2011. Explorer with typical appointments, korina body. This guitar was produced with a variety of specs, ranging from maple tops to spruce tops, different inlay markers were also used, different pickup combinations have been seen, natural or sunburst finish.

1998-2011		$600	$900

1958 Gothic Explorer/Flying V

2002-2012. Flat black finish, V ends in 2010.

2002-2012		$500	$800

Firebird

1995-2000. Two mini-humbuckers, Firebird Red, dot markers.

1995-2000		$700	$1,000

Firebird 300

1986-1988. Korean import, Firebird Red.

1986-1988		$600	$900

Firebird 500

1986-1988. Korean import, Firebird Red.

1986-1988		$800	$1,200

1963 Firebird VII/Firebird VII

2000-2010. Reverse body, 3 mini-humbuckers, gold hardware, Maestro-style vibrato, block markers, Firebird Red. 1963 dropped from name in '03.

2000-2010		$900	$1,500

Firebird I Joe Bonamassa

2016. Artist Limited Edition, modeled after his Gibson '63 Firebird I (nicknamed "Treasure"), Tobacco Sunburst or Polymist Gold.

2016		$800	$1,200

Firebird Studio

2006-2011. Two humbuckers, with worn cherry finish.

2006-2011		$500	$800

Flamekat

1999-2005. Archtop, double dice position markers, 2 mini-humbuckers, Epiphone Bigsby, flame finish.

1999-2005		$600	$900

Flying V/'67 Flying V

1989-1998, 2003-2005. '67 or '58 specs, alder body, natural.

1989-1998	'67 specs	$600	$900
2003-2005	'58 specs	$500	$800

MODEL YEAR	FEATURES	EXC. COND. LOW	HIGH

1958 Korina Flying V

1998-2011, 2016. Typical Flying V configuration, korina body, veneer top. Limited Edition offered in '16 with solid korina, 2 humbucker pickups and gold hardware.

1998-2011	Factory, veneer	$600	$900
2016	Limited Edition	$900	$1,500

1958 Korina Flying V Joe Bonamassa

2017-2018. Limited Edition, modeled from his first '58 Korina Flying V (nicknamed "Amos"), '50s-style Flying V case, hand-signed COA.

2017-2018		$1,200	$1,800

Flying V Prophecy

2020-present. AAA figured maple top, Yellow Tiger or Black with aged gloss finish.

2020-2024		$700	$1,000

FT 30

1941-1949. Acoustic flat-top, brown stain, mahogany back and sides, reintroduced as Gibson-made FT 30 Caballero in '58.

1941-1943		$2,000	$3,000
1944-1949		$1,800	$2,800

FT 30 Caballero

1959-1970. Reintroduced from Epiphone-made FT 30, Gibson-made acoustic flat-top, natural, all mahogany body, dot inlay, tenor available '63-'68.

1959-1961		$1,200	$1,800
1962-1964		$900	$1,500
1965		$800	$1,200
1966-1970		$700	$1,100

FT 45

1941-1948. Acoustic flat-top, walnut back and sides, cherry neck, rosewood 'board, natural top, reintroduced as Gibson-made FT 45 Cortez in '58.

1941-1943		$2,500	$3,800
1944-1948		$2,000	$3,000

FT 45 Cortez

1958-1969. Reintroduced from Epiphone-made FT 45, Gibson-made acoustic flat-top, 16.5", mahogany back and sides, sunburst or natural top (sunburst only in '59-'62).

1958-1959	Sunburst	$1,600	$2,500
1960-1964	Sunburst, natural	$1,600	$2,500
1965-1966	Sunburst, natural	$1,300	$2,000
1967-1969	Sunburst, natural	$1,000	$1,500

FT 79

1941-1958. Acoustic 16" flat-top, square shoulder dreadnought, walnut back and sides until '49 and laminated maple back and sides '49 on, natural, renamed FT 79 Texan by Gibson in '58.

1941-1943	Walnut	$3,000	$4,500
1944-1949	Walnut	$2,500	$3,800
1949-1958	Maple	$2,000	$3,000

FT 79 Texan

1958-1970, 1993-1995. Renamed from Epiphone FT 79, Gibson-made acoustic flat-top, mahogany back and sides, sunburst or natural top, Gibson Montana made 170 in '93-'95.

1958-1959		$3,500	$5,500
1960-1964		$3,200	$4,800
1965		$3,000	$4,500

MODEL YEAR	FEATURES	EXC. COND. LOW	HIGH
1966-1967		$2,800	$4,200
1968-1969		$2,500	$3,800
1970		$2,200	$3,500

Paul McCartney 1964 Texan (U.S.A.)

2005-2006. Reproduction of McCartney's '64 Texan made in Gibson's Montana plant, two runs, one of 40 guitars ('05), second of 250 ('05-'06). The first 40 were hand-aged and came with Sir Paul's autograph, display case and certificate; the 250 run were not-hand aged, but have signed labels.

2005-2006 — $3,500 — $7,000

Paul McCartney 1964 Texan (Japan)

2006-2010. Limited run of 1,964 guitars.

2006-2010 — $2,000 — $4,500

1964 Texan (Inspired By Series)

2010-2019. Imported production model, acoustic/ electric, non-adjustable bridge.

2010-2019 — $400 — $600

FT 85 Serenader 12-String

1963-1969. 12 strings, mahogany back and sides, dot inlay, natural.

Year	Features	Low	High
1963-1964		$1,800	$2,800
1965		$1,600	$2,500
1966-1969		$1,400	$2,200

FT 90 El Dorado

1963-1970. Dreadnought flat-top acoustic, mahogany back and sides, multi-bound front and back, natural.

Year	Features	Low	High
1963-1964		$2,000	$3,000
1965		$1,700	$2,500
1966-1967		$1,500	$2,300
1968-1970		$1,500	$2,300

FT 95 Folkster

1966-1969. 14" small body, mahogany back and sides, natural, double white 'guards.

1966-1969 — $1,000 — $1,500

FT 98 Troubadour

1963-1969. 16" square shouldered drednought, maple back and sides, gold-plated hardware, classical width 'board.

Year	Features	Low	High
1963-1964		$1,800	$2,800
1965		$1,700	$2,500
1966-1969		$1,600	$2,400

FT 110

1941-1958. Acoustic flat-top, natural, renamed the FT 110 Frontier by Gibson in '58.

Year	Features	Low	High
1941-1943	Square shoulder	$3,500	$5,300
1944-1949	Square shoulder	$3,300	$5,000
1949-1958	Round shoulder	$2,700	$4,000

FT 110 Frontier

1958-1970, 1994. Renamed from FT 110, acoustic flat-top, natural or sunburst, Gibson Montana made 30 in '94. Reintroduced '21, Antique Natural or Frontier Burst.

Year	Features	Low	High
1958-1959		$4,800	$7,500
1960-1964		$4,500	$6,500
1965		$3,500	$5,000
1966-1970		$3,700	$5,500

FT Deluxe

1939-1941. Acoustic flat-top, 16.5".

1939-1941 — $5,000 — $7,500

FT Deluxe Cutaway (FT 210)

1954-1957. Acoustic flat-top, cutaway, 16.5". Some labeled FT 210.

1954-1957 — $5,000 — $7,500

FT Series (Flat-Tops Japan)

1970s. In '70 Epiphone moved production to Japan. Various 6- to 12-string models were made, nearly all with bolt necks and small rectangular blue labels on the inside back, ranging from the budget FT 120 to the top-of-the-line FT 570 Super Jumbo.

1970s — Various models — $600 — $1,200

G 310

1989-2019. SG-style model with large 'guard and gig bag.

1989-2019 — $300 — $500

G 400

1989-2013. SG-style, 2 humbuckers, crown inlays.

1989-2013 — $400 — $600

G 400 Custom

1998-2000, 2003-2011. 3 humbucker version, gold hardware, block inlays.

1998-2011 — $600 — $900

G 400 Deluxe

1999-2007. Flame maple top version of 2 humbucker 400.

1999-2007 — $500 — $800

G 400 Limited Edition

2001-2002. 400 with Deluxe Maestro lyra vibrola, cherry red.

2001-2002 — $700 — $1,000

G 400 Tony Iommi

2003-2011. SG-style model with cross 'board inlay markers, black finish.

2003-2011 — $900 — $1,500

G 1275 Custom Double Neck

1996-2011. SG-style alder body, 6- & 12-string, maple top, mahogany neck, cherry red, set neck. Also offered as bolt-neck Standard for '96-'98.

1996-2011 — $1,200 — $1,800

Genesis

1979-1980. Double-cut solidbody, 2 humbuckers with coil-taps, carved top, red or black, available as Custom, Deluxe, and Standard models, Taiwan import.

1979-1980 — $1,000 — $1,500

Granada (Non-cutaway Thinbody)

1962-1969. Non-cut thinline archtop, 1 f-hole, 1 pickup, trapeze tailpiece, sunburst finish.

Year	Features	Low	High
1962-1964		$1,500	$2,500
1965-1969		$1,200	$1,800

Granada (Cutaway)

1965-1970. Single-cut version.

1965-1970 — $1,300 — $2,000

Harry Volpe (E721/E722)

1955-1957. Hollow body, 1 pickup.

Year	Features	Low	High
1955-1957	E721, Shaded	$2,000	$3,500
1955-1957	E722, Blonde	$2,000	$3,500

Hollywood Masterbilt Tenor

1931-1936. Tenor version of the Triumph, acoustic archtop 15.4", 19-fret Brazilian rosewood 'board, diagonal diamond markers.

1931-1936 — $2,000 — $2,500

1963 Epiphone FT 85 Serenader
Rivington Guitars

1965 Epiphone FT 110 Frontier
Carter Vintage Guitars

GUITARS

Epiphone Hummingbird Pro

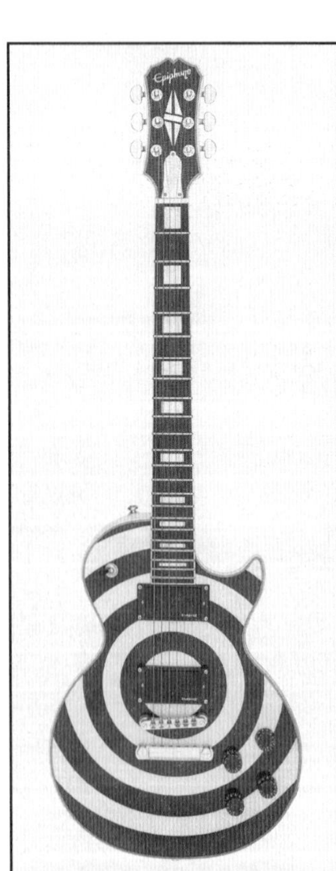

2004 Epiphone Zakk Wylde Les Paul Custom

MODEL YEAR	FEATURES	EXC. COND. LOW	HIGH

Howard Roberts Standard

1964-1970. Single-cut acoustic archtop, bound front and back, cherry or sunburst finish, listed in catalog as acoustic but built as electric.

1964-1970		$2,500	$5,000

Howard Roberts Custom

1965-1970. Single-cut archtop, bound front and back, 1 pickup, walnut finish (natural offered '66 only).

1965-1970		$3,000	$6,000

Howard Roberts III

1987-1991. Two pickups, various colors.

1987-1991		$1,000	$1,500

Hummingbird/Pro/Studio

1994-present. Twin parallelogram inlays, hummingbird 'guard, replaced by Pro, with added electronics, in '13. Pro dropped from name in 2020, named Hummingbird Studio in 23.

1994-2024		$400	$600

Inspiration Style A Tenor

1928-1929. Banjo resonator style body with round sound hole, A headstock logo, spruce top, walnut back, sides and neck.

1928-1929		$2,500	$4,000

Joe Pass/Joe Pass Emperor II

1995-2019. Single-cut archtop jazz guitar, 2 humbuckers, blocks, gold hardware, natural or sunbusrt, renamed from Emperor II (see that listing). Limited Edition all-gold finish or Wine Red were available early on.

1995-2019		$500	$800

Johnny A Signature Custom Outfit

2017-2018. Artist Signature series, Limited Edition, double-cut hollowbody, flamed maple top, 2 pickups, Bigsby tail, Sunset Glow gloss finish.

2017-2018		$1,200	$1,800

Les Paul 100/LP-100

1993-2019. Affordable single-cut Les Paul, bolt-on neck.

1993-2019		$300	$500

Les Paul '56 Goldtop

1998-2013. Made in China, based on '56 Goldtop specs with 2 P-90s. Black finish was offered starting in '09.

1998-2013	Gold	$600	$900
2009-2013	Black	$700	$1,000

Les Paul Ace Frehley

2001. Les Paul Custom 3-pickups, Ace's signature on 22nd fret, lightning bolt markers.

2001		$1,200	$1,800

Les Paul Alabama Farewell Tour

2003. Limited production, 1 pickup single-cut Jr., American flag and Alabama logo graphics and band signatures on body, Certificate of Authenticity.

2003		$800	$1,200

Les Paul Black Beauty

1997-2019. Classic styling with three gold plated pickups, black finish, block markers.

1997-2019		$600	$900

Les Paul Classic

2003-2005. Classic Les Paul Standard specs, figured maple top, sunburst.

2003-2005		$500	$800

MODEL YEAR	FEATURES	EXC. COND. LOW	HIGH

Les Paul Custom

1989-2011. Various colors.

1989-2011		$600	$900

Les Paul Custom Plus (Flame Top)

1998-2010. Flamed maple top version of 2 pickup Custom, gold hardware, sunburst.

1998-2010		$700	$1,000

Les Paul Custom Silverburst

2007-2008. 2 humbuckers, silverburst finish.

2007-2008		$800	$1,200

Les Paul Dale Earnhardt

2003. Dale Earnhardt graphics, 1 humbucker.

2003		$800	$1,200

Les Paul Deluxe

1998-2000. Typical mini-humbucker pickups.

1998-2000		$700	$1,000

Les Paul ES Limited Edition

1999-2000. Les Paul semi-hollow body with f-holes, carved maple top, gold hardware, cherry sunburst and other color options.

1999-2000	Custom	$800	$1,200
1999-2000	Standard	$600	$900

Les Paul Gold Top

1994-1998. Goldtop, 2 humbuckers. Listed as Les Paul Standard Goldtop in '94.

1994-1998		$600	$900

Les Paul Joe Bonamassa Goldtop

2010. Limited Edition, 1,000 made, LP Standard specs with metallic gold finish and black trim rings.

2010		$1,200	$1,800

Les Paul Joe Perry Boneyard

2004-2006. Boneyard logo on headstock, figured Boneyard finish.

2004-2006		$1,000	$1,500

Les Paul Jr. '57 Reissue

2006. '57 Reissue on truss rod cover, logo and script Les Paul Junior stencil on headstock, lower back headstock states 'Epiphone Limited Edition Custom Shop'.

2006		$500	$800

Les Paul Music Rising

2006-2007. Music Rising (Katrina charity) graphics, LP Studio, 2 humbuckers.

2006-2007		$500	$800

Les Paul Prophecy

2020-present. Modern Collection, mahogany body, AAA flame maple veneer top in Red Tiger or Olive Tiger aged gloss, or plain top in black aged gloss.

2020-2024		$700	$1,000

Les Paul Sparkle L.E.

2001. Limited Edition LP Standard, silver, purple, red (and others) glitter finish, optional Bigsby.

2001		$800	$1,200

Les Paul Special

1994-2000, 2020-present. Double-cut, bolt neck. Reintroduced in '20 with P-90 Pro pickups, CTS electronics, TV yellow finish.

1994-2000		$300	$500

MODEL YEAR	FEATURES	EXC. COND. LOW	HIGH

Les Paul Special II

1996-2019. Economical Les Paul, 2 pickups, single-cut, various colors.

1996-2016	Guitar and amp	$200	$300
1996-2019	Guitar only	$150	$250

Les Paul Special/TV Special

2006. Copy of single-cut late '50s Les Paul Special with TV finish.

2006		$400	$600

Les Paul Standard

1989-2019. Solid mahogany body, carved maple top, 2 humbuckers.

1989-2019	Various colors	$500	$800

Les Paul Standard Baritone

2004-2005. 27-3/4" long-scale baritone model.

2004-2005		$800	$1,200

Les Paul Standard Plus FMT

2003-2012. LP Standard figured curly maple sunburst top.

2003-2012		$600	$900

Les Paul Standard Ultra/Ultra II

2005-2012. LP Standard with chambered and contoured body, quilted maple top.

2005-2012	Ultra	$600	$900
2005-2012	Ultra II	$700	$1,000

Les Paul Studio

1995-present. Epiphone's version of Gibson LP Studio.

1995-2024		$400	$600

Les Paul XII

1998-2000. 12-string solidbody, trapeze tailpiece, flamed maple sunburst, standard configuration.

1998-2000		$800	$1,200

Slash Les Paul

1997-2000. Slash logo on body.

1997-2000		$1,000	$1,500

Slash Les Paul Goldtop

2008-2012. Limited Edition 2,000 made, goldtop finish, Seymour Duncan exposed humbuckers, Slash logo on truss rod cover, includes certificate of authenticity.

2008-2012	With COA	$1,000	$1,500

Slash Les Paul Standard Plus Top

2008-2012. Figured top, exposed humbuckers, includes certificate of authenticity.

2008-2012	With COA	$1,200	$1,800

Zakk Wylde Les Paul Custom

2002-2019. Bull's-eye graphic, block markers, split diamond headstock inlay.

2002-2019		$900	$1,500

Madrid (Classical)

1962-1969. Classical, natural.

1962-1964		$800	$1,200
1965-1969		$700	$1,000

MD-30

1993. D-size, round metal resonator, spruce top with dual screens.

1993		$500	$800

Melody Tenor

1931-1937. 23" scale, bound body.

1931-1937	Masterbilt	$1,500	$2,200

Moderne

2000. Copy of '58 Gibson Moderne design, dot markers, Moderne script logo on 'guard, black.

2000		$600	$900

Navarre

1931-1940. Hawaiian flat-top, mahogany back and sides, bound top and back, dot inlay, brown finish.

1931-1937	Masterbilt label	$2,500	$4,000
1938-1940	Standard label	$2,200	$3,500

Nighthawk Standard

1995-2000. Epiphone's version of the Gibson Nighthawk, single-cut, bolt neck, figured top.

1995-2000		$400	$600

Noel Gallagher Union Jack/Super Nova

1997-2005. Limited edition, higher-end ES-335. Union Jack with British flag finish (introduced '99) or Supernova in solid blue.

1997-2005		$1,200	$1,800

Olympic (Acoustic Archtop)

1931-1949. Mahogany back and sides.

1931-1936	Smaller body	$2,500	$3,500
1937-1939	Larger body	$2,000	$3,000
1940-1949		$2,000	$3,000

Olympic Tenor (Acoustic Archtop)

1937-1949. 4-string version of the Olympic.

1937-1949		$1,500	$2,500

Olympic Single (Solidbody)

1960-1970. Slab body, the same as the mid-'60s Coronet, Wilshire and Crestwood Series, single-cut '60-'62, asymmetrical double-cut '63-'70, 2 Melody maker single-coil pickups, vibrato optional in '64 and standard by '65.

1960-1962	Single-cut	$1,500	$2,500
1963-1964	Double-cut	$1,200	$1,800
1965-1970		$1,000	$1,500

Olympic Double (Solidbody)

1960-1969. Slab body, the same as the mid-'60s Coronet, Wilshire and Crestwood Series, single-cut '60-'62, asymmetrical-cut '63-'70, 2 Melody Maker single-coils, vibrato optional in '64 and standard by '65.

1960-1963	Single-cut	$2,500	$3,500
1963-1964	Double-cut	$2,000	$3,000
1965-1969	Cherry, sunburst	$1,800	$2,800

Olympic (3/4 Scale Solidbody)

1960-1963. 22" scale, sunburst.

1960-1963		$1,500	$2,500

Olympic Special (Solidbody)

1962-1970. Short neck with neck body joint at the 16th fret (instead of the 22nd), single Melody Maker-style single-coil bridge pickup, small headstock, double-cut slab body, dot markers, Maestro or Epiphone vibrato optional '64-'65, slab body contour changes in '65 from symmetrical to asymmetrical with slightly longer bass horn, sunburst.

1962-1964	Symmetrical	$1,000	$1,500
1965-1970	Asymmetrical	$900	$1,200

PR Series

1980-2004. Budget acoustics, mainly D size but some smaller, cut and non-cut bodies.

1980-2004	Various models	$250	$1,200

1965 Epiphone Olympic Special

Marc Freidenberg

1990 Epiphone PR-325

Dave Mullikin

GUITARS

1967 Epiphone Riviera 12-string
Dean Nissen

1965 Epiphone Sorrento (1 pickup)
Tom Pfeifer

MODEL YEAR	FEATURES	EXC. COND. LOW	HIGH

Pro 1

1989-1996. Solidbody, double-cut, 1 single-coil and 1 humbucking pickup, bolt-on neck, various colors.

1989-1996		$400	$600

Pro 2

1995-1998. Higher-end Pro I with Steinberger DB bridge, set-neck, 2 humbuckers, various colors.

1995-1998		$450	$700

Professional

1962-1967. Double-cut, thinline archtop, 1 pickup, mahogany finish. Values include matching Professional amp.

1962-1964	With matching amp	$2,500	$3,500
1965	With matching amp	$2,200	$3,300
1966-1967	With matching amp	$2,000	$3,000

Prophecy Extura

2020-present. Modern Collection, mahogany body, AAA flame maple veneer top, 2 Fishman pickups, various colors with aged gloss finish.

2020-2024		$700	$1,000

Recording A

1928-1931. Asymmetrical body flat-top with exaggerated treble bout cutaway, celluloid headstock veneer, dot inlays. All Recording models were offered in concert or auditorium body sizes.

1928-1931	Standard 6-string	$2,500	$4,000
1928-1931	Tenor 4-string	$2,200	$3,500

Recording B

1928-1931. As Recording A but with arched back, bound fingerboard, fancier body binding and zigzagging double slotted-diamond inlays.

1928-1931		$3,000	$5,000

Recording C

1928-1931. As Recording B but with arched top.

1928-1931		$3,500	$6,000

Recording D

1928-1931. As Recording C, but with large cross-hatched block inlays.

1928-1931		$4,000	$7,000

Recording E

1928-1931. As Recording D, but with large floral engraved block inlays.

1928-1931		$5,000	$8,000

Ritz

1940-1949. 15.5" acoustic archtop, large cello f-holes, dot inlays, no headstock ornamentation other than script Epiphone inlay, blond finish.

1940-1949		$1,500	$2,500

Riviera

1962-1970. Double-cut thinline archtop, 2 mini-humbuckers, Royal Tan standard finish changing to sunburst in '65, cherry optional by '66-'70, additional 250 were made in Nashville in '93-'94, a Riviera import was available in '82 and for '94-'06.

1962-1964	Tan or cherry	$4,500	$7,000
1964	Sunburst	$4,000	$6,000
1965	Sunburst, cherry	$3,700	$5,500
1966-1967	Sparkling Burgundy	$3,700	$5,500
1966-1970	Sunburst, cherry	$3,500	$5,500
1967-1968	Walnut	$3,500	$5,500

MODEL YEAR	FEATURES	EXC. COND. LOW	HIGH

Riviera (U.S.A.)

1993-1994. Made in U.S.A. on back of headstock.

1993-1994		$1,500	$2,200

Riviera Reissue (Korea)

1994-2006. Korean-made contemporary reissue, natural.

1994-2006		$600	$900

Riviera 12-String

1965-1970. Double-cut, 12 strings, thinline archtop, 2 mini-humbuckers, sunburst or cherry.

1965-1970		$3,500	$4,500

Riviera 12-String Reissue (Korea)

1997-2000. Korean-made reissue, natural.

1997	Humbuckers	$800	$1,200
1998-2000	Mini-hums	$600	$900

Royal

1931-1935. 15 1/2" acoustic archtop, mahogany back and sides, dot markers, sunburst, bound top, back and neck, Masterbilt headstock logo.

1931-1935		$2,500	$4,000

S-900

1986-1989. Neck-thru-body, locking Bender tremolo system, 2 pickups with individual switching and a coil-tap control.

1986-1989		$500	$800

SC350

1976-1979. Mahogany solidbody, scroll bass horn, rosewood 'board, dot inlays, bolt neck, 2 humbuckers, made in Japan.

1976-1979	Mahogany	$800	$1,200

SC450

1976-1979. Like SC350, but with maple body, glued neck, and coil tap.

1976-1979	Maple	$900	$1,400

SC550

1976-1979. Like SC450, but with gold hardware, block inlays, neck and body binding, and ebony 'board.

1976-1979	Maple, gold hdwr	$900	$1,400

Seville EC-100 (Classical)

1938-1941, 1961-1969 (Gibson-made). Classical guitar, mahogany back and sides, natural, the '61-'63 version also available with a pickup.

1961-1964		$800	$1,200
1965-1969		$700	$1,000

Prophecy SG

2020-present. Modern Collection, mahogany body, AAA flame maple veneer top, 2 Fishman pickups, various colors with aged gloss finish.

2020-2024		$700	$1,000

SG Special

2000-present. SG body, dot markers, 2 open-coil humbuckers, later P-90s.

2000-2016	Guitar and amp	$250	$350
2000-2024	Guitar only	$200	$300

Sheraton

1958-1970. Double-cut thinline archtop, 2 New York pickups '58-'60, 2 mini-humbuckers '61 on, frequensator tailpiece, multi-bound, gold-plated hardware, sunburst or natural finish with cherry optional by '65. Reissued '93-'94.

1958-1960	Natural, NY pus	$8,000	$12,000

MODEL YEAR	FEATURES	EXC. COND. LOW	HIGH
1959-1964	Sunburst, mini-hums	$7,000	$10,500
1961-1964	Natural, mini-hums	$8,000	$12,000
1962	Cherry, few made	$7,500	$11,500
1965	Cherry, natural	$5,500	$8,500
1965	Sunburst	$4,500	$8,000
1966-1967	Natural	$5,000	$7,500
1966-1970	Cherry, sunburst	$4,000	$6,000

Sheraton (Japan)

1982-1983. Early reissue, not to be confused with Sheraton II issued later, natural or sunburst.

MODEL YEAR	FEATURES	EXC. COND. LOW	HIGH
1982-1983		$1,200	$1,800

Sheraton (Reissue U.S.A.)

1993-1994, 2005. An additional 250 American-made Sheratons were built from '93-'94.

MODEL YEAR	FEATURES	EXC. COND. LOW	HIGH
1993-1994		$1,800	$2,800
2005		$2,000	$3,000

Sheraton II/Sheraton II PRO

1986-present. Contemporary archtop reissue, natural or sunburst.

MODEL YEAR	FEATURES	EXC. COND. LOW	HIGH
1986-2024		$500	$800

Slasher

2001. Reverse offset double cut solidbody, bolt neck, six-on-a-side tuners, 2 pickups, dot markers.

MODEL YEAR	FEATURES	EXC. COND. LOW	HIGH
2001		$400	$600

Sorrento (1 pickup)

1960-1970. Single-cut thinline archtop, 1 pickup in neck position, tune-o-matic bridge, nickel-plated hardware, sunburst, natural or Royal Olive finish, (cherry or sunburst by '68).

MODEL YEAR	FEATURES	EXC. COND. LOW	HIGH
1960-1964		$2,500	$3,500
1965		$2,200	$3,200
1966-1970		$2,000	$3,000

Sorrento (2 pickups)

1960-1970. Single-cut thinline archtop, 2 pickups, tune-o-matic bridge, nickel-plated hardware, sunburst, natural or Royal Olive finish, (cherry or sunburst by '68).

MODEL YEAR	FEATURES	EXC. COND. LOW	HIGH
1960-1964		$3,000	$4,500
1965		$2,800	$4,200
1966-1970		$2,500	$3,800

Sorrento (Reissue)

1994-2000. Reissue of 2 pickup model, import.

MODEL YEAR	FEATURES	EXC. COND. LOW	HIGH
1994		$800	$1,200
1995-2000		$600	$900

Spartan

1934-1949. Acoustic archtop, 16 3/8", laminated maple body, multi-bound, trapeze tailpiece, sunburst or natural.

MODEL YEAR	FEATURES	EXC. COND. LOW	HIGH
1934-1939	Sunburst	$1,800	$2,800
1940-1949	Sunburst	$1,500	$2,200
1941-1947	Natural	$1,500	$2,200

Special/SG Special (U.S.A.)

1979-1983. SG Special body style, dot markers, 2 exposed humbuckers, Special logo on truss rod cover.

MODEL YEAR	FEATURES	EXC. COND. LOW	HIGH
1979-1983		$1,000	$1,500

Spider/The Spider

1997-2000. Wood body resonator, spider bridge, square neck.

MODEL YEAR	FEATURES	EXC. COND. LOW	HIGH
1997-2000		$400	$600

Spirit I/Spirit II

1982. U.S.-made electric solidbody, double-cut, flat-top with 1 (I) or 2 (II) humbuckers, Epiphone U.S.A. script logo on headstock, Spirit logo on truss rod cover.

MODEL YEAR	FEATURES	EXC. COND. LOW	HIGH
1982		$1,000	$1,500

SST

2007-2011. Acoustic/electric solidbody, either Classic (nylon) or Studio (steel). Chet Atkins model also available.

MODEL YEAR	FEATURES	EXC. COND. LOW	HIGH
2007-2011		$400	$600

Tom Delonge Signature ES-333

2008-2019. One humbucker, dot inlays.

MODEL YEAR	FEATURES	EXC. COND. LOW	HIGH
2008-2019		$800	$1,200

Trailer Park Troubadour Airscreamer

2003-2005. Airstream trailer-shaped body, identifying logo on headstock.

MODEL YEAR	FEATURES	EXC. COND. LOW	HIGH
2003-2005		$700	$1,000

Triumph

1931-1957. 15 1/4" '31-'33, 16 3/8" '33-'36, 17 3/8" '36-'57, walnut back and sides until '33, laminated maple back and sides '33, solid maple back and sides '34, natural or sunburst.

MODEL YEAR	FEATURES	EXC. COND. LOW	HIGH
1931-1932	Sunburst, laminated walnut	$3,000	$4,500
1933	Sunburst, laminated maple	$3,000	$4,500
1934-1935	Sunburst, solid maple	$3,300	$5,000
1936-1940	Sunburst 17 3/8" body	$3,300	$5,000
1941-1957	Natural	$3,300	$5,000
1941-1957	Sunburst	$3,300	$5,000

Triumph Regent (Cutaway)

1948-1969. Acoustic archtop, single-cut, F-holes, renamed Triumph Cutaway in '53, then Gibson listed this model as just the Triumph from '58-'69.

MODEL YEAR	FEATURES	EXC. COND. LOW	HIGH
1948-1952	Regent, natural	$4,000	$6,000
1948-1952	Regent, sunburst	$4,000	$6,000
1953-1957	Cutaway, natural	$3,800	$5,500
1953-1957	Cutaway, sunburst	$3,500	$5,200
1958-1964	Sunburst	$4,000	$6,000
1965	Sunburst	$3,800	$5,800
1966-1969	Sunburst	$3,500	$5,500

USA Map Guitar

1982-1983. U.S.-made promotional model, solidbody electric, mahogany body shaped like U.S. map, 2 pickups, natural.

MODEL YEAR	FEATURES	EXC. COND. LOW	HIGH
1982-1983		$2,500	$3,500

USA Map Guitar Limited Edition

MODEL YEAR	FEATURES	EXC. COND. LOW	HIGH
2007	Import	$600	$900

Vee-Wee (Mini Flying V)

2003. Mini Flying V, single bridge pickup, gig bag.

MODEL YEAR	FEATURES	EXC. COND. LOW	HIGH
2003		$200	$300

Wildkat

2001-2019. Thinline, single-cut, hollow-body, 2 P-90s, Bigsby tailpiece, various colors.

MODEL YEAR	FEATURES	EXC. COND. LOW	HIGH
2001-2019		$500	$800

Wilshire

1959-1970. Double-cut solidbody, 2 pickups, tune-o-matic bridge, cherry.

MODEL YEAR	FEATURES	EXC. COND. LOW	HIGH
1959	Symmetrical	$5,000	$7,500
1960-1962	Thinner-style, P-90s	$4,000	$6,000

1961 Epiphone Triumph Regent

Carter Vintage Guitars

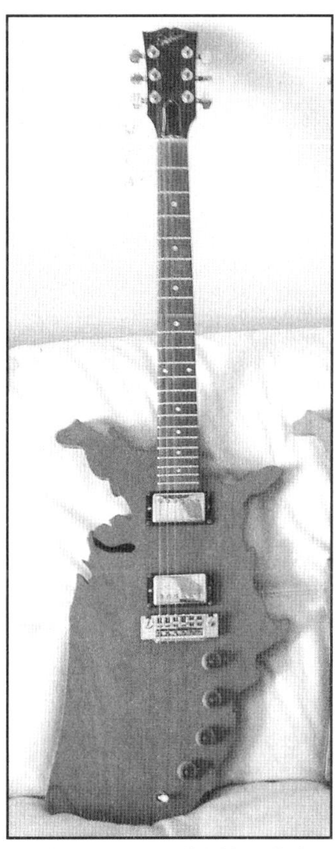

1983 Epiphone USA Map Guitar

James Seldin

1948 Epiphone Zenith
Edward Sparks

1961 Epiphone Zephyr Electric (Cutaway)
Jim Sliff

MODEL YEAR	FEATURES	EXC. COND. LOW	HIGH
1962-1963	Symmetrical, mini-hums	$4,000	$6,000
1963-1964	Asymmetrical, mini-hums	$3,500	$5,500
1965-1966	Custom color	$4,000	$6,000
1965-1966	Standard color	$3,000	$4,500
1967-1970		$2,700	$4,000

Wilshire 12-String

1966-1968. Solidbody, 2 pickups, cherry.

1966-1968		$3,000	$4,500

Wilshire II

1984-1985. Solidbody, maple body, neck and 'board, 2 humbuckers, 3-way switch, coil-tap, 1 tone and 1 volume control, various colors.

1984-1985		$800	$1,200

Windsor (1 Pickup)

1959-1962. Archtop, 1 or 2 pickups, single-cut thinline, sunburst or natural finish.

1959-1960	Natural, NY pu	$3,000	$4,500
1959-1960	Sunburst, NY pu	$2,800	$4,200
1961-1962	Natural, mini-hum	$2,200	$3,300
1961-1962	Sunburst, mini-hum	$2,000	$3,000

Windsor (2 Pickups)

1959-1962. Archtop, 1 or 2 pickups, single-cut thinline, sunburst or natural finish.

1959-1960	Natural, NY pu	$3,300	$5,000
1959-1960	Sunburst, NY pu	$3,000	$4,500
1961-1962	Natural, mini-hum	$2,800	$4,200
1961-1962	Sunburst, mini-hum	$2,200	$3,300

X-1000

1986-1989. Electric solidbody, Korean-made, various colors.

1986-1989		$500	$800

Zenith

1931-1969. Acoustic archtop, bound front and back, f-holes, sunburst.

1931-1933		$1,400	$1,800
1934-1935	14 3/4" body	$1,700	$2,200
1936-1949	16 3/8" body	$1,700	$2,200
1950-1957	Natural	$1,800	$2,300
1950-1957	Sunburst	$1,700	$2,200
1958-1969		$1,600	$2,100

Zephyr

1939-1957. Non-cut electric archtop, 1 pickup, bound front and back, blond or sunburst (first offered '53), called Zephyr Electric starting in '54.

1939-1940	Natural, metal handrest pu	$2,000	$3,000
1941-1943	Natural, no metal handrest	$2,000	$3,000
1944-1946	Natural, top mounted pu	$2,000	$3,000
1947-1948	17 3/8", metal covered pu	$2,000	$3,000
1949-1957	Natural, NY pu	$1,800	$2,700
1953-1957	Sunburst, NY pu	$1,700	$2,600

Zephyr Regent

1950-1953. Single-cut electric archtop, 1 pickup, natural or sunburst, called Zephyr Cutaway for '54-'57.

1950-1953	Natural	$3,200	$4,800
1950-1953	Sunburst	$2,500	$3,800

Zephyr Cutaway

1954-1957. Cutaway version of Zephyr Electric, called Zephyr Regent for 1950-'53.

1954-1957	Natural	$3,200	$4,800
1954-1957	Sunburst	$2,800	$4,200

Zephyr Electric (Cutaway)

1958-1964. Gibson-made version, thinline archtop, single-cut, 2 pickups, natural or sunburst.

1958-1959	Natural	$4,000	$5,500
1958-1959	Sunburst	$3,500	$4,500
1960-1964	Natural	$5,000	$6,000
1960-1964	Sunburst	$4,500	$5,500

Zephyr De Luxe (Non-cutaway)

1941-1942, 1945-1954. Non-cut electric archtop, 1 or 2 pickups, multi-bound front and back, gold-plated hardware, natural or sunburst.

1941-1942	Natural	$2,800	$5,000
1945-1949	Natural, 1 pu	$3,200	$5,000
1945-1954	Natural, 2 pus	$3,500	$5,500
1950-1954	Sunburst, 2 pus	$3,200	$5,000

Zephyr De Luxe Regent (Cutaway)

1948-1954. Single-cut electric archtop, 1 or 2 pickups until '50, then only 2, gold-plated hardware, sunburst or natural finish. Renamed Deluxe Electric in '54.

1948-1949	Natural, 1 pu	$3,500	$6,500
1948-1949	Natural, 2 pus	$4,200	$7,000
1948-1949	Sunburst, 1 pu	$3,200	$5,000
1948-1949	Sunburst, 2 pus	$4,000	$6,000
1950-1954	Natural, 2 pus	$4,200	$7,000
1950-1954	Sunburst, 2 pus	$4,000	$6,000

Zephyr Emperor Regent

1950-1954. Archtop, single rounded cutaway, multi-bound body, 3 pickups, sunburst or natural finish, renamed Emperor Electric in '54.

1950-1954	Natural	$7,000	$12,000
1950-1954	Sunburst	$5,500	$9,500

Zephyr Tenor

1940-1950. Natural, figured top.

1940-1950		$2,000	$3,000

Zephyr Blues Deluxe

1999-2005. Based on early Gibson ES-5, 3 P-90 pickups.

1999-2005		$900	$1,500

Epoch

Economy level imports made by Gibson and sold through Target stores.

Equator Instruments

2006-present. Production/custom, professional and premium grade, solidbody, hollowbody, acoustic and classical guitars built in Chicago, Illinois by luthier David Coleman.

Erlewine

1979-present. Professional and premium grade, production/custom guitars built by luthier Mark Erlewine in Austin, Texas. Erlewine also produces the Chiquita brand travel guitar.

MODEL YEAR	FEATURES	EXC. COND. LOW	HIGH

Esoterik Guitars

Professional grade, production/custom, electric guitars built in San Luis Obispo, California by luthier Ryan Cook. He began with guitars in 2010 and plans to add basses.

ESP

1983-present. Intermediate, professional, and premium grade, production/custom, Japanese-made solidbody guitars and basses. Hisatake Shibuya founded Electronic Sound Products (ESP), a chain of retail stores, in '75. They began to produce replacement parts for electric guitars in '83 and in '85 started to make custom-made guitars. In '87 a factory was opened in Tokyo. In '86 ESP opened a sales office in New York, selling custom guitars and production models. From around '98 to ca. '02 they operated their California-based USA custom shop. In '96, they introduced the Korean-made LTD brand and in '03 introduced the Xtone brand, which was folded into LTD in '10. Hisatake Shibuya also operated 48th Street Custom Guitars during the '90s but he closed that shop in 2003.

20th Anniversary

1995. Solidbody, double-cut, ESP95 inlaid at 12th fret, gold.

1995 $2,000 $3,000

25th Anniversary

2000. Slab body, single-cut.

2000 $2,500 $5,000

Eclipse Custom (U.S.A.)

1998-2002. U.S. Custom Shop-built, single-cut, mahogany body and maple top, various colors offered.

1998-2002 $1,200 $1,800

Eclipse Custom/Custom T (Import)

1986-1988, 2003-2010. Single-cut mahogany solidbody, earliest model with bolt dot marker neck, 2nd version with neck-thru and blocks, the Custom T adds locking trem. Current has quilt maple top.

1986-1987 Bolt-on, dots $1,000 $2,000
1987-1988 Neck-thru, blocks $1,200 $3,000
1987-1988 Neck-thru, Custom T $1,500 $2,500

Eclipse Deluxe

1986-1988. Single-cut solidbody, 1 single-coil and 1 humbucker, vibrato, black.

1986-1988 $900 $1,500

Eclipse Series

1995-present. Recent Eclipse models.

1995-2000 Eclipse/Eclipse I $1,000 $1,500
1996-2000 Eclipse Archtop $1,000 $1,500

George Lynch Flaming Skull

1994. Carved flaming skull solid body, only 50 made.

1994 $5,000 $10,000

George Lynch M-1

1996-2021. Signature series, sunburst tiger finish.

1996-2021 $2,000 $3,000

Horizon (Import)

1986, 1996-2001. Double-cut neck-thru, bound ebony 'board, 1 single-coil and 1 humbucker, buffer preamp, various colors, reintroduced '96-'01with bolt neck, curved rounded point headstock.

1986 $900 $2,000
1996-2001 $1,000 $1,500

Horizon Classic (U.S.A.)

1993-1995. U.S.-made, carved mahogany body, setneck, dot markers, various colors, optional mahogany body with figured maple top also offered.

1993-1995 $2,500 $4,000

Horizon Custom (U.S.A.)

1998-2001. U.S. Custom Shop-made, mahogany body, figured maple top, bolt-on neck, mostly translucent finish in various colors.

1998-2001 $2,500 $4,000

Horizon Deluxe (Import)

1989-1992. Horizon Custom with bolt-on neck, various colors.

1989-1992 $1,000 $2,200

Hybrid I (Import)

1986 only. Offset double-cut body, bolt maple neck, dots, six-on-a-side tuners, vibrato, various colors.

1986 $800 $1,200

Hybrid II (Import)

1980s. Offset double-cut, rosewood 'board on maple bolt neck, lipstick neck pickup, humbucker at bridge, Hybrid II headstock logo.

1980s $900 $1,500

James Hetfield Custom Explorer MX-250

1992. Limited production.

1992 $8,000 $12,000

Jeff Hanneman S & Key Inlay

2004. Only 12 made, camo or black.

2004 $20,000 $25,000

LTD EC-GTA Guitarsonist

2008. Flame graphic by Matt Touchard, 100 made.

2008 $1,500 $3,000

LTD EC-SIN Sin City

2008. Vegas graphic by Matt Touchard, 100 made.

2008 $1,500 $3,000

LTD Series

1998-present. Various Limited Edition models, range of prices due to wide range of specs.

1998-2024 Various models $300 $500

Maverick/Maverick Deluxe

1989-1992. Offset double-cut, bolt maple or rosewood cap neck, dot markers, double locking vibrola, six-on-a-side tuners, various colors.

1989-1992 $800 $1,800

Metal I

1986 only. Offset double-cut, bolt maple neck, rosewood cap, dots, various colors.

1986 $900 $1,500

Metal II

1986 only. Single horn V body, bolt on maple neck with rosewood cap, dot markers, various colors.

1986 $900 $1,500

Metal III

1986 only. Reverse offset body, bolt maple neck with maple cap, dot markers, gold hardware, various colors.

1986 $900 $1,500

Esoterik DR1

ESP Eclipse I

ESP Vintage Plus
Tom Nicholson

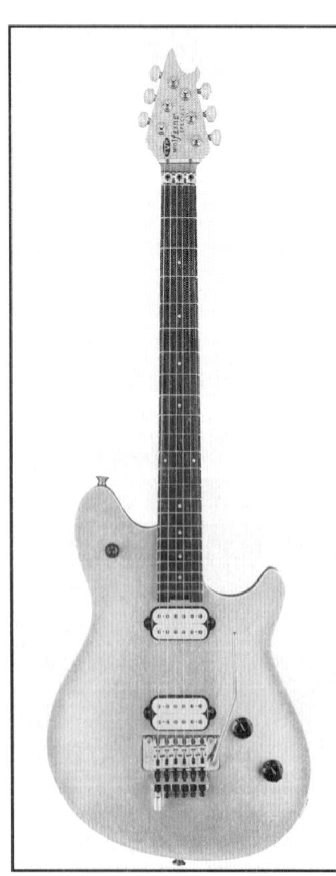
EVH Wolfgang Special

MODEL YEAR	FEATURES	EXC. COND. LOW	HIGH

M-I Custom

1987-1994. Offset double-cut thru-neck body, offset block markers, various colors.

1987-1994		$1,200	$1,800

M-I Deluxe

1987-1989. Double-cut solidbody, rosewood 'board, 2 single-coils and 1 humbucker, various colors.

1987-1989		$1,200	$1,800

M-II

1989-1994, 1996-2000. Double-cut solidbody, reverse headstock, bolt-on maple or rosewood cap neck, dot markers, various colors.

1989-1994		$1,000	$1,500

M-II Custom

1990-1994. Double-cut solidbody, reverse headstock, neck-thru maple neck, rosewood cap, dot markers, various colors.

1990-1994		$1,200	$1,800

M-II Deluxe

1990-1994. Double-cut solidbody, reverse headstock, Custom with bolt-on neck, various colors.

1990-1994		$1,200	$1,800

Mirage Custom

1986-1990. Double-cut neck-thru solidbody, 2-octave ebony 'board, block markers, 1 humbucker and 2 single-coil pickups, locking trem, various colors.

1986-1990		$1,200	$1,800

Mirage Standard

1986 only. Single pickup version of Mirage Custom, various colors.

1986		$800	$1,200

Phoenix

1987 only. Offset, narrow waist solidbody, thru-neck mahogany body, black hardware, dots.

1987		$1,200	$1,800

Phoenix Contemporary

Late-1990s. 3 pickups vs. 2 on the earlier offering.

1998		$1,000	$1,500

S-454/S-456

1986-1987. Offset double-cut, bolt maple or rosewood cap neck, dot markers, various colors.

1986-1987		$900	$1,500

S-500

1991-1993. Double-cut figured ash body, bolt-on neck, six-on-a-side tuners, various colors.

1991-1993		$1,200	$1,800

SV-II

2009-2012. Part of Standard Series, made in Japan, neck-thru offset v-shaped solidbody, 2 pickups, dot inlays.

2009-2012		$2,000	$2,500

Traditional

1989-1990. Double-cut, 3 pickups, tremolo, various colors.

1989-1990		$900	$1,500

Vintage/Vintage Plus S

1995-1998. Offset double-cut, bolt maple or rosewood cap neck, dot markers, Floyd Rose or standard vibrato, various colors.

1995	20th Anniv Ed	$2,000	$3,000
1995-1998		$1,200	$1,800

MODEL YEAR	FEATURES	EXC. COND. LOW	HIGH

Viper Series

2004-present. Offset double-cut SG style, 2 humbuckers, various models

2010	300M	$500	$800

Espana

1963-ca. 1973. Primarily acoustic guitars distributed by catalog wholesalers Bugeleisen & Jacobson. Built by Watkins in England.

Classical

1963-1973. Guitars with white spruce fan-braced tops with walnut, mahogany, or rosewood back and sides.

1963-1973		$300	$600

EL (Electric) Series

1963-1973. Various double-cut models, 2 or 3 pickups, tremolo, '63-ca. '68 with nitro finish, ca. '69-'73 poly finish.

1963-1973	EL-30, 2 pickups	$500	$800
1963-1973	EL-31, 3 pickups	$600	$900
1963-1973	EL-32, 12-string	$500	$800
1963-1973	EL-36, 2 pickups	$500	$800

Jumbo Folk

1969-1973. Natural.

1969-1973		$300	$500

Essex (SX)

1985-present. Budget grade, production, electric and acoustic guitars imported by Rondo Music of Union, New Jersey. They also offer basses.

Solidbody Electric

1980s-1990s. Copies of classic designs like the Les Paul and Telecaster.

1980s		$200	$400

Este

1909-1939. Luthier Felix Staerke's Este factory built classical and archtop guitars in Hamburg, Germany. They also built high-end banjos. The plant ceased instrument production in '39 and was destroyed in WW II.

Esteban

2002-present. Budget grade, production, acoustic and classical import guitars sold as packages with classical guitarist Esteban's (Stephen Paul) guitar lesson program, other miscellany and sometimes a small amp.

Steel and Nylon Acoustics

2002-2024	Various models	$50	$100

EtaVonni

2008-2010. Luthier Ben Williams built premium grade, production/custom, carbon fiber and aluminum electric guitars in Kentwood, Michigan.

Euphonon

1930-1944. A Larson brothers brand, most Euphonons date from 1934-'44. Body sizes range from 13 ½" to the 19" and 21" super jumbos. The larger body 14-fret neck sizes have body woods of Brazilian rosewood, mahogany, or maple. Ornamentation

MODEL YEAR	FEATURES	EXC. COND. LOW	HIGH

and features are as important to value as rosewood vs. mahogany. Production also included mandolins, and most models were A-style, with teardrop body and flat backs.

Everett Guitars

1977-present. Luthier Kent Everett builds his premium and presentation grade, production/custom, steel-string and classical guitars in Atlanta, Georgia. From '01 to '03, his Laurel Series guitars were built in conjunction with Terada in Japan and set up in Atlanta. He has also built archtops, semi-hollow and solidbody electrics, resonators, and mandolins.

Evergreen Mountain

1971-present. Professional grade, custom, flat-top and tenor guitars, basses and mandolins built by luthier Jerry Nolte in Cove, Oregon. He also built over 100 dulcimers in the '70s.

Everly Guitars

1982-2001. Luthier Robert Steinegger built these premium grade, production/custom flat-tops in Portland, Oregon (also see Steinegger Guitars).

EVH

2007-present. Eddie Van Halen worked with FMIC to create a line of professional and premium grade, production, solidbody guitars built in the U.S. and imported from other countries. Van Halen died October 2020, but the brand continues. They also build amps.

Wolfgang Special

2010-present. Made in Japan, offset double-cut solidbody, figured maple top over basswood body, birdseye maple 'board, 2 pickups, tremolo, opaque finish. Some more recent models made in Mexico.

2010-2024		$1,200	$1,800

Excelsior

The Excelsior Company started offering accordions in 1924 and had a large factory in Italy by the late '40s. They started building guitars around '62, which were originally plastic covered, switching to paint finishes in the mid '60s. They also offered classicals, acoustics, archtops and amps. By the early '70s they were out of the guitar business.

The Excelsior brand was also used ca.1885-ca.1890 on guitars and banjos by Boston's John C. Haynes & Co.

Dyno and Malibu

1960s. Offset, double cut, 2 or 3 pickups, vibrato.

1960s	Dyno I	$500	$800
1960s	Dyno II	$600	$900
1960s	Malibu I	$600	$900
1960s	Malibu II	$600	$900

Exlusive

2008-2013. Intermediate grade, production, electric guitars and basses, imported from Asia and finished in Italy by luthier Galeazzo Frudua.

MODEL YEAR	FEATURES	EXC. COND. LOW	HIGH

Fairbuilt Guitar Co.

2000-present. Professional and premium grade, custom guitars and mandolins, built by luthier Martin Fair in Loudoun County, Virginia.

Falk

1989-2017. Professional and premium grade, production/custom archtop guitars, mandolins and dulcimers built by luthier Dave Falk, originally in Independence, Missouri, then Amarillo, Texas and finally in Kansas City. Falk died in 2017.

Fano

1995-present. Professional grade, production/custom, solidbody electric guitars and basses originally built by luthier Dennis Fano in Fleetwood, Pennsylvania. In 2009 Dennis sold the Fano brand to Premier Builders Guild (PBG) in Arroyo Grande, California. Since 2017, the brand is owned by Desert Son Musical in Phoenix, Arizona.

Farnell

1989-present. Luthier Al Farnell builds his professional grade, production, solidbody guitars and basses in Ontario, California. He also offers his intermediate grade, production, C Series which is imported from China.

Fat Cat Custom Guitars

2004-present. Intermediate to premium grade, production/custom, solidbody and chambered electric guitars and basses built in Carpentersville, Illinois by luthier Scott Bond.

Favilla

1890-1973. Founded by the Favilla family in New York, the company began to import guitars in 1970, but folded in '73. American-made models have the Favilla family crest on the headstock. Import models used a script logo on the headstock.

Acoustic Classical

1960s-1973. Various nylon-string classical models.

1960s-1973		$200	$500

Acoustic Flat-Top

1960s-1973. Various flat-top models, 000 to D sizes, mahogany to spruce.

1960s-1973		$200	$500

Fell

One of the many guitar brands built by Japan's Matsumoku company.

Fender

1946 (1945)-present. Budget, intermediate, professional, and premium grade, production/custom, electric, acoustic, acoustic/electric, classical, and resonator guitars built in the U.S. and overseas. They also build amps, basses, mandolins, bouzoukis, banjos, lap steels, ukes, violins, and PA gear. Ca. 1939 Leo Fender opened a radio and record store called Fender Radio Service, where he

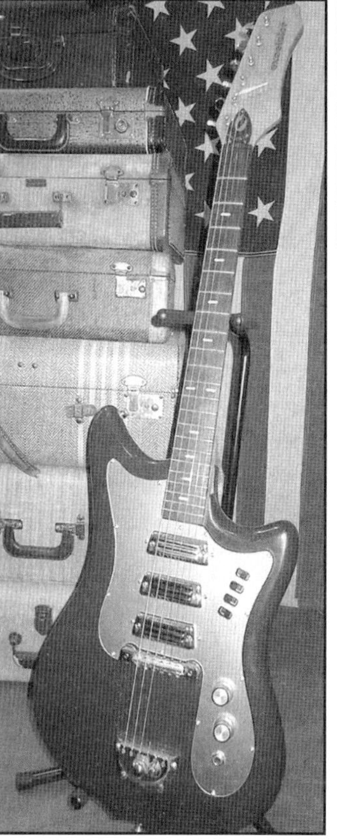

1968 Excelsior Dyno III
Rivington Guitars

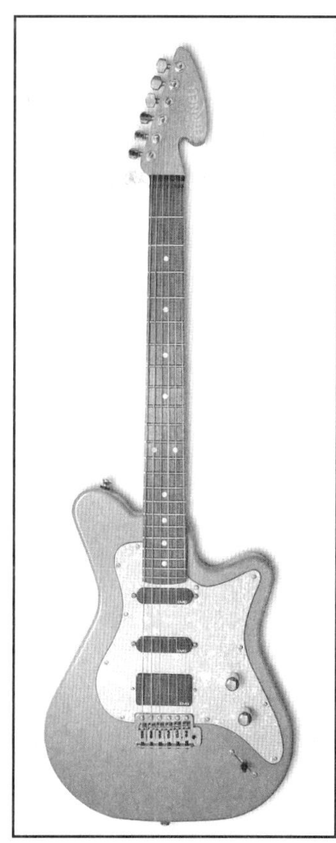

Farnell

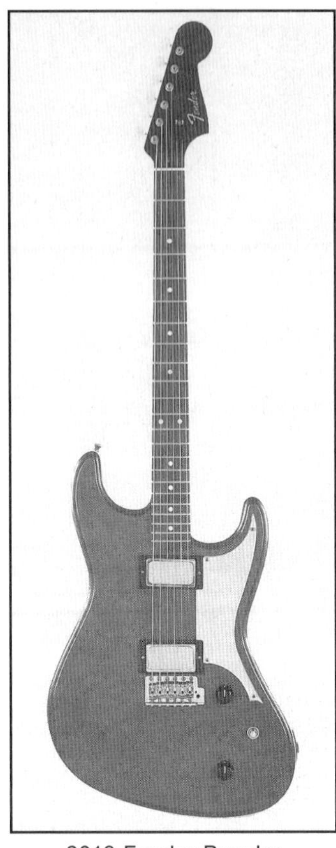
2019 Fender Brawler Baritone (Custom Shop)

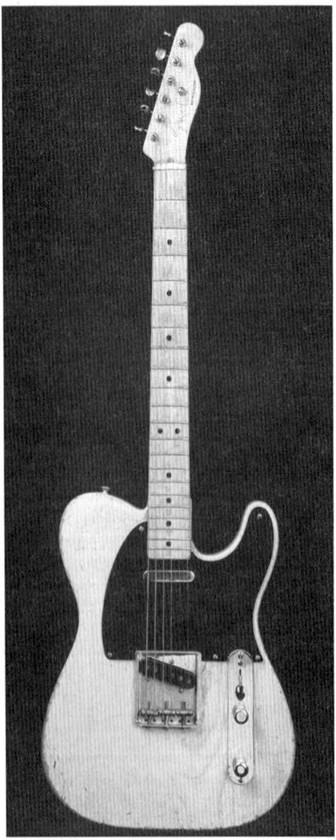
1951 Fender Broadcaster
John Amaral

met Clayton Orr 'Doc' Kauffman, and in '45 they started KF Company to build lap steels and amps. In '46 Kauffman left and Fender started the Fender Electric Instrument Company.

In January '65 CBS purchased the company and renamed it Fender Musical Instruments Corporation. The CBS takeover is synonymous with a perceived decline in quality among musicians and collectors, and Pre-CBS Fenders are more valuable. Fender experienced some quality problems in the late-'60s. Small headstock is enlarged in '65 and the 4-bolt neck is replaced by the 3-bolt in '71. With high value and relative scarcity of Pre-CBS Fenders, even CBS-era instruments are now sought by collectors. Leo Fender was kept on as consultant until '70 and went on to design guitars for Music Man and G&L.

In '82 Fender Japan is established to produce licensed Fender copies for sale in Japan. Also, in '82, the Fender Squier brand debuts on Japanese-made instruments for the European market and by '83 they were imported into U.S. In March '85, the company was purchased by an investor group headed by Bill Schultz but the purchase does not include the Fullerton factory. While a new factory was being established at Corona, California, all Fender Contemporary Stratocasters and Telecasters were made either by Fender Japan or in Seoul, Korea. U.S. production resumes in late '85. The Fender Custom Shop, run by Michael Stevens and John Page, opens in '87. The Mexican Fender factory is established in '90. In '95, Fender purchased the Guild guitar company. On January 3, 2002, Fender Musical Instruments Corporation (FMIC) recapitalized a minority portion of common stock, with partners including Roland Corporation U.S. and Weston Presidio, a private equity firm in San Francisco. In 2003, Fred Gretsch Enterprises, Ltd granted Fender the exclusive rights to develop, produce, market, and distribute Gretsch guitars worldwide. Around the same time, Fender also acquired the Jackson/Charvel Guitar Company. In October, '04, Fender acquired Tacoma Guitars. On January 1, '08, Fender acquired Kaman Music Corporation and the Hamer, Ovation, and Genz Benz brands. The Groove Tubes brand was purchased by Fender in June, '08.

Dating older Fender guitars is an imprecise art form at best. While serial numbers were used, they were frequently not in sequence, although a lower number will frequently be older than a substantially higher number. Often necks were dated, but only with the date the neck was finished, not when the guitar was assembled. Generally, dating requires triangulating between serial numbers, neck dates, pot dates, construction details and model histories.

From '50 through roughly '65, guitars had more-or-less sequential numbers in either 4 or 5 digits, though some higher numbers may have an initial 0 or - prefix. These can range from 0001 to 99XXX.

From '63 into '65, some instruments had serial numbers beginning with an L prefix plus 5 digits (LXXXXX). Beginning in '65 with the CBS takeover into '76, 6-digit serial numbers were stamped on F neckplates roughly sequentially from 10XXXX to 71XXXX. In '76 the serial number was shifted to the headstock decal. From '76-'77, the serial number began with a bold-face 76 or S6 plus 5 digits (76XXXXX).

From '77 on, serial numbers consisted of a 2-place prefix plus 5 digits (sometimes 6 beginning in '91): '77 (S7, S8), '78 (S7, S8, S9), '79 (S9, E0), '80-'81 (S9, E0, E1), '82 (E1, E2, E3), '84-'85 (E4), '85-'86 (no U.S. production), '87 (E4), '88 (E4, E8), '89 (E8, E9), '90 (E9, N9, N0), '91 (N0), '92 (N2).

Serial numbers on guitars made by Fender Japan consist of either a 2-place prefix plus 5 digits or a single prefix letter plus 6 digits: '82-'84 (JV), '83-'84 (SQ), '85-'86+ (A, B, C), '86-'87 (F), '87-'88+ (G), '88-'89 (H), '89-'90 (I, J), '90-'91 (K), '91-'92 (L), '92-'93 (M).

Factors affecting Fender values: All Fender instruments shipped originally with a maple one-piece neck. A walnut "skunk stripe" plug was used on the back of the neck to cover the truss rod channel. The use of a rosewood fretboard beginning in 1959 changes the value of some models significantly. The sale to CBS in '65 is also a major point in Fender instrument values as CBS made many changes collectors feel affected quality. The '70s introduced the 3-bolt neck and other design changes that aren't as popular with guitarists. Custom color instruments, especially Strats from the '50s and early-'60s, can be valued much more than the standard sunburst finishes. In '75 Fender dropped the optional custom colors and started issuing the guitars in a variety of standard colors.

Custom colors are worth more than standard colors. For a Stratocaster, Telecaster Custom and Esquire Custom the standard color is sunburst, while the Telecaster and Esquire standard color is blond. The first Precision Bass standard color was blond but changed to sunburst in the late 1950s. The Jazz Bass standard color is sunburst. The Telecaster Thinline standard color is natural. All Fender guitars were available in a custom DuPont Duco or DuPont Lucite color. Some custom colors are rarer than others. Below is a list of the custom colors offered in 1960. They are sorted in ascending order with the most valuable color, Shell Pink, listed last. For example, Fiesta Red is typically worth 12% more than a Black or Blond, though all are in the Common Color category. In the Rare Color group, Foam Green is normally worth 8% more than Shoreline Gold. The two Very Rare colors are often worth 30% more than Shoreline Gold. In our pricing information we will list the standard color, then the relative value of a common custom color, and then the value of a rare custom color. Remember that the amount of fade also affects the price. These prices are for custom colors with slight or no fade, which implies a lighter color, but some examples can also be much darker in color due to the yellowing of the nitrocellulose clearcoat. Blue can fade to dark green. White can fade to deep yellow. The prices in the Guide are for factory original finishes only. It is important to understand that custom-colored

GUITARS

MODEL YEAR	FEATURES	EXC. COND. LOW	HIGH

Fenders are commonly forged. It is recommended to always buy from a reputable dealer when adding a custom-colored Pre-CBS Fender to your collection.

The various Telecaster and Stratocaster models are grouped under those general headings.

Common Color: Black, Blond, Candy Apple Red, Olympic White, Lake Placid Blue, Dakota Red, Daphne Blue, Fiesta Red

Rare Color: Shoreline Gold, Inca Silver, Burgundy Mist, Sherwood Green, Sonic Blue, Foam Green

Rare (Very Rare) Pastel Color: Surf Green, Shell Pink

1960 - 1962: Black, Blond, Burgundy Mist, Dakota Red, Daphne Blue, Fiesta Red, Foam Green, Inca Silver, Lake Placid Blue, Olympic White, Shell Pink, Sherwood Green, Shoreline Gold, Sonic Blue, Sunburst, Surf Green

1963 - 1964: Black, Blond, Burgundy Mist, Candy Apple Red, Dakota Red, Daphne Blue, Fiesta Red, Foam Green, Inca Silver, Lake Placid Blue, Olympic White, Sherwood Green, Shoreline Gold, Sonic Blue, Sunburst, Surf Green

1965 - 1969: Black, Blond, Blue Ice, Candy Apple Red, Charcoal Frost, Dakota Red, Fiesta Red, Firemist Gold, Firemist Silver, Foam Green, Lake Placid Blue, Ocean Turquoise, Olympic White, Sonic Blue, Sunburst, Teal Green

1970 - 1971: Black, Blond, Candy Apple Red, Firemist Gold, Firemist Silver, Lake Placid Blue, Ocean Turquoise, Olympic White, Sonic Blue, Sunburst

1972: Black, Blond, Candy Apple Red, Lake Placid Blue, Olympic White, Sonic Blue, Sunburst

1973: Black, Blond, Candy Apple Red, Lake Placid Blue, Natural, Olympic White, Sunburst, Walnut

1974 - 1977: Black, Blond, Natural, Olympic White, Sunburst, Walnut

1978 - 1979: Antigua, Black, Blond, Natural, Olympic White, Sunburst, Walnut, Wine

Arrow

1969-1972. See listing for Musiclander.

Avalon

1985-1995. California Series, acoustic import, 6-on-a-side tuners, mahogany neck, back and sides (nato after '93), spruce top, various colors.

1985-1995		$250	$350

Balboa

1983-1987. California Series, acoustic import.

1983-1987		$400	$600

Brawler Baritone (Custom Shop)

2019-2020. Journeyman Relic, masterbuilt by Carlos Lopez.

2019-2020		$7,000	$10,000

Broadcaster

Mid-1950-early-1951. For a short time in early-'51, before being renamed the Telecaster, models had no Broadcaster decal; these are called No-casters by collectors.

1950	Blond	$150,000	$250,000
1951	Clipped decal, "No Caster"	$85,000	$125,000

Broadcaster Leo Fender Custom Shop

1999 only. Leo Fender script logo signature replaces Fender logo on headstock, Custom Shop certificate signed by Phyllis Fender, Fred Gretsch, and William Schultz, includes glass display case and poodle guitar case.

1999	50 made	$8,000	$12,000

'50s Relic/'51 NoCaster Custom Shop

1995-2014. Called the '50s Relic NoCaster for '96-'99, and '51 NoCaster in NOS, Relic, or Closet Classic versions 2000-'10, with the Relic Series being the highest offering. From June '95 to June '99 Relic work was done outside of Fender by Vince Cunetto and included a certificate noting model and year built, an instrument without the certificate is worth less than the value shown. Blonde or Honey Blonde finish. Also, in '09, the Limited '51 NoCaster Relic was offered with Twisted Tele neck pickup, 50 each in 2-tone sunburst or Dakota Red.

1995-1997	Cunetto built Relic	$5,000	$8,000
1997-1999	Cunetto era Closet Classic	$5,000	$8,000
1997-1999	Cunetto era NOS	$5,000	$8,000
1998-1999	Cunetto era Relic	$5,000	$7,500
2000-2009	Closet Classic	$3,000	$4,500
2000-2014	NOS	$3,000	$4,500
2000-2014	Relic	$3,000	$4,500

'51 NoCaster Limited Edition

2009. Custom Shop Limited Edition, as above but with Twisted Tele neck pickup, 50 each in 2-tone sunburst or Dakota Red.

2009	Relic	$3,000	$4,500

70th Anniversary Broadcaster Limited Edition

2020 only. Production model has ash body, black 'guard, '50s spaghetti logo, blonde lacquer finish. Custom Shop model available with aging Relic, Heavy Relic, NOS Time Capsule and Journeyman Relic.

2020	Custom Shop	$3,000	$4,500
2020	Production	$1,800	$2,800

Bronco

1967-1980. Slab solidbody, 1 pickup, tremolo, red.

1967-1968	Nitro	$2,000	$3,000
1969-1980	Poly	$1,200	$2,200

Buddy Miller Signature

2007-2009. Artist Design series, flat-top, Fishman Ellipse Aura, signature on headstock.

2007-2009		$700	$1,000

Bullet/Bullet Deluxe

1981-1983. Solidbody, came in 2- and 3-pickup versions (single-coil and humbucker), and single- and double-cut models, various colors. Becomes Squire Bullet in '85.

1981-1983	Various models	$800	$1,500

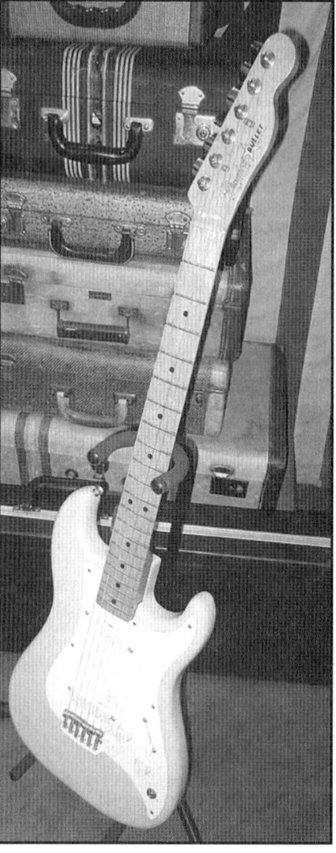

1981 Fender Bullet
Rivington Guitars

Fender CC-60SCE Concert

GUITARS

1964 Fender Duo Sonic
Robbie Keene

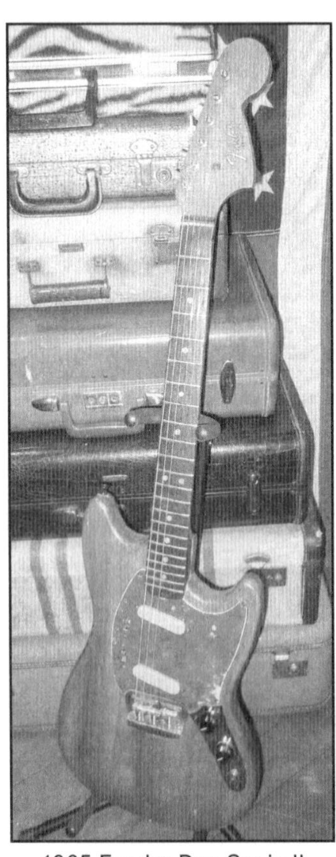
1965 Fender Duo Sonic II
Rivington Guitars

MODEL YEAR	FEATURES	EXC. COND. LOW	HIGH

Catalina

1983-1995. California Series, acoustic dreadnought, import.

1983-1995		$300	$500

CC-60SCE Concert

2020-present. Single-cut, spruce top, mahogany back and sides, Fishman pickup, black or natural.

2020-2024		$250	$400

CD (Classic Design) Series

2006-present. Imported, intermediate grade, various models, acoustic or acoustic-electric, steel or nylon string.

2006-2024	Various models	$200	$300

CG (Classical Guitar) Series

1995-2005. Imported, various nylon-string classical acoustic and acoustic/electric models, label on the inside back clearly indicates the model number, back and sides of rosewood, mahogany or other woods.

1995-2005	Various models	$100	$300

Concert

1963-1970. Acoustic flat-top slightly shorter than King/Kingman, spruce body, mahogany back and sides (optional Brazilian or Indian rosewood, zebrawood, or vermillion), natural, sunburst optional by '68.

1963-1970	Natural or sunburst	$800	$1,200

Concord

1986-1995. Dreadnought flat-top, 6-on-a-side headstock, natural.

1986-1995		$250	$400

Coronado I

1966-1969. Thinline semi-hollowbody, double-cut, tremolo, 1 pickup, single-bound, dot inlay.

1966-1969	Various colors	$1,800	$2,200

Coronado II

1966-1969 (Antigua finish offered until '70). Thinline semi-hollowbody, double-cut, tremolo optional, 2 pickups, single-bound, block inlay, available in standard finishes but special issues offered in Antigua and 6 different Wildwood finishes (labeled on the pickguard as Wildwood I through Wildwood VI to designate different colors). Wildwood finishes were achieved by injecting dye into growing trees.

1966-1969	Various colors	$2,000	$2,500
1966-1969	Wildwood	$2,800	$3,500
1967-1970	Antigua	$2,000	$2,500

Coronado XII

1966-1969 (Antigua finish offered until '70). Thinline semi-hollowbody, double-cut, 12 strings, 2 pickups, block inlay, standard, Antigua and Wildwood finishes available.

1966-1969	Various colors	$2,200	$3,000
1966-1969	Wildwood	$2,800	$3,500
1967-1970	Antigua	$2,200	$3,000

Custom

1969-1971. Six-string solidbody that used up parts from discontinued Electric XII, asymmetrical-cut, long headstock, 2 split pickups, sunburst. Also marketed as the Maverick.

1969-1971		$5,500	$8,000

Cyclone

1998-2006. Mexican import, solidbody, contoured offset waist, poplar body, various colors.

1998-2006	Various options	$800	$1,200

MODEL YEAR	FEATURES	EXC. COND. LOW	HIGH

D'Aquisto Elite

1984, 1989-1994, 1994-2002. Part of Fender's Master Series, 16" laminated maple-side archtop, single-cut, glued neck, 1 pickup, gold hardware, made in Japan until '94, in '94 the Fender Custom Shop issued a version that retailed at $6,000, various colors.

1984-1994		$2,200	$3,300

D'Aquisto Standard

1984 (Serial numbers could range from 1983-1985). Like D'Aquisto Elite, but with 2 pickups.

1984		$1,800	$2,500

D'Aquisto Ultra

1984, 1994-2000. USA Custom Shop, made under the supervision of James D'Aquisto, solid flamed maple back and sides, spruce top, ebony tailpiece, bridge and 'guard, all hand carved.

1994-2000		$5,000	$8,500

DG (Dreadnought Guitar) Series

1995-1999, 2002-2014. Made in China, various lower-end acoustic and acoustic/electric models.

1995-2014	Various models	$100	$200

Duo-Sonic/Player Duo-Sonic

1956-1969, 2016-present. Solidbody, 3/4-size, 2 pickups, Desert Sand ('56-'61), sunburst ('61-'63), blue, red or white after, short- and long-scale necks, short-scale necks listed here (see Duo-Sonic II for long-scale), reissued Mexican-made in '94. In 2016 it becomes part of Player Series.

1956-1958	Desert Sand	$4,000	$5,500
1959	Maple neck	$4,000	$5,500
1960	Rosewood 'board	$3,200	$4,200
1961-1963	Desert Sand	$3,200	$4,200
1963	Sunburst (rare)	$2,800	$3,800
1964-1965	Blue, red, sunburst, white	$2,800	$3,800
1966-1969	Blue, red or white	$2,000	$2,600

Duo-Sonic II

1965-1969. Solidbody, 2 pickups, blue, red or white, long-scale neck, though the long-scale neck Duo-Sonic was not known as the Duo-Sonic II until '65, we have lumped all long-scales under the II for the purposes of this Guide.

1965-1969		$2,500	$3,500

Duo-Sonic Reissue

1993-1997. Made in Mexico, black, red or white.

1993-1997		$400	$600

Duo-Sonic HS/Player Duo-Sonic HS

2017-present. Player Series, humbucker and single-coil pickups.

2017-2024		$500	$800

Electric XII

1965-1969. Solidbody, 12 strings, long headstock, 2 split pickups. Please refer to the Fender Guitar Intro Section for details on Fender color options.

1965-1969	Common color	$8,000	$10,500
1965-1969	Rare color	$10,000	$13,000
1965-1969	Sunburst	$5,500	$7,200

Electric XII Alternate Reality

2019. Modern updated reissue.

2019		$800	$1,200

MODEL YEAR	FEATURES	EXC. COND. LOW	HIGH

Ensenada Series

2005-2007. Made in Mexico acoustics, solid top, back and sides, A (grand auditorium), D (dreadnought), M (mini jumbo) and V (orchestra) sizes, E suffix denotes on-board electronics.

2005-2007	Acoustic	$400	$600
2005-2007	Acoustic-electric	$450	$700

Esprit Elite

1984. Master Series, made in Japan, double-cut, semi-hollow, carved maple top, 2 humbuckers, 4 controls, bound rosewood 'board, snowflake inlays.

1983-1985		$1,500	$2,200

Esprit Standard

1984. Like Esprit Elite, but with dot inlays, 2 controls.

1983-1985		$1,000	$1,500

Esprit Ultra

1984. Like Esprit Elite, but with bound ebony 'board, split-block inlays, gold hardware.

1984		$1,800	$2,800

Esquire

1950-1970. Ash body, single-cut, 1 pickup, maple neck, black 'guard '50-'54, white 'guard '54 on. Please refer to the Fender Guitar Intro Section for details on Fender color options.

1950-1951	Blond, black 'guard	$50,000	$65,000
1952-1953	Blond, black 'guard	$45,000	$60,000
1954	Blond, black 'guard	$40,000	$52,000
1954-1955	Blond, white 'guard	$30,000	$40,000
1956-1957	Blond	$30,000	$40,000
1958	Blond, backloader	$25,000	$35,000
1958	Blond, toploader	$22,500	$30,000
1959	Blond, maple 'board	$22,500	$30,000
1959	Blond, rosewood 'board	$22,500	$30,000
1960	Blond	$22,000	$30,000
1960	Sunburst	$22,500	$30,000
1961	Blond, slab 'board	$18,000	$23,500
1961	Custom color	$45,000	$60,000
1961	Sunburst, slab	$22,500	$30,000
1962	Blond, curved 'board	$16,500	$22,000
1962	Blond, slab	$18,000	$23,500
1962	Custom color	$40,000	$55,000
1962	Sunburst, curved	$22,500	$30,000
1962	Sunburst, slab	$22,500	$30,000
1963	Blond	$16,500	$21,500
1963	Common color	$27,000	$35,000
1963	Rare color	$40,000	$50,000
1963	Sunburst	$20,000	$26,000
1964	Blond	$15,500	$20,000
1964	Common color	$27,000	$35,000
1964	Rare color	$40,000	$50,000
1964	Sunburst	$20,000	$26,000
1965	Blond	$13,500	$18,000
1965	Common color	$22,500	$30,000
1965	Rare color	$35,000	$45,000
1965	Sunburst	$18,000	$23,500
1966	Blond	$11,500	$15,000
1966	Common color	$18,000	$25,000
1966	Rare color	$30,000	$40,000
1966	Sunburst	$13,500	$18,000
1967	Blond	$10,500	$14,000
1967	Blond, smuggler cavity	$11,500	$15,000
1967	Common color	$16,500	$22,000
1967	Rare color	$24,000	$32,000
1967	Sunburst	$11,500	$15,000
1968	Blond, nitro	$10,000	$13,000
1968	Common color, nitro	$16,500	$22,000
1968	Rare color, nitro	$24,000	$32,000
1968	Sunburst, nitro	$11,500	$15,000
1969	Blond, poly	$7,500	$10,000
1969	Common color, poly	$11,500	$15,000
1969	Rare color, poly	$15,500	$22,000
1969	Sunburst, poly	$10,500	$14,000
1970	Blond	$7,000	$9,500
1970	Common color	$10,500	$14,000
1970	Rare color	$13,500	$20,000
1970	Sunburst	$7,000	$9,500

Esquire (Japan)

1985-1994. Made in Japan, '54 specs.

1985-1986		$1,200	$1,800
1987-1989	'50s Esquire	$1,000	$1,500
1990-1994	'50s Esquire	$900	$1,400

'50s Esquire (Mexico)

2005-2010. Maple neck, ash body.

2005-2010		$500	$800

'52 Esquire

2012. Custom Shop, price includes Certificate of Authenticity.

2012	NOS	$3,000	$4,500

'53 Esquire

2012. Custom Shop, price includes Certificate of Authenticity.

2012	NOS	$3,000	$4,500

'59 Esquire

2003-2007, 2013-2016. Custom Shop, Relic version lasted to '07, then came back in '13 for limited run.

2003-2013	Closet Classic	$3,000	$4,500
2003-2013	NOS	$3,000	$4,500
2003-2016	Relic	$3,000	$4,500

'60 Esquire

Custom Shop, NOS.

2010		$3,000	$4,500

'70 Esquire

2008. Custom Shop, only 20 made.

2008	Heavy Relic	$3,000	$4,500
2008	Relic	$3,000	$4,500

70th Anniversary Esquire

2020 only. Roasted pine body, 1-piece maple neck, 1 pickup, Anniversary neck plate, white blond.

2020		$1,500	$2,200

Custom Esquire '95

1995. Custom Shop, limited run of 12 for Sam Ash Music, stealth pickup under 'guard, bird's-eye maple neck.

1995		$10,000	$15,000

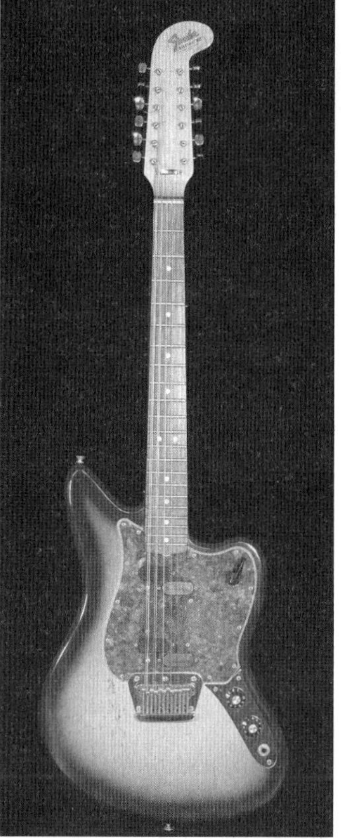

1965 Fender Electric XII

Thel Rountree

1986 Fender Esquire

Michael Alonzi

GUITARS

1959 Fender Esquire Custom
John Andrews

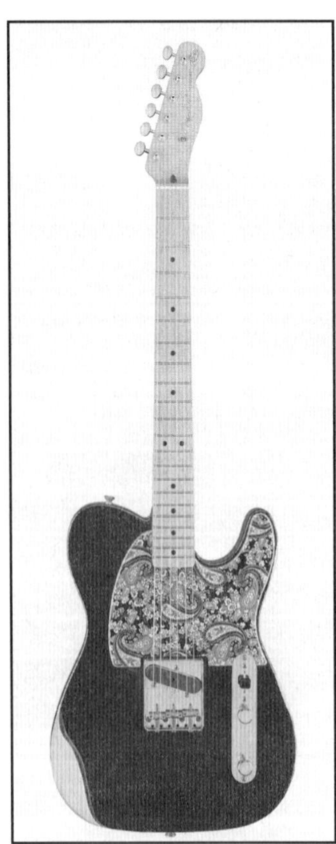
Fender Brad Paisley Esquire

MODEL YEAR	FEATURES	EXC. COND. LOW	HIGH

Esquire Custom

1959-1970. Same as Esquire, but with bound alder sunburst body and rosewood 'board.

1959	Sunburst	$28,000	$40,000
1960	Custom color	$42,000	$65,000
1960	Sunburst	$28,000	$40,000
1961	Custom color	$36,000	$55,000
1961	Sunburst	$26,000	$35,000
1962	Custom color	$36,000	$50,000
1962	Sunburst, curve	$24,000	$35,000
1962	Sunburst, slab	$26,000	$40,000
1963	Custom color	$36,000	$50,000
1963	Sunburst	$24,000	$35,000
1964	Custom color	$30,000	$40,000
1964	Sunburst	$20,000	$30,000
1965	Custom color	$22,500	$30,000
1965	Sunburst	$18,000	$25,000
1966	Custom color	$20,000	$30,000
1966-1970	Sunburst	$12,500	$20,000

Esquire Custom (Import)

1983-1994. Made in Japan with all the classic bound Esquire features, sunburst.

1983-1987		$1,200	$1,800
1988-1994		$1,000	$1,500

Esquire Custom GT/Celtic/Scorpion

2003. Made in Korea, single-cut solidbody, 1 humbucker, 1 knob (volume), set-neck, solid colors.

2003		$800	$1,200

Esquire Z

2001. Custom Shop, black body and headstock, curly maple neck, ebony 'board, 25 made.

2001		$10,000	$15,000

Brad Paisley Esquire

2020-present. Spruce top and back, 2 single-coil pickups, black and silver paisley 'guard, road worn black sparkle finish.

2020-2024		$1,200	$1,800

Jeff Beck Tribute Esquire (Custom Shop)

2006. Also called Beck Artist Esquire or Tribute Series Jeff Beck Esquire, specs include an extremely lightweight 2-piece offset ash body with Beck's original contours, distressed for an appearance like Beck's original Esquire that was used on many Yardbird records, 150 made.

2006		$8,000	$12,000

F (Flat-Top) Series

1969-1981. The F-Series were Japanese-made flat-top acoustics, included were Concert- and Dreadnought-size instruments with features running from plain to bound necks and headstocks and fancy inlays, there was also a line of F-Series classical, nylon-string guitars. A label on the inside indicates the model. FC-20 is a classical with Brazilian rosewood. There was also an Asian (probably Korean) import Standard Series for '82-'90 where the models start with a F.

1969-1981	Dreadnought, laminated	$250	$400
1969-1981	Dreadnought, solid top	$400	$600
1972-1981	Classical (FC)	$250	$500

FA (Fender Alternative) Series

2009-present. Entry-level acoustic series, various Concert, Dreadnought and Auditorium sized models.

2009-2024	FA-115, FA-125	$150	$300
2018-2024	FA-345CE	$300	$500

Flame Elite

1984. Master Series, made in Japan, neck-thru, offset double-cut, solidbody, 2 humbuckers, rosewood 'board, snowflake inlays.

1984-1988		$1,800	$3,000

Flame Standard

1984-1988. Like Flame Elite, but with dot inlays.

1984-1988		$1,500	$2,200

Flame Ultra

1984. Like Flame Elite, but with split block inlays (some with snowflakes), gold hardware.

1984-1988		$2,200	$3,300

FR-48 Resonator

2003-2009. Made in Korea, steel body.

2003-2009		$300	$500

FR-50 Resonator

2000-2015. Spruce top, mahogany back and sides, sunburst, optional square-neck.

2000-2015		$350	$600

FR-50CE Resonator

2000-2015. Same as FR-50 with cutaway and pickups.

2009-2015		$400	$650

FR-55 Hawaiian Resonator

2012-2013. Bell brass nickel-plated body etched with scenes of South Seas.

2012-2013		$450	$700

GA (Grand Auditorium) Series

2001-2009. Various grand auditorium models made in Korea, an oval label on the inside back clearly indicates the model number.

2001-2009		$250	$500

GC (Grand Concert) Series

1997-2009. Various concert-sized models, an oval label on the inside back clearly indicates the model number.

1997-2009		$200	$400

GD (Grand Dreadnought) Series

1997-2009. Various dreadnought-sized models, an oval label on the inside back clearly indicates the model number.

1997-2009		$250	$500

GDO (Global Design Orchestra) Series

2004-2008. Various orchestra-sized acoustic models, an oval label on the inside back clearly indicates the model number.

2004-2008		$350	$600

Gemini Series

1983-1990. Korean-made flat-tops, label on inside indicates model. I is classical nylon-string, II, III and IV are dreadnought steel-strings, there is also a 12-string and an IIE acoustic/electric.

1984-1987	Gemini II	$200	$300
1984-1988	Gemini I	$180	$300
1987-1988	Gemini III	$300	$500
1987-1990	Gemini IIE	$300	$500
1987-1990	Gemini IV	$300	$500

MODEL YEAR	FEATURES	EXC. COND. LOW	HIGH

GN (Grand Nylon) Series

2001-2007. Various grand nylon acoustic models, an oval label on the inside back clearly indicates the model number.

2001-2007		$300	$450

Harmony-Made Series

Late-1960s-1973. Various Harmony-made models, with white stencil Fender logo, mahogany, natural or sunburst.

1960s	D-style model	$400	$800
1970-1973	Stella model	$200	$300

Jag-Stang

1996-1999, 2003-2004. Made in Japan, designed by Curt Cobain, body similar to Jaguar, tremolo, 1 pickup, oversize Strat peghead, Fiesta Red or Sonic Blue. First year has 50th Anniversary label.

1996-2004		$900	$1,500

Jaguar

1962-1975. Reintroduced as Jaguar '62 in '95-'99. Please refer to the Fender Guitar Intro Section for details on Fender color options.

1962-1964	Common color	$9,000	$12,000
1962-1964	Rare color	$13,000	$20,000
1962-1964	Sunburst	$5,500	$7,500
1965	Common color	$8,500	$11,000
1965	Rare color	$11,000	$15,000
1965	Sunburst	$4,500	$6,000
1966	Common color	$7,500	$10,000
1966	Rare color	$11,000	$15,000
1966	Sunburst	$4,500	$6,000
1967-1969	Common color	$7,000	$9,500
1967-1969	Rare color	$10,000	$13,000
1967-1969	Sunburst	$4,500	$6,000
1970	Common color	$6,500	$8,500
1970	Rare color	$8,000	$12,000
1970-1975	Sunburst	$4,000	$5,500
1971-1974	Custom color	$6,000	$8,000
1975	Custom color	$4,500	$6,000

Jaguar '62

1986-2012. Reintroduction of Jaguar, Japanese-made until '99, then U.S.-made American Vintage series, basswood body, rosewood 'board, various colors.

1986-1999	Import	$1,200	$1,800
1999-2012	USA	$1,800	$2,800

50th Anniversary Jaguar

2012. USA, modeled after '62, classic 24" scale, new one-degree neck-angle pocket, repositioned tremolo plate, redesigned hot Jaguar single-coils, lacquer finish in Lake Placid Blue, Candy Apple Red, or burgundy.

2012		$1,800	$3,000

American Professional Jaguar

2017-2020. Double-cut, alder body, maple or rosewood 'board, V-Mod single-coil pickups, tremolo tailpiece, various colors.

2017-2020		$1,200	$1,800

American Vintage '62 Jaguar

2000. Export version, Lake Placid Blue, Candy Apple Red, Shell Pink, Burgundy Mist Metallic and Ice Blue Metallic with matching headstocks, a special run for Yamano, Japan. Limited to 50 in each color.

2000		$2,000	$3,000

Blacktop Jaguar 90

2012-2014. Alder body, maple neck, rosewood 'board, 2 single-coil pickups, 2-tone sunburst or Candy Apple Red.

2012-2014		$800	$1,200

Blacktop Jaguar HH

2010-2014. Stripped-down electronics with 2 humbuckers, 1 volume, 1 tone, single 3-way switch, maple neck, rosewood 'board, black 'guard, black or silver.

2010-2014		$800	$1,200

Jaguar Baritone Special HH

2005-2010. Japan, limited edition, Baritone Special logo on matching headstock, 2 humbuckers, no trem, black.

2005-2010		$900	$1,500

Jaguar Classic Player Special

2009-2019. Classic Player series, classic Jag look, tremolo, 2 single-coils

2009-2019		$800	$1,200

Jaguar Classic Player Special HH

2009-2019. Classic Player series. 2 humbucker version.

2009-2019		$900	$1,500

Jaguar FSR Classic '66 Reissue

2008-2010. Fender Special Run, '66 specs, block inlays, black logo, custom colors, limited edition.

2008-2010		$1,500	$2,200

Jaguar FSR Thinline

2012. Limited Edition, semi-hollowbody with f-hole, 2 vintage-style single-coil pickups.

2012		$1,800	$2,800

Jaguar HH/Special Edition Jaguar HH

2005-2014. Japan, 2 Dragster humbuckers, matching headstock, chrome knobs and pickup covers.

2005-2014		$800	$1,200

Jaguar Limited Edition Classic Series

2002-2003. Crafted in Japan.

2002-2003	Various models	$1,000	$1,500

Johnny Marr Signature Jaguar

2012-present. Artist series, based on Marr's '65 Jaguar, Olympic White or Metallic KO.

2012-2024		$1,800	$2,800

Kurt Cobain Signature Jaguar

2011-present. Artist Series, based on Cobain's '65 Jaguar, 3-color sunburst.

2011-2024		$1,500	$2,200

Modern Player Jaguar

2012-2014. Mahogany body, maple neck, rosewood 'board, 2-color chocolate burst, trans red or trans black.

2012-2014		$400	$600

Pawn Shop Jaguarillo

2012-2013. Alder body, maple neck, rosewood 'board, HSS pickups, various colors.

2012-2013		$800	$1,200

Player Jaguar

2018-present. Alder body, maple neck, 1 humbucker and 1 single-coil, various colors with gloss finish.

2018-2024		$600	$900

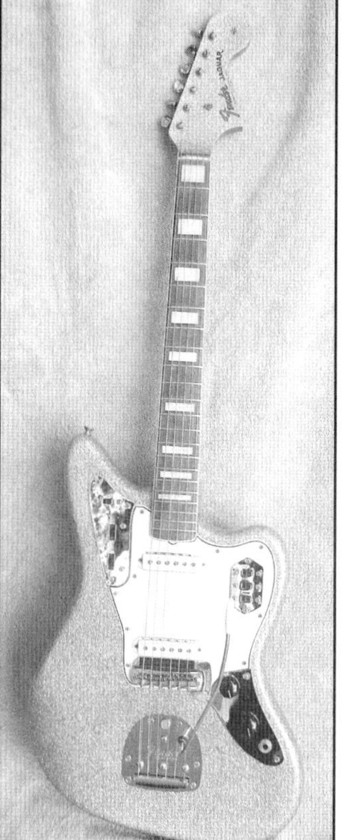

1966 Fender Jaguar
Rob Zolezzi

2010 Fender American Vintage '62 Jaguar
Rivington Guitars

GUITARS

1962 Fender Jazzmaster

Kevin Rush

Fender American Performer Jazzmaster

Jazzmaster

1958-1980. Contoured body, 2 pickups, rosewood 'board, clay dot inlay, reintroduced as Japanese-made Jazzmaster '62 in '94. Please refer to the Fender Guitar Intro Section for details on Fender color options.

MODEL YEAR	FEATURES	EXC. COND. LOW	HIGH
1958	Sunburst, anodized guard	$20,000	$25,000
1958	Sunburst	$13,500	$17,500
1958	Sunburst, maple 'board	$16,500	$21,500
1959	Custom color, includes rare	$25,500	$50,000
1959	Sunburst	$13,500	$17,500
1960-1961	Common color	$18,000	$25,000
1960-1961	Rare color	$22,500	$45,000
1960-1961	Sunburst	$10,500	$14,000
1962-1964	Common color	$18,000	$25,000
1962-1964	Rare color	$22,500	$45,000
1962-1964	Sunburst	$10,500	$13,500
1965	Common color	$10,500	$14,000
1965	Rare color	$18,000	$25,000
1965	Sunburst	$7,000	$9,000
1966-1969	Common color	$10,500	$15,000
1966-1969	Rare color	$18,000	$25,000
1966-1969	Sunburst	$6,500	$8,500
1970	Common color	$7,500	$10,000
1970	Rare color	$9,000	$12,500
1970-1980	Sunburst	$4,000	$5,500
1971-1974	Custom color	$6,500	$8,500
1975	Custom color	$6,000	$7,500
1976-1980	Custom color	$5,000	$6,500

Road Worn '60s Jazzmaster

2015-2019. '60s style with aged/worn alder body and maple neck, worn nitro-lacquer finish. Replaced by American Original '60s Jazzmaster.

MODEL YEAR	FEATURES	EXC. COND. LOW	HIGH
2015-2019		$900	$1,500

Limited Edition 60th Anniversary Classic Jazzmaster

Introduced July 2018. 'Limited Edition 60th Anniversary Jazzmaster' logo etched into neck plate, matching painted headstock, block markers, nitro finish.

MODEL YEAR	FEATURES	EXC. COND. LOW	HIGH
2018		$1,200	$1,800

Jazzmaster '62

1986-2012. Japanese-made reintroduction of Jazzmaster, basswood body, rosewood 'board, from '99 U.S.-made American Vintage series, various colors.

MODEL YEAR	FEATURES	EXC. COND. LOW	HIGH
1986-1989	Import	$1,200	$1,800
1990-1998	Import	$1,000	$1,500
1999-2012	USA	$1,800	$2,800

Jazzmaster '65/American Vintage '65

2013-2018. Alder body, maple neck, mid-'60s neck profile, rosewood 'board. Part of American Vintage series in '16.

MODEL YEAR	FEATURES	EXC. COND. LOW	HIGH
2013-2018		$1,800	$2,500

Jazzmaster '69

1986-1990s. Made in Japan.

MODEL YEAR	FEATURES	EXC. COND. LOW	HIGH
1986-1989		$1,200	$2,000
1990-1999		$1,000	$1,800

American Performer Jazzmaster

Introduced Dec. 2018-present. Made in the US, new features include Yosemite single-coil pickups, Greasebucket tone system, various colors.

MODEL YEAR	FEATURES	EXC. COND. LOW	HIGH
2018-2024		$900	$1,500

American Ultra Jazzmaster

2019-present. Alder or ash body, maple neck, rosewood 'board, 2 pickups.

MODEL YEAR	FEATURES	EXC. COND. LOW	HIGH
2019-2024		$1,800	$2,500

Blacktop Jazzmaster HS

2010-2014. Stripped-down electronics with a single-coil and a humbucker, 1 volume, 1 tone, single 3-way switch, maple neck, rosewood 'board, black or sunburst.

MODEL YEAR	FEATURES	EXC. COND. LOW	HIGH
2010-2014		$800	$1,200

Classic Player Jazzmaster Special

2008-2019. Alder body, maple neck, rosewood 'board, 2 single-coils, 3-color sunburst or black.

MODEL YEAR	FEATURES	EXC. COND. LOW	HIGH
2008-2019		$800	$1,200

Elvis Costello Jazzmaster

2008-2010. Artist series, walnut stain, '70s neck, vintage style tremolo.

MODEL YEAR	FEATURES	EXC. COND. LOW	HIGH
2008-2010		$1,800	$2,800

J Mascis Jazzmaster

2007-2009. Artist series, purple sparkle finish, matching headstock, Adjusto-Matic bridge, reinforced tremolo arm.

MODEL YEAR	FEATURES	EXC. COND. LOW	HIGH
2007-2009		$1,200	$1,800

Jazz Tele

June 2018. Parallel Universe series, limited edition, 2 American Vintage '65 Jazzmaster single-coil pickups.

MODEL YEAR	FEATURES	EXC. COND. LOW	HIGH
2018		$1,500	$2,200

Noventa Jazzmaster

2021. Alder body, maple neck, 3 single-coil pickups, Fiesta Red, Surf Green, or Walnut.

MODEL YEAR	FEATURES	EXC. COND. LOW	HIGH
2021		$800	$1,200

Pinup Girl Jazzmaster

1997. Custom Shop Limited Edition, pinup girl art on body, figured maple neck, 3 pickups, certificate of authenticity.

MODEL YEAR	FEATURES	EXC. COND. LOW	HIGH
1997		$2,500	$4,000

Select Jazzmaster

2012-2013. Chambered alder body with a carved flame maple top, Fender Select headstock medallion, various finish options.

MODEL YEAR	FEATURES	EXC. COND. LOW	HIGH
2012-2013		$2,000	$3,000

Sonic Youth Signature Jazzmaster

2009-2014. Lee Ranaldo and Thurston Moore Signature models based on their modified Jazzmasters which basically removed the standard control layout and replaced it with a 3-way switch.

MODEL YEAR	FEATURES	EXC. COND. LOW	HIGH
2009-2014	Lee Ranaldo	$1,800	$2,800
2009-2014	Thurston Moore	$1,800	$2,800

The Ventures Limited Edition Jazzmaster

1996. Japanese-made, ash body, 2 pickups, block inlay, transparent purple/black.

MODEL YEAR	FEATURES	EXC. COND. LOW	HIGH
1996		$1,800	$2,800

Troy Van Leeuwen Jazzmaster

2014-present. Alder body, maple neck, Oxblood finish, red tortoiseshell 'guard, matching headstock, various custom colors.

MODEL YEAR	FEATURES	EXC. COND. LOW	HIGH
2014-2024		$1,200	$1,800

MODEL YEAR	FEATURES	EXC. COND. LOW	HIGH

White Opal Jazzmaster HH

2016. Special Edition, made in Mexico, white opal body and headstock, pearloid 'guard, 2 humbuckers.

2016		$600	$900

JZM Deluxe

2007-2009. Electracoustic Series, acoustic/electric, Jazzmaster/Jaguar body styling, Fishman and Tele pickups, sunburst or trans amber.

2007-2009		$600	$900

Katana

1985-1986. Japanese-made wedge-shaped body, 2 humbuckers, set neck, triangle inlays, black.

1985-1986		$2,500	$4,000

King

1963-1965. Full-size 15 5/8" wide acoustic, natural. Renamed Kingman in '65.

1963-1965	Brazilian rosewood	$2,500	$3,500
1963-1965	Indian, Zebra, Vermillion	$1,500	$2,000

Kingman

1965-1971. Full-size 15 5/8" wide acoustic, slightly smaller by '70, offered in 3 Wildwood colors, referred to as the Wildwood acoustic which is a Kingman with dyed wood. Reissued as import in '06.

1965-1968		$1,300	$1,800
1969-1971		$1,000	$1,500

Kingman Antigua

1968-1971. Kingman in Antigua finish (silver to black sunburst).

1968-1971		$1,200	$1,800

Kingman ASCE

2008-2017. Cutaway acoustic-electric, mahogany back and sides.

2008-2017		$400	$600

Kingman SCE

2008-2017. Cutaway acoustic-electric, mahogany back and sides.

2008-2017		$450	$650

Kingman Tom Petty Signature

2014. Custom Shop Limited Edition, signature on headstock back, Indian rosewood 'board, ivoroid binding, gold 'guard, nitro gloss black.

2014		$2,500	$3,500

Kingman USA Pro Custom

2013-2014. Custom Shop Pro series, limited run of 50, AA sitka spruce top, maple back/sides/neck, Firemist Gold.

2013-2014		$1,500	$2,500

Kingman USA Select

2012. All solid woods, rosewood 'board, Fishman electronics, 3-color sunburst.

2012		$1,500	$2,500

Kingman USA Select C

2012. Custom Shop limited edition of 150, Engelmann spruce top, mahogany back and sides, vintage C-shaped maple neck, rosewood 'board, Fiesta Red.

2012		$1,800	$2,800

Kingman/Elvis Kingman

2012-2013. Wildwood model as used by Elvis Presley in the '67 film 'Clambake', spruce top, mahogany back and sides, rosewood 'board, natural.

2012-2013		$500	$800

MODEL YEAR	FEATURES	EXC. COND. LOW	HIGH

Lead I

1979-1982. Double-cut solidbody with 1 humbucker, maple or rosewood 'board, black or brown.

1979-1982		$1,000	$1,500

Lead II

1979-1982. Lead with 2 pickups, black or brown.

1979-1982		$1,200	$1,800

Lead III

1982. Lead with 2 split-coil humbuckers, 2 3-way switches, various colors.

1982		$1,300	$2,000

Player Lead II

2020-2024. Reintroduced using late-70s and updated model features.

2020-2024		$500	$800

Player Lead III

2020-2024. Reintroduced using late-70s and updated model features.

2020-2024		$500	$800

LTD

1969-1975. Archtop electric, single-cut, gold-plated hardware, carved top and back, 1 pickup, multi-bound, bolt-on neck, sunburst.

1969-1975		$7,500	$12,000

Malibu

1965-1971. Flat-top, spruce top, mahogany back and sides, black, mahogany or sunburst. Later version is import.

1965-1971		$800	$1,200

Malibu (California Series)

1983-1995. Made first in Japan, then Korea in '85.

1983-1995		$300	$500

Malibu SCE

2006-2013. Imported single-cut acoustic/electric, solid spruce top, laminated mahogany back and sides, block inlays.

2006-2013		$300	$500

Marauder

1965 only. The Marauder has 3 pickups, and some have slanted frets, only 8 were made, thus it is very rare. 1st generation has hidden pickups, 2nd has exposed.

1965	1st generation	$11,500	$17,000
1965	2nd generation	$9,000	$12,500

Marauder (Modern Player)

2011-2014. Jazzmaster-type body, 1 Jazzmaster pickup and 1 Triple Bucker, rosewood 'board.

2011-2014		$500	$800

Maverick Dorado (Parallel Universe)

2020. Parallel Universe Vol. II series, alder body, 22-fret maple neck, 2 pickups, Bigsby vibrato, Mystic Pine Green, Ultraburst and Firemist Gold.

2020		$1,500	$2,200

Meteora (Parallel Universe)

November 2018-2019. Parallel Universe Vol. II series, sleek offset body with both Jazzmaster and Telecaster features.

2018-2019		$800	$1,200

Mod Shop

2016-present. Models designed by customer by choosing options from a menu and built by Fender, 4 models offered - Jazz Bass, Precision Bass, Strato-

1963 Fender King

Rivington Guitars

1971 Fender Kingman

Imaged by Heritage Auctions, HA.com

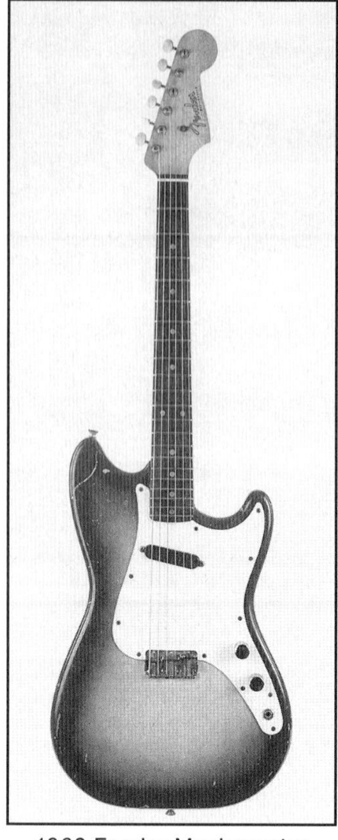
1963 Fender Musicmaster
Cream City Music

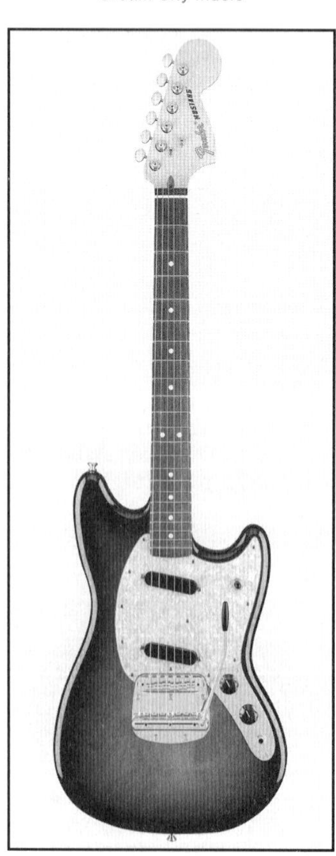
Fender American Performer Mustang

MODEL YEAR	FEATURES	EXC. COND. LOW	HIGH

caster and Telecaster. Values should be determined on case-by-case basis.

2016-2024		$1,500	$2,500

Montara (California Series)

1990-1995. Korean-made single-cut acoustic/electric flat-top, natural, sunburst or black. Maple with flamed sides starting '92.

1990-1995		$400	$600

Montego I/II

1968-1975. Electric archtop, single-cut, bolt-on neck, 1 pickup (I) or 2 pickups (II), chrome-plated hardware, sunburst.

1968-1975	I	$6,500	$9,500
1968-1975	II	$7,000	$10,000

Musiclander

1969-1972. Also called Swinger and Arrow, solidbody, 1 pickup, arrow-shaped headstock, no model name on peghead, red, white, and blue. Fender used '66-'68 dated necks but final assembly did not begin until '69.

1969-1972		$4,000	$5,500

Musicmaster

1956-1980. Solidbody, 1 pickup, short-scale (3/4) neck, Desert Sand ('56-'61), sunburst ('61-'63), red, white, or blue after. Regular-scale necks were optional and are called Musicmaster II from '64 to '69, after '69 II is dropped and Musicmaster continues with regular-scale neck.

1956-1959	Blond	$3,000	$4,000
1960-1964	Blond	$1,800	$2,400
1964-1965	Nitro, red, white, blue	$1,800	$2,400
1966-1968	Nitro, red, white, blue	$1,500	$2,000
1969-1972	Poly, red, white, blue	$1,500	$2,000
1973-1980	Red, white, blue	$1,500	$2,000

Musicmaster II

1964-1969. Solidbody, 1 pickup, long regular-scale neck version of Musicmaster, red, white, or blue.

1964-1965		$1,800	$2,800
1966-1969		$1,500	$2,200

Mustang/Player Mustang

1964-1982, 1997-1998, 2016-present. Solidbody, 2 pickups. Reissued as '69 Mustang in 1990s, name changed back to Mustang '97-'98. Dakota Red, Daphne Blue and Olympic White with Competition Red, Blue and Orange finishes with a racing stripe on the front of the body added '69-'73 (with matching headstock for '69-'70). Named Player Mustang in '16.

1964-1965	Red, white or blue	$3,000	$4,000
1966-1969	Red, white or blue	$2,500	$3,200
1969-1970	Competition blue or red	$3,000	$4,000
1969-1970	Competition orange	$5,000	$6,500
1970-1979	Contour body, poly	$2,000	$2,500
1978-1980	Antigua	$2,000	$2,500
1980-1982	Various colors	$1,500	$2,000

Vintera '60s Mustang

2019-present. Alder body, '60s C-neck, 2 single-coils, 3-color sunburst, Lake Placid Blue or Seafoam Green.

2019-2024		$600	$900

MODEL YEAR	FEATURES	EXC. COND. LOW	HIGH

Mustang '65 Reissue

2006-2016. Made in Japan, Classic Series.

2006-2016		$800	$1,200

Mustang '69 Reissue

1986-1998, 2005. Japanese-made, blue or white.

1986-1998		$1,200	$1,800

Mustang 90/Player Mustang 90

2016-present. Made in Mexico, 2 MP-90 pickups. Named Player series in '20.

2016-2024		$600	$900

American Performer Mustang

Introduced Dec. 2018-present. Made in U.S.A., Yosemite single-coil pickups, Greasebucket tone system, various colors.

2018-2024		$1,000	$1,500

American Special Mustang

2017-2018. FSR model, 2 humbucking pickups, ash body with natural finish or alder Olympic White Pearl.

2017-2018		$1,200	$1,800

Ben Gibbard Mustang

2021-present. Artist series, chambered ash body, natural poly gloss finish.

2021-2024		$1,000	$1,500

Kurt Cobain Mustang

2012-2016. Artist Series, rosewood 'board, Fiesta Red finish.

2012-2016		$1,000	$1,500

Mustang Special

2011-2013. Pawn Shop series, 2 humbucker pickups. 3-color sunburst, Candy Apple Red or Lake Placid Blue.

2011-2013		$600	$900

Newporter

1965-1971. Acoustic flat-top, mahogany back and sides. Reissued as import.

1965-1968	Spruce top	$800	$1,200
1968-1971	Mahogany top	$600	$900

Newporter (California Series)

1983-1995. Made first in Japan, then Korea in '85.

1983-1995		$300	$600

Newporter (Custom Shop USA)/ USA Select Newporter

2013-2014. Fishman electronics, 150 offered, certificate of authenticity.

2013-2014		$2,000	$3,000

Newporter Classic

2018-present. Spruce top, matching headstock, natural mahogany back and sides, pau ferro 'board.

2018-2024		$400	$600

Newporter Player

2018-present. California series, solid spruce top, mahogany back and sides, walnut 'board, various colors with gloss poly finish.

2018-2024		$300	$500

Palomino

1968-1971. Acoustic flat-top, spruce top, mahogany back and sides, triple-bound, black or mahogany.

1968-1971		$700	$1,000

Paramount Series

2016-2022. Various Standard and Deluxe acoustic models introduced at Jan. '16 NAMM.

2016-2022		$550	$1,000

MODEL YEAR	FEATURES	EXC. COND. LOW	HIGH

Pawn Shop Series

2011-2014. All-new designs with diverse Fender components and the philosophy "guitars that never were but should have been".

2011-2014	Various models	$800	$2,000

Performer

1985-1986. Imported Swinger-like body design, 2 slanted humbuckers.

1985-1986		$1,500	$2,200

Prodigy

1991-1993. US-made, electric solidbody, double-cut, chrome-plated hardware, 2 single-coil and 1 humbucker pickups, blue or black.

1991-1993		$1,000	$1,500

Redondo

1969-1970. Mid-size flat-top, 14 3/8" wide, replaces Newport spruce top model.

1969-1970		$800	$1,200

Redondo (California Series)

1983-1995. Made first in Japan, then Korea in '85.

1983-1995		$300	$500

Redondo Player

2018-present. California series, solid Sitka spruce top, mahogany back and sides, walnut 'board, various colors with gloss poly finish.

2018-2024		$300	$500

Robben Ford Signature

1989-1994. Symmetrical double-cut, 2 pickups, glued-in neck, solidbody with tone chambers, multi-bound, gold-plated hardware, sunburst. After '94 made in Fender Custom Shop.

1989-1994		$2,000	$3,000
1995	Custom Shop	$3,500	$5,500

San Luis Rey (California Series)

1990-1995. Acoustic flat-top, solid spruce top, rosewood back and sides.

1990-1995		$300	$600

San Miguel (California Series)

1990-1992. Acoustic cutaway flat-top, spruce top, mahogany back and sides.

1990-1992		$250	$400

Santa Maria (California Series)

1988-1992. Acoustic flat-top 12-string, spruce top, mahogany back and sides.

1988-1992		$300	$500

Santa Marino (California Series)

1990-1992. Acoustic flat-top, solid spruce top, mahogany back and sides.

1990-1992		$250	$400

Sergio Vallin Signature

2015-2017. New offset double-cut body shape, HSS pickups.

2015-2017		$700	$1,000

Shenandoah 12-String

1965-1971. Acoustic flat-top, spruce top, mahogany back and sides.

1965-1971	Antigua	$1,200	$1,800
1965-1971	Blond	$1,000	$1,500

Showmaster (Import)

2003-2007. Off-set double-cut solidbody, set neck, various models.

2003	Celtic, 1 bridge hum	$600	$900
2003-2007	HH, 2 hums	$600	$900
2004-2006	3 single coils	$600	$900

Showmaster FMT (Custom Shop)

2000-2007. Bound figured maple top (FMT), 2 single-coil pickups and a bridge position humbucker, maple neck, Custom Shop certificate.

2000-2007		$2,500	$4,000

Sonoran SCE (California Series)

2006-2018. Cutaway flat-top acoustic, 6-on-a-side tuners, spruce top, laminated mahogany back and sides, rosewood 'board, electronics options.

2006-2018		$300	$500

Squier Series

The following are all Squier Series instruments from Fender, listed alphabetically. Fender Japan was established in '82 with Squier production beginning that same year. Production was shifted to Korea in '87 and later allocated to China, India (Squier II '89-'90), Mexico and other countries.

Squier '51

2004-2006. Korean-made, Strat-style body with a Tele-style neck, various colors.

2004-2006		$300	$600

Squier Bullet

1983-1988, 1995-1996, 2000-2011. Strat style, early with Tele headstock, 1980s' models include H-2 ('83-'86, 2 humbuckers), S-3 ('83-'86, 3 single-coils), S-3T ('83-'88, 3 single-coils, vibrato). Name revived in 1995 (3 SC, vib.) and in 2000 on various models with 3 SC or 2 HB pickups.

1983-1984	S-3, T	$500	$800
1983-1986	H-2	$600	$900
1985-1988	S-3, T	$400	$600
2000-2011		$150	$350

Squier Bullet Stratocaster HT HSS

2017-present. Thin poplar body, maple neck, 1 humbucker and 2 single coil pickups, Shell Pink, Brown Sunburst or black.

2017-2024		$100	$250

Squier Duo-Sonic '50s (Classic Vibe Series)

2008-2010. Classic Vibe Series, made in China.

2008-2010		$200	$300

Squier Jaguar HH ST (Contemporary Series)

2021-present. Poplar body, roasted maple neck, Indian Laurel 'board, 2 humbucker pickups, stop tailpiece, Shorline Gold or Sky Burst Metallic.

2021-2024		$300	$500

Squier Jazzmaster (Classic Vibe Series)

2010-present. Includes both '60s ('10-present) and '70s ('10-'20) Jazzmaster, inspired by vintage-era models, various colors with gloss poly finish.

2010-2024	'60s or '70s	$250	$400

Squier Katana

1985-1987. Wedge-shaped body, 1 humbucker, bolt neck, dot inlays.

1985-1987		$650	$1,000

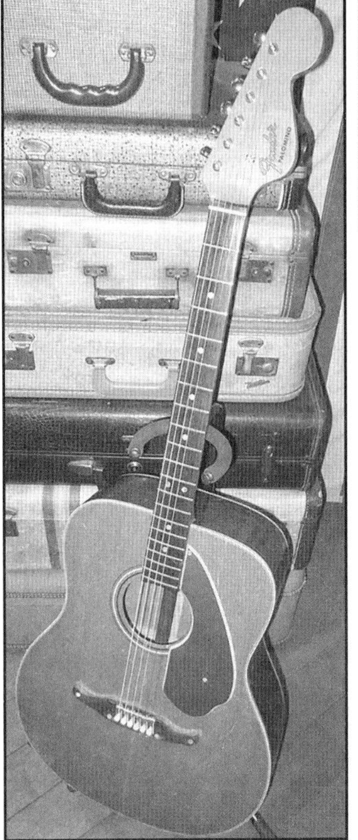

1969 Fender Palomino
Rivington Guitars

2005 Fender Squier '51
Fred Schweng

GUITARS

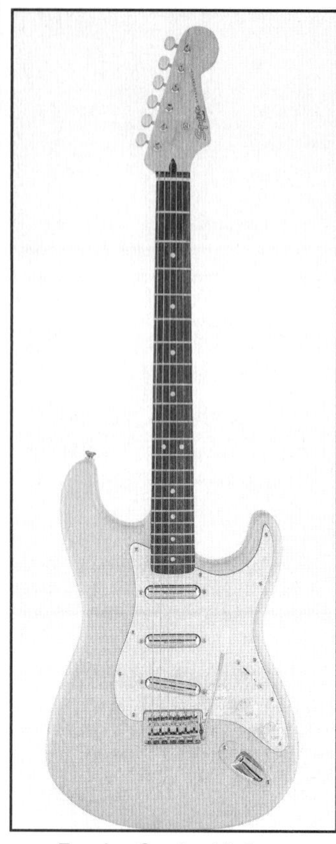

Fender Squire Vintage Modified Surf Stratocaster

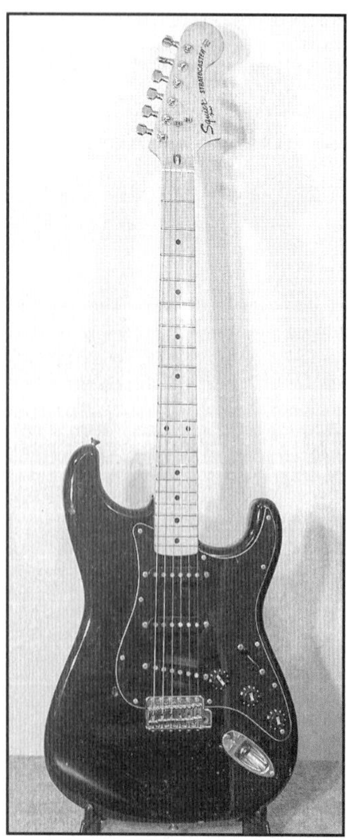

1983 Fender Squier Standard Stratocaster

Tom Pfeifer

MODEL YEAR	FEATURES	EXC. COND. LOW	HIGH

Squier Mini Stratocaster

2020-present. Poplar body, maple neck, 3 single-coil pickups, various colors. Dual humbucker pickups (HH) available.

2020-2024		$100	$200

Squier Showmaster Series

2002-2005. Made in China, various pickup configs.

2002-2005	Various models	$150	$250

Squier Stagemaster HH

1999-2002. 2 humbuckers, reverse headstock, 6- or 7-string.

1999-2002		$150	$250

Squier Standard Double Fat Strat

1999-2007. 2 humbucker pickups.

1999-2007		$100	$200

Squier Standard Fat Strat

1996-2006. Hum/single/single pickups. Replaced by the HSS.

1996-2006		$100	$200

Squier Standard Floyd Rose Strat

1992-1996. Floyd Rose tailpiece, black, white or foto flame finish, Fender and Squier headstock logos.

1992-1996		$400	$600

Squier Standard Stratocaster

1982-2019. Standard Series represent the classic designs.

1982-1984	1st logo, JV serial	$1,200	$1,800
1985-1989	2nd logo, SQ serial	$600	$900
1990-1999	Mexico	$350	$550
2000-2019	Indonesia	$150	$250

Squier II Stratocaster

1988-1992. Squier II models were targeted at a lower price point than regular Squier series. Mainly built in Korea but some early ones from India. Line was replaced by other models under regular Squier instruments.

1988-1992		$200	$300

Squier Stratocaster (Affinity Series)

1997-present. Lower priced version, made in China.

1997-2024		$150	$250

Squier Stratocaster (Contemporary Series)

2020-present. Poplar body, roasted maple neck, 2 humbucker pickups, various colors with gloss poly finish. Floyd Rose tremolo available.

2020-2022	HH	$250	$400
2020-2024	HH FR, Floyd Rose	$300	$500

Squier Stratocaster '50s (Classic Vibe Series)

2008-present. China, alder body, maple 'board, white pickguard, 2-tone sunburst, Lake Placid Blue or Oly White.

2008-2024		$250	$400

Squier Stratocaster '60s (Classic Vibe Series)

2008-present. China, as '50s Classic Vibe but with rosewood 'board, tortoise pickguard, 3-tone sunburst or candy apple red.

2008-2024		$250	$400

Squier Stratocaster Pro-Tone

1996-1998. Korean-made, higher-end Squier series with solid ash bodies, one-piece maple necks, alnico single-coils.

1996-1998		$450	$700

Squier Stratocaster Special (Contemporary Series)

2021-present. Poplar body, roasted maple neck, 3 single-coil pickups, painted headstock with chrome logo, various colors with gloss poly finish. Hardtail bridge (HT) available.

2021-2024		$300	$500

Squier Tom Delonge Stratocaster

2002-2003. Hardtail, 1 humbucker.

2002-2003		$300	$500

Squier Standard Telecaster

1982-2019. Standard Series represent classic designs.

1982-1984	1st logo, JV serial	$1,200	$1,800
1985-1989	2nd logo, SQ serial	$600	$900
1990-1999	Mexico	$350	$550
2000-2019	Indonesia	$150	$250

Squier Standard Telecaster Special

2004-2007. Made in Indonesia, 1 humbucker, 1 single-coil.

2004-2007		$150	$250

Squier Telecaster (Affinity Series)

1998-present. Lower priced version, made in China.

1998-2024		$150	$250

Squier Telecaster HH/RH

2020-present. Contemporary series, poplar body, maple neck, 2 dual humbucking (HH) pickups, in '22 changed to RH (rail humbucker, hum), black metallic with pearl white 'guard or pearl white with black 'guard.

2020-2024		$300	$500

Squier Telecaster Custom/Custom II

2003-2012. 2 humbuckers, Custom II has 2 soapbar single-coils. Changed to Vintage Modified series in '12.

2003-2012		$150	$250

Squier J5 (John 5) Telecaster

2009-2020. Artist Series, black with chrome hardware or Frost Gold with gold hardware (introduced '14), matching headstock.

2014-2020		$300	$500

Squier Telecaster Thinline (Classic Vibe Series)

2014-2020. Semi-hollow mahogany body with f-hole.

2004-2020		$200	$300

Squier Venus

1997-1998. Offset double-cut solidbody, 2 pickups, co-designed by Courtney Love, also offered as 12-string.

1997-1998		$700	$1,000

Squier Vintage Modified Series

2012-2020. Imported, various models, large script Squier logo and small Fender logo on headstock.

2012-2016	Jaguar	$275	$450
2012-2016	Jazzmaster Special	$275	$450
2012-2016	Surf Stratocaster	$250	$400
2012-2016	Telecaster Special	$250	$400
2012-2020	'70s Stratocaster	$250	$400
2012-2020	Stratocaster HSS	$250	$400

MODEL YEAR	FEATURES	EXC. COND. LOW	HIGH

Starcaster

1974-1980, 2014-2017. Offset double-cut, thinline semi-hollowbody, arched maple top and back, 2 humbuckers, 5 knobs (2 tone, 2 volume, 1 master volume), originally offered in tobacco sunburst, natural, walnut, black, white or custom blond finish. Model revived in Modern Player Series in '14 without master volume. Fender also used the Starcaster name as a brand on a line of budget guitars in the 2000s.

1974-1980	Various colors	$3,500	$6,000
2014-2017	Modern Player	$600	$1,000

Starcaster by Fender

2000s. Fender used the Starcaster brand on a line of budget versions of the Strat, Tele, and J- and P-Bass. They also offered small solid state amps and guitar packages with nylon- or steel-string acoustic or a Strat/amp combo. Sold in Costco and other discounters.

2000s	Acoustic	$100	$150
2000s	Electric guitar only	$100	$150
2000s	Guitar with amp & stand	$100	$150

Stratacoustic Series

2000-2019. Thinline acoustic/electric, single-cut, spruce top, fiberglass body, various colors. Stratacoustic discontinued '05, Deluxe begins '07 and Standard added in '09. Both Plus and Premier '14-'17.

2000-2019		$325	$800

Stratocaster

The following are all variations of the Stratocaster. The first six listings are for the main American-made line. All others are listed alphabetically after that in the following order:

Stratocaster
Standard Stratocaster
American Standard Stratocaster
American Series Stratocaster
American Professional Stratocaster
American Professional II Stratocaster
20th Century American Standard Stratocaster
21st Century American Standard Stratocaster
25th Anniversary Stratocaster
30th Anniversary Guitar Center Stratocaster
35th Anniversary Stratocaster
40th Anniversary 1954 Stratocaster Limited Edition
40th Anniversary American Standard Stratocaster
40th Anniversary Stratocaster Diamond Dealer
40th Anniversary Stratocaster ST62 (Japan)
'50s Stratocaster/Classic Series '50s Stratocaster
American Original '50s Stratocaster
Classic Player '50s Stratocaster
Classic Series '50s Stratocaster Lacquer
Road Worn '50s Stratocaster
50th Anniversary 1954 Stratocaster
50th Anniversary American Deluxe Stratocaster
50th Anniversary American Standard Stratocaster
50th Anniversary American Vintage 1957 Stratocaster
50th Anniversary Stratocaster
50th Anniversary Stratocaster Relic
'54 Stratocaster (Custom Shop)
'54 Stratocaster FMT
'55 Stratocaster (Custom Shop)
'55 Dual-Mag Strat Journeyman Relic
'55 Historic 1955 NOS Stratocaster
'55 Rocking Dog Stratocaster
'55 Stratocaster Journeyman Relic
'56 Stratocaster (Custom Shop)
'56 Stratocaster Heavy Relic
'56 Stratocaster Journeyman Closet Classic
American Vintage '56 Stratocaster
American Vintage '56 Stratocaster Limited Edition Roasted Ash
'57 Stratocaster (Custom Shop)
'57 Stratocaster (CS)
'57 Stratocaster (USA)
'57 Special Stratocaster
'57 Vintage Stratocaster (Japan)
American Vintage '57 Commemorative Stratocaster
Time Machine 1957 Stratocaster Relic
Vintage Custom 1957 Stratocaster NOS
Wildwood "10s" 1957 Limited Stratocaster Relic
'58 Stratocaster (Custom Shop)
'58 Stratocaster (Dakota Red)
'58 Limited Edition MIJ Stratocaster
'58 Stratocaster Journeyman Relic
Time Machine 1958 Stratocaster Heavy Relic
'59 Rocking Dog Stratocaster
'59 Stratocaster (Custom Shop)
1959 Stratocaster LTD Journeyman
American Vintage '59 Pine Stratocaster
American Vintage '59 Stratocaster
Time Machine 1959 Stratocaster
Wildwood "10s" 1959 Limited Stratocaster Relic
'60 Stratocaster (Custom Shop)
'60 Stratocaster FMT (Custom Shop)
Custom 1960 Stratocaster
'60s Stratocaster/Classic Series '60s Stratocaster
'60s Stratocaster/Time Machine 1960 Stratocaster
American Original '60s Stratocaster
Classic Player '60s Stratocaster
Classic Series '60s Stratocaster Lacquer
Limited Edition '60s Daybreak Stratocaster
Road Worn '60s Stratocaster
60th Anniversary '54 Stratocaster (Custom Shop)
60th Anniversary American Stratocaster
60th Anniversary American Vintage 1954 Stratocaster
60th Anniversary Commemorative Stratocaster
60th Anniversary Presidential Stratocaster
'61 Stratocaster (Custom Shop)
Wildwood "10s" 1961 Limited Stratocaster

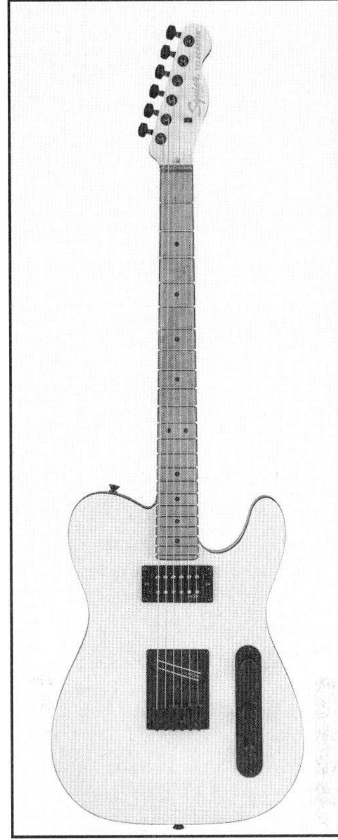

Fender Squier Telecaster RH

1976 Fender Starcaster
James Seldin

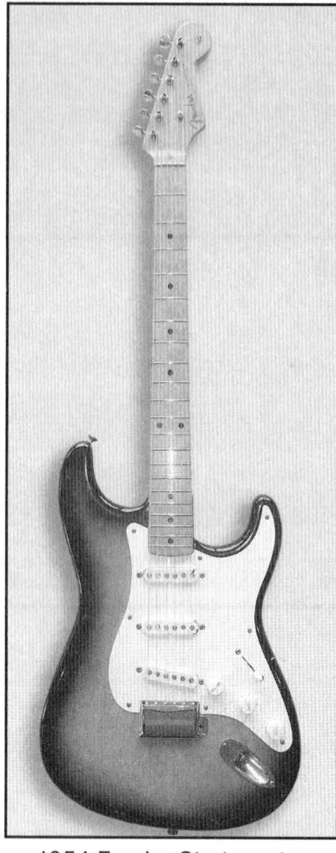

1954 Fender Stratocaster

Tony Sheedy

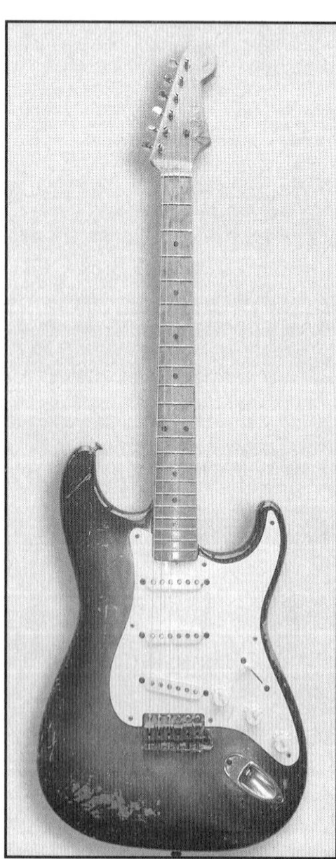

1954 Fender Stratocaster

Tony Sheedy

George Harrison Rocky Stratocaster
Gold Stratocaster
Gold Elite Stratocaster
Gold Stratocaster (Custom Shop)
GT11 Stratocaster
H.E.R. Stratocaster
Hank Marvin Stratocaster
Hank Marvin 40th Anniversary Stratocaster
Harley-Davidson 90th Anniversary Stratocaster
Highway One Stratocaster/HSS
HM Strat (USA/Import)
HM Strat Limited Edition
Homer Haynes HLE Stratocaster
Hot Wheels Stratocaster
HRR Stratocaster/Floyd Rose HRR (Japan)
Ike Turner Tribute Stratocaster
Jeff Beck Signature Stratocaster (CS)
Jeff Beck Stratocaster
Jerry Donahue Hellecaster Stratocaster
Jim Root Stratocaster
Jimi Hendrix Limited Edition Stratocaster (Custom Shop)
Jimi Hendrix Monterey Pop Stratocaster
Jimi Hendrix Monterey Stratocaster
Jimi Hendrix Stratocaster
Jimi Hendrix Tribute Stratocaster
Jimi Hendrix Voodoo 29th Anniversary (Guitar Center) Stratocaster
Jimi Hendrix Voodoo Child Signature Stratocaster NOS
Jimi Hendrix Voodoo Child Stratocaster Journeyman Relic
Jimi Hendrix Voodoo Stratocaster
Jimmie Vaughan Tex-Mex Stratocaster
John Jorgenson Hellecaster Stratocaster
John Mayer Limited Edition Black1 Stratocaster
John Mayer Limited Edition Cypress Mica Stratocaster
John Mayer Stratocaster
Kenny Wayne Shepherd Stratocaster
Koa Stratocaster
Kon Tiki Stratocaster
Lenny Stratocaster
Limited Roasted Tomatillo Stratocaster Relic
Lincoln Brewster Signature Stratocaster
Lite Ash Stratocaster Special Edition
Lone Star Stratocaster
Mark Kendrick Master Design '65 Stratocaster
Mark Knopfler Stratocaster
Masterbuilt Custom Shop Stratocaster
Matthias Jabs Signature Stratocaster
Michael Landau Signature Relic Stratocaster 1963/1968
Milonga Deluxe Stratocaster
MLB Major League Baseball Stratocaster
Mod Shop Stratocaster
Modern Player Stratocaster HSH/HSS
Moto Limited Edition Stratocaster
Moto Set Stratocaster
Noventa Stratocaster
Orange Krush Limited Edition Stratocaster
Paisley Stratocaster
Parallel Universe Volume II Strat Jazz Deluxe
Parallel Universe Volume II Strat-Tele Hybrid
Playboy 40th Anniversary Stratocaster
Player Plus Stratocaster
Player Series Stratocaster
Post Modern Stratocaster (Custom Shop)
Post Modern Stratocaster Closet Classic (Custom Shop)
Post Modern Stratocaster Journeyman Relic (Custom Shop)
Post Modern Stratocaster NOS (Custom Shop)
Powerhouse/Powerhouse Deluxe Stratocaster
Rarities Stratocaster
Richie Sambora Stratocaster
Ritchie Blackmore Stratocaster
Ritchie Blackmore Tribute Stratocaster
Roadhouse Stratocaster
Robert Cray Signature Stratocaster
Robert Cray Stratocaster (Mexico)
Robin Trower Signature Stratocaster
Rory Gallagher Tribute Stratocaster
Sandblasted Stratocaster
Select Stratocaster
Set-Neck Stratocaster
Short-Scale (7/8) Stratocaster
So-Cal J.W. Black Stratocaster
So-Cal Speed Shop Stratocaster
Special Edition David Lozeau Art Stratocaster
Special Edition Stratocaster
Special Edition Stratocaster (Matching Headstock)
Special Edition White Opal Stratocaster
Splatter Stratocaster
Standard Roland Ready Stratocaster
Standard Stratocaster (Japan)
Standard Stratocaster (Mexico)
Standard Stratocaster Plus Top
Standard Stratocaster Satin Finish
Steve Miller The Joker American Stratocaster
Stevie Ray Vaughan Signature Stratocaster
Stevie Ray Vaughan Signature Stratocaster (Custom Shop)
Stevie Ray Vaughan Tribute #1 Stratocaster
Strat Plus
Stratocaster Junior
Stratocaster Pro Closet Classic (Custom Shop)
Stratocaster Pro NOS (Custom Shop)
Stratocaster Special
Stratocaster XII
Strat-o-Sonic
Sub Sonic Stratocaster
Super Stratocaster
Supreme Stratocaster
Tanqurey Tonic Stratocaster
Tash Sultana Stratocaster
Texas Special Stratocaster
The Edge Stratocaster
The Strat
Tie-Dye Stratocaster
Tom Delonge Stratocaster
Tom Morello "Soul Power" Stratocaster
Tree of Life Stratocaster
Turquoise Sparkle Stratocaster
U.S. Ultra/Ultra Plus Stratocaster

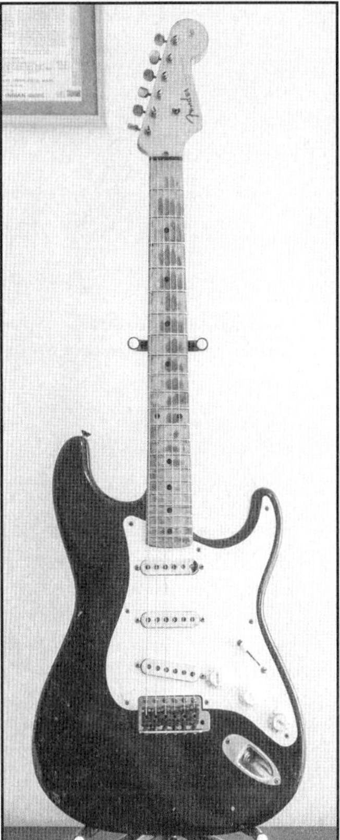

1956 Fender Stratocaster
David Stone

1956 Fender Stratocaster
Trey Rabinek

GUITARS

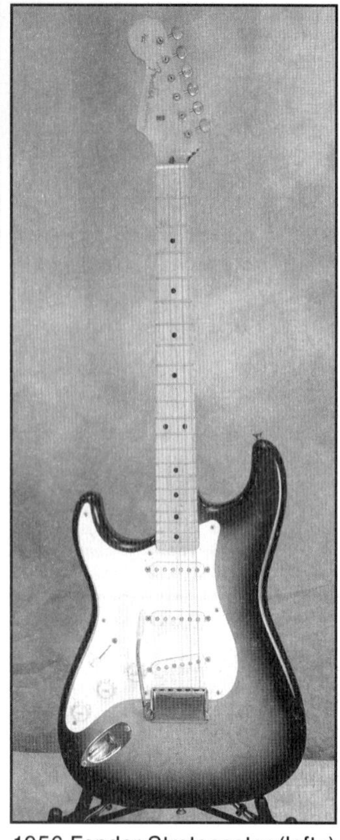
1956 Fender Stratocaster (lefty)
HI Guitars

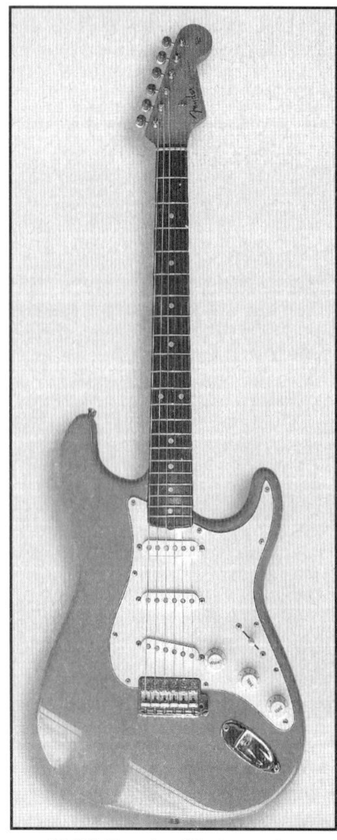
1962 Fender Statocaster
Tony Sheedy

MODEL YEAR	FEATURES	EXC. COND. LOW	HIGH

Ventures Limited Edition Stratocaster
VG Stratocaster
Vintage Hot Rod Stratocaster
Vintera Series Stratocaster
Walnut Elite Stratocaster
Walnut Stratocaster
Wayne Kramer Signature/MC5 Stratocaster
Western Stratocaster
Whiteguard Stratocaster Limited Edition
Yngwie Malmsteen Double-neck Stratocaster
Yngwie Malmsteen Signature Stratocaster (Custom Shop)
Yngwie Malmsteen Stratocaster
Yngwie Malmsteen Tribute Stratocaster

Stratocaster

1954-1981. Two-tone sunburst until '58, 3-tone after. Please refer to the Fender Guitar Intro Section for details on Fender color options.

Three-bolt neck '72-'81, otherwise 4-bolt. Unless noted, all Stratocasters listed have the Fender tremolo system. Non-tremolo models (aka hardtails) typically sell for less. Many guitarists feel the tremolo block helps produce a fuller range of sound. On average, many more tremolo models were made. One year, '58, seems to be a year where a greater percentage of non-tremolo models were made.

From '63-'70, Fender offered both the standard Brazilian rosewood fretboard and an optional maple fretboard. Prices listed here, for those years, are for the rosewood 'board models. Currently, the market considers the maple 'board (commonly referred to as a 'maple cap') to be a premium. The use of maple 'boards on Stratocasters was very rare and they can be worth up to 20% more than the values shown.

Renamed Standard Stratocaster for '82-'84 (see following listings), American Standard Stratocaster for '86-2000, the American Series Stratocaster for '00-'07, and the American Standard Stratocaster (again) for '08-'16. Currently called the American Professional Stratocaster.

MODEL YEAR	FEATURES	EXC. COND. LOW	HIGH
1954	Very first '54, rare features	$200,000	$275,000
1954	Early-mid '54, typical features	$100,000	$210,000
1954	Sunburst, later production	$75,000	$120,000
1955	Late-'55, blond, nickel hw	$65,000	$125,000
1955	Sunburst, ash body	$50,000	$75,000
1956	Blond, nickel hw	$65,000	$150,000
1956	Mary Kaye, gold hw	$100,000	$165,000
1956	Sunburst, alder body	$48,500	$65,000
1956	Sunburst, ash body	$50,000	$75,000
1956	Sunburst, non-trem	$40,000	$55,000
1957	Blond, nickel hw	$60,000	$150,000
1957	Mary Kaye, gold hw	$100,000	$165,000
1957	Sunburst	$42,500	$55,000
1957	Sunburst, non-trem	$35,000	$45,000
1958	Blond, nickel hw	$55,000	$150,000
1958	Mary Kaye gold hw	$85,000	$165,000
1958	Sunburst 2-tone, maple	$42,500	$55,000
1958	Sunburst 2-tone, non-trem	$35,000	$45,000
1958	Sunburst 3-tone, maple	$40,000	$50,000
1958	Sunburst 3-tone, non-trem	$32,500	$42,500
1959	Blond, nickel hw, maple 'board	$50,000	$150,000
1959	Blond, nickel hw, slab 'board	$42,500	$85,000
1959	Custom color	$80,000	$175,000
1959	Mary Kaye, gold hw, maple	$80,000	$165,000
1959	Mary Kaye, gold hw, slab	$80,000	$150,000
1959	Sunburst 3-tone, maple	$35,000	$45,000
1959	Sunburst, non-trem, slab	$25,000	$35,000
1959	Sunburst, slab, 1-ply 'guard	$30,000	$40,000
1959	Sunburst, slab, 3-ply 'guard	$30,000	$40,000
1960	Common color	$50,000	$75,000
1960	Rare color	$75,000	$200,000
1960	Sunburst	$30,000	$40,000
1961	Common color	$45,000	$75,000
1961	Rare color	$75,000	$200,000
1961	Sunburst	$30,000	$40,000
1962	Common color, early slab	$45,000	$75,000
1962	Common color, late curve	$40,000	$55,000
1962	Rare color, early slab	$65,000	$175,000
1962	Rare color, late curve	$55,000	$175,000
1962	Sunburst, early slab	$30,000	$40,000
1962	Sunburst, late curve	$27,500	$38,000
1963	Common color	$40,000	$55,000
1963	Rare color	$55,000	$175,000
1963	Sunburst	$27,500	$38,000
1964	Common color	$40,000	$55,000
1964	Rare color	$55,000	$175,000
1964	Sunburst, spaghetti logo	$27,500	$38,000
1964	Sunburst, transition logo	$21,500	$30,000
1965	Common color	$35,000	$45,000
1965	Rare color	$50,000	$65,000
1965	Sunburst, early-'65 green 'guard	$21,500	$30,000

MODEL YEAR	FEATURES	EXC. COND. LOW	HIGH
1965	Sunburst, late-'65 F-plate	$17,000	$22,500
1965	Sunburst, white 'guard	$19,500	$25,000
1966	Common color	$30,000	$40,000
1966	Common color, bound 'board (rare)	$35,000	$45,000
1966	Rare color	$45,000	$75,000
1966	Sunburst, block markers	$21,500	$30,000
1966	Sunburst, dot markers	$17,000	$22,500
1967	Common color	$30,000	$40,000
1967	Rare color	$45,000	$75,000
1967	Sunburst	$17,000	$22,500
1968	Common color, nitro	$30,000	$40,000
1968	Common color, poly	$25,000	$35,000
1968	Common color, poly body, nitro neck	$24,000	$32,000
1968	Rare color, nitro	$40,000	$75,000
1968	Rare color, poly	$35,000	$50,000
1968	Rare color, poly body, nitro neck	$35,000	$50,000
1968	Sunburst, nitro	$17,000	$22,500
1968	Sunburst, poly	$12,500	$16,500
1968	Sunburst, poly body, nitro neck	$13,500	$18,000
1969	Common color	$25,000	$30,000
1969	Rare color	$30,000	$50,000
1969	Sunburst	$12,500	$16,500
1970	Common color, 4-bolt	$15,500	$20,000
1970	Rare color, 4-bolt	$21,500	$30,000
1970	Sunburst, 4-bolt	$11,000	$14,500
1971	Common color, 4-bolt	$15,000	$20,000
1971	Early-mid '71, sunburst, 4-bolt	$10,500	$14,500
1971	Late '71, sunburst, 3-bolt	$5,000	$6,500
1971	Rare color, 4-bolt	$18,000	$25,000
1972	Common color, 3-bolt	$5,500	$8,500
1972	Rare color, 3-bolt	$9,500	$12,000
1972	Sunburst, 3-bolt	$4,500	$6,500
1973	Common color	$5,500	$7,500
1973	Natural	$4,000	$5,500
1973	Rare color	$8,000	$10,000
1973	Sunburst	$4,500	$6,000
1973	Walnut	$4,250	$5,500
1974	Black, blond, white (white parts)	$4,500	$6,000
1974	Natural (white parts)	$3,500	$5,000
1974	Sunburst (white parts)	$4,000	$5,500
1974	Walnut (white parts)	$4,000	$5,500
1975	Black, blond, white (black parts)	$4,000	$5,500
1975	Black, blond, white (white parts)	$4,500	$6,000
1975	Early-'75, sunburst (white parts)	$4,000	$5,500
1975	Late-'75, sunburst (black parts)	$3,500	$4,500
1975	Natural (black parts)	$3,000	$4,000
1975	Walnut (black parts)	$2,800	$3,600
1976-1977	Various colors	$3,000	$4,000
1978	Various colors	$2,500	$3,500
1979	Antiqua	$3,000	$4,000
1979	Various colors	$2,500	$3,500
1980	Various colors	$2,500	$3,500
1980-1981	International colors	$2,800	$3,800
1981	Various colors	$2,500	$3,500

Standard Stratocaster (includes "Smith Strat")

1981-1984. Replaces the Stratocaster. Renamed the American Standard Stratocaster for '86-'00 (see next listing). Renamed American Series Stratocaster in '00. From '81/'82 to mid-'83, 3 knobs same as regular Strat but with 4-bolt neck. In August '81, Dan Smith was hired by Bill Schultz and Fender produced an alder body, 4-bolt neck, 21-fret, small headstock Standard Stratocaster that has been nicknamed the Smith Strat (made from Dec. '81-'83). Mid-'83 to the end of '84 2 knobs and 'guard mounted input jack. Not to be confused with current Standard Stratocaster, which is made in Mexico.

MODEL YEAR	FEATURES	EXC. COND. LOW	HIGH
1981-1983	Various colors	$2,000	$3,000
1983-1984	Sunburst, 2-knob	$1,200	$1,500
1983-1984	Various colors, 2-knob	$1,200	$1,500

American Standard Stratocaster

1986-1999, 2008-2016. Fender's new name for the American-made Strat when reintroducing it after CBS sold the company. The only American-made Strats made in 1985 were the '57 and '62 models. See Stratocaster and Standard Stratocaster for earlier models. Name used again for '08-'16, various pickup options including SSS, HH, HSH, HSS, Fat and HSS plus. Renamed American Series Stratocaster in 2000 and again renamed the American Professional Series Stratocaster in 2017.

MODEL YEAR	FEATURES	EXC. COND. LOW	HIGH
1986-1999	Various colors & options	$900	$1,500
2008-2016	Various colors & options	$900	$1,500

American Series Stratocaster

2000-2007. Ash or alder body, rosewood or maple 'board, dot markers, various pickup options including HSS and HH, 5-way switch. Renamed the American Standard Stratocaster again in '08.

MODEL YEAR	FEATURES	EXC. COND. LOW	HIGH
2000-2007	Various colors & options	$900	$1,200
2004	50th Anniversary	$1,000	$1,500

1963 Fender Stratocaster
Scott Dailey

1983 Fender "Smith Strat"
Bill Beals

GUITARS

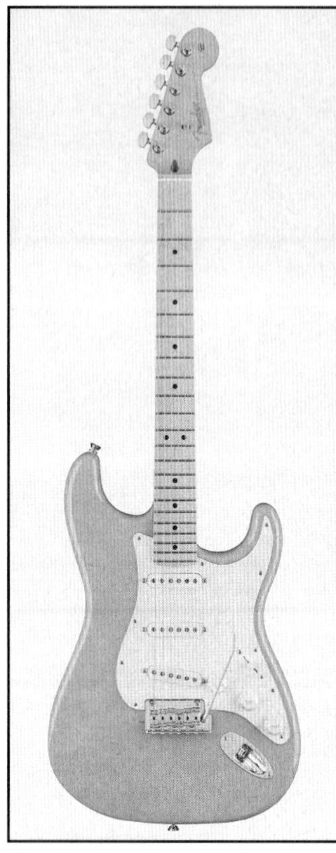

Fender American Professional II Stratocaster

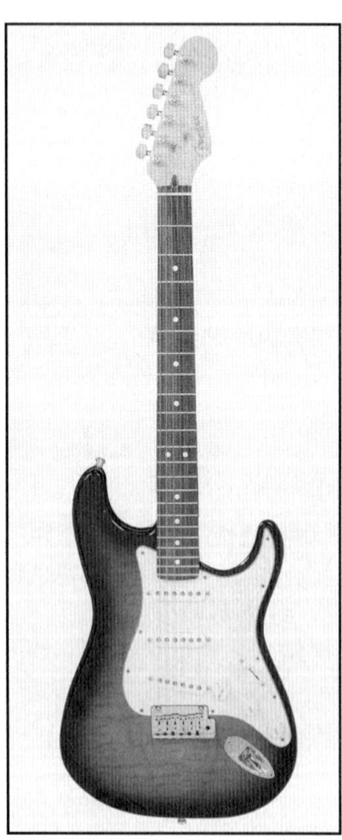

1996 Fender 50th Anniversary Stratocaster

Imaged by Heritage Auctions, HA.com

MODEL YEAR	FEATURES	EXC. COND. LOW	HIGH

American Professional Stratocaster

2017-2020. Model replaces American Standard Series Strat, redesign includes new V-Mod pickups, narrow-tall frets, new 'deep C' neck profile, genuine bone nut, various colors. Also available left-hand model. Renamed American Professional II in '20.

2017-2020	High-end features	$1,200	$1,800
2017-2020	Low-end features	$900	$1,200

American Professional II Stratocaster

2020-present. Various pickup options, woods and various colors.

2020-2024	HSS	$1,000	$1,500
2020-2023	Roasted Pine	$1,100	$1,600
2020-2023	Roasted Pine HSS	$1,100	$1,600
2020-2024	SSS	$1,100	$1,600

20th Century American Standard Stratocaster

1999. Limited Edition of the last 100 Strats off the line in 1999. COA signed by William Schultz. "20th Century American Standard" headstock stamp and neckplate.

1999		$1,200	$1,800

21st Century American Standard Stratocaster

2000. Limited Edition of the first 100 Strats off the line in 2000. COA signed by William Schultz. "21st Century American Standard" headstock stamp and neckplate.

2000		$1,200	$1,800

25th Anniversary Stratocaster

1979-1980. Limited Edition, 4-bolt neck plate, standard truss rod, has ANNIVERSARY on upper body horn, early-'79 has pearlescent finish which flaked, late-'79-'80 was changed to silver metallic.

1979	Early run pearlescent	$2,000	$3,000
1979-1980	Silver	$2,200	$3,500

30th Anniversary Guitar Center Stratocaster

1994		$1,500	$2,500

35th Anniversary Stratocaster

1989-1991. Custom Shop, 500 made, figured maple top, Lace Sensor pickups, Eric Clapton preamp circuit.

1989-1991		$2,800	$4,500

40th Anniversary 1954 Stratocaster Limited Edition

1994. Standard production (not Custom Shop), 1,954 made, "40th Anniversary STRATOCASTER 1994" neck plate, serial number series xxxx of 1954, spaghetti logo, tremolo, Kluson tuners, solid maple neck, 2-tone sunburst semi-transparent finish on ash body.

1994		$3,000	$4,500

40th Anniversary American Standard Stratocaster

1994 only. US-made, American Standard model (not Custom Shop), plain top, appearance similar to a '54 maple-neck Strat, sunburst, 2 neck plates offered "40th Anniversary" and "40th Anniversary and still rockin'".

1994		$1,200	$1,800

40th Anniversary Stratocaster Diamond Dealer

1994 only. Custom Shop model, 150 made, 40th Anniversary headstock inlay, flamed maple top on ash body, '54-'94 inlay at 12th fret, gold etched 'guard, gold hardware, sunburst.

1994		$4,500	$6,000

40th Anniversary Stratocaster ST62 (Japan)

1994 only. Made in Japan, '62 reissue specs.

1994		$1,000	$1,500

'50s Stratocaster/Classic Series '50s Stratocaster

1985-2019. 'Made in Japan' logo until 'Crafted in Japan' logo mid-'97, basswood body, then mid-'99 made in Mexico with poplar or alder body. Foto-Flame finish offered '92-'94.

1985-1996	Made in Japan	$1,200	$1,800
1997-1999	Crafted in Japan	$700	$1,000
1999-2019	Mexico	$600	$900

American Original '50s Stratocaster

2018-2023. Vintage-style appointments, 3 pickups, alder or ash body (White Blonde only), 2-color sunburst or Aztec Gold.

2018-2023		$1,500	$2,200

Classic Player '50s Stratocaster

2006-2019. U.S.-made components but assembled in Mexico, alder body, maple neck and 'board, vintage-style pickups.

2006-2019		$600	$900
2014	50th Anniversary	$800	$1,200

Classic Series '50s Stratocaster Lacquer

2014-2019. Candy Apple Red nitro-lacquer finish.

2014-2019		$700	$1,000

Road Worn '50s Stratocaster

2009-2019. Made in Mexico, maple 'board, '50s specs, aged finish.

2009-2019		$800	$1,200

50th Anniversary 1954 Stratocaster

2004-2005. Custom Shop, celebrates 50 years of the Strat, 1954 specs and materials, replica form-fit case, certificate, Fender took orders for these up to December 31, 2004.

2004-2005		$3,000	$4,500

50th Anniversary American Deluxe Stratocaster

2004-2005. Deluxe series features, engraved neck plate, tweed case.

2004-2005		$1,200	$1,800

50th Anniversary American Standard Stratocaster

2004. Mexico, engraved neck plate, '54 replica pickups, tweed case.

2004		$800	$1,200

50th Anniversary American Vintage 1957 Stratocaster

1996. V serial number, 50th decal back of headstock.

1996		$1,500	$2,200

MODEL YEAR	FEATURES	EXC. COND. LOW	HIGH

50th Anniversary Stratocaster

1995-1996. Custom Shop, 2500 made, flame maple top, 3 vintage-style pickups, gold hardware, gold 50th Anniversary (of Fender) coin on back of the headstock, sunburst.

1995-1996		$2,500	$4,000

50th Anniversary Stratocaster Relic

1995-1996. Custom Shop relic model, aged played-in feel, diamond headstock inlay, Shoreline Gold finish.

1995-1996		$3,000	$4,500

'54 Stratocaster (Custom Shop)

1992-1998. Classic reissue, ash body, Custom '50s pickups, gold-plated hardware.

1992-1998		$3,000	$4,500

'54 Stratocaster FMT

1992-1998. Custom Classic reissue, Flame Maple Top, also comes in gold hardware edition.

1992-1998		$3,000	$4,500

'55 Stratocaster (Custom Shop)

2006, 2013. 1st version is Limited Edition of 100 Relics with 2-tone sunburst; 2nd version is Closet Classic. Both include certificate of authenticity.

2006	Relic	$3,000	$4,500
2013	Closet Classic	$3,000	$4,500

'55 Dual-Mag Strat Journeyman Relic

2017-2019. Custom Shop Limited Edition, certificate of authenticity.

2017-2019		$4,000	$6,000

'55 Historic 1955 NOS Stratocaster

2018-2020. Custom Shop NOS, certificate of authenticity.

2018-2020		$3,000	$4,500

'55 Rocking Dog Stratocaster

2007. Custom Shop, commissioned by Garrett Park Guitars, various colors.

2007		$3,500	$5,500

'55 Stratocaster Journeyman Relic

2017. Custom Shop, vintage-correct appointments, certificate of authenticity.

2017		$4,000	$6,000

'56 Stratocaster (Custom Shop)

1996-2016. Most detailed replica (and most expensive to date) of '56 Strat, including electronics and pickups, offered with rosewood or maple 'board, gold hardware is +$100.

1996-1998	Cunetto built Relic	$6,000	$9,000
1997-1998	Cunetto era (staff built)	$3,000	$4,500
1999-2010	Closet Classic	$3,000	$4,500
1999-2010	NOS	$3,000	$4,500
1999-2014	Relic	$3,000	$4,500
2014-2016	Heavy relic	$3,000	$4,500

'56 Stratocaster Heavy Relic

2020. Custom Shop, certificate of authenticity.

2020		$3,000	$4,500

'56 Stratocaster Journeyman Closet Classic

2020. Custom Shop, certificate of authenticity.

2020		$4,000	$6,000

American Vintage '56 Stratocaster

2013-2018. Vintage '56 style, maple 'board, black, Shell Pink or aged white blonde.

2013-2018		$1,500	$2,200

MODEL YEAR	FEATURES	EXC. COND. LOW	HIGH

American Vintage '56 Stratocaster Limited Edition Roasted Ash

2017. Roasted ash body, roasted maple neck and 'board, nitro lacquer finish.

2017		$1,800	$2,800

'57 Stratocaster (Custom Shop)

1994-1996. Custom Shop models can be distinguished by the original certificate that comes with the guitar. Replaced by the more authentic, higher-detailed '56 Custom Shop Stratocaster by '99.

1994-1996	Various colors	$3,000	$4,500

'57 Stratocaster (CS)

2007, 2010-2016. Custom Shop models, Relic ('07), Closet Classic ('10-'13), Heavy Relic ('15-'16), NOS Dealer Select program ('13-'16) where models are built for specific dealers.

2007	Relic	$3,000	$4,500
2010-2013	Closet Classic	$3,000	$4,500
2013-2016	NOS	$3,000	$4,500
2015-2016	Heavy relic	$3,000	$4,500

'57 Stratocaster (USA)

1982-2012. U.S.-made at the Fullerton, California plant ('82-'85) and at the Corona, California plant ('85-'12), American Vintage series.

1982-1984	SN: V series	$3,000	$4,500
1986-1989	Common color	$1,800	$3,000
1986-1989	Rare color	$2,500	$3,500
1990-1999		$1,600	$2,500
1990-1999	Rare color	$2,200	$3,000
2000-2012	Various colors	$1,500	$2,500

'57 Special Stratocaster

1992-1993. Custom Shop, limited run of 60, flamed maple top, birdseye maple neck, sunburst.

1992-1993		$2,000	$3,000

'57 Vintage Stratocaster (Japan)

1982-1998. Made in Japan logo, JV serial numbers '82-'84, E serial '84-'87, Crafted in Japan logo by '98, various colors.

1982-1985	MIJ logo	$1,200	$2,000
1998	CIJ logo	$800	$1,200

American Vintage '57 Commemorative Stratocaster

2007. Limited production, 1957-2007 Commemorative logo neckplate.

2007-2012		$1,500	$2,200

Time Machine 1957 Stratocaster Relic

2020. Custom Shop Time Machine series, certificate of authenticity.

2020		$3,000	$4,500

Vintage Custom 1957 Stratocaster NOS

2019-present. Custom Shop, maple 'board, aged white blonde with gold hardware.

2019-2024		$3,000	$4,500

Wildwood "10s" 1957 Limited Stratocaster Relic

2014-2015. Custom Shop Dealer Select model for Wildwood Music, '57 specs with 3 single coil or HSS pickups, certificate of authenticity.

2014-2015		$3,000	$4,500

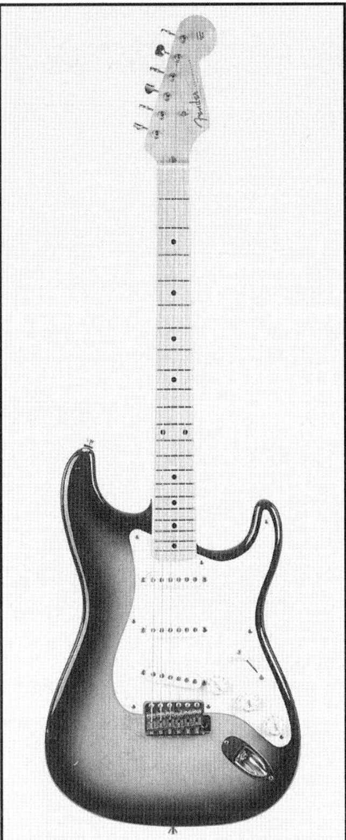

2002 Fender '56 Stratocaster NOS (Custom Shop)
Cream City Music

Fender Vintage Custom 1957 Stratocaster NOS

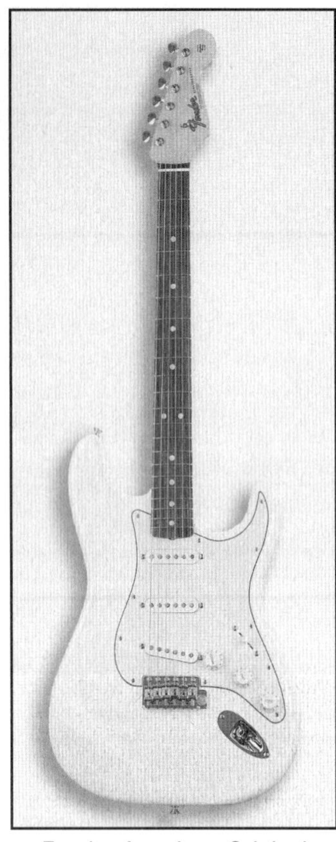

Fender American Original '60s Stratocaster

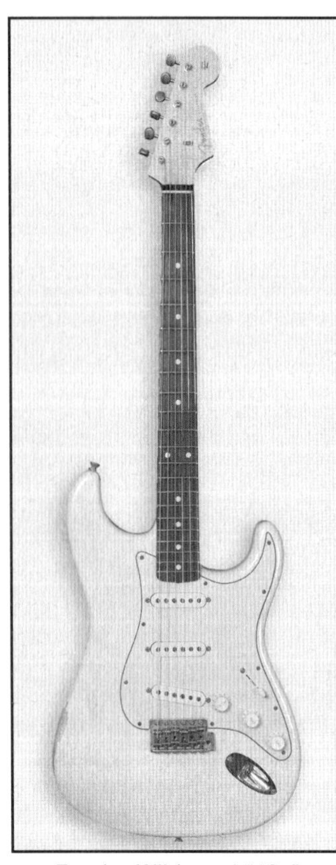

Fender Wildwood "10s" 1961 Limited Stratocaster

MODEL YEAR	FEATURES	EXC. COND. LOW	HIGH

'58 Stratocaster (Custom Shop)

1996-1999. Ash body, Fat '50s pickups, chrome or gold hardware (gold is +$100.), Custom Shop models have certificate of authenticity.

1996-1999	Various colors	$3,000	$4,500

'58 Stratocaster (Dakota Red)

1996. Custom Shop, run of 30 made in Dakota Red with matching headstock, maple neck, Texas special pickups, gold hardware.

1996		$3,000	$4,500

'58 Limited Edition MIJ Stratocaster

2013. Made in Japan logo, 252 offered.

2013		$1,500	$2,200

'58 Stratocaster Journeyman Relic

2016. Custom Shop, vintage-correct appointments, certificate of authenticity.

2016		$3,000	$4,500

Time Machine 1958 Stratocaster Heavy Relic

2020. Custom Shop Time Machine series, certificate of authenticity.

2020		$3,000	$4,500

'59 Rocking Dog Stratocaster

2007. Custom Shop, commissioned by Garrett Park Guitars, based on '59 rosewood 'board Strat, various colors.

2007		$3,500	$5,500

'59 Stratocaster (Custom Shop)

2010-2013. Rosewood 'board, vintage appointments, COA, various colors with Relic or Heavy Relic finish.

2010-2013	Relic	$3,000	$4,500
2013	Heavy Relic	$3,000	$4,500

1959 Stratocaster LTD Journeyman

2019-2020. Custom Shop, limited edition, vintage and modern appointments, COA, various colors with Relic or Heavy Relic lacquer finish.

2019	Relic	$3,000	$4,500
2019-2020	Heavy Relic	$3,000	$4,500

American Vintage '59 Pine Stratocaster

2017. Limited Edition neck plate, pine body built from re-claimed 100-year-old wood, 3 vintage '59 single-coil pickups.

2017		$1,800	$2,800

American Vintage '59 Stratocaster

2013-2018. Maple or slab rosewood 'board.

2012-2018		$1,500	$2,200

Time Machine 1959 Stratocaster

2019-2021. Custom Shop Time Machine series, vintage and modern appointments, COA, various colors with Relic or Heavy Relic lacquer finish.

2019-2020	Relic	$3,000	$4,500
2020-2021	Heavy Relic	$3,000	$4,500

Wildwood "10s" 1959 Limited Stratocaster Relic

2011-2017. Custom Shop, quartersawn maple neck, Brazilian rosewood 'board, 3 pickups, faded 3-color sunburst. Limited Edition neck plate decal, and certificate of authenticity.

2011	Maple 'board	$4,000	$6,000
2011-2017	Brazilian 'board	$5,000	$8,000

'60 Stratocaster (Custom Shop)

1992-1999. 3 Texas Special pickups, various colors, optional gold hardware is +$100, with certificate of authenticity. In 2000 the '60 Stratocaster name was applied to the Time Machine model (see following).

1992-1999		$3,000	$4,500

'60 Stratocaster FMT (Custom Shop)

1997-1999. Flame maple top (FMT).

1997-1999		$3,000	$4,500

Custom 1960 Stratocaster

1994. Short run of 20 custom ordered and specified instruments that have 1960 specs along with other specs such as a pearloid 'guard, matching headstock color, came with certificate of authenticity.

1994		$3,000	$4,500

'60s Stratocaster/Classic Series '60s Stratocaster

1985-2019. 'Made in Japan' logo until 'Crafted in Japan' logo mid-'97, basswood body, then mid-'99 made in Mexico with poplar or alder body. Foto-Flame finish offered '92-'94.

1985-1996	Made in Japan	$1,200	$1,800
1997-1999	Crafted in Japan	$700	$1,000
1999-2019	Mexico	$600	$900

'60s Stratocaster/Time Machine 1960 Stratocaster

1996-2020. Custom Shop Relic/Time Machine. For '96-'99 was called the '60s Stratocaster, in 2000 name was changed to Time Machine 1960 Stratocaster. Heavy Relic began late-'15. Optional gold hardware is +$100. Vince Cunetto and company did the aging of the guitars to mid-1999. The price includes the original Certificate of Authenticity, a guitar without the original COA is worth less than the values shown.

1996-1998	Cunetto built Relic	$6,000	$9,000
1997-1999	Cunetto era (staff built)	$3,000	$4,500
1999-2010	Closet Classic	$3,000	$4,500
1999-2010	NOS	$3,000	$4,500
1999-2015	Relic	$3,000	$4,500
2015-2020	Heavy relic	$3,000	$4,500

American Original '60s Stratocaster

2018-2023. Vintage-style appointments, 3 pickups, alder body, 3-color sunburst. Candy Apple Red or Olympic White.

2018-2023		$1,500	$2,200

Classic Player '60s Stratocaster

2006-2019. U.S.-made components but assembled in Mexico, alder body, maple neck, rosewood 'board, vintage-style pickups.

2006-2019		$600	$900

Classic Series '60s Stratocaster Lacquer

2014-2019. Made in Mexico, 3-color sunburst nitro-lacquer finish.

2014-2019		$700	$1,000

Limited Edition '60s Daybreak Stratocaster

2019-2020. Traditional series, made in Japan, Olympic White with matching headstock, gold hardware.

2019-2020		$800	$1,200

MODEL YEAR	FEATURES	EXC. COND. LOW	HIGH

Road Worn '60s Stratocaster

2009-2020. Rosewood 'board, '60s specs, aged finish. Renamed Vintera Road Worn '60s Strat in '20.

2009-2020		$800	$1,200

60th Anniversary '54 Stratocaster (Custom Shop)

2014. Heavy relic, certificate of authenticity, 60th guitar case.

2014		$3,000	$4,500

60th Anniversary American Stratocaster

2006-2007. Celebrates Fender's 60th, US-made, 'Sixty Years' decal logo on headstock, engraved 60th Anniversary neck plate, Z-series serial number, coin on back of headstock, sunburst only, paperwork.

2006-2007	American flag logo	$1,200	$1,800

60th Anniversary American Vintage 1954 Stratocaster

2014-2016. 1,954 built, came with reproduction 1954 paperwork and 1954 Anniversary Strat Certificate.

2014-2016		$1,500	$2,200

60th Anniversary Commemorative Stratocaster

2014. Celebrates the Strat's 60th, US-made, 60th Anniversary neckplate, 60th medallion on back of headstock, gold hardware, special case, commemorative book.

2014		$1,500	$2,200

60th Anniversary Presidential Stratocaster

2006. Custom Shop, Diamond (60th) anniversary, limited to 100, bookmatched maple top stained using grapes from Hill Family Winery (California), '1946-2006' logo on neck, 'Limited Edition 60th Anniv. Presidential' neck plate logo, certificate of authenticity.

2006		$5,000	$8,000

'61 Stratocaster (Custom Shop)

2001-2012. Relic, certificate of authenticity.

2001-2012		$3,000	$4,500

Wildwood "10s" 1961 Limited Stratocaster

2010-2024. Custom Shop, NOS, relic or heavy relic, quartersawn maple and AA flame maple necks, 3 pickups, "faded" thin nitro finishes in multiple colors.

2010-2016	NOS	$3,000	$4,500
2010-2024	Relic	$3,000	$4,500

'62 Stratocaster (USA)

1982-1984, 1986-2012. Made at Fullerton plant ('82-'84) then at Corona plant ('86-2012), American Vintage series.

1982-1984	SN: V series	$3,000	$4,500
1986-1989	Common color	$1,800	$3,000
1986-1989	Rare color	$2,500	$3,500
1990-1999	Common color	$1,600	$2,500
1990-1999	Rare color	$2,200	$3,000
2000-2012	Common color	$1,500	$2,500

'62 Heavy Relic Stratocaster

2007-2010. Custom Shop Dealer Select series, extreme Relic work.

2007-2010		$3,000	$4,500

'62 Stratocaster ST62D/ST54 DEX2

1996. Made in Japan, '54 maple neck, '62 body.

1996		$1,200	$1,800

'62 Stratocaster ST62US Reissue

2008-2012. Crafted in Japan, US-made 'vintage' pickups.

2008-2012		$800	$1,200

'62 Vintage Stratocaster (Japan)

1982-1984. Made in Japan, JV serial numbers, various colors.

1982-1984		$1,200	$1,800

Dave's Guitar Shop American 1962 Stratocaster

2019-2020. Limited Edition, various colors with nitro lacquer finish.

2019-2020		$1,500	$2,500

Deluxe Vintage Player '62 Stratocaster

2005-2006. Limited Edition, vintage and modern features based upon '62 specs, 3 Samarium Cobalt Noiseless pickups, Deluxe American Standard electronics, Olympic White or Ice Blue Metallic.

2005-2006		$1,000	$1,500

Vintage Custom 1962 Stratocaster

2019-present. Custom Shop, NOS finish, alder body, maple neck and 'board, 3-color sunburst.

2019-2024		$3,000	$4,500

Willcutt Guitars True '62 Stratocaster

2016-2020. Custom Shop, limited run for Bob Willcutt Guitars, 4 models; 'V' neck, '59 'C' neck, '60s 'C' neck and large 'C' neck.

2016-2020		$3,000	$4,500

'63 Stratocaster (Custom Shop)

2015-2018. Time Machine series, Relic in '15-'17, Heavy Relic '18.

2015-2017	Relic	$3,000	$4,500
2018	Heavy Relic	$3,000	$4,500

'63 Stratocaster Journeyman Relic

2015. Custom Shop, vintage-correct appointments, alder body, bird's-eye maple neck, rosewood 'board, 3 single-coil pickups, certificate of authenticity.

2015		$4,000	$6,000

'64 Stratocaster (Custom Shop)

2009-2014. Relic or Closet Classic, certificate of authenticity.

2009-2012	Relic	$3,000	$4,500
2011-2014	Closet Classic	$3,000	$4,500

Time Machine 1964 Stratocaster Journeyman Relic

2018-2020. Custom Shop Time Machine series, vintage-correct appointments, certificate of authenticity.

2018-2020		$4,000	$6,000

'65 Stratocaster (Custom Shop)

1998-1999, 2003-2006, 2010 (no Closet Classic). Custom Shop model, '65 small-headstock specs, rosewood or maple cap 'board, transition logo, offered in NOS, Relic, or Closet Classic versions.

1998-1999	Cunetto era (staff built)	$3,000	$4,500
2003-2006	Closet Classic	$3,000	$4,500
2003-2010	NOS	$3,000	$4,500
2003-2010	Relic	$3,000	$4,500

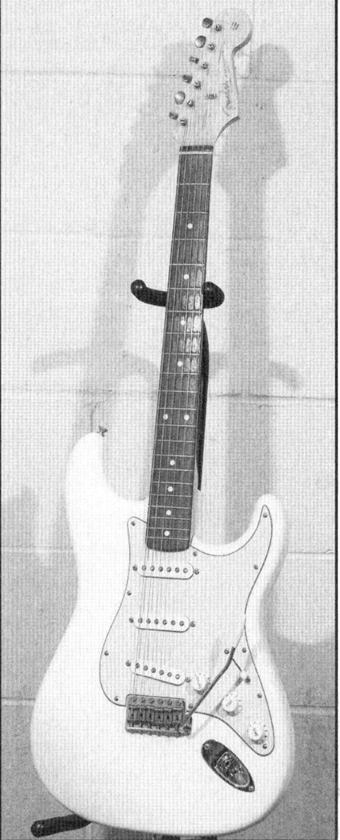

2003 Fender '62 Stratocaster

Tom Pfeifer

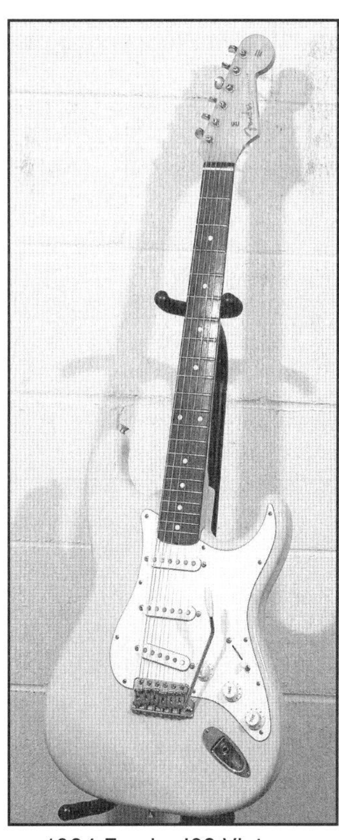

1984 Fender '62 Vintage Stratocaster

Tom Pfeifer

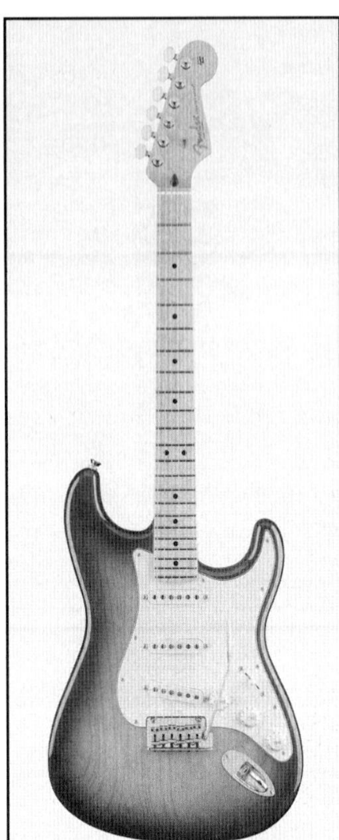

Fender 75th Anniversary Commemorative Stratocaster

Fender American Custom Stratocaster

MODEL YEAR	FEATURES	EXC. COND. LOW	HIGH

'65 Stratocaster Journeyman Closet Classic

2019-2020. Custom Shop, vintage-correct appointments, certificate of authenticity.

2019-2020		$4,000	$6,000

American Vintage '65 Stratocaster

2013-2017. V serial number, flash coat finish, various colors, some with matching headstock.

2013-2017		$1,500	$2,200

Time Machine 1965 Stratocaster Journeyman Relic

2010. Custom Shop Time Machine series, vintage-correct appointments, certificate of authenticity.

2010		$4,000	$6,000

Total Tone '65 Stratocaster Relic

2013. Custom Shop Limited Edition, alder body, maple neck, reverse wound middle pickup for noise reduction, various colors with Relic nitro lacquer finish.

2013		$3,000	$4,500

'66 Stratocaster (Custom Shop)

2004-2008. Custom Shop model, offered in Closet Classic, NOS or Relic versions.

2004-2008	Closet Classic	$3,000	$4,500
2004-2008	NOS	$3,000	$4,500
2004-2008	Relic	$3,000	$4,500

Time Machine 1967 Stratocaster Journeyman Relic Aged

2020. Custom Shop Time Machine series, vintage-correct appointments.

2020		$4,000	$6,000

Time Machine 1967 Stratocaster Journeyman Relic Custom Top

2020. Custom Shop Time Machine series, vintage-correct appointments.

2020		$4,000	$6,000

'68 Heavy Relic Stratocaster

2007-2010. Custom Shop Dealer Select, extreme relic work.

2007-2010		$3,500	$5,000

'68 Reverse Strat Special (USA)

2001-2002. With special reverse left-hand neck, large headstock (post-CBS style).

2001-2002		$2,200	$3,500

'68 Stratocaster (Japan)

1996-1999, 2013. Part of Collectables Series, '68 specs including large headstock, sunburst, natural or Olympic White.

1996-1999		$900	$1,400
2013		$900	$1,300

'69 Stratocaster (Custom Shop)

1997-2012, 2016. Large headstock, U-shaped maple neck with rosewood or maple cap options, '69-style finish, gold hardware is +$100, since 2000, offered in NOS, Relic, or Closet Classic (no CC after '08) versions. Heavy Relic in '16.

1997-1999	Cunetto era (staff built)	$3,000	$4,500
2000-2008	Closet Classic	$3,000	$4,500
2000-2009	NOS	$3,000	$4,500
2000-2012	Relic	$3,000	$4,500
2016	Heavy Relic	$3,000	$4,500

MODEL YEAR	FEATURES	EXC. COND. LOW	HIGH

Wildwood "10s" 1969 Limited Stratocaster

2014. Custom Shop, Relic, Jimi Hendrix specs, certificate of authenticity.

2014		$3,500	$5,000

'70s Stratocaster/Classic Series '70s Stratocaster

1999-2019. Made in Mexico, large headstock, white pickups and knobs, rosewood 'board.

1999-2019		$600	$900

American Vintage '70s Stratocaster

2009-2012. Large '70s headstock, early '70s white pickups and knobs, 3-bolt neck. Hardtail version in '15.

2009-2012		$1,500	$2,200

American Vintage '70s Stratocaster Hardtail

2015. Hardtail bridge version.

2015		$1,500	$2,200

'72 Stratocaster (Japan)

1985-1996. Basswood body, maple 'board, large headstock, various colors (does not include the Paisley '72).

1985-1996		$1,200	$1,800

'72 Stratocaster Limited Edition

2013. Made in Japan for US domestic sales, 144 made, large headstock, bullet truss rod, 3-bolt maple neck, 21 frets, 3 Alnico pickups.

2013		$900	$1,400

75th Anniversary Commemorative Stratocaster

2021-2023. US-made, limited edition, inlaid 75th Anniversary ingot back of headstock, gold hardware, 2-color Bourbon Burst gloss finish. Includes custom Inca Silver case with Lake Placid Blue interior.

2021-2023		$1,800	$2,800

75th Anniversary Stratocaster

2021-2023. Made in Mexico, 75th Anniversary neck plate, Diamond Anniversary satin finish with matching painted headstock.

2021-2023		$800	$1,200

Acoustasonic Stratocaster

2003-2009. Hollowed out alder Strat body with braceless graphite top, 3 in-bridge Fishman piezo pickups, acoustic sound hole.

2003-2009		$600	$900

Aerodyne Classic Stratocaster

2020. Limited run made in Japan, figured maple top, rosewood 'board, 3 pickups, various colors with gloss poly finish.

2020		$1,000	$1,500

Aerodyne Stratocaster

2004-2009. Import Strat with Aerodyne body profile, bound body, black.

2004-2009		$600	$900

Albert Hammond Jr. Signature Stratocaster

2018-2024. Made in Mexico, styled after his 1985 reissue of a '72 Strat.

2018-2024		$800	$1,200

MODEL YEAR	FEATURES	EXC. COND. LOW	HIGH

Aluminum Stratocaster (Custom Shop)

1994. Custom Shop aluminum bodies, chrome body with black 'guard, black body with chrome 'guard, or green with black lines and red swirls. There are also several Custom Shop one-offs with aluminum bodies.

1993-1994		$4,500	$7,500

Aluminum Stratocaster American Standard

1994-1995. Aluminum-bodied American Standard with anodized finish in blue marble, purple marble or red, silver and blue stars and stripes. Some with 40th Anniversary designation. There is also a Custom Shop version.

1994-1995	Various patterns & options	$3,000	$4,500

American Acoustasonic Stratocaster

2019-present. Solid A sitka spruce top, mahogany back and sides, ebony 'board, various colors. Also offered with cocobolo and ziricote top.

2019-2024		$1,200	$1,800
2020-2024	Cocobolo top	$1,500	$2,200

American Classic Holoflake Stratocaster

1992-1993. Custom Shop model, splatter/sparkle finish, pearloid 'guard.

1992-1993		$2,500	$4,000

American Classic Stratocaster

1992-1999. Custom Shop version of American Standard, 3 pickups, tremolo, rosewood 'board, nickel or gold-plated hardware, various colors.

1992-1999	Various options	$2,500	$4,000

American Custom Stratocaster (Custom Shop)

2020-present. Custom Shop American Custom series, various woods and colors.

2020-2024		$2,800	$4,500

American Deluxe Stratocaster

1998-2016. Premium alder or ash body, maple neck, various pickup options including SSS, HSS, HSH, HSS Plus, Fat and Shawbucker, various colors.

1998-2016	Various options	$1,000	$1,500

American Deluxe Stratocaster Dealer Event

2013. Sold at private dealer event at Fender Corona, various premium tonewoods, various colors and finishes.

2013		$2,000	$3,000

American Deluxe Stratocaster Designer Series

2004-2015. Limited production, various upgrades such as flamed maple top, mahogany, etc.

2004-2015		$1,500	$2,200

American Deluxe Stratocaster FMT HSS

2004-2009. Flame maple top version of the HSS.

2004-2009		$1,200	$1,800

American Deluxe Stratocaster HSS Mahogany

2015-2016. Limited Edition 10 for 15 series, 2-piece mahogany body.

2015-2016		$1,500	$2,200

American Elite Stratocaster

2016-2019. Alder body, 3 single-coil pickups or HSS with Shawbucker.

2016-2019		$1,200	$1,800

American Elite Stratocaster Limited Edition

2016. Various color options with matching headstock.

2016		$1,500	$2,200

American Longboard Stratocaster HSS

2015. Part of Fender's limited edition 10 for 15 series, vintage surfboard laminate top design.

2015		$1,500	$2,200

American Performer Stratocaster

2018-present. Made in the US, new features include 3 Yosemite single-coil pickups, Greasebucket tone system, various colors.

2018-2024		$900	$1,400

American Special Stratocaster

2010-2018. Limited Edition, '70s headstock with post-CBS black Stratocaster logo, Texas Special pickups (SSS or HSS), satin (early were gloss) finish.

2010-2018		$900	$1,400

American Standard Stratocaster Limited Edition

1990s-2019. American Standard series, various limited-edition models.

1995-2000	Matching hdstk	$1,200	$1,800
2001	Standard hdstk	$1,000	$1,500
2009	Matching hdstk, Seafoam/Surf Green	$1,500	$2,200
2014-2017	Channel Bound	$1,200	$1,800
2015	Mystic Black	$1,300	$2,000
2015-2016	Mystic Aztec Gold	$1,400	$2,100
2015-2016	Oiled Ash	$1,500	$2,200
2015-2016	Vintage White	$1,300	$2,000
2017	Rosewood neck	$1,500	$2,200
2019	Pale Moon Quilt	$1,800	$2,800

American Ultra Luxe Stratocaster

2021-present. Pickups options and various colors.

2021-2024	Floyd Rose HHS	$1,200	$1,800
2021-2024	SSS	$1,200	$1,800

American Ultra Stratocaster

2019-present. Various options and colors.

2019-2024		$1,200	$1,800

Ancho Poblano Stratocaster Journeyman Relic

2018-2019. Custom Shop Limited Edition series, alder body, 2-color sunburst or opaque white blonde, with Journeyman Relic nitro lacquer finish.

2018-2019		$4,000	$6,000

Ancho Poblano Roasted Stratocaster Relic

2019-2020. Custom Shop Limited Edition series, roasted alder body with Relic lacquer finish, various colors.

2019-2020		$3,000	$4,500

Antigua Stratocaster

2004. Made in Japan, limited-edition reissue, '70s features and antigua finish.

2004		$1,000	$1,500

2010 Fender American Deluxe Stratocaster
Cream City Music

Fender Artisan Series Spalted Maple Thinline Stratocaster

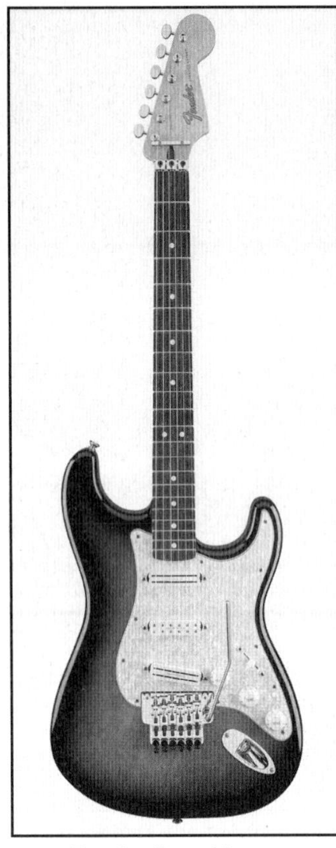

Fender Dave Murray Stratocaster

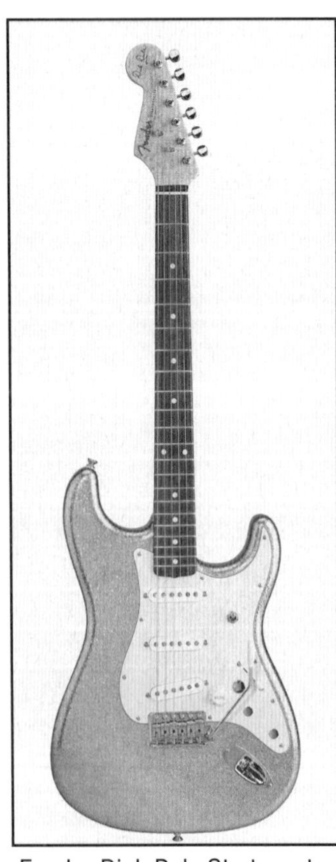

Fender Dick Dale Stratocaster

MODEL YEAR	FEATURES	EXC. COND. LOW	HIGH

Artisan Series Stratocaster (Custom Shop)

2015-present. Features distinctively figured woods, gold hardware, hand-rubbed oil finishes, certifiicate of authenticity, various models: Okoume, Claro Walnut, Figured Rosewood, Spalted Maple, Tamo Ash, Thinline Koa.

2015	Okoume	$3,500	$5,500
2016-2019	Tamo Ash	$3,500	$5,500
2016-2022	Spalted Maple	$3,500	$5,500
2020-2024	Maple Burl	$3,500	$5,500

Big Apple Stratocaster

1997-2000. Two humbucking pickups, 5-way switch, rosewood 'board or maple neck, non-tremolo optional.

1997-2000	Various colors	$1,000	$1,500

Big Block Stratocaster

2005-2006. Pearloid block markers, black with matching headstock, 2 single coils (neck, middle) 1 humbucker (bridge), vintage style tremolo.

2005-2006		$800	$1,200

Big Head Stratocaster

2020. Custom Shop Limited Edition series.

2020		$3,000	$4,500

Bill Carson Stratocaster

1992. Based on the '57 Strat, birdseye maple neck, Cimarron Red finish, 1 left-handed and 100 right-handed produced, serial numbers MT000-MT100, made in Fender Custom Shop, and initiated by The Music Trader (MT) in Florida.

1992		$3,500	$5,500

Billy Corgan Stratocaster

2008-2012. US-made, 3 DiMarzio pickups, string-thru hardtail bridge.

2008-2012		$1,200	$1,800

Blackie Stratocaster (Custom Shop)

1987, 2006. Includes Certificate of Authenticity, 12 made in '87, in '06 185 made for U.S. market and 90 for export.

1987	12 made	$20,000	$30,000
2006	Blackie Tribute	$5,000	$7,500

Black Paisley Stratocaster

2020. Made in Japan, Limited Edition, run of 300, silver and black paisley-print design on basswood body, rosewood 'board, 3 single-coil pickups.

2020		$800	$1,200

Blacktop Stratocaster

2011-2015. Alder body, maple neck, rosewood or maple 'board, various pickup options including HH and HSH, various finish options. Floyd Rose version is also available.

2011-2015		$600	$900

Mahogany Blacktop Stratocaster Limited Edition

2019. 2 or 3 Alnico humbuckers, mahogany body, black headstock, Oly White, black or crimson red, chrome or gold hardware.

2019		$600	$900

Blue Flower Stratocaster

1984-1997, 2002-2004. Made in Japan, '72 Strat reissue with a '68 Tele Blue Floral finish.

1984-1987	1st issue	$1,800	$2,800
1988-1994	MIJ	$1,200	$1,800
1995-1997	CIJ	$1,000	$1,500
2002-2004	2nd issue	$800	$1,200

Bonnie Raitt Stratocaster

1995-2001. Alder body, often in blueburst, Bonnie Raitt's signature on headstock.

1995-2001		$1,800	$2,800

Bowling Ball/Marble Stratocaster

1983-1984. Standard Strat with 1 tone and 1 volume control, jack on 'guard, called Bowling Ball due to the swirling color, blue, red or gold.

1983-1984	Blue or red	$4,000	$5,000
1983-1984	Gold	$4,500	$9,500

Buddy Guy Signature Stratocaster

1995-2009. Maple neck, 3 Gold Lace Sensor pickups, ash body, blond or sunburst.

1995-2009		$1,500	$2,200

Buddy Guy Standard Stratocaster

1996-present. Made in Mexico, maple neck, polka-dot finish.

1996-2024		$800	$1,200

Buddy Holly Tribute Stratocaster

2014. Custom Shop, 50 made, '55 specs, with certificate of authenticity.

2014		$6,000	$10,000

California Stratocaster/ California Fat Stratocaster

1997-1999. Made in the U.S., painted in Mexico, 3 single coils, Fat has HSS, various colors.

1997-1999	SSS or HSS	$600	$900

Carroll Shelby Limited Edition Stratocaster

2009. Built for Ford Motor Co. as tribute to Shelby's life, graphic photo montage on front, engraved Shelby Automobiles logo on 'guard, only 100 produced.

2009		$4,500	$7,500

Carved Top Stratocaster HSS (Custom Shop)

1995-1998. Carved figured maple top, HSS (HH offered in '98), certificate of authenticity, various colors.

1995-1998		$1,800	$2,800

Classic Player Stratocaster

2000. Custom Shop, Standard Stratocaster with useful 'player-friendly features' such as noiseless stacked single-coil pickups and factory Sperzel locking tuners, black, gold anodized 'guard.

2000		$2,500	$4,000

Classic Player Stratocaster HH

2015-2016. Alder body, maple neck, bound rosewood 'board, 2 humbuckers, dark Mercedes Blue gloss finish with matching headstock.

2015-2016		$700	$1,000

Collector's Edition Stratocaster ('62 Reissue)

1997. Pearl inlaid '97 on 12th fret, rosewood 'board, alder body, gold hardware, tortoise 'guard, nitro finish, sunburst, 1997 made.

1997		$2,200	$3,500

Contemporary Stratocaster (Custom Shop)

1989-1998. 7/8 scale body, hum/single/single pickups, various colors.

1989-1998		$2,500	$4,000

MODEL YEAR	FEATURES	EXC. COND. LOW	HIGH

Contemporary Stratocaster (Import)

1985-1987. Import model used while the new Fender reorganized, black or natural headstock with silver-white logo, black or white 'guard, 2 humbucker pickups or single-coil and humbucker, 2 knobs and slider switch.

1985-1987		$900	$1,400

Crash Stratocaster

2005-2007. Master Built Custom Shop, hand painted by John Crash Matos, approximately 50, comes with a certificate, the prices shown include the original certificate.

2005-2007		$4,500	$6,500

Custom Classic Stratocaster

2000-2008. Custom Shop version of American Standard Strat.

2000-2008		$3,000	$4,500

Custom Deluxe Stratocaster

2009-2014. Custom Shop, birdseye maple neck, rosewood or maple 'board, certificate. Model also available with flame maple top.

2009-2014		$3,000	$4,500

Custom Shop Limited Edition Stratocaster

1992. Only 100 made, flame maple top, birdseye maple neck, rosewood 'board, gold hardware, trans red finish.

1992		$4,000	$6,000

Dave Murray Stratocaster

2009-present. Alder body, maple neck, rosewood 'board, 3 pickups, 2-color sunburst.

2009-2024		$800	$1,200

David Gilmour Signature Stratocaster

2008-2019. Custom Shop, NOS or Relic, based on Gilmour's '70 black Stratocaster, certificate of authenticity.

2008-2019		$4,000	$6,000

Deluxe Lone Star Stratocaster

2007-2016. Reissue of Lone Star Strat, made in Mexico, 1 humbucker and 2 single-coils, rosewood 'board.

2007-2016		$600	$900

Deluxe Players Special Edition Stratocaster

2007. Made in Mexico, Special Edition Fender oval sticker on back of headstock along with 60th Anniversary badge.

2007		$650	$1,000

Deluxe Players Stratocaster

2004-2016. Made in Mexico, 3 noiseless single-coils, push-button switching system.

2004-2016		$700	$1,000

Deluxe Roadhouse Stratocaster

2008-2021. Deluxe series reissue, Texas Special pickups.

2008-2021		$700	$1,000

Deluxe Stratocaster

2016-2021. Mexico-made, double-cut, 3 vintage noiseless single-coils or 1 humbucker and 2 single-coils.

2016-2021	SSS or HSS	$700	$1,000

Deluxe Stratocaster HSS Plus Top With IOS Connectivity

2014-2016. Deluxe series, plugs into iOS devices.

2014-2016		$700	$1,000

Deluxe Stratocaster Plus

1987-1998. Alder (poplar earlier) with ash veneer front and back, 3 Lace Sensor pickups, Floyd Rose, various colors. Becomes American Deluxe Strat Plus.

1987-1998		$1,200	$1,800

Dick Dale Stratocaster

1994-present. Custom Shop signature model, alder body, reverse headstock, sparkle finish.

1994-2024		$3,500	$5,500

Elite Stratocaster

1983-1984. The Elite Series features active electronics and noise-cancelling pickups, push buttons instead of 3-way switch, Elite script logo on 4-bolt neck plate, various colors. Also see Gold Elite Stratocaster and Walnut Elite Stratocaster.

1983-1984		$1,800	$2,800

EOB (Ed O'Brien) Sustainer Stratocaster

2017-present. Alder body, maple neck and 'board, 3 pickups (Sustainer in neck position), custom "Flower of Life" neck plate, gloss poly white finish.

2017-2024		$1,000	$1,500

Eric Clapton Crossroads Stratocaster

2007. Custom Shop Limited Edition of 100, Crossroads graphic, 50 sold with matching '57 Twin amp autographed by Clapton (and with other goodies) retailed at $30,000. The other 50 sold guitar alone (with less goodies) at $20,000.

2007	Guitar & Twin Amp	$15,000	$20,000
2007	Guitar only	$10,000	$15,000

Eric Clapton Gold Leaf Stratocaster

2004. Custom Shop model, special build for Guitar Center, 50 made, 23k gold leaf finish/covering.

2004		$7,500	$12,000

Eric Clapton Signature Journeyman Relic Stratocaster

2020-present. Custom Shop, Clapton's signature on the headstock, 2-color sunburst or aged white blonde.

2024		$4,000	$6,000

Eric Clapton Signature Stratocaster (Custom Shop)

2019-present. Alder body, maple neck, three Vintage Noiseless pickups, Clapton's signature on headstock, black or Mercedes Blue.

2019-2024		$3,500	$5,000

Eric Clapton Stratocaster

1988-present. U.S.-made, '57 reissue features, had Lace Sensor pickups until '01, when switched to Vintage Noiseless. Black versions have added "Blackie" decal on headstock.

1988-1999	Lace Sensors	$1,200	$1,800
2000	Lace Sensors	$1,200	$1,800
2001-2024	Noiseless	$1,000	$1,500

Eric Clapton Stratocaster (Custom Shop)

2004-2016 Custom Shop model, standard non-active single-coil pickups, black or blue finish

2004-2016		$3,500	$5,000

Fender EOB (Ed O'Brien) Sustainer Stratocaster

Fender Eric Clapton Signature Journeyman Relic Stratocaster

Tyler Willison

Fender H.E.R. Stratocaster

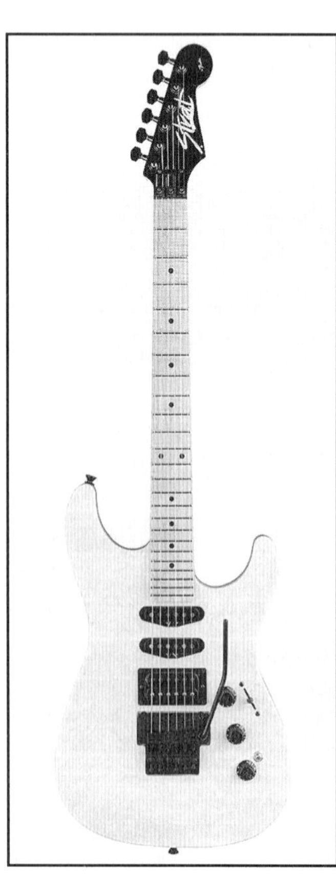
Fender HM Strat
Limited Edition

MODEL YEAR	FEATURES	EXC. COND. LOW	HIGH

Eric Johnson 1954 "Virginia" Stratocaster

2020-present. Stories Collection, limited numbers offered from both Custom Shop (see Masterbuilt listing) and Corona production.

2020-2024	Fender Corona	$2,000	$3,000

Eric Johnson Signature Stratocaster Thinline

2018-2020. Alder body, maple neck and 'board, 3 single-coil pickups, 2-color sunburst or vintage white.

2017-2020		$1,800	$2,800

Eric Johnson Stratocaster

2005-present. '57 spec body and 1-piece maple soft-v-neck, or, for '09 to '15, rosewood 'board, special design pickups, vintage tremolo with 4 springs, EJ initials and guitar-player figure engraved neck plate. Also listed as Eric Johnson Stratocaster Maple or Rosewood.

2005-2024	Maple or rosewood	$1,500	$2,200

Floyd Rose Classic Relic Stratocaster

1998. Custom Shop, late '60s large headstock, 1 humbucker and 1 Strat pickup.

1998		$3,500	$5,000

Floyd Rose Classic Stratocaster (Strat HSS) (Strat HH)

1992-2002. Two single-coils, bridge humbucker, Floyd Rose tremolo, became Floyd Rose Classic Strat HSS or HH (2 humbuckers) in '98.

1992-2002		$1,200	$1,800

Ford Shelby GT Stratocaster

2007. 200 made, black with silver Shelby GT racing stripe.

2007	200 made	$3,000	$4,500

Foto Flame Stratocaster

1994-1996, 2000. Japanese-made Collectables model, alder and basswood body with Foto Flame (simulated woodgrain) finish on top cap and back of neck.

1994-2000		$1,000	$1,500

Freddy Tavares Aloha Stratocaster

1993-1994. Custom Shop, hollow aluminum body with hand engraved Hawaiian scenes, custom inlay on neck, 153 made.

1993-1994		$5,000	$7,500

FSR Stratocaster

2012-2019. Factory Special Run models might be 'dealer exclusive' or open to all dealers as limited run. FSR have a special set of appointments that are not standard to the core lineup.

2012	Antigua Strat	$900	$1,400
2013	Hot Rod Strat	$700	$1,000
2013-2017	Classic '60s Strat	$700	$1,000
2015-2016	Amer Std '54 Strat	$1,500	$2,200
2017-2019	Classic '50s Strat	$700	$1,000
2018-2019	Traditional '50s Strat	$900	$1,400

George Fullerton 50th Anniversary '57 Strat Ltd. Ed. Set

2007. Limited Edition, 150 made, '57 Strat with matching relic Pro Junior tweed amp, 2 certificates of authenticity signed by Fullerton, commemorative neck plate.

2007		$6,000	$9,000

MODEL YEAR	FEATURES	EXC. COND. LOW	HIGH

George Harrison Rocky Stratocaster

2020-present. Custom Shop Limited Edition, 2-piece alder body, 5A flame maple neck, 3 '60s Strat pickups, finish is designed from Harrison's psychedelic paint job including the "Grimwoods" decal, Sonic Blue with custom Rocky graphics top.

2020-2024		$18,000	$25,000

Gold Stratocaster

1981-1983. Gold metallic finish, gold-plated brass hardware, 4-bolt neck, maple 'board, skunk strip, trem.

1981-1983		$2,000	$3,000

Gold Elite Stratocaster

1983-1984. The Elite series features active electronics and noise-cancelling pickups, the Gold Elite has gold hardware and pearloid tuner buttons, also see Elite Stratocaster and Walnut Elite Stratocaster.

1983-1984		$1,800	$2,800

Gold Stratocaster (Custom Shop)

1989. Custom Shop, 500 made, gold finish with gold anodized and white 'guards included.

1989		$4,000	$6,000

GT11 Stratocaster

2019-2020. Custom Shop, exclusive models for Sweetwater, relic and heavy relic.

2019-2020	Heavy Relic	$4,000	$6,000
2019-2020	Relic	$3,000	$4,500

H.E.R. Stratocaster

2020-present. Made in Mexico, Artist Signature series, alder body with Chrome Glow finish, matching painted headstock.

2020-2024		$1,000	$1,500

Hank Marvin Stratocaster

1995-1996. Custom Shop, Feista Red.

1995-1996		$3,500	$5,500

Hank Marvin 40th Anniversary Stratocaster

1998. Custom Shop logo with '40 Years 1958-1998' marked on back of headstock, Fiesta Red, only 40 made, COA.

1998		$8,000	$12,000

Harley-Davidson 90th Anniversary Stratocaster

1993. Custom Shop, 109 total made, Harley-Davidson and Custom Shop V logo on headstock (Diamond Edition, 40 units), 9 units produced for the Harley-Davidson company without diamond logo, 60 units were not Diamond Edition, chrome-plated engraved metal body, engraved 'guard, COA necessary.

1993		$25,000	$40,000

Highway One Stratocaster/HSS

2002-2014. U.S.-made, alder body, satin lacquer finish, 3 single-coil pickups or HSS version has humbucker/single/single.

2002-2014		$800	$1,500

HM Strat (USA/Import)

1988-1992 ('88 Japanese-made, '89-'90 U.S.- and Japanese-made, '91-'92 U.S.-made). Heavy Metal Strat, Floyd Rose, regular or pointy headstock, black hardware, H, HH, SH, or SSH pickup options. Later models have a choice of SHH or SSH.

1988-1990	Import	$1,000	$1,500
1989-1992	USA	$1,200	$1,800

MODEL YEAR	FEATURES	EXC. COND. LOW	HIGH

HM Strat Limited Edition

2020-2021. '88-'92 HM specs, available in era-correct Day-Glo colors, Frozen Yellow, Flash Pink, Ice Blue and Bright White.

2020-2021		$1,000	$1,500

Homer Haynes HLE Stratocaster

1988-1989. Custom Shop, limited edition of 500, '59 Strat basics with gold finish, gold anodized guard and gold hardware.

1988-1989		$4,000	$6,000

Hot Wheels Stratocaster

2003. Custom Shop model commissioned by Hot Wheels, 16 made, orange flames over blue background, large Hot Wheels logo.

2003		$1,500	$2,200

HRR Stratocaster/Floyd Rose HRR (Japan)

1990-1994. Made in Japan, hot-rodded vintage-style Strat, Floyd Rose tremolo system, H/S/S pickups, maple neck, sunburst or colors. Called the Floyd Rose HRR for '92-'94 (with optional Foto Flame finish).

1990-1994		$900	$1,400

Ike Turner Tribute Stratocaster

2005. Custom Shop model, 100 made, replica of Ike Turner's Sonic Blue Strat.

2005		$3,500	$5,500

Jeff Beck Signature Stratocaster (CS)

2004-present. Custom Shop, 3 Noiseless dual-coils, Olympic White or Surf Green.

2004-2019		$3,000	$4,500
2020-2024		$4,000	$6,000

Jeff Beck Stratocaster

1991-present. Alder body, originally 3 Lace Sensors (HSS) changing to 3 Noiseless dual-coils in '01, rosewood 'board, Olympic White and Surf Green (Midnight Purple until '02).

1991	1st issue, Lace Sensors	$2,250	$3,000
1992-1993	Lace Sensors	$2,000	$2,500
1994-2000	Lace Sensors	$1,500	$2,000
2001-2009	Noiseless	$1,500	$2,000
2010-2024	Artist Series	$1,500	$2,000

Jerry Donahue Hellecaster Stratocaster

1997. Made in the Fender Japan Custom Shop as one part of the 3-part Hellecasters Series, limited edition, Seymour Duncan pickups, maple, blue with blue sparkle guard.

1997		$1,200	$1,800

Jim Root Stratocaster

2010-present. Artist series, mahogany body, ebony or maple 'board, 2 active pickups, black hardware, black or white finish.

2010-2024		$1,000	$1,500

Jimi Hendrix Limited Edition Stratocaster (Custom Shop)

2019-2021. Custom Artist series, designed from Hendrix's modified '68 Strat used at Woodstock ('69), aged Olympic White.

2019-2021		$4,000	$6,000

Jimi Hendrix Monterey Pop Stratocaster

1997-1998. Custom Shop, near replica of Monterey Pop Festival sacrifice guitar, red psychedelic-style finish.

1997-1998		$18,000	$25,000

Jimi Hendrix Monterey Stratocaster

2017-2018. Body art like Hendrix's hand-painted original that he destroyed at Monterey Pop Festival, custom neck plate, signature on headstock rear.

2017-2018		$900	$1,400

Jimi Hendrix Stratocaster

2015-present. Reverse headstock, silhouette and engraved 'Authentic Hendrix' on neckplate.

2015-2024		$800	$1,200

Jimi Hendrix Tribute Stratocaster

1997-2000. Left-handed guitar strung right-handed, maple cap neck, Olympic White. Fender headstock logo positioned upside down, made for right-handed player to look as if they are playing a left-handed guitar flipped over.

1997-2000		$2,000	$3,000

Jimi Hendrix Voodoo 29th Anniversary (Guitar Center) Stratocaster

1993. Custom Shop made only 35 for Guitar Center, large 'Guitar Center 29th Anniversary' logo on neckplate, right-handed body with reverse left-handed headstock and reversed Fender headstock logo, purple sparkle finish.

1993		$4,000	$6,500

Jimi Hendrix Voodoo Child Signature Stratocaster NOS

2018-present. Custom Shop, Custom Artist series, 2-piece alder body, maple neck and 'board, 3 pickups, Olympic White or black, with NOS nitro lacquer finish.

2018-2024		$3,500	$5,500

Jimi Hendrix Voodoo Child Stratocaster Journeyman Relic

2020-present. Custom Shop, Olympic White or black with aged relic finish.

2020-2024		$4,000	$6,500

Jimi Hendrix Voodoo Stratocaster

1997-2002. Right-handed body with reverse headstock, maple neck, Olympic White, sunburst or black.

1997-2002		$2,500	$3,500

Jimmie Vaughan Tex-Mex Stratocaster

1997-present. Poplar body, maple 'board, signature on headstock, 3 Tex-Mex pickups, various colors.

1997-2024		$800	$1,200

John Jorgenson Hellecaster Stratocaster

1997. Fender Japan Custom Shop, part of the 3-part Hellecasters Series, limited edition, Seymour Duncan pickups, gold sparkle 'guard, gold hardware, split single-coils, rosewood 'board.

1997		$1,500	$2,200

John Mayer Limited Edition Black1 Stratocaster

2010. Custom Shop, 83 made, black finish NOS or extreme relic option, JC serial number, Custom Shop/John Cruz logo on back of headstock includes personal letter from John Mayer.

2010	Extreme Relic	$12,000	$18,000
2010	NOS	$2,200	$3,300

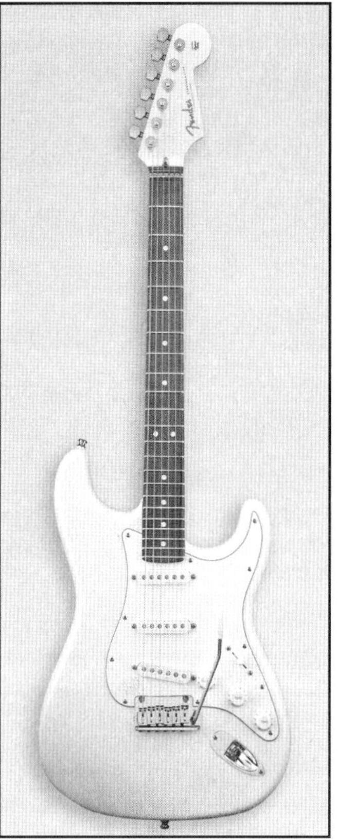

Fender Jeff Beck Signature Stratocaster (CS)

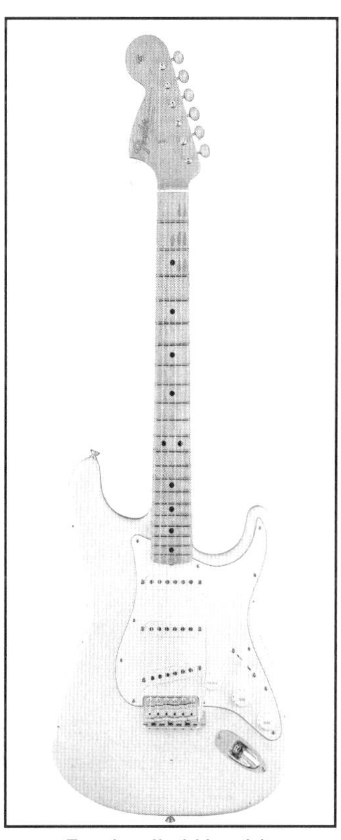

Fender Jimi Hendrix Voodoo Child Stratocaster Journeyman Relic

2006 Fender Masterbuilt Stratocaster
David Stone

Fender Noventa Stratocaster

MODEL YEAR	FEATURES	EXC. COND. LOW	HIGH

John Mayer Limited Edition Cypress Mica Stratocaster

2007. Limited run of 500, alder body, maple neck, 3 single-coil pickups, Cypress Mica finish.

2007		$2,500	$5,000

John Mayer Stratocaster

2005-2014. Alder body, special scooped mid-range pickups, vintage tremolo, special design gig bag with pocket for laptop computer.

2005-2014		$1,500	$2,200

Kenny Wayne Shepherd Stratocaster

2009-2016, 2020-present. Artist series, based on Shepherd's '61, rosewood 'board, jumbo frets, Artic White with cross, black with racing stripes or 3-color sunburst. Reintroduced '20, chambered ash body, 3 single-coil pickups, trans Faded Sonic Blue with matching painted headstock.

2009-2016	Import	$800	$1,200
2020-2024	US-made	$1,800	$2,800

Koa Stratocaster

2006-2008. Made in Korea, Special Edition series, sunburst over koa veneer top, plain script Fender logo, serial number on back of headstock with.

2006-2008		$700	$1,000

Kon Tiki Stratocaster

2003. Custom Shop, limited run of 25, Tiki Green including Tiki 3-color artwork on headstock.

2003		$5,000	$8,000

Lenny Stratocaster

Introduced Dec. 12, 2007 by Guitar Center stores, Custom Shop model, 185 guitars made, initial product offering price was 17K.

2007		$9,000	$15,000

Limited Roasted Tomatillo Stratocaster Relic

2019-2020. Custom Shop Limited Edition series, roasted alder body and 4A flame maple neck, various colors with Relic lacquer finish.

2019-2020		$3,500	$5,000

Lincoln Brewster Signature Stratocaster

2019-present. Ash body, 1-piece maple neck, 3 single-coil pickups, gold with lacquer finish.

2019-2024		$1,000	$1,500

Lite Ash Stratocaster Special Edition

2004-2007. Korea, light ash body, birds-eye maple neck.

2004-2007		$600	$900

Lone Star Stratocaster

1996-2001. Alder body, 1 humbucker and 2 single-coil pickups, rosewood 'board or maple neck, various colors.

1996	50th Anniv Badge	$1,200	$1,800
1997-2001		$1,000	$1,500

Mark Kendrick Master Design '65 Stratocaster

2004. Custom Shop Limited Edition, run of 65, alder body, maple neck, African rosewood 'board, Lake Placid Blue over Olympic White.

2004		$3,500	$5,000

Mark Knopfler Stratocaster

2003-2013. '57 body with '62 maple neck.

2003-2013		$1,800	$2,800

Masterbuilt Custom Shop Stratocaster

2006-present. Builder Select series, various models and builders, specific identification to builder, must include certificate of authenticity.

2006-2024	Various models	$5,000	$25,000

Matthias Jabs Signature Stratocaster

1998. Made in Japan, 200 offered, Candy Apple Red.

1998		$1,500	$2,200

Michael Landau Signature Relic Stratocaster 1963/1968

2014-present. Custom Shop Artist series, Relic, alder body, rosewood 'board, '63 is worn Fiesta Red over 3-color sunburst, '68 is black or bleached 3-color sunburst.

2014-2024	1963 Relic	$3,500	$5,500
2014-2024	1968 Relic	$3,500	$5,500

Milonga Deluxe Stratocaster

2005. Special Edition made in Mexico, Vintage Noiseless pickups, rosewood 'board, Olympic White, gold hardware.

2005		$800	$1,200

MLB Major League Baseball Stratocaster

2014. Official team logos and imagery unique to each, licensed by Major League Baseball Properties.

2014	Various models	$900	$1,400

Mod Shop Stratocaster

2017-present. Mod Shop allows you to create your own factory-customized electric guitar or bass.

2017-2024		$1,500	$2,200

Modern Player Stratocaster HSH/HSS

2013-2015. Made in China, hum-single-hum or hum-single-single.

2013-2015		$500	$800

Moto Limited Edition Stratocaster

1995. Custom Shop model, pearloid cover in various colors, includes Certificate of Authenticity, not to be confused with white pearloid Moto Strat which is part of a guitar and amp set (as listed below).

1995		$2,000	$3,000

Moto Set Stratocaster

1995-1996. Custom Shop set including guitar, case, amp, and amp stand, white pearloid finish.

1995-1996	Red (few made)	$7,500	$12,000
1995-1996	White	$6,000	$9,000

Noventa Stratocaster

2021-2024. Alder body, maple neck, Pau Ferro 'board, 2 single-coil pickups, Crimson Red Trans, Daphne Blue or Surf Green.

2021-2024		$800	$1,200

Orange Krush Limited Edition Stratocaster

1995. Custom Shop, 25 made, based on '57 Strat, orange finish with matching headstock, certificate of authenticity.

1995		$4,000	$6,000

Paisley Stratocaster

1984-1997, 2003-2004, 2008. Japanese-made '72 Strat reissue with a reissue '68 Tele Pink Paisley finish, large headstock until mid-'94, 'Made in Japan' logo used until early-'97, 'Crafted in Japan' after.

1984-1987	1st issue	$2,000	$3,000
1988-1994	MIJ	$1,800	$2,800

MODEL YEAR	FEATURES	EXC. COND. LOW	HIGH
1995-1997	MIJ	$1,500	$2,200
2003-2004	CIJ	$1,200	$1,800
2008	2nd issue, 200 made	$1,200	$1,800

Parallel Universe Volume II Strat Jazz Deluxe

2019-2021. Limited Edition, alder body, 2 pickups, Mystic Surf Green with nitro lacquer finish.

2019-2021		$1,500	$2,200

Parallel Universe Volume II Strat-Tele Hybrid

2017-2018. Limited Edition, Tele body, Strat neck and headstock, 3 single-coil Strat pickups, 2-color sunburst with gloss nitro lacquer finish.

2017-2018		$1,500	$2,200

Playboy 40th Anniversary Stratocaster

1994. Custom Shop, 175 made, nude Marilyn Monroe graphic on body.

1994		$20,000	$30,000

Player Plus Stratocaster

2021-present. Alder body, maple neck, 3 Noiseless Stat pickups, various colors.

2021-2024		$800	$1,200

Player Series Stratocaster

2017-present. Various models include SSS, HSS, HSH, HSS Plus, Floyd Rose, SSS LH and SSS Plus, various colors and finishes.

2017-2024	SSS, HSS, HSH	$600	$1,000
2018-2023	Floyd Rose HSS	$800	$1,200
2018-2024	Plus Top SSS, HSS	$600	$1,000

Post Modern Stratocaster (Custom Shop)

2015-2019. Offered in Journeyman Relic, NOS, and lush Closet Classic finishes.

2015-2017	NOS	$3,000	$4,500
2016-2019	Journeyman Relic	$4,000	$6,000
2019	Closet Classic	$3,000	$4,500

Post Modern Stratocaster Closet Classic (Custom Shop)

2019-2020. Made exclusive for Sweetwater, certificate.

2019-2020	Aged natural	$3,500	$5,500

Post Modern Stratocaster Journeyman Relic (Custom Shop)

2019-2020. Made exclusively for Sweetwater, alder or ash, certificate.

2019-2020	Alder or ash	$4,000	$6,000

Post Modern Stratocaster NOS (Custom Shop)

2019-2020. Made exclusive for Sweetwater, certificate.

2019-2020	Aged natural	$3,000	$4,500

Powerhouse/Powerhouse Deluxe Stratocaster

1997-2010. Made in Mexico, Standard Strat configuration with pearloid 'guard, various colors.

1997-2010		$700	$1,000
2005	Powerbridge, TRS stereo	$700	$1,000

Rarities Stratocaster

2019-2020. Rarities Collection series, limited edition, models include Flame Maple Top, Flame KOA Top, Quilt Maple Top.

2019-2020	Various models	$2,500	$3,800

Richie Sambora Stratocaster

1993-2002. U.S. and Mexico models offered, alder body, Floyd Rose tremolo, maple neck, various colors.

1993-2002	USA	$2,500	$4,000
1994-2002	Mexico	$800	$1,200
1995-1997	Mexico, swirl color	$1,000	$1,500

Ritchie Blackmore Stratocaster

2009-present. Based on Blackmore's '70s large headstock model, scalloped rosewood 'board, Duncan Quarter Pound Flat pickups, Olympic White.

2009-2024		$900	$1,400

Ritchie Blackmore Tribute Stratocaster

2014. Custom Shop, '68 specs, maple neck.

2014		$4,000	$6,000

Roadhouse Stratocaster

1997-2000. U.S.-made, poplar body, tortoise shell 'guard, maple 'board, 3 Texas Special pickups, various colors.

1997-2000		$800	$1,200

Robert Cray Signature Stratocaster

1991-present. Custom Shop, rosewood 'board, chunky neck, lighter weight, non-trem, alder body, gold-plated hardware, various colors.

1991-2024		$3,500	$5,000

Robert Cray Stratocaster (Mexico)

1996-present. Artist series, chrome hardware.

1996-2024		$800	$1,200

Robin Trower Signature Stratocaster

2004-present. Custom Shop Custom Artist series, 100 made, large headstock (post '65-era), with '70s logo and 3-bolt neck, bullet truss rod, white.

2004-2024		$3,500	$5,500

Rory Gallagher Tribute Stratocaster

2004-present. Custom Shop, based on Gallagher's '61 model, heavily distressed, price includes the original certificate.

2004-2024		$4,000	$6,500

Sandblasted Stratocaster

2014-2015, 2019-2020. Limited Edition series, ash body, sandblasted finish. Limited run '19-'20 exclusive for Sweetwater USA.

2014-2015		$900	$1,400
2019-2020	Sweetwater	$1,000	$1,500

Select Stratocaster

2012-2015. Select Series, figured top, rear-headstock 'Fender Select' medallion, gloss-lacquer finish, various colors.

2012-2015		$2,000	$3,000

Set-Neck Stratocaster

1992-1999. Custom Shop model, mahogany body and figured maple top, 4 pickups, glued-in neck, active electronics, by '96 ash body.

1992-1999		$4,500	$6,500

Short-Scale (7/8) Stratocaster

1989-1995. Similar to Standard Strat, but with 2 control knobs and switch, 24" scale vs. 25" scale, sometimes called a mini-Strat, Japanese import, various colors.

1989-1995		$800	$1,200

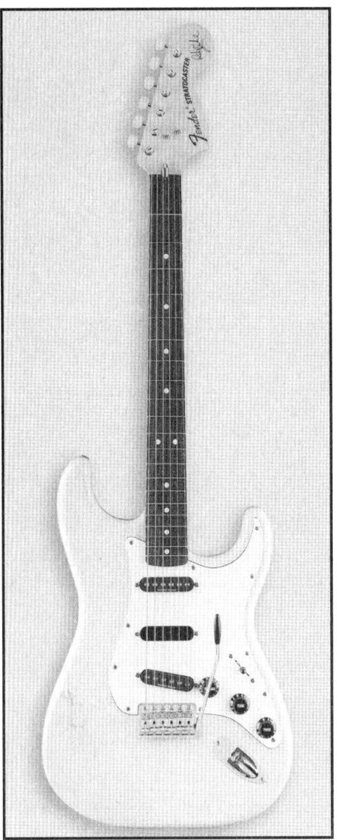

Fender Ritchie Blackmore Stratocaster

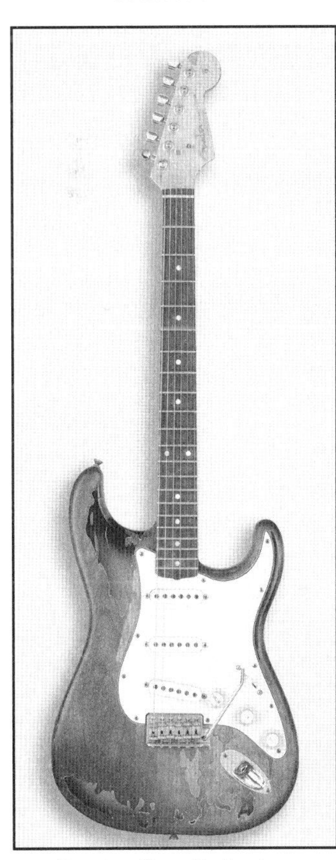

Fender Rory Gallagher Tribute Stratocaster

GUITARS

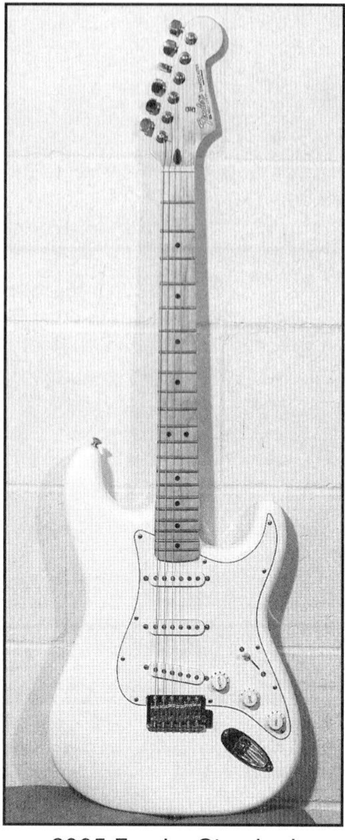
2005 Fender Standard Stratocaster (Mexico)
Tom Pfeifer

1988 Fender Strat Plus
Scott Anderson

MODEL YEAR	FEATURES	EXC. COND. LOW	HIGH

So-Cal J.W. Black Stratocaster

2000-2001. Custom Shop, So-Cal logo art on body, 20 offered.

2000-2001		$7,500	$12,000

So-Cal Speed Shop Stratocaster

2005-2006. Limited Edition for Musician's Friend, red, white, and black So-Cal paint job, basswood body, rosewood 'board, 1 humbucker, So-Cal Speed Shop decal.

2005-2006		$800	$1,200

Special Edition David Lozeau Art Stratocaster

2015-2016. Finishes include orange Tree of Life, blue Dragon, yellow Rose Tattoo and red Sacred Heart, etched David Lozeau neck plate.

2015-2016		$600	$900

Special Edition Stratocaster

2004-2009. Import model, Special Edition oval logo on back of headstock, various styles offered, '50s or '60s vintage copy specs, maple 'board, ash or koa body, see-thru or opaque finish.

2004-2009		$600	$900

Special Edition Stratocaster (Matching Headstock)

2016-2017. Made in Mexico, various colors with matching headstock.

2016-2017		$600	$900

Special Edition White Opal Stratocaster

2016. Made in Mexico, white opal body and headstock, pearloid 'guard, 3 humbuckers.

2016		$600	$900

Splatter Stratocaster

2003. Made in Mexico, splatter paint job, various color combinations, with gig bag.

2003		$800	$1,200

Standard Roland Ready Stratocaster

1998-2011. Made in Mexico, built-in Roland pickup system and 3 single-coils.

1998-2011		$600	$900

Standard Stratocaster (Japan)

1985-1989. Interim production in Japan while the new Fender reorganized, standard pickup configuration and tremolo system, 3 knobs with switch, traditional style input jack, traditional shaped headstock, offered in black, red or white.

1985-1989		$1,000	$1,500

Standard Stratocaster (Mexico)

1990-2018. Made in Mexico, renamed Player Series in '18. Not to be confused with the American-made Standard Stratocaster of '81-'84. Various models and colors, high-end range includes a hard guitar case, while low-end includes only a gig bag.

1990-2018	Various models	$500	$1,200

Standard Stratocaster Plus Top

2014-2018. Made in Mexico, alder body with flamed maple top. Renamed Player Series Plus Top in '18.

2014-2018		$600	$900

Standard Stratocaster Satin Finish

2003-2006. Basically Mexico-made Standard with satin finish.

2003-2006		$500	$800

MODEL YEAR	FEATURES	EXC. COND. LOW	HIGH

Steve Miller The Joker American Stratocaster

2000s. Alder body, maple neck, rosewood 'board, black with "Joker" graphic.

2000s		$20,000	$30,000

Stevie Ray Vaughan Signature Stratocaster

1992-present. U.S.-made, alder body, sunburst, gold hardware, SRV 'guard, lefty tremolo, Brazilian rosewood 'board (pau ferro by '93).

1992	1st year, Brazilian	$5,000	$8,000
1992-2024	Pau Ferro	$2,200	$3,500

Stevie Ray Vaughan Signature Stratocaster (Custom Shop)

2019-present. Custom Artist series, 3-color sunburst with NOS or aged relic lacquer finish.

2019-2024	NOS	$4,000	$6,000
2019-2024	Relic	$5,000	$7,000

Stevie Ray Vaughan Tribute #1 Stratocaster

2004. Custom Shop Limited Edition, recreation of SRV's #1 made by Master Builder John Cruz in the Custom Shop, 100 made, $10,000 MSRP, includes flight case stenciled "SRV - Number One," and other goodies.

2004		$20,000	$30,000

Strat Plus

1987-1999. Three Lace Sensor pickups, alder (poplar available earlier) body, tremolo, rosewood 'board or maple neck, various colors. See Deluxe Strat Plus for ash veneer version.

1987-1999	Various colors	$1,200	$1,800

Stratocaster Junior

2004-2006. Import, short 22.7" scale, Alder body, non-trem hardtail bridge.

2004-2006		$600	$900

Stratocaster Pro Closet Classic (Custom Shop)

2006-2013. Ash body, early '60s neck, rosewood or maple board, solid or sunburst finish.

2006-2013		$3,000	$4,500

Stratocaster Pro NOS (Custom Shop)

2012-2016. Ash body, maple neck, rosewood 'board, solid or 3-tone sunburst.

2012-2016		$3,000	$4,500

Stratocaster Special

1993-1995. Made in Mexico, a humbucker and a single-coil pickup, 1 volume, 1 tone.

1993-1995		$500	$800

Stratocaster XII

1988-1997, 2003-2010. 1st version Japanese-made, alder body, 22-fret rosewood 'board. 2nd version is 21-fret Classic Series model for 2 years then Classic Series.

1988-1997	1st version	$1,200	$1,800
2003-2010	2nd version	$1,000	$1,500

Strat-o-Sonic

2003-2006. American Special Series, Stratocaster-style chambered body, includes Strat-o-Sonic Dove I (1 pickup, '03 only), Dove II/DV II (2 black P-90s, '03-'06) and HH (2 humbuckers, '05-'06).

2003	Dove I	$1,200	$1,800
2003-2006	Dove II/DV II	$1,200	$1,800
2003-2006	HH	$1,200	$1,800

MODEL YEAR	FEATURES	EXC. COND. LOW	HIGH

Sub Sonic Stratocaster

2000-2001. Baritone model, offered in 2 production models - HH (2 humbuckers, 2000-'01), HSS (hum-single-single, '01) - and in a Custom Shop version of the HSS (2000-'01).

2000-2001		$1,200	$1,800
2000-2001	Custom Shop, COA	$3,000	$4,500

Super Stratocaster

1997-2003. Deluxe series, made in Mexico, 3 Super Fat single-coils, Super Switching gives 2 extra pickup options, gold tremolo.

1997-2003		$600	$900

Supreme Stratocaster

2017. Limited Edition, collaboration with Supreme (NY-based fashion brand), all white color with red Supreme logo on front.

2017		$5,000	$6,500

Tanqurey Tonic Stratocaster

1988. Made for a Tanqurey Tonic liquor ad campaign giveaway in '88, Tanqurey Tonic Green; many were given to winners around the country, ads said that they could also be purchased through Tanqurey, but that apparently didn't happen.

1988		$2,500	$4,500

Tash Sultana Stratocaster

2020-present. Artist series, all gold hardware, aged white pearl 'guard, trans cherry finish with matching painted headstock.

2020-2024		$1,000	$1,500

Texas Special Stratocaster

1991-1992. Custom Shop, 50 made, state of Texas map stamped on neck plate, Texas Special pickups, maple fretboard, sunburst.

1991-1992		$2,000	$3,000

The Edge Stratocaster

2016-2020. U2 guitarist The Edge signature on large '70s-style headstock, alder body, 1-piece quartersawn maple neck and 'board, 3 pickups, black.

2016-2020		$1,800	$2,800

The Strat

1980-1983. Alder body, 4-bolt neck, large STRAT on painted peghead, gold-plated brass hardware, various colors.

1980-1983		$1,500	$2,200

Tie-Dye Stratocaster

2004-2005. Single-coil neck and humbucker bridge pickups, Band of Gypsies or Hippie Blue tie-dye pattern, poly finish.

2004-2005		$600	$900

Tom Delonge Stratocaster

2001-2004. 1 humbucker, rosewood back and sides. Also in Squier version.

2001-2004		$800	$1,200

Tom Morello "Soul Power" Stratocaster

2020-2024. Alder body, rosewood 'board, black with white 'guard. Shipped with "Soul Power" decal for face of guitar.

2020-2024		$1,000	$1,500

Tree of Life Stratocaster

1993. Custom Shop, 29 made, tree of life fretboard inlay, 1-piece quilted maple body.

1993		$7,500	$12,000

Turquoise Sparkle Stratocaster

2001. Custom Shop, limited run of 75 for Mars Music, turquoise sparkle finish.

2001		$5,000	$7,500

U.S. Ultra / Ultra Plus Stratocaster

1990-1997. Alder body with figured maple veneer on front and back, single Lace Sensor pickups in neck and middle, double Sensor at bridge, ebony 'board, sunburst.

1990-1997		$1,800	$2,800

Ventures Limited Edition Stratocaster

1996. Japanese-made tribute model, matches Jazzmaster equivalent, black.

1996		$1,800	$2,800

VG Stratocaster

2007-2009. American Series, modeling technology using Roland's VG circuitry, 5 guitar tone banks deliver 16 sounds.

2007-2009		$1,200	$1,800

Vintage Hot Rod Stratocaster

2007-2014. Vintage styling with modern features, '07-'13 named '57 Strat and '62 Strat, in '14 changed to '50s and '60s.

2007-2014	All models	$1,500	$2,200

Vintera Series Stratocaster

2019-2024. Modified and non-modified '50s, '60s and '70s Strat models, various options and colors.

2019-2020	'70s	$800	$1,200
2019-2020	'70s modified	$800	$1,200
2019-2024	'50s	$800	$1,200
2019-2024	'50s modified	$800	$1,200
2019-2024	'60s	$800	$1,200
2019-2024	'60s modified	$800	$1,200

Walnut Elite Stratocaster

1983-1984. The Elite Series features active electronics and noise-cancelling pickups, Walnut Elite has a walnut body and neck, gold-plated hardware and pearloid tuner buttons. Also see Elite Stratocaster and Gold Elite Stratocaster.

1983-1984		$2,000	$3,000

Walnut Stratocaster

1981-1983. American black walnut body and 1-piece neck and 'board.

1981-1983		$1,800	$2,800

Wayne Kramer Signature/MC5 Stratocaster

2011. Red-white-blue paint graphics, humbucking pickup in center position.

2011		$1,500	$2,200

Western Stratocaster

1995. Custom Shop, only 5 made, featured in Fender Custom Shop book from the 1990s.

1995		$10,000	$15,000

Whiteguard Stratocaster Limited Edition

2018. Limited Edition neck plate, ash body, Tele hardware and white 'guard, 2 single-coil pickups, lacquer finish.

2018		$1,200	$1,800

Yngwie Malmsteen Double-Neck Stratocaster

1992-1993. Japan, less than 200 made, 12- and 6-string, scalloped necks, basswood body.

1992-1993		$5,000	$12,000

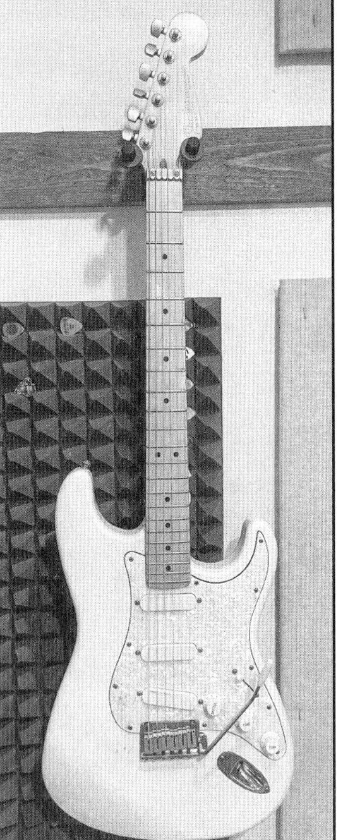

1991 Fender Strat Plus
David Mullins.

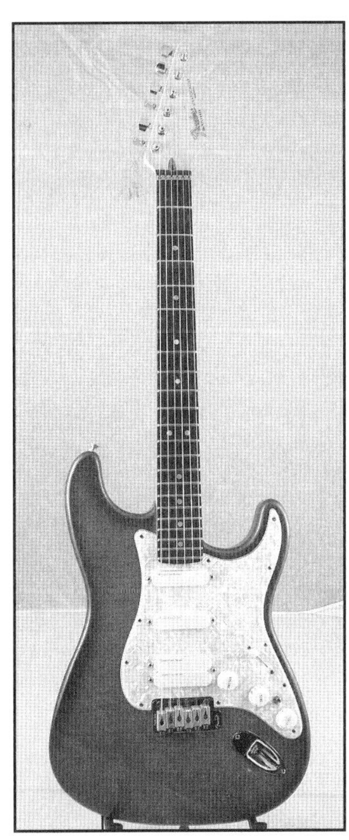

1993 Fender U.S. Ultra Stratocaster
Keith Myers

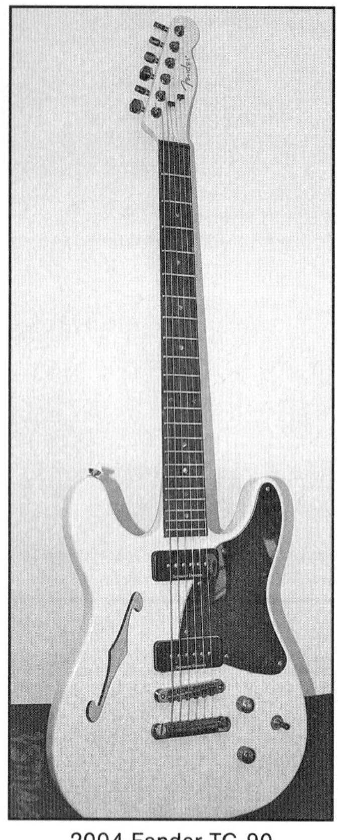

2004 Fender TC-90
Dave Meyer

1952 Fender Telecaster
Trey Rabinek

MODEL YEAR	FEATURES	EXC. COND. LOW	HIGH

Yngwie Malmsteen Signature Stratocaster (Custom Shop)

2020-present. Custom Artist series, 2-piece select alder body, flat sawn maple neck, various colors with nitro lacquer finish.

2020-2024		$4,000	$6,000

Yngwie Malmsteen Stratocaster

1988-present. U.S.-made, maple neck, scalloped 'board, 3 single-coil pickups, Vintage White.

1988-2024		$1,200	$1,800

Yngwie Malmsteen Tribute Stratocaster

2008-2009. Custom Shop, heavy relic version of Malmsteen's '71 blond Strat with maple neck.

2008-2009		$4,000	$6,000

Swinger

1969-1972. See listing for Musiclander.

SX Series

1992-1995. Dreadnought and jumbo acoustics, ply or solid spruce tops with various wood options on back and sides, E models with electronics.

1992-1995	Various models	$200	$1,000

T-Bucket 300CE

2016-2018. Acoustic/electric, D-size, cutaway.

2016-2018		$225	$350

TC-90/TC-90 Thinline

2004-2007. Made in Korea, 2 single-coil P90s, double-cut, Vintage White or Black Cherry Burst.

2004-2007		$500	$750

Telecaster

The following are all variations of the Telecaster. Broadcaster and Nocaster models are under Broadcaster. The first five listings are for the main American-made line. All others are listed alphabetically after that in the following order:

Telecaster
Standard Telecaster
American Standard Telecaster
American Series Telecaster
American Professional/Professional II Telecaster
30th Anniversary Guitar Center Tree of Life Telecaster
40th Anniversary Telecaster
'50 Custom Telecaster
'50s Telecaster/Classic Series '50s Telecaster
Road Worn '50s Telecaster
50th Anniversary Spanish Guitar Set
50th Anniversary Telecaster
'52 Telecaster/American Vintage '52 Telecaster
American Vintage '52 Telecaster Korina (U.S.A.)
'52 Telecaster (Custom Shop)
'52 LTD Telecaster NOS
'52 Vintage Telecaster (Japan)
'54 Telecaster (Custom Shop)
'56 Telecaster (JC Serial Number)
'58 Telecaster (Custom Shop)
American Vintage '58 Telecaster (U.S.A.)
'60s Telecaster Custom
'60s Telecaster/Classic Series '60s Telecaster
American Original '60s Telecaster
American Original '60s Telecaster Thinline
'60 Telecaster Custom
60th Anniversary American Telecaster
60th Anniversary Telecaster (U.S.A.)
60th Anniversary Telecaster Limited Edition
'61 Telecaster Custom
'62 Telecaster Custom (Import)
'62 Telecaster Custom (U.S.A.)
'62 Mod Squad Custom Telecaster
'62 Telecaster Reissue (Japan)
Junkyard Dog 1962 Telecaster Relic
'63 Telecaster (Custom Shop)
'63 Telecaster Custom Relic LTD
'64 Telecaster Limited Relic
American Vintage '64 Telecaster
'67 Telecaster (Custom Shop)
'68 Telecaster Rosewood
'69 Tele/Telecaster Thinline (Import)
'69 Telecaster Thinline (Custom Shop)
'72 Telecaster Custom/Classic Series '72 Telecaster Custom
'72 Telecaster Deluxe/Classic Series '72 Telecaster Deluxe
'72 Telecaster Thinline American Vintage
'72 Telecaster Thinline/Classic Series Telecaster Thinline
1972 Telecaster Custom Closet Classic
75th Anniversary Commemorative Telecaster
75th Anniversary Telecaster
'90s Telecaster Deluxe
'90s Telecaster Thinline
1998 Collectors Edition Telecaster
Aerodyne Telecaster
Albert Collins Telecaster
Aluminum Telecaster
American Acoustasonic Telecaster
American Classic Holoflake Telecaster
American Classic Telecaster
American Deluxe HH Telecaster
American Deluxe Power Telecaster
American Deluxe Telecaster
American Deluxe B Bender Telecaster
American Deluxe/Elite Telecaster Thinline
American Elite Telecaster
American Nashville B-Bender Telecaster
American Performer Telecaster
American Professional II Telecaster Deluxe
American Professional Telecaster Deluxe Shawbucker
American Rustic Ash Telecaster
American Special Telecaster
American Standard Telecaster Limited Edition
American Standard Telecaster Special Edition
American Ultra Luxe Telecaster
American Ultra Telecaster
Andy Summers Masterbuilt Tribute Telecaster
Antigua Telecaster
Big Block Telecaster
Bigsby Telecaster
Blacktop Telecaster Series
Blue Flower Telecaster
Bowling Ball/Marble Telecaster
Britt Daniel Telecaster Thinline

Brown's Canyon Redwood Telecaster
Buck Owens Limited Edition Telecaster
Cabronita Telecaster (American Standard)
Cabronita Telecaster (Classic Player)
Cabronita Telecaster Thinline
California Fat Telecaster
California Telecaster
Chrissie Hynde Telecaster
Clarence White Telecaster (Custom Shop)
Classic Player Baja Telecaster
Collector's Edition Telecaster
Contemporary Telecaster (Import)
Custom Carved Telecaster HH
Custom Classic Telecaster
Custom Deluxe Telecaster
Custom Plus Telecaster
Custom Telecaster
Danny Gatton Signature Telecaster
Deluxe Nashville Power Telecaster
Deluxe Nashville Telecaster (Mexico)
Deluxe Telecaster (U.S.A.)
Elite Nashville Telecaster
Elite Telecaster
Fat Telecaster
GD (Global Designs) Telecaster
G.E. Smith Telecaster
Graham Coxon Special Run Telecaster
GT11 Telecaster
Highway One Telecaster/Texas Telecaster
HMT Telecaster (Import)
J5 Triple Telecaster Deluxe
J5/John 5 Signature Telecaster (Custom Shop)
James Burton Standard Telecaster
James Burton Telecaster
Jason Isbell Custom Telecaster
Jerry Donahue JD Telecaster
Jerry Donahue Telecaster
Jim Adkins JA-90 Telecaster Thinline
Jim Root Telecaster
Jimmy Bryant Tribute Telecaster
Jimmy Page Mirror Telecaster
Jimmy Page Telecaster
Joe Strummer Telecaster
John Jorgenson Telecaster
Jr. Telecaster
La Cabronita Especial Telecaster
Mahogany Offset Telecaster
Marty Stuart Telecaster
Merle Haggard Signature Telecaster
Mod Shop Telecaster
Modern Player Telecaster Plus
Moto Limited Edition Telecaster
Muddy Waters Signature Telecaster Custom
Muddy Waters Tribute Telecaster
Nashville Telecaster
NHL Premier Edition Telecaster
Nokie Edwards Telecaster
Noventa Telecaster
Old Pine Telecaster
Paisley Telecaster
Palo Escrito Telecaster
Parallel Universe Jazz-Tele
Parallel Universe Troublemaker Telecaster

MODEL YEAR	FEATURES	EXC. COND. LOW	HIGH

Parallel Universe Volume II Tele Mágico
Player Telecaster
Player II Telecaster
Plus Telecaster
Rarities Telecaster
Richie Kotzen Telecaster
Rosewood Telecaster
Rosewood Telecaster (Japan)
Rosewood Telelcaster Limited Edition
Select Telecaster
Select Telecaster Thinline
Set-Neck Telecaster
Snakehead Telecaster
Sparkle Telecaster
Special Edition Custom Telecaster FMT HH
Special Edition Deluxe Ash Telecaster
Special Edition Koa Telecaster
Special Edition White Opal Telecaster
Special Telecaster/Telecaster Special
Standard Telecaster (Japan)
Standard Telecaster (Mexico)
Telecaster (Japanese Domestic)
Telecaster Custom
Telecaster Custom (Japan)
Telecaster Custom FMT HH (Korea)
Telecaster Stratocaster Hybrid
Telecaster Thinline
Tele-Sonic
Texas Special Telecaster
TV Jones Telecaster/Custom Shop Double TV Jones Telecaster NOS
Twisted Telecaster Limited Edition
Two-Tone Telecaster Thinline
Vintage Hot Rod Telecaster
Voodoo Lounge Supreme Telecaster
Waylon Jennings Tribute Telecaster
Will Ray Signature Jazz-A-Caster
Will Ray Signature Mojo Telecaster

Telecaster

1951-1982. See Standard Telecaster (following listing) for '82-'85, American Standard Telecaster for '88-'00, the American Series Telecaster for '00-'07. and the American Standard Telecaster (again) for '08-'16. Currently called the American Professional Telecaster. Please refer to the Fender Guitar Intro Section for details on Fender color options.

In the late '60s and early '70s Fender began to increase their use of vibrato tailpieces. A vibrato tailpiece for this period is generally worth about 13% less than the values shown.

From '63-'70, Fender offered both the standard Brazilian rosewood fretboard and an optional maple fretboard. Prices listed here, for those years, are for the rosewood 'board models. Currently, the market considers the maple 'board to be a premium, so Telecasters with maple, for those years, are worth 10% to 15% more than the values shown.

1951	Blond, black 'guard	$60,000	$80,000
1952	Blond, black 'guard	$50,000	$75,000
1953	Blond, black 'guard	$50,000	$75,000
1954	Blond, black 'guard	$50,000	$75,000

1956 Fender Telecaster
Frank Manno

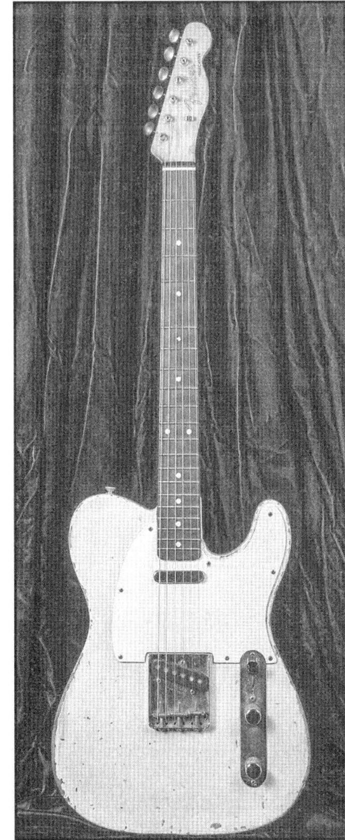

1961 Fender Telecaster
Gordon Kennedy

GUITARS

1966 Fender Telecaster
Rivington Guitars

1967 Fender Telecaster
Lynn Rose

MODEL YEAR	FEATURES	EXC. COND. LOW	HIGH
1954	Blond, white 'guard	$35,000	$50,000
1955	Blond, white 'guard	$35,000	$50,000
1956	Blond	$35,000	$50,000
1957	Blond, backloader	$30,000	$45,000
1958	Blond, backloader	$27,000	$40,000
1958	Blond, top loader	$25,000	$35,000
1958	Sunburst, backloader	$30,000	$45,000
1958	Sunburst, top loader	$27,000	$45,000
1959	Blond, maple	$25,000	$35,000
1959	Blond, slab	$25,000	$35,000
1959	Custom color	$65,000	$85,000
1959	Sunburst, maple	$30,000	$45,000
1959	Sunburst, slab	$30,000	$45,000
1960	Blond, slab	$24,000	$35,000
1960	Common color	$40,000	$55,000
1960	Rare color	$50,000	$75,000
1960	Sunburst, slab	$28,000	$40,000
1961	Blond, slab	$22,000	$32,000
1961	Common color	$35,000	$50,000
1961	Rare color	$50,000	$65,000
1961	Sunburst, slab	$25,000	$35,000
1962	Blond, curve	$18,000	$25,000
1962	Blond, slab	$20,000	$30,000
1962	Common color	$30,000	$45,000
1962	Rare color	$40,000	$60,000
1962	Sunburst, curve	$20,000	$30,000
1962	Sunburst, slab	$22,500	$35,000
1963	Blond	$18,000	$25,000
1963	Common color	$30,000	$45,000
1963	Rare color	$40,000	$60,000
1963	Sunburst	$20,000	$30,000
1963-1964	Mahogany, see-thru cherry	$35,000	$45,000
1964	Blond	$15,500	$22,000
1964	Common color	$25,000	$35,000
1964	Rare color	$30,000	$45,000
1964	Sunburst	$18,000	$25,000
1965	Blond	$13,500	$20,000
1965	Common color	$20,000	$30,000
1965	Early '65, Sunburst	$16,500	$23,000
1965	Late '65, Sunburst	$15,500	$20,000
1965	Rare color	$30,000	$40,000
1966	Blond	$11,500	$18,000
1966	Common color	$18,000	$25,000
1966	Rare color	$20,000	$30,000
1966	Sunburst	$12,500	$18,000
1967	Blond	$10,500	$16,000
1967	Blond, smuggler	$13,500	$20,000
1967	Common color	$16,000	$22,000
1967	Rare color	$20,000	$30,000
1967	Sunburst	$12,500	$18,000
1968	Blond	$10,000	$15,000
1968	Blue Flora	$20,000	$30,000
1968	Common color	$15,000	$20,000
1968	Pink Paisley	$20,000	$30,000
1968	Rare color	$20,000	$30,000
1968	Sunburst	$12,000	$18,000
1969	Blond, poly	$8,000	$12,000
1969	Blue Flora	$20,000	$25,000
1969	Common color, poly	$12,000	$18,000
1969	Pink Paisley	$20,000	$25,000
1969	Rare color, poly	$18,000	$25,000
1969	Sunburst, poly	$9,000	$15,000
1970	Blond, poly	$7,500	$10,000
1970	Common color, poly	$10,000	$15,000
1970	Rare color, poly	$15,000	$20,000
1970	Sunburst, poly	$7,500	$11,000
1971	Blond	$6,500	$8,500
1971	Common color	$8,000	$12,000
1971	Rare color	$10,000	$15,000
1971	Sunburst	$6,500	$8,500
1972	Blond	$5,800	$7,500
1972	Common color	$8,000	$10,000
1972	Natural	$4,800	$6,000
1972	Rare color	$12,000	$15,000
1972	Sunburst	$5,800	$7,500
1973	Black, white	$4,200	$5,500
1973	Blond	$4,200	$5,500
1973	Natural	$3,800	$5,000
1973	Rare color	$8,000	$11,000
1973	Sunburst	$4,200	$5,500
1973	Walnut	$3,800	$5,000
1974	Blond, black, white	$4,000	$5,000
1974	Natural	$3,300	$4,500
1974	Sunburst	$4,200	$5,500
1974	Walnut	$3,300	$4,500
1975	Blond, black, white	$3,800	$5,000
1975	Natural	$3,300	$4,500
1975	Sunburst	$3,800	$5,000
1975	Walnut	$3,300	$4,500
1976	Blond, black, white	$3,300	$4,500
1976	Natural	$3,000	$4,000
1976	Sunburst	$3,300	$4,500
1976	Walnut	$3,000	$4,000
1977	Black, blond, white	$3,300	$4,500
1977	Natural	$3,000	$4,000
1977	Sunburst	$3,300	$4,500
1977	Walnut	$3,000	$4,000
1978-1979	All colors	$3,300	$4,500
1980-1981	All colors	$2,300	$3,000
1980-1981	International colors	$3,000	$3,800

Standard Telecaster

1982-1984. See Telecaster for '51-'82, and American Standard Telecaster (following listing) for '88-2000. Not to be confused with the current Standard Telecaster, which is made in Mexico.

MODEL YEAR	FEATURES	EXC. COND. LOW	HIGH
1982	Blond, sunburst	$2,300	$3,000
1983-1984	Blond, sunburst	$1,400	$2,000

American Standard Telecaster

1988-2000, 2008-2016. Name used when Fender reissued the standard American-made Tele after CBS sold the company. The only American-made Tele available for '86 and '87 was the '52 Telecaster. See Telecaster for '51-'81, and Standard Telecaster for '82-'84. All '94 models have a metal 40th Anniversary pin on the headstock but should not be confused with the actual 40th Anniversary Telecaster model (see separate listing), all standard colors. Renamed the American Series Tele-

MODEL YEAR	FEATURES	EXC. COND. LOW	HIGH

caster in 2000, then back to American Standard Series Telecaster in '08. Becomes American Professional in '17.

1988-2000		$900	$1,400
2008-2016		$900	$1,400

American Series Telecaster

2000-2007. See Telecaster for '51-'81, Standard Telecaster for '82-'84, and American Standard for '88-'99. Renamed American Standard again in '08.

2000-2007		$900	$1,400

American Professional/ Professional II Telecaster

2017-present. Model replaces American Standard Tele, redesign includes 2 V-Mod pickups, narrow-tall frets, new 'deep C' neck profile, various colors. Also available left-hand model. Renamed American Professional II in '20.

2017-2020	Pro	$900	$1,400
2020-2024	Pro II	$900	$1,400

30th Anniversary Guitar Center Tree of Life Telecaster

1994. Limited Edition, produced for 30th anniversary of Guitar Center, engraved neckplate with GC logo, tree-of-life 'board inlay.

1994		$7,500	$12,000

40th Anniversary Telecaster

1988, 1999. Custom Shop, limited edition run of 300, 2-piece flamed maple top, gold hardware ('88), flamed maple top over ash body, gold hardware ('99).

1988	1st run, high-end	$5,000	$7,500
1999	2nd run, plain top	$4,000	$6,000

'50 Custom Telecaster

1997. Custom Shop, limited run of 10, humbucker neck pickup, standard unbound body, highly figured maple neck, blackguard specs.

1997		$2,500	$4,000

'50s Telecaster/Classic Series '50s Telecaster

1990-2019. Made in Japan (basswood body) until mid '99, then in Mexico with ash body. Foto-Flame finish offered in '94 (see separate listing).

1990-1999	Japan	$1,200	$1,800
1999-2019	Mexico	$600	$900

Road Worn '50s Telecaster

2009-2019. Maple 'board, '50s specs, aged finish.

2009-2019		$800	$1,200

50th Anniversary Spanish Guitar Set

1996. Custom Shop, 50 sets made, Tele Prototype reproduction with similar era copy of woodie amp.

1996		$8,000	$12,000

50th Anniversary Telecaster

1995-1996. Custom Shop, flame maple top, 2 vintage-style pickups, gold hardware, sunburst, gold 50th Anniversary coin on back of the headstock, 1250 made.

1995-1996		$3,000	$4,500

'52 Telecaster/American Vintage '52 Telecaster

1982-1984, 1986-2017. Ash body, maple neck or rosewood 'board, blond. Replaced by the American Original '50s Telecaster.

1982-1984		$3,000	$4,500
1986-1999		$1,800	$2,800
1990-1999	Copper (limited)	$2,000	$3,000
2000-2009		$1,500	$2,200
2010-2017		$1,500	$2,200

American Vintage '52 Telecaster Korina (U.S.A.)

2015. Part of Fender's limited edition 10 for 15 series, Korina body, '52 specs.

2015		$2,500	$3,800

'52 Telecaster (Custom Shop)

2004-2018. Custom Shop Dealer Select model, NOS, Relic and Closet Classic offered, changed to Heavy Relic in '15.

2004-2012	NOS	$3,000	$4,500
2004-2014	Relic	$3,000	$4,500
2010-2011	Closet Classic	$3,000	$4,500
2015-2018	Heavy Relic	$3,000	$4,500
2007	Relic, LTD Copper	$5,000	$7,500

'52 LTD Telecaster NOS

2020. Custom Shop, ash body, maple neck, faded blonde, lacquer finish.

2020		$3,000	$4,500

'52 Vintage Telecaster (Japan)

1982-1984. Made in Japan, JV serial numbers.

1982-1984		$1,800	$2,800

'54 Telecaster (Custom Shop)

1997-1998, 2013-2016. Relic, Closet Classic available with more recent model.

2013-2016	Relic	$3,000	$4,500

'56 Telecaster (JC Serial Number)

2006. Made by General Master Builder John Cruz, JC serial number, super relic finish.

2006		$6,000	$12,000

'58 Telecaster (Custom Shop)

2008. Custom Shop, relic and heavy relic.

2008	Heavy relic	$3,000	$4,500
2008	NOS	$3,000	$4,500
2008	Relic	$3,000	$4,500

American Vintage '58 Telecaster (U.S.A.)

2013-2018. Ash body, white 'guard, Aged White Blonde.

2013-2018		$1,500	$2,200

'60s Telecaster Custom

1997-1999. Custom Shop, bound alder body, sunburst, black or custom colors, nickel or gold hardware.

1997-1999		$3,000	$4,500

'60s Telecaster/Classic Series '60s Telecaster

1992-2019. Made in Japan (basswood body) until mid '99, then in Mexico with ash body. Foto-Flame finish offered in '94 (see separate listing). '06 version may have 60th Anniversary Badge on back of headstock.

1992-1996	Made in Japan	$900	$1,400
1997-1999	Crafted in Japan	$800	$1,200
1999-2019	Mexico	$600	$900

American Original '60s Telecaster

2018-2023. '60s specs, rosewood 'board, alder body.

2018-2023		$1,200	$1,800

American Original '60s Telecaster Thinline

2020-2023. '60s specs, ash body, maple neck, aged natural, 3-color sunburst or Surf Green.

2020-2023		$1,200	$1,800

1970 Fender Telecaster

W. H. Stephens

2012 Fender American Standard Telecaster

Steve Alvito

GUITARS

2006 Fender 60th Anniversary Telecaster Limited Edition
Imaged by Heritage Auctions, HA.com

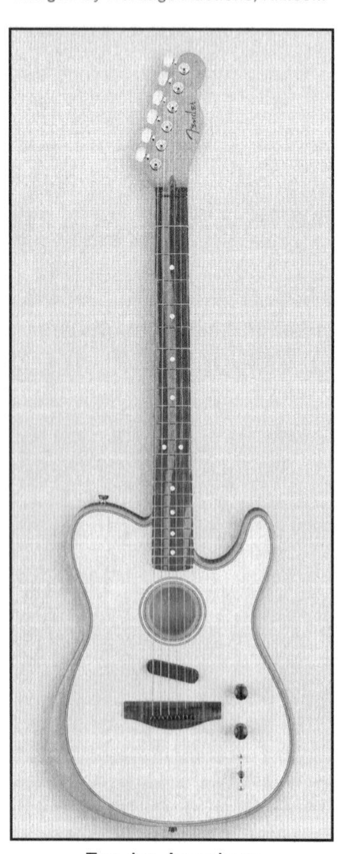
Fender American Acoustasonic Telecaster

MODEL YEAR	FEATURES	EXC. COND. LOW	HIGH

'60 Telecaster Custom
2003-2004. Custom Shop Time Machine, bound alder body, offered in NOS, Closet Classic and Relic versions and in sunburst, CA Red and Sonic Blue.

2003-2004	Closet Classic	$3,000	$4,500
2003-2004	NOS	$3,000	$4,500
2003-2004	Relic	$3,000	$4,500

60th Anniversary American Telecaster
2006-2007. Special Edition commemorating Fender's 60th year, banner headstock 60th logo, neck plate reads Diamond Anniversary 1946-2006, made in U.S.A., rosewood 'board, sunburst.

2006-2007		$1,200	$1,800

60th Anniversary Telecaster (U.S.A.)
2011-2012. Celebrating 60 years of the Tele, commemorative chrome neck plate, ash body, blonde thin-skin finish.

2011-2012		$1,500	$2,200

60th Anniversary Telecaster Limited Edition
2006. Limited Edition of 1,000, 60 Diamond Anniversary 1946-2006 logo engraved in neck plate, American Flag logo on pickguard, '51 NoCaster pickup layout, 60 wood inlay on the face below bridge, clear nitro finish on natural ash body, silver guitar case with Fender 60 logo on inside lid.

2006		$2,500	$4,000

'61 Telecaster Custom
2010-2012. Custom Shop Dealer Select model, bound body Custom, NOS, Relic or Heavy Relic.

2010-2012	Closet Classic	$3,000	$4,500
2010-2012	NOS	$3,000	$4,500
2010-2012	Relic	$3,000	$4,500

'62 Telecaster Custom (Import)
1985-1999. Made in Japan, bound top and back, rosewood 'board, sunburst or red.

1985-1989		$1,500	$2,200
1990-1999		$1,200	$1,800

'62 Telecaster Custom (U.S.A.)
1999-2012. American Vintage Series, rosewood board.

1999-2012		$1,800	$2,800

'62 Mod Squad Custom Telecaster
2013. Custom Shop, Broadcaster bridge pickup and Duncan neck humbucker.

2013		$3,000	$4,500

'62 Telecaster Reissue (Japan)
1989-1990, 2005-2006. Made by Fender Japan.

1989-1990		$1,500	$2,200
2005-2006		$1,200	$1,800

Junkyard Dog 1962 Telecaster Relic
2014-2015. Custom Shop Dealer Select series, ash body, rosewood neck and 'board, white guard, Vintage Blonde.

2014-2015		$3,000	$4,500

'63 Telecaster (Custom Shop)
1999-2010, 2018-2019. Alder body (or blond on ash), original spec pickups, C-shaped neck, rosewood 'board. Relic offered in '07 and later heavy relic in '18.

1999-2010	Closet Classic	$3,000	$4,500
1999-2010	NOS	$3,000	$4,500
2007	Relic	$3,000	$4,500
2018-2019	Heavy relic	$3,000	$4,500

'63 Telecaster Custom Relic LTD
2006. Custom Shop, Limited Edition.

2006		$3,500	$5,000

'64 Telecaster Limited Relic
2009. Custom Shop, rosewood 'board, thin nitro finish, 50 each of black, aged white, and 3-tone chocolate sunburst.

2009		$3,500	$5,000

American Vintage '64 Telecaster
2013-2018. Ash body, mid-'60s 'C' neck profile, rounded rosewood 'board, 2 vintage single-coil pickups, White Blonde.

2013-2018		$1,500	$2,200

'67 Telecaster (Custom Shop)
2005-2008, 2010-2011. Alder body, rosewood or maple 'board, Relic, NOS or Closet Classic, 2010 and later is rosewood 'board, Relic or NOS.

2005-2008	Closet Classic	$3,000	$4,500
2005-2011	NOS	$3,000	$4,500
2005-2011	Relic	$3,000	$4,500

'68 Telecaster Rosewood
Custom Shop, rosewood body.

2007	NOS	$4,000	$6,000

'69 Tele/Telecaster Thinline (Import)
1986-2015. Import, Classic Series, 2 Tele pickups.

1986-1996	Made in Japan	$1,200	$1,800
1997-1999	Crafted in Japan	$1,000	$1,500
2000-2015	Mexico	$600	$900

'69 Telecaster Thinline (Custom Shop)
2005-2006. Semi-hollow mahogany body, maple neck with maple 'board.

2005-2006		$3,000	$4,500

'72 Telecaster Custom/Classic Series '72 Telecaster Custom
1986-2019. Import, 1 humbucker and 1 single-coil, 2 humbuckers after '99.

1986-1989	Japan	$1,500	$2,200
1990-1999	Japan	$1,200	$1,800
2000-2019	Mexico	$600	$900

'72 Telecaster Deluxe/Classic Series '72 Telecaster Deluxe
2004-2019. Made in Mexico, alder body, large Deluxe 'guard, 2 humbuckers.

2004-2019		$600	$900

'72 Telecaster Thinline American Vintage
2012-2013. US-made, American Vintage FSR model, f-hole, 2 humbuckers.

2012-2013		$1,500	$2,200

'72 Telecaster Thinline/Classic Series Telecaster Thinline
1986-2019. Import, 2 humbuckers, f-hole.

1986-1999	Japan	$1,200	$1,800
2000-2019	Mexico	$600	$900

1972 Telecaster Custom Closet Classic
2013. Custom Shop, ash body, maple neck and 'board, 2 pickups, black finish.

2013		$3,000	$4,500

MODEL YEAR	FEATURES	EXC. COND. LOW	HIGH

75th Anniversary Commemorative Telecaster

2021. US-made, limited edition, inlaid 75th Anniversary ingot back of headstock, gold hardware, 2-color Bourbon Burst gloss finish. Includes custom Inca Silver case with Lake Placid Blue interior.

2021		$1,800	$2,800

75th Anniversary Telecaster

2021. Made in Mexico, 75th Anniversary neck plate, Diamond Anniversary satin finish with matching painted headstock.

2021		$700	$1,000

'90s Telecaster Deluxe

1995-1998. Import, 1 Tele-style bridge pickup and 2 Strat-style pickups, rosewood 'board, Foto Flame '95-'97 and standard finishes '97-'98.

1995-1997	Foto-Flame	$1,000	$1,500
1997-1998	Standard finish	$900	$1,400

'90s Telecaster Thinline

1998-2001. Bound semi-hollow ash body, f-hole, white or brown shell 'guard, 2 single-coils, sunburst, black, natural, or transparent crimson.

1998-2001		$1,800	$2,800

1998 Collectors Edition Telecaster

1998. 1,998 made, 1998 logo inlay on 'board, maple, gold hardware.

1998		$2,200	$3,300

Aerodyne Telecaster

2004-2009. Imported Tele with Aerodyne body profile, bound body, black.

2004-2009		$1,000	$1,500

Albert Collins Telecaster

1990-2018. Custom Shop signature model, bound swamp ash body, humbucker pickup in neck position, natural or silver sparkle.

1990-2018		$4,000	$6,000

Aluminum Telecaster

1994-1995. Aluminum-bodied American Standard with anodized finish in blue marble, purple marble or red, silver and blue stars and stripes.

1994-1995	Flag option	$3,000	$4,500
1994-1995	Marble patterns	$3,000	$4,500

American Acoustasonic Telecaster

2019-present. Solid A Sitka spruce top, mahogany back, sides and neck, various colors.

2019-2024		$1,200	$1,800

American Classic Holoflake Telecaster

1996-1999. Custom Shop, splatter/sparkle finish, pearloid 'guard.

1996-1999		$2,500	$4,000

American Classic Telecaster

1996-1999. Custom Shop model, handcrafted version of American Standard, thin lacquer-finished ash body, maple or rosewood 'board, various options and colors, earlier versions had gold hardware and custom-color options.

1996-1999		$2,500	$4,000

American Deluxe HH Telecaster

2004-2006. Rosewood, maple top, 2 humbucker pickups.

2004-2006		$1,200	$1,800

MODEL YEAR	FEATURES	EXC. COND. LOW	HIGH

American Deluxe Power Telecaster

1999-2001. Made in USA, with Fishman power bridge piezo pickups.

1999-2001		$1,500	$2,200

American Deluxe Telecaster

1998-2017. Premium ash or alder body with see-thru finishes.

1998-2017		$1,200	$1,800

American Deluxe B Bender Telecaster

1996-2000s. Production version of Clarence White's Tele, factory B Bender, '96-'97 with 2 pickups, '98-2000s 3 pickups.

1996-2000s		$2,000	$3,000

American Deluxe/Elite Telecaster Thinline

2015-2019. Single-cut, alder body, f-hole, maple neck, 2 Noiseless pickups, various colors.

2015-2019		$1,500	$2,200

American Elite Telecaster

2016-2020. Single-cut, alder body, maple neck, rosewood 'board, 2 single-coil pickups, various colors.

2016-2020		$1,200	$1,800

American Nashville B-Bender Telecaster

1998-2015. US-made, alder body, added Texas Special Strat pickup in middle position, white pearloid 'guard, Parsons-Fender B-string bender, 5-way switch.

1998-2015		$2,000	$3,000

American Performer Telecaster

Introduced Dec. 2018-present. Made in the US, new features include Yosemite single-coil pickups, Greasebucket tone system, various colors.

2018-2024		$800	$1,200

American Professional II Telecaster Deluxe

2020-present. Alder body, maple neck, 2 humbucking pickups, various colors with gloss finish.

2020-2024		$1,200	$1,800

American Professional Telecaster Deluxe Shawbucker

2017-2018. With 2 ShawBucker humbucking pickups, various colors.

2017-2018		$1,000	$1,500

American Rustic Ash Telecaster

2013. Limited Edition, single-cut solidbody, ash body, maple neck, 2 single-coil pickups.

2013		$1,500	$2,200

American Special Telecaster

2010-2018. Alder body, gloss finish, Texas Special pickups.

2010-2018		$800	$1,200

American Standard Telecaster Limited Edition

1990s-2019. American Standard series, various limited-edition models.

1995-1997	B-Bender	$2,000	$3,000
2009	Matching hdstk	$1,500	$2,200
2014-2015	Channel Bound	$1,800	$2,800
2015	Double-cut	$1,800	$2,800
2015	Rosewood neck	$2,000	$3,000
2015-2016	HH	$1,500	$2,200

2001 Fender American Deluxe Telecaster
Cream City Music

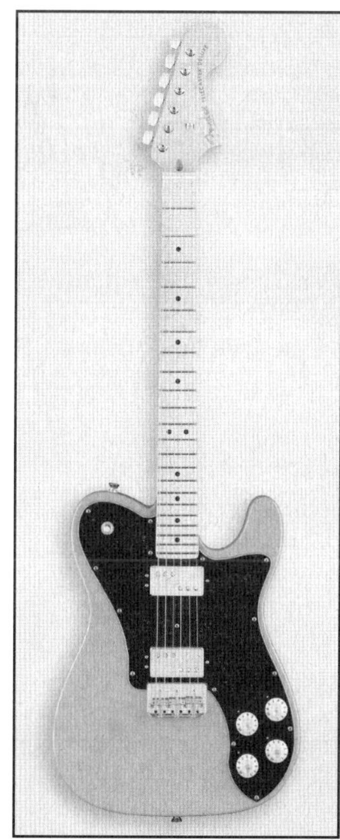

Fender American Professional II Telecaster Deluxe

GUITARS

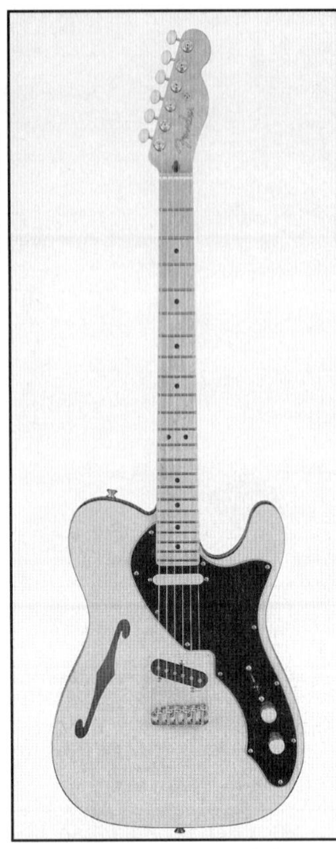

Fender Britt Daniel Telecaster Thinline

1974 Fender Custom Telecaster

Scott Casey

MODEL YEAR	FEATURES	EXC. COND. LOW	HIGH

American Standard Telecaster Special Edition

2009. Surf Green, Fiesta Red or Daphne Blue with matching headstock.

2009		$1,500	$2,200

American Ultra Luxe Telecaster

2021-present. 2 Noiseless single-coil or Floyd Rose with 2 humbucker, 2-color sunburst, trans Surf Green or black.

2021-2024	Floyd Rose HH	$1,800	$2,800
2021-2024	SS	$1,600	$2,500

American Ultra Telecaster

2019-present. Alder or ash body, upgrades include 2 Ultra Noiseless Vintage Tele single-coil pickups and 7 new colors with gloss poly finish.

2019-2024		$1,500	$2,200

Andy Summers Masterbuilt Tribute Telecaster

2009. Custom shop, based on Summer's '61 Tele, heavy relic, 250 made, custom electronics rear-mounted overdrive unit controlled by a third knob, includes DVD, strap and Andy Summer's logo travel guitar case.

2009		$10,000	$15,000

Antigua Telecaster

2004. Made in Japan, limited edition, 400 made, '70s features and antigua finish.

2004		$1,800	$2,800

Big Block Telecaster

2005-2006. Pearloid block markers, black with matching headstock, 3 single-coils with center pickup reverse wound.

2005-2006		$1,000	$1,500

Bigsby Telecaster

2003. Made in Mexico, standard Tele specs with original Fender-logo Bigsby tailpiece.

2003		$800	$1,200

Blacktop Telecaster Series

2012-2015. Includes 2 humbucker HH and hum-single-single Baritone.

2012-2015	Various models	$600	$900

Blue Flower Telecaster

1985-1993, 2003-2004. Import, Blue Flower finish.

1985-1993	1st issue	$1,500	$2,200
2003-2004	2nd issue	$1,000	$1,500

Bowling Ball/Marble Telecaster

1983-1984. Standard Tele, called Bowling Ball Tele due to the swirling color, blue, red or gold.

1983-1984	Blue or red	$5,000	$8,000
1983-1984	Gold	$6,000	$9,000

Britt Daniel Telecaster Thinline

2019-present. Ash body, maple neck, 2 single-coil pickups, Amarillo Gold lacquer finish.

2019-2024		$1,500	$2,200

Brown's Canyon Redwood Telecaster

2011. For Fender's 60th anniversary in 2011, they released 12 limited edition U.S.-made Tele-bration Telecasters, including this one with body made from 1890s California redwood.

2011		$2,800	$4,000

Buck Owens Limited Edition Telecaster

1998-1999. Red, white and blue sparkle finish, 250 made, gold hardware, gold 'guard, rosewood 'board.

1998-1999		$3,000	$4,500

Cabronita Telecaster (American Standard)

2011. For Fender's 60th anniversary in 2011, American Standard series, they released 12 limited edition U.S.-made Tele-bration Telecasters, including this one with 2 TV Jones Filter'Trons.

2011		$1,500	$2,200

Cabronita Telecaster (Classic Player)

2014-2015. Mexico version, Classic Player series.

2014-2015		$700	$1,000

Cabronita Telecaster Thinline

2012-2013. Made in Mexico, ash body, maple neck, 2 Fideli'Tron humbucking pickups, 2-Color Sunburst, Shoreline Gold or White Blonde.

2012-2013		$700	$1,000

California Fat Telecaster

1997-1998. Alder body, maple fretboard, Tex-Mex humbucker and Tele pickup configuration.

1997-1998		$1,200	$1,800

California Telecaster

1997-1998. Alder body, maple fretboard, sunburst, Tex-Mex Strat and Tele pickup configuration.

1997-1998		$1,000	$1,500

Chrissie Hynde Telecaster

2021-present. Artist series, alder body with Faded Ice Blue Metallic Road Worn finish, chrome mirror 'guard.

2021-2024		$1,200	$1,800

Clarence White Telecaster (Custom Shop)

1994-2000. Parsons-White B-Bender and Scruggs-style tuners on both E strings, sunburst.

1994-2000		$6,000	$9,000

Classic Player Baja Telecaster

2007-2019. Made in Mexico, Custom Shop designed neck plate logo, thin gloss poly blond finish.

2007-2019		$600	$900

Collector's Edition Telecaster

1998. Mid-1955 specs including white 'guard, offered in sunburst with gold hardware (which was an option in '55), 1,998 made, Collector's Edition neck plate with serial number.

1998		$2,200	$3,300

Contemporary Telecaster (Import)

1985-1987. Japanese-made while the new Fender reorganized, 2 or 3 pickups, vibrato, black chrome hardware, rosewood 'board.

1985-1987		$1,000	$1,500

Custom Carved Telecaster HH

2013. Figured maple top, carved back, 2 humbucking pickups.

2013		$1,800	$2,800

Custom Classic Telecaster

2000-2008. Custom Shop, maple or rosewood 'board, certificate of authenticity.

2000-2008		$3,000	$4,500

GUITARS

MODEL YEAR	FEATURES	EXC. COND. LOW	HIGH

Custom Deluxe Telecaster

2009-2014. Custom Shop model, ash body, AA birdseye maple neck, rosewood or maple 'board, abalone dot inlays, 2 pickups, certificate, black Bakelite 'guard, Aged White Blonde, Dakota Red or faded 2-color sunburst.

2009-2014		$3,000	$4,500

Custom Plus Telecaster

1991. Player Plus Noiseless single-coil pickups, various colors.

1991		$2,500	$4,000

Custom Telecaster

1972-1981. One humbucking and 1 Tele pickup, standard colors, see Telecaster Custom for 2 Tele pickup/bound body version.

1972		$3,600	$5,500
1973-1974		$3,200	$4,200
1975-1977		$3,200	$4,200
1978-1979		$2,700	$3,500
1980-1981		$2,700	$3,500

Danny Gatton Signature Telecaster

1990-2018. Custom Shop, like '53 Telecaster, maple neck, 2 humbuckers.

1990-1999	Frost Gold	$3,000	$4,500
2000-2018	Various colors	$3,000	$4,500

Deluxe Nashville Power Telecaster

1999-2014. Like Deluxe Nashville, but with piezo transducer in each saddle.

1999-2014		$900	$1,400

Deluxe Nashville Telecaster (Mexico)

1997-2021. Tex-Mex Strat and Tele pickup configuration, various colors.

1997-2021		$600	$900

Deluxe Telecaster (U.S.A.)

1972-1981. Two humbuckers, various colors. Mexican-made version offered starting in 2004.

1972	Common color	$3,800	$5,000
1972	Less common color	$4,200	$5,500
1973-1974	Common color	$3,400	$4,500
1973-1974	Less common color	$4,200	$5,500
1975	Common color	$2,800	$4,000
1975	Less common color	$3,800	$5,000
1976-1977	Common color	$2,800	$4,000
1978-1979	Common color	$2,500	$3,500
1980-1981	Common color	$2,200	$3,000

Elite Nashville Telecaster

Custom Shop Limited Edition, ash body, 3 pickups, Antique Cherry Burst.

2016		$1,500	$2,200

Elite Telecaster

1983-1985. Two active humbucker pickups, 3-way switch, 2 volume knobs, 1 presence and filter controls, chrome hardware, various colors.

1983-1985		$2,000	$3,000

Fat Telecaster

1999-2001. Humbucker pickup in neck, Tele bridge pickup.

1999-2001		$1,000	$1,500

GD (Global Design) Telecaster

2004-2006. Dreadnought acoustic, various models starting with GD, solid wood tops.

2004-2006		$800	$1,200

G.E. Smith Telecaster

2007-2014. Swamp ash body, vintage style hardware, U-shaped neck, oval and diamond inlays.

2007-2014		$1,500	$2,200

Graham Coxon Special Run Telecaster

2011, 2013-2014. Blond, Tele bridge and humbucker neck pickup, rosewood 'board, limited run in 2011.

2011-2014		$1,000	$1,500

GT11 Telecaster

2019. Custom Shop, alder body, maple neck, rosewood 'board, 2 single-coil pickups, various aged colors.

2019		$3,500	$5,000

Highway One Telecaster/ Texas Telecaster

2003-2011. U.S.-made, alder body, satin lacquer finish, Texas version (introduced in '04) has ash body and Hot Vintage pickups.

2003-2011		$800	$1,200

HMT Telecaster (Import)

1990-1993. Japanese-made Heavy Metal Tele, available with or without Floyd Rose tremolo, 1 Fender Lace Sensor pickup and 1 DiMarzio bridge humbucker pickup, black.

1990-1993		$800	$1,200

J5 Triple Telecaster Deluxe

2007-2017. John 5 model, made in Mexico, 3 humbuckers, medium jumbo frets.

2007-2017		$800	$1,200

J5/John 5 Signature Telecaster (Custom Shop)

2003-present. Custom Artist, ash body, maple neck, rosewood 'board, 1 humbucker and 1 Tele pickup, black with matching headstock.

2003-2024		$3,500	$5,500

James Burton Standard Telecaster

1995-2016. Mexico, 2 Texas Special Tele pickups, standard colors (no paisley).

1995-2016		$700	$1,000

James Burton Telecaster

1990-present. Ash body, 3 Fender Lace pickups, available in black with Gold Paisley, black with Candy Red Paisley, Pearl White, and Frost Red until '05. In '06 in black with red or blue flame-shaped paisley, or Pearl White.

1990-2005	Black & gold paisley, gold hw	$2,500	$3,800
1990-2005	Black & red paisley, black hw	$2,500	$3,800
1990-2010	Frost Red or Pearl White	$1,800	$2,800
1994	Blue Paisley, gold hw	$3,000	$4,500
2006-2024	Paisley flames	$1,800	$2,800

Jason Isbell Custom Telecaster

2021-present. Artist series, double-bound body, aged hardware, Road Worn Chocolate Sunburst with lacquer finish.

2021-2024		$1,500	$2,200

Jerry Donahue JD Telecaster

1993-1999. Made in Japan, Custom Strat neck pickup and Custom Tele bridge pickup, basswood body, special "V" shaped maple neck.

1993-1999		$1,200	$1,800

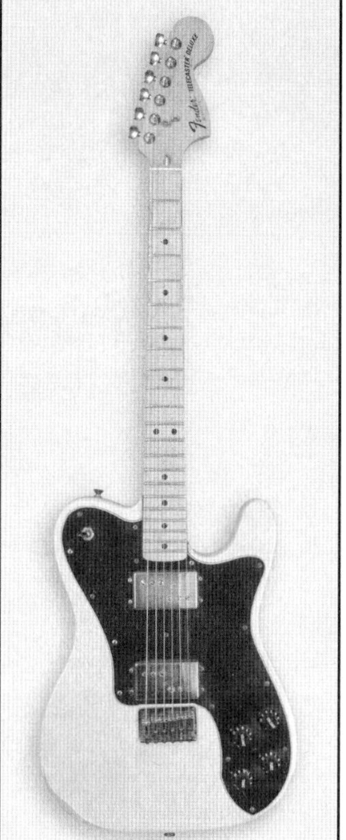

1977 Fender Deluxe Telecaster
Rivington Guitars

Fender Jason Isbell Custom Telecaster

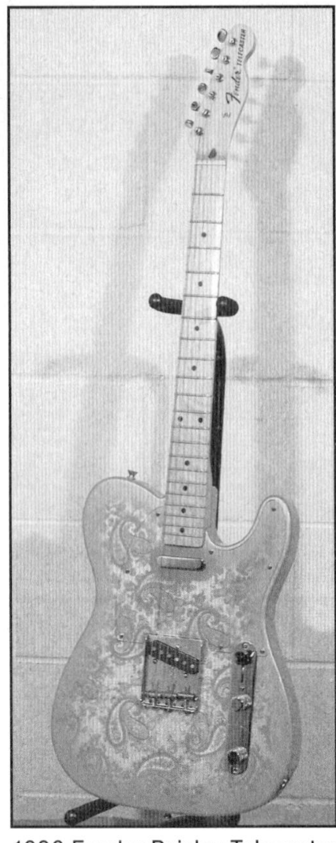

1996 Fender Paisley Telecaster
Tom Pfeifer

Fender Richie Kotzen Telecaster

MODEL YEAR	FEATURES	EXC. COND. LOW	HIGH

Jerry Donahue Telecaster

1992-2001. Custom Shop model designed by Donahue, Tele bridge pickup and Strat neck pickup, birdseye maple neck, top and back, gold hardware, passive circuitry, sunburst, transparent Crimson Red or Sapphire Blue. There was also a Japanese-made JD Telecaster.

1992-2001	Various colors	$1,800	$2,700

Jim Adkins JA-90 Telecaster Thinline

2008-present. Rosewood 'board, vintage-style P-90 soapbars.

2008-2024		$700	$1,000

Jim Root Telecaster

2007-present. Made in Mexico, black hardware, mahogany body.

2007-2024		$800	$1,200

Jimmy Bryant Tribute Telecaster

2004-2005. Custom Shop, hand-tooled leather 'guard overlay with JB initials.

2004-2005		$4,000	$6,000

Jimmy Page Mirror Telecaster

2019-present. Ash body with white blonde lacquer finish, rosewood 'board, 2 single-coil pickups, vintage-style tweed case, shipped with 8 round mirrors.

2019-2024		$2,500	$3,800

Jimmy Page Telecaster

2020-present. Ash body with gloss finish over Page's artwork, maple neck with Road Worn nitro finish, rosewood 'board.

2020-2024		$1,500	$2,500

Joe Strummer Telecaster

2007-2009. Limited edition, heavily relic'd based on Strummer's '66 Tele, Fender offered a limited-edition art customization kit as part of the package.

2007	Limited Edition	$1,000	$1,500
2007-2009	Standard run	$800	$1,200

John Jorgenson Telecaster

1998-2001. Custom Shop, korina body, double-coil stacked pickups, sparkle or black finish.

1998-2001	Sparkle	$2,500	$3,800

Jr. Telecaster

1994, 1997-2000. Custom Shop, transparent blond ash body, 2 P-90-style pickups, set neck, 11 tone chambers, 100 made in '94, reintroduced in '97.

1994		$3,500	$5,000
1997-2000		$3,000	$4,500

La Cabronita Especial Telecaster

2009-2010. Custom Shop relics, 1 or 2 TV Jones pickups. In '09, 10 each with 1 pickup in black or Shoreline Gold and 20 each with 2 pickups in black or Shoreline Gold. In '10, 10 each with 1 pickup in Candy Apple Red or Sonic Blue and 20 each with 2 pickups in Candy Apple Red or Sonic Blue.

2009-2010	Various colors	$4,500	$6,500

Mahogany Offset Telecaster

2020. Made in Japan series, mahogany body and neck, rosewood 'board, 2 pickups, natural finish.

2020		$1,000	$1,500

Marty Stuart Telecaster

2001. Custom Shop, 30 made, blue sparkle finish.

2001		$7,500	$10,000

Merle Haggard Signature Telecaster

2009-2018. Custom Shop, figured maple body and neck, maple 'board, 2-color sunburst.

2009-2018		$5,000	$7,500

Mod Shop Telecaster

2017-present. Mod Shop allows you to create your own factory-customized electric guitar or bass.

2017-2024		$1,500	$2,200

Modern Player Telecaster Plus

2012-2018. Import, pine body, maple neck, HSS pickups, Honey Burst or Trans Charcoal.

2012-2018		$500	$800

Moto Limited Edition Telecaster

1990s. Custom Shop, pearloid cover in various colors. There were also Strat and Jag versions.

1990s		$2,000	$3,000

Muddy Waters Signature Telecaster Custom

2001-2009. Mexico, Fender amp control knobs, Telecaster Custom on headstock, Muddy Waters signature logo on neck plate, Candy Apple Red.

2001-2009		$800	$1,200

Muddy Waters Tribute Telecaster

2000. Custom Shop, 100 made, Fender amp control knobs, rosewood 'board, relic Candy Apple Red finish, certificate of authenticity.

2000		$4,000	$6,000

Nashville Telecaster

1995. Custom Shop model, 3 pickups.

1995		$3,000	$4,500

NHL Premier Edition Telecaster

1999-2000. Limited edition of 100 guitars with NHL hockey art logo on the top.

1999-2000	All models	$1,500	$2,200

Nokie Edwards Telecaster

1996. Made in Japan, limited edition, book matched flamed top, multi-lam neck, Seymour Duncan pickups, gold hardware, zero fret, tilted headstock.

1996		$1,200	$1,800

Noventa Telecaster

2021-2024. Alder body, maple neck, maple or pau ferro 'board, single-coil pickup, 2-Color Sunburst, Fiesta Red or Vintage Blonde.

2021-2024		$600	$900

Old Pine Telecaster

2011. For Fender's 60th anniversary in 2011, they released 12 limited edition U.S.-made Tele-bration Telecasters, including this one with 100-year-old pine body, 300 made.

2011		$2,200	$3,300

Paisley Telecaster

1986-1998, 2003-2004, 2008. Import, 'Made in Japan' logo used until '98, 'Crafted in Japan' after, Pink Paisley finish.

1986-1994		$1,500	$2,200
1995-1998		$1,200	$1,800
2003-2004		$1,000	$1,500
2008	600 made	$1,000	$1,500

Palo Escrito Telecaster

2006-2007. Mexico, Classic series, palo escrito is tonewood from Mexico with unique grain patterns, natural finish.

2006-2007		$800	$1,200

MODEL YEAR	FEATURES	EXC. COND. LOW	HIGH

Parallel Universe Jazz-Tele

June 2018. Parallel Universe series, limited edition, Tele body, 2 Jazzmaster single-coil pickups, 2-Color Sunburst or Surf Green.

2018		$1,500	$2,200

Parallel Universe Troublemaker Telecaster

July 2018. Parallel Universe series, limited edition, mahogany body, maple top, custom Cabronita 'guard, 2 Shaw-Bucker (1T and 2T) humbucking pickups. Bigsby optional.

2018		$1,800	$2,800
2018	with Bigsby	$2,000	$2,800

Parallel Universe Volume II Tele Mágico

2020-2021. Parallel Universe Volume II series, limited edition, ash body, flame maple neck and 'board, Daphane Blue or Surf Green.

2020-2021		$1,500	$2,200

Player Telecaster

2018-present. Alder body, maple neck, 2 SS or HH pickups, various colors with gloss finish.

2018-2024		$500	$800

Player II Telecaster

2006-present. Offered in alder, chambered ash or chambered mahogany body, maple or rosewood 'board, 2 single-coil pickups, various colors.

2006-2024	Chambered ash	$1,500	$2,200
2006-2024	Chambered mahogany	$1,800	$2,800

Plus Telecaster

1994-1997. Lace Sensor pickups, various colors.

1994-1997		$1,500	$2,200

Rarities Telecaster

2019-2020. Rarities Collection series, limited edition, models include Flame Maple Top, Quilt Maple Top, Red Mahogany Top.

2019-2020		$2,000	$2,800

Richie Kotzen Telecaster

2017-present. Ash body, bound flame maple top, 2 DiMarzio pickups, gold hardware, signature on headstock.

2017-2024		$1,200	$1,800

Rosewood Telecaster

1969-1972. Rosewood body and neck.

1969-1972		$16,500	$25,000

Rosewood Telecaster (Japan)

1986-1996. Japanese-made reissue, rosewood body and neck.

1986-1996		$1,500	$2,200

Rosewood Telelcaster Limited Edition

2014. Custom Shop, Limited Edition neck plate, based on George Harrison's rosewood Tele.

2014		$4,000	$6,000

Select Telecaster

2012-2013. Select Series, figured maple top, rear-headstock 'Fender Select' medallion, gloss-lacquer finish, chrome or gold hardware.

2012-2013		$1,500	$2,200

Select Telecaster Thinline

2012-2013. Select Series, rear-headstock 'Fender Select' medallion, chrome or gold hardware, various finish options.

2012-2013		$1,800	$2,800

MODEL YEAR	FEATURES	EXC. COND. LOW	HIGH

Set-Neck Telecaster

1990-1996. Glued-in neck, Custom Shop, 2 humbucking pickups, Set-Neck CA (Country Artist) has 1 humbucker and 1 Tele pickup, various colors.

1990-1996		$4,500	$6,500

Snakehead Telecaster

Custom Shop Limited Edition, 45 offered.

2010		$7,500	$12,000

Sparkle Telecaster

1993-1995. Custom Shop model, poplar body, white 'guard, sparkle finish: champagne, gold, silver.

1993-1995		$2,500	$4,000

Special Edition Custom Telecaster FMT HH

2020-present. Mahogany body with carved flame maple top, 2 Seymour Duncan pickups, various colors with matching headstock.

2020-2024		$700	$1,000

Special Edition Deluxe Ash Telecaster

2009-2016. Mexico, butterscotch finish, ash body, 1-piece maple neck.

2009-2016		$600	$900

Special Edition Koa Telecaster

2006-2008. Made in Korea, standard Tele specs, koa veneer top over basswood body, pearloid 'guard, sunburst.

2006-2008		$700	$1,000

Special Edition White Opal Telecaster

2016. Made in Mexico, white opal body and headstock, pearloid 'guard.

2016		$700	$1,000

Special Telecaster/Telecaster Special

2004-2008. Made in Mexico, Special Edition logo with star logo sticker on back of headstock, special features like 6-way bridge and modern tuners.

2004-2008		$600	$900

Standard Telecaster (Japan)

1985-1989. In '85, the only Teles were interim production in Japan while the new Fender reorganized, no serial number, Japan headstock logo in '85, back of neck '86-'89.

1985-1989		$1,200	$1,800

Standard Telecaster (Mexico)

1990-2018. Guitar production at the Mexico facility started in '90. High end of range includes a hard guitar case, while the low end of the range includes only a gig bag, various colors. Replaced by Player Series.

1990-2018		$500	$800

Telecaster (Japanese Domestic)

1982-1997. Made in Japan for Japanese domestic market (not for export), suffix serial numbers JV5 ('82-'84) and A6 through V6 ('84-'97).

1982-1984	JV serial	$1,500	$2,200
1985-1989		$1,200	$1,800
1990-1997		$1,000	$1,500

Telecaster Custom

1959-1972. Body bound top and back, rosewood 'board, 2 Tele pickups, see Custom Telecaster for the 1 Tele/1 humbucker version. Please refer to the Fender Guitar Intro Section for details on Fender color options.

1959	Sunburst, maple	$35,000	$45,000
1960	Custom color	$50,000	$65,000

1969 Fender Rosewood Telecaster
Keith Hardie

1975 Fender Custom Telecaster
Michael Alonzi

GUITARS

Fender Telecaster Custom

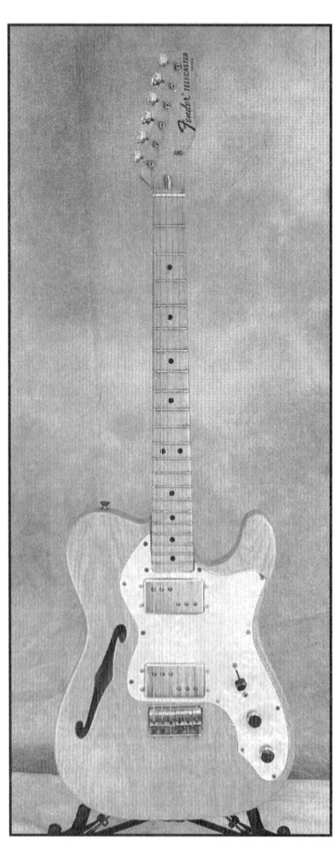
1972 Fender Telecaster Thinline

MODEL YEAR	FEATURES	EXC. COND. LOW	HIGH
1960	Sunburst	$33,500	$44,000
1961	Custom color	$45,000	$60,000
1961	Sunburst	$32,500	$42,500
1962	Custom color	$45,000	$60,000
1962	Sunburst, curve	$30,500	$40,000
1962	Sunburst, slab	$32,500	$42,500
1963	Custom color	$45,000	$60,000
1963	Sunburst	$30,000	$40,000
1964	Custom color	$40,000	$55,000
1964	Sunburst	$25,000	$32,500
1965	Custom color	$30,000	$40,000
1965	Sunburst	$23,500	$30,000
1966	Custom color	$25,000	$35,000
1966	Sunburst	$15,000	$20,000
1967	Custom color	$25,000	$35,000
1967	Sunburst	$15,000	$20,000
1968	Custom color	$25,000	$35,000
1968	Sunburst	$15,000	$20,000
1969	Custom color	$25,000	$35,000
1969	Sunburst	$15,000	$20,000
1970	Custom color	$16,000	$20,000
1970	Sunburst	$13,500	$17,500
1971	Custom color, 4-bolt	$16,000	$20,000
1971	Sunburst, 3-bolt	$4,200	$5,500
1971	Sunburst, 4-bolt	$12,500	$17,000
1972	Custom color, 3-bolt	$8,500	$11,000
1972	Sunburst, 3-bolt	$4,200	$5,500

Telecaster Custom (Japan)

1985. Made in Japan during the period when Fender suspended all USA manufacturing in '85, Tele Custom specs including bound body.

1985		$1,500	$2,200

Telecaster Custom FMT HH (Korea)

2003-2019. Korean-made, flamed maple top, 2 humbuckers.

2003-2019		$800	$1,200

Telecaster Stratocaster Hybrid

2006. Tele body shape, Strat pickup system and wiring, Strat headstock shape, dot markers on rosewood board, reissue tremolo, includes Custom Shop COA that reads "Telecaster Stratocaster Hybrid".

2006		$3,000	$4,500

Telecaster Thinline

1968-1980. Semi-hollowbody, 1 f-hole, 2 Tele pickups, ash or mahogany body, in late-'71 the tilt neck was added and the 2 Tele pickups were switched to 2 humbuckers. Please refer to the Fender Guitar Intro Section for details on Fender color options.

MODEL YEAR	FEATURES	EXC. COND. LOW	HIGH
1968	Common color	$16,000	$20,000
1968	Natural ash	$11,000	$15,000
1968	Natural mahogany	$11,000	$15,000
1968	Rare color	$20,000	$30,000
1968	Sunburst	$12,000	$16,000
1969	Common color	$15,000	$20,000
1969	Natural ash	$11,000	$15,000
1969	Natural mahogany	$11,000	$15,000
1969	Rare color	$20,000	$25,000
1969	Sunburst	$12,000	$16,000
1970	Common color	$15,000	$20,000
1970	Natural ash	$11,000	$15,000
1970	Natural mahogany	$11,000	$15,000
1970	Rare color	$20,000	$25,000
1970	Sunburst	$12,000	$16,000
1971	Color option, 3-bolt, hums	$9,000	$12,000
1971	Color option, 4-bolt, singles	$14,000	$18,000
1971	Natural ash, 3-bolt	$5,000	$7,000
1971	Natural ash, 3-bolt, hums	$5,000	$7,000
1971	Natural ash, 4-bolt, singles	$11,000	$15,000
1971	Natural mahogany, 3-bolt	$5,000	$7,000
1971	Natural mahogany, 3-bolt, hums	$5,000	$7,000
1971	Natural mahogany, 4-bolt, singles	$11,000	$15,000
1971	Sunburst, 3-bolt, hums	$5,000	$7,000
1971	Sunburst, 4-bolt, singles	$6,500	$9,000
1972	Color option	$8,000	$11,000
1972	Mahogany	$4,500	$6,000
1972	Natural ash	$4,500	$6,000
1972	Sunburst	$5,000	$6,500
1973	Color option	$6,000	$8,500
1973	Mahogany	$4,500	$6,000
1973	Natural ash	$4,500	$6,000
1973	Sunburst	$5,000	$6,500
1974	Color option	$4,500	$6,000
1974	Mahogany	$3,500	$5,000
1974	Natural ash	$3,500	$5,000
1974	Sunburst	$4,000	$5,500
1975	Color option	$4,500	$6,000
1975	Natural ash	$3,500	$5,000
1975	Sunburst	$4,000	$5,500
1976	Color option	$3,200	$4,200
1976	Natural ash	$3,200	$4,200
1976	Sunburst	$3,200	$4,200
1977	Color option	$3,200	$4,200
1977	Natural ash	$3,200	$4,200
1977	Sunburst	$3,200	$4,200
1978	Color option	$3,000	$4,000
1978	Natural ash	$3,000	$4,000
1978	Sunburst	$3,000	$4,000

Tele-Sonic

1998-2000. U.S.A., chambered Telecaster body, 2 DeArmond pickups, dot markers, upper bass bout 3-way toggle switch.

1998-2000		$1,800	$2,800

Texas Special Telecaster

1991-1992. Custom Shop, 60 made, state of Texas outline on the 'guard, ash body with Texas Orange transparent finish, large profile maple neck, with certificate of authenticity.

1991-1992		$3,000	$4,500

MODEL YEAR	FEATURES	EXC. COND. LOW	HIGH

TV Jones Telecaster/Custom Shop Double TV Jones Telecaster NOS

2013-2014. Alder body, maple neck, ebony 'board, 2 TV Jones pickups, NOS finish in various colors.

2013-2014		$3,500	$5,500

Twisted Telecaster Limited Edition

2005. Custom Shop, 50 built by Master Builder Yuriy Shishkov, 100 built by the Custom Shop team, top loaded Bigsby.

2005	Shishkov built	$4,000	$6,000
2005	Team built	$3,500	$5,500

Two-Tone Telecaster Thinline

2019-2020. FSR Limited Edition, alder body, various top colors with matching headstock and white back and sides.

2019-2020		$1,000	$1,500

Vintage Hot Rod Telecaster

2007-2014. Vintage styling with modern features, '07-'13 named '52 Tele and '62 Tele, in '14 changed to '50s, and '60s.

2007-2014	All models	$1,500	$2,200

Voodoo Lounge Supreme Telecaster

2008-2009. Custom Shop, premium transparent butterscotch blond finish.

2008-2009		$4,000	$6,000

Waylon Jennings Tribute Telecaster

1995-2003. Custom Shop, black with white leather rose body inlays.

1995-2003		$5,000	$7,500

Will Ray Signature Jazz-A-Caster

1997. Made in Fender Japan Custom Shop as one part of the three-part Hellecasters Series, limited edition, Strat neck on a Tele body with 2 soap-bar Seymour Duncan Jazzmaster-style pickups, gold leaf finish.

1997		$1,500	$2,200

Will Ray Signature Mojo Telecaster

1998-2001. Custom Shop, ash body, flamed maple Strat neck, locking tuners, rosewood 'board, skull inlays, double coil pickups, optional Hipshot B bender.

1998-2001		$3,000	$4,500

Telecoustic Series

2000-2016. Thinline acoustic/electric, single-cut, spruce top, fiberglass body, various colors. Telecoustic discontinued '05, Deluxe begins '07-'09 and Standard added in '09-'16. Both Plus and Premier '14-'16.

2000-2016	Various models	$350	$550

Toronado/Deluxe/HH/Highway 1/GT HH

1998-2006. American Special series, various models and colors. Deluxe model made in Mexico.

1998-2006		$600	$900

Villager 12-String

1965-1969, 2011-present. Acoustic flat-top, spruce top, mahogany back and sides, 12 strings, natural. Reintroduced in '11 (California Series) with on-board Fishman System, made in China.

1965-1969		$900	$1,500
2011-2024	Reintroduced	$300	$450

Violin - Electric

1958-1976, 2013. Violin-shape, solidbody, sunburst is the standard finish.

1958-1976		$2,500	$4,000
2013		$600	$900

Wildwood

1963-1971. Acoustic flat-top with Wildwood dyed top.

1966-1971	Various (unfaded)	$2,000	$3,000

Fenix

Late 1980s-mid 1990s. Brand name of Korean manufacturer Young Chang, used on a line of original-design and copy acoustic, electric and bass guitars. They also built Squier brand guitars for Fender during that period.

Fenton-Weill

See info under Burns-Weill.

Fernandes

1969-present. Established in Tokyo. Early efforts were classical guitars, but they now offer a variety of intermediate grade, production, imported guitars and basses.

Fina

Production classical and steel-string guitars and acoustic basses built in Huiyang City, Guang Dong, China.

Finck, David

1986-present. Luthier David Finck builds custom, professional, and premium grade, acoustic guitars, presently in Valle Crucis, North Carolina. In the past, he has built in Pittsburg, Kansas and Reader, West Virginia.

Fine Resophonic

1988-present. Professional and premium grade, production/custom, wood and metal-bodied resophonic guitars (including reso-electrics) built by luthiers Mike Lewis and Pierre Avocat in Vitry Sur Seine, France. They also build ukes and mandolins.

Firefly

Independent brand, budget models produced in China.

Electric

Various copy models made in China.

2019-2024		$200	$300

First Act

1995-present. Budget and professional grade, production/custom, acoustic, solid and semi-hollow body guitars built in China and in their Custom Shop in Boston. They also make basses, violins, and other instruments.

Firth Pond & Company

1822-1867. An east coast retail distributor that sold Martin and Ashborn private brand instruments. The

2011 Fender Telecoustic
Rivington Guitars

1968 Fender Villager 12-String
Imaged by Heritage Auctions, HA.com

GUITARS

Flowers

Frame Works

company operated as Firth and Hall from 1822-1841 (also known as Firth, Hall & Pond) in New York City and Litchfield, Connecticut. Most instruments were small parlor size (11" lower bout) guitars, as was the case for most builders of this era. Sometimes the inside back center seam will be branded Firth & Pond. Brazilian rosewood sides and back instruments fetch considerably more than most of the other tone woods and value can vary considerably based on condition. Guitars from the 1800s are sometimes valued more as antiques than working vintage guitars. In 1867 Firth & Sons sold out to Oliver Ditson Company.

Flammang Guitars

1990-present. Premium grade, custom/production, steel string guitars built by luthier David Flammang in Greene, Iowa and previously in East Hampton and Higganum, Connecticut.

Flaxwood

2004-present. Professional grade, production/custom, solid and semi-hollow body guitars built in Finland, with bodies of natural fiber composites.

Fleishman Instruments

Introduced in 1974, premium and presentation grade, custom flat-tops made by luthier Harry Fleishman in Sebastopol, California. He also offers basses and electric uprights. Fleishman is the director of Luthiers School International.

Fletcher Brock Stringed Instruments

1992-present. Custom flat-tops and archtops made by luthier Fletcher Brock originally in Ketchum, Idaho, and currently in Seattle, Washington. He also builds mandolin family instruments.

Flowers Guitars

1993-present. Premium grade, custom, archtop guitars built by luthier Gary Flowers in Baltimore, Maryland.

Floyd Rose

2004-2006. Floyd Rose, inventor of the Floyd Rose Locking Tremolo, produced a line of intermediate and professional grade, production, solidbody guitars from '04 to '06. They continue to offer bridges and other accessories.

Foggy Mountain

Intermediate grade, production, steel and nylon string acoustic and acoustic/electric guitars imported from China.

Fontanilla Guitars

1987-present. Luthier Allan Fontanilla builds his premium grade, production/custom, classical guitars in San Francisco, California.

Fouilleul

1978-present. Production/custom, classical guitars made by luthier Jean-Marie Fouilleul in Cuguen, France.

MODEL YEAR	FEATURES	EXC. COND. LOW	HIGH

Fox Hollow Guitars

2004-present. Luthier Don Greenough builds his professional and premium grade, custom, acoustic and electric guitars in Eugene, Oregon. He also builds mandolins.

Fox or Rocking F

1983-present. Premium grade, custom, steel string acoustic guitars built in Seattle, Washington by luthier Cat Fox.

Foxxe

1990-1991. Short-lived brand of solidbodies offered by the same company that produced Barrington guitars, Korean-made.

Frame Works

1995-present. Professional grade, production/custom, steel- and nylon-string guitars built by luthier Frank Krocker in Burghausen, Germany. The instruments feature a neck mounted on a guitar-shaped frame. Krocker has also built traditional archtops, flat-tops, and classicals.

Framus

1946-1977, 1996-present. Professional and premium grade, production/custom, guitars made in Markneukirchen, Germany. They also build basses, amps, mandolins, and banjos. Frankische Musikindustrie (Framus) founded in Erlangen, Germany by Fred Wilfer, relocated to Bubenreuth in '54, and to Pretzfeld in '67. Begun as an acoustic instrument manufacturer, Framus added electrics in the mid-'50s. Earliest electrics were mostly acoustics with pickups attached. Electric designs began in the early-'60s. A unique feature was a laminated maple neck with many thin plies. By around '64-'65 upscale models featured the organtone, often called a spigot, a spring-loaded volume control that allowed you to simulate a Leslie speaker effect. Better models often had mutes and lots of switches.

In the '60s, Framus instruments were imported into the U.S. by Philadelphia Music Company. Resurgence of interest in ca. '74 with the Jan Akkermann hollowbody followed by original mid-'70s design called the Nashville, the product of an alliance with some American financing.

The brand was revived in '96 by Hans Peter Wilfer, the president of Warwick, with production in Warwick's factory in Germany.

Amateur

Early-1960s to mid-1970s. Model 5/1, small flat-top, early without pickguard, plain, dot markers.

1960s-70s	Model 5/1	$200	$400

Atilla Zoller AZ-10

Early-1960s-early-1980s. Single-cut archtop, 2 pickups, neck glued-in until the '70s, bolt-on after, sunburst. Model 5/65 (rounded cutaway, made until late '60s) and Model 5/67 (sharp cutaway).

1960s	Model 5/65	$1,000	$1,500
1960s-70s	Model 5/67	$1,000	$1,500

GUITARS

MODEL YEAR	FEATURES	EXC. COND. LOW	HIGH

Atlantic

Ca. 1965-ca. 1970. Model 5/110, single-cut thin body electric archtop, 2 pickups, tremolo optional.

1965-1970	Model 5/110	$800	$1,500

Atlantic Elec-12

Mid- to late-1960s. Model 5/011 and 5/013, double cut semi-hollow, 2 pickups, 12-string.

1960s	Model 5/011 & /013	$1,000	$1,500

Big 18 Doubleneck

Late-1960s. Model 5/200 is a solidbody and Model 5/220 is acoustic.

1960s	Model 5/200 & /220	$1,200	$1,800

Caravelle

Ca.1965-ca. 1975. Double-cut archtop, tremolo, model 5/117-52 has 2 pickups and 5/117-54 has 3.

1965-1975	Model 5/117	$800	$1,500

Gaucho

1967 to mid-1970s. Lower grade flat-top, concert size, spruce top, mahogany sides and back, rosewood bridge and 'board, sunburst or natural finish.

1967-70s	Model 5/194	$300	$600

Guitar-Banjo 6/76 Dixi, SL-76

Ca. 1957-early 1970s. Banjo body, guitar neck, silver hardware.

1957-1970s		$600	$1,200

Hollywood

1960s. Double-cut, 3 pickups, red sunburst.

1960s	Model 5/132	$800	$1,500

Jan Akkerman

1974-1977. Single-cut semi-hollowbody, 2 pickups, gold hardware.

1974-1977		$800	$1,200

Jumbo

1963 to late-1970s. Models earlier 5/97, later 5/197, jumboflat-top, mahogany or maple sides and back.

1960s-70s		$800	$1,200

Jumbo 12-String

Late-1960s to mid-1970s. 12-string version.

1960s-70s	Model 5/297	$800	$1,200

Missouri (E Framus Missouri)

Ca.1955-ca. 1975. Originally non-cut acoustic archtop until early '60s when single-cut archtop with 1 or 2 pickups added.

1960s	Model 5/60	$500	$750

New Sound Series

1960s. Double-cut semi-hollowbody, model 5/116-52 has 2 pickups and 5/116-54 has 3.

1960s		$800	$1,500

Sorella Series

Ca.1955 to mid-1970s. Single-cut, Model 5/59 is acoustic archtop (with or without single pickup), 5/59-50 is 1-pickup electric archtop, 5/59-52 is electric 2-pickup.

1955-1975	Model 5/59	$800	$1,500
1965-1972	Model 5/59-50	$800	$1,500
1965-1972	Model 5/59-52	$800	$1,500

Sorento

Ca.1963-ca. 1970. Thinline archtop, single-cut, 2 pickups, organ effect, f-holes.

1963-1970	Model 5/112-53	$800	$1,500

MODEL YEAR	FEATURES	EXC. COND. LOW	HIGH

Sorento 12

Ca.1963-ca. 1970. 12-string version.

1963-1970	Model 5/012	$1,000	$2,000

Sport

Early 1950s-mid-1970s. Small beginner flat-top, plain appointments, dot markers.

1950s-70s	Model 50/1	$200	$400

Strato de Luxe 12 String

Ca. 1963-ca. 1970. Model 5/067(metal pickguard) and 5/068 (wood grain pickguard and large gold cover plates), 2 pickups, tremolo.

1963-1970	Model 5/068	$800	$1,500

Strato de Luxe Series

Ca.1964-ca. 1970. Various models, 1 or 2 pickups (5/155, 5/167-52, 5/168-52), 3 pickups (5/167-54, 5/168-54), some models have gold hardware.

1964-1970	2 pickups	$600	$1,200
1964-1970	3 pickups	$800	$1,500

Strato Super

Early to late-1960s. Offset double-cut, 2 pickups.

1960s	Model 5/155-52	$800	$1,500

Studio Series

Late-1950s to mid-1970s. Model 5/51 (a.k.a. 030) is non-cut acoustic archtop (some with pickup - 5/51E), 5/108 is electric archtop, 1 pickup.

1960s-70s	Model 5/51	$300	$600
1960s-70s	Model 5/51E	$300	$600

Television Series

Early to late-1960s. Model 5/118-52 2 pickups and 5/118-54 3 pickups, offset double-cut thinline hollowbody.

1960s	Model 5/118-52	$800	$1,500
1960s	Model 5/118-54	$800	$1,500

Texan Series

Late-1960s to early-1980s. Model 5/196, 5/196E (with pickup) and 5/296 12-string flat-top, mahogany back and sides. 6-string ends in late '70s.

1960s-70s	6-string	$500	$800
1960s-80s	12-string	$500	$800

Western

1960s. Model 5/195, grand concert size, lower grade flat-top, spruce top, maple sides and back.

1960s	Model 5/195	$300	$600

Franklin Guitar Company

1974-present. Premium and presentation grade, custom, flat-top steel string guitars built first in Franklin, Michigan and since 2003 in Rocheport, Missouri by luthier Nick Kukich. He also built in Idaho, Washington and Oregon.

Fraulini

2001-present. Luthier Todd Cambio builds his professional and premium grade, primarily custom, early 20th century style guitars, in Madison, Wisconsin.

FreeNote

Intermediate to professional grade, the innovative FreeNote 12-Tone Ultra Plus provides two frets for every traditional fret placement which provides an unlimited number of playable notes.

1962 Framus Sorella Model 5/59-50
Rivington Guitars

Fraulini Francesca Auditorium

Futurama III

1995 G&L ASAT Classic
Robbie Keene

MODEL YEAR	FEATURES	EXC. COND. LOW	HIGH

Fresher

1973-1985. The Japanese-made Fresher brand models were mainly copies of popular brands and limited numbers were imported into the U.S. They also made basses.

Solidbody Electric

1970s. Import from Japan, various models.

1970s		$300	$500

Fret-King

2008-present. Luthier Trev Wilkinson builds professional and premium grade, production, solidbody and semi-hollow electric guitars and basses in Yorkshire, U.K., and offers a line imported from Korea.

Fritz Brothers

1988-present. Premium grade, production/custom, acoustic, semi-hollow, and solidbody guitars and basses built by luthier Roger Fritz, originally in Mobile, Alabama, then in Mendocino, California. In 2013 he again relocated to Mobile.

Froggy Bottom Guitars

1974-present. Luthier Michael Millard builds his premium and presentation grade, production/custom flat-tops in Newfane, Vermont (originally in Hinsdale, New York, and until '84 production was in Richmond, New Hampshire).

Frudua Guitar Works

1988-present. Luthier Galeazzo Frudua builds his intermediate to premium grade, production/custom, electric guitars, basses and amps in Imola, Italy.

Fukuoka Musical Instruments

1993-present. Custom steel- and nylon-string flat-tops and archtops built in Japan.

Furch

See listing for Stonebridge.

Furnace Mountain Guitar Works

1995-1999. Instruments built by luthier Martin Fair in New Mexico. He currently builds under the Fairbuilt Guitar Co. brand.

Fury

1962-2017. Founded by Glenn McDougall in Saskatoon, Saskatchewan, Fury offered production, hollow, semi-hollow and solidbody electric guitars and basses. McDougall died in early '17.

Futurama

1957-mid to late 1960s. Futurama was a brand name used by Selmer in the United Kingdom. Early instruments made by the Drevokov Cooperative in Czechoslovakia, models for '63-'64 made by Sweden's Hagstrom company. Some later '60s instruments may have been made in Japan. Beatles fans will recognize the brand name as Beatle George Harrison's first electric.

Futurama I/II/III

1957-1969. Offset double-cut, 2- or 3-pickup versions available, large Futurama logo on headstock with the reverse capital letter F. George Harrison purchased his Futurama in '59; maple neck, 3 pickups, 3 push button levels, 2 knobs, Futurama logo on 'guard. The price shown for the Harrison model assumes an all-original, excellent condition that exactly matches his '59 model.

1960-1969	III, Harrison, maple	$2,000	$5,000
1960-1969	III, rosewood	$1,000	$1,800

Fylde Guitars

1973-present. Luthier Roger Bucknall builds his professional and premium grade, production/custom acoustic guitars, basses, mandolins, mandolas, bouzoukis, and citterns in Penrith, Cumbria, UK.

G&L

1980-present. Intermediate and professional grade, production/custom, solidbody and semi-hollowbody electric guitars made in the U.S. and overseas. They also make basses. Founded by Leo Fender and George Fullerton following the severance of ties between Fender's CLF Research and Music Man. Company sold to John MacLaren and BBE Sound when Leo Fender died in '91. In '98 they added their Custom Creations Department. In '03 G&L introduced the Korean-made G&L Tribute Series. George Fullerton died in July, '09.

ASAT

1986-1998. Called the Broadcaster in '85. Two or 3 single-coil or 2 single-coil/1 humbucker pickup configurations until early-'90s, 2 single-coils after.

1986		$1,250	$1,750
1987	Leo sig on headstock	$1,250	$1,750
1988-1991	Leo sig on body	$1,250	$1,750
1992-1998	BBE era	$1,000	$1,500

ASAT 20th Anniversary

2000. Limited Edition run of 50, ash body, tinted birdseye maple neck, 2-tone sunburst.

2000		$1,250	$1,750

ASAT '50

1999. Limited edition of 10.

1999		$1,250	$1,750

ASAT Bluesboy Limited Edition

1999. Limited edition of 20.

1999		$1,250	$1,750

ASAT Bluesboy Semi-Hollow Limited Edition

1999. Limited edition of 12, thin semi-hollow.

1999		$1,250	$1,750

ASAT Classic

1990-present. Two single-coil pickups, individually adjustable bridge saddles, neck-tilt adjustment and tapered string posts.

1990-1991	Leo sig on body	$1,000	$1,250
1992-1997	3-bolt neck	$800	$1,125
1997-2024	4-bolt neck	$800	$1,125

MODEL YEAR	FEATURES	EXC. COND. LOW	HIGH

ASAT Classic B-Bender

1997. 12 made with factory-original B-Bender.

1997		$1,125	$1,500

ASAT Classic Bluesboy

2001-present. Humbucker neck pickup, single-coil at bridge.

2001-2024		$1,000	$1,250

ASAT Classic Bluesboy Rustic

2010-2015. Classic Bluesboy with Rustic aging and refinements.

2010-2015		$1,125	$1,500

ASAT Classic Bluesboy Semi-Hollow

1997-present. Chambered Classic with f-hole.

1997-2024		$1,125	$1,500

ASAT Classic Commemorative/ Commemorative

1991-1992. Leo Fender signature and birth/death dating, Australian lacewood (6 made) and Cherryburst or Sunburst (1,000 made).

1991-1992	Australian	$5,500	$7,000
1991-1992	Cherryburst	$1,500	$1,875
1991-1992	Sunburst	$1,500	$1,875

ASAT Classic Custom

1996-1997, 2002-2013. Large rectangular neck pickup, single-coil bridge pickup. 2nd version has 4-bolt neck.

1996-1997	1st version	$1,000	$1,500
2002-2013	2nd version	$1,000	$1,500

ASAT Classic Custom Semi-Hollow

2002-2013. Custom with f-hole.

2002-2013		$950	$1,250

ASAT Classic S

2007. Limited run of 50, certificate, swamp ash body, 3 single-coil pickups, Nashville pickup configuration.

2007		$1,000	$1,250

ASAT Classic Semi-Hollow

1997-2021. With f-hole.

1997-2021		$1,000	$1,250

ASAT Classic Signature

1988-1991. Leo Fender signature on upper cutaway horn.

1988-1991	Various colors	$1,500	$1,875

ASAT Classic Three

1998. Limited Edition run of 100.

1998		$1,125	$1,500

ASAT Custom

1996. No pickguard, 25 to 30 made.

1996		$900	$1,250

ASAT Deluxe

1997-present. Flamed maple top, bound body, 2 humbuckers.

1997	3-bolt neck	$1,125	$1,500
1997-2024	4-bolt neck	$1,125	$1,500

ASAT Deluxe Semi-Hollow

1997-2018. Two humbuckers.

1997-2018		$1,125	$1,500

ASAT III

1988-1991, 1996-1998. Single-cut body, 3 single-coil pickups.

1988-1991	Leo era, 150 made	$1,125	$1,500
1996-1998	Post Leo era	$1,000	$1,250

ASAT JD-5/Jerry Donahue JD-5

2004-2007. Jerry Donahue model, single-cut, 2 single-coils, special wired 5-way switch.

2004-2007		$1,125	$1,500

ASAT Junior

1998-1999. Limited Edition run of 250, single-cut semi-hollowbody, 2 single-coils.

1998-1999		$1,000	$1,250

ASAT S-3

1998-2000. Three soap-bar single-coil pickups, limited production.

1998-2000		$700	$875

ASAT Special

1992-present. Like ASAT, but with 2 larger P-90-type pickups, chrome hardware, various colors.

1992-1997	3-bolt neck	$900	$1,125
1997-2019	4-bolt neck	$900	$1,125

ASAT Special Semi-Hollow

1997-2018. Semi-hollow version of ASAT Special.

1997-2018		$700	$875

ASAT Special Deluxe

2001-2015. No 'guard version of the Special with figured maple top.

2001-2015		$1,000	$1,250

ASAT Special Detroit Muscle Series

2015. Classic automobile colors include; Daytona Yellow, Hugger Orange, Cranberry Red and Marina Blue.

2015		$900	$1,500

ASAT Z-2 Limited Edition

1999. Limited run of 10, semi-hollow construction, natural ash, tortoise bound, engraved neckplate.

1999		$1,000	$1,250

ASAT Z-3

1998-2020. Three offset-style Z-3 high output pickups, sunburst.

1998-2020		$900	$1,125

ASAT Z-3 Semi-Hollow

1998-2020. F-hole version of Z-3.

1998-2020		$900	$1,125

Broadcaster

1985-1986. Solidbody, 2 single coils with adjustable polepieces act in humbucking mode with selector switch in the center position, black parts and finish, name changed to ASAT in early-'86.

1985-1986	Kahler	$2,250	$3,000
1985-1986	Signed by Leo	$2,500	$3,250

Cavalier

1983-1986. Offset double-cut, 2 humbuckers, 700 made, sunburst.

1983-1986		$1,125	$1,500

Climax

1992-1996. Offset double-cut, bolt maple neck, six-on-a-side tuners, double locking vibrato, blue.

1992-1996		$800	$1,000

Climax Plus

1992-1996. Two humbuckers replace single-coils of the Climax, plus 1 single-coil.

1992-1996		$800	$1,000

Climax XL

1992-1996. Two humbuckers only.

1992-1996		$800	$1,000

G&L ASAT Classic Bluesboy

Emmitt Omar

G&L ASAT Special

GUITARS

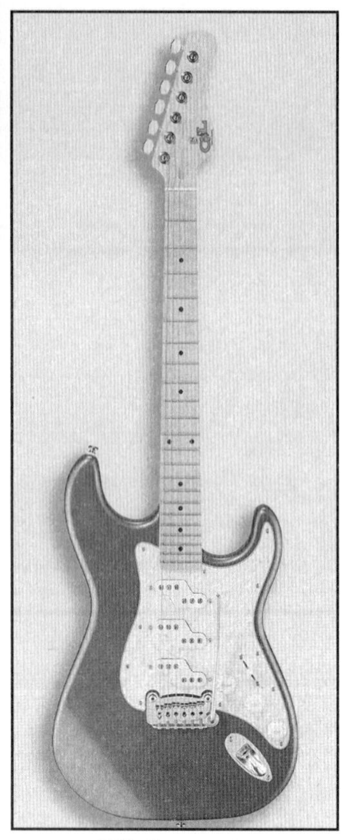
G&L Comanche

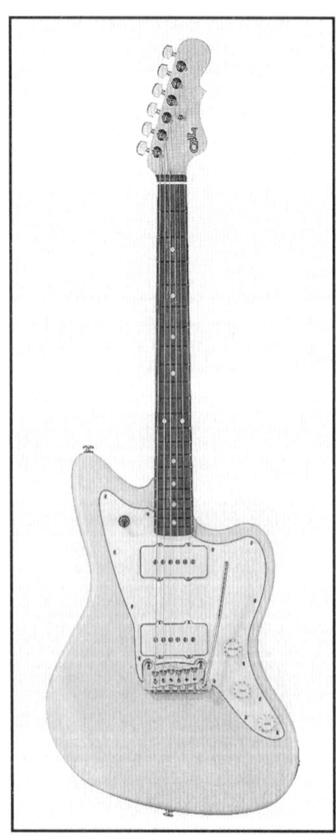
G&L Fullerton Deluxe Dohney

MODEL YEAR	FEATURES	EXC. COND. LOW	HIGH

Comanche V

1988-1991. Solidbody, 3 Z-shaped single-coil humbuckers, maple neck in choice of 3 radii, rosewood 'board, vibrato, fine tuners, Leo Fender's signature on the body, sunburst.

1988-1991		$1,375	$1,750

Comanche VI

1990-1991. Leo Fender's signature on the body, 6 mini-toggles.

1990-1991		$1,250	$1,750

Comanche (Reintroduced)

1998-2024. Reissue with either swamp ash or alder body, bolt-on maple neck, 3 Z-coil pickups, standard or premium finish options.

1998-2024	Premium finish	$1,000	$1,250
1998-2024	Standard finish	$900	$1,125

Comanche Deluxe (Reintroduced)

2018-present. Fullerton Deluxe series, old style double-cut, 3 Z-coil pickups, alder or swamp ash top, various colors with vintage tint satin finish.

2018-2024		$900	$1,125

F-100 (Model I and II)

1980-1986. Offset double-cut solidbody, 2 humbuckers, natural. Came in an I and II model - only difference is the radius of the 'board.

1980-1986		$800	$1,000

F-100E (Model I and II)

1980-1982. Offset double-cut solidbody, 2 humbuckers, active electronics, pre-amp, natural. Came in an I and II model - only difference is the radius of the 'board.

1980-1982		$800	$1,000

Fallout

2013-2024. SC-2 body style, P-90 and humbucker, swamp ash body on premier and alder on standard finishes, maple neck, maple or rosewood 'board.

2013-2024		$900	$1,125

Fullerton Deluxe Dohney

2018-present. Fullerton Deluxe series, old style, 2 pickups, alder or swamp ash top, various colors with vintage tint satin finish.

2018-2024		$900	$1,125

G-200/G-201

1981-1982. Mahogany solidbody, maple neck, ebony 'board, 2 humbucking pickups, coil-split switches, natural or sunburst, 209 made.

1981-1982	Front load	$1,875	$2,500
1981-1982	Rear load	$2,750	$3,500

GBL-LE (Guitars by Leo Limited Edition)

1999. Limited edition of 25, semi-hollowbody, 3 pickups.

1999		$1,000	$1,250

George Fullerton Signature

1995-2007. Double-cut solidbody, sunburst.

1995-1997	3-bolt neck	$1,125	$1,500
1997-2007	4-bolt neck	$1,125	$1,500

HG-1

1982-1983. Offset double-cut, 1 humbucker, dot inlays. Very rare as most were made into HG-2s.

1982-1983	5 made	$1,500	$1,870

HG-2

1982-1984. 2-humbucker HG, body changes to classic offset double-cut in '84.

1982-1983	Mustang-body	$1,250	$1,625
1984	Double-cut	$1,250	$1,625

Interceptor

1983-1991. To '86 an X-shaped solidbody, either 3 single-coils, 2 humbuckers, or 1 humbucker and 2 single-coils, '87-'91 was an offset double-cut solidbody.

1983-1985	1st X-body, 70 made	$2,250	$3,000
1985-1986	2nd X-body, 12 made	$2,250	$3,000
1987-1991	Double-cut	$1,250	$1,625

Invader

1984-1991, 1998-2018. Double-cut solidbody, 2 single-coil and 1 humbucker pickups.

1984-1991	1st version	$1,000	$1,250
1998-2018	2nd version	$1,000	$1,250

Invader Plus

1998-2018. Two humbuckers and single blade pickup in the middle position.

1998-2018		$900	$1,125

Invader XL

1998-2018. Fancy top, 2 humbuckers.

1998-2018		$1,000	$1,250

John Jorgenson Signature ASAT

1995. About 190 made, Silver Metalflake finish.

1995		$1,000	$1,250

Legacy

1992-2024. Classic double-cut configuration, USA logo, 3-bolt neck until '97, 4-bolt after, various colors.

1992-1994	3-bolt, Duncans	$800	$1,000
1995-1997	3-bolt, Alnicos	$800	$1,000
1996-1997	Swirl finish	$900	$1,125
1998-2024	4-bolt, Alnicos	$800	$1,000

Legacy Deluxe

2001-present. No 'guard, figured maple top.

2001-2024		$800	$1,000

Legacy HH

2001-2022. Two humbucker pickups.

2001-2022		$800	$1,000

Legacy HSS

2001-present. One humbucker pickup at bridge position plus 2 single-coil pickups.

2001-2024		$800	$1,000

Legacy Special

1993-2023. Legacy with 3 humbuckers, various colors.

1992-1997	3-bolt neck	$800	$1,000
1998-2023	4-bolt neck	$800	$1,000

Limited Edition 25th Anniversary

2006. G&L Custom Creations, 250 made, combines appearance of '81 F-100 with contours and control layout of ASAT Super, single-cut mahogany body, 2 custom wound MFD humbuckers, custom blend 'root beer' finish.

2006		$1,000	$1,250

Nighthawk

1983. Offset double-cut solidbody, 269 made, 3 single-coil pickups, sunburst, name changed to Skyhawk in '84.

1983		$900	$1,125

GUITARS

MODEL YEAR	FEATURES	EXC. COND. LOW	HIGH

Rampage

1984-1991. Offset double-cut solidbody, hard rock maple neck, ebony 'board, 1 bridge-position humbucker pickup, sunburst. Currently available as Jerry Cantrell Signature Model.

1984-1991	Common color	$1,000	$1,250
1984-1991	Rare color	$1,500	$1,875

Rampage (Reissue)

2000. Limited Edition run of 70, supplied with gig bag and not hard case, ivory finish.

2000		$600	$750

Rampage Jerry Cantrell Limited Edition

2011. Limited Edition run of 50, blue dress decal.

2011		$2,000	$3,500

S-500

1982-2024. Double-cut mahogany or ash solidbody, maple neck, ebony or maple 'board, 3 single-coil pickups, vibrato.

1982-1987		$1,000	$1,250
1988-1991	Mini-toggle, Leo sig on body	$900	$1,125
1992-1997	3-bolt neck	$725	$1,000
1997-2024	4-bolt neck	$725	$1,000

S-500 Deluxe

2001-present. Deluxe Series features, including no 'guard and flamed maple top, natural.

2001-2024		$900	$1,125

SC-1

1982-1983. Offset double-cut solidbody, 1 single-coil pickup, tremolo, sunburst, 250 made.

1981-1982		$900	$1,125

SC-2

1982-1983, 2010-2018. Offset double-cut solidbody, shallow cutaways change to deeper pointed in '83, 2 MFD soapbar pickups, about 600 made in original run. Reissue maple or rosewood 'board.

1982-1983		$1,250	$1,625
2010-2018	Reissue	$550	$750

SC-3

1982-1991. Offset double-cut solidbody, shallow cutaway changes to deeper pointed in '84, 3 single-coil pickups, tremolo.

1982-1987	No 'guard	$1,000	$1,250
1988-1991	With 'guard	$1,000	$1,250

Skyhawk

1984-1991. Renamed from Nighthawk, offset double-cut, 3 single-coils, signature on headstock '84-'87, then on body '88-'91.

1984-1987	Dual-Fulcrum or saddle lock	$800	$1,000
1984-1987	Kahler	$650	$850
1988-1991	Dual-Fulcrum or saddle lock	$700	$875
1988-1991	Kahler	$625	$800

Superhawk

1984-1987. Offset double-cut, maple neck, ebony 'board, G&L or Kahler tremolos, 2 humbuckers, signature on headstock.

1984-1987		$1,000	$1,250

Tribute Series

2003-present. Imported versions of regular models.

2003-2024	Various models	$225	$750

Trinity

2006. Only 25 made, ASAT-style with 3 new style single-coils, designed by Tim Page of Buffalo Brothers, the last G&L to have COA signed by George Fullerton.

2006		$1,500	$1,875

Will Ray Signature

2002-2018. Will Ray signature on headstock, 3 Z-coil pickups, Hipshot B-Bender.

2002-2018		$700	$875

G.L. Stiles

1960-1994. Built by Gilbert Lee Stiles primarily in the Miami, Florida area. First solidbody, including pickups and all hardware, built by hand in his garage. Stiles favored scrolls, fancy carving, and walnut fingerboards. His later instruments were considerably fancier and more refined. He moved to Hialeah, Florida by '63 and began making acoustic guitars and other instruments. Only his solidbodies had consecutive serial numbers. Stiles, who died in '94, made approximately 1000 solidbodies and 500 acoustics.

Gadotti Guitars

Luthier Jeanfranco Biava Gadotti, began in 1997, builds premium grade, custom/production, nylon- and steel-string, carved, chambered solidbodies in Orlando, Florida.

Gadow Guitars

2002-2019. Luthier Ryan Gadow built his professional and premium grade, custom/production, solid and semi-hollow body guitars and basses in Durham, North Carolina.

Gagnon

Luthier Bill Gagnon began building his premium and presentation grade, production/custom, archtop guitars in Beaverton, Oregon, starting in 1998.

Galanti

Ca.1962-ca.1967. Electric guitars offered by the longtime Italian accordion maker, some built by Zero Sette. They may have also offered acoustics.

Electric

1962-1967. Solidbody or hollowbody.

1962-1967	Fancy features	$800	$1,800
1962-1967	Plain features	$400	$800

Galiano

New Yorkers Antonio Cerrito and Raphael Ciani offered guitars under the Galiano brand during the early part of the last century. They used the brand both on guitars built by them and others, including The Oscar Schmidt Company. They also offered mandolins.

G&L Tribute ASAT Classic

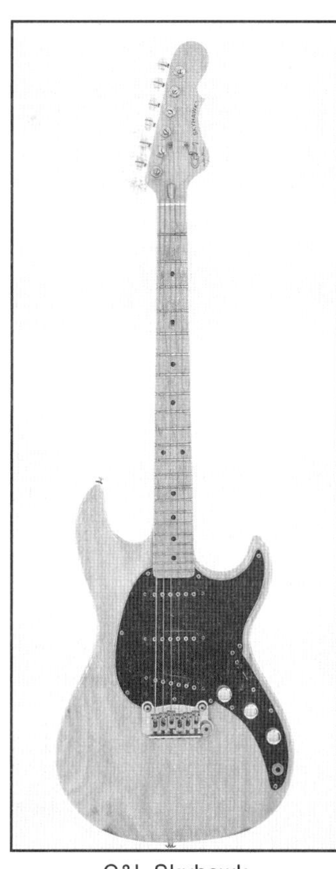

G&L Skyhawk

Imaged by Heritage Auctions, HA.com

Gallaher Doc Watson Signature

Gallagher G-70

MODEL YEAR	FEATURES	EXC. COND. LOW	HIGH

Gallagher

1965-present. Professional and premium grade, production/custom, flat-top guitars built in Wartrace, Tennessee. J. W. Gallagher started building Shelby brand guitars in the Slingerland Drum factory in Shelbyville, Tennessee in '63. In '65 he and his son Don made the first Gallagher guitar, the G-50. Doc Watson began using Gallagher guitars in '68. In '76, Don assumed operation of the business when J. W. semi-retired, J. W. died in '79. In 2019 the brand was sold to David Mathis.

71 Special

1970s-2015. Rosewood back and sides, spruce top, herringbone trim, bound ebony 'board, natural.

1970s-2015		$2,000	$3,000

72 Special

1977-2016. Rosewood back and sides, spruce top, abalone trim, bound ebony 'board, natural.

1977-2016		$3,000	$4,500

A-70 Ragtime Special

1978-2015. Smaller auditorium/00 size, spruce top, mahogany back and sides, G logo, natural.

1978-2015		$2,000	$3,000

Custom 12-String

Introduced in 1965-present. Mahogany, 12-fret neck, natural.

1965		$2,200	$3,000

Doc Watson

1968-present. Spruce top, mahogany back and sides, scalloped bracing, ebony 'board, herringbone trim, natural.

1968-2024		$2,500	$4,000

Doc Watson (Cutaway)

1975-2010. Spruce top, mahogany back and sides, scalloped bracing, ebony 'board, herringbone trim, natural.

1975-2010		$3,000	$4,500

Doc Watson 12-String

1995-2000. Natural.

1995-2000		$3,000	$4,000

Doc Watson Signature

2000-present. Signature inlay 12th fret.

2000-2024		$3,500	$4,500

G-45

1970-2008. Mahogany back and sides, spruce top, ebony 'board, natural.

1970-1979		$1,500	$2,500
1980-2008		$1,200	$1,800

G-50

1960s-2015. Mahogany back and sides, spruce top, ebony 'board, natural.

1960s		$2,000	$3,000
1970-2015		$1,800	$2,500

G-65

1980s-2015. Rosewood back and sides, spruce top, ebony 'board, natural.

1980s-2015		$2,000	$3,000

G-70

1978-present. Rosewood back and sides, herringbone purfling on top and sound hole, mother-of-pearl diamond 'board inlays, bound headstock, natural.

1978-2024		$2,500	$4,000

G-71

1970s. Indian rosewood, gold tuners.

1970s		$2,000	$3,000

Gallagher, Kevin

1996. Kevin Gallagher, luthier, changed name brand to Omega to avoid confusion with J.W. Gallagher. See Omega listing.

Gallotone

1950s-1960s. Low-end foreign brand similar to 1950s Stellas, the Gallotone Champion, a 3/4 size student flat-top, is associated with John Lennon as his early guitar.

Galloup Guitars

1994-present. Luthier Bryan Galloup builds his professional and premium grade, production/custom flat-tops in Big Rapids, Michigan. He also operates the Galloup School of Lutherie and The Guitar Hospital repair and restoration business.

Galveston

Budget and intermediate grade, production, imported acoustic, acoustic/electric, resonator and solidbody guitars. They also offer basses and mandolins.

Gamble & O'Toole

1978-present. Premium grade, custom classical and steel string guitars built by luthier Arnie Gamble in Sacramento, California, with design input and inlay work from his wife Erin O'Toole.

Ganz Guitars

1995-present. Luthier Steve Ganz builds his professional grade, production/custom classical guitars in Bellingham, Washington.

Garcia

Made by luthier Federico Garcia in Spain until late-1960s or very early-'70s when production moved to Japan.

Classical

1960s-1970s. Mid-level, '60s model is solid spruce top with solid mahogany, rosewood or walnut back and sides, '70s model is Spanish pine top with walnut back and sides.

1960s-70s	Various wood	$300	$500
1970s	Spanish pine/Brazilian	$600	$1,000

Garrison

2000-2007. Intermediate and professional grade, production, acoustic and acoustic/electric guitars designed by luthier Chris Griffiths using his Active Bracing System (a single integrated glass-fiber bracing system inside a solid wood body). He started Griffiths Guitar Works in 1993 in St. John's, Newfoundland, and introduced Garrison guitars in 2000. In '07, the Garrison facility was acquired by Gibson.

GUITARS

MODEL YEAR	FEATURES	EXC. COND. LOW	HIGH

Gary Kramer

2006-present. Intermediate and professional grade, production/custom, solidbody electric guitars built by luthier Gary Kramer in El Segundo, California, and imported. Kramer was one of the founders of the Kramer guitar company in the '70s.

Gauge Guitars

Luthier Aaron Solomon builds custom, professional and premium grade, solidbody and semi-solid electric guitars in New Jersey, starting in 2002.

Gemelli

Early 1960s-ca. 1966. European-made (likely Italian) guitars. Similar to Bartolini guitars, so most likely from the same manufacturer. Originally plastic covered, they switched to paint finishes by around '65.

Gemunder

1870s-1910s. New York shop that specialized in reproduction-aged violins, but also made parlor-sized guitars that were similar to Martin guitars of the era. An original label on the inside back identifies August Gemunder and Sons, New York.

Parlor

1870s-1910s. Style 28 appointments, rosewood body, spruce top.

1870-1910s		$1,500	$2,500

George

See listing under Chris George.

German Guitars

2001-present. Luthier Greg German builds his premium grade, custom/production, acoustic archtop guitars in Broomfield, Colorado.

Giannini

1900-present. Classical, acoustic, and acoustic/electric guitars built in Salto, SP, Brazil near Sao Paolo. They also build violas, cavaquinhoes and mandolins. Founded by guitar-builder Tranquillo Giannini, an Italian who traveled to Brazil in 1890 and discovered the exotic woods of Brazil. The company was producing 30,000 instruments a year by '30. They began exporting their acoustic instruments to the U.S. in '63. They added electric guitars in '60, but these weren't imported as much, if at all. Gianninis from this era used much Brazilian Rosewood.

Classical

Early-1970s. Nylon string import, small body.

1970s	Brazilian rosewood	$700	$1,000
1970s	Pau ferro, mahogany	$300	$500

CraViolia

1972-1974, 2004-present. Kidney bean-shaped rosewood body, acoustic, natural, line included a classical, a steel string, and a 12-string.

1972-1974		$800	$1,500

CraViolia 12-String

1972-1974, 2004-2024. Kidney bean-shaped body, 12 strings.

1972-1974		$800	$1,500

Gibson

1890s (1902)-present. Intermediate, professional, and premium grade, production/custom, acoustic and electric guitars made in the U.S. They also build basses, mandolins, amps, and banjos. Gibson also offers instruments under the Epiphone, Kramer, Steinberger, Dobro, Tobias, Valley Arts, Garrison, Slingerland (drums), Baldwin (pianos), Trace Elliot, Electar (amps), Maestro, Gibson Labs, Oberheim, and Echoplex brands.

Founded in Kalamazoo, Michigan by Orville Gibson, a musician and luthier who developed instruments with tops, sides and backs carved out of solid pieces of wood. Early instruments included mandolins, archtop guitars and harp guitars. By 1896 Gibson had opened a shop. In 1902 Gibson was bought out by a group of investors who incorporated the business as Gibson Mandolin-Guitar Manufacturing Company, Limited. The company was purchased by Chicago Musical Instrument Company (CMI) in '44. In '57 CMI also purchased the Epiphone guitar company, transferring production from Philadelphia to the Gibson plant in Kalamazoo. Gibson was purchased by Norlin in late-'69 and a new factory was opened in Nashville, Tennessee in '74. The Kalamazoo factory ceased production in '84. In '85, Gibson was sold to a group headed by Henry Juskewiscz. Gibson purchased the Flatiron Company in '87 and built a new factory in '89, moving acoustic instrument production to Bozeman, Montana. In '18 Gibson went into Chapter 11 bankruptcy, emerging later in the year with KKR as new majority owner and James "JC" Curleigh as CEO.

The various models of Firebirds, Flying Vs, Les Pauls, SGs, and Super 400s are grouped together under those general headings. Custom Shop and Historic instruments are listed with their respective main model (for example, the '39 Super 400 Historical Collection model is listed with the Super 400s).

Model specifications can cross model years. For example, it is possible that an early '60 Gibson guitar might have a specification, such as a wider-rounder neck, which is typically a '59 spec. In that case it is possible for the early '60 model to be valued more closely to the late '59 model than to a mid to late '60 model with a thinner-flatter neck profile.

Orville Gibson

1894-1902. Hand-made and carved by Orville Gibson, various models and sizes most with standard printed white rectangle label "O.H. Gibson" with photo of Orville Gibson and lyre-mandolin. Prices are for fully functional, original or refurbished examples. It is almost expected that a black Orville Gibson instrument has been refinished, and most of those were done by Gibson.

1894-1902	Very rare, hand made	$60,000	$85,000

German DB6

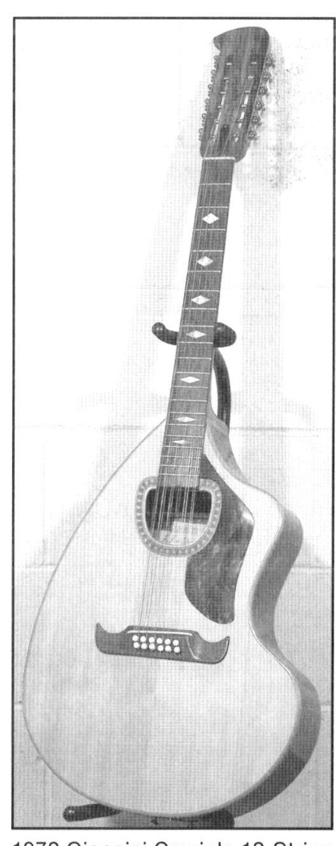

1972 Giannini Craviola 12-String

Tom Pfeifer

1980 Gibson 335-S DeLuxe Professional
Ken MacSwan

1938 Gibson Advanced Jumbo
Imaged by Heritage Auctions, HA.com

MODEL YEAR	FEATURES	EXC. COND. LOW	HIGH

335 S Custom

1980-1981. Solidbody, 335-shaped, mahogany body, unbound rosewood 'board, 2 exposed Dirty Finger humbuckers, coil-tap, TP-6 tailpiece. Also available in natural finish, branded headstock Firebrand version.

1980-1981		$1,500	$2,000

335 S Deluxe

1980-1982. Same as 335 S Custom but with bound ebony 'board, brass nut.

1980-1982		$1,500	$2,000

335 S Limited Run

2011-2013. Maple body and neck, rosewood 'board, nitro-finish sunburst.

2011-2013		$1,200	$1,600

335 S Standard

1980-1981. Same as 335 S Custom except stop tailpiece, no coil-tap. Also available in natural finish, branded headstock Firebrand version.

1980-1981		$1,500	$2,000

Advanced Jumbo

1936-1940. Dreadnought, 16" wide, round shoulders, Brazilian rosewood back and sides, sunburst, reintroduced '90-'97.

1936-1940		$75,000	$85,000

Advanced Jumbo (Reissue)

1990-1999, 2002-2018. Issued as a standard production model, but soon available only as a special order for most of the '90s; currently offered as standard production. Renamed 1936 Advanced Jumbo for 1997-1998. There were also some limited-edition AJs offered during the '90s.

1990-1999	Reissue	$2,500	$4,500
2002-2018	Reintroduced	$2,000	$3,800

Advanced Jumbo 12

2015. 12-fret neck.

2015		$2,800	$4,200

Advanced Jumbo 75th Anniversary

2011-2012. 75th Anniversary label, 2nd edition 75 made with on-board electronics.

2011	1st edition	$3,800	$6,000
2012	2nd edition	$3,500	$5,500

1935 Advanced Jumbo

2013. Limited run of 35, Adirondack red spruce top, Indian rosewood back and sides, Vintage Sunburst.

2013		$7,000	$10,000

Advanced Jumbo Koa

2006. Custom Shop, koa back and sides, Adirondack top.

2006		$4,500	$7,500

Advanced Jumbo Luthier's Choice

2000-2008. Custom Shop, various wood options.

2000-2005	Brazilian	$7,000	$10,000
2008	Cocobolo	$5,000	$7,500

Advanced Jumbo Pro

2011-2013. Made for Guitar Center, Baggs pickup, Sitka top, solid rosewood back and sides.

2011-2013		$2,200	$3,500

Advanced Jumbo Red Spruce/ AJ Red Spruce

2013. Limited Edition, Adirondack red spruce top, rosewood back and sides.

2013		$3,800	$6,000

Advanced Jumbo Supreme

2007. Custom Shop, Madagascar rosewood back and sides, Adirondack spruce top.

2007		$4,000	$6,500

Iron Mountain Advanced Jumbo

2014. Custom Shop model, limited run of 65, Adirondack red spruce top, Birdseye maple back and sides, Honeyburst finish.

2014		$2,800	$4,000

Randy Scruggs Advanced Jumbo Limited Edition

2010-2018. Sitka spruce top, East Indian rosewood body, king's crown headstock logo on, crown markers, Fishman pickup, vintage sunburst.

2010-2018		$3,500	$5,500

All American I

1995-1997. Solidbody electric with vague double-cut Melody Maker body style, 1 pickup. Renamed the SG-X in '98.

1995-1997		$800	$1,200

All American II

1996-1997. As American I with 2 pickups.

1996-1997		$900	$1,400

B.B. King Custom

1980-1988. Lucille on peghead, 2 pickups, multi-bound, gold-plated parts, Vari-tone, cherry or ebony, renamed B.B. King Lucille in '88.

1980-1988		$3,500	$5,500

B.B. King Lucille

1988-2019. Introduced as B.B. King Custom, renamed B.B. King Lucille. Lucille on peghead, 2 pickups, multi-bound, gold-plated parts, Vari-tone, cherry or ebony. In '07 B.B. King logo and large king's crown on headstock with Lucille logo on truss rod cover.

1988-2019		$3,000	$5,000
2007-2009	King logo	$3,500	$5,500

B.B. King Standard

1980-1985. Like B.B. King Custom, but with stereo electronics and chrome-plated parts, cherry or ebony.

1980-1985		$2,500	$3,800

B.B. King Limited Edition (70th Birthday)

1995. Issued to celebrate B.B. King's 70th birthday, 150 made.

1995		$6,000	$9,000

B.B. King 80th Birthday Lucille

2005. Custom Shop, limited run of 80, 'guard engraved with crown and signature, headstock engraved with artwork from King's birthday tribute album.

2005		$7,500	$11,500

B.B. King Super Lucille

2002-2004. Signed guard, abalone inlays, custom black sparkle finish.

2002-2004		$4,500	$6,500

B-15

1967-1971. Mahogany, spruce top, student model, natural finish.

1967-1971		$1,200	$1,600

B-20

1971-1972. 14.5" flat-top, mahogany back and sides, dot markers, decal logo, strip in-line tuners with small buttons.

1971-1972		$1,300	$2,000

MODEL YEAR	FEATURES	EXC. COND. LOW	HIGH

B-25 3/4 / B-25N 3/4

1962-1968. Short-scale version, flat-top, mahogany body, cherry sunburst (natural finish is the B-25 3/4N).

1962	Wood bridge	$1,300	$1,800
1963-1964	Plastic bridge	$1,300	$1,800
1965		$1,200	$1,500
1966-1968		$1,000	$1,300

B-25/B-25N

1962-1977, 2008-2012. Flat-top, mahogany, bound body, upper belly on bridge (lower belly '68 on), cherry sunburst or black (natural finish is B-25N). Reissued in '08.

1962	Wood bridge	$2,500	$3,200
1963-1964	Plastic bridge	$2,500	$3,300
1965		$1,800	$2,300
1966-1968	Above belly bridge	$1,700	$2,200
1968	Black, white 'guard	$3,600	$4,800
1968	Red, white 'guard	$3,200	$4,200
1969	Below belly bridge	$1,400	$1,800
1970-1977		$1,400	$1,800
2008-2012	Reissue, black	$1,700	$2,200

B-25-12/B-25-12N

1962-1977. Flat-top 12-string version, mahogany, bound body, cherry sunburst (natural finish is the B-25-12N).

1962-1964	No tailpiece	$2,300	$3,000
1965	Trapeze tailpiece	$1,800	$2,500
1966-1968	Trapeze tailpiece	$1,700	$2,200
1969	Below belly bridge	$1,500	$2,000
1970-1977		$1,500	$2,000

B-45-12/B-45-12N

1960-1979. Flat-top 12-string, mahogany, round shoulders for '60-'61, square after, sunburst (natural finish is the B-45-12N).

1960	Early specs	$3,200	$4,500
1961-1962	Round shoulder	$2,700	$3,500
1962-1963	Square shoulder	$2,500	$3,400
1964	No tailpiece	$2,500	$3,400
1965	Trapeze tailpiece	$1,800	$2,500
1966-1968		$1,800	$2,500
1969	Below belly bridge	$1,500	$2,000
1970-1979		$1,400	$1,800

B-45-12 Limited Edition

1991-1992. Limited edition reissue with rosewood back and sides, natural.

1991-1992		$1,800	$2,500

Barney Kessel Custom

1961-1973. Double-cut archtop, 2 humbuckers, gold hardware, cherry sunburst.

1961	PAFs	$9,000	$12,000
1962	Pat #	$5,000	$6,500
1963-1964		$5,000	$6,500
1965		$4,500	$6,000
1966-1969		$4,300	$5,500
1970-1973		$3,200	$4,200

Barney Kessel Regular

1961-1974. Double-cut archtop, 2 humbuckers, nickel hardware, cherry sunburst.

1961	PAFs	$8,500	$11,000
1962	Pat #	$4,800	$6,500
1963-1964		$4,800	$6,500
1965		$4,300	$5,500
1966-1969		$4,000	$5,200
1970-1974		$3,200	$4,200

Blue Ridge

1968-1979, 1989-1990. Flat-top, dreadnought, laminated rosewood back and sides, natural finish, reintroduced for '89-'90.

1968-1969	Brazilian	$1,800	$3,000
1970-1979		$1,000	$1,500

Blue Ridge 12

1970-1978. Flat-top, 12 strings, laminated rosewood back and sides, natural finish.

1970-1978		$1,200	$2,000

Blues King

2012-2013. Acoustic/electric, non-cut, bubinga back and sides, dot inlays.

2012-2013		$1,800	$2,800

Blueshawk

1996-2006. Small single-cut, f-holes, 2 single-coil hum cancelling Blues 90 pickups, 6-way Varitone dial, gold hardware, Bigsby option starts '98.

1996-2006		$1,200	$2,000

B-SJ Blue Ridge

1989. Model name on the label is B-SJ, truss rod covers logo is Blue Ridge, SJ appointments but with narrow peghead shape.

1989		$1,500	$2,500

Byrdland

1955-1992. Thinline archtop, single-cut (rounded until late-'60, pointed '60-late-'69, rounded after '69, rounded or pointed '98-present), 2 pickups, now part of the Historic Collection.

1956-1957	Natural, Alnicos	$12,000	$15,500
1956-1957	Sunburst, Alnicos	$10,000	$13,000
1958-1959	Natural, PAFs	$18,000	$25,000
1958-1959	Sunburst, PAFs	$15,000	$20,000
1960-1962	Natural, PAFs	$15,000	$20,000
1960-1962	Sunburst, PAFs	$12,500	$18,000
1963-1964	Natural, pat #	$10,000	$15,000
1963-1964	Sunburst, pat #	$9,000	$12,000
1965	Natural	$7,500	$10,000
1965	Sunburst	$7,000	$9,500
1966-1969	Natural	$6,000	$8,000
1966-1969	Sunburst	$6,000	$8,000
1970-1992	Various colors	$4,500	$6,000

Byrdland Historic Collection

1993-2018. Custom shop, various colors.

1993-2018	Sunburst, Natural	$6,000	$9,000
2010	Custom Shop	$6,500	$9,500
2013	Collection Edition	$7,000	$11,000

C-0 Classical

1962-1971. Spruce top, mahogany back and sides, bound top, natural.

1962-1964		$600	$1,000
1965		$500	$900
1966-1971		$400	$800

C-1 Classical

1957-1971. Spruce top, mahogany back and sides, bound body, natural.

1957-1959		$800	$1,400
1960-1964		$700	$1,200
1965		$600	$1,000
1966-1971		$500	$900

1963 Gibson Byrdland
Paul Lutzke

1967 Gibson C-O
Imaged by Heritage Auctions, HA.com

GUITARS

1982 Gibson Chet Atkins CE
Geoff Barker

1984 Gibson Corvus II
Imaged by Heritage Auctions, HA.com

MODEL YEAR	FEATURES	EXC. COND. LOW	HIGH

C-1 D Laredo

1963-1971. Natural spruce top, mahogany sides and back, upgrade to standard C-1.

1963-1965		$1,200	$2,500

C-1 E Classical Electric

1960-1967. C-1 with ceramic bridge pickup, catalog notes special matched amplifier that filters out fingering noises.

1960-1964		$800	$1,500
1965		$700	$1,200
1966-1967		$600	$1,000

C-1 S Petite Classical

1961-1966. Petite 13 1/4" body, natural spruce top, mahogany back and sides.

1961-1964		$700	$1,200
1965		$600	$1,000
1966-1967		$500	$900

C-2 Classical

1960-1971. Maple back and sides, bound body, natural.

1960-1964		$900	$1,600
1965		$800	$1,400
1966-1971		$700	$1,200

C-4 Classical

1962-1968. Maple back and sides, natural.

1962-1964		$1,000	$1,800
1965		$900	$1,600
1966-1968		$800	$1,400

C-6 Classical/Richard Pick

1958-1971. Rosewood back and sides, gold hardware, natural.

1958-1959	Brazilian	$3,000	$6,000
1960-1964	Brazilian	$2,800	$5,500
1965	Brazilian	$2,500	$5,000
1966-1969	Brazilian	$2,300	$4,500
1970-1971	Indian	$1,800	$3,500

C-8 Classical

1962-1969. Rosewood back and sides, natural.

1962-1964		$1,200	$2,500
1965		$1,000	$2,200
1966-1969		$900	$2,000

C-100 Classical

1971-1972. Slotted peghead, spruce top, mahogany back and sides, ebony 'board, Gibson Master Model label, non-gloss finish.

1971-1972		$400	$800

C-200 Classical

1971-1972. C-100 with gloss finish.

1971-1972		$500	$900

C-300 Classical

1971-1972. Similar to C-100, but with rosewood 'board, wood binding, wider sound hole ring.

1971-1972		$600	$1,000

C-400 Classical

1971-1972. Rosewood sides and back, spruce top, high-end appointments, chrome hardware.

1971-1972		$800	$1,400

C-500 Classical

1971-1972. C-400 with gold hardware.

1971-1972		$1,000	$1,800

MODEL YEAR	FEATURES	EXC. COND. LOW	HIGH

CF-100

1950-1958. Flat-top, pointed cutaway, mahogany back and sides, bound body, sunburst finish.

1950-1958		$3,500	$5,500

CF-100 E

1951-1959, 2009. CF-100 with a single-coil pickup. Also offered in '94 1950 CF-100 E limited edition and in '07 as a Custom Shop model.

1950-1959		$4,500	$7,000

CF-100 E Reissue

2007. Custom Shop, all maple body, ebony 'board, 24 made.

2007		$3,500	$5,500

Challenger I

1983-1985. Single-cut Les Paul-shaped solidbody, 1 humbucker, bolt-on maple neck, rosewood 'board, dot markers, silver finish standard.

1983-1985		$600	$1,200

Challenger II

1983-1985. 2 humbucker version.

1983-1985		$700	$1,500

Challenger III

1984. 3 single-coil version, never cataloged so could be very limited.

1984		$1,000	$1,800

Chet Atkins CE

1981-2005. CE stands for Classical Electric, single-cut, multi-bound body, rosewood 'board until '95, then ebony, standard width nut, gold hardware, various colors.

1981-2005		$1,500	$3,000

Chet Atkins CEC

1981-2005. Same as CE, but with ebony 'board and 2" classical width nut, black or natural.

1981-2005		$1,800	$3,500

Chet Atkins Country Gentleman

1986-2005. Thinline archtop, single rounded cutaway, 2 humbuckers, multi-bound, gold hardware, Bigsby. Part of Gibson's Custom line.

1986-2005		$3,000	$5,500

Chet Atkins SST

1987-2006. Steel string acoustic/electric solidbody, single-cut, bridge transducer pickup, active bass and treble controls, gold hardware.

1987-1993	White	$1,800	$3,000
1987-2006	Black	$1,500	$2,800
1987-2006	Natural	$1,500	$2,800
1993	Red Wine or Antique	$2,000	$3,500
1994	Cherry Sunburst	$2,000	$3,500

Chet Atkins SST Celebrity

1991-1993. Gold hardware, 200 made, black body with unique white 'guard.

1991-1993		$2,500	$4,500

Chet Atkins SST-12

1990-1994. 12-string model similar to 6-string, mahogany/spruce body, preamp circuit controls single transducer pickup, natural or ebony finish.

1990-1994		$2,000	$3,800

MODEL YEAR	FEATURES	EXC. COND. LOW	HIGH

Chet Atkins Super 4000

1997-2000. Custom Shop, figured curly maple back and sides, orange amber finish, 25 built, COA.

1997-2000		$20,000	$25,000

Chet Atkins Tennessean

1990-2005. Single rounded cutaway archtop, 2 humbuckers, f-holes, bound body. Part of Gibson's Custom line.

1990-2005		$2,500	$4,500

Chicago 35

1994-1995. Flat-top dreadnought, round shoulders, mahogany back and sides, prewar script logo.

1994-1995		$1,200	$2,000

Citation

1969-1971. 17" full-depth body, single-cut archtop, 1 or 2 floating pickups, fancy inlay, natural or sunburst. Only 8 shipped for '69-'71, reissued the first time '79-'83 and as part of the Historic Collection in '93.

1969-1971		$20,000	$35,000

Citation (1st Reissue)

1979-1983. Reissue of '69-'71 model, natural or sunburst. Reintroduced in '93 as part of Gibson's Historic Collection.

1979-1983		$18,000	$25,000

Citation (2nd Reissue)

1993-2018. Limited production via Gibson's Historic Collection, natural or sunburst.

1994-2018		$15,000	$20,000

Citation Vanderbilt Rose

2015. Custom Shop, very few made, Vanderbilt Rose lacquer finish with matching maple 'guard.

2015		$13,500	$25,000

CJ-165/CJ-165 Modern Classic

2006-2008. Called J-165 in first year of production, classic small body non-cutaway flat-top, solid spruce top, maple or rosewood back and sides.

2006-2008		$2,000	$3,200

CJ-165 EC Modern Classic

2007-2009. As above, but with single-cut, electronics, maple or rosewood back and sides.

2007-2009		$2,000	$3,000

CL-10 Standard

1997-1998. Flat-top, solid spruce top, laminated mahogany back and sides.

1997-1998		$1,200	$2,000

CL-20 Standard Plus

1997-1998. Flat-top, laminated back and sides, 4-ply binding with tortoiseshell appointments, abalone diamond inlays.

1997-1998		$1,400	$2,200

CL-30 Deluxe

1997-1998. J-50 style dreadnought, solid spruce top, bubinga back and sides, factory electronics.

1997-1998		$1,800	$2,800

CL-35 Deluxe

1998. Single cutaway CL-30.

1998		$1,900	$3,000

CL-40 Artist

1997-1998. Flat-top, gold hardware, rosewood back and sides.

1997-1998		$2,000	$3,200

CL-45 Artist

1997-1998. Single cutaway CL-40.

1997-1998		$2,200	$3,500

CL-50

1997-1999. Custom Shop model, D-style body, higher-end appointments, offered with Brazilian rosewood.

1997-1999		$4,000	$7,500

Corvus I

1982-1984. Odd-shaped solidbody with offset V-type cut, bolt maple neck, rosewood 'board, 1 humbucker, standard finish was silver gloss, but others available at an additional cost.

1982-1984		$800	$1,500

Corvus II

1982-1984. Same as Corvus I, but with 2 humbuckers, 2 volume controls, 1 master tone control.

1982-1984		$900	$1,800

Corvus III

1982-1984. Same as Corvus I, but with 3 single-coil pickups, master volume and tone control, 5-way switch.

1982-1984		$1,200	$2,500

Crest Gold

1969-1971. Double-cut thinline archtop, Brazilian rosewood body, 2 pickups, bound top and headstock, bound f-holes, gold-plated parts. The Crest name was also used on a few (3-6) custom guitars based on the L-5CT built in 1959-'61.

1969-1971		$9,000	$15,000

Crest Silver

1969-1972. Silver-plated parts version of Crest.

1969-1972		$8,000	$12,000

CS Series

2002-2017. Custom Shop, scaled down ES-335 body style, plain top or F indicates figured top.

2002-2003	CS-356	$3,000	$4,500
2002-2012	CS-336F	$3,500	$5,500
2002-2014	CS-356F	$3,800	$6,000
2002-2017	CS-336	$3,200	$4,800

Dave Grohl DG-335

2007-2008. Custom Shop Inspired By series, Trini Lopez Standard specs, Certificate of Authenticity, Pelham Blue or black finish.

2007-2008		$5,500	$8,500

Dove

1962-1996, 1999-2013. Flat-top acoustic, maple back and sides, square shoulders, natural or sunburst.

1962-1964		$9,000	$12,000
1965	Early '65	$6,000	$8,000
1965	Late '65	$4,500	$6,000
1966-1969		$4,000	$5,500
1970-1979	Various colors	$2,800	$3,800
1980-1984	Double X	$2,500	$3,500
1985-1988	Single X	$2,500	$3,500
1989	New specs	$2,500	$3,500
1990-1996	Various colors	$2,500	$3,500
1999-2013	Reissue model	$2,500	$3,500

'60s Dove

1997-2004. Spruce top, maple back and sides, Dove appointments.

1997-2004		$2,500	$4,000

1969 Gibson Crest Silver

Gary's Classic Guitars

1968 Gibson Dove

Tom Gingrich

GUITARS

Gibson Doves in Flight

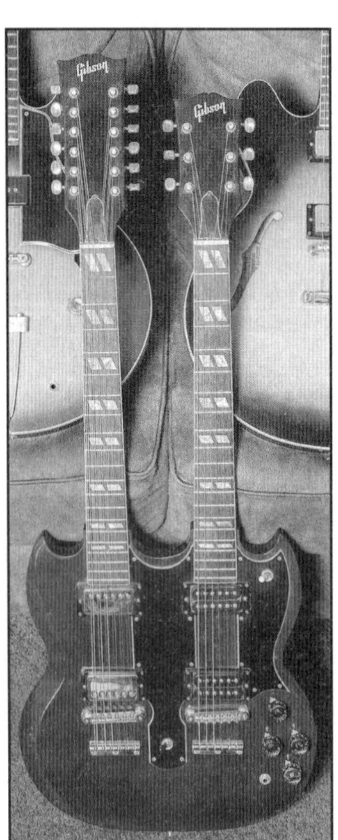
1964 Gibson EDS-1275
John Wesley

MODEL YEAR	FEATURES	EXC. COND. LOW	HIGH

'60s Dove Limited Edition

2014. Sitka spruce top, flame maple back and sides, Indian rosewood 'board, Vintage Cherryburst finish.

2014	50 offered	$4,500	$7,000

Dove Artist

1999-2005. Sitka spruce, Indian rosewood.

1999-2005		$2,800	$4,500

Dove Commemorative

1994-1996. Commemorates Gibson's 100th anniversary, Heritage or Antique Cherry finish, 100 built.

1994-1996		$3,500	$5,500

Dove In Flight Limited Edition

1996-1997. Custom Shop, 250 made, figured maple sides and back, Adirondack top, Certificate of Authenticity, dove inlays on headstock.

1996-1997		$4,500	$7,500

Doves In Flight (Brazilian)

2003. Custom Shop, only 2 made.

2003		$15,000	$25,000

Doves In Flight (Production Model)

1996-present. Gibson Custom model, maple back and sides, doves in flight inlays.

1996-2024		$3,500	$5,500

Dove Elvis Presley Signature

2008-2010. Artist Series, Certificate of Authenticity, black.

2008-2010		$3,500	$6,000

Super Dove

2009-2012. Cutaway, on-board electronics, sold through certain retailers.

2009-2012		$3,000	$4,800

Duane Eddy Signature

2004-2009. Single rounded cut, flamed maple top and back, 2 single-coils and piezo, pearl 'moustache' markers, signature engraved on 'guard, Bigsby, Rockabilly Brown finish.

2004-2009		$3,500	$5,500

EAS Deluxe

1992-1994. Single-cut flat-top acoustic/electric, solid flamed maple top, bound rosewood 'board, trapezoid inlays, 3-band EQ, Vintage Cherry Sunburst.

1992-1994		$1,500	$2,200

EAS Standard/Classic

1992-1995. Like EAS Deluxe, but with spruce top, unbound top, dot inlays, called EAS Classic for '92.

1992-1995		$1,200	$1,800

EBS(F)-1250 Double Bass

1962-1968. Double-cut SG-type solidbody, doubleneck with bass and 6-string, originally introduced as the EBSF-1250 because of a built-in fuzztone, which was later deleted, only 22 made.

1962-1964	Various colors	$40,000	$50,000
1965	Various colors	$20,000	$25,000
1966-1968	Various colors	$18,000	$22,500

EC-10 Standard

1997-1998. Jumbo single-cut, on-board electronics, solid spruce top, maple back and sides.

1997-1998		$1,200	$2,000

MODEL YEAR	FEATURES	EXC. COND. LOW	HIGH

EC-20 Starburst

1997-1998. Jumbo single-cut, on-board electronics, solid spruce top, maple back and sides, renamed J-185 EC in '99.

1997-1998		$1,800	$3,000

EC-30 Blues King Electro (BKE)

1995-1998. Jumbo single-cut, on-board electronics, solid spruce top, maple back and sides, double parallelogram inlays, renamed J-185 EC in '99.

1995-1998		$2,000	$3,500

EDS-1275 Double 12

1958-1967, 1977-1990. Double-cut doubleneck with one 12- and one 6-string, thinline hollowbody until late-'62, SG-style solidbody '62 on.

1958-1961	Custom order	$150,000	$200,000
1962-1964	SG body	$40,000	$50,000
1965	SG body	$30,000	$40,000
1966-1967	SG body	$25,000	$35,000
1977-1979	Various colors	$10,000	$15,000
1977-1979	White	$10,000	$15,000
1980-1989	Various colors	$5,000	$6,500
1990	Various colors	$5,000	$6,500

EDS-1275 Double 12 (Historic Collection)

1991-2018. Custom Shop Historic Collection reissue.

1991-2018	Various colors	$6,000	$10,000

EDS-1275 Double 12 Centennial

1994. Guitar of the Month (May), gold medallion on back of headstock, cherry with gold hardware.

1994		$7,000	$12,000

EDS-1275 Double 12 Jimmy Page VOS Signature

2008. Custom Shop model with Certificate of Authenticity, 250 made.

2008	Signed	$30,000	$50,000
2008	Unsigned	$10,000	$15,000

EDS-1275 Double Neck Alex Lifeson

2015-2016. Custom Shop model based on Lifeson's '70s Gibson, limited run of 100, first 25 signed and played by Alex, aged Arctic White.

2015-2016		$10,000	$15,000

EDS-1275 Double Neck Don Felder 'Hotel California'

2015-2016. Custom Shop limited edition, 50 aged/signed, 100 aged/unsigned, 1 set of exposed pickups (VI), 1 set of covered pickups (XII), aged faded white nitro finish.

2010	Signed	$25,000	$40,000
2010	Unsigned	$12,000	$18,000

EDS-1275 "Slash" 1966 Doubleneck

2019. Custom Shop limited, 125 made and signed, authentic '66 replica, aged ebony.

2019	Signed	$18,000	$28,000
2019	Unsigned	$8,000	$12,000

EMS-1235 Double Mandolin

1958-1963, 1965-1967. Double-cut, doubleneck with 1 regular 6-string and 1 short 6-string (the mandolin neck), thinline hollowbody until late-1962, SG-style solidbody '62-'68, black, sunburst or white, total of 61 shipped.

1958-1961	Custom order	$40,000	$50,000
1962-1963	SG body	$30,000	$40,000
1965	SG body	$25,000	$32,500
1966-1967	SG body	$24,000	$30,000

MODEL YEAR	FEATURES	EXC. COND. LOW	HIGH

ES-5/ES-5N

1949-1955. Single-cut archtop, 3 P-90 pickups, sunburst or natural (5N). Renamed ES-5 Switchmaster in '55.

1949-1955	Natural	$9,000	$15,000
1949-1955	Sunburst	$8,000	$10,000

ES-5 Switchmaster/ES-5N Switchmaster

1956-1962. Renamed from ES-5, single-cut (rounded until late-'60, pointed after) archtop, 3 P-90s until end of '57, humbuckers after, switchmaster control.

1956-1957	Natural, P-90s	$10,000	$12,500
1956-1957	Sunburst, P-90s	$9,000	$11,500
1957-1960	Natural, hums	$16,000	$20,000
1957-1960	Sunburst, hums	$15,000	$19,000
1960-1962	Pointed Florentine cutaway	$11,500	$14,500

ES-5/ES-5 Switchmaster Historic

1995-2006. Custom Shop Historic Collection.

1995-2002	ES-5, sunburst, P-90s	$4,500	$7,000
1995-2002	Switchmaster, Wine Red, hums	$5,000	$7,500
1995-2006	Switchmaster, natural, hums	$5,500	$8,500
1995-2006	Switchmaster, sunburst, hums	$4,800	$7,200

ES-100

1938-1941. Archtop, 1 pickup, bound body, sunburst, renamed ES-125 in '41.

1938-1941		$1,800	$2,500

ES-120 T

1962-1970. Archtop, thinline, 1 f-hole, bound body, 1 pickup, sunburst.

1962-1964		$1,500	$2,000
1965		$1,400	$1,800
1966-1970		$1,400	$1,800

ES-125

1941-1943, 1946-1970. Archtop, non-cut, 1 pickup, sunburst, renamed from ES-100.

1941-1943	Blade pickup	$2,400	$3,200
1947-1949	1st non-adj, P-90s	$2,400	$3,200
1950	1st non-adj, P-90s	$2,300	$3,000
1951-1959	Adj P-90s with poles	$2,300	$3,000
1960-1964		$1,600	$2,100
1965		$1,500	$2,000
1966-1970		$1,400	$1,800

ES-125 C

1966-1970. Wide body archtop, single pointed cutaway, 1 pickup, sunburst.

1965		$1,700	$2,200
1966-1970		$1,600	$2,100

ES-125 CD

1965-1970. Wide body archtop, single-cut, 2 pickups, sunburst.

1965		$2,500	$3,300
1966-1970		$2,300	$3,000

ES-125 D

1957. Limited production (not mentioned in catalog), 2 pickup version of thick body ES-125, sunburst.

1957		$2,600	$3,400

MODEL YEAR	FEATURES	EXC. COND. LOW	HIGH

ES-125 T

1956-1968. Archtop thinline, non-cut, 1 pickup, bound body, sunburst.

1956-1959		$2,300	$3,000
1960-1964		$2,000	$2,600
1965		$1,800	$2,300
1966-1968		$1,600	$2,100

ES-125 T 3/4

1957-1968. Archtop thinline, short-scale, non-cut, 1 pickup, sunburst.

1957-1960		$2,300	$3,000
1961-1964		$2,300	$3,000
1965		$2,300	$3,000
1966-1968		$2,300	$3,000

ES-125 TC

1960-1970. Archtop thinline, single pointed cutaway, bound body, 1 P-90 pickup, sunburst.

1960-1964		$2,300	$3,000
1965		$2,100	$2,700
1966-1970		$2,000	$2,600

ES-125 TD

1957-1963. Archtop thinline, non-cut, 2 pickups, sunburst.

1957-1963		$2,700	$3,500

ES-125 TDC or ES-125 TCD

1960-1971. Archtop thinline, single pointed cutaway, 2 P-90 pickups, sunburst.

1960-1964		$3,500	$4,500
1965	Early '65	$3,300	$4,300
1965	Late '65	$2,800	$3,600
1966-1971		$2,800	$3,600

ES-130

1954-1956. Archtop, non-cut, 1 pickup, bound body, sunburst, renamed ES-135 in '56.

1954-1959		$2,500	$4,500

ES-135

1956-1958. Renamed from ES-130, non-cut archtop, 1 pickup, sunburst, name reused on a thin body in the '90s.

1957-1959		$2,700	$3,500

ES-135 (Thinline)

1991-2005. Single-cut archtop, laminated maple body, 2 humbuckers or 2 P-100s, stoptail or trapeze, chrome or gold hardware.

1991-2005	Stoptail	$1,800	$3,000
1991-2005	Trapeze	$1,600	$2,800

ES-137 Classic

2002-2015. Thin-body electric single cut, trapezoid inlays, 2 humbuckers, f-holes, gold hardware.

2002-2015		$1,800	$2,500

ES-137 Custom

2002-2011. Like Classic, but with split-diamond inlays and varitone.

2002-2011		$1,800	$2,500

ES-137 P (Premier)

2002-2005. Like Classic, but with exposed humbuckers, chrome hardware and very small trapezoid inlays.

2002-2005		$2,200	$3,500

ES-139

2013-2016. Semi-hollow Les Paul style body, 2 humbuckers, Guitar Center model.

2013-2016		$1,800	$2,800

1961 Gibson ES-125 TC

Jim King

2002 Gibson ES-135 (Thinline)

Rivington Guitars

GUITARS

1957 Gibson ES-140 3/4

Robbie Keene

1953 Gibson ES-175

Alex Clarke

MODEL YEAR	FEATURES	EXC. COND. LOW	HIGH

ES-140 (3/4) or ES-140N (3/4)

1950-1956. Archtop, single-cut, 1 pickup, bound body, short-scale, sunburst or natural option (N).

1950-1956	Natural option	$3,000	$5,000
1950-1956	Sunburst	$2,500	$4,500

ES-140 (3/4) T or ES-140N (3/4) T

1957-1968. Archtop thinline, single-cut, bound body, 1 pickup, short-scale, sunburst or natural option (140N).

1957-1959	Natural option	$2,500	$4,500
1957-1959	Sunburst	$2,200	$4,000
1960-1964	Sunburst	$2,000	$3,500
1965	Sunburst	$1,800	$3,200
1966-1968	Sunburst	$1,700	$3,000

ES-150

1936-1942, 1946-1956. Historically important archtop, non-cut, bound body, Charlie Christian bar pickup from '36-'39, various metal covered pickups starting in '40, sunburst.

1936-1939	Charlie Christian pu	$7,500	$10,000
1940-1942	Metal covered pu	$6,500	$8,000
1946-1949	P-90 pickup	$3,500	$5,500
1950-1956	P-90 pickup	$2,800	$5,000

ES-150 DC

1969-1975. Archtop, double rounded cutaway, 2 humbuckers, multi-bound, cherry, natural or walnut.

1969-1975		$3,000	$4,000

ES-165 Herb Ellis

1991-2011. Single pointed cut hollowbody, 1 humbucker, gold hardware.

1991-2011		$2,500	$3,500

ES-175 or ES-175N

1949-1971. Archtop, single pointed cutaway, 1 pickup (P-90 from '49-early-'57, humbucker early-'57-'71), multi-bound, sunburst or natural option (175N).

1949-1956	Natural, P90	$6,200	$8,500
1949-1956	Sunburst, P-90	$6,000	$8,000
1957-1959	Natural, hum	$9,500	$12,000
1957-1963	Sunburst, PAF	$9,250	$11,500
1964	Sunburst, pat #	$7,000	$9,000
1965	Sunburst, hum	$4,500	$7,000
1966-1969	Sunburst, pat #	$4,000	$6,500
1967-1969	Black	$4,500	$5,500
1970-1971	Various colors	$3,800	$6,000

ES-175 CC

1978-1979. 1 Charlie Christian pickup, sunburst or walnut.

1978-1979		$3,500	$5,500

ES-175 D or ES-175N D

1952-2016. Archtop, single-cut, 2 pickups (P-90s from '53-early-'57, humbuckers early-'57 on), sunburst or natural option (175N D). Humbucker pickups were converted from PAF-stickers to Pat. No.-stickers in '62. Different models were converted at different times. An ES-175 model, made during the transitional time, with PAFs, will fetch more. In some of the electric-archtop models, the transition period may have been later than '62. Cataloged as the ES-175 Reissue in the '90s, currently as the ES-175 under Gibson Memphis.

1952-1956	Natural, P-90s	$6,500	$9,000
1952-1956	Sunburst, P-90s	$6,000	$8,000
1957-1963	Natural, PAFs	$16,000	$20,000
1957-1963	Sunburst, PAFs	$15,000	$19,000
1964	Natural, pat #	$7,500	$10,000
1964	Sunburst, pat #	$6,500	$9,000
1965	Natural, pat #	$6,500	$9,000
1965	Sunburst, hums	$6,000	$8,000
1966	Natural, pat #	$5,000	$7,000
1966	Sunburst, hums	$5,000	$7,000
1967-1969	Black	$5,000	$7,000
1967-1969	Various colors	$4,500	$7,000
1970-1979	Various colors	$4,000	$6,500
1980-2016	Various colors	$3,500	$6,000

ES-175 D Tenor

1966. Rare custom ordered tenor version, sunburst.

1966		$4,000	$5,500

ES-175 D-AN

1999-2000. Limited run, P-90s, Antique Natural finish.

1999-2000		$4,000	$6,500

ES-175 SP

2006. Single humbucker version, sunburst.

2006		$3,000	$5,000

ES-175 Steve Howe

2001-2007. Maple laminate body, multi-bound top, sunburst.

2001-2007		$4,500	$7,500

ES-175 T

1976-1980. Archtop thinline, single pointed cutaway, 2 humbuckers, various colors including international colors.

1976-1980		$2,800	$4,500

ES-225 T or ES-225N T

1955-1959. Thinline, single pointed cutaway, 1 P-90 pickup, bound body and neck, sunburst or natural option (225N T).

1955-1959	Natural	$5,000	$6,500
1955-1959	Sunburst	$3,500	$4,500

ES-225 TD or ES-225N TD

1956-1959. Thinline, single-cut, 2 P-90s, bound body and neck, sunburst or natural option (225N TD).

1956-1959	Natural	$7,500	$9,500
1956-1959	Sunburst	$5,500	$7,500

1959 ES-225 Historic

2014-2016. Single-cut TD reissue with 2 P-90s, sunburst.

2014-2016		$3,000	$5,000

ES-235 Gloss

2018-2020. Semi-hollow single-cut, maple neck, rosewood 'board, 2 pickups.

2018-2020		$1,800	$3,000

ES-250 or ES-250N

1939-1940. Archtop, carved top, special Christian pickup, multi-bound, high-end appointments, stairstep headstock '39 and standard in '40, sunburst or natural option (250N).

1939	Natural, stairstep hs	$35,000	$45,000
1939	Sunburst, stairstep hs	$25,000	$35,000
1940	Natural, standard hs	$35,000	$45,000
1940	Sunburst, standard hs	$25,000	$35,000

MODEL YEAR	FEATURES	EXC. COND. LOW	HIGH

ES-275

2016-2019. Hollowbody archtop, single-cut, 2 humbucker pickups standard or optional P-90s, various colors and finishes, certificate of authenticity.

2016	Gloss, opaque	$2,500	$4,000
2016-2019	Gloss, figured	$3,500	$5,500
2017	Gloss, P-90s	$3,200	$5,200
2018	Custom metallic	$4,500	$7,000
2019	Satin, opaque	$2,200	$3,800

ES-295

1952-1958. Single pointed cutaway archtop, 2 pickups (P-90s from '52-late-'57, humbuckers after), gold finish, gold-plated hardware.

1952-1957	P-90s	$12,000	$20,000
1957-1958	Humbuckers	$20,000	$25,000

ES-295 Historic Collection

1990-2000. Custom Shop, 2 P-90 pickups, Bigsby, Antique Gold finish.

1990-2000		$3,000	$5,000

ES-295 '52 Historic Collection

2013-2015. Custom Shop. Limited VOS Vintage Cherry offered in '15.

2013-2015		$3,500	$5,500
2015	Limited Cherry	$4,500	$7,000

ES-295 Scotty Moore Signature

1999. Custom Shop, 15 produced, 12 with Scotty's actual signature on lower bout, Bullion Gold, trapeze tailpiece.

1999		$8,000	$15,000

ES-300 or ES-300N

1940-1942, 1945-1953. Archtop, non-cut, f-holes, had 4 pickup configurations during its run, sunburst or natural (300N).

1940	Natural, oblong diagonal pu	$5,000	$6,500
1940	Sunburst, oblong diagonal pu	$4,000	$5,000
1941-1942	Natural, 1 pu	$5,000	$6,500
1941-1942	Sunburst, 1 pu	$4,000	$5,000
1945	Black, 1 pu	$3,750	$4,750
1945-1949	Sunburst, 1 pu	$3,750	$4,750
1945-1953	Natural, 1 pu	$4,500	$6,000
1949-1953	Natural, 2 pus	$5,000	$6,500
1949-1953	Sunburst, 2 pus	$4,000	$5,000

ES-320 TD

1971-1974. Thinline archtop, double-cut, 2 single-coil pickups, bound body, cherry, natural, or walnut.

1971-1974		$1,800	$3,000

ES-325 TD

1972-1978. Thinline archtop, double-cut, 2 mini-humbuckers, 1 f-hole, bound body, top mounted control panel, cherry or walnut.

1972-1978		$2,000	$3,500

ES-330 L

2009-2015. Custom Shop, classic 330 design, 2 dog-ear P-90 pickups, sunburst or black. 2015 model has humbuckers.

2009-2015		$2,800	$4,500

ES-330 T or ES-330N T

1959-1963. Double rounded cutaway, thinline, 1 pickup, bound body and neck, sunburst, cherry or natural option (330N T). In the '60s came with either an original semi-hard case (better than chip board) or a hardshell case. Prices quoted are for hardshell case; approximately $100 should be deducted for the semi-hard case.

1959-1961	Natural	$10,000	$12,000
1959-1963	Cherry	$6,500	$9,000
1959-1963	Sunburst	$5,500	$8,000

ES-330 TD or ES-330N TD

1959-1972. Double rounded cutaway, thinline, 2 pickups, bound body and neck, dot markers early then blocks, sunburst, cherry or natural option (330N TD). In the '60s came with either an original semi-hard case (better than chip board) or a hardshell case. Prices noted for the hardshell case; approximately $100 should be deducted for the semi-hard case.

1959-1961	Natural	$14,000	$18,000
1959-1962	Cherry, dots	$8,500	$11,000
1959-1962	Sunburst, dots	$8,500	$11,000
1963-1964	Cherry, blocks	$7,200	$9,500
1963-1964	Sunburst, blocks	$7,200	$9,500
1965	Cherry, sunburst	$6,200	$8,000
1966-1968	Cherry, sunburst	$4,800	$6,500
1967-1968	Burgundy Metallic	$5,200	$7,000
1968	Walnut option	$5,000	$6,500
1969-1972	Various colors	$4,800	$6,300

ES-330 TDC

1998-2000. Custom Shop model, block markers.

1998-2000		$2,500	$4,000

1959 ES-330 Historic VOS

2012-2019. Gibson Memphis, Historic series, P-90 pickups, trapeze tailpiece, certificate, VOS finish in sunburst, natural or cherry.

2012-2019		$3,000	$5,000

1959 ES-330 Wildwood Spec

2015. Gibson Memphis, Limited Edition, figured top, natural, certificate.

2015		$4,500	$6,500

1964 ES-330 Historic VOS

2015-2019. Historic series, vintage specs, P-90 pickups, trapeze tailpiece, certificate.

2015-2019		$3,200	$5,200

ES-333

2002-2005. Economy ES-335, no 'guard, no headstock inlay, exposed coils, stencil logo, satin finish.

2002-2005		$1,800	$3,000

ES-335 TD or ES-335N TD

1958-1981. The original design ES-335 has dot 'board inlays and a stop tailpiece, sunburst, cherry or natural option (335N). Block inlays replaced dots in mid-'62, in late-'64 the stop tailpiece was replaced with a trapeze tailpiece. Replaced by the ES-335 DOT in '81.

1958	Natural, bound neck	$100,000	$125,000
1958	Natural, bound neck, Bigsby	$80,000	$100,000
1958	Natural, unbound neck	$95,000	$125,000
1958	Natural, unbound neck, Bigsby	$75,000	$90,000
1958	Sunburst, bound neck	$50,000	$70,000

1956 Gibson ES-225 T

1953 Gibson ES-295
Adam Turton

GUITARS

1965 Gibson ES-335
K.C. Cormack

1968 Gibson ES-335 TD
Bruce Cohen

MODEL YEAR	FEATURES	EXC. COND. LOW	HIGH
1958	Sunburst, bound neck, Bigsby	$40,000	$55,000
1958	Sunburst, unbound neck	$45,000	$60,000
1958	Sunburst, unbound neck, Bigsby	$36,000	$45,000
1959	Cherry (early), stop tail	$100,000	$125,000
1959	Natural, bound neck	$150,000	$175,000
1959	Natural, bound neck, Bigsby	$120,000	$150,000
1959	Sunburst, bound neck	$65,000	$85,000
1959	Sunburst, bound neck, Bigsby	$55,000	$70,000
1960	Cherry, factory Bigsby	$35,000	$45,000
1960	Cherry, factory stop tail	$40,000	$50,000
1960	Natural, factory Bigsby	$75,000	$100,000
1960	Natural, factory stop tail	$95,000	$125,000
1960	Sunburst, factory Bigsby	$35,000	$45,000
1960	Sunburst, factory stop tail	$40,000	$50,000
1961	Cherry, factory Bigsby	$22,000	$30,000
1961	Cherry, factory stop tail	$30,000	$40,000
1961	Sunburst, factory Bigsby	$22,000	$30,000
1961	Sunburst, factory stop tail	$30,000	$40,000
1962	Cherry, blocks, PAFs	$20,000	$25,000
1962	Cherry, blocks, pat#	$16,000	$20,000
1962	Cherry, dots, PAFs	$26,500	$35,000
1962	Cherry, vibrola, pat#	$15,000	$20,000
1962	Sunburst, blocks, PAFs	$20,000	$25,000
1962	Sunburst, blocks, pat#	$16,000	$20,000
1962	Sunburst, dots, PAFs	$26,500	$35,000
1962	Sunburst, dots, pat#	$16,500	$21,500
1962	Sunburst, vibrola, pat#	$14,500	$18,500
1963-1964	Cherry, factory Bigsby	$16,000	$20,000
1963-1964	Cherry, factory Maestro	$16,000	$20,000
1963-1964	Cherry, factory stop tail	$20,000	$25,000
1963-1964	Sunburst, factory Bigsby	$16,000	$20,000
1963-1964	Sunburst, factory Maestro	$16,000	$20,000
1963-1964	Sunburst, factory stop tail	$18,500	$24,000
1965	Early '65, wide neck	$12,000	$15,000
1965	Mid '65, narrow neck	$7,000	$9,000
1966	Cherry, sunburst	$6,500	$8,500
1966	Pelham Blue	$15,000	$20,000
1966	Sparkling Burgundy	$8,000	$12,000
1967	Black	$10,000	$14,000
1967	Cherry, sunburst	$6,500	$8,500
1967	Pelham Blue	$14,000	$17,500
1967	Sparkling Burgundy	$8,000	$12,000
1968	Cherry, sunburst	$6,500	$8,500
1968	Pelham Blue	$14,000	$17,500
1968	Sparkling Burgundy	$8,000	$11,000
1969	Cherry, sunburst	$5,500	$7,500
1969	Walnut option	$6,000	$9,000
1970-1976	Cherry, sunburst	$3,500	$5,500
1970-1976	Walnut option	$4,000	$6,000
1977-1979	All colors	$3,200	$5,000
1980-1981	All colors	$3,000	$4,800

ES-335 Dot

1981-1990. Reissue of '60 ES-335 and replaces ES-335 TD. Name changed to ES-335 Reissue. Various color options including highly figured wood.

MODEL YEAR	FEATURES	LOW	HIGH
1981	Black	$2,500	$4,000
1981-1984	Natural	$2,500	$4,000
1981-1990	Cherry, sunburst	$2,000	$3,500
1985-1990	Natural	$2,300	$3,800

ES-335 Dot CMT (Custom Shop)

1983-1985. Custom Shop ES 335 Dot with curly maple top and back, full-length center block, 2 PAF-labeled humbuckers, natural or sunburst.

MODEL YEAR	FEATURES	LOW	HIGH
1983-1985		$3,500	$5,500

ES-335 Reissue/ES-335 '59 Dot Reissue/ES-335

1991-present. Replaced the ES-335 DOT, dot inlays, various color options including highly figured wood. Renamed the 1959 ES-335 Dot Reissue in '98 and currently just ES-335 followed by options - Dot, Block (added in '98), Fat Neck (added in '08), Figured (added in '06), Plain, Satin (added in '06).

MODEL YEAR	FEATURES	LOW	HIGH
1991-2020	Cherry, sunburst, walnut, black	$2,500	$4,000
1991-2024	Natural	$3,000	$4,500
2006-2017	Satin	$2,000	$3,200

ES-335 Dot P-90

2007. Custom Shop limited edition with black dog-ear P-90s, stop tailpiece.

MODEL YEAR	FEATURES	LOW	HIGH
2007		$3,000	$4,800

ES-335-12

1965-1971. 12-string version of the 335.

MODEL YEAR	FEATURES	LOW	HIGH
1965-1968		$4,000	$7,000

MODEL YEAR	FEATURES	EXC. COND. LOW	HIGH

ES-335 '59 Dot Historic

1999-2000, 2002-2016. Custom Shop Historic Collection, based upon 1959 ES-335 dot neck, figured maple top on early series, plain on later, nickel hardware.

1999-2016	Figured top	$4,500	$7,000
2002-2016	Plain top	$3,500	$5,500

1959 ES-335 Dot Reissue Limited Edition

2009-2017. Custom Shop, plain laminated maple top/back/sides, rounded '59 neck profile, '57 Classic humbuckers, Certificate of Authenticity, 250 each to be made in Antique Vintage Sunburst or Antique Natural (standard gloss or V.O.S. treatments).

2009-2017		$4,000	$6,500

1959 ES-335 Ultra Heavy Aged/Ultra Light Aged

2021-present. Custom Shop Murphy Lab Collection, ultra heavy aged (Vintage Natural) and ultra light (Ebony or Vintage Natural). Ultra light ends in '22.

2021-2024	Ultra Heavy Aged	$6,000	$9,000
2021-2024	Ultra Light Aged	$5,000	$7,500

ES-335 '60s Block Inlay

2004-2007. Made in Memphis facility, plain maple top, small block markers.

2004-2007		$3,500	$5,500

50th Anniversary 1958 ES-335

2008. Custom Shop logo on back of neck, 200 made, plain top, sunburst nitro finish, includes COA.

2008		$5,500	$8,500

50th Anniversary 1960 ES-335

2009-2010. Custom Shop, dot markers, natural.

2009-2010		$4,500	$7,000

1961 ES-335 Heavy Aged/ Ultra Light Aged

2021-2022. Custom Shop Murphy Lab Collection, heavy or ultra light aged, Sixties Cherry finish. Ultra light ends in '22.

2021-2022	Heavy Aged	$6,500	$9,500
2021-2022	Ultra Light Aged	$5,500	$8,000

1961 ES-335 Reissue (Custom Shop)

2020-present. Historic series, 3-Ply maple/poplar/maple body, solid mahogany neck, Indian rosewood 'board, 2 Alnico pickups, Sixties Cherry or Vintage Burst.

2020-2024		$4,500	$6,500

50th Anniversary 1963 Block ES-335TD/ES-335TDC

2010-2013. Memphis Custom Shop, block markers, double-ring vintage-style tuners, Antique Vintage Sunburst (TD), Antique Faded Cherry (TDC).

2010-2013	TD, sunburst	$4,000	$6,000
2010-2013	TDC, cherry	$4,500	$6,500

ES-335 '63 Block Historic

1998-2000, 2002-2018. Custom Shop Historic Collection, based upon 1963 ES-335 with small block markers, figured maple top on early series, plain on later, nickel hardware.

1998-2000	1st release, figured top	$4,500	$7,000
2002-2018	2nd release, figured top	$4,000	$6,000
2002-2018	Plain top	$3,500	$5,000

1964 ES-335 Ultra Light Aged

2021-2022. Custom Shop Murphy Lab Collection, Sixties Cherry finish.

2021-2022		$5,500	$8,000

ES-335 Alvin Lee

2006-2007. Custom Division Nashville, 50 made, features reflect Alvin Lee's Big Red ES-335 complete with decal art, cherry red, includes certificate of authenticity (if missing value is reduced). There is also an unlimited version without a certificate.

2006-2007	With certificate	$4,500	$7,000

ES-335 Andy Summers

2002. Custom Shop, 50 made, script signature on 'guard, early dot neck specs, nitro cherry finish, certificate of authenticity.

2002		$4,000	$6,500

ES-335 Artist

1981. Off-set dot markers, large headstock logo, metal truss rod plate, gold hardware, 3 control knobs with unusual toggles and input specification.

1981		$3,500	$6,000

ES-335 Canadian Custom

2007. Custom Shop Canadian exclusive, run of 50, maple leaf 'Limited Edition' decal on back of headstock, 'Custom Made' engraved plate on guitar front, solid mahogany neck, pearloid block inlays, antique cherry finish with aged binding.

2007		$3,500	$5,500

ES-335 Centennial

1994. Centennial edition, gold medallion in headstock, diamond inlay in tailpiece, cherry.

1994		$5,000	$8,000

ES-335 Chris Cornell

2012-2016. Olive Drab Green or black.

2012-2016		$4,500	$7,000

ES-335 CRR/CRS

1979. Country Rock Regular with standard wiring and CRR logo. Country Rock Stereo with stereo wiring and CRS logo, 300 of each built, 2 pickups, coil-tap.

1979	CRR	$2,500	$4,000
1979	CRS	$2,500	$4,000

ES-335 Diamond Edition

2006. Trini Lopez style diamond f-holes, Bigsby tailpiece option, gold hardware, Pelham Blue, pearl white or black pearl.

2006		$4,200	$6,500

ES-335 Eric Clapton Crossroads '64 Reissue

2005. Reissue of EC's, with certificate of authenticity.

2005		$7,500	$11,500

ES-335 Goldtop

2013-2016. Gibson Memphis, limited edition, 2 Burstbucker humbuckers, gold finish.

2013-2016		$3,800	$6,000

ES-335 Gothic

1998-1999. Gothic appointments including ebony 'board and black satin finish.

1998-1999		$2,200	$3,500

2001 Gibson ES-335 '59 Dot Reissue

Cream City Music

Gibson ES-335 '63 Block Historic

Ted Mottor

GUITARS

1979 Gibson ES-335 Pro
Michael Campbell

1959 Gibson ES-345 TD
Trey Rabinek

MODEL YEAR	FEATURES	EXC. COND. LOW	HIGH

ES-335 Government Series

2015-2016. Made from guitar bodies, necks and 'boards returned from Federal Government after '11 raid on Gibson, special run of 300 built, each with Certificate of Authenticity.

2015-2016		$3,800	$6,000

ES-335 Jim Beam Limited Edition

1999. Promotional Custom Shop model, approximately 18 made, large Jim Beam notation on body, comes with certificate.

1999		$3,800	$6,000

ES-335 Jimmy Wallace Reissue

Special order by Texas Gibson dealer Jimmy Wallace.

1980		$3,500	$6,000

ES-335 Joe Bonamassa Signature

2012. Custom Shop, based on Joe's '61 335, VOS sunburst.

2012		$4,500	$7,000

ES-335 King of the Blues

2006. Offered through Guitar Center, 150 made, based on B.B.'s Lucille, King of the Blues logo on 'guard.

2006		$4,500	$6,500

ES-335 Larry Carlton

2002-2016. Mr. 335 logo on truss rod cover, block neck like Larry's guitar, vintage (faded) sunburst.

2002-2016		$4,000	$6,500

ES-335 Lee Ritenour

2008. Custom Shop, COA, 50 signed and 100 unsigned, Antique Cherry finish.

2008	Signed	$5,000	$7,500
2008	Unsigned	$4,000	$6,000

ES-335 Limited Edition (P-90s)

2001. ES-335 style crown inlay on headstock, P-90 pickups.

2001		$3,500	$5,000

ES-335 Nashville

1994. All serial numbers begin with 94, first year Custom Shop run (not the Centennial).

1994		$4,000	$6,000

ES-335 Pro

1979-1981. Two humbucking pickups with exposed coils, bound 'board, cherry or sunburst.

1979-1981		$1,800	$3,000

ES-335 Rich Robinson

2014-2016. Bigsby, small blocks, Cherry VOS finish.

2014-2016		$4,000	$6,500

ES-335 Roy Orbison

2006. About 70 made, RO serial number, black finish.

2006		$6,000	$9,000

ES-335 Rusty Anderson

2013. Figured maple, natural, dot neck specs.

2013		$4,500	$7,000

ES-335 Showcase Edition

1988. Guitar of the Month series, limited production, black gothic-style hardware, EMG pickups, transparent white/beige finish.

1988		$3,000	$4,500

ES-335 Studio

1986-1991, 2013-2020. Bound body, 2 Dirty Finger humbuckers, cherry or ebony. Reissued in '13 by Gibson Memphis using '58 specs but with Vintage Sunburst or ebony finish.

1986-1991		$1,800	$3,000
2013-2020	Memphis	$1,800	$2,800

ES-335 Warren Haynes

2013-2015. Custom Shop model.

2013-2015	500 made	$4,500	$7,000
2014	1961 Ltd Ed	$5,000	$7,500

ESDT-335

2001-2009. Memphis Custom Shop, flame maple top and back, 2 humbucking pickups, various colors.

2001-2009		$4,000	$6,500

ES-336

1996-1998. Custom Shop smaller sized ES-335 with smaller headstock, dot markers.

1996-1998	All options	$3,500	$5,500

ES-339

2007-present. Modern series, smaller-sized bound 335 body, 2 humbuckers, block inlays, various colors.

2007-2024	All options	$2,800	$4,500

ES-339 Studio

2013-2018. Stripped-down 339, no binding or pickguard, dot inlays.

2013-2018		$1,700	$2,500

ES-339 Traditional Pro

2013. Figured or plain, cherry or vintage sunburst.

2013		$2,800	$4,500

ES-340 TD

1968-1973. The 335 with a laminated maple neck, master volume and mixer controls, various colors.

1968-1973	Natural, Walnut	$3,500	$5,500

ES-345 TD or ES-345 TDSV

1959-1983. The 335 with Vari-tone, stereo, 2 humbuckers, gold hardware, double parallelogram inlays, stop tailpiece '59-'64 and '82-'83, trapeze tailpiece '65-'82. Cataloged as ES-345 TDSV by '80.

1959	Cherry, Bigsby	$27,500	$35,000
1959	Cherry, stud tail	$30,000	$40,000
1959	Natural, Bigsby	$55,000	$75,000
1959	Natural, stud tail	$75,000	$100,000
1959	Sunburst, Bigsby	$24,000	$30,000
1959	Sunburst, stud tail	$30,000	$37,500
1960	Cherry, Bigsby	$22,500	$30,000
1960	Cherry, stud tail	$28,500	$36,000
1960	Natural, Bigsby	$60,000	$75,000
1960	Natural, stud tail	$70,000	$95,000
1960	Sunburst, Bigsby	$22,500	$30,000
1960	Sunburst, stud tail	$28,500	$40,000
1961	Cherry, Bigsby	$15,000	$20,000
1961	Cherry, stud tail	$20,000	$25,000
1961	Sunburst, Bigsby	$15,000	$20,000
1961	Sunburst, stud tail	$20,000	$25,000
1962	Bigsby, PAF	$13,500	$20,000
1962	Stud tail, PAF	$17,500	$25,000
1963-1964	Bigsby, pat #	$11,500	$15,000
1963-1964	Stud tail, pat #	$13,500	$20,000
1965	Early '65 wide neck	$7,500	$9,500
1965	Mid '65 narrow neck	$4,500	$6,000

MODEL YEAR	FEATURES	EXC. COND. LOW	HIGH
1966-1969	Various colors	$4,500	$6,000
1970-1976	Various colors	$3,500	$5,500
1977-1979	Various colors	$3,200	$5,000
1980-1983	Various colors	$3,000	$4,500

ES-345 Historic

1998-1999. Custom Shop Historic Collection, stopbar, Bigsby or Maestro tailpiece, Viceroy Brown, Vintage Sunburst, Faded Cherry or natural.

1998-1999		$3,500	$5,500

ES-345 Reissue

2002-2010. 6-position Varitone selector, gold hardware, stop tailpiece, various colors.

2002-2010		$3,800	$6,000

1959 ES-345 TD

2014-2015. Period-correct '59 specs with VOS aged look, certificate of authenticity, Historic Burst or natural (TDN) finish.

2014	'59 reissue	$4,500	$7,000
2015	VOS	$4,800	$7,500

ES-346 Paul Jackson Jr.

1997-2006. Custom Shop, 335-like with figured or plain maple top, rosewood 'board, double-parallelogram inlays.

1997-2006		$4,000	$6,500

ES-347 TD or ES-347 S

1978-1985, 1987-1993. 335-style with gold hardware, tune-o-matic bridge, 2 Spotlight double-coil pickups, coil-tap, bound body and neck, S added to name in '87.

1978-1985	TD	$2,500	$4,000
1987-1993	S	$2,800	$4,500

ES-350 or ES-350N

1947-1956. Originally the ES-350 Premier, full body archtop, single-cut, 1 P-90 pickup until end of '48, 2 after, sunburst or natural (350N).

1947-1948	Natural, 1 pu	$8,500	$11,000
1947-1948	Sunburst, 1 pu	$8,000	$10,000
1949-1956	Natural, 2 pu	$9,000	$12,000
1949-1956	Sunburst, 2 pu	$8,500	$11,000

ES-350 Centennial

1994. Guitar of the Month, sunburst, gold hardware, gold medallion on back of headstock, diamond accents, 101 made with serial numbers from 1984-1994. Included a gold signet ring.

1994		$5,000	$8,000

ES-350 T or ES-350N T

1955-1963, 1977-1981, 1992-1993. Called the ES-350 TD in early-'60s, thinline archtop, single-cut (round '55-'60 and '77-'81, pointed '61-'63), 2 P-90 pickups '55-'56, humbuckers after, gold hardware. Limited runs were done in 1992-1993.

1956	Natural, P-90s	$8,500	$11,000
1956	Sunburst, P-90s	$8,000	$10,000
1957-1959	Natural, PAFs	$13,500	$17,000
1957-1959	Sunburst, PAFs	$13,500	$17,000
1960-1963	Natural, PAFs	$13,500	$17,000
1960-1963	Sunburst, PAFs	$13,500	$17,000
1977-1981	Natural, sunburst	$3,500	$4,500

ES-350 T Historic

1998-2000. Custom Shop Historic Collection reissue.

1998-2000		$4,500	$7,000

Chuck Berry 1955 ES-350 T

2019. Limited to 55, antique natural with VOS finish.

2019		$8,000	$12,000

ES-355 TD

1958-1970. 335-style with large block inlays, multi-bound body and headstock, 2 humbuckers, the 355 model was standard with a Bigsby, sideways or Maestro vibrato, non-vibrato models were an option. The prices shown assume a vibrato tailpiece, a factory stop tailpiece was considered an advantage and will fetch more. Early examples have factory Bigsby vibratos, early '60s have sideways vibratos, and late '60s have Maestro vibratos, cherry finish was the standard finish.

1958-1959	Cherry, PAFs, Bigsby, vibrato	$28,000	$35,000
1960-1962	Cherry, PAFs, Bigsby, vibrato	$20,000	$25,000
1962	Cherry, PAFs, side-pull, vibrato	$20,000	$25,000
1963-1964	Cherry, pat#, Bigsby, vibrato	$12,500	$16,000
1965	Early '65, wide neck	$9,000	$11,500
1965	Mid '65, narrow neck	$6,000	$7,500
1966-1968	Cherry or sunburst	$6,000	$7,500
1966-1968	Sparkling Burgundy	$9,000	$11,500
1969-1970	Cherry or sunburst	$5,000	$6,500

ES-355 TDSV

1959-1982. The stereo version of ES-355 with Varitone switch, a mono version was available, but few were made, the 355 model was standard with a Bigsby, sideways or Maestro vibrato, non-vibrato models were an option. The prices shown assume a vibrato tailpiece. A factory stop tailpiece was considered an advantage and will fetch more, early examples have factory Bigsby vibratos, early-'60s have sideways vibratos and late-'60s have Maestro vibratos, cherry finish was standard, walnut became available in '69.

1959	Bigsby	$20,000	$25,000
1959	Factory stop tail	$60,000	$75,000
1960	Bigsby	$16,500	$20,000
1961-1963	Sideways, late PAFs	$16,500	$20,000
1962	Maestro, late PAFs	$16,500	$20,000
1963-1964	Maestro, pat #	$11,500	$14,500
1965	Early '65 wide neck	$9,000	$11,500
1965	Mid '65 narrow neck	$6,000	$7,500
1966	Sparkling Burgundy	$9,000	$11,500
1966-1967	Cherry or sunburst, Maestro	$5,000	$6,500
1968	Various colors, Maestro	$5,000	$6,500
1969	Various colors, Bigsby	$4,500	$6,000
1970-1982	Various colors, Bigsby	$4,250	$5,500

ES-355/ES-355 TD (Custom Shop)

1994, 1997, 2006-2010. Mono, Bigsby or stop tail.

1994-2010		$4,000	$6,000

1967 Gibson ES-345

Scott Anderson

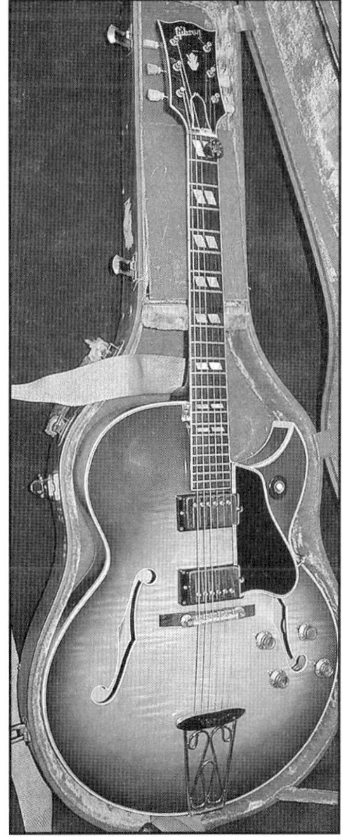

1962 Gibson ES-350 T

Landy Hardy

GUITARS

1958 Gibson Explorer

1996 Gibson Explorer '76
Rivington Guitars

MODEL YEAR	FEATURES	EXC. COND. LOW	HIGH

1959 ES-355 Light Aged/Ultra Light Aged

2021-present. Custom Shop Murphy Lab Collection, light aged (Watermelon Red) and ultra light (Ebony or Vintage Natural). Ultra light ends in '22.

2021-2024	Light Aged	$6,000	$9,000
2021-2022	Ultra Light Aged	$5,500	$8,000

ES-355 Alex Lifeson

2008-2010. Custom Shop Inspired By series, gold hardware, Alpine White finish.

2008-2010		$5,500	$8,500

ES-355 Centennial

1994. Guitar of the Month, sunburst, gold hardware, gold medallion on back of headstock, diamond accents, 101 made with serial numbers from 1984-1994. Included a gold signet ring.

1994		$5,500	$8,500

ES-355 Curly Maple Limited Edition

2010-2012. Figured flamed maple top, stop tailpiece, natural finish.

2010-2012		$4,500	$7,000

ES-355 Limited Edition (VOS)

2015-2018. Gibson Memphis, Bigsby, gold hardware, various colors with VOS finish.

2015-2018		$4,000	$6,000

ES-355 Summer Jam Series

2011. Custom Shop Summer Jam series, 25 made in Bourbon Burst.

2011		$5,000	$8,000

ES-359

2008-2016. Custom Shop, ES-335/ES-339 style with LP Custom style appointments, minor-figured top and back, sunburst.

2008-2016		$3,000	$4,500

ES-369

1981-1982. A 335-style with 2 exposed humbucker pickups, coil-tap, sunburst.

1981-1982		$2,500	$4,500

ES-390

2014-2018. Memphis model, thinline hollow-body, rosewood 'board, 2 P-90s, Vintage Dark Burst finish.

2014-2018		$2,800	$4,500

ES-446

1999-2003. Single cut semi-hollow, 2 humbuckers, Bigsby, Custom Shop.

1999-2003	Various colors	$3,500	$5,500

ES-775

1990-1993. Single-cut hollowbody, 2 humbuckers, gold hardware, ebony, natural or sunburst.

1990-1993		$4,000	$6,500

ES-Artist

1979-1985. Double-cut thinline, semi-hollowbody, no f-holes, 2 humbuckers, active electronics, gold hardware, ebony, fireburst or sunburst. Moog electronics includes 3 mini-switches for compressor, expander, and bright boost.

1979-1985		$2,500	$4,000

EST-150

1937-1939. Tenor version of ES-150, Charlie Christian pickup, sunburst, renamed ETG-150 in '40.

1937-1939		$5,000	$10,000

ETG-150

1940-1942, 1947-1971. Renamed from EST-150, tenor version of ES-150, 1 metal-covered pickup '40-'42, P-90 after, sunburst.

1940-1942		$3,500	$6,500
1947-1959		$2,500	$4,500
1960-1971		$2,000	$3,500

Everly Brothers

1962-1972. Jumbo flat-top, huge double 'guard, star inlays, natural was optional in '63 and became the standard color in '68, reintroduced as the J-180 Everly Brothers in '86.

1962-1964	Black	$20,000	$30,000
1963	Natural option	$20,000	$30,000
1965	Early '65, black, large neck	$15,000	$20,000
1965	Late '65, black, small neck	$10,000	$15,000
1966-1967	Black	$8,000	$12,000
1968-1969	Natural	$7,000	$10,000
1970-1972	Natural	$6,000	$8,000

Explorer

1958-1959, 1963. Some '58s shipped in '63, korina body, 2 humbuckers. The Explorer market is a very specialized and very small market, with few genuine examples available and a limited number of high-end buyers. The slightest change to the original specifications can mean a significant drop in value. The narrow price ranges noted are for all original examples that have the original guitar case.

1958-1959		$1,000,000	$1,350,000
1963		$500,000	$750,000

Explorer (Mahogany)

1975-1982. Mahogany body, 2 humbuckers, black, white or natural.

1975-1982	Black or white	$5,000	$6,500
1975-1982	Natural	$5,000	$6,500

Explorer I

1981-1982. Replaces Explorer (Mahogany), 2 Dirty Finger humbuckers, stoptail or Kahler vibrato, becomes Explorer 83 in '83.

1981-1982		$2,000	$3,500

Explorer 83 or Explorer (Alder)

1983-1989. Renamed Explorer 83 from Explorer I, changed to Explorer in '84, alder body, 2 humbuckers, maple neck, ebony 'board, dot inlays, triangle knob pattern.

1983-1984		$2,200	$3,800
1985-1989	Custom color, limited run	$2,800	$4,500
1985-1989	Standard finishes	$2,000	$3,500

Explorer II (E/2)

1978-1983. Five-piece maple and walnut laminate body sculptured like V II, ebony 'board with dot inlays, 2 humbuckers, gold-plated hardware, natural finish.

1978-1983	Figured top	$3,000	$4,500
1978-1983	Various colors	$2,800	$4,200

Explorer III

1984-1985. Alder body, 3 P-90 pickups, 2 control knobs, chrome or black hardware ('85 only), optional locking trem.

1984-1985	All options	$2,500	$5,000

MODEL YEAR	FEATURES	EXC. COND. LOW	HIGH

Explorer '76/X-plorer/Explorer

1990-2014, 2019-2024. Mahogany body and neck, rosewood 'board, dot inlays, 2 humbucking pickups, name changed to X-plorer in 2002 and to Explorer in '09. Reintroduced in '19.

1990-2014	Various colors	$1,800	$3,000
2019-2024	Various colors	$1,600	$2,800

Explorer 90 Double

1989-1990. Mahogany body and neck, 1 single-coil and 1 humbucker, strings-thru-body.

1989-1990		$2,500	$4,000

Explorer Baritone

2011-2013. 28"-scale, 2 exposed humbuckers.

2011-2013		$2,200	$3,500

Explorer Centennial

1994 only. Les Paul Gold finish, 100 year banner inlay at 12th fret, diamonds in headstock and gold-plated knobs, Gibson coin in rear of headstock, only 100 made.

1994		$5,000	$7,500

Explorer CMT/The Explorer

1981-1984. Flamed maple body, bound top, exposed-coil pickups, TP-6 tailpiece.

1981-1984		$2,800	$4,500

Explorer Custom Shop

2003-2012. Custom Shop model with Certificate of Authenticity, Korina body, gold hardware.

2003-2012		$4,500	$7,000

Explorer Designer Series

1983-1985. Custom paint finish.

1983-1985		$2,800	$4,500

Explorer Gothic

1998-2003. Gothic Series with black finish and hardware.

1998-2003		$2,200	$3,500

Explorer Government Series

2012-2016. Made from guitar bodies, necks and 'boards returned from Federal Government after '11 raid on Gibson, special run of 300 built, each with Certificate of Authenticity.

2013		$2,000	$3,000

Explorer Heritage

1983. Reissue of '58 Explorer, korina body, gold hardware, inked serial number, limited edition.

1983	Black, white, red	$5,000	$8,000
1983	Natural	$10,000	$15,000

Explorer Korina

1982-1984. Korina body and neck, 2 humbucking pickups, gold hardware, standard 8-digit serial (versus the inked serial number on the Heritage Explorer of the same era).

1982-1984		$4,500	$7,000

Explorer 1958 Korina/Split Headstock

1994. Split headstock, 50 made.

1994		$8,000	$12,000

Explorer 50th Anniversary '58 Korina

2007-2008. Custom Shop, natural korina, includes custom colors.

2007-2008		$9,500	$12,000

Explorer 50-Year Brimstone Commemorative

2008. Guitar of the month Oct. '08, solid mahogany body, AA figured maple top, higher-end appointments, 50th logo on truss rod cover, Brimstone Burst finish.

2008		$4,500	$7,000

Explorer 120

2014. 120th Anniversary inlay at 12th fret, mahogany body, cherry or black.

2014		$3,000	$5,000

Explorer Pro

2002-2005, 2007-2008. Explorer model updated with smaller, lighter weight mahogany body, 2 humbuckers, ebony or natural.

2002-2008		$2,300	$3,500

Allen Collins Tribute Explorer

2003. Custom Shop, limited production, korina body and neck, rosewood 'board, 2 humbucker pickups.

2003		$8,500	$15,000

Dethklok "Thunderhorse" Explorer

2011-2012. Limited Edition of 400, Thunderhorse logo on truss rod cover, silverburst finish.

2011-2012		$3,000	$5,000

Explorer Limited Edition (Korina)

1976. Limited edition korina body replaces standard mahogany body, natural.

1976		$6,000	$10,000

Explorer Limited Edition (Mahogany)

1999. Mahogany with natural finish.

1999		$2,800	$4,500

Explorer Robot

2008-2012. Announced Sept. '08, Robot Tuning System, trapezoid markers, 2 exposed humbuckers, red finish.

2008-2012		$2,500	$4,000

Explorer Split Headstock Collection

2001. Custom Shop model, 25 made, Explorer body with V-split headstock.

2001		$6,000	$9,000

Explorer T/Explorer 2016 T/2017 T

2016-2018. Mahogany body, rosewood 'board, white 'guard, ebony or cherry finish.

2016-2018		$1,800	$3,000

Explorer Voodoo

2002-2004. Juju finish, red and black pickup coils.

2002-2004		$2,200	$3,000

Explorer XPL

1985. Factory Gibson Kahler tremolo, Cherry Sunburst or Ivory.

1985		$1,800	$2,800

Explorer XPL Custom

1985. Gibson Custom Shop logo on back of headstock, factory Gibson Kahler tremolo, extra cutaway on lower treble bout.

1985		$2,200	$3,500

Holy Explorer

2009-2011. Explorer body 7 routed holes, 1 knob, 2 exposed humbuckers, Limited Run Series certificate of authenticity, 350 made.

2009-2011		$2,200	$3,500

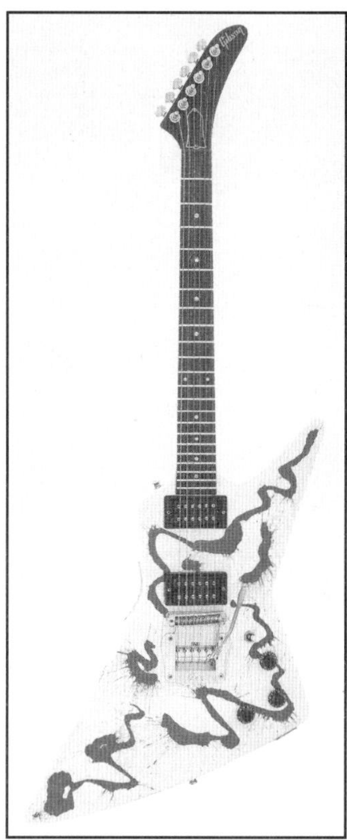

1984 Gibson Explorer Designer Series

Imaged by Heritage Auctions, HA.com

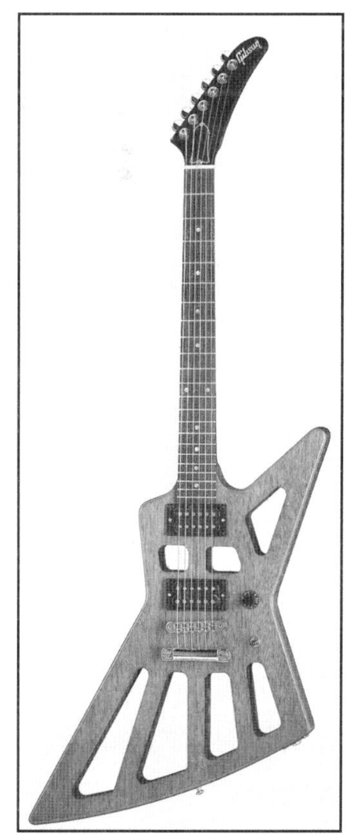

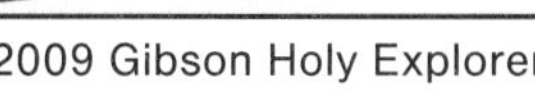

2009 Gibson Holy Explorer

GUITARS

1965 Gibson Firebird I
Matt Carleson

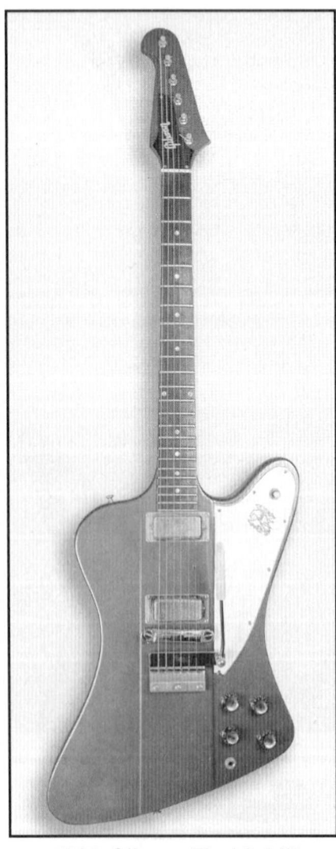
1964 Gibson Firebird III
Dave Rogers

MODEL YEAR	FEATURES	EXC. COND. LOW	HIGH

Reverse Explorer

2008. Guitar of the Month Sept. '08, 1,000 made, Antique Walnut finish, includes custom guitar case.

2008		$2,500	$4,500

Sammy Hagar Signature Explorer

2011-2013. Mahogany with Red Rocker finish, ghosted Chickenfoot logo on back.

2011-2013		$3,000	$5,000

Shred X Explorer

2008. Guitar of the Month June '08, 1,000 made, ebony finish, black hardware, 2 EMG 85 pickups, Kahler.

2008		$2,000	$3,500

Tribal Explorer

2009-2011. Black tribal graphics on white body. Limited run of 350.

2009-2011		$2,200	$3,500

X-Plorer/X-Plorer V New Century

2006-2007. Full-body mirror 'guard, mahogany body and neck, 2 humbuckers, mirror truss rod cover.

2006-2007		$1,800	$3,000

Eye Guitar

Announced April 2009. Nashville Limited Run series, 350 made, double-cut solid mahogany body, 2 humbucker pickups, volume/tone, Fire Engine Red finish with matching headstock, with COA.

2009		$3,000	$5,000

Firebird I

1963-1969. Reverse body and 1 humbucker '63-mid-'65, non-reversed body and 2 P-90s mid-'65-'69.

1963	Sunburst, reverse, hardtail	$17,500	$25,000
1963	Sunburst, reverse, trem	$11,000	$15,000
1964	Cardinal Red, reverse	$22,500	$30,000
1964	Sunburst, reverse, hardtail	$16,000	$25,000
1964	Sunburst, reverse, trem	$9,500	$15,000
1965	Cardinal Red, reverse	$16,500	$25,000
1965	Custom color, non-reverse	$12,500	$16,000
1965	Sunburst, non-reverse, 2 P-90s	$5,000	$7,000
1965	Sunburst, reverse	$8,000	$10,000
1966	Custom color, non-reverse	$9,000	$12,000
1966	Sunburst, non-reverse	$5,000	$6,500
1967	Custom color, non-reverse	$9,000	$12,000
1967	Sunburst, non-reverse	$5,000	$6,500
1968-1969	Sunburst, non-reverse	$5,000	$6,500

Firebird I (Custom Shop)

1991-1992		$3,000	$5,000

Firebird I 1963 Reissue Historic

2000-2006. Custom Shop Historic Collection, neck-thru, reverse body, Firebird logo on 'guard, various colors including sunburst and Frost Blue.

2000-2006	Various colors	$2,500	$4,500

Eric Clapton 1964 Firebird I

2019. Custom Shop, limited run of 100, mahogany body, mahogany/walnut neck, Indian rosewood 'board, signed backplate, 1 Alnico pickup, Vintage Sunburst, certificate.

2019		$6,500	$9,500

Firebird 76

1976-1978. Reverse body, gold hardware, 2 pickups.

1976	Bicentennial	$5,500	$7,500
1976	Black	$5,000	$7,000
1976	Sunburst, red/white/blue 'guard logo	$5,500	$7,500
1977-1978	Sunburst	$5,000	$7,000
1977-1978	White	$5,000	$7,000

Firebird I/ Firebird 76

1980-1982. Reintroduced Firebird 76 but renamed Firebird I.

1980-1982		$3,500	$4,500

Firebird II/Firebird 2

1981-1982. Maple body with figured maple top, 2 full size active humbuckers, TP-6 tailpiece.

1981-1982		$4,500	$6,000

Firebird III

1963-1969. Reverse body and 2 humbuckers '63-mid-'65, non-reversed body and 3 P-90s mid-'65-'69, various colors.

1963	Cardinal Red	$22,500	$30,000
1963	Golden Mist	$22,500	$30,000
1963	Pastel Color	$60,000	$80,000
1963	Polaris White	$18,000	$24,000
1963	Sunburst	$12,000	$16,000
1964	Cardinal Red, reverse	$18,000	$25,000
1964	Golden Mist, reverse	$18,000	$25,000
1964	Pelham Blue	$18,000	$25,000
1964	Polaris White, reverse	$16,500	$22,000
1964	Sunburst, reverse	$12,000	$16,000
1965	Cherry, non-reverse, 3 P-90s	$7,000	$9,000
1965	Cherry, reverse	$12,000	$16,000
1965	Frost Blue, non-reverse	$12,000	$16,000
1965	Frost Blue, reverse	$15,000	$20,000
1965	Golden Mist, reverse	$15,000	$20,000
1965	Inverness Green, non-reverse	$12,000	$16,000
1965	Inverness Green, reverse	$15,000	$20,000
1965	Sunburst, non-reverse, 2 P-90s	$5,500	$7,000
1965	Sunburst, non-reverse, 3 P-90s	$6,000	$8,000

MODEL YEAR	FEATURES	EXC. COND. LOW	HIGH
1965	Sunburst, reverse, 2 P-90s	$9,000	$12,000
1965	Sunburst, reverse, mini hums	$9,500	$12,500
1966	Frost Blue	$12,000	$16,000
1966	Pelham Blue	$12,000	$16,000
1966	Polaris White	$11,500	$15,000
1966-1969	Sunburst	$6,000	$8,000
1967	Cherry	$6,000	$8,000
1967	Frost Blue	$13,000	$16,000
1967-1969	Pelham Blue	$13,000	$16,000

Firebird III 1964 Reissue Historic

2000-2013. Custom Shop Historic Collection, Maestro, mini-humbuckers, sunburst or color option.

2000-2013		$3,000	$5,000

Firebird III 1965 Reissue Historic

2009. Custom Shop Historic Collection, reverse body, Maestro, 2 mini-humbuckers, sunburst.

2009		$3,500	$5,000

Firebird Non-Reverse

2002-2004. Non-reverse body, 2 humbuckers, standard finishes. There was also a limited edition in '02 with swirl finishes.

2002-2004		$2,500	$4,000

Firebird Studio Non-Reverse

2011-2012. Non-reverse body, 3 tapped P-90 pickups, 5-way pickup selector switch, dot markers, Vintage Sunburst or Pelham Blue nitro finish.

2011-2012		$1,800	$2,800

Firebird Studio Tribute/Studio T

2012-2017. Reverse mahogany body, '70s profile maple neck, 2 mini-humbuckers.

2012-2017		$1,500	$2,500

Firebird Studio/Firebird III Studio

2004-2010. Two humbuckers, dot markers, tune-o-matic and bar stoptail, reverse body, dark cherry finish.

2004-2010		$1,800	$2,800

Firebird V

1963-1969. Two humbuckers, reverse body '63-mid-'65, non-reversed body mid-'65-'69.

1963	Sunburst, reverse	$18,000	$25,000
1963-1964	Pelham Blue, reverse	$30,000	$40,000
1964	Cardinal Red, reverse	$22,500	$30,000
1964	Sunburst, reverse	$18,000	$25,000
1965	Cardinal Red, reverse	$22,500	$30,000
1965	Sunburst, non-reverse	$8,500	$12,000
1965	Sunburst, reverse	$13,000	$17,000
1965	Pastel Color, reverse	$40,000	$50,000
1966-1967	Cardinal Red, non-reverse	$13,000	$18,000
1966-1969	Sunburst	$7,000	$9,000

Firebird V/Firebird V Reissue/ Firebird V 2010

1986-1987, 1990-2018. Based on Firebird V specs, reverse body, 2 pickups, tune-o-matic bridge, vintage sunburst, classic white or ebony with Cardinal Red optional in '91. Called Reissue for '90-'93, renamed V in '94, then V 2010 in '10.

1986-1987	Sunburst, white, black	$3,000	$4,000
1990	Sunburst, white, black	$3,000	$4,000
1991	Cardinal Red	$3,000	$4,000
1991-1999	Sunburst, white, black	$2,200	$3,000
2000-2018	Sunburst, white, black	$1,800	$2,500

Firebird V-12

1966-1967. Non-reverse Firebird V-style body with standard six-on-a-side headstock and split diamond headstock inlay (like ES-335-12 inlay), dot markers, special twin humbucking pickups (like mini-humbuckers).

1966-1967	Custom color	$12,000	$18,000
1966-1967	Sunburst	$6,000	$9,500

Firebird V 1963 Aged (Custom Shop)

2016. Reverse body, Vintage Sunburst, aged hardware.

2016		$4,000	$6,000

Firebird V 1963 Johnny Winter

2008. Johnny Winter script logo, certificate of authenticity.

2008		$6,000	$9,000

1963 Firebird V (Maestro Vibrola) Murphy Lab Aged

2021-present. Custom Shop Murphy Lab Collection, heavy aged (Antique Frost Blue), light aged (Cardinal Red) and ultra light (Ember Red or Pelham Blue).

2021-2024	Heavy aged	$5,500	$7,500
2021-2024	Light aged	$5,000	$6,500
2021-2024	Ultra Light aged	$4,800	$6,200

Firebird V 1964 Johnny Winter

2021-2023. Mahogany/walnut body, Indian rosewood 'board, 2 Alnico pickups, banjo tuners, Murphy Lab aged Polaris White finish.

2021-2023		$5,000	$7,500

Firebird V 1965 Reissue (Custom Shop)

2000-2013. Reverse body, 2 mini-humbuckers, Maestro tremolo, certificate, sunburst or colors.

2000-2013		$3,500	$5,500

Firebird V 50th Anniversary

2013. Gold hardware, '50th Anniversary 1963-2013' on 'guard, gold finish.

2013		$3,800	$5,500

Firebird V Celebrity Series

1990-1993. Reverse body, gold hardware, 2 humbuckers, various colors.

1990-1993		$3,000	$4,500

Firebird V Guitar Trader Reissue

1982. Guitar Trader commissioned Firebird reissue, only 15 made, sunburst or white.

1982		$6,000	$10,000

Firebird V Limited Edition Zebrawood

2007. Limited edition from Gibson USA, Guitar of the Week #12, 400 made, zebrawood reverse body.

2007		$3,500	$5,500

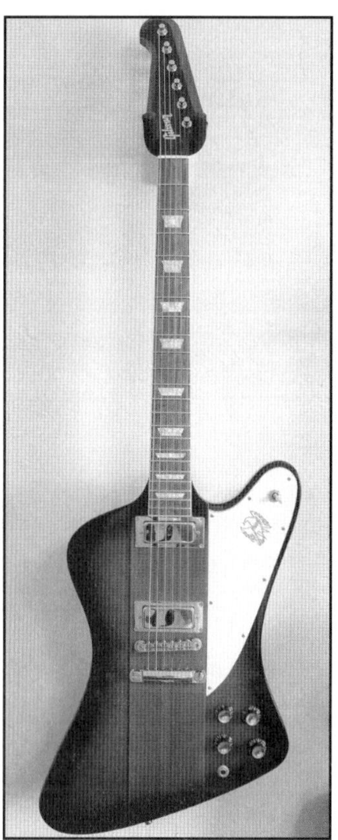

2002 Gibson Firebird V Reissue

Johnny Zapp

Gibson 1963 Firebird V Murphy Lab Aged

GUITARS

1959 Gibson Flying V
Kris Blakely

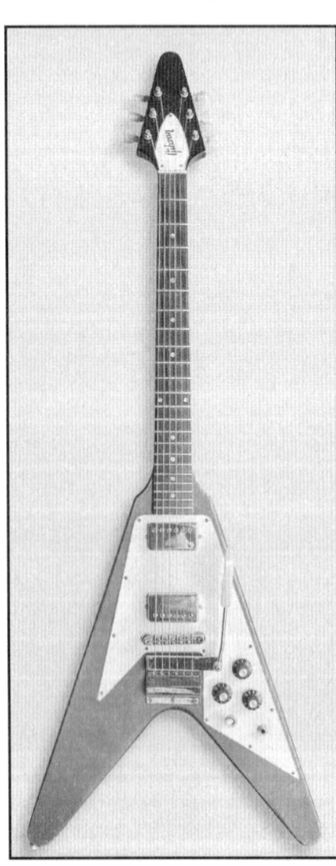

1967 Gibson Flying V (Mahogany)
Jeff Lisec

MODEL YEAR	FEATURES	EXC. COND. LOW	HIGH

Firebird V Medallion

1972-1973. Reverse body, 2 humbuckers, Limited Edition medallion mounted on body.

1972-1973		$8,500	$12,000

Firebird VII

1963-1969. Three humbuckers, reverse body '63-mid-'65, non-reversed body mid-'65-'69, sunburst standard.

1963-1964	Sunburst, reverse	$27,000	$35,000
1964	Custom color, reverse	$45,000	$60,000
1965	Custom color, non-reverse	$27,000	$35,000
1965	Custom color, reverse	$40,000	$52,000
1965	Sunburst, non-reverse	$9,000	$12,000
1965	Sunburst, reverse	$17,000	$22,000
1966-1967	Custom color, non-reverse	$18,000	$25,000
1966-1969	Sunburst, non-reverse	$8,500	$12,000
1968	Custom color, non-reverse	$15,000	$20,000

Firebird VII (Reissue)

2002-2007. Designer collection, various production models, reverse and non-reverse, 3 pickups, block markers, vibrola, various color options with matching headstock.

2002-2007	All colors	$3,300	$5,000

Firebird VII 1965 Historic

1998-2013. Custom Shop Historic Collection, 3 mini-humbuckers, Vintage Sunburst or solid colors.

1998-2013		$4,000	$6,500

20th Anniversary 1965 Firebird VII

2014. Custom Shop, '65 specs, gold hardware, Golden Mist finish, certificate of authenticity.

2014		$5,500	$8,000

Firebird VII Centennial

1994 only. Headstock medallion, sunburst.

1994		$4,500	$7,000

Firebird X Limited Edition Robot

2011-2018. 1800 to be made, lightweight swamp ash body, 1-piece maple neck, curly maple 'board, 3 pickups, robot electronics, nitro lacquer finish in Redolution or Bluevolution.

2011-2018		$2,500	$4,000

Elliot Easton "Tikibird" Firebird

2013-2018. Reverse body, mahogany, rosewood 'board, 2 pickups, Tiki graphic on 'guard, signature on headstock back, Gold Mist Poly finish.

2013-2018		$4,000	$6,500

Firebird Custom Acoustic

2004-2018. Sitka spruce top, quilted maple back and sides, ebony 'board, mother-of-pearl headstock logo with MOP and abalone flames inlay, antique natural finish.

2004-2018		$2,500	$4,500

Firebird Zero

2016-2018. S Series, new body design, 2 pickups, poplar body, maple neck, rosewood 'board, various colors.

2016-2018		$1,000	$1,500

Flamenco 2

1963-1967. Natural spruce top, 14 3/4", cypress back and sides, slotted headstock, zero fret.

1963-1967		$1,500	$2,000

Flying V

1958-1959, 1962-1963. Only 81 shipped in '58 and 17 in '59, guitars made from leftover parts and sold in '62-'63, natural korina body, string-thru-body design. The original case with oxblood interior adds $2,500.

As with any ultra high-end instrument, each instrument should be evaluated on a case-by-case basis. The Flying V market is a very specialized market, with few untouched examples available, and a limited number of high-end buyers. The price ranges noted are for all-original, excellent condition guitars with the original Flying V case. The slightest change to the original specifications can mean a significant drop in value.

1958-1959		$500,000	$750,000

Flying V (Mahogany)

1966-1970, 1975-1981. Mahogany body, around 200 were shipped for '66-'70. Gibson greatly increased production of Flying Vs in '75. See separate listing for the '71 Medallion V version.

1966	Cherry, sunburst	$65,000	$85,000
1967-1970	Cherry, sunburst, sparkling burgundy, walnut	$55,000	$80,000
1975-1981	Various colors	$8,000	$12,000
1979	Silverburst	$8,000	$12,000
1980-1981	Silverburst	$8,000	$12,000

Flying V (Mahogany String-through-body)

1982. Mahogany body, string-thru-body design, only 100 made, most in white, some red or black possible.

1982	All colors	$3,500	$5,500

Flying V (Custom Shop)

2004-2008. A few made each year, figured maple top, options include standard point-headstock or split-headstock.

2004-2008	All options	$5,000	$6,500

Flying V Limited Registered Edition

1980. All gold.

1980		$9,000	$15,000

Flying V Heritage

1981-1982. Limited edition based on '58 specs, korina body, 4 colors available.

1981-1982	Natural	$6,000	$9,000
1981-1982	Various colors	$6,500	$10,000

Flying V I/V '83/Flying V (no pickguard)

1981-1988. Introduced as Flying V I, then renamed Flying V '83 in 1983, called Flying V from '84 on. Alder body, 2 exposed humbuckers, maple neck, ebony 'board, dot inlays, black rings, no 'guard, ebony or ivory finish, designed for lower-end market.

1981-1988		$2,500	$4,500

Flying V Korina

1983. Name changed from Flying V Heritage, korina body, various colors.

1983		$6,000	$9,000

MODEL YEAR	FEATURES	EXC. COND. LOW	HIGH

Flying V Reissue/'67/Factor X/Flying V

1990-2014. Mahogany body, called Flying V Reissue first year, then '67 Flying V '91-'02, V Factor X '03-'08, Flying V '09-'14.

1990-2014	Various colors	$2,000	$3,500

Flying V II

1979-1982. Five-piece maple and walnut laminate sculptured body (1980 catalog states top is either walnut or maple), ebony 'board with dot inlays, 2 V-shaped pickups (2 Dirty Fingers humbuckers towards end of run), gold-plated hardware, natural.

1979-1982		$3,500	$5,500
1982	Silverburst	$4,000	$6,000

Flying V 50th Anniversary

2008. Built as replica of '58 square shoulder V, 100 made, natural finish on korina body and neck, rosewood 'board, 8-series serial number, price includes original certificate.

2008		$6,500	$8,500

Flying V '58 Historic

1991-2013. Custom Shop Historic Collection, based on '58 Flying V, gold hardware, natural korina.

1991-1999		$6,500	$8,500
2000-2013		$5,000	$8,000

Flying V 1958 Mahogany

2021-2024. Custom Shop Designer series, mahogany with walnut finish.

2021-2024		$4,000	$6,500

Flying V '59 (Custom Shop)

2001	Natural	$4,500	$6,500
2004	Cherry	$4,800	$6,800
2013	Natural	$4,500	$6,500
2014	Pelham Blue, 20 offered	$6,000	$9,000
2020	TV Black Gold	$4,500	$6,500

Flying V 1959 Mahogany

2014-2020. Custom Shop Designer series, mahogany with various colors.

2014-2020		$3,000	$4,500

Flying V '67 Historic

1997-2004. Custom Shop Historic Collection, '67 Flying V specs, korina body, natural or opaque colors.

1997-2004		$3,500	$5,000

Flying V '84 Silverburst

2007. Limited Edition Guitar of the Week.

2007		$2,800	$4,200

Flying V '90 Double

1989-1990. Mahogany body, stud tailpiece, 1 single-coil and 1 double-coil humbucker, Floyd Rose tremolo, ebony, silver or white.

1989-1990		$2,500	$4,000

Flying V '98

1998. Mahogany body, '58 style controls, gold or chrome hardware.

1998		$2,500	$3,800

Flying V 120

2014. Mahogany body and neck, 120th Anniversary inlay at 12th fret, rosewood 'board, 2 BurstBucker pickups, ebony, classic white or Heritage Cherry.

2014		$2,800	$4,000

MODEL YEAR	FEATURES	EXC. COND. LOW	HIGH

Flying V 50-Year Commemorative

2008. Guitar of the Month March '08, 1,000 made, AA flamed maple top, higher-end appointments, 50th logo on truss rod cover, Brimstone Burst finish.

2008		$3,000	$4,500

Flying V Brendon Small Snow Falcon

2013. Snow Falcon decal on headstock back, 2 Burstbucker pickups, chrome hardware, Snow Burst finish, limited run.

2013		$3,500	$5,500

Flying V Centennial

1994 only. 100th Anniversary Series, all gold, gold medalion, other special appointments.

1994		$4,500	$7,000

Flying V CMT/The V

1981-1985. Maple body with a curly maple top, 2 pickups, stud tailpiece, natural or sunburst.

1981-1985		$3,500	$5,500

Flying V Custom

2002. Limited Edition, appointments similar to Les Paul Custom, including black finish, only 40 made.

2002		$4,500	$7,500

Flying V Designer Series

1983-1984. Custom paint finish.

1983-1984		$3,000	$5,000

Flying V Faded

2002-2012. Worn cherry finish.

2002-2012		$1,200	$2,000

Flying V Gothic/'98 Gothic

1998-2003. Satin black finish, black hardware, moon and star markers.

1998-2003		$2,000	$3,500

Flying V Government Series

2012-2016. Made from guitar bodies, necks and 'boards returned from Federal Government after '11 raid on Gibson, special run of 300 built, each with Certificate of Authenticity.

2013		$2,200	$3,500

Flying V Hendrix Hall of Fame

Late-1991-1993. Limited Edition (400 made), numbered, black.

1991-1993		$5,000	$8,000

Flying V Hendrix Psychedelic

2005-2006. Hand-painted 1967 Flying V replica, 300 made, includes certificate, instruments without the certificate are worth less than the amount shown.

2005-2006		$8,000	$10,000

Flying V Kirk Hammett Signature

2012. Custom Shop, '76 specs, aged ebony.

2012		$6,000	$9,000

Flying V Lenny Kravitz

2002. Custom Shop, 125 made.

2002		$4,000	$5,500

Flying V Lonnie Mack

1993-1995. Mahogany body with Lonnie Mack-style Bigsby vibrato, cherry.

1993-1995		$5,500	$7,000

Flying V LTD

2001. Limited Edition logo, certificate of authenticity.

2001		$3,000	$4,500

1982 Gibson Flying V Heritage

Steve Evans

1998 Gibson Flying V '98

K.C. Cormack

GUITARS

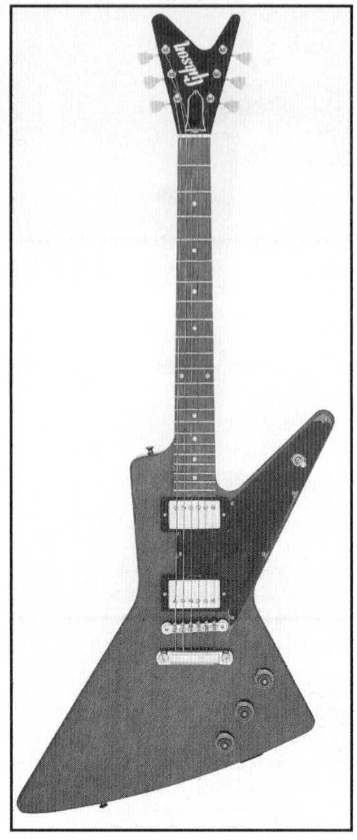

1999 Gibson Historic Korina Futura

Imaged by Heritage Auctions, HA.com

Gibson G-00

MODEL YEAR	FEATURES	EXC. COND. LOW	HIGH

Flying V Medallion

1971, 1973-1974. Mahogany body, stud tailpiece, numbered Limited Edition medallion on bass side of V, 350 made in '71 (3 more were shipped in '73-'74).

1971-1974		$20,000	$25,000

Flying V New Century

2006-2007. Full-body mirror 'guard, mahogany body and neck, 2 humbuckers, Flying V style neck profile, mirror truss rod cover.

2006-2007		$2,000	$3,500

Flying V Pearl Block Marker

1979-1980. Pearl block inlays, various colors.

1979-1980		$9,000	$15,000

Flying V Primavera

1994. Primavera (light yellow/white mahogany) body, gold-plated hardware.

1994		$3,500	$5,500

Flying V Robot

2008-2011. Robot Tuning System.

2008-2011		$2,000	$3,000

Flying V T

2016-2017. Mahogany body, thicker 1-piece 'board.

2016-2017		$2,000	$3,500

Flying V The Holy V

2009. Guitar of the month for Jan. '09, large triangular cutouts in bouts, split diamond markers, 1 humbucker, 1 control knob.

2009		$2,200	$3,500

Flying V Voodoo

2002-2003. Black finish, red pickups.

2002-2003		$2,800	$4,000

Flying V XPL

1984-1986. Various colors with Purple 'Burst being rarest.

1984-1986		$1,800	$2,800

Limited Edition Flying V

2016. Dirty Fingers, faded amber finish, gig bag.

2016		$1,000	$1,500

Reverse Flying V

2006-2008. Introduced as part of Guitar of the Week program, reintroduced by popular demand in a '07 limited run, light colored solid mahogany body gives a natural Korina appearance or opaque white or black, V-shaped reverse body, traditional Flying V neck profile.

2006-2007		$3,000	$4,000
2008	Guitar of the Week	$2,800	$4,500

Rudolf Schenker Flying V

1993. Only 103 made, black and white body and headstock, signature on 'guard.

1993		$3,500	$5,500

Rudolf Schenker Scorpions Flying V

1984. Custom Shop model, Kahler tremolo, mother-of-pearl inlays, black and white.

1984		$4,000	$6,500

Shred V

2008. Guitar of the Month, 1000 made, EMG humbuckers, Kahler, black.

2008		$2,500	$3,800

Tribal V

2009-2011. Black tribal graphics on white body. Limited run of 350.

2009-2011		$1,800	$2,500

MODEL YEAR	FEATURES	EXC. COND. LOW	HIGH

Zakk Wylde Flying V

2007-2011. Custom Shop, with Floyd Rose and typical bullseye finish.

2007-2011		$4,500	$6,500

F-25 Folksinger

1963-1971. 14-1/2" flat-top, mahogany body, most have double white 'guard, natural.

1963-1964		$1,800	$2,500
1965		$1,500	$2,200
1966-1971		$1,400	$2,200

FJN Folk Singer

1963-1967. Jumbo flat-top, square shoulders, natural finish with deep red on back and sides.

1963-1964		$2,200	$3,200
1965		$2,000	$2,800
1966-1967		$1,800	$2,500

Futura

1982-1984. Deep cutout solidbody, 2 humbucker pickups, gold hardware, black, white or purple.

1982-1984		$2,000	$3,000

Futura (Custom Shop)

2008. Only 4 made.

2008		$15,000	$25,000

Historic Korina Futura

1998-1999. Custom Shop Historic Collection, Explorer body with V headstock.

1998-1999		$8,000	$12,000

G-00

2021-2024. Generation Collection, parlor-sized, Sitka spruce top, walnut back and sides, natural finish.

2021-2024		$800	$1,200

G-45 (Standard/Studio)

2019-2024. Slim body, Fishman pickup, solid Sitka spruce top, walnut back and sides, Antique Natural satin finish (standard) or gloss (studio).

2019-2021	Gloss	$1,000	$1,500
2019-2024	Satin	$900	$1,400

GB Series Guitar Banjos

See listings in Banjo section of the Price Guide.

GGC-700

1981-1982. Slab single-cut body, 2 exposed humbuckers, dots.

1981-1982		$1,200	$1,800

GK-55 Active

1979-1980. LP body style, 2 exposed Dirty Fingers humbuckers, bolt neck, dot markers.

1979-1980		$1,200	$1,800

Gospel

1973-1979. Flat-top, square shoulders, laminated maple back and sides, arched back, Dove of Peace headstock inlay, natural.

1973-1979		$1,500	$2,500

Gospel Reissue

1992-1997. Laminated mahogany back and sides, natural or sunburst (walnut added in '94, blue and red in '95), changes to old-style script logo and headstock ornamentation in '94.

1992-1993	Reissue specs	$1,800	$2,800
1994-1997	Old-style specs	$1,500	$2,500

MODEL YEAR	FEATURES	EXC. COND. LOW	HIGH

GS-1 Classical

1950-1956. Mahogany back and sides.

1950-1956		$700	$1,000

GS-2 Classical

1950-1956. Maple back and sides.

1950-1959		$700	$1,000

GS-5 Custom Classic/C-5 Classical

1954-1960. Brazilian rosewood back and sides, renamed C-5 Classical in '57.

1954-1960		$1,500	$2,200

GS-35 Classical/Gut String 35

1939-1942. Spruce top, mahogany back and sides, only 39 made.

1939-1942		$1,800	$2,800

GS-85 Classical/Gut String 85

1939-1942. Brazilian rosewood back and sides.

1939-1942		$3,500	$5,500

GY (Army-Navy)

1918-1921. Slightly arched top and back, low-end budget model, Sheraton Brown.

1918-1921		$900	$1,500

Harley Davidson LTD

1994-1995. Limited Edition, 16" wide body, flat-top, Harley Davidson in script and logo, black, 1500 sold through Harley dealers to celebrate 100th Anniversary of Harley.

1994-1995		$2,800	$4,500

Heritage

1965-1982. Flat-top dreadnought, square shoulders, rosewood back and sides (Brazilian until '67, Indian '68 on), bound top and back, natural finish.

1965-1967	Brazilian	$4,000	$7,000
1968-1982	Indian	$2,500	$4,500

Heritage-12

1968-1971. Flat-top dreadnought, 12 strings, Indian rosewood back and sides, bound top and back, natural finish.

1968-1971		$2,500	$3,800

HG-00 (Hawaiian)

1932-1942. Hawaiian version of L-00, 14 3/4" flat-top, mahogany back and sides, bound top, natural.

1932-1947		$4,500	$6,000

HG-20 (Hawaiian)

1929-1933. Hawaiian, 14 1/2" dreadnought-shaped, maple back and sides, round sound hole and 4 f-holes.

1929-1933		$4,500	$6,000

HG-22 (Hawaiian)

1929-1932. Dreadnought, 14", Hawaiian, round sound hole and 4 f-holes, white paint logo, very small number produced.

1929-1932		$4,800	$7,000

HG-24 (Hawaiian)

1929-1932. 16" Hawaiian, rosewood back and sides, round sound hole plus 4 f-holes, small number produced.

1929-1932		$6,500	$9,500

HG-Century (Hawaiian)

1937-1938. Hawaiian, 14 3/4" L-C Century of Progress, pearloid 'board.

1937-1938		$4,500	$6,500

Howard Roberts Artist

1976-1980. Full body single-cut archtop, sound hole, 1 humbucking pickup, gold hardware, ebony 'board, various colors.

1976-1980		$2,500	$4,000

Howard Roberts Artist Double Pickup

1979-1980. Two pickup version of HR Artist.

1979-1980		$2,800	$4,500

Howard Roberts Custom

1975-1981. Full body single-cut archtop, sound hole, 1 humbucking pickup, chrome hardware, rosewood 'board, various colors.

1975-1981		$3,000	$5,000

Howard Roberts Fusion/ Fusion II/Fusion III

1979-2009. Single-cut, semi-hollowbody, 2 humbucking pickups, chrome hardware, ebony 'board (unbound until '78), TP-6 tailpiece, various colors, renamed Howard Roberts Fusion II in late-'88, and Howard Roberts Fusion III in '91.

1979-2009		$2,000	$3,500

HP-415 W

2017-2018. High Performance series, slimmer round shoulder cutaway, Sitka spruce top, walnut back and sides.

2017-2018		$900	$1,200

Hummingbird

1960-2020. Flat-top acoustic, square shoulders, mahogany back and sides, bound body and neck. Name changes to Hummingbird Standard in '20.

1960	Cherry Sunburst	$9,000	$12,000
1961-1964	Cherry Sunburst	$9,000	$12,000
1963-1965	Natural	$8,000	$10,000
1965	Cherry Sunburst	$6,000	$8,500
1966	Cherry Sunburst	$4,500	$6,000
1966	Natural	$4,500	$6,000
1967-1968	Natural, screwed 'guard	$4,500	$6,000
1967-1968	Sunburst, screwed 'guard	$4,000	$5,500
1969	Natural, screwed 'guard	$3,500	$5,000
1969	Sunburst, screwed 'guard	$3,500	$5,000
1970-1971	Natural, sunburst	$3,000	$4,000
1972-1979	Double X, block markers	$3,000	$4,000
1980-1985	Double X, block markers	$2,500	$3,500
1985-1988	Single X	$2,000	$3,500
1989	25 1/2" scale	$2,200	$3,200
1990-2020		$2,200	$3,200
1994	100 Years 1894-1994 label	$3,500	$4,500
2015-2020	Custom Shop, ebony	$3,500	$4,500

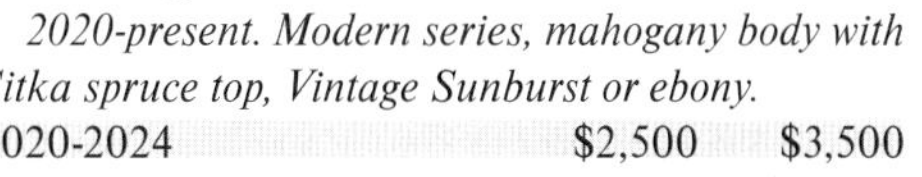

Hummingbird Standard

2020-present. Modern series, mahogany body with Sitka spruce top, Vintage Sunburst or ebony.

2020-2024		$2,500	$3,500

1937 Gibson HG-Century
Imaged by Heritage Auctions, HA.com

1963 Gibson Hummingbird
Craig Brody

GUITARS

Gibson Hummingbird Studio Rosewood

1985 Gibson Invader

Imaged by Heritage Auctions, HA.com

MODEL YEAR	FEATURES	EXC. COND. LOW	HIGH

Hummingbird Historic

2005-2006. Custom Shop Historic Collection, Vintage Honeyburst.

2005-2006		$3,000	$4,500

50th Anniversary 1960 Hummingbird

2010-2012. Limited Edition, 200 made, 50th Anniversary logo on truss rod cover.

2010-2012		$3,500	$5,000

Hummingbird 12

2005-2011. Custom Shop, 12-string, Vintage Sunburst.

2005-2011		$3,500	$5,500

Hummingbird Artist

2007-2011. Plain (no Hummingbird) small 'guard, L.R. Baggs Element, sold through Guitar Center.

2007-2011		$2,000	$3,000

Hummingbird Custom Koa

2004, 2009-2018. Highly flamed koa back and sides, spruce top, gloss finish.

2004-2018		$5,000	$8,000

Hummingbird Limited Edition

1993-1994. Only 30 made, quilted maple top and back.

1993-1994		$4,500	$7,000

Hummingbird Madagascar Honeyburst

2009. Limited run of 20, figured Madagascar rosewood back and sides, factory electronics, certificate of authenticity.

2009		$4,000	$6,000

Hummingbird Modern Classic

2010-2012. Cherry sunburst or ebony finish, L.R. Baggs Element Active pickup system.

2010-2012		$2,500	$3,500

Hummingbird Pro

2010-2013. Non-cut, plain (no Hummingbird) small 'guard, L.R. Baggs Element, Guitar Center.

2010-2013		$2,200	$3,200

Hummingbird Pro EC

2010-2013. Cutaway version, Fishman Prefix Plus-T, Guitar Center.

2010-2013		$2,200	$3,300

Hummingbird Pro 12-String

2018. Custom Shop Limited Edition, Sitka spruce top, mahogany back and sides, Vintage Sunburst or Heritage Cherry Sunburst.

2018		$2,500	$3,800

Hummingbird Quilt Series

2007-2014	Custom Shop	$4,000	$6,000

Hummingbird Silverburst

2007. Silverburst finish, 25 made.

2007		$3,800	$5,500

Hummingbird Studio

2019-2020. Slim body, on-board electronics, Antique Natural or Walnut Burst.

2019-2020		$1,800	$2,800

Hummingbird Studio Rosewood

2020-present. Sitka spruce top, rosewood back and sides, Antique Natural or Rosewood Burst.

2020-2024		$2,500	$3,500

Hummingbird Studio Walnut

2020-present. Sitka spruce top, walnut back and sides, Antique Natural or Walnut Burst.

2020-2024		$1,800	$2,800

MODEL YEAR	FEATURES	EXC. COND. LOW	HIGH

Hummingbird True Vintage

2007-2013. Sitka spruce top, Madagascar rosewood bridge and 'board, special '60s Heritage Cherry or sunburst finish.

2007-2013		$3,500	$5,000

Invader

1983-1988. Single cutaway solid mahogany body, two humbucker pickups, four knobs with three-way selector switch, stop tailpiece, bolt-on maple neck.

1983-1988	All colors	$1,000	$1,500

J-15/J-15 Standard

2014-2021. Acoustic-electric dreadnought, slope shoulder, walnut back and sides, Antique Natural.

2014-2021		$1,400	$2,200

J-25

1983-1985. Flat-top, laminated spruce top, synthetic semi-round back, ebony 'board, natural or sunburst.

1983-1985		$800	$1,200

J-29 Rosewood

2014-2016. Sitka spruce top, solid rosewood back and sides.

2014-2016		$1,800	$2,700

J-30

1985-1993. Dreadnought-size flat-top acoustic, mahogany back and sides, sunburst, Renamed J-30 Montana in '94.

1985-1993		$1,200	$2,000

J-30 Cutaway

1990-1995. Cutaway version of J-30, transducer pickup.

1990-1995		$1,400	$2,200

J-30 Montana

1994-1997. Renamed from J-30, dreadnought-size flat-top acoustic, mahogany back and sides, sunburst.

1994-1997		$1,500	$2,500

J-30 RCA Limited Edition

1991. Limited edition for RCA Nashville, RCA logo on headstock.

1991		$2,500	$4,000

J-35

1936-1942, 2012-2018. Sitka spruce top, mahogany back, sides and neck, rosewood 'board.

1936-1942	Original	$15,000	$25,000
2012-2018	Reissue	$2,000	$3,200

J-40

1971-1982. Dreadnought flat-top, mahogany back and sides, economy satin finish.

1971-1982		$1,500	$2,500

J-45

1942-1982, 1984-present. Dreadnought flat-top, mahogany back and sides, round shoulders until '68 and '84 on, square shoulders '69-'82, sunburst finish (see J-50 for natural version) then natural finish also available in '90s, renamed J-45 Western in '94, renamed Early J-45 in '97 then renamed J-45 Standard in '99. The prices noted are for all-original crack free instruments. A single professionally repaired minor crack that is nearly invisible will reduce the value only slightly. Two or more, or unsightly repaired cracks will devalue an otherwise excellent original acoustic instrument. Repaired cracks should be evaluated on a case-by-case basis.

MODEL YEAR	FEATURES	EXC. COND. LOW	HIGH
1942-1945	Banner, Adirondack	$13,000	$18,000
1942-1945	Banner, mahogany	$12,000	$17,000
1945	Banner, Sitka	$10,000	$14,000
1946-1948	Script, Sitka	$10,000	$14,000
1949	Small 'guard	$8,500	$12,000
1950-1954		$8,000	$11,000
1955-1959	Big 'guard	$7,000	$9,500
1960-1964	Round shoulders	$5,000	$6,500
1965	Early '65, wide nut	$4,500	$6,000
1965	Late '65, slim nut	$3,500	$5,000
1966-1967	Round shoulders	$3,300	$4,500
1968	Black, Cherry	$5,500	$7,500
1968	Blue, Green	$7,000	$9,500
1968-1969	Sunburst, Gibson 'guard	$3,200	$4,500
1969	Square D-shape, late '69	$3,000	$4,000
1970	Square, sunburst	$2,300	$3,500
1971-1975	Deluxe, sunburst	$2,000	$3,500
1976-1979	Sunburst	$2,000	$3,500
1980-1982	Sunburst	$2,000	$3,500
1984-1993	Various Colors	$2,000	$3,500
1994-1997	Western	$2,000	$3,500
1997-1998	Early J-45	$2,000	$3,500
1999-2024	Standard	$2,000	$3,500

J-45 1942 Legend

2006-2014. Early J-45 specs, Adirondack red spruce body, mahogany back/sides/neck, rosewood 'board, Vintage Sunburst finish, certificate of authenticity.

2006-2014		$4,500	$6,500

J-45 1968 Reissue

2004-2007. Limited Edition, special run using '68 specs including Gibson logo 'guard, black or cherry finish.

2004-2007		$2,500	$3,800

J-45 20th Anniversary

2009. Custom Shop, African Zebrawood, only 20 made.

2009		$5,000	$7,500

J-45 Brad Paisley

2010-2016. Adirondack red spruce top, mahogany back and sides, cherry sunburst.

2010-2016		$4,000	$6,000

J-45 Buddy Holly

1995-1996. Limited Edition, 250 made.

1995-1996		$4,500	$7,000

J-45 Celebrity

1985. Acoustic introduced for Gibson's 90th anniversary, spruce top, rosewood back and sides, ebony 'board, binding on body and 'board, only 90 made.

1985		$3,000	$4,500

J-45 Custom

1999-2020. Custom logo on truss rod, maple, mahogany or rosewood body, abalone trim, fancy headstock inlay.

1999-2020	Various options	$2,800	$8,000

J-45 Custom Vine

1999-2010. Custom Shop, Indian rosewood back and sides, fancy pearl and abalone vine inlay in ebony 'board, pearl Gibson logo and crown, natural gloss finish.

1999-2010		$4,000	$6,000

J-45 Elite Mystic

2014. Figured back, limited edition, rosewood back and sides.

2014		$3,500	$5,500

J-45 Heart of Texas Rosewood

2004. Custom Shop, sound hole label signed by Master Luthier Ren Ferguson, Indian rosewood back and sides, abalone top trim.

2004		$3,500	$5,500

J-45 Historic

2005. Limited edition, 670 made, Historic Collection logo rear headstock, sunburst.

2005		$3,000	$4,500

J-45 John Hiatt

2010-2011. Signature on truss rod cover, 100 offered, Tri Burst top with Tobacco Brown back and sides.

2010-2011		$4,000	$6,000

J-45 Natural Anniversary

2009. Custom Shop Limited Edition, decal on headstock back, 20 made, spruce top, maple neck, zebrawood back and sides, natural finish.

2009		$4,500	$7,000

J-45 Quilt

2001. Custom Shop, quilted maple back.

2001		$3,500	$5,500

J-45 Red Spruce Edition

2007. Custom Shop limited edition, only 50 made.

2007		$4,500	$6,500

J-45 Rosewood

1999-2006. Indian rosewood body, spruce top.

1999-2006		$2,800	$4,000

J-45 Studio Rosewood

2020-present. Sitka spruce top, rosewood back and sides, Antique Natural or Rosewood Burst.

2020-2024		$2,000	$3,000

J-45 Studio Sustainable

2019-2020. Sitka spruce top, sustainably harvested North American walnut back and sides, hand-rubbed beeswax finish, Antique Natural.

2019-2020		$1,800	$2,800

J-45 Studio Walnut

2020-present. Sitka spruce top, walnut back and sides, Antique Natural or Walnut Burst.

2020-2024		$1,800	$2,800

J-45 True Vintage/J-45 Vintage

2007-2019. Part of Vintage Series, vintage sunburst finish. True dropped from name in '19.

2007-2019		$3,500	$5,000

J-45 Walnut Limited Edition

2015. Adirondack, flamed walnut.

2015		$3,000	$4,500

Working Man 45 (J-45)

1998-2005. Soft shoulder J-45 style, gloss finish spruce top, satin finish mahogany back and sides, dot markers, natural.

1998-2005		$1,500	$2,500

J-50

1942, 1945-1981, 1990-1995, 1998-2008 (present). Dreadnought flat-top, mahogany back and sides, round shoulders until '68, square shoulders after, natural finish (see J-45 for sunburst version). Though not

1958 Gibson J-45

John Wesley

Gibson J-45 Studio Walnut

GUITARS

1994 Gibson J-100
Edward Sparks

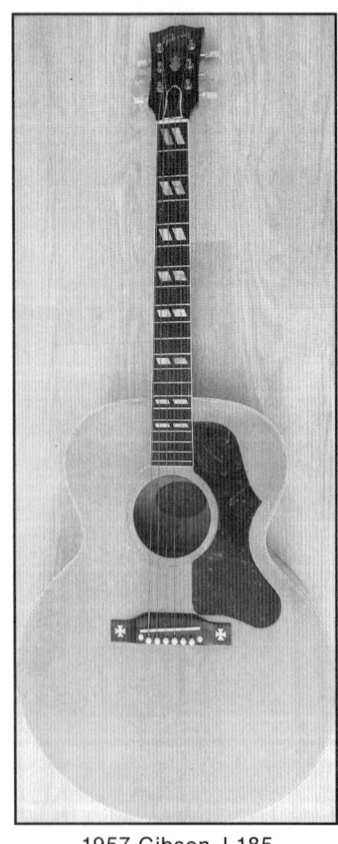
1957 Gibson J-185
Daniel Hess

MODEL YEAR	FEATURES	EXC. COND. LOW	HIGH

labeled J-50, the J-45 Standard is now also available in natural finish.

1945	Banner logo	$11,500	$17,500
1946-1948	Script logo	$10,000	$15,000
1949	Small 'guard	$9,000	$13,500
1950-1954	Small 'guard	$6,500	$9,500
1955	Big 'guard	$6,000	$9,000
1956-1959	Standard fixed bridge	$6,000	$9,000
1960-1964	Round shoulders	$5,000	$7,500
1965	Early '65, wide nut	$4,500	$6,000
1965	Late '65, slim nut	$3,500	$5,500
1966-1969	Round shoulders	$3,200	$4,800
1969	Late '69, square D-shape	$2,800	$4,200
1970-1979	Square shoulders	$2,200	$3,500
1980-2008		$2,200	$3,500

J-55

1935-1942. Mahogany.

1935-1942		$20,000	$25,000

J-55 (Jumbo 55) Limited Edition

1994 only. 16" flat-top, spruce top, mahogany back and sides, 100 made, sunburst.

1994		$3,000	$4,500

J-55 (Reintroduced)

1973-1982. Flat-top, laminated mahogany back and sides, arched back, square shoulders, sunburst. See Jumbo 55 listing for '39-'43 version.

1973-1982		$1,500	$2,500

J-60 Curly Maple

1993 and 1996. Curly maple back and sides, limited edition from Montana shop, natural.

1993,1996		$2,500	$4,000

J-60/J-60 Traditional

1992-1999. Solid spruce top dreadnought, square shoulders, Indian rosewood back and sides, ebony 'board, multiple bindings, natural or sunburst.

1992-1999		$2,000	$3,500

J-100/J-100 Custom

1970-1974, 1985-1997. Flat-top jumbo, multi-bound top and back, black 'guard, dot inlays, mahogany back and sides, '80s version has maple back and sides, dot inlays and tortoise shell 'guard, '90s model has maple back and sides, no 'guard, and J-200 style block inlays.

1970-1974	Mahogany	$2,000	$3,500
1985-1997	Maple	$2,200	$3,500

J-100 Xtra

1991-1997, 1999-2006. Jumbo flat-top, mahogany back and sides, moustache bridge, dot inlays, various colors, J-100 Xtra Cutaway also available, reintroduced in '99 with maple back and sides and single-bound body.

1991-2006		$2,000	$3,500

J-150/SJ-150 Maple

1999-2008. Super jumbo body, solid spruce top, figured maple back and sides (rosewood in '05), MOP crown inlays, moustache bridge with transducer. Renamed SJ-150 in 2006.

1999-2005	J-150	$2,500	$4,000
2006-2008	SJ-150	$2,800	$4,200

MODEL YEAR	FEATURES	EXC. COND. LOW	HIGH

J-160E

1954-1979. Flat-top jumbo acoustic, 1 bridge P-90 pickup, tone and volume controls on front, sunburst finish, reintroduced as J-160 in '90.

1954-1964		$6,000	$8,500
1965		$4,500	$7,000
1966-1969		$3,500	$6,500
1970-1979		$2,500	$4,000

J-160E Reissue/Standard/VS

1990-1997, 2003-2008. Reintroduced J-160E with solid spruce top, solid mahogany back and sides.

1990-2008		$2,500	$4,000

J-160E John Lennon Peace

2003-2013. J-160E with tortoise 'guard, natural, signature on truss rod cover.

2003-2013		$3,500	$5,500

J-160E John Lennon Peace Limited Edition

2009. Certificate of authenticity, 750 made.

2009		$4,000	$6,000

J-160E Montana Special

1995 only.

1995		$3,000	$4,500

J-160VS/John Lennon 70th

2010. Commemorative edition for John Lennon's 70th birthday, 500 made, vintage sunburst gloss finish.

2010		$4,000	$6,000

J-165 (Maple)

See CJ-165 listing.

J-180

2000s. Limited Edition, star logo on headstock, star position markers, black finish.

2000s		$2,500	$4,000

J-180 Billie Jo Armstrong

2011. Certificate of authenticity, 100 made.

2011		$4,500	$6,500

J-180/Everly Brothers/ The Everly Brothers

1986-2005. Everly Brothers flat-top model discontinued '72, but was reissued in '86 as the J-180. Star logo on headstock, star position markers, black finish. From '92-'93 was again called The Everly Brothers and in '94 name went back to J-180.

1986-2005		$3,000	$4,500

J-180 Special Edition

1993. Gibson Bozeman, only 36 made, Everly Brother specs, large double white pearloid 'guard.

1993		$4,500	$6,500

J-185/J-185N

1951-1959. Flat-top jumbo, figured maple back and sides, bound body and neck, sunburst (185) or natural (185N).

1951-1959	Natural, sunburst	$20,000	$25,000

J-185 Reissue

1990-1995, 1999-2018. Flat-top jumbo, figured maple back and sides, bound body and neck, natural or sunburst, limited run of 100 between '91-'92.

1990-2018		$2,500	$4,000

J-185-12

2001-2004. 12-string J-185, flamed maple sides and back.

2001-2004		$3,000	$4,500

MODEL YEAR	FEATURES	EXC. COND. LOW	HIGH

1951 J-185 Limited Edition

1994-1995. Oct. '94 Centennial model, limited run of 100.

1994-1995		$4,000	$6,000

J-185 Custom Vine

2004-2012. Limited Edition, only 50 made, abalone and mother-of-pearl vine inlays.

2004-2012		$4,500	$7,000

J-185 EC

1999-2018. Acoustic/electric, rounded cutaway, flamed maple back and sides. Replaced EC-30 Blues King.

1999-2018		$2,800	$4,200

J-185 EC Custom

2005. Limited Edition, 200 made, spruce top, figured maple sides and back, pearl double parallelogram markers, Fishman Prefix Plus on-board electronics.

2005		$3,000	$4,500

J-185 EC Rosewood

2006-2018. Acoustic/electric, rounded cutaway, Indian rosewood back and sides.

2006-2018		$3,000	$4,500

J-185 EC Modern Rosewood

2020-2022. Slim body, Sitka spruce top, rosewood back and sides, Antique Natural or Rosewood Burst.

2020-2022		$2,800	$4,000

J-185 EC Modern Walnut

2020-2022. Slim body, Sitka spruce top, walnut back and sides, Antique Natural or Walnut Burst.

2020-2022		$2,500	$3,500

J-185 EC Quilt

2002. Quilted maple top, flamed maple body.

2002		$3,500	$5,500

J-190 EC Super Fusion

2001-2004. Jumbo single cut acoustic/electric, spruce top, curly maple back and sides, neck pickup and Fishman Piezo.

2001-2004		$3,000	$4,500

J-200/SJ-200/J-200N/SJ-200N

1946-present. Labeled SJ-200 until ca.'54. Super Jumbo flat-top, maple back and sides, see Super Jumbo 200 for '38-'42 rosewood back and sides model, called J-200 Artist for a time in the early-'70s, renamed '50s Super Jumbo 200 in '97 and again renamed SJ-200 Reissue in '99. Currently called the SJ-200 Original. 200N indicates natural option.

1946-1949	Natural, sunburst	$18,000	$24,000
1950-1959	Natural, sunburst	$15,000	$20,000
1960-1964	Natural, sunburst	$12,000	$18,000
1965	Natural, sunburst	$8,000	$12,000
1966-1969	Natural, sunburst	$6,000	$9,000
1970-1979	Natural, sunburst	$4,200	$6,500
1972	Artist (label)	$4,200	$6,500
1980-1989	Natural, sunburst	$3,800	$5,800
1990-1999	Natural, sunburst	$3,800	$5,800
2000-2009	Natural, sunburst	$3,800	$5,800
2010-2024	Natural, sunburst	$3,600	$5,500

J-200 Celebrity

1985-1987. Acoustic introduced for Gibson's 90th anniversary, spruce top, rosewood back, sides and 'board, binding on body and 'board, sunburst, only 90 made.

1985-1987		$5,000	$8,000

J-200 Custom/SJ-200 Custom

2009-2013. Additional abalone trim, gold hardware, sunburst or natural. Model name also used in 1993 on J-200 with tree-of-life fingerboard inlay.

2009-2013		$4,000	$6,000

J-200 Deluxe Rosewood

1993-1996. Rosewood back and sides, abalone trim, gold hardware, sunburst or natural.

1993-1996		$4,500	$7,000

J-200 E

1986-1987. Built in Nashville, on-board volume control, sunburst.

1986-1987		$3,000	$4,500

J-200 Elvis Presley Signature

2002. Only 250 made, large block letter Elvis Presley name on 'board, figured maple sides and back, gloss natural spruce top, black and white custom designed 'guard after one of Presley's personal guitars.

2002		$5,000	$8,000

J-200 Jr.

1991-1996, 2002. Smaller 16" body, sunburst, natural, black or cherry.

1991-1996		$2,000	$3,500

J-200 Koa

1994-2013. Figured Hawaiian Koa back and sides, spruce top, natural.

1994-2013		$4,500	$6,500

J-200 M Trophy 75th Anniversary

2012-2013. Limited Edition, 75 made, quilt maple back and sides, rosewood 'board, abalone crown inlays, antique natural or vintage sunburst nitro finish.

2012-2013		$5,500	$8,000

J-200 Montana Gold Flame Maple

1998-2012. SJ-200 design, 100 made, AAA Sitka spruce top with Eastern curly maple back and sides, ebony 'board, Custom Montana Gold banner peghead logo, antique natural.

1998-2012		$5,000	$7,500

J-200 Montana Western Classic

2016. Spruce top, rosewood back and sides, maple neck, Sunset Burst finish.

2016		$3,500	$5,000

J-200 Ron Wood/SJ-200 Ron Wood

1997. Based on a '57 SJ-200 with Wood's oversized double 'guard on either side of the sound hole, flame-pattern fretboard inlays, script signature inlay on headstock, 100 made, natural.

1997		$5,000	$7,500

J-200 Rose

1994-1995. Centennial Series, 100 made, based on Emmylou Harris' guitar, black finish, rose 'guard, gold tuners.

1994-1995		$5,000	$7,500

J-200 Rosewood

1991, 1994-1996. Made in Bozeman, rosewood back and sides.

1991-1996		$4,000	$6,000

J-200 Studio

2009-2018. Studio logo on truss rod cover, unbound 'board, plain 'guard.

2009-2018		$2,000	$3,500

2000 Gibson J-185 EC

Cream City Music

1964 Gibson J-200N

Smyth Jones

GUITARS

2015 Gibson Jackson Browne Signature

Gibson Johnny A Signature Series

Imaged by Heritage Auctions, HA.com

MODEL YEAR	FEATURES	EXC. COND. LOW	HIGH

J-200 Western Classic Pre-War

1999-2012. Indian rosewood.

1999-2012		$4,500	$6,500

J-200 Western Classic Pre-War 200 Brazilian

2003. Custom Shop, very few made, based on Ray Whitley's '37 J-200, Brazilian rosewood back and sides.

2003		$8,000	$12,000

J-250 Monarch/SJ-250 Monarch

1995-2018. Rosewood back and sides, maple neck, ebony 'board, abalone trim, certificate of authenticity.

1995-2018		$10,000	$15,000

J-250 R

1972-1973, 1976-1978. A J-200 with rosewood back and sides, sunburst, only 20 shipped from Gibson.

1972-1978		$3,500	$5,500

J-1000/SJ-1000

1992-1994. Jumbo cutaway, spruce top, rosewood back and sides, on-board electronics, diamond-shape markers and headstock inlay.

1992-1994		$2,500	$4,000

J-1500

1992. Jumbo cutaway flat-top, higher-end appointments including Nick Lucas-style position markers, sunburst.

1992		$2,000	$3,500

J-2000/J-2000 Custom/J-2000R

1986, 1992-1999. Cutaway acoustic, rosewood back and sides (a few had Brazilian rosewood or maple bodies), ebony 'board and bridge, Sitka spruce top, multiple bindings, sunburst or natural. Name changed to J-2000 Custom in '93 when it became available only on a custom-order basis.

1986-1999	All models	$3,500	$5,500

Jackson Browne Signature

2011-2016. Based on '30s Jumbo style with increased body depth and upgraded tonewoods, Model 1 without pickup, Model A with pickups, Adirondack red spruce top, English walnut back and sides, nitro lacquer sunburst finish.

2011-2016	Model 1	$4,000	$5,500
2011-2016	Model A	$4,500	$6,500

JG-0

1970-1972. Economy, square shouldered jumbo, follows Jubilee model in '70.

1970-1972		$1,200	$2,000

JG-12

1970. Economy square shouldered jumbo 12-string, follows Jubilee-12 model in '70.

1970		$1,500	$2,500

Johnny A Signature Series

2004-2013. Thinline semi-hollow, sharp double-cut, flamed maple top, humbuckers, gold hardware, Bigsby, sunburst, includes certificate of authenticity.

2004-2013	Includes rare color option	$3,500	$5,500

Johnny Smith/Johnny Smith Double

1961-1989. Single-cut archtop, 1 or 2 humbucker pickups, gold hardware, multiple binding front and back, natural or sunburst. By '80 cataloged as JS and JSD models.

1961-1964		$13,500	$17,000
1965		$8,500	$11,000

MODEL YEAR	FEATURES	EXC. COND. LOW	HIGH
1966-1969		$8,000	$10,500
1970-1989		$7,500	$10,000

Jubilee

1969-1970. Flat-top, laminated mahogany back and sides, single bound body, natural with black back and sides.

1969-1970		$1,800	$2,800

Jubilee Deluxe

1970-1971. Flat-top, laminated rosewood back and sides, multi-bound body, natural finish.

1970-1971		$1,800	$2,800

Jubilee-12

1969-1970. Flat-top, 12 strings, laminated mahogany back and sides, multi-bound, natural.

1969-1970		$1,800	$2,800

Jumbo

1934-1936. Gibson's first Jumbo flat-top, mahogany back and sides, round shoulders, bound top and back, sunburst, becomes the 16" Jumbo 35 in late-'36.

1934	Unbound	$30,000	$40,000
1935-1936	Bound	$25,000	$35,000

Jumbo 35/J-35

1936-1942. Jumbo flat-top, mahogany back and sides, silkscreen logo, sunburst, reintroduced as J-35, square-shouldered dreadnought, in '83.

1936-1938	Sunburst, 3 tone bars	$20,000	$25,000
1939	Natural, 3 tone bars	$20,000	$25,000
1940-1942	Sunburst, 2 tone bars	$15,000	$20,000

Jumbo 55/J-55

1939-1943. Flat-top dreadnought, round shoulders, mahogany back and sides, pearl inlaid logo, sunburst, reintroduced in '73 as J-55.

1939-1940	Stairstep	$20,000	$25,000
1941-1943	Non-stairstep	$20,000	$25,000

Jumbo Centennial Special

1994. Reissue of 1934 Jumbo, natural, 100 made.

1994		$3,500	$5,500

Junior Pro

1987-1989. Single-cut, mahogany body, KB-X tremolo system 1 humbucker pickup, black chrome hardware, various colors.

1987-1989		$900	$1,500

Kalamazoo Award Model

1978-1981. Single-cut archtop, bound f-holes, multi-bound top and back, 1 mini-humbucker, gold-plated hardware, woodgrain 'guard with bird and branch abalone inlay, highly figured natural or sunburst.

1978-1981	Natural	$15,000	$20,000
1978-1981	Sunburst	$15,000	$20,000

Keb' Mo' Royale

2016. Limited to 50, aged Adirondack red spruce top, vintage sunburst finish, label signed by artist, includes certificate of authenticity.

2016		$4,000	$6,000

Keb' Mo' Signature Bluesmaster

2010-2015. Limited run of 300, small-bodied flat-top acoustic, Baggs pickup, sound hole-mounted volume control, vintage sunburst or antique natural finish.

2010-2015		$3,500	$5,500

MODEL YEAR	FEATURES	EXC. COND. LOW	HIGH

Kiefer Sutherland KS-336

2007. Custom Shop Inspired By Artist series.

2007		$3,500	$5,500

KZ II

1980-1981. Double-cut solidbody, 2 humbuckers, 4 knob and toggle controls, tune-o-matic, dot markers, stencil Gibson logo on headstock, KZ II logo on truss rod cover, walnut stain finish.

1980		$1,500	$2,500

L-0

1926-1933, 1937-1942. Acoustic flat-top, maple back and sides '26-'27, mahogany after. Reissued '37 with spruce top.

1926-1928	13 1/2", maple	$5,500	$7,000
1928-1930	13 1/2", mahogany	$5,500	$7,000
1931-1933	14 3/4"	$6,000	$8,000
1937-1942	14 3/4", spruce	$6,000	$8,000

L-00

1932-1946. Acoustic flat-top, mahogany back and sides, bound top to '36 and bound top and back '37 on.

1932-1946		$6,000	$7,500

L-00 1937 Legend

2006-2016. Part of the Vintage Series.

2006-2016		$4,000	$6,000

L-00 Standard

2016-present. Small body, Sitka spruce top, mahogany back and sides, Vintage Sunburst nitro finish.

2016-2024		$2,200	$3,200

L-00 Studio Walnut

2020-2023. Walnut back and sides, Fishman pickup, nitro finish, Antique Natural or Walnut Burst.

2020-2023		$1,500	$2,500

L-00 Studio/Montana Studio

2019-2020. Sitka spruce top, walnut back and sides, Fishman pickup, aged nitro finish.

2019-2020		$1,500	$2,500

L-00 Sustainable

2018-2021. Sitka spruce top, richlite 'board and bridge made from recycled trees pulp, Antique Natural.

2018-2021		$1,800	$3,000

L-00/Blues King

1991-1997, 1999-2019. Reintroduced as L-00, called Blues King L-00 for '94-'97, back as L-00 for '99-'02, called Blues King '03-present.

1991-1997		$2,200	$3,500
2003-2019		$2,000	$3,200

L-1 (Archtop)

1902-1925. Acoustic archtop, single-bound top, back and sound hole, name continued on flat-top model in '26.

1902-1907	12 1/2"	$3,000	$4,000
1908-1919	13 1/2"	$3,000	$4,000
1920-1925	13 1/2", Loar era	$3,000	$4,000

L-1 (Flat-Top)

1926-1937. Acoustic flat-top, maple back and sides '26-'27, mahogany after.

1926-1929	13 1/2", 12-fret	$7,000	$9,000
1930-1931	14 3/4", 13-fret	$7,500	$9,500
1932-1937	14-fret	$8,000	$10,000

MODEL YEAR	FEATURES	EXC. COND. LOW	HIGH

L-1 1928 Blues Tribute

2014-2018. Adirondack red spruce top, mahogany back and sides, rosewood 'board, faded Vintage Sunburst.

2014-2018		$2,800	$4,500

L-1 CM Montana Special

1991-1993. Special Edition from Bozeman, Montana, limited run of 31, curly maple back and sides, Vintage Sunburst finish.

1991-1993		$4,000	$6,000

L-1 Robert Johnson

2007-2016. 1926 specs, Robert Johnson inlay at end of 'board.

2007-2016		$3,000	$4,500

L-1 Special

2016. Adirondack red spruce top, limited edition of 75.

2016		$3,500	$5,500

L-2 (Archtop)

1902-1926. Round sound hole archtop, pearl inlay on peghead, 1902-'07 available in 3 body sizes: 12 1/2" to 16", '24-'26 13 1/2" body width.

1902-1907	12 1/2"	$3,000	$4,000
1924-1926	13 1/2"	$3,000	$4,000

L-2 (Flat-Top)

1929-1935. Acoustic flat-top, rosewood back and sides except for mahogany in '31, triple-bound top and back, limited edition model in '94.

1929-1933	Brazilian	$20,000	$25,000
1931-1932	Mahogany	$16,500	$22,000

L-2 1929 Reissue

1994 only. Spruce top, Indian rosewood back and sides, raised 'guard.

1994		$3,500	$5,500

L-3 (Archtop)

1902-1933. Acoustic archtop, available in 3 sizes: 12 1/2", 13 1/2", 16".

1902-1907	12 1/2", round hole	$4,000	$5,000
1908-1919	13 1/2", round hole	$4,000	$5,000
1920		$4,000	$5,000
1921-1926	Loar era	$4,000	$5,000
1927-1928	13 1/2", oval hole	$4,000	$5,000
1929-1933	13 1/2", round hole	$4,000	$5,000

L-4

1912-1956. Acoustic archtop, 16" wide.

1912-1919	12-fret, oval hole	$4,000	$5,000
1920		$4,000	$5,000
1921-1924	Loar era	$4,000	$5,000
1925-1927	12-fret, oval hole	$4,000	$5,000
1928-1934	14-fret, round hole	$4,000	$5,000
1935-1946	Fleur-de-lis, f-holes	$5,000	$6,500
1947-1949	Crown, double-parallel	$5,000	$6,500
1950-1956		$4,500	$5,500

L-4 A or L-4 A EC

2003-2008. 15 3/4" lower bout, mid-size jumbo, rounded cutaway, factory electronics with preamp.

2003-2008		$2,800	$4,000

1942 Gibson L-0

David Stone

1935 Gibson L-00

David Stone

GUITARS

1953 Gibson L4-C

Ray Bohlken

1976 Gibson L-5 S

Frank Manno

MODEL YEAR	FEATURES	EXC. COND. LOW	HIGH

L-4 C or L-4 CN

1949-1971. Single-cut acoustic archtop, sunburst or natural (CN).

1949-1959	Natural	$6,000	$8,000
1949-1959	Sunburst	$5,500	$7,000
1960-1964	Natural	$5,500	$7,000
1960-1964	Sunburst	$4,500	$5,500
1965	Natural	$4,000	$5,000
1965	Sunburst	$3,500	$4,500
1966-1969	Natural, sunburst	$3,000	$4,000
1970-1971	Natural, sunburst	$2,500	$3,500

L-4 CES/L-4 CES Mahogany

1958, 1969, 1986-2018. Single pointed cutaway archtop, 2 humbuckers, gold parts, natural or sunburst, maple back and sides '58 and '69, mahogany laminate back and sides for '86-'93, became part of Gibson's Historic Collection (Custom Shop) with laminated maple back and sides for '94, renamed L-4 CES Mahogany with solid mahogany back and sides in '04.

1958	Natural, PAFs	$15,000	$20,000
1958	Sunburst, PAFs	$12,000	$17,000
1969	Natural, sunburst	$5,000	$7,500
1986-1993	Laminate mahogany	$4,000	$6,000
1994-2003	Laminate maple	$4,000	$6,000
2004-2018	Solid mahogany	$4,500	$7,000

L-4 Special Tenor/Plectrum

Late-1920s. Limited edition 4-string flat-top.

1929		$3,000	$4,000

L-5 '34 Non-Cutaway Historic

1994. 1934 specs including block pearl inlays, bound snakehead peghead, close grained solid spruce top, figured solid maple sides and back, replica Grover open back tuners, Cremona Brown Sunburst finish.

1994		$6,000	$9,000

L-5 Premier/L-5 P/L-5 PN

1939-1947. Introduced as L-5 Premier (L-5 P) and renamed L-5 C in '48, single rounded cutaway acoustic archtop, sunburst or natural option (PN).

1939-1947	Natural option	$22,500	$30,000
1939-1947	Sunburst	$18,000	$23,500

L-5/L-5N

1924-1958. Acoustic archtop, non-cut, multiple bindings, Lloyd Loar label in '24, 17" body by '35, Master Model label until '27, sunburst with natural option later.

1924	'24 ship date, Loar era	$60,000	$75,000
1925	Early '25, value per specs	$55,000	$65,000
1925	Late '25, value per specs	$32,000	$42,000
1926	'26 ship date, value per specs	$32,000	$42,000
1927	'27 ship date, value per specs	$32,000	$42,000
1928-1932	Value per specs	$27,000	$35,000
1933-1934	Value per specs	$13,500	$18,000
1935-1940	Value per specs	$9,000	$12,000
1939-1940	Natural option, value per specs	$12,000	$16,000
1946-1949	Natural option, value per specs	$11,000	$15,000
1946-1949	Sunburst, value per specs	$9,000	$12,000
1950-1958	Natural, value per specs	$9,000	$12,000
1950-1958	Sunburst, value per specs	$7,000	$9,500

L-5 C/L-5 CN

1948-1982. Renamed from L-5 Premier (L-5 P), single rounded cutaway acoustic archtop, sunburst or natural option (CN)

1948-1949	Natural	$15,000	$20,000
1948-1949	Sunburst	$13,000	$18,000
1950-1959	Natural	$13,000	$18,000
1950-1959	Sunburst	$10,500	$13,500
1960-1964	Natural	$10,500	$13,500
1960-1964	Sunburst	$9,500	$12,000
1965	Natural	$8,500	$11,000
1965	Sunburst	$8,500	$11,000
1966-1969	Natural	$7,000	$9,000
1966-1969	Sunburst	$7,000	$9,000
1970-1982	Natural, sunburst	$5,000	$6,500

L-5 CES/L-5 CESN

1951-2018. Electric version of L-5 C, single round cutaway (pointed mid-'60-'69), archtop, 2 pickups (P-90s '51-'53, Alnico Vs '54-mid-'57, humbuckers after), sunburst or natural (CESN), now part of Gibson's Historic Collection.

1951-1957	Natural, single coils	$20,000	$25,000
1951-1957	Sunburst, single coils	$18,000	$25,500
1958-1959	Natural, PAFs	$22,500	$30,000
1958-1959	Sunburst, PAFs	$21,500	$28,000
1960-1962	Natural, PAFs	$21,500	$28,000
1960-1962	Sunburst, PAFs	$18,000	$22,500
1963-1964	Natural, pat #	$16,000	$20,000
1963-1964	Sunburst, pat #	$13,000	$16,500
1965	Natural, sunburst	$10,500	$13,000
1966-1969	Natural	$8,500	$11,000
1966-1969	Sunburst	$8,500	$11,000
1970-1979	Natural, sunburst	$7,000	$9,500
1980-1984	Kalamazoo made	$6,500	$9,000
1985-1992	Nashville made	$6,500	$9,000

L-5 CES Historic

1994-1997. Custom Shop Historic Collection series, sunburst or natural.

1994	100th Anniv, black	$7,000	$10,000
1994-1996	Natural, highly figured	$6,500	$9,000
1994-1996	Sunburst	$6,000	$8,500
1997	Wine Red	$5,500	$8,000

L-5 CT (George Gobel)

1959-1961. Single-cut, thinline archtop acoustic, some were built with pickups, cherry.

1959-1961		$20,000	$30,000

L-5 CT Reissue

1998-2007. Historic Collection, acoustic and electric versions, natural, sunburst, cherry.

1998-2007		$5,000	$7,500

MODEL YEAR	FEATURES	EXC. COND. LOW	HIGH

L-5 S

1972-1985, 2004-2005. Single-cut solidbody, multi-bound body and neck, gold hardware, 2 pickups (low impedance '72-'74, humbuckers '75 on), offered in natural, cherry sunburst or vintage sunburst. 1 humbucker version issued in '04 from Gibson's Custom, Art & Historic division.

1972-2005	All options	$4,500	$7,000

L-5 S Ron Wood

2015. Custom Shop, limited run of 250 with 1st 50 signed by Ron, certificate of authenticity, 2 Burstbucker pickups, ebony gloss finish.

2015		$6,000	$9,000

L-5 Signature

2001-2004. Carved spruce top, AAA maple back, tangerineburst or vintage sunburst.

2001-2004		$5,000	$7,500

L-5 Studio

1996-2000. Normal L-5 dual pickup features, marble-style 'guard, translucent finish, dot markers.

1996-2000		$3,500	$5,500

L-5 Wes Montgomery

1993-2018. Custom Shop, various colors.

1993-2018		$6,000	$9,000

L-6 S

1973-1975. Single-cut solidbody, 2 humbucking pickups, 6 position rotary switch, stop tailpiece, cherry or natural. Renamed L-6 S Custom in '75.

1973-1975	Cherry, natural	$2,000	$3,500

L-6 S Custom

1975-1980. Renamed from the L-6 S, 2 humbucking pickups, stop tailpiece, cherry or natural.

1975-1980		$2,500	$4,000
1978-1980	Silverburst option	$3,000	$5,000

L-6 S Deluxe

1975-1981. Single-cut solidbody, 2 humbucking pickups, no rotary switch, strings-thru-body design, cherry or natural.

1975-1981		$2,000	$3,500

L-6 S Reissue

2011-2012. With rotary switch, 2 humbuckers, natural or silverburst.

2011-2012		$1,500	$2,200

L-7/L-7N

1932-1956. Acoustic archtop, bound body and neck, fleur-de-lis peghead inlay, 16" body '32-'34, 17" body X-braced top late-'34, sunburst or natural (N).

1932-1934	16" body	$5,000	$6,500
1935-1939	17" body, X-braced	$5,000	$6,500
1940-1949	Natural	$4,500	$6,000
1940-1949	Sunburst	$4,500	$6,000
1950-1956	Natural	$4,500	$6,000
1950-1956	Sunburst	$4,200	$5,500

L-7 C/L-7 CN

1948-1972. Single-cut acoustic archtop, triple-bound top, sunburst or natural (CN). Gibson revived the L-7 C name for a new acoustic archtop in 2002.

1948-1949	Natural	$6,000	$8,000
1948-1949	Sunburst	$5,000	$7,000
1950-1959	Natural	$5,000	$7,000
1950-1959	Sunburst	$4,500	$6,000

MODEL YEAR	FEATURES	EXC. COND. LOW	HIGH
1960-1964	Natural	$4,200	$5,500
1960-1964	Sunburst	$4,000	$5,500
1965	Natural	$4,200	$5,500
1965	Sunburst	$3,800	$5,000
1966-1972	Natural	$4,000	$5,500
1966-1972	Sunburst	$3,500	$5,000

L-7 Custom Electric

1936. L-7 with factory Christian-style pickup, limited production, often custom ordered.

1936		$10,000	$13,000

L-7 E/L-7 CE

1948-1954. L-7 and L-7 C with "McCarty" assembly of pickguard-mounted pickups (1 or 2), sunburst only.

1948-1954	L-7 CE, cutaway	$5,500	$8,000
1948-1954	L-7 E, non-cut	$4,500	$7,000

L-7 C (Custom Shop)

2002-2013. Custom Shop logo, Certificate of Authenticity.

2002-2013		$5,500	$8,500

L-10

1923-1939. Acoustic archtop, single-bound body and 'board, black or sunburst (added in '35).

1923-1934	16", F-holes	$6,000	$8,000
1935-1939	17", X-braced	$6,000	$8,000

L-12

1930-1955. Acoustic archtop, single-bound body, 'guard, neck and headstock, gold-plated hardware, sunburst.

1930-1934	16"	$6,500	$8,500
1935-1939	17", X-braced	$6,500	$8,500
1940-1941	Parallel top braced	$6,500	$8,500
1946-1949	Post-war	$4,000	$5,000
1950-1955		$3,500	$4,500

L-12 Premier/L-12 P

1947-1950. L-12 with rounded cutaway, sunburst.

1947-1950		$5,000	$6,500

L-20 20th Anniversary Limited Edition

2009. Custom Shop, 20 made, "20th Anniversary" logo on back of headstock and on label, Certificate of Authenticity.

2009		$4,500	$7,000

L-20 Special/L-20 K International Special

1993-1994. Rosewood or mahogany back and sides (Koa on the K), ebony 'board, block inlays, gold tuners, multi-bound.

1993-1994	L-20, mahogany	$2,500	$3,800
1993-1994	L-20, rosewood	$3,000	$4,500
1993-1994	L-20K, koa	$3,200	$4,800

L-30

1935-1943. Acoustic archtop, single-bound body, black or sunburst.

1935-1943		$2,200	$3,000

L-37

1937-1941. 14 3/4" acoustic archtop, flat back, single-bound body and 'guard, sunburst.

1937-1941		$2,200	$3,000

L-47

1940-1942. Acoustic archtop.

1940-1942		$2,500	$3,500

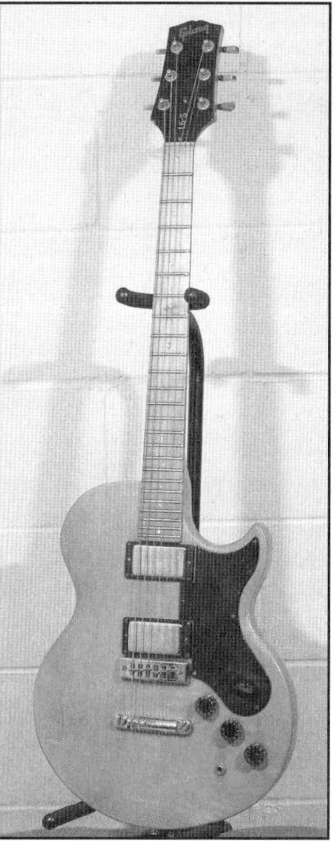

1973 Gibson L-6 S

Tom Pfeifer

1935 Gibson L-30

Tyler Willison

GUITARS

1934 Gibson L-50
Guitar Maniacs,

1936 Gibson L-75
David Stone

MODEL YEAR	FEATURES	EXC. COND. LOW	HIGH

L-48

1946-1971. 16" acoustic archtop, single-bound body, mahogany sides, sunburst.

1946-1949		$2,000	$2,500
1950-1959		$2,000	$2,500
1960-1964		$1,800	$2,300
1965		$1,500	$2,000
1966-1969		$1,200	$1,600
1970-1971		$1,000	$1,500

L-50

1932-1971. 14 3/4" acoustic archtop, flat or arched back, round sound hole or f-holes, pearl logo pre-war, decal logo post-war, maple sides, sunburst, 16" body late-'34.

1932-1934	14 3/4" body	$2,800	$3,800
1934-1943	16" body	$2,800	$3,800
1946-1949	16", trapezoids	$2,700	$3,500
1950-1959		$2,200	$2,800
1960-1964		$2,000	$2,600
1965		$1,700	$2,200
1966-1969		$1,500	$2,000
1970-1971		$1,500	$2,000

L-75

1932-1939. 14 3/4" archtop with round sound hole and flat back, size increased to 16" with arched back in '35, small button tuners, dot markers, lower-end style trapeze tailpiece, pearl script logo, sunburst.

1932	14 3/4", dot neck	$3,500	$4,500
1933-1934	14 3/4", pearloid	$3,500	$4,500
1935-1939	16" body	$3,500	$4,500

L-130

1999-2005. 14 7/8" lower bout, small jumbo, solid spruce top, solid bubinga back and sides, rosewood 'board, factory electronics with preamp.

1999-2005		$1,800	$2,800

L-140

1999-2005. Like L-130 but with rosewood back and sides, ebony 'board.

1999-2005		$2,200	$3,500

L-200 Emmylou Harris

2001-2016. Smaller and thinner than standard 200, flamed maple sides and back, gold hardware, crest markers, natural or sunburst.

2001-2016		$3,500	$5,000

L-C Century

1933-1939. Curly maple back and sides, bound body, white pearloid 'board and peghead (all years) and headstock (until '38), sunburst.

1933-1938	Pearloid	$9,500	$12,500
1939		$9,000	$12,000

L-C Century Elvis Costello Limited

2016. Signed custom label, pearloid 'board, Adirondack red spruce top, AAA flamed maple back and sides, 300 made.

2016		$4,000	$6,000

L-C Century Reissue

1994. Pearloid headstock and 'board.

1994		$3,500	$5,500

L-Jr.

1918-1927. Archtop, solid carved spruce top, carved figured birch back, Sheraton Brown or natural finish.

1918-1927		$2,500	$3,500

LC-1 Cascade

2002-2006. LC-Series acoustic/electric, advanced L-00-style, solid quilted maple back and sides.

2002-2006		$2,200	$3,500

LC-2 Sonoma

2002-2006. Released November '02, LC-Series acoustic/electric, advanced L-00-style, solid walnut back and sides.

2002-2006		$2,800	$4,000

LC-3 Caldera

2003-2004. 14 3/4" flat-top, soft cutaway, solid cedar top, solid flamed Koa back and sides, fancy appointments.

2003-2004		$3,000	$4,500

Le Grande

1993-2010. Electric archtop, 17", formerly called Johnny Smith.

1993-2010		$7,000	$10,000

LES PAUL

The following are models bearing the Les Paul name. In order to keep certain models grouped together, subheadings have been included for Classic, Custom, Deluxe, Goldtop, Junior, Special, Standard and Studio models. All others are then listed pretty much alphabetically as follows:

'60 Les Paul Corvette
Les Paul 25/50 Anniversary
Les Paul 40th Anniversary (from 1952)
Les Paul (All Maple)
Les Paul Artisan and Artisan/3
Les Paul Artist/L.P. Artist/Les Paul Active

LES PAUL CLASSIC

Following are Les Paul Classic models listed alphabetically.

Les Paul Classic
Les Paul Classic 1960 Mars Music
Les Paul Classic Antique Mahogany
Les Paul Classic Custom
Les Paul Classic H-90
Les Paul Classic Limited Edition
Les Paul Classic Mark III/MIII
Les Paul Classic Plus
Les Paul Classic Premium Plus
Les Paul Classic Premium Plus (Custom Shop)
Les Paul Classic Tom Morgan Limited Edition

LES PAUL CUSTOM

Following are Les Paul Custom models listed alphabetically.

Les Paul Custom
Les Paul Custom 25
Les Paul Custom '54
Les Paul Custom Historic '54
Les Paul Custom Historic '57 Black Beauty
1957 Les Paul Custom (2-Pickup) Ultra Light Aged
1957 Les Paul Custom (3-Pickup) Light Aged
Les Paul Custom Historic '68
1968 Les Paul Custom Reissue (Custom Shop)

1968 Les Paul Custom Ultra Light Aged
20th Anniversary Les Paul Custom
25th Anniversary (Guitar Center) Les Paul Custom
50th Anniversary Les Paul Custom Limited Edition
35th Anniversary Les Paul Custom
120th Anniversary Les Paul Custom
120th Anniversary Les Paul Custom Lite
Les Paul Custom Ace Frehley "Budokan"
Les Paul Custom Adam Jones 1979
Les Paul Custom F (Custom Shop)
Les Paul Custom Jeff Beck 1954 Oxblood
Les Paul Custom Jimmy Page
Les Paul Custom John Sykes 1978
Les Paul Custom Lite
Les Paul Custom Lite (Show Case Edition)
Les Paul Custom Mick Ronson '68
Les Paul Custom Music Machine
Les Paul Custom Peter Frampton Signature
Les Paul Custom Plus
Les Paul Custom Randy Rhoads
Les Paul Custom Showcase Edition
Les Paul Custom Silverburst
Les Paul Custom Steve Jones 1974
Les Paul Custom Zakk Wylde Signature

Les Paul Dale Earnhardt
Les Paul Dale Earnhardt Intimidator
Les Paul Dark Fire
Les Paul Dark Knight Quilt Top
Les Paul DC AA
Les Paul DC Classic
Les Paul DC Pro
Les Paul DC Standard (Plus)
Les Paul DC Studio

LES PAUL DELUXE

Following are Les Paul Deluxe models listed alphabetically.

Les Paul Deluxe
Les Paul Deluxe 30th Anniversary
Les Paul Deluxe '69 Reissue
Les Paul Deluxe Hall of Fame
Les Paul Deluxe Limited Edition
Les Paul Deluxe Limited Edition AMS
Les Paul Deluxe Reissue
Les Paul Deluxe #1 Pete Townshend
Les Paul Deluxe #3 Pete Townshend
Les Paul Deluxe #9 Pete Townshend
Les Paul Pro Deluxe

Les Paul Dusk Tiger
Les Paul ES-Les Paul
Les Paul ES-Les Paul Custom
Les Paul ES-Les Paul Standard
Les Paul ES-Les Paul Studio
Les Paul Florentine Plus
Les Paul Supreme Florentine
Les Paul Futura
Les Paul Goddess

LES PAUL GOLDTOP

Following are Les Paul Goldtop models listed alphabetically.

Les Paul Model
'52 Les Paul Goldtop
'52 Les Paul Tribute
'54 Les Paul Goldtop
'54 Les Paul Wildwood
1954 Les Paul Goldtop Heavy Aged
'55 Les Paul Goldtop Hot-Mod Wraptail
'56 Les Paul Goldtop
1956 Les Paul Goldtop "CME Spec"
1956 Les Paul Goldtop Reissue
1956 Les Paul Goldtop Ultra Light Aged
'57 Les Paul Goldtop
'57 Les Paul Goldtop (R-7 wrap-around)
1957 Les Paul Goldtop Darkback Light Aged
1957 Les Paul Goldtop Reissue
1957 Les Paul Goldtop Ultra Light/Ultra Heavy Aged
True Historic 1957 Les Paul Goldtop
Les Paul 30th Anniversary
Les Paul 50th Anniversary 1956 Les Paul Standard Goldtop
Les Paul 50th Anniversary 1957 Les Paul Standard Goldtop
Les Paul Billy F. Gibbons Goldtop
Les Paul Centennial ('56 LP Standard Goldtop)
Les Paul Dickey Betts Goldtop
Les Paul Joe Bonamassa Aged Goldtop
Les Paul LP-295 Goldtop
Les Paul Pro Showcase Edition
Les Paul Reissue Goldtop
Les Paul Slash Signature Goldtop

Les Paul Government Series I
Les Paul Government Series II
Les Paul GT
Les Paul HD.6-X Pro Digital
Les Paul Indian Motorcycle
Les Paul Jumbo

LES PAUL JUNIOR

Following are Les Paul Junior models listed alphabetically.

Les Paul Junior
Les Paul Junior 3/4
1957 Les Paul Junior (Single-Cut) Ultra Light Aged/Heavy Aged
1957 Les Paul Junior (Single-Cut) VOS
1958 Les Paul Junior (Double-Cut) VOS
'60 Les Paul Junior
1960 Les Paul Junior (Double-Cut) Ultra Heavy Aged
Les Paul J / LPJ
Les Paul Junior Billie Joe Armstrong Signature
Les Paul Junior DC Hall of Fame
Les Paul Junior Double Cutaway
Les Paul Junior Faded
Les Paul Junior II
Les Paul Junior John Lennon LTD
Les Paul Junior Lite

1978 Gibson Les Paul Custom

Kevin Okanos

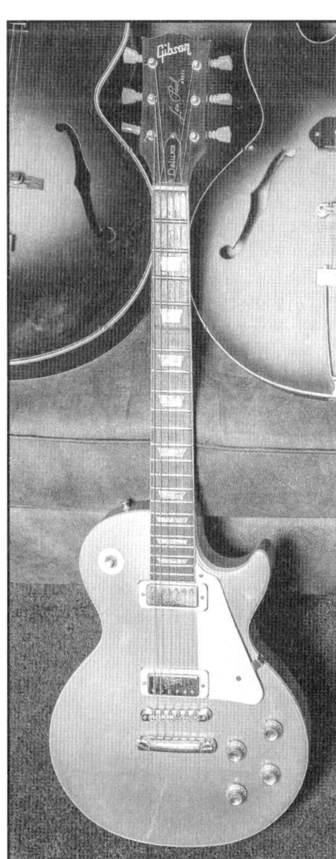

1969 Gibson Les Paul Deluxe

John Wesley

1953 Gibson Les Paul Model

1959 Gibson Les Paul Special 3/4
Alex Sauceda

Les Paul Junior Special
Les Paul Junior Special Robot
Les Paul Junior Tenor/Plectrum
Les Paul TV
Les Paul TV 3/4
Les Paul TV Junior

Les Paul Limited Run 2016 Series
Les Paul Lou Pallo Signature
Les Paul Marc Bolan
Les Paul Menace
Les Paul Old Hickory
Les Paul Personal
Les Paul 'Push Tone'
Les Paul Professional
Les Paul Recording
Les Paul Richard Petty LTD
Les Paul Signature/L.P. Signature
Les Paul Silver Streak
Les Paul SM
Les Paul SmartWood Exotic
Les Paul SmartWood Standard
Les Paul SmartWood Studio

LES PAUL SPECIAL

Following are Les Paul Special models listed alphabetically.

Les Paul Special
Les Paul 55
1957 Les Paul Special (Single-Cut) Ultra Light Aged
'60 Les Paul Special
Les Paul Special (Reissue)
Les Paul Special 3/4
Les Paul Special Centennial
Les Paul Special Double Cutaway
Les Paul Special Faded
Les Paul Special New Century
Les Paul Special Peter Frampton
Les Paul Special Robot
Les Paul Special SL
Les Paul Special Tenor
Les Paul Special Worn Cherry

LES PAUL STANDARD

Following are Les Paul Standard models, beginning with the original model, then listed alphabetically.

Les Paul Standard (Sunburst)
Les Paul Standard (SG body)
Les Paul Standard (reintroduced)
'50s Les Paul Standard
'58 Les Paul Figured Top
'58 Les Paul Plaintop (VOS)
1958 Les Paul Standard "CME Spec"
1958 Les Paul Standard Light Aged/Heavy Aged
1958 Les Paul Standard Ultra Light Aged
'59 Les Paul Flametop/Reissue/Standard
'59 Les Paul Burst Brothers
'59 Les Paul Korina Reissue
'59 Les Paul Plaintop (VOS)
1959 Les Paul Standard "CME Spec"
1959 Les Paul Standard Heavy Aged
1959 Les Paul Standard Light Aged
1959 Les Paul Standard Reissue
1959 Les Paul Standard Ultra Heavy Aged
1959 Les Paul Standard Ultra Light Aged
True Historic 1959 Les Paul
'60s Les Paul Standard
'60 Les Paul Flametop/Standard '60s
'60 Les Paul Plaintop (VOS)
1960 Les Paul Standard Heavy Aged
1960 Les Paul Standard Light Aged
1960 Les Paul Standard Reissue
1960 Les Paul Standard Ultra Light Aged
True Historic 1960 Les Paul
'82 Les Paul Standard
Les Paul 10th Anniversary Chambered '58 Reissue
Les Paul 40th Anniversary (from 1959)
Les Paul 50th Anniversary (Historic)
Les Paul 50th Anniversary 1956 Les Paul Standard
Les Paul 50th Anniversary 1959 Les Paul Standard
Les Paul 50th Anniversary 1960 Les Paul Standard
Les Paul 50th Anniversary DaPra
Les Paul 50th Anniversary Korina Tribute
Les Paul 50th Anniversary Les Paul Standard (Sweetwater)
Les Paul 60th Anniversary 1960 Les Paul Standard "CME Spec"
Les Paul 120th Anniversary
Les Paul Axcess Alex Lifeson
Les Paul Axcess Dave Amato
Les Paul Axcess Standard
Les Paul BFG
Les Paul Bird's-Eye Standard
Les Paul Carved Series
Les Paul Catalina
Les Paul Centennial ('59 LP Special)
Les Paul Class 5
Les Paul Cloud 9 Series
Les Paul Collector's Choice Series
Les Paul Dickey Betts Red Top
Les Paul Don Felder Hotel California 1959
Les Paul Duane Allman
Les Paul Duane Allman Hot 'Lanta
Les Paul Elegant
Les Paul Eric Clapton 1960
Les Paul Gary Moore BFG
Les Paul Gary Moore Signature
Les Paul Gary Rossington Signature
Les Paul Guitar Trader Reissue
Les Paul Heritage 80
Les Paul Heritage 80 Award
Les Paul Heritage 80 Elite
Les Paul Heritage 80/Standard 80
Les Paul Hot Rod Magazine '58 Standard
Les Paul Jim Beam (Custom Shop)
Les Paul Jimmy Page "Number Two"

Les Paul Jimmy Page (Custom Authentic)
Les Paul Jimmy Page Signature
Les Paul Jimmy Page Signature (Custom Shop)
Les Paul Jimmy Wallace Reissue
Les Paul Joe Bonamassa Bonabyrd
Les Paul Joe Bonamassa Skinnerburst 1959
Les Paul Joe Bonamassa 'Tomato Soup Burst' Limited Edition
Les Paul Joe Perry 1959
Les Paul Joe Perry Signature
Les Paul KM (Kalamazoo Model)
Les Paul Korina
Les Paul Leo's Reissue
Les Paul Limited Edition (3-tone)
Les Paul Modern
Les Paul Music Machine 25th Anniversary
Les Paul Music Machine Brazilian Stinger
Les Paul Music Rising Limited Edition
Les Paul Neal Schon Signature
Les Paul Peace
Les Paul Reissue Flametop
Les Paul SG '61 Reissue
Les Paul SG Standard Authentic
Les Paul SG Standard Reissue
Les Paul Signature "T"
Les Paul Slash Appetite
Les Paul Slash Signature
Les Paul Slash Snakepit
Les Paul Southern Rock Tribute 1959
Les Paul Spider-Man
Les Paul Spotlight Special
Les Paul Standard 100
Les Paul Standard 2008
Les Paul Standard 2010 Limited
Les Paul Standard Billy Gibbons 'Pearly Gates'
Les Paul Standard F
Les Paul Standard Faded
Les Paul Standard HP
Les Paul Standard Limited Edition Series
Les Paul Standard Limited Edition Sparkle
Les Paul Standard Lite Double Cutaway
Les Paul Standard Lite Limited Edition
Les Paul Standard Michael Bloomfield 1959
Les Paul Standard Mike McCready 1959
Les Paul Standard Music Zoo 25th Anniversary
Les Paul Standard Paul Kossoff 1959
Les Paul Standard Plus
Les Paul Standard Premium Plus
Les Paul Standard Raw Power
Les Paul Standard Rick Nielsen 1959
Les Paul Standard Robot
Les Paul Standard RSM 1959/RSM '59 Les Paul Standard
Les Paul Standard Showcase Edition
Les Paul Strings and Things Standard
Les Paul Tie Dye (St. Pierre)
Les Paul Tie Dye Custom Shop
Les Paul Traditional Pro/Pro II
Les Paul Traditional/Plus
Les Paul Ultima
Les Paul Ultra-Aged

MODEL YEAR	FEATURES	EXC. COND. LOW	HIGH

Les Paul Warren Haynes
Les Paul Zebra Wood

LES PAUL STUDIO

Following are Les Paul Studio models listed alphabetically.

Les Paul Studio
Les Paul Studio 120th Anniversary
Les Paul Studio '50s Tribute
Les Paul Studio '60s Tribute
Les Paul Studio '70s Tribute
Les Paul Studio Baritone
Les Paul Studio BFD
Les Paul Studio Custom
Les Paul Studio Deluxe '60s
Les Paul Studio Deluxe II
Les Paul Studio Faded Vintage Mahogany
Les Paul Studio Faded/Pro Faded
Les Paul Studio Gem
Les Paul Studio Gothic
Les Paul Studio Gothic Morte
Les Paul Studio Joe Bonamassa
Les Paul Studio Limited Edition
Les Paul Studio Lite
Les Paul Studio Lite Mark III/M3/M III
Les Paul Studio MLB Baseball
Les Paul Studio Platinum
Les Paul Studio Platinum Plus
Les Paul Studio Plus
Les Paul Studio Premium Plus
Les Paul Studio Raw Power
Les Paul Studio Robot
Les Paul Studio Robot Limited Edition
Les Paul Studio Roland Synthesizer
Les Paul Studio Shred
Les Paul Studio Special
Les Paul Studio Special Limited Edition
Les Paul Studio Standard
Les Paul Studio Swamp Ash
Les Paul Studio USA Anniversary Flood

Les Paul Supreme
Les Paul Vixen
Les Paul Voodoo/Voodoo Les Paul
Les Paul XR-I / II / III
The Les Paul
The Paul
The Paul Firebrand Deluxe
The Paul II

'60 Les Paul Corvette

1995-1997. Custom Shop Les Paul, distinctive Chevrolet Corvette styling from '60, offered in 6 colors.

1995-1997		$4,500	$7,000

Les Paul 25/50 Anniversary

1978-1979. Split-block inlays, five- or seven- piece maple and walnut neck, gold and silver hardware, 2 humbuckers, coil splitter, TP-6 tailpiece, antique sunburst, natural, wine red, black, and white finishes offered, 8-digit SN followed by 4-digit limited edition number, 1,106 made in '78, 2,305 in '79.

1978-1979		$4,500	$6,500

2019 Gibson Les Paul Traditional

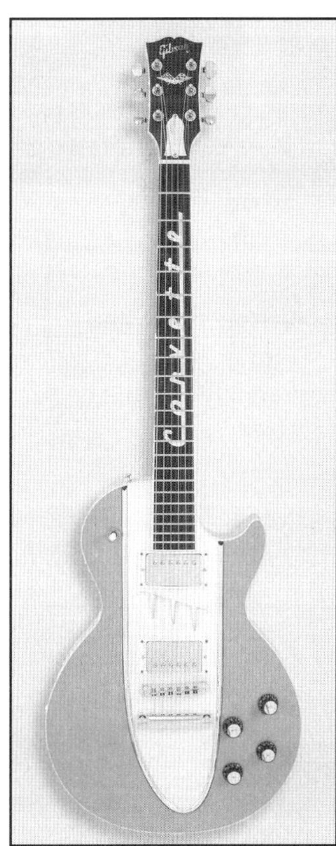

1996 '60 Les Paul Corvette

1978 Gibson Les Paul Artisan
Gary's Classic Guitars

2018 Gibson Classic Player Plus
Dan Lussier

MODEL YEAR	FEATURES	EXC. COND. LOW	HIGH

Les Paul 40th Anniversary (from 1952)

1991-1992. Black finish, 2 soapbar P-100 pickups, gold hardware, stop tailpiece, 40th Anniversary inlay at 12th fret.

1991-1992		$4,000	$6,000

Les Paul (All Maple)

1984. Limited run, all maple body, Super 400-style inlay, gold hardware.

1984		$2,500	$3,800

Les Paul Artisan and Artisan/3

1976-1982. Carved maple top, 2 or 3 humbuckers, gold hardware, hearts and flowers inlays on 'board and headstock, ebony, sunburst or walnut.

1976-1982	2 pickups	$4,200	$6,500
1976-1982	3 pickups	$4,200	$6,500

Les Paul Artist/L.P. Artist/ Les Paul Active

1979-1982. Two humbuckers (3 optional), active electronics, gold hardware, 3 mini-switches, multi-bound, Fireburst, ebony or sunburst.

1979-1982		$2,500	$5,000

LES PAUL CLASSIC

Following are Les Paul Classic models listed alphabetically.

Les Paul Classic

1990-1998, 2000-2008, 2014-present. Early models have 1960 on pickguard, 2 exposed humbuckers, Les Paul Model on peghead until '93, Les Paul Classic afterwards. Limited run of Ebony finish in 2000, 2014 and 2015 have those years in the model name.

1990-2008	Various colors	$2,000	$3,000
2014-2024	Various colors	$1,800	$2,500

Les Paul Classic 1960 Mars Music

2000. All black.

2000		$2,200	$3,500

Les Paul Classic Antique Mahogany

2007. All mahogany body, exposed humbuckers, Guitar of the Week, limited run of 400 each of cherry (week 27) and sunburst (week 33).

2007		$2,000	$2,800

Les Paul Classic Custom

2007-2008, 2011-2012. Mahogany body with carved maple top, 2 exposed humbuckers in '07-'08, covered afterwards, various colors.

2007-2012		$3,000	$4,000

Les Paul Classic H-90

2008. Guitar of the Week, 400 made, gold hardware, H-90 soapbar pickups.

2008		$2,200	$3,500

Les Paul Classic Limited Edition

2000. Limited Edition logo on back of headstock, Les Paul Classic stencil logo, 3 exposed humbuckers, gold hardware, black finish.

2000		$3,000	$4,000

Les Paul Classic Mark III/MIII

1991-1993. Les Paul Classic features, no 'guard, exposed-coil humbuckers at neck and bridge and single-coil at middle position, 5-way switch, coil-tap.

1991-1993		$2,800	$3,800

Les Paul Classic Plus

1991-1996, 1999-2003. Les Paul Classic with fancier maple top, 2 exposed humbucker pickups. Price depends on top figure.

1991-2003		$2,200	$3,000

Les Paul Classic Premium Plus

1993-1996, 2001-2002. Les Paul Classic with AAA-grade flame maple top, 2 exposed humbucker pickups. Price depends on top figure.

1993-2002		$2,500	$3,500

Les Paul Classic Premium Plus (Custom Shop)

1994-1998. Custom Shop version, quilted maple top, Custom Shop logo, various colors.

1994-1998		$3,500	$4,500

Les Paul Classic Tom Morgan Limited Edition

2007. 400 made, custom finish top, black finish back/sides, Classic logo on truss rod cover.

2007		$3,000	$4,000

LES PAUL CUSTOM

Following are Les Paul Custom models listed alphabetically.

Les Paul Custom

1953-1963 (renamed SG Custom late-1963), 1968-present (production moved to Custom Shop in 2004). Les Paul body shape except for SG body '61-'63, 2 pickups (3 humbuckers mid-'57-'63 and '68-'70, 3 pickups were optional various years after), '75 Price List shows a Les Paul Custom (B) model which is equipped with a Bigsby tailpiece versus a wraparound. By '80 offered as Les Paul Custom/Gold Parts and / Nickel Parts, because gold plating wears more quickly and is therefore less attractive there is no difference in price between an '80s Gold Parts and Nickel Parts instrument.

1953	Very early NSN model	$35,000	$50,000
1954-1957	Single coils	$35,000	$50,000
1954-1957	Single coils, factory Bigsby	$30,000	$40,000
1957-1961	Bigsby	$70,000	$90,000
1957-1961	Stoptail	$95,000	$150,000
1957-1961	Stoptail, only 2 pu	$200,000	$250,000
1961-1963	White, SG body Maestro	$25,000	$33,000
1961-1963	White, SG body, side-pull vibrato	$18,500	$25,000
1962-1963	Black option, SG body, factory stop tail	$28,000	$36,500
1962-1963	Black option, SG body, side-pull vibrato	$18,500	$25,000
1962-1963	White, SG body, factory stop tail	$28,000	$36,500
1968	Black, 1-piece body	$20,000	$26,000
1969	Black, 1-piece body	$16,000	$21,000

MODEL YEAR	FEATURES	EXC. COND. LOW	HIGH
1969	Black, 3-piece body	$12,000	$16,000
1970-1973	Various colors, 3 pu	$6,500	$8,500
1970-1974	Various colors, 2 pu	$6,500	$8,500
1974	Black, white, 3 pu	$6,500	$8,500
1974	Natural, cherry sunburst	$5,000	$6,500
1975-1976	Maple 'board, 2 pu	$5,000	$6,500
1975-1976	Maple 'board, 3 pu	$5,000	$6,500
1975-1978	Volute, 2 pu	$4,800	$6,200
1975-1978	Volute, 3 pu	$4,800	$6,200
1977	Maple 'board, black, 2 pu	$5,000	$6,500
1977-1978	Maple 'board, blond, 2 pu	$5,000	$6,500
1979	2 or 3 pickups	$4,800	$6,500
1979	Silverburst, 2 pu	$8,000	$11,000
1980-1984	Silverburst, 2 pu	$6,500	$8,500
1980-1986	2 or 3 pickups	$4,800	$6,500
1987-1989	Various colors	$4,800	$6,500
1990-1999	Limited Edition color series	$4,200	$5,500
1990-1999	Various colors	$3,800	$5,000
2000-2024	Various colors	$3,800	$5,000

Les Paul Custom 25

2007. Custom Shop Limited Edition run of 100, Les Paul "25" logo on truss rod cover, COA name Custom 25, triple-split block inlays, mahogany body with flame maple top, gold hardware, sunburst.

2007		$4,000	$6,000

Les Paul Custom '54

1972-1973. Reissue of 1954 Custom, black finish, Alnico V and P-90 pickups.

1972-1973		$6,500	$10,000

Les Paul Custom Historic '54

1991-2013. Custom Shop Historic Collection, 1954 appointments and pickup configuration, black, gold hardware.

1991-2013		$4,500	$6,500

Les Paul Custom Historic '57 Black Beauty

1991-2013. Black finish, gold hardware, 2 or 3 humbucker pickups, part of Gibson's Historic Collection.

1991-2012	2 pickups	$4,000	$6,500
1991-2013	3 pickups	$4,500	$7,000
2007	Goldtop, 3 pu	$5,000	$7,500
2007	Murphy aged, 3 pu	$5,500	$8,500

1957 Les Paul Custom (2-Pickup) Ultra Light Aged

2021-2024. Custom Shop Murphy Lab Collection, Ebony finish.

2021-2024		$5,000	$7,500

1957 Les Paul Custom (3-Pickup) Light Aged

2021-present. Custom Shop Murphy Lab Collection, with Bigsby vibrato, Ebony finish.

2021-2024		$5,500	$8,000

Les Paul Custom Historic '68

1999-2008. Custom Shop Historic Collection, flamed maple top, 2 pickups.

1999-2007	Flamed maple	$4,500	$6,000
2000	Black	$4,000	$5,500
2007-2008	Reissue, chambered	$4,000	$5,500

1968 Les Paul Custom Reissue (Custom Shop)

2020-present. Solid maple top, mahogany back, 2 humbucker pickups, gold hardware, Ebony gloss nitro finish. Limited slightly aged Silverburst in '20.

2020	Aged Silverburst	$6,000	$7,500
2020-2024	Ebony	$5,000	$6,500

1968 Les Paul Custom Ultra Light Aged

2021-2022. Custom Shop Murphy Lab Collection, Ebony finish.

2021-2022		$5,000	$7,500

20th Anniversary Les Paul Custom

1974. Regular 2-pickup Custom, with 20th Anniversary inlay at 15th fret, cherry sunburst, natural, black or white.

1974	Black, white	$5,500	$7,500
1974	Cherry Sunburst, natural	$6,000	$9,000

25th Anniversary (Guitar Center) Les Paul Custom

1977-1978. Guitar Center Silver Anniversary, 50 made, 'Les Paul Custom' logo on truss rod cover, special 'Les Paul Custom Made in USA' on back of headstock, silver finish.

1977-1978		$6,000	$9,000

35th Anniversary Les Paul Custom

1989. Gold hardware, 3 pickups, carved, solid mahogany body and neck, 35th Anniversary inlay on headstock, black.

1989		$4,500	$6,000

50th Anniversary Les Paul Custom Limited Edition

2007. Gold finish,large 50th Anniversary logo on headstock, high-end appointments, COA.

2007		$5,500	$8,000

120th Anniversary Les Paul Custom

2014. Custom Shop, 120th Anniversary neck inlay.

2014		$4,500	$6,500

120th Anniversary Les Paul Custom Lite

2014. Custom Shop, 120th Anniversary neck inlay.

2014		$3,500	$5,500

Les Paul Custom Ace Frehley "Budokan"

2012-2013. Custom Shop, limited edition of 50 hand-aged signed by Frehley, 100 hand-aged unsigned and 150 additional with VOS finish.

2012-2013	Hand-aged, signed	$18,000	$25,000
2012-2013	Hand-aged	$12,000	$16,000
2012-2013	VOS	$9,000	$12,000

Les Paul Custom Adam Jones 1979

2021-2024. Custom Shop Limited Edition, recreates Jones' '79 LP Custom, 1st 79 aged and signed by Jones, Antique Silverburst VOS finish.

2021-2024	Signed	$8,000	$12,000
2021-2024	Unsigned	$6,000	$9,000

Gibson 1957 Les Paul Custom Light Aged

Gibson Les Paul Custom Adam Jones 1979

GUITARS

2008 Gibson Les Paul Custom Jimmy Page
Imaged by Heritage Auctions, HA.com

Gibson Les Paul Dark Knight Quilt Top

MODEL YEAR	FEATURES	EXC. COND. LOW	HIGH

Les Paul Custom F (Custom Shop)

2014-2018. Figured maple top, various colors.

2014-2018		$4,500	$6,500

Les Paul Custom Jeff Beck 1954 Oxblood

2009. Custom Shop, limited run of 150, 1st 50 aged, hand-signed and played by Beck, next 100 VOS, mahogany body, carved maple top, rosewood 'board, Burstbucker humbucking pickups, Oxblood VOS finish.

2009	Signed	$18,000	$25,000
2009	VOS	$8,500	$12,000

Les Paul Custom Jimmy Page

2008. Based on Page's '60 LP Custom with 3 pickups, stop tailpiece or Bigsby option, certificate of authenticity, black VOS finish.

2008	Signed	$30,000	$45,000
2008	VOS	$11,500	$18,000

Les Paul Custom John Sykes 1978

2006. Custom Shop Limited Edition, run of 66, recreates Sykes' '78 LP Custom including mods he made, aged Ebony finish.

2006	Limited, aged	$6,500	$9,000
2006	VOS	$5,000	$7,000

Les Paul Custom Lite

1987-1990, 2013-2016. Carved maple top, ebony 'board, pearl block inlays, gold hardware, PAF pickups, bound neck, headstock and body. Reissue in '13 with new options and colors.

1987-1990	Floyd Rose, opaque	$2,800	$4,500
1987-1990	Other colors	$2,500	$4,000
1987-1990	Sunburst, mild figure	$2,800	$4,500
2013-2016		$3,300	$5,000

Les Paul Custom Lite (Show Case Edition)

1988. Showcase Edition, only 200 made, gold top.

1988		$3,800	$6,000

Les Paul Custom Mick Ronson '68

2007. Custom Shop, includes certificate and other authentication material.

2007		$5,000	$7,000

Les Paul Custom Music Machine

2003. Custom run for dealer Music Machine with special serial number series, chambered body style for reduced body weight, quilt tops.

2003	Figured Brazilian	$8,000	$12,000
2003	Quilted	$5,200	$8,000

Les Paul Custom Peter Frampton Signature

2008. Limited Edition 3-pickup version of Frampton's LP Custom, PF serial number series, black.

2008		$5,500	$8,000

Les Paul Custom Plus

1991-1998. Regular Custom with figured maple top, sunburst finish or colors.

1991-1998		$3,800	$5,800

Les Paul Custom Randy Rhoads

2010-2011. Custom Shop, recreation of Rhoad's '74 LP Custom, 100 hand-aged and 200 VOS made.

2010-2011	Aged	$7,000	$10,000
2010-2011	VOS	$5,500	$8,000

MODEL YEAR	FEATURES	EXC. COND. LOW	HIGH

Les Paul Custom Showcase Edition

1988. Showcase Edition logo on back of headstock, goldtop, black hardware.

1988		$4,500	$7,000

Les Paul Custom Silverburst

2007-2014. Custom Shop Limited Edition.

2007-2014		$4,500	$6,500

Les Paul Custom Steve Jones 1974

2008. Custom Shop Limited Edition, recreates Jones' '74 LP Custom including pin-up girl stickers, aged white finish.

2008		$5,000	$7,500

Les Paul Custom Zakk Wylde Signature

1999, 2003-2016. Black and antique-white bullseye graphic finish. Green Camo bullseye option.

1999-2016	Black/white	$5,000	$7,500
2003-2016	Green Camo	$5,500	$8,500
2010	Custom Shop	$6,000	$9,000

Les Paul Dale Earnhardt

1999. 333 made, Dale's image and number 3 on front and headstock, signature script on fretboard, several pieces of literature and an original certificate are part of the overall package, a lower serial number may add value.

1999		$3,500	$5,500

Les Paul Dale Earnhardt Intimidator

2000. 333 made, Dale's 'Goodwrench' car on the front of the body, The Intimidator inlay on the fretboard, includes certificate, chrome hardware.

2000		$5,000	$8,000

Les Paul Dark Fire

2009. Limited edition, 1st run of Les Pauls with Robot 2 Chameleon tone Technology designed to produce various classic guitar tones, completely computer interactive, Burstbucker3 bridge pickup, P-90H neck pickup and 6 Piezo pickups.

2009		$3,000	$4,500

Les Paul Dark Knight Quilt Top

2019. Exclusive limited run made for Guitar Center, trans black satin finish over quilted maple top.

2019		$3,500	$5,500

Les Paul DC AA

2007. Double A flamed top.

2007		$2,500	$4,000

Les Paul DC Classic

1992-1993. Gold finish.

1992-1993		$2,500	$3,800

Les Paul DC Pro

1997-1998, 2006-2007. Custom Shop, body like a '59 Les Paul Junior, carved highly figured maple top, various options. Name revived in '06 but not a Custom Shop model.

1997-1998		$3,500	$5,000
2006-2007		$2,200	$3,500

Les Paul DC Standard (Plus)

1998-1999, 2001-2006. Offset double-cut, highly flamed maple top, translucent lacquer finishes in various colors, reintroduced as Standard Lite in '99 but without Les Paul designation on headstock or truss rod cover.

1998-1999		$2,500	$4,000
2001-2006		$2,500	$4,000

MODEL YEAR	FEATURES	EXC. COND. LOW	HIGH

Les Paul DC Studio

1997-1999. DC Series double-cut like late '50s models, carved maple top, 2 humbucker pickups, various colors.

1997-1999		$1,800	$2,800

LES PAUL DELUXE

Following are Les Paul Deluxe models listed alphabetically.

Les Paul Deluxe

1969-1985. In 1969, the Goldtop Les Paul Standard was renamed the Deluxe. Two mini-humbuckers (regular humbuckers optional in mid-'70s). Mid-'70s sparkle tops are worth more than standard finishes. The market slightly favors the Goldtop finish, but practically speaking condition is more important than finish, such that all finishes fetch about the same amount (with the exception of the sparkle finish). Initially, the Deluxe was offered only as a Goldtop and the first year models are more highly prized than the others. Cherry sunburst was offered in '71, cherry in '71-'75, walnut in '71-'72, brown sunburst in '72-'79, natural in '75, red sparkle in '73-'75 only, blue sparkle in '73-'77, wine red/see-thru red offered '75-'85. In '99, the Deluxe was reissued for its 30th anniversary.

1969	Goldtop	$8,500	$11,000
1970	Goldtop	$7,000	$9,000
1971-1975	Goldtop	$6,500	$8,500
1971-1975	Natural	$4,000	$5,500
1971-1975	Red (solid)	$4,000	$5,500
1971-1975	Sunburst	$4,000	$5,500
1971-1975	Wine	$4,000	$5,500
1973-1975	Red sparkle, few made	$7,500	$10,000
1973-1977	Blue sparkle, more made	$7,000	$9,500
1976-1979	All other colors	$3,500	$5,000
1976-1979	Goldtop	$5,000	$6,500
1976-1979	Natural	$3,800	$5,000
1976-1979	Sunburst	$3,800	$5,000
1980-1985	Various colors	$3,500	$4,500

Les Paul Deluxe 30th Anniversary

1999. Limited Edition logo on the lower back of the headstock, Deluxe logo on truss rod cover, Wine Red.

1999		$2,200	$3,500

Les Paul Deluxe '69 Reissue

2000-2005. Mini-humbuckers, gold top

2000-2005		$2,500	$4,000

Les Paul Deluxe Hall of Fame

1991. All gold finish.

1991		$3,000	$4,500

Les Paul Deluxe Limited Edition

1999-2002. Limited edition reissue with Les Paul Standard features and Deluxe mini-humbuckers, black.

1999-2002		$2,500	$3,500

Les Paul Deluxe Limited Edition AMS

2014. Limited edition chocolate finish, offered only by American Musical Supply.

2014		$2,500	$3,500

Les Paul Deluxe Reissue

2012. Mini-humbuckers, chambered body.

2012		$3,000	$4,800

Les Paul Deluxe #1 Pete Townshend

2006. Limited to 75, red.

2006		$7,000	$10,000

Les Paul Deluxe #3 Pete Townshend

2006. Limited to 75, goldtop.

2006		$7,500	$10,500

Les Paul Deluxe #9 Pete Townshend

2006. Limited to 75, cherry burst.

2006		$7,000	$10,000

Les Paul Pro Deluxe

1978-1982. Chrome hardware, 2 P-90s, various colors. Les Pauls could vary significantly in weight during the '70s and '80s and lighter-weight examples may be worth up to 25% more than these values.

1978-1982		$3,500	$5,500

Les Paul Dusk Tiger

Late-2009-2012. Limited edition, 1000 to be made, features Gibson's Robot Technology, Burstbucker bridge, P-90H neck and 6 Piezo pickups.

2009-2012		$3,000	$5,000

Les Paul ES-Les Paul

2014-2018. Semi-hollow Les Paul body with f-holes, 3-ply maple/basswood/maple top and back, mahogany neck with maple spline, dark rosewood 'board, 2 pickups, light burst or black.

2014-2018		$2,800	$4,500

Les Paul ES-Les Paul Custom

2015. Memphis Shop, limited run, semi-hollow maple/poplar/maple body, f-holes, high gloss Ebony finish.

2015		$4,000	$6,000

Les Paul ES-Les Paul Standard

2016. Memphis Shop, limited run, semi-hollow, figured maple, various colors.

2016		$3,000	$4,800

Les Paul ES-Les Paul Studio

2016. Memphis Shop, limited run, semi-hollow maple body, f-holes, Ginger Burst or Wine Red.

2016		$2,200	$3,500

Les Paul Florentine Plus

1997-2001. Custom Shop model, hollowbody with f-holes, higher-end appointments.

1997-2001		$4,000	$6,000

Les Paul Supreme Florentine

2009-2015. Les Paul Standard with sharp Florentine cutaway, 350 made, Bigsby tailpiece, chambered mahogany body, highly figured maple top and back, Caribbean Blue finish.

2009-2015		$4,500	$6,500

Les Paul Futura

2014-2015. Light weight, unbound, Min-Etune, various bright colors.

2014-2015		$1,200	$2,000

Les Paul Goddess

2006-2007. Maple carved top, trapezoid inlays, smaller body, 2 humbuckers, 2 controls, tune-a-matic bridge.

2007		$2,500	$3,500

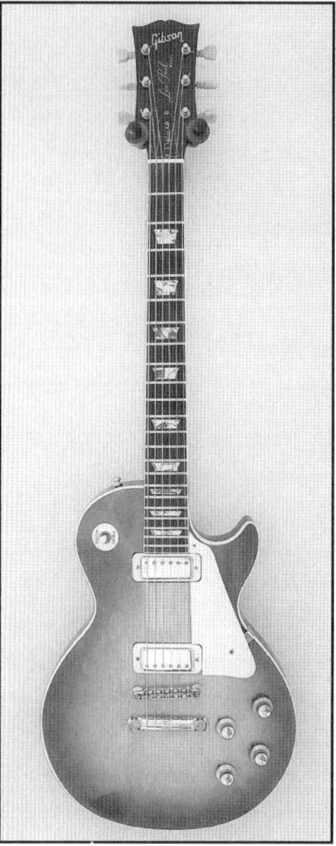

1973 Gibson Les Paul Deluxe

Rich Goldman

1997 Gibson Les Paul Florentine Plus

GUITARS

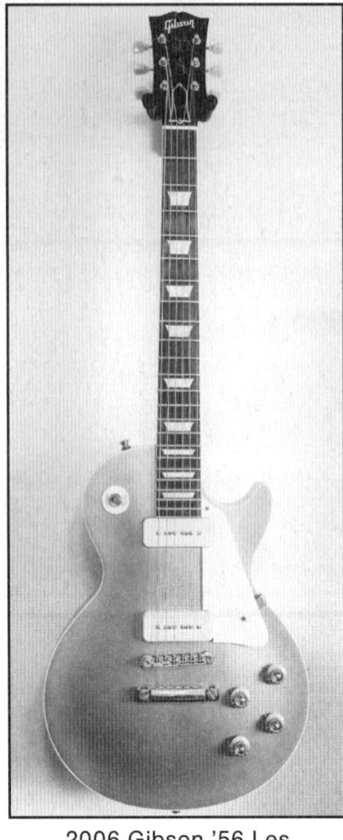

2006 Gibson '56 Les Paul Goldtop
Johnny Zapp

1994 Gibson '57 Les Paul Goldtop
W. H. Stephens

MODEL YEAR	FEATURES	EXC. COND. LOW	HIGH

LES PAUL GOLDTOP

Following are Les Paul Goldtop models listed alphabetically.

Les Paul Model

1952-1958. The "goldtop", 2 P-90 pickups until mid-'57, humbuckers after, trapeze tailpiece until late-'53, stud tailpiece/bridge '53-mid-'55, Tune-o-matic bridge '55-'58, renamed Les Paul Standard in '58. All gold option add +10% if the neck retains 90% of the gold paint. All gold option with ugly green wear on the neck is equal to or below the value of a standard paint job. Some instruments had all mahogany bodies which did not have the maple cap. The all-mahogany version, although rarer, has a 10% lower value. A factory installed Bigsby tailpiece will reduce value by 30%. A non-factory installed Bigsby will reduce value up to 50%.

1952	1st made, unbound neck	$35,000	$45,000
1952	5/8" knobs, bound neck	$30,000	$40,000
1953	1/2" knobs, trapeze tailpiece	$30,000	$40,000
1953	Late-'53, 1/2" knobs, stud tailpiece	$40,000	$60,000
1954	Stud tailpiece, wrap-around	$40,000	$60,000
1955	Early-'55, stud tailpiece, wrap-around	$40,000	$60,000
1955	Late-'55, tune-o-matic tailpiece	$80,000	$100,000
1956	Tune-o-matic tailpiece	$80,000	$100,000
1957	Early-'57, P-90s	$80,000	$100,000
1957	PAFs, black plastic	$160,000	$250,000
1957-1958	PAFs, white plastic	$165,000	$250,000

'52 Les Paul Goldtop

1997-2002. Goldtop finish, 2 P-90s, '52-style trapeze tailpiece/bridge.

1997-2002		$3,000	$4,800
1997-2002	Murphy aged	$3,800	$6,000

'52 Les Paul Tribute

2009. Recreation of '52 Les Paul Goldtop model, 564 made, special serialization, each guitar has 'prototype' impressed on back of headstock, Tribute designation logo on truss rod, includes COA booklet with serialized COA and tribute dates 1915-2009.

2009		$3,500	$5,500

'54 Les Paul Goldtop

1996-2013. Goldtop finish, 2 P-90s, '53-'54 stud tailpiece/bridge.

1996-2013		$3,500	$5,500
2003	Brazilian, COA	$6,000	$9,000

'54 Les Paul Wildwood

2012. Wildwood guitars special run, '54 specs, wrap-around tailpiece, 2 P-90 pickups, plaintop sunburst.

2012		$4,500	$6,500

1954 Les Paul Goldtop Heavy Aged

2021. Custom Shop Murphy Lab Collection, Double Gold finish.

2021		$6,500	$9,000

'55 Les Paul Goldtop Hot-Mod Wraptail

2010. Musician's Friend, based on '55 LP Humbucking Pickup Test Guitar, '55 specs, aged nitrocellulose gold finish, includes COA.

2010		$4,000	$6,000

'56 Les Paul Goldtop

1991-2016. Renamed from Les Paul Reissue Goldtop. Goldtop finish, 2 P-90 pickups, Tune-o-matic, now part of Gibson's Historic Collection, Custom Authentic aging optional from '01, Vintage Original Specs aging optional from '06.

1991-2016		$3,500	$5,500
2003	Brazilian	$6,000	$9,000

1956 Les Paul Goldtop "CME Spec"

2019-2020. Custom Shop special run for Chicago Music Exchange, Double Gold with VOS finish.

2019-2020		$4,500	$6,500

1956 Les Paul Goldtop Reissue

2020-present. Custom Shop, authentic replica parts, Double Gold with VOS finish.

2020-2024		$4,000	$6,000

1956 Les Paul Goldtop Ultra Light Aged

2021-2022. Custom Shop Murphy Lab Collection, Double Gold finish.

2021-2022		$5,500	$8,000

'57 Les Paul Goldtop

1993-2018. Goldtop finish, 2 humbuckers, now part of Gibson's Historic Collection.

1993-2018		$3,800	$5,800
2003	Brazilian	$6,500	$9,500

'57 Les Paul Goldtop (R-7 wrap-around)

2007. Special run with wrap-around bar tailpiece/bridge similar to tailpiece on an original '54 Les Paul Goldtop.

2007		$4,500	$6,500

1957 Les Paul Goldtop Darkback Light Aged

2021-present. Custom Shop Murphy Lab Collection, Double Gold finish with dark back.

2021-2024		$6,500	$9,000

1957 Les Paul Goldtop Reissue

2020-present. Custom Shop, authentic replica parts, all Double Gold or Double Gold with dark back.

2020-2024		$4,000	$6,000

1957 Les Paul Goldtop Ultra Light/Ultra Heavy Aged

2021-present. Custom Shop Murphy Lab Collection, ultra light or heavy aged, Double Gold finish. Ultra light ended in '22.

2021-2024	Ultra light	$5,000	$7,500
2021-2024	Heavy	$6,000	$9,000

True Historic 1957 Les Paul Goldtop

2015. Custom Shop, Murphy aged, certificate of authenticity.

2015		$5,000	$8,000

MODEL YEAR	FEATURES	EXC. COND. LOW	HIGH

Les Paul 30th Anniversary

1982-1984. Features of a 1958 Les Paul Goldtop, 2 humbuckers, 30th Anniversary inlay on 19th fret.

1982-1984		$4,000	$5,500

Les Paul 50th Anniversary 1956 Les Paul Standard Goldtop

2006. Custom Shop, '56 tune-o-matic P-90 specs.

2006		$4,000	$5,500

Les Paul 50th Anniversary 1957 Les Paul Standard Goldtop

2007. Custom Shop, limited run of 150, humbucker pickups, large gold 50th Anniversary headstock logo.

2007		$4,500	$6,500

Les Paul Billy F. Gibbons Goldtop

2014-2018. Custom Shop, mahogany neck with maple spline, rosewood 'board, holly headstock, 2 Duncan Pearly Gates pickups, Goldtop VOS or Goldtop Aged.

2014-2018	Signed, aged	$10,000	$15,000
2014-2018	VOS	$7,000	$9,500

Les Paul Centennial ('56 LP Standard Goldtop)

1994. Historic Collection reissue, limited run of 100, Goldtop mahogany body, gold hardware, gold truss rod plate, gold medallion, engraved light-gold 'guard, with COA.

1994		$3,500	$6,000

Les Paul Dickey Betts Goldtop

2001-2003. Aged gold top.

2001-2003		$6,000	$9,000

Les Paul Joe Bonamassa Aged Goldtop

2008. Inspired By Series, LP Standard aged goldtop with black trim (including black pickup rings), serial number starts with BONAMASSA.

2008	Signed	$8,500	$10,000
2008	Unsigned	$5,500	$8,500

Les Paul LP-295 Goldtop

2008. Guitar of the Month (April, '08), limited run of 1000, Les Paul body style, goldtop, 2 humbuckers, ES-295 appointments such as 'guard and fretboard markers, Bigsby tailpiece option.

2008		$3,500	$5,500

Les Paul Pro Showcase Edition

1988. Goldtop 1956 specs, Showcase Edition decal, 200 made.

1988		$3,500	$5,500

Les Paul Reissue Goldtop

1983-1991. Goldtop finish, 2 P-100 pickups, renamed '56 Les Paul Goldtop in '91.

1983-1991		$3,500	$5,500

Les Paul Slash Signature Goldtop

2008. Limited Edition, 1000 made, LP Standard model, Slash logo truss rod cover, Limited Edition logo back of headstock, certificate of authenticity.

2008		$5,000	$7,500

Les Paul Government Series I

2013. Limited Edition, fretboard made from rosewood that was seized by US Government in 2011 and eventually returned, 2 Dirty Fingers pickups, gunmetal gray finish, with COA.

2013		$1,500	$3,000

Les Paul Government Series II

2013-2018. 2 Dirty Fingers pickups, Government Tan finish, with COA.

2013-2018		$1,200	$2,500

Les Paul GT

2007. Includes over/under dual truss rods, GT logo on truss rod cover, several specs designed to add durability during heavy professional use.

2007		$1,500	$2,500

Les Paul HD.6-X Pro Digital

2008-2009. Digital sound system, hex pickups.

2008-2009		$1,800	$2,800

Les Paul Indian Motorcycle

2002. 100 made, has Indian script logo on fretboard and chrome cast war bonnet on the body, crimson red and cream white.

2002		$5,000	$6,500

Les Paul Jumbo

1969-1970. Single rounded cutaway, flat-top dreadnought acoustic/electric, 1 pickup, rosewood back and sides, natural.

1969-1970		$4,000	$8,000

LES PAUL JUNIOR

Following are Les Paul Junior models listed alphabetically.

Les Paul Junior

1954-1963, 1986-1992, 2001-2002, 2005-2013. One P-90 pickup, single-cut solidbody '54-mid-'58, double-cut '58-early-'61, SG body '61-'63, renamed SG Jr. in '63, reintroduced as single-cut for '86-'92, reissued as the 1957 Les Paul Jr. Single Cutaway in '98. Headstock repair reduces the value by 40%-50%. Reinstalled tuners reduces the value by 5% to 10%. Replaced tuner buttons reduces the value by 5% to 10%.

1954-1958	Sunburst, single-cut	$10,000	$12,500
1958-1961	Cherry, double-cut	$9,000	$12,000
1961-1963	Cherry, SG body	$6,000	$8,000
1986-1992	Sunburst, single-cut, tune-o-matic	$1,500	$2,500
1998-2013	Sunburst, single-cut, stop tail	$1,500	$2,500

Les Paul Junior 3/4

1956-1961. One P-90 pickup, short-scale, single-cut solidbody '54-mid-'58, double-cut '58-early-'61.

1956-1958	Sunburst, single-cut	$4,500	$7,000
1958-1961	Cherry, double-cut	$3,800	$5,800

1957 Les Paul Junior (Single-Cut) Ultra Light Aged/Heavy Aged

2021-present. Custom Shop Murphy Lab Collection, ultra light or heavy aged, TV Yellow finish on both.

2021-2024	Heavy aged	$4,000	$6,500
2021-2024	Ultra Light aged	$3,500	$5,500

1957 Les Paul Junior (Single-Cut) VOS

1998-2014. Custom Shop, nickel-plated hardware, Vintage Original Spec aging optional from '06.

1998-2014		$2,500	$4,500

Gibson Les Paul 50th Anniversary 1957 Les Paul Standard Goldtop

Matt Carleson

1961 Gibson Les Paul Junior

Michael Alonzi

GUITARS

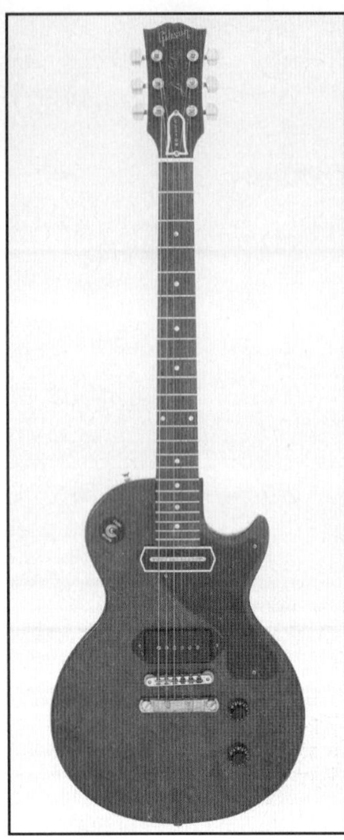

2008 Gibson Les Paul Junior John Lennon LTD
Imaged by Heritage Auctions, HA.com

Gibson Les Paul TV Junior
Bill Miller

MODEL YEAR	FEATURES	EXC. COND. LOW	HIGH

1958 Les Paul Junior (Double-Cut) VOS

1998-2013. Custom Shop, nickel plated hardware, Vintage Original Spec aging optional from '06.

1998-2013		$2,800	$4,800

'60 Les Paul Junior

1992-2003. Historic Collection reissue.

1992-2003		$2,200	$4,000

1960 Les Paul Junior (Double-Cut) Ultra Heavy Aged

2021. Custom Shop Murphy Lab Collection, Ebony finish.

2021		$4,500	$7,000

Les Paul J / LPJ

2013-2018. Mahogany body with carved maple top, '50s profile maple neck, rosewood 'board, 2 Modern Classics humbucking pickups, various finishes.

2013-2018		$600	$1,200

Les Paul Junior Billie Joe Armstrong Signature

2006-2013. 1956 LP Junior specs.

2006-2013		$1,200	$2,500

Les Paul Junior DC Hall of Fame

1990-1992. Part of Hall of Fame Series, limited run of LP Junior Double Cutaway but with P-100 pickup.

1990-1992		$1,000	$1,800

Les Paul Junior Double Cutaway

1986-1992, 1995-1996. Copy of '50s double-cut Jr., cherry or sunburst, reissued as the 1958 Les Paul Jr. Double Cutaway in '98.

1986-1989		$1,200	$2,000

Les Paul Junior Faded

2010-2012. Single-cut, faded cherry finish.

2010-2012		$800	$1,400

Les Paul Junior II

1989. Single-cut solidbody, 2 P90 Soapbar pickups, Heritage Cherry or ebony finish.

1989		$1,000	$1,800

Les Paul Junior John Lennon LTD

2008. Custom Shop Inspired By series, 300 made, Charlie Christian neck pickup and P-90 bridge as per Lennon's modified Junior, aged-relic finish, certificate, book and New York t-shirt.

2008		$3,500	$5,500

Les Paul Junior Lite

1999-2002. Double-cut, Tune-o-matic, 2 P-100 pickups, stop tail, mini-trapezoid markers, burnt cherry gloss finish.

1999-2002		$900	$1,500

Les Paul Junior Special

1999-2004. LP Jr. single-cut slab body with 2 P-90s (making it a Special) instead of the standard single P-90, double pickup controls, cherry, tinted natural or sunburst.

1999-2004		$1,000	$1,800

Les Paul Junior Special Robot

2008. P-90s, TV Yellow.

2008		$1,200	$2,000

Les Paul Junior Tenor/Plectrum

Late-1950s. Four string neck on Junior body, cherry.

1959		$6,000	$10,000

MODEL YEAR	FEATURES	EXC. COND. LOW	HIGH

Les Paul TV

1954-1959. Les Paul Jr. with limed mahogany (TV Yellow) finish, single-cut until mid-'59, double-cut after, renamed SG TV (see that listing for more) in late-'59.

1954-1959	Single-cut	$15,000	$25,000
1958-1959	Double-cut	$14,500	$20,000

Les Paul TV 3/4

1954-1957. Limed mahogany (TV Yellow) Les Paul Jr. 3/4, short-scale, single-cut.

1954-1957		$8,500	$12,000

Les Paul TV Junior

2001-2016. Custom Shop, TV Yellow.

2001-2016		$1,800	$3,500

Les Paul Limited Run 2016 Series

Various Les Paul limited edition models released in 2016.

2016-2018	Fort Knox	$3,000	$5,000
2016-2018	Mahogany Limited	$3,000	$4,500
2016-2018	Pete Townshend Deluxe	$4,000	$6,500
2016-2018	Redwood	$3,000	$5,000
2016-2018	Standard Figured Walnut	$3,000	$5,000
2016-2018	Sunken Treasure	$3,000	$5,000

Les Paul Lou Pallo Signature

2010. Maple top, mahogany back and neck, rosewood 'board, 2 pickups, ebony finish.

2010		$3,300	$5,000

Les Paul Marc Bolan

2011. Artist model with certificate of authenticity, limited run of 100 hand-aged and 350 VOS, Bolan Chablis finish.

2011	VOS	$4,000	$6,500
2011	Hand-aged	$7,000	$12,000

Les Paul Menace

2006-2007. Carved mahogany body, 2 humbucker pickups.

2006-2007		$1,000	$1,500

Les Paul Old Hickory

1998 only. Limited run of 200, tulip poplar body wood from The Hermitage, Custom-style trim.

1998		$4,000	$6,500

Les Paul Personal

1969-1972. Two angled, low impedance pickups, phase switch, gold parts, walnut finish.

1969-1972		$3,800	$6,000

Les Paul 'Push Tone'

2008. Guitar of the Month, allows for 'pushing' different pickups (humbucking or P90) into the guitar, AAA tight pin-stripe flamed top.

2008		$3,500	$5,500

Les Paul Professional

1969-1971, 1977-1979. Single-cut, 2 angled, low impedance pickups, carved top, walnut or white.

1969-1971	Walnut	$4,200	$6,500
1969-1971	White	$4,000	$6,000

Les Paul Recording

1971-1979. Two angled, low impedance pickups, high/low impedance selector switch, walnut '71-'77, white added '75, natural, ebony and sunburst added '78.

MODEL YEAR	FEATURES	EXC. COND. LOW	HIGH
1971-1977	Walnut	$3,500	$5,500
1975-1979	White	$4,000	$6,000
1978-1979	Black, Natural, Sunburst	$4,000	$6,000

Les Paul Richard Petty LTD

2003. Richard Petty's image on front and back, 'The King' inlay on fretboard, 43 made.

2003		$5,200	$8,000

Les Paul Signature/L.P. Signature

1973-1978. Thin semi-hollowbody, double-cut, 2 low impedance pickups, f-holes, various colors. The Price List refers to it as L.P. Signature.

1973-1978		$3,200	$5,000

Les Paul Silver Streak

1982. Custom Shop decal, silver finish.

1982		$4,000	$6,500

Les Paul SM

1980. Solid mahogany, single-cut with coil-tap, Les Paul SM truss rod logo, burgundy or silverburst finish.

1980		$2,500	$4,000

Les Paul SmartWood Exotic

1998-2001. Full-depth Les Paul-style built with eco-friendly woods, Muiracatiara (or Muir) top, mahogany back, Preciosa 'board, pearloid dots.

1998-2001		$1,800	$3,000

Les Paul SmartWood Standard

1996-2002. Smartwood Series, figured maple top, mahogany body, Smartwood on truss rod cover, antique natural.

1996-2002		$1,800	$2,800

Les Paul SmartWood Studio

2002-2006. Muiracatiara (Muir) top and mahogany back, Preciosa (Prec) 'board, Studio appointments including pearl-style dot markers.

2002-2006		$1,500	$2,500

LES PAUL SPECIAL

Following are Les Paul Special models listed alphabetically.

Les Paul Special

1955-1959. Slab solidbody, 2 pickups (P-90s in '50s, P-100 stacked humbuckers on later version), single-cut until end of '58, double in '59, renamed SG Special in late-'59.

1955-1958	TV Yellow, single-cut	$15,000	$20,000
1959	Cherry, double-cut	$11,000	$14,500
1959	TV Yellow, double-cut	$20,000	$25,000

Les Paul 55

1974, 1976-1981. Single-cut Special reissue, 2 pickups. By '78 the catalog name is Les Paul 55/78.

1974-1981	Sunburst	$2,000	$3,000
1974-1981	TV Yellow (limed)	$2,500	$4,000
1976-1981	Wine	$2,500	$4,000

1957 Les Paul Special (Single-Cut) Ultra Light Aged

2021-present. Custom Shop, solid mahogany body, Murphy lab, TV Yellow.

2021-2024		$4,000	$6,000

'60 Les Paul Special

1998-2012. Historic Collection reissue, limited edition, single-cut or double-cut.

1998-2012		$2,500	$4,000
2007	Murphy aged	$4,000	$6,000

Les Paul Special (Reissue)

1989-1998, 2002-2006. Briefly introduced as Les Paul Junior II but name changed to Special in the first year, single-cut, 2 P-100 stacked humbuckers, TV Yellow, in '90 there was a run of 300 with LE serial number, renamed Special SL in '98.

1989-1998	P-100s	$1,200	$1,800
2002-2006	Humbuckers	$1,200	$1,800

Les Paul Special 3/4

1959. Slab solidbody, 2 P-90 pickups, double-cut, short-scale, cherry finish, renamed SG Special 3/4 in late-'59.

1959		$7,500	$12,000

Les Paul Special Centennial

1994 only. 100 made, double-cut, cherry, 100 year banner at the 12th fret, diamonds in headstock and in gold-plated knobs, gold-plated Gibson coin in back of headstock.

1994		$3,500	$5,500

Les Paul Special Double Cutaway

1976-1979, 1993-1994, 2015. Double-cut, 2 P-90s, 1990s version was made in Custom Shop and was reintroduced as the '60 Les Paul Special Historic in '98. 2015 version was limited run wth 'Les Paul 100' script logo on headstock.

1976-1979		$2,000	$3,500
1993-1994	Custom Shop	$2,200	$3,500
2015	Les Paul 100 logo	$1,200	$1,800

Les Paul Special Faded

2005-2012. Double- or single-cut, dot markers, 2 P-90s, Special logo on truss rod cover, faded TV limed mahogany or cherry finish.

2005-2012		$1,200	$2,000

Les Paul Special New Century

2006-2008. Full-body mirror 'guard, 2 exposed humbuckers, single-cut LP Special body, mirror truss rod cover.

2006-2008		$1,800	$3,000

Les Paul Special Peter Frampton

2005-2007. Inspired By series, mahogany body and neck, rosewood 'board.

2005-2007		$3,500	$6,000

Les Paul Special Robot

2008. Two P-90 pickups, various colors.

2008		$1,500	$2,500

Les Paul Special SL

2003-2004. Sans lacquer (SL) finish, 2 humbucker pickups.

2003-2004		$1,800	$3,500

Les Paul Special Tenor

1959. Four-string electric tenor, LP Special body, TV Yellow.

1959		$8,000	$15,000

Les Paul Special Worn Cherry

2003-2006. Single-cut, non-bound LP Special with 2 humbuckers.

2003-2006		$1,000	$1,500

1969 Gibson Les Paul Personal

Frank Manno

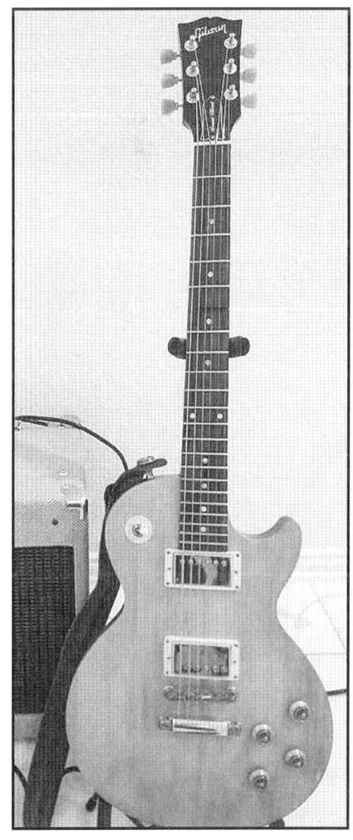

2002 Gibson Les Paul Smartwood Studio

Joseph Atkins

GUITARS

1959 Gibson Les Paul Standard
Gordon Kennedy

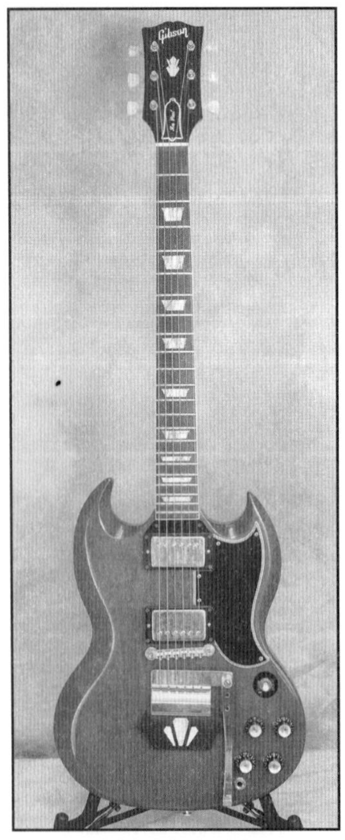

1962 Gibson Les Paul Standard

LES PAUL STANDARD

Following are Les Paul Standard models, beginning with the original model, then listed alphabetically.

Les Paul Standard (Sunburst)

1958-1960, special order 1972-1975. Les Paul Sunbursts from '58-'60 should be individually valued based on originality, color and the amount and type of figure in the maple top, changed tuners or a Bigsby removal will drop the value. Approximately 15% came with the Bigsby tailpiece. The noted price ranges are guidance valuations. Each '58-'60 Les Paul Standard should be evaluated on a case-by-case basis. As is always the case, the low and high ranges are for an all original, excellent condition, undamaged guitar. About 70% of the '58-'60 Les Paul Standards have relatively plain maple tops. The majority of '58-'60 Les Paul Standards have moderate or extreme color fade.

Wider fret wire was introduced in early-'59. White bobbins were introduced in early- to mid-'59. Double ring Kluson Deluxe tuners were introduced in late-'60. It has been suggested that all '58-'60 models have 2-piece centerseam tops. This implies that 1-piece tops, 3-piece tops and off-centerseam tops do not exist.

The terminology of the 'Burst includes: arching medullary grain, swirling medullary grain, ribboncurl, chevrons, Honey-Amber, receding red aniline, pinstripe, bookmatched, double-white bobbins, zebra bobbins, black bobbins, fiddleback maple, sunburst finish, Honeyburst, lemon drop, quarter sawn, blistered figure, width of gradation, flat sawn, Teaburst, Bigsby-shadow, rift sawn, heel size, aged clear lacquer, 3-dimensional figure, intense fine flame, tag-shadow, red pore filler, Eastern maple fleck, medium-thick flame, shrunk tuners, wave and flame, flitch-matched, elbow discoloration, ambered top coat, natural gradation, grain orientation, script oxidation, asymmetrical figure Tangerineburst, Greenburst, and birdseye.

The bobbins used for the pickup winding were either black or white. The market has determined that white bobbin PAFs are the most highly regarded. Generally speaking, in '58 bobbins were black, in '59 the bobbin component transitioned to white and some guitars have 1 white and 1 black bobbin (aka zebra). In '60, there were zebras and double blacks returned.

Rather than listing separate line items for fade and wood, the Guide lists discounts and premiums as follows. The price ranges shown below are for instruments with excellent color, excellent wood, with the original guitar case. The following discounts and premiums should be considered.

An instrument with moderate or total color fade should be discounted about 10%.

One with a factory Bigsby should be discounted about 10%-15%.

Original jumbo frets are preferred over original small frets and are worth +10%.

MODEL YEAR	FEATURES	EXC. COND. LOW	EXC. COND. HIGH
1958	Highly figured	$450,000	$550,000
1958	Minor figured	$375,000	$475,000
1958	Plain top, no figuring	$275,000	$350,000
1959	Highly figured	$550,000	$750,000
1959	Minor figured	$450,000	$600,000
1959	Plain top, no figuring	$300,000	$400,000
1960	Early '60, fat neck, highly figured	$550,000	$750,000
1960	Early '60, fat neck, minor figured	$450,000	$600,000
1960	Early '60, fat neck, plain top	$300,000	$400,000
1960	Late '60, flat neck, highly figured	$400,000	$500,000
1960	Late '60, flat neck, minor figured	$300,000	$400,000
1960	Late '60, flat neck, plain top	$250,000	$350,000

Les Paul Standard (SG body)

1961-1963 (SG body those years) Renamed SG Standard in late-'63

MODEL YEAR	FEATURES	EXC. COND. LOW	EXC. COND. HIGH
1961-1963	Cherry, side vibrola, PAFs	$22,500	$28,000
1962	Cherry, Bigsby, 1 pat #, 1 PAF	$18,000	$22,500
1962-1963	Cherry, side vibrola, pat #	$16,500	$22,000
1962-1963	Ebony block, SG, PAFs, dlx vibrola	$22,500	$28,500
1962-1963	Ebony block, SG, pat #, dlx vibrola	$18,000	$22,500

Les Paul Standard (reintroduced then renamed)

1968-1969. Comes back as a goldtop with P-90s for '68-'69 (renamed Les Paul Deluxe, '69), available as special order Deluxe '72-'76.

MODEL YEAR	FEATURES	EXC. COND. LOW	EXC. COND. HIGH
1968	P-90s, small hdsk, no volute	$20,000	$25,000
1968-1969	P-90s, large hdsk	$16,500	$20,500

Les Paul Standard (reintroduced)

1971-July 2008, 2012-2018. Available as special order Deluxe '72-'76, reintroduced with 2 humbuckers '76-present. The '75 Price List shows a Les Paul Standard (B) model which is equipped with a Bigsby tailpiece versus a wraparound, also shows a Les Paul Standard (B) with palm pedal. Replaced by Les Paul Standard 2008 in August '08. Name revived in '12 on chambered-body version with tapped Burstbucker pickups, available in AAA tops, black, Gold Top or Blue Mist finishes.

MODEL YEAR	FEATURES	EXC. COND. LOW	EXC. COND. HIGH
1971	Early special order goldtop, P-90s	$12,000	$15,000
1972-1974	Special order goldtop, P-90s	$9,500	$12,000

MODEL YEAR	FEATURES	EXC. COND. LOW	HIGH
1972-1974	Special order sunburst, P-90s	$7,500	$9,500
1974-1975	Special order, hums	$7,500	$9,500
1976	Sunburst, 4-piece pancake body	$4,500	$6,000
1976-1978	Other colors	$3,750	$5,000
1977-1978	Sunburst	$4,500	$6,000
1978-1979	Natural	$3,750	$5,000
1979	Brown Sunburst	$4,500	$6,000
1979	Cherry Sunburst	$4,500	$6,000
1979	Goldtop	$4,500	$6,000
1979	Wine Red	$3,750	$5,000
1980-1984	Other colors	$3,500	$5,000
1980-1984	Sunburst	$3,500	$5,000
1980-1984	White (RRhoads)	$3,500	$5,000
1985-1989	Various colors	$3,000	$4,000
1985-1989	White (RRhoads)	$3,000	$4,000
1990-1993	Ltd Ed colors with sticker	$3,000	$4,000
1990-1999	White (RRhoads)	$2,500	$3,500
1990-2018	Figured top	$2,500	$3,500
1990-2018	Plain top	$2,200	$3,200
2000-2018	Opaque solid color	$2,200	$3,500

'50s Les Paul Standard

2005-present. Originally an AMS exclusive with AA (later AAA) maple top and various finishes. In '19, Gibson introduced a regular production model with the same name with standard maple top finished in Goldtop, Heritage Cherry Sunburst or Tobacco Burst.

2005-2024	AA & AAA top	$2,500	$4,000
2019-2024	Standard top	$2,000	$3,000

'58 Les Paul Figured Top

1996-2000, 2002-2003, 2009-2012. Custom Shop, less top figure than '59 Reissue, sunburst.

1996-2000		$3,500	$5,500
2002-2012		$3,500	$5,500
2003	Brazilian	$9,500	$14,500

'58 Les Paul Plain Top

1994-1999, 2003-2013. Custom Shop model, plain maple top version of '58 Standard reissue, sunburst, VOS model starts in '04. Replaced by the 1958 Les Paul Reissue with a non-chambered body.

1994-1999	Non-VOS	$2,800	$4,500
2003-2013	VOS, non-chambered	$3,000	$5,000
2006-2013	VOS, chambered	$2,800	$4,500

1958 Les Paul Standard "CME Spec"

2019-2020. Custom Shop special run for Chicago Music Exchange, various colors with VOS finish.

2019-2020		$4,000	$6,500

1958 Les Paul Standard Light Aged/Heavy Aged

2021-present. Custom Shop Murphy Lab Collection, light or heavy aged, Lemon Burst.

2021-2024		$6,000	$9,000

1958 Les Paul Standard Ultra Light Aged

2021-2022. Custom Shop Murphy Lab Collection, Bourbon Burst or Washed Cherry Sunburst.

2021-2022		$4,500	$7,000

'59 Les Paul Flametop/Reissue/Standard

1993-2016. Renamed from Les Paul Reissue Flametop, for 2000-'05 called the 1959 Les Paul Reissue, in '06 this model became part of Gibson's Vintage Original Spec series and is called the '59 Les Paul Standard VOS. Flame maple top, 2 humbuckers, thick '59-style neck, sunburst finish, part of Gibson's Historic Collection, the original certificate authenticity adds value, an instrument without the matching certificate has less value. By '98 Gibson guaranteed only AAA Premium grade maple tops would be used.

Collectors of Historic Collection instruments tend to buy and store these instruments, maintaining them in near mint to New Old Stock (NOS) mint condition. In recent years, NOS instruments that are up to five years old, but in like-new mint condition, have been sold at prices that are higher than instruments in excellent condition, which is the usual condition that VG Price Guide values are given. Because of that trend, the prices shown here give consideration to the numerous NOS instruments that have sold. The inclusion of both excellent condition instruments and mint NOS instruments creates a wider than normal price range, but the high-side of the range is very realistic for NOS instruments.

1993	Custom Shop decal, early '93	$5,500	$8,500
1993	Historic decal, late '93	$4,500	$6,800
1994-1995	Murphy aged	$5,000	$8,000
1994-1999	Aged, figured top	$4,500	$6,800
1996-1999	Figured top	$4,500	$6,800
2000-2016	Aged, figured top	$4,200	$6,500
2000-2016	Figured top	$3,800	$6,000
2003	Brazilian, aged, figured	$10,500	$16,000
2003	Brazilian, highly figured	$9,500	$14,500
2003	Brazilian, low figured	$8,500	$13,000

'59 Les Paul Burst Brothers

2009-2010. Limited edition created with Dave Belzer and Drew Berlin, sold through Guitar Center, wood-figure was selected to reflect the nature of a '50s LP Standard rather than using only AAA best-quality flame, 1st run of 34 (ser. # series BB 9 001-034) with dark Madagascar rosewood 'board, 2nd run had 37 (ser. # series BB 0 001-037).

2009	1st run, 34 made	$12,500	$20,000
2010	2nd run, 37 made	$10,000	$15,000

'59 Les Paul Korina Reissue

2008. Custom Shop Limited Edition, korina body and neck, quilted maple top, rosewood 'board, natural finish.

2008		$5,000	$8,000

'59 Les Paul Plaintop (VOS)

2006-2013. Custom Shop, very little or no-flame.

2006-2013		$3,000	$5,000

1959 Les Paul Standard "CME Spec"

2019-2020. Custom Shop special run for Chicago Music Exchange, various colors with VOS finish.

2019-2020		$5,000	$7,500

Gibson '50s Les Paul Standard

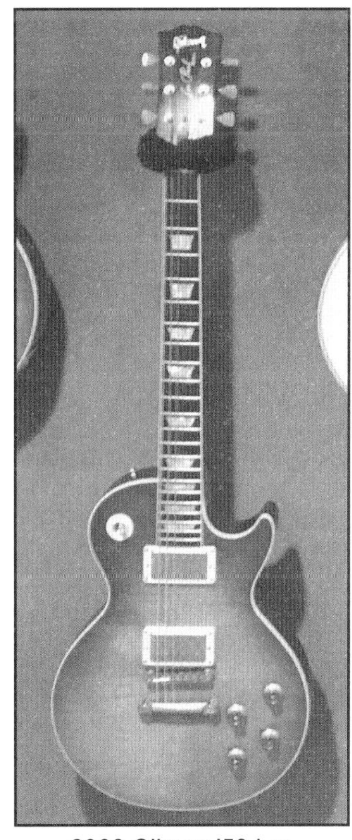

2009 Gibson '59 Les Paul Burst Brothers

Anthony Perrotta

Gibson '60 Les Paul Flametop

Tyler Willison

Gibson Les Paul Custom Shop VOS 1960

Dudley Taft

MODEL YEAR	FEATURES	EXC. COND. LOW	HIGH

1959 Les Paul Standard Heavy Aged

2021-present. Custom Shop Murphy Lab Collection, Green Lemon Fade, Golden Poppy Burst or Slow Iced Tea Fade.

2021-2024		$6,000	$9,000

1959 Les Paul Standard Light Aged

2021-present. Custom Shop Murphy Lab Collection, Cherry Tea Burst, Lemon Burst or Royal Tea Burst.

2021-2024		$5,000	$7,500

1959 Les Paul Standard Reissue

2020-present. Custom Shop, authentic replica parts, Washed Cherry Sunburst, Iced Tea Burst or Dirty Lemon, all colors with VOS finish.

2020-2024		$4,000	$6,500

1959 Les Paul Standard Ultra Heavy Aged

2021-present. Custom Shop Murphy Lab Collection, Kindred Burst or Lemon Burst.

2021-2024		$7,000	$10,000

1959 Les Paul Standard Ultra Light Aged

2021-2022. Custom Shop Murphy Lab Collection, Factory Burst, Southern Fade Burst or Sunrise Teaburst.

2021-2022		$4,500	$7,000

True Historic 1959 Les Paul

2015-2018. Figured maple top, Indian rosewood 'board, certificate of authenticity, various vintage finishes including Murphy aged option.

2015-2018		$6,000	$9,000

'60s Les Paul Standard

2005-present. Originally an AMS exclusive with AA (later AAA) maple top and various finishes. In '19, Gibson introduced a regular production model with the same name with standard maple top finished in Ice Tea, Bourbon Burst, or Unburst.

2005-2024	AA & AAA top	$2,500	$4,000
2019-2024	Standard top	$2,000	$3,000

'60 Les Paul Flametop/Standard '60s

1991-present. Renamed from Les Paul Reissue Flametop, flame maple top, 2 humbuckers, thinner neck, sunburst finish, part of Gibson's Historic Collection. In '06 this model became part of Gibson's Vintage Original Spec series and called '60 Les Paul Standard VOS, then in '17 the name changed to Les Paul Standard '60s.

1991-1999	Figured top	$4,500	$7,000
1994-1999	Aged, figured	$4,500	$7,000
2000-2016	Aged, figured	$3,800	$6,000
2000-2024	Figured top	$3,400	$5,000
2003	Brazilian, aged, figured	$10,000	$15,000
2003	Brazilian, figured	$9,500	$14,500

'60 Les Paul Plaintop (VOS)

2006-2010. Plain maple top version of '60 Standard reissue, certificate of authenticity, VOS cherry sunburst.

2006-2010		$3,000	$5,000

1960 Les Paul Standard Heavy Aged

2020-present. Custom Shop Murphy Lab Collection, heavy aged Tangerine Burst.

2020-2024		$6,000	$9,000

1960 Les Paul Standard Light Aged

2020-present. Custom Shop Murphy Lab Collection, light aged Tomato Soup Burst.

2020-2024		$5,000	$7,500

1960 Les Paul Standard Reissue

2020-present. Custom Shop, authentic reproduction, vintage-style appointments, various colors with VOS finish.

2020-2024		$4,000	$6,500

1960 Les Paul Standard Ultra Light Aged

2020-2022. Custom Shop Murphy Lab Collection, ultra light aged Orange Lemon Fade Burst or Wide Tomato Burst.

2020-2022		$4,500	$7,000

True Historic 1960 Les Paul

2015-2018. Figured maple top, Indian rosewood 'board, certificate of authenticity, various vintage finishes including Murphy aged option.

2015-2018		$6,000	$9,000

'82 Les Paul Standard

1982. Standard 82 on truss rod cover, made in Kalamazoo, Made in USA stamp on back of the headstock, generally quilted maple tops.

1982		$3,500	$6,000

Les Paul 10th Anniversary Chambered '58 Reissue

2014. Custom Shop, chambered mahogany body, carved maple top, '50s neck profile, rosewood 'board.

2014		$4,000	$6,500

Les Paul 40th Anniversary (from 1959)

1999. Reissue Historic, humbuckers, highly figured top, price includes 40th Anniversary Edition Certificate of Authenticity with matching serial number, a guitar without the certificate is worth less.

1999		$5,000	$8,000

Les Paul 50th Anniversary (Historic)

2002. From Gibson Custom Art & Historic Division, 50 made, carved figured koa top, figured maple back and sides, 3-piece figured maple neck, abalone cloud inlay markers, pearl split-diamond headstock inlay and pearl Gibson logo, Antique Natural.

2002		$10,000	$15,000

Les Paul 50th Anniversary 1956 Les Paul Standard

2006.Custom Shop, highly figured top, certificate of authenticity.

2006		$4,000	$6,500

Les Paul 50th Anniversary 1959 Les Paul Standard

2009-2011. Custom Shop, highly figured top, certificate of authenticity.

2009-2011		$5,000	$8,000

Les Paul 50th Anniversary 1960 Les Paul Standard

2010-2011. Limited Edition, offered in Heritage Cherry Sunburst, Heritage Dark Burst, Sunset Tea Burst and Cherry Burst.

2010-2011		$4,500	$7,000

Les Paul 50th Anniversary DaPra

2009. Limited run of 25 made for Vic DaPra of Guitar Gallery, '59 Historic (R9).

2009		$5,000	$7,500

MODEL YEAR	FEATURES	EXC. COND. LOW	HIGH

Les Paul 50th Anniversary Korina Tribute

2009. Custom Shop model, 100 made, single-cut Korina natural finish body, 3 pickups, dot markers, V-shaped Futura headstock, Custom logo on truss rod cover, slanted raised Gibson logo on headstock.

2009		$5,000	$8,000

Les Paul 50th Anniversary Les Paul Standard (Sweetwater)

2009. Custom Shop, limited run of 25 for Sweetwater Music, exclusive custom Ruby 'Burst finish.

2009		$4,500	$7,000

Les Paul 60th Anniversary 1960 Les Paul Standard "CME Spec"

2020. Custom Shop, special run for Chicago Music Exchange, Orange Lemon Fade or Tomato Soup Burst, with VOS finish.

2020		$4,500	$7,000

Les Paul 120th Anniversary

2014. Custom Shop, 120th Anniversary neck inlay, heavy quilted top.

2014		$4,000	$6,500

Les Paul Axcess Alex Lifeson

2011-2018. Custom Shop, push-pull volume pots, nitrocellulose lacquer finish in Royal Crimson or Viceroy Brown Sunburst, first 25 of each color signed by Lifeson with additional production unsigned, certificate of authenticity.

2011	Signed	$7,000	$10,000
2011-2018	Unsigned	$4,500	$7,000

Les Paul Axcess Dave Amato

2016. Custom Shop, figured maple top, mahogany back and neck, single '57 Classic Plus pickup, Floyd Rose tailpiece, TV yellow.

2016		$4,000	$6,500

Les Paul Axcess Standard

2009-present. Custom Shop, new neck joint carve allows access to high frets, Floyd Rose, slightly thinner body, nitro lacquer Iced Tea Burst or Gun Metal Gray. In '20 DC Rust (unique stain) only.

2009-2024		$3,500	$5,500

Les Paul BFG

2006-2008, 2018. Burstbucker 3 humbucker at bridge and P-90 at neck, 2 volume and 1 tone knobs, figured maple top over mahogany body. Reissued in '18.

2006-2008		$1,500	$2,500
2018		$1,800	$3,000

Les Paul Bird's-Eye Standard

1999. Birdseye top, gold hardware, 2 humbucking pickups, transparent amber.

1999		$3,500	$5,500

Les Paul Carved Series

2003-2005. Custom Shop Standards with relief-carved tops, one in diamond pattern, one with flame pattern.

2003-2005		$3,200	$4,800

Les Paul Catalina

1996-1997. Large Custom Shop logo on headstock.

1996-1997		$3,500	$5,500

Les Paul Centennial ('59 LP Special)

1994. Guitar of the Month, limited edition of 100, slab body Special-style configuration, gold hardware, P-90s, gold medallion, commemorative engraving in 'guard, cherry, with COA.

1994		$3,500	$5,500

Les Paul Class 5

2001-2017. Custom Shop, various woods, highly flamed or quilt top, or special finish, 1960 profile neck, weight relieved body, Burst Bucker humbucking pickups, several color options.

2001-2017	All models	$3,500	$5,500

Les Paul Cloud 9 Series

2003-2006. Special lightweight Les Paul series run for three dealers, Music Machine, Dave's Guitar Shop, and Wildwood Guitars, '59 Les Paul body specs, CR serial series number, '59 or '60 neck profile options, various colors, other reissue models available.

2003-2006	All models	$3,500	$5,500

Les Paul Collector's Choice Series

2010-2018. Custom Shop models based on Gibson replicas of one-of-a-kind historic guitars.

2010-2018	All models	$5,000	$18,000

Les Paul Dickey Betts Red Top

2003. Transparent red, gold hardware.

2003		$5,000	$8,000

Les Paul Don Felder Hotel California 1959

2010. Custom Shop, '59 sunburst specs, 50 Murphy aged and signed by Felder, 100 aged, and 150 in VOS finish.

2010	Aged, signed	$11,000	$14,000
2010	Aged, unsigned	$8,500	$11,000
2010	VOS	$6,500	$8,500

Les Paul Duane Allman

2013. Custom Shop certificate, Murphy Aged or VOS, 150 made of each.

2013	Aged	$7,000	$10,000
2013	VOS	$5,000	$7,500

Les Paul Duane Allman Hot 'Lanta

2003. "DUANE" spelled out in fret wire on back, Custom Shop certificate, 55 made.

2003		$18,500	$28,000

Les Paul Elegant

1994-2004. Custom Shop, highly flamed maple top, abalone crown markers and Custom Shop headstock inlay.

1994-2004		$4,000	$6,500

Les Paul Eric Clapton 1960

2011. Nicknamed the Beano Burst, '60 thinner 'Clapton' neck profile, Custom Bucker pickups, nickel-plated Grover kidney button tuners, lightly figured maple cap, traditional 17-degree angled headstock, total of 500 made; 55 Murphy Aged and signed by Clapton, 95 unsigned Murphy Aged, 350 finished with Gibson's VOS treatment.

2011	Aged, signed	$25,000	$35,000
2011	Aged, unsigned	$10,000	$13,000
2011	VOS	$6,500	$8,500

Les Paul Gary Moore BFG

2009-2012. Plain appointment BFG specs, P-90 neck pickup and Burstbucker 3 bridge pickup.

2009-2012		$2,000	$3,000

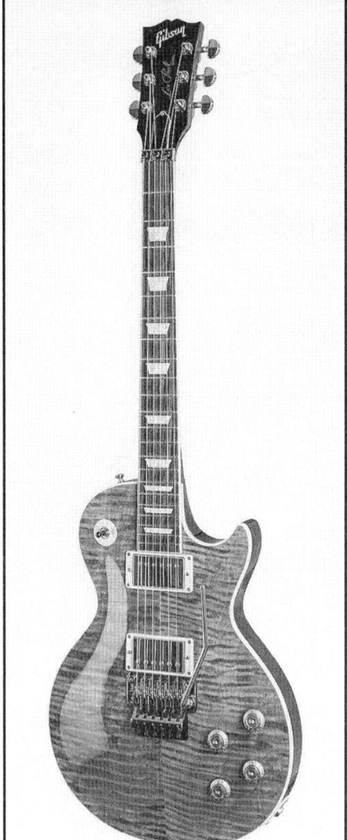

Gibson Les Paul Axcess Standard

2009 Gibson Les Paul Gary Moore BFG

James Magrini

GUITARS

1996 Gibson Les Paul Jimmy Page Signature

Tony Jones

1982 Gibson Les Paul Jimmy Wallace Reissue

MODEL YEAR	FEATURES	EXC. COND. LOW	HIGH

Les Paul Gary Moore Signature

2000-2002. Signature Series model, Gary Moore script logo on truss rod cover, flamed maple top.

2000-2002		$4,000	$6,500

Les Paul Gary Rossington Signature

2002. GR serial number, replica of his '59 LP Standard, Custom Shop, aged finish, 250 made, includes display case with backdrop photo of Rossington, price includes certificate with matching serial number.

2002		$8,500	$11,000

Les Paul Guitar Trader Reissue

1982-1983. Special order flametop Les Paul by the Guitar Trader Company, Redbank, New Jersey. Approximately 47 were built, the first 15 guitars ordered received original PAFs, all were double black bobbins (except 1 Zebra and 1 double white), 3 of the guitars were made in the '60-style. The PAF equipped models were based on order date and not build date. The serial number series started with 9 1001 and a second serial number was put in the control cavity based upon the standard Gibson serial number system, which allowed for exact build date identification. Gibson's pickup designer in the early-'80s was Tim Shaw and the pickups used for the last 32 guitars have been nicknamed Shaw PAFs. After Gibson's short run for Guitar Trader, 10 non-Gibson replica Les Pauls were made. These guitars have a poorly done Gibson logo and other telltale issues.

1982-1983	Actual PAFs installed	$22,500	$35,000
1982-1983	Shaw PAFs, highly flamed	$11,500	$18,000
1982-1983	Shaw PAFs, low flame	$8,500	$12,500

Les Paul Heritage 80

1980-1982. Copy of '59 Les Paul Standard, curly maple top, mahogany body, rosewood 'board, nickel hardware, sunburst. In '80 cataloged as Les Paul Standard-80 without reference to Heritage, the catalog notes that the guitar has Heritage Series truss rod cover.

1980-1982	Figured top	$4,500	$7,000
1980-1982	Plain top	$3,000	$4,800

Les Paul Heritage 80 Award

1982. Ebony 'board, 1-piece mahogany neck, gold-plated hardware, sunburst.

1982	Figured	$5,000	$7,500
1982	Highly figured	$6,000	$9,500

Les Paul Heritage 80 Elite

1980-1982. Copy of '59 Les Paul Standard, quilted maple top, mahogany body and neck, ebony 'board, chrome hardware, sunburst. In '80 cataloged as Les Paul Standard-80 Elite without reference to Heritage, the catalog notes that the guitar has the distinctive Heritage Series truss rod cover.

1980-1982		$5,000	$7,500

Les Paul Heritage 80/Standard 80

1982. Based on '57 Les Paul Standard Goldtop, Heritage Series Standard 80 logo on truss rod cover.

1982		$3,200	$5,000

MODEL YEAR	FEATURES	EXC. COND. LOW	HIGH

Les Paul Hot Rod Magazine '58 Standard

2008. Custom Shop, 150 made, Hot Rod inspired flames over a figured-maple top, Hot Rod truss rod cover.

2008		$5,000	$8,000

Les Paul Jim Beam (Custom Shop)

Ca. 2002-2003. JBLP serial number series, several versions of Jim Beam logo art on top of guitar, award-ribbon-style B Bean logo on headstock, 100 made.

2002-2003		$3,000	$4,500

Les Paul Jimmy Page "Number Two"

2009-2010. Custom Shop, 1st 25 aged and signed, 100 aged and unsigned, 200 VOS.

2009-2010	Aged, signed	$30,000	$45,500
2009-2010	Aged, unsigned	$12,000	$16,000
2009-2010	VOS	$10,000	$15,000

Les Paul Jimmy Page (Custom Authentic)

2004-2006. Custom Shop, includes certificate.

2004-2006	Aged, signed	$13,500	$25,000
2004-2006	Aged, unsigned	$10,000	$14,000
2004-2006	VOS	$7,500	$10,000

Les Paul Jimmy Page Signature

1995-1999. Jimmy Page signature on 'guard, mid-grade figured top, push-pull knobs for phasing and coil-tapping, Grover tuners, gold-plated hardware. This is not the '04 Custom Shop Jimmy Page Signature Series Les Paul (see separate listing).

1995	1st year, highly figured	$6,000	$9,000
1995	1st year, low figure	$4,500	$7,000
1995	1st year, moderate figure	$5,000	$7,500
1996-1999	Highly figured	$5,000	$7,500
1996-1999	Low figure	$4,000	$6,500
1996-1999	Moderate figure	$4,500	$7,000

Les Paul Jimmy Page Signature (Custom Shop)

2004. January '04 NAMM Show, 175 planned production, the first 25 were personally inspected, played-in, and autographed by Jimmy Page. Initial retail price for first 25 was $25,000, the remaining 150 instruments had an initial retail price of $16,400. Cosmetically aged by Tom Murphy to resemble Page's No. 1 Les Paul in color fade, weight, top flame, slab cut attribution on the edges, neck size and profile.

2004	1st 25 made	$25,000	$40,000
2004	Next 26-150	$12,000	$20,000
2004	Over 151	$7,500	$10,000

Les Paul Jimmy Wallace Reissue

1978-1997. Les Paul Standard '59 reissue with Jimmy Wallace on truss rod cover, special order by dealer Jimmy Wallace, figured maple top, sunburst.

1978-1982	Kalamazoo, low flame	$7,500	$10,000
1978-1983	Kalamazoo, high flame	$8,500	$12,000
1983-1997	Nashville-made	$5,000	$7,500

Les Paul Joe Bonamassa Bonabyrd

2015-2016. Limited Edition, 100 made each signed by Joe, plain maple top, retro Firebird headstock, Indian rosewood 'board, 2 Custom Bucker pickups, Antique Pelham Blue finish.

2015-2016		$7,000	$12,000

MODEL YEAR	FEATURES	EXC. COND. LOW	HIGH

Les Paul Joe Bonamassa Skinnerburst 1959

2014. Custom Shop, recreation of '59 Les Paul, 150 Murphy aged (first 50 signed by Joe) and 150 VOS, faded Dirty Lemon finish.

2014	Aged, signed	$12,000	$15,000
2014	Aged, unsigned	$9,500	$12,000
2014	VOS	$7,000	$9,000

Les Paul Joe Bonamassa 'Tomato Soup Burst' Limited Edition

2016. Limited run of 150, AAA flamed maple top, mahogany back and neck, rosewood 'board, Tomato Soup Burst finish.

2016		$5,000	$7,500

Les Paul Joe Perry 1959

2013. Custom Shop, recreation of '59 Les Paul, 150 Murphy aged (first 50 signed by Perry) and 150 VOS, faded Tobacco Sunburst finish.

2013	Aged, signed	$12,000	$15,000
2013	Aged, unsigned	$8,500	$11,000
2013	VOS	$6,500	$8,500

Les Paul Joe Perry Signature

1997-2001. Unbound slab body with push-pull knobs and Joe Perry signature below bridge, Bone-Yard logo model with typical Les Paul Standard bound body, configuration and appointments.

1997-2001	Bone-Yard option	$3,000	$4,500
1997-2001	Unbound standard	$3,000	$4,500

Les Paul KM (Kalamazoo Model)

1979. Regular Les Paul Standard with 2 exposed humbuckers, KM on headstock, sunburst, approximately 1500 were made in the Kalamazoo plant.

1979		$3,500	$5,500

Les Paul Korina

1999. Custom Shop logo on back of headstock, limited run with figured Korina top.

1999		$5,000	$8,000

Les Paul Leo's Reissue

1980-1985. Special order from Gibson's Nashville facility for Leo's Music, Oakland, California. Identified by serial number with L at the beginning, flamed maple top. About 800 guitars were made, with about 400 being exported to Japan. Kalamazoo-made Leo's have a 2nd serial number in the control cavity, Nashville-made Leo's do not have a 2nd serial number.

1980-1983	Kalamazoo, high flame	$8,500	$12,000
1980-1983	Kalamazoo, low flame	$7,500	$10,000
1983-1985	Nashville-made	$6,000	$9,500

Les Paul Limited Edition (3-tone)

1997. Limited Edition stamped on the back of the headstock, Les Paul Standard configuration with cloud inlay markers, 2-piece 3-tone sunburst finish over non-figured maple top.

1997		$3,000	$5,000

Les Paul Modern

2017-present. New light-weight features, mahogany body with maple top, back is natural finish, top with faded pelham blue, sparkling burgundy or graphite black.

2017-2024		$2,500	$4,000

MODEL YEAR	FEATURES	EXC. COND. LOW	HIGH

Les Paul Music Machine 25th Anniversary

2002. Custom run for dealer Music Machine with special serial number series, 14 flame top and 14 quilt top instruments were produced, Music Machine 25th Anniversary logo on truss rod cover, special cherry sunburst finish.

2002	Flame top	$7,500	$10,000
2002	Quilt top	$8,000	$12,000

Les Paul Music Machine Brazilian Stinger

2003. Custom run for dealer Music Machine with special serial number series, Brazilian rosewood 'board, black stinger paint on back of neck-headstock, '59 or '60 reissue body and neck profile options, highly figured flame or quilt top options, other reissue options available.

2003	'54, '56 or '58, figured flame or quilt	$10,000	$15,000
2003	'54, '56 or '58, goldtop	$8,000	$11,000
2003	'59 or '60, figured flame or quilt	$10,500	$16,000
2003	'59 or '60, plain top	$10,000	$15,000

Les Paul Music Rising Limited Edition

2005. Built for U2's Music Rising campaign to raise funds to replace instruments lost to hurricane Katrina. Multi-colored Mardi Gras motif, less than 300 made, no two finishes the same. Wood back plate, pickguard, toggle cover, and truss rod cover. Music Rising logo etched into pickguard.

2005	Signed by The Edge	$4,500	$7,000
2005	Unsigned	$4,000	$6,500

Les Paul Neal Schon Signature

2005. Custom Shop, 80 made, Floyd Rose tremolo, signature on truss rod cover, COA, black.

2005		$10,000	$15,000

Les Paul Peace

2014-2015. AA top, rosewood 'board, 2 pickups, various color finishes.

2014-2015		$3,000	$5,000

Les Paul Reissue Flametop

1983-1990. Flame maple top, 2 humbuckers, thicker '59-style neck, sunburst finish, renamed '59 Les Paul Flametop in '91.

1983-1990	Highly figured	$6,000	$9,000

Les Paul SG '61 Reissue

1993-2003. Renamed the Les Paul SG '61 Reissue from SG '62 Reissue, early '60s Les Paul Standard SG specs with small guard, trapezoid markers, heritage cherry finish, by 2003 the Les Paul script marking was not on the truss rod cover, renamed to SG '61 Reissue.

1993-2003	Stud tail	$3,000	$4,500

Les Paul SG Standard Authentic

2005. SG '61 specs, small guard, Les Paul truss rod logo, stud tailpiece.

2005		$3,000	$5,000

Les Paul SG Standard Reissue

2000-2004. Reissue of early-'60s specs including Deluxe Maestro vibrato with lyre tailpiece (stop bar tp offered), small 'guard, holly head veneer, standard color faded cherry, available in Classic White or TV Yellow, becomes the SG Standard Reissue by '05.

2000-2004	Maestro	$3,000	$5,000

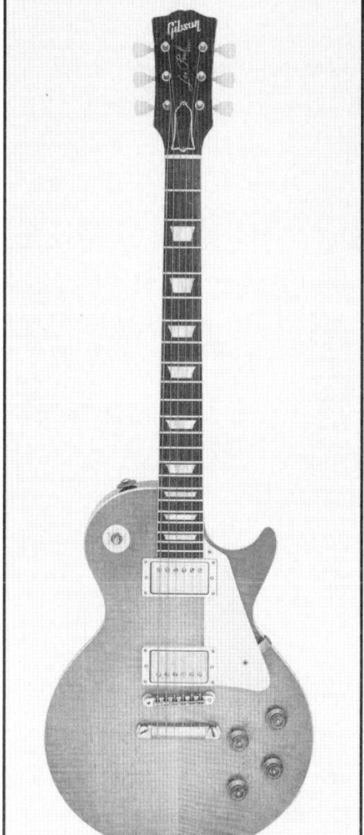

2014 Gibson Les Paul Joe Bonamassa Skinnerburst 1959

Imaged by Heritage Auctions, HA.com

Gibson Les Paul Modern

1983 Gibson Les Paul Spotlight Special

2011 Gibson Les Paul Standard Plus
Rivington Guitars

MODEL YEAR	FEATURES	EXC. COND. LOW	HIGH

Les Paul Signature "T"

2014-2018. Chambered solidbody, 2 exposed split-coil humbuckers, "Les Paul" signature on 'guard, Mini-Etune.

2014-2018		$2,000	$3,000

Les Paul Slash Appetite

2010-2012. Figured maple top, Slash artwork headstock logo, 2 Alnico II Pro Slash pickups, Appetite Amber finish.

2010-2012	Aged, signed	$8,500	$12,500
2010-2012	Aged, unsigned	$4,500	$5,500
2010-2012	VOS	$5,500	$7,000

Les Paul Slash Signature

2008. Slash logo on truss rod, Darkburst, SL serial number series, Darkburst. Sunburst or Goldtop option.

2008	Aged, signed	$5,500	$8,500
2008	Aged, unsigned	$6,500	$8,000
2008	VOS	$5,500	$7,000
2008	Sunburst or Goldtop	$4,500	$5,500

Les Paul Slash Snakepit

1996-1997. Custom Art Historic, 100 made, highly figured top, cobra inlay neck, snake and hat on body.

1996-1997		$22,500	$35,000

Les Paul Southern Rock Tribute 1959

2014-2018. Limited Edition, commemorative medallion on switch-cavity cover, first 50 aged and signed by Southern Rock Ambassadors (Dickey Betts, Charlie Daniels, Gary Rossington, Jimmy Hall), remainder are VOS, reverse burst finish.

2014-2016	Aged, signed	$8,000	$12,000
2014-2018	VOS	$4,200	$6,500

Les Paul Spider-Man

2002. Custom Shop, superhero depicted on the body, red spider logo, gold hardware, Standard appointments. 15 guitars were produced as a Gibson/Columbia TriStar Home Entertainment/Tower Records promotion, while a larger batch was sold at retail.

2002		$5,000	$8,000

Les Paul Spotlight Special

1983-1984. Curly maple and walnut top, 2 humbuckers, gold hardware, multi-bound top, Custom Shop Edition logo, natural or sunburst.

1983-1984	Figured top	$7,500	$10,000

Les Paul Standard 100

2015. Les Paul 100 on headstock (facsimile of his actual signature) honoring his 100th birthday, Les Paul hologram back of headstock, G-Force tuning, various new colors with high gloss finish.

2015		$2,500	$4,000

Les Paul Standard 2008

August 2008-2012. 2008 added to name, chambered mahogany body, new asymmetrical neck profile, locking grovers, plain or AA flamed maple top, Ebony, Gold Top, various sunbursts.

2008-2012	Figured top	$2,500	$4,000
2008-2012	Gold top	$2,800	$4,500
2008-2012	Plain top	$2,000	$3,000

Les Paul Standard 2010 Limited

2010. Robot tuning technology, 2 pickups, scripted "Limited Edition" logo on headstock, Fireball Sunburst finish.

2010		$3,000	$4,500

MODEL YEAR	FEATURES	EXC. COND. LOW	HIGH

Les Paul Standard Billy Gibbons 'Pearly Gates'

2009-2011. Aged - 50 made, Aged and signed - 50 made, V.O.S. - 250 made.

2009-2011	Aged, signed	$20,000	$30,000
2009-2011	Aged, unsigned	$12,000	$15,000
2009-2011	VOS	$8,000	$12,000

Les Paul Standard F

2010-2017. Custom Shop, also called LPS-F, 5A flame maple top, 2 Burstbucker pickups, various new colors with gloss nitro finish.

2010-2017		$2,500	$3,800

Les Paul Standard Faded

2005-2008. Figured top, exposed humbuckers, faded satin finish.

2005-2008		$2,000	$3,000

Les Paul Standard HP

2016-2018. Solidbody, figured maple top, mahogany back and sides, 2 humbucker pickups, G-Force automatic tuners, various colors with gloss nitro finish.

2016-2018		$2,500	$4,000

Les Paul Standard Limited Edition Series

2004-2007. Various models and colors.

2004-2007		$3,000	$5,000

Les Paul Standard Limited Edition Sparkle

2001. Models with sparkle colors.

2001		$4,000	$6,500

Les Paul Standard Lite Double Cutaway

1999-2001, 2004. Double-cut body, renamed from DC Standard in '99, reintroduced as Les Paul Standard DC Plus in 2001, various translucent finishes, available in 2004 under this name also.

1999-2004		$2,200	$3,500

Les Paul Standard Lite Limited Edition

2014. Thin body LP, Burstbuckers, 3 knobs, coil tap switch, "120th Anniversary" on 12th fret, highly figured flame top or plain top offered.

2014	Flame top	$3,000	$5,000
2014	Plain top	$1,800	$2,500

Les Paul Standard Michael Bloomfield 1959

2009-2011. Custom Shop, limited production of 100 Murphy-aged and 200 VOS, matching certificate of authenticity.

2009-2011	Aged, estate signed	$12,000	$15,000
2009-2011	Aged, unsigned	$8,000	$12,000
2009-2011	VOS	$5,500	$7,000

Les Paul Standard Mike McCready 1959

2010-2016. Custom Shop, limited to 50 aged and signed, 100 VOS finish.

2010-2016	Aged, signed	$11,000	$14,000
2010-2016	Aged, unsigned	$7,500	$11,500
2010-2016	VOS	$5,500	$7,000

Les Paul Standard Music Zoo 25th Anniversary

2019. Custom Shop special run for Music Zoo, MZ serial number, less than 50 made, styled from '59 LP Standard, figured maple top, mahogany body and neck, Indian rosewood 'board, VOS Orange Drop finish.

2019		$6,000	$9,000

MODEL YEAR	FEATURES	EXC. COND. LOW	HIGH

Les Paul Standard Paul Kossoff 1959

2012-2013. Custom Shop, 100 aged and 250 VOS, green lemon finish, certificate of authenticity.

2012-2013	Aged	$9,500	$12,000
2012-2013	VOS	$5,500	$7,000

Les Paul Standard Plus

1995-2012. Gibson USA model, figured maple top, non-chambered, Vintage Sunburst, Heritage Cherry Sunburst or Honeyburst finish.

1995-2012		$2,500	$4,000

Les Paul Standard Premium Plus

1999-2007. Premium plus flamed maple top.

1999-2007		$3,000	$5,000

Les Paul Standard Raw Power

2000-2001, 2006-2007. Natural gloss finish on maple top, appears to have been a Musician's Friend version in '06-'07.

2000-2001		$2,000	$3,000

Les Paul Standard Rick Nielsen 1959

2016-2017. Custom Shop, first 50 aged and signed, figured maple top, mahogany back and neck, Indian rosewood 'board, aged or vintage gloss finish.

2016-2017	Aged, signed	$12,000	$16,000
2016-2017	Aged, unsigned	$8,000	$10,000
2016-2017	VOS	$5,500	$7,000

Les Paul Standard Robot

2007. Blueburst finish, robot tuning.

2007		$1,800	$2,500

Les Paul Standard RSM 1959 / RSM '59 Les Paul Standard

2018 and 2020. Custom Shop special run for Rumble Seat Music, recreation of the original 1959 LP Standard, limited run of 5 each year, highly flamed top, Brazilian rosewood 'board.

2018		$15,000	$25,000
2020		$15,000	$25,000

Les Paul Standard Showcase Edition

1988. Showcase Edition logo on back of neck, Guitar of the Month, silverburst.

1988		$4,000	$6,500

Les Paul Strings and Things Standard

1975-1978. Special order flamed maple top Les Paul Standard model, built for Chris Lovell, owner of Strings and Things, a Gibson dealer in Memphis, approximately 24 were built, sunburst. Authentication of a Strings and Things Les Paul is difficult due to no diffinitive attributes, valuation should be on a case-by-case basis.

1975-1978	24 made	$13,500	$20,000

Les Paul Tie Dye (St. Pierre)

1996-1997. Hand colored by George St. Pierre, 103 made.

1996-1997		$4,000	$6,000

Les Paul Tie Dye Custom Shop

2002. Limited series of one-off colorful finishes, Custom Shop logo.

2002		$4,000	$6,500

Les Paul Traditional Pro/Pro II

2010-2014. Exposed tapped coil humbuckers, sunbursts, goldtop, ebony or wine red.

2010-2014	Various colors	$2,000	$3,000

MODEL YEAR	FEATURES	EXC. COND. LOW	HIGH

Les Paul Traditional/Plus

2008-2019. Traditional on truss rod, '80s styling with weight-relief holes in an unchambered body, standard appointments. Figured maple (Plus) or opaque color top.

2008-2014	Opaque	$2,000	$3,000
2008-2019	Plain sunburst	$2,000	$3,000
2008-2019	Plus, figured maple	$2,500	$4,000

Les Paul Ultima

1996-2007. Custom Shop, flame or quilt sunburst, abalone and mother-of-pearl tree of life, harp, or flame fingerboard inlay, multi abalone bound body.

1996-2007		$5,500	$7,500

Les Paul Ultra-Aged

2011-2012. Custom Shop, '59 specs, Bigsby optional, aged by Tom Murphy.

2011-2012		$6,000	$9,000

Les Paul Warren Haynes

2007. Custom Shop, Inspired by Artist series.

2007		$4,500	$7,000

Les Paul Zebra Wood

2007. Zebrawood top, mahogany back and neck, rosewood 'board, 2 '57 Classic pickups, natural satin zebrawood finish.

2007		$3,200	$5,000

LES PAUL STUDIO

Following are Les Paul Studio models listed alphabetically.

Les Paul Studio

1983-present. Unbound mahogany body, (early models have alder body), 2 humbuckers, various colors.

1983-2009		$1,200	$1,800
2009-2012	Silverburst	$1,500	$2,500
2010-2019		$1,200	$1,800
2020-2024		$1,200	$1,800

Les Paul Studio 120th Anniversary

2014. Figured maple top, 120th Anniversary badge on 12th fret, vintage gloss finish on various colors.

2014		$1,800	$3,000

Les Paul Studio '50s Tribute

2010-2016. '56 LP Goldtop specs, P-90s, '50s neck, Tune-o-matic, stopbar tailpiece, chambered unbound body.

2010-2016		$1,200	$1,800

Les Paul Studio '60s Tribute

2011-2016. Similar to '50s Tribute except for '60 slim taper neck.

2011-2016		$1,200	$1,800

Les Paul Studio '70s Tribute

2012-2016. Similar to '50s Tribute except for '70s neck profile with volute.

2012-2016		$1,200	$1,800

Les Paul Studio Baritone

2004-2012. 28" baritone scale, maple top, mahogany back and neck, 2 pickups, nitro gloss honeyburst finish.

2004-2012		$2,000	$3,000

Les Paul Studio BFD

2007. Studio specs but with BFD electronics.

2007		$1,200	$1,800

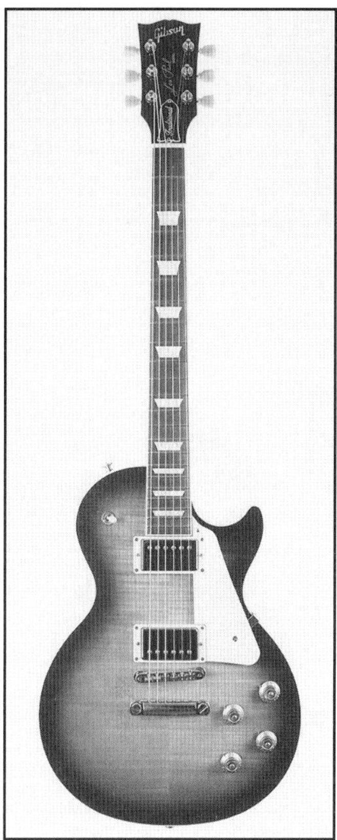

2017 Gibson Les Paul Traditional

Cream City Music

Gibson Les Paul Studio '60s Tribute

GUITARS

2003 Gibson Les Paul Studio Plus
Imaged by Heritage Auctions, HA.com

2012 Gisbon Les Paul Studio Shred

MODEL YEAR	FEATURES	EXC. COND. LOW	HIGH

Les Paul Studio Custom
1981-1985. 2 humbucking pickups, multi-bound top, gold-plated hardware, various colors.
1981-1985 $2,200 $3,500

Les Paul Studio Deluxe '60s
2010-2012. Exposed pickups, Deluxe logo on truss rod cover, sunburst.
2010-2012 $1,500 $2,500

Les Paul Studio Deluxe II
2008-2013. Carved flame maple top, mahogany back, 2 pickups, various colors.
2008-2013 $1,500 $2,500

Les Paul Studio Faded Vintage Mahogany
2007-2010. Vintage mahogany with faded satin.
2007-2010 $1,200 $1,800

Les Paul Studio Faded/Pro Faded
2005-2012. Faded sunburst tops. Name changes to Studio Pro Faded in '12, then ends production.
2005-2012 $1,200 $1,800

Les Paul Studio Gem
1996-1998. Limited edition with Les Paul Studio features, but using P-90 pickups instead of humbucker pickups, plus trapezoid markers and gold hardware.
1996-1998 $1,800 $2,800

Les Paul Studio Gothic
2000-2001. Orville Gibson image on back of headstock, single Gibson crescent and star neck marker, Gothic Black with black hardware.
2000-2001 $1,200 $1,800

Les Paul Studio Gothic Morte
2011-2012. All-mahogany body, African Obeche 'board, 2 humbuckers, satin ebony finish.
2011-2012 $1,200 $1,800

Les Paul Studio Joe Bonamassa
2011-2013. Maple top, mahogany back and neck, 2 Alnico II pickups, goldtop finish.
2011-2013 $2,500 $4,000

Les Paul Studio Limited Edition
1997. P-100 pickups, black.
1997 $1,500 $2,500

Les Paul Studio Lite
1987-1998. Carved maple top, mahogany back and neck, 2 humbucker pickups, various colors.
1987-1998 $1,200 $1,800

Les Paul Studio Lite Mark III/M3/M III
1991-1994. HSH pickup configuration, trans finishes.
1991-1994 $1,500 $2,500

Les Paul Studio MLB Baseball
2008. Major League Baseball graphics on body, only 30 made, satin finish, dot markers.
2008 $2,500 $4,000

Les Paul Studio Platinum
2004-2006. 2 Humbuckers, no position markers, brushed metal hardware, body, neck and headstock in satin platinum finish, matching platinum hardshell case.
2004-2006 $1,500 $2,500

Les Paul Studio Platinum Plus
2004-2006. Same as Platinum but with trapezoid markers and black hardshell case.
2004-2006 $1,800 $2,800

Les Paul Studio Plus
2002-2007. Two-piece AA flamed unbound top, gold hardware, Desert Burst or see-thru black.
2002-2007 $1,500 $2,500

Les Paul Studio Premium Plus
2006-2008. AAA flamed-maple top.
2006-2008 $2,000 $3,000

Les Paul Studio Raw Power
2009-2012. Unbound maple top, chambered maple body, 2 humbuckers, dots, satin finishes.
2009-2012 $1,200 $1,800

Les Paul Studio Robot
2007-2011. Robot tuning, trapezoid inlays, silverburst, fireburst, wine red, black, red metallic, green metallic.
2007-2011 All colors $1,500 $2,500

Les Paul Studio Robot Limited Edition
2012. 'Chameleon' tone circuit.
2012 $1,500 $2,500

Les Paul Studio Roland Synthesizer
1985. With Roland 700 synth.
1985 $1,500 $2,500

Les Paul Studio Shred
2012. Unbound body, trapazoid markers, 2 humbuckers. Floyd Rose, high-gloss ebony nitro finish.
2012 $1,800 $2,800

Les Paul Studio Special
2001. Solidbody, single-cut, 2 pickups, various colors.
2001-2020 $1,200 $1,800

Les Paul Studio Special Limited Edition
2019-2020. Limited Edition, nitro finish in Lemon Burst or Desert Burst.
2019-2020 $1,500 $2,500

Les Paul Studio Standard
1984-1987. Cream top and neck binding, dots.
1984-1987 $2,500 $3,500

Les Paul Studio Swamp Ash
2004-2012. Studio model with swamp ash body.
2004-2012 $1,800 $2,800

Les Paul Studio USA Anniversary Flood
2011. Commemorating the Nashville flood of May, 2010, blue or green swirl.
2011 $1,800 $3,000

Les Paul Supreme
2003-2018. Highly figured AAAA maple top and back on translucent finishes only, custom binding, deluxe pearl markers, chambered mahogany body, globe logo or "Supreme" on headstock, solid colors available by '06.
2003-2018 Various tops & colors $3,500 $5,000

Les Paul Supreme Goldtop (Hand-Signed 90th Birthday Limited Edition)
2005. Custom Shop limited edition for Les Paul's 90th birthday, 90 made Les Paul signed.
2005 $5,000 $7,500

Les Paul Vixen
2006-2007. Les Paul Special single-cut slab body, dot markers, 2 humbuckers, 2 controls, wrap-around bridge.
2006-2007 Various colors $1,500 $2,500

MODEL YEAR	FEATURES	EXC. COND. LOW	HIGH

Les Paul Voodoo/Voodoo Les Paul

2004-2005. Single-cut, swamp ash body, 2 exposed humbuckers, black satin finish.

2004-2005		$2,500	$3,500

Les Paul XR-I / II / III

1981-1983. No frills model with Dirty Finger pickups, dot markers, Les Paul stencil logo on headstock, goldburst, silverburst and cherryburst finishes.

1981-1983	All models	$2,250	$3,500

The Les Paul

1976-1979. Figured maple top, 2 humbuckers, gold hardware, rosewood binding, 'guard, 'board, knobs, cover plates, etc., fewer than 100 made, natural or rosewood finishing, natural only by '79.

1976-1979	Natural or rosewood	$15,000	$25,000

The Paul

1978-1982. Offered as The Paul Standard with solid walnut body and The Paul Deluxe with solid mahogany body, 2 exposed humbuckers.

1978-1982	Walnut or mahogany	$1,500	$2,000

The Paul Firebrand Deluxe

1980-1982. Single-cut mahogany solidbody, Gibson branded in headstock, 2 exposed humbuckers, black, Pelham Blue or rough natural finish.

1980-1982	All colors	$2,000	$3,000

The Paul II

1996-1998. Mahogany body, 2 humbucking pickups, rosewood dot neck, renamed The Paul SL in '98.

1996-1998		$1,000	$1,500

LG-0

1958-1974. Flat-top acoustic, mahogany, bound body, rosewood bridge '58-'61 and '68-'74, plastic bridge '62-'67, natural.

1958-1961	Rosewood bridge	$1,400	$1,800
1962-1964	Plastic bridge	$1,100	$1,500
1965	Plastic bridge	$1,000	$1,300
1966	Plastic bridge	$900	$1,200
1967-1969	Rosewood bridge	$900	$1,200
1970-1974		$800	$1,000

LG-1

1943-1968. Flat-top acoustic, spruce top, mahogany back and sides, bound body, rosewood bridge '43-'61, plastic bridge after, examples seen to '74, sunburst.

1943-1945		$3,000	$4,000
1946-1949		$3,000	$4,000
1950-1959	Rosewood bridge	$2,500	$3,500
1960-1961	Rosewood bridge	$2,300	$3,000
1962-1964	Plastic bridge	$2,000	$2,500
1965		$1,800	$2,400
1966-1968		$1,800	$2,400

LG-2

1942-1962. Flat-top acoustic, spruce top, mahogany back and sides (some with maple '43-'46), banner headstock '42-'46, bound body, X-bracing, sunburst finish, replaced by B-25 in '62.

1942-1945	Banner, mahogany	$4,500	$6,000
1942-1945	Banner, spruce	$6,000	$8,000
1946-1949	Sitka	$5,000	$7,000
1950-1959		$4,500	$6,000
1960-1961	Rosewood bridge	$3,000	$4,000
1962	Adjustable bridge	$3,000	$4,000

LG-2 3/4

1949-1962. Short-scale version of LG-2 flat-top, wood bridge, sunburst.

1949	Rosewood bridge	$2,700	$3,500
1950-1959	Rosewood bridge	$2,500	$3,200
1960-1961	Rosewood bridge	$2,200	$2,800
1962	Adjustable bridge	$2,200	$2,800

LG-2 3/4 Arlo Guthrie

2003, 2005-2018. Vintage replica finish.

2003-2018		$2,200	$3,500

LG-2 American Eagle

2013-2018. Sitka top, mahogany back and sides, L.R. Baggs.

2013-2018		$2,000	$3,200

LG-2 Banner

2013. All mahogany, only 50 made.

2013		$3,000	$4,000

LG-2 H

1945-1955. Flat-top, Hawaiian, natural or sunburst.

1944-1945		$4,500	$6,000
1946-1949		$3,500	$4,500
1950-1955		$3,000	$4,000

LG-3

1942-1964. Flat-top acoustic, spruce top, mahogany back and sides, bound body, natural finish, replaced by B-25 N.

1942-1945	Banner	$6,000	$8,000
1946-1949		$5,500	$7,000
1950-1959		$4,000	$5,000
1960-1961	Last wood bridge	$3,500	$4,500
1962-1964	Plastic bridge	$3,200	$4,200

Longhorn Double Cutaway

2008. Guitar of the Month for July '08, AA figured maple top, 2 active pickups, piezo pickup, sunburst or transparent finishes.

2008		$2,500	$4,000

M III Series

1991-1996, 2013-2018. Double-cut solidbody with extra long bass horn, six-on-a-side tuners on a reverse pointy headstock, dot markers, reverse Gibson decal logo. Reissued in '13 with natural finish on 'board and choice of Cosmic Cobalt, Electric Lime, Vibrant Red, or Orange Glow.

1991-1992	Deluxe	$2,500	$3,500
1991-1996	Standard	$2,200	$3,000
2013-2018	Reissue	$1,500	$2,500

M IV Series

1993-1995. M III with Steinberger vibrato.

1993-1995	S Deluxe	$2,200	$3,500
1993-1995	S Standard	$2,000	$3,800

Mach II

1990-1991. Renamed from U-2, offset double-cut, 2 single coils and 1 humbucking pickup.

1990-1991		$1,500	$2,500

Map Guitar

1983, 1985. Body cutout like lower 48, 2 humbuckers, limited run promotion, '83 version in natural mahogany or red, white and blue, '85 version red, white and blue stars and stripes on a white background. This

1964 Gibson LG-1
Johnny Zapp

1946 Gibson LG-2
David Stone

1983 Gibson Map Guitar
James Seldin

2011 Gibson Melody Maker Joan Jett Signature Blackheart

MODEL YEAR	FEATURES	EXC. COND. LOW	HIGH

model can often be found in better than excellent condition because the instrument is as much a show piece as it is a player guitar, and the price range reflects that.

1983	Natural	$3,500	$5,000
1983	Red, white & blue	$4,000	$5,500

Marauder

1975-1980. Single-cut solidbody, pointed headstock, 2 pickups, bolt-on neck, various colors.

1975-1980		$1,800	$2,500

Marauder Custom

1976-1977. Marauder with 3-way selector switch, bound 'board, block markers, bolt-on neck, Marauder logo on truss rod cover, sunburst.

1976-1977		$2,500	$4,500

Melody Maker

1959-1971, 1986-1993. Slab solidbody, 1 pickup, single-cut until '61, double '61-'66, SG body '66-'71, reintroduced as single-cut in '86-'93. A single-cut Les Paul Melody Maker was offered from '03-'06.

1959-1961	Sunburst, single-cut	$2,200	$3,000
1962-1964	Sunburst, cherry, double-cut	$2,000	$2,500
1965-1966	Cherry, double cut	$1,800	$2,300
1966-1971	Various colors, SG body	$2,200	$3,000
1986-1993	Reintroduced as single-cut	$800	$1,100

Melody Maker 3/4

1959-1963. Short-scale version.

1959-1963		$2,000	$2,500

Melody Maker D

1960-1970. Two pickup version of Melody Maker, reintroduced as Melody Maker Double in '77.

1960-1961	Sunburst, single-cut	$2,800	$3,800
1961-1964	Sunburst, cherry, double-cut	$2,500	$3,300
1965-1966	Sunburst, cherry, double-cut	$2,000	$2,800
1966-1970	Various colors, SG body	$2,200	$3,000

Melody Maker Double

1977-1983. Reintroduction of Melody Maker D, double-cut solidbody, 2 pickups, cherry or sunburst.

1977-1983	Bolt-on	$1,200	$1,800
1977-1983	Set-neck	$1,500	$2,200

Melody Maker III

1967-1971. SG-style double-cut solidbody, 3 pickups, various colors.

1967-1971		$2,500	$3,500

Melody Maker 12

1967-1971. SG-style solidbody, 12 strings, 2 pickups, red, white or Pelham Blue.

1967-1971		$2,500	$3,500

Melody Maker Faded

2003. Les Paul Jr. styling, single-cut, 1 P-90 style pickup, Nashville tune-o-matic bridge, black satin finish.

2003		$700	$1,000

Les Paul Melody Maker

2003-2008. Slab single-cut solidbody, one P-90, tune-o-matic bridge, dot markers, 2 knobs. Revised in '07 with 1 single-coil (2 also offered), wrap around tailpiece, 1 knob, pickguard mounted jack.

2003-2006	1 pickup	$800	$1,200
2007-2008	1 pickup, revised specs	$800	$1,200
2007-2008	2 pickup option	$800	$1,200

Les Paul Melody Maker 120th Anniversary

2014. Custom Shop, 120th Anniversary neck inlay, maple top, mahogany back, Charcoal, TV Yellow, Wine Red or Manhattan Midnight, all with satin finish.

2014		$1,200	$1,800

Melody Maker Joan Jett Signature

2008-2012. Double-cut, worn-white (til '11), 1 Burstbucker 3. Blackheart version in black with red dots starts '10.

2008-2012		$1,300	$1,800

Melody Maker Jonas Brothers

2010-2011. Limited run of 300, single-cut slab body, slim taper neck profile, trademark "JB" shield graphic signed 'guard, 2 P90 Soapbar pickups, satin white finish.

2010-2011		$1,800	$2,500

Melody Maker Pro II

1989. Limited production, single-cut slab body, banana Explorer headstock, 2 humbucking pickups.

1989		$2,200	$3,000

Midnight Special

1974-1975. L-6S body style, maple 'board, dot markers, 2 humbucker pickups, custom colors.

1974-1975		$2,200	$3,500

Midtown Custom

2012-2014. 335-style semi-hollow, 2 humbuckers, block markers.

2012-2014		$1,500	$2,200

Midtown Kalamazoo

2013-2015. Limited run of 600, maple top, mahogany back and sides, 2 pickups, 165-style tailpiece, Vintage Sunburst.

2013-2015		$1,800	$2,500

Midtown Standard P-90

2011-2014. Like Midtown Custom but with P-90s.

2011-2014		$1,500	$2,000

MK-35

1975-1978. Mark Series flat-top acoustic, mahogany back and sides, black-bound body, natural or sunburst, 5226 made.

1975-1978		$1,200	$1,800

MK-53

1975-1978. Mark Series flat-top acoustic, maple back and sides, multi-bound body, natural or sunburst, 1424 made.

1975-1978		$1,500	$2,200

MK-72

1975-1978. Mark Series flat-top acoustic, rosewood back and sides, black-bound body, chrome tuners, natural or sunburst, 1229 made.

1975-1978		$2,000	$3,000

MODEL YEAR	FEATURES	EXC. COND. LOW	HIGH

MK-81

1975-1978. Mark Series flat-top acoustic, rosewood back and sides, multi-bound body, gold tuners, high-end appointments, natural or sunburst, 431 made.

1975-1978		$3,000	$4,500

Moderne

2012. Limited run, mahogany body and neck, dual '57 Classic humbuckers, trans amber or ebony finish.

2012		$3,500	$4,800

Moderne Heritage

1981-1983. Limited edition, korina body, 2 humbucking pickups, gold hardware, natural, black or white.

1981-1983	Black or white	$12,000	$18,000
1981-1983	Natural	$15,000	$20,000

Nick Lucas / Gibson Special

1926-1941. Though they were shipped into '41, the last year of production was '37. Mahogany 13 ½" L-1 body ('26-'29), 14 ¾" L-00 body ('30-'41), parallel bracing '26-'27, X-braced '28-'41, 12 frets early (13 and 14 later), banjo tuners early (guitar style later), black (rare) or sunburst finish. Reintroduced in '91.

1926-1941	Various specs	$20,000	$60,000

Nick Lucas Reissue Limited Edition

1991-1992. 100 made, label signed by Ren Ferguson.

1991-1992		$3,000	$5,500

Nick Lucas Tenor

1928-1938. 14 3/4", 12-fret, early models have mahogany, later maple, The Gibson headstock logo.

1928-1930	Mahogany	$6,500	$9,500
1931-1938	Maple	$5,000	$8,000

Nick Lucas Elite

1999-2002. Ebony 'board, abalone inlay and inlays.

1999-2002		$4,000	$5,500
2001	Elite Custom	$5,500	$7,500

Nick Lucas Grande

2015-2016. Limited Edition of 50, Sitka spruce top, English walnut back and sides, COA, Honeyburst finish.

2015-2016		$4,500	$6,000

Nick Lucas Koa Elite

2015. Limited to 50, Adirondack and koa, COA.

2015		$5,000	$7,000

Nick Lucas Supreme

2015. Limited to 40, Adirondack red spruce top, AAA flame koa back and sides, abalone trim, certificate of authenticity, Honeyburst finish.

2015		$4,500	$6,000

Nighthawk 2009 Limited

2009. Limited series, AAA figured maple top, mahogany body, Translucent Amber finish.

2009		$1,600	$2,200

Nighthawk Custom

1993-1998. Flame maple top, ebony 'board, gold hardware, fireburst, single/double/mini pickups.

1993-1998		$2,500	$3,500

Nighthawk Special

1993-1998. Single-cut solidbody, figured maple top, double-coil and mini-pickup or with additional single-coil options, dot marker inlay, cherry, ebony or sunburst.

1993-1998		$1,600	$2,200

Nighthawk Standard

1993-1998. Single-cut solidbody, figured maple top, 2 or 3 pickups, double-parallelogram inlay, amber, fireburst or sunburst.

1993-1998		$2,000	$2,800

Nighthawk Standard 2010 Limited

2010-2012. Limited Run series, AAA quilted maple top, chambered poplar body, 3 pickups, Memphis Mojo, St. Louis Sauce or Chicago Blue finishes.

2010-2012		$1,800	$2,500

Nighthawk Studio

2011-2012. AAA quilted maple top, dots.

2011-2012		$1,000	$1,500

Nouveau NV6T-M

1986-1987. Hybrid USA/Japan, a line of Gibson flat-tops with imported parts assembled and finished in the U.S., acoustic dreadnought, bound maple body, natural.

1986-1987		$800	$1,200

NR-336F

2012. Custom Shop, 25 made, double-cut, non-reverse (NR) Firebird headstock, flamed maple top, rosewood 'board, antique sunburst top, cherry back.

2012		$2,500	$3,500

OP-25

1991-1992. Acoustic-electric, limited production run, synthetic back.

1991-1992		$900	$1,300

Original Jumbo (Custom Shop)

2003. 16" jumbo body, Adirondack top, mahogany sides and back, butterbean tuner buttons, deep sunburst finish on complete body, Custom Art Historic.

2003		$3,000	$4,200

Pat Martino Custom/Signature

1999-2006. Sharp single-cut thinline, f-holes, 2 humbuckers, flamed cherry sunburst maple top, small snakehead style headstock, Pat Martino logo on truss rod cover.

1999-2006		$4,000	$5,500

PG-00

1932-1937. Plectrum neck, flat-top.

1932-1937		$3,000	$5,000

PG-1

1928-1938. Plectrum neck, flat-top.

1929		$3,000	$5,000

PG-175

1950. Acoustic/electric with ES-175 bobdy and 4-string plectrum neck, bow-tie markers, sunburst.

1950		$4,000	$7,000

Q-100

1985-1986. Offset double-cut solidbody, Kahler trem, 6-on-a-side tuners, 1 humbucker, black hardware.

1985-1986		$1,200	$1,800

Q-200/Q2000

1985-1986. Like Q-100, but with 1 single and 1 hum, black or chrome hardware. Name changed to 2000 late '85.

1985-1986		$1,300	$2,000

Q-300/Q3000

1985-1986. Like Q-100, but with 3 single-coils, black or chrome hardware. Name changed to 3000 late '85.

1985-1986		$1,500	$2,000

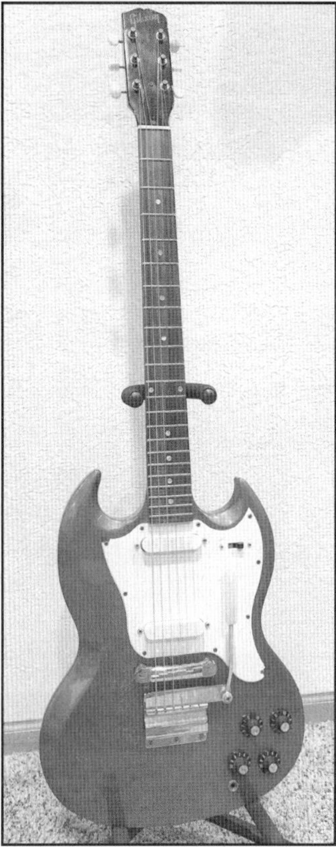

1967 Gibson Melody Maker D

Tim McClutchy

1936 Gibson Nick Lucas

M. Mattingly

1972 Gibson SG II
Rivington Guitars

2006 Gibson SG '61 Reissue

MODEL YEAR	FEATURES	EXC. COND. LOW	HIGH

Q-3000 Custom Shop

1985. Limited Custom production, 3 single-coil pickups.

1985		$2,500	$3,500

Q-4000/Q400

Late-1985-1987. Limited custom production, like Q-100, but with 2 singles and 1 hum, black hardware, Name changed to 400 late '85. Ferrari Red or Pink Panther finish as 4000, ebony as 400.

1985-1987		$1,800	$2,500

RD Artist CMT

1981. Figured top.

1981		$3,500	$5,000

RD Artist/77

1980. The 77 model has a 25.5" scale versus 24.75".

1980		$3,000	$4,500

RD Artist/79

1978-1982. Double-cut solidbody, 2 humbuckers, TP-6 tailpiece, active electronics, ebony 'board, block inlays, gold-plated parts, various colors, called just RD (no Artist) in '81 and '82.

1978-1982		$4,000	$6,000

RD Custom

1977-1979. Double-cut solidbody, 2 humbuckers, stop tailpiece, active electronics, dot inlays, maple 'board, chrome parts, natural or walnut.

1977-1979		$3,000	$4,500

RD Standard

1977-1979. Double-cut solidbody, 2 humbuckers, stop tailpiece, rosewood 'board, dot inlays, chrome parts, natural, sunburst or walnut.

1977-1979		$2,500	$3,500

RD Standard Reissue

2007, 2009, 2011. 400 Silverburst made in '07. Black or Trans Amber Red versions offered as limited run in '09 in Japan and in U.S. in '11.

2007-2011	Various colors	$2,500	$3,500

Roy Smeck Radio Grande Hawaiian

1934-1939. Dreadnought acoustic flat-top, rosewood back and sides, bound body and neck, natural.

1934-1939	Brazilian, Spanish converted	$18,000	$25,000
1934-1939	Brazilian, unconverted	$12,000	$18,000

Roy Smeck Radio Grande Hawaiian Limited

1994. Centennial Guitar of the Month in '94, 100 made, Indian rosewood.

1994		$3,500	$4,800

Roy Smeck Radio Grande Hawaiian Reissue

1996. Part of SmartWood Series, Grenadillo back and sides.

1996		$3,800	$5,000

Roy Smeck Stage Deluxe Hawaiian

1934-1942. Dreadnought acoustic flat-top, mahogany back and sides, bound body, natural.

1934-1942	Spanish converted	$9,000	$12,000
1934-1942	Unconverted	$7,000	$9,000

MODEL YEAR	FEATURES	EXC. COND. LOW	HIGH

S-1

1976-1980. Single-cut solidbody, pointed headstock, 3 single-coil pickups, similar to the Marauder, various colors.

1976-1980		$1,800	$2,500

SG

Following are models, listed alphabetically, bearing the SG name.

SG I

1972-1978. Double-cut, mahogany body, 1 mini-humbucker (some with SG Jr. P-90), wraparound bridge/tailpiece, cherry or walnut.

1972-1978		$1,500	$2,200

SG II

1972-1979. SG I with 2 mini-humbuckers (some in '75 had regular humbuckers), 2 slide switches, cherry or walnut.

1972-1979		$1,800	$2,500

SG III

1972-1977. SG II with sunburst and tune-o-matic.

1972-1977		$2,200	$3,000

SG-3

2007-2008. SG styling, SG Standard appointments, 3 gold humbuckers or 3 single coils, 1 rotor switch, 2 knobs, stop tail.

2007-2008	3 humbuckers	$1,500	$2,000
2007-2008	3 single coils	$1,500	$2,000

SG '61 Reissue

2003-2015. Renamed from Les Paul SG '61 Reissue, no Les Paul script on truss rod, small 'guard, stop bar tailpiece (no Deluxe Maestro vibrato), '60 slim-taper neck profile.

2003-2015		$1,800	$2,500

SG '62 Reissue/SG Reissue

1986-1991. Trapezoid markers, stop bar, 2 humbuckers, called SG Reissue '86-'87, SG '62 Reissue '88-'91. Reintroduced as Les Paul SG '61 Reissue for '93-'03 and SG '61 Reissue '03-present, cherry.

1986-1991		$2,200	$3,000

SG '62 Reissue Showcase Edition

1988. Guitar of the Month, bright blue opaque finish, 200 made.

1988		$2,500	$3,500

Les Paul '63 Corvette Sting Ray

1995-1997. Custom Shop SG-style body carved to simulate split rear window on '63 Corvette, Sting Ray inlay, 150 made, offered in black, white, silver or red.

1995-1997		$8,000	$12,000

SG-90 Double

1988-1990. SG body, updated electronics, graphite reinforced neck, 2 pickups, cherry, turquoise or white.

1988-1990		$3,500	$5,000

SG-90 Single

1988-1990. SG body, updated electronics, graphite reinforced neck, 1 humbucker pickup, cherry, turquoise or white.

1988-1990		$2,200	$3,000

SG-100

1971-1972. Double-cut solidbody, 1 pickup, cherry or walnut.

1971-1972	Melody Maker pu	$1,200	$1,800

GUITARS

MODEL YEAR	FEATURES	EXC. COND. LOW	HIGH
1971-1972	P-90 pu option	$1,500	$2,000
1971-1972	Sam Ash model	$1,800	$2,200

SG-200

1971-1972. Two pickup version of SG-100 in black, cherry or walnut finish, replaced by SG II.

1971-1972	2 Melody Makers	$1,500	$2,200

SG-250

1971-1972. Two-pickup version of SG-100 in cherry sunburst, replaced by SG III.

1971-1972	2 Melody Makers	$1,800	$2,500

SG-400/SG Special 400

1985-1987. SG body with 3 toggles, 2 knobs (master volume, master tone), single-single-humbucker pickups, available with uncommon opaque finishes.

1985-1987		$1,800	$2,500

SG Angus Young

2010-2016. Like Angus Signature but with small guard, stop tailpiece and tune-o-matic, Aged Cherry.

2010-2016		$2,000	$2,800

SG Angus Young Signature

2000-2009. Custom Shop, late-'60s Std specs with large 'guard, Deluxe Maestro lyre vibrato with Angus logo, aged cherry finish.

2000-2009		$3,000	$4,000

SG Baritone

2013-2016. Longer 27" scale, 2 exposed humbuckers, ebony 'board, Alpine White finish.

2013-2016		$1,600	$2,200

SG Carved Top - Autumn Burst

2009. Limited run of 350, highly flamed carved maple top, rosewood 'board, certificate of authenticity.

2009		$2,000	$2,800

SG Classic/SG Classic Faded

1999-2001, 2003-2013. Late '60s SG Special style, Classic on truss rod cover, large 'guard, black soapbar single-coil P-90s, dot markers, stop bar tailpiece, cherry or ebony stain.

1999-2013		$1,500	$2,200

SG Custom

1963-1980. Renamed from Les Paul Custom, 3 humbuckers, vibrato, made with Les Paul Custom plate from '61-'63 (see Les Paul Custom), white finish until '68, walnut and others after.

1963-1964	White, pat #, Maestro	$22,500	$30,000
1965	Early '65, white, large neck	$15,000	$20,000
1965	Late '65, white, small neck	$14,000	$18,500
1966-1968	White, large 'guard	$10,500	$14,000
1969	Walnut, lyre, 1-piece neck	$6,500	$8,500
1969	Walnut, lyre, 3-piece neck	$4,800	$6,500
1969	White, lyre, 1 piece neck	$6,500	$8,500
1969	White, lyre, 3 piece neck	$5,200	$7,000
1970	Walnut, lyre	$4,000	$5,500
1970	White, lyre	$4,000	$5,500
1970-1973	Walnut, Bigsby	$3,200	$4,500
1970-1973	White option, Bigsby	$4,000	$5,500
1974-1975	Brown, dark cherry	$2,800	$3,800
1974-1975	White option	$3,500	$4,500
1976-1979	Brown, dark cherry	$2,500	$3,500
1976-1979	White option	$3,200	$4,200
1980	Various colors	$2,300	$3,000

SG Custom '67 Reissue/ Les Paul SG '67 Custom

1991-1993. The SG Custom '67 Reissue has a wine red finish, the Les Paul SG '67 Custom ('92-'93) has a wine red or white finish.

1991-1993		$2,500	$4,500

SG Custom Elliot Easton Signature

2006-2007. Custom Shop, SG Custom specs, Maestro deluxe vibrola, Pelham Blue or white, includes Certificate of Authenticity.

2006-2007		$3,500	$6,000

SG Deluxe

1971-1972, 1981-1985, 1998-1999, 2013-2018. The '70s models were offered in cherry, natural or walnut finishes, reintroduced in '98 with 3 Firebird mini-humbucker-style pickups in black, red or Ice Blue finishes, in 2013 with 3 '57 Classic humbuckers in Cobalt Fade, Lime Burst, Orange Burst or Red Fade.

1971-1972	Cherry	$2,200	$2,800
1971-1972	Natural, walnut	$2,200	$2,800
1981-1985	Various colors	$1,800	$2,500
1998-1999	Various colors	$1,400	$1,800
2013-2018	New specs, all colors	$1,800	$2,300

SG Diablo

2008. Guitar of the Month for Dec. '08, 1,000 made, '61 specs, metallic silver finish with matching headstock, 1 volume, 1 tone knob, 3-way toggle, 24 frets.

2008		$1,800	$2,500

SG Diablo Premium Plus

2012-2013. AAA maple top.

2012-2013		$2,000	$2,800

SG Diablo Tremolo

2012-2013. Diablo with Floyd Rose.

2012-2013		$2,200	$3,000

SG Dickey Betts

2012. Custom Shop, 75 hand-aged include a leather certificate of authenticity signed by Betts, 250 VOS include unsigned COA, Vintage Red finish.

2012	Aged, signed	$8,000	$10,000
2012	VOS, unsigned	$5,000	$6,500

SG Elegant

2004-2013. Custom Shop, quilt maple top, gold hardware, Blue Burst, Firemist and Iguana Burst finishes.

2004-2013		$2,800	$3,800

SG Elite

1987-1989. SG Custom specs, 3 humbuckers, gold hardware, ebony 'board, various colors.

1987-1989		$2,200	$3,000

SG Exclusive

1979. SG with humbuckers, coil-tap and rotary control knob, block inlay, pearl logo (not decal), black/ebony finish.

1979		$3,500	$5,000

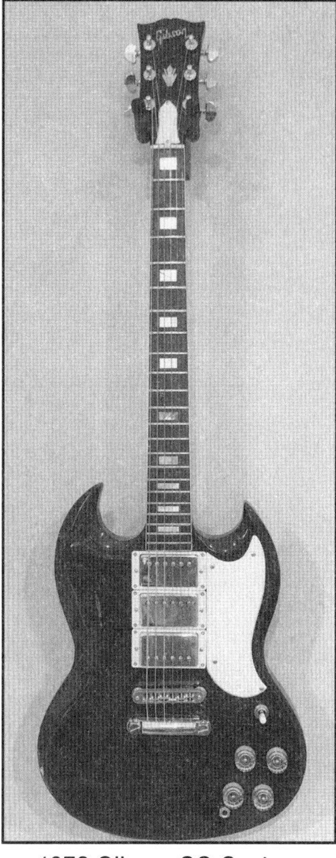

1972 Gibson SG Custom
Tom Allen

1972 Gibson SG Deluxe
Imaged by Heritage Auctions, HA.com

GUITARS

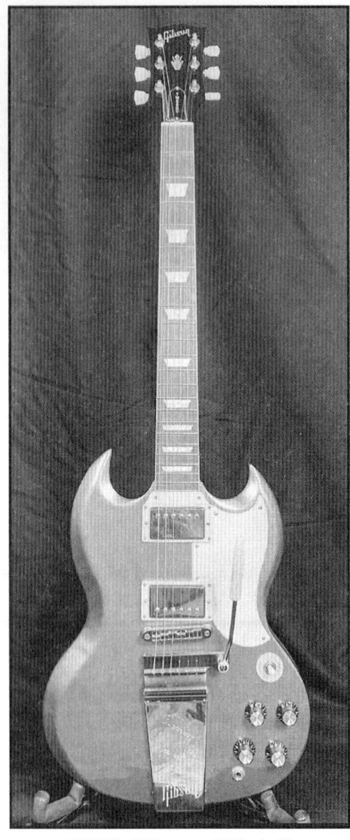
2012 Gibson SG Jeff Tweedy Signature
Matt Carleson

1965 Gibson SG Junior
Tim Fleck

MODEL YEAR	FEATURES	EXC. COND. LOW	HIGH

SG Firebrand

1980-1982. Double-cut mahogany solidbody, rough natural finish, Gibson branded in headstock, 2 exposed humbuckers, Firebrand logo on The SG (Standard) model.

1980-1982		$2,200	$3,000

SG Frank Zappa "Roxy"

2013. 400 offered, Maestro vibrola, 2 exposed-coil humbuckers.

2013		$5,500	$7,500

SG Futura

2013-2014. Mahogany body, maple neck, rosewood 'board, 2 pickups, various colors.

2013-2014		$1,500	$2,500

SG Goddess

2007. SG Goddess logo on truss rod cover, only 2 control knobs versus standard 4, exposed humbuckers.

2007		$2,000	$2,800

SG Gothic

2000-2003. SG Special with satin black finish, moon and star marker on 12th fret, black hardware.

2000-2003		$1,500	$2,500

SG Gothic Morte

2011-2012. Solid mahogany body, African Obeche 'board, 2 pickups, satin ebony finish

2011-2012		$1,200	$1,800

SG Government Series

2013-2016. Made from guitar bodies, necks and 'boards returned from Federal Government after '11 raid on Gibson, with Certificate of Authenticity.

2013-2016		$1,800	$2,500

SG GT

2006-2007. '61 specs with racing stripes paint job and removable tailpiece hood scoop, locking tuners, Candy Apple Red, Daytona Blue, or Phantom Black.

2006-2007		$1,800	$2,500

SG Jeff Tweedy Signature

2012. SG Standard with Maestro vibrola, mahogany body and neck, rosewood 'board, Blue Mist.

2012		$3,500	$4,800

SG Jimi Hendrix '67 Custom

2020. Custom Shop Limited Edition, 150 made, Murphy lab, Aged Polaris White.

2020		$10,000	$15,000

SG Judas Priest Signature

2003. Custom Shop, 30 made, dot markers, exposed '57 classic humbucker and EMG58 pickups, black, large chrome metal 'guard, also sold as a set with Flying V Judas Priest, includes certificate of authenticity.

2003		$2,800	$3,800

SG Judas Priest Signature Set With Flying V

2003. Custom Shop, 30 sets made.

2003		$8,000	$12,000

SG Junior

1963-1971, 1991-1994. One pickup, solidbody. Prices are for an unfaded finish, cherry finish faded to brown reduces the value by 30%.

1963-1964	Cherry	$5,500	$7,000
1964	White	$6,000	$7,500
1965	Early-'65, cherry	$4,800	$6,200
1965	Late-'65, cherry	$3,500	$4,500
1965	Pelham Blue	$7,000	$9,500
1965	White	$4,500	$6,500
1966-1969	Cherry	$3,300	$4,300
1966-1969	White	$4,300	$5,500
1970-1971	Cherry or walnut	$2,800	$3,800
1991-1994	Various colors	$1,200	$1,500

SG Junior (Reintroduced)

2018-2024. Gibson Original series, '60s design, mahogany body, P-90 single-coil pickup, Vintage Cherry gloss nitro finish.

2018-2024		$1,500	$2,200

SG Junior Limited

2018. Double-cut, mahogany body and neck, rosewood 'board, 1 single-coil pickup, Vintage Cherry.

2018		$1,800	$2,500

SG Junior P-90

2006-2007. Single P-90 pickup, large 'guard, stop tail, cherry finish.

2006-2007		$1,200	$1,800

SG Kirk Douglas Signature

2019-2023. Mother-of-pearl headstock logo, 3 Burst-Bucker pickups, ebony or Inverness Green.

2019-2023		$2,500	$3,500

SG Les Paul '61 Custom

1997-2005. 1961 specs, SG body style, 3 humbuckers, Deluxe Maestro vibrato or stud with tune-o-matic bridge, white or silver option.

1997-2005		$4,000	$5,500

SG Les Paul '62 Custom

2003. Custom Shop, Maestro vibrato, small 'guard, white.

1986-1990		$3,500	$5,000

SG Les Paul '62 Custom (Historic Collection)

2003. Custom Shop, Maestro vibrato, small 'guard, white.

2003		$4,000	$6,500

SG Les Paul '90 Custom

1990-1992. 1962 specs, 3 humbuckers.

1990-1992		$3,500	$5,000

SG Les Paul Custom 30th Anniversary

1991. SG body, 3 humbuckers, gold hardware, TV Yellow finish, 30th Anniversary on peghead.

1991		$5,500	$7,500

SG Menace

2006-2007. Carved mahogany body, 2 exposed humbuckers, flat black finish, black hardware, single brass knuckle position marker, gig bag.

2006-2007		$1,500	$2,200

SG Music Machine Stinger

2003. Custom run for dealer Music Machine, special serial number series, SG Custom with 2 pickups and SG Standard models available, 10 of each made, black stinger paint job on neck/headstock, various colors.

2003	SG Custom	$12,000	$18,000
2003	SG Standard	$8,000	$12,000

SG Original

2013-2019. Mahogany body, slim '60s neck profile, Lyre vibrato, '57 classic pickups, Vintage Cherry. Replaced by SG Standard '61 Maestro Vibrola in '19.

2013-2019		$1,600	$2,200

MODEL YEAR	FEATURES	EXC. COND. LOW	HIGH

SG Pete Townshend Signature

2001. Signature on back of headstock.

2001		$2,800	$4,000

SG Pete Townshend Signature (Custom Shop)

2000. Custom Shop Limited Edition, 250 made, SG Special with '69 specs, large 'guard, 2 cases, cherry red, COA.

2000		$5,500	$7,500

SG Platinum

2005. A mix of SG Special and SG Standard specs, platinum paint on the body, back of neck, and headstock, no crown inlay, Gibson stencil logo, exposed humbucker pickups, large plantium-finish 'guard, special plantinum colored Gibson logo guitar case.

2005		$2,000	$2,800

SG Pro

1971-1974. Tune-o-matic bridge, vibrato, 2 P-90 pickups, cherry, mahogany or walnut.

1971-1974		$2,500	$3,500

SG R1/SG Artist

1980-1982. Active RD-era electronics. SG style but thicker body, no 'guard, ebony 'board, black finish, dot markers, renamed SG Artist in '81.

1980	SG-R1	$3,500	$5,000
1981-1982	SG Artist	$4,000	$5,500

SG Raw Power

2009-2012. All maple body, neck and 'board, 2 exposed-coil humbuckers, offered in 9 satin finishes, including natural.

2009-2012		$1,500	$2,500

SG Select

2007. Made in Nashville, TN, carved solid book-matched AAA flame maple, 3-piece flamed maple neck, described as the most exquisite SG offered to date, 2 humbuckers, gold hardware.

2007		$2,000	$2,800

SG Special

1960-1978. Rounded double-cut for '60, switched to SG body early-'61, 2 P-90s '59-'71, 2 mini-humbuckers '72-'78, 2 regular humbuckers on current version, redesigned in '85. Prices are for an unfaded finish, cherry finish faded to brown reduces the value by 20%-30%. Instruments with stop tailpieces vs. Maestro tailpiece have the same value.

1960	Cherry, slab, low neck pu	$9,500	$12,000
1961-1962	Cherry, SG body	$7,000	$9,000
1961-1962	TV Yellow, SG body	$20,000	$25,000
1962	White, SG body	$8,000	$10,500
1963-1964	Cherry, Maestro or stop	$7,000	$9,000
1963-1964	White	$8,000	$10,000
1965	Cherry, Maestro or stop	$4,800	$6,300
1965	White	$6,200	$8,000
1966	Cherry, large 'guard	$4,300	$5,500
1966	Cherry, small 'guard	$4,300	$5,500
1966	White, large 'guard	$5,200	$6,800
1966	White, small 'guard	$5,700	$7,000
1967	Cherry, large 'guard	$4,300	$5,500
1967	White, large 'guard	$4,200	$5,500
1968-1969	Cherry, large 'guard	$4,300	$5,500
1970-1971	Cherry	$3,800	$5,000
1972-1978	Mini-hums	$2,000	$2,500

SG Special (redesigned)

1985-1996. In mid-'85 Gibson introduced a redesigned SG Special model with 2 control knobs (1 pickup) or 3 control knobs (2 pickups) versus the previously used 4-knob layout.

1985-1986	1 pu, 2 knobs	$1,200	$1,800
1985-1989	2 pus, 3 knobs	$1,300	$2,000
1990-1996	2 pus, 3 knobs	$1,200	$1,800

SG Special (reintroduced)

1996-present. In '96 Gibson reintroduced the original 4-knob layout, 2 humbucker pickups, dot markers.

1996-2024		$1,200	$1,800

SG Special 3/4

1961. Only 61 shipped.

1961		$6,500	$9,500

SG Special '60s Tribute

2011-2018. '60s specs including small guard, dot markers, dual P-90s, Slim Taper '60s neck profile, 4 worn-finish options.

2011-2018		$1,200	$1,800

1963 SG Special Ultra Light Aged

2021. Custom Shop Murphy Lab Collection, Classic White finish.

2021		$4,500	$6,500

SG Special Faded (3 pickups)

2007. Made in Nashville, TN, 3 exposed 490 humbuckers, dot markers, stop tail, SG initials on truss rod cover, 2 knobs and 6-position selector switch, hand-worn satin finish.

2007		$1,200	$1,800

SG Special Faded/Faded SG Special

2002-2018. Aged worn cherry finish.

2002-2005	Half moon markers	$1,000	$1,500
2003-2018	Dot markers	$1,000	$1,500

SG Special I

1983-1985. Dot markers, 1 exposed-coil humbucker pickup with 2 knobs, called by various names including Gibson Special ('83), Special I, and SG Special I.

1983-1985		$1,000	$1,500

SG Special II

1983-1985. Dot markers, 2 exposed-coil humbucker pickups with 3 knobs, called by various names including Gibson Special ('83), Special II, SG Special II.

1983-1985		$1,200	$1,800

SG Special II EMG

2007. EMG humbucker pickups, no position markers, standard 4-knob and 3-way toggle switch SG format, black satin finish over entire guitar, black hardware.

2007		$1,200	$2,000

SG Special 400

1985-1986. Double-cut solidbody, mahogany body and neck, HSS pickups, Ferrari Red, ebony, olive green metallic, pink or white.

1985-1986		$1,200	$1,800

2023 Gibson SG Kirk Douglas Signature

1969 Gibson SG Special

Landon Furlong

GUITARS

1984 Gibson SG Standard

Rivington Guitars

1969 Gibson SG Standard

W. H. Stephens

MODEL YEAR	FEATURES	EXC. COND. LOW	HIGH

SG Special New Century

2006-2008. Full-body mirror 'guard, 2 exposed humbuckers, SG body, mirror truss rod cover.

2006-2008		$1,600	$2,200

SG Special Robot

2008-2012. Dot markers, robot tuning.

2008-2012		$1,600	$2,200

SG Special Robot Limited

2008. Limited run with trapezoid markers, robot tuning.

2008		$1,800	$2,500

SG Special Robot Limited Silverburst

2008. Limited run of 400.

2008		$3,000	$4,500

SG Special VOS Reissue

2006-2013. Custom Shop, mahogany body and neck, bound rosewood 'board, dot inlays, 2 P-90s, certificate, white, TV yellow, or faded cherry finish.

2006-2013		$2,800	$4,000

SG Standard

1963-1981, 1983-present. Les Paul Standard changes to SG body, 2 humbuckers, some very early models have optional factory Bigsby. Prices are for an unfaded finish, a cherry finish faded to brown reduces the value by 30% or more.

1963-1964	Cherry, sm 'guard, dlx vibr or Bigsby	$19,000	$25,000
1964	Pelham Blue, sm 'guard, dlx vibr	$25,000	$35,000
1965	Cherry, sm 'guard, dlx vibr, lg neck	$16,000	$20,000
1965	Cherry, sm 'guard, dlx vibr, sm neck	$15,000	$20,000
1965	Pelham Blue,sm 'guard, dlx vibr	$24,000	$32,000
1966	Early '66, cherry, vibr, sm 'guard, dlx vibrato	$10,500	$13,500
1966	Late '66, cherry, lg 'guard	$8,000	$10,500
1967	Burgundy Metallic	$8,500	$11,000
1967	Cherry	$7,800	$10,000
1967	White	$9,500	$12,500
1968	Cherry, engraved lyre	$6,700	$8,500
1969	Engraved lyre, 1-piece neck	$6,700	$8,500
1969	Engraved lyre, 3-piece neck	$5,200	$7,000
1970	Engraved lyre, 3-piece neck	$4,800	$6,500
1970	Walnut, non-lyre tailpiece	$3,300	$4,500
1970-1971	Cherry, non-lyre tailpiece	$3,300	$4,300
1971	Engraved lyre, 3-piece neck	$4,300	$5,500
1972-1979	Blocks, mini 'guard, top mount	$2,800	$3,800
1980-1986	New colors, sm blocks	$2,200	$2,800
1992-1999	New specs	$1,300	$1,800
2000-2024	Standard colors	$1,300	$1,800
2006-2012	Silverburst	$1,500	$2,000

SG Standard '61 Reissue

2004-2008. Small 'guard, stop tail, Nashville tune-o-matic bridge, Gibson Deluxe Keystone tuners, standard Gibson logo and crown inlay, no Les Paul logo, Vintage Original Spec aging optional from '06. Reintroduced in '19.

2004-2008		$2,500	$3,500

SG Standard '61

2019-present. Classic '61 design, 3 models offered - Maestro vibrola, Sideways or Stop Bar, mahogany body and neck, rosewood 'board, vintage cherry finish.

2019-2025	Maestro vibrola	$2,000	$2,800
2019-2024	Sideways vibrola	$2,000	$2,800
2019-2024	Stop Bar vibrola	$2,000	$2,800

1964 SG Standard (Maestro Vibrola) Murphy Lab Aged

2021-present. Custom Shop Murphy Lab Collection, heavy aged (Faded Cherry), light aged (Pelham Blue) and ultra light (Cherry Red or Pelham Blue).

2021-2024	Heavy aged	$8,000	$10,000
2021-2024	Light aged	$7,000	$9,000
2021-2022	Ultra Light aged	$6,500	$8,500

SG Standard 24 50th Anniversary

2011. Limited run, mother-of-pearl Gibson logo with gold 50th Anniversary silkscreen, 2 '57 classic pickups, antique ebony finish.

2011		$3,000	$4,000

SG Standard (Etune)

2014-2018. Min-Etune robot tuners, Etune logo on truss rod.

2014-2018		$1,600	$2,200

SG Standard Brian Ray '63 (Custom Shop)

2015. Silver Fox finish, Bigsby, certificate of authenticity.

2015		$4,500	$6,500

SG Standard Celebrity Series

1991-1992. SG Standard with large 'guard, gold hardware, black finish.

1991-1992		$2,500	$3,500

SG Standard Gary Rossington Signature

2004. '63-'64 SG Standard specs with Deluxe Maestro vibrola, '60 slim taper neck, limited edition, Brazilian (1st run) or Indian rosewood 'board, Murphy aged, faded cherry.

2004	1st run, Brazilian	$10,000	$15,000
2004	Indian	$8,000	$10,000

SG Standard HP (High Performance)

2016-2019. Solid mahogany body and neck, AA figured maple top, 2 pickups, different colors offered each year.

2016-2019		$2,000	$2,800

SG Standard Korina (Custom Shop)

2008-2009. Custom Shop limited reissue of '60s SG Standard, 2 BurstBucker pickups, black.

2008-2009		$3,500	$4,800

SG Standard Korina Limited Edition

1993-1994. Korina version of SG Standard, limited run, natural.

1993-1994		$4,000	$5,500

MODEL YEAR	FEATURES	EXC. COND. LOW	HIGH

SG Standard Korina/SG Standard K (Custom Shop)

2001-2008. Custom Shop serial number, large 'guard, no SG logo on truss rod, CS logo back of headstock, natural finish.

2001-2008		$3,800	$5,200

SG Standard Limited Edition

2000. Limited Edition logo back of headstock, 2 humbuckers, large pearloid guard, gold hardware, dark opaque finish.

2000		$1,800	$2,500

SG Standard Limited Edition (3 pickups)

2007. Guitar of the Week, 400 made, 3 single-coil blade pickups, 6-position rotator switch with chickenhead knob, SG logo on truss rod cover, large 'guard, satin finish.

2007		$2,000	$2,800

SG Standard Reissue

2004-2018. Reissue of near '63-'64 specs with Deluxe Maestro lyre vibrato and small 'guard, also offered with stop bar tailpiece, cherry finish, '60 slim taper neck, smooth neck heel joint, trapezoid markers, unmarked truss rod cover without Les Paul designation, formerly called Les Paul SG Standard Reissue, by 2005 part of Gibson's 'Vintage Original Spec' Custom Shop series, certificate of authenticity.

2004-2007	VOS, Maestro	$3,000	$4,500
2007-2018	VOS, stoptail	$3,000	$4,500
2008-2009	Maestro, LP logo	$3,000	$4,500

SG Standard VOS Historic

2003-2014. Custom Shop, Vintage Original Specs.

2003-2014		$3,500	$4,500

SG Standard Robby Krieger

2009. Custom Shop model, Inspired By series, based on Krieger's '67 SG, limited run of 150 with 50 aged and signed, 100 with V.O.S. finish treatment, certificate of authenticity.

2009	Aged, signed	$8,000	$10,000
2009	VOS	$5,000	$6,500

SG Standard 50th Anniversary Robby Krieger

2012. Mahogany body and neck, rosewood 'board, 2 '57 classic Alnico II pickups, Maestro tailpiece, Heritage Cherry finish.

2012		$4,000	$6,000

SG Supreme

2004-2007. '57 humbuckers, flamed maple top, split-diamond markers, various colors.

2004-2007		$3,000	$4,500

SG Tony Iommi Signature (Historic/Custom Shop)

2001-2003. Custom Shop Historic Collection, higher-end, signature humbuckers without poles, cross inlays, ebony or Wine Red.

2001-2003	Signed	$7,000	$9,500
2001-2003	Unsigned	$5,000	$6,500

SG Tony Iommi Signature (Production)

2002-2003. Standard production model.

2002-2008		$2,500	$3,500

SG TV

1959-1961. See Les Paul TV.

SG Voodoo/Voodoo SG

2002-2004. Carved top, black hardware, voodoo doll inlay at 5th fret, Juju finish (black with red wood filler).

2002-2004		$1,600	$2,200

SG-X

1998-2000. Previously part of the All American series, SG body with single bridge humbucker, various colors.

1998-2000		$1,200	$1,800

SG-X Tommy Hilfiger

1998. Hilfiger logo on front, dot markers, plain headstock like a SG Special, dark blue finish, 100 made.

1998		$4,000	$6,000

SG Zoot Suit

2007-2010. Body of individual dyed strips of birch.

2007-2010		$2,000	$2,800

SG-Z

1998. Z-shaped string-thru tailpiece, 2 humbuckers, split diamond markers.

1998		$1,600	$2,200

The SG

1979-1983. Offered as The SG Standard (walnut body) and The SG Deluxe (mahogany), ebony 'board, 2 humbuckers, 'The SG' truss rod logo.

1979-1983	Walnut or mahogany	$1,800	$2,500

Sheryl Crow Country Western Supreme

2019-2022. Artist series, aged Sitka spruce top, mahogany back and sides, Antique Cherry finish.

2019-2022		$3,800	$5,000

Sheryl Crow Signature

2001-2018. Artist Series, based on Sheryl Crow's 1962 Country and Western with Hummingbird influences.

2001 2018		$2,800	$4,000

Sheryl Crow Southern Jumbo Special Edition

2013-2018. Adirondack red spruce top, mahogany back and sides, rosewood 'board, with signed certificate of authenticity, Montana Sunsetburst finish. Limited production in '13.

2013-2018		$3,500	$4,800

SJ (Southern Jumbo)

1942-1969,1991-1996. Flat-top, sunburst standard, natural optional starting in '54 (natural finish version called Country-Western starting in '56), round shoulders (changed to square in '62), catalog name changed to SJ Deluxe in '70, refer to that listing.

1942-1944	Banner, Adirondack	$19,000	$25,000
1942-1944	Banner, mahogany	$15,000	$20,000
1945	Script, Sitka	$16,000	$20,000
1946	Script, Sitka	$14,000	$18,000
1947	Script, Sitka	$13,000	$16,000
1948-1949	Script, Sitka	$11,500	$14,500
1950-1953		$7,500	$10,000
1954-1956	Natural option	$7,500	$10,000
1954-1959	Sunburst	$7,500	$10,000
1960-1962	Round shoulder (ends)	$6,500	$8,500
1962-1964	Square shoulder (begins)	$6,000	$8,000

Gibson 1964 SG Standard (Maestro Vibrola) Murphy Lab Aged

1960 Gibson SJ

David Stone

1959 Gibson SJN Country Western
Rod Highsmith

Gibson SJ Woody Guthrie
Bill Miller

MODEL YEAR	FEATURES	EXC. COND. LOW	HIGH
1965	Cherry Sunburst	$3,600	$5,500
1965	Tobacco Sunburst	$4,500	$6,000
1966	Tobacco Sunburst	$4,000	$5,500
1966-1968	Cherry Sunburst	$3,600	$5,000
1969	Below belly bridge	$2,800	$4,500

SJ Deluxe (Southern Jumbo)

1970-1978. SJ name changed to SJ Deluxe in catalog, along with a series of engineering changes.

1970-1971	Non-adj saddle	$2,000	$3,000
1972-1973	Unbound 'board	$1,800	$3,500
1974-1978	4-ply to binding	$1,800	$3,500

SJN (Country-Western)

1956-1969. Flat-top, natural finish version of SJ, round shoulders '56-'62, square shoulders after, called the SJN in '60 and '61, the SJN Country Western after that, catalog name changed to SJN Deluxe in '70, refer to that listing.

1956-1959		$7,000	$9,500
1960-1962	Round shoulder (ends)	$6,800	$9,000
1962-1964	Square shoulder (begins)	$6,300	$8,200
1965		$4,500	$6,000
1966-1968		$4,000	$5,500
1969	Below belly bridge	$3,200	$4,000

SJN Deluxe (Country-Western Jumbo)

1970-1978. SJN name changed to SJN Deluxe in catalog, along with a series of engineering changes.

1970-1971	Non-adj saddle	$2,000	$3,000
1972-1973	Unbound 'board	$2,000	$3,000
1974-1978	4-ply to binding	$2,000	$3,000

SJ 1942 Reissue (Southern Jumbo)

2000. Custom Shop, mahogany back and sides, '42 SJ appointments, 'Only A Gibson is Good Enough' banner logo.

2000		$3,000	$4,000

SJ Reissue (Southern Jumbo)

2003-2007. Sunburst.

2003-2007		$2,800	$4,000

SJ Hank Williams Jr. Hall of Fame

1997. Custom Shop, mahogany back and sides, SJ appointments.

1997		$3,500	$4,800

SJ Hank Williams Sr.

1993. Custom Shop, 25 offered.

1993		$4,000	$5,500

SJ Kristofferson

2009-2012. Limited run of 300, first 50 signed, AAA Sitka top, mahogany back and sides, Indian rosewood 'board, aged vintage sunburst.

2009-2012	Signed	$4,800	$6,500
2009-2012	Unsigned	$3,500	$4,800

SJ True Vintage

2007-2008. "Only A Gibson Is Good Enough" headstock banner, Sitka spruce top, dark mahogany back and sides, dual parallelogram markers.

2007-2008		$3,500	$4,800

SJ Woody Guthrie

2003-2018. Single-bound round shoulder body, mahogany back and sides, parallelogram inlays.

2003-2018		$2,800	$4,000

SJ-100

2008. Jumbo body, dot markers, crown headstock inlay, inlaid Gibson logo, natural.

2008		$2,500	$3,500

1939 SJ-100 Centennial

1994. Acoustic flat-top, limited edition, sunburst.

1994		$4,000	$6,500

1941 SJ-100

2013-2018. Sitka spruce top, mahogany back, sides and neck, rosewood 'board, Vintage Sunburst or Antique Natural.

2013-2018		$3,000	$4,200

SJ-150

Listed with J-150.

SJ-200

Listed with J-200.

1957 SJ-200 (Custom Shop)

2020-present. Aged Sitka spruce top, flamed maple back and sides, 4 bar moustach bridge, VOS finish, Antique Natural or Vintage Sunburst.

2020-2024		$5,000	$8,000

SJ-200 Bob Dylan Autographed Collector's Edition

2015-2018. Exact replica of Dylan's personal highly-customized SJ-200, Indian rosewood, Sitka spruce, Dylan eye logo inlaid on headstock, abalone inlay on 'guard, label signed by Bob Dylan, 175 made, case with embroidered eye logo.

2015-2018		$15,000	$20,000

SJ-200 Bob Dylan Player's Edition

2015-2018. Adirondack red spruce, flamed maple, eye logo headstock inlay, LR Baggs Anthem pickup.

2015-2018		$5,000	$6,500

SJ-200 Centennial Limited Edition

1994. Made in Bozeman, Montana, 100 made, 'guard specs based on '38 design, inside label "Gibson 100 Years 1894-1994", includes certificate of authenticity.

1994		$5,000	$7,500

SJ-200 Custom Rosewood

2007. Custom shop, certificate of authenticity.

2007		$4,500	$7,500

SJ-200 Custom Vine

2000. Custom shop, extremely figured maple sides and back, vine inlay on 'board.

2000		$6,000	$10,000

SJ-200 Deluxe

2020-2024. Custom Shop, Sitka spruce top, rosewood back and sides, mother-of-pearl crown inlays, Rosewood Burst finish.

2020-2024		$4,000	$6,500

SJ-200 Elite

1998-2007. Gibson Custom Shop Bozeman, maple sides and back.

1998-2007		$4,000	$6,500

SJ-200 Elite Brazilian

2001. Gibson Custom Shop Bozeman, Brazilian rosewood sides and back.

2001		$8,000	$12,000

MODEL YEAR	FEATURES	EXC. COND. LOW	HIGH

SJ-200 Elite Custom Koa

2004. Figured koa, ebony board with abalone crown inlays, Antique Natural.

2004		$5,000	$8,000

SJ-200 Elvis Presley "King of Rock" Limited Edition

2008. Custom Shop, 250 made, mother-of-pearl crown inlays, black finish.

2008		$6,000	$10,000

SJ-200 Pete Townshend Limited

2004-2012. Gibson Custom Shop Bozeman, maple sides and back.

2004	Signed, 1st 50 made	$9,000	$12,000
2004-2012		$5,000	$8,000

SJ-200 Ray Whitley/J-200 Custom Club

1994-1995. Based on Ray Whitley's late-1930s J-200, including engraved inlays and initials on the truss rod cover, only 37 made, one of the limited edition models the Montana division released to celebrate Gibson's 100th anniversary.

1994-1995		$11,500	$18,000

SJ-200 Ron Wood

Listed with J-200 Ron Wood.

SJ-200 Sea Green Limited Edition

2016. Bozeman Custom Shop, 40 made, Sitka spruce top, AAA flamed maple back and sides, mother-of-pearl crown inlays.

2016		$6,000	$10,000

SJ-200 Standard

2015-present. AAA flamed maple body, on-board electronics, Wine Red or Autumnburst.

2015-2024		$3,500	$6,000

SJ-200 Summer Jam Koa

2006. Custom Shop, only 6 made, offered to attendees of Gibson Guitar Summer Jam, highly figured koa back/sides.

2006		$4,500	$7,500

SJ-200 True Vintage/SJ-200 Vintage

2007-2019. AAA Adirondack red spruce top, AAA Eastern curly maple back and sides, rosewood 'board, tortoise 'guard, nitro finish. True dropped from name in '19.

2007-2019		$4,000	$6,500

SJ-200 Vine

2002-2018. Custom Shop, Sitka spruce top, Eastern curly maple back/sides, abalone vine inlay in 'board, abalone body trim. Limited Edition in '15, 30 made.

2002-2018		$5,000	$8,000

SJ-250 Monarch

Listed with J-250 Monarch.

SJ-300

2007-2010. Super Jumbo with Indian rosewood back and sides, ebony 'board, abalone crown inlays and rosette, gold imperial tuners, active transducer.

2007-2010		$2,500	$4,500

SJ-1000

Listed with J-1000.

Sonex Artist

1981-1985. Active electronics, 3 mini switches, 2 humbuckers.

1981-1985		$1,200	$1,800

MODEL YEAR	FEATURES	EXC. COND. LOW	HIGH

Sonex-180 Custom

1980-1982. Two Super humbuckers, coil-tap, maple neck, ebony 'board, single-cut, body of Multi-Phonic synthetic material, black or white.

1980-1982		$1,200	$1,800

Sonex-180 Deluxe

1980-1984. Hardwood neck, rosewood 'board, single-cut, body of Multi-Phonic synthetic material, 2 pickups, no coil-tap, various colors.

1980-1984	Various colors	$1,200	$1,800
1982-1984	Silverburst	$1,500	$2,500

Sonex-180 Standard

1980. Dirty-fingers pickups, rosewood 'board, ebony finish.

1980		$1,200	$1,800

Songbird Deluxe

1999-2002. Solid rosewood back, sides and 'board, on-board electronics. Renamed Songwriter Deluxe.

1999-2002		$2,000	$3,500

Songmaker Series

2008. Acoustic, various models and woods, natural finish.

2008	DSM-CE	$1,800	$3,200

Songwriter

2003-2020. Sitka spruce top, rosewood back, sides and 'board, mahogany neck, Antique Natural or Rosewood Burst. Becomes Songwriter Standard in '20.

2003-2020		$2,000	$3,500

Songwriter 12-String Rosewood

2019-2020. Sitka spruce top, rosewood back and sides, Antique Natural or Rosewood Burst.

2019-2020		$2,500	$4,500

Songwriter Deluxe

2003-2011. Solid rosewood back and sides, trapezoid inlays, cutaway or non-cutaway, on-board electronics.

2003-2011		$2,500	$4,500

Songwriter Deluxe 12-String

2006-2022. 12-string version, non-cut.

2006-2022		$2,800	$4,000

Songwriter Deluxe Koa

2009. Custom Shop, all koa, cutaway.

2009		$3,500	$6,000

Songwriter Deluxe Standard

2009-2012. Solid rosewood back and sides, bound ebony 'board, diamond and arrows inlays, cutaway or non-cutaway.

2009-2012		$2,500	$4,500

Songwriter Deluxe Studio

2009-2018. Like Standard, but with bound rosewood 'board and double parallelogram inlays, cutaway or non-cutaway.

2009-2018		$2,500	$4,500

Songwriter Modern EC Mahogany

2020-2021. Cutaway, Sitka spruce top, mahogany back, sides and neck, Light Cherry Burst with nitro finish.

2020-2021		$2,000	$3,500

Songwriter Modern EC Rosewood

2020-2021. Cutaway, Sitka spruce top, rosewood back and sides, mahogany neck, Rosewood Burst with nitro finish.

2020-2021		$2,500	$4,500

1982 Gibson Sonex-180 Deluxe

Imaged by Heritage Auctions, HA.com

2019 Gibson Songwriter

1921 Gibson Style O
Imaged by Heritage Auctions, HA.com

1917 Gibson Style U Harp Guitar

MODEL YEAR	FEATURES	EXC. COND. LOW	HIGH

Songwriter Special

2007. Mahogany sides and back, dark opaque finish.

2007		$2,000	$3,500

Songwriter Special Deluxe

2003. Custom Shop, Brazilian rosewood.

2003		$2,500	$4,500

Songwriter Standard EC Rosewood

2020-present. Cutaway, Sitka spruce top, rosewood back and sides, Antique Natural or Rosewood Burst finish.

2020-2024		$2,500	$4,500

Songwriter Standard Rosewood

2020-present. Non-cut, Sitka spruce top, rosewood back and sides, Antique Natural or Rosewood Burst finish.

2020-2024		$2,000	$3,500

Songwriter Studio

2003-2019. Non-cutaway or cutaway.

2003-2019		$2,000	$3,500

Spirit I

1982-1987. Double rounded cutaway, 1 pickup, chrome hardware, various colors.

1982-1987		$1,200	$1,800

Spirit I XPL

1985-1986. Spirit I with 6-on-a-side Explorer-style headstock.

1985-1986		$2,000	$3,800

Spirit II

1982-1987. Spirit I with 2 pickups, bound top.

1982-1987		$1,500	$2,500

Spirit II XPL

1985-1987. 2 pickup version.

1985-1987		$2,500	$4,500

SR-71

1987-1989. Floyd Rose tremolo, 1 humbucker, 2 single-coil pickups, various colors, Wayne Charvel designed.

1987-1989		$2,000	$3,800

Star

1992. Star logo on headstock, star position markers, single sharp cutaway flat-top, sunburst.

1991-1992		$1,500	$2,500

Starburst Standard/Flame

1992-1994. Single-cut acoustic/electric, star inlays, figured maple back and sides.

1992-1994		$2,000	$3,800

Style O

1902-1925. Acoustic archtop, oval sound hole, bound top, neck and headstock, various colors.

1902-1906	Paddle headstock	$7,000	$8,500
1902-1906	Paddle headstock, fancy	$8,500	$10,500
1906-1908	Slotted headstock	$8,500	$10,500
1908-1913	Solid headstock	$8,500	$10,500
1914-1921	Scroll variation	$8,500	$10,500
1922-1924	Loar era	$10,000	$12,500
1925	Scroll, truss rod	$9,000	$11,500

Style O-1

1902. Acoustic archtop, celluloid binding.

1902		$6,500	$10,000

Style O-2

1902. Acoustic archtop, pearl/ebony binding.

1902		$7,000	$12,000

Style O-3

1902. Acoustic archtop, green/white binding.

1902		$7,000	$12,000

Style R Harp Guitar

1902-1907. Acoustic 6-string, with 6 sub-bass strings, walnut back and sides, bound sound hole.

1902-1907		$9,000	$15,000

Style R-1 Harp Guitar

1902. Style R with fancier pearl and ivory rope pattern binding.

1902		$9,000	$15,000

Style U Harp Guitar

1902-1939. Acoustic 6-string, with 10 or 12 sub-bass strings, walnut (until about '07) or birch back and sides, bound sound hole, black.

1902-1939		$9,500	$15,000

Style U-1 Harp Guitar

1902-1907, 1915, 1917. Slightly fancier Style U.

1902-1917		$10,000	$15,000

Super 300

1948-1955. Acoustic archtop, non-cut, bound body, neck and headstock, sunburst.

1948-1955		$4,000	$7,500

Super 300 C

1954-1958. Acoustic archtop, rounded cutaway, bound body, neck and headstock, sunburst with natural option.

1954-1958	Sunburst	$5,000	$9,000

Super 400

1935-1941, 1947-1955. Introduced early '35 as Super L-5 Deluxe. Acoustic archtop, non-cut, maple, multi-bound, f-holes, sunburst (see Super 400 N for natural version).

1935	Early, L-5, highly flamed	$19,000	$25,000
1935	Early, L-5, plain	$16,500	$22,000
1935	Late, 400, highly flamed	$17,500	$23,000
1935	Late, 400, plain	$13,000	$17,000
1936-1941	Highly flamed	$14,500	$20,000
1936-1941	Plain	$11,500	$15,000
1947-1949	Highly flamed	$9,000	$12,000
1947-1949	Plain	$7,000	$9,500
1950-1955		$6,500	$8,500

Super 400 N

1940, 1948-1955. Natural finish version of Super 400, highly flamed, non-cut, acoustic archtop.

1940		$19,000	$25,000
1948-1949		$14,500	$20,000
1950-1955		$11,500	$15,000

Super 400 P (Premier)

1939-1941. Acoustic archtop, single rounded cutaway, '39 model 'board rests on top, sunburst finish.

1939-1941		$23,500	$30,000

Super 400 PN (Premier Natural)

1939-1940. Rounded cutaway, '39 'board rests on top, natural finish.

1939-1940		$33,500	$45,000

MODEL YEAR	FEATURES	EXC. COND. LOW	HIGH

Super 400 C

1948-1982. Introduced as Super 400 Premier, acoustic archtop, single-cut, sunburst finish (natural is called Super 400 CN).

1948-1949		$15,500	$20,500
1950-1959		$15,000	$20,000
1960-1964		$14,000	$18,500
1965		$9,500	$12,500
1966-1969		$8,000	$10,500
1970-1982		$6,200	$8,000

Super 400 CN

1950-1987. Natural finish version of Super 400 C.

1950-1959		$16,500	$21,500
1960-1964		$14,500	$20,000
1965		$13,500	$17,500
1966-1969		$12,000	$15,500

Super 400 CES

1951-2018. Electric version of Super 400 C, archtop, single-cut (round '51-'60 and '69-present, pointed '60-'69), 2 pickups (P-90s '51-'54, Alnico Vs '54-'57, humbuckers '57 on), sunburst (natural version called Super 400 CESN), now part of Gibson's Historic Collection.

1951-1953	P-90s	$20,000	$25,000
1954-1957	Alnico Vs	$20,000	$25,000
1957-1960	PAFs	$28,500	$37,000
1961-1962	PAFs, sharp cut	$25,000	$32,500
1963-1964	Pat #	$19,000	$25,000
1965		$13,000	$17,000
1966-1969		$11,500	$15,000
1970-1979		$9,500	$12,500
1980-2018		$9,500	$12,500

Super 400 CESN

1952-2016. Natural version of Super 400 CES, now part of Gibson's Historic Collection.

1952-1953	P-90s	$20,500	$26,000
1954-1956	Alnico Vs	$20,500	$26,000
1957-1960	PAFs	$28,500	$37,000
1961-1962	PAFs, sharp cut	$25,000	$35,000
1963-1964	Pat #	$19,000	$25,000
1965		$13,000	$17,000
1966-1969		$11,500	$15,000
1970-1979		$9,500	$12,500
1980-2016		$9,500	$12,500

Super 400 CESN Thin

2003. Custom Shop, thinner body, natural finish.

2003		$8,000	$12,000

Super 400 (Custom Shop)

2009. Non-cutaway, natural.

2009		$8,000	$12,000

'39 Super 400 Historic

1993-1997. Custom Shop Historic Collection, reissue of non-cut '39 version, various colors.

1993-1997		$8,000	$12,000

Super 4000 Chet Atkins

2000. Limited run of 25. AAA Sitka spruce carved top, highly figured carved maple back, antique natural and faded cherry sunburst.

2000		$15,000	$20,000

Super Jumbo 100

1939-1943. Jumbo flat-top, mahogany back and sides, bound body and neck, sunburst, reintroduced as J-100 with different specs in '84.

1939-1941	Early '41	$25,000	$40,000
1941-1943	Late '41	$25,000	$35,000

Super Jumbo/Super Jumbo 200

1938-1942. Initially called Super Jumbo in '38 and named Super Jumbo 200 in '39. Name then changed to J-200 (see that listing) by '47 (with maple back and sides) and SJ-200 by the '50s. Named for super large jumbo 16 7/8" flat-top body, double braced with rosewood back and sides, sunburst finish.

1938-1940		$125,000	$175,000
1941-1942		$115,000	$145,000

Super V BJB

1978-1983. A Super V CES but with a single floating pickup.

1978-1983		$4,500	$7,500

Super V CES

1978-1993. Archtop, L-5 with a Super 400 neck, 2 humbucker pickups, natural or sunburst.

1978-1993		$4,500	$7,500

Tal Farlow

1962-1971, 1993-2018. Full body, single-cut archtop, 2 humbuckers, triple-bound top, reintroduced '93 as part of Gibson's Historic Collection.

1962-1964	Viceroy Brown	$8,000	$12,000
1965	Viceroy Brown	$7,800	$10,000
1966-1971	Viceroy Brown	$7,200	$9,500
1993-2018	Various colors	$4,200	$6,500

TG-0

1927-1933, 1960-1974. Acoustic tenor based on L-0, mahogany body, light amber.

1927-1933		$3,000	$4,500
1960-1964		$1,500	$2,500
1965		$1,200	$1,800
1966-1969		$1,200	$1,800
1970-1974		$1,000	$1,500

TG-00

1932-1943. Tenor flat-top based on L-00.

1932-1943		$3,000	$4,500

TG-1/L-1 Tenor/L-4 Tenor

1927-1937. Acoustic flat-top, tenor or plectrum guitar based on L-1, mahogany back and sides, bound body, sunburst.

1927-1937		$3,000	$4,500
1928-1932	Rare Lucas/ Johnson body	$5,000	$7,500

TG-2/L-2 Tenor

1929-1930. Acoustic tenor guitar.

1929-1930		$4,000	$7,500

TG-7

1934-1940. Tenor based on the L-7, sunburst.

1934-1940		$3,500	$7,500

TG-25/TG-25 N

1962-1970. Acoustic flat-top, tenor guitar based on B-25, mahogany back and sides, sunburst or natural (25 N).

1962-1964		$1,500	$2,500
1965		$1,500	$2,500
1966-1969		$1,500	$2,500
1970		$1,200	$2,000

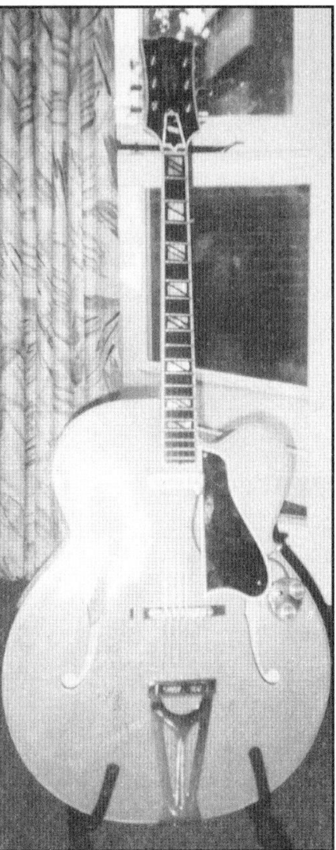

1969 Gibson Super 400 CN
Loek Van Schooten

Gibson Super 400 CES

GUITARS

GUITARS

Giffin T Deluxe

Gitane DG-255

MODEL YEAR	FEATURES	EXC. COND. LOW	HIGH

TG-50

1934-1940, 1947-1961, 1963. Acoustic archtop, tenor guitar based on L-50, mahogany back and sides, sunburst.

1934-1940		$3,000	$4,500
1947-1963		$3,000	$4,500

Traveling Songwriter EC

2005-2015. Solid spruce top, solid mahogany sides and back, soft cutaway, on-board electronics and EQ.

2005-2015		$1,800	$2,500

Trini Lopez Standard

1964-1970. Double rounded cutaway, thinline archtop, 2 humbuckers, tune-o-matic bridge, trapeze tailpiece, single-bound, cherry, Sparkling Burgundy and Pelham Blue finishes.

1964	Cherry	$10,000	$13,000
1965	Cherry	$9,000	$12,000
1965	Pelham Blue	$13,500	$18,000
1965	Sparkling Burgundy	$10,000	$13,000
1966	Pelham Blue	$11,000	$14,500
1966-1970	Cherry	$8,000	$10,500
1966-1970	Sparkling Burgundy	$8,000	$10,500

Trini Lopez Standard (Custom Shop)

2010-2011. Custom Shop reissue of thinline Trini Lopez Standard, diamond f-holes, 6-on-a-side tuners, trapeze tailpiece, Certificate of Authenticity, cherry red.

2010-2011		$4,500	$6,000

Trini Lopez Deluxe

1964-1970. Double pointed cutaway archtop, 2 humbuckers, triple-bound, sunburst.

1964		$7,800	$10,000
1965		$7,200	$9,500
1966-1970		$6,800	$9,000

U-2

1987-1989. Double-cut, 1 humbucker and 2 single-coil pickups, ebony or red, renamed Mach II in '90-'91.

1987-1991		$1,800	$2,500

U-2 Showcase Edition

1988. November 1988 Guitar of the Month series, 250 made.

1988		$2,000	$3,000

US-1/US-3

1986-1991. Double-cut maple top with mahogany back, 3 humbucker pickups (US-1), or 3 P-90s (US-3), standard production and Custom Shop.

1986-1991		$1,500	$2,200

Vegas Standard

2006-2007. Flat-top semi-hollowbody thinline, slim neck, 2 humbuckers, f-holes, split diamond inlays.

2006-2007		$2,500	$3,500

Vegas High Roller

2006-2007. Upgraded version, AAA maple top, gold hardware and frets, block inlays.

2006-2007		$3,500	$4,800

Victory MV II (MV 2)

1981-1984. Asymetrical double-cut with long horn, 3-way slider, maple body and neck, rosewood 'board, 2 pickups.

1981-1984		$1,500	$2,200

Victory MV X (MV 10)

1981-1984. 3 humbuckers, 5-way switch, various colors.

1981-1984		$1,800	$2,500

WRC

1987-1988. Designed for Gibson by Wayne R. Charvel (WRC), earlier models had Kahler trem, later Floyd Rose, offered in red, black or white.

1987-1988		$1,500	$2,200

XPL Custom

1985-1986. Explorer-like shape, exposed humbuckers, locking tremolo, bound maple top, sunburst or white.

1985-1986		$1,500	$2,200

Y2K Dwight Yoakam Signature

1999-2000. Limited run of 200, small body jumbo, spruce top, highly figured maple sides and back, 2-piece flamed maple neck, double 'guard, gloss natural finish.

1999-2000		$2,500	$3,500

Zakk Wylde ZV Buzzsaw

2008. Custom Shop Inspired By series, limited run of 50, Flying V wings with SG horns, 2 humbuckers.

2008		$5,500	$7,500

Gibson Baldwin

2005-ca. 2013. Entry-level electric and acoustic guitars, basses, amps and accessories made in China for discount store market and sold under the Signature, Maestro, Echelon, and Genesis brand names. Models include Les Paul and SG copies. Guitars have Music - Gibson logo on neckplate and brand logo on headstock.

Giffin

1977-1988, 1997-present. Professional and premium grade, production/custom, hollow-, semi-hollow-, and solidbody guitars built by luthier Roger Giffin in West San Fernando Valley, California. For '77-'88, Giffin's shop was in London. From '88 to '93, he worked for the Gibson Custom Shop in California as a Master Luthier. In '97, Giffin set up shop in Sweden for a year, moving back to California in the Spring of '98. He also built small numbers of instruments during '67-'76 and '94-'96 (when he had a repair business).

Gigliotti

2000-present. Premium grade, production/custom, electric guitars with a metal plate top and tone chambers and designed by Patrick Gigliotti in Tacoma, Washington.

Gila Eban Guitars

Premium grade, custom, classical guitars built by luthier Gila Eban in Riverside, Connecticut, starting in 1979.

Gilbert Guitars

1965-present. Custom classical guitars by luthiers John Gilbert and William Gilbert in Paso Robles, California. Son William has handled all production since '91. John died early 2012.

MODEL YEAR	FEATURES	EXC. COND. LOW	HIGH

Gilchrist

1977-present. Currently known more for his mandolins, luthier Steve Gilchrist, of Warrnambool, Australia, has also built premium and presentation grade, custom, guitars.

Acoustic Archtop

1990s-present. Very limited production.

1990s-2024		$20,000	$25,000

Gilet Guitars

1976-present. Luthier Gerard Gilet builds production/custom, premium grade, acoustic, classical, flamenco, and wooden bodied resonator guitars in Botany, Sydney, New South Wales, Australia. He also builds lap steels.

Girl Brand Guitars

1996-2012. Premium-grade, production/custom, guitars built by luthier Chris Larsen in Tucson, Arizona. Larson now builds under the Larsen Guitar Mfg. name.

Gitane

2003-present. Intermediate and professional grade, production, classic Selmer-Maccaferri style jazz guitars made in China for Saga.

Gittler

1974-ca.1985. Minimalistic electric guitar designed by Allan Gittler, consisting basically of a thin rod with frets welded to it. A total of 560 were built, with Gittler making the first 60 in the U.S. from '74 to the early '80s. The remainder were made around '85 in Israel by the Astron corporation under a licensing agreement. Three Gittler basses were also built. Gittler emigrated to Israel in the early '80s and changed his name to Avraham Bar Rashi. He died in 2002. A U.S.-made Gittler is the only musical instrument in the Museum of Modern Art in New York.

Metal Skeleton

1971-1982		$3,000	$5,000
1982-1999		$2,500	$4,500

Giulietti

1962-1965. The Giulietti Accordion Company, New York, offered guitars and amps in the '60s.

GJ2

Gold Jackson Enterprises LLC, a partnership between luthier Grover Jackson and Jon Gold, established 2012, builds professional and premium grade, production/custom, solidbody electric guitars in Laguna Hills, California.

Glendale

2004-present. Professional grade, production/custom, solidbody guitars built by luthier Dale Clark in Arlington, Texas.

GLF

1991-1997. Solidbody electric guitars built by luthier Kevin Smith in Minnesota. In '97 he started building his ToneSmith line of guitars.

Glick Guitars

Premium grade, production/custom, acoustic and electric archtop, and acoustic guitars built in Santa Barbara, California by luthier Mike Glick, starting in '96.

Global

Late-1960s-1970s. Budget copy models, not unlike Teisco, imported from Asia for the student market. They also offered amps.

Electric Solidbody

Late-1960s-1970s.

1968		$250	$400

GMP

1990-2005. Professional and premium grade solidbody electric guitars built by GM Precision Products, Inc. of San Dimas, California. Original owners were Gary and Cameron Moline, Dave Pearson and Glenn Matjezel. Many guitars featured fancy tops or custom graphics. They also made basses. Overall production is estimated at 1120 guitars and basses. GMP reopened in '10 under new ownership (see following).

GMP (Genuine Musical Products)

2010-present. The GMP brand was acquired by Dan and Kim Lawrence in '08. Since '10, Dan along with fellow luthiers Glenn Matjezel and William Stempke build professional and premium grade, production/custom, electric guitars in San Dimas, California. They also build basses.

GMW

1998-present. Professional grade, production/custom, solidbody guitars from Lee Garver's GMW Guitarworks of Glendora, California.

Godin

1987-present. Intermediate and professional grade, production, solidbody electrics and nylon and steel string acoustic/electrics from luthier Robert Godin. They also build basses and mandolins. Necks and bodies are made in La Patrie, Quebec with final assembly in Berlin, New Hampshire. Godin is also involved in the Seagull, Norman, Richmond, Art & Lutherie, and Patrick & Simon brand of guitars. SA on Godin models stands for Synth Access.

5th Avenue Kingpin

2008-present. Full-size non-cut electric archtop, 1 or 2 P-90 pickups, plain or highly flamed top, premium price for highly flamed.

2008-2024		$900	$1,300

Glendale

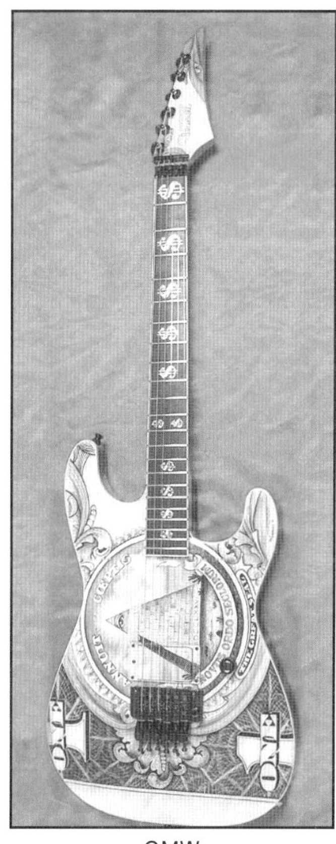

GMW

GUITARS

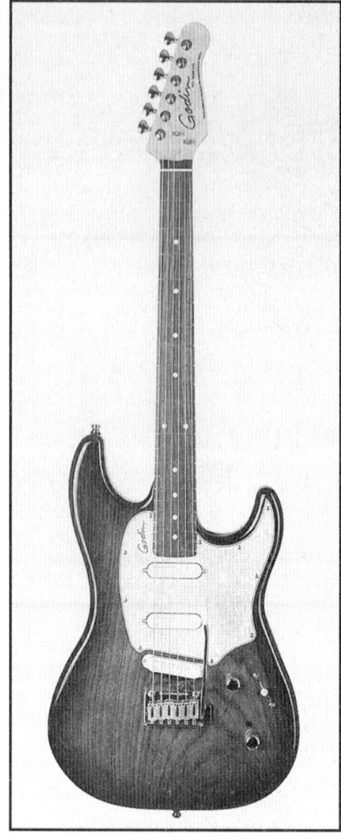
Godin Passion RG-3

Gold Tone Mastertone PBR-D

MODEL YEAR	FEATURES	EXC. COND. LOW	HIGH

5th Avenue Uptown

2012-present. Archtop cutaway with Bigsby, f-holes, Canadian wild cherry top, back and sides, silver leaf maple neck, various colors.

2012-2024		$950	$1,500

A Series

1990s-present. Electric-acoustic nylon strings, single-cut, chambered body, 6-, 11-, 12-string, various wood and colors.

1990s-2024	A12, 12-string	$1,000	$1,500
1990s-2024	A6, 6-string	$700	$1,000
2000-2017	A11 Glissentar, 11-string	$1,000	$1,500

Acousticaster (6)

1987-2020. Thin line single-cut chambered maple body, acoustic/electric, maple neck, 6-on-a-side tuners, spruce top.

1987-2020		$700	$1,000

Acousticaster 6 Deluxe

1994-2008. Acousticaster 6 with mahogany body.

1994-2008		$800	$1,200

Artisan ST I/ST I

1992-1998. Offset double-cut solidbody, birdseye maple top, 3 pickups.

1992-1998		$900	$1,200

Flat Five X

2002-2004. Single-cut, semi-hollow with f-holes, 3-way pickup system (magnetic to transducer).

2002-2004		$1,000	$1,500

Freeway Classic/Freeway Classic SA

2004-2015. Offset double-cut solidbody, birdseye maple top on translucent finishes, hum-single-hum pickups.

2004-2015		$700	$1,000

G-1000/G-2000/G-3000

1993-1996. Offset double-cut solidbody, extra-large bass horn, various pickup options.

1993-1996		$450	$550

Jeff Cook Signature

1994-1995. Quilted maple top, light maple back, 2 twin rail and 1 humbucker pickups.

1994-1995		$700	$900

L.R. Baggs Signature

1990s. Single-cut chambered thinline electric, spruce top, mahogany body, EQ.

1990s		$700	$900

LG/LGT

1995-2011. Single-cut carved slab mahogany body, 2 Tetrad Combo pickups ('95-'97) or 2 Duncan SP-90 pickups ('98-present), various colors, satin lacquer finish. LGT with tremolo.

1995-2011		$500	$700

LGX/LGXT/LGX-SA

1996-2018. Single-cut maple-top carved solidbody, 2 Duncan humbuckers, various quality tops offered. LGXT with tremolo.

1996-2018	Standard top	$900	$1,200
1997-2018	SA synth access	$1,200	$1,500
1998-2018	AA top	$1,200	$1,800
1998-2018	AAA top	$1,500	$1,800

MODEL YEAR	FEATURES	EXC. COND. LOW	HIGH

Montreal Series

2004-present. Chambered body carved from solid mahogany, f-holes, 2 humbuckers, saddle transducer, stereo mixing output.

2004-2024		$1,000	$1,500

Multiac Series

1994-present. Single-cut, thinline electric with solid spruce top, RMC Sensor System electronics, available in either nylon string or steel string versions, built-in EQ, program up/down buttons.

1994-2024	Various models	$800	$2,000

Passion RG-3

2011-2022. Double-cut, 3 single-coil pickups, swamp ash body, rosewood neck (RN) or maple (MN), Indigo Burst finish with artic white pearloid 'guard.

2011-2022		$1,500	$2,200

Radiator

1999-2013. Single-cut, dual pickup, pearloid top, dot markers.

1999-2013		$400	$600

Redline Series

2007-2015. Maple body and neck, rosewood 'board, Redline 1 has 1 pickup, 2 and 3 have 2 pickups (3 has Floyd Rose), various colors.

2007-2011	Redline 1	$550	$900
2008-2015	Redline 2 & 3	$600	$900

SD Series

1990s-2012. Performance series, figured maple veneer top, maple neck, maple or rosewood 'board, various colors.

1990-2012	SD22, SD24	$450	$700

Solidac - Two Voice

2000-2009. Single-cut, 2-voice technology for electric or acoustic sound.

2000-2009		$500	$750

TC Signature

1987-1999. Single-cut, quilted maple top, 2 Tetrad Combo pickups.

1987-1999		$900	$1,200

Velocity

2007-2011. Offset double-cut, hum/single/single.

2007-2011		$800	$1,200

Gold Tone

1993-present. Wayne and Robyn Rogers build their intermediate and professional grade, production/custom guitars and basses in Titusville, Florida. They also build lap steels, mandolins, ukuleles, banjos and banjitars.

Goldbug Guitars

1997-present. Presentation grade, production/custom, acoustic and electric guitars built by luthier Sandy Winters in Delavan, Wisconsin.

Golden Hawaiian

1920s-1930s. Private branded lap guitar most likely made by one of the many Chicago makers for a small retailer, publisher, cataloger, or teaching studio.

MODEL YEAR	FEATURES	EXC. COND. LOW	HIGH

Guitars

1920-1930s	Various models	$500	$1,000

Goldentone

1960s. Guitars made by Ibanez most likely in the mid to late '60s. Often have a stylized I (for Ibanez) on the tailpiece or an Ibanez logo on the headstock.

Goldon

German manufacturer of high-quality archtops and other guitars before and shortly after WW II. After the war, they were located in East Germany and by the late 1940s were only making musical toys.

Goodall

1972-present. Premium grade, custom flat-tops and nylon-strings, built by luthier James Goodall originally in California and, since '92, in Kailua-Kona, Hawaii.

Classical

1986. Brazilian and cedar.

1986	BC425	$6,000	$8,500

Concert Jumbo

1998-present. Various woods.

2007-2024	Red cedar/ Indian rw	$3,500	$4,500
2007-2024	Sitka/figured Koa	$3,500	$4,500

Concert Jumbo Cutaway

2004-2018. Rosewood.

2004-2018		$4,000	$5,500

Jumbo KJ

1995-2011. Sitka, Koa.

1995-2011		$4,000	$5,500

RS Rosewood Standard

1989-1997. Indian rosewood back and sides.

1989-1997		$4,000	$5,500

Standard

1980s-present. Jumbo-style with wide waist, mahogany back and sides, Sitka spruce top.

1980s-2024		$3,000	$4,500

Goodman Guitars

1975-present. Premium grade, custom/production, archtop, flat-top, classical, and electric guitars built by luthier Brad Goodman in Brewster, New York. He also builds mandolins.

Goran Custom Guitars

1998-present. Luthier Goran Djuric builds his professional and premium grade, custom, electric guitars in Belgrade, Serbia. He also builds effects.

Gordon-Smith

1979-present. Intermediate and professional grade, production/custom, semi-hollow and solidbody guitars built by luthier John Smith in Partington, England.

Gower

1955-1960s. Built in Nashville by Jay Gower, later joined by his son Randy. Gower is also associated with Billy Grammer and Grammer guitars.

G-55-2 Flat-Top

1955-1968. Square shoulder-style flat-top, triple abalone rosette, abalone fretboard trim, dot markers, natural.

1955-1968		$1,200	$2,000

G-65 Flat-Top

1955-1968. Square shoulder-style flat-top, lower belly bridge with pearl dots on bridge, dot markers, sunburst.

1955-1968		$1,200	$1,800

G-100 Flat-Top

1955-1968	Brazilian rosewood	$1,800	$2,800

Goya

1952-1996. Brand initially used by Hershman Musical Instrument Company of New York City, New York, in mid-'50s for acoustic guitars made in Sweden by Levin, particularly known for its classicals. From '58 to '61 they imported Hagstrom- and Galanti-made electrics labeled as Goya; in '62 they offered electrics made by Valco. In '67 they again offered electrics, this time made by Zero Sette in Castelfidardo, Italy. By '63 the company had become the Goya Musical Instrument Corporation, marketing primarily Goya acoustics. Goya was purchased by Avnet, Inc., prior to '66, when Avnet purchased Guild Guitars. In '69, Goya was purchased by Kustom which offered the instruments until '71. Probably some '70s guitars were made in Japan. The brand name was purchased by C.F. Martin in '76, with Japanese-made acoustic guitars, solidbody electric guitars and basses, banjos and mandolins imported in around '78 and continuing into the '90s.

Classical

1955-1960s. Various models.

1955-1960s	G Series	$300	$500
1970s-80s	Japan	$450	$600

Flamenco

1955-1960s. Various models.

1955-1960s	FL Series	$300	$500

Folk

1950s-1980s. Various models.

1955-1960s	F Series	$300	$500

Model 80/Model 90

1959-1962. Single-cut body, replaceable modular pickup assembly, sparkle top.

1959-1962		$800	$1,200

Panther S-3

1967-1968. Double-cut solidbody, 3 pickups, Panther S-3 Goya logo, volume and tone knobs with 6 upper bass bout switches, bolt-on neck.

1967-1968		$800	$1,200

Rangemaster

1967-1968. Wide variety of models.

1967-1968		$800	$1,500

Steel

1955-1960s. Various models.

1955-1960s	M and S Series	$200	$400

Gordon-Smith Gatsby

Goya G-13

Imaged by Heritage Auctions, HA.com

GUITARS

1966 Grammer
Bill Lawlor

1982 Greco Silverburst
Mike Greco

MODEL YEAR	FEATURES	EXC. COND. LOW	HIGH

Graf

See listing under Oskar Graf Guitars.

Grammer

1965-1971. Acoustic guitars built in Nashville. Founded by country guitarist Bill Grammer, music store owner Clyde Reid and luthier J.W. Gower (who also built his own line). Grammer sold the company to Ampeg in '68 who sold it again in '71, but it quickly ceased business. Originally the Grammer headstock logo had an upper-case G, Ampeg-made instruments have a lower-case one.

G-10

1965-1970. Solid Brazilian rosewood back and sides, solid spruce top, large crown-shaped bridge, pearl dot markers, natural.

1965-1967	Grammer era	$2,500	$3,500
1968-1970	Ampeg era	$1,800	$2,500

G-20

1965-1970. Flamed maple, natural.

1965-1967	Grammer era	$2,000	$3,000
1968-1970	Ampeg era	$1,800	$2,800

G-30

1965-1970. Ribbon mahogany, natural.

1965-1967	Grammer era	$2,000	$3,000
1968-1970	Ampeg era	$1,800	$2,800

G-50

1965-1970. Top-of-the-line Grammer, Brazilian rosewood back and sides, Adirondack spruce top.

1965-1967	Grammer era	$3,000	$4,000
1968-1970	Ampeg era	$3,000	$4,000

S-30

1965-1970. Solid spruce top, solid ribbon mahogany back and sides.

1965-1967	Grammer era	$1,800	$2,500
1968-1970	Ampeg era	$1,500	$2,200

Granada

Late 1960s-1980s. Japanese-made acoustic, electric solid, semi-hollow and hollowbody guitars, many copies of classic American models. They also offered basses.

Acoustic

1970-1979. Import from Japan, various copy models.

1970-1979		$200	$500

Electric

1970-1979. Import from Japan, various copy models.

1970-1979		$300	$450

Granata Guitars

1989-present. Luthier Peter Granata builds his professional grade, custom, flat-top and resonator guitars in Oak Ridge, New Jersey.

Graveel

Production/custom, solidbody guitars built by luthier Dean Graveel in Indianapolis, Indiana.

Grazioso

1950s. Grazioso was a brand name used by Selmer in England on instruments made in Czechoslovakia. They replaced the brand with their Futurama line of guitars.

GRD

1978-1982. High-end acoustic and electric guitars produced in Charles Fox's Guitar Research & Design Center in Vermont. GRD introduced the original thin-line acoustic-electric guitar to the world at the '78 Winter NAMM show.

Great Divide Guitars

2009-2011. Budget and intermediate grade, production, flat-top guitars imported from China, designed by luthier Tom Bedell, Dan Mills and Sophia Yang. They also offer Bedell Guitars.

Greco

1960s-present. Brand name used in Japan and owned by Kanda Shokai. Fuji Gen Gakki, maker of many Hoshino/Ibanez guitars, also made many Greco models during the '70s; thus often Greco guitars are similar to Ibanez. During the '70s the company sold many high-quality copies of American designs, though by '75 they offered many weird-shaped original designs, including the Iceman and carved people shapes. By the late-'70s they were offering neck-through-body guitars. Currently offering solidbody, hollowbody and acoustic guitars and basses, including models licensed by Zemaitis.

Green, Aaron

1990-present. Premium and presentation grade, custom, classical and flamenco guitars built by luthier Aaron Green in Waltham, Massachusetts.

Greene & Campbell

2002-2005. Luthier Dean Campbell built his intermediate and professional grade, production/custom, solidbody guitars in Westwood, Massachusetts. Founding partner Jeffrey Greene left the company in '04; Greene earlier built guitars under his own name. In '05, Campbell changed the name to Campbell American Guitars.

Greene, Jeffrey

2000-2002. Professional grade, production/custom, electric solidbody guitars built by luthier Jeffrey Greene in West Kingston, Rhode Island. He went to work with Dean Campbell building the Greene & Campbell line of guitars.

Greenfield Guitars

1996-present. Luthier Michael Greenfield builds his production/custom, presentation grade, acoustic steel string, concert classical and archtop guitars in Montreal, Quebec.

Gretsch

1883-present. Currently Gretsch offers intermediate, professional, and premium grade, production, acoustic, solidbody, hollowbody, double neck, resonator and Hawaiian guitars. They also offer basses, amps and lap steels. In 2012 they again started offering

MODEL YEAR	FEATURES	EXC. COND. LOW	HIGH

mandolins, ukuleles, and banjos.

Previous brands included Gretsch, Rex, 20th Century, Recording King (for Montgomery Ward), Dorado (Japanese imports). Founded by Friedrich Gretsch in Brooklyn, New York, making drums, banjos, tambourines, and toy instruments which were sold to large distributors including C. Bruno and Wurlitzer. Upon early death of Friedrich, son Fred Gretsch, Sr. took over business at age 15. By the turn of the century the company was also making mandolins. In the '20s, they were distributing Rex and 20th Century brands, some made by Gretsch, some by others such as Kay. Charles "Duke" Kramer joined Gretsch in '35. In '40 Gretsch purchased Bacon & Day banjos. Fred Gretsch, Sr. retired in '42 and was replaced by sons Fred, Jr., and Bill. Fred departs for Navy and Bill runs company until his death in '48, when Fred resumes control. After the war the decision was made to promote the Gretsch brand rather than selling to distributors, though some jobbing continues. Kramer becomes Chicago branch manager in '48. Gretsch's most successful innovations occurred during the Jimmie Webster era in the mid-50s. This would include straying from traditional sunburst finishes, marketing humbucking pickups, and employing a bridge that could be precisely intoned before Gibson or Fender.

The change from single-cut to double-cut bodies beginning in 1961 significantly lowers the value of most models.

In '67 Baldwin of Cincinnati bought Gretsch. During '70-'72 the factory relocated from Brooklyn to Booneville, Arkansas and company headquarters are moved to Cincinnati. A '72 factory fire drastically reduced production for next two years. In '78 Baldwin bought Kustom amps and sold Gretsch to Kustom's Charlie Roy, and headquarters are moved to Chanute, Kansas. Duke Kramer retired in '80. Guitar production ends '80-'81. Ca. '83 ownership reverted back to Baldwin and Kramer was asked to arrange the sale of the company. In '84 Fred Gretsch III was contacted and in '85 Gretsch guitars came back to the Gretsch family and Fred Gretsch Enterprises, Ltd (FGE). Initial Gretsch Enterprise models were imports made by Japan's Terada Company. In '95, some U.S.-made models were introduced. In 2003, Gretsch granted Fender the rights to develop, produce, market, and distribute Gretsch guitars worldwide, including development of new products.

Binding rot can be a problem on 1950s models and prices shown are for fully original, unrestored bindings.

12-String Electric Archtop (6075/6076)

1967-1972. 16" double-cut, 2 Super Tron pickups, 17" body option available, sunburst (6075) or natural (6076).

1967-1972		$2,500	$4,500

12-String Flat-Top (6020)

1969-1972. 15 1/5" body, mahogany back and sides, spruce top, slotted headstock, dot markers.

1969-1972		$1,500	$3,000

Anniversary (6124/6125)

1958-1972, 1993-1999. Single-cut hollow body archtop, 1 pickup (Filtron '58-'60, Hi-Lo Tron '61 on), bound body, named for Gretsch's 75th anniversary. 6125 is 2-tone green with 2-tone tan an option, 6124 sunburst. Model numbers were revived in '90s.

1958-1959	Green 2-tone	$3,000	$5,000
1958-1959	Sunburst	$3,000	$5,000
1960-1961	Green 2-tone or tan	$3,000	$3,500
1960-1961	Sunburst	$3,000	$3,500
1962-1964	Green 2-tone or tan	$2,500	$3,500
1962-1964	Sunburst	$2,500	$3,500
1965-1966	Various colors	$1,750	$2,250
1967-1969	Various colors	$1,500	$2,000
1970-1972	Various colors	$1,375	$1,750

Anniversary Tenor (6124)

1958-1971. Gretsch offered many models with the 4-string tenor option and also made small batches of tenors, with the same colors and pickups as standard models.

1958-1971		$1,500	$2,000

Anniversary Reissue (6124/6125)

1993-1999. 1 pickup Anniversary reissue, 6124 in sunburst, 6125 2-tone green.

1993-1999		$1,750	$2,500

Anniversary Reissue (6117/6118)

1993-present. 2 pickup like Double Anniversary, 6118 in 2-tone green with (T) or without Bigsby, 6117 is sunburst.

1993-2015	6117	$1,750	$2,500
1993-2024	6118	$1,750	$2,500

120th Anniversary (6118T-120)

2003. Limited Edition, single-cut hollow body electric, maple body and neck, rosewood 'board, 2 pickups, 2-tone bamboo yellow/copper finish.

2003		$2,000	$3,500

Astro-Jet (6126)

1965-1967. Solid body electric, double-cut, 2 pickups, vibrato, 4/2 tuner arrangement, red top with black back and sides.

1965-1967		$2,000	$2,500

Atkins Axe (7685/7686)

1976-1980. Solid body electric, pointed single-cut, 2 pickups, ebony stain (7685) or red rosewood stain (7686), called the Super Axe with added on-board effects.

1976-1980		$2,000	$3,500

Atkins Super Axe (7680/7681)

1976-1981. Pointed single-cut solid body with built-in phaser and sustain, five knobs, three switches, Red Rosewood (7680) or Ebony (7681) stains.

1976-1981		$2,500	$4,000

Bikini (6023/6024/6025)

1961-1962. Solid body electric, separate 6-string and bass neck-body units that slide into 1 of 3 body butterflies - 1 for the 6-string only (6023), 1 for bass only (6024), 1 for double neck (6 and bass - 6025). Components could be purchased separately.

1961-1962	6023/6024, single	$1,500	$2,000
1961-1962	6025, double	$3,500	$4,500

Greenfield Andy McKee Model

1961 Gretsch Bikini (6025)

Randy Barnett

GUITARS

Gretsch Brian Setzer Hot Rod (6120SHx)

Gretsch Eddie Cochran Signature Hollow Body (6120)

MODEL YEAR	FEATURES	EXC. COND. LOW	HIGH

Billy-Bo Jupiter Thunderbird (6199)

2005-present. Billy Gibbons and Bo Diddley influenced, chambered mahogany body, laminate maple top, 2 pickups.

2005-2024		$2,000	$3,500

Black Falcon (6136BK/TBK/DSBK)

1992-1997, 2003-2015. Black version of Falcon, single-cut, 2.75" body, oversize f-holes, G tailpiece, DSBK with DynaSonic pickups replaces Filter'Tron BK in '06. Had the Limited Edition 1955 designation for '96-'97. Bigsby-equipped TBK offered '04-present.

1992-2015		$2,250	$3,500

Black Falcon (7594BK)

1992-1998. Black version of G7594 Falcon, double-cut, 2" thick body, Bigsby.

1992-1998		$2,250	$3,500

Black Falcon I (7593BK)

1993-1998, 2003-2005. G63136BK with Bigsby and standard f-holes. Came back in '03 as Black Falcon I with wire handle Gretsch Bigsby tailpiece.

1993-1998		$2,250	$3,500

Black Hawk (6100/6101)

1967-1972. Hollow body archtop, double-cut, 2 pickups, G tailpiece or Bigsby vibrato, bound body and neck, sunburst (6100) or black (6101).

1967-1972	6100, sunburst	$2,000	$3,500
1967-1972	6101, black	$2,000	$3,500

Black Penguin (6134B)

2003-2015. Jet black version.

2003-2015		$2,500	$4,000

Blue Penguin (6134CSRSBP)

2010. Custom Shop Masterbuilt, blue finish.

2010		$7,000	$10,000

Bo Diddley (1810/5810)

2000-2015. Korean-made version.

2000-2015		$500	$900

Bo Diddley (6138)

1999-present. Reproduction of rectangle-shaped, semi-hollow guitar originally made for Diddley by Gretsch, Firebird Red.

1999-2024		$2,000	$3,500

Broadkaster (Hollow Body)

1975-1980. Double-cut archtop, hollow body, 2 pickups, natural or sunburst. Red available '77-'80.

1975-1977	7603, Bigsby, natural	$1,500	$2,000
1975-1977	7604, Bigsby, sunburst	$1,500	$2,000
1975-1977	7607, G tailpiece, natural	$1,500	$2,000
1975-1977	7608, G tailpiece, sunburst	$1,500	$2,000
1977-1980	7609, red	$1,500	$2,000

Broadkaster (Solid Body)

1975-1979. Double-cut, maple body, 2 pickups, bolt-on neck, natural (7600) or sunburst (7601).

1975-1979	7600 and 7601	$1,250	$2,000

BST 1000 Beast

1979-1980. Single-cut solid body, bolt-on neck, mahogany body, available with 1 pickup in walnut stain (8210) or red stain (8216) or 2 pickups in walnut (7617, 8215, 8217) or red stain (8211).

1979-1980		$1,250	$2,000

BST 2000 Beast

1979. Symmetrical double-cut solid body of mahogany, 2 humbucking pickups, bolt-on neck, walnut stain (7620 or 8220) or red stain (8221).

1979		$1,250	$2,000

BST 5000 Beast

1979-1980. Asymmetrical double-cut solid body, neck-thru, walnut and maple construction, 2 humbucker pickups, stud tailpiece, natural walnut/maple (8250).

1979-1980		$1,250	$2,000

Burl Ives (6004)

1949-1955. Flat-top acoustic, mahogany back and sides, bound body, natural top (6004).

1949-1955		$1,500	$2,500

Chet Atkins Country Gentleman (6122/7670)

1958-1981. Hollow body, single-cut to late-'62 and double after, 2 pickups, painted f-holes until '72, real after, mahogany finish (6122). Model number changes to 7670 in '71. Guitars made during and after '64 might have replaced body binding which reduces the value shown by about 10% or more.

1958-1959		$7,500	$10,000
1960		$6,500	$9,000
1961		$6,500	$9,000
1962-1963	George Harrison specs	$6,500	$9,000
1964		$3,250	$4,000
1965		$3,250	$4,000
1966-1970		$2,750	$3,500
1971-1981	7670	$2,750	$3,500

Chet Atkins Country Gentleman (6122-1958)

2007-2015. Single-cut reissue of '58.

2007-2015		$2,000	$3,500

Chet Atkins Country Gentleman (6122-1962)

2007-2015. Double-cut reissue of '62, double muffler (mutes) system, Filter'Trons.

2007-2015		$2,000	$3,500

Chet Atkins Hollow Body (6120)

1954-1966, 2007-2015. Archtop electric, single-cut to '61, double after, 2 pickups, vibrato, f-holes (real to '61 and fake after), cactus and cows engraved block inlays '54-early '56, G brand on top '54-'56, orange finish (6120). Renamed Chet Atkins Nashville in '67. Reissued single-cut in '07.

1954-1955	G brand, Western	$20,000	$25,000
1955-1956	Non-engraved, amber red	$15,000	$18,000
1957-1959	No G-brand	$10,000	$15,000
1960-1961	Single-cut	$8,000	$12,500
1961-1966	Double-cut	$4,500	$7,000
2007-2015	Single-cut	$2,000	$2,750

Chet Atkins Nashville (6120/7660)

1967-1980. Replaced Chet Atkins Hollow Body (6120), electric archtop, double-cut, 2 pickups, amber red (orange). Renumbered 7660 in '72, reissued in '90 as the Model 6120 Nashville.

1967-1969	6120	$3,000	$4,000

GUITARS

MODEL YEAR	FEATURES	EXC. COND. LOW	HIGH
1970-1971	6120	$2,250	$3,000
1972-1980	7660	$2,000	$2,500

Chet Atkins Nashville (6120DC)

2007-2016. Double-cut hollow body based on '62 model, gold plated 'guard with Atkin's signature.

2007-2016		$1,750	$3,000

Chet Atkins Hollow Body (6120W-1957)

2007-2009. Western Maple Stain, western block inlays, Bigsby.

2007-2009		$2,250	$3,500

Brian Setzer Black Phoenix (6136-SLBP)

2005-2015. Artist Signature Series, nitro gloss black.

2005-2015		$2,500	$4,000

Brian Setzer Hot Rod (6120SHx)

1999-present. Like SSL, but with only pickup switch and 1 master volume control, various colors.

1999-2024		$2,000	$3,500

Brian Setzer Nashville (6120SSL, etc.)

1993-present. Hollow body electric, double-cut, 2 Alnico PAF Filtertron pickups, based on the classic Gretsch 6120.

1993-2024	Western Orange	$2,000	$4,000

Brian Setzer Tribute (6120SSC)

2009. Made in Fender Custom Shop, Limited Edition, 59 made, replica of Setzer's 1959 (6120) model, special decal-logos.

2009		$8,000	$12,000

Duane Eddy (6210DE)

1997-2003. 6120 style, 2 DeArmond single coils, Bigsby, orange.

1997-2003		$2,000	$3,500

Duane Eddy Signature Hollow Body (6120DE)

2011-present. Single-cut, Western Orange stain lacquer finish.

2011-2024		$2,250	$3,750

Eddie Cochran Signature Hollow Body (6120)

2011-present. Artist Signature Edition, maple body, rosewood 'board, Bigsby, Western maple stain.

2011-2024		$2,250	$3,750

Keith Scott Nashville (6120KS)

1999-2013. Hump-back inlays, gold hardware, metallic gold finish.

1999-2013		$2,000	$3,500

Nashville 1955 (6120-1955)

1995-2018. Custom Shop, recreation of original '55 with G brand, curly maple top, orange stain finish.

1995-2018		$1,750	$3,500

Nashville Double Neck 6/12 (6120)

1997-2002. Built in Japan, few made, all gold hardware, necks are maple with ebony 'boards, orange finish.

1997-2002		$3,500	$6,000

Nashville Jr. (6120-JR/JR2)

1998-2004. Orange, 2 pickups.

1998-2004		$1,750	$3,000

New Nashville (6120N)

2001-2003. Single-cut, humptop inlays, gold hardware.

2001-2003		$1,750	$3,000

Reverend Horton Heat (6120RHH)

2005-present. Cows and cactus inlays, TV jones pickups.

2005-2024		$2,500	$4,000

Chet Atkins Solid Body (6121)

1955-1963. Solid body electric, single-cut, maple or knotty pine top, 2 pickups, Bigsby vibrato, G brand until '57, multi-bound top, brown mahogany, orange finish (6121).

1955-1956	Full Western	$12,000	$14,000
1957	G brand	$10,000	$12,500
1957-1959	No G brand	$5,500	$8,000
1960	Single-cut	$5,500	$8,000
1961-1963	Double-cut	$5,000	$7,000

Chet Atkins Solid Body (6121-1955)

2007-2021. Reissue of '55 6121 with G brand, leather trim, cactus and cows block inlays.

2007-2021		$2,250	$4,000

Chet Atkins Solid Body (6121-1959)

2007-2021. Reissue of '59 6121, no G brand or leather trim, thumbnail inlays.

2007-2021		$2,000	$3,500

Chet Atkins Tennessean (6119/7655)

1958-1980. Archtop electric, single-cut, 1 pickup until early-'61 and 2 after, vibrato. Renumbered as the 7655 in '71.

1958-1960	1 Fil 'tron	$4,500	$6,500
1960-1961		$4,000	$6,000
1961-1964	2 Hi-Lo	$4,500	$6,000
1965-1967	2 pickups	$3,250	$4,500
1968-1970	2 pickups	$3,250	$4,500
1971-1980	7655	$3,000	$4,000

Chet Atkins Tennessee Rose (6119-1959, 1962)

1995-2015. Import, 16" maple body, maple neck, dual FilterTron pickups.

1995-2015	1959 and 1962	$2,000	$3,500

Clipper (6185/6186/6187/7555)

1958-1975. Archtop electric, single-cut, sunburst, 1 pickup (6186) until '72 and 2 pickups (6185) from '72-'75, also available in 1 pickup natural (6187) from '59-'61.

1958-1961	6186	$1,250	$1,750
1959-1961	6187	$1,375	$2,000
1962-1967	6186	$1,250	$1,750
1968-1971	6186	$1,125	$1,750
1972-1975	7555	$1,375	$2,000

Committee (7628)

1977-1980. Neck-thru electric solid body, double-cut, walnut and maple body, 2 pickups, 4 knobs, natural.

1977-1980		$1,500	$2,750

Constellation (6030/6031)

1955-1960. Renamed from Synchromatic 6030 and 6031, archtop acoustic, single-cut, G tailpiece, humped block inlay.

1955-1960		$2,250	$3,000

Convertible (6199)

1955-1958. Archtop electric, single-cut, 1 pickup, multi-bound body, G tailpiece, renamed Sal Salvador in '58.

1955-1958		$2,750	$3,500

1956 Gretsch Chet Atkins Hollow Body 6120

Jim Hilmar

1962 Gretsch Chet Atkins Tennessean (6119/7655)

Matt Carleson

1963 Gretsch Country Club
Geoff Barker

1964 Gretsch Double Anniversary Mono (6117/6118)
Guitar Maniacs

MODEL YEAR	FEATURES	EXC. COND. LOW	HIGH

Corsair

1955-1960. Renamed from Synchromatic 100, archtop acoustic, bound body and headstock, G tailpiece, available in sunburst (6014), natural (6015) or burgundy (6016).

1955-1960	6014, 6015, 6016	$1,250	$1,625

Corvette (Hollow Body)

1955-1959. Renamed from Electromatic Spanish, archtop electric, 1 pickup, f-holes, bound body, Electromatic on headstock, non-cut, sunburst (6182), Jaguar Tan or natural (6184), and ivory with rounded cutaway (6187).

1955-1959	6182, sunburst	$1,125	$1,500
1955-1959	6184, Jaguar Tan	$1,500	$2,000
1955-1959	6184, natural	$1,750	$2,250
1957-1959	6187, ivory	$2,250	$3,000

Corvette (Solid Body)

1961-1972, 1976-1978. Double-cut slab solid body. Mahogany 6132 and cherry 6134 1 pickup for '61-'68. 2 pickup mahogany 6135 and cherry 7623 available by '63-'72 and '76-'78. From late-'61 through '63 a Twist option was offered featuring a red candy stripe 'guard. Platinum Gray 6133 available for '61-'63 and the Gold Duke and Silver Duke sparkle finishes were offered in '66.

1961-1962	Mahogany, cherry	$1,250	$1,750
1961-1963	Platinum Gray	$1,750	$2,250
1961-1963	Twist 'guard	$1,750	$2,250
1963-1965	Custom color, 1 pu	$1,750	$2,250
1963-1965	Custom color, 2 pu	$2,000	$2,500
1963-1965	Mahogany, cherry, 1 pu	$1,000	$1,250
1963-1965	Mahogany cherry, 2 pu	$1,250	$1,750
1966	Gold Duke	$1,750	$2,250
1966	Silver Duke	$1,750	$2,250
1966-1968	Mahogany, cherry, 1 pu	$1,000	$1,250
1966-1968	Mahogany, cherry, 2 pu	$1,125	$1,500
1969-1972	Mahogany, cherry, 2 pu	$1,125	$1,500
1976-1978	7623, 2 pu	$1,000	$1,250

Corvette/CVT (5135)

2006-2018. Like double-cut solid body Corvette, 2 Mega'Tron pickups, Bigsby, becomes the CVT in '10.

2006-2018		$600	$1,250

Country Classic

1989-1992. Both single- and double-cut versions of the Country Gentleman, 2 Filtertron pickups, painted F-holes.

1989-1992		$2,000	$3,500

Country Classic I/II (6122 Reissue)

1989-2006. Country Gentleman reissue with '58 (I) and '62 (II) specs. Also cataloged as G6122-1958 and G6122-1962 Country Classic.

1989-2006	'58, single-cut	$2,000	$3,500
1989-2006	'62, double-cut	$2,000	$3,500

Country Classic II Custom Edition (6122)

2005. Reissue of George Harrison's 2nd 6122 Country Gentleman, the Custom Edition has TV Jones Filtertron pickups.

2005		$2,750	$4,500

Country Club

1954-1981. Renamed from Electro II Cutaway, archtop electric, single-cut, 2 pickups (Filter Trons after '57), G tailpiece, multi-bound, various colors.

1954-1958	Sunburst	$4,500	$6,000
1954-1959	Cadillac Green	$5,500	$7,500
1954-1959	Natural	$4,500	$6,000
1959	Sunburst	$5,500	$7,000
1960-1964	Cadillac Green	$5,500	$7,000
1960-1964	Sunburst	$4,000	$5,500
1961-1962	Natural	$4,000	$5,500
1965-1969	Sunburst or walnut	$3,250	$4,500
1970-1981	Various colors	$3,000	$4,000

Country Club 1955 (6196-1955) (FGE)

1995-1999. U.S.-made reissue of Country Club, single-cut, 2 DeArmond pickups, hand-rubbed lacquer finish.

1995-1999		$2,250	$3,750

Country Club (6196, etc.)

2001-present. Includes Cadillac Green (G6196, '01-present), sunburst (G6192, '03-'08), amber natural (G6193,'03-'08), Bamboo Yellow (G6196TSP-BY, '09-'13), and smoky gray and violet 2-tone (G6196TSP-2G, '09-'12), G6196T-59GE Golden Era Edition ('16-present), T means Bigsby.

2001-2024	Cadillac Green	$2,250	$3,750
2009-2013	Bamboo Yellow	$2,250	$3,750

Country Roc (7620)

1974-1978. Single-cut solid body, 2 pickups, belt buckle tailpiece, western scene fretboard inlays, G brand, tooled leather side trim.

1974-1978		$1,750	$3,500

Custom (6117)

1964-1968. Limited production, smaller thinner version of Double Anniversary model, 2 pickups, cat's eye sound holes, red or black finish.

1964		$3,750	$5,000
1965-1966		$3,250	$4,500
1967-1968		$3,250	$4,500

Deluxe Chet (7680/7681)

1972-1974. Electric archtop with rounded cutaway, Autumn Red (7680) or brown walnut (7681) finishes.

1972-1974		$2,500	$4,000

Deluxe Flat-Top (7535)

1972-1978. 16" redwood top, mahogany back and sides.

1972-1978		$800	$1,750

Double Anniversary Mono (6117/6118)

1958-1976. Archtop electric, single-cut, 2 pickups, stereo optional until '63, sunburst (6117) or green 2-tone (6118). Reissued in '93 as the Anniversary 6117 and 6118.

1958-1959	Green 2-tone	$5,000	$7,000
1958-1959	Sunburst	$5,000	$7,000
1960-1961	Green 2-tone	$4,000	$5,000
1960-1961	Sunburst	$4,000	$5,000
1962-1964	Green 2-tone or tan	$3,000	$4,000
1962-1964	Sunburst	$2,500	$3,250
1965-1966	Various colors	$1,750	$2,250
1967-1969	Various colors	$1,500	$2,000
1970-1976	Various colors	$1,350	$1,750

MODEL YEAR	FEATURES	EXC. COND. LOW	HIGH

Double Anniversary Stereo (6111/6112)

1961-1963. One stereo channel/signal per pickup, sunburst (6111) or green (6112).

1961-1963	Green	$3,000	$4,000
1961-1963	Sunburst	$2,500	$3,500

Duo-Jet (6128)

1953-1971. Solid body electric, single-cut until '61, double after, 2 pickups, block inlays to late '56, then humptop until early '58, then thumbprint inlays, black (6128) with a few special-order Cadillac Green, sparkle finishes were offered '63-'66, reissued in '90.

1953	Black, single-cut, script logo	$8,000	$10,000
1955-1956	Black, blocks	$6,000	$8,000
1956-1958	Black, humptop	$8,000	$10,000
1957	Cadillac Green	$15,000	$18,000
1958-1960	Black, thumbprint	$6,000	$8,000
1961-1964	Black, double-cut	$5,000	$6,000
1963-1966	Sparkle, double-cut	$10,000	$12,000
1965-1971	Black	$4,000	$5,000

Duo-Jet (6128TCG)

2005-2016. Cadillac Green, gold hardware, Bigsby.

2005-2016		$2,000	$3,500

Duo-Jet Custom Edition (6128TSP)

2004-2006. Reissue of '57 model, originally called the Duo Jet Special.

2004-2006		$2,500	$4,000

Duo-Jet Reissue (6128/6128T)

1990-2017. Reissue of the '50s solid body, optional Bigsby (G6128T). Replaced by Vintage Select Edition series.

1990-2017		$1,750	$3,250

Duo-Jet Tenor (6127)

1954-1960. Electric tenor, 4 strings, block inlays, black.

1954-1960		$3,500	$4,500

Duo-Jet Vintage Select Edition '59 (6128T-59)

2017-present. Bigsby, TV Jones Filter 'Trons, black.

2017-2024		$2,500	$4,000

Elliot Easton Signature Duo-Jet (6128TEE)

2000-2005. Bigsby, gold hardware, Cadillac Green (TEE), red (TREE), black (TBEE).

2000-2005		$2,250	$3,750

George Harrison Tribute Duo-Jet (6128GH)

2011. USA Custom Shop, master luthier Stephen Stern, 60 made, relic aged to replicate Harrison's '57 Duo-Jet.

2011		$15,000	$25,000

Eldorado (6040/6041)

1955-1970, 1991-1997. This is the larger 18" version, renamed from Synchromatic 400, archtop acoustic, single-cut, triple-bound fretboard and peghead, sunburst (6040) or natural (6041). Reintroduced in '91, made by Heritage in Kalamazoo, as the G410 Synchromatic Eldorado in sunburst or natural (G410M).

1955-1959	Natural	$3,250	$4,250
1955-1959	Sunburst	$2,500	$3,500
1960-1963	Natural	$2,375	$3,250
1960-1963	Sunburst	$2,125	$3,000
1964	Natural	$2,000	$2,625
1964	Sunburst	$1,750	$2,500
1965-1997	Natural, sunburst	$1,625	$2,250

Eldorado (6038/6039)

1959-1968. The smaller 17" version, named Fleetwood from '55 to '58, sunburst (6038) or natural (6039), also available as a full body non-cutaway.

1959-1964	Natural, sunburst	$1,500	$2,000
1965-1968	Natural, sunburst	$1,375	$1,750

Electro Classic (6006/6495)

1969-1973. Classical flat-top with piezo pickup.

1969-1970	6006	$800	$1,750
1971-1973	6495	$800	$1,750

Electro II Cutaway (6192/6193)

1951-1954. Archtop electric, single-cut, Melita bridge by '53, 2 pickups, f-holes, sunburst (6192) or natural (6193). Renamed Country Club in '54.

1951-1954	6192, sunburst	$4,250	$5,500
1951-1954	6193, natural	$4,750	$6,125

Electro II Non-Cutaway (6187/6188)

1951-1954. 16" electric archtop, 2 DeArmonds, large f-holes, block markers, 6187 sunburst, 6188 natural, label is Model 6187-8, vertical Electromatic logo on headstock.

1951-1954	6187, sunburst	$3,750	$5,000
1951-1954	6188, natural	$3,750	$5,000

Electromatic (5420T)

2013-present. Hollow body, single-cut, Bigsby.

2013-2024		$500	$1,250

Electromatic (5422-12)

2013-present. 12-string 5422.

2013-2024		$500	$1,250

Electromatic (5422T)

2013-present. Hollow body, double-cut, Bigsby.

2013-2024		$500	$1,250

Electromatic Hollow Body (5120/5125-29/5420)

2005-2020. Single-cut, 2 dual-coils, Bigsby, black, Aspen Green, sunburst or orange. With Filter'Tron pickups in '13 (5420).

2005-2020		$500	$1,250

Electromatic Hollow Body (5122/5422)

2009-2014. Double-cut version of G5120, 2 dual-coils, Bigsby, black, trans red or walnut. With Filter'Tron pickups in '13 (5422). Replaced with G5422T.

2009-2014		$500	$1,250

Tim Armstrong Signature Electromatic (5191BK-TA)

2010-present. Hollow body, single-cut, gold hardware.

2010-2024		$800	$1,500

Electromatic Spanish (6185/6185N)

1940-1955. Hollow body, 17" wide, 1 pickup, sunburst (6185) or natural (6185N). Renamed Corvette (hollowbody) in '55.

1940-1949	Sunburst	$1,625	$2,125
1950-1955	Natural	$1,625	$2,125
1950-1955	Sunburst	$1,500	$2,000

Gretsch Duo-Jet Vintage Select Edition '59 (6128T-59)

2015 Gretsch Electromatic (5422T)
David Mullins

1958 Gretsch Grand Concert (6003)
Imaged by Heritage Auctions, HA.com

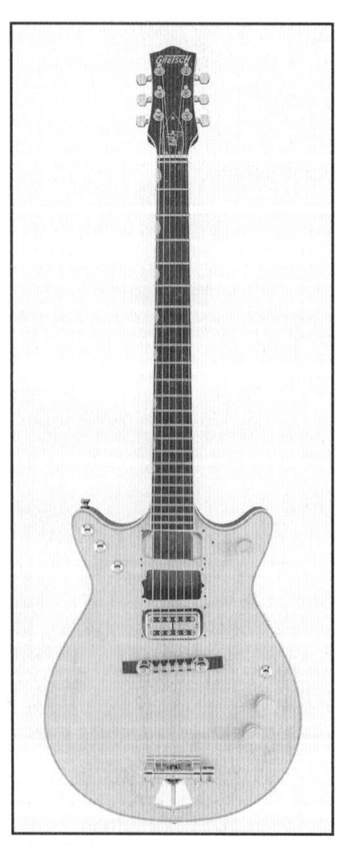

2019 Gretsch Malcom Young Signature Jet (6131-MY)

MODEL YEAR	FEATURES	EXC. COND. LOW	HIGH

Fleetwood (6038/6039)

1955-1958. Named Synchromatic prior to '55, single-cut, sunburst (6038) or natural (6039). Renamed Eldorado in '59, available by custom order.

1955-1958	Natural	$3,750	$5,000
1955-1958	Sunburst	$3,000	$4,000

Folk/Folk Singing (6003/7505/7506)

1963-1975. Lower-model of Gretsch flat-tops, 14 1/4", mahogany back and sides. Renamed from Jimmie Rodgers model, renamed Folk Singing in '63.

1963-1964		$875	$1,125
1965-1969		$750	$975
1970-1975		$650	$850

Golden Classic (Hauser/6000)

1961-1969. Grand Concert body size, nylon-string classical, 14 1/4" spruce top, mahogany back and sides, multiple inlaid sound hole purfling, inlaid headstock.

1961-1969		$575	$750

Grand Concert (6003)

1955-1959. Lower-model of Gretsch flat-tops, 14 1/4", mahogany back and sides. Renamed from Model 6003 and renamed Jimmie Rodgers in '59.

1955-1959		$900	$1,250

Guitar-Banjo

1920s. 6-string guitar neck on banjo body, slotted headstock, open back.

1920s		$675	$900

Jet 21

Late-1940s. 16" acoustic archtop, Jet 21 engraved logo on headstock, bound top and back, white 'guard, jet black finish.

1947-1948		$850	$1,125

Jet Firebird (6131)

1955-1971. Solid body electric, single-cut until '61, double '61-'71, 2 pickups, black body with red top, block inlays to late '56, then humptop until early '58, then thumbprint inlays.

1955-1956	Single-cut	$8,000	$10,000
1957-1958	Single-cut	$8,500	$10,000
1959-1960	Single-cut	$6,000	$9,000
1961-1964	Double-cut	$5,000	$6,500
1965-1967		$4,000	$5,500
1968-1971	Super Trons	$4,000	$5,500

Jet Firebird Reissue/Power Jet Firebird (6131/6131T)

1989-1997, 2003-2019. Single-cut '58 specs, red top, 2 FilterTrons, thumbprint markers, gold hardware for '91-'05, currently chrome. Bigsby available (T). Non-Bigsby 6131 ends in '05. DynaSonic-equipped TDS starts in '05 and TV Jones PowerTrons (TVP) in '06.

2003-2019		$2,000	$3,500

Jet/Pearl Jet/Blue Pearl Jet (6129/6129T)

1996-2011. Chambered mahogany body with maple top, unique Pearl or Blue Pearl finish.

1996-2011		$1,750	$3,500

Jimmie Rodgers (6003)

1959-1962. 14" flat-top with round hole, mahogany back and sides, renamed from Grand Concert and renamed Folk Singing in '63.

1959-1962		$1,000	$2,000

MODEL YEAR	FEATURES	EXC. COND. LOW	HIGH

Jumbo Flat-Top (6009)

1969-1971. Flat-top acoustic, sunburst.

1969-1971		$1,250	$2,500

Jumbo Synchromatic (125F)

1947-1955. 17" flat-top, triangular sound hole, bound top and back, metal bridge anchor plate, adjustable wood bridge, natural top with sunburst back and sides or optional translucent white-blond top and sides.

1947-1955	Natural	$2,500	$3,250
1947-1955	White-blond	$2,750	$3,500

Malcom Young Signature Jet (6131-MY)

2018-present. Professional Collection series, double-cut mahogany body, maple top, aged white binding, semi-gloss natural finish.

2018-2024		$2,500	$4,000

Model 25 (Acoustic)

1933-1939. 16" archtop, no binding on top or back, dot markers, sunburst.

1933-1939		$775	$1,000

Model 30 (Acoustic)

1939-1949. 16" archtop, top binding, dot markers, sunburst.

1939-1949		$850	$1,125

Model 35 (Acoustic)

1933-1949. 16" archtop, single-bound top and back, dot markers, sunburst.

1933-1949		$1,000	$1,500

Model 40 Hawaiian (Acoustic)

1936-1949. Flat-top, bound top and neck, diamond inlays.

1936-1949		$1,000	$1,500

Model 50/50R (Acoustic)

1936-1949. Acoustic archtop, f-holes. Model 50R ('36-'39) has round sound hole.

1936-1939	TG-50 Tenor	$800	$1,125
1936-1949	50/50R	$1,250	$1,625

Model 65 (Acoustic)

1933-1939. Archtop acoustic, bound body, amber.

1933-1939		$1,250	$1,625

Model 75 Tenor (Acoustic)

1933-1949. 4-string tenor.

1933-1949		$850	$1,125

Model 6003

1951-1955. 14 1/4", mahogany back and sides, renamed Grand Concert in '55.

1951-1954		$1,000	$1,500

Monkees

Late 1966-1968. Hollow body electric, double-cut, 2 pickups, Monkees logo on 'guard, bound top, f-holes and neck, vibrato, red.

1966-1968		$3,000	$5,000

New Yorker

Ca.1949-1970. Archtop acoustic, f-holes, sunburst.

1949-1959		$750	$975
1960-1964		$700	$950
1965-1969		$600	$800
1970		$500	$650

New Yorker Tenor (6050)

1950s. 4-string tenor version.

1950s		$500	$650

MODEL YEAR	FEATURES	EXC. COND. LOW	HIGH

Ozark/Ozark Soft String (6005)

1965-1968. 16" classical, rosewood back and sides.

1965-1968		$500	$650

Princess (6106)

1963. Corvette-type solid body double-cut, 1 pickup, vibrato, gold parts, colors available were white/grape, blue/white, pink/white, or white/gold, often sold with the Princess amp.

1963		$2,750	$3,500

Rally (6104/6105)

1967-1969. Archtop, double-cut, 2 pickups, vibrato, racing stripe on truss rod cover and pickguard, Rally Green (6104) or Bamboo Yellow (6105).

1967-1969	6104 or 6105	$2,500	$3,250

Rambler (6115)

1957-1961. Small body electric archtop, single-cut, 1 DeArmond pickup '57-59, then 1 Hi-Lo 'Tron '60-'61, G tailpiece, bound body and headstock.

1957-1959	DeArmond	$2,750	$3,500
1960-1961	Hi-Lo 'Tron	$2,250	$3,000

Rancher

1954-1980. Flat-top acoustic, triangle sound hole, Western theme inlay, G brand until '61 and '75 and after, Golden Red (orange), reissued in '90.

1954-1957	G brand	$5,500	$7,500
1958-1961	G brand	$5,000	$7,000
1962-1964	No G brand	$4,000	$5,500
1965-1969	No G brand	$3,250	$4,250
1970-1974	No G brand	$2,750	$4,000
1975-1980	G brand	$2,750	$4,000

Rancher (6022C)

2005-2006. Made in Japan.

2005-2006		$1,250	$2,250

Rancher (6022E)

2005-2007. US-made, laminated spruce top, 3-piece maple neck, Fishman electronics, G brand.

2005-2007		$1,250	$2,250

Roc I/Roc II (7635/7621)

1974-1976. Electric solid body, mahogany, single-cut, Duo-Jet-style body, 1 pickup (7635) or 2 pickups (7621), bound body and neck.

1974-1976	Roc I	$1,750	$3,250
1974-1977	Roc II	$2,000	$3,750

Roc Jet

1970-1980. Electric solid body, single-cut, 2 pickups, adjustamatic bridge, black, cherry, pumpkin or walnut.

1970-1980		$2,000	$3,500

Round-Up (6130)

1954-1960. Electric solid body, single-cut, 2 pickups, G brand, belt buckle tailpiece, maple, pine, knotty pine or orange. Reissued in '90.

1954-1956	Knotty pine (2 knots)	$15,000	$20,000
1954-1956	Knotty pine (4 knots)	$20,000	$25,000
1954-1956	Mahogany (few made)	$12,000	$15,000
1954-1956	Pine	$15,000	$18,000
1957-1960	Orange	$8,000	$10,000

Round-Up Reissue (6121/6121W)

1989-1995, 2003-2006. Based on the '50s model, Bigsby, Western Orange.

1989-2006		$1,750	$3,500

Round-Up Western Leather Trim (6130)

2006-2007. Higher-end reissue of '55 Round-Up, G brand, tooled leather trim around edge, cactus and cows inlays.

2006-2007		$2,500	$4,000

Round-Up Knotty Pine (6130KPW)

2008-2010. Like '06 6130 but with belt buckle tailpiece and knotty pine top.

2008-2010		$3,500	$5,500

Sal Fabraio (6117)

1964-1968. Double-cut thin electric archtop, distinctive cats-eye f-holes, 2 pickups, sunburst, ordered for resale by guitar teacher Sal Fabraio.

1964-1968		$2,250	$3,000

Sal Salvador (6199)

1958-1968. Electric archtop, single-cut, 1 pickup, triple-bound neck and headstock, sunburst.

1958-1959		$2,500	$3,250
1960-1962		$2,250	$3,000
1963-1964		$2,000	$2,500
1965-1968		$1,750	$2,250

Sho Bro (Hawaiian/Spanish)

1969-1978. Flat-top acoustic, multi-bound, resonator, Lucite fretboard, Hawaiian version non-cut, square neck and Spanish version non- or single-cut, round neck.

1969-1978	Hawaiian	$1,250	$2,000
1969-1978	Spanish	$1,500	$2,500

Sierra Jumbo (3700)

1999-2005. Historic series, single-cut jumbo body, triangular sound hole, sunburst finish.

1999-2005		$600	$950

Silver Classic (Hauser/6001)

1961-1969. Grand Concert body size, nylon-string classical. Similar to Golden Classic but with less fancy appointments.

1961-1969		$500	$1,250

Silver Falcon (6136SL) (1955) (T)

1995-1999, 2003-2005. Black finish, silver features, single cut, G tailpiece available until '05, T for Bigsby available starting '05. Had the 1955 designation in the '90s.

1995-1999		$2,000	$3,000

Silver Falcon (7594SL)

1995-1999. Black finish and silver features, double-cut, 2" thick body.

1995-1999		$1,750	$2,500

Silver Jet (6129)

1954-1963. Solid body electric, single-cut until '61, double '61-'63, 2 pickups, Duo-Jet with silver sparkle top, reissued in '89. Optional sparkle colors were offered but were not given their own model numbers; refer to Duo-Jet listing for optional colors.

1954-1956	Single-cut	$8,000	$10,000
1957-1958	Single-cut	$8,000	$10,000
1959-1960	Single-cut	$8,000	$10,000
1961-1963	Double-cut	$7,500	$9,500
1961-1963	Double-cut, Burgandy	$13,000	$15,500

1955 Gretsch New Yorker

Tim Fleck

1970 Gretsch Sho Bro

GUITARS

Gretsch Streamliner Center Block Jr. (G2655T)

1955 Gretsch Syncromatic
Pete Mann

MODEL YEAR	FEATURES	EXC. COND. LOW	HIGH

Silver Jet 1957 Reissue (6129-1957)

1989-2019. Reissue of single-cut '50s Silver Jet, silver sparkle. '1957' added to name in '94.

1989-2019		$1,500	$2,250

Silver Jet 1962 Reissue (6129-1962)

1996-2009. Reissue of '60s double-cut Silver Jet, silver sparkle.

1996-2009		$1,500	$2,000

Songbird (Sam Goody 711)

1967-1968. Standard body thinline double-cut with G sound holes, offered by Sam Goody of New York.

1967-1968		$2,500	$4,000

Southern Belle (7176)

1983. Electric archtop, walnut, parts from the late-'70s assembled in Mexico and U.S., 5 made with all original parts, several others without pickguard and case.

1983		$2,000	$3,000

Sparkle Jet (6129/6129T/6129TG)

1995-2019. Duo-Jet with sparkle finishes other than Silver, single-cut, 2 pickups. Many different colors offered over the years.

1995-2019		$1,500	$2,250

Streamliner Single Cutaway (6189/6190/6191)

1955-1959. Electric archtop, single-cut, maple top, G tailpiece, 1 pickup, multi-bound, Jaguar Tan (6189), sunburst (6190), or natural (6191). Name reintroduced as a double-cut in '68.

1955-1959	6189, Jaguar Tan	$2,750	$3,500
1955-1959	6190, Sunburst	$2,500	$3,250
1955-1959	6191, Natural	$3,250	$4,000

Streamliner Center Block Jr. (2655T)

2016-present. Double-cut, spruce center block, Bigsby, black, walnut stain or Golddust.

2016-2024		$450	$600

Streamliner Double Cutaway (6102/6103)

1968-1973. Reintroduced from single-cut model, electric archtop, double-cut, 2 pickups, G tailpiece, cherry or sunburst.

1968-1973		$2,000	$2,500

Sun Valley (6010/7515/7514)

1959-1977. Flat-top acoustic, laminated Brazilian rosewood back and sides, multi-bound top, natural or sunburst.

1959-1964	6010	$1,250	$1,625
1965-1970	6010	$1,000	$1,375
1971-1972	7515	$900	$1,125
1973-1977	7514	$900	$1,125

Super Chet (7690/7690-B/7691/7691-B)

1972-1980. Electric archtop, single rounded cutaway, 2 pickups, gold hardware, mini control knobs along edge of 'guard, Autumn Red or walnut.

1972-1980		$2,000	$3,000

Supreme (7545)

1972-1978. Flat-top 16", spruce top, mahogany or rosewood body options, gold hardware.

1972-1978	Mahogany	$2,500	$4,000
1972-1979	Rosewood	$2,500	$4,000

Synchromatic (6030/6031)

1951-1955. 17" acoustic archtop, becomes Constellation in '55.

1951-1955	6030 or 6031	$1,500	$2,000

MODEL YEAR	FEATURES	EXC. COND. LOW	HIGH

Synchromatic (6038/6039)

1951-1955. 17" acoustic archtop, single-cut, G tailpiece, multi-bound, sunburst (6038) or natural (6039), renamed Fleetwood in '55.

1951-1955	6038 or 6039	$1,750	$2,250

Synchromatic 75

1939-1949. Acoustic archtop, f-holes, multi-bound, large floral peghead inlay. Tenor available.

1939-1949		$1,000	$1,500
1939-1949	Tenor	$700	$950

Synchromatic Jr. (3900)

1990-2003. Historic Series, 15" single-cut archtop acoustic.

1990-2003		$800	$1,250

Synchromatic 100 (6014/6015)

1939-1955. Renamed from No. 100F, acoustic archtop, double-bound body, amber, sunburst (6014) or natural (6015), renamed Corsair in '55.

1939-1949	Natural	$1,125	$1,500
1939-1949	Sunburst	$900	$1,125
1950-1955	Natural	$950	$1,250

Synchromatic 160 (6028/6029)

1939-1943, 1947-1951. Acoustic archtop, cats-eye sound holes, maple back and sides, triple-bound, natural or sunburst.

1939-1943	Sunburst	$1,500	$2,000
1947-1951	Sunburst	$1,250	$1,625
1948-1951	Natural	$1,500	$2,000

Synchromatic 200

1939-1949. Acoustic archtop, cats-eye sound holes, maple back and sides, multi-bound, gold-plated hardware, amber or natural.

1939-1949		$1,500	$2,000

Synchromatic 300

1939-1955. Acoustic archtop, cats-eye sound holes until '51 and f-holes after, multi-bound, natural or sunburst.

1939-1949	Natural	$2,750	$3,500
1939-1949	Sunburst	$2,500	$3,250
1950-1955	Natural	$2,500	$3,250
1950-1955	Sunburst	$2,250	$3,000

Synchromatic 400

1940-1955. Acoustic archtop, cats-eye sound holes until '51 and f-holes after, multi-bound, gold hardware, natural or sunburst.

1940-1949	Natural	$5,750	$7,500
1940-1949	Sunburst	$5,250	$6,750
1950-1955	Natural	$5,250	$6,750
1950-1955	Sunburst	$6,250	$8,000

Synchromatic 400F/6042 Flat-Top

1947-1955. 18" flat-top, renamed 6042 in the late '40s.

1947-1948	400F	$5,750	$7,500
1949-1955	6042	$5,750	$7,500

Synchromatic G400/400C

1990-2008. Acoustic archtop, full-body, non-cut (400) or single-cut (C), sunburst.

1990-2008	G400	$1,125	$1,750
1990-2008	G400C	$1,125	$1,750

MODEL YEAR	FEATURES	EXC. COND. LOW	HIGH

Synchromatic Limited (G450/G450M)

1997. Acoustic archtop, hand carved spruce (G450) or maple (G450M) top, floating pickup, sunburst, only 50 were to be made.

1997	Maple	$1,500	$2,000
1997	Spruce	$1,250	$1,750

Synchromatic Sierra

1949-1955. Renamed from Synchromatic X75F (see below), acoustic flat-top, maple back and sides, triangular sound hole, sunburst.

1949-1955		$1,750	$2,250

Synchromatic X75F

1947-1949. Acoustic flat-top, maple back and sides, triangular sound hole, sunburst, renamed Synchromatic Sierra in '49.

1947-1949		$1,750	$2,250

TK 300 (7624/7625)

1977-1981. Double-cut maple solid body, 1 humbucker, bolt-on neck, six-on-a-side tuners, hockey stick headstock, Autumn Red or natural.

1977-1981		$1,500	$2,500

Town and Country (6021)

1954-1959. Renamed from Jumbo Synchromatic 125 F, flat-top acoustic, maple back and sides, triangular sound hole, multi-bound.

1954-1959		$3,500	$4,500

Traveling Wilburys (TW300T)

1988-1990. Promotional guitar, solid body electric, single-cut, 1 and 2 pickups, 6 variations, graphics.

1988-1990		$800	$1,250

Van Eps 6-String (6081/6082)

1968-1971. Electric archtop, single-cut, 2 pickups, 6 strings.

1968-1971		$3,000	$5,500

Van Eps 7-String (6079/6080/7580/7581)

1968-1978. 7-string version, sunburst (6079) or walnut (6080), model numbers change to 7580 (sunburst) and 7581 (walnut) in '72.

1968-1971	6079 or 6080	$3,000	$4,500
1972-1978	7580 or 7581	$2,750	$4,000

Viking

1964-1975. Archtop, double-cut, 2 pickups, vibrato, sunburst (6187), natural (6188) or Cadillac Green (6189). Re-designated 7585 (sunburst) and 7586 (natural) in '72.

1964	Cadillac Green	$5,500	$7,000
1964	Natural	$5,000	$6,000
1964	Sunburst	$3,500	$4,500
1965-1971	Cadillac Green	$4,000	$5,000
1965-1971	Natural	$4,000	$5,000
1965-1971	Sunburst	$3,000	$4,000
1972-1975	Sunburst, natural	$2,750	$3,500

Wayfarer Jumbo (6008)

1969-1971. Flat-top acoustic dreadnought, non-cut, maple back and sides, multi-bound, Wayfarer and sailing ship logo on 'guard.

1969-1971		$1,250	$2,000

White Falcon Jr.

1999-2003. Import.

1999-2003		$1,500	$2,500

MODEL YEAR	FEATURES	EXC. COND. LOW	HIGH

White Falcon Mono (6136/7594)

1955-1981. Includes the single-cut 6136 of '55-'61, the double-cut 6136 of '62-'70, and the double-cut 7594 of '71-'81.

1955	6136, single-cut, gold leaf	$50,000	$65,000
1956-1961	6136, single-cut, sparkle binding	$45,000	$55,000
1962-1964	6136, double-cut	$25,000	$30,000
1965-1969		$15,000	$20,000
1970		$10,000	$12,500
1971-1972	7594	$7,500	$10,000
1973-1981	7594	$7,000	$9,000

White Falcon Stereo (6137)

1958-1964. Features Project-O-Sonic Stereo, gold sparkle trim.

1958-1961	Single-cut	$45,000	$60,000
1962-1964	Double-cut	$25,000	$30,000

White Falcon (Import)

1989-2021. Various imported models.

1989-2021	Various models	$2,500	$3,500

White Falcon Custom U.S.A. (6136-1955)

1995-1999. U.S.-made, single-cut, DynaSonic pickups, gold sparkle appointments, rhinestone embedded knobs, white. In '04, Current U.S. model called G6136CST is released. The import White Falcon has sometimes been listed with the 1955 designation and is not included here.

1995-1999		$6,000	$8,500

White Penguin (6134)

1955-1962. Electric solid body, single-cut until '61, double '61-'62, 2 pickups (DeArmond until '58 then Filter Tron), fewer than 100 made, white, gold sparkle bound, gold-plated parts. More than any other model, there seems a higher concern regarding forgery.

1956-1962		$150,000	$175,000

White Penguin (G6134)

1993, 2003-2018. White, single-cut, metalflake binding, gold hardware, jeweled knobs, Cadillac G tailpiece.

2003-2018		$2,750	$4,000

Greven

1969, 1975-2021. Luthier John Greven builds his premium grade, production/custom, acoustic guitars in Portland, Oregon.

Grez

2009-present. Production/custom, professional and premium grade, electric solid body, semi-hollowbody, archtop and acoustic guitars, built by Barry Grzebik in Petaluma, California.

Griffin String Instruments

1976-present. Luthier Kim Griffin builds his professional and premium grade, production/custom, parlor, steel-string, and classical guitars in Greenwich, New York.

Grimes Guitars

1972-present. Premium and presentation grade, custom, flat-tops, nylon-strings, archtops, semi-

Grez Guitars OM-1C

Grimes Custom Archtop

GUITARS

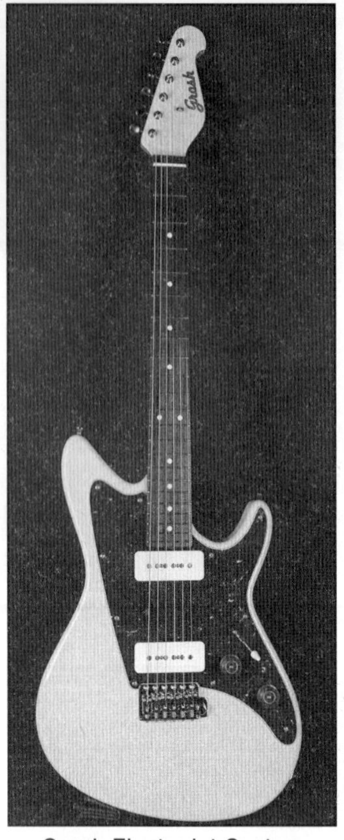

Grosh ElectraJet Custom

1967 Gruggett

MODEL YEAR	FEATURES	EXC. COND. LOW	HIGH

hollow electrics made by luthier Steve Grimes originally in Port Townsend, Washington, and since '82 in Kula, Hawaii. He also made mandolins early on.

Grinnell

Late 1930s-early 1940s. Private brand made by Gibson for Grinnell Music of Detroit and Southeast Michigan, which at the time, was the largest music chain in the Detroit area.

KG-14

1940. Gibson-made L-00 flat-top style with maple sides and back, tortoise-style binding on top and back, ladder bracing.

1940	$2,000	$3,000

Groehsl

1890-1921. Chicago's Groehsl Company made guitars for Wards and other mass-marketers. In 1921 the company became Stromberg-Voisinet, which in turn became the Kay Musical Instrument Company.

Groove Tools

2002-2004. Korean-made, production, intermediate grade, 7-string guitars that were offered by Conklin Guitars of Springfield, Missouri. They also offered basses.

Grosh

1993-present. Professional and premium grade, production/custom, solid and semi-hollow body guitars and basses built by luthier Don Grosh originally in Santa Clarita, California and, since '05 in Broomfield, Colorado. He also builds basses. Grosh worked in production for Valley Arts from '84-'92. Guitars generally with bolt necks until '03 when set-necks were added to the line.

Classical Electric

1990s. Single-cut solidbody with nylon strings and piezo-style hidden pickup, highly figured top.

1990s	$1,800	$2,500

Custom S Bent Top/Bent Top Custom

2003-2019. Offset double-cut, figured maple carved top, 2 pickups.

2003-2019	$1,800	$2,500

Custom T Carve Top

2003-2012. Single-cut, figured maple carved top, 2 pickups.

2003-2012	$1,800	$2,500

ElectraJet Custom

2009-present. Modified offset double-cut, 2 P-90s, 2 hums, or single-single-hum pickups.

2009-2024	$1,800	$2,500

Retro Classic

1993-present. Offset double-cut, 3 pickups.

1993-2024	$1,800	$2,500

Retro Classic Vintage T

1993-present. Single-cut, black 'guard.

1993-2024	$1,800	$2,500

Gruen Acoustic Guitars

Luthier Paul Gruen builds professional grade, custom steel-string guitars, starting in 1999, in Chapel Hill, North Carolina.

Gruggett

Mid 1960s-2012. In the 1960s, luthier Bill Gruggett worked with Mosrite and Hallmark guitars as well as building electric guitars under his own name in Bakersfield, California. He continued to make his Stradette model for Hallmark guitars until his death in October 2012.

Guernsey Resophonic Guitars

Production/custom, resonator guitars built by luthier Ivan Guernsey in Marysville, Indiana, starting in 1989.

Guild

1952-present. Professional and premium grade, production/custom, acoustic and acoustic/electric guitars. They have built solid, hollow and semi-hollowbody guitars in the past. Founded in New York City by jazz guitarist Alfred Dronge, employing many ex-Epiphone workers. The company was purchased by Avnet, Inc. in '66 and the Westerly, Rhode Island factory was opened in '68. Hoboken factory closed in '71 and headquarters moved to Elizabeth, New Jersey. The company was in bankruptcy in '88 and was purchased by Faas Corporation, New Berlin, Wisconsin. The brand was purchased by Fender in '95 and production was moved from Westerly to the Fender plant in Corona, California in 2001. In '05, Fender moved Guild production to their newly acquired Tacoma plant in Washington. In '08, production moved to the Ovation/Hamer plant in New Hartford, Connecticut. With the 2001 move to the Fender Corona plant, Bob Benedetto and Fender veteran Tim Shaw (who previously ran the Nashville-based custom shop) created a line of Guild acoustic guitars that were primarily based on vintage Guild Hoboken designs.

Designs of Tacoma-built Guild product were nothing like Tacoma guitars. The new Guilds were dovetail neck based with nitrocellulose finishes. Later, FMIC Guild introduced the Contemporary Series giving the Tacoma factory another line in addition to the vintage-based F and D model Traditional Series. In '14 Fender sold Guild to Cordoba Music Group, manufacturer of Cordoba acoustic guitars who moved production to Oxnard, California.

A-50

1994-1996. Original A-50 models can be found under the Cordoba A-50 listing, the new model drops the Cordoba name, size 000 flat-top, spruce top, Indian rosewood body.

1994-1996	$1,200	$2,000

MODEL YEAR	FEATURES	EXC. COND. LOW	HIGH

Aragon F-30

1954-1986. Acoustic flat-top, spruce top, laminated maple arched back (mahogany back and sides by '59), reintroduced as just F-30 in '98.

1954-1959		$2,000	$3,000
1960-1969		$1,800	$2,800
1970-1986		$1,500	$2,200

Aragon F-30 NT

1959-1985. Natural finish version of F-30.

1959-1969		$2,200	$3,300
1970-1985		$2,000	$3,000

Aragon F-30 R

1973-1995. Rosewood back and sides version of F-30, sunburst.

1973-1979		$2,000	$3,000

Aristocrat M-75

1954-1963. Electric archtop, routed semi-hollow single-cut body, 2 pickups, sunburst, natural (added '59) or cherry (added '61), reintroduced as Bluesbird M-75 in '67.

1954-1959		$4,500	$6,500
1960-1963		$4,000	$6,000

Aristocrat M-75 Tenor

Mid-late 1950s. Tenor version of 6-string Aristocrat electric, dual soapbar pickups, 4 knobs.

1950s		$3,000	$4,500

Artist Award

1961-1999. Renamed from Johnny Smith Award, single-cut electric archtop, floating DeArmond pickup (changed to humbucker in '80), multi-bound, gold hardware, sunburst or natural.

1961-1969		$7,000	$12,000
1970-1999		$6,000	$9,000

Bluegrass D-25/D-25M

1968-1999. Flat-top, mahogany top until '76, spruce after, mahogany back and sides, various colors, called Bluegrass D-25 M in late-'70s and '80s, listed as D-25 in '90s.

1968-1969		$1,200	$1,800
1970-1999		$800	$1,200

Bluegrass D-25-12

1987-1992, 1996-1998. 12-string version of D-25.

1987-1998		$1,000	$1,500

Bluegrass D-35

1966-1988. Acoustic flat-top, spruce top and mahogany back and sides, rosewood 'board and bridge, natural.

1966-1969		$1,800	$2,800
1970-1988		$1,200	$1,800

Bluegrass F-40/Valencia F-40

1954-1963, 1973-1983. Acoustic flat-top, spruce top, maple back and sides, rosewood 'board and bridge, natural or sunburst.

1954-1963	Valencia F-40	$3,500	$5,500
1973-1983	Bluegrass F-40	$1,500	$2,200

Bluegrass F-47

1963-1976. 16" narrow-waist style, mahogany sides and back, acoustic flat-top, spruce top, mahogany back and sides, bound rosewood 'board and bridge, natural.

1963-1969	Horses-art 'guard	$2,800	$4,200
1970-1976		$2,200	$3,300

Bluegrass Jubilee D-40

1963-1992. Acoustic flat-top, spruce top, mahogany back and sides, rosewood 'board and bridge, natural. Has been reissued.

1963-1969		$2,000	$3,000
1970-1992		$1,500	$2,200

Bluegrass Jubilee D-40C

1975-1991. Acoustic flat-top, single Florentine cutaway, mahogany back and sides, rosewood 'board and bridge, natural.

1975-1991		$1,500	$2,200

Bluegrass Jubilee D-44

1965-1972. Acoustic flat-top, spruce top, pearwood back and sides, ebony 'board, rosewood bridge.

1965-1969		$2,500	$4,000
1970-1972		$2,000	$3,000

Bluegrass Jubilee D-44M

1971-1985. Acoustic flat-top, spruce top, maple back & sides, ebony fingerboard, rosewood bridge.

1971-1985		$1,800	$2,800

Bluegrass Special D-50

1963-1993. Acoustic flat-top, spruce top, rosewood back and sides, ebony fretboard, multi-bound. Reissued in '99.

1963-1968	Brazilian rosewood	$5,000	$7,500
1969-1979	Indian rosewood	$2,200	$3,500
1980-1993	Indian rosewood	$2,000	$3,000

Bluegrass Special D-50 (Reissue)/D-50

1999-2004. Also available with pickup system, initially listed as D-50. Reintroduced in '06.

1999-2004		$1,200	$1,800

Bluegrass Special D-50 (Reintroduced)

2006-2014. New specs, sitka spruce top, rosewood back and sides, ebony 'board, natural.

2006-2014		$1,500	$2,500

Blues 90

2000-2002. Bluesbird single-cut, chambered body, unbound rosewood 'board, dots, 2 Duncan P-90s.

2000-2002		$1,000	$1,500

Bluesbird M-75 (Hollow Body)

1967-1970. Reintroduced from Aristocrat M-75, thinbody electric archtop of maple, spruce ('67) or mahogany, single-cut, 2 pickups, Deluxe has gold hardware, Standard chrome. A solidbody Bluesbird was also introduced in '70.

1967-1970		$2,500	$4,000

Bluesbird M-75 (Solid Body)

1970-1978. Solid body version of Bluesbird M-75, mahogany body, rounded cutaway, 2 pickups, CS with plain top and chrome hardware, GS flamed top and gold hardware.

1970-1978	CS	$2,000	$3,000
1970-1978	GS	$2,500	$3,800

Bluesbird M-75 (Solid Body) Reintroduced

1984-1988. Various pickups; 3 single-coil ('84-'85), 3 EMG ('86), 3 DiMarzio ('87-'88).

1984-1985	Single-coil	$1,200	$1,800
1986	EMG	$1,300	$2,000
1987-1988	DiMarzio	$1,200	$1,800

1975 Guild Bluegrass D-35

Daniel Malone

1973 Guild Bluesbird M-75

Cream City Music

1977 Guild Capri CE-100D
Greg Gagliono

Guild D4-12
Imaged by Heritage Auctions, HA.com

MODEL YEAR	FEATURES	EXC. COND. LOW	HIGH

Bluesbird (Reintroduced)

1994-2003. Single-cut chambered solid body, 2 humbuckers, block inlays, available with AAA flamed maple top.

1994-2003		$1,500	$2,200
2001	Fender CS	$2,500	$4,000

Bluesbird

2011-2012. Single-cut solid body, Chesterfield headstock logo, flame maple top, block markers, 2 humbuckers, natural finish.

2011-2012		$1,000	$1,500

Brian May BHM-1

1984-1987. Electric solid body, double-cut, vibrato, 3 pickups, bound top and back, red or green, Brian May Pro, Special and Standard introduced in '94.

1984-1987		$3,000	$4,500

Brian May Pro

1994-1995. Electric solid body, double-cut, vibrato, 3 pickups, bound top and back, various colors.

1994-1995		$3,000	$4,500

Brian May Signature Red Special

1994. Signature initials on truss rod cover, script signature on back of headstock, BM serial number, dot markers, custom Duncan pickups, custom vibrola, red special finish.

1994		$3,000	$4,500

CA-100 Capri

1956-1973. Acoustic archtop version of CE-100, sharp Florentine cutaway, solid spruce top, laminated maple back and sides, rosewood 'board and bridge, nickel-plated metal parts, natural or sunburst.

1956-1959		$1,800	$2,800
1960-1973		$1,500	$2,200

Capri CE-100

1956-1985. Electric archtop, single Florentine cutaway, 1 pickup (2 pickups by '83), maple body, Waverly tailpiece, sunburst, in '59-'82 CE-100 D listed with 2 pickups.

1956-1959		$2,000	$3,000
1960-1985		$1,500	$2,200

Capri CE-100D

1956-1982. Electric archtop, single Florentine cutaway, 2 pickups, maple body, sunburst, Waverly tailpiece (D dropped, became the Capri CE-100 in '83).

1956-1959		$2,500	$3,800
1960-1982		$2,000	$3,000

Capri CE-100T Tenor

1950s. Electric-archtop Capri 4-string tenor guitar, sunburst.

1956		$2,000	$3,000

CO-1/CO-1C

2006-2008. Contemporary series, F-30 style, red cedar top, solid mahogany neck/back/sides, rosewood 'board, natural. CO-1C with soft cutaway.

2006-2008	CO-1	$700	$1,000
2006-2008	CO-1C	$900	$1,400

CO-2/CO-2C

2008. Contemporary series, as CO-1 but with red spruce top, ebony 'board, and offered in blonde, Antique Burst or Ice Tea Burst. CO-2C with soft cutaway.

2008	CO-2	$1,000	$1,500
2008	CO-2C	$1,200	$1,800

MODEL YEAR	FEATURES	EXC. COND. LOW	HIGH

Cordoba A-50

1961-1972. Acoustic archtop, lowest-end in the Guild archtop line, named Granada A-50 prior to '61.

1961-1965		$1,500	$2,200
1966-1972		$1,200	$1,800

Cordoba T-50 Slim

1961-1973. Thinbody version of Cordoba X-50.

1961-1965		$1,200	$1,800
1966-1969		$1,200	$1,800
1970-1972		$1,000	$1,500

Cordoba X-50

1961-1970. Electric archtop non-cut, laminated maple body, rosewood 'board, 1 pickup, nickel-plated parts.

1961-1965		$1,500	$2,200
1966-1970		$1,200	$1,800

CR-1 Crossroads Single E/Double E

1993-2000. Single-cut solid body acoustic, humbucker (S2 in '93) neck pickup and Piezo bridge, 97 single necks (Single E, '93-'97) and very few 6/12 double necks (Double E, '93, '98-'00) made by Guild custom shop.

1993-1997	Single neck	$1,500	$2,200
1993-2000	Double neck	$3,500	$5,500

Custom F-412 12-String

1968-1986. Special order only from '68-'74, then regular production, 17" wide body 12-string version of F-50 flat-top, spruce top, maple back and sides, arched back, 2-tone block inlays, gold hardware, natural finish.

1968-1969		$2,500	$4,000
1970-1986		$1,800	$2,800

Custom F-512 12-String

1968-1986, 1990. Indian rosewood back and sides version of F-412. See F-512 for reissue.

1968-1969		$3,000	$4,500
1970-1979		$2,500	$3,500
1980-1986		$2,000	$3,000

Custom F-612 12-String

1972-1973. Acoustic 12-string, similar to Custom F-512, but with 18" body, fancy mother-of-pearl inlays, and black/white marquee body, neck and headstock binding.

1972-1973	Brazilian rosewood	$5,000	$7,500
1972-1973	Indian rosewood	$3,500	$5,500

Custom Shop 45th Anniversary

1997. Built in Guild's Nashville Custom Shop, all solid wood, spruce top, maple back and sides, high-end appointments, gold hardware, natural.

1997		$2,500	$4,000

CV-1/CV-1C

2006-2008. Contemporary Vintage series, F-40 style, solid Indian rosewood back/sides, rosewood 'board. CV-1C with sharp cutaway.

2006-2008	CV-1	$800	$1,200
2006-2008	CV-1C	$900	$1,400

CV-2/CV-2C

2008. Contemporary Vintage series, as CV-1 but with flamed maple back/sides, ebony 'board. CV-2C with sharp cutaway.

2008	CV-2	$1,000	$1,500
2008	CV-2C	$1,100	$1,600

MODEL YEAR	FEATURES	EXC. COND. LOW	HIGH

D-4 Series

1991-2002. Dreadnought flat-top, mahogany sides, dot markers.

1991-2002	6-String	$600	$900
1992-1999	12-String	$600	$900

D-6 (D-6E/D-6HG/D-6HE)

1992-1995. Flat-top, 15 3/4", mahogany back and sides, natural satin non-gloss finish, options available.

1992-1995		$600	$900

D-15 Mahogany Rush

1983-1988. Dreadnought flat-top, mahogany body and neck, rosewood 'board, dot inlays, stain finish.

1983-1988		$600	$900

D-15 12-String

1983-1985. 12-string version of Mahogany Rush D-15.

1983-1985		$600	$900

D-16 Mahogany Rush

1984-1986. Like D-15, but with gloss finish.

1984-1986		$800	$1,200

D-17 Mahogany Rush

1984-1988. Like D-15, but with gloss finish and bound body.

1984-1988		$800	$1,200

D-25/D-25M

2003. Solid mahogany body. Refer to Bluegrass D-25 for earlier models. Reintroduced in '06 as GAD-25.

2003		$800	$1,200

D-26 (Guitar Center)

1995. Made for Guitar Center, spruce top, mahogany back and sides, natural finish.

1995		$800	$1,200

D-30

1987-1999. Acoustic flat-top, spruce-top, laminated maple back and solid maple sides, rosewood 'board, multi-bound, various colors.

1987-1999		$1,200	$1,800

D-40

1999-2007. Solid spruce top, mahogany back and sides, rosewood 'board. See earlier models under Bluegrass Jubilee D-40.

1999-2007		$1,200	$1,800

D-40 Bluegrass Jubilee

2006-2014. Indian rosewood, red spruce top, mahogany back and sides, 3-piece neck (mahogany/walnut/mahogany).

2006-2014	No pickup	$1,200	$1,800
2006-2014	With Duncan D-TAR	$1,000	$1,500

D-40 Richie Havens

2003-2014. Richie Havens signature logo on truss rod cover, mahogany sides and back, Fishman Matrix, natural.

2003-2014		$1,200	$1,800

D-40C NT

1975-1991. Pointed cutaway version.

1975-1991		$1,500	$2,200

D-46

1980-1985. Dreadnought acoustic, ash back, sides and neck, spruce top, ebony 'board, ivoroid body binding.

1980-1985		$1,500	$2,200

D-50

See Bluegrass Special Model.

D-55

See TV Model.

D-55 50th Anniversary

2003. Brazilian rosewood, 1953-2003 Anniversary logo.

2003		$4,000	$6,000

D-60

1987-1990, 1998-2000. Renamed from D-66, rosewood back and sides ('87-'90), maple ('98-'00), scalloped bracing, multi-bound top, slotted diamond inlay, G shield logo.

1987-1990	Rosewood	$2,200	$3,300
1998-1999	Maple	$2,200	$3,300

D-64

1984-1986. Maple back and side, multi-bound body, notched diamond inlays, limited production.

1984-1986		$2,200	$3,300

D-66

1984-1987. Amber, rosewood back and sides, 15 3/4", scalloped bracing, renamed D-60 in '87.

1984-1987		$2,200	$3,300

D-70

1981-1985. Dreadnought acoustic, spruce top, Indian rosewood back and sides, multi-bound, ebony 'board with mother-of-pearl inlays.

1981-1985		$3,000	$4,500

D-70-12E

1981-1985. Only 2 made, 12-string version, Fishman electronics.

1981-1985		$3,200	$4,800

D-80

1983-1987. Non-carved heel.

1983-1987		$3,200	$4,800

D-100

1990-1998. Top-of-the-line dreadnought-size acoustic, spruce top, rosewood back and sides, scalloped bracing.

1990-1998		$3,200	$4,800

D-125

2011-2014. All mahogany with Indian rosewood 'board, natural or cherry red.

2011-2014		$400	$600

D-212 12-String/D-25-12/D-212

1981-1983, 1987-1992, 1996-2022. 12-string version of D-25, laminated mahogany back and sides, natural, sunburst or black. Renamed D-25-12 for '87-'92, reintroduced as D-212 '96.

1981-1983		$600	$900

D-412 12-String

1990-1997. Dreadnought, 12 strings, mahogany sides and arched back, satin finished, natural.

1990-1997		$1,200	$1,800

DC-130

1994-1995. US-made, limited run, D-style cutaway, flamed maple top/back/sides.

1994-1995		$2,500	$3,800

DCE True American

1993-2000. Cutaway flat-top acoustic/electric, 1 with mahogany back and sides, 5 with rosewood.

1993-2000	DC-1, DCE-1 True Amer	$600	$900
1994-2000	DCE-5	$700	$1,000

1968 Gretsch Guild D-25

Imaged by Heritage Auctions, HA.com

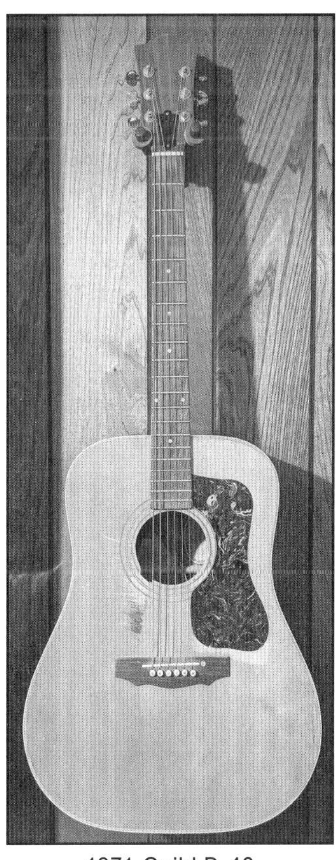

1971 Guild D-40

Richard Potter

GUITARS

1963 Guild Duane Eddy DE-300
Earl Ward

Guild DV-6

MODEL YEAR	FEATURES	EXC. COND. LOW	HIGH

Del Rio M-30

1959-1964. Flat-top, 15", all mahogany body, satin non-gloss finish.

1959		$2,200	$3,300
1960-1964		$2,000	$3,000

Detonator

1987-1990. Electric solid body, double-cut, 3 pickups, bolt-on neck, Guild/Mueller tremolo system, black hardware.

1987-1990		$800	$1,200

DK-70 Peacock Limited Edition

1995-1996. Limited run of 50, Koa, peacock 'guard.

1995-1996		$5,000	$10,000

Duane Eddy Deluxe DE-500

1962-1974, 1984-1987. Electric archtop, single rounded cutaway, 2 pickups (early years and '80s version have DeArmonds), Bigsby, master volume, spruce top with maple back and sides, available in blond (BL) or sunburst (SB).

1962-1964	Natural	$6,000	$9,000
1962-1964	Sunburst	$5,000	$7,500
1965	Natural	$5,000	$7,500
1965	Sunburst	$4,500	$7,000
1966	Natural	$5,000	$7,500
1966	Sunburst	$4,500	$7,000
1967-1969	Various colors	$4,500	$7,000
1970-1974	Various colors	$4,000	$6,000
1984-1987	Various colors	$3,000	$4,500

Duane Eddy Standard DE-400

1963-1974. Electric archtop, single rounded cutaway, 2 pickups, vibrato, natural or sunburst, less appointments than DE-500 Deluxe.

1963	Cherry (option)	$4,500	$6,500
1963	Natural	$4,500	$6,500
1963	Sunburst	$3,500	$5,500
1964	Cherry (option)	$4,000	$6,000
1964	Natural	$4,000	$6,000
1964	Sunburst	$3,500	$5,500
1965	Natural	$3,500	$5,500
1965	Sunburst	$3,000	$4,500
1966	Natural	$3,000	$4,500
1966	Sunburst	$2,500	$4,000
1967-1969	Various colors	$2,500	$4,000
1970-1974	Various colors	$2,200	$3,500

DV Series

1992-2001, 2007-2011. Acoustic flat-tops, mahogany or rosewood back and sides, ebony or rosewood 'board, satin or gloss finish.

1992-2001	DV-52S	$1,200	$2,000
1992-2001	DV-52HG (high gloss)	$1,500	$2,200
1993-1994	DV-76	$2,800	$4,000
1993-1995	DV-62	$1,200	$1,800
1994-1995	DV-72	$2,500	$4,000
1994-1995	DV-73	$2,500	$4,000
1994-1995	DV-82	$1,500	$2,200
1995-1996	DV-74 Pueblo	$2,800	$4,200
1995-1999	DV-6	$700	$1,000
1999-2000	DV-25	$900	$1,400
1995-1999	DV-6HG (high gloss)	$1,000	$1,500
1999-2001	DV-4	$500	$800
1999-2001	DV-4HG (high gloss)	$800	$1,200

Economy M-20

1958-1965, 1969-1973. Mahogany body, acoustic flat-top, natural or sunburst satin finish.

1958-1959		$2,000	$3,000
1960-1969		$1,800	$2,800
1970-1973		$1,500	$2,200

F-4CEHG

1992-2002. High Gloss finish, single-cut flat-top, acoustic/electric.

1992-2002		$600	$900

F-5CE

1992-2001. Acoustic/electric, single-cut, rosewood back and sides, dot inlays, chrome tuners.

1992-2001		$600	$900

F-30

1990-2001. Formerly the Aragon F-30, made in Westerly, Rhode Island.

1990-2001		$1,200	$1,800

F-30R-LS

1990s. Custom Shop, limited production, bearclaw spruce top, rosewood sides and back.

1990s		$1,500	$2,200

F-44

1984-1987. Acoustic flat-top, maple, designed by George Gruhn.

1984-1987		$1,800	$2,800

F-45CE

1983-1992. Acoustic/electric, single-cut, mahogany or maple back and sides, rosewood 'board, on-board electronics, natural. Early '87 model was named GF-45CE (flamed maple), by mid '87 it was back to F-45CE.

1983-1984	Laminated mahogany	$800	$1,200
1985-1986	Flamed maple	$1,000	$1,500
1987	Early '87, GF-45CE	$1,000	$1,500
1987-1992	Mid '87, F-45CE	$1,000	$1,500

F-46

1984. Jumbo body style flat-top, designed for Guild by George Gruhn.

1984		$2,500	$3,800

F-47M/F-47MC

2007-2016. Made in the USA, solid flamed maple sides and back, MC with cutaway.

2007-2016	F-47M	$1,800	$2,800
2007-2016	F-47MC	$1,800	$2,800

F-47R/F-47RC

2008-2014. Solid rosewood sides and back, available with electronics, RC with cutaway.

2008-2014		$1,800	$2,800

F-47RCE Grand Auditorium

1999-2003. Cutaway acoustic/electric, rosewood back and sides, block inlays.

1999-2003		$1,800	$2,800

F-50/F-50R

2002-2016. Jumbo, solid spruce top, solid maple sides, arched laminated maple back, abalone rosette. See Navarre F-50/F-50R for earlier models.

2002-2016	F-50, maple	$2,000	$3,000
2002-2016	F-50R, rosewood	$2,000	$3,000

MODEL YEAR	FEATURES	EXC. COND. LOW	HIGH

F-65CE

1992-2001. Acoustic/electric, single-cut, rosewood back and sides, block inlay, gold tuners.

1992-2001		$2,000	$3,000

F-212 12-String/F-212XL

1964-1986, 1998-2000. Acoustic flat-top jumbo, 12 strings, spruce top, mahogany back and sides, 16" body. Named F-212XL in '66, then XL dropped from name in '98.

1964-1965	F-212	$1,200	$1,800
1966-1986	F-212XL	$1,200	$1,800
1998-2000	F-212	$900	$1,400

F-312 Artist 12-String

1964-1973. Flat-top, rosewood back and sides, spruce top, no board inlay (but some in '72 may have dots).

1964-1968	Brazilian rosewood	$4,500	$6,500
1969-1973	Indian rosewood	$2,000	$3,000

F-412

2002-2016. Solid spruce top, solid maple back and sides, block inlays, 12-string. See Custom F-412 for earlier models.

2002-2016		$1,800	$2,800

F-512

2002-present. Solid spruce top, rosewood back and sides, 12-string. See Custom F-512 for earlier models.

2002-2024		$2,000	$3,000

Freshman M-65

1958-1973. Electric archtop, single-cut, mahogany back and sides, f-holes, 1 single-coil (some with 2), sunburst or natural top.

1958-1959		$2,000	$3,000
1960-1969		$1,500	$2,200
1970-1973		$1,300	$2,000

Freshman M-65 3/4

1958-1973. Short-scale version of M-65, 1 pickup.

1958-1959		$1,500	$2,200
1960-1969		$1,200	$1,800
1970-1973		$1,200	$1,800

FS-20CE

1986-1987. Solid body acoustic, routed mahogany body.

1986-1987		$700	$1,000

FS-46CE

1983-1986. Flat-top acoustic/electric, pointed cutaway, mahogany, black, natural or sunburst.

1983-1986		$800	$1,200

G-5P

1988-ca.1989. Handmade in Spain, cedar top, gold-plated hardware.

1988-1989		$1,200	$1,800

G-37

1973-1986. Acoustic flat-top, spruce top, laminated maple back and sides, rosewood 'board and bridge, sunburst or natural top.

1973-1986		$1,200	$1,800

G-41

1974-1978. Acoustic flat-top, spruce top, mahogany back and sides, rosewood 'board and bridge, 20 frets.

1975-1978		$1,200	$1,800

G-45 Hank Williams Jr.

1982-1986, 1993-1996. Hank Williams Jr. logo on 'guard, flat-top.

1982-1996		$1,300	$2,000

G-75

1975-1977. Acoustic flat-top, 3/4-size version of D-50, spruce top, rosewood back and sides, mahogany neck, ebony 'board and bridge.

1975-1977		$1,200	$1,800

G-212 12-String

1974-1983. Acoustic flat-top 12-string version of D-40, spruce top, mahogany back and sides, natural or sunburst.

1974-1983		$1,200	$1,800

G-212XL 12-String

1974-1983. 17" version of G-212 12-String.

1974-1983		$1,200	$1,800

G-312 12-String

1974-1987. Acoustic flat-top 12-string version of the D-50, spruce top, rosewood back and sides. Renamed D-50-12 in '87.

1974-1987		$1,200	$1,800

GAD (Guild Acoustic Design) Series

2004-2014. Imported, all models begin with GAD, various woods, some with electronics (E).

2004-2014	Various models	$500	$1,200

George Barnes AcoustiLectric

1962-1972. Electric archtop, single-cut, solid spruce top, curly maple back and sides, multi-bound, 2 humbuckers, gold-plated hardware, sunburst or natural finish.

1962-1972		$4,000	$6,000

George Barnes Guitar in F

1963-1973. Smaller electric archtop at 13.5", 2 humbuckers, chrome hardware.

1963-1973		$4,000	$6,000

GF-25

1987-1992. Acoustic flat-top, mahogany back and sides.

1987-1992		$700	$1,000

GF-25C

1988-1991. Cutaway GF-25.

1988-1991		$1,000	$1,500

GF-30

1987-1991. Acoustic flat-top, maple back/sides/neck, multi-bound.

1987-1991		$1,100	$1,600

GF-40

1987-1991. Mahogany back and sides, multi-bound.

1987-1991		$1,200	$1,800

GF-50

1987-1991. Acoustic flat-top, rosewood back and sides, mahogany neck, multi-bound.

1987-1991		$1,200	$1,800

GF-55

1990-1991. Jumbo acoustic, spruce top, rosewood back and sides, natural.

1990-1991		$1,800	$2,800

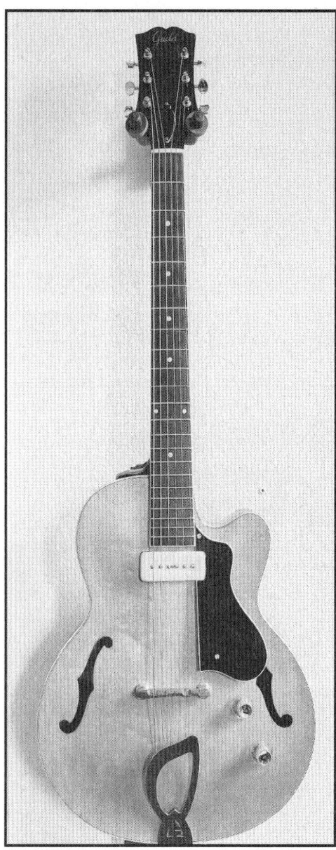

1958 Guild Freshman M-65

Charlie Apicella

1957 Guild Grenada/ Cordova X-50

Imaged by Heritage Auctions, HA.com

GUITARS

1993 Guild JF-30
Imaged by Heritage Auctions, HA.com

1958 Guild Johnny Smith Award
Richard Sarmento

MODEL YEAR	FEATURES	EXC. COND. LOW	HIGH

GF-60

1987-1989. Jumbo size, rosewood or maple sides and back, diamond markers. Cutaway version available.

1987-1989	GF-60C, cutaway	$2,200	$3,300
1987-1989	GF-60M, maple	$2,200	$3,300
1987-1989	GF-60R, rosewood	$2,200	$3,300

Granada A-50 (Acoustic Archtop)

1956-1960. Lowest-end acoustic archtop in the Guild line, renamed Cordoba A-50 in '61.

1956-1960		$1,200	$1,800

Granada X-50

1954-1961. Electric archtop, non-cut, laminated all maple body, rosewood 'board and bridge, nickel-plated metal parts, 1 pickup, sunburst. Renamed Cordoba X-50 in '61.

1954-1959		$1,500	$2,200
1960-1961		$1,200	$1,800

GV (Guild Vintage) Series

1993-1995. Flat-top, rosewood back and sides, various enhancements.

1993-1995	GV-52, rw, gloss	$1,100	$1,600
1993-1995	GV-52, rw, satin	$1,000	$1,500
1993-1995	GV-70, abalone, gloss	$1,100	$1,600
1993-1995	GV-72, herring-bone, gloss	$1,100	$1,600

Jet Star S-50

1963-1970. Electric solid body, double-cut, mahogany or alder body, 1 pickup, vibrato optional by '65, asymmetrical headstock until '65. Reintroduced as S-50 in '72-'78 with body redesign.

1963-1965	3-on-side	$2,000	$3,000
1966-1969	6-in-line	$1,500	$2,200
1970	6-in-line	$1,500	$2,200

JF-4NT

1992-1995. Jumbo flat-top, mahogany, natural.

1992-1995		$900	$1,400

JF-30

1987-2004. Jumbo 6-string acoustic, spruce top, laminated maple back, solid maple sides, multi-bound. Becomes GAD-JF30 in '04.

1987-2004		$1,200	$1,800

JF-30-12

1987-2004. 12-string version of the JF-30.

1987-2004		$1,200	$1,800

JF-30E

1994-2004. Acoustic/electric version.

1994-2004		$1,200	$1,800

JF-50R

1987-1988. Jumbo 6-string acoustic, rosewood back and sides, multi-bound.

1987-1988		$1,200	$1,800

JF-55

1989-2000. Jumbo flat-top, spruce top, rosewood body.

1989-2000		$1,800	$2,800

JF-55-12

1991-2000. 12-string JF-55.

1991-2000		$1,800	$2,800

JF-65

1987-1994. Renamed from Navarre F-50, Jumbo flat-top acoustic, spruce top, R has rosewood back and sides and M has maple.

1987-1994	JF-65M, maple	$2,200	$3,300
1987-1994	JF-65R, rosewood	$2,200	$3,300

JF-65-12

1987-2001. 12-string, version of JF-65.

1987-2001	JF-65M-12, maple	$2,200	$3,300
1987-2001	JF-65R-12, rosewood	$2,200	$3,300

JF-100

1992-2000. Jumbo, maple top, rosewood back and sides, abalone trim, natural. Carved heel available '94-'00.

1992-1995		$3,000	$4,500

JF-100-12

1992-2000. Jumbo 12-string version, non-carved or carved heel.

1994-2000	Carved heel	$3,000	$4,500

Johnny Smith Award

1956-1961. Single-cut electric archtop, floating DeArmond pickup, multi-bound, gold hardware, sunburst or natural, renamed Artist Award in '61.

1956-1961		$6,500	$10,000

Johnny Smith Award - Benedetto

2004-2006. Only 18 custom made under the supervision of Bob Benedetto, signed by Johnny Smith, with certificate of authenticity signed by Smith and Benedetto.

2004-2006	18 made	$5,000	$7,500

JV-72

1993-1999. Jumbo acoustic, custom turquoise inlay.

1993-1999		$2,200	$3,300

Liberator Elite

1988. Limited Edition, set-neck, offset double-cut solid body, figured maple top, mahogany body, rising-sun inlays, 3 active pickups, last of the Guild solidbodies.

1988		$1,000	$1,500

M-80CS/M-80

1975-1984. Solidbody, double-cut, 2 pickups, introduced as M-80CS with bound rosewood 'board and block inlays, shortened to M-80 in '80 with unbound ebony 'board and dots.

1975-1980		$1,500	$2,200

Manhattan X-170 (Mini-Manhattan X-170)

1985-2002. Called Mini-Manhattan X-170 in '85-'86, electric archtop hollow body, single rounded cutaway, maple body, f-holes, 2 humbuckers, block inlays, gold hardware, natural or sunburst.

1985-2002		$2,000	$3,000

Manhattan X-175 (Sunburst)

1954-1985. Electric archtop, single rounded cutaway, laminated spruce top, laminated maple back and sides, 2 pickups, chrome hardware, sunburst. Reissued as X-160 Savoy.

1954-1959		$2,200	$3,300
1960-1969		$2,000	$3,000
1970-1985		$1,800	$2,800

MODEL YEAR	FEATURES	EXC. COND. LOW	HIGH

Manhattan X-175 B (Natural)

1954-1976. Natural finish X-175.

1954-1959		$2,200	$3,300
1960-1969		$2,000	$3,000
1970-1976		$2,000	$3,000

Mark I

1961-1972. Classical, Honduras mahogany body, rosewood 'board, slotted headstock.

1961-1969		$400	$600
1970-1973		$300	$500

Mark II

1961-1987. Like Mark I, but with spruce top and body binding.

1961-1969		$600	$900
1970-1979		$400	$600
1980-1987		$300	$500

Mark III

1961-1987. Like Mark II, but with Peruvian mahogany back and sides and floral sound hole design.

1961-1969		$600	$900
1970-1979		$500	$800
1980-1987		$400	$600

Mark IV

1961-1985. Like Mark III, but with flamed pearwood back and sides (rosewood offered in '61, maple in '62).

1961-1969	Pearwood	$700	$1,000
1970-1979	Pearwood	$600	$900
1980-1985	Pearwood	$500	$800

Mark V

1961-1987. Like Mark III, but with rosewood back and sides (maple available for '61-'64).

1961-1968	Brazilian rw	$1,800	$2,800
1969-1979	Indian rw	$700	$1,000
1980-1987	Indian rw	$500	$800

Mark VI

1962-1973. Rosewood back and sides, spruce top, wood binding.

1962-1968	Brazilian rw	$2,500	$3,800
1969-1973	Indian rw	$800	$1,200

Mark VII Custom

1968-1973. Special order only, spruce top, premium rosewood back and sides, inlaid rosewood bridge, engraved gold tuners.

1962-1968	Brazilian rw	$2,800	$4,200
1969-1973	Indian rw	$1,000	$1,500

Navarre F-48

1972-1975. 17", mahogany, block markers.

1972-1975		$1,500	$2,200

Navarre F-50/F-50

1954-1986, 1994-1995. Acoustic flat-top, spruce top, curly maple back and sides, rosewood 'board and bridge, 17" rounded lower bout, laminated arched maple back, renamed JF-65 M in '87. Reissued in '94 and again in '02 as the F-50.

1954-1956		$5,500	$8,000
1957-1962	Pearl block markers	$5,500	$8,000
1963-1969	Ebony 'board	$5,000	$7,500
1970-1995		$2,500	$3,800

Navarre F-50R/F-50R

1965-1987. Rosewood back and side version of F-50, renamed JF-65 R in '87. Reissued in '02 as F-50R.

1965-1968	Brazilian rw	$7,500	$10,000
1969-1987	Indian rw	$3,000	$4,500

Nightbird

1985-1987. Single-cut solid body, tone chambers, 2 pickups, multi-bound, black or gold hardware, renamed Nightbird II in '87.

1985-1987		$2,000	$3,000

Nightbird I

1987-1988. Like Nightbird but with chrome hardware, less binding and appointments.

1987-1988		$2,000	$3,000

Nightbird II

1987-1992. Renamed from Nightbird, with black hardware, renamed Nightbird X-2000 in '92.

1987-1992		$2,000	$3,000

Nightbird X-2000

1992-1996. Renamed from Nightbird II.

1992-1996		$2,000	$3,000

Park Ave X-180

2005. Cutaway acoustic archtop, 2 pickups, block markers.

2005		$1,200	$1,800

Peregrine

1999-2005. Solid body acoustic, cutaway, Fishman.

1999-2005	Custom	$1,000	$1,500
1999-2005	Flamed maple	$1,100	$1,600
1999-2005	S7CE, (CS)	$1,100	$1,600
1999-2005	S7CE, (CS), quilted	$1,100	$1,600
1999-2005	Standard	$900	$1,400

Polara S-100

1963-1970. Double-cut mahogany or alder solid body, rosewood 'board, 2 single coils, built-in stand until '70, asymmetrical headstock, in '70 Polara dropped from title (see S-100), renamed Polara S-100 in '97.

1963-1970	2 or 3 pickups	$2,000	$3,000

Roy Buchanan T-200

1986. Single-cut solid body, 2 pickups, pointed six-on-a-side headstock, poplar body, bolt-on neck, gold and brass hardware.

1986		$600	$900

S-50

1972-1978. Double-cut solid body, 1 single-coil (switched to humbucker in '74), dot inlay.

1972-1978		$1,100	$1,600

S-60/S-60D

1976-1981. Double-cut solid body with long bass horn, 1 humbucker (60) or 2 single-coils (60D), mahogany body, rosewood 'board.

1976-1981		$1,000	$1,500

S-65D

1980-1981. S-60 but with 1 DiMarzio Super Distortion pickup.

1980-1981		$1,000	$1,500

S-70D/S-70AD

1979-1981. Solid body (mahogany D, ash AD), rosewood 'board, 3 single-coils.

1979-1981	S-70AD	$1,200	$1,800
1979-1981	S-70D	$1,200	$1,800

1963 Guild S-50

Rivington Guitars

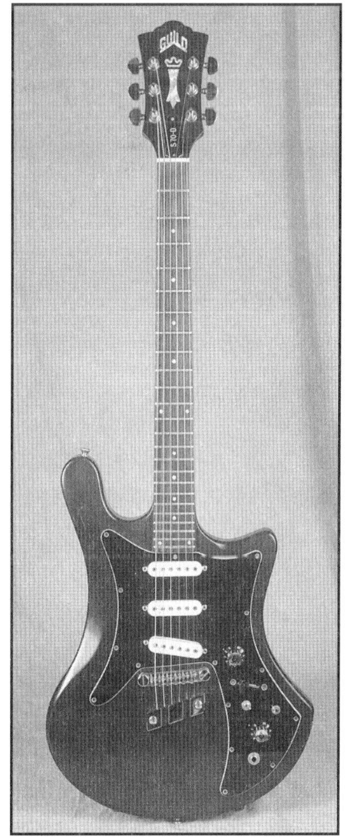

1979 Guild S-70D

GUITARS

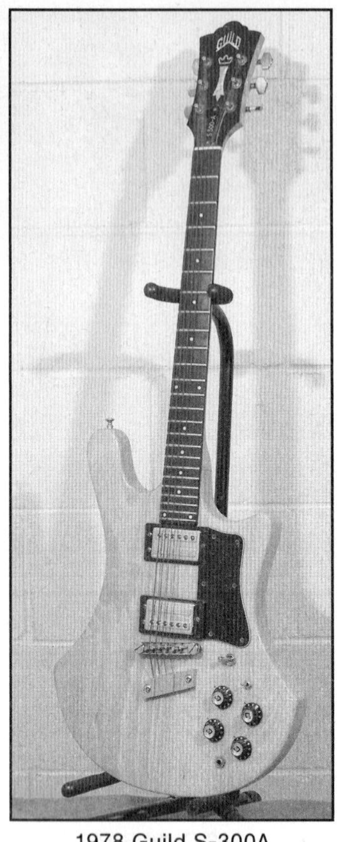
1978 Guild S-300A
Tom Pfeifer

1962 Guild Slim Jim T-100D
Brian Chambers

MODEL YEAR	FEATURES	EXC. COND. LOW	HIGH

S-90

1972-1977. Double-cut SG-like body, 2 humbuckers, dot inlay, chrome hardware.

1972-1977		$1,200	$1,800

S-100

1970-1978, 1994-1996. S-100 Standard is double-cut solid body, 2 humbuckers, block inlays. Deluxe of '72-'75 had added Bigsby. Standard Carved '74-'77 has acorns and oakleaves carved in the top.

1970-1978	Standard	$2,000	$3,000
1972-1975	Deluxe	$2,000	$3,000
1974-1977	Standard Carved	$2,000	$3,000

S-100 Reissue

1994-1997. Renamed Polara in '97.

1994-1997		$800	$1,200

S-250

1981-1983. Double-cut solid body, 2 humbuckers.

1981-1983		$500	$800

S-261

Ca.1985. Double-cut, maple body, black Kahler tremolo, 1 humbucker and 2 single-coil pickups, rosewood 'board.

1985		$500	$800

S-270 Runaway

1985. Offset double-cut solid body, 1 humbucker, Kahler.

1985		$500	$800

S-271 Sprint

1986. Replaced the S-270.

1986		$500	$800

S-275

1982-1983. Offset double-cut body, 2 humbuckers, bound figured maple top, sunburst or natural.

1982-1983		$500	$800

S-280 Flyer

1983-1984. Double-cut poplar body, 2 humbuckers or 3 single-coils, maple or rosewood neck, dot markers.

1983-1984		$500	$800

S-281 Flyer

1983-1988. Double-cut poplar body S-280 with locking vibrato, optional pickups available.

1983-1988		$500	$800

S-284 Starling/Aviator

1984-1988. Starling (early-'84) and Aviator (late-'84-'88), double-cut, 3 pickups.

1984	Starling	$500	$800
1984-1988	Aviator	$500	$800

S-285 Aviator

1986. Deluxe Aviator, bound 'board, fancy inlays.

1986		$500	$800

S-300 Series

1976-1983. Double-cut mahogany solid body with larger bass horn and rounded bottom, 2 humbuckers. S-300 A has ash body, D has exposed DiMarzio humbuckers.

1976-1983	S-300	$1,100	$1,600
1977-1982	S-300D	$1,100	$1,600
1977-1983	S-300A	$1,100	$1,600

S-400/S-400A

1980-1981. Double-cut solid body, mahogany (400) or ash (400A), 2 humbuckers.

1980-1981		$1,000	$1,500

Savoy A-150

1958-1973, 2013-present. Acoustic archtop version of X-150, available with floating pickup, natural or sunburst finish. Reissued in '13, part of Newark St. Collection.

1958-1961	Natural	$2,200	$3,300
1958-1961	Sunburst	$2,000	$3,000
2013-2024		$1,200	$1,800

Savoy X-150

1954-1965. Electric archtop, rounded single-cut, spruce top, maple back and sides, rosewood 'board and bridge, 1 single-coil pickup, sunburst, blond or sparkling gold finish. Reissued in '98 as X-150 Savoy.

1954	Sunburst	$2,800	$4,200
1955-1959	Sunburst	$2,500	$3,800
1960-1965	Sunburst	$2,200	$3,300

Slim Jim T-100

1958-1973. Electric archtop thinline, single-cut, laminated all-maple body, rosewood 'board and bridge, Waverly tailpiece, 1 pickup, natural or sunburst.

1958-1959		$2,300	$3,300
1960-1964		$2,000	$3,000
1965-1969		$1,800	$2,800
1970-1973		$1,500	$2,500

Slim Jim T-100D

1958-1973. Semi-hollow body electric, single Florentine cutaway, thinline, 2-pickup version of the T-100, natural or sunburst.

1958-1959		$2,500	$3,800
1960-1964		$2,200	$3,300
1965-1969		$2,000	$3,000
1970-1973		$1,800	$2,800

Songbird S Series

1984-1991. Designed by George Gruhn, flat-top, mahogany back, spruce top, single pointed cutaway, pickup with preamp, multi-bound top, black, natural or white. Renamed S-4 later in run.

1984-1991		$1,000	$1,500

Standard (STD) Series

2010-2014. Imported flat-top acoustics based on various classic Guild models.

2010-2014		$1,100	$1,600

Standard F-112 12-String

1968-1982. Acoustic flat-top, spruce top, mahogany back, sides and neck.

1968-1969		$1,200	$1,800
1970-1982		$1,000	$1,500

Starfire I

1960-1964. Electric archtop, single-cut thinline, laminated maple or mahogany body, bound body and neck, 1 pickup, Starfire Red finish.

1960-1961		$1,500	$2,200
1962-1964		$1,500	$2,200

Starfire II

1960-1976, 1997-2001. Electric archtop, single-cut thinline, laminated maple or mahogany body, bound body and rosewood neck, 2 pickups, various colors.

1960-1961	Sunburst	$2,400	$3,600
1962	Emerald Green	$2,400	$3,600
1962-1966	Special color options	$2,600	$4,000

MODEL YEAR	FEATURES	EXC. COND. LOW	HIGH
1962-1966	Sunburst, Starfire Red	$2,400	$3,600
1967-1969	Sunburst, Starfire Red	$2,200	$3,300
1970-1976	Sunburst, Starfire Red	$2,000	$3,000
1997-2001	Reissue	$1,400	$2,100

Starfire III

1960-1974, 1997-2005, 2013-present. Electric archtop, single-cut thinline, laminated maple or mahogany body, bound body and rosewood neck, 2 pickups, Guild or Bigsby vibrato, Starfire Red. Reissued in '13, part of Newark St. Collection.

1960-1966		$3,000	$4,500
1967-1974		$2,800	$4,200
1997-2005	Reissue	$1,500	$2,200
2013-2024	Newark St	$900	$1,400

Starfire IV

1963-1987, 1991-2005. Thinline, double-cut semi-hollow body, laminated maple or mahogany body, f-holes, 2 humbuckers, rosewood 'board, cherry or sunburst.

1963-1966		$3,000	$4,500
1967-1975		$2,800	$4,200
1976-1987		$2,500	$3,800
1991-2005	Reissue	$1,500	$2,200

Starfire IV Special (Custom Shop)

2001-2002. Nashville Custom Shop.

2001-2002		$1,800	$2,800

Starfire V

1963-1973, 1999-2001. Same as Starfire IV but with block markers, Bigsby and master volume, natural or sunburst finish, reissued in '99.

1963-1966		$3,000	$4,500
1967-1973		$2,800	$4,200
1999-2001	Reissue	$1,500	$2,200

Starfire VI

1964-1979. Same as Starfire IV but with higher appointments such as ebony 'board, pearl inlays, Guild/Bigsby vibrato, natural or sunburst.

1964-1966		$3,000	$4,500
1967-1975		$2,800	$4,200
1976-1979		$2,500	$3,800

Starfire XII

1966-1973. Electric archtop, 12-string, double-cut, maple or mahogany body, set-in neck, 2 humbuckers, harp tailpiece.

1966-1969		$2,200	$3,300
1970-1973		$2,200	$3,300

Stratford A-350

1956-1973. Acoustic archtop, rounded single-cut, solid spruce top with solid curly maple back and sides, rosewood 'board and bridge (changed to ebony by '60), sunburst.

1956-1959		$3,000	$4,500
1960-1965		$2,800	$4,200
1966-1969		$2,500	$3,800
1970-1973		$2,500	$3,800

Stratford A-350B

1956-1973. A-350 in blond/natural finish option.

1956-1959		$3,500	$5,000
1960-1965		$3,000	$4,500
1966-1969		$2,800	$4,200
1970-1973		$2,500	$3,800

Stratford X-350

1954-1965. Electric archtop, rounded single-cut, laminated spruce top with laminated maple back and sides, rosewood 'board, 6 push-button pickup selectors, sunburst finish (natural finish is X-375).

1954-1959		$3,800	$6,000
1960-1965		$3,200	$5,000

Stratford X-375/X-350B

1953-1965. Natural finish version of X-350, renamed X-350B in '58.

1953-1958	X-375	$4,000	$6,000
1959-1965	X-350B	$3,500	$5,500

Stuart A-500

1956-1969. Acoustic archtop single-cut, 17" body, A-500 sunburst, available with Guild logo, floating DeArmond pickup.

1956-1959		$3,500	$5,500
1960-1965		$3,500	$5,500
1966-1969		$3,000	$4,500

Stuart A-550/A-500B

1956-1969. Natural blond finish version of Stuart A-500, renamed A-500B in '60.

1956-1959		$3,500	$5,500
1960-1965		$3,200	$5,000
1966-1969		$3,000	$4,500

Stuart X-500

1953-1995. Electric archtop, single-cut, laminated spruce top, laminated curly maple back and sides, 2 pickups, sunburst.

1953-1959		$4,000	$6,000
1960-1965		$3,800	$5,500
1966-1969		$3,500	$5,000
1970-1995		$3,200	$4,800

Stuart X-550/X-500B

1953-1995. Natural blond finish Stuart X-550, renamed X-500B in '60.

1953-1959		$4,000	$6,000
1960-1964		$3,800	$5,500
1965-1969		$3,500	$5,000
1970-1995		$3,200	$4,800

Studio 301/ST301

1968-1970. Thinline, semi-hollow archtop Starfire-style but with sharp horns, 1 single-coil pickup, 2 humbuckers in '70, dot inlays, cherry or sunburst.

1968-1969	1 single-coil	$1,200	$1,800
1970	2 humbuckers	$1,500	$2,200

Studio 302/ST302

1968-1970. Like Studio 301, but with 2 pickups.

1968-1969	2 single-coils	$1,800	$2,800
1970	2 humbuckers	$1,800	$2,800

Studio 303/ST303

1968-1970. Like Studio 301, but with 2 pickups and Guild/Bigsby.

1968-1969	2 single-coils	$2,000	$3,000
1969-1970	2 humbuckers	$2,000	$3,000

Studio 402/ST402

1969-1970. Inch thicker body than other Studios, 2 pickups, block inlays.

1969-1970	2 humbuckers	$2,500	$3,800
1969-1970	2 single-coils	$2,500	$3,800

1975 Standard F-112
Rivington Guitars

1967 Guild Starfire V lefty
Paul Swanson

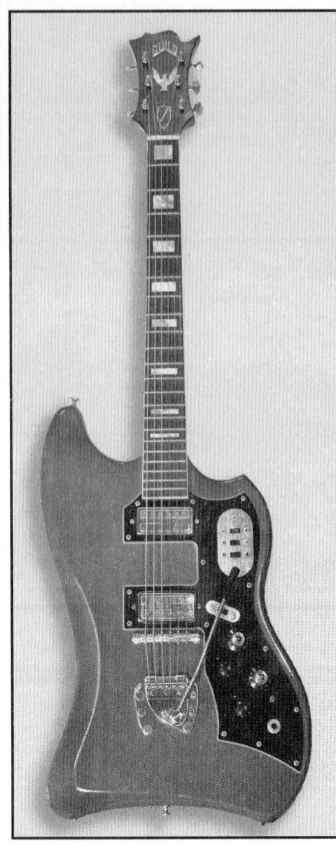

1963 Guild Thunderbird S-200

Ben Rogers

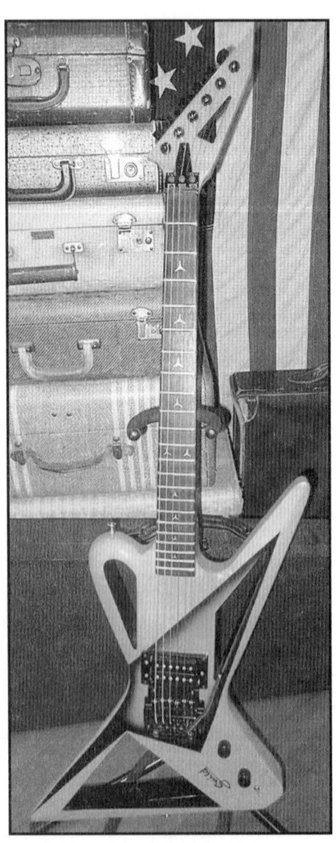

1985 Guild X-100 Bladerunner

Rivington Guitars

T-250

1986-1988. Single-cut body and pickup configuration with banana-style headstock.

MODEL YEAR	FEATURES	EXC. COND. LOW	HIGH
1986-1988		$500	$800

Thunderbird S-200

1963-1968. Electric solid body, offset double-cut, built-in rear guitar stand, AdjustoMatic bridge and vibrato tailpiece, 2 humbucker pickups, changed to single-coils in '66.

MODEL YEAR	FEATURES	EXC. COND. LOW	HIGH
1963-1965	Humbuckers	$4,500	$6,500
1966-1968	Single-coils	$4,000	$6,000

Troubadour F-20

1956-1987. Acoustic flat-top, spruce top with maple back and sides (mahogany '59 and after), rosewood 'board and bridge, natural or sunburst.

MODEL YEAR	FEATURES	EXC. COND. LOW	HIGH
1956-1959		$2,200	$3,300
1960-1964		$2,000	$3,000
1965-1969		$2,000	$3,000
1970-1979		$1,500	$2,200
1980-1987		$1,200	$1,800

TV Model D-55/D-65/D-55

1968-1987, 1990-present (special order only for 1968-1973). Dreadnought acoustic, spruce top, rosewood back and sides, scalloped bracing, gold-plated tuners, renamed D-65 in '87. Reintroduced as D-55 in '90.

MODEL YEAR	FEATURES	EXC. COND. LOW	HIGH
1968-1969		$2,200	$3,300
1970-1987		$2,200	$3,300
1988-1989	D-65	$2,200	$3,300
1990-1999	D-55	$2,200	$3,300
2000-2024	D-55	$2,200	$3,300

Willy Porter Signature

2007-2008. AAA Sitka spruce top, solid flamed maple sides and back, special appointments, Fishman Ellipse system.

MODEL YEAR	FEATURES	EXC. COND. LOW	HIGH
2007-2008		$1,200	$1,800

X-79 Skyhawk

1981-1986. Four-point solid body, 2 pickups, coil-tap or phase switch, various colors. Custom graphics available '84-'86.

MODEL YEAR	FEATURES	EXC. COND. LOW	HIGH
1981-1986		$1,000	$1,500

X-80 Skylark/Swan

1982-1985. Solid body with 2 deep cutaways, banana-style 6-on-a-side headstock, renamed Swan in '85.

MODEL YEAR	FEATURES	EXC. COND. LOW	HIGH
1982-1985		$1,000	$1,500

X-82 Nova/Starfighter

1981-1986. Solid body, XR-7 humbuckerss, also available with 3 single-coil pickups, Quick Change SP-6 tailpiece, Adjusto-Matic bridge, Deluxe tuning machine.

MODEL YEAR	FEATURES	EXC. COND. LOW	HIGH
1981-1983	Nova	$1,000	$1,500
1984-1986	Starfighter	$1,000	$1,500

X-88 Flying Star Motley Crue

1984-1986. Pointy 4-point star body, rocket ship meets spearhead headstock on bolt neck, 1 pickup, optional vibrato.

MODEL YEAR	FEATURES	EXC. COND. LOW	HIGH
1984-1986		$1,000	$1,500

X-88D Star

1984-1987. 2 humbucker version X-88.

MODEL YEAR	FEATURES	EXC. COND. LOW	HIGH
1984-1987		$1,000	$1,500

X-92 Citron

1984. Electric solid body, detachable body section, 3 pickups.

MODEL YEAR	FEATURES	EXC. COND. LOW	HIGH
1984		$900	$1,400

X-100/X-110

1953-1954. Guild was founded in 1952, so this is a very early model, 17" non-cut, single-coil soapbar neck pickup, X-100 sunburst, X-110 natural blond.

MODEL YEAR	FEATURES	EXC. COND. LOW	HIGH
1953-1954	X-100	$2,000	$3,000
1953-1954	X-110	$2,200	$3,300

X-100 Bladerunner

1985-1987. 4-point body with large cutouts, 1 humbucker, Kahler, script Guild logo on body, cutout headstock.

MODEL YEAR	FEATURES	EXC. COND. LOW	HIGH
1985-1987		$2,500	$3,800

X-150 Savoy/X-150D Savoy

1998-2013. Replaces Savoy X-150, 1 pickup, D has 2 pickups.

MODEL YEAR	FEATURES	EXC. COND. LOW	HIGH
1998-2005	X-150	$1,100	$1,600
1998-2013	X-150D	$1,200	$1,800

X-160 Savoy

1989-1993. No Bigsby, black or sunburst.

MODEL YEAR	FEATURES	EXC. COND. LOW	HIGH
1989-1993		$1,500	$2,200

X-161 Savoy/X-160B Savoy

1989-1994. X-160 Savoy with Bigsby, sunburst or black.

MODEL YEAR	FEATURES	EXC. COND. LOW	HIGH
1989-1994		$1,500	$2,200

X-200/X-220

1953-1954. Electric archtop, spruce top, laminated maple body, rosewood 'board, non-cut, 2 pickups. X-200 is sunburst and X-220 blond.

MODEL YEAR	FEATURES	EXC. COND. LOW	HIGH
1953-1954	X-200	$2,200	$3,300
1953-1954	X-220	$2,500	$3,800

X-300/X-330

1953-1954. No model name, non-cut, 2 pickups, X-300 is sunburst and X-330 blond. Becomes Savoy X-150 in '54.

MODEL YEAR	FEATURES	EXC. COND. LOW	HIGH
1953-1954	X-300	$2,200	$3,300
1953-1954	X-330	$2,500	$3,800

X-400/X-440

1953-1954. Electric archtop, single-cut, spruce top, laminated maple body, rosewood 'board, 2 pickups, X-400 in sunburst and X-440 in blond. Becomes Manhattan X-175 in '54.

MODEL YEAR	FEATURES	EXC. COND. LOW	HIGH
1953-1954	X-400	$3,000	$4,500
1953-1954	X-440	$3,200	$4,800

X-600/X-660

1953. No model name, single-cut, 3 pickups, X-600 in sunburst and X-660 in blond. Becomes Stratford X-350 in '54.

MODEL YEAR	FEATURES	EXC. COND. LOW	HIGH
1953	X-600	$4,000	$6,000
1953	X-660	$4,500	$6,500

X-700

1994-1999. Rounded cutaway, 17", solid spruce top, laminated maple back and sides, gold hardware, natural or sunburst.

MODEL YEAR	FEATURES	EXC. COND. LOW	HIGH
1994-1999		$2,200	$3,300

Guillermo Roberto Guitars

Professional grade, solidbody electric bajo quintos made in San Fernando, California starting in the year 2000.

MODEL YEAR	FEATURES	EXC. COND. LOW	HIGH

Guitar Company of America

1971-2015. Professional grade, custom, acoustic guitars and mandolins built by luthier Dixie Michell. Originally built in Tennessee, then Missouri and finally in Tulsa, Oklahoma. Michell died in '15.

Guitar Mill

2006-2011. Luthier Mario Martin built his production/custom, professional grade, semi-hollow and solidbody guitars and basses in Murfreesboro, Tennessee. He also built basses. In '11, he started branding his guitars as Mario Martin.

Gurian

1965-1981. Luthier Michael Gurian started making classical guitars on a special-order basis, in New York City. In '69, he started building steel-string guitars as well. 1971 brought a move to Hinsdale, Vermont, with increased production. In February, '79 a fire destroyed his factory, stock, and tools. He reopened in West Swanzey, New Hampshire, but closed the doors in '81. Around 2,000 Gurian instruments were built. The guitars have unusual neck joint construction and can be difficult, if not impossible, to repair. Dealers have reported that '70s models sometimes have notable wood cracks which require repair.

CL Series

1970-1981. Classical Series, mahogany (M), Indian rosewood (R), or Brazilian rosewood (B).

1970-1981	CLB, Brazilian rw	$3,000	$4,000
1970-1981	CLM, mahogany	$1,500	$2,000
1970-1981	CLR, Indian rw	$1,800	$2,500

FLC

1970-1981. Flamenco guitar, yellow cedar back and sides, friction tuning pegs.

1970-1981		$1,800	$2,500

JB3H

1970-1981	Brazilian rosewood	$3,000	$4,000

JM/JMR

1970-1981. Jumbo body, mahogany (JM) or Indian rosewood (JMR), relatively wide waist (versus D-style or SJ-style).

1970-1981	JM	$1,800	$2,500
1970-1981	JMR	$2,000	$3,000

JR3H

1970-1981. Jumbo, Indian rosewood sides and back, 3-piece back, herringbone trim.

1970-1981		$2,800	$3,500

S2B3H

1970-1981	Brazilian rosewood	$3,000	$4,000

S2M

1970-1981. Size 2 guitar with mahogany back and sides.

1970-1981		$1,500	$2,000

S2R/S2R3H

1970-1981. Size 2 with Indian rosewood sides and back, R3H has 3-piece back and herringbone trim.

1970-1981	S2R	$1,800	$2,500
1970-1981	S2R3H	$1,500	$2,500

MODEL YEAR	FEATURES	EXC. COND. LOW	HIGH

S3B3H

1981	Brazilian rosewood	$3,000	$4,000

S3M

1970-1981	Mahogany	$1,500	$2,000

S3R/S3R3H

1970-1981. Size 3 with Indian Rosewood, S3R3H has 3-piece back and herringbone trim.

1970-1981	S3R	$2,200	$3,500
1970-1981	S3R3H	$2,200	$3,500

Guyatone

1933-present. Made in Tokyo by Matsuki Seisakujo, founded by Hawaiian guitarists Mitsuo Matsuki and Atsuo Kaneko (later of Teisco). Made Guya brand Rickenbacker lap steel copies in '30s. After a hiatus for the war ('40-'48), Seisakujo resumes production of laps and amps as Matsuki Denki Onkyo Kenkyujo. In '51 the Guyatone brand was first used on guitars and basses, and in '52 they changed the company name to Tokyo Sound Company. Guyatones are among the earliest U.S. imports, branded as Marco Polo, Winston, Kingston and Kent. Other brand names included LaFayette and Bradford. Production and exports slowed after '68.

Hagenlocher, Henner

1996-present. Luthier Henner Hagenlocher builds his premium grade, custom, nylon-string guitars in Granada, Spain.

Hagstrom

1958-1983, 2004-present. Intermediate, professional, and premium grade, production/custom, solidbody, semi-hollowbody and acoustic guitars made in the U.S. and imported. Founded by Albin Hagström of Älvdalen, Sweden, who began importing accordions in 1921. Electric guitar and bass production began in '58 with plastic-covered hollowbody De Luxe and Standard models. The guitars were imported into the U.S. by Hershman Music of New York as Goya 90 and 80 from '58-'61. Bass versions were imported in '61. Following a year in the U.S., Albin's son Karl-Erik Hagström took over the company as exclusive distributor of Fender in Scandinavia; he changed the U.S. importer to Merson Musical Instruments of New York (later Unicord in '65), and redesigned the line. The company closed its doors in '83. In 2004 American Music & Sound started manufacturing and distributing the Hagstrom brand under license from A.B. Albin Hagstrom. In 2009 U.S. Music became involved via its acquisition of JAM, and the 'new' Hagstrom established a Swedish office. A new line of instruments under the Vintage Series (made in China) included classic '60s models. Later the Northen series was introduced with instruments made entirely in Europe.

Corvette/Condor

1963-1967. Offset double-cut solidbody, 3 single-coils, multiple push-button switches, spring vibrato, called the Condor on U.S. imports.

1963-1967		$1,000	$1,5000

1970 Gurian JM

Imaged by Heritage Auctions, HA.com

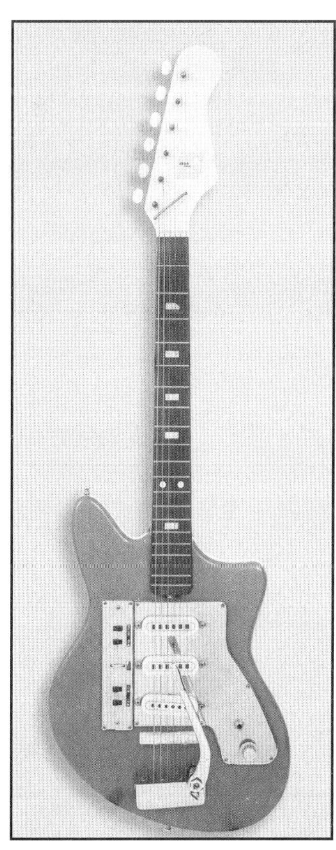

Guyatone

GUITARS

1965 Hagstrom Model I
Rivington Guitars

Hahn Model 112

MODEL YEAR	FEATURES	EXC. COND. LOW	HIGH

D'Aquisto Jimmy

1969-1975, 1976-1979. Designed by James D'Aquisto, electric archtop, f-holes, 2 pickups, sunburst, natural, cherry or white. The '69 had dot inlays, the later version had blocks. From '77 to '79, another version with an oval soundhole (no f-holes) was also available.

1969-1975	1st design	$1,500	$2,200
1976-1979	2nd design	$1,200	$2,000

Deluxe 90

1958-1962. Carved single-cut mahogany body, set-neck, 2 humbuckers, sparkle tops or sunburst.

1958-1962	Sparkle top	$1,500	$2,500

F Series

2004-2015. Made in China, offset double-cut basswood body, 2 or 3 pickups.

2004-2015	Various models	$250	$850

H-12 Electric/Viking XII

1965-1967. Double-cut, 2 pickups, 12 strings.

1965-1967		$700	$1,000

H-22 Folk

1965-1967. Flat-top acoustic.

1965-1967		$400	$600

Impala

1963-1967. Two-pickup version of the Corvette, sunburst.

1963-1967		$800	$1,200

Kent

1962-1967. Offset double-cut solidbody, 2 pickups.

1962-1967		$600	$900

Model I

1965-1971. Small double-cut solidbody, 2 single-coils, early models have plastic top.

1965-1971		$750	$1,100

Model II/F-200 Futura/H II

1965-1972, 1975-1976. Offset double-cut slab body with beveled edge, 2 pickups, called F-200 Futura in U.S., Model II elsewhere, '75-'76 called H II. F-200 reissued in 2004.

1965-1976		$800	$1,200

Model III/F-300 Futura/H III

1965-1972, 1977. Offset double-cut slab body with beveled edge, 3 pickups, called F-300 Futura in U.S., Model III elsewhere, '77 called H III.

1965-1969		$850	$1,300
1970-1977		$600	$900

Swede

1970-1982, 2004-present. Bolt-on neck, single-cut solidbody, black, cherry or natural, '04 version is set-neck.

1979-1982		$900	$1,400

Super Swede

1979-1983, 2004-present. Glued-in neck upgrade of Swede, '04 version is maple top upgrade of Swede.

1979-1983		$1,000	$1,500
1979-1983	Custom color	$1,200	$1,800
2004-2020	Reissue	$500	$800

Viking/V1

1965-1975, 1978-1979, 2004-present. Double-cut thinline, 2 f-holes, 2 pickups, chrome hardware, dot inlays, also advertised as the V-1. '60s had 6-on-side headstock, '70s was 3-and-3, latest version back to 6-on-side.

1965-1979		$1,000	$1,500
2004-2024	Reissue	$450	$700

MODEL YEAR	FEATURES	EXC. COND. LOW	HIGH

Viking Deluxe/V2

1967-1968, 2004-present. Upscale version, gold hardware, block inlays, bound headstock and f-holes. Current version upgrades are blocks and flame maple.

1967-1968		$1,100	$1,600
2004-2024	Reissue	$450	$700

Hahn

2007-present. Professional and premium grade, custom electric guitars built by luthier Chihoe Hahn in Garnerville, New York.

Haight

1989-present. Premium and presentation grade, production/custom, acoustic (steel and classical) guitars built in Scottsdale, Arizona by luthier Norman Haight. He also builds mandolins.

Halfling Guitars and Basses

Luthier Tom Ribbecke builds premium grade, production/custom, pin bridge, thinline and jazz guitars and basses, starting in 2003, in Healdsburg, California.

Hallmark

1965-1967, 2004-present. Imported and U.S.-made, intermediate and premium grade, production/custom, guitars and basses from luthiers Bob Shade and Bill Gruggett, and located in Greenbelt, Maryland. They also make basses. The brand was originally founded by Joe Hall in Arvin, California, in '65. Hall had worked for Semie Moseley (Mosrite) and had also designed guitars for Standel in the mid-'60s. Bill Gruggett, who also built his own line of guitars, was the company's production manager. Joe Hall estimates that less than 1000 original Hallmark guitars were built. The brand was revived by Shade in '04.

Sweptwing

1965-1967, 2000s. Pointed body, sorta like a backwards Flying V.

1965-1967		$3,000	$4,000
2000s	Reissue	$600	$900

Hamblin Guitars

Luthier Kent Hamblin built his premium grade, production/custom, flat-top acoustic guitars in Phoenix, Arizona and Telluride, Colorado, and presently builds in Colorado Springs. He began building in 1996.

Hamer

1974-2012, 2017-present. Intermediate grade, production, electric guitars. Hamer previously made basses and the Slammer line of instruments. Founded in Arlington Heights, Illinois, by Paul Hamer and Jol Dantzig. Prototype guitars built in early-'70s were on Gibson lines, with first production guitar, the Standard (Explorer shape), introduced in '75. Hamer was puchased by Kaman Corporation (Ovation) in '88. The Illinois factory

MODEL YEAR	FEATURES	EXC. COND. LOW	HIGH

was closed and the operations were moved to the Ovation factory in Connecticut in '97. On January 1, '08, Fender acquired Kaman Music Corporation and the Hamer brand. In '90, they started the Korean-import Hamer Slammer series which in '97 became Hamer Import Series (no Slammer on headstock). In '05 production was moved to China and name changed to XT Series (in '07 production moved to Indonesia). The U.S.-made ones have U.S.A. on the headstock. The less expensive import Slammer brand (not to be confused with the earlier Slammer Series) was introduced in '99 (see that listing). Fender suspended production of the Hamer brand at the end of 2012, later selling KMC (and Hamer brand) to Jam Industries, which relaunched Hamer in '17.

Archtop P-90

Solidbody double-cut, archtop sloping on top, P-90 pickups.

1993		$1,100	$1,600

Artist/Archtop Artist/Artist Custom

1995-2012. U.S.-made, similar to Sunburst Archtop with semi-solid, f-hole design, sunburst, named Archtop Artist, then renamed Artist (with stop tailpiece)/Artist Custom in '97.

1995-2012	Higher-end specs	$1,800	$2,500
1995-2012	Standard specs	$1,200	$1,800

Artist 25th Anniversary Edition

1998. Made in USA, 25th Anniversary Edition script logo on headstock.

1998		$1,200	$2,200

Artist Korina

2001-2012. Double-cut, bass f-hole, korina (limba) body and neck, 2 P 90s or 2 humbuckers (HB), natural gloss finish.

2001-2012		$1,800	$2,500

Artist Ultimate

1998-2012. Figured maple top, deluxe binding, gold hardware.

1998-2012		$2,000	$3,000

Blitz

1982-1984 (1st version), 1984-1990 (2nd version). Explorer-style body, 2 humbuckers, 3-on-a-side peghead, dot inlays, choice of tremolo or fixed bridge, second version same except has angled 6-in-line peghead and Floyd Rose tremolo.

1982-1984	3-on-a-side	$2,200	$3,000
1984-1990	6-in-line	$1,500	$2,200

Californian

1987-1997. Made in the USA, solidbody double cut, bolt neck, 1 humbucker and 1 single-coil, Floyd Rose tremolo.

1987-1989	Various features	$2,200	$3,000
1990-1997	Various features	$2,000	$3,000

Californian Custom

1987-1997. Made in the USA, downsized contoured body, offset double-cut, neck-thru-body, optional figured maple body, Duncan Trembucker and Trem-single pickups.

1987-1989		$2,200	$3,000
1990-1997		$2,000	$3,000

Californian Elite

1987-1997. Made in the USA, downsized contoured body, offset double-cut, optional figured maple body, bolt-on neck, Duncan Trembucker and Trem-single pickups.

1987-1989		$2,200	$3,000
1990-1997		$2,000	$3,000

Centaura

1989-1995. Alder or swamp ash offset double-cut, bolt-on neck, 1 humbucker and 2 single-coils, Floyd Rose, sunburst.

1989-1995		$1,200	$1,800

Chaparral

1985-1987 (1st version), 1987-1994 (2nd version). Offset double-cut, glued neck, angled peghead, 1 humbucker and 2 single-coils, tremolo, second version has bolt neck with a modified peghead.

1985-1987	Set-neck	$1,800	$2,500
1987-1994	Bolt-on neck	$1,200	$1,800

Daytona

1993-1997. Offset double-cut, bolt neck, dot inlay, 3 single-coils, Wilkinson tremolo.

1993-1997		$1,100	$1,600

Diablo/Diablo II

1992-1997. Offset double-cut, bolt neck, rosewood 'board, dot inlays, reversed peghead '92-'94, 2 pickups, tremolo. Diablo II has 3 pickups.

1992-1997		$1,100	$1,600

DuoTone

1993-2003. Semi-hollowbody, double-cut, bound top, glued-in neck, rosewood 'board, 2 humbuckers, EQ.

1993-2003		$850	$1,200

Echotone/Echotone Custom

2000-2002. Thinline semi-hollow archtop, f-holes, 2 humbuckers, trapezoid inlays, gold hardware.

2000-2002		$450	$700

Eclipse

1994-1996. Asymmetrical double-cut slab mahogany body, glued neck, rosewood 'board, 2 Duncan Mini-Humbuckers, cherry.

1994-1996		$850	$1,200

Eclipse (Import)

1997-1999. Import version.

1997-1999		$300	$500

Eclipse 12-String

1994-1996. 12-string version of Eclipse.

1995		$800	$1,200

FB I

1986-1987. Reverse Firebird-style body, glued-in neck, reverse headstock, 1 pickup, rosewood 'board with dot inlays, also available in non-reverse body.

1986-1987		$2,800	$4,500

FB II

1986-1987. Reverse Firebird-style, glued-in neck, ebony 'board with boomerang inlays, angled headstock, 2 humbuckers, Floyd Rose tremolo, also available as a 12-string.

1986-1987		$3,200	$5,000

Korina Standard

1995-1996. Limited run, 100 made, Korina Explorer-type body, glued-in neck, angled peghead, 2 humbuckers.

1995-1996		$3,800	$6,000

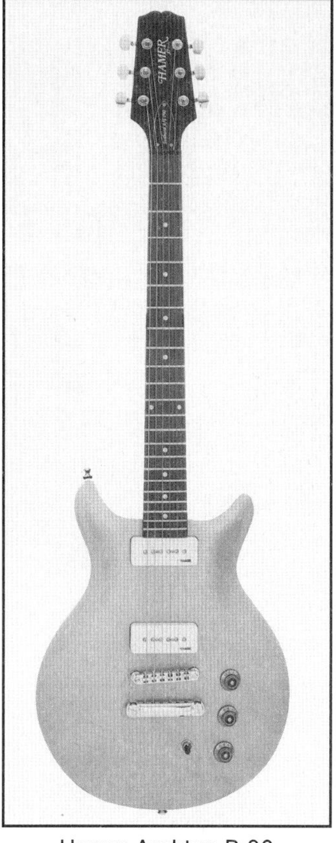

Hamer Archtop P-90

Imaged by Heritage Auctions, HA.com

Hamer Artist Korina

1993 Hamer Special
Paul Johnson

1938 Harmony Cremona
George Cox

MODEL YEAR	FEATURES	EXC. COND. LOW	HIGH

Korina V

1995-1996. Limited run, 72 made, Korina Explorer-type body, 2 humbuckers.

1995-1996		$4,200	$6,500

Maestro

1990. Offset double-cut, 7 strings, tremolo, bolt-on maple neck, 3 Seymour Duncan rail pickups.

1990		$1,200	$1,800

Mirage

1994-1998. Double-cut carved figured Koa wood top, transparent flamed top, initially with 3 single-coil pickups, dual humbucker option in '95.

1994-1998		$1,200	$1,800

Monaco III

2003-2007. Single-cut semi-hollow, 3 P90 pickups.

2003-2007		$1,800	$2,800

Newport Series

1999-2012. USA, double-cut thinline, center block, f-holes, 2 humbuckers (Newport 90 has P-90s), wrap-around bridge tailpiece.

1999-2012	Newport	$1,200	$1,800
1999-2012	Newport Pro	$1,200	$1,800

Phantom A5

1982-1884, 1985-1986 (2nd version). Offset double-cut, glued neck, 3-on-a-side peghead, 1 triple-coil and 1 single-coil pickup, second version same but with 6-in-line peghead and Kahler.

1982-1984		$1,200	$1,800

Phantom GT

1984-1986. Contoured body, offset double-cut, glued-in fixed neck, 6-in-line peghead, 1 humbucker, single volume control.

1984-1986		$1,200	$1,800

Prototype

1981-1985. Contoured mahogany body, double-cut with 1 splitable triple-coil pickup, fixed bridge, three-on-a-side peghead, Prototype II has extra pickup and tremolo.

1981-1985		$1,200	$1,800

Scarab I

1984-1986. Multiple cutaway body, 6-in-line peghead, 1 humbucker, tremolo, rosewood or ebony 'board, dot inlays.

1984-1986		$1,800	$2,500

Scarab II

1984-1986. Two humbucker version of the Scarab.

1984-1986		$1,800	$2,500

Scepter

1986-1990. Futuristic-type body, ebony 'board with boomerang inlays, angled 6-in-line peghead, Floyd Rose tremolo.

1986-1990		$3,000	$4,500

Slammer Series

1990-1997. Various models imported from Korea, not to be confused with Hamer's current Slammer budget line started in '98.

1990-1997		$300	$500

Special Series

1980-1983 (1st version), 1984-1985 (Floyd Rose version), 1992-1997 (2nd version), 2017-present. Double-cut solidbody, flame maple top, glued neck, 3-on-a-side peghead, 2 humbuckers, Rose version has mahogany body with ebony 'board, the 2nd version is all mahogany and has tune-o-matic bridge, stop tailpiece and Duncan P-90s, cherry red.

1980-1983	1st version	$2,000	$3,000
1984-1985	With Floyd Rose	$2,000	$3,000
1992-1997	2nd version	$1,500	$2,200
2017-2024	Reissue	$1,500	$2,200

Standard

1974-1985, 1995-2005. Futuristic body, maple top, bound or unbound body, glued neck, angled headstock, either unbound neck with dot inlays or bound neck with crown inlays, 2 humbuckers. Reissued in '95 with same specs but unbound mahogany body after '97. Higher dollar Standard Custom still available.

1974-1975	Pre-production, 20 made	$18,000	$25,000
1975-1977	Production, 50 made, PAFs	$13,500	$20,000
1977-1979	Dimarzio PAF-copy	$10,500	$15,000
1980-1985		$8,000	$12,000
1995-1999		$4,500	$6,500
2000-2005	USA, flamed top	$2,800	$4,500

Standard (Import, XT)

1998-2012. Import version, 2 humbuckers.

1998-2012		$400	$600

Standard Custom GSTC

2007-2012. Made in the USA, flamed maple top, mahogany neck, rosewood 'board.

2007-2012		$4,000	$6,000

Stellar 1

1999-2000. Korean import, double-cut, 2 humbuckers.

1999-2000		$200	$300

Steve Stevens I

1984-1992. Introduced as Prototype SS, changed to Steve Stevens I in '86, contoured double-cut, 6-in-line headstock, dot or crown inlays, 1 humbucker and 2 single-coil pickups.

1984-1992		$1,800	$2,800

Steve Stevens II

1986-1987. One humbucker and 1 single-coil version.

1986-1987		$1,800	$2,800

Studio

1993-2012. Double-cut, flamed maple top on mahogany body, 2 humbuckers, cherry or natural.

1993-2012		$1,100	$1,600

Studio Custom

1997-2012. Carved figured maple, humbuckers, tune-o-matic bridge, stop tailpiece, sunburst.

1997-2012		$1,500	$2,200

Sunburst

1977-1979, 1990-1992. Double-cut bound solidbody, flamed maple top, glued-in neck, bound neck and crown inlays optional, 3-on-a-side headstock, 2 humbuckers.

1977	1st 100, thin body	$4,500	$6,500
1978-1979		$2,800	$4,500
1990-1992		$1,800	$2,800

MODEL YEAR	FEATURES	EXC. COND. LOW	HIGH

Sunburst (Import, XT)

1997-2012. Import version of Sunburst, flat-top or archtop, 2 pickups.

1997-2012		$300	$500

Sunburst Archtop

1991-1997. Sunburst model with figured maple carved top, 2 humbuckers, offered under various names: Standard - unbound neck and dot inlays, tune-o-matic and stop tailpiece '91-'93 (replaced by the Studio). Custom - bound neck and crown inlays '91-'93, which became the Archtop for '94-'97 (replaced by the Studio Custom). Archtop GT - Gold top with P-90 soapbar-style pickups '93-'97.

1991-1997	Various models	$1,800	$2,800

T-51

1993-1997. Classic single-cut southern ash body, 2 single-coils.

1993-1997		$900	$1,500

T-62

1991-1995. Classic offset double-cut solidbody, tremolo, pau ferro 'board, Lubritrak nut, locking tuners, 3-band active EQ, various colors.

1991-1995		$900	$1,500

TLE

1986-1992. Single-cut mahogany body, maple top, glued neck, 6-in-line headstock, rosewood 'board, dot inlays, 3 pickups.

1986-1992		$2,200	$3,300

TLE Custom

1986-1992. Bound, single-cut solidbody with maple top, glued-in neck, angled headstock, ebony 'board with boomerang inlays, 3 pickups.

1986-1992		$2,200	$3,300

Vector

1982-1985. V-style body (optional flame maple top), 3-on-a-side peghead, rosewood 'board, 2 humbuckers, Sustain Block fixed bridge (Kahler or Floyd Rose tremolos may also be used).

1982-1985		$1,200	$1,800

Vector Limited Edition Korina

1997. 72 built in Hamer's Arlington Heights, Illinois shop, price includes original Hamer certificate of authenticity with matching serial number, Flying-V Vector style body, gold hardware, natural finish.

1997		$3,500	$5,000

Hanson

2009-present. Founders John and Bo Pirruccello import intermediate grade, electric guitars which are set up in Chicago, Illinois.

Harden Engineering

1999-present. Professional grade, custom, solidbody guitars built by luthier William Harnden in Chicago, Illinois. He also builds effects pedals.

Harmony

1892-1976, late 1970s-present. Huge, Chicago-based manufacturer of fretted instruments, mainly budget models under the Harmony name or for many other American brands and mass marketers. Harmony was at one time the largest guitar builder in the world. In its glory days, Harmony made over one-half of the guitars built in the U.S., with '65 being their peak year. But by the early-'70s, the crash of the '60s guitar boom and increasing foreign competition brought an end to the company. The Harmony brand appeared on Asian-built instruments starting in the late '70s to the '90s with sales mainly through mass-retail stores. In 2000, the Harmony brand was distributed by MBT International. In '02, former MBT marketing director Alison Gillette launched Harmony Classic Reissue Guitars and Basses and in '09 the trademark was acquired by Westheimer Corporation. Many Harmony guitars have a factory order number on the inside back of the guitar which often contains the serial number. Most older Harmony acoustics and hollowbodies have a date ink-stamped inside the body. DeArmond made most of the electronic assemblies used on older Harmony electrics, and they often have a date stamped on the underside.

Amplifying Resonator Model 27

1930s. Dobro-licensed with Dobro metal resonator, wood body.

1930s		$700	$875

Cremona

1930s-1952. Full-size archtop line, Harmony and Cremona logo on headstock, natural. Cutaways became available in '53.

1940-1952		$275	$350

D Series (Electric)

Late-1980s-Early-1990s. Classic electric copy models including offset double- and single-cut solidbody and double-cut thin hollowbody (D720), 1 to 3 pickups. All models begin with D, some models part of Harmony Electric series and others the Harmony Igniter series.

1980s-90s	Various models	$95	$175

H/HG Series (Electric)

Late-1980s-Early-1990s. Classic electric copy models including offset double-cut, single-cut and double-cut semi-hollow, 1 to 3 pickups, with or without tremolo. All models begin with H or HG, some models part of Harmony Electric series and others the Harmony Igniter series.

1980s-90s	Various models	$100	$175

H14/H15 Bob Kat

1968. Replaces Silhouette solidbody, H14 has single pickup and 2 knobs, H15 has 2 pickups. When vibrato is added it becomes the H16 model.

1968	H14	$450	$600
1968	H15	$550	$750

H14/H15/H17 Silhouette

1963-1967. Double-cut solidbody, H14 single pickup, H15 dual pickup, H17 dual with vibrato (offered until '66).

1963-1967	H14	$400	$600
1963-1967	H15	$500	$700
1963-1967	H17	$600	$800

H19 Silhouette De Luxe Double

1965-1969. Double-cut solidbody, deluxe pickups, block markers, advanced vibrato, sunburst.

1965-1969		$725	$1,000

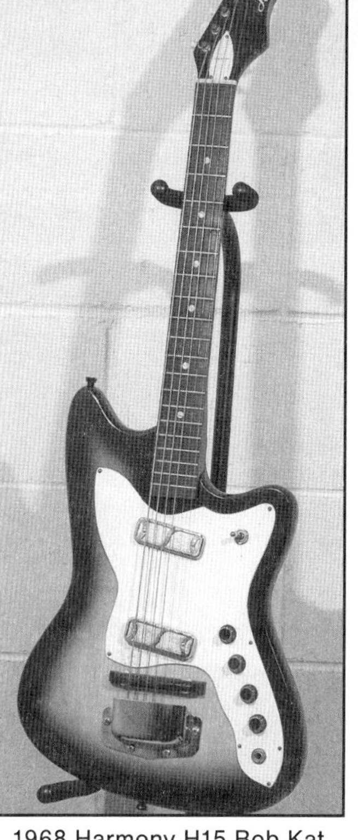

1968 Harmony H15 Bob Kat

Tom Pfeifer

1967 Harmony H19 Silhouette De Luxe Double

Tom Pfeifer

1967 Harmony H79 Double Cutaway Hollowbody 12-string
Bill Ruxton

1969 Harmony H954 Broadway
Edward Sparks

MODEL YEAR	FEATURES	EXC. COND. LOW	HIGH

H37 Hollywood

1960-1961. Electric archtop, auditorium size 15.75" body, 1 pickup, Harmony and Hollywood logo on headstock, 2-tone gold metallic finish.

1960-1961		$450	$650

H39 Hollywood

1960-1965. Like H37 but with sunburst.

1960-1965		$400	$650

H41 Hollywood

1960-1965. Like H37 but with 2 pickups, sunburst.

1960-1965		$550	$800

H42/1 and H42/2 Stratotone Newport

1957-1958. Brightly colored, single-cut, Newport headstock logo, 1 single-coil. 42/1 in sunshine yellow, /2 in metallic green.

1957-1958		$1,375	$1,750

H44 Stratotone

1953-1957. First edition models had small bodies and rounded cutaway, 1 pickup with plain cover using 2 mounting rivets, sometimes called Hershey Bar pickup, '60s models had slightly larger bodies and sharp cutaways, some with headstock logo Harmony Stratotone with atomic note graphic.

1953-1957		$1,500	$1,875

H45/H46 Stratotone Mars Electric

1958-1968. Single-cut, tone chamber construction, sunburst finish, H45 with 1 pickup, H46 with 2 pickups.

1960s	H45	$675	$900
1960s	H46	$900	$1,250

H47/48 Stratotone Mercury Electric

1958-1968. Single-cut, tone chamber construction, H47 with 1 pickup, block inlay and curly maple sunburst top, H48 is the same with a blond top.

1960s	H47	$900	$1,250
1960s	H48	$900	$1,250

H49 Stratotone Deluxe Jupiter

1958-1965. Single-cut, tone chamber construction, 2 pickups, bound spruce top, curly maple back and 6 control knobs, blond finish.

1958-1965		$1,125	$1,500

H53 Rocket I

1959-1973. Single-cut, f-holes, 1 pickup, trapeze, 2-tone brown sunburst ('59-'62) or red sunburst ('63 on).

1959-1969		$450	$600
1970-1973		$400	$500

H54 Rocket II

1959-1973. Same as H53 but with 2 pickups.

1959-1969		$750	$950
1970-1973		$450	$600

H59 Rocket III

1960-1973. Same as H53 but with 3 pickups.

1960-1969		$1,125	$1,500
1970-1973		$1,000	$1,250

H59 Rocket Reissue

2000s. Import, double-cut, 3 pickups, 6 knobs.

2000s		$500	$700

H60 Double Cutaway Hollowbody

1968-1970. Thinline double-cut, 2 pickups, trapeze tailpiece, sunburst.

1968-1970		$950	$1,250

H62 Blond

1950s-1965. Thin body, dual pickup archtop, curly maple back and sides, spruce top, block markers, blond.

1950s-1965		$1,875	$2,500

H62VS (Reissue)

2000s. H62 with sunburst finish.

2000s		$850	$1,125

H63 Espanada

1950s-1965. Thick body, single-cut, jazz-style double pickups, black finish with white appointments, by early '60s 'Espanada' logo on lower bass bout.

1950s-1965		$1,375	$1,750

H64 Double Cutaway Electric

1968-1970. Double-cut electric, factory Bigsby, dot markers, sunburst.

1968-1970		$1,125	$1,500

H65 Modern Trend

1956-1960. Short-scale electric thin body archtop, 1 single-coil, block inlays, Sherry Blond finish on curly maple grain.

1956-1960		$1,000	$1,250

H66 Vibra-Jet

1962-1966. Thinline single-cut, 2 pickups, built-in tremolo circuit and control panel knobs and selection dial, sunburst.

1962-1966		$1,250	$1,750

H68 Deep Body Electric

1968-1971. Full-body single-cut electric archtop, 2 pickups, trapeze bridge, block markers.

1968-1971		$1,250	$1,750

H70/H71 Meteor

1958-1966. Single rounded cutaway 2" thin body, 2 pickups, 3-part f-holes, block inlays, bolt neck, H70 sunburst, H71 natural (ended '65), lefty offered '65-'66, reintroduced as H661 and H671 (without Meteor name) in '72-'74.

1958-1965	H71, natural	$1,375	$1,750
1958-1966	H70, sunburst	$1,375	$1,750

H72/H72V Double Cutaway Hollowbody

1966-1971. Multiple bindings, 2 pickups, cherry red, H72V has Bigsby.

1966-1971		$1,250	$1,750

H73 Roy Smeck

1963-1964. Electric hollowbody, single neck silver bar-style pickup or 2 Harmony pickups.

1963-1964		$1,250	$1,750

H74 Neo-Cutaway

1961-1967. Modified double-cut, 2 pickups, Bigsby, 3-part F-holes, dot inlays.

1961-1967		$1,375	$1,750

H75 Double Cutaway Hollowbody

1960-1970. Three pickups, multi-bound body, 3-part f-holes, block inlays, bolt neck, brown sunburst.

1960-1970		$1,375	$1,750

H76 Double Cutaway Hollowbody

1960-1962. H75 with Bigsby.

1960-1962		$1,375	$1,750

H77 Double Cutaway Hollowbody

Late-1960s. Same as H75, but in cherry sunburst.

1960s		$1,375	$1,750

MODEL YEAR	FEATURES	EXC. COND. LOW	HIGH

H78 Double Cutaway Hollowbody

Late-1960s. H77 with Bigsby.

1960s		$1,375	$1,750

H79 Double Cutaway Hollowbody 12-String

1966-1970. Unique slotted headstock, cherry finish.

1966-1970		$1,375	$1,750

H81 Rebel

1968-1971. Single pickup version of Rebel, brown sunburst.

1968-1971		$400	$500

H82/H82G Rebel

Listed as a new model in 1971. Thin body, hollow tone chamber, double-cut, 2 pickups, H82 sunburst, H82G greenburst avacado shading (renumbered as H682 and H683 in '72).

1970s	H82	$600	$750
1970s	H82G	$600	$750

H88 Stratotone Doublet

1954-1957. Basically 2-pickup H44.

1954-1957		$1,250	$1,500

H150 Student

1963-1969. Parlor-size acoustic.

1963-1969		$150	$200

H162 Folk

1950s-1971. Grand concert size acoustic, spruce top, mahogany body.

1950s-1971		$400	$500

H165 Grand Concert

1948-1957. Flat-top, all mahogany body. Body changed to square-shoulder in '58 (see Folk H165).

1948-1957		$375	$475

H165/H6365 Folk

1958-1974. Square-shouldered flat-top, all mahogany body. Renamed the H6365 in '72.

1958-1974		$400	$500

H169 Buck Owens

1969. Acoustic flat-top, red, white and blue. The price shown is for a guitar that has an unblemished finish, paint wear will reduce the price, prices vary considerable due to the condition of the finish.

1969		$2,250	$3,500

H600 Roy Rogers

1954-1958. 3/4 size, stencil, sold through Sears.

1954-1958		$325	$425

H910 Classical

1970s. Beginner guitar, natural.

1970s		$75	$95

H945 Master

1965-1966. 15" Auditorium-sized acoustic archtop, block markers, music note painted logo on headstock, sunburst.

1965-1966		$275	$350

H950/H952/H1325/H1456/H1457/H6450

1930s-1974. Line of Auditorium and Grand Auditorium acoustic archtop models.

1950s	H950 Monterey	$300	$400
1950s	H952 Colorama	$400	$500
1950s-60s	Other models	$275	$450
1970s	H6450	$175	$250

H954 Broadway

1930s-1971. 15-3/4" body, acoustic archtop, dot markers, sunburst.

1930s-1971		$250	$450

H1057 Singing Cowboys

1950s. Western chuck-wagon scene stencil top, Singing Cowboys stenciled on either side of upper bouts, brown background versus earlier Supertone version that had black background.

1950s		$325	$500

H1200 Auditorium Series

1948-1975. Acoustic archtop, treble-clef artwork on headstock, model 1213 & 1215 (shaded brown sunburst) and 1214 (blond ivory, ends in '64). Model 1215 was renamed H6415 in '72 and lasted until '75.

1948-1975	Various models	$250	$450

H1203 Sovereign Western Special Jumbo

1960s-1970s. 15" wide body, 000-style.

1960s		$600	$750

H1215 Archtone

1950-1960s. Lower-end archtop, 6-string, sunburst.

1950-60s		$400	$550

H1215 Archtone Tenor

1950-1960s. Lower-end archtop tenor, 4-string, sunburst.

1950-60s		$350	$450

H1250 Roy Smeck Vita Standard

1928-1931. Pear shaped body, seal-shaped sound holes.

1928-1931		$900	$1,125

H1252 Professional Hawaiian

1940. Hawaiian acoustic jumbo, high-end appointments, Professional logo on headstock, figured Koa or mahogany back and sides, spruce top, Brazilian rosewood fretboard, various-shaped fretboard markers.

1940		$2,000	$2,500

H1260 Sovereign Jumbo

1960s-1970s. Jumbo shape, 16" wide body, natural.

1960s		$700	$1,000
1970s		$500	$650

H1265 Sovereign Jumbo Deluxe

1965-1969. Jumbo D-style, 16" fancy.

1965-1969		$1,125	$1,500

H1266 Sovereign Jumbo Deluxe

Late-1960s-1970s. Jumbo nearly D-style, 16" wide body with out-sized 'guard, natural.

1960s		$1,250	$1,750
1970s		$700	$900

H1270 Flat-Top 12-String

1965. 16" deluxe acoustic 12-string flat-top, spruce top, mahogany sides and back, dot markers.

1965		$800	$1,250

H1310 Brilliant Cutaway

1953-1973. Grand Auditorium acoustic archtop, single rounded cutaway, block inlays, sunburst. Called H6510 in '72.

1953-1973		$575	$725

H1311 Brilliant Cutaway

1953-1962. As H1310, but in blond.

1953-1963		$800	$1,000

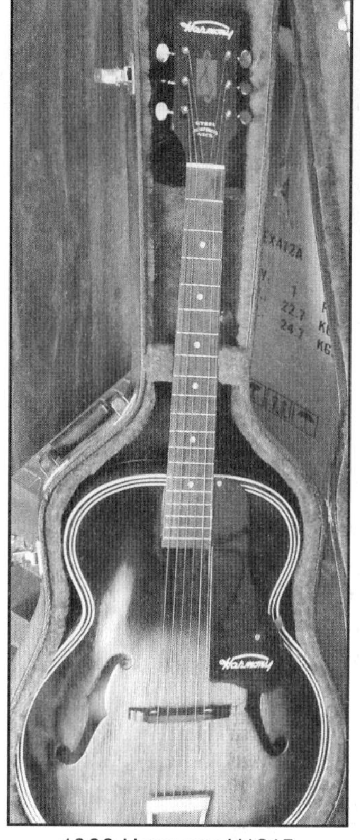

1963 Harmony H1215 Auditorium

Douglas Morissette

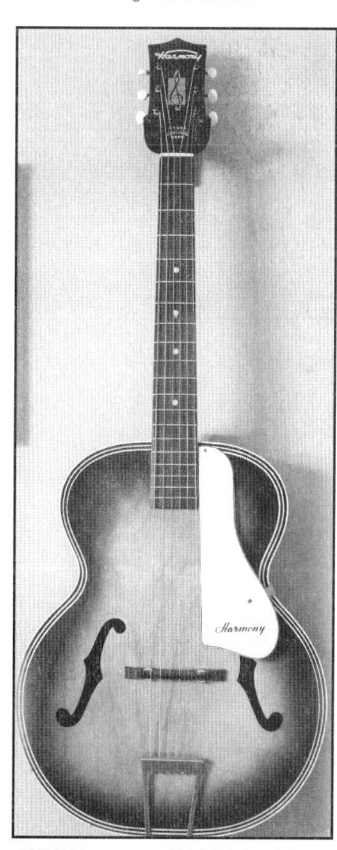

1958 Harmony H1215 Archtone

Johnny Zapp

Harrison Classic GB Guitar

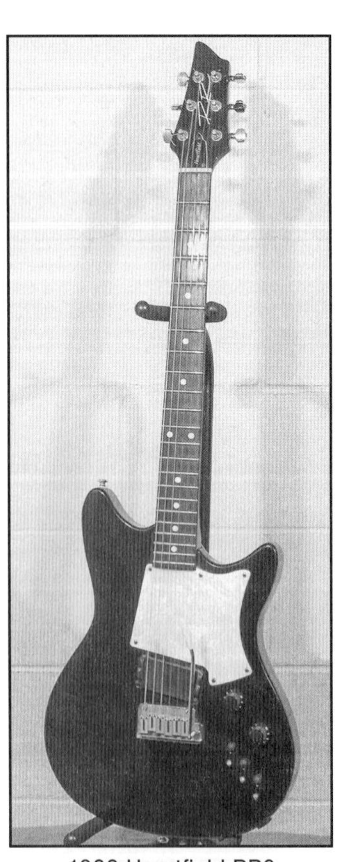
1988 Heartfield RR9
Tom Pfeifer

MODEL YEAR	FEATURES	EXC. COND. LOW	HIGH

H1407/H1414/H1418 Patrician

1932-1973. Model line mostly with mahogany bodies and alternating single/double dot markers (later models with single dots), introduced as flat-top, changed to archtop in '34. In '37 line expanded to 9 archtops (some with blocks) and 1 flat-top. Flat-tops disappeared in the '40s, with various archtops offered up to '73.

1932-1973		$350	$450

H1442 Roy Smeck Artiste

1939-ca. 1942. Grand auditorium acoustic archtop, Roy Smeck Artiste logo on headstock, split rectangle markers, black with white guard.

1939-1942		$550	$700

H4101 Flat-Top Tenor

1950s-1970s. Mahogany body, 4-string.

1950s-70s		$350	$450

Holiday Rocket

Mid-1960s. Similar to H59 Rocket III but with push-button controls instead of rotary selector switch, 3 Goldentone pickups, pickup trim rings, Holiday logo on 'guard, higher model than standard Rocket.

1960s		$1,000	$1,250

Igniter Series (D/H/HG)

Late-1980s to early-1990s. Pointy-headstock electric copy models, offset double-cut, all models begin with D, H, or HG.

1980s-90s	Various models	$100	$225

Lone Ranger

1950-1951. Lone Ranger headstock stencil, Lone Ranger and Tonto stencil on brown body. This model was first introduced in 1936 as the Supertone Lone Ranger with the same stencil on a black body.

1950-1951		$300	$400

TG1201 Tenor

1950s. Spruce top, two-on-a-side tuners, Sovereign model tenor, natural.

1950s		$325	$425

Harptone

1893-ca. 1975. The Harptone Manufacturing Corporation was located in Newark, New Jersey. They made musical instrument cases and accessories and got into instrument production from 1934 to '42, making guitars, banjos, mandolins, and tiples. In '66 they got back into guitar production, making the Standel line from '67 to '69. Harptone offered flat-tops and archtops under their own brand until the mid-'70s when the name was sold to the Diamond S company, which owned Micro-Frets.

Acoustic

1966-mid-1970s. Various models.

1966-1970s	Deluxe/Custom	$1,200	$1,800
1966-1970s	Standard	$1,000	$1,500

Electric

1966-mid-1970s. Various models.

1966-1970s		$1,200	$1,800

Harrison Guitars

1992-present. Luthier Douglas Harrison builds premium grade, production/custom, archtop and semi-hollowbody jazz guitars in Toronto, Ontario.

MODEL YEAR	FEATURES	EXC. COND. LOW	HIGH

Harwood

Harwood was a brand introduced in 1885 by Kansas City, Missouri instrument wholesalers J.W. Jenkins & Sons (though some guitars marked Harwood, New York). May have been built by Jenkins until circa 1905, but work was later contracted out to Harmony.

Parlor

1890s. Slotted headstocks, most had mahogany bodies, some with Brazilian rosewood body, considered to be well made.

1890s	Brazilian rosewood	$900	$1,500
1890s	Mahogany	$550	$850

Hascal Haile

Late 1960s-1986. Luthier Hascal Haile started building acoustic, classical and solidbody guitars in Tompkinsville, Kentucky, after retiring from furniture making. He died in '86.

Hauver Guitar

2001-present. Professional and premium grade, custom, acoustic guitars, built in Sharpsburg, Maryland by luthier Michael S. Hauver.

Hayes Guitars

Professional and premium grade, production/custom, steel and nylon string guitars made by luthier Louis Hayes in Paonia, Colorado. He began building in 1993.

Hayman

1970-1973. Solid and semi-hollowbody guitars and basses developed by Jim Burns and Bob Pearson for Ivor Arbiter of the Dallas Arbiter Company and built by Shergold in England.

Haynes

1865-early 1900s. The John C. Haynes Co. of Boston also made the Bay State brand.

Heartfield

1989-1994. Founded as a joint venture between Fender Musical Instrument Corporation (U.S.A.) and Fender Japan (partnership between Fender and distributors Kanda Shokai and Yamano Music) to build and market more advanced designs (built by Fuji Gen-Gakki). First RR and EX guitar series and DR Bass series debut in '90. Talon and Elan guitar series and Prophecy bass series were introduced in '91. The brand was dead by '94.

Electric Solidbody

1989-1994	Various models	$700	$1,000

Heiden Stringed Instruments

1974-present. Luthier Michael Heiden builds his premium grade, production/custom, flat-top guitars in Chilliwack, British Columbia. He also builds mandolins.

GUITARS

MODEL YEAR	FEATURES	EXC. COND. LOW	HIGH

Heit Deluxe

Ca. 1967-1970. Imported from Japan by unidentified New York distributor. Many were made by Teisco, the most famous being the Teisco V-2 Mosrite copy. They also had basses.

Acoustic

1967-1970	Various models	$200	$300

Electric

1967-1970	Various models	$325	$500

Hembry Guitars

2002-present. Professional grade, production/custom, solidbody electric guitars built by luthier Scott Hembry in Shelton, Washington. He also builds basses.

Hemken, Michael

1993-2021. Luthier Michael Hemken built his premium grade, custom, archtops in St. Helena, California. He died January 2021.

HenBev

Premium grade, production, solid and hollow body electric guitars and basses built by luthier Scotty Bevilacqua in Oceanside, California, starting in 2005.

Henderson Guitars

Luthier Wayne C. Henderson builds premium and presentation grade, custom acoustic guitars in Rugby, Virginia. He produces around 20 guitars per year and has also made mandolins, banjos and fiddles.

Hendrick

1982-1985. Solidbody guitars built by luthier Kurt Hendrick in Texas, Ohio and Michigan. Less than 100 built, the most popular model was the Generator. Hendrick also worked with Schecter, Fender, Jackson and Epiphone.

Henman Guitars

2010-present. Owners Graham and Paris Henman offer premium grade, production/custom, solidbody and chambered electric guitars and basses built by luthier Rick Turner in Santa Cruz, California.

Heritage

1985-present. Professional, premium, and presentation grade, production/custom, hollow, semi-hollow, and solidbody guitars built in Kalamazoo, Michigan. They have also made banjos, mandolins, flat-tops, and basses in the past.

Founded by Jim Deurloo, Marvin Lamb, J.P. Moats, Bill Paige and Mike Korpak, all former Gibson employees who did not go to Nashville when Norlin closed the original Gibson factory in '84. In 2007, Vince Margol bought out Paige. In '16, a private group of local Kalamazoo investors bought the business with Deurloo, Lamb and Paige remaining active in the company.

MODEL YEAR	FEATURES	EXC. COND. LOW	HIGH

Eagle

1986-2009. Single rounded cut semi-hollowbody, mahogany body and neck, bound body, 1 jazz pickup, f-holes, sunburst or natural.

1986-2009		$2,500	$4,000

Eagle Classic

1992-present. Standard Collection, Eagle with maple body and neck, bound neck and headstock, gold hardware, sunburst or natural.

1992-2024		$3,000	$4,500

Gary Moore

1989-1991. Single-cut solidbody, 2 pickups, chrome hardware, sunburst.

1989-1991		$2,000	$3,000

Golden Eagle

1985-2019. Single-cut hollowbody, back inlaid with mother-of-pearl eagle and registration number, multi-bound ebony 'board with mother-of-pearl cloud inlays, bound f-holes, gold-plated parts, ebony bridge inlaid with mother-of-pearl, mother-of-pearl truss rod cover engraved with owner's name, 1 Heritage jazz pickup, multi-bound curly maple 'guard.

1985-2019	Floating pickup	$4,000	$6,000
1985-2019	Mounted pickup	$3,500	$5,500

Groove Master

2004-2018. 16" hollow-body, single rounded cutaway, neck pickup, sunburst.

2004-2018		$2,800	$4,500

H-137

1980s-2021. Standard Collection, single-cut solidbody, 2 P-90s, sunburst, natural lime (early) or TV yellow (later).

1980s-2018	Sunburst or natural lime	$1,200	$1,800
2019-2021	Sunburst or TV yellow	$1,500	$2,500

H-137 AA

2018-2021. Artisan Aged Collection, sunburst or TV yellow with aged finish.

2018-2021		$1,800	$2,800

H-140/H-140 CM

1985-2005, 2007-2016. Single pointed cutaway solidbody, bound curly maple ('85-'04) or solid gold top ('94-'05), 2 humbuckers, chrome parts.

1985-1996	Black	$1,200	$1,800
1985-2004	CM, curly maple	$1,500	$2,200
1994-2005	Goldtop	$1,400	$2,100
2001	CM, flamed maple	$1,600	$2,400
2007-2016	2nd edition, goldtop	$1,500	$2,200

H-147

1990-1991. Single-cut solidbody, 2 humbuckers, mahogany body, mother-of-pearl block inlays, black with black or gold hardware.

1990-1991		$1,200	$1,800

H-150

1990s-present. Standard Collection, solid carved figured maple top, mahogany back, various colors.

1990s-2024	Cherry Sunburst	$1,800	$3,000
1990s-2024	Ebony	$1,800	$3,000
1990s-2024	Goldtop	$1,800	$3,000
1990s-2024	Sunburst	$1,800	$3,000

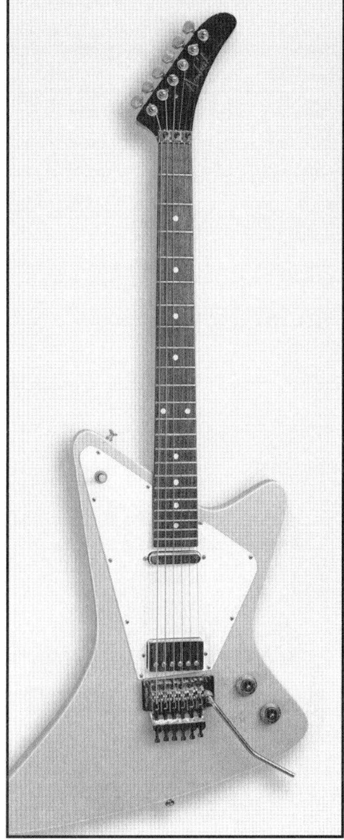

Hendrick Generator

Heritage H-150

Cream City Music

GUITARS

Heritage H-535

Heritage H-575

MODEL YEAR	FEATURES	EXC. COND. LOW	HIGH

H-150 AA

2018-2023. Artisan Aged Collection, sunburst, ebony, various colors with aged finish.

2018-2023		$2,200	$3,500

H-150 C/H-150 CM

1985-2018. Single rounded cutaway solidbody, curly maple top, 2 pickups, chrome parts, cherry sunburst.

1985-2018	Flamed	$2,000	$3,000
1985-2018	Goldtop	$2,000	$3,000

H-150 Deluxe Limited Edition

1992. 300 made.

1992		$2,800	$4,500

H-157

1989-2004. Mahogany body with maple top, natural, sunburst or black.

1989-2004		$2,000	$3,000

H-157 Ultra

1993-1994. Single-cut solidbody, large block markers, highly figured maple top.

1993-1994		$2,500	$4,000

H-160

1986, 2007. Limited production.

1986		$1,800	$2,800
2007	2nd Edition	$1,800	$2,800

H-170

1980s-1997. Double-cut solidbody, 2 humbuckers, bound carved top, was also a later curly maple top version (H-170CM).

1980s-1997		$1,800	$2,800

H-204 DD

1986-1989. Single-cut solidbody of mahogany, curly maple top, 1-piece mahogany neck, 22-fret rosewood 'board.

1986-1989		$1,200	$1,800

H-207 DD

1986-1989. Double-cut solidbody of mahogany, curly maple top, 1-piece mahogany neck, 22-fret rosewood 'board.

1986-1989		$1,200	$1,800

H-357

1989-1994. Asymmetrical solidbody, neck-thru.

1989-1994		$1,500	$2,200

H-516 Thin

1999-2015. Single-cut, thin all maple body, mahogany neck, 2 humbucking pickups, various colors.

1999-2015		$1,800	$2,800

H-530

2016-present. Standard Collection, double-cut hollowbody, sunburst, trans cherry or antique natural.

2016-2024		$1,800	$2,800

H-535

1987-present. Standard Collection, double-cut semi-hollowbody, curly maple top and back, 2 pickups, various colors.

1987-2018		$2,000	$3,000
2019-2024		$2,000	$3,000

H-535 AA

2018-2021. Artisan Aged Collection, various colors with aged finish.

2018-2021		$2,500	$3,800

H-537

1990. Single-cut, thinline, dots.

1990		$1,800	$2,800

H-550

1990-2018. Single-cut hollowbody, laminated maple top and back, multiple bound top, white bound 'guard, f-holes, 2 humbuckers.

1990-2018		$2,200	$3,300

H-555

1989-2018. Like 535, but with maple neck, ebony 'board, pearl and abalone inlays, gold hardware.

1989-2018		$2,200	$3,300

H-575

1987-present. Standard Collection, sharp single-cut hollowbody, solid maple top and back, cream bound top and back, wood 'guard, f-holes, 2 humbuckers.

1987-2019		$2,500	$4,000
2020-2024		$2,500	$4,000

H-575 AA

2018-2020. Artisan Aged Collection, various colors with aged finish.

2018-2020		$3,000	$4,500

H-576

1990-2004. Single rounded cut hollowbody, laminated maple top and back, multiple bound top, single bound back and f-holes and wood 'guard, 2 humbuckers.

1990-2004		$2,200	$3,300

Henry Johnson (HJ) Signature

2005-2018. Pointed single cut curly maple back and sides hollowbody, 2 humbuckers, block inlays, multi-bound.

2005-2018		$2,800	$4,000

HFT-445

1987-2000. Flat-top acoustic, mahogany back and sides, spruce top, maple neck, rosewood 'board.

1987-2000		$1,500	$2,500

Johnny Smith

1989-2001. Custom hand-carved 17" hollowbody, single-cut, f-holes, 1 pickup, various colors.

1989-2001	Various options	$4,000	$7,500

Kenny Burrell (KB) Groove Master

2004-2018. Single-cut 16" hollow body, 1 humbucker, gold hardware, block inlays.

2004-2018		$2,800	$4,500

Millennium Eagle 2000

2000-2009. Single-cut semi-solidbody, multiple bound curly maple top, single-bound curly maple back, f-holes, 2 humbuckers, block inlays.

2000-2009		$3,000	$5,000

Millennium Eagle Custom

2000-2009. Like ME 2000 but with curlier maple, multiple bound neck, split block inlays.

2000-2009		$3,500	$5,500

Millennium SAE

2000-2009. Single-cut semi-solidbody, laminated arch top, single cream bound top and back, f-holes, 2 humbuckers.

2000-2009		$2,000	$3,500

MODEL YEAR	FEATURES	EXC. COND. LOW	HIGH

Millennium Ultra/Standard Ultra

2004-2016. Single-cut, ultra curly maple top, mahogany back and sides, 1-piece mahogany neck, f-holes, mother-of-pearl block inlays.

2004-2016		$2,800	$4,500

Parsons Street

1989-1992. Offset double-cut, curly maple top on mahogany body, single/single/hum pickups, pearl block markers, sunburst or natural.

1989-1992		$1,200	$1,800

Roy Clark

1992-2018. Thinline, single-cut semi-hollow archtop, gold hardware, 2 humbuckers, block markers, cherry sunburst.

1992-2018		$3,000	$4,500

SAE Custom

1992-2000. Single-cut maple semi-hollowbody, f-holes, 2 humbuckers and 1 bridge pickup.

1992-2000		$2,000	$3,000

Super Eagle

1988-2018. 18" body, single-cut electric archtop, 2 humbuckers.

1989-2018		$4,000	$6,000

Super KB Kenny Burrell

2005-2011. Carved spruce top, tiger-flame maple back and sides, 2 pickups, natural or Antique Sunburst.

2005-2011		$4,000	$6,000

Sweet 16

1987-2018. Single-cut maple semi-hollowbody, spruce top, 2 pickups, pearl inlays.

1987-2018		$3,500	$5,500

Hermann Hauser

Born in 1882, Hauser started out building zithers and at age 23 added classical guitars and lutes, most built in his shop in Munich, Germany. He died in 1952. Hermann I instruments are linked with Andres Segovia. Hermann II Era instruments with modern players like Julian Bream. Hermann III builds Segovia style and custom-made instruments. Kathrin Hauser, daughter of Hermann III, is a fourth-generation builder. The original Hauser shop in Munich was destroyed during the war in 1946 and was moved to Reisbach. Labels often stipulate the city of construction as well as the Hermann Hauser name. Labels are easily removed and changed, and an original instrument should be authenticated. Beautiful violin-like clear varnish finish ends in '52, approximately 400 instruments were made by Hermann I. Under Hermann II nitrocellulose lacquer spray replaces varnish in '52, bracing patterns change in the '60s. He built 500-600 instruments from '52 to '88. Hermann III took over the business upon the death of his father in '88. Instruments should be evaluated on a case-by-case basis.

Hess

1872-ca. 1940. Located in Klingenthal, Germany, Hess built acoustic and harp guitars, as well as other stringed instruments and accordians.

Hewett Guitars

1994-present. Luthier James Hewett builds his professional and premium grade, custom/production, steel string, archtop jazz, solidbody and harp guitars in Panorama Village, Texas.

Hill Guitar Company

1972-1980, 1990-present. Luthier Kenny Hill builds his professional and premium grade production/custom, classical and flamenco guitars in Felton, California and Michoacan, Mexico.

Hirade Classical

1968-present. Professional grade, production, solid top, classical guitars built in Japan by Takamine. The late Mass Hirade was the founder of the Takamine workshop. He learned his craft from master luthier Masare Kohno. Hirade represents Takamine's finest craftsmanship and material.

HML Guitars

Introduced in 1997, Howard Leese custom-designs, premium grade, electric guitars, built by luthier Jack Pimentel in Puyallup, Washington.

Hoffman Guitars

1971-present. Premium grade, custom flat-tops and harp guitars built by luthier Charles Hoffman in Minneapolis, Minnesota.

Hoffman Small Jumbo

Höfner

1887-present. Budget, intermediate, professional and premium grade, production, solidbody, semi-hollow, archtop, acoustic, and classical guitars built in Germany and the Far East. They also produce basses and bowed instruments. Founded by Karl Höfner in Schonbach, Germany. The company was already producing guitars when sons Josef and Walter joined the company in 1919 and '21 and expanded the market worldwide. They moved the company to Bavaria in '50 and to Hagenau in '97. The S in Hofner model names usually denotes cutaway.

Beatle Electric Model 459TZ

1966-1967. Violin-shaped 500/1 body, block-stripe position markers, transistor-powered flip-fuzz and treble boost, sunburst.

1966-1967		$1,500	$2,500

Beatle Electric Model 459VTZ

1966-1967. Same as Model 459TZ except with vibrato tailpiece, brown (standard) or blond option.

1966-1967	Blond option	$1,800	$2,800
1966-1967	Brown	$1,500	$2,200

Beatle Electric Model G459TZ Super

1966-1967. Deluxe version of Model 459TZ, flamed maple sides, narrow grain spruce top, gold hardware, elaborate inlays and binding, natural blond.

1966-1967		$1,800	$2,800

Beatle Electric Model G459VTZ Super

1966-1967. Same as G459TZ Super but with vibrato tailpiece.

1966-1967		$1,800	$2,800

1967 Höfner Beatle Electric Model 459VTZ
Imaged by Heritage Auctions, HA.com

GUITARS

1965 Höfner Deluxe Model 176
Rivington Guitars

1969 Höfner Model 457/12
Imaged by Heritage Auctions, HA.com

MODEL YEAR	FEATURES	EXC. COND. LOW	HIGH

Club Model 40

1959-1962. Lowest-level of the Club Series, single-cut, 2 pickups, sunburst.

1959-1962		$2,200	$3,300

Club Model 40 John Lennon Limited Edition

2008. Limited run of 120, single-cut, spruce top, maple back and sides, neck pickup, vertical Höfner logo on headstock, Lennon signature on 'guard.

2008		$1,500	$2,200

Club Model 50

1959-1962. Mid-level of the 'Club Series', single-cut, 2 pickups, sunburst.

1959-1962		$1,800	$2,800

Club Model 60

1959. Highest model of 'Club Series', single-cut, 2 black bar pickups, 2 knobs and 2 slider switches on control panel, high-end split-diamond style markers, natural blond finish.

1959-1962		$2,000	$3,000

Club Model 126

1954-1970. Mid-sized single-cut solidbody, dot markers, flamed maple back and sides, spruce top, sunburst. Listed with Höfner Professional Electric Series.

1954-1970		$1,300	$2,000

Committee Model 4680 Thin Electric

1961-1968. Thinline single-cut archtop, 2 pickups, split-arrowhead markers, no vibrato, sunburst.

1961-1968		$1,500	$2,200

Deluxe Model 176

1964-1983. Double-cut, 3 pickups, polyester varnished sunburst finish, vibrola tailpiece, similar to Model 175 polyester varnished red and gold version.

1964-1966		$1,000	$1,500
1967-1969		$800	$1,200
1970-1983		$600	$900

Galaxy Model 175

1963-1966. Double-cut, 3 pickups, red and gold vinyl covering, fancy red-patch 'guard, vibrola, similar to Model 176 polyester varnished sunburst version.

1963-1966		$1,000	$1,500

Golden Höfner

1959-1963. Single-cut archtop, blond, 2 pickups, f-holes.

1959-1963		$6,000	$8,500

Jazzica Custom

2000-2010. Full body, single soft cutaway, acoustic/electric archtop, carved German spruce top, sunburst.

2000-2010		$1,500	$2,200

Model 165

1975-1976. Offset double-cut, S-style body, 2 single-coil pickups, bolt-on neck.

1975-1976		$400	$600

Model 171

1975-1976. Copy of Tele-Thinline.

1975-1976		$400	$600

Model 172 II (R) (S) (I)

1962-1963. Double-cut body, polyester varnished wood (S) or scuff-proof red (R) or white (I) vinyl, 2 pickups, vibrato.

1962-1963		$500	$800

MODEL YEAR	FEATURES	EXC. COND. LOW	HIGH

Model 173 II (S) (I)

1962-1963. Double-cut body, polyester varnished wood (S) or scuff-proof vinyl (I), 3 pickups, vibrato.

1962-1963		$500	$800

Model 178

1967-ca. 1969. Offset double-cut solidbody, 2 pickups with an array of switches and push button controls, fancy position markers, vibrola, sunburst. 178 used on different design in the '70s.

1967-1969		$500	$800

Model 180 Shorty Standard

1982. Small-bodied travel guitar, single-cut, solidbody, 1 pickup. The Shorty Super had a built-in amp and speaker.

1982		$300	$500

Model 450S Acoustic Archtop

Mid-1960s. Economy single-cut acoustic archtop in Hofner line, dot markers, Höfner logo on 'guard, sunburst.

1960s		$500	$800

Model 455S Acoustic Archtop

1950s-1970. Archtop, single-cut, block markers.

1950s-1970		$700	$1,000

Model 456 Acoustic Archtop

1950s-1962. Full body acoustic archtop, f-holes, laminated maple top, sides, back, large pearloid blocks, two color pearloid headstock laminate.

1950s-1962		$700	$1,000

Model 457 President

1959-1972. Single-cut thinline archtop, 2 pickups, non-vibrato.

1959-1972		$800	$1,200

Model 457/12 12-String Electric

1969-1970. Comfort-thin cutaway archtop, shaded brown.

1969-1970		$600	$900

Model 462 Acoustic Archtop

Ca. 1952-1960s. Single-cut archtop, bound cat's-eye soundholes, 3-piece pearloid headstock overlay, 3-piece large block inlays. Also offered with fingerboard mounted pickup with no controls (EG) and by mid '50s with 1, 2, or 3 pickups with volume and tone knobs/switches (462S/E1, 2, or 3).

1952-1960s	462S	$600	$900
1952-1960s	462SEG	$900	$1,400

Model 463 Electric Archtop

1958-1960. Archtop electric, 2 or 3 pickups.

1958-1960		$1,100	$1,600

Model 470SE2 Electric Archtop

1961-1994. Large single rounded cutaway electric archtop on Höfner's higher-end they call "superbly flamed maple (back and sides), carved top of best spruce," 2 pickups, 3 control knobs, gold hardware, pearl inlay, natural finish only.

1961-1994		$800	$1,200

Model 471SE2 Electric Archtop

1969-1977. Large single pointed cutaway electric archtop, flamed maple back and sides, spruce top, black celluloid binding, ebony 'board, pearl inlays, sunburst version of the 470SE2.

1969-1977		$800	$1,200

MODEL YEAR	FEATURES	EXC. COND. LOW	HIGH

Model 490 Acoustic Flat-Top

Late 1960s. 16" body, 12-string, spruce top, maple back and sides, dot markers, natural.

1960s		$300	$500

Model 490E Electric Flat-Top

Late 1960s. Flat-top 12-string with on-board pickup and 2 control knobs.

1960s		$400	$600

Model 491 Acoustic Flat-Top

1960s-1970s. Slope shoulder body style, spruce top, mahogany back and sides, shaded sunburst.

1970s		$400	$600

Model 492 Acoustic

Late-1960s. 16" body, 12-string, spruce top, mahogany back and sides, dot markers.

1960s		$300	$500

Model 492E Acoustic Electric

Late 1960s. Flat-top 12-string with on-board pickup and 2 control knobs.

1960s		$300	$500

Model 496 Jumbo Flat-Top

1960s. Jumbo-style body, selected spruce top, flamed maple back and sides, gold-plated hardware, vine pattern 'guard, sunburst.

1960s		$500	$800

Model 514-H Classical Concert

1960s. Concert model, lower end of the Höfner classical line, natural.

1960s		$200	$300

Model 4500 Thin Electric

Late-1960s-early-1970s. Thinline archtop, single-cut, 3 options, laminated maple top and back, dot markers, top mounted controls, brown sunburst.

1960s-70s	E1, 1 pickup	$500	$800
1960s-70s	E2, 2 pus	$600	$900
1960s-70s	V2, 2 pus, vibrato	$600	$900

Model 4560 Thin Electric

Late-1960s-early-1970s. Thinline archtop, single-cut, 2 options, laminated maple top and back, 2-color headstock, large block markers, top mounted controls, brown sunburst.

1960s-70s	E2	$700	$1,000
1960s-70s	V2, vibrato	$700	$1,000

Model 4574VTZ Extra Thin

Late-1960s-early-1970s. Extra thinline acoustic, 2 pickups, vibrato arm, treble boost and flip-fuzz.

1960s-70s		$800	$1,200

Model 4575VTZ Extra Thin

Late-1960s-early-1970s. Extra-thinline acoustic, double-cut with shallow rounded horns, 3 pickups, vibrato arm, treble boost and flip-fuzz.

1960s-70s		$1,000	$1,500

Model 4578TZ President

1959-1970. Double-cut archtop. 'President' dropped from name by late-'60s and renamed Model 4578 Dual Cutaway, also added sharp horns.

1959-1965		$800	$1,200
1966-1970		$700	$1,000

Model 4600 Thin Electric

Late-1960s-early-1970s. Thinline acoustic, double-cut, 2 pickups, dot markers, sunburst, V2 with vibrato.

MODEL YEAR	FEATURES	EXC. COND. LOW	HIGH
1960s-70s	E2	$600	$900
1960s-70s	V2, vibrato	$650	$950

Model 4680 Thin Electric

Late-1960s-early-1970s. Single-cut thinline electric, 2 pickups, 3-in-a-line control knobs, ornate inlays, spruce top, brown sunburst, V2 with vibrato.

1960s-70s	E2	$900	$1,400
1960s-70s	V2, vibrato	$1,000	$1,500

Model 4700 Thin Electric

Late-1960s-early-1970s. Deluxe version of Model 4680, gold plated appointments and natural finish, V2 with vibrato.

1960s-70s	E2	$1,000	$1,500
1960s-70s	V2, vibrato	$1,100	$1,600

Senator Acoustic Archtop

1958-1960s. Full body archtop, floating pickup option available, f-holes, made for Selmer, London.

1958-1960		$500	$800

Senator E1

1961. Senator full body archtop jazz, single top mounted pickup and controls.

1961		$700	$1,000

Verythin Standard

2001-2008. Update of the 1960s Verythin line, 2 humbuckers, f-holes, dot inlays.

2001-2008		$725	$1,000

Hohner

1857-present. Budget and intermediate grade, production, acoustic and electric guitars and basses. They also have mandolins, banjos and ukuleles. Matthias Hohner, a clockmaker in Trossingen, Germany, founded Hohner in 1857, making harmonicas. Hohner has been offering guitars and basses at least since the early '70s. HSS was founded in 1986 as a distributor of guitars and other musical products. By 2000, Hohner was also offering the Crafter brands of guitars.

Alpha Standard

1987. Designed by Klaus Scholler, solidbody, stereo outputs, Flytune tremolo.

1987		$250	$400

G 2T/G 3T Series

1980s-1990s. Steinberger-style body, 6-string, neck-thru, locking tremolo.

1980s-90s		$400	$600

Jacaranda Rosewood Dreadnought

1978. Flat-top acoustic.

1978		$800	$1,200

Jack

1987-1990s. Mate for Jack Bass. Headless, tone circuit, tremolo, 2 single-coils and 1 humbucker.

1987-1992		$300	$500

L 59/L 75 Series

Late-1970s-1980s. Classic single-cut solidbody, 2 humbuckers, glued neck, sunburst, 59 has upgrade maple body with maple veneer top.

1970s-80s		$400	$600

Mad Cat

1972-1973. Tele-style, associated with Prince, walnut strip in the middle, leopard print 'guard.

1972-1973		$5,500	$8,500

1966 Höfner 4570 E2

Heinz Rebellius

1950s Höfner Senator Acoustic Archtop

Paul Johnson

GUITARS

Hollingworth Guitars

1980 Hondo II
Rivington Guitars

MODEL YEAR	FEATURES	EXC. COND. LOW	HIGH

Miller Beer Guitar

1985. Solidbody, shaped like Miller beer logo.

1985	$225	$400

Professional

1980s. Single-cut solidbody, maple neck, extra-large 'guard, natural.

1980s	$300	$500

Professional Series - TE Custom

1980s-1990s. Single-cut solidbody, bolt neck.

1980s-90s	$800	$1,200

Professional Series - TE Prinz

Late 1980s-early 1990s. Based on Prince's No. 1 guitar, 2 single-coils, bolt neck, Professional The Prinz headstock logo, natural.

1989-1990	$800	$1,200

SE 35

1989-mid-1990s. Semi-hollow thinline, 2 humbuckers, natural.

1989	$300	$500

SG Lion

1980s-1990s. Offset double-cut, pointy headstock, glued neck.

1980s-90s	$250	$400

ST Series

1986-1990s. Includes the bolt neck ST 57, ST Special, ST Special S, Viper I, Viper II (snakeskin finish option), ST Victory, ST Metal S, and the ST Custom.

1986-1992	$300	$500

Standard Series - EX Artist

1970s-1980s. Solidbody, 2 humbuckers, gold hardware, neck-thru, solid maple body, rosewood 'board, tremolo.

1970s-80s	$300	$500

Standard Series - RR Custom

1970s-1980s. Randy Rhoads V body, 2 humbuckers, chrome hardware, glued neck, mahogany body, rosewood 'board, tremolo.

1970s-80s	$300	$500

Standard Series - SR Heavy

1970s-1980s. Hybrid body, 2 humbuckers, neck-thru, solid maple body, rosewood 'board, tremolo.

1970s-80s	$300	$500

Holiday

1960s. Electric, acoustic and bass guitars sold by Aldens, a Chicago catalog company. Most models built by Harmony. They also offered mandolins and banjos.

Silhouette Bobcat

1964-1967. Solidbody electric made by Harmony, similar to Harmony Silhouette, offset double-cut, 2 pickups, 4-in-a-row control knobs.

1964-1967	$425	$700

Hollenbeck Guitars

1970-2008. Luthier Bill Hollenbeck built his premium grade, production/custom, hollow and semi-hollow body acoustics and electric guitars in Lincoln, Illinois. Bill passed away in '08.

Hollingworth Guitars

1995-present. Luthier Graham Hollingworth builds his production/custom, premium grade, electric, acoustic and archtop guitars in Mermaid Beach, Gold Coast, Queensland, Australia. He also builds lap steels.

Holman

1966-1968. Built by the Holman-Woodell guitar factory in Neodesha, Kansas. The factory was started to build guitars for Wurlitzer, but that fell through by '67.

Holst

1984-present. Premium grade, custom, archtop, flat-top, semi-hollow, and classical guitars built in Creswell, Oregon by luthier Stephen Holst. He also builds mandolins. Until '01 he was in Eugene, Oregon.

Holzapfel (Holzapfel & Beitel)

1898-1930s. Carl C. Holzapfel and Clemence Beitel built guitars, banjos, and mandolins in Baltimore, but are best-known as early innovators of the 12-string guitar. Beitel left the company in 1905 and Holzapfel continued to build instruments up to the depression. He, and later his son, Carl M., mainly repaired instruments after that (up to 1988), but still would do custom builds.

Hondo/Hondo II

1969-1987, 1991-2005. Budget grade, production, imported acoustic, classical and electric guitars. They also offered basses, banjos, and mandolins. Originally imported by International Music Corporation (IMC) of Fort Worth, Texas, founded by Jerry Freed and Tommy Moore and named after a small town near San Antonio, Texas. Early pioneers of Korean guitar making, primarily targeted at beginner market. Introduced their first electrics in '72. Changed brand to Hondo II in '74. Some better Hondos made in Japan '74-'82/'83. In '85 IMC purchased major interest in Jackson/Charvel, and the Hondo line was supplanted by Charvels. 1987 was the last catalog before hiatus. In '88 IMC was sold and Freed began Jerry Freed International and in '91 he revived the Hondo name. Acquired by MBT International in '95, currently part of Musicorp.

Acoustic Flat-Top

1969-1987, 1991-2005.

1969-2005	$100	$150

Electric Hollowbody

1969-1987, 1991-2005.

1969-2005	$200	$600

Electric Solidbody

1969-1987, 1991-2005.

1969-1987	$200	$600
1991-1999	$200	$600
2000-2005	$100	$200

MODEL YEAR	FEATURES	EXC. COND. LOW	HIGH

Hondo Chiquita Travel Guitar

See Chiquita brand.

Longhorn

Ca. 1978-1980s. Copy of Danelectro Long Horn guitar, Dano Coke bottle-style headstock, brown-copper.

1978-80s		$600	$800

Longhorn 6/12 Doubleneck

Ca. 1978s-1980s. Copy of Danelectro Longhorn 6/12 Doubleneck guitar, Dano coke bottle-style headstock, white sunburst.

1978s-80s		$750	$1,000

M 16 Rambo-Machine Gun

1970s-1980s. Machine gun body-style, matching machine gun-shaped guitar case, black or red. Price includes original case with form-fit interior; deduct as much as 40% less for non-original case.

1970s-80s		$500	$850

Hopf

1906-present. Intermediate, professional, premium, and presentation grade, production/custom, classical guitars made in Germany. They also make basses, mandolins and flutes.

The Hopf family of Germany has a tradition of instrument building going back to 1669, but the modern company was founded in 1906. Hopf started making electric guitars in the mid-'50s. Some Hopf models were made by others for the company. By the late-'70s, Hopf had discontinued making electrics, concentrating on classicals.

Explorer Standard

1960s. Double-cut semi-hollow, sharp horns, center block, 2 mini-humbuckers.

1960s		$900	$1,500

Saturn Archtop

1960s. Offset cutaway, archtop-style sound holes, 2 pickups, white, says Saturn on headstock.

1960s		$1,100	$1,600

Super Deluxe Archtop

1960s. Archtop, 16 3/4", catseye sound holes, carved spruce top, flamed maple back and sides, sunburst.

1960s		$1,200	$1,800

Hopkins

1998-present. Luthier Peter Hopkins builds his presentation grade, custom, hand-carved archtop guitars in British Columbia.

Horabe

Classical and Espana models made in Japan.

Classical

1960-1980s	Various models	$350	$600

Hottie

In 2009, amp builders Jean-Claude Escudie and Mike Bernards added production/custom, professional and premium grade, solidbody electric guitars built by luthier Saul Koll in Portland, Oregon.

House Guitars

2004-present. Luthier Joshua House builds his production/custom, premium grade, acoustic guitars and guitar-bouzoukis in Goderich, Ontario.

Howe-Orme

1897-ca. 1910. Elias Howe and George Orme's Boston-based publishing and distribution buisness offered a variety of mandolin family instruments and guitars and received many patents for their designs. Many of their guitars featured detachable necks.

Hoyer

1874-1987. Intermediate grade, production, flat-top, classical, electric, and resonator guitars. They also build basses. Founded by Franz Hoyer, building classical guitars and other instruments. His son, Arnold, added archtops in the late-1940s, and solidbodies in the '60s. In '67, Arnold's son, Walter, took over, leaving the company in '77. The company changed hands a few times over the following years. Walter started building guitars again in '84 under the W.A. Hoyer brand, which is not associated with Hoyer.

Acoustic

1960s. Acoustic archtop or flat-top.

1960s		$450	$700

Junior

Early-1960s. Solidbody with unusual sharp horn cutaway, single neck pickup, bolt-on neck, dot markers, Arnold Hoyer logo on headstock, shaded sunburst.

1960s		$600	$900

Soloist Electric

1960-1962. Single-cut acoustic-electric archtop, 2 pickups, teardrop f-holes, sunburst.

1960-1962		$600	$900

Special 24

1950s-1960s. Single-cut acoustic archtop, Hoyer Special script logo on headstock, pickups added in '60s. SL was the deluxe version.

1950s-60s		$1,800	$2,500

Huerga

Introduced in 1995, professional to presentation grade, production/custom, archtop, flat-top, and metal-front solidbody electric guitars built by luthier Diego Huerga in Buenos Aires, Argentina.

Humming Bird

1947-ca.1975. Japanese manufacturer offering acoustics and electrics. By 1968 making pointy Mosrite inspirations. Probably not imported into the U.S.

Electric Solidbody

1950s		$200	$300

Humphrey, Thomas

1970-2008. Premium and presentation grade, custom, nylon-string guitars built by luthier Thomas Humphrey in Gardiner, New York. In 1996 Hum-

1963 Hopf Saturn

Dudley Taft

Hopkins Contessa

GUITARS

GUITARS

Ian A

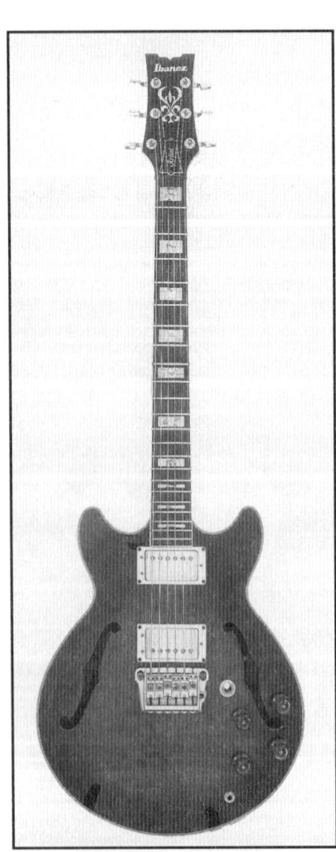
Ibanez AM-225 Artist
Imaged by Heritage Auctions, HA.com

MODEL YEAR	FEATURES	EXC. COND. LOW	HIGH

phrey began collaborating with Martin Guitars, resulting in the Martin C-TSH and C-1R. Often the inside back label will indicate the year of manufacture. Humphrey died in April 2008.

Classical

1976-1984. Brazilian or Indian rosewood back and sides, spruce top, traditionally-based designs evolved over time with Millenium becoming a benchmark design in 1985, values can increase with new designs. Valuations depend on each specific instrument; each instrument should be evaluated on a case-by-case basis.

1976-1984		$5,500	$7,500

Millennium (Classical)

1985-2008. Professional performance-grade high-end classical guitar with innovative taper body design and elevated 'board, tops are generally spruce (versus cedar) with rosewood back and sides.

1995-2008		$10,000	$15,000

Steel String

1974. D-style, only 4 made.

1974		$3,000	$4,500

Huss and Dalton Guitar Company

1995-present. Luthiers Jeff Huss and Mark Dalton build their professional and premium grade flat-tops and banjos in Staunton, Virginia.

Hutchins

2006-present. Gary Hutchins in Sussex, U.K. imports intermediate and professional grade, production, acoustic and electric guitars and basses from China, Germany and Korea.

Ian A. Guitars

1991-present. In the early 1990s luthier Ian Anderson built guitars under his name, in 2005 he began using the Ian A. brand. He builds premium grade, production/custom, solidbody electric guitars in Poway, California.

Ibanez

1932-present. Budget, intermediate, and professional grade, production/custom, acoustic and electric guitars. They also make basses, amps, mandolins, and effects.

Founded in Nagoya, Japan, by Matsujiro Hoshino as book and stationary supply, started retailing musical instruments in 1909, importing them by '21. The company's factories were destroyed during World War II, but the business was revived in '50. The Ibanez name was in use by 1957. Junpei Hoshino, grandson of founder, became president in '60; a new factory opened called Tama Seisakusho (Tama Industries). Brand names by '64 included Ibanez, Star, King's Stone, Jamboree and Goldentone, supplied by 85 factories serving global markets. Sold acoustic guitars to Harry Rosenblum of Elger Guitars ('59-ca.'65) in Ardmore, Pennsylvania, in early-'60s. Around '62 Hoshino purchased a 50% interest in Elger Guitars, and ca. '65 changed the name to Ibanez.

Jeff Hasselberger headed the American guitar side beginning '73-'74, and the company headquarters were moved to Cornwells Heights, Pennsylvania in '74. By '75 the instruments were being distributed by Chesbro Music Company in Idaho Falls, Idaho, and Harry Rosenblum sells his interest to Hoshino shortly thereafter. Ca. '81, the Elger Company becomes Hoshino U.S.A. An U.S. Custom Shop was opened in '88.

Most glued-neck guitars from '70s are fairly rare.

Dating: copy guitars begin ca. '71. Serial numbers begin '75 with letter (A-L for month) followed by 6 digits, the first 2 indicating year, last 4 sequential (MYYXXXX). By '88 the month letter drops off. Dating code stops early-'90s; by '94 letter preface either F for Fuji or C for Cort (Korean) manufacturer followed by number for year and consecutive numbers (F4XXXX=Fuji, C4XXXX=Cort, 1994).

Pickups on Asian import electric guitars from the '50s-'70s are often considered to be the weakest engineering specification on the instrument. Old Ibanez pickups can become microphonic and it is not unusual to see them replaced.

AE (Acoustic Electric) Series

1983-present. Flat-top models include AE, AEF, AEG, AEL, AES, (no archtops).

1983-2024	Various models	$250	$1,200

AH10 Allan Holdsworth

1985-1987. Offset double-cut solidbody, bolt neck, bridge humbucker, dots, various colors.

1985-1987	1 pickup	$1,200	$2,000

AH20 Allan Holdsworth

1986	2 pickups	$1,500	$2,200

AM (Archtop) Series

1985-1991. Small body archtops, models include AM70, 75, 75T, 100, 225. Becomes Artstar in '92.

1985-1991	Various models	$1,200	$1,800

AM Stagemaster Series

1983-1984, 1989-1990. Made in Japan, small double-cut semi-hollow body, 2 humbuckers, models include AM50, 100, 205, 255. Model name used again, without Stagemaster in '89-'90.

1983-1984	Various models	$1,200	$2,200

Artcore Series

2002-present. Made in China, hollowbody electric, models include AF, AG, AK, AM, AS, AWD, FWD, and TM.

2002-2024	Various models	$250	$2,000

Artist AR50 (Jr. Artist)

1979-1983. Double-cut solidbody, dot markers, 2 humbuckers.

1979-1983		$900	$1,400

Artist AR100

1979-1984. Double-cut solidbody, set neck, maple top, 2 humbuckers.

1979-1984		$1,000	$1,500

Artist AR200

1997-1999, 2004-2005. Symmetrical double-cut solidbody, maple top, 2 humbucker pickups.

2004-2005		$700	$1,000

MODEL YEAR	FEATURES	EXC. COND. LOW	HIGH

Artist AR250

1999-2004. Double-cut solidbody, flamed maple top, 2 humbuckers.

1999-2004 | | $1,000 | $1,500

Artist AR300

1979-1982. Symmetrical double-cut, carved maple top.

1979-1982 | | $1,500 | $2,200

Artist AR500

1979-1982. 2 humbuckers, EQ.

1979-1982 | | $1,800 | $2,800

Artist AS50

1980-1981. Made in Japan, semi-acoustic.

1980-1981 | | $800 | $1,200

Artist AS100

1979-1981. Set neck, gold hardware.

1979-1981 | | $1,200 | $1,800

Artist AS200

1979-1986. Double-cut semi-acoustic, flamed maple, block markers, gold hardware, 2 humbuckers, replaced Artist 2630. Artist dropped from name when model becomes hollowbody archtop in '82.

1979-1986 | | $1,800 | $2,800

Artstar AS50

1998-1999. Laminated maple body, bound rosewood 'board, dot inlays, 2 humbuckers.

1998-1999 | | $700 | $1,000

Artstar AS80

1994-2002. Double-cut semi-hollow body, dots, 2 humbuckers.

1994-2002 | | $800 | $1,200

Artstar AS180

1997-1999. Double-cut semi-hollow body, plain top, dots, 2 humbuckers.

1997-1999 | | $700 | $1,000

Artstar AS200

1992-2000. Flame maple top, gold hardware, 2 humbuckers, block inlays.

1992-2000 | | $1,500 | $2,200

Artwood Series

1979-present. Electric-acoustics, various AW, AC models.

1979-2024 | Various models | $250 | $2,000

Blazer Series

1980-1982, 1997-1998. Offset double-cut, 10 similar BL models in the '80s with different body woods and electronic configurations. Series name returns on 3 models in late '90s.

1980-1998 | Various BL models | $500 | $800

Bob Weir (2681)

1975-1980, 1995. Double-cut ash solidbody, ebony 'board, tree-of-life inlay, gold-plated pickups, limited numbers. Reintroduced as a limited run in '95.

1975-1980 | | $2,500 | $3,800

Bob Weir Standard (2680)

1976-1980. Standard production model of 2681.

1976-1980 | | $2,000 | $3,000

Bob Weir Model One BWM1 (Cowboy Fancy)

2005. Limited run of 30, double-cut swamp ash solidbody, ebony 'board, pearl vine inlay down neck and part way around body.

2005 | | $4,000 | $6,000

Challenger (2552ASH)

1977-1978. T-style ash solidbody.

1977-1978 | | $600 | $900

CN100 Concert Standard

1978-1979. Double-cut solidbody, set neck, 2 humbuckers, chrome hardware, dot markers.

1978-1979 | | $400 | $600

CN200 Concert Custom

1978-1979. Carved maple top, mahogany body, 7 layer black/white binding, bolt-on neck, gold hardware, block inlays, 2 Super 80 pickups.

1978-1979 | | $600 | $900

CN250 Concert

1978-1979. Like CN200 but with vine inlay.

1978-1979 | | $700 | $1,000

DG350 Destroyer II

1986-1987. X Series, modified X-shaped basswood body, flame maple top, 2 humbuckers, trem.

1986-1987 | | $1,000 | $1,500

DT50 Destroyer II

1980-1982. Modified alder Explorer body, 6-in-line headstock, bolt neck, 2 humbuckers, thick paint.

1980-1982 | | $800 | $1,200

DT150 Destroyer II

1982-1984. Like DT50 but birch/basswood, 1 humbucker.

1982-1984 | | $800 | $1,200

DT155 Destroyer II

1982-1984. Like DT150 but with 3 humbuckers.

1982-1984 | | $1,000 | $1,500

DT350 Destroyer II

1984-1985. X Series, opaque finish, 1 humbucker, trem.

1984-1985 | | $800 | $1,200

DT400 Destroyer II

1980-1982. Modified mahogany Explorer body, flame maple top, 6-in-line headstock, set-neck, 2 humbuckers, cherry sunburst. Model changed to DT500 in '82.

1980-1982 | | $1,000 | $1,800

DT500 Destroyer II

1982-1984. Replaced the DT400, flame maple top.

1982-1984 | | $1,000 | $1,800

DT555 Destroyer II Phil Collen

1983-1987. Bound basswood solidbody, 3 humbuckers, vibrato, black.

1983-1987 | | $2,200 | $3,500

DTX120 Destroyer

2000-2004. X Series, known as the Millennium Destroyer, 2 humbuckers.

2000-2004 | | $400 | $800

EX Series

1988-1993. Double-cut electric solidbodies with long thin horns.

1988-1993 | Various models | $180 | $1,200

FA/FG (Full Acoustic) Series

1973-1987. Single-cut full body jazz-style.

1973-1987 | Various models | $1,250 | $2,500

Flash (I, II, III)

1975. The Iceman was first introduced as the Flash at the Frankfurt Trade Show in West Germany in '75, it was renamed the Iceman prior to its introduction in the U.S. See Iceman 2663 listing.

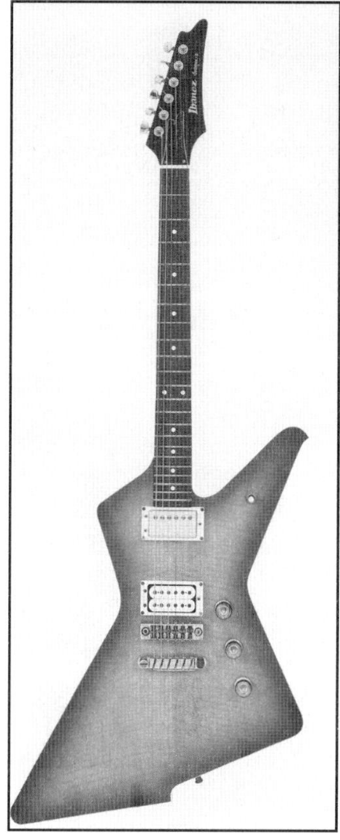

1981 Ibanez DT50 Destroyer II

Imaged by Heritage Auctions, HA.com

1993 Ibanez EX160

Imaged by Heritage Auctions, HA.com

GUITARS

Ibanez George Benson GB10

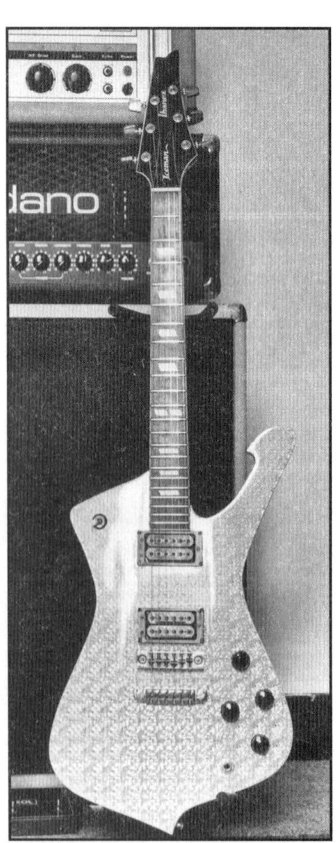
1979 Ibanez Iceman IC400
Eric Van Gansen

MODEL YEAR	FEATURES	EXC. COND. LOW	HIGH

FR1620/Prestige FR1620

2008-2014. Ash body, maple/walnut neck, rosewood 'board, 2 pickups, Prestige logo on headstock, black or red finish.

2008-2014		$800	$1,200

GAX Series

1998-2009. Symmetrical double-cut (Gibson SG style) with 2 humbuckers, lower cost of the AX line.

1998-2009	Various models	$150	$300

George Benson GB10

1977-present. Single-cut, laminated spruce top, flame maple back and sides, 2 humbuckers, 3-piece set-in maple neck, ebony 'board, sunburst or blond.

1977-1989		$2,000	$3,000
1990-1999		$2,000	$3,000
2000-2024		$1,800	$2,800

George Benson GB15

2006-2010. Like GB10, but with 1 humbucker.

2006-2010		$1,800	$2,500

George Benson GB20

1978-1982. Larger than GB10, laminated spruce top, flame maple back and sides.

1978-1982		$2,500	$3,800

George Benson GB100 Deluxe

1993-1996. GB-10 with flamed maple top, pearl binding, sunburst finish 'guard, pearl vine inlay tailpiece, gold hardware.

1993-1996		$2,500	$3,500

GSA Series

2000-2011. Offset double-cut body.

2000-2011	GSA20/GSA60	$150	$250

Iceman 2663/2663TC/2663SL

1975-1978. The original Iceman Series models, called the Flash I, II and III respectively, I has 2 humbuckers, II (TC) and III (SL) have 1 triple-coil pickup.

1975-1978		$3,500	$5,500

Iceman PS10 Paul Stanley

1978-1981. Limited edition Paul Stanley model, abalone trim, Stanley's name engraved at 21st fret, reissued in '95 with upgraded model names.

1978-1981	Korina finish	$2,500	$3,500
1978-1981	Sunburst or black	$2,000	$3,000

Iceman PS10 II Paul Stanley

1995-1996. Reissue of original PS-10.

1995-1996	Black	$1,800	$2,800

Iceman PS10LTD Paul Stanley

1995-1996. Limited edition, gold mirror appointments, gold hardware, black pearl metalflake finish.

1995-1996		$2,000	$3,000

Iceman Series

1975-2010. Ibanez unique body styles with hooked lower treble horn body.

1978-1979	IC250	$1,000	$1,500
1978-1979	IC300 (Korina)	$1,000	$1,500
1978-1980	IC210	$1,000	$1,500
1978-1982	IC400	$1,100	$1,600
1978-1990	IC200	$800	$1,200
1979-1980	IC50	$800	$1,200
1981-1982	IC400 CS	$900	$1,400
1994	IC500	$900	$1,400
1994-2003	IC300	$400	$600
1995-1996	IC350	$400	$600

MODEL YEAR	FEATURES	EXC. COND. LOW	HIGH

IMG-2010 Guitar Controller MIDI

1985-1987. Similar to Roland GR-707, slim triangle-wedge body with treble horn.

1985-1987	Guitar only	$600	$900

JEM7 Series

1988-2010. Basswood or alder body, various models, alder 7V offered until '10.

1988-2010	Various models	$1,800	$2,500

JEM77 Series

1988-1999, 2003-2010. Basswood body, monkey grip handle, 3 pickups, 'board with tree of life or pyramids inlay, finishes include floral pattern or multicolor swirl. Current version has dot inlays and solid finish. The JEM 77BRMR Bad Horsie was introduced in '05 with a mirror finish.

1980-2010	Various models	$2,800	$3,500

JEM555

1994-2000. Basswood, dots and vine inlay, 3 pickups.

1994-2000		$600	$1,000

JEM777 Series

1987-1996. Basswood body, monkey grip 3 pickups, pyramids or vine inlay.

1987-1996	Various models	$4,500	$7,500

JEM 10th Anniversary

1996. Limited Edition signature Steve Vai model, bolt neck, vine metal 'guard, vine neck inlays and headstock art.

1996		$5,500	$8,000

JEM 20th Anniversary

2007. Steve Vai 20th Anniversary JEM model, green acrylic illuminating body, celebrates the 20th year (1987-2007) of the Ibanez JEM series, limited edition.

2007		$5,500	$8,000

JEM 90th Anniversary

1997. Limited Edition signature Steve Vai model, textured silver finish, chrome 'guard.

1997		$3,500	$4,500

JEM Y2KDNA (Limited Edition)

2000. Red Swirl marble finish using Steve Vai's blood in the paint.

2000		$9,000	$12,000

Joe Pass JP20

1981-1990. Full body, single-cut, 1 pickup, abalone and pearl split block inlay, JP inlay on headstock.

1981-1990	Sunburst	$1,500	$2,500

Joe Satriani JS1

1993. Limited production, JS Series headstock logo.

1993		$1,200	$1,800

Joe Satriani JS2 Chrome Boy

1990. Extremely rare.

1990		$6,500	$9,000

Joe Satriani JS3 Donnie Hunt

1990. Limited to 300, hand painted by Donnie Hunt.

1990		$6,500	$9,000

Joe Satriani JS4 Electric Rainbow

1992. Only 22 made, hand painted by Joan Satriani.

1992		$6,500	$9,000

Joe Satriani JS5 Rain Forest

1995. Limited production, rain forest graphic.

1995		$6,500	$9,000

MODEL YEAR	FEATURES	EXC. COND. LOW	HIGH

Joe Satriani JS6

1993. Limited production, lightweight mahogany body, non-gloss stained oil finish, JS Series headstock logo.

1993		$1,500	$2,500

Joe Satriani JS100

1994-2014. Offset double cut basswood body, 2 humbuckers, vibrato, red, black, white or custom finish.

1994-2014	Custom finish	$500	$800
1994-2014	Standard finish	$400	$600

Joe Satriani JS1000

1994-1996, 1998-2012. 2 DiMarzio humbuckers, lightweight body.

1994-2012	Various colors	$1,000	$2,000

Joe Satriani JS1200

2004-2016. Candy Apple Red.

2004-2016		$1,200	$1,800

Joe Satriani JS 10th Anniversary

1998. Chrome-metal body, Satriani Anniversary script on back cover plate.

1998		$3,500	$5000

Joe Satriani JS 20th Anniversary

2008. Opaque finish with alien surfer graphic.

2008		$3,500	$5,000

Joe Satriani Y2K

2000. Clear see-thru plexi-style body.

2000		$3,500	$5,000

John Petrucci JPM100 P2

1996. Offset double-cut solidbody, 2 pickups, multi-color graphic.

1996		$2,000	$3,000

John Petrucci JPM100 P3

1997. As P2 but with same graphic in black and white.

1997		$2,500	$3,500

John Petrucci JPM100 P4

1998. As P2 but with same graphic in camo colors.

1998		$2,200	$3,000

John Scofield JSM100

2001-present. Double-cut semi hollow body, 2 humbuckers, ebony 'board, gold hardware.

2001-2024		$1,800	$2,800

Lee Ritenour LR10

1981-1987. Flame maple body, bound set neck, Quick Change tailpiece, 2 pickups, dark red sunburst, foam-filled body to limit feedback.

1981-1987		$1,500	$2,500

M310

1982. D-size flat-top, maple back and sides, rosewood 'board.

1982		$200	$300

M340

1978-1979. D-size flat-top, flamed maple back and sides, maple 'board.

1978-1979		$400	$600

Maxxas

1987-1988. Solidbody (MX2) or with internal sound chambers (MX3, '88 only), 2 pickups, all-access neck joint system.

1987-1988	MX2	$1,000	$1,500
1988	MX3	$1,200	$1,800

MC Musician Series

1978-1982. Solidbodies, various models.

1978-1980	MC500, carved top	$1,800	$2,800
1978-1980	Neck-thru body	$1,500	$2,500
1978-1982	Bolt-neck	$1,000	$1,800

Mick Thompson MTM-1

2006. Seven logo on fretboard, MTM1 logo on back of headstock.

2006		$800	$1,200

Model 600 Series

1974-1978. Copy era acoustic flat-tops with model numbers in the 600 Series, basically copies of classic American square shoulder dreadnoughts. Includes the 683, 684, 693 and the 6-in-line 647; there were 12-string copies as well.

1974-1978	Various models	$700	$1,000

Model 700 Series

1974-1977. Upgraded flat-top models such as the Brazilian Scent 750, with more original design content than 600 Series.

1974-1977	Various models	$700	$1,000

Model 900 Series

1963-1964. Offset double-cut solidbody with sharp curving horns, Burns Bison copy.

1963-1964	901, 1 pickup	$600	$900
1963-1964	992, 2 pickups	$650	$950

Model 1453

1971-1973. Copy of classic single-cut hollowbody, replaced by Model 2355 in '73.

1971-1973		$1,200	$1,800

Model 1800 Series

1962-1963. Offset double-cut solidbody (Jazzmaster-style), models came with bar (stud) or vibrato tailpiece, and 2, 3 or 4 pickups.

1962-1963	Various models	$400	$2,500

Model 1912

1971-1973. Double-cut semi-hollow body, sunburst finish.

1971-1973		$1,000	$1,500

Model 2020

1970. Initial offering of the copy era, offset double-cut, 2 unusual rectangular pickups, block markers, raised nailed-on headstock logo, sunburst.

1970		$800	$1,200

Model 2240M

Early 1970s. Thick hollowbody electric copy, single pointed cutaway, double-parallelogram markers, 2 humbuckers, natural finish.

1971-1973		$1,500	$2,200

Model 2336 Les Jr.

1974-1976. Copy of classic slab solidbody, TV Lime.

1974-1976		$500	$800

Model 2340 Deluxe '59er

1974-1977. Copy of classic single-cut solidbody, Hi-Power humbuckers, opaque or flametop.

1974-1977	Flametop	$900	$1,500
1974-1977	Opaque	$900	$1,500

Model 2341 Les Custom

1974-1977. Copy of classic single-cut solidbody.

1974-1977		$850	$1,200

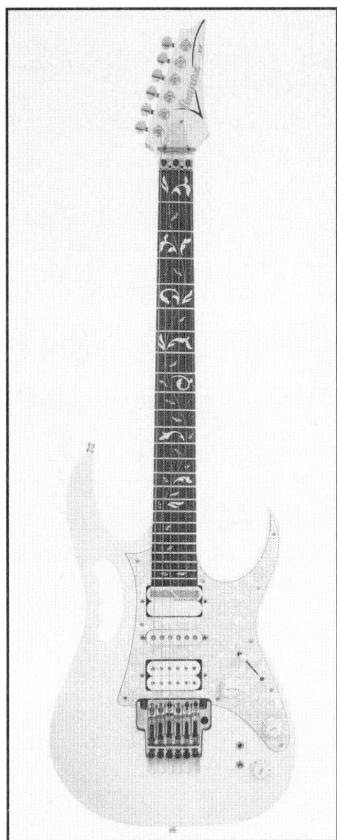

2004 Ibanez JEM 77

Imaged by Heritage Auctions, HA.com

1978 Ibanez MC Musician

Rivington Guitars

1976 Ibanez 2355
Stoeffu Vogt

Ibanez Model 2404 Double Axe
Greg Perrine

MODEL YEAR	FEATURES	EXC. COND. LOW	HIGH

Model 2342 Les Moonlight/ Sunlight Special

1974-1977. Copy of classic slab solidbody, black (Moonlight) or ivory (Sunlight).

1974-1977	$850	$1,200

Model 2343 FM Jr.

1974-1976. Copy of LP TV Jr.

1974-1976	$800	$1,200

Model 2343 Jr.

1974-1976. Copy of classic Jr., cherry mahogany.

1974-1976	$800	$1,200

Model 2344

1974-1976. Copy of classic double-cut solidbody.

1974-1976	$500	$800

Model 2345

1974-1976. Copy of classic sharp double-cut solidbody, set neck, walnut or white, vibrato, 3 pickups.

1974-1976	$850	$1,200

Model 2346

1974. Copy of classic sharp double-cut solidbody, vibrato, set neck, 2 pickups.

1974	$800	$1,200

Model 2347

1974-1976. Copy of classic sharp double-cut solidbody, set-neck, 1 pickup.

1974-1976	$600	$900

Model 2348 Firebrand

1974-1977. Copy of classic reverse solidbody, mahogany body, bolt neck, 2 pickups.

1974-1977	$1,000	$1,500

Model 2350 Les

1971-1977. Copy of classic single-cut solidbody, bolt neck, black, gold hardware, goldtop version (2350G Les) also available. A cherry sunburst finish (2350 Les Custom) was offered by '74.

1971-1977	$1,000	$2,000

Model 2351 Les

1974-1977. Copy of classic single-cut solidbody, gold top, 2 pickups.

1974-1977	$1,200	$1,800

Model 2351DX

1974-1977. Copy of classic single-cut solidbody, gold top, 2 mini-humbuckers.

1974-1977	$1,000	$1,500

Model 2351M Les

1974-1977. LP Standard style, sunburst.

1974-1977	$1,000	$2,000

Model 2352 Telly

1974-1978. Copy of early classic single-cut solidbody, 1 bridge pickup, white finish.

1974-1978	$700	$1,000

Model 2352CT

1974-1978. Copy of classic single-cut solidbody, single-coil bridge and humbucker neck pickup.

1974-1978	$700	$1,000

Model 2352DX Telly

1974-1978. Copy of classic single-cut solidbody, 2 humbuckers.

1974-1978	$700	$1,000

Model 2354

1974-1977. Copy of classic sharp double-cut solidbody, 2 humbuckers, vibrato.

1974-1977	$1,000	$1,500

Model 2354S

1972-1977. Stop tailpiece version of 2354.

1972-1977	$900	$1,400

Model 2355/2355M

1973-1977. Copy of classic single-cut hollowbody, sunburst or natural maple (M).

1973-1977	$1,200	$1,800

Model 2356

1973-1975. Copy of classic double pointed cutaway hollowbody, bowtie markers, sunburst. There was another Model 2356 in '74, a copy of a different hollowbody.

1973-1975	$1,000	$1,500

Model 2363R

1973-1974. Cherry finish copy of classic varitone double-cut semi-hollow body.

1973-1974	$1,000	$1,500

Model 2364 Ibanex

1971-1973. Dan Armstrong see-thru Lucite copy, 2 mounted humbuckers.

1971-1973	$1,200	$1,800

Model 2368 Telly

1973-1978. Copy of classic single-cut thinline, chambered f-hole body, single coil pickup, mahogany body.

1974-1978	$700	$1,000

Model 2368F

1973-1974. Classic single-cut black 'guard copy.

1973-1974	$700	$1,000

Model 2370

1972-1977. Sunburst version of Model 2363R.

1972-1977	$1,000	$1,500

Model 2372 Les Pro/2372DX Les Pro

1972-1977. Copy of classic single-cut solidbody, bolt neck, low impedance pickups, DX with gold hardware available for '73-'74.

1972-1977	$900	$1,400

Model 2374 Crest

1974-1976. Copy of classic double-cut semi-hollow body, walnut finish.

1974-1976	$1,200	$1,800

Model 2375 Strato

1971-1978. Strat copy, 3 single-coils, sunburst.

1971-1978	$700	$1,000

Model 2375 Strato 6/12

1974-1975. Double neck, 6 and 12 strings.

1974-1975	$1,500	$2,500

Model 2375ASH Strato

1974-1978. 2375 with ash body.

1974-1978	$700	$1,000

Model 2375WH/N/BK Strato

1974-1978. 2375 in white (WH), natural (N), and black (BK) finishes.

1974-1978	$1,200	$2,000

Model 2377

1974-1975. Copy of classic double sharp-cut solidbody, short production run, dot markers.

1974-1975	$900	$1,400

MODEL YEAR	FEATURES	EXC. COND. LOW	HIGH

Model 2380
1973-1977. Copy of LP Recording, single-cut solidbody, low impedence pickups, small block markers.

1973-1977		$800	$1,200

Model 2383
1974-1976. Copy of classic double sharp cut solidbody, white or walnut, 3 humbuckers, gold hardware.

1974-1976		$800	$1,200

Model 2384 Telly
1974-1976. Copy of classic single-cut, f-holes, 2 humbuckers, ash body.

1974-1976		$700	$1,000

Model 2387 Rocket Roll/Rocket Roll Sr.
1975-1977. V copy, bolt-neck (2387) or set-neck (2387DX/2387CT), dot markers, gold-covered pickups.

1975-1977	All models	$4,000	$6,000

Model 2390
1974-1976. Copy of classic double-cut semi-hollow body, maple 'board, walnut finish.

1974-1976		$1,000	$1,500

Model 2394
Ca. 1974-ca. 1976. SG style, 2 humbuckers, maple 'board, black block inlays.

1974-1976		$800	$1,200

Model 2395
1974-1976. Natural finished 2390.

1974-1976		$1,000	$1,500

Model 2397
1974-1976. Double-cut semi-hollow body, low impedance electronics, trapezoid markers, goldtop.

1974-1976		$1,000	$1,500

Model 2399DX Jazz Solid
1974-1976. Single-cut solidbody, sunburst, set-neck, gold hardware.

1974-1976		$1,000	$1,500

Model 2401 Signature
1974-1976. Double-cut semi-hollow archtop, gold top, bolt neck.

1974-1976		$1,200	$2,000

Model 2402/2402DX Double Axe
1974-1977. Double sharp cut solidbody 6/12 doubleneck, cherry or walnut, DX model has gold hardware and white finish.

1974-1977	All models	$2,000	$4,500

Model 2404 Double Axe
1974-1977. Double sharp cut solidbody guitar/bass doubleneck copy, walnut, white available '75 only.

1974-1977		$1,500	$2,500

Model 2405 Custom Agent
1974-1977. Single-cut solidbody, set neck, scroll headstock, pearl body inlay, 2 humbuckers.

1974-1977		$1,500	$2,500

Model 2406 Double Axe
1974-1977. Double sharp cut solidbody doubleneck, two 6-strings, cherry or walnut.

1974-1977		$1,500	$2,500

Model 2407 Stratojazz 4/6
1974-1975. Half Strat, half Jazz bass, all rock and roll!

1974-1975		$1,500	$2,500

MODEL YEAR	FEATURES	EXC. COND. LOW	HIGH

Model 2451
1974-1977. Single-cut solidbody, maple 'board, black or natural, set neck.

1974-1977		$1,000	$1,500

Model 2453 Howie Roberts
1974-1977. Single-cut archtop, round soundhole, maple body, set neck, rosewood 'board, block markers, 1 pickup, gold hardware, burgundy or sunburst.

1974-1977		$1,200	$1,800

Model 2454
1974-1977. Copy of classic double-cut semi-hollow body, set-neck, small block markers, cherry finish over ash.

1974-1977		$1,000	$1,500

Model 2455
1974-1977. L-5 copy, sharp single-cut archtop, blocks, natural.

1974-1977		$2,000	$3,000

Model 2459 Destroyer
1975-1977. Korina finished mahogany body.

1975-1977		$5,000	$7,500

Model 2460
1975-1977. L-5 copy, rounded cut laminated archtop, blocks, natural.

1975-1977		$2,000	$3,000

Model 2461
1975-1977. Copy of classic single-cut archtop, laminated spruce top, curly maple body, set-neck, ebony 'board, pearl blocks, 2 pickups, gold hardware, sunburst or natural.

1975-1977		$2,000	$3,000

Model 2464
1975-1977. Byrdland copy, rounded single-cut, blocks, natural.

1975-1977		$2,000	$3,000

Model 2469 Futura
1976-1977. Korina finished futuristic model copy.

1976-1977		$4,000	$6,000

Model 2601 to 2604 Artist
1976-1978. Upgrade acoustic flat-tops, higher end than 600 and 700 series, less of a copy model, original headstock decal.

1976-1978	All models	$500	$800

Model 2612 Artist
1974-1975. Rounded double-cut solidbody, black finish, birch top, gold hardware, bound rosewood 'board, 2 humbuckers, fleur-de-lis inlay.

1974-1975		$1,200	$1,800

Model 2613 Artist
1974-1975. Natural version of 2612.

1974-1975		$1,200	$1,800

Model 2616 Artist Jazz
1974-1975. Single-cut curly maple hollow body, f-holes, fleur-de-lis, 2 humbuckers.

1974-1975		$2,000	$3,000

Model 2617 Artist
1976-1980. Pointed double-cut natural ash solidbody, set-neck, German carved top, spilt block inlays, bound ebony 'board, 2 humbuckers, later would evolve into the Professional model.

1976-1980		$1,500	$2,200

1976 Ibanez Model 2405 Custom Agent

1977 Ibanez Model 2460
Imaged by Heritage Auctions, HA.com

Ibanez Model 2671
Randy Scruggs
Greg Perrine

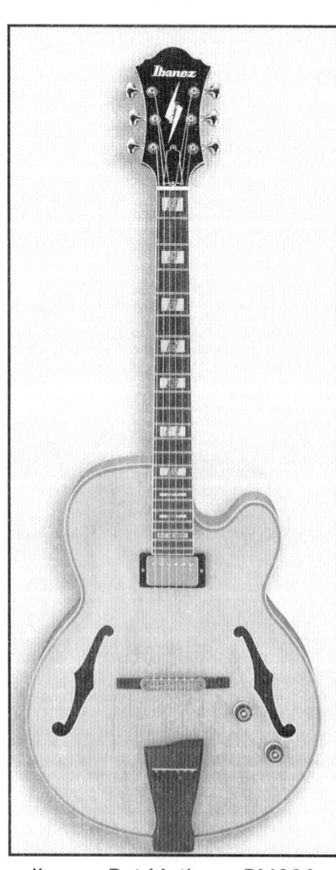

Ibanez Pat Metheny PM200

MODEL YEAR	FEATURES	EXC. COND. LOW	HIGH

Model 2618 Artist

1976-1979. Like 2617, but with maple and mahogany body and dot markers. Becomes AR200 in '79.

1976-1979		$1,200	$1,800

Model 2619 Artist

1976-1979. Like 2618, but with split block markers. Becomes AR300 in '79.

1976-1979		$1,200	$1,800

Model 2622 Artist EQ

1977-1979. EQ, Steve Miller model. Becomes AR500 in '79.

1977-1979		$1,200	$1,800

Model 2630 Artist Deluxe

1976-1979. Double cut semi-hollow body, sunburst, name changed to AS200 in '79.

1976-1979		$1,500	$2,200

Model 2640 Artist/AR1200 Doubleneck

1977-1984. Double-cut solidbody, set 6/12 necks, 4 humbuckers, gold hardware. Called 2640 until '79 when changed to AR1200.

1977-1984		$1,500	$2,200

Model 2662 Super Cutaway

1974-1976. Solidbody, set neck, 2 dramatic cutaways, block inlays, 2 humbuckers.

1974-1976		$1,500	$2,200

Model 2671 Randy Scruggs

1976-1978. Single-cut solidbody, tree-of-life inlay, German-carve top.

1976-1978		$1,200	$1,800

Model 2700 Artist Custom

1977-1978. Cutaway, dot markers, gold hardware, natural, black, antique violin or dark satin finish.

1977-1978		$1,800	$2,800

Model 2710 Artist Custom

1978. Like Model 2700 with exotic wood and Anvil case.

1978		$1,800	$2,800

Model 2800 Andorra Series

1974-1979. Classical nylon-string guitars, part of Ibanez Andorra Series, all with 2800-2899 model numbers.

1974-1979	Various models	$400	$600

Model 2900 Andorra Professional Series

1974-1979. Steel-string dreadnought models with solid spruce tops, all with 2909-2912 model numbers.

1974-1979	Various models	$400	$600

Pat Metheny PM

1996-present. Acoustic-electric archtops, single or single/half cutaway, 1 or 2 humbuckers.

1996-2010	PM100	$1,800	$2,800
1997-1999	PM20	$1,000	$1,500
2000-2015	PM120	$1,800	$2,800

Paul Gilbert PGM

1992-2011. Superstrat body style, painted f-holes, appointments vary with model numbers.

1997-2011	PGM300 WH	$1,200	$1,800
1998	PGM 90th	$2,000	$3,000
1998	PGM200 FB	$1,500	$2,200

PF Performer Series Acoustics

1987-present. Mostly dreadnought size flat-tops.

1987-2024	Various models	$100	$600

PF100 Performer Standard

1978-1979. Single-cut solidbody, plain birch top, mahogany body, bolt neck, dot inlays, 2 humbuckers.

1978-1979		$700	$1,000

PF200 Performer Custom

1978-1979. Maple top PF100.

1978-1979		$900	$1,400

PF300 Performer

1978-1980. Single-cut solidbody, maple top, mahogany body, set neck, 2 humbuckers, Tri-Sound.

1978-1980		$900	$1,400

PF400 Performer

1978-1979. Single cut solidbody, flame maple top, alder body, set neck, block inlays, 2 humbuckers, Tri-Sound.

1978-1979		$1,000	$1,500

PL Pro Line Series

1985-1987. Pro Line models begin with PL or PR.

1985-1987	Various models	$400	$1,200

PR Pro Line Series

1985-1987. Pro Line models begin with PL or PR.

1985-1987	Various models	$400	$1,200

Reb Beach Voyager RBM1

1991-1996. Unusual cutaway lower bout, extreme upper bout cutaways, RBM Series logo on headstock.

1991-1996		$1,200	$2,000

RG/RS Roadster/Roadstar Series

1979-present. A large family of guitars whose model identification starts with prefix RS ('79-'81) or RG ('82-present), includes the Roadstar Standard, Roadstar Deluxe and Roadstar II models.

1979-2024	Higher-range	$600	$900
1979-2024	Highest-range	$900	$1,400
1979-2024	Low to mid-range	$300	$500
1979-2024	Lower-range	$200	$300
1979-2024	Mid-range	$400	$600

Rocket Roll II RR550

1982-1984. Flying V body, six-on-side headstock, pearloid blocks, cherry sunburst, maple top, set neck.

1982-1984		$1,200	$1,800

RT Series

1992-1993. Offset double-cut, bolt neck, rosewood 'board, dot markers.

1992-1993	Various models	$350	$650

RX Series

1994-1997. Offset double-cut, solidbodies.

1994-1997	Various models	$150	$350

S Models

1987-present. In '87 Ibanez introduced a new line of highly tapered, ultra-thin body, offset double-cut guitars that were grouped together as the S Models. Initially the S Models were going to be called the Sabre models but that name was trademarked by Music Man and could not be used. The S models will carry an S suffix or S prefix in the model name.

1987-2024	Various models	$450	$1,250

ST Studio Series

1978-1982. Double-cut solidbodies, lots of natural finishes, various models, even a doubleneck.

1979-1981	Various models	$375	$800

MODEL YEAR	FEATURES	EXC. COND. LOW	HIGH

STW Double

1999. Double neck with 7-string and 6-string neck, limited edition.

1999		$2,200	$3,500

TC/TV Talman Series

1994-1998. Softer double-cut solidbodies.

1994-1998	Various models	$300	$500

USRG U.S.A. Custom Series

1994-1995. RG style guitars built in the U.S. by PBC Guitar Technology.

1994-1995	Various models	$1,200	$1,800

UV7PBK Steve Vai Universe

1990-1994. Black, green dot inlays.

1990-1994		$2,000	$3,000

UV7PWH Steve Vai Universe

1990-1993. White, pyramid inlays.

1990-1993		$2,000	$3,500

UV77MC Steve Vai Universe

1990-1997. Multi-colored.

1990-1997		$4,500	$10,000

UV777BK Steve Vai Universe

1998-2000s. Black, mirrored 'guard.

1998-2000s		$1,500	$2,500

UV777GR Steve Vai Universe

1998-2000s. Green, pyramid inlays.

1998-2000s		$3,500	$6,500

V300 Vintage Series

1978-1991. Vintage Series acoustic dreadnought, spruce top, mahogany back and sides, sunburst or various colors.

1978-1991		$200	$300

Xiphos Series

2007-2015. Part of the X Series, various XP and XPT models, X-shaped solidbody electric, neck-thru construction. Replaced by Iron Label (XPIR) series in '15.

2007-2015	Various models	$900	$1,400

XV500

1985-1987. Sharply pointed X-body with scalloped bottom.

1985-1987		$900	$1,400

Ibanez, Salvador

1875-1920. Salvador Ibanez was a Spanish luthier who operated a small guitar-building workshop. In the early 1900s he founded Spain's largest guitar factory. In 1929 Japan's Hoshino family began importing Salvador Ibanez guitars. Demand for the Salvador Ibanez guitars became so great that the Hoshino family began building their own guitars, which ultimately became known as the Ibanez brand. Guitars from 1875-1920 were mostly classical style and often can be identified by a label on the inside back which stipulates Salvador Ibanez.

Ignacio Rozas

1987-2008. Luthier Ignacio M. Rozas built his classical and flamenco guitars in Madrid, Spain. He also offered factory-made guitars built to his specifications. He retired in '08.

Illusion Guitars

1992-present. Luthier Jeff Scott builds his premium grade, production/custom, solidbody guitars in Fallbrook, California.

Imperial

Ca.1963-ca.1970. Imported by the Imperial Accordion Company of Chicago, Illinois. Early guitars made in Italy by accordion builder Crucianelli. By ca. '66 switched to Japanese guitars. They also made basses.

Imperial (Japan)

1957-1960. Early, budget grade, Japanese imports from the Hoshino company which was later renamed Ibanez.

Infeld

2003-2005. Solidbody guitars and basses offered by string-maker Thomastik-Infeld of Vienna.

Infinox

1980s. Infinox by JTG, of Nashville, offered a line of 'the classic shapes of yesterday and the hi-tech chic of today', including copies of many classic American solidbody designs with special metallic grafteq paint finish, space-age faux graphite-feel neck, Gotoh tuning machines, Gotoh locking nut tremolo with fine tuners, all models with 1 or 2 humbuckers.

Interdonati

1920s-1930s. Guitars built by luthier Philip Interdonati, in New York City, originally professional grade. He also built mandolins.

Isana

1951-1974. Acoustic and electric archtop guitars built by luthier Josef Sandner in Nauheim, Germany. Elvis played one while in the army in Germany.

Acoustic Archtop

1951-1974	Various models	$450	$1,500

Island Instruments

2010-present. Luthier Nic Delisle builds professional and premium grade, production/custom, small-bodied acoustic and electric guitars in Montreal, Quebec. He also builds basses.

Italia

1999-present. Intermediate grade, production, solid, semi-solid, and hollow body guitars and basses designed by Trevor Wilkinson and made in Korea.

J Backlund Design

2008-present. Professional and premium grade, custom, electric guitars and basses designed by J. Backlund in Hixson, Tennessee, starting in 2008. He also imports Korean-made guitars under the Retronix brand.

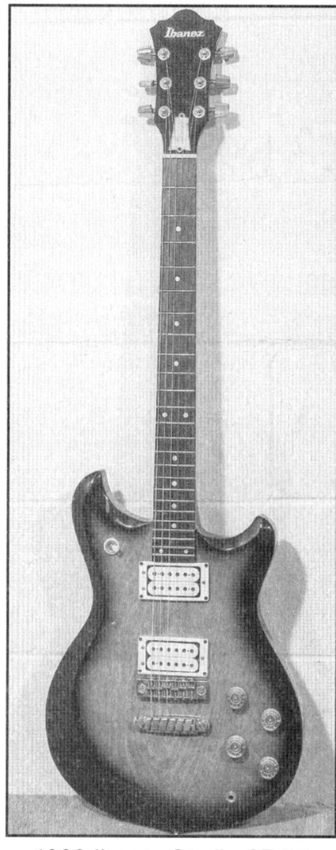

1980 Ibanez Studio ST-55

Tom Pfeifer

1979 Ibanez V302

Peter Busch

Jackson Phil Collen PC1 (U.S.A.)

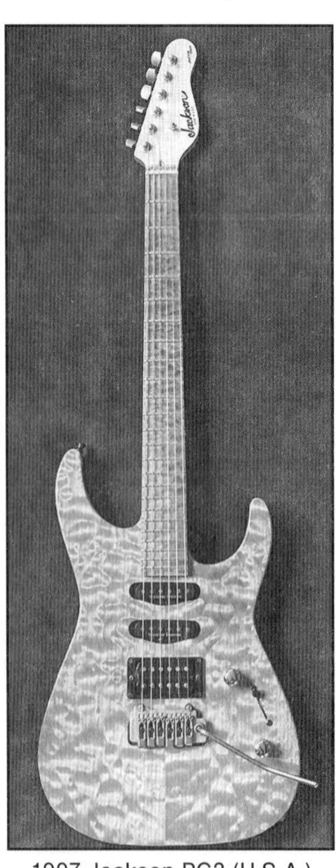

1997 Jackson PC3 (U.S.A.)
Ian Vatet

J Burda Guitars

Flat-top guitars built by luthier Jan Burda in Berrien Springs, Michigan.

J. Frog Guitars

1978-present. Professional and premium grade, production/custom, solidbody guitars made by Ed Roman Guitars. Custom orders only in 2025.

J.B. Player

1980s. Budget and intermediate grade, production, imported acoustic, acoustic/electric, and solidbody guitars and basses. They also offer banjos and mandolins. Founded in United States. Moved production of guitars to Korea but maintained a U.S. Custom Shop. MBT International/Musicorp took over manufacture and distribution in '89, then Kamen acquired MBT in 2005.

J.R. Zeidler Guitars

1977-2002. Luthier John Zeidler built premium and presentation grade, custom, flat-top, 12-string, and archtop guitars in Wallingford, Pennsylvania. He also built mandolins. He died in '02 at age 44.

J.S. Bogdanovich

1996-present. Production/custom, premium grade, classical and steel string guitars built by luthier John S. Bogdanovich in Swannanoa, North Carolina.

J.T. Hargreaves Basses & Guitars

1995-present. Luthier Jay Hargreaves builds his premium grade, production/custom, classical and steel string guitars and basses in Seattle, Washington.

Jack Daniel's

2004-2017. Acoustic and electric guitars and basses, some with Jack Daniel's artwork on the body and headstock, built by Peavey for Jack Daniel's Distillery. There is also an amp model.

Jackson

1980-present. Currently Jackson offers intermediate, professional, and premium grade, production, electric guitars. They also offer basses. In '78 Grover Jackson bought out Charvel Guitars and moved it to San Dimas. Jackson made custom-built bolt-on Charvels. In '82 the pointy, tilt-back Jackson headstock became standard. The Jackson logo was born in '80 and used on a guitar designed as Randy Rhoad's first flying V. Jacksons were neck-through construction. The Charvel trademark was licensed to IMC in '85. IMC moved the Jackson factory to Ontario, California in '86.

Grover Jackson stayed with Jackson/Charvel until '89 (see Charvel). On October 25, 2002, Fender Musical Instruments Corp (FMIC) took ownership of Jackson/Charvel Manufacturing Inc.

MODEL YEAR	FEATURES	EXC. COND. LOW	HIGH
Dinky Reverse DR2			
1996-1998. US-made, reverse headstock, no inlay, 2 Duncan humbuckers, ebony 'board.			
1996-1998		$850	$1,200
Dinky Reverse DR3/DR5			
1992-2001. Import, reverse headstock, 2 humbuckers, dots (DR5) or sharkfin inlays (DR3), locking trem.			
1992-1997	Dots	$400	$600
1995-2001	Sharkfin	$500	$800
DX Series			
2000-2007. Standard offset double-cut body, reverse headstock.			
2000-2007		$300	$500
Fusion Pro			
Late 1980s-early 1990s. Import from Japan.			
1980s-90s		$550	$800
Fusion U.S.A.			
1992-1994. Jackson with Made In USA logo on headstock, graphics.			
1992-1994		$1,800	$2,800
Jenna II RX10D Rhoads			
2009. Limited production, Rhoads body style, named after performer Jenna Jameson.			
2009		$700	$1,000
JSX94			
1994-1995. Offset double-cut solidbody, single/single/hum, rosewood 'board, dot markers.			
1994-1995		$300	$500
JTX			
1993-1995. Partial offset double-cut, single-coil neck pickup, humbucker bridge pickup, Jackson-Rose double lock vibrato, bolt-on neck, dot markers on maple fretboard, JTX truss rod cover logo.			
1993-1995		$400	$600
Kelly Custom			
1984-early 1990s. Solidbody, Kahler tremolo, 2 humbuckers, ebony 'board with shark's tooth inlays, bound neck and headstock.			
1984-1993		$3,800	$5,000
Kelly Pro			
1994-1995. Pointy-cut solidbody, neck-thru, 2 humbuckers, bound ebony 'board, sharkfin inlays.			
1994-1995		$2,800	$4,000
Kelly Standard			
1993-1995. Pointy cutaway solidbody, bolt neck, 2 humbuckers, dot markers.			
1993-1995		$1,800	$2,800
Kelly U.S.A. (KE2)			
1998-2021. Alder solidbody, flame maple top, neck-thru.			
1998-2021		$1,800	$2,800
Kelly XL			
1994-1995. Pointy cutaway solidbody, bolt neck, 2 humbuckers, bound rosewood 'board, sharkfin inlays.			
1994-1995		$600	$900
King V Dave Mustaine (KV1)			
1998. Dave Mustaine (Megadeth) signature, sharkfin inlays, 2 pickups.			
1998		$2,800	$4,200

MODEL YEAR	FEATURES	EXC. COND. LOW	HIGH

King V (KV2)

2003-2024. King V Pro reissue, neck-thru, shark-fin markers, Floyd Rose, U.S.-made.

2003-2024		$900	$1,500

King V Pro

1993-1995. Soft V-shaped neck-thru solidbody, sharkfin markers, 2 humbuckers.

1993-1995		$600	$900

King V STD

1993-1995. Bolt neck version of King V.

1993-1995		$300	$500

Phil Collen

1989-1991, 1993-1995. Offset double-cut maple neck-thru solidbody, 6-in-line tuners, 1 volume, bound ebony 'board, U.S.-made, early version has poplar body, 1 humbucker; later version with basswood body, 1 single-coil and 1 humbucker.

1989-1995		$2,800	$4,000

Phil Collen PC1 (U.S.A.)

1996-present. Quilt maple top, bolt-on maple neck, maple board, koa body '96-'00, mahogany body '01-present, 1 humbucker and 1 single coil '96-'97, humbucker, stacked humbucker, and single coil '98-present.

1996-2024		$2,200	$3,300

Phil Collen PC3 (Import)

1996-2001. Downscale version of Collen model, poplar body, bolt neck, humbucker\single\single.

1996-2001		$500	$800

PS Performers Series

1994-2003. Some with PS model number on truss rod cover.

1994-2003	Various models	$300	$500

Randy Rhoads (Import)

1992-2011. Bolt neck import version.

1992-2011		$450	$700

Randy Rhoads Limited Edition

1992 only. Shark fin-style maple neck-thru body, gold hardware, white with black pinstriping, block inlays, 6-in-line tuners, U.S.-made, only 200 built.

1992		$5,500	$8,500

Randy Rhoads Pro Series RR3 and RR5

1995-2012. Made in Japan, various finishes.

1995-2012	RR3, bolt-on	$1,200	$2,000
2001-2011	RR5, neck-thru	$1,200	$2,000

Randy Rhoads Relic Tribute

2009. Custom Shop limited edition to celebrate the 30th anniversary of the Randy Rhoads Concorde, 60 made, exacting dimension and design of Rhoads' original custom-made Concorde guitar, relic-treatment to mimic the original.

2009		$7,000	$10,500

Randy Rhoads Roswell

1996-1999. Mother-of-pearl crop circle inlays.

1996-1999		$9,000	$12,000

Randy Rhoads U.S.A.

1983-2024. V-shaped (also referred to as Concorde-shaped) neck-thru solidbody, 2 humbuckers, originally made at San Dimas plant, serial numbers RR 0001 to RR 1929, production moved to the Ontario plant by '87, serial numbers RR 1930 to present in sequential order.

1983	Early serial #, no trem	$7,000	$10,000
1983	Mid serial #, no trem	$6,000	$8,500
1983-1986	Late serial #, Kahler trem	$4,500	$6,500
1983-1986	Rose trem or string-thru	$4,000	$6,000
1987-1989	Early Ontario-built	$3,200	$4,500
1990-1992	Early '90s vintage	$2,800	$4,000
1993-2002		$2,800	$4,000
2003-2019	RR5	$2,200	$3,500
2003-2024	RR1	$3,200	$4,500

RX Series

2000-2011. Bolt-on, shark fin inlays.

2000-2008	RX10D Rhoads	$275	$450

San Dimas Serialized Plated

1980-1982. Various custom-built solidbody models, values vary depending on each individual instrument. The values are true for so-called "Serialized Plated" with Jackson neck plate, Jackson logo and serial number.

1980-1982		$5,500	$7,500

Soloist Custom

1993-1995. U.S.-made, double-cut, neck-thru solidbody, 1 humbucker and 2 single-coils, bound ebony 'board, shark's tooth inlays.

1993-1995		$3,000	$4,000

Soloist Pro

1990-1995. Imported version of Soloist, with, shark's tooth inlays.

1990-1995		$750	$1,200

Soloist Shannon

1998. Shark fin inlays, single-single-hum pickups, Rose, signed by Mike Shannon.

1998		$3,200	$4,500

Soloist Student J1 (U.S.A.)

1984-1999. Double-cut neck-thru solidbody, Seymour Duncan single-single-hum pickups, rosewood 'board, dot inlays, no binding.

1984-1986	San Dimas-built	$2,200	$3,500
1986-1999	Ontario-built	$2,200	$3,500

Soloist/Soloist USA/X Series

1984-present. U.S.-made, double-cut, neck-thru, string-thru solidbody, 2 humbuckers, bound rosewood 'board, standard vibrato system on Soloist is Floyd Rose locking vibrato, a guitar with Kahler vibrato is worth less. Replaced by the Soloist USA in '90, then X Series in 2023.

1984-1986	Custom order, Floyd Rose	$5,500	$7,500
1984-1986	Custom order, Kahler	$3,800	$5,500
1984-1986	San Dimas-built, Floyd Rose	$4,800	$7,000
1984-1986	San Dimas-built, Kahler	$3,800	$5,500
1986-1990	Custom order features	$3,800	$5,500
1986-1990	Ontario-built	$2,800	$4,000
1990-2024	Various models, includes SL1 & SL2	$2,200	$3,500

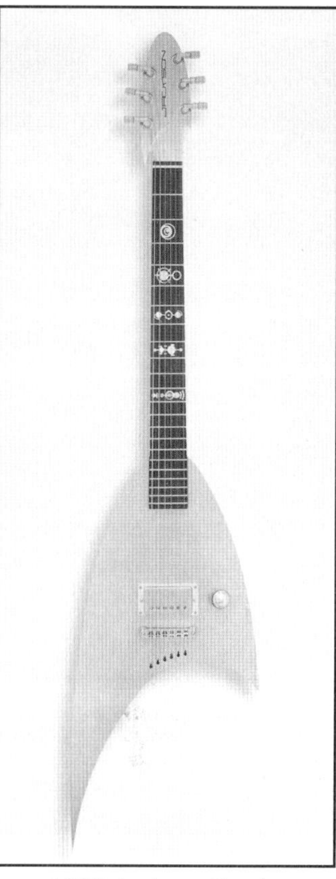

1997 Jackson Randy Rhoads Roswell

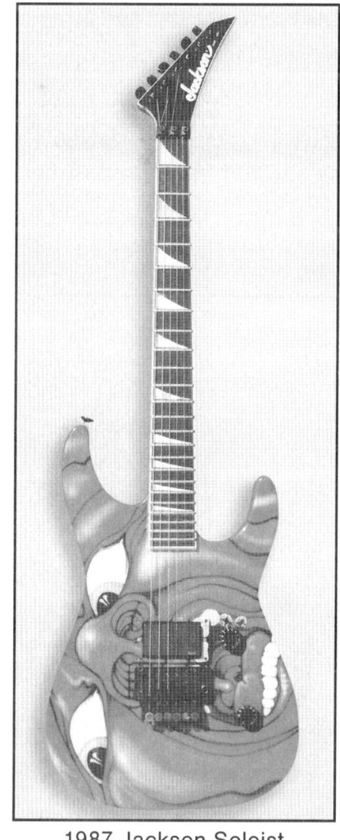

1987 Jackson Soloist
John DeSilva

GUITARS

2005 James Trussart Steel Deville
Rivington Guitars

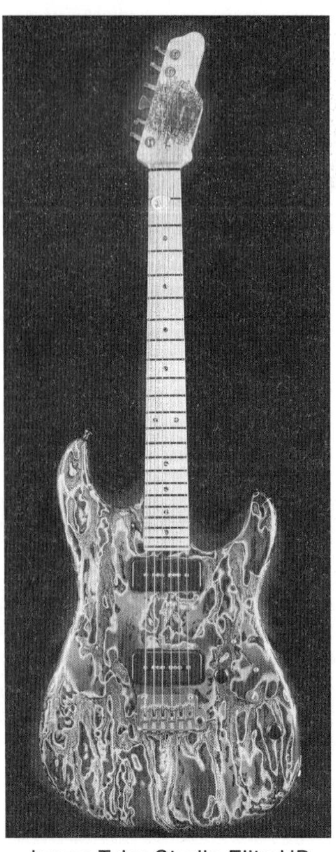
James Tyler Studio Elite HD
Frank Manno

MODEL YEAR	FEATURES	EXC. COND. LOW	HIGH

Stealth EX

1992-late 1990s. Offset double-cut, pointed headstock, H/S/S pickups, offset dot markers, tremolo, Jackson Professional logo.

1990s		$450	$700

Stealth HX

1992-1995. 3 humbucker version of Stealth, string-thru body.

1992-1995		$450	$700

Stealth XL

1993. Stealth XL truss rod cover logo, 1 humbucker, 2 single-coils, left edge dot markers.

1993		$450	$700

Surfcaster SC1

1998-2001. Jackson logo on headstock, Charvel Surfcaster styling.

1998-2001		$1,000	$1,600

Warrior Pro (Import)

1990-1992. Japanese version.

1990-1992		$350	$600

Warrior U.S.A.

1990-1992. Four-point neck-thru solidbody, 1 humbucker and 1 single-coil, triangle markers, active electronics, U.S.-made, the Warrior Pro was Japanese version.

1990-1992	Red	$900	$1,500

Y2KV Dave Mustaine Signature

2000-2002. V-shaped body, shark tooth markers, neck-thru, 2 humbuckers.

2000-2002		$4,500	$6,500

Jackson-Guldan/ Jay G Guitars

1920s-1960s. The Jackson-Guldan Violin Company, of Columbus, Ohio, mainly built inexpensive violins, violas, cellos, etc. but also offered acoustic guitars in the 1950s and early '60s, some of which were distributed by Wards. Their sales flyers from that era state - Made in America by Jackson-Guldan Craftsman. Very similar to small (13"-14") Stella economy flat-tops. Jay G name with quarter-note logo is sometimes on the headstock. They also offered lap steels and small tube amps early on.

Jacobacci

1930s-1994. Founded in France by Italian Vincent Jacobacci and originally building basso-guitars, banjos, and mandolins. Sons Roger and Andre joined the company and encouraged pop to add lapsteels and electric and regular acoustic guitars around '52. The guitars are sometimes labeled Jaco and, from ca. '54 to ca. '66, as Jaco Major. In '58 the company introduced aluminum neck models, and in '59 their first solidbodies. In the '60s they also made instruments branded Royal, Texas, Ohio, Star and made instruments for Major Conn and other companies. By the mid '60s, they were producing mainly jazz style guitars.

Jamboree

1960s. Guitar brand exported by Japan's Hoshino (Ibanez).

James Einolf Guitars

1964-2017. Production/custom, professional grade, flat-top guitars built first in Denver, then Castle Rock, Colorado by luthier James Einolf.

James R. Baker Guitars

1996-present. Luthier James R. Baker builds his premium grade, custom, archtops in Shoreham, New York.

James Trussart

1980-present. Luthier James Trussart builds his premium grade, custom/production, solid and semi-hollow body electric guitars and basses in Los Angeles, California.

James Tyler

Early 1980s-present. Luthier James Tyler builds his professional and premium grade, custom/production, solidbody guitars and basses in Van Nuys, California, and also has a model built in Japan.

Janofsky Guitars

Production classical and flamenco guitars built by luthier Stephen Janofsky in Amherst, Massachusetts starting in 1978.

Jaros

Beginning in 1995 these professional and premium grade, production/custom, solidbody and acoustic/electric guitars were originally built by father and son luthiers Harry and Jim Jaros in Rochester, Pennsylvania. In '01 Ed Roman in Las Vegas, bought the brand. He sold it in '04 to Dave Weiler in Nashville. Serial numbers under 1000 were made by the Jaros', numbers 1001-2000 were made by Ed Roman, over 2000 made by Dave Weiler.

Jasmine

1994-2019. Budget and intermediate grade, production, steel and classical guitars offered by Takamine Jasmine or Jasmine by Takamine. Student level instruments.

Jason Z. Schroeder Guitars

1994-present. Luthier Jason Schroeder builds professional and premium grade, production/custom, electric guitars in Redding, California.

Jay Turser

1997-present. Budget and intermediate grade, production, imported acoustic, acoustic/electric, electric and resonator guitars and basses. They also have amps. Designed and developed by Tommy Rizzi for Music Industries Corp.

JBG (Joe Bochar Guitars)

2009-present. Production/custom, professional grade, solidbody electric guitars built by luthier Joe Bochar in Santa Clarita, California.

MODEL YEAR	FEATURES	EXC. COND. LOW	HIGH

JD Bluesville

John Schappell and luthier Davis Millard build their professional grade, custom/production, solidbody electric guitars in Allentown, Pennsylvania. They began in 2005.

Jeff Traugott Guitars

1991-present. Premium and presentation grade, custom, flat-top, nylon-string, and acoustic/electric guitars built by luthier Jeff Traugott, in Santa Cruz, California.

Jeremy Locke Guitars

Premium grade, production/custom, classical and flamenco guitars built by luthier Jeremy Locke in Coomera, South East Queensland, Australia, starting in 1985.

Jeronimo Pena Fernandez

1967-2002. Luthier Jeronimo Pena Fernandez started building classical guitars in Marmolejo, Spain, in the '50s. In '67, he went full-time and soon became well-known for his fine work. He is now retired, but still builds a few guitars a year. Prices can vary depending on model specs, each instrument should be evaluated on a case-by-case basis.

Jerry Jones

1981-2011. Intermediate grade, production, semi-hollowbody electric guitars and sitars from luthier Jerry Jones, built in Nashville, Tennessee. They also built basses. Jones started building custom guitars in '81 and launched his Danelectro-inspired line in '87. He retired in 2011.

Electric

Various models include Baritone 6-string ('89-'11); Electric Sitar ('90-'11) with buzz-bar sitar bridge, individual pickup for sympathetic strings and custom color gator finish; Longhorn Guitarlin ('89-'00, '05-'11) with large cutaway Guitarlin-style body, 24 frets in '89 and 31 after; and the Neptune 12-string ('81-'11) single-cut with 3 pickups.

1981-2011	Neptune 12-string	$1,800	$2,800
1981-2011	Neptune 6/12 Double Neck	$2,800	$4,200
1989-2011	Baritone 6-string	$1,800	$2,800
1989-2011	Longhorn Guitarlin	$1,800	$2,800
1989-2011	Neptune, baritone 6-string	$2,200	$3,300
1990-2011	Baby Sitar	$1,800	$2,800
1990-2011	Shorthorn	$1,800	$2,800
1990-2011	Sitar	$1,800	$2,800
1990-2011	U-3, 3 pickups	$1,800	$2,800

Jersey Girl

1991-present. Premium grade, production/custom, solidbody guitars made in Japan. They also build effects.

JET

1998-present. Premium grade, custom/production, chambered solidbody electric guitars built by luthier Jeffrey Earle Terwilliger in Raleigh, North Carolina.

Jewel

1920s. Instruments built by the Oscar Schmidt Co. and possibly others. Most likely a brand made for a distributor.

JG Guitars

1991-present. Luthier Johan Gustavsson builds his premium and presentation grade, production/custom, solidbody electric guitars in Malmö, Sweden.

Jim Dyson

1972-2015. Intermediate, professional and premium grade, production/custom electric guitars and basses built by luthier Jim Dyson in Torquay, Southern Victoria, Australia. He also built lap steels.

Jim Redgate Guitars

1992-present. Luthier Jim Redgate builds his premium grade, custom, nylon-string classical guitars in Belair, Adelaide, South Australia.

John Le Voi Guitars

1970-present. Production/custom, gypsy jazz, flat-top, and archtop guitars built by luthier John Le Voi in Lincolnshire, United Kingdom. He also builds mandolin family instruments.

John Page Guitars and John Page Classic

2006-present. Luthier John Page builds his custom, premium grade, chambered and solidbody electric guitars in Sunny Valley, Oregon.

John Price Guitars

Custom classical and flamenco guitars built by luthier John Price, starting in 1984, in Australia.

Johnson

Mid-1990s-2025. Budget, intermediate, and professional grade, production, acoustic, classical, acoustic/electric, resonator and solidbody guitars and basses imported by The Music Link, Brisbane, California. Johnson also offers amps, mandolins, ukuleles and effects.

Jon Kammerer Guitars

1997-present. Luthier Jon Kammerer builds his professional and premium grade, custom/production, solidbody, chambered, hollowbody, and acoustic guitars and basses in Keokuk, Iowa.

Jones

See TV Jones listing.

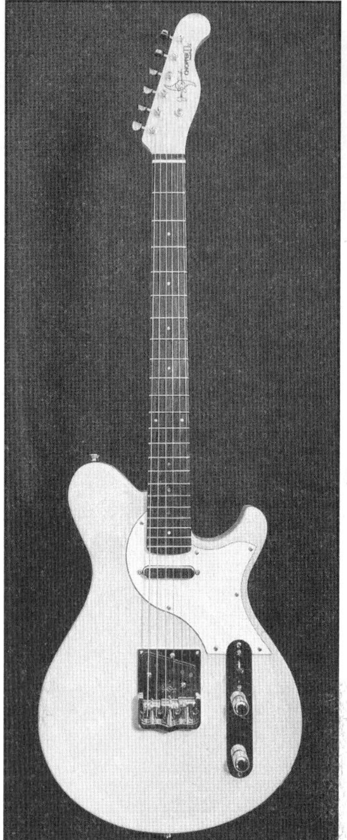

Jason Z. Schroeder
The Chopper TL

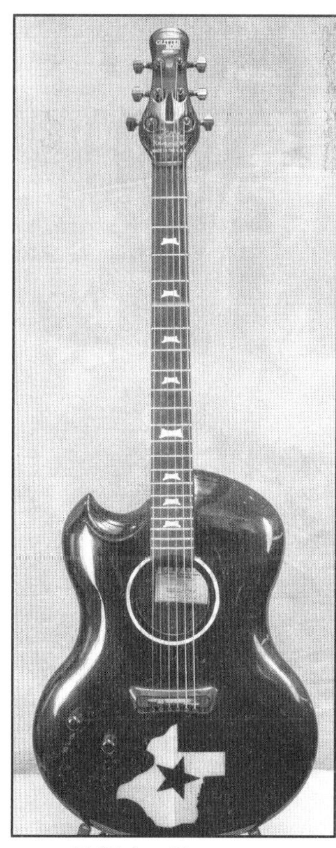

2007 Jon Kammerer
Glitter Rose Series

GUITARS

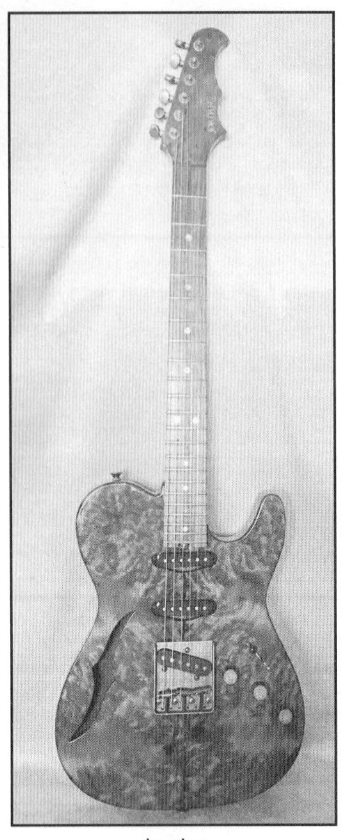

Jordan

JY Jeffery Yong JJ Special Model 2017

MODEL YEAR	FEATURES	EXC. COND. LOW	HIGH

Jordan

1981-present. Professional and premium grade, custom, flat-top and archtop guitars built by luthier John Jordan in Concord, California. He also builds electric violins and cellos.

Jose Oribe

1962-present. Presentation grade, production, classical, flamenco, and steel-string acoustic guitars built by luthier Jose Oribe in Vista, California.

Jose Ramirez

See listing under Ramirez, Jose.

Juliett

1960s. Guitars built by Zerosette (or Zero-Sette), an accordion builder near Castelfidardo, Italy.

JY Jeffrey Yong Guitars

2003-present. Professional and premium grade, production/custom, classical, acoustic and electric guitars and basses and harp guitars built by Jeffrey Yong in Kuala Lumpur, Malaysia.

K & S

1992-1998. Hawaiian-style and classical guitars distributed by George Katechis and Marc Silber and handmade in Paracho, Mexico. A few 16" wide Leadbelly Model 12-strings were made in Oakland, California by luthier Stewart Port. K & S also offered mandolins, mandolas and ukes. In '98, Silber started marketing guitars under the Marc Silber Guitar Company brand and Katechis continued to offer instruments under the Casa Montalvo brand.

Kakos, Stephen

Luthier Stephen Kakos builds his premium grade, production/custom, classical guitars in Mound, Minnesota starting in 1972.

Kalamazoo

1933-1942, 1965-1970. Budget brand built by Gibson. Made flat-tops, solidbodies, mandolins, lap steels, banjos, and amps. Name revived for a line of amps, solidbodies and basses in '65-'67. Playability and string tension will affect values of '60s electrics.

KG-1/KG-1A

1965-1969. Offset double-cut (initial issue) or SG-shape (second issue), 1 pickup, Model 1A with spring vibrato, red, blue, or white.

1965-1969		$500	$700

KG-2/KG-2A

1965-1970. Offset double-cut (initial shape) or SG-shape, 2 pickups, Model 2A with spring vibrato, red, blue, or white.

1965-1970		$550	$800

KG-11

1933-1941. Flat-top, all mahogany, 14" with no 'guard, sunburst.

1933-1941		$1,600	$2,500

MODEL YEAR	FEATURES	EXC. COND. LOW	HIGH

KTG-11 Tenor

1936-1940. Tenor version of 11.

1936-1940		$750	$1,000

KG-12

1940-1941. Rare model, L-00, sunburst.

1940-1941		$2,500	$3,500

KG-14/KG-14N

1936-1940. Flat-top L-0-size, mahogany back and sides, with 'guard, sunburst or natural (N).

1936-1940		$2,500	$3,500

KTG-14 Tenor

1936-1940. Tenor version of 14.

1936-1940		$1,200	$1,500

KG-16

1939-1940. Gibson-made archtop, small body, f-hole.

1939-1940		$1,200	$1,500

KG-21

1936-1941. Early model 15" archtop (bent, not curved), dot markers, bound top, sunburst.

1936-1941		$1,200	$1,500

KTG-21 Tenor

1935-1939. Tenor version of 21.

1935-1939		$700	$1,000

KG-22

1940-1942. Early model 16" archtop.

1940-1942		$1,300	$2,000

KG-31

1935-1940. Archtop L-50-size, 16" body, non-carved spruce top, mahogany back and sides.

1935-1940		$1,300	$2,000

KG-32

1939-1942. Archtop, 16" body.

1939-1942		$1,600	$2,500

KG Senior

1933-1934. Senior Model logo, fire stripe guard, bound top and bottom, rope rose.

1933-1934		$2,300	$3,500

KG Sport

1937-1942. Small body, ¾ size, Sport Model logo.

1937-1942		$2,300	$3,500

KGN-12 Oriole

1940-1941. Flat-top, same body as KG-14, but with maple back and sides, stencil Oriole picture on headstock, natural.

1940-1941		$2,500	$3,500

KGN-32 Oriole

1940-1941. Archtop, maple back and sides, stencil Oriole picture on headstock, natural.

1940-1941		$2,500	$3,500

KHG Series

1936-1941. Acoustic Hawaiian guitar (HG), some converted to Spanish set-up.

1936-1940	KHG-11	$1,600	$2,500
1936-1941	KHG-14	$2,500	$3,500

Kamico

1947-1951. Flat-top acoustic guitars. Low-end budget brand made by Kay Musical Instrument Company and sold through various distributors. They also offered lap steel and amp sets.

MODEL YEAR	FEATURES	EXC. COND. LOW	HIGH

K Stratotone Thin Single

1950-1951. Similar to Kay Stratotone-style neck-thru solidbody, single slim-tube pickup.

1950-1951		$900	$1,300

Kapa

Ca. 1962-1970. Begun by Dutch immigrant and music store owner Koob Veneman in Hyattsville, Maryland whose father had made Amka guitars in Holland. Kapa is from K for Koob, A for son Albert, P for daughter Patricia, and A for wife Adeline. Crown shield logo from Amka guitars. The brand included some Hofner and Italian imports in '60. Ca. '66 Kapa started offering thinner bodies. Some German Pix pickups ca. '66. Thinlines and Japanese bodies in '69. Kapa closed shop in '70 and the parts and equipment were sold to Micro-Frets and Mosrite. Later Veneman was involved with Bradley copy guitars imported from Japan. Approximately 120,000 Kapa guitars and basses were made.

Electric

1962-1970. Various models include Challenger with 3-way toggle from '62-'66/'67 and 2 on/off switches after; Cobra with 1 pickup; Continental and Continental 12-string; Minstrel and Minstrel 12-string with teardrop shape, 3 pickups; and the Wildcat, mini offset double-cut, 3 pickups and mute.

1962-1970	Various models	$400	$2,000

Karol Guitars

2001-present. Luthier Tony Karol builds his custom, premium grade, acoustic and electric guitars in Mississauga, Ontario.

Kasha

1967-1997. Innovative classical guitars built by luthier Richard Schneider in collaboration with Dr. Michael Kasha. Schneider also consulted for Gibson and Gretsch. Schneider died in '97.

Kathy Wingert Guitars

1996-present. Luthier Kathy Wingert builds her premium grade, production/custom, flat-tops in Rancho Palos Verdes, California. Discontinued custom orders in 2024.

Kawai

1927-present. Kawai is a Japanese piano and guitar maker. They started offering guitars around '56 and they were imported into the U.S. carrying many different brand names, including Kimberly and Teisco. In '67 Kawai purchased Teisco. Odd-shaped guitars were offered from late-'60s through the mid-'70s. Few imports carrying the Kawai brand until the late-'70s; best known for high quality basses. By '90s they were making plexiglass replicas of Teisco Spectrum 5 and Kawai moon-shaped guitar. Kawai quit offering guitars and basses around 2002.

Acoustic

1956-2002		$300	$500

MODEL YEAR	FEATURES	EXC. COND. LOW	HIGH

Electric

1956-2002	Common model	$325	$500
1956-2002	Rare model	$600	$2,500

Kay

Ca. 1931 (1890)-present. Originally founded in Chicago, Illinois as Groehsl Company (or Groehsel) in 1890, making bowl-backed mandolins. Offered Groehsl, Stromberg, Kay Kraft, Kay, Arch Kraft brand names, plus made guitars for S.S.Maxwell, Old Kraftsman (Spiegel), Recording King (Wards), Supertone (Sears), Silvertone (Sears), National, Dobro, Custom Kraft (St.Louis Music), Hollywood (Shireson Bros.), Oahu and others.

In 1921 the name was changed to Stromberg-Voisinet Company. Henry Kay "Hank" Kuhrmeyer joined the company in '23 and was secretary by '25. By the mid-'20s the company was making many better Montgomery Ward guitars, banjos and mandolins, often with lots of pearloid. First production electric guitars and amps are introduced with big fanfare in '28; perhaps only 200 or so made. Last Stromberg instruments seen in '32. Kuhrmeyer becomes president and the Kay Kraft brand was introduced in '31, probably named for Kuhrmeyer's middle name, though S-V had used Kay brand on German Kreuzinger violins '28-'36. By '34, if not earlier, the company is changed to the Kay Musical Instrument Company. A new factory was built at 1640 West Walnut Street in '35. The Kay Kraft brand ends in '37 and the Kay brand is introduced in late-'36 or '37.

Violin Style Guitars and upright acoustic basses debuted in '38. In '40 the first guitars for Sears, carrying the new Silvertone brand, were offered. Kamico budget line introduced in '47 and Rex flattops and archtops sold through Gretsch in late-'40s. Kuhrmeyer retires in '55 dies a year later. A new gigantic factory in Elk Grove Village, Illinois opens in '64. Seeburg purchased Kay in '66 and sold it to Valco in '67. Valco/Kay went out of business in '68 and its assets were auctioned in '69. The Kay name went to Sol Weindling and Barry Hornstein of W.M.I. (Teisco Del Rey) who began putting Kay name on Teisco guitars. By '73 most Teisco guitars are called Kay. Tony Blair, president of Indianapolis-based A.R. Musical Enterprises Inc. (founded in '73) purchased the Kay nameplate in '79 and currently distributes Kay in the U.S. Currently Kay offers budget and intermediate grade, production, acoustic, semi-hollow body, solidbody, and resonator guitars. They also make amps, basses, banjos, mandolins, ukes, violins.

K11/K8911 Rhythm Special

1953-1961. Single-cut 17" acoustic archtop, "eighth note" headstock logo, large position markers, white 'guard, became K8911 in '57, sunburst or blond (B).

1953-1961	Blond	$1,000	$1,500
1953-1961	Sunburst	$850	$1,200

K20 Super Auditorium

1939-1942. 16" archtop, solid spruce top, maple back and sides, sunburst.

1939-1942		$300	$500

1941 Kalamazoo KGN-32 Oriole

David Stone

1953 Kay K11

John Neff

GUITARS

1950s Kay K-21
Donald DiLoreto

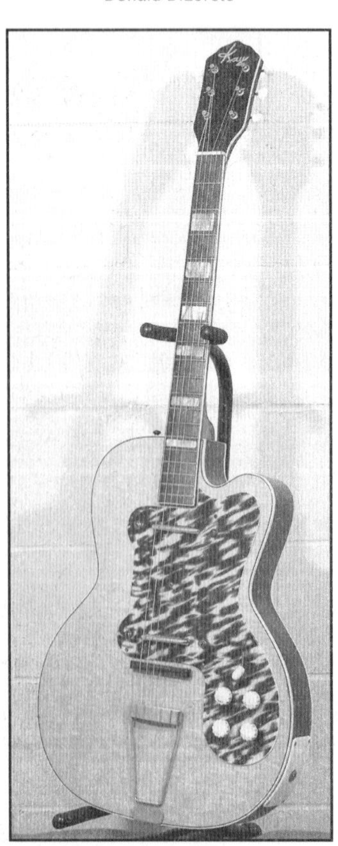
1953 Kay K161 Thin Twin
Tom Pfeifer

MODEL YEAR	FEATURES	EXC. COND. LOW	HIGH

K20T

1970s. Japanese-made solidbody, 2 pickups, tremolo, model number on neck plate, circle-capital K logo on headstock.

1970s		$150	$300

K21/K21B Cutaway Professional

1952-1956. Single-cut 17" acoustic archtop, split block markers, sunburst or blond (B).

1952-1956	Blond	$1,200	$1,800
1952-1956	Sunburst	$1,200	$1,800

K22 Artist Spanish

1947-1956. Flat-top similar to Gibson J-100 17", spruce top, mahogany back and sides.

1947-1956		$600	$900

K26 Artist Spanish

1947-1951. Flat-top, block markers, natural.

1947-1951		$700	$1,000

K27 Jumbo

1952-1956. 17" Jumbo flat-top, fancy appointments.

1952-1956		$1,200	$1,800

K37T Spanish Tenor

1952-1956. Mahogany bodied archtop, tenor.

1952-1956		$300	$500

K39 Super Grand Auditorium

1947-1951. Full size acoustic archtop, faux rope binding on top, Kay script logo.

1947-1951		$400	$600

K44 Artist Archtop

1947-1951. Non-cut archtop, solid spruce top, 17" curly maple veneered body, block markers, sunburst.

1947-1951		$600	$900

K45 Professional Master Size Archtop

1952-1954. Non-cut archtop, 17" body, engraved tortoiseshell-celluloid headstock, large block markers, natural.

1952-1954		$600	$900

K45 Travel Guitar

1981. Made in Korea, known as the 'rifle guitar', 'travel guitar', or 'Austin-Hatchet copy', circle K logo.

1981		$400	$600

K46 Artist Master Size Archtop

1947-1951. Non-cut archtop, solid spruce top, 17" curly maple-veneered body, double-eighth note headstock inlay, sunburst.

1947-1951		$600	$900

K48 Artist Master Size Archtop

1947-1951. Non-cut archtop, 17" solid spruce top with figured maple back and sides, split block inlays, sunburst or black.

1947-1951		$850	$1,200

K48/K21 Jazz Special

Late-1960s. Slim solidbody with 3 reflective pickups, garden spade headstock, fancy position Circle K headstock logo, white.

1968		$500	$800

K100 Vanguard

1961-1966. Offset double-cut slab solidbody, genuine maple veneered top and back over hardwood body, sunburst.

1961-1966		$300	$500

K102 Vanguard

1961-1966. Double pickup version of the K100, sunburst.

1961-1966		$400	$600

K136 (aka Stratotone)

1955-1957. Small single-cut slab solidbody electric, similar to Harmony Stratotone style, set neck, 1 pickup, trapeze tailpiece, triangle paint graphic in Spring Green and White Mist, matching green headstock, attractive finish adds value to this otherwise lower-end student model.

1955-1957		$1,000	$1,500

K142 (aka Stratotone)

1955-1957. Small slab solidbody, introduced in '55 along with the K136, offered with 1 pickup or 2 pickups (more rare), trapeze tailpiece, copper finish.

1955-1957	1 pickup	$1,000	$1,500
1955-1957	2 pickups	$1,000	$1,500

K161 Thin Twin/Jimmy Reed

1952-1958. Single-cut semi-hollow body, 2 pickups.

1952-1958		$1,000	$1,500

K161V/VB Thin Twin

2009-present. Vintage Reissue series, single-cut hollowbody, 2 pickups.

2009-2024		$800	$1,200

K300 Double Cutaway Solid Electric

1962-1966. Two single-coils, block inlays, some with curly maple top and some with plain maple top, natural.

1962-1966		$500	$800

K360 Apollo/K365 Apollo II

1965-1968. Solidbody, 2 pickups, block inlays, vibrato.

1965-1968		$1,000	$1,500

K535 Double Cutaway Thinline

1961-1965. Thinline double-cut, 2 pickups, vibrato, sunburst.

1961-1965		$600	$900

K550 Dove

1970s. Square shoulder D-style, 2 Dove-style 'guards, capital K logo.

1970s		$200	$300

K571/K572/K573 Speed Demon

1961-1965. Thinline semi-acoustic/electric, single pointed cutaway, some with Bigsby vibrato, with 1 (K571), 2 (K572) or 3 (K573) pickups. There was also a Speed Demon solidbody.

1961-1965	571, 1 pickup	$400	$600
1961-1965	572, 2 pickups	$500	$800
1961-1965	573, 3 pickups	$500	$800

K580 Galaxy

1961-1966. Thinline, single-cut, 1 pickup.

1961-1966		$500	$800

K592 Double Cutaway Thinline

1962-1966. Thinline semi-acoustic/electric, double Florentine cut, 2 or 3 pickups, Bigsby vibrato, pie-slice inlays, cherry.

1962-1966		$500	$800

K672/K673 Swingmaster

1961-1965. Single rounded cutaway semi-hollowbody, with 2 (K672) or 3 (K673) pickups.

1961-1965	672, 2 pickups	$1,000	$1,500
1961-1965	673, 3 pickups	$1,100	$1,600

GUITARS

MODEL YEAR	FEATURES	EXC. COND. LOW	HIGH

K682 Galaxie II

1966-1968. Hollowbody, 2 pickups, vibrato tailpiece.

1966-1968		$550	$900

K775/K776 Jazz II

1961-1966. Electric thinline archtop, double-cut, standard Bigsby vibrato, 2 Gold K pickups, 4 knobs with toggle controls. Replaces Barney Kessel series as top-of-the-line model.

1961-1966	775, shaded	$1,300	$2,000
1961-1966	776, blond	$1,300	$2,000

K797 Acoustic Archtop

1930s. Full size student-intermediate acoustic archtop, 3-on-a-strip tuners, dot markers, sunburst.

1935-1937		$300	$500

K1160 Standard

1957-1964. Small 13" (standard) flat-top, laminated construction.

1957-1964		$75	$150

K1452 Aristocrat

1952. Acoustic-electric archtop, 2 pickups, sunburst.

1952		$800	$1,200

K1700/K1701 Barney Kessel Pro

1957-1960. 13" hollowbody, single-cut, Kelvinator headstock, ebony 'board with pearl inlays, white binding, 1 (K1701) or 2 (K1700) pickups, sunburst.

1957-1960	1700, 2 pickups	$1,800	$2,800
1957-1960	1701, 1 pickup	$1,600	$2,500

K1961/K1962/K1963 Value Leader

1960-1965. Part of Value Leader line, thinline single-cut, hollowbody, identified by single chrome-plated checkered, body-length guard on treble side, laminated maple body, maple neck, dot markers, sunburst, with 1 (K1961), 2 (K1962) or 3 (K1963) pickups.

1960-1965	1961, 1 pickup	$425	$650
1960-1965	1962, 2 pickups	$500	$800
1960-1965	1963, 3 pickups	$500	$800

K1982/K1983 Style Leader/Jimmy Reed

1960-1965. Part of the Style Leader mid-level Kay line. Sometimes dubbed Jimmy Reed of 1960s. Easily identified by the long, brushed copper dual guard plates on either side of the strings. Brown or gleaming golden blond (natural) finish, laminated curly maple body, simple script Kay logo, with 2 (K1982) or 3 (K1983) pickups.

1960-1965	1982, 2 pickups	$600	$900
1960-1965	1983, 3 pickups	$700	$1,000

K3500 Studio Concert

1966-1968. 14 1/2" flat-top, solid spruce top, laminated maple back and sides.

1966-1968		$100	$150

K5113 Plains Special

1968. Flat-top, solid spruce top, laminated mahogany back and sides.

1968		$200	$300

K5160 Auditorium

1957-1965. Flat-top 15" auditorium-size, laminated construction.

1957-1965		$200	$300

K6100 Country

1950s-1960s. Jumbo flat-top, spruce x-braced top, mahogany back and sides, natural.

1957-1962		$425	$650

K6116 Super Auditorium

1957-1965. Super Auditorium-size flat-top, laminated figured maple back and sides, solid spruce top.

1957-1965		$250	$400

K6120 Western

1960s. Jumbo flat-top, laminated maple body, pin less bridge, sunburst.

1962		$225	$350

K6130 Calypso

1960-1965. 15 1/2" flat-top with narrow waist, slotted headstock, natural.

1960-1965		$300	$500

K6533/K6535 Value Leader

1961-1965. Value Leader was the budget line of Kay, full body archtop, with 1 (K6533) or 2 (K6535) pickups, sunburst.

1961-1965	6533, 1 pickup	$400	$600
1961-1965	6535, 2 pickups	$425	$650

K6700/K6701 Barney Kessel Artist

1956-1960. Single-cut, 15 1/2" body, 1 (K6701) or 2 (K6700) pickups, Kelvinator headstock, sunburst or blond.

1956-1960	6700, 2 pickups	$2,700	$4,000
1956-1960	6701, 1 pickup	$2,500	$3,800

K6878 Style Leader

1966-1968. Full size (15.75) acoustic archtop, circle K logo on 'guard, sunburst.

1966-1968		$300	$500

K7000 Artist

1960-1965. Highest-end of Kay classical series, fan bracing, spruce top, maple back and sides.

1960-1965		$350	$550

K7010 Concerto

1960-1965. Entry level of Kay classical series.

1960-1965		$100	$150

K7010 Maestro

1960-1965. Middle level of Kay classical series.

1960-1965		$225	$350

K8110 Master

1957-1960. 17" master-size flat-top which was largest of the series, laminated construction.

1957-1960		$180	$300

K8127 Solo Special

1957-1965. Kay's professional grade flat-top, narrow waist jumbo, block markers.

1957-1965		$450	$700

K8700/K8701 Barney Kessel Jazz Special

1956-1960. Part of the Gold K Line, top-of-the-line model, 17" single-cut archtop, 1 (K8701) or 2 (K8700) pickups, 4 controls and toggle, Kelvinator headstock with white background, natural or shaded sunburst, Barney Kessel signature logo on acrylic scalloped 'guard, no signature logo on '60 model.

1956-1960	8700, 2 pickups	$2,700	$4,000
1956-1960	8701, 1 pickup	$2,300	$3,500

K8990/K8995 Upbeat

1956/1958-1960. Less expensive alternative to Barney Kessel Jazz Special, 2 (K8990) or 3 (K8995) pickups, Gold K Line, Kelvinator headstock, sunburst.

1956-1960	8990, 2 pickups	$1,500	$2,200
1958-1960	8995, 3 pickups	$1,500	$2,200

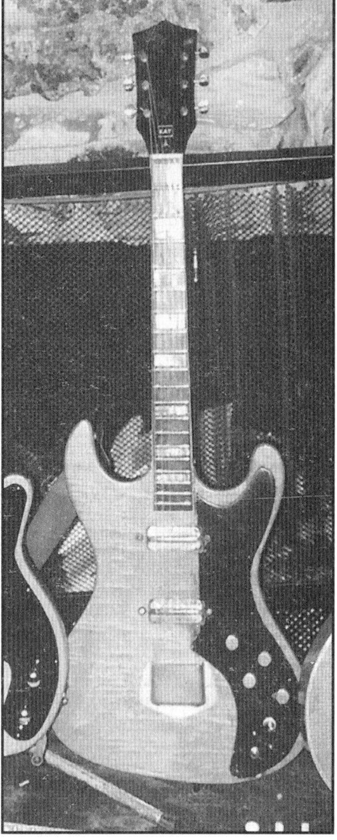

1963 Kay K300
Richard Kregear

1963 Kay K6535 Value Leader
Rivington Guitars

GUITARS

Kelly Guitar

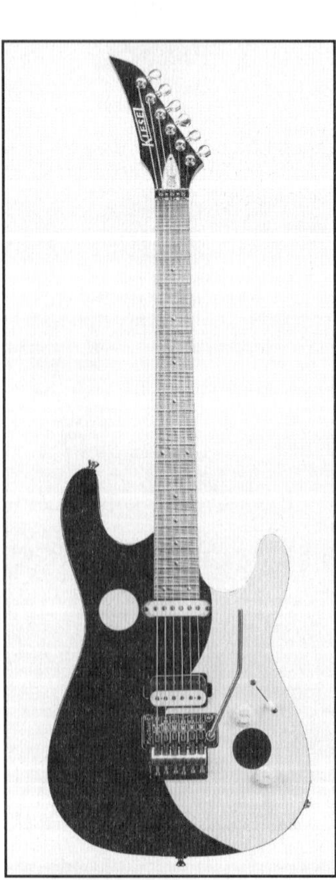

Kiesel Jason Becker Yin Yang

MODEL YEAR	FEATURES	EXC. COND. LOW	HIGH

Wood Amplifying Guitar

1934. Engineered after Dobro/National metal resonator models except the resonator and chamber on this model are made of wood, small production.

1934		$1,600	$2,500

Kay Kraft

1927-1937. First brand name of the Kay Musical Instrument Company as it began its transition from Stromberg-Voisinet Company to Kay (see Kay for more info).

Recording King

1931-1937		$600	$900

Venetian Archtop

1930s. Unique Venetian cutaway body style, acoustic with round soundhole, flower-vine decal art on low bout.

1930s		$1,200	$1,800

KB

1989-present. Luthier Ken Bebensee builds his premium grade, custom, acoustic, and electric guitars and basses in North San Juan, California. He was in San Luis Obispo from '89-'01. He also builds mandolins.

Kel Kroydon (by Gibson)

1930-1933. Private branded budget level instruments made by Gibson. They also had mandolins and banjos. The name has been revived on a line of banjos by Tom Mirisola and made in Nashville.

KK-1

1932. 14 3/4" L-0 sytle body, colorful parrot stencils on body.

1932		$4,000	$6,000

Keller Custom Guitars

Professional grade, production/custom, solidbody guitars built by luthier Randall Keller in Mandan, North Dakota. He began in 1994.

Keller Guitars

1975-2022. Premium grade, production/custom, flat-tops made by luthier Michael L. Keller in Rochester, Minnesota.

Kelly Guitars

1968-present. Luthier Rick Kelly builds professional grade, custom, solidbody electric guitars in New York, New York.

Ken Franklin

2003-present. Luthier Ken Franklin builds his premium grade, production/custom, acoustic guitars and ukuleles in Ukiah, California.

Kendrick

1989-present. Premium grade, production/custom, solidbody guitars built in Texas. Founded by Gerald Weber in Pflugerville, Texas and currently located in Kempner, Texas. Mainly known for their handmade tube amps, Kendrick added guitars in '94 and also offers speakers and effects. Weber died in 2024, wife Jill and daughter Helen plan to continue his Kendrick amps.

Kenneth Lawrence Instruments

1986-present. Luthier Kenneth Lawrence builds his premium grade, production/custom, electric solidbody and chambered guitars and basses in Arcata, California.

Kent

1961-1969. Imported from Japan by Buegeleisen and Jacobson of New York, New York. Manufacturers unknown but many early guitars and basses were made by Guyatone and Teisco.

Acoustic Flat-Top

1962-1969. Various models.

1962-1969		$200	$300

Acoustic/Electric

1962-1969. Various models.

1962-1969		$300	$500

Electric 12-String

1965-1969. Thinline electric, double pointy cutaways, 12 strings, slanted dual pickup, sunburst.

1965-1969		$500	$800

Semi-Hollow Electric

1962-1969. Thinline electric, offset double pointy cutaways, slanted dual pickups, various colors.

1962-1969		$500	$800

Solidbody Electric

1962-1969. Models include Polaris I, II and III, Lido, Copa and Videocaster.

1962-1969	Common model	$300	$500
1962-1969	Rare model	$500	$800

Kevin Ryan Guitars

1989-present. Premium grade, custom, flat-tops built by luthier Kevin Ryan in Westminster, California.

KeyKord

Ca. 1929-mid 1930s. Keykord offered guitars, ukes and banjos that had a push-button mechanism mounted over the fingerboard that "fingered" a different chord for each button. The guitars were built by Chicago's Stromberg-Voisinet (Kay).

Tenor

1920s-1930s. Venetian mahogany body, 4-string, pearloid headstock overlay.

1920s-30s		$500	$800

Kiesel

1946-present. Founded by Lowell C. Kiesel in '46. Refer to Carvin listing for more info regarding the early years. Prior to his death in 2009, L.C. had turned the business over to his sons and it was located in several different California cities over the years.

In 2015, son Mark and grandson Jeff Kiesel began

MODEL YEAR	FEATURES	EXC. COND. LOW	HIGH

the new independent Kiesel Custom Guitars. They build professional and premium grade, acoustic and electric guitars and basses in Escondido, California.

Kimbara

1970s-1980s. Japanese line of guitars and basses mainly imported into the U.K. Models were the same as the Fresher brand.

Kimberly

Late-1960s-early-1970s. Private branded import made in the same Japanese factory as Teisco. They also made basses.

Longhorn

1960s. S-style, deep double-cut, 2 pickups.

1960s		$450	$800

May Queen

1960s. Same as Teisco May Queen with Kimberly script logo on headstock and May Queen Teisco on the 'guard.

1960s		$550	$900

Kinal

1969-present. Production/custom, professional and premium grade, solid body electric and archtop guitars and basses built and imported by luthier Michael Kinal in Vancouver, British Columbia.

King's Stone

1960s. Guitar brand exported by Japan's Hoshino (Ibanez).

Kingsley

1960s. Early Japanese imports, Teisco-made.

Soldibody Electric

1960s. Four pickups with tremolo.

1960s		$400	$600

Kingslight Guitars

1980-2015. Luthier John Kingslight built his premium grade, custom/production, steel string guitars and basses in Portage, Michigan (in Taos, New Mexico for '80-'83).

Kingston

Ca. 1958-1967. Guitars and basses imported from Japan by Jack Westheimer and Westheimer Importing Corporation of Chicago, Illinois. Early examples made by Guyatone and Teisco. They also offered mandolins and banjos.

Electric

1958-1967. Various models include B-1, soldibody, 1 pickup; B-2T/B-3T/B-4T, solidbodies, 2/3/4 pickups and tremolo; SA-27, thin hollowbody, 2 pickups, tremolo.

1958-1967	Common model	$400	$600
1958-1967	Rare model	$650	$1,000

Kinscherff Guitars

1990-present. Luthier Jamie Kinscherff builds his premium grade, production/custom, flat-top guitars in Austin, Texas.

MODEL YEAR	FEATURES	EXC. COND. LOW	HIGH

Kleartone

1930s. Private brand made by Regal and/or Gibson.

Small Flat-Top

1930s		$500	$800

Klein Acoustic Guitars

First produced in 1972, luthiers Steve Klein and Steven Kauffman build their production/custom, premium and presentation grade flat-tops and basses outside Sonoma, California.

Klein Electric Guitars

1988-2007. Steve Klein added electrics to his line in '88. In '95, he sold the electric part of his business to Lorenzo German, who continued to produce professional grade, production/custom, solidbody guitars and basses in Linden, California.

K-Line Guitars

2005-present. Professional grade, production/custom, T-style and S-style guitars and basses built by luthier Chris Kroenlein in St. Louis, Missouri. He also builds basses.

Klira

1887-1980s. Founded by Johannes Klira in Schoenbach, Germany, mainly made violins, but added guitars in the 1950s. The guitars of the '50s and '60s were original designs, but by the '70s most models were similar to popular American models. The guitars of the '50s and '60s were aimed at the budget market, but workmanship improved with the '70s models. They also made basses.

Electric

1950s-60s	Common model	$500	$800
1950s-60s	Rare model	$900	$1,500

Knaggs

2010-present. Luthiers Joseph Knaggs and Peter Wolf build premium and presentation grade, production/custom, acoustic and electric guitars and basses in Greensboro, Maryland.

Knox

Early-mid-1960s. Budget grade guitars imported from Japan, script Knox logo on headstock.

Electric Solidbody

1960s. Student models, 2 pickups, push buttons.

1960s	Various models	$400	$600

Knutsen

1890s-1920s. Luthier Chris J. Knutsen of Tacoma and Seattle, Washington, experimented with and perfected Hawaiian and harp guitar models. He moved to Los Angeles, California around 1916. He also made steels, mandolins and ukes. Dealers state the glue used on Knutsen instruments is prone to fail and instruments may need repair.

1967 Kingston
Tom Pfeifer

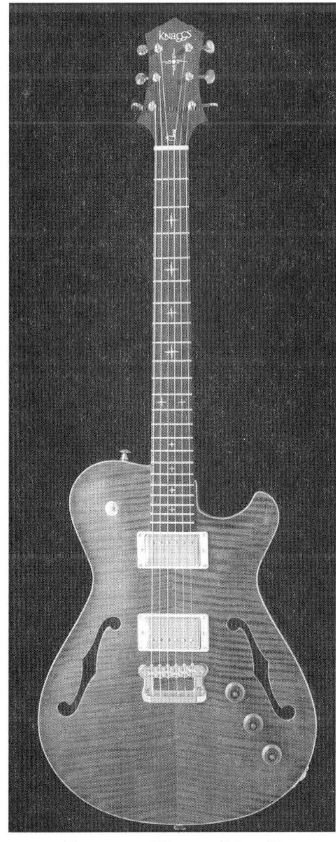

Knaggs Chena Tier 2

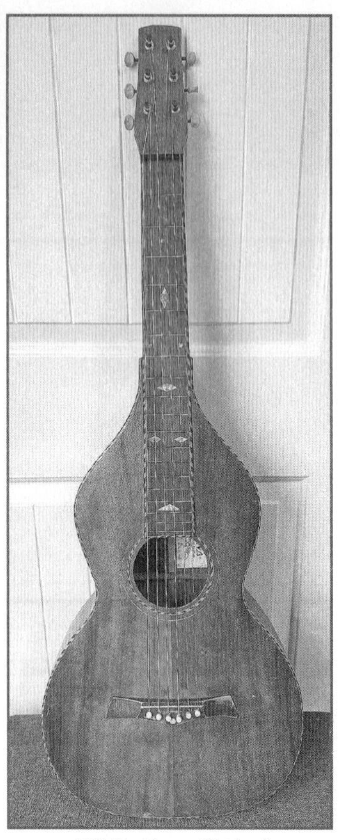

1920s Kona Style 3

Terrel Albright

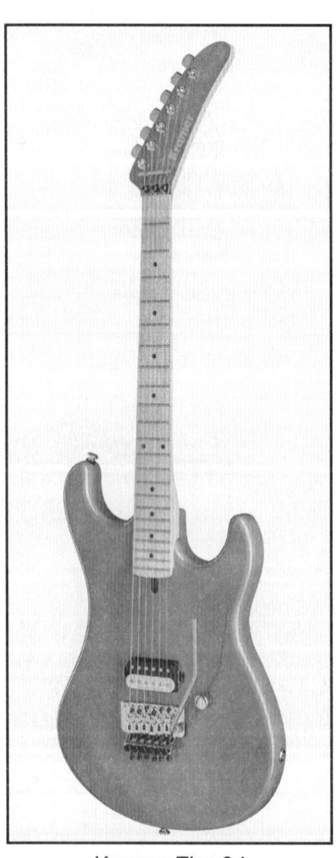

Kramer The 84

MODEL YEAR	FEATURES	EXC. COND. LOW	HIGH

Convertible

1909-1914. Flat-top model with adjustable neck angle that allowed for a convertible Hawaiian or Spanish setup.

1909-1914		$4,000	$5,000

Harp Guitar

1900s. Normally 11 strings with fancy purfling and trim.

1900-1910		$3,500	$4,500

Knutson Luthiery

1981-present. Professional and premium grade, custom, archtop and flat-top guitars built by luthier John Knutson in Forestville, California. He also builds basses, lap steels and mandolins.

Kohno

1960-present. Luthier Masaru Kohno built his classical guitars in Tokyo, Japan. When he died in '98, production was taken over by his nephew, Masaki Sakurai.

Koll

1990-present. Professional and premium grade, custom/production, solidbody, chambered, and archtop guitars and basses built by luthier Saul Koll, originally in Long Beach, California, and since '93, in Portland, Oregon.

Kona

1910s-1920s. Acoustic Hawaiian guitars sold by C.S. Delano and others, with later models made by the Herman Weissenborn Co. Weissenborn appointments are in line with style number, with thicker body and solid neck construction. Kona name is currently used on an import line offered by M&M Merchandisers.

Style 2

1927-1928		$2,500	$3,500

Style 3

1920s	Koa	$3,500	$5,000

Style 4

1920s	Hawaiian	$3,500	$5,000
1920s	Spanish	$3,500	$5,000

Kona Guitar Company

2000-present. Located in Fort Worth, Texas, Kona imports budget and intermediate grade, production, nylon and steel string acoustic and solid and semi-hollow body electric guitars and basses. They also offer amps, mandolins and ukes.

Koontz

1970-late 1980s. Luthier Sam Koontz started building custom guitars in the late '50s. Starting in '66 Koontz, who was associated with Harptone guitars, built guitars for Standel. In '70, he opened his own shop in Linden, New Jersey, building a variety of custom guitars. Koontz died in the late '80s. His guitars varied greatly and should be valued on a case-by-case basis.

Kopp String Instruments

Located in Republic, Ohio from 2000-2004, luthier Denny Kopp presently builds his professional and premium grade, production/custom, semi-hollow archtop electric and hand-carved archtop jazz guitars in Catawba Island, Ohio. He started in 2000.

Kopy Kat

1970s. Budget copy-era solidbody, semi-hollow body and acoustic guitars imported from Japan. They also made basses and mandolins.

Acoustic

1970s	J-200 copy	$300	$500

Kragenbrink

Premium grade, production/custom, steel string acoustic guitars built by luthier Lance Kragenbrink in Vandercook Lake, Michigan, starting in the year 2001.

Kramer

1976-1990, 1995-present. Currently Kramer offers budget and intermediate grade, production, imported acoustic, acoustic/electric, semi-hollow and solidbody guitars. They also offer basses, amps, and effects.

Founded by New York music retailer Dennis Berardi, ex-Travis Bean partner Gary Kramer and ex-Norlin executive Peter LaPlaca. Initial financing provided by real estate developer Henry Vaccaro. Parent company named BKL Corporation (Berardi, Kramer, LaPlaca), located in Neptune City, New Jersey. The first guitars were designed by Berardi and luthier Phil Petillo and featured aluminum necks with wooden inserts on the back to give them a wooden feel. Guitar production commenced in late-'76. Control passed to Guitar Center of Los Angeles for '79-'82, which recommended a switch to more economical wood necks. Most wooden necks from Kramer's Golden Era (1981-1986) we made in Japan by ESP and shipped to the U.S.A. for final guitar assembly. Aluminum necks were phased out during the early-'80s and were last produced in '85. In '84 they added their first import models, the Japanese-made Focus line, followed by the Korean-made Striker line. By 1986 Kramer was the top American electric guitarmaker. In '89, a new investment group was brought in with James Liati as president, hoping for access to Russian market, but the company went out of business in late-'90. In '95 Henry Vaccaro and new partners revived the company and designed several new guitars in conjunction with Phil Petillo. However, in '97 the Kramer brand was sold to Gibson. In '98, Henry Vaccaro released his new line of aluminum-core neck, split headstock guitars under the Vacarro brand. From 1997 to 2009, sales of Kramer instruments were only through Gibson's MusicYo website. In 2010, Gibson began to distribute the brand through traditional music retail channels with new issues and 1980s legacy models. Non-U.S.-

GUITARS

MODEL YEAR	FEATURES	EXC. COND. LOW	HIGH

made models include the following lines: Aerostar, Ferrington, Focus, Hundred (post-'85 made with 3 digits in the 100-900), Showster, Striker, Thousand (post-'85 made with 4 digits in the 1000-9000), XL (except XL-5 made in '80s).

Serial numbers for import models include:

Two alpha followed by 4 numbers: for example AA2341 with any assortment of letters and numbers.

One alpha followed by 5 numbers: for example B23412.

Five numbers: for example 23412.

Model number preceding numbers: for example XL1-03205.

The notation "Kramer, Neptune, NJ" does indicate U.S.A.-made production.

Most post-'85 Kramers were ESP Japanese-made guitars. American Series were ESP Japanese components that were assembled in the U.S.

The vintage/used market makes value distinctions between U.S.-made and import models.

Headstock and logo shape can help identify U.S. versus imports as follows:

Traditional or Classic headstock with capital K as Kramer: U.S.A. '81-'84.

Banana (soft edges) headstock with all caps KRAMER: U.S.A. American Series '84-'86.

Pointy (sharp cut) headstock with all caps KRAMER: U.S.A. American Series '86-'87.

Pointy (sharp cut) headstock with downsized letters Kramer plus American decal: U.S.A. American Series '87-'94.

Pointy (sharp cut) headstock with downsized letters Kramer but without American decal, is an import.

1984 Reissue

2003-2007. Made in the U.S., based on EVH's Kramer, single Gibson humbucker, Rose tremolo, various colors.

2003-2007		$650	$850

The 84 (Original Collection)

2019-present. Alder body, maple neck, Seymour Duncan pickup, Floyd Rose trem, various colors with gloss finish.

2019-2024		$550	$700

250-G Special

1977-1979. Offset double-cut, tropical woods, aluminum neck, dot markers, 2 pickups.

1977-1979		$1,000	$1,250

350-G Standard

1976-1979. Offset double-cut, tropical woods, aluminum neck, tuning fork headstock, ebonol 'board, zero fret, 2 single coils, dot inlays. The 350 and 450 were Kramer's first models.

1976-1979		$1,500	$1,875

450-G Deluxe

1976-1980. Like 350-G, but with block inlays, 2 humbuckers. Became the 450G Deluxe in late '77 with dot inlays.

1976-1980		$1,500	$1,875

650-G Artist

1977-1980. Aluminum neck, ebonol 'board, double-cut solidbody, 2 humbuckers.

1977-1980		$1,750	$2,250

Assault 220FR/Assault 220 (Modern Collection)

2010-present. Mahogany body, 2 humbucker pickups, Floyd Rose trem, white or black gloss finish. FR dropped from name in '20.

2010-2019	FR	$350	$500
2020-2024		$275	$350

Assault Plus (Modern Collection)

2020-present. Mahogany body with flame maple veneer top, reverse headstock, 2 Seymour Duncan pickups, Floyd Rose trem, Bengal Burst or Trans Purple Burst.

2020		$400	$600

Baretta

1984-1990. Offset double-cut, banana six-on-a-side headstock, 1 pickup, Floyd Rose tremolo, black hardware, U.S.A.-made.

1984-1985		$2,000	$2,500
1986-1987		$1,750	$2,250
1988-1990	Standard opaque	$725	$1,000
1988-1990	With graphics	$850	$1,125
1988-1990	More desirable graphics	$3,500	$5,500
1990	Baretta III hybrid	$650	$850

Baretta '85 Reissue

2006. Made in the U.S., based on 1985 banana headstock model, Rose tremolo.

2006		$750	$950

Baretta II/Soloist

1986-1990. Soloist sleek body with pointed cutaway horns.

1986-1990		$750	$950

Baretta (Original Collection)

2020-present. Maple body and neck, Seymour Duncan pickup, Floyd Rose trem, Pewter Gray or Ruby Red.

2020-2024		$450	$600

Baretta Special (Original Collection)

2020-present. Mahogany body, maple neck, Alnico humbucker pickup, traditional trem, gloss finish in Candy Blue, Ruby Red or Purple.

2020-2024		$125	$175

Classic Series

1986-1987. Solidbody copies of the famous Southern California builder, including offset contoured double-cut (Classic I) and slab body single-cut designs (Classic II and Classic III).

1986-1987	Classic I	$550	$750
1986-1987	Classic II	$800	$1,000
1986-1987	Classic III	$800	$1,000

Condor

1985-1986. Futuristic 4-point body with large upper bass horn and lower treble horn.

1985-1986		$650	$850

DMZ Custom Series

1978-1981. Solidbody double-cut with larger upper horn, bolt-on aluminum T-neck, slot headstock, models include the 1000 (super distortion humbuckers), 2000

1978 Kramer 450-G Deluxe

Carter Vintage Guitars

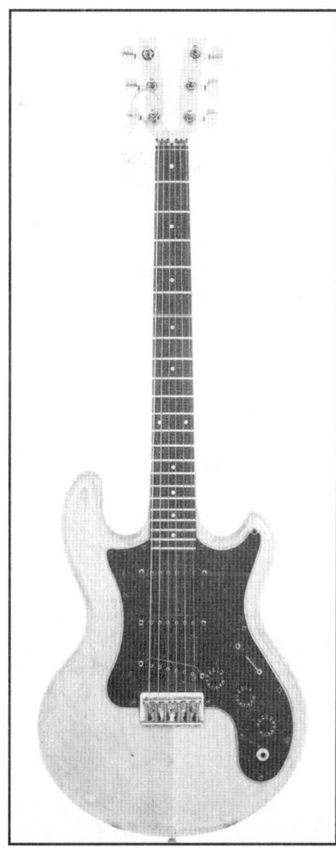

1979 Kramer DMZ-3000

GUITARS

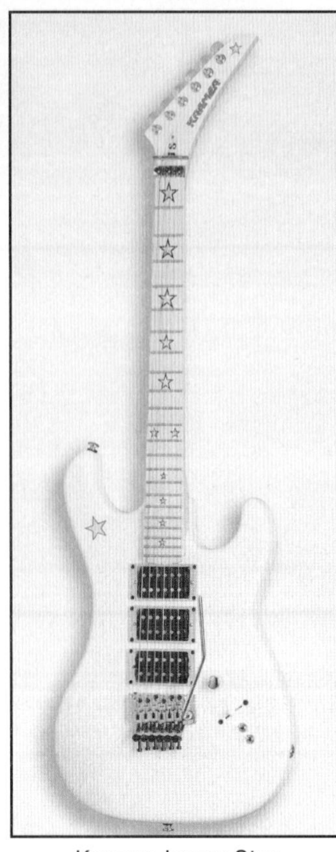
Kramer Jersey Star

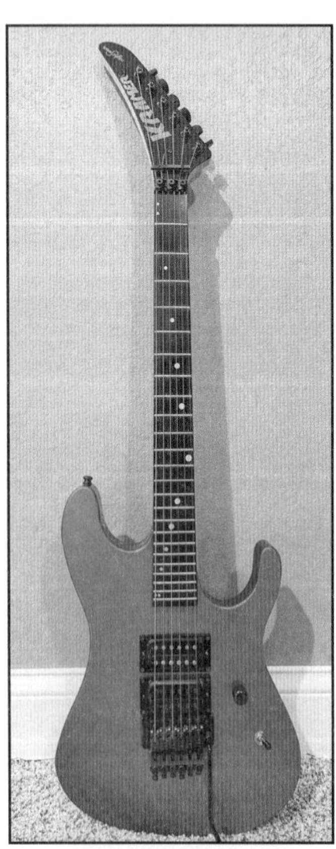
1988 Kramer Nightswan
Jamie Wetsch

MODEL YEAR	FEATURES	EXC. COND. LOW	HIGH

(dual-sound humbuckers), 3000 (3 SDS single-coils), 6000 (dual-sound humbuckers, active DBL).

1978-1981	DMZ-1000	$1,250	$1,750
1978-1981	DMZ-2000	$1,250	$1,750
1978-1981	DMZ-3000	$1,500	$1,875
1978-1981	DMZ-6000	$1,750	$2,250

Duke Custom/Standard

1981-1982. Headless aluminum neck, 22-fret neck, 1 pickup, Floyd Rose tremolo.

1981-1982		$500	$700

Duke Special

1982-1985. Headless aluminum neck, two pickups, tuners on body.

1982-1985		$500	$700

Elliot Easton Pro I

1987-1988. Designed by Elliot Easton, offset double-cut, six-on-a-side headstock, Floyd Rose tremolo, 2 single-coils and 1 humbucker.

1987-1988		$850	$1,125

Elliot Easton Pro II

1987-1988. Same as Pro I, but with fixed-bridge tailpiece, 2 single-coils.

1987-1988		$750	$950

Ferrington

1985-1990. Acoustic-electric, offered in single- and double-cut, bolt-on electric-style neck, transducers, made in Korea.

1985-1990		$450	$600

Floyd Rose Signature Edition

1983-1984. Four pointed-bout body with deep cutawaybelow tremolo assembly, Floyd Rose vibrato system.

1983-1984		$1,000	$1,250

Focus/F Series (Import)

1983-1989. Kramer introduced the Focus series as import copies of their American-made models like the Pacer, Baretta, Vanguard (Rhoads-V), and Voyager (star body). Model numbers were 1000-6000, plus the Focus Classic I, II, and III. Most models were offset, double-cut solidbodies. In '87 the Focus line was renamed the F-Series. In '88 a neck-through body design, which is noted as NT, was introduced for a short time. The Classic series was offered with over a dozen color options.

1983-1989	Various models	$350	$900

Gene Simmons Axe

1980-1981. Axe-shaped guitar, aluminum neck, 1 humbucker, slot headstock, stop tailpiece, 25 were made.

1980-1981		$5,500	$7,500

Gorky Park (Import)

1986-1989. Triangular balalaika, bolt-on maple neck, pointy droopy six-on-a-side headstock, 1 pickup, Floyd Rose tremolo, red with iron sickle graphics, tribute to Russian rock, reissued in late-'90s.

1986-1989		$450	$600

Hundred Series

1988-1990. Import budget line, most with offset double-cut 7/8th solidbody.

1988-1990	Various models	$200	$400

Jersey Star

2004-2007. A reissue of the Richie Sambora model.

2004-2007		$850	$1,125

Jersey Star (Original Collection)

2020-present. Alder body, maple neck, mother-of-pearl Jersey Star logo, 3 pickups, Floyd Rose trem, Candy Apple Red or Alpine White.

2020		$700	$875

Liberty '86 Series

1986-1987. Offset double cut arched-top solidbody, pointy head, 2 humbuckers, black, white or flame-maple bound body.

1986-1987	Black or white	$3,000	$4,000
1986-1987	Flame maple	$3,500	$4,500

Metalist/Showster Series

1989-1990. Korean-made offset double-cut solidbody, metal trim in body design, pointy droopy six-on-a-side headstock, various pickup options, Floyd Rose.

1989-1990		$500	$700

Night Rider

2000-2007. Inexpensive import double-cut semi-hollow, 2 humbuckers.

2000-2007		$100	$150

Nightswan

1987-1990. Offset double-cut, six-on-a-side headstock, 2 Duncan humbuckers, Floyd Rose tremolo, blue metallic.

1987-1990		$1,500	$2,000
1987-1990	Custom color/finish	$1,750	$2,500
1987-1990	More desirable graphics	$3,500	$5,500

Nightswan (Original Collection)

2020-present. Mahogany body, maple neck, 2 pickups, Floyd Rose trem, jet black metallic, vintage white with Aztec graphic or black with blue polka dots.

2020-2024		$550	$700

Night-V (Modern Collection)

2020-present. Mahogany body, maple neck, 2 pickups, Floyd Rose trem, satin black finish.

2020-2024		$275	$350

Night-V Plus (Modern Collection)

2020-present. Mahogany body, maple neck, 2 pickups, Floyd Rose trem, Alpine white.

2020-2024		$450	$600

Pacer (Original Collection)

2020-present. Double-cut offset maple body, 2 Seymour Duncan pickups, Floyd Rose trem, pearl white or orange tiger finish.

2020-2024		$500	$700

Pacer Carrera

1982-1986. Offset double-cut, wood neck, classic six-on-a-side headstock, ebonized 22-fret rosewood 'board, 2 pickups, 3-way switch, black Rockinger, restyled body with Floyd Rose in '83, banana headstock in '85.

1982-1985		$850	$1,125
1986		$750	$950

Pacer Custom

1983-1987. Offset double-cut, bolt-on maple neck with maple cap, 2 humbuckers, translucent finish, gold hardware.

1983-1985		$1,250	$1,500
1986-1987		$900	$1,125

MODEL YEAR	FEATURES	EXC. COND. LOW	HIGH

Pacer Custom I

1987-1989. Custom with slanted hum and 2 single coils, various colors.

1987-1989		$900	$1,125

Pacer Custom II

1987-1989. Custom with hum and 2 single coils, various colors.

1987-1989		$900	$1,125

Pacer Deluxe

1983-1987. Offset double-cut, six-on-a-side headstock, hum/single/single pickups, bolt-on maple neck.

1983-1985		$950	$1,250
1986-1987		$900	$1,125

Pacer Imperial

1981-1989. Offset double cut, bolt-on maple neck with maple cap, 2 humbuckers.

1981-1985		$950	$1,250
1986-1989		$900	$1,125

Pacer Special

1981-1985. Various headstocks, 1 humbucker pickup, EVH trem.

1981-1985		$950	$1,250

The Pacer

1982-1985. Pacer with 3 single coils.

1982-1985		$950	$1,250

Paul Dean

1986-1988. Offset double cut, neck-thru, hum/single/single pickups, droopy pointy head.

1986-1988		$900	$1,125

ProAxe (U.S.A.)

1989-1990. U.S.A.-made, offset double-cut, sharp pointy headstock, dot markers, 2 or 3 pickups, smaller 7/8ths size body, 3 models offered with slightly different pickup options. The model was discontinued when Kramer went out of business in 1990.

1989-1990	Deluxe	$1,125	$1,500
1989-1990	Special	$1,125	$1,500
1989-1990	Standard	$1,125	$1,500

Richie Sambora

1987-1989. Designed by Sambora, mahogany offset double-cut, maple neck, pointy droopy 6-on-a-side headstock, gold hardware, Floyd Rose, 3 pickups, 2 coil-taps.

1987-1989		$1,250	$1,500

Ripley RSG-1

1984-1987. Offset double-cut, banana six-on-a-side headstock, 22 frets, hexophonic humbucking pickups, panpots, dual volume, Floyd Rose tremolo, black hardware, stereo output, pointy droopy headstock in '87.

1984-1985		$950	$1,250
1986-1987		$850	$1,125

Savant/Showster Series

1989-1990. Offset double-cut solidbody, pointy headstock, various pickup options.

1989-1990	Various models	$850	$1,125

SM-1 (Original Collection)

2020-present. Double-cut mahogany body, 3 pickups, Floyd Rose trem, gloss finish in Orange Crush, Candy Blue or Maximum Steel.

2020-2024		$700	$875

Stagemaster Series

1983-1987. Offset double-cut neck-thru solidbody models, smaller 7/8th body.

1983-1987	Various models	$950	$3,000

Striker Series

1984-1989. Offset double-cut, various pickup options, series included Striker 100, 200, 300, 400, 600 and 700 Bass.

1984-1989	Various models	$250	$400

Sustainer

1989. Offset double-cut solidbody, reverse pointy headstock, Floyd Rose tremolo.

1989		$950	$1,250

Triax

1986. Rare, odd shape, 2 humbuckers, Floyd Rose trem, Pearlescent Red.

1986		$3,000	$4,000

Vanguard Series

1981-1986. U.S.-made or American Series (assembled in U.S.). V shape, 1 humbucker, aluminum (Special '81-'83) or wood (Custom '81-'83) neck. Added for '83-'84 were the Imperial (wood neck, 2 humbuckers) and the Headless (alum neck, 1 humbucker). For '85-'86, the body was modified to a Jackson Randy Rhoads style V body, with a banana headstock and 2 humbuckers. In '99 this last design was revived as an import.

1981-1986	Various models	$900	$1,500

Vanguard (Reissue)

1999-2014. Pointy headstock, 2 humbuckers, licensed Floyd Rose.

1999-2014		$400	$550

Voyager

1982-1985. Wood neck, classic headstock, rosewood 'board, 1 pickup (2 optional), Floyd Rose tremolo, black.

1982-1985		$1,125	$1,500

XKG-10

1980-1981. Aluminum neck, V-shaped body.

1980-1981		$950	$1,250

XKG-20

1980-1981. More traditional double-cut body with small horns.

1980-1981		$950	$1,250

XL Series

1980-1981, 1987-1990. The early-'80s U.S.-made models had aluminum necks and were completely different than the late-'80s wood neck models, which were inexpensive imports.

1980-1981	Aluminum neck	$950	$1,500
1987-1990	Wood neck	$300	$400

ZX Aero Star Series

1986-1989. Offset double-cut solidbodies, pointy six-on-a-side headstock. Models include the 1 humbucker ZX-10, 2 humbucker ZX-20, 3 single coil ZX-30, and hum/single/single ZX-30H.

1986-1989		$150	$250

Kramer-Harrison, William

Luthier William Kramer-Harrison began building in 1977, premium grade, custom, classical, and flat-top guitars in Kingston, New York.

Kramer Night V

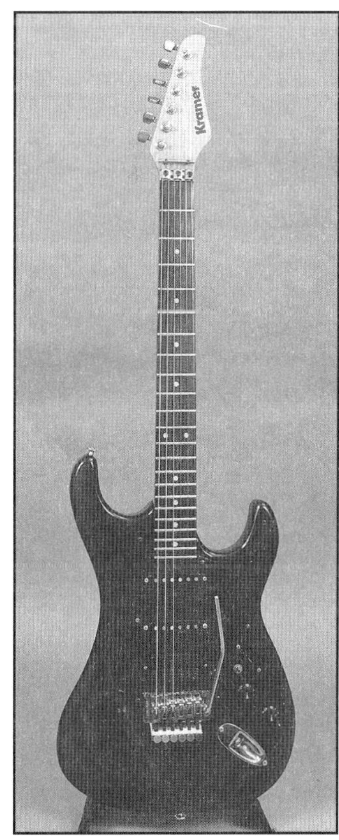

1983 Kramer Pacer

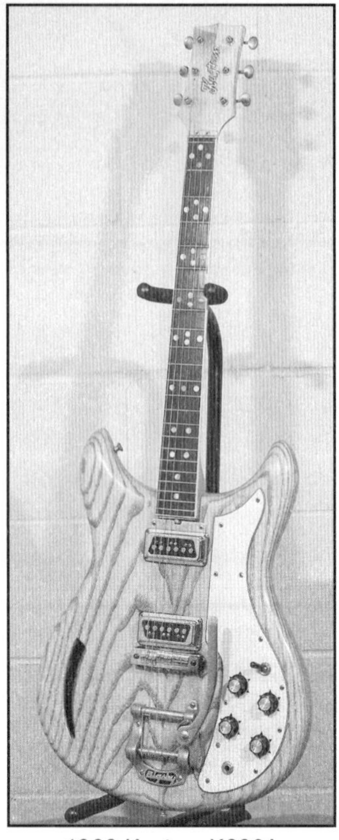
1968 Kustom K200A
Tom Pfeifer

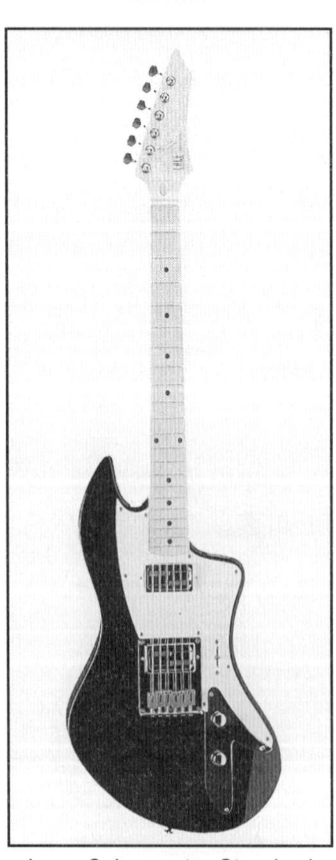
Lace Cybercaster Standard

MODEL YEAR	FEATURES	EXC. COND. LOW	HIGH

KSM

Luthier Kevin S. Moore, starting in 1988, premium grade, custom/production, solidbody electric guitars in Logan, Utah.

Kubicki

1973-present. Kubicki is best known for their Factor basses but did offer a few guitar models in the early '80s. See Bass section for more company info.

Kustom

1968-present. Founded by Bud Ross in Chanute, Kansas, and best known for the tuck-and-roll amps, Kustom also offered guitars from '68 to '69. See Amp section for more company info.

Electric Hollowbody

1968-1969. Hollowed-out 2-part bodies; includes the K200A (humbucker, Bigsby), the K200B (single-coils, trapeze tailpiece), and the K200C (less fancy tuners), various colors.

1968-1969	$1,200	$1,800

Kwasnycia Guitars

1997-present. Production/custom, premium grade, acoustic guitars built by luthier Dennis Kwasnycia in Chatham, Ontario.

Kyle, Doug

Premium grade, custom, Selmer-style guitars made by luthier Doug Kyle in the U.K., starting in 1990.

L Benito

Professional grade, steel and nylon string acoustics from luthier Lito Benito and built in Chile starting in 2001.

La Baye

1967. Designed by Dan Helland in Green Bay, Wisconsin and built by the Holman-Woodell factory in Neodesha, Kansas. Introduced at NAMM and folded when no orders came in. Only 45 prototypes were made. A few may have been sold later as 21st Century. They also had basses.

2x4 6-String

1967. Narrow plank body, controls on top, 2 pickups, tremolo, 12-string version was also made.

1967	$2,500	$3,500

La Mancha

Professional and premium grade, production/custom, classical guitars made in Mexico under the supervision of Kenny Hill and Gil Carnal and distributed by Jerry Roberts of Nashville, Tennessee. They began in 1996.

La Patrie

Production, classical guitars. Founded by luthier Robert Godin, who also has the Norman, Godin, Seagull, and Patrick & Simon brands of instruments.

La Scala

Ca. 1920s-1930s. La Scala was another brand of the Oscar Schmidt Company of New Jersey, and was used on guitars, banjos, and mandolins. These were often the fanciest of the Schmidt instruments. Schmidt made the guitars and mandolins; the banjos were made by Rettberg & Lang.

Lace Music Products

1979-present. Intermediate and professional, production, electric guitars from Lace Music Products of Cypress, California, a division of Actodyne General Inc. which was founded by Don Lace Sr., inventor of the Lace Sensor Pickup. In '96, Lace added amplifiers, followed by guitars in 2001 and Rat Fink guitars in '02.

Lacey Guitars

1974-present. Luthier Mark Lacey builds his premium and presentation archtops and flat-tops in Nashville, Tennessee.

Lado

1973-present. Founded by Joe Kovacic, Lado builds professional and premium grade, production/custom, solidbody guitars and basses in Lindsay, Ontario. Some model lines are branded J. K. Lado.

Lafayette

Ca. 1963-1967. Sold through Lafayette Electronics catalogs. Early Japanese-made guitars and basses from pre-copy era, generally shorter scale beginner instruments. Many made by Guyatone, some possibly by Teisco.

Electric

1963-1967. Various models.

1963-1967	$500	$800

Laguna

2008-present. Guitar Center private label, budget and intermediate grade, production, imported electric and acoustic guitars price range.

Lakeside (Lyon & Healy)

Early-1900s. Mainly catalog sales of guitars and mandolins from the Chicago maker. Marketed as a less expensive alternative to the Lyon & Healy Washburn product line.

Harp Guitar

Early-1900s. Spruce top, rosewood finished birch back and sides, two 6-string necks with standard tuners, 1 neck is fretless without dot markers, rectangular bridge.

1900s	$2,000	$3,000

Parlor

Early-1900s. Spruce top, oak back and sides, cedar neck.

1900s	$550	$850

GUITARS

MODEL YEAR	FEATURES	EXC. COND. LOW	HIGH

Lakewood

1986-present. Luthier Martin Seeliger builds his professional and premium grade, production/custom, steel and nylon string guitars in Giessen, Germany. He has also built mandolins.

Langdon Guitars

Luthier Jeff Langdon, began in 1997, builds professional and premium grade, production/custom, flat-top, archtop, and solidbody guitars in Eureka, California.

Langejans Guitars

1971-2016. Premium grade, production/custom, flat-top, 12-string, and classical guitars built by luthier Delwyn Langejans in Holland, Michigan. He retired in '16.

Larrivee

1968-present. Professional and premium grade, production/custom, acoustic, acoustic/electric, and classical guitars built in Vancouver, British Columbia and, since '01, in Oxnard, California. They also offered several acoustic and a few electric basses over the years as well as ukes. Founded by Jean Larrivee, who apprenticed under Edgar Monch in Toronto. He built classical guitars in his home from '68-'70 and built his first steel string guitar in '71. Moved company to Victoria, BC in '77 and to Vancouver in '82. In '83, he began building solidbody electric guitars until '89, when focus again returned to acoustics.

Up to 2002, Larrivee used the following model designations: 05 Mahogany Standard, 09 Rosewood Standard, 10 Deluxe, 19 Special, 50 & 60 Standard (unique inlay), 70 Deluxe, and 72 Presentation. Starting in '03 designations used are: 01 Parlor, 03 Standard, 05 Select Mahogany, 09 Rosewood Artist, 10 Rosewood Deluxe, 19 California Anniv. Special Edition Series, 50 Traditional Series, 60 Traditional Series, E = Electric, R = Rosewood.

Larrivee also offers Limited Edition, Custom Shop, and Custom variations of standard models although the model name is the same as the standard model. These Custom models are worth more than the values shown.

0-60

2005. Small fancy rosewood.

2005		$2,500	$4,500

00-05

1996. 14.25", all mahogany.

1996		$1,800	$3,200

00-09

2000s		$2,000	$3,500

00-10

2000s. 00-size 14" lower bout, spruce top, rosewood back and sides, gloss finish.

2000s		$2,500	$4,000

000-40R

2014-present. Legacy series, sitka spruce top, Indian rosewood back and sides, satin finish.

2014-2024		$2,000	$3,800

000-50

2008-present. Mahogany back and sides.

2008-2024		$2,000	$3,500

000-60

2006-present. Traditional Series, Indian rosewood.

2006-2024		$2,500	$4,500

000-60K

Traditional Series, figured koa.

2012		$3,000	$5,000

C-10 Deluxe

Late-1980s-1990s. Sitka spruce top, Indian rosewood back and sides, sharp cutaway, fancy binding.

1980s		$3,000	$5,500

C-72 Presentation

1990s. Spruce top, Indian rosewood back and sides, non-cut Style D, ultra-fancy abalone and pearl hand-engraved headstock.

1990s	Jester headstock	$4,000	$7,500

C-72 Presentation Cutaway

1990s. Spruce top, Indian rosewood back and sides, sharp cutaway, ultra-fancy abalone and pearl hand-engraved headstock.

1990s	Mermaid headstock	$4,500	$8,000

D-02/D-02E

1998-2013. Sitka spruce top, mahogany back and sides, satin finish, E with electronics.

1998-2013		$1,000	$2,000

D-03E

2008-present. Solid mahogany back and sides, spruce top, satin finish, electronics.

2008-2024		$1,200	$2,500

D-03R

2002-present. Rosewood.

2002-2024		$1,600	$3,000

D-03RE

2010-present. Rosewood, on-board electronics.

2010-2024		$1,600	$3,000

DV-03K

Venetian cutaway, koa back and sides.

2000s		$2,000	$3,800

D-04E

2000-2004, 2013-2014. Mahogany, on-board electronics.

2000-2014		$1,600	$3,000

D-05-12E

2008-2013	12 strings	$2,000	$3,500

D-09

2001-present. Rosewood, spruce top, gloss finish.

2001-2012	Indian or walnut	$2,000	$3,500
2001-2024	Brazilian	$5,000	$10,000

D-10 Deluxe

1995-present. Sitka spruce top, Indian rosewood back and sides, abalone top and sound hole trim.

1995-2024		$2,800	$4,800

D-50

2003-present. Traditional Series, mahogany back and sides.

2003-2024		$2,200	$3,800

Larrivee D-03R

Larrivee D-09

GUITARS

Larrivee OM-10

Larrivee OM-10
Tim Page

MODEL YEAR	FEATURES	EXC. COND. LOW	HIGH

D-60

2003-present. Brazilian or Indian rosewood back and sides.

2000s	Brazilian	$5,000	$12,000
2003-2024	Indian	$2,500	$4,500

D-70

1992-1995. Horsehead headstock inlay, ebony 'board, rosewood back and sides.

1992-1995		$3,200	$6,000

D-Style Classical

1970s. Rosewood body, unicorn inlays.

1970s		$2,000	$4,500

J-05-12

2000s. Jumbo acoustic-electric 12-string, spruce top, mahogany back and sides.

2000s		$2,200	$3,800

J-09

2002-2009. Jumbo, rosewood back and sides, Sitka spruce top.

2002-2009		$2,200	$3,800

J-09-12K

Jumbo 12-string, rosewood back and sides.

2000s		$2,800	$4,800

J-70

1990s. Jumbo, Sitka spruce top, solid Indian rosewood back and sides, presentation grade fancy appointments, limited production.

1990s		$3,000	$5,500

JV-05 Mahogany Standard

Mahogany back and sides, Venetian cutaway.

2000s		$1,800	$3,200

L Series

1980s-present. Various models, mahogany or rosewood (R) back and sides, some with on-board electronics (E).

1980s-90s	L-11	$3,000	$5,500
1990s	L-50	$2,200	$4,000
1990s-2024	L-72 (Presentation)	$4,000	$8,000
2000s	L-30 (Classical)	$2,000	$3,800
2004	L-19	$3,000	$5,500
2013-2024	L-10-12	$2,800	$4,800

L-0 Standard Series

1983-present. Various models, 6- or 12-string, mahogany, rosewood (R) or Koa (K), some with on-board electronics (E), satin or gloss finish.

1983-2024	L-03/03E	$1,500	$3,000
1983-2024	L-05/05E	$2,000	$3,500
1983-2024	L-09/09E	$2,200	$4,000
2000s	L-01	$1,200	$2,500
2000s	L-04	$1,500	$2,800
2008-2012	L-03K, Koa	$2,200	$4,000
2008-2024	L-03R, rosewood	$2,000	$3,500
2008-2024	L-03R-12, 12-string	$2,000	$3,500
2008-2024	L-03RE	$1,800	$3,200

LS Series

1990s-2011. Various models.

1990s-2011	LS-05, mahogany	$1,800	$3,200
2008-2011	LS-03R, rosewood	$2,000	$3,500

LV Series

1990s-present. Various models.

1990s-2024	LV-05/05E	$2,200	$3,800
1990s-2024	LV-09/09E	$2,500	$4,200
2002	LV-19 Special Vine	$3,500	$6,500
2007-2024	LV-03/03E	$1,800	$3,300
2007-2024	LV-10/10E	$3,000	$5,000

OM Series

1990s-present. Various models.

1990-2000s	OM-02	$1,200	$2,500
1990-2000s	OM-09R, rosewood	$2,200	$3,800
1990s-2024	OM-03/03E	$1,600	$3,000
1990s-2024	OM-10 Deluxe	$2,800	$4,800
1999-2024	OM-05/05E	$2,000	$3,500
2000-2024	OM-03R, rosewood	$2,000	$3,500
2000-2024	OM-40/40E	$2,200	$3,800
2000-2024	OM-50/50E	$2,500	$4,200
2000s	OM-09K, Koa	$2,800	$4,500
2008-2024	OM-60/60E	$2,500	$4,200

OMV Series

1990s-present. Various models.

2000s	OMV-13	$2,200	$3,800
2000s-2024	OMV-40/40E	$2,400	$4,000
2000s-2024	OMV-09/09E	$2,500	$4,200
2000s-2024	OMV-50/50E	$2,800	$4,500
2009-2024	OMV-60/60E	$3,200	$5,000

Parlor Walnut

Early-2000s. Spruce top, solid walnut back and sides.

2000s		$1,200	$2,500

PV Series

2007-present. Various Parlor models.

2007	PV-09, maple	$2,000	$3,500
2007-2024	PV-09/09E, rosewood	$2,500	$3,800

RS-2 Ventura

2010-2015. Mahogany solidbody, rosewood 'board, 1 or 2 pickups, satin finish various colors.

2010-2015		$1,200	$2,500

RS-4 CM Carved Top

1988-1989. Carved top solidbody, curly maple top, single-single-humbucker pickups, sunburst or translucent finishes.

1988-1989		$2,000	$4,000

SD Series

2008-present. Various models.

2008-2012	SD-03R	$2,000	$3,500
2008-2024	SD-50/50E	$2,500	$4,200
2008-2024	SD-60/60E	$2,500	$4,500

Larry Alan Guitars

2003-present. Professional and premium grade, production/custom, acoustic and electric guitars and basses, built by luthier Larry Alan Daft in Lansing, Michigan. He also builds effects pedals.

Larson Brothers

1900-1944. Chicago's Carl and August Larson bought Maurer & Company in 1900 where they built guitars and mandolin family instruments until 1944. Their house brands were Maurer, Prairie State and Euphonon and they also built for catalog companies Wm. C. Stahl and W. J. Dyer & Bro., adding brands like Stetson, a house brand of Dyer. See brand listings for more information.

GUITARS

Laskin

1973-present. Luthier William "Grit" Laskin builds his premium and presentation grade, custom, steel-string, classical, and flamenco guitars in Toronto, Ontario. Many of his instruments feature extensive inlay work.

Laurie Williams Guitars

1983-present. Luthier Laurie Williams builds his premium and presentation grade, custom/production, steel string, classical and archtop guitars on the North Island of New Zealand. He also builds mandolins.

Leach Guitars

1980-present. Luthier Harvey Leach builds his professional and premium grade, custom, flat-tops, archtops, and solidbody electrics, travel guitars and basses in Cedar Ridge, California.

Lehmann Stringed Instruments

1971-present. Luthier Bernard Lehmann builds his professional and premium grade, production/custom, flat-top, archtop, classical and Gypsy guitars in Rochester, New York. He also builds lutes, vielles and rebecs.

Lehtela

1993-present. Professional and premium grade, custom/production, acoustic, acoustic/electric, archtop, and solidbody guitars and basses built by luthier Ari Lehtela in Newell, North Carolina.

Lentz

1975-present. Luthier Scott Lentz builds his professional, premium, and presentation grade, custom/production, solidbody electric guitars in San Marcos, California.

Les Stansell Guitars

1980-present. Luthier Les Stansell builds his premium grade, custom, nylon-string guitars in Pistol River, Oregon.

Levin

1900-1973. Founded by Herman Carlson Levin and located in Gothenburg, Sweden, Levin was best known for their classical guitars, which they also built for other brands, most notably Goya from ca. 1955 to the mid '70s. They also built mandolins and ukes.

Levy-Page Special

1930s. Acoustic guitars likely built by Gibson, having many features of Kalamzoo guitars of the era. Possibly made for a distributor.

Lewis

1981-present. Luthier Michael Lewis builds his premium and presentation grade, custom/production, archtop guitars in Grass Valley, California. He also builds mandolins. He also built guitars under the D'Angelico name.

Linc Luthier

1991-present. Professional and premium grade, custom/production, electric and acoustic guitars, basses and double-necks built by luthier Linc Luthier in Upland, California.

Lindberg

Ca. 1950s. Line of guitars produced by Hoyer for Germany's Lindberg music store.

Lindert

1986-2002. Luthier Chuck Lindert made his intermediate and professional grade, production/custom, Art Deco-vibe electric guitars in Chelan, Washington.

Line 6

1996-present. Professional grade, production, imported solidbody and acoustic modeling guitars able to replicate the tones of a variety of instruments. Line 6 also builds effects and amps.

Lion

1960s. One of the brand names of guitars built for others by Egmond in Holland.

Lipe Guitars USA

1983-1989, 2000-2018. Luthier Michael Lipe built custom, professional grade, guitars and basses in Sun Valley, California. Lipe died Dec. '18.

Liscombe

1992-2013. Professional grade, production and limited custom, chambered electric guitars built by luthier Ken Liscombe in Burlington, Ontario.

Loar (The)

2005-present. Professional grade, production, imported archtop acoustic guitars designed by Greg Rich for The Music Link, which also has Johnson and other brands of instruments. They also offer mandolins.

Lollar

1979-present. Luthier Jason Lollar builds his premium grade, production/custom, solidbody and archtop guitars in Vashon, Washington.

Lopez, Abel Garcia

Luthier Abel Garcia Lopez builds his premium grade, custom, classical guitars in Mexico starting in 1985.

Loprinzi

1972-present. Professional and premium grade, production/custom, classical and steel-string guitars built in Clearwater, Florida. They also build ukes. Founded by Augustino LoPrinzi and his brother Thomas in New Jersey. The guitar operations were taken over by AMF/Maark Corp. in '73. LoPrinzi

Larrivee PV-09

Loar LH-309-VS

LSL Instruments Del Rey

LTD SN-1000HT

MODEL YEAR	FEATURES	EXC. COND. LOW	HIGH

left the company and again started producing his own Augustino Guitars, moving his operations to Florida in '78. AMF ceased production in '80, and a few years later, LoPrinzi got his trademarked name back.

Classical

1970s. Various models.

1970s	Brazilian rosewood	$2,500	$6,000
1970s	Indian rosewood	$1,800	$3,500
1970s	Mahogany	$1,500	$3,000

Lord

Mid-1960s. Acoustic and solidbody electric guitars imported by Halifax.

Acoustic or Electric Soldibody

1960s	Various models	$300	$500

Lotus

Late-1970s-2004. Budget grade acoustic and electric guitars and basses imported originally by Midco International, of Effingham, Illinois, and most recently by Musicorp. They also offered banjos and mandolins.

Louis Panormo

Early to mid-1800s. Spanish guitars made in London, England by luthier Louis (Luis) Panormo. He was born in Paris in 1784, and died in 1862.

Lowden

1973-present. Luthier George Lowden builds his premium and presentation grade, production/custom, steel and nylon string guitars in Downpatrick, Northern Ireland. From '80 to '85, he had some models made in Japan.

Flat-Top

1980s-present. Standard models include D, F, O, and S sizes and models 10 through 32.

1980s-2024	Premium models	$4,000	$8,000
1980s-2024	Standard models	$2,500	$5,000

LsL Instruments

2008-present. Luthier Lance Lerman builds his production, professional grade, solidbody electric guitars and basses in Los Angeles, California.

LSR Headless Instruments

1988-present. Professional and premium grade, production/custom, solidbody headless guitars and basses made by Ed Roman Guitars.

LTD

1995-present. Intermediate grade, production, Korean-made solidbody guitars and basses offered by ESP.

Lucas Custom Instruments

1989-present. Premium and presentation grade, production/custom, flat-tops built by luthier Randy Lucas in Columbus, Indiana.

Lucas, A. J.

1990-present. Luthier A. J. Lucas builds his production/custom, classical and steel string guitars in Lincolnshire, England.

Luis Feu de Mesquita

2000-present. Professional and premium grade, custom, acoustic and flat-top guitars including Spanish, classical and flamenco built in Toronto, Ontario by luthier Luis Feu de Mesquita.

Luna Guitars

2005-present. Located in Tampa, Florida, Yvonne de Villiers imports her budget to professional grade, production, acoustic and electric guitars and basses from Japan, Korea and China. She also added ukuleles in '09 and amps in '10.

Luttrell Guitars

1993-present. Professional and premium grade, production/custom, acoustic, electric and resonator guitars built by luthier Ralph H. Luttrell in Sandy Springs, Georgia.

Lyle

Ca. 1969-1980. Imported by distributor L.D. Heater of Portland, Oregon. Generally higher quality Japanese-made copies of American designs by unknown manufacturers, but some early ones, at least, were made by Arai and Company. They also had basses and mandolins.

Lyon & Healy

1864-present. Founded by George Washburn Lyon and Patrick Joseph Healy, Lyon & Healy was an industry giant, operating a chain of music stores, and manufacturing harps (their only remaining product), pianos, Washburn guitars and a line of brass and wind instruments. See Washburn, American Conservatory, Lakeside, and College brands.

Lyon by Washburn

1990s-2000s. Budget grade, production, solidbody guitars and basses sold by mass merchandisers such as Target.

Lyra

1920s. Instruments built by the Oscar Schmidt Co. and possibly others. Most likely a brand made for a distributor.

Lyric

Luthier John Southern started building his professional and premium grade, custom, semi-hollow and solidbody and bass guitars in Tulsa, Oklahoma in 1996.

M. Campellone Guitars

See listing under Campellone Guitars.

M.Zaganin and N.Zaganin

1989-present. Luthier Márcio Zaganin began his career using the M.Zaganin brand, in 2004 it was changed to N. He builds professional and premium grade, production/custom, semi-hollow and solidbody electric guitars in São Paulo, Brazil. He also builds basses.

Maccaferri

1923-1990. Built by luthier and classical guitarist Mario Maccaferri (b. May 20, 1900, Cento, Italy; d. 1993, New York) in Cento, Italy; Paris, France; New York, New York; and Mount Vernon, New York. Maccaferri was a student of Luigi Mozzani from '11 to '28. His first catalog was in '23 and included a cutaway guitar. He also made mandolins. His Europe-era instruments are very rare. He designed Selmer guitars in '31. Maccaferri invented the plastic clothespin during World War II and used that technology to produce plastic ukes starting in '49 and Dow Styron plastic guitars in '53. He made several experimental plastic electrics in the '60s and plastic violins in the late-'80s.

Plastic (Dow Styron)

1950s. Plastic construction, models include Deluxe (archtop, crown logo), Islander (Islander logo), TV Pal (4-string cutaway) and Showtime (Showtime logo).

MODEL YEAR	FEATURES	EXC. COND. LOW	HIGH
1950s	Deluxe	$200	$350
1950s	Islander	$200	$400
1950s	Romancer	$200	$350
1950s	Showtime	$200	$350
1950s	TV Pal	$150	$300

Madeira

1973-ca. 1984, ca. 1990. Imported budget and intermediate grade acoustic and electric guitars distributed by Guild. The Japanese-made electrics were basically copies of Gibson, Fender, and Guild models, the acoustics originally copies of Martin. The electrics were only offered first year or so during the '70s run. Name revived again around '90 on imported acoustics and electrics. They also offered mandolins and banjos.

Madrid

1996-present. Luthier Brandon Madrid builds his production/custom, professional and premium grade, acoustic and solidbody electric guitars, in San Diego, California. Prior to 2009 he built in Portland, Oregon.

Maestro

1950s-1970s, 2001-2012, 2022-present. Maestro is a brand name Gibson first used on 1950s accordion amplifiers. The first Maestro effects were introduced in the early-'60s and they used the name until the late-'70s. In 2001, Gibson revived the name for a line of effects, banjos and mandolins. Those were dropped in '09, when imported budget and intermediate, production, acoustic and electric guitars and amps were added. By '12 the brand was no longer listed but was reintroduced on a line of Gibson effects in '22. Since '04, the brand has also been used on an unrelated line of acoustic guitars and ukes built in Singapore.

Electric

2009-2012. Various student models, Maestro headstock logo, 'By Gibson' logo on truss rod cover.

MODEL YEAR	FEATURES	EXC. COND. LOW	HIGH
2009-2012		$100	$200

Magnatone

Ca.1937-1971, 2013-present. Founded as Dickerson Brothers in Los Angeles, California and known as Magna Electronics from '47, with Art Duhamell president. Brands include Dickerson, Oahu (not all), Gourley, Natural Music Guild, Magnatone. In '59 Magna and Estey merged and in '66 the company relocated to Pennsylvania. In '71, the brand was taken over by a toy company. Between 1957 and '67, the company produced four different model lines of Spanish electrics. In 2013, Ted Kornblum revived the Magnatone name on a line of tube amps built in St. Louis, Missouri.

Cyclops

1930s. Dobro-made resonator guitar.

MODEL YEAR	FEATURES	EXC. COND. LOW	HIGH
1930s	Round neck	$1,300	$2,000
1930s	Square neck	$1,300	$2,000

Mark Artist Series

MODEL YEAR	FEATURES	EXC. COND. LOW	HIGH
1959-1961	More common	$1,000	$1,500
1959-1961	Rare	$1,300	$2,000

Mark Series

1955-1960. Solidbody series made by Paul Bigsby in small quantities, then taken over by Paul Barth at Magnatone in '59.

MODEL YEAR	FEATURES	EXC. COND. LOW	HIGH
1955-1959	Mark II	$1,800	$2,800
1955-1959	Mark III	$1,800	$2,800
1955-1959	Mark IV	$2,200	$3,300
1955-1959	Mark V	$2,200	$3,300

Model Series

MODEL YEAR	FEATURES	EXC. COND. LOW	HIGH
1962	Model 100	$400	$600
1962	Model 150	$400	$600
1962	Model 200, 2 pus	$400	$600

X-5 Zephyr

1965-1966. Double-cut with 2 DeArmond single-coil pickups, vibrato, metallic finish.

MODEL YEAR	FEATURES	EXC. COND. LOW	HIGH
1965-1966		$600	$900

X-15 Tornado

1965-1966. Offset double-cut body, 2 pickups, various options.

MODEL YEAR	FEATURES	EXC. COND. LOW	HIGH
1965-1966		$850	$1,200

X-20 Typhoon

1965-1966. Double-cut solidbody, 3 pickups, various options.

MODEL YEAR	FEATURES	EXC. COND. LOW	HIGH
1965-1966		$1,000	$1,500

Magno-Tone

1930s. Brand most likely used by a music studio (or distributor) on instruments made by others, including Regal-built resonator instruments.

Luttrell Guitars

Maestro 12-String
Rivington Guitars

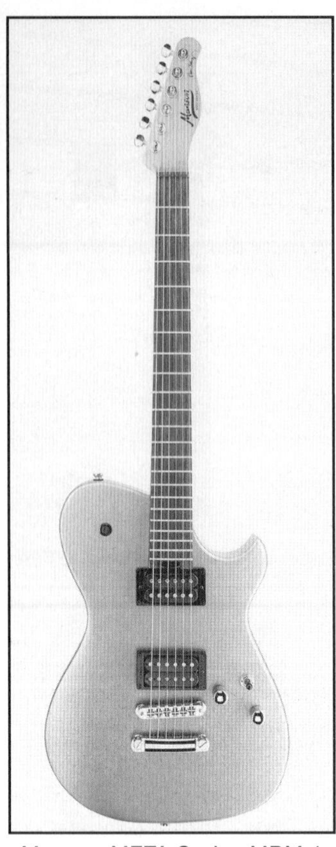
Manson META Series MBM-1

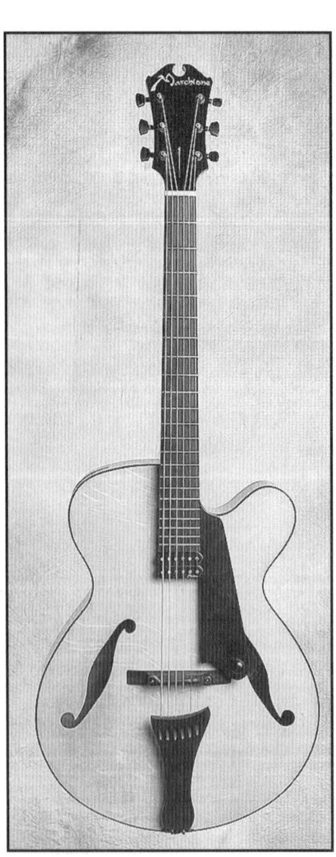
Marchione 16" Archtop

MODEL YEAR	FEATURES	EXC. COND. LOW	HIGH

Mai Kai

1910s. Line of Hawaiian guitars built in Los Angeles, California by the Shireson Brothers.

Mako

1985-1989. Line of budget to lower-intermediate solidbody guitars from Kaman (Ovation, Hamer). They also offered basses and amps.

Solidbody

1985-1989	Various models	$175	$300

Mal n' Sal

See listing for Alternative Guitar and Amplifier Company.

Malinoski

1986-present. Luthier Peter Malinoski builds his production/custom, professional and premium grade, solidbody electric guitars and basses in Hyattsville, Maryland.

Mann

Ca. 1971-ca. 1985. A brand name used in Canada by Japan's Hoshino company on some of the same acoustic and electric models as their Ibanez guitars.

Manne

1987-present. Professional and premium grade, production/custom, semi-acoustic and electric guitars and basses built by luthier Andrea Ballarin in Italy.

Manson Guitar Works

1979-present. Premium grade, production/custom, electric guitars built by luthiers Hugh Manson and Adrian Ashton in Exeter, Devon UK. They also offer a line of professional grade, guitars crafted in the Czech Republic and assembled in UK. They also build basses.

Manuel & Patterson

1993-present. Luthiers Joe Manuel and Phil Patterson build professional, premium and presentation grade, production/custom, flat-top, archtop and solidbody electric guitars in Abita Springs, Louisiana. They also offer mandolins.

Manuel Contreras

1962-1994. Luthier Manuel Gonzalez Contreras worked with José Ramírez III, before opening his own shop in Madrid, Spain, in '62.

Manuel Contreras II

1986-present. Professional grade, production/custom, nylon-string guitars made in Madrid, Spain, by luthier Pablo Contreras, son of Manuel.

Manuel Ramirez

See listing under Ramirez, Manuel.

Manuel Rodriguez and Sons, S.L.

1905-present. Professional, premium, and presentation grade, custom flat-top and nylon-string guitars from Madrid, Spain.

Manuel Velázquez

1933-2014. Luthier Manuel Velázquez (d. 2014) built his classical guitars in Puerto Rico ('72-'82), New York City, Virginia, and Florida. His son Alfredo continues to build guitars.

Manzanita Guitars

1993-present. Custom, steel-string, Hawaiian, and resonator guitars built by luthiers Manfred Pietrzok and Moritz Sattler in Rosdorf, Germany.

Manzer Guitars

1976-present. Luthier Linda Manzer builds her premium and presentation grade, custom, steel-string, nylon-string, and archtop guitars in Toronto, Ontario.

Maple Lake

2003-present. Intermediate grade, production, flat-top and acoustic/electric imported guitars from luthier Abe Wechter. Wechter also builds guitars under his own name.

MapleTree Guitars Canada

2011-present. Steve Maric, owner and luthier from Toronto, Canada, works with luthier Fulu Wang, Beijing, China to build production/custom, professional grade, acoustic guitars.

Mapson

1995-present. Luthier James L. Mapson builds his premium and presentation grade, production/custom, archtops in Santa Ana, California.

Marc Silber Guitar Company

1998-present. Intermediate and professional grade, production, flat-top, nylon-string, and Hawaiian guitars designed by Marc Silber and made in Mexico. These were offered under the K & S Guitars and/or Silber brands for 1992-'98. Silber also has ukuleles.

Marchione Guitars

1993-present. Premium and presentation grade, custom, archtops and solidbodies built by Stephen Marchione originally in New York City, but currently in Houston, Texas.

Marcia

1920s. Instruments built by the Oscar Schmidt Co. and possibly others. Most likely a brand made for a distributor.

Marco Polo

1960-ca. 1964. Imported from Japan by Harry Stewart and the Marco Polo Company of Santa Ana,

GUITARS

MODEL YEAR	FEATURES	EXC. COND. LOW	HIGH

California. One of the first American distributors to advertise inexpensive Japanese guitars and basses. Manufacturers unknown, but some acoustics by Suzuki, some electrics by Guyatone.

Acoustic Hollowbody

1960-1964	Various models	$150	$300

Mario Martin Guitars

2011-present. Luthier Mario Martin builds his production/custom, professional grade, semi-hollow and solidbody guitars and basses in Murfreesboro, Tennessee. From 2006 to '11, he built guitars under the Guitar Mill brand name.

Mark Wescott Guitars

Premium grade, custom, flat-tops, built by luthier Mark Wescott, starting in 1980, in Somers Point, New Jersey.

Marling

Ca. 1975. Budget line guitars and basses marketed by EKO of Recanati, Italy; probably made by them, although possibly imported.

Acoustic

1975. Includes the steel-string S.110, and the dreadnoughts W.354 Western, and W.356 Western.

1975		$150	$300

Electric Soldibody

1975. Includes the E.400 (semi-acoustic/electric), E.490 (solidbody), E.480 (single-cut), and the 460 (Manta-style).

1975		$150	$300

Martelle

1934. Private brand attributed to Gibson and some to Kay.

De Luxe

1934. Gibson 12-fret round shoulder Jumbo construction, laminate maple or mahogany back and sides, sunburst, Hawaiian or Spanish option.

1934		$10,000	$12,000

Martin

1833-present. Intermediate, professional, premium, and presentation grade, production/custom, acoustic, acoustic/electric, archtop and resonator guitars. Founded in New York City by Christian Frederick Martin, former employee of J. Staufer in Vienna, Austria. Moved to Nazareth, Pennsylvania in 1839. Early guitars were made in the European style, many made with partners John Coupa, Charles Bruno and Henry Schatz. Scalloped X-bracing was introduced in the late-1840s. The dreadnought was introduced in 1916 for the Oliver Ditson Company, Boston; and Martin introduced their own versions in 1931.

Martin model size and shape are indicated by the letter prefix (e.g., 0, 00, 000, D, etc.); materials and ornamentation are indicated by number, with the higher the number, the fancier the instrument (e.g., 18, 28, 35, etc.). Martin offered electric thinline guitars from '61-'68 and electric solidbodies from '78-'82. The Martin Shenandoah was made in Asia and assembled in U.S. Japanese Martin Sigma ('72-'73) and Korean Martin Stinger ('85 on) imported solidbodies.

Most Martin flat-top guitars, particularly Style 18 and above, came with a standard natural finish, therefore Martin guitar finish coloring is generally not mentioned because it is assumed to be see-through natural. Conversely, Gibson's standard finish for their flat-tops during their Golden Era was sunburst. Martin introduced their shaded (sunburst) finish as an option on their Style 18 in 1934 and their Style 28 in 1931. Values for a shaded finish should be considered on a case-by-case basis. Braced for steel strings specifications described under certain models are based on current consensus information and data provided by the late Martin employee-historian Mike Longworth and is for guidance only. Variations from these specs have been found, so "bracing" should be considered on a case-by-case basis.

0-15

1935, 1940-1943, 1948-1961. Maple or birch in '35, all mahogany after, unbound rosewood 'board, slotted peghead and 12-fret neck until '34, solid peghead and 14-fret neck thereafter, natural mahogany.

1935	Maple or birch	$3,500	$4,500
1940-1949	Mahogany begins	$3,500	$4,500
1950-1959		$3,250	$4,000
1960-1961		$2,800	$3,500

0-15H

1940. Hawaiian neck, all mahogany.

1940		$3,500	$5,500

0-15M Elderly Instruments 40th Anniversary

2011-2012. Limited Edition, 10 made, solid mahogany body and neck, special appointments, inside label signed by Elderly Instruments president Stan Werbin and Martin CEO Chris Martin.

2011-2012		$2,000	$3,000

0-15T

1960-1963. Tenor with Style 15 appointments, natural mahogany.

1960-1963		$1,800	$2,800

0-16

1961 only. Six made.

1961		$2,500	$4,000

0-16NY

1961-1977, 1979-1992, 1994. Mahogany back and sides, 12 frets, slotted peghead, unbound extra-wide rosewood 'board, natural.

1961-1969		$3,200	$4,800
1970-1979		$2,800	$4,000
1980-1989		$2,200	$3,500
1990-1994		$2,000	$3,000

0-17

1906-1917, 1929-1948, 1966-1968. The first version has mahogany back and sides, 3 black sound hole rings, rosewood bound back, unbound ebony 'board, 12 frets, slotted peghead. The second version ('29 and

1941 Martin 0-15

Imaged by Heritage Auctions, HA.com

1937 Martin 0-17

David Stone

GUITARS

1919 Martin 0-18
David Stone

1926 Martin 0-21
Imaged by Heritage Auctions, HA.com

MODEL YEAR	FEATURES	EXC. COND. LOW	HIGH

on) is all mahogany, 3 white-black-white sound hole rings, top bound until '30, thin black backstripe, 12 frets and slotted peghead until '34, solid peghead and 14 frets beginning in '33, natural mahogany.

1906-1917	Gut	$3,200	$4,500
1929-1933	Steel, 12-fret	$4,000	$6,000
1933-1934	Flat natural, 14-fret	$5,000	$7,500
1934-1938	Gloss dark, 14-fret	$5,000	$7,500
1939	Early '39, 175 neck	$5,000	$7,500
1939	Late '39, 168 neck	$5,000	$7,500
1940-1946		$4,800	$7,000
1947-1948		$4,000	$5,500
1966-1968	Special order	$3,800	$5,000

0-17H

1930, 1935-1940. Hawaiian, mahogany back and sides, 12 frets clear of body, natural.

1930	12-fret	$4,500	$6,500
1935-1940	14-fret	$5,000	$7,500

0-17S

Early 1930s. Limited production style 17 with spruce top, unique 'guard.

1931		$7,000	$10,000

0-17T

1932-1960. Mahogany back and sides, tenor, natural.

1932-1933		$1,800	$2,500
1934-1939		$2,500	$3,500
1940-1947		$2,000	$2,500
1948-1949		$1,800	$2,500
1950-1960		$1,800	$2,500

0-18

1898-1994, 2017-2024. Rosewood back and sides until 1917, mahogany back and sides after, Adirondack spruce top until 1946, slotted peghead and 12 frets until 1934, solid peghead and 14 frets after 1934, braced for steel strings in 1923, improved neck in late-1934, non-scalloped braces appear late-'44, natural. Reintroduced '17, Sikta spruce, mahogany.

1898-1917	Brazilian	$5,000	$6,500
1918-1922	Mahogany, gut	$4,000	$5,000
1923-1934	12-fret, steel	$7,000	$9,000
1932-1938	14-fret	$8,000	$10,000
1939	Early '39, 175 neck	$8,000	$10,000
1939	Later '39, 168 neck	$7,000	$9,000
1940-1944		$6,500	$8,500
1945-1946		$5,500	$7,000
1947-1949		$5,000	$6,500
1950-1959		$4,500	$6,000
1960-1964		$4,200	$5,500
1965		$4,000	$6,000
1966-1969		$3,500	$4,500
1970-1979		$3,000	$4,000
1980-1989		$2,500	$3,500
1990-1994		$2,500	$3,500
2017-2024	Reintroduced	$1,800	$2,800

0-18G

1960s. Special order classical nylon-string model, natural.

1961		$2,000	$2,800

MODEL YEAR	FEATURES	EXC. COND. LOW	HIGH

0-18K

1918-1935. Hawaiian, all Koa wood, T-frets and steel T-bar neck in late-1934, natural.

1918-1933		$6,500	$8,500
1934-1935		$7,500	$9,500

0-18KH

1927-1928. Hawaiian, Koa.

1927-1928		$7,500	$9,500

0-18T

1929-1932, 1936-1989, 1991-1992, 1994-1995. Mahogany body, spruce top, tenor, natural.

1929-1939		$2,800	$4,000
1940-1946		$2,500	$3,500
1947-1949		$2,200	$3,000
1950-1959		$2,000	$2,800
1960-1969		$1,800	$2,500
1970-1979		$1,200	$1,800
1980-1989		$1,000	$1,500
1991-1995		$1,000	$1,500

0-18T Nick Reynolds

2010-2011. Custom Artist Edition, mahogany.

2010-2011		$3,000	$4,000

0-18TE

1959, 1962. Only 2 made, tenor, 1 pickup.

1959, 1962		$5,000	$6,500

0-18VS Elderly Instruments 40th Anniversary Limited Edition

2012-2014. Mahogany body, Sikta spruce top, slotted headstock, 12-fret neck, inside label signed by C. F. Martin IV and Elderly founder Stan Werbin.

2012-2014		$3,500	$6,500

0-20

1850-1859		$6,000	$8,000

0-21

1898-1931, 1934-1938, 1941, 1944, 1946-1948. Rosewood back and sides, Adirondack spruce top until 1946, 12 frets, T-frets and steel T-bar neck in late-1934, non-scalloped braces in late-1944, natural.

1898-1926	Gut	$8,500	$11,000
1927-1929	Steel	$10,500	$14,500
1930	14-fret (only year)	$10,500	$14,500
1930	Belly bridge	$10,500	$14,500
1931-1938		$10,500	$14,500
1941		$10,000	$13,000
1944	Non-scalloped	$9,500	$12,000
1946	Adirondack	$7,500	$9,500
1947-1948	Sikta	$7,200	$9,000

0-21K

1919-1929. Koa top, back and sides.

1919-1929		$10,000	$12,500

0-21T

1929-1930, 1935, 1961.

1929-1935		$4,500	$6,000
1961		$2,000	$2,500

0-26

1895. Only 1 made, rosewood back and sides, ivory-bound top, rope-style purfling.

1895		$8,000	$11,000

MODEL YEAR	FEATURES	EXC. COND. LOW	HIGH

0-27

1850s-1890s. Rosewood back and sides, ivory-bound top.

1850s	Antiqu market value	$12,000	$15,000
1860s-90s		$9,000	$12,000

0-28

1874-1931, 1937 (6 made), 1969 (1 made). Brazilian rosewood back and sides, herringbone binding until 1937, natural.

1874-1895		$10,000	$15,000
1896-1897	Dark orange (rare)	$10,000	$15,000
1898-1923		$10,000	$15,000
1924-1927	Gut	$10,000	$15,000
1925-1927	Steel option	$14,500	$20,000
1928-1929	Steel (standard)	$14,500	$20,000
1930-1931	Belly bridge, 12-fret	$17,500	$22,500
1937	Belly bridge, 14-fret	$20,000	$26,000
1969	Brazilian	$9,000	$12,000

0-28H

1927-1928. One made each year, Hawaiian, Koa.

1927-1928		$10,500	$15,000

0-28IA Ian Anderson

2004. Limited Edition 87 made, Adirondack spruce top, Indian rosewood sides and back, slotted headstock, can be converted from nylon to light steel strings.

2004		$4,000	$5,000

0-28K

1917-1931, 1935. Hawaiian, all Koa wood, braced for steel strings in '23, natural.

1917-1924		$11,500	$15,000
1925-1929		$12,500	$15,500
1930-1935		$13,500	$18,000

0-28T

1930-1931, 1941. Tenor neck.

1930-1931	Steel option	$5,500	$7,500
1941		$4,200	$6,000

0-28VS

2009-2019. Rosewood back and sides, slotted head, 12 fret neck.

2009-2019		$2,800	$4,000

0-30

1899-1921. Brazilian rosewood back and sides, ivory-bound body, neck and headstock.

1899-1921		$9,500	$15,000

0-34

1885, 1898-1899, 1907. Brazilian rosewood.

1885-1907		$9,000	$11,500

0-40

1860s-1898, 1912-1913. Indian rosewood.

1880-1913		$11,500	$14,500

0-42

1870s-1924, 1926-1930, 1 each in '34, '38,'42. Brazilian rosewood back and sides, 12 frets, natural.

1890-1924		$22,000	$30,000
1926-1927	Gut	$22,000	$30,000
1928-1942	Steel	$35,000	$45,000

0-44 Soloist/Olcott-Bickford Artist

1911-1931. Vahdah Olcott-Bickford Artist Model, run of 17 style-44 guitars made, Brazilian rosewood, ivory or faux-ivory-bound ebony 'board.

1911-1931		$30,000	$40,000

MODEL YEAR	FEATURES	EXC. COND. LOW	HIGH

0-45

1904-1908, '11, '13, '15, '17-'20, '22-'24, '26-'30, '39. Brazilian rosewood back and sides, natural, special order only for '31-'39.

1904-1927	Gut	$42,500	$60,000
1927-1939	Steel	$65,000	$85,000

0-45JB Joan Baez

1998. Indian rosewood, 59 made.

1998		$8,000	$10,500

0-45S Stephen Stills

2007. Madagascar rosewood sides and back, Adirondack spruce top, 91 made.

2007		$8,000	$12,000

0-X1E

2020-2023. Concert size, figured mahogany laminate, Fishman electronics.

2020-2023		$400	$600

00-1

1995-2002. Grand Concert, mahogany.

1995-2002		$800	$1,000

00-1R

1995-1999. Rosewood version.

1995-1999		$800	$1,000

00-15

1999-2010. Sapele/mahogany.

1999-2010		$1,000	$1,500

00-15E Retro

2017-2018. Solid mahogany top, back and sides, electronics.

2017-2018		$1,500	$2,000

00-15M

2009-present. All mahogany.

2009-2024		$1,000	$1,500

00-15M Custom Elderly Instruments

2010-2014. All mahogany, diamond and square inlays, custom-made for Elderly Instruments, about 10 offered each year.

2010-2014		$2,000	$3,000

00-15M Elderly Instruments 40th Anniversary Limited Edition

2012. Only 12 made, mahogany body and neck, label signed by Elderly's president Stan Werbin and Martin CEO Chris Martin.

2012		$2,500	$4,000

00C-15AE

2000-2002. Built-in electronics, natural finish.

2000-2002		$1,200	$1,800

00-16C

1962-1977, 1980-1981. Classical, mahogany back and sides, 5-ply bound top, satin finish, 12 frets, slotted peghead, natural.

1962-1969		$2,000	$3,000
1970-1977		$1,500	$2,200
1980-1981	2 made	$1,200	$1,800

00-16DB

1997. Women and Music series, limited run of 97, deep body (DB), Sitka spruce top, mahogany back and sides, natural.

1997		$1,200	$1,800

1903 Martin 0-28

Martin 0-X1E

GUITARS

1952 Martin 00-18
Billy White Jr.

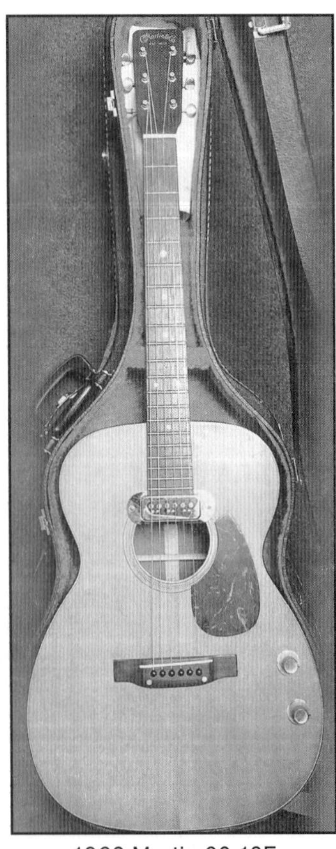
1963 Martin 00-18E
Greg Perrine

MODEL YEAR	FEATURES	EXC. COND. LOW	HIGH

00-16DBFM

2006. Women and Music series, deep body (DB), flamed maple (FM), slotted headstock.

2001-2003		$1,500	$2,200

00-16DBM

2000-2005. Women and Music series, deep body (DB), mahogany (M), slotted headstock, gloss finish.

2000-2005		$1,300	$2,000

00-16DBR

1998-2000. Women and Music series, deep body (DB), rosewood ®, 14-fret slotted headstock, gloss natural finish.

1998-2000		$1,500	$2,200

00C-16DB

1999-2002. Women in Music series, cutaway, deep body (DB), mahogany, slotted headstock.

1999-2002		$1,500	$2,200

00C-16DBRE

2005-2007. Women and Music series, rounded cutaway, deep body (DB), rosewood (R), electronics (E).

2005-2007		$1,800	$2,800

00-17

1908-1917, 1930-1960, 1982-1988, 2001-2004. Mahogany back and sides, 12 frets and slotted headstock until '34, solid headstock and 14 frets after '34, natural mahogany, reissued in 2001 with a high gloss finish.

1908-1917	Gut strings	$4,200	$5,500
1930-1933	Steel, 12-fret	$6,200	$8,000
1934	14-fret, flat natural	$6,500	$8,500
1935-1938	14-fret, gloss dark	$6,500	$8,500
1939	Early '39, 175 neck	$6,500	$8,500
1939	Later '39, 168 neck	$6,000	$8,000
1940-1944		$6,000	$8,000
1945-1946		$5,500	$7,000
1947-1949		$5,000	$6,500
1950-1960		$4,500	$6,000
1982-1988		$2,200	$3,000
2001-2004	Reissue	$1,500	$2,500

00-17 Authentic 1931

2018-2020. Mahogany top, back and sides, Brazilian rosewood 'board, vintage gloss finish.

2018-2020		$2,500	$3,500

00-17H

1934-1935. Hawaiian set-up, mahogany body, no binding.

1934-1935		$6,500	$8,000

00-17S Black Smoke/Whiskey Sunset

2015-2020. Sikta spruce top, mahogany back and sides, rosewood 'board and bridge, on-board electronics (E) optional.

2015-2020	No electronics	$1,200	$1,800
2016-2020	With electronics	$1,500	$2,200

00-17SO Sing Out! 50th Anniversary

2000. Limited Edition, 50 made for 50th anniversary of Sing Out! Magazine, folk era logo inlays, SING OUT inlay on 20th fret, mahogany body.

2000		$2,000	$3,000

00-18

1898-1995, 2016-present. Rosewood back and sides until 1917, mahogany after, braced for steel strings in '23, improved neck in late-'34, war-time design changes '42-'46, non-scalloped braces in late-'44, Adirondack spruce top until '46, natural. Reissued 2016 with Sikta spruce top and mahogany back and sides.

1898-1917	Brazilian	$6,800	$9,000
1918-1922	Mahogany	$6,800	$9,000
1923-1929		$9,000	$12,000
1930-1932	12-fret	$13,500	$18,000
1933	14-fret, bar fret	$18,000	$24,000
1934-1937	14-fret	$18,000	$24,000
1938	175 neck	$18,000	$24,000
1939	Early '39, 175 neck	$18,000	$24,000
1939	Late '39, 168 neck	$16,500	$22,000
1940-1941		$16,500	$22,000
1942-1944	Scalloped	$16,500	$22,000
1944-1946	Non-scalloped	$11,500	$15,000
1947-1949		$9,000	$12,000
1950-1953		$5,000	$6,500
1954-1959		$5,000	$6,500
1960-1964		$4,200	$5,500
1965		$4,000	$5,500
1966-1969		$3,600	$5,000
1970-1979		$3,200	$4,500
1980-1989		$2,700	$3,500
1990-1995		$2,500	$3,200
2016-2024		$1,800	$2,500

00-18 Authentic 1931

2016-2018. Adirondack spruce top, mahogany back and sides, ebony 'board, Vintage Tone System (VTS), natural finish.

2016-2018		$3,500	$5,500

00-18 Custom

2008. Custom Shop run of 75 or more made.

2008		$2,000	$3,000

00-18 Gruhn Limited Edition

1995. Sikta spruce top, C-shaped neck profile, 25 made.

1995		$2,500	$4,000

00-18 Tim O'Brien Signature

2008-2011. Limited Edition, 25.5" scale, label signed by O'Brien.

2008-2011		$3,500	$5,500

00-18C

1962-1995. Renamed from 00-18 G in '62, mahogany back and sides, classical, 12 frets, slotted headstock, natural.

1962-1969		$2,200	$3,500
1970-1979		$1,800	$2,800
1980-1995		$1,500	$2,200

00-18CTN Elizabeth Cotton

2001. Commemorative Edition, 76 made.

2001		$3,000	$5,000

00-18E

1959-1964. Flat-top Style 18, single neck pickup and 2 knobs, heavier bracing, natural.

1959-1964		$5,500	$8,000

00-18G

1936-1962. Mahogany back and sides, classical, natural, renamed 00-18 C in '62.

1936-1939		$3,200	$4,500
1940-1949		$2,200	$3,500
1950-1959		$2,200	$3,500
1960-1962		$2,200	$3,500

MODEL YEAR	FEATURES	EXC. COND. LOW	HIGH

00-18H

1935-1941. Hawaiian, mahogany back and sides, 12 frets clear of body, natural. The Price Guide is generally for all original instruments. The H conversion is an exception, because converting from H (Hawaiian-style) to 00-18 specs is considered by some to be a favorable improvement and something that adds value.

1935-1941		$11,000	$14,500

00-18H Geoff Muldaur

2006-2011. Solid Adirondack spruce top, solid mahogany sides and back, sunburst.

2006-2011		$3,000	$4,500

00-18K

1918-1925, 1934. All Koa.

1918-1921		$5,000	$6,500
1922-1925		$7,500	$9,500
1934		$8,000	$10,000

00-18S John Mellencamp

2009-2010. Limited run of 78, slotted, 12-fret, satin finish.

2009-2010		$3,000	$4,500

00-18SH Steve Howe

1999-2000. Limited edition run of 250.

1999-2000		$2,500	$4,000

00-18T

1931, 1936, 1938-1940. Tenor version.

1931-1940		$3,000	$4,000

00-18V

1984, 2003-2015. Vintage Series, mahogany back and sides, spruce top.

1984	9 made	$3,500	$5,500
2003-2015		$2,000	$3,000

00-18V/VS Elderly Instruments 40th Anniversary

2012-2013. Limited Edition, solid (V) or slotted (VS) headstock, 12-fret, low profile.

2012-2013	V	$2,500	$4,000
2013	VS, 10 made	$3,000	$5,000

00-21

1898-1996. Brazilian rosewood back and sides, changed to Indian rosewood in 1970, dark outer binding, unbound ebony 'board until 1947, rosewood from 1947, slotted diamond inlays until '44, dot after, natural.

1898-1926	Gut bracing	$8,500	$12,000
1927-1939	Steel bracing	$15,500	$20,000
1940-1943	Scalloped	$15,500	$20,000
1944-1947	Non-scalloped	$12,000	$16,000
1948-1949		$11,500	$15,000
1950-1959		$10,500	$14,000
1960-1964		$8,500	$11,000
1965		$6,500	$8,500
1966-1969	Brazilian	$6,000	$8,000
1970-1979	Indian	$3,500	$4,500
1980-1989	Indian	$3,500	$4,500
1990-1996	Indian	$3,000	$4,000

00-21 Custom

2005-2006. Custom order size 00 style 21, Brazilian rosewood sides and back.

2005-2006		$4,000	$6,500

MODEL YEAR	FEATURES	EXC. COND. LOW	HIGH

00-21 Kingston Trio LTD

2007. 50th Anniversary of the Kingston Trio, inspired by Dave Guard's 00-21, 100 made, 12-fret, Indian rosewood, Kingston Trio label and notation "In Memory of Dave Guard 1934-1991".

2008-2009		$3,000	$5,000

00-21G

1937-1938. Gut string, Brazilian rosewood sides and back.

1937-1938		$4,000	$5,000

00-21GE Golden Era

1998-2000		$3,500	$5,500

00-21H

Hawaiian, special order, limited production.

1914	1 made	$10,000	$15,000
1934		$16,500	$25,000
1952, 1955	1 made each year	$11,500	$18,000

00-21LE

1987. Guitar of the Month, Limited Edition, 19 made.

1987		$2,500	$4,000

00-21NY

1961-1965. Brazilian rosewood back and sides, no inlay, natural.

1961-1964		$7,000	$9,500
1965		$6,500	$8,500

00-21S

1968. Slotted headstock, Brazilian rosewood sides and back.

1968		$6,000	$9,000

00-21T

1934. Tenor, Brazilian rosewood back and sides, only 2 made.

1934		$5,000	$7,000

00-25K

1980, 1985, 1988. Spruce top, Koa back and sides.

1980-1988		$2,500	$3,500

00-25K2

1980, 1982-1984, 1987-1989. Koa top, back and sides.

1980-1989		$3,000	$4,000

00-28

Mid-1880s-1931, 1934, 1936-1941, 1958 (1 made), 1977 (1 made), 1984 (2 made), 2017-present. Brazilian rosewood back and sides, changed to Indian rosewood in 1977, herringbone purfling through 1941, white binding and unbound 'board after 1941, no inlays before 1901, diamond inlays from 1901-'41, dot after, natural. Reintroduced 2017, Sikta spruce top, modified low oval neck.

1880s-1924	Gut	$14,000	$18,000
1925-1931	Steel	$28,000	$38,000
1934	Few made	$37,500	$50,000
1936-1941	Few made	$37,500	$50,000
1958	Special order	$15,500	$20,000
1977	Special order	$3,800	$5,000
1984	Special order	$3,200	$4,500
2017-2024	Reissue	$2,200	$3,000

1983 Martin 00-25K

1925 Martin 00-28

Izzy Miller

GUITARS

2015 Martin 00-DB Jeff Tweedy

Rodger Reed

Martin 00-X2E

MODEL YEAR	FEATURES	EXC. COND. LOW	HIGH

00-28C

1966-1995. Renamed from 00-28 G, Brazilian rosewood back and sides, changed to Indian rosewood in '70, classical, 12 frets, natural.

1966-1969	Brazilian	$3,800	$6,000
1970-1979	Indian	$2,000	$3,000
1980-1989		$1,500	$2,200
1990-1995		$1,500	$2,200

00-28G

1936-1962. Brazilian rosewood back and sides, classical, natural, reintroduced as 00-28 C in '66.

1936-1946		$6,000	$8,000
1947-1949		$5,000	$6,500
1950-1959		$4,500	$6,000
1960-1962		$4,200	$5,500

00-28K

1919-1921, 1926, 1928-1931, 1933. Hawaiian, Koa back and sides.

1919-1921	34 made	$15,000	$20,000
1926-1933	1 made per year	$25,000	$32,000

00-28T

1931, 1940. Tenor, Brazilian rosewood back and sides, tenor 4-string neck, only 2 made.

1931, 1940		$7,500	$10,000

00-28VS

2009-2019. Rosewood back and sides.

2009-2019		$2,500	$3,500

00-28VS Custom Shop

2009-2013. Various Custom Shop options.

2009-2013		$3,500	$5,500

00-30

1890s-1921. Rosewood.

1899-1921		$15,500	$22,000

00-34

1898-1899. 6 made.

1898-1899		$18,000	$25,000

00-37K2 Steve Miller

2001. Flamed Koa back and sides, solid Engelmann spruce top, limited run of 68.

2001		$4,500	$6,500

00-40

1913, 1917. 4 made.

1913	Brazilian	$35,000	$45,000
1917	Koa	$35,000	$45,000

00-40 Martin Stauffer

1997. Rosewood/spruce, 35 made.

1997		$6,000	$8,500

00-40H

1928-1939. Hawaiian, Brazilian rosewood back and sides, 12 frets clear of body, natural. H models are sometimes converted to standard Spanish setup, in higher-end models this can make the instrument more valuable to some people.

1928-1929	Pyramid bridge	$30,000	$40,000
1930-1939	Belly bridge	$30,000	$40,000

00-40K

Few were made (only 6), figured Koa, natural.

1918	1 made	$30,000	$40,000
1930	5 made	$30,000	$40,000

MODEL YEAR	FEATURES	EXC. COND. LOW	HIGH

00-41 Custom

2005. Custom Shop model, parlor size.

2005		$4,500	$6,000

00-42

1898-1943, 1973 (1 made). Brazilian rosewood back and sides, Indian rosewood in 1973, pearl top borders, 12 frets, ivory bound peghead until 1918, ivoroid binding after 1918, natural.

1898-1927	Pyramid bridge	$32,500	$45,000
1927-1943	Steel bracing	$52,000	$75,000
1973	1 made	$5,000	$7,000

00-42 Linda Ronstadt Limited Edition

2009-2010. Madagascar rosewood, slotted headstock.

2009-2010		$5,500	$8,500

00-42G

1936-1939. Gut string slotted headstock classical, only 3 made.

1936-1939	3 made	$12,000	$15,000

00-42JM-C John Mayer Crossroads

2019. Limited run of 50 for Guitar Center, designed by John Mayer to benefit Crossroads Centre in Antigua, Sikta spruce top, Cocobolo back and sides, gloss finish.

2019		$6,500	$9,000

00-42K

1919. Koa body, only 1 made.

1919	1 made	$50,000	$65,000

00-42K2 Robbie Robertson

2008-2009. Limited Edition, all Koa body (K2), 00-12 fret style, high-end appointments.

2008-2009		$5,000	$7,500

00-42SC John Mayer

2012-2019. Sikta spruce top, cocobolo back, sides and headplate, ebony 'board.

2012-2019		$5,000	$7,500

00-44 Soloist/Olcott-Bickford Artist

1913-1939. Custom-made in small quantities, Brazilian rosewood, ivory or faux-ivory-bound ebony 'board.

1913-1939	6 made	$45,000	$60,000

00-44G

1938. Set up with gut strings, 1 made.

1938	1 made	$35,000	$45,000

00-45

1904-1929, 1970-1982, 1984-1987, 1989-1990, 1992-1993. Brazilian rosewood back and sides, changed to Indian rosewood in '70, 12 frets and slotted headstock until '34 and from '70 on 14 frets, and solid headstock from '34-'70, natural.

1904-1927	Gut	$52,000	$75,000
1927-1929	Steel	$100,000	$125,000
1970-1979	Reintroduced	$7,500	$9,500
1980-1993		$6,500	$8,500

00-45 Custom

1980-1985. Spruce top, rosewood back and sides, pearl inlays, natural.

1980-1984		$3,500	$5,500
1985	Brazilian	$6,000	$9,000

00-45K

1919. Koa body, 1 made.

1919		$75,000	$95,000

MODEL YEAR	FEATURES	EXC. COND. LOW	HIGH

00-45S

1970. Slotted headstock.

1970		$7,500	$11,500

00-45S Limited Edition

2002. 1902 vintage-pattern with fancy inlays, 00 size style 45, 50 made.

2002		$12,000	$18,000

00-45SC John Mayer

2012-2013. Limited Edition, 25 made, slotted headstock, cocobolo.

2012-2013		$10,000	$14,000

00-45ST Stauffer Commemorative

1997-1998. Limited Edition, 25 made, six-on-a-side headstock, 45-style appointments, 00 body, Sikta top, Brazilian rosewood back and sides.

1997-1998		$9,000	$15,000

00-45S "1902"

2002-2004. Reissue of 1902 prototype model, 60 made, Adirondack spruce top, Brazilian rosewood back and sides, natural.

2002-2004		$7,000	$10,000

00-55

1935. 12 made for Rudnick's Music of Akron, Ohio.

1935		$12,000	$18,000

00CMAE

1999-2001. Single-cut acoustic-electric flat-top, laminate back and sides, made in U.S.

1999-2001		$800	$1,200

00CXAE

2000-2013. Single-cut acoustic-electric flat-top, composite laminate back and sides, made in U.S.

2000-2013	Various colors	$400	$700

00L Earth

2021-2023. Dedicated to climate control, 100% FSC-certified and 100% plastic-free, graphic art by Robert Goetzl, gig bag made from hemp.

2021-2023		$1,200	$1,800

00L Fly Fishing

2019-2021. Limited Edition, run of 100, artwork by William Matthews, Sikta spruce top, Goncalo Alves back and sides, gloss finish.

2019-2021		$1,500	$2,200

00L-17 Black Smoke/Whiskey Sunset

2016-2019. Sikta spruce top, mahogany back and sides, on-board electronics optional.

2016-2019	17, No electronics	$1,200	$1,800
2016-2019	17E, Electronics	$1,300	$2,000

00L-X1AE

2017-2019		$400	$600

00L-X2E

2020-2022. Sikta spruce top, figured mahogany laminate back and sides, Fishman electronics, natural finish.

2020-2022		$500	$800

00-DB Jeff Tweedy Signature

2011-2019. Custom Shop Signature Edition with solid FSC® Certified Mahogany and mahogany burst finish.

2011-2019		$2,000	$3,000

00-X1AE

2015-2019		$400	$600

00-X2E

2020-present. Sikta spruce top, figured mahogany laminate back and sides, Fishman electronics, natural finish.

2020-2024		$500	$800

000-1

1994-2005. Solid spruce top with laminated mahogany back and sides.

1994-2005		$700	$1,000

000-1E

1994-2005. 000-1 with electronics.

1994-2005		$800	$1,200

000-1R

1994-2003. 000-1 with Indian rosewood back and sides.

1994-2003		$900	$1,400

000-10E

2019-present. Road Series, updated version of 000RS1, sapele top, back and sides, Fishman electronics, satin finish.

2019-2024		$600	$900

000-12E Koa

2019-present. Road Series, Sikta spruce top, Koa veneer back and sides, Fishman electronics, gloss finish.

2019-2024		$900	$1,400

000-13E

2017-2018. Road Series, updated version of 000RSG, Sikta spruce top, siris back and sides, Fishman electronics, natural gloss.

2017-2018		$800	$1,200

000-15/000-15S

1999-2009. Mahogany body, headstock is solid or slotted (S, first offered in '00). Renamed 000-15M with solid headstock in '10.

1999-2009	000-15	$1,000	$1,500
2000-2009	000-15S	$1,200	$1,800

000-15M

2010-present. All mahogany, satin finish.

2010-2024		$800	$1,200

000-15M Burst

2016-2018. Solid mahogany, 14-fret, satin finish with added burst to top.

2016-2018		$1,000	$1,500

000-15M Elderly Instruments 40th Anniversary

2011-2012. 10 made, mahogany body and neck, label signed by Elderly Instruments president Stan Werbin and Martin CEO Chris Martin

2011-2012		$2,500	$4,000

000-15M StreetMaster

2017-present. Same specs as 000-15M but with distressed mahogany satin finish.

2017-2024		$1,000	$1,500

000-15SM

2011-present. Solid mahogany, slotted headstock, 12-fret neck, satin finish.

2011-2024		$1,000	$1,500

000-16 Series

1989-2024. Mahogany back and sides, diamonds and squares inlay, sunburst, name changed to 000-16 T Auditorium with higher appointments in '96, in

Martin 000-10E

Martin 000-15M StreetMaster

2012 Martin 000-16GT
Cream City Music

Martin 000-17 Black Smoke

2000-2005 slotted (000-16 S) and gloss finish (000-16 SGT) were offered.

MODEL YEAR	FEATURES	EXC. COND. LOW	HIGH
1989	000-16M	$1,200	$1,800
1989-1995	000-16	$1,300	$2,000
1989-2024	000-16GT	$1,000	$1,500
1995-1998	000-16T	$1,200	$1,800
1996	000-16TR	$1,000	$1,500
1996-2002	000-16R	$1,200	$1,800
2001-2005	000-16RGT	$1,000	$1,500
2002-2003	000-16SRGT	$1,200	$1,800
2003-2004	000-16SGT	$1,200	$1,800
2019-2024	000-16E	$1,500	$2,200

000-17

1911, 1952. Mahogany back and sides, 1 made in 1911, 25 more in '52.

MODEL YEAR	FEATURES	EXC. COND. LOW	HIGH
1911		$9,000	$12,000
1952		$4,000	$5,500

000-17 Black Smoke/Whiskey Sunset

2016-2023. Sikta spruce top, mahogany back and sides, rosewood 'board and bridge, on-board electronics (000-17E) optional.

MODEL YEAR	FEATURES	EXC. COND. LOW	HIGH
2016-2023	17, No electronics	$1,000	$1,500
2016-2023	17E, Electronics	$1,100	$1,600

000-17S

2002-2004. All mahogany, slotted headstock, 12 fret neck.

MODEL YEAR	FEATURES	EXC. COND. LOW	HIGH
2002-2004		$1,200	$1,800

000-17SM

2013-2015. Sikta spruce top, mahogany back and sides, East Indian rosewood headplate, vintage slotted headstock.

MODEL YEAR	FEATURES	EXC. COND. LOW	HIGH
2013-2015		$1,200	$1,800

000-18

1906, 1911-present (none in 1932-1933). Maple back and sides in '06, then rosewood until '17, and mahogany since, longer scale in '24-'34, 12-fret neck until '33, changed to 14 in '34. Improved neck late-'34, war-time changes '41-'46, non-scalloped braces in late-'44, switched from Adirondack spruce to Sikta spruce top in '46 (though some Adirondack tops in '50s and '60s), natural. Now a part of the Standard Series.

MODEL YEAR	FEATURES	EXC. COND. LOW	HIGH
1906	Maple	$13,500	$18,000
1911-1917	Rosewood	$13,500	$18,000
1920-1922	Gut, mahogany	$12,000	$16,000
1923-1931	Steel	$20,000	$28,000
1934	Early '34, long scale	$31,500	$40,000
1934-1938	14-fret	$31,500	$40,000
1939	Early '39 175 neck	$21,000	$28,000
1939	Late '39, 168 neck	$17,000	$22,500
1940-1941		$16,000	$22,000
1942-1943	Scalloped braces	$16,000	$22,000
1944	Scalloped braces	$13,500	$18,000
1944-1947	Non-scalloped	$10,000	$14,000
1948-1949		$8,500	$11,000
1950-1953		$8,000	$10,500
1954-1959		$6,500	$8,500
1960-1964		$5,500	$7,000
1965		$5,000	$6,500
1966-1969		$4,000	$5,500
1970-1979		$3,000	$4,000
1980-1989		$2,200	$3,300
1990-1999		$2,200	$3,300
2000-2013		$2,000	$3,000
2014-2024	Standard Series	$1,750	$2,500

000-18 Authentic 1937

2008-2011. Natural or sunburst, high-X bracing.

MODEL YEAR	FEATURES	EXC. COND. LOW	HIGH
2008-2011		$4,000	$6,000

000-18 Kenny Sultan Signature

2007-2009. Flamed mahogany sides, diamond and squares inlays, label signed by Sultan, less than 100 made.

MODEL YEAR	FEATURES	EXC. COND. LOW	HIGH
2007-2009		$3,000	$4,500

000-18 Marquis

2010-2011. Like Golden Era but with Madagascar rosewood headplate, not Brazilian, 63 made, sunburst.

MODEL YEAR	FEATURES	EXC. COND. LOW	HIGH
2010-2011		$3,500	$5,500

000-18 Norman Blake Signature

2006-2011. 12 fret neck on 14-fret body.

MODEL YEAR	FEATURES	EXC. COND. LOW	HIGH
2006-2011		$3,000	$4,500

000-18E Retro

2012-2019. Sikta spruce top, mahogany back and sides.

MODEL YEAR	FEATURES	EXC. COND. LOW	HIGH
2012-2019		$1,800	$2,500

000-18G

1955. Classical, 1 made.

MODEL YEAR	FEATURES	EXC. COND. LOW	HIGH
1955		$5,000	$7,500

000-18GE Golden Era 1934 Special Edition

2007. Adirondack red spruce top, scalloped and forward shifted X-bracing, 14-fret V-shaped mahogany neck, 20-fret ebony 'board, old style decal logo.

MODEL YEAR	FEATURES	EXC. COND. LOW	HIGH
2007		$3,500	$5,000

000-18GE Golden Era 1937 Special Edition

2006-2014. Natural or sunburst. 1937 dropped from name in '12.

MODEL YEAR	FEATURES	EXC. COND. LOW	HIGH
2006-2014	Natural or sunburst	$3,000	$4,500

000-18GE Golden Era Sunburst

2006-2014. Sunburst version, Adirondack.

MODEL YEAR	FEATURES	EXC. COND. LOW	HIGH
2006-2014		$3,000	$4,500

000-18P

1930. Plectrum neck.

MODEL YEAR	FEATURES	EXC. COND. LOW	HIGH
1930		$6,000	$8,000

000-18S

1976-1977. Slotted, 12-fret.

MODEL YEAR	FEATURES	EXC. COND. LOW	HIGH
1976-1977		$3,500	$4,500

000-18T

1930, '34, '36, '38, '41. Tenor.

MODEL YEAR	FEATURES	EXC. COND. LOW	HIGH
1930		$6,500	$8,500
1934-1938		$12,000	$15,000
1941		$7,000	$9,000

000-18V/VS Elderly Instruments 40th Anniversary

2012-2013. Limited Edition, solid (V) or slotted (VS) headstock, Sikta top, label signed by C.F. Martin IV and Stan Werbin, includes matching wood guitar stand.

MODEL YEAR	FEATURES	EXC. COND. LOW	HIGH
2012-2013	V	$3,000	$4,000
2013	VS, 10 made	$3,500	$5,500

GUITARS

MODEL YEAR	FEATURES	EXC. COND. LOW	HIGH

000-18WG Woody Guthrie

1999. Signed label including artwork and model identification.

1999		$2,500	$3,500

000-21

1902-1923 (22 made over that time), 1931(2), 1938-1959, 1965 (1), 1979 (12). Brazilian rosewood back and sides, changed to Indian rosewood in '79, natural.

1902-1923		$18,000	$24,000
1931	12-fret	$21,500	$28,000
1938-1939	Early '39, 175 neck	$32,500	$43,000
1939	Late '39, 168 neck	$27,000	$35,000
1940-1941		$21,500	$30,000
1942-1943		$20,000	$26,000
1944-1945		$18,000	$23,500
1946		$12,500	$16,500
1947-1949		$10,500	$14,000
1950-1954		$10,500	$14,000
1955-1959		$10,000	$13,000
1965	Last Brazilian	$9,000	$12,000
1979	Indian	$3,500	$4,500

000-21 10-String/Harp Guitar

1902. Only 2 made, 10 strings, Brazilian rosewood back and sides.

1902		$6,000	$8,000

000-28

1902-present. Brazilian rosewood back and sides, changed to Indian rosewood in '70, herringbone purfling through '41, white binding and unbound 'board after '41, no inlays before '01, slotted diamond inlays from '01-'44, dot after, 12 frets until '32, 14 frets '31 on (both 12 and 14 frets were made during '31-'32), natural through '93, sunburst or natural after.

1902-1927	Gut	$23,500	$30,000
1925-1927	Steel	$42,000	$55,000
1928		$42,000	$55,000
1929	Pyramid bridge	$42,000	$55,000
1930	Belly bridge	$42,000	$55,000
1931-1933		$42,000	$55,000
1934	Early '34 long scale	$70,000	$95,000
1934-1937	Not long scale	$65,000	$85,000
1938-1939	Early '39, 175 neck	$60,000	$80,000
1939	Late '39, 168 neck	$55,500	$75,000
1940-1941		$47,000	$60,000
1942-1944	Scalloped, herringbone	$47,000	$60,000
1944-1946	Non-scalloped, herringbone	$32,500	$42,500
1947-1949	Non-herringbone	$18,500	$24,000
1950-1952		$15,500	$20,000
1953-1955	Kluson	$15,500	$20,000
1956-1958	Kluson	$14,000	$18,000
1958-1959	Late '58, Grover	$14,000	$18,000
1960-1962		$11,000	$14,500
1964		$10,500	$14,000
1965		$8,200	$11,000
1966-1969	Early '66, Tortoise 'guard	$8,200	$11,000
1970-1979		$4,000	$5,500
1980-1989		$3,200	$4,500
1990-1999		$3,000	$4,000
2000-2024		$2,800	$3,800

000-28 Martin/Mandolin Brothers 25th Anniversary

1997-1998. Limited Edition, 25 made, mandolin 12th fret inlay, signed label.

1997-1998		$4,500	$6,500

000-28 Modern Deluxe

2019-present. Sikta spruce top, Vintage Tone System, Indian rosewood back and sides. Electronics are optional (000-28E).

2019-2024	28, No electronics	$2,500	$3,500
2019-2024	28E, Electronics	$3,000	$4,500

000-28 Norman Blake

2004-2008. Signature Edition, 12-fret neck on 14-fret body, B version is Brazilian rosewood.

2004-2008	Brazilian	$6,500	$10,000
2004-2008	Indian	$3,000	$4,500

000-28 Perry Bechtel

2007. East Indian rosewood back and sides, 29 made.

2007		$4,500	$6,500

000-28C

1962-1967. Classical, Brazilian rosewood back and sides, slotted peghead, natural.

1962-1967		$5,000	$7,500

000-28EC

1996-present. Custom Signature Edition, Eric Clapton specs, Sikta spruce top, Indian rosewood back and sides, herringbone trim, natural or sunburst.

1996-2024	Natural	$2,500	$4,000
1996-2024	Sunburst	$2,800	$4,200

000-28EC Eric Clapton Crossroads Madagascar

2013. Limited to 150 in collaboration with Guitar Center, sound hole label hand-signed by Clapton and Chris Martin, Crossroads symbol inlaid (mother-of-pearl) into bridge, Clapton signature between 19th-20th frets, Clapton signature case and strap.

2013		$5,000	$7,500

000-28ECB Eric Clapton

2002-2003. Limited edition, EC 000-28 with Brazilian rosewood, certificate of authenticity, label hand-signed by Eric Clapton and Chris Martin.

2002-2003		$7,000	$10,000

000-28G

1937, 1939-1940, 1946-1947, 1949-1950, 1955. Special order classical guitar, very limited production.

1937-1940		$9,500	$12,000
1946		$8,800	$11,000
1947, 1949		$7,000	$9,000
1950, 1955		$6,000	$8,000

000-28GE Golden Era

1996 only. Sikta spruce top, rosewood back and sides, scalloped braces, herringbone trim, 12-fret model, natural.

1996		$4,000	$6,000

1936 Martin 000-18

M. Mattingly

Martin 000-28

Martin 000-28VS

Martin 000-42 Authentic 1939

MODEL YEAR	FEATURES	EXC. COND. LOW	HIGH

000-28H

2000-2017. Herringbone top trim, production model for '00-'02, Custom Shop model made for Elderly Instruments after that (stamped Custom on neck block).

2000-2002		$2,200	$3,300
2003-2017	Custom Shop	$3,000	$4,500

000-28HB Brazilian 1937 Reissue

1997. Pre-war specs including scalloped bracing, Brazilian rosewood.

1997 — $7,000 — $10,000

000-28K

1921. Non-catalog special order model, only 2 known to exist, Koa top, back and sides.

1921 — Rare model — $50,000 — $65,000

000-28K Authentic 1921

2014-2015. Slotted, 12-fret, highly figured Koa body.

2014-2015 — $5,000 — $7,500

000-28LD Lonnie Donegan

2002. Sitka spruce top, Indian rosewood back and sides, mahogany neck, sunburst.

2002 — $2,500 — $4,000

000-28LSH/LSH Custom

2008. Large sound hold (LSH), style 28 appointments, wild grain East Indian sides and back.

2008 — $2,800 — $4,200

000-28M Eric Clapton

2009. Limited Edition run of 461, Madagascar rosewood back and sides, Carpathian spruce top, signature between 19th and 20th frets, interior label hand-signed by Clapton, natural or sunburst.

2009 — $5,000 — $7,500

000-28NY

1962. 2 made.

1962 — $8,000 — $10,000

000-28S

1974-1977. Slotted headstock, 12-fret neck.

1974-1977 — $3,500 — $5,000

000-28SO Sing Out! 40th Anniversary

1990. Limited Edition, 40 made for 40th Anniversary of Sing Out! Magazine.

1990 — $3,500 — $5,500

000-28VS

1999-2019. Vintage Series, spruce top with aging toner, scalloped bracing, rosewood sides and back, slotted diamond markers, herringbone top trim.

1999-2019 — $2,500 — $3,500

000-30 Authentic 1919

2017-2018. Adirondack spruce top, Vintage Tone System, Madagascar rosewood back and sides.

2017-2018 — $4,500 — $6,500

000-38

1980. Rosewood back and sides, 3 made.

1980 — $2,500 — $4,000

000-40

1909. Ivoroid bound top and back, snowflake inlay, 1 made.

1909 — $40,000 — $50,000

000-40Q2GN Graham Nash

2003. Limited edition of 147 guitars, quilted mahogany top/back/sides, flying-heart logo on headstock, Graham Nash signature on frets 18-20.

2003 — $3,500 — $4,500

000-40S Mark Knopfler "Ragpicker's Dream" Signature

2006-2007. Limited run of 155, Italian Alpine spruce top, East Indian rosewood back and sides, natural.

2006-2007 — $4,000 — $6,000

000-40SPR Peter Rowan "Midnight Moonlight" Signature

2001-2002. Limited run of 87, Sikta spruce top, mahogany back and sides, phases of the moon inlays.

2001-2002 — $3,000 — $4,500

000-42

1918, 1921-1922, 1925, 1930, 1932, 1934, 1938-1943, 2004-present. Brazilian rosewood back and sides, natural. The 1918-1934 price range is wide due to the variety of specifications.

1918-1925	Limited production	$55,000	$70,000
1930, 1932	2 made, 14 fret	$90,000	$112,500
1934	1 made	$112,000	$140,000
1938	27 made	$100,000	$125,000
1939	Early '39, 175 neck	$100,000	$125,000
1939	Late '39, 168 neck	$95,000	$120,000
1940-1943	Last pearl border	$100,000	$125,000
2004-2024		$4,500	$6,500

000-42 Authentic 1939

2017-2019. Adirondack spruce top with Vintage Tone System (VTS), Madagascar rosewood back and sides, ebony 'board and bridge.

2017-2019 — $8,500 — $12,000

000-42 Marquis

2007-2009. Indian rosewood.

2007-2009 — $5,000 — $7,500

000-42EC Eric Clapton

1995. Style 45 pearl-inlaid headplate, ivoroid bindings, Eric Clapton signature, 24.9" scale, flat-top, sunburst top price is $8320 ('95 price), only 461 made; 433 natural, 28 sunburst.

1995 — $7,500 — $11,500

000-42ECB Eric Clapton

2000-2001. With Brazilian rosewood, 200 made.

2000-2001 — $12,000 — $18,000

000-42EC-Z Eric Clapton Crossroads

2019-2021. Ziricote back and sides, 50 made to benefit Crossroads Centre.

2019-2021 — $10,000 — $15,000

000-42M Eric Clapton Limited Edition

2008-2009. Limited Edition, 250 made, Madagascar rosewood sides and back, Carpathian spruce top.

2008-2009 — $6,500 — $10,000

000-42SB

2004. 1935 style with sunburst finish, Indian rosewood back and sides.

2004 — $3,500 — $5,500

000-44 Soloist/Olcott-Bickford Artist

1917-1919. Style 44 guitars were made for guitarist Vahdah Olcott-Bickford, rosewood back and sides, 3 made.

1917-1919 — $50,000 — $65,000

MODEL YEAR	FEATURES	EXC. COND. LOW	HIGH

000-45

1906, 1911-1914, '17-'19, '22-'29, '34-'42, '70-'94. Brazilian rosewood back and sides, changed to Indian rosewood in '70, 12-fret neck and slotted headstock until '34 (but 7 were made in '70 and 1 in '75), 14-fret neck and solid headstock after '34, natural.

1906-1919		$85,000	$110,000
1922-1927	Gut	$85,000	$110,000
1926-1929	Steel	$165,000	$200,000
1930-1931	000-45 designated	$165,000	$200,000
1934	Early '34, long scale	$250,000	$325,000
1934	Late '34, short scale	$225,000	$300,000
1935-1937	14 fret, CFM inlay	$225,000	$300,000
1938	Early '38	$225,000	$300,000
1938	Late '38	$200,000	$250,000
1940-1942		$165,000	$200,000
1970-1977		$7,500	$10,500
1980-1989		$6,000	$7,500
1990-1994		$5,500	$8,500

000-45 7-String

1911, 1929, 1931. 1 made each year.

1911-1931 $50,000 $60,000

000-45EC Eric Clapton Crossroads Brazilian

2013. Limited to 18 in collaboration with Guitar Center, Brazilian rosewood, Crossroads symbol inlaid both ends of bridge, Crossroads case and strap.

2013 $30,000 $40,000

000-45EC Eric Clapton Crossroads Madagascar

2013. Limited to 55 in collaboration with Guitar Center, Crossroads symbol inlaid both ends of bridge, Crossroads case and strap.

2013 $8,500 $12,500

000-45H

1937. Brazilian rosewood, Hawaiian, 2 made.

1937 $225,000 $375,000

000-45JR Jimmie Rodgers

1997-1998. Adirondack spruce top, Brazilian rosewood back and sides, scalloped high X-braces, abalone trim, natural, 52 made. Sometimes referred to as Blue Yodel.

1997-1998 $12,500 $20,000

000-45S

1974-1976. 12-fret.

1974-1976 $8,500 $12,000

000-45S Stephen Stills

2005. Only 91 made, Indian rosewood.

2005 $11,500 $18,000

000C David Gray Custom

2005-2006. Custom Artist Edition, 000-size cutaway, Italian spruce top, mahogany back and sides, 23 made, interior label signed by David Gray.

2005-2006 $4,500 $7,000

000C Nylon

2012-2018. Cutaway, 12-fret, Sikta spruce top, sapele back and sides, slotted headstock, Fishman.

2012-2018 $1,200 $1,800

MODEL YEAR	FEATURES	EXC. COND. LOW	HIGH

000C Steve Miller Pegasus

2005-2006. Cutaway, mahogany back and sides, Pegasus logo.

2005-2006 $3,500 $5,000

000C12-16E Nylon

2020-present. Gloss Sikta spruce top, satin mahogany back and sides, Fishman electronics.

2020-2024 $1,200 $1,800

000C-15E

1999-2002. Cutaway, mahogany back and sides, Fishman.

1999-2002 $1,000 $1,500

000C-16 (T Auditorium)

1990-1998. Cutaway acoustic, mahogany back and sides, diamonds and squares inlay, name changed to 000-C16T Auditorium in '96.

1990-1998 $1,200 $1,800

000C-16GTE

1999-2003. Cutaway, mahogany.

1999-2003 $1,300 $2,000

000C-16GTE Premium

2003-2009. Mahogany back and sides.

2003-2009 $1,500 $2,200

000C-16RB (Baby Face)

2000-2002. Cutaway acoustic, East Indian rosewood back and sides.

2000-2002 $2,000 $3,000

000C-16RGTE

2000-2010. Cutaway, rosewood back and sides.

2000-2010 $1,200 $1,800

000C-16SGTNE

2003-2006. Classical electric, nylon string, cutaway, mahogany body, 12-fret cedar neck, slotted headstock.

2003-2006 $1,200 $1,800

000C-16SRNE

2003-2005. Classical cutaway, rosewood body, 12-fret cedar neck, slotted headstock.

2003-2005 $1,400 $2,100

000C-16T

1996-1997. Sikta spruce top, mahogany back, sides and neck, rosewood 'board.

1996-1997 $1,200 $1,800

000C-1E Auditorium

1997-1999. Cutaway, mahogany back and sides, transducer pickup.

1997-1999 $800 $1,200

000C-28 Andy Summers

2006. Cutaway, rosewood back and sides, Buddhist Mudra inlays.

2006 $3,500 $5,000

000C-28SMH Merle Haggard

2001-2002. Cutaway, 12-fret neck, Blue Yodel No. 13 inlay, 122 made.

2001-2002 $4,000 $6,000

000CDB Dion The Wanderer

2002. Cutaway acoustic/electric, 57 made, scalloped bracing, mahogany sides and back, slotted diamond and square markers, Dion logo on headstock, gloss black finish.

2002 $4,000 $6,000

1936 Martin 000-45

Imaged by Heritage Auctions, HA.com

Martin 000C12-16E Nylon

GUITARS

Martin 000Jr-10

Martin 000-X2E

MODEL YEAR	FEATURES	EXC. COND. LOW	HIGH

000CDG Doug Greth Commemorative Edition

2011. Nylon string cutaway, slotted headstock, mahogany back and sides, 48 made.

2011		$2,000	$3,000

000CJR-10E

2019-2022. Junior Series, 000JR-10 model with Fishman electronics.

2019-2022		$600	$900

000CME

1999-2002. Laminate back and sides, on-board electronics, satin finish.

1999-2002		$800	$1,200

000CXE Black

2003-2013. Acoustic-electric, cutaway, laminated body, black finish.

2003-2013		$500	$800

000E Black Walnut Ambertone

2020. Limited Edition, run of 125, Sikta spruce top with gloss amber burst finish, satin black walnut back and sides, Fishman electronics.

2020		$1,500	$2,200

000-ECHF Bellezza Bianca

2005-2006. Eric Clapton and Hiroshi Fujiwara White Beauty model, Engleman spruce top, flamed Pacific big-leaf maple back and sides, model name logo on 20th fret, white finish, all-white case, 410 made.

2005-2006		$5,500	$7,500

000-ECHF Bellezza Nera

2004-2005. Eric Clapton and Hiroshi Fujiwara Black Beauty Model, 476 made, Italian Alpine spruce top, Indian rosewood back and sides, black finish.

2004-2005		$6,000	$8,000

000-JBP Jimmy Buffett Pollywog

2003. Model name and number on label inside back, 168 made.

2003		$3,000	$4,500

000JR-10

2019-present. Junior Series, Sikta spruce top, sapele back and sides, satin finish.

2019-2024		$400	$600

000-M

1997-2009. Road Series, mahogany or sapele back and sides.

1997-2009		$900	$1,400

000-MMV Custom

2005-2018. Guitar Center model, spruce, rosewood, gloss finish.

2005-2018		$1,500	$2,200

000RS1

2014-2018. Road Series, made in Mexico, sapele top, back and sides, Fishman Sonitone electronics. Replaced by 000-10E in '19.

2014-2018		$600	$900

000RS2

2014-2015. Road Series as above with spruce top.

2014-2015		$500	$800

000RS25 Navojoa 25th Anniversary

2014-2016. Made in Mexico, celebrates 25th Anniversary of Martin's Navojoa facility, headstock Anniversary logo, Sikta spruce top, sapele back and sides, East Indian rosewood 'board.

2014-2016		$700	$1,000

000X Hippie

2007. Limited Edition of 200, celebrates the 40th Anniversary of the 'Summer of Love'.

2007		$1,200	$1,800

000X1

2000-2010. Mahogany grained HPL (high pressure laminate) back and sides, solid spruce top.

2000-2010		$400	$600

000X1AE

2010-2019. 000X1 with electronics. Replaced by 000-X2E in '20.

2010-2019		$500	$800

000-X2E

2020-present. X Series, Sikta spruce top, figured mahogany laminate back and sides, Fishman electronics.

2020-2024		$500	$800

000XM Auditorium

1999-2002. Spruce top, Indian rosewood back and sides, natural finish.

1999-2002		$400	$600

0000-1

1997-2001. 0000-size, mahogany.

1997-2001		$800	$1,200

0000-18 Custom/Custom 0000-18 (Gruhn 35th Anniversary)

2005-2009. Commissioned for Gruhn Guitars 35th Anniversary, 35 made, 1st year models have signed Anniversary labels, 16" lower bout, high X-brace, mahogany back and sides.

2005-2009		$3,500	$5,500

0000-21S Custom (Gruhn 45th Anniversary)

2015. Commissioned for Gruhn Guitars 45th Anniversary, 50 made, label signed by CF Martin IV and George Gruhn, Adirondack spruce top, Cocobolo or Guatemalan rosewood back and sides.

2015		$5,000	$7,500

0000-28 Series

1997-2011. Several models, jumbo-size 0000 cutaway body, models include H (herringbone trim, Sikta spruce top), Custom (Indian rosewood, Sikta), H-AG (Arlo Guthrie 30th anniversary, Indian rosewood, only 30 made), HA (herringbone trim, Adirondack).

1997-2000	0000-28H	$2,500	$3,500
1998-2006	0000-28 Custom	$2,500	$3,500
1999	0000-28H-AG	$2,500	$3,500
2011	0000-28HA	$2,500	$3,500

0000-38 (M-38)

1997-1998. Called M-38 in '77-'97 and '07-present (see that listing), 0000-size, Indian rosewood back and sides, multi-bound.

1997-1998		$3,000	$4,500

1-17

1906-1917 (1st version), 1931-1934 (2nd version). The first version has spruce top, mahogany back and sides, second version has all mahogany with flat natural finish.

1906-1934		$3,500	$5,200

MODEL YEAR	FEATURES	EXC. COND. LOW	HIGH

1-17P

1928-1931, 1939. Mahogany back and sides, plectrum neck, 272 made.

1928-1939		$1,800	$2,800

1-18

1899-1903, 1906-1907, 1909-1921, 1923-1927. Brazilian rosewood or mahogany back and sides.

1899-1917	Brazilian	$4,500	$6,800
1918-1927	Mahogany	$3,200	$4,800

1-18H

1918. Hawaiian, only 3 made.

1918		$3,200	$4,800

1-18K

1917-1919. Koa.

1917-1919		$5,000	$7,500

1-18P

1929. 5-string plectrum, 1 made.

1929		$2,500	$3,800

1-18T

1927. Tenor 5-string, only 3 made.

1927		$2,200	$3,300

1-20

1860s. Parlor guitar, rosewood back and sides.

1867		$6,000	$9,000

1-21

1860s-1907, 1911, 1913-1921, 1925-1926. Initially offered in size 1 in the 1860s, ornate sound hole rings. A beautiful crack-free instrument is worth twice as much as a worn model with repaired cracks.

1860s-1926		$6,000	$9,000

1-21P

1930. Plectrum.

1930		$2,800	$4,200

1-22

1850s. Antique market value.

1850s		$9,000	$13,500

1-26

1855, 1874, 1890, 1903. Rosewood back and sides, ivory-bound top, rope-style purfling, antique market value.

1855-1903		$9,000	$13,500

1-27

1880s-1907, 1911, 1913-1921, 1925-1926. Antique market value.

1880-1926		$9,000	$13,500

1-28

1880s-1904, 1906-1907, 1909, 1911-1920, 1923. Style 28 appointments including Brazilian rosewood back and sides, antique market value.

1880s-1923		$9,000	$13,500

1-28P

1928-1930. Plectrum.

1928-1930		$3,500	$5,300

1-30

1860s-1904, 1906-1907, 1911-1914, 1916-1917, 1919. Size 1 Style 30 with pearl sound hole trim, cedar neck, antique market value.

1860s-1919		$7,800	$11,000

MODEL YEAR	FEATURES	EXC. COND. LOW	HIGH

1-42

1858-1919. Rosewood back and sides, ivory-bound top and 'board.

1858-1919		$12,500	$18,000

1-45

1904-1905, 1911-1913, 1919. Only 6 made, slotted headstock and Style 45 appointments.

1904-1919		$30,000	$35,000

1/4 - 28

1973, 1979. 14 made.

1973, 1979		$5,800	$8,500

2-15

1939-1964. All mahogany body, dot markers.

1939-1964		$2,500	$3,800

2-17

1910, 1922-1934, 1936-1938. The 1910 version has spruce top, mahogany back and sides. '22 on, all mahogany body, no body binding after '30.

1867		$3,000	$4,500
1910		$2,800	$4,200
1922-1938		$2,800	$4,200

2-17H

1927-1929, 1931. Hawaiian, all mahogany, 12 frets clear of body.

1927-1931		$2,800	$4,200

2-17T

1927-1928. Tenor, 45 made.

1927-1928		$1,300	$2,000

2-18

1857-1900, 1902-1903, 1907, 1925, 1929, 1934, 1938. Rosewood back and sides, changed to mahogany from 1917, dark outer binding, black back stripe, no dot inlay until 1902.

1857-1938		$3,800	$5,500

2-18T

1928-1930. Tenor.

1928-1930		$2,300	$3,500

2-20

1855-1897. Rare style only offered in size 2.

1855-1897		$4,500	$6,500

2-21

1850s-1900, 1903-1904, 1909, 1925, 1928-1929. Rosewood back and sides, herringbone sound hole ring.

1885-1929		$3,600	$5,500

2-21T

1928. Tenor.

1928		$1,800	$2,700

2-24

1857-1898. Antique market value.

1857-1898		$6,300	$9,500

2-27

1857-1880s, 1898-1900, 1907. Brazilian rosewood back and sides, pearl ring, zigzag back stripe, ivory bound ebony 'board and peghead.

1857-1907		$7,200	$10,000

2-28

Brazilian rosewood back and sides, slot head.

1880		$7,200	$10,000

1930 Martin 1-17P

Bernunzio Uptown Music

1890s Martin 2-24

Cody Lindsey

GUITARS

1880s Martin 2 1/2-21
Imaged by Heritage Auctions, HA.com

1950 Martin 5-15 T
David Stone

MODEL YEAR	FEATURES	EXC. COND. LOW	HIGH

2-28T

1928-1929. Tenor neck, Brazilian rosewood back and sides, herringbone top purfling.

1928-1929		$3,600	$5,500

2-30

1874, 1902-1904, 1909-1910, 1921. Similar to 2-27, only 7 made.

1874-1921		$7,800	$11,000

2-34

1850s-1898. Similar to 2-30.

1850s-1898		$8,200	$12,000

2-40

1850s-1898, 1909.

1850s-1898		$8,500	$12,000

2-42

1858-1900.

1874		$10,000	$15,000

2-44

1930. Style 44, Olcott-Bickford Soloist custom order, only 4 made.

1930		$16,500	$25,000

2-45T

1927-1928. Tenor style 45, 2 made.

1927-1928		$7,800	$12,000

2 1/2-17

1856-1897, 1909, 1911-1914. The first Style 17s were small size 2 1/2 and 3, these early models use Brazilian rosewood.

1856-1914		$3,600	$5,500

2 1/2-18

1865-1898, 1901, 1909-1914, 1916-1923. Parlor-size body with Style 18 appointments.

1865-1917	Brazilian	$3,600	$5,500
1918-1923	Mahogany	$3,200	$4,800

2 1/2-21

1880s, 1909, 1911-1913, 1917-1921. Brazilian rosewood back and sides.

1880s-1921		$4,000	$6,000

2 1/2-42

1880s, 1911. Style 42 size 2 1/2 with Brazilian rosewood. Only 1 made 1911.

1880s-1911		$10,500	$16,000

3-16

1850. Adirondack spruce top, Indian rosewood back and sides, natural.

1850		$2,800	$4,200

3-17

1856-1897, 1908 (1 made). The first Style 17s were small size 2 1/2 and 3. The early models use Brazilian rosewood, spruce top, bound back, unbound ebony 'board.

1856-1870s	Brazilian	$3,300	$4,800
1880s-1908	Mahogany	$2,800	$4,200

3-21

1885. Brazilian rosewood.

1885		$3,600	$5,500

3-24

1860. Brazilian rosewood.

1860		$5,800	$9,000

3-34

1860. Brazilian rosewood.

1860		$7,800	$12,000

5-15

2003-2007. Sapele or mahogany body, shorter scale.

2003-2007		$1,000	$1,500

5-15T

1949-1963. Tenor neck, all mahogany, non-gloss finish.

1927-1930		$2,000	$3,000
1949-1963		$1,500	$2,200

5-16

1962-1963. Mahogany back and sides, unbound rosewood 'board.

1962-1963		$2,800	$4,200

5-17

1912-1914, 1916, 1927-1928, 1930-1931, 1933-1943. Special order 1912-'36, standard production '37-'43.

1912-1916		$2,700	$4,000
1927-1928		$4,000	$6,000
1930-1939		$3,200	$4,800
1940-1943		$2,800	$4,200

5-17T

1949-1958. Tenor neck, all mahogany.

1949-1958		$1,300	$2,000

5-18

1898-1899, 1912-1914, 1917, 1919-1921, 1923-1924, 1926-1932, 1934-1937, 1940-1941, 1943-1962, 1965, 1968-1977, 1979-1981, 1983-1989. Rosewood back and sides (changed to mahogany from 1917 on), 12 frets, slotted headstock.

1898-1917		$4,000	$6,000
1919-1921		$3,200	$4,800
1923-1937		$5,800	$8,700
1940-1946		$5,400	$8,500
1948-1949		$5,000	$7,500
1950-1959		$4,500	$6,500
1960-1962		$3,800	$5,500
1965		$3,200	$4,800
1966-1969		$3,000	$4,500
1970-1979		$2,800	$4,200
1980-1989		$2,500	$3,500

5-18 Marty Robbins

2009-2011. Custom Edition, 12-fret, Adirondack top, mahogany back and sides.

2009-2011		$2,500	$3,500

5-18T

1940, 1954, 1960-1961. Tenor, only 1 made each year.

1940		$1,500	$2,200
1954		$1,300	$2,000
1960-1961		$1,200	$1,800

5-21

1890s, 1902, 1912-1914, 1916-1920, 1927, 1977. Rosewood back and sides.

1890s-1977		$4,500	$6,500

5-21T

1927-1928. Tenor guitar with 21-styling.

1927-1928		$2,000	$3,000

5-28

1901-1902, 1904, 1918, 1920-1921, 1923, 1935, 1939, 1969-1970, 1977, 1980-1981, 1988, 2001-2002. Special edition, 1/2-size parlor guitar, rosewood back and sides.

1901-1923		$3,500	$4,500

MODEL YEAR	FEATURES	EXC. COND. LOW	HIGH
1935-1939		$6,000	$9,000
1969-1988		$4,800	$7,500
2001-2002		$2,500	$3,500

7-28

1980-1995, 1997-2002. 7/8-body-size of a D-model, Style 28 appointments.

1980-1989		$2,200	$3,300
1990-2002		$2,000	$3,000

7-37K

1980-1987. 7/8-size baby dreadnought acoustic, Koa back and sides, spruce top, oval sound hole.

1980-1987		$2,200	$3,300

Alternative II Resonator

2004-2007. Metal top, Dobro-style, Fishman pickup.

2004-2007		$800	$1,200

Alternative X

2001-2013. OO-Grand Concert body shape, textured aluminum top, matching headstock overlay, spun aluminum cone resonator, Fishman pickup.

2001-2013		$500	$800

Alternative XT

2002-2005. Alternative with DiMarzio humbucker, volume & tone controls, coil tap, Bigsby.

2003-2005		$500	$800

American Chopper Custom

2020. Limited Edition run of 7, designed for TV show 'American Chopper' with special features and appointments.

2020		$20,000	$30,000

America's Guitar 175th Anniversary

2008. D-style, 14-fret, Adirondack spruce top, Madagascar rosewood sides and back, 175 made, 'America's Guitar' headstock inlay, '175th Anniversary 1833-2008'.

2008		$3,500	$5,500

Arts and Crafts

2006-2007. Limited run of 100, bearclaw spruce top, figured mahogany back and sides.

2006-2007		$3,500	$4,500

AS-D41 Australian Series

2005. Tasmanian Blackwood sides and back, Sikta spruce top, Australian theme appointments and label.

2005		$3,500	$5,500

Backpacker

1992-present. Small-bodied travel guitar, nylon called Classical Backpacker.

1992-2024	Steel strings	$200	$300
1994-2021	Nylon strings	$250	$400

Backpacker 25th Anniversary

2017 only. Sapele.

2017		$300	$500

Bentley Snowflake First Edition

2021-2024. Custom Shop Limited Edition, 75 made, Sikta spruce top, Madagascar rosewood back and sides, exclusive Wilson A. Bentley (photomicrography) snowflake images for neck and pickguard inlays.

2021-2024		$8,500	$12,500

Bigsby/Martin D-28 Bigsby

2018-2019. Martin partnered with Gretsch to build, Merle Travis inspired, 100 made, Sikta spruce top, East Indian rosewood back and sides, Bigsby headstock, natural finish.

2018-2019		$3,200	$5,000

MODEL YEAR	FEATURES	EXC. COND. LOW	HIGH

C-1

1931-1942. Acoustic archtop, mahogany back and sides, spruce top, round hole until '33 (449 made), f-holes appear in '32 (786 made), bound body, sunburst.

1931-1933	Round hole	$2,800	$4,200
1932-1942	F-hole	$2,800	$4,200

C-1-12

1932. Only 1 made, 12-string version.

1932		$2,800	$4,200

C-1P

1931-1933, 1939. Archtop, plectrum.

1931-1933	Round hole	$2,200	$3,300
1939	F-hole	$2,200	$3,300

C-1R Humphrey

1997-2000. Solid cedar top, laminated rosewood back and sides, satin finish.

1997-2000		$1,500	$2,500

C-1T

1931-1934, 1936-1938. Archtop, tenor, round hole (71 made) or f-hole (83 made).

1931-1933	Round hole	$2,200	$3,300
1933-1938	F-hole	$2,200	$3,300

C-2

1931-1942. Acoustic archtop, Brazilian rosewood back and sides, carved spruce top, round hole until '33 (269 made), f-holes appear in '32 (439 made), zigzag back stripe, multi-bound body, slotted-diamond inlay, sunburst.

1931-1933	Round hole	$3,800	$5,500
1932-1942	F-hole	$3,300	$5,000

C-2-12

1932. Only 1 made, 12-string version.

1932		$3,200	$4,800

C-2P

1931. Archtop, plectrum, round hole, 2 made.

1931		$3,000	$4,500

C-2T

1931-1936. Archtop, tenor, round or f-hole.

1931-1934	Round hole	$2,800	$4,200
1934-1936	F-hole	$2,200	$3,300

C-3

1931-1934. Archtop, Brazilian rosewood back and sides, round sound hole until early '33 (53 made), f-holes after (58 made).

1931-1933	Round hole	$6,200	$9,500
1933-1934	F-hole	$4,800	$7,200

C-3T

1933. Archtop, tenor, 1 made.

1933		$4,000	$6,000

Car Talk Special Edition

2008-2010. Limited run of 25, D-size, East Indian rosewood back and sides, car parts and tools inlay, Car Talk credits on 'guard.

2008-2010		$5,000	$7,000

CEO Series

1997-present. Chief Executive Officer (C.F. Martin IV), Special Edition (CEO-1 through CEO-6) and Custom Signature Edition (CEO-7 through CEO-9), various woods and specs. CEO-1/1R ('97-'98), 2 ('98), 3 ('99-'00), 4 ('01-'04), 4R ('02-'10), 5 ('01-'04), 6 ('11-'13), 7 ('15-present), 8 ('15-'17), 8.2/E ('17-'18), 9 ('19-present).

1967 Martin 5-18

Imaged by Heritage Auctions, HA.com

Martin Bentley Snowflake First Edition

GUITARS

Martin CEO

CS-CF Martin Outlaw-17

MODEL YEAR	FEATURES	EXC. COND. LOW	HIGH
1997-2016	CEO-1 to CEO-6	$2,000	$3,000
2014-2024	CEO-7	$2,000	$3,000
2015-2017	CEO-8	$3,000	$4,500
2017-2018	CEO-82	$4,000	$6,000
2017-2018	CEO-82E	$3,000	$4,500

CF-1 American Archtop

2004-2009. 17", solid maple sides, laminated maple back, ebony 'board, dot markers, 1 pickup, sunburst, natural or black.

2004-2009		$2,000	$3,000

CF-2 American Archtop

2004-2009. CF-1 with 2 humbuckers, sunburst, natural or black.

2004-2009		$2,000	$3,000

Claire's Guitar

2005-2006. Made to celebrate the birth of Claire Frances Martin, limited to 100, small parlor size, Sikta spruce top, Brazilian rosewood back and sides, fancy appointments, comes with pink-lined hard case.

2005-2006		$5,000	$7,500

Concept J

2003. U.S.-made, solid spruce top, solid mahogany back and sides, cutaway, on-board electronics, sparkle-mist finish.

2003		$1,800	$2,800

Cowboy 2015 Limited Edition/ LE Cowboy 2015

2015. Limited to number sold in '15, 000, 12-fret, Sikta spruce top, solid Goncalo Alves back and sides, cowboy on horse artwork by William Matthews.

2015		$2,500	$3,500

Cowboy 2016 Limited Edition/LE Cowboy 2016

2016. Limited to number sold in '16, auditorium, 12-fret, Sikta spruce top, mahogany back and sides, cowboy on bucking bronco artwork by William Matthews.

2016		$2,500	$3,500

Cowboy Series

2000-2009. Models include Cowboy X (2000, 250 made), Cowboy II ('01, 500 made), Cowboy III ('03, 750 made), and Cowboy IV ('05-'06, 250 made), Cowboy V ('06-'09, 500 made).

2001-2009	Various models	$600	$900

CS-21-11

2011. Limited Edition, 171 made, Madagascar rosewood.

2011		$4,000	$6,000

CS-Bluegrass-16

2016-2020. Limited to 100, Adirondack spruce top, Guatemalan rosewood back and sides, vintage gloss finish.

2016-2020		$3,500	$5,500

CS-CF Martin Outlaw-17

2017-2020. Limited to 100 made, Adirondack spruce top, mahogany back and sides, natural gloss finish.

2017-2020		$3,500	$5,500

CSN (Gerry Tolman Tribute)

2007-2009. Crosby, Stills & Nash, CSN logo on headstock, D-style, high-end appointments, East Indian rosewood back and sides. Tolman was CSN's longtime manager and was killed in car wreck in '06.

2007-2009		$3,000	$4,500

C-TSH (Humphrey/Martin)

1997-2002. Designed by classical guitar luthier Thomas Humphrey, based on his Millenium model, arched Englemann spruce top, rosewood back and sides.

1997-2002		$2,500	$3,500

Custom 15

1991-1994. Renamed HD-28V Custom 15 in ca. 2001.

1991-1994		$2,000	$3,000

Custom D Classic Mahogany

2006-2014. D body, spruce top, mahogany back and sides.

2006-2014		$1,000	$1,500

Custom D Classic Rosewood

2006-2011. D body, spruce top, rosewood back and sides.

2006-2011		$1,200	$1,800

Custom Shop 18 Style 0000

2019-2020. Adirondack, Sinker mahogany back and sides, Sinker is old growth from 1900-1920, specs can vary.

2019-2020		$3,000	$4,500

Custom Shop 18 Style Dreadnought

2019-2020. Adirondack, Sinker mahogany back and sides, specs can vary.

2019-2020		$3,000	$4,500

Custom Shop 18 Style OM

2020. Adirondack, Sinker mahogany back and sides, 14-fret, specs can vary.

2020		$3,000	$4,500

Custom Shop 28 Style Dreadnought

2020. Adirondack, Indian rosewood back and sides.

2020		$3,500	$5,000

Custom Shop 28 Style OM

2020. Adirondack, Indian rosewood back and sides, sunburst or natural.

2020		$3,500	$5,000

D-1

1992-2006, 2009. Current model with mahogany body, A-frame bracing, available as an acoustic/electric.

1992-2006		$800	$1,200
2009	Reintroduced	$900	$1,400

D12-1

1996-2001. Mahogany, satin finish, 12-string.

1996-2001		$1,000	$1,500

D-1 Authentic 1931

2016-2019. Adirondack spruce top, dark mahogany back and sides, Vintage Gloss finish.

2016-2019		$3,500	$5,000

D-1E

1994-1998, 2009. Acoustic/electric version, current model solid Sikta with sapele.

1994-1998		$900	$1,400
2009		$1,000	$1,500

D-1GT

2011-2014. Double bound body, gloss finish top, satin back and sides.

2011-2014		$900	$1,400

MODEL YEAR	FEATURES	EXC. COND. LOW	HIGH

D-1R

1994-2003, 2012. D-1 with laminated rosewood back and sides.

1994-2003		$1,000	$1,500
2012	Reintroduced	$1,000	$1,500

D-1RE

1994-1995, 1998. D-1R with various electronics.

1994-1998		$1,000	$1,500

D-2

1931-1932, 1934. Earliest version of the D-28, Brazilian rosewood.

1931-1934		$250,000	$325,000

D-2R

1996-2002. Style 28 appointments, laminated rosewood back and sides, natural satin finish.

1996-2002		$1,000	$1,500

D3-18

1991. Limited Edition, run of 80, Sikta spruce top, 3-piece mahogany back.

1991		$2,000	$3,000

D-10E

2019-present. Road Series, updated version of DSR1/DSR2, Sikta spruce or sapele top, sapele back and sides, Fishman electronics, satin finish.

2019-2024		$700	$1,000

D-12E

2019-present. Sikta spruce top, sapele back and sides, Fishman.

2019-2024		$900	$1,200

D-12E Koa

2020. Sikta spruce top, Koa veneer back and sides, gloss finish.

2020		$1,000	$1,500

D-12 David Crosby

2009-2011. D-size 12-string, less than 100 made, quilted mahogany body, Carpathian spruce top.

2009-2011		$4,000	$6,000

D-13E

2019-present. Updated version of DRSG, Sikta spruce top, siris back and sides, Fishman.

2019-2024		$1,000	$1,500

D-15/D-15M

1997-present. The body is all mahogany up to 2002, mahogany or sapele (which is like mahogany) up to '10. Becomes the all-mahogany D-15M in '11.

1997-2010		$1,000	$1,500
2011-2024	M	$1,000	$1,500

D-15M Burst

2015-2018. Shaded mahogany top, back and sides, satin finish.

2015-2018		$1,200	$1,800

D-15M Elderly Instruments 40th Anniversary

2012. Only 10 made, solid mahogany body, special appointments, label signed by Elderly president Stan Werbin and Chris Martin.

2012		$2,500	$4,000

D-15M StreetMaster

2017-present. Distressed mahogany satin finish.

2017-2024		$1,000	$1,500

D-15S

2001-2009. Slotted headstock D-15, body is solid sapele or mahogany.

2001-2009		$1,200	$1,800

D-16 Adirondack

2009-2013. Adirondack spruce top, mahogany back and sides.

2009-2013		$2,000	$3,000

D-16 50th Anniversary

2011. Adirondack spruce top, rosewood back and sides, natural.

2011		$2,200	$3,300

D-16 Lyptus

2003-2005. Lyptus back and sides.

2003-2005		$1,200	$1,800

D-16A

1987-1990. North American ash back and sides, scalloped bracing.

1987-1990		$1,500	$2,200

D-16E Burst

2019-2021. Mahogany burst ovangkol gloss top, satin ovangkol back and sides, Fishman electronics.

2019-2021		$1,500	$2,200

D-16E Rock The Vote

2019-2021. Special Edition, designed by David Crosby, custom artwork by Robert F. Goetzl, Sikta spruce gloss top, satin sycamore back and sides, Fishman electronics.

2019-2021		$1,800	$2,700

D-16E Rosewood

2019-2021. Gloss Sikta spruce top, satin East Indian rosewood back and sides, Fishman electronics.

2019-2021		$1,500	$2,200

D-16E/D-16E Mahogany

2017-present. Gloss Sikta spruce top, satin sycamore back and sides, Fishman electronics. Mahogany in '20.

2017-2020		$1,500	$2,200
2020-2024	Mahogany	$1,500	$2,200

D-16GT

1999-2019. D-16 with gloss top.

1999-2019		$1,000	$1,500

D-16GTE

1999-2015. D-16GT with Fishman electronics.

1999-2015		$1,200	$1,800

D-16H (1991, 1992, 1993)

1990-1994. D-16 with herringbone sound hole ring, replaced by D-16T in '94.

1990-1994		$1,500	$2,200

D-16K Koa

1986. Koa back and sides.

1986		$1,800	$2,800

D-16M Mahogany

1986-1990. Mahogany back and sides.

1986-1990		$1,200	$1,800

D-16O Oak

1999. Red oak or white oak, 4 made.

1999		$1,200	$1,800

D-16R/D-16TR/D-16TRG

1995-2009. Spruce top, Indian rosewood back and sides, satin finish (R), gloss (TR) or full gloss (TRG).

1995-2009		$1,500	$2,200

Martin D-10E

Martin D-13E

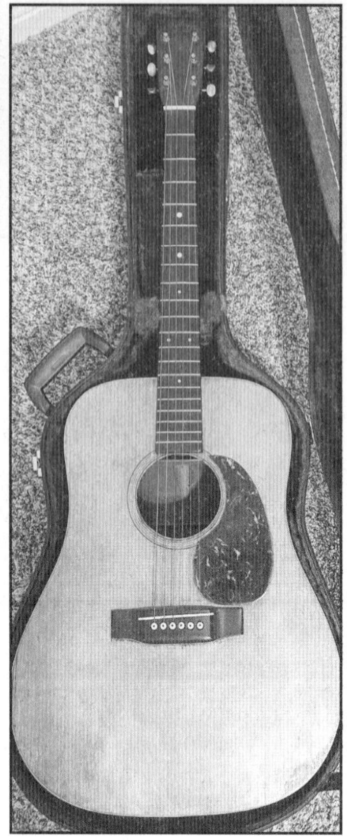
Martin D-18 Authentic 1937

1947 Martin D-18
Folkway Music

MODEL YEAR	FEATURES	EXC. COND. LOW	HIGH

D-16RGT

1999-2019. D-16 T specs with rosewood back and sides, gloss finish.

1999-2019		$1,000	$1,500

D-16RGT Ryman Auditorium

2007. Custom designed by George Gruhn, oak 'guard, headplate and fret markers made from original Ryman Auditorium pews, laser-etched image of Ryman on headplate, spruce top, Indian rosewood back and sides, special Ryman label.

2007		$2,500	$4,000

D-16T/D-16TG

1994-1998. Mahogany back and sides, satin finish (T) or gloss (TG).

1994-1998	T	$1,200	$1,800
1995-1997	TG	$1,000	$1,500

D-16W Walnut

1987, 1990. Walnut back and sides.

1987, 1990		$1,200	$1,800

D-17

2001-2005. All solid mahogany back, sides and top, natural brown mahogany finish.

2001-2005		$1,000	$1,500

D-17E

2002-2003. With on-board electronics.

2002-2003		$1,200	$1,800

D-17M

2013-2016. Shaded spruce top, solid mahogany back and sides.

2013-2016		$1,000	$1,500

D-18

1931-present. Standard Series, mahogany back and sides, spruce top, black back stripe, 12-fret neck, changed to 14 frets in '34.

1931-1934	12-fret	$90,000	$110,000
1934	14-fret, dark top	$140,000	$180,000
1934-1937	14-fret	$80,000	$100,000
1938	Early '38, Advanced X	$75,000	$95,000
1938	Late '38, Rear X	$55,000	$75,000
1939	Early '39, 175 neck	$50,000	$65,000
1939	Late '39, 168 neck	$40,000	$50,000
1940-1941		$40,000	$50,000
1942-1944	Scalloped	$35,000	$45,000
1944-1946	Non-scalloped	$25,000	$30,000
1947-1949		$11,000	$15,000
1950-1959		$8,500	$11,500
1960-1964		$6,000	$8,500
1965		$5,500	$7,500
1966-1969		$4,000	$5,500
1970-1979		$2,800	$4,000
1980-1989		$2,300	$3,000
1983	50th Ann 1833-1983	$2,300	$3,000
1990-1999		$2,300	$3,000
2000-2024		$2,000	$2,800

D12-18

1973-1995. Mahogany back and sides, 12 strings, 14 frets clear of body, solid headstock.

1973-1979		$2,000	$3,000
1980-1989		$1,800	$2,800
1990-1995		$1,800	$2,800

CS-D18-12

2012-2014. Custom Shop, based on 1929 Ditson 111 (12-string), 75 made, 12-fret mahogany neck, Adirondack spruce top, Madagascar rosewood binding.

2012-2014		$4,500	$6,500

D-18 1955 CFM IV

2010. Celebrates C. F. Martin IV birthday, 55 made.

2010		$4,000	$6,000

D-18 75th Anniversary Edition

2009. '75th Anniversary Edition 1934-2009' noted on label and headstock stencil.

2009		$3,000	$4,500

D-18 Andy Griffith

2003. Bear claw spruce top, Andy's script signature on 18th fret.

2003		$3,000	$4,500

D-18 Authentic 1937

2006-present. Authentic pre-war specs, Adirondack spruce, forward X-brace and scalloped Adirondack bracing, 14-fret neck.

2006-2024		$4,000	$6,000

D-18 Authentic 1939

2013-2024. Adirondack spruce top, mahogany back, sides and neck, ebony 'board, vintage gloss finish.

2013-2019		$4,000	$5,500
2019-2024	VTS	$4,500	$6,000

D-18 Authentic 1939 Aged

2020-2024. New design, Torrefied Adirondack.

2020-2024		$3,500	$5,500

D-18 Custom Adirondack

2016. Adirondack spruce top, mahogany back and sides.

2016		$3,000	$4,500

D-18 Del McCoury 50th Anniversary Custom Edition

2010. Adirondack spruce top, mahogany sides and back, interior label signed by Del McCourey, 50 made.

2010		$4,000	$6,000

D-18 Modern Deluxe

2019-present. Sikta spruce top with Vintage Tone System (VTS), mahogany back and sides, gloss finish.

2019-2024		$2,500	$3,800

D-18 Special

1989. Guitar of the Month, 28 made, first Martin to use rosewood for binding, heel cap and endpiece since 1932, scalloped top, mahogany back and sides, slotted-diamond markers.

1989		$3,000	$4,500

D-18CW Clarence White Commemorative Edition

2001. Rare Appalachian spruce top, 2-piece quilted mahogany back and sides, Clarence White's signature between 19th - 20th frets, aged gloss lacquer finish.

2001		$3,500	$5,500

D-18D

1975. Frap pickup.

1975		$2,500	$3,500

D-18DC David Crosby

2002. David Crosby signature at 20th fret, Englemann spruce top, quilted mahogany back and sides, 250 made.

2002		$4,000	$6,000

MODEL YEAR	FEATURES	EXC. COND. LOW	HIGH

D-18E

1958-1959. D-18 factory built with DeArmond pickups which required ladder bracing (reducing acoustic volume and quality).

1958-1959		$10,000	$15,000

D-18E 2020

2020. Limited Edition, 2,020 offered, Sikta spruce top, mahogany back and sides, electronics, gloss finish.

2020		$2,500	$3,500

D-18E Modern Deluxe

2020-2021. Torrified Sikta spruce top, Fishman electronics.

2020-2021		$3,000	$4,000

D-18E Retro

2012-2019. Sikta spruce top, mahogany back and sides.

2012-2019		$2,000	$3,000

D-18GE Golden Era

1995, 2000-2016. The 1995 version is a copy of a '37 D-18, 272 made. The current model is based on '34 model, natural or sunburst.

1995	320 made	$3,500	$5,000
2000-2016		$3,000	$4,500

D-18GE Golden Era 1934 Special Edition

1999-2012. Specs from '34 D-18, red Adirondack spruce top, mahogany back and sides, aged finish.

1999-2012		$3,500	$5,000

D-18GL Gordon Lightfoot

2001. Only 61 made, higher-end inlays and figured wood.

2001		$4,000	$6,000

D-18H

1934-1935. Hawaiian, 3 made.

1934-1935		$90,000	$125,000

D-18H Huda

1966. Huda wood, Hawaiian, 2 made.

1966		$5,000	$7,500

D-18LE

1986-1987. Limited Edition, 65 made, quilted or flamed mahogany back and sides, scalloped braces, gold tuners with ebony buttons.

1986-1987		$3,000	$4,500

D-18MB

1990. Limited Edition Guitar of the Month, flame maple binding, Engelmann spruce top signed by shop foremen, X-brace, total of 99 sold.

1990		$3,000	$4,500

D-18P

2010-2011. Fishman electronics.

2010-2011		$2,000	$3,000

D-18S

1967-1994. Mahogany back and sides, 12-fret neck, slotted headstock, majority of production before '77, infrequent after that.

1967-1969		$6,000	$9,000
1970-1979		$5,000	$7,500
1980-1989		$4,000	$6,000
1990-1994		$4,000	$6,000

D-18V/D-18 Vintage

1985 (V), 1992 (Vintage). Low-profile neck, scalloped braces, bound, total of 218 sold, Guitar of the Month in '85, Vintage Series in '92.

1985	V, 56 made	$3,500	$5,000
1992	Vintage	$3,000	$4,500

D-18VE

2004-2007. D-18 V with Fishman Ellipse.

2004-2007		$2,500	$3,500

D-18VM/D-18V/D-18VO

1995-2011. Vintage Series, 14-fret, mahogany (M) back and sides, tortoise binding, V-neck. M dropped from name in '99. Natural finish. 48 sunburst (D-18VO) made in '95.

1995	VO	$2,500	$3,500
1995-1998	VM	$2,800	$4,200
1999-2011	V	$2,500	$3,500

D-18VMS/D-18VS

1996-2011. Vintage Series, 12-fret version of D-18 VM/V, M dropped from name in '99.

1996-1999	VMS	$3,000	$4,500
2000-2011	VS	$2,800	$4,000

D-19

1977-1988. Deluxe mahogany dreadnought, optional mahogany top, multi-bound but unbound rosewood 'board.

1977-1979		$2,500	$3,500
1980-1988		$2,000	$3,000

D12-20

1964-1991. Mahogany back and sides, 12 strings, 12 frets clear of body, slotted headstock.

1964-1969		$2,500	$3,500
1970-1979		$2,200	$3,300
1980-1991		$2,000	$3,000

D-21

1955-1969. Brazilian rosewood back and sides, rosewood 'board, chrome tuners.

1955-1959		$11,500	$14,500
1960-1964		$10,000	$13,000
1965		$8,500	$11,000
1966-1969		$7,500	$10,000

D-21 Special/D-21S

2008-2020. Sikta spruce top, Indian rosewood back and sides, herringbone sound hole.

2008-2020		$2,500	$3,500

D-21JC Jim Croce Signature

1999-2000. Jim Croce signature and 1973 dime inlaid on neck, Indian rosewood back and sides, 73 made.

1999-2000		$3,500	$5,000

D-21JCB Jim Croce Limited Edition

1999-2001. Same as above but with Brazilian rosewood back and sides.

1999-2001		$8,000	$12,000

D-21LE

1985. Limited Edition, 75 made.

1985		$3,500	$5,500

D-25K

1980-1989. Dreadnought-size, Koa back and sides, spruce top.

1980-1989		$2,500	$3,500

D-25K2

1980-1989. Same as D-25K, but with Koa top and black 'guard.

1980-1989		$2,800	$4,200

1968 Martin D-12-20

W. H. Stephens

1956 Martin D-21

David Stone

1947 Martin D-28
Terry White

Martin D-28 Authentic 1937

MODEL YEAR	FEATURES	EXC. COND. LOW	HIGH

D-28

1931-present. Brazilian rosewood back and sides (changed to Indian rosewood in '70), '36 was the last year for the 12-fret model, '44 was the last year for scalloped bracing, '47 was the last year herringbone trim was offered, natural. Ultra high-end D-28 Martin guitar (pre-'47) valuations are very sensitive to structural and cosmetic condition. Finish wear and body cracks for ultra high-end Martin flat-tops should be evaluated on a case-by-case basis. Small variances within the 'excellent condition' category can lead to notable valuation differences.

1931-1936	12-fret	$300,000	$350,000
1934-1937	14-fret, dark top	$225,000	$275,000
1934-1937	14-fret	$175,000	$225,000
1938	Early '38, Advanced X	$175,000	$225,000
1938	Late '38, Rear X	$165,000	$215,000
1939	Early '39, 175 neck	$165,000	$215,000
1939	Late '39, 168 neck	$150,000	$175,000
1940-1941		$115,000	$150,000
1942	Scalloped	$115,000	$150,000
1943	Scalloped	$100,000	$125,000
1944	Scalloped, herringbone	$95,000	$120,000
1944-1945	Herringbone, non-scalloped	$47,500	$62,000
1946-1947	Early '47, herringbone, non-scalloped	$43,000	$55,000
1947-1949	Late '47, non-herringbone	$20,000	$28,000
1950-1952		$14,000	$20,000
1953-1957	Kluson	$14,000	$20,000
1958-1959	Grover	$14,000	$20,000
1960-1962		$9,500	$12,500
1963-1964		$9,000	$12,000
1965		$8,000	$10,500
1966-1969	Brazilian	$7,500	$10,000
1970-1979	Indian	$3,800	$5,000
1980-1989		$2,800	$4,000
1990-1999		$2,500	$3,500
2000-2009		$2,300	$3,000
2010-2017	Standard X	$2,300	$3,000
2018-2024	Forward-shifted X	$2,300	$3,000

D12-28

1970-2018. Indian rosewood back and sides, 12 strings, 14 frets clear of body, solid headstock.

1970-1979		$2,500	$3,800
1980-1989		$2,000	$3,000
1990-1999		$2,000	$3,000
2000-2018		$2,000	$3,000

D-28 1935 Special

1993. Guitar of the Month, 1935 features, Indian rosewood back and sides, peghead with Brazilian rosewood veneer.

1993		$3,500	$5,000

MODEL YEAR	FEATURES	EXC. COND. LOW	HIGH

D-28 1955 CFM IV

2009-2010. Limited Edition, 55 made celebrating Chris Martin IV birthyear 1955, Madagascar rosewood.

2009-2010		$4,500	$6,500

D-28 50th Anniversary

1983. Stamped inside '1833-1983 150th Anniversary', Indian rosewood back and sides.

1983		$3,000	$4,500

D-28 75th Anniversary

2009 only. Limited production celebrating 1934 to 2009, Madagascar rosewood back and sides, Adirondack spruce top.

2009		$4,000	$6,000

D-28 75th Anniversary Brazilian

1983. Brazilian rosewood back and sides.

1983		$8,000	$12,000

D-28 150th Anniversary

1983-1985. Limited production of 268, only '83 vintage have the anniversary stamp, Brazilian rosewood sides and back.

1983	150th stamp	$8,000	$12,000
1984-1985	No stamp	$7,500	$11,500

D-28 Authentic 1931

2013-2015. Adirondack spruce top, Madagascar rosewood back and sides, authentic '31 appointments, vintage gloss finish.

2013-2015		$4,500	$6,500

D-28 Authentic 1937

2005-2009, 2014-present. First 50 made with '37 specs and Brazilian rosewood. Reintroduced '14 with Madagascar rosewood and Vintage Tone System (VTS).

2005-2024		$10,000	$15,000

D-28 Authentic 1941

2013-2016. Adirondack, Madagascar rosewood.

2013-2016		$4,500	$6,500

D-28 Custom

1984. Guitar of the Month Nov. '84, double bound D-body, multi-ring rosette, rosewood back/sides, spruce top, 43 made.

1984		$4,000	$6,000

D-28 Dan Tyminski

2010-2013. Custom Artist limited edition, Indian rosewood back and sides, Adirondack spruce top, other bracing specs.

2010-2013		$3,500	$5,000

D-28CW/CWB Clarence White

2003-2014. CW has Indian rosewood back and sides, the CWB Brazilian, only 150 CWBs were to be built.

2003-2004	CWB	$8,000	$12,000
2003-2014	CW	$4,000	$6,000

D-28DM Del McCoury Signature

2003. Limited edition of 115, natural.

2003		$4,000	$6,000

D-28E

1959-1964. Electronics, Brazilian rosewood back and sides, 2 DeArmond pickups, natural.

1959-1964		$15,000	$22,500

GUITARS

MODEL YEAR	FEATURES	EXC. COND. LOW	HIGH

D-28E Modern Deluxe

2020-2021. Sikta spruce VTS aged top, East Indian rosewood back and sides, Fishman electronics, gloss finish.

2020-2021		$3,000	$4,000

D-28 Elvis Presley Commemorative Edition

2008-2010. Carpathian spruce top, East Indian rosewood back and sides, tooled leather cover.

2008-2010		$4,000	$6,000

D-28 Elvis Presley Limited Edition

2008-2010. Carpathian spruce top, East Indian rosewood back and sides.

2008-2010		$6,000	$8,000

D-28 John Lennon Signature Edition

2017-2018. Custom Signature Edition, Sikta spruce top with Vintage Tone System, East Indian rosewood back and sides, back inlaid with a peace sign, Lennon's self-portrait illustration beneath Martin logo on headstock.

2017-2018		$3,500	$5,000

D-28 John Lennon 75th Anniversary

2016. Limited Edition to commemorate Lennon's 75th birthday (10/9/2015), 75 made, Adirondack spruce top, Madagascar rosewood back and sides, headplate includes Lennon's famous self-portrait illustration.

2016		$7,000	$10,500

D-28 John Prine

2017-2020. Custom Signature Edition, only 70 offered, Engelmann spruce top, Madagascar rosewood back and sides, inlaid pearl angel wings on headstock.

2017-2020		$4,000	$6,000

D-28 Louvin Brothers

2015-2020. Limited run of 50, Sikta spruce top, East Indian rosewood back and sides, printed Louvin Brothers artwork from "Satan is Real" album.

2015-2020		$3,000	$4,500

D-28 Marquis

2004-2017. Golden Era appointments, Adirondack top, Indian rosewood, natural or sunburst.

2004-2017	Natural	$3,500	$5,000
2004-2017	Sunburst	$3,700	$5,500
2007-2009	Madagascar option	$4,500	$6,500

D-28 Modern Deluxe

2019-present. Sikta spruce top with Vintage Tone System (VTS), East Indian rosewood back and sides, gloss finish.

2019-2024		$2,800	$4,200

D-28 Museum Edition 1941

2009-2012. Based on '41 model located in Martin's PA museum, 48 made, Adirondack spruce top, Madagascar rosewood back and sides, natural finish.

2009-2012		$6,000	$8,500

D-28 Rich Robinson

2022-present. Custom Signature Edition, styled from Robinson's '54 D-28, Sikta spruce top, East Indian rosewood back and sides, aged vintage gloss finish.

2022-2024		$4,000	$6,000

MODEL YEAR	FEATURES	EXC. COND. LOW	HIGH

D-28GE Golden Era

1999-2005. GE Golden Era, Brazilian rosewood, herringbone trim.

1999-2005		$8,000	$12,000

D-28HW Hank Williams

1998. Limited Edition, 150 made, replica of Hank Williams' 1944 D-28, Brazilian rosewood sides and back, scalloped braces, herringbone.

1998		$8,000	$12,000

D-28KTBS Bob Shane

2003. Bob Shane of the Kingston Trio, Signature Edition with 51 offered, Sikta spruce top, East Indian rosewood back and sides, The Kingston Trio logo between 11th-13th frets, Shane's pearl signature 19th-20th frets.

2003		$4,500	$6,500

D-28LF Lester Flatt

1998. Limited Edition, 50 made, Brazilian rosewood.

1998		$8,000	$12,000

D-28LSH

1991. Guitar of the Month, Indian rosewood back and sides, herringbone trim, snowflake inlay, zigzag back stripe.

1991		$3,500	$5,000

D-28LSV

1999-2005. Large sound hole model.

1999-2005		$2,800	$4,000

D-28M Elvis Presley

2008-2010. Limited Edition, 175 made, Madagascar rosewood back and sides, Adirondack top, tooled leather cover.

2008-2010		$6,000	$8,500

D-28M Merle Travis

2008-2010. 100 made, Adirondack top, Madagascar rosewood back and sides, curly maple neck, 6-on-a-side Bigsby-style headstock, heart-diamond-spade-club inlays.

2008-2010		$5,000	$7,500

D-28M The Mamas and The Papas

2012-2014. Custom Artist, 100 made, Madagascar rosewood back and sides.

2012-2014		$3,500	$5,500

D-28P

1988-1990, 2011-2012. P indicates low-profile neck, Indian rosewood back and sides. Reintroduced 2011 with high performance neck.

1988-1990		$2,000	$3,000
2011-2012		$2,200	$3,300

D-28S

1954-1994. Rosewood back and sides, 12-fret neck.

1954-1959	Special order	$20,000	$25,000
1960-1965	Special order	$15,000	$20,000
1966-1969	Brazilian	$13,500	$18,000
1970-1979	Indian	$3,800	$5,500
1980-1989		$2,800	$4,000
1990-1994		$2,800	$4,000

D-28SW Wurlitzer

1962-1965, 1968. Made for the Wurlitzer Co.

1962-1965	Less than 30 made	$12,000	$18,000
1968		$10,000	$15,000

2009 Martin D-28 Elvis Presley Commemorative Edition

Imaged by Heritage Auctions, HA.com

Martin D-28 Modern Deluxe

GUITARS

1974 Martin D12-35

Peter Van Wagner

1968 Martin D-35S

David Stone

MODEL YEAR	FEATURES	EXC. COND. LOW	HIGH

D-28V

1983-1985. Limited Edition, Brazilian rosewood back and sides, herringbone trim, slotted diamond inlay.

YEAR	FEATURES	LOW	HIGH
1983-1985		$8,000	$12,000

D-35

1965-present. Brazilian rosewood sides and 3-piece back, changed to Brazilian wings and Indian center in '70, then all Indian rosewood in '71, natural with sunburst option. For a brief time, on the back side, the center panel was Brazilian and the two side panels were Indian.

YEAR	FEATURES	LOW	HIGH
1965	Brazilian	$9,500	$12,000
1966-1970	Brazilian	$9,000	$12,000
1970	Center panel only	$4,200	$5,500
1970-1979	Indian	$3,800	$5,000
1980-1989		$3,200	$4,500
1983	150th center strip	$3,200	$4,500
1990-1999		$2,800	$4,000
2000-2024		$2,800	$3,800
2015	50th Anniv Label	$2,800	$3,800

D12-35

1965-1995. Brazilian rosewood back and sides, changed to Indian rosewood in '70, 12 strings, 12 frets clear of body, slotted headstock.

YEAR	FEATURES	LOW	HIGH
1965-1969	Brazilian	$7,000	$10,000
1970-1979	Indian	$3,000	$4,500
1980-1989		$2,800	$4,200
1990-1995		$2,800	$4,200

D12-35 50th Anniversary Limited Edition

2015-2016. Limited to 183 (the quantity of 1st production run in '65), European spruce top, 3-piece East Indian rosewood back and sides, natural gloss finish.

YEAR	FEATURES	LOW	HIGH
2015-2016		$4,000	$6,000

D-35 30th Anniversary

1995. Limited Edition, 207 made, D-35 with '1965-1995' inlay on 20th fret, gold hardware.

YEAR	FEATURES	LOW	HIGH
1995		$3,500	$5,000

D-35 Bicentennial

1975-1976. Limited Edition, 197 made, Sikta spruce top, 3-piece Indian rosewood back, eagle inlay on headstock, 13 star inlay on 'board.

YEAR	FEATURES	LOW	HIGH
1975-1976		$3,500	$5,000

D-35 David Gilmour

2021. Custom Signature Artist Edition, 250 total split between both 6- and 12-string models.

YEAR	FEATURES	LOW	HIGH
2021	6-String	$4,500	$6,500

D-35 Ernest Tubb

2003. Indian rosewood back and sides, special inlays, 90 built.

YEAR	FEATURES	LOW	HIGH
2003		$4,000	$6,000

D-35 Seth Avett

2013-2019. Swiss spruce top, East Indian rosewood/flamed Koa back, copper snowflake inlay.

YEAR	FEATURES	LOW	HIGH
2013-2019		$3,000	$5,000

D-35E Retro

2012-2019. Sikta spruce top, East Indian rosewood back and sides.

YEAR	FEATURES	LOW	HIGH
2012-2019		$2,500	$3,500

D-35JC Johnny Cash

2006-present. Rosewood back and sides.

YEAR	FEATURES	LOW	HIGH
2006-2024		$3,000	$4,500

MODEL YEAR	FEATURES	EXC. COND. LOW	HIGH

D-35MP

2011-2012. Madagascar rosewood back and sides, high performance neck.

YEAR	FEATURES	LOW	HIGH
2011-2012		$3,000	$4,500

D-35P

1986-1990. P indicates low-profile neck.

YEAR	FEATURES	LOW	HIGH
1986-1990		$2,200	$3,300

D-35S

1966-1993. Brazilian rosewood back and sides, changed to Indian rosewood in '70, 12-fret neck, slotted peghead.

YEAR	FEATURES	LOW	HIGH
1966-1969	Brazilian	$10,000	$15,000
1970-1979	Indian	$4,000	$6,000
1980-1989		$3,500	$5,500
1990-1993		$2,800	$4,500

D-35SW Wurlitzer

1966, 1968. Made for the Wurlitzer Co., Brazilian rosewood.

YEAR	FEATURES	LOW	HIGH
1966, 1968		$10,000	$15,000

D-35V

1984. Limited Edition, 10 made, Brazilian rosewood back and sides.

YEAR	FEATURES	LOW	HIGH
1984		$8,000	$12,000

D-37K

1980-1994. Dreadnought-size, Koa back and sides, spruce top.

YEAR	FEATURES	LOW	HIGH
1980-1994		$2,500	$3,800

D-37K2

1980-1994. Same as D-37 K but has a Koa top and black 'guard.

YEAR	FEATURES	LOW	HIGH
1980-1994		$3,000	$4,500

D-37W Lucinda Williams

2003. Only 4 made, never put into production, Aztec pearl inlay favored by Lucinda Williams, quilted mahogany sides and back.

YEAR	FEATURES	LOW	HIGH
2003		$8,000	$12,000

D-40

1997-2005. Indian rosewood back and sides, hexagon inlays.

YEAR	FEATURES	LOW	HIGH
1997-2005		$2,500	$3,500

D-40BLE

1990. Limited Edition Guitar of the Month, 50 made, Brazilian rosewood back and sides, pearl top border except around 'board.

YEAR	FEATURES	LOW	HIGH
1990		$8,000	$12,000

D-40DM Don McLean

1998. Englemann spruce top, 71 made.

YEAR	FEATURES	LOW	HIGH
1998		$4,500	$6,500

D-40FMG

1995-1996. Figured mahogany back and sides, 150 made.

YEAR	FEATURES	LOW	HIGH
1995-1996		$3,500	$5,000

D-40FW Limited Edition

1996. Figured claro walnut sides and back, 'Limited Edition D-40FW' label, 148 made.

YEAR	FEATURES	LOW	HIGH
1996		$3,500	$5,000

D-40QM Limited Edition

1996. Limited Edition, 200 made, quilted maple body.

YEAR	FEATURES	LOW	HIGH
1996		$3,500	$5,000

GUITARS

MODEL YEAR	FEATURES	EXC. COND. LOW	HIGH

D-41

1969-present. Brazilian rosewood back and sides for the first ones in '69 then Indian rosewood, bound body, scalloped braces, natural.

1969	Brazilian	$25,500	$35,000
1970-1979	Indian	$4,500	$6,500
1980-1989		$4,000	$6,000
1990-1999		$4,000	$6,000
2000-2009		$4,000	$6,000
2010-2024		$3,800	$5,800

D-41 Porter Wagoner

2008-2011. Custom Artist series, 50 made, Indian rosewood back and sides.

2008-2011		$4,000	$6,000

D-41 Special

2004-2011. D-41 with snowflake inlays.

2004-2011		$4,000	$5,500

D-41A Turbo Mandolin Brothers

2011, 2013. Two Custom Shop models made for Mandolin Bros., Adirondack top. Similar except 10 40th Anniversary models which have abalone and pearl mandolin 12th-fret inlay and label signed by Stan Jay and Chris Martin.

2011		$4,500	$6,500

D-41DF Dan Fogelberg

2001. 141 made, East Indian rosewood back and sides, hexagon 'board inlays, pearl snowflakes inlaid on bridge.

2001		$4,500	$6,500

D-41GJ George Jones

2001. Style 41 appointments, limited run of 100, label signed by the Opossum.

2001		$4,500	$6,500

D-41K Purple Martin

2013-2020. Limited to 50 with labels signed by C.F. Martin IV, highly flamed Koa back and sides, purple martin-inspired inlay on 'board, bridge, and 'guard.

2013-2020		$8,500	$12,000

D-41LE

1989. Limited Edition Guitar of the Month, Brazilian rosewood back and sides, pearl top border except around 'board.

1989		$8,000	$12,000

D-41S/SD-41S

1970-1994. Sunburst, Indian rosewood, 12-fret neck, slotted peghead.

1970-1979		$4,500	$6,500
1980-1994		$4,000	$6,000

D-42

1973-1988, 1995-present. Limited production '73-'88, Indian rosewood back and sides, spruce top, pearl rosette and inlays, snowflake 'board inlays, gold tuners, gloss finish.

1995-2024		$4,000	$5,500

D-42E

1996-2008. With Fishman Ellipse VT pickup system.

1996-2008		$3,500	$5,000

D-42 Amazon Rosewood Limited Edition

2002-2003, 2007. Only 30 made in '02-'03 with Swiss spruce top, Amazon rosewood back and sides, abalone trim, natural finish. Run of 35 in '07 with Adirondack spruce top.

2002-2003	30 made	$6,000	$8,500
2007	35 made	$6,000	$8,500

D-42 Blackwood

2009-2010. Limited Edition, 10 made, Adirondack spruce top, Tasmanian blackwood back and sides, abalone trim, natural.

2009-2010		$6,500	$9,500

D-42 Flamed Mahogany

2006. Adirondack, figured mahogany, 30 made with tree-of-life inlay.

2006		$6,000	$8,500

D-42 Peter Frampton

2006-2007. Indian rosewood back and sides, Style 45 features.

2006-2007		$5,000	$7,500

D-42 Purple Martin Flamed Myrtle

2018-2021. Flamed myrtle back and sides, limited to 100 made.

2018-2021		$8,500	$12,000

D-42JC Johnny Cash

1997. Rosewood back and sides, gloss black lacquer on body and neck, Cash signature inlaid at 19th fret, have label signed by Cash and C.F. Martin IV, 80 sold.

1997		$5,000	$7,500

D-42K Limited Edition

1998. Limited production, highly flamed Koa back and sides, Sikta top with aging toner, high X-brace design, 45-style abalone snowflake inlays.

1998		$4,000	$6,000

D-42K/D-42K2

1998-2006. K has Koa back and sides, the all Koa body K2 was discontinued in '05.

1998-2006	D-42K	$4,000	$6,000
2000-2005	D-42K2	$4,500	$6,500

D-42LE

1988 only. Limited Edition (75 sold), D-42-style, scalloped braces, low profile neck.

1988		$5,500	$8,500

D-42SB

2006-2007. Sunburst finish, Sikta spruce top, 45-style appointments.

2006-2007		$4,500	$6,000

D-42V

1985. Vintage Series, 12 made, Brazilian rosewood, scalloped braces.

1985		$10,000	$15,000

D-45

1933-1942 (96 made), 1968-present. Brazilian rosewood back and sides, changed to Indian rosewood during '69. The pre-WW II D-45 is one of the holy grails. A pre-war D-45 should be evaluated on a case-by-case basis. The price ranges are for all-original guitars in excellent condition and are guidance pricing only. These ranges are for a crack-free guitar. Unfortunately, many older acoustics have a crack or two and this can make ultra-expensive acoustics more difficult to evaluate than ultra-expensive solidbody electrics. Technically, a repaired body crack makes a guitar non-original, but the vintage market generally considers a professionally repaired crack to be original. Crack width, length and

Martin D-41

2000 Martin D-42
Rivington Guitars

GUITARS

1941 Martin D-45

1968 Martin D-45
Wayne Stephens

MODEL YEAR	FEATURES	EXC. COND. LOW	HIGH

depth can vary, therefore extra attention is suggested.

YEAR	FEATURES	LOW	HIGH
1936-1938		$550,000	$675,000
1939	Early, wide neck	$550,000	$675,000
1939	Late, thin neck	$500,000	$600,000
1940-1942		$450,000	$550,000
1968	European spruce, Brazilian	$55,000	$70,000
1969	Sikta, Brazilian	$50,000	$65,000
1970-1979		$9,000	$12,000
1980-1989		$9,000	$12,000
1990-1999		$8,500	$11,000
2000-2017		$8,500	$11,000
2018-2024	New specs	$8,500	$11,000

D12-45

1970s-1987. Special order instrument, not a standard catalog item, with D-45 appointments, Indian rosewood.

YEAR	FEATURES	LOW	HIGH
1970-1979		$7,000	$10,000
1980-1987		$6,500	$9,500

D-45 100th Anniversary Limited Edition

1996. Label reads '1896-1996 C.F. Martin Commemorative Anniversary Model'.

1996		$10,000	$15,000

D-45 150th Anniversary

1983. Brazilian rosewood back and sides, Sikta spruce top, '150th' logo stamp.

1983		$20,000	$30,000

D-45CFMB CMR Sr. (200th Anniversary, Brazilian)

1996. Commemorating the 200th Anniversary of C.F. Martin Sr. birthday, Brazilian rosewood back and sides, style 45 Deluxe pearl bordering, fossilized ivory nut and saddle, 14-fret neck, gold hardware.

1996		$25,000	$40,000

D-45CFM CMR Sr. (200th Anniversary, East Indian)

1996. Commemorating the 200th Anniversary of C.F. Martin Sr. birthday, East Indian rosewood back and sides, style 45 pearl bordering, bone nut and saddle, 14-fret neck, gold hardware.

1996		$12,000	$18,000

D-45 (1939 Reissue Mandolin Brothers)

1990. Commissioned by Mandolin Brothers, 5 made, figured Brazilian rosewood. Original name "The Reissue 1939 Martin D-45." Said to be the first reissue of the era and the seed for the '90s Martin Custom Shop.

1990		$25,000	$40,000

D-45 (1939 Reissue)

1992. High-grade spruce top, figured Brazilian rosewood back and sides, high X and scalloped braces, abalone trim, natural, gold tuners.

1992		$20,000	$35,000

D-45 Celtic Knot

2004-2005. Brazilian rosewood, Celtic knot 'board inlays, 30 built.

2004-2005		$25,000	$40,000

D-45 Custom Shop

1984, 1991-1992. Various options and models, Indian rosewood back and sides in '84, then Brazilian rosewood.

YEAR	FEATURES	LOW	HIGH
1984	Indian	$8,000	$12,000
1991-1992	Brazilian	$20,000	$35,000

D-45 Deluxe

1993 only. Guitar of the Month, Brazilian rosewood back and sides, figured spruce top, inlay in bridge and 'guard, tree-of-life inlay on 'board, pearl borders and back stripe, gold tuners with large gold buttons, total of 60 sold.

1993		$15,000	$25,000

D-45 Deluxe CFM Sr. (200th Anniversary, Brazilian)

1996. Commemorating the 200th Anniversary of C.F. Martin Sr. birthday, 91 made, Brazilian rosewood back and sides, style 45 Deluxe pearl bordering, fossilized-ivory nut and saddle, 14-fret neck, gold hardware.

1996		$15,000	$25,000

D-45 Gene Autry

1994 only. Gene Autry inlay (2 options available), natural.

YEAR	FEATURES	LOW	HIGH
1994	Gene Autry 'board	$20,000	$30,000
1994	Snowflake 'board option	$20,000	$30,000

D-45 Marquis

2006-2008. Rosewood back and sides.

2006-2008		$8,000	$12,000

D-45 Mike Longworth Commemorative Edition

2004-2006. East Indian rosewood back and sides, Adirondack spruce top, 91 made, label signed by Mike's wife Sue and C.F. Martin IV.

2004-2006		$12,000	$18,000

D-45 Woodstock 50th Anniversary

2019-2020. Limited Edition, run of 50, East Indian rosewood back and sides, abalone inlay, Woodstock dove on headstock, '1969-2019' on 'board, peace sign on heelcap.

2019-2020		$8,000	$12,000

D-45B Brazilian

1994. Brazilian rosewood.

1994		$20,000	$35,000

D-45E Aura

2010. With Fishman Electronics Ellipse Aura technology.

2010		$6,000	$9,000

D-45E Retro

2013-2019. East Indian rosewood, Fishman.

2013-2019		$6,000	$9,000

D-45GE Golden Era

2001-2004. 167 made, '37 specs, Brazilian rosewood.

2001-2004		$25,000	$40,000

D-45K

2006-2008. Flamed Koa back and sides.

2006-2008		$12,000	$20,000

D-45KLE

1991. Limited Edition Koa, Engelmann, bear claw, 54 made.

1991		$10,000	$15,000

D-45LE

1987. Limited Edition, 44 made, Guitar of the Month, September '87.

1987		$20,000	$35,000

GUITARS

MODEL YEAR	FEATURES	EXC. COND. LOW	HIGH

D-45S Authentic 1936

2013-present. Adirondack spruce top, Vintage Tone System, Brazilian rosewood back and sides, '36 style appointments and specs.

2013-2024		$35,000	$50,000

D-45S Deluxe

1992. Limited Edition, 50 made, Indian rosewood, spruce top, high-end appointments.

1992		$9,000	$13,500

D-45S/SD-45S

1969-1994. Brazilian rosewood back and sides in '69, Indian rosewood after, 12-fret neck, S means slotted peghead, only 50 made.

1969	Brazilian	$40,000	$60,000
1970-1979	Indian	$10,000	$15,000
1980-1994	Indian	$9,500	$12,000

D-45SS Steven Stills

1998. Brazilian rosewood back and sides, 91 made.

1998		$30,000	$50,000

D-45V Brazilian

1983. Brazilian rosewood back and sides, scalloped braces, snowflake inlay, natural.

1983		$20,000	$35,000

D-45VR/D-45V

1997-2020. Vintage specs, Indian rosewood back and sides, vintage aging toner, snowflake inlay. Name changed to D-45V in '99 (not to be confused with Brazilian rosewood D-45V of the '80s).

1997-1998	VR	$8,000	$12,000
1999-2020	V	$7,500	$10,000

D-50 Deluxe/D-50DX

2001-2003. Deluxe limited edition, 50 made, one of the most ornate Martin models ever made, Brazilian rosewood back and sides, highly ornate pearl inlay.

2001-2003		$30,000	$45,000

D-50K Deluxe/D-50K2 Deluxe

2003-2006. As D-50 Deluxe with ornate pearl inlay and highly flamed Koa back and sides (K, 45 made) or highly flamed Koa top, back and sides (K2, 5 made).

2003-2006	K Deluxe	$30,000	$45,000
2003-2006	K2 Deluxe	$30,000	$45,000

D-60

1989-1995. Birdseye maple back and sides, snowflake inlays, tortoiseshell binding and 'guard.

1989-1995		$3,500	$5,500

D-62

1987-1995. Flamed maple back and sides, chrome-plated enclosed Schaller tuners.

1987-1995		$3,500	$5,500

D-62LE

1986. Limited Edition, Guitar of the Month October '86, flamed maple back and sides, spruce top, snowflake inlays, natural.

1986		$3,500	$5,500

D-64LE

1985-1995. Flamed maple top, low profile neck.

1985-1995		$3,500	$5,500

D-76 Bicentennial Limited Edition

1975-1976. Limited to 200 made in '75 and 1,976 made in '76, Indian rosewood back and sides, 3-piece back, herringbone back stripe, pearl stars on 'board, eagle on peghead.

1975-1976		$6,000	$10,000

D-93

1993. Mahogany, spruce, 93 pertains to the year, not a style number.

1993		$2,000	$3,000

D-100 Deluxe

2004. Limited Edition, guitars have the first 50 sequential serial numbers following the millionth Martin guitar (1,000,001 to 1,000,050), fancy pearl inlay on back, 'guard, headstock, 'board and bridge. Herringbone top and rosette inlay, Adirondack spruce top, Brazilian rosewood back and sides.

2004		$50,000	$65,000

D-200 Deluxe

2017-present. Celebration of Martin's two-millionth serial number, limited to 50 offered, watch-themed highly decorative, comes with renowned watchmaker Roland G Murphy watch with matching serial no., premium case has built-in hygrometer.

2017-2024		$95,000	$120,000

D-222 100th Anniversary

2016. Commemorates 100th anniversary of the dreadnought, limited to 100, Sikta spruce top, mahogany back and sides, ivoroid binding, slotted headstock.

2016		$4,000	$6,000

D-420

2017-2019. Top with custom legal weed illustration by artist Robert Goetzl, mahogany back and sides.

2017-2019		$2,500	$4,000

D-3532 Shenandoah

1984-1993. Dreadnought, built-in electronics, spruce top, rosewood back and sides, natural.

1984-1993		$1,000	$1,500

DJr / DJrE

2015-2018. Dreadnought Junior, Sikta spruce top, sapele back and sides. DJrE with Fishman electronics.

2015-2018	No electronics	$500	$800
2015-2018	With electronics	$600	$900

DJr-10 / DJr-10E

2020-present. Dreadnought Junior, thinner 000-sized body, Sikta spruce or sapele top, satin sapele back and sides. Fishman electronics available (DJr-10E).

2020-2024	No electronics	$500	$800
2020-2024	With electronics	$600	$900

DJr-10E StreetMaster

2021-present. Dreadnought Junior with thinner body and tapered neck, Fishman electronics, dark mahogany finish.

2021-2024		$600	$900

DC Series

1980s-2021. Dreadnought cutaway versions, E models have electronics, GT is gloss top, R indicates rosewood back and sides. Replaced by DC-X Series starting in '20.

1981-1997	DC-28	$2,500	$4,000
1996-2010	DC-1E	$700	$1,000
1997-2000	DCM	$600	$900
1997-2005	DC-1M	$600	$900
1997-2006	DCME	$700	$1,000

Martin D-45S Authentic 1936

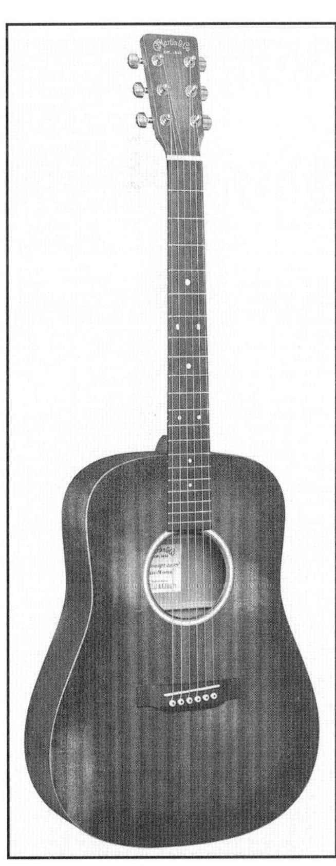

Martin DJr-10E StreetMaster

GUITARS

Martin DC-X2E

Martin DR Centennial LE

MODEL YEAR	FEATURES	EXC. COND. LOW	HIGH
1998	DCXM	$500	$800
1998-2001	DCXME	$500	$800
1998-2010	DC-15E	$700	$1,000
1999-2000	DC-1R	$600	$900
2000	DCRE	$700	$1,000
2000-2013	DCX1E	$500	$800
2001-2005	DCXE Black	$500	$800
2002-2003	DC-16RE	$700	$1,000
2003-2005	DC-16GTE Premium	$1,200	$1,800
2003-2016	DC-16GTE	$1,000	$1,500
2003-2019	DC-16E	$1,000	$1,500
2004-2013	DCX1KE	$500	$800
2004-2013	DCX1RE	$500	$800
2005	DC Trey Anastasio	$4,500	$7,000
2005	DC-16RE Aura	$800	$1,200
2005	DC-16RGTE Aura	$1,000	$1,500
2005-2007	DC-16E Koa	$1,000	$1,500
2005-2008	DC-16RGTE	$1,000	$1,500
2005-2010	DC-Aura	$2,200	$3,300
2006-2019	DC-28E	$2,200	$3,300
2009-2016	DCPA1/ DCPA1 Plus	$2,000	$3,000
2011	DCPA2/DCPA3	$1,000	$1,500
2011-2016	DCPA4 Shaded	$1,000	$1,500
2011-2017	DCPA4 Rosewood	$1,200	$1,800
2013-2016	DCPA5	$500	$800
2013-2016	DCPA5 Black	$500	$800
2013-2016	DCPA5K Koa	$500	$800
2016-2019	DC-15ME	$700	$1,000
2016-2019	DC-35E	$2,200	$3,300
2017-2018	DCRSG	$800	$1,200
2017-2019	DC-18E	$2,000	$3,000
2017-2019	DCPA4	$1,000	$1,500
2017-2019	DCX1AE/ DCX1AE Macassar	$500	$800
2017-2019	DCX1RAE	$500	$800
2019-2021	DC-13E	$600	$900

DC-X Series

2020-present. Replaces the DC Series, dreadnought models with various woods, some with electronics.

2020-2022	DC-X2E	$500	$850

Ditson Dreadnaught 111

2007-2009. Based on 1929 Ditson 111, 12-fret neck, slot head, mahogany back and sides, Brazilian rosewood binding.

2007-2009		$4,000	$6,000

DM

1996-2009. Solid Sikta spruce top, laminated mahogany back and sides, dot markers, natural satin.

1996-2009		$500	$800

DM-12

1996-2009. 12-string DM.

1996-2009		$600	$900

DM3MD Dave Matthews

1999-2001. Three-piece back of Indian rosewood, African padauk center wedge, Englemann spruce top, high-end appointments.

1999-2001		$4,000	$6,500

Doobie-42 Tom Johnston

2007. Signature Edition, D-42 style, 35 made, solid Indian rosewood back and sides, abalone and catseye markers, other special appointments.

2007		$5,000	$8,000

DR

1997-2008. Road Series Dreadnought, rosewood back and sides.

1997-2008		$600	$900

DR Centennial LE

2016-2020. Limited Edition celebrates '100 Years of the Dreadnought', Adirondack, East Indian rosewood, antique white binding, satin finish.

2016-2020		$2,500	$4,500

DRS1 (Road/1 Series)

2011-2019. D-size, sapele top, back and sides, satin finish, Fishman. Replaced by D-10E in '19.

2011-2019		$600	$900

DRS2 (Road/1 Series)

2012-2018. DRS1 with spruce top. Replaced by D-10E in '19.

2012-2018		$700	$1,000

DRSG

2017-2018. Sikta spruce top, siris back and sides, Fishman Sonitone. Replaced by D-13E in '19.

2017-2018		$800	$1,200

DRSGT

2014-2015. Sikta spruce top, sapele back and sides, Fishman with USB port.

2014-2015		$700	$1,000

DSR Sugar Ray

2003. Limited Edition of 57 made, D-17 style, all mahogany, signed by C.F. Martin IV and all members of Sugar Ray band.

2003		$4,000	$6,000

DSS-17

2018-present. Slope-shoulder dreadnought, Sikta spruce top, mahogany back and sides with antique white binding, satin Black Smoke or Whiskey Sunset Burst.

2018-2019	Black Smoke	$1,200	$1,800
2019-2024	Whiskey Sunset	$1,300	$2,000

DVM Veterans

2002-2008. D-style, spruce top, rosewood back and sides, special veterans' ornamentation.

2002-2008		$2,000	$3,500

Dwight Yoakam DD28

2017-2018. Custom Signature Edition, Sikta spruce top, East Indian rosewood back and sides, inlaid mother-of-pearl and recon stone playing cards.

2017-2018		$3,000	$5,000

DX 175th Anniversary

2008. Rosewood HPL back and sides, founder's picture on top.

2008		$500	$800

DX Johnny Cash

2019-present. D-sized, Jett black HPL top, back and sides, custom 'board inlaid with stars and CASH logo, Cash's signature on rosette and label, Fishman electronics.

2019-2024		$800	$1,200

GUITARS

MODEL YEAR	FEATURES	EXC. COND. LOW	HIGH

DX Series

1996-2020. D-size, high pressure wood laminate (HPL) backs and sides, exterior wood-grain image with gloss finish. M is for mahogany woodgrain, R rosewood and K Koa. A 1 indicates a solid spruce top with Series 1 bracing, otherwise the top is wood-patterned HPL. C indicates cutaway and E Fishman Presys Plus and AE Fishman Sonitone. Replaced by D-X Series starting in '20.

1996-2009	DXM / DMX	$450	$700
1998-2012	DXME	$450	$700
1999-2000	D12XM 12-String	$450	$700
1999-2019	DXMAE	$450	$700
2000-2014	DX1 / DX1E	$400	$600
2000-2019	DX1AE	$450	$700
2001-2009	DX1R	$450	$700
2002-2009	DXK2	$450	$700
2004-2009	DX1K	$450	$700
2008-2010	D12X1 12-String	$450	$700
2010-2020	DX1KAE	$450	$700
2011-2019	D12X1AE 12-String	$500	$800
2014-2019	DXAE Black	$450	$700
2014-2020	DXK2AE	$450	$700
2015-2019	DX1RAE	$450	$700
2017	DX420	$950	$1,500
2017-2019	DX2AE Macassar	$450	$700

D-X Series

2020-present. New spec dreadnought models to replace the DX Series. Various options, woods and finishes.

2020-2024	D-X1E	$500	$800
2020-2024	D-X2E	$550	$900
2020-2024	D-X2E 12-String	$600	$1,000

E-18

1979-1983. Offset double-cut, maple and rosewood laminate solidbody, 2 DiMarzio pickups, phase switch, natural.

1979-1983		$1,500	$2,500

E-28

1980-1983. Double-cut electric solidbody, carved top, ebony 'board, 2 humbuckers.

1980-1983		$1,800	$2,800

EM-18

1979-1983. Offset double-cut, maple and rosewood laminate solidbody, 2 exposed-coil humbucking pickups, coil split switch.

1979-1983		$1,500	$2,500

EMP-1

1998-1999. Employee series designed by Martin employee team, cutaway solid spruce top, ovangkol wood back and sides with rosewood middle insert (D-35-style insert), on-board pickup.

1998-1999		$2,000	$2,500

EMP-2 Limited Edition

1999. D size, tzalam body, flying saucer inlays.

1999		$1,500	$2,200

F-1

1940-1942. Archtop, mahogany back and sides, carved spruce top, multi-bound, f-holes, sunburst, 91 made.

1940-1942		$4,500	$6,500

F-1-12

1941. F-1 12 string.

1941		$4,000	$6,000

F-2

1940-1942. Carved spruce top, maple or rosewood back and sides, multi-bound, f-holes, 46 made.

1940-1942		$5,000	$7,500

F-5

1940. 2 made.

1940		$8,000	$12,000

F-7

1935-1939, 1941-1942. Brazilian rosewood back and sides, f-holes, carved top, back arched by braces, multi-bound, sunburst top finish.

1935-1938		$10,000	$15,000
1941-1942		$9,500	$14,500

F-9

1935-1942. Highest-end archtop, Brazilian rosewood, Martin inlaid vertically on headstock, 7-ply top binding, 45-style back strip, sunburst.

1935-1942		$20,000	$30,000

F-50

1961-1965. Single-cut thinline archtop with laminated maple body, 1 pickup.

1961-1965		$2,000	$3,000

F-55

1961-1965. Single-cut thinline archtop with laminated maple body, 2 pickups.

1961-1965		$3,000	$4,500

F-65

1961-1965. Electric archtop, double-cut, f-holes, 2 pickups, square-cornered peghead, Bigsby, sunburst.

1961-1965		$3,000	$4,500

Felix The Cat

2004-2010. Felix the Cat logo art, Don Oriolo logo, red body, Felix gig bag.

2004	Felix I, 756 made	$600	$900
2005-2006	Felix II, 625 made	$600	$900
2007-2010	Felix III, 1000 made	$600	$900

GCD-16CP (Guitar Center)

1998. 15 5/8" Style D.

1998		$1,500	$2,500

GPC Series

2010-present. Standard Series (GPC-), Performing Artist (GPCPA) and X Series (GPCX), Grand Performance size, cutaway, acoustic/electric, various woods.

2010-2016	GPCPA1/Plus	$2,000	$3,000
2011	GPCPA2	$1,200	$1,800
2011-2012	GPCPA3	$1,200	$1,800
2012-2016	GPCPA5K Koa	$450	$700
2013-2016	GPCPA4	$1,000	$1,500
2013-2016	GPCPA5	$450	$700
2013-2016	GPCPA5 Black	$450	$700
2013-2019	GPC12PA4 12-string	$1,000	$1,500
2013-2019	GPCPA4 Rosewood	$1,000	$1,500
2013-2019	GPCPA4 Sapele	$1,200	$1,800
2016-2018	GPC-35E	$2,200	$3,300
2016-2020	GPC-18E	$2,200	$3,300
2016-2020	GPC-28E	$2,200	$3,300

Martin DSS-17

Martin GPC-13E

1966 Martin GT-75
Izzy Miller

Martin HD12-28

MODEL YEAR	FEATURES	EXC. COND. LOW	HIGH
2017-2018	GPC-15ME	$1,000	$1,500
2017-2018	GPCRSG	$800	$1,200
2017-2018	GPCRSGT	$600	$900
2017-2018	GPCXAE Black	$400	$600
2017-2019	GPCX1RAE	$425	$650
2017-2021	GPCX1AE	$425	$650
2017-2021	GPCX2AE Macassar	$425	$650
2017-2024	GPC-X2E	$550	$850
2019-2024	GPC-11E	$750	$1,200
2019-2024	GPC-13E	$850	$1,200
2020-2021	GPC-16E Rosewood	$1,200	$1,800
2020-2024	GPC-16E	$1,200	$1,800

Grand J12-40E Special

2009-2011. J12-40 with D-TAR Multi-source electronics.

2009-2011		$3,000	$4,000

Grand J-28LSE

2011-2014. Baritone.

2011-2014		$2,500	$3,500

Grand J-35E

2009-2011. Grand jumbo size, rosewood back and sides.

2009-2011		$2,500	$3,500

Grand Ole Opry/HDO Grand Ole Opry

1999-2007. Custom Shop Limited Edition, 650 made, 'Grand Ole Opry 75th Anniversary' on neck block, WSM microphone headstock logo, off-white Micarta fingerboard, Sikta spruce top, East Indian rosewood back and sides.

1999-2007		$3,500	$5,500

Gruhn 50th Anniversary 0000 (Custom Shop)

2020. Celebrates Gruhn Guitar 50 years in business, interior label signed by George Gruhn, 12- or 14-fret, limited to 50 each in natural or sunburst.

2020		$5,000	$8,000

GT-70

1965-1966. Electric archtop, bound body, f-holes, single-cut, 2 pickups, tremolo, burgundy or black finish.

1965-1966		$2,500	$3,500

GT-75

1965-1967. Electric archtop, bound body, f-holes, double-cut, 2 pickups, tremolo, burgundy or black finish. There is also a 12-string version.

1965-1967		$3,000	$4,000

Hawaiian X

2002-2004. Hawaiian scene painted on top, similar to the Cowboy guitar model, limited edition of 500.

2002-2004		$800	$1,200

HD-7 Roger McGuinn

2005-2008. Rosewood back and sides, herringbone top trim, 7-string with double G.

2005-2008		$3,500	$5,500

HD12-28

2018-present. Sikta spruce top, East Indian rosewood back and sides, natural.

2018-2024		$2,500	$3,500

HD-16R Adirondack

2008-2016. Rosewood back and sides, Adirondack top.

2010-2016		$2,200	$3,500

HD-16R LSH

2007-2013. Indian rosewood (R), large sound hole (LSH).

2007-2013		$2,000	$3,000

HD-18JB Jimmy Buffett

1998. 424 made, solid mahogany back and sides, herringbone trim, palm tree headstock logo, Style 42 markers, Buffett pearl signature.

1998		$5,000	$8,000

HD-18LE

1987. Indian rosewood.

1987		$3,000	$5,000

HD-28

1976-present. Standard Series, Indian rosewood back and sides, scalloped bracing, herringbone purfling, sunburst. Ambertone added in '22.

1976-1979		$3,500	$5,000
1980-1989		$2,500	$4,000
1990-1999		$2,000	$3,500
2000-2017	Last Standard X	$2,000	$3,000
2018-2024	Forward X	$2,200	$3,200

HD-28 1935 Special

1993. 'HD-28 1935 Special' model name on label.

1993		$3,500	$5,500

HD-28 2R

1991, 1993-1997. 2R specification for 2 herringbone sound hole rings, larger sound hole.

1991-1997		$3,000	$5,000

HD-28 Custom 150th Anniversary

1983. 150th Anniversary, Martin Custom Shop, Indian rosewood sides and back, '1833-1983 150th Year' stamped on inside backstrip.

1983		$4,000	$6,000

HD-28 Custom/Custom HD-28

1994. Custom Shop model.

1994-1995		$3,000	$4,500

HD-28AWB Custom

2008-2013. Elderly Instruments Custom model, Adirondack spruce top, rosewood back and sides, white-bound body, gloss natural finish.

2008-2013		$3,000	$4,500

HD-28BLE

1990. Guitar of the Month, 100 made, Brazilian rosewood back and sides, herringbone sound hole ring, low profile neck (LE), chrome tuners, aging toner finish.

1990		$10,000	$15,000

HD-28BSE

1987-1999. Brazilian rosewood, 93 made.

1987-1999		$10,000	$15,000

HD-28CTB

1992. Guitar of the Month, herringbone top trim/back stripe, fancy peghead inlay, tortoise binding, gold hardware, label signed by CF Martin IV.

1992		$3,500	$5,000

HD-28E Retro

2013-2019. Solid Sikta spruce top, East Indian rosewood back and sides.

2013-2019		$2,500	$3,500

MODEL YEAR	FEATURES	EXC. COND. LOW	HIGH

HD-28GM

1989. Grand Marquis, Guitar of the Month, scalloped braced Sikta spruce top with 1930s-era bracing pattern that replaced the X-brace below the sound hole, herringbone top purfling, sound hole ring and back stripe, gold tuners.

1989		$3,500	$5,500

HD-28GM LSH

1994. Grand Marquis, Guitar of the Month, rosewood back and sides, large sound hole with double herringbone rings, snowflake inlay in bridge, natural (115 made) or sunburst (36 made).

1994		$3,500	$5,500

HD-28KM Keb Mo

2001-2002. Signature Edition, Hawaiian Koa back and sides, 252 made.

2001-2002		$4,000	$6,000

HD-28LE

1985. Limited Edition, Guitar of the Month, rosewood back and sides, scalloped bracing, herringbone top purfling, diamonds and squares 'board inlay, V-neck.

1985		$3,500	$5,500

HD-28LSV

1997-2005. Vintage Series, large diameter soundhole, patterned after Clarence White's modified '35 D-28.

1997-2005		$2,500	$3,500

HD-28LSVA

2005. Custom Shop, Adirondack spruce top with aging toner, high X-brace, large soundhole, rosewood back and sides.

2005		$3,000	$4,500

HD-28M

1988. Standard profile.

1988		$2,500	$4,000

HD-28MP

1990-1991, 2011-2012. Bolivian rosewood back and sides, herringbone top trim, low profile neck. Reissued in 2011 with Madagascar rosewood and modern-style neck.

1990-1991		$2,500	$4,000
2011-2012		$3,000	$4,000

HD-28P

1987-1989. Rosewood back and sides, scalloped braces, herringbone, low profile neck (P), zigzag back stripe.

1987-1989		$2,500	$4,000

HD-28PSE

1988. Signature Edition, Guitar of the Month, rosewood back and sides, signed by C.F. Martin IV and foremen, scalloped braces, herringbone top purfling, low profile neck, squared peghead, ebony tuner buttons.

1988		$3,500	$5,500

HD-28S Custom

1995. Slotted headstock.

1995		$3,000	$4,500

HD-28SB/HD-28 Ambertone/ HD-28SB-AMB

2016-2022. Sikta, East Indian rosewood, natural, sunburst or ambertone. SB and Ambertone dropped from name in '22 and ambertone finish added to HD-28.

2016-2022		$2,500	$3,500

MODEL YEAR	FEATURES	EXC. COND. LOW	HIGH

HD-28SE

1986-1987. Signature Edition, rosewood back and sides, signed by C. F. Martin and foremen/supervisors, '87 model was a Guitar of the Month with Brazilian rosewood.

1986		$3,000	$4,500
1987	Brazilian	$7,500	$12,000

HD-28SO Sing Out!

1996. Limited edition, 45 made, Indian rosewood back and sides.

1996		$3,500	$5,500

HD-28V Custom

2007-2012. Indian rosewood back and sides, Adirondack top, wide nut, Elderly Instruments special issue.

2007-2012		$3,500	$5,000

HD-28V/HD-28VR

1996-2019. 14-fret, Indian rosewood body, R dropped from name in '99.

1996-1999	HD-28VR	$2,500	$3,500
2000-2019	HD-28V	$2,200	$3,200

HD-28VE

2004-2006. HD-28 V with Fishman Ellipse Blend system.

2004-2006		$2,500	$3,500

HD-28VS

1996-2016. Slotted headstock, 12-fret, spruce top with aging toner, Indian rosewood sides and back.

1996-2016		$3,000	$4,500

HD-35

1978-present. Indian rosewood back and sides, herringbone top trim, zipper back stripe.

1978-1979		$3,500	$5,000
1980-1999		$2,500	$4,000
2000-2024		$2,200	$3,200

HD-35 CFM IV 60th

2016-2020. Celebrates C.F. Martin IV's 60th birthday, limited to 60, European spruce top, 3-piece back of siris wings and East Indian rosewood wedge, personally signed label.

2016-2020		$6,500	$8,500

HD-35 Custom

2009. Custom Designed on neck block, Adirondack spruce top, East Indian rosewood sides and back.

2009		$3,000	$4,500

HD-35 Nancy Wilson

2006-2007. Englemann spruce top, 3-piece back with bubinga center wedge, 101 made.

2006-2007		$4,000	$6,000

HD-35P

1987-1989. HD-35 with low profile neck.

1987-1989		$2,500	$4,000

HD-35SJC Judy Collins Signature Edition

2002. Collins signature headstock logo, wildflower headstock inlay, East Indian rosewood, 3-piece back with figured maple center, 50 made.

2002		$4,000	$6,000

HD-40 Tom Petty Signature Edition

2004-2006. Limited run of 274, Indian rosewood sides and back, high-end appointments, inside label with signature.

2004-2006		$5,000	$7,500

Martin HD-28VR

2002 Martin HD-28LSV

Martin HD-40MS Marty Stuart

Imaged by Heritage Auctions, HA.com

Martin J-16E 12-String

MODEL YEAR	FEATURES	EXC. COND. LOW	HIGH

HD-40MK Mark Knopfler

2001-2002. Limited Edition of 251 made, Mark Knopfler signature inlay 20th fret, herringbone trim, fancy marquetry sound hole rings.

2001-2002		$6,000	$9,000

HD-40MS Marty Stuart

1996. Indian rosewood, 250 made, pearl/abalone inlay.

1996		$6,000	$9,000

HD-41

1999-2001. Like D-41, but with herringbone rosette, binding.

1999-2001		$3,000	$4,500

HD-282R

1992-1996. Large sound hole with 2 herringbone rings, zigzag backstripe.

1992-1996		$3,000	$4,500

HD Dierks Bentley

2013-2014. Rosewood.

2013-2014		$4,000	$6,000

HD Elliot Easton Custom Edition

2006-2008. Limited Edition, 40 made, Adirondack spruce top with aging tone, Fishman Ellipse Aura pickup available on HDE.

2006-2008		$5,500	$8,500

HDN Negative Limited Edition

2003. Limited to 135 made, unusual appointments include pearloid headstock and black finish, HDN Negative Limited Edition notation on the inside label.

2003		$4,000	$6,000

HJ-28

1992, 1996-2000. Limited Edition Guitar of the Month in '92, regular production started in '96. Jumbo, non-cut, spruce top, Indian rosewood sides and back, herringbone top purfling, with or without on-board electronics.

1992	Limited Edition	$3,500	$5,500
1996-2000		$2,000	$3,000

HJ-28M

1994. Mahogany/spruce, herringbone top purfling, Guitar of the Month, 72 made.

1994		$2,000	$3,000

HJ-38 Stefan Grossman

2008-2011. Custom Edition, Madagascar rosewood back and sides.

2008-2011		$4,000	$6,000

HM Ben Harper

2008-2009. Special Edition, 62 made, M-style width, 000-style depth, solid Adirondack spruce top, solid East Indian rosewood sides and back, onboard Fishman Ellipse Matrix Blend.

2008-2009		$5,000	$8,000

HOM-35

1989. Herringbone Orchestra Model, Guitar of the Month, scalloped braces, 3-piece Brazilian rosewood back, book matched sides, 14-fret neck, only 60 built.

1989		$7,000	$12,000

HTA Kitty Wells 'Honky Tonk Angel'

2002. D-size with 000-size depth, Indian rosewood back and sides, Queen of Country Music inlay logo on headstock (no Martin headstock logo).

2002	70 made	$4,500	$7,500

MODEL YEAR	FEATURES	EXC. COND. LOW	HIGH

J-1

1997-2001. Jumbo body with mahogany back and sides.

1997-2001		$800	$1,200

J12-15

2000-2008. 12-string version of J-15.

2000-2008		$1,500	$2,500

J12-16GT

2000-2013. 16" jumbo 12-string, satin solid mahogany back and sides, gloss solid spruce top.

2000-2013		$1,200	$2,000

J12-16GTE

2014-2015. Jumbo 12-string, Fishman.

2014-2015		$1,300	$2,200

J12-40/J12-40M

1985-1996. Called J12-40M from '85-'90, rosewood back and sides, 12 strings, 16" jumbo size, 14-fret neck, solid peghead, gold tuners.

1985-1990	J12-40M	$3,500	$5,500
1991-1996	J12-40	$3,000	$4,500

J12-65

1985-1995. Called J12-65M for '84-'90, 12-string, figured maple back and sides.

1985-1995		$3,000	$4,500

J-15

1999-2010. Jumbo 16" narrow-waist body, solid mahogany top, sides, and back, satin finish.

1999-2010		$1,500	$2,000

J-15E

2000-2001. Acoustic/electric J-15.

2000-2001		$1,800	$2,800

J-16E 12-String

2021-present. Grand 14-fret, Sikta spruce top, rosewood back and sides.

2021-2024		$2,000	$3,000

J-18/J-18M

1987-1996. Called J-18M for '87-'89, J-size body with Style 18 appointments, natural.

1987-1989	J-18M	$2,000	$3,000
1990-1996	J-18	$1,800	$2,800

J-21/J-21M

1985-1996. Called J-21M prior to '90, Indian rosewood back and sides, black binding, rosewood 'board, chrome tuners.

1985-1989	J-21M	$2,500	$3,500
1990-1996	J-21	$2,200	$3,200

J-21MC

1986. J cutaway, oval sound hole, Guitar of the Month.

1986		$3,000	$4,500

J-40

1990-present. Called J-40M from '85-'89, Jumbo, Indian rosewood back and sides, triple-bound 'board, hexagonal inlays.

1990-2024		$2,500	$4,000

J-40 Custom

1993-1996. J-40 with upgrades including abalone top trim and rosette.

1993-1996		$3,500	$5,500

J-40BK

1990-1997. Black finish and 'guard, gold hardware.

1990-1997		$3,000	$4,500

MODEL YEAR	FEATURES	EXC. COND. LOW	HIGH

J-40M/J-40MBK

1985-1989. Jumbo, Indian rosewood back and sides, triple-bound 'board, hexagonal inlays, MBK ('88-'89) indicates black, name changed to J-40 in '90.

1985-1989	J-40M	$2,500	$4,000
1988-1989	J-40MBK	$3,000	$4,500

J-40MBLE

1987. Brazilian rosewood, Style 45 snowflakes, 17 made.

1987		$8,500	$12,000

J-40MC

1987-1989. Rounded Venetian cutaway version of J-40 M, oval sound hole, gold-plated enclosed tuners. Becomes JC-40 in '90.

1987-1989		$3,000	$4,500

J-41 Special

2004-2007. East Indian rosewood back and sides, Style 45 snowflake inlays.

2004-2007		$3,500	$5,000

J-45M Deluxe

1986. Guitar of the Month, 17 made, East Indian rosewood back and sides, tortoise-colored binding, mother-of-pearl and abalone, gold tuners with ebony buttons.

1986		$8,000	$12,000

J-65 Custom/J-65FM

1993-1996. White binding, herringbone. Available with MEQ electronics.

1993-1996		$3,500	$5,500
1993-1996	With MEQ	$4,000	$6,000

J-65/J-65E/J-65M

1985-1995. Jumbo, maple back and sides, gold-plated tuners, scalloped bracing, ebony 'board, tortoise shell-style binding.

1985-1995		$3,000	$4,500

JC Buddy Guy Signature

2006-2007. Only 36 made, rosewood back and sides.

2006-2007		$5,500	$8,500

JC-1E

1999-2002. Jumbo, mahogany, cutaway, pickup.

1999-2002		$800	$1,200

JC-16GTE

2000-2003. Jumbo, cutaway, mahogany back and sides, gloss top, Fishman.

2000-2003		$1,500	$2,500

JC-16GTE Premium

2003-2005. Fishman Prefix Stereo Blender pickup system.

2003-2005		$1,800	$2,800

JC-16KWS Kenny Wayne Shepherd Signature

2001-2002. Cutaway, blue lacquer top, back and sides in gloss black, on-board electronics, 198 made.

2001-2002	198 made	$3,500	$6,000

JC-16ME Aura

2006-2009. JC-16 with maple back and sides, Fishman Aura.

2006-2009		$2,000	$3,000

JC-16RE Aura

2006-2011. Like ME, but with rosewood back and sides.

2006-2011		$2,500	$3,500

JC-16RGTE Aura

2000-2003. Like RE Aura, but with gloss top.

2000-2003		$1,200	$1,800

JC-16WE

2002-2003		$1,000	$1,500

JC-40

1990-1997. Renamed from J-40 MC, cutaway flat-top, oval sound hole.

1990-1997		$3,000	$4,500

JSO Sing Out! 60th Pete Seeger

2011. Triangular sound hole, Sikta top, East Indian rosewood back and sides, 2 'guards, 60 made. There was also a 12-string model (J12SO!).

2011		$5,000	$7,500

LE-HMSD 2015 (HMS Dreadnought Battleship)

2015. Limited Edition, HMS Dreadnought Battleship (British Royal Navy) illustrated by artist Robert Goetzl is printed on the Sikta spruce top, dark mahogany back and sides, ebony 'board.

2015		$3,500	$5,500

LX Series

2003-present. The LX series is the Little Martin models, featuring small bodies with high pressure wood laminate (HPL) backs and sides with an exterior woodgrain image with a gloss finish. M is for mahogany woodgrain, R for rosewood and K for Koa. They are also offered in all solid colors. A 1 indicates a HPL spruce top, 2 is HPL Koa top. E indicates electronics.

2003-2019	LXM	$300	$500
2004-2025	LX1	$300	$500
2004-2025	LXK2	$300	$500
2009	LX Elvis Presley	$550	$900
2009-2021	LX1E	$400	$700
2013-2014	LX1E Ed Sheeran	$550	$900
2013-2019	LXME	$400	$700
2017-2024	LX Black	$300	$500
2019-2021	LX1RE	$500	$900
2019-2025	LX1R	$500	$900

M2C-28

1988. Double-cut, Guitar of the Month, 22 made.

1988		$6,000	$10,000

M-3H Cathy Fink

2005. M 0000-size body, gloss finish, rosewood sides, 3-piece back with flamed Koa center panel, torch headstock inlay, herringbone top trim, no Martin logo on headstock.

2005		$4,000	$6,000

M-3M George Martin

2005-2006. M Model, Style 40 appointments with Style 42 snowflake inlays, 127 made.

2005-2006		$4,000	$6,000

M-3SC Shawn Colvin

2002-2003. M 0000-size body, 120 made, mahogany sides, 3-piece mahogany/rosewood back, Fishman, Shawn Colvin & C.F.M. III signed label.

2002-2003		$4,000	$6,500

M-16GT

2001-2003. M-size single cut, gloss top, mahogany sides and back.

2001-2003		$1,500	$2,500

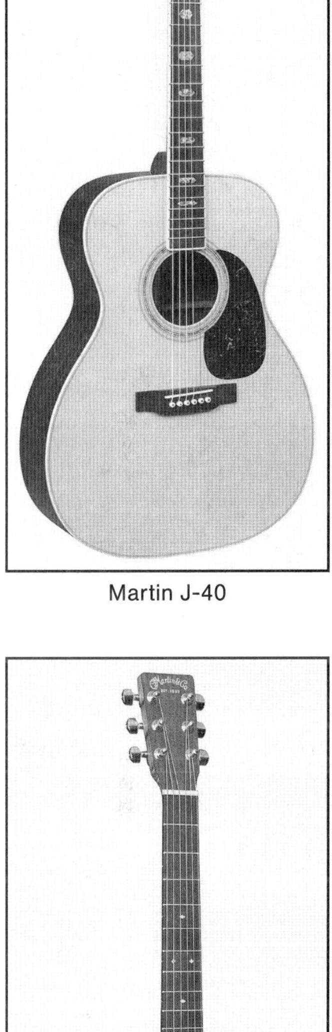

Martin J-40

Martin LX1R

GUITARS

Martin M-30 Jorma Kaukonen

1979 Martin M-38
Gantt Kushner

MODEL YEAR	FEATURES	EXC. COND. LOW	HIGH

M-18

1984-1988. M size, mahogany, 106 made.

1984-1988		$4,000	$6,000

M-21 Custom

December 1984. Guitar of the Month, fewer than 100 made, low profile neck M-Series, Indian rosewood back and sides, special ornamentation.

1984		$3,500	$6,000

M-21 Steve Earle

2008-2011. Custom Edition, 154 made, East Indian rosewood back and sides, Italian Alpine spruce top.

2008-2011		$5,000	$7,500

M-30 Jorma Kaukonen

2010-2013. Custom Artist Edition, 157 made, M 0000-size body, Style 30 appointments, East Indian rosewood back and sides, Maltese diamond/square inlays, optional electronics.

2010-2013		$5,000	$7,000

M-35/M-36

1978-1997, 2007-2024. First 26 labeled as M-35, Indian rosewood back and sides, bound 'board, low profile neck, multi-bound, white-black-white back stripes.

1978	M-35, 26 made	$4,000	$6,500
1978-1979		$3,500	$5,000
1980-1989		$2,500	$4,000
1990-2024		$2,200	$3,200
2008	175th Anniv	$3,500	$5,500

M-36B

1985. Brazilian rosewood.

1985		$10,000	$15,000

M-38 (0000-38)

1977-1997, 2007-2011. Called 0000-38 (see that listing) in '97-'98, 0000-size, Indian rosewood back and sides, multi-bound.

1977-1979		$3,500	$5,000
1980-1997		$2,500	$4,000
2007-2011		$2,200	$3,200

M-38 Koa Special

2009-2010. Sikta spruce top, highly flamed Koa back and sides.

2009-2010		$4,000	$6,000

M-38B

1985. Brazilian rosewood.

1985		$10,000	$15,000

M-42 David Bromberg

2005-2006. 0000-14 body, rosewood back and sides, snowflakes, 83 made.

2005-2006		$6,500	$9,500

M-64

1985-1996. Flamed maple back and sides, tortoise-shell-style 'guard and binding. The 11 made in '85 were labeled M-64R.

1985-1996		$2,500	$4,000

MC12-41 Richie Sambora

2006. 12-string version of OMC-41 Richie Sambora, Brazilian rosewood, planned 200 combined models made.

2006		$10,000	$15,000

MC-16GTE

2002-2004. M-16 GT with single-cut and Fishman.

2002-2004		$1,200	$1,800

MC-16GTE Premium

2003-2005. Fishman Prefix Stereo Blender pickup system.

2003-2005		$1,500	$2,500

MC-28

1981-1996. Rosewood back and sides, single-cut, oval sound hole, scalloped braces.

1981-1996		$2,500	$4,000

MC-37K

1981-1982, 1987-1994. Cutaway, Koa back and sides, 53 made.

1981-1994		$2,500	$3,500

MC-38 Steve Howe Special Edition

2009-2011. Indian rosewood back and sides, cutaway, slot headstock.

2009-2011		$4,000	$6,000

MC-40 Eric Johnson

2003. Limited run of 90, Engelmann spruce top, East Indian rosewood back and sides, abalone angel inlay on headstock.

2003		$5,000	$8,000

MC-68/MC-68R/MC-68+

1985-1996. Auditorium-size, single-cut, maple back and sides, scalloped bracing, vertical logo, natural or sunburst. In '85 it was called the MC-68 R (for adjustable truss-rod), 7 with sunburst shaded top option called MC-68+.

1985	MC-68R	$3,000	$4,500
1986-1996	MC-68	$2,500	$4,000
1986-1996	MC-68+	$2,800	$4,500

MC-DSM

2007-2010. Limited Edition of 100, cutaway, designed by District Sales Manager (DSM), spruce top, figured Koa back and sides.

2007-2010		$4,000	$6,000

Mini-Martin Limited Edition

1999-2009. Size 5 Terz body, solid Sikta spruce top, rosewood sides and back, vintage style Martin Geib case with green interior.

1999-2009		$1,200	$1,800

MMV

2008-2012. D-style, rosewood sides and back, nitro finish.

2008-2012		$2,000	$3,000

Model America 1

2018. Limited Edition D-body, United States sourced woods, Adirondack spruce top, sycamore back and sides, cherry neck, black walnut 'board, gloss finish.

2018		$2,500	$4,000

MTV-1 Unplugged

1996. The body is 1/2 rosewood and 1/2 mahogany, scalloped bracing, MTV logo on headstock, gloss (588 sold) or satin (73 sold) finish.

1996	Gloss finish	$3,200	$5,000
1996	Satin finish	$3,000	$4,500

MTV-2 Unplugged

2003-2004. The body is 1/2 rosewood and 1/2 maple, scalloped bracing, MTV logo on headstock.

2003-2004		$3,200	$5,000

GUITARS

MODEL YEAR	FEATURES	EXC. COND. LOW	HIGH

N-10

1968-1993. Classical, mahogany back and sides, fan bracing, wood marquetry sound hole ring, unbound rosewood 'board, 12-fret neck and slotted peghead from '70.

1968-1970	Short-scale	$3,500	$4,500
1970-1979	Long-scale	$3,200	$4,200
1980-1993	Long-scale	$3,000	$4,000

N-20

1968-1992. Classical, Brazilian rosewood back and sides (changed to Indian rosewood in '69), multi-bound, 12-fret neck, solid headstock (changed to slotted in '70), natural.

1968-1969	Brazilian, short-scale	$11,500	$18,000
1969	Prismatone pu & Baldwin C-1 Amp	$12,000	$20,000
1970	Indian, short-scale	$5,000	$6,500
1970-1979	Indian, long-scale	$5,000	$6,500
1980-1992	Long-scale	$5,000	$6,500

N-20B

1985-1986. Brazilian rosewood N-20.

1985-1986		$8,000	$12,000

N-20WNB 'Trigger'

1998-1999. Designed after Willie Nelson's famous N-20 he named Trigger, 100 made, Brazilian rosewood (30) or Indian (70).

1998-1999	Brazilian	$12,000	$18,000
1998-1999	Indian	$5,000	$8,000

OM-1

1999-2002, 2009-2010. Sikta spruce top, sapele back and sides, East Indian rosewood 'board, natural satin finish.

1999-2010		$800	$1,200

OM-1GT

2011-2014. OM-1 with gloss top.

2011-2014		$900	$1,400

CS-OM-13

2013. Custom Shop Limited Edition, 80 made, Swiss spruce top, Madagascar rosewood back and sides, gloss natural finish.

2013		$5,000	$7,500

OM-15

2001-2003. Mahogany body, cutaway.

2001-2003		$1,500	$2,500

OM-15M

2015. All mahogany, natural satin finish.

2015		$1,800	$2,800

OM-16GT

2001-2005. Spruce top, mahogany back, sides and neck, natural gloss finish.

2001-2005		$1,500	$2,500

OM-18

1930-1934. Orchestra Model, mahogany back and sides, 14-fret neck, solid peghead, banjo tuners (changed to right-angle in '31).

1930-1931	Banjo tuners, small 'guard	$40,000	$50,000
1931	Standard tuners, small 'guard	$35,000	$45,000
1932-1933	Standard tuners, large 'guard	$25,000	$30,000

MODEL YEAR	FEATURES	EXC. COND. LOW	HIGH

OM-18 Authentic 1933

2013-2019. Period-correct (1933) appointments, Vintage Tone System, vintage gloss finish.

2013-2019		$4,500	$6,500

OM-18 Special

2012. Custom Shop model.

2012		$2,500	$4,000

OM-18GE Golden Era

2003-2009. Mahogany back and sides, Brazilian rosewood purfling and binding.

2003-2009		$3,500	$5,500

OM-18P

1930-1931. Plectrum.

1930-1931		$8,000	$12,000

OM-18V

1999-2009. Vintage features.

1999-2009		$2,500	$4,000

OM-18VLJ Laurence Juber

2002, 2008-2009. Cutaway, Adirondack spruce top, 133 made.

2002-2009		$4,500	$7,000

OM-21

1994-2024. Indian rosewood back and sides, herringbone back stripe and sound hole ring, 14-fret neck, chrome tuners, natural or sunburst.

1994-1999		$2,000	$3,500
2000-2024		$2,200	$3,200

OM-21 Special

1991, 2007-2011. Upgrade to ebony 'board, rosewood bindings.

1992-2011		$3,000	$4,500

OM-21 Special Limited Edition

1991. Custom Shop, prototype to '92 production.

1991	36 made	$5,000	$8,000

OM-28

1929-1933, 1990-1997, 2015-present. Brazilian rosewood back and sides, 14-fret neck, solid peghead, banjo tuners (changed to right-angle in '31), reintroduced with Indian rosewood for '90-'97 and again in 2015.

1929	Banjo pegs, small 'guard, pyramid end bridge	$135,000	$175,000
1930	Early '30, banjo tuners, small 'guard, pyramid bridge	$125,000	$150,000
1930	Late '30, banjo tuners, small 'guard, belly bridge	$100,000	$125,000
1931	Early '31, banjo tuners, small 'guard, belly bridge	$100,000	$125,000
1931	Late '31, standard tuners, large 'guard	$85,000	$110,000
1931	Mid '31, banjo tuners, large 'guard	$100,000	$125,000

1933 Martin OM-18
Jet City Guitars

1930 Martin OM-28
Jet City Guitars

Martin OM-28 Modern Deluxe

Martin OM-28E Retro

MODEL YEAR	FEATURES	EXC. COND. LOW	HIGH
1932-1933	Standard tuners, full-size 'guard	$85,000	$110,000
1990-1997		$2,800	$4,000
2015-2024		$2,300	$3,000

OM-28 Authentic 1931

2015-2019. Adirondack spruce top, Madagascar rosewood back and sides, Vintage Tone System (VTS).

2015-2019		$6,000	$9,000

OM-28 Marquis

2005-2015. Pre-war appointments, Adirondack top, East Indian rosewood back, sides and headplate.

2005-2015		$3,500	$5,000

OM-28 Marquis Adirondack

2011-2013. Adirondack spruce top.

2011-2013		$4,500	$6,500

OM-28 Marquis Madagascar

2007-2008. Madagascar rosewood.

2007-2008		$5,000	$7,500

OM-28 Modern Deluxe

2019-present. Sikta spruce top with Vintage Tone System (VTS), East Indian rosewood back and sides, '30s style script logo on headstock, gloss finish. Electronics available (OM-28E).

2019-2024		$3,500	$5,000
2019-2024	OM-28E	$4,000	$5,500

OM-28E Retro

2012-2019. Sikta top, Indian rosewood back and sides, herringbone binding, Fishman.

2012-2019		$3,000	$4,500

OM-28GE Golden Era

2003-2004. Brazilian rosewood back and sides, Adirondack spruce top.

2003-2004		$15,000	$25,000

OM-28GE Golden Era Guatemalan Rosewood

2015. Custom Shop model, Guatemalan rosewood back and sides.

2015		$7,000	$10,000

OM-28JM John Mayer

2003. Limited Edition, 404 made.

2003		$7,000	$10,000

OM-28LE

1985. Limited Edition only 40 made, Guitar of the Month, Indian rosewood back and sides, herringbone top binding, V-neck.

1985		$5,000	$8,000

OM-28M Roseanne Cash

2008. Signature Edition, Madagascar rosewood back and sides, 100 made.

2008		$4,500	$6,500

OM-28PB Perry Bechtel

1993. Guitar of the Month, signed by Perry Bechtel's widow Ina, Indian rosewood back and sides, zigzag back stripe, chrome tuners, V-neck, 50 made.

1993		$6,000	$9,000

OM-28SO Sing Out! 35th Anniversary

1985. For Sing Out! Magazine's 35th anniversary, label signed by Pete Seeger.

1985		$4,000	$6,500

OM-28V Custom Shop (Brazilian/Adirondack)

2000-2001. Brazilian rosewood back and sides, Adirondack "red" spruce top, ca. 1933 prewar features including Martin gold headstock decal logo.

2000-2001		$8,000	$12,000

OM-28VR/OM-28V

1984-1990, 1999-2014. VR suffix until '99, then just V (Vintage Series), rosewood back and sides.

1984-1999	OM-28VR	$3,000	$5,000
1999-2014	OM-28V	$2,500	$4,000

OM-35

2003-2007. 000-size body, Indian rosewood sides and 3-piece back, spruce top, gloss natural finish.

2003-2007		$2,500	$4,000

OM-40 Rory Block

2004. Limited Edition, 38 made, 000-size, Indian rosewood back and sides, Englemann spruce top, 'the road' inlay markers, vintage-auto inlay on headstock.

2004		$5,500	$8,500

OM-40BLE

1990. Limited Edition, 50 made, Brazilian rosewood back and sides.

1990		$8,000	$12,000

OM-40LE

1994. Limited Edition, Guitar of the Month, Indian rosewood back and sides, double pearl borders, snowflake inlay on 'board, gold tuners, natural (57 sold) or sunburst (29 sold).

1994		$5,000	$8,000

OM-41 Special

2005-2006. Rosewood back and sides, Style 45 snowflake inlays.

2005-2006		$4,000	$6,000

OM-42

1930, 1999-present. Indian rosewood back and sides, Style 45 snowflake inlays, there were 2 guitars labeled OM-42 built in 1930.

1930	2 made	$125,000	$165,000
1999-2024		$5,000	$7,500

OM-42 Flamed Mahogany

2006. Limited Edition, 30 made, flamed mahogany back and sides, vines.

2006		$7,000	$10,000

OM-42 Koa

2005-2008. Koa sides and back.

2006-2008		$6,000	$9,000

OM-42PS Paul Simon

1997. Book matched Sikta spruce top, Indian rosewood back and sides, 42- and 45-style features, low profile PS neck, 500 planned but only 223 made.

1997		$6,000	$9,000

OM-45

1930-1933. OM-style, 45 level appointments. Condition is critically important on this or any ultra high-end instrument, minor flaws are critical to value.

1930	Banjo pegs	$500,000	$625,000
1931	Right-angle tuners	$350,000	$450,000
1932-1933		$350,000	$450,000

MODEL YEAR	FEATURES	EXC. COND. LOW	HIGH

OM-45/SOM-45/Special OM-45

1977-1994. First batch labeled SOM-45, 2 labeled OM-45N in '94 that had square tube bar in neck and without scalloped braces.

1977-1979		$8,000	$12,000
1980-1989		$7,500	$10,000
1990-1994		$7,000	$9,500
1994	OM-45 N option	$7,000	$9,500

OM-45 Custom Deluxe

1998-1999. Limited custom shop run of 14, Adirondack spruce and typical Style 45 appointments.

1998-1999		$20,000	$30,000

OM-45 Deluxe

1930. Only 14 made, Brazilian rosewood back and sides, zipper pattern back stripe, pearl inlay in 'guard and bridge. Condition is critically important on this or any ultra high-end instrument, minor flaws are critical to value.

1930		$500,000	$750,000

OM-45 Deluxe (Special)

1999. 4 made on special order, highly figured Brazilian rosewood.

1999		$25,000	$40,000

OM-45 Deluxe Golden Era

1998. Brazilian, few made.

1998		$25,000	$40,000

OM-45 Tasmanian Blackwood

2005. Limited Edition, 29 made, Tasmanian Blackwood (Koa-family) back and sides with curly grain, 000-size, OM and 45 style appointments.

2005		$6,000	$9,000

OM-45/OM-45B Roy Rogers

2006. Limited Edition, based on Roy's 1930 OM-45 Deluxe, Indian rosewood (84 made) or Brazilian rosewood (45B, 14 made).

2006	OM-45, Indian	$7,000	$10,000
2006	OM-45B, Brazilian	$20,000	$30,000

OM-45GE Golden Era

1999, 2001-2005. Red spruce top, Brazilian rosewood.

1999-2005		$15,000	$25,000

OM 1833 Custom Shop Limited Edition

2006. Italian alpine spruce top, flamed claro walnut back and sides, 000-size, low profile 14-fret neck, fancy inlay and appointments, natural gloss finish.

2006		$6,000	$9,000

OM Chris Hillman

2009-2010. Adirondack top, Indian rosewood back and sides, sunburst.

2009-2010	21 made	$6,000	$9,000

OM Jeff Daniels

2012-2013. Based on Daniels 1934 C-2 archtop conversion, Adirondack, Madagascar rosewood back and sides, sunburst.

2012-2013	57 made	$4,500	$7,000

OM Negative

2007-2008. Limited Edition, 60 made, black body and white 'board, black inside label signed Dick Boak, gloss finish.

2007-2008		$5,000	$7,500

MODEL YEAR	FEATURES	EXC. COND. LOW	HIGH

OM Night Dive

2004. Limited Edition, 20 built, bearclaw sitka spruce top, Brazilian rosewood back and sides, inlay design work by luthier Grit Laskin.

2004		$25,000	$40,000

OM True North-16/CS-OM True North-16

2016. Custom Shop Limited Edition, 50 made, Adirondack spruce top, figured Koa back and sides, back features a compass design inlaid with flamed jarrah, Claro walnut, waterfall bubinga and Paua pearl, ebony headplate has True North design inlaid with mother of pearl.

2016		$8,000	$12,000

OMC Aura

2004-2011. OM size, cutaway, rosewood back and sides, Fishman Aura.

2004-2011		$2,500	$4,000

OMC Cherry

2008-2013. Sustainable wood program, solid cherry back and sides, solid rescued spruce top, 000 body, cutaway, Fishman electronics.

2008-2013		$1,800	$3,000

OMC Fingerstyle 1

2005-2008. Cutaway, Spanish cedar back and sides, no inlays.

2005-2008		$2,500	$4,000

OMC Red Birch

2005-2009. Sustainable Series, rescued spruce top, solid red birch back and sides, Fishman electronics.

2005-2009		$2,000	$3,500

OMC-1E

2009-2010. Style 28 appointments, cutaway, onboard Fishman.

2009-2010		$800	$1,200

OMC-15E

2001-2007. All solid mahogany body.

2001-2007		$1,500	$2,500

OMC-15ME

2016-2022. Mahogany top, back and sides, East Indian rosewood 'board, Fishman electronics.

2016-2022		$1,800	$3,000

OMC-16E Burst

2019-2022. Mahogany burst ovangkol gloss top, satin ovangkol back and sides, Fishman electronics.

2019-2022		$1,800	$3,000

OMC-16E Koa

2005-2009. Koa back and sides, on-board electronics.

2005-2009		$1,500	$2,200

OMC-16E Maple

2005-2009. Maple, on-board electronics.

2005		$2,500	$4,000

OMC-16E/E Premium

2003-2007, 2017-2019. Sikta spruce top, sapele back and sides, on-board electronics. Premium model with Prefix Premium Blend electronics. Reintroduced '17 with cherry back and sides and Fishman® Matrix VT.

2003-2007		$2,000	$3,500
2017-2019	16E, Reintroduced	$1,800	$3,000

1998 Martin OM-28VR

Imaged by Heritage Auctions, HA.com

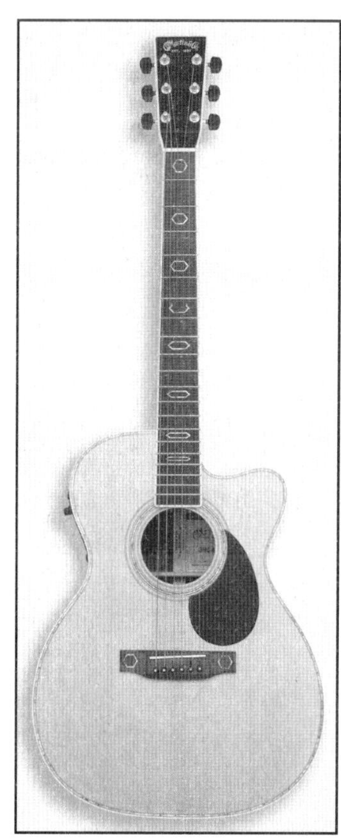

2008 Martin OMC Aura

GUITARS

Martin OMCPA4

Martin OMJM John Mayer

MODEL YEAR	FEATURES	EXC. COND. LOW	HIGH

OMC-16GTE

2010-2013. Gloss top, satin sapele back and sides.

2010-2013		$2,000	$3,000

OMC-16RE Aura

2005-2009. East Indian rosewood back and sides, gloss body.

2005-2009		$2,500	$4,000

OMC-16RE/RE Premium

2003-2005. Solid rosewood back and sides, on-board electronics.

2003-2005		$2,200	$3,500

OMC-16WE

2002-2003. Walnut back and sides.

2002-2003		$2,200	$3,500

OMC-18 Laurence Juber Custom Edition

2008. Venetian cutaway 000 body, Adirondack spruce top, gloss natural finish.

2008		$3,500	$5,500

OMC-18E

2017-2019. Sikta spruce top, mahogany back and sides, ebony 'board, Fishman electronics.

2017-2019		$2,000	$3,200

OMC-18LJ Laurence Juber

2008-2010. Cutaway 000, Adirondack spruce top.

2008-2010		$4,500	$7,000

OMC-28

1990. Guitar of the Month, 81 made, Indian rosewood, low profile neck, label signed by C.F. Martin IV.

1990		$5,000	$8,000

OMC-28 Laurence Juber

2004-2005. OM size, cutaway, Indian rosewood.

2004-2005		$4,500	$6,500

OMC-28BLJ Laurence Juber

2004. Brazilian rosewood, 50 made.

2004		$10,000	$15,000

OMC-28E

2006-2009, 2017-2019. OMC-28 with Fishman Ellipse. Reintroduced '17 with Fishman Aura.

2006-2009		$2,500	$4,000
2017-2019		$3,000	$4,500

OMC-28M Laurence Juber

2006-2011. Madagascar rosewood.

2006-2011		$5,000	$7,500

OMC-35E

2016-2017. Sikta spruce top, East Indian rosewood back & sides, ebony 'board and 'guard, Fishman electronics.

2016-2017		$3,000	$4,500

OMC-41 Richie Sambora

2006-2009. Madagascar rosewood sides and back, combination Style 45 and 41 appointments, 12-string is MC12-41 Richie Sambora, planned 200 made combined models.

2006-2009		$8,000	$10,000

OMC-LJ Pro Laurence Juber

2013. Custom Shop Artist Edition, Adirondack spruce top, flamed maple back and sides.

2013		$5,000	$7,500

OMCPA Series

2010-2019. Performing Artist Series, OM size, cutaway, acoustic/electric, various woods.

2010-2016	OMCPA1/1 Plus	$2,000	$3,000
2011	OMCPA2	$1,200	$1,800
2011-2013	OMCPA3	$1,200	$1,800
2011-2019	OMCPA4 Sapele	$1,200	$1,800
2012-2019	OMCPA4 Rosewood	$1,000	$1,500

OMCRE

2008-2009. Carpathian spruce top, East Indian rosewood sides and back, Babicz adjustable neck joint, Fishman, gloss finish.

2008-2009		$2,500	$4,000

OMC-X1E Black

2020-2023. Replaces OMCXAE Black. Jett black HPL top, back and sides, Fishman electronics.

2020-2023		$500	$800

OMCXK2E

2006-2009. Hawaiian Koa HPL (high pressure laminate) textured finish.

2006-2009		$600	$900

OMJM John Mayer

2003-present. Indian rosewood sides and back.

2003-2024		$3,500	$5,500

OMM

2000-2003. Solid spruce top, mahogany back and sides.

2000-2003		$800	$1,200

OMM John Renbourne

2011-2013. Madagascar rosewood sides and back.

2011-2013		$4,500	$7,000

OMXAE Black

2014-2019. Black HPL back and sides, black Richlite 'board.

2014-2019		$500	$800

Philadelphia Folk Festival 40th Anniversary

2002. Commemorating 40th Anniversary of Martin Philly Folk Festival, 85 made, 0000-14 fret, Englemann spruce top, Indian rosewood back and sides, PFF logo inlays, one label signed by CF Martin IV and David Baskin, one signed by festival participants, blue denim-covered hard case.

2002		$4,000	$6,500

POW MIA

2006-2010. POW MIA logo position marker lettering on fretboard, D-style body, dark finish.

2006-2010		$4,000	$6,000

PS2 Paul Simon Signature

2003. Paul Simon signature logo at bottom of fretboard, 200 made.

2003		$4,500	$7,000

R-15

1934. Archtop, sunburst.

1934	2 made	$3,000	$4,500

R-17

1934-1942. All mahogany, arched top and back, 3-segment f-holes (changed to 1-segment in '37).

1934-1942		$3,000	$4,500

R-18P

1934-1936. Only 4 made, plectrum neck.

1934-1936		$3,000	$4,500

R-18S/R-18

1932-1942. Spruce arched top (carved top by 1937), mahogany back and sides, bound top, sunburst.

1932-1942		$3,500	$5,500

MODEL YEAR	FEATURES	EXC. COND. LOW	HIGH

R-18T

1934-1941. Tenor archtop, 14 3/8" lower bout, 2 f-holes, dot markers, sunburst.

1934-1941		$2,500	$3,500

R-21

1938. 000 body archtop, 1 made.

1938		$6,500	$8,500

SC Series

2020-present. Road Series, patented Sure Align® neck system, Sikta spruce top with various wood back and sides, 10E/13E (Koa), 13E Special (ziricote), CS-SC-2022 (Custom Shop, rosewood).

2020-2024	SC-13E	$1,200	$1,800
2022	CS-SC-2022	$6,000	$9,000
2022-2024	SC-10E	$800	$1,200
2022-2024	SC-13E Special	$1,400	$2,000
2022-2024	SC-13E Special Burst	$1,600	$2,200

Schoenberg Soloist by C.F. Martin

1987-1994. Designed by Eric Schoenberg with help from luthier Dana Bourgeois, OM body, Brazilian rosewood back and sides.

1987-1994		$7,000	$9,000

Shenandoah Series

1983-1993. Bodies and necks were built in Japan with final assembly and finishing in Nazareth and a Thinline piezo added, styled after U.S. models with a 32 added to the model name.

1983-1993	Various models	$1,000	$2,000

SP000 Series

1996-2002. Special Edition 000-size, spruce top with aging toner, scalloped bracing, rosewood or mahogany body.

1996-1997	SP000C-16TR	$1,800	$2,800
1996-2002	SP000-16	$1,500	$2,500
1996-2002	SP000-16R	$1,600	$2,800
1996-2002	SP000-16T	$1,800	$3,000
1996-2002	SP000-16TR	$2,000	$3,200
1997-2002	SP000C-16R	$2,000	$3,200
1999-2002	SP000C-16	$1,800	$3,000
1999-2002	SP000C-16E	$2,000	$3,500
2003	SP000C-16R (CS)	$3,000	$5,000

SP00-16RST Stauffer

2000-2002. Stauffer 6-on-a-side headstock, 12-fret neck, rosewood back and sides.

2000-2002		$2,500	$4,000

SPD12-16R

1997-2004. 12-string, solid rosewood body, abalone sound hole ring, Style-45 backstripe.

1999-2000		$2,000	$3,500

SPD-16 Series

1997-2004. D-16 Series Special models.

1996-1999	SPD-16TR	$2,000	$3,500
1997-2004	SPD-16	$1,500	$2,500
1997-2004	SPD-16T	$1,500	$2,500
1999-2001	SPD-16B Black	$1,500	$2,000
1999-2002	SPD-16M Maple	$1,200	$1,800
1999-2002	SPD-16W Walnut	$1,200	$1,800
2000	SPD-16E	$1,500	$2,200
2000-2002	SPD-16R	$1,500	$2,200
2000-2005	SPD-16K	$2,000	$3,000
2000-2005	SPD-16K2	$2,000	$3,000

SPDC-16 Series

1997-2001. Cutaway version of SPD-16.

1997-1999	SPDC-16TR	$2,000	$2,500
1997-2001	SPDC-16RE Rosewood	$2,000	$2,500
2000-2002	SPDC-16R	$2,000	$2,500

SPJC-16RE

2000-2003. Single-cut, East Indian rosewood body, 000-size, on-board electronics.

2000-2003		$2,000	$2,500

SPOM-16

1999-2001. Mahogany.

1999-2001		$1,800	$2,800

SS-0041GB-17

2017-2020. Limited Edition of 50, Grand Concert 12-fret, European spruce top with Vintage Tone System (VTS), Guatemalan rosewood back and sides, gloss finish.

2017-2020		$6,000	$9,000

SS-00L41-16

2016-2020. Limited Edition, Adirondack spruce top with Vintage Tone System (VTS), moabi back and sides, mahogany neck, hand-rubbed finish.

2016-2020		$5,000	$8,000

SS-OMVine-16

2016. Limited Edition of 35, NAMM show special, figured English walnut, aluminum vine inlay on ebony 'board.

2016		$7,000	$10,000

Stauffer

1830s-ca.1850s. One of C.F. Martin's earliest models, distinguished by the scrolled, six-on-a-side headstock, ornamentation varies. Each instrument should be evaluated on a case-by-case basis, those in truly original excellent condition may be worth more than the values shown.

1835	Fancy (2nd highest)	$40,000	$55,000
1835	Fancy (highest)	$145,000	$165,000
1835	Mid-level	$25,000	$35,000
1835	Plain (2nd lowest)	$20,000	$25,000
1835	Plain (lowest)	$16,500	$22,500

Sting Mini

2006. 100 made, Size 5, Western red cedar top, Solomon padauk body.

2005-2006		$6,500	$8,000

Stinger

1980s-1990s. Import copy offset S-style electric solidbody.

1980s-90s		$300	$500

SW00-D8 Machiche

2006-2007. Smartwood Limited Edition, 125 made, rescued solid spruce top, sustainable machiche sides and back.

2006-2007		$2,500	$4,000

SWC

1998. Smartwood 'The Sting Signature Classical Model', machiche wood body.

1998		$1,800	$3,500

Martin SC-10E

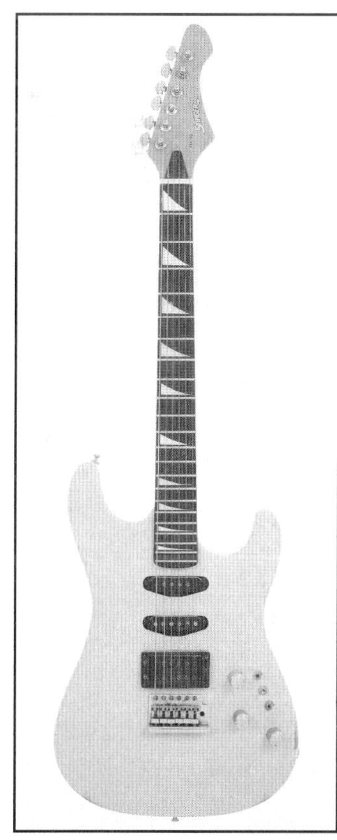

1987 Martin Stinger SSX-10

GUITARS

1930s May Bell

Imaged by Heritage Auctions, HA.com

1962 Maton EG240SE

MODEL YEAR	FEATURES	EXC. COND. LOW	HIGH

SWD

1998-2001. Smartwood D-size, built from wood material certified by the Forest Stewardship Council, Sikta top, cherry back and sides, natural satin finish.

1998-2001		$1,500	$2,500

SWD Red Birch

2003-2005. Red Birch.

2003-2005		$1,800	$3,000

SWDGT

2001-2016. Gloss top SWD.

2001-2016		$1,500	$2,500

SWDTG

2000-2007. Cherry back and sides, gloss finish.

2000-2007		$1,500	$2,500

SWMGT

2002-2003. M size, cherry back and sides, gloss finish.

2002-2003		$1,800	$3,000

SWOM

2000-2001. Sustainable Woods Series.

2000-2001		$1,800	$3,000

SWOMGT

2001-2018. Smartwood OM, rescued solid Sikta spruce top, sustainable cherry sides and back, gloss finish.

2001-2018		$1,500	$2,500

Yuengling 180th Anniversary Custom

2008. Celebrating 180th company anniversary, limited production, large company logo on top of body, fancy D-41 style appointments, certificate.

2008		$4,000	$6,000

Maruha

1960s-1970s. Japanese-made acoustic, classical, archtop and solidbody guitars, often copies of American brands. Probably not imported into the U.S.

Marvel

1950s-mid-1960s. Brand name used for budget guitars and basses marketed by Peter Sorkin Company in New York, New York. Sorkin manufactured and distributed Premier guitars and amplifiers made by its Multivox subsidiary. Marvel instruments were primarily beginner-grade. Brand disappears by mid-'60s. The name was also used on archtop guitars made by Regal and marketed by the Slingerland drum company in the 1930s to early 1940s.

Electric

1950s-60s	Various models	$300	$500

Marveltone by Regal

1925-1930. Private branded by Regal, Marveltone pearl style logo on headstock.

Guitar

1925-1930. 14" Brazilian rosewood.

1925-1930		$2,200	$3,300

Masaki Sakurai

See Kohno brand.

MODEL YEAR	FEATURES	EXC. COND. LOW	HIGH

Mason

1936-1939. Henry L. Mason on headstock, wholesale distribution, similar to Gibson/Cromwell, pressed wood back and sides.

Student/Intermediate Student

1936-1939. Various flat-top and archtop student/budget models.

1936-1939		$500	$800

Mason Bernard

1990-1991. Founded by Bernie Rico (BC Rich founder). During this period BC Rich guitars were licensed and controlled by Randy Waltuch and Class Axe. Most Mason models were designs similar to the BC Rich Assassin, according to Bernie Rico only the very best materials were used, large MB logo on headstock. Around 225 guitars were built bearing this brand.

Maton

1946-present. Intermediate and professional grade, production/custom, acoustic, acoustic/electric, hollowbody and solidbody guitars built in Box Hill, Victoria, Australia. Founded by Bill May and his brother Reg and still run by the family. Only available in USA since '82.

Matsuda Guitars

See listing for Michihiro Matsuda.

Matsuoka

1970s. Ryoji Matsuoka from Japan built intermediate grade M series classical guitars that often featured solid tops and laminated sides and back.

Matt Pulcinella Guitars

1998-present. Production/custom, professional grade, electric guitars and basses built in Chadds Ford, Pennsylvania by luthier Matt Pulcinella.

Mauel Guitars

Luthier Hank Mauel builds his premium grade, custom, flat-tops in Auburn, California. He began in 1995.

Maurer

Late 1880s-1944. Robert Maurer built guitars and mandolins in the late 1880s under the Maurer and Champion brands in his Chicago shop. Carl and August Larson bought the company in 1900 and retained the Maurer name. The Larsons also built under the Prairie State, Euphonon, W. J. Dyer and Wm. C. Stahl brands.

Max B

Luthier Sebastien Sulser builds professional grade, production/custom, electric guitars and basses, starting in 2000, in Kirby, Vermont.

GUITARS

May Bell

1923-1940s. Brand of flat-top guitars, some with fake resonators, marketed by the Slingerland Company. Most were made by Regal.

Maya

See El Maya.

McAlister Guitars

Premium grade, custom, flat-tops built by luthier Roy McAlister, starting in 1997, in Watsonville, California.

McCollum Guitars

1994-2009. Luthier Lance McCollum builds his premium grade, custom, flat-top and harp guitars in Colfax, California. McCollum died in 2009.

McCurdy Guitars

1983-present. Premium grade, production/custom, archtops built by luthier Ric McCurdy originally in Santa Barbara, California and, since '91, New York, New York.

McElroy

1995-present. Premium grade, custom, classical and flat-top steel string acoustic guitars built by luthier Brent McElroy in Seattle, Washington.

McGill Guitars

1976-present. Luthier Paul McGill builds his premium grade, production/custom, classical, resonator, and acoustic/electric guitars in Nashville, Tennessee.

McGlincy

Ca. 1974-ca. 1978. Custom flat-tops built by luthier Edward McGlincy in Toms River, New Jersey. Only 12 instruments made, and owners included Gordon Lightfoot and David Bromberg. He later offered uke and guitar kits. He also operated Ed's Musical Instruments. McGlincy died in '97.

McGlynn Guitars

2005-2007. Luthier Michael J. McGlynn built his premium and presentation grade, custom, solidbody guitars in Henderson, Nevada. McGlynn died in '07.

McGowan Guitars

Luthier Brian McGowan builds his production/custom, premium grade, steel-string acoustic guitars in Hampton, Virginia. He began in 2004.

MCI, Inc

1967-1988. MusiConics International (MCI), of Waco, Texas, introduced the world to the GuitOrgan, invented by Bob Murrell. Later, they also offered effects and a steel guitar. In the '80s, a MIDI version was offered. MCI was also involved with the Daion line of guitars in the late '70s and early '80s. MCI also built a double-neck lap steel.

MODEL YEAR	FEATURES	EXC. COND. LOW	HIGH

GuitOrgan B-35

1970s (ca. 1976-1978?). Duplicated the sounds of an organ and more. MCI bought double-cut semi-hollow body guitars from others and outfitted them with lots of switches and buttons. Each fret has 6 segments that correspond to an organ tone. There was also a B-300 and B-30 version, and the earlier M-300 and 340.

1970s	Fully functional	$1,300	$2,000

McInturff

1996-present. Professional and premium grade, production/custom, solidbody guitars built by luthier Terry C. McInturff originally in Holly Springs, North Carolina, and since '04, in Moncure, North Carolina. McInturff spent 17 years doing guitar repair and custom work before starting his own guitar line.

McKnight Guitars

1992-present. Luthier Tim McKnight builds his custom, premium grade, acoustic steel string guitars in Morral, Ohio.

McPherson Guitars

1981-present. Premium grade, production, flat-tops built by luthier Mander McPherson in Sparta, Wisconsin.

Mean Gene

1988-1990. Heavy metal style solidbodies made by Gene Baker, who started Baker U.S.A. guitars in '97, and Eric Zoellner in Santa Maria, California. They built around 30 custom guitars. Baker currently builds b3 guitars.

Megas Guitars

1989-present. Luthier Ted Megas builds his premium grade, custom, archtop and solidbody guitars, originally in San Franciso, and currently in Portland, Oregon.

Melancon

Professional and premium grade, custom/production, solid and semi-hollow body guitars and basses built by luthier Gerard Melancon, beginning in 1995, in Thibodaux, Louisiana.

Mello, John F.

1973-present. Premium grade, production/custom, classical and flat-top guitars built by luthier John Mello in Kensington, California.

Melophonic

1960s. Brand built by the Valco Company of Chicago, Illinois.

Resonator

1965		$900	$1,300

Melville Guitars

1988-present. Luthier Christopher Melville builds his premium grade, custom, flat-tops in Milton, Queensland, Australia.

1930s May Bell
Imaged by Heritage Auctions, HA.com

Late-'70s MCI B-35 Guitorgan
Tom Pfeifer

1997 Metropolitan Glendale
Imaged by Heritage Auctions, HA.com

Michael Kelly Hybrid Special
Cream City Music

MODEL YEAR	FEATURES	EXC. COND. LOW	HIGH

Memphis

One of the many guitar brands built by Japan's Matsumoku company.

Mercurio

2002-2005. Luthier Peter Mercurio built his custom/production solidbody guitars, featuring his interchangeable PickupPak system to swap pickups, in Chanhassen, Minnesota.

Mermer Guitars

Luthier Richard Mermer, started building in 1983, premium grade, production/custom, steel-string, nylon-string, and Hawaiian guitars in Sebastian, Florida.

Merrill Brothers

Premium grade, production/custom, steel-string and harp guitars built by luthiers Jim and Dave Merrill in Williamsburg, Virginia, starting in 1998.

Mesrobian

1995-present. Luthier Carl Mesrobian builds his professional and premium grade, custom, archtop guitars in Salem, Massachusetts.

Messenger

1967-1968. Built by Musicraft, Inc., originally of 156 Montgomery Street, San Francisco, California. The distinguishing feature of the Messengers is a metal alloy neck which extended through the body to the tailblock, plus mono or stereo outputs. Sometime before March '68 the company relocated to Astoria, Oregon. Press touted "improved" magnesium neck, though it's not clear if this constituted a change from '67. Brand disappears after '68. They also made basses.

Electric Hollowbody Archtop

1967-1968. Symmetrical double-cut body shape, metal neck with rosewood 'boards, stereo.

1967-1968		$2,500	$3,500

Metropolitan

1995-2008. Professional and premium grade, production/custom, retro-styled solidbodies designed by David Wintz reminiscent of the '50s National Res-o-glas and wood body guitars. They featured full-scale set-neck construction and a wood body instead of Res-o-glas. Wintz also made Robin and Alamo brand instruments.

Electric Solidbody

1995-2008	Various models	$2,000	$2,500

Meyers Custom Guitars

Professional grade, custom, solidbody electric guitars built by luthier Donald Meyers in Houma, Louisiana, beginning 2005.

Miami

1920s. Instruments built by the Oscar Schmidt Co. and possibly others. Most likely a brand made for a distributor.

Michael Collins Custom Guitars

Premium grade, custom/production, classical, flamenco and steel string guitars built in Argyle, New York, by luthier Michael Collins, starting in 1975.

Michael Collins Guitars

Luthier Michael Collins builds his professional and premium grade, custom, Selmer style, archtop and flat-top guitars, starting in 2002, in Keswick, Ontario. He also builds mandolins.

Michael Cone

1968-present. Presentation grade, production/custom, classical guitars built previously in California and currently in Kihei Maui, Hawaii by luthier Michael Cone. He also builds ukuleles.

Michael Dunn Guitars

Luthier Michael Dunn begins in 1968, builds production/custom Maccaferri-style guitars in New Westminster, British Columbia. He also offers a harp uke and a Weissenborn- or Knutsen-style Hawaiian guitar and has built archtops.

Michael Kelly

1999-present. Founded by Tracy Hoeft and offering intermediate and professional grade, production, acoustic, solidbody and archtop guitars. The brand was owned by the Hanser Music Group from 2004-'15. They also offer mandolins and basses.

Michael Lewis Instruments

1992-present. Luthier Michael Lewis builds his premium and presentation grade, custom, archtop guitars in Grass Valley, California. He also builds mandolins.

Michael Menkevich

Luthier Michael Menkevich builds his professional and premium grade, production/custom, flamenco and classical guitars in Elkins Park, Pennsylvania, starting in 1970.

Michael Silvey Custom Guitars

2003-ca. 2007. Solidbody electric guitars built by Michael Silvey in North Canton, Ohio.

Michael Thames

1972-present. Luthier Michael Thames builds his premium grade, custom/production, classical guitars in Taos, New Mexico.

Michael Tuttle

2003-present. Professional and premium grade, custom, solid and hollowbody guitars and basses built by luthier Michael Tuttle in Saugus, California.

Michihiro Matsuda

1997-present. Presentation grade, production/custom, steel and nylon string acoustic guitars built by luthier Michihiro Matsuda in Oakland, California. He also builds harp guitars.

MODEL YEAR	FEATURES	EXC. COND. LOW	HIGH

Microfrets

1967-1975, 2004-2005. Professional grade, production, electric guitars built in Myersville, Maryland. They also built basses. Founded by Ralph S. Jones, Sr. in Frederick, Microfrets offered over 20 models of guitars that sported innovative designs and features, with pickups designed by Bill Lawrence. The brand was revived, again in Frederick, by Will Meadors and Paul Rose in '04.

Serial numbers run from about 1000 to about 3800. Not all instruments have serial numbers, particularly ones produced in '75. Serial numbers do not appear to be correlated to a model type but are sequential by the general date of production.

Instruments can be identified by body styles as follows; Styles 1, 1.5, 2, and 3. An instrument may be described as a Model Name and Style Number (for example, Covington Style 1). Style 1 has a wavey-shaped pickguard with control knobs mounted below the guard and the 2-piece guitar body has a particle board side gasket. Style 1.5 has the same guard and knobs, but no side body gasket. Style 2 has an oblong pickguard with top mounted control knobs and a pancake style seam between the top and lower part of the body. Style 3 has a seamless 2-piece body and a Speedline neck.

Baritone Signature

1971. Baritone version of Signature Guitar, sharply pointed double-cut, with or without f-holes, single- or double-dot inlays.

1971		$2,000	$3,000

Baritone Stage II

1971-ca. 1975. Double-cut, 2 pickups.

1971-1975		$2,500	$3,800

Calibra I

1969-1975. Double-cut, 2 pickups, f-hole.

1969-1975		$1,500	$2,200

Covington

1967-1969. Offset double-cut, 2 pickups, f-hole.

1967-1969		$1,500	$2,200

Golden Comet

1969. Double-cut, 2 pickups, f-hole, name changed to Wanderer.

1969		$2,000	$3,000

Golden Melody

1969, 2004-2005. Offset double-cut, 2 pickups, f-hole, name changed to Stage II in '69.

1969-1971		$2,000	$3,000

Huntington

1969-1975. Double-cut, 2 pickups.

1969-1975		$2,000	$3,000

Orbiter

1967-1969. Odd triple cutaway body, thumbwheel controls on bottom edge of 'guard.

1967-1969		$1,800	$2,800

Plainsman

1967-1969. Offset double-cut, 2 pickups, f-hole, thumbwheel controls on bottom edge of 'guard.

1967-1969		$1,500	$2,200

MODEL YEAR	FEATURES	EXC. COND. LOW	HIGH

Signature

1967-1969. Double-cut, 2 pickups.

1967-1969		$2,000	$3,000

Spacetone

1969-1971, 2004-2005. Double-cut semi-hollow body, 2 pickups.

1969-1971		$2,500	$4,000

Stage II

1969-1975. Renamed from Golden Melody, offset double-cut, 2 pickups.

1969-1975		$2,000	$3,000

Swinger

1971-1975. Offset double-cut, 2 pickups.

1971-1975		$1,800	$2,800

Voyager/The Voyager

1967-1968. Early model, less than a dozen made, Voyager headstock logo (no Microfrets logo), 2 DeArmond-style single-coils, offset double-cut body, FM transmitter on upper bass bout facilitates wireless transmission to Microfrets receiver or FM radio.

1967-1968		$2,000	$3,000

Wanderer

1969-1971. Renamed from Golden Comet, double-cut, 2 pickups.

1969-1971		$1,800	$2,800

Mike Lull Custom Guitars

1995-present. Professional and premium grade, production/custom, guitars and basses built by luthier Mike Lull in Bellevue, Washington.

Milburn Guitars

1990-present. Orville and Robert Milburn, father and son luthiers, build their premium grade, custom, classical guitars in Sweet Home, Oregon. Orville died in 2017.

Miller

1960s. One of the brand names of guitars built for others by Egmond in Holland.

Minarik

2002-present. Luthier M.E. Minarik builds his professional and premium grade, custom/production, solid and chambered body guitars in Van Nuys, California.

Minerva

1930s. Resonator and archtop guitars sold through catalog stores, likely made by one of the big Chicago builders of the era.

Mirabella

1997-present. Professional and premium grade, custom archtops, flat-tops, hollowbody, and solid-body guitars and basses built by luthier Cristian Mirabella in Babylon, New York. He also builds mandolins and ukes.

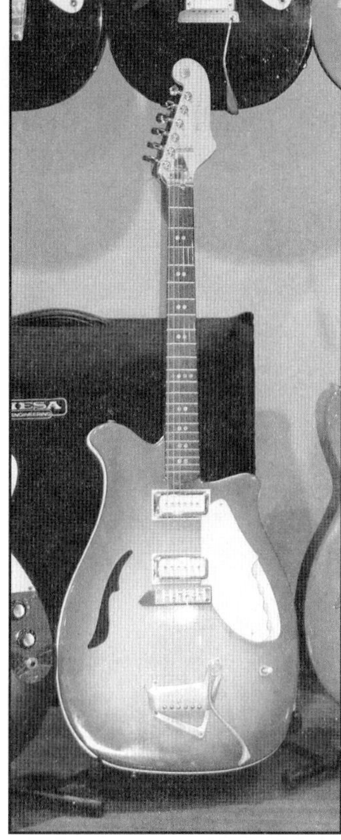

Microfrets Plainsman

Michael Kellum

Microfrets Spacetone

Michael Kellum

Modulus Blackknife
Joseph Fradella

Moll Custom Instruments

MODEL YEAR	FEATURES	EXC. COND. LOW	HIGH

Miranda Guitars

Owner Phil Green uses components made by various shops in California to assemble and set-up, professional grade, full-size travel/silent-practice guitars in Palo Alto, California. He started in 2002.

Mitre

1983-1985. Bolt neck, solidbody guitars and basses made in Aldenville (or East Longmeadow), Massachusetts, featuring pointy body shapes, 2 humbuckers, active or passive electronics.

MJ Guitar Engineering

1993-present. Professional and premium grade, production/custom, hollowbody, chambered and solidbody guitars and basses built by luthier Mark Johnson in Rohnert Park, California.

Mobius Megatar

2000-2019. Professional grade, production, hybrid guitars designed for two-handed tapping, built in Mount Shasta, California. Founded by Reg Thompson, Henri Dupont, and Traktor Topaz in '97, they released their first guitars in '00.

Modulus

1978-2013. Founded by Geoff Gould in the San Francisco area, and later built in Novato, California. Modulus built professional grade, production/custom, solidbody electric guitars up to '05.

Genesis 2/2T

1996-2005. Double-cut, extended bass horn alder body, bolt-on carbon fiber/red cedar neck, hum-single-single pickups, locking vibrato (2T model).

1996-2005		$2,000	$3,000

Moll Custom Instruments

1996-present. Luthier Bill Moll builds his professional and premium grade, archtops in Springfield, Missouri. He has also built violins, violas and cellos.

Monrad, Eric

1993-present. Premium, custom, flamenco and classical guitars built by luthier Eric Monrad in Healdsburg, California.

Monroe Guitars

Luthier Matt Handley builds his custom, professional grade, solidbody electric guitars and basses in State Center, Iowa. He started in 2004.

Montalvo

See the listing under Casa Montalvo.

Montaya

Late 1970s-1980s. Montaya Hyosung 'America' Inc., Korean acoustic and electric import copies.

Monteleone

1976-present. Presentation grade, production/custom, archtop guitars built by Luthier John Monteleone in Islip, New York. He also builds mandolins. Instruments should be evaluated on a case-by-case basis.

Eclipse

1990s. Very rare archtop.

1990s		$50,000	$65,000

Montgomery Ward

The mail-order and retail giant offered a variety of instruments and amps from several different U.S. and overseas manufacturers.

Model 8379/H44 Stratotone

Mid-1950s. Private branded Harmony Stratotone, some without logo but with crown-style stencil/painted logo on headstock, many with gold-copper finish, 1 pickup.

1950s	Various models	$1,200	$1,800

Monty

1980-present. Luthier Brian Monty builds his professional, premium and presentation grade, production/custom, archtop, semi-hollow, solidbody, and chambered electric guitars originally in Lennoxville, Quebec, and currently in Anne de Prescott, Ontario.

Moog

1964-present. Moog introduced its premium grade, production, Harmonic Control System solidbody guitar in 2008. They also offer guitar effects.

Moon (Japan)

1979-present. Professional and premium grade, production/custom, guitars and basses made in Japan.

Moon (Scotland)

1979-present. Intermediate, professional and premium grade, production/custom, acoustic and electric guitars built by luthier Jimmy Moon in Glasgow, Scotland. They also build mandolin family instruments.

Moonstone

1972-2020. Professional, premium, and presentation grade production/custom flat-top, solid and semi-hollow electric guitars, built by luthier Steve Helgeson in Eureka, California. He also built basses. Higher unit sales in the early-'80s. Some models have an optional graphite composite neck built by Modulus. Steve passed away in June 2020.

Earth Axe

1974-1976. Limited production, solidbody, natural finish.

1974-1976		$6,000	$8,000

Eclipse Deluxe

1979-1983. Figured birdseye maple body, offset double-cut, neck-thru, gold hardware, diamond markers, natural finish.

1979-1983		$3,000	$4,500

MODEL YEAR	FEATURES	EXC. COND. LOW	HIGH

Eclipse Standard

1979-1983. Figured wood body, offset double-cut, neck-thru, standard maple neck, dot markers, natural finish, 12-string (XII) available.

1979-1983		$2,500	$3,500
1979-1983	XII	$2,500	$3,500

Exploder

1980-1983. Figured wood solidbody, neck-thru, standard maple neck, natural finish.

1980-1983		$2,500	$3,500

Flaming V

1980-1984. Figured wood body, V-shaped, neck-thru, standard maple neck, natural finish.

1980-1984		$2,500	$3,500

M-80

1980-1984. Figured wood double-cut semi-hollow body, standard maple or optional graphite neck, natural finish.

1980s	Maple or graphite	$3,000	$3,500

Vulcan Deluxe

1979-1983. Figured maple carved-top body, offset double-cut, diamond markers, standard maple or optional graphite neck, natural finish.

1979-1983	Maple or graphite	$3,000	$3,500

Vulcan Standard

1979-1983. Mahogany carved-top body, offset double-cutaway, dot markers, standard maple or optional graphite neck, natural finish.

1979-1983	Maple or graphite	$3,000	$3,500

Morales

Ca.1967-1968. Guitars and basses made in Japan by Zen-On, not heavily imported into the U.S., if at all.

Solidbody Electric

1967-1968	Various models	$175	$300

More Harmony

1930s. Private branded by Dobro for Dailey's More Harmony Music Studio. Private branding for catalog companies, teaching studios, publishers, and music stores was common for the Chicago makers. More Harmony silk-screen logo on the headstock.

Dobro

1930s. 14" wood body with upper bout f-holes and metal resonator, sunburst.

1930s		$900	$1,300

Morgaine Guitars

1994-2004. Luthier Jorg Tandler built his professional and premium grade, production/custom electrics in Germany, until 2004. He started using Tandler name in '05.

Morgan Monroe

Intermediate grade, production, acoustic, acoustic/electric and resonator guitars and basses made in Korea and distributed by SHS International of Indianapolis, Indiana. They also offer mandolins and banjos.

Morris

1967-present. Intermediate, professional and premium grade, production, acoustic guitars imported by Moridaira of Japan. Morris guitars were first imported into the U.S. from the early '70s to around '90. They are again being imported into the U.S. starting in 2001. They also offered mandolins in the '70s.

000 Copy

1970s. Brazilian rosewood laminate body.

1970s		$900	$1,300

Acoustic-Electric Archtop

1970s	Various models	$900	$1,300

D-45 Copy

1970s. Brazilian rosewood laminate body.

1970s		$900	$1,300

Mortoro Guitars

1992-present. Luthier Gary Mortoro builds his premium grade, custom, archtop guitars in Miami, Florida.

Mosrite

The history of Mosrite has more ups and downs than just about any other guitar company. Founder Semie Moseley had several innovative designs and had his first success in 1954, at age 19, building doubleneck guitars for super picker Joe Maphis and protégé Larry Collins. Next came The Ventures, who launched the brand nationally by playing Mosrites and featuring them on album covers. At its '60s peak, the company was turning out around 1,000 guitars a month. The company ceased production in '69, and Moseley went back to playing gospel concerts and built a few custom instruments during the '70s.

In the early-'80s, Mosrite again set up shop in Jonas Ridge, North Carolina, but the plant burned down in November '83, taking about 300 guitars with it. In early-'92, Mosrite relocated to Booneville, Arkansas, producing a new line of Mosrites, of which 96% were exported to Japan, where the Ventures and Mosrite have always been popular. Semie Moseley died, at age 57, on August 7, '92 and the business carried on until finally closing its doors in '93. The Mosrite line has again been revived, offering intermediate and premium grade, production, reissues.

Throughout much of the history of Mosrite, production numbers were small and model features often changed. As a result, exact production dates are difficult to determine.

Balladeer

1964-1965. Mid-size flat-top, slope shoulder, natural or sunburst.

1964-1965		$1,500	$2,200

Brass Rail

1970s. Double-cut solidbody, has a brass plate running the length of the 'board.

1970s		$2,000	$3,000

1957 Montgomery Ward
Donald Kuntze

Moonstone Vulcan Deluxe

GUITARS

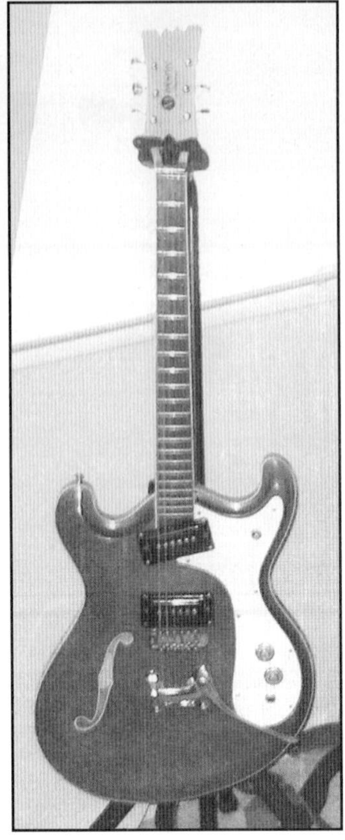
1968 Mosrite Combo
Dave Mullikin

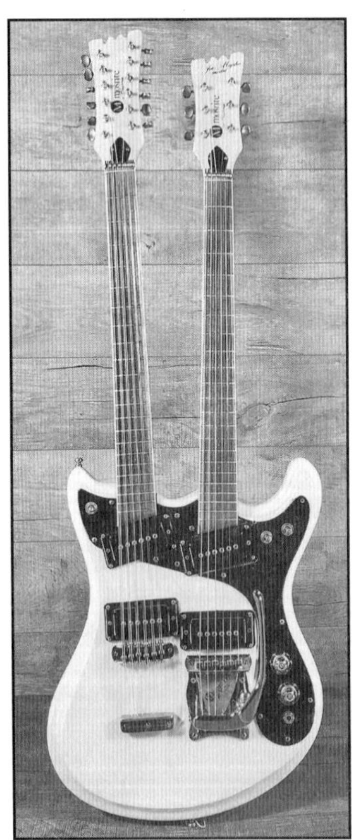
1968 Mosrite Joe Maphis Mark XVIII
Mathew A. Dirjish

MODEL YEAR	FEATURES	EXC. COND. LOW	HIGH

Celebrity 1

Late-1960s-1970s. Thick hollowbody, 2 pickups, sunburst.

1960s-70s		$2,000	$3,000

Celebrity 2 Standard

Late-1960s-1970s. Thin hollowbody, 2 pickups, in the '70s, it came in a Standard and a Deluxe version.

1960s-70s		$2,200	$3,300

Celebrity 3

Late-1960s-1970s. Thin hollowbody, double-cut, 2 pickups, f-holes.

1960s-70s		$2,000	$3,000

Combo Mark 1

1966-1968. Bound body, 1 f-hole.

1966-1968		$2,500	$3,800

Custom-Built

1952-1962. Pre-production custom instruments hand built by Semie Moseley, guidance pricing only, each instrument will vary. A wide variety of instruments were made during this period. Some were outstanding, but others, especially those made around '60, could be very basic and of much lower quality. Logos would vary widely and some '60 logos looked especially homemade.

1952-1959	Rare, high-end	$8,000	$12,000
1960-1962	Common, low-end	$2,000	$4,500

D-40 Resonator

1960s. Symmetrical double-cut thinline archtop-style body with metal resonator in center of body, 2 pickups, 2 control knobs and toggle switch.

1960s		$2,200	$3,300

D-100 Californian

1960s. Double-cut, resonator guitar with 2 pickups.

1967		$2,500	$3,800

Gospel

1967. Thinline double-cut, f-hole, 2 pickups, vibrato, Gospel logo on headstock.

1967	Sunburst	$2,500	$3,800
1967	White	$3,000	$4,500

Joe Maphis Doubleneck

1963-1968. Limited Edition reissue of the guitar Semie Moseley made for Maphis, with the smaller octave neck, sunburst.

1963-1968	Octave 6/standard 6	$5,000	$10,000
1963-1968	Standard 6/12	$5,000	$10,000

Joe Maphis Mark 1

1959-1972. Semi-hollow double-cut, 2 single-coils, spruce top, walnut back, rosewood 'board, natural.

1959-1972		$3,000	$4,500

Joe Maphis Mark XVIII

1960s. 6/12 doubleneck, double-cut, 2 pickups on each neck, Moseley tremolo on 6-string.

1960s		$5,000	$10,000

Mosrite 1988

1988-early-1990s. Has traditional Mosrite body styling, Mosrite pickups and bridge.

1988		$1,800	$2,800

Octave Guitar

1963-1965. 14" scale, 1 pickup, Ventures Mosrite body style, single neck pickup, very few made.

1963-1965		$3,500	$6,000

Stereo 350

1974-1975. Single-cut solidbody, 2 outputs, 2 pickups, 4 knobs, slider and toggle, black.

1974-1975		$2,500	$3,800

Ventures Model

1963-1968. Double-cut solidbody, triple-bound body '63, no binding after, Vibramute for '63-'64, Moseley tailpiece '65-'68.

1963	Blue or red, bound	$7,000	$9,500
1963	Sunburst, bound	$5,500	$8,000
1964	Blue or red, Vibramute	$5,000	$7,000
1964	Sunburst, Vibramute	$5,500	$8,000
1965	Moseley (2 screws)	$3,000	$4,500
1965	Vibramute, (3 screws)	$4,000	$6,000
1966-1968	Moseley	$2,800	$4,000

Ventures (Jonas Ridge/Boonville)

1982-1993. Made in Jonas Ridge, NC or Booneville, AR, classic Ventures styling.

1982-1993		$2,000	$4,500

Ventures Mark V

1963-1967. Double-cut solidbody.

1963-1967		$3,500	$5,500

Ventures Mark XII

1966-1967. Double-cut solidbody, 12 strings.

1966-1967		$3,000	$4,500

Mossman

Professional and premium grade, production/custom, flat-top guitars built in Sulphur Springs, Texas, starting in 1965. They have also built acoustic basses. Founded by Stuart L. Mossman in Winfield, Kansas. In '75, fire destroyed one company building, including the complete supply of Brazilian rosewood. They entered into an agreement with C.G. Conn Co. to distribute guitars by '77. 1200 Mossman guitars in a Conn warehouse in Nevada were ruined by being heated during the day and frozen during the night. A disagreement about who was responsible resulted in cash flow problems for Mossman. Production fell to a few guitars per month until the company was sold in '86 to Scott Baxendale. Baxendale sold the company to John Kinsey and Bob Casey in Sulphur Springs in '89.

Flint Hills

1970-1979. Flat-top acoustic, East Indian rosewood back and sides.

1970-1979	Indian rosewood	$2,500	$3,500

Flint Hills Custom

1970-1979	Indian rosewood	$3,000	$4,000

Golden Era

1970-1977. D-style, vine inlay and other high-end appointments, Brazilian rosewood back and sides until '76, then Indian rosewood.

1970-1975	Brazilian rosewood	$6,000	$8,000
1976-1977	Indian rosewood	$4,500	$5,500

Golden Era Custom

1970-1975	Brazilian rosewood	$7,500	$10,000

MODEL YEAR	FEATURES	EXC. COND. LOW	HIGH

Great Plains

1970-1979. Flat-top, Brazilian rosewood until '75 then Indian rosewood, herringbone trim.

1970-1975	Brazilian rosewood	$4,500	$7,000
1976-1979	Indian rosewood	$3,500	$4,500

Great Plains Custom

1970-1975	Brazilian rosewood	$6,500	$8,500

Southwind

1976-ca. 1986, mid-1990s-2002. Flat-top, abalone trim top.

1976-1979	Indian rosewood	$3,000	$4,000

Tennessee

1972-1979. D-style, spruce top, mahogany back and sides, rope marquetry purfling, rope binding.

1972-1979		$2,000	$3,000

Tennessee 12-String

1975-1979	Mahogany	$2,500	$3,500

Timber Creek

1976-1979. D-style, Indian rosewood back and sides, spruce top.

1976-1979	Indian rosewood	$3,000	$4,500

Winter Wheat

1976-1979, mid-1990s-2000s. Flat-top, Indian rosewood back and sides, abalone trim, natural finish.

1976-1979	Indian rosewood	$3,000	$4,500

Winter Wheat 12-String

1976-1979. 12-string version of Winter Wheat, natural.

1976-1979	Indian rosewood	$3,500	$5,000

MotorAve Guitars

2002-present. Luthier Mark Fuqua builds his professional and premium grade, production, electric guitars originally in Los Angeles, California, and currently in Durham, North Carolina.

Mouradian

1983-present. Luthiers Jim and Jon Mouradian build their professional and premium grade, production/custom, electric guitars and basses in Winchester, Massachusetts. Jim died in 2017.

Mozart

1930s. Private brand made by Kay.

Hawaiian (Square Neck)

1930s. Spruce top, solid mahogany sides and back, pearloid overlay on peghead with large Mozart inscribed logo, small jumbo 15 1/2" body.

1935-1939		$1,100	$1,600

Mozzani

Built in shops of Luigi Mozzani (b. March 9, 1869, Faenza, Italy; d. 1943) who opened lutherie schools in Bologna, Cento and Rovereto in 1890s. By 1926 No. 1 and 2 Original Mozzani Model Mandolin (flat back), No. 3 Mandola (flat back), No. 4 6-String Guitar, No. 5 7-, 8-, and 9-String Guitars, No. 6 Lyre-Guitar.

M-Tone Guitars

2009-present. Professional and premium grade, production/custom, solidbody electric guitars built in Portland, Oregon by luthier Matt Proctor.

MODEL YEAR	FEATURES	EXC. COND. LOW	HIGH

Muiderman Guitars

1997-present. Custom, premium grade, steel string and classical guitars built by luthier Kevin Muiderman currently in Grand Forks, North Dakota, and previously in Beverly Hills, Michigan, 1997-2001, and Neenah, Wisconsin, '01-'07. He also builds mandolins.

Murph

1965-1967. Mid-level electric semi-hollow and solidbody guitars built by Pat Murphy in San Fernado, California. Murph logo on headstock. They also offered basses and amps.

Electric Solidbody

1965-1967		$1,200	$1,800

Electric XII

1965-1967		$1,200	$1,800

Music Man

1972-present. Professional grade, production, solidbody guitars built in San Luis Obispo, California. They also build basses. Founded by ex-Fender executives Forrest White and Tom Walker in Orange County, California. Music Man originally produced guitar and bass amps based on early Fender ideas using many former Fender employees. They contracted with Leo Fender's CLF Research to design and produce a line of solidbody guitars and basses. Leo Fender began G & L Guitars with George Fullerton in '80. In '84, Music Man was purchased by Ernie Ball and production was moved to San Luis Obispo.

Albert Lee Signature

1993-present. Swamp ash body, figured maple neck, 3 pickups, white pearloid 'guard, Pinkburst.

1993-2024	Pinkburst	$2,000	$3,500
1996-2019	Tremolo option	$1,800	$2,800

Axis

1996-present. Offset double-cut solidbody, figured maple top, basswood body, 2 humbucker pickups, Floyd Rose.

1996-2024		$1,500	$2,200

Axis Sport

1996-2002. Two P-90s.

1996-2002		$1,200	$1,800

Axis Super Sport

2003-present. Figured top.

2003-2024		$1,800	$3,200

Edward Van Halen

1991-1996. Basswood solidbody, figured maple top, bolt-on maple neck, maple 'board, binding, 2 humbuckers, named changed to Axis.

1991-1996	6,000 made	$5,500	$7,000
1991-1996	Rare color (purple & black)	$6,000	$10,000

John Petrucci 6/JP-6

2008-2021. Standard model, basswood body, maple neck, rosewood 'board, various colors with high gloss finish.

2008-2021		$2,000	$3,000

1976 Mossman Flint Hills

Allen Boudreaux

1976 Mossman Southwind

GUITARS

1976 Music Man Stingray II
Cream City Music

Music Man Steve Morse Signature

MODEL YEAR	FEATURES	EXC. COND. LOW	HIGH

John Petrucci BFR

2011-2020. Ball Family Reserve (BFR).

2011-2020		$2,800	$4,500

Reflex

2011-2017. Referred to as The Game Changer, patent-pending pickup switching system, maple or rosewood neck with matching headstock, black finish.

2011-2017		$1,200	$1,800

S.U.B 1

2004-2006. Offset double-cut solidbody.

2004-2005		$600	$900

Sabre I

1978-1982. Offset double-cut solidbody, maple neck, 2 pickups, Sabre I comes with a flat 'board with jumbo frets.

1978-1982		$2,500	$4,500

Sabre II

1978-1982. Same as Sabre I, but with an oval 7 1/2" radius 'board.

1978-1982		$2,500	$4,500

Silhouette

1986-present. Offset double-cut, contoured beveled solidbody, various pickup configurations.

1986-2024		$1,200	$1,800
2006	20th Anniversary	$1,800	$2,800

Silhouette 6/12 Double Neck

2009-2014. Alder body, maple or rosewood 'boards, 4 humbuckers.

2009-2014		$3,000	$4,500

Silhouette Special

1995-present. Silhouette with Silent Circuit.

1995-2024		$1,200	$1,800

Steve Morse Signature

1987-present. Solidbody, 4 pickups, humbuckers in the neck and bridge positions, 2 single-coils in the middle, special pickup switching, 6-bolt neck mounting, maple neck.

1987-2024		$1,500	$2,200

Stingray I

1976-1982. Offset double-cut solidbody, flat 'board radius.

1976-1982		$3,000	$5,000

Stingray II

1976-1982. Offset double-cut solidbody, rounder 'board radius.

1976-1982		$3,000	$5,000

Musicvox

1996-2001, 2011-present. Intermediate grade, production, imported retro-vibe guitars and basses from Matt Eichen of Cherry Hill, New Jersey.

Myka

2003-present. Luthier David Myka builds his professional and premium grade, custom/production, solidbody, semi-hollowbody, hollowbody, archtop, and flat-top guitars in Seattle, Washington. Until '07 he was located in Orchard Park, New York.

Nady

1976-present. Wireless sound company Nady Systems offered guitars and basses with built-in wireless systems for 1985-'87. Made by Fernandes in Japan until '86, then by Cort in Korea.

Lightning/Lightning II

1985-1987. Double-cut, neck-thru, solidbody, 24 frets, built-in wireless, labeled as just Lightning until cheaper second version (bolt-neck) came out in '86.

1985-1987		$350	$600

Napolitano Guitars

1993-2010. Luthier Arthur Napolitano built professional and premium grade, custom, archtop guitars in Allentown, New Jersey.

NashGuitars

2001-present. Luthier Bill Nash builds his professional grade, production/custom, aged solidbody electric guitars and basses in Olympia, Washington.

Nashville Guitar Company

1985-present. Professional and premium grade, custom, flat-top guitars built by luthier Marty Lanham in Nashville, Tennessee. He has also built banjos.

National

Ca. 1927-present. Founded in Los Angeles as the National String Instrument Corporation by John Dopyera, George Beauchamp, Ted Kleinmeyer and Paul Barth. In '29 Dopyera left to start the Dobro Manufacturing Company with Rudy and Ed Dopyera and Vic Smith. The Dobro company competed with National until the companies reunited. Beauchamp and Barth then left National to found Ro-Pat-In with Adolph Rickenbacker and C.L. Farr (later becoming Electro String Instrument Corporation, then Rickenbacher). In '32 Dopyera returns to National and National and Dobro start their merger in late-'33, finalizing it by mid-'34. Throughout the '30s, National and Dobro maintained separate production, sales, and distribution. National Dobro moved to Chicago in '36 where archtop and flat-top bodies are built primarily by Regal and Kay; after '37 all National resonator guitar bodies made by Kay. L.A. production is maintained until around '37, although some assembly of Dobros continued in L.A. (primarily for export) until '39 when the L.A. offices are finally closed. By ca. '39 the Dobro brand disappears.

In '42, the company's resonator production ceased, and Victor Smith, Al Frost and Louis Dopyera buy the company and change name to Valco Manufacturing Company. Post-war production resumed in '46. Valco was purchased by treasurer Robert Engelhardt in '64. In '67, Valco bought Kay, but in '68 the new Valco/Kay company went out of business. In the Summer of '69 the assets, including brand names, were auctioned off and the National and Supro names were purchased by Chicago-area distributor/importer Strum 'N Drum (Noble, Norma brands). The National brand is used on copies in the early- to mid-'70s, and the brand went into hiatus by the '80s.

In '88 National Resophonic Guitars is founded

MODEL YEAR	FEATURES	EXC. COND. LOW	HIGH

in San Luis Obispo, California, by Don Young, with production of National-style resonator guitars beginning in '89 (see following). In the '90s, the National brand also resurfaces on inexpensive Asian imports.

National Resonator guitars are categorized by materials and decoration (from plain to fancy): Duolian, Triolian, Style 0, Style 1, Style 2, Style 3, Style 4, Don #1, Style 97, Don #2, Don #3, Style 35.

National guitars all have serial numbers which provide clues to date of production. This is a complex issue. This list combines information included in George Gruhn and Walter Carter's Gruhn's Guide to Vintage Guitars, which was originally provided by Bob Brozman and Mike Newton, with new information provided by Mike Newton.

Pre Chicago numbers:
A101-A450 1935-1936.

Chicago numbers:
A prefix (some may not have the prefix) 1936-mid-1997. B prefix Mid-1937-1938. C prefix Late-1938-1940. G prefix up to 200 Ea. 1941-ea. 1942. G suffix under 2000 Ea. 1941-ea. 1942. G suffix 2000-3000s (probably old parts) 1943-1945. G suffix 4000s (old parts) Late 1945-mid-1947.

V100-V7500 1947. V7500-V15000 1948. V15000-V25000 1949. V25000-V35000 1950. V35000-V38000 1951. X100-X7000 1951. X7000-X17000 1952. X17000-X30000 1953. X30000-X43000 1954. X43000-X57000 1955. X57000-X71000 1956. X71000-X85000 1957. X85000-X990001958.

T100-T5000 1958. T5000-T25000 1959. T25000-T50000 1960. T50000-T75000 1961. T75000-T90000 1962. G100-G5000 1962. T90000-T99000 1963. G5000-G15000 1963. G15000-G40000 1964. 1 prefix 1965-ea. 1968. 2 prefix Mid-1968.

Aragon De Luxe
1939-1942. Archtop with resonator (the only archtop resonator offered), spruce top and maple back and sides, light brown.
1939-1942 $8,500 $11,000

Big Daddy LP-457-2
1970s. Strum & Drum import, single-cut, LP-style, 2 pickups, gold hardware, black.
1970s $325 $450

Bluegrass 35
1963-1965. Acoustic, non-cut single-cone resonator, Res-O-Glas body in Arctic White.
1963-1965 $1,750 $2,250

Bobbie Thomas
Ca.1967-1968. Double-cut thinline hollowbody, bat-shaped f-holes, 2 pickups, Bobbie Thomas on 'guard, vibrato.
1967-1968 $1,250 $1,500

Cameo
1957-1958. Renamed from Model 1140 in '57, full-body acoustic archtop with carved top.
1957-1958 $850 $1,125

MODEL YEAR	FEATURES	EXC. COND. LOW	HIGH

Collegian
1942-1943. Metal body resonator similar to Duolian, 14-fret round or square neck, yellow.
1942-1943 $1,500 $2,000

Don Style 1
1934-1936. Plain body with engraved borders, pearl dot inlay, 14 frets, single-cone, silver (nickel-plated).
1934-1936 $9,000 $11,500

Don Style 2
1934-1936. Geometric Art Deco body engraving, 14 frets, single-cone, fancy square pearl inlays and pearloid headstock overlay, silver (nickel-plated).
1934-1936 $10,500 $13,500

Don Style 3
1934-1936. Same as Style 2 but more elaborate floral engravings, fancy pearl diamond inlays, 14 frets, single-cone, silver (nickel-plated), only a very few made.
1934-1936 $18,500 $25,000

Duolian
1930-1939. Acoustic steel body, frosted paint finish until '36, mahogany-grain paint finish '37-'39, round neck, square neck available in '33, 12-fret neck until '34 then 14-fret.
1930-1934 Round neck $3,500 $4,500

EG 685 Hollow Body Electric
1970s. Strum & Drum distributed, double-cut hollowbody copy, 2 pickups.
1970s $550 $700

El Trovador
1933 only. Wood body, 12 frets.
1933 $3,000 $4,000

Electric Spanish
1935-1938. 15 1/2" archtop with Pat. Appl. For bridge pickup, National crest logo, fancy N-logo 'guard, black and white art deco, sunburst, becomes New Yorker Spanish '39-'58.
1935-1938 $2,250 $2,750

Estralita
1934-1942. Acoustic with single-cone resonator, f-holes, multi-bound, 14-fret, mahogany top and back, shaded brown.
1934-1942 $1,250 $1,750

Glenwood 95
1962-1964. Glenwood 98 without third bridge-mount pickup, Vermillion Red or Flame Red.
1962-1964 $3,500 $4,500

Glenwood 98
1964-1965. USA map-shaped solidbody of molded Res-O-Glas, 2 regular and 1 bridge pickup, vibrato, 3 tailpiece options, Pearl White.
1964-1965 $3,500 $4,500

Glenwood 99
1962-1965. USA map-shaped solidbody of molded Res-O-Glas, 2 regular and 1 bridge pickups, butterfly inlay.
1962-1963 Snow White $3,500 $4,500
1964-1965 Green/Blue $9,000 $11,500

Glenwood Deluxe
1959-1961. Renamed from Glenwood 1105, Les Paul-shaped solidbody, wood body, not fiberglass, multi-bound, 2 pickups, factory Bigsby, vibrato, natural.
1959-1961 $2,250 $3,000

Nash T52
Jonh Childs

National Don Style 1
Imaged by Heritage Auctions, HA.com

GUITARS

1937 National Duolian
Imaged by Heritage Auctions, HA.com

1954 National Model N-66/1155
Imaged by Heritage Auctions, HA.com

MODEL YEAR	FEATURES	EXC. COND. LOW	HIGH

Havana

1938-1942. Natural spruce top, sunburst back and sides.

1938-1942	Round neck	$1,250	$1,500
1938-1942	Square neck	$800	$1,000

Model 1100 California

1949-1955. Electric hollowbody archtop, multi-bound, f-holes, trapeze tailpiece, 1 pickup, natural.

1949-1955		$950	$1,250

Model 1103 Del-Mar

1954-1957. Electric archtop, 2 pickups, adjustable bridge, sunburst finish.

1954-1957		$1,000	$1,250

Model 1104 Town and Country

1954-1958. Model just below Glenwood 1105, dots, 2 or 3 pickups, plastic overlay on back, natural finish.

1954-1958	2 pickups	$1,750	$2,250
1954-1958	3 pickups	$2,000	$2,500

Model 1105 Glenwood

1954-1958. Les Paul-shaped solidbody, wood body, not fiberglass, single-cut, multi-bound, 2 pickups, natural, renamed Glenwood Deluxe with Bigsby in '59.

1954-1958		$2,500	$3,000

Model 1106 Val-Trol Baron

1959-1960. Single-cut solidbody, 2 pickups, 1 piezo, block inlays, black.

1959-1960		$1,500	$2,500

Model 1107 Debonaire

1953-1960. Single rounded-cutaway full-depth 16" electric archtop, single neck pickup, Debonaire logo on 'guard (for most models), large raised National script logo on headstock, sunburst.

1953-1960		$1,000	$1,250

Model 1109/1198 Bel-Aire

1953-1960. Single pointed cut archtop, 2 (1109) pickups until '57, 3 (1198) after, master tone knob and jack, bound body, sunburst.

1953-1957	1109, 2 pickups	$1,500	$1,875
1958-1960	1198, 3 pickups	$1,750	$2,250

Model 1110/1111 Aristocrat

1941-1954. Electric full body non-cut archtop, 1 pickup, 2 knobs, early model with triple backslash markers, later with block markers, National-crest headstock inlaid logo, natural finish only until model numbers added to name in '48, shaded sunburst finish (1110) and natural (1111).

1941-1948	Natural	$900	$1,125
1948-1955	1110, sunburst	$1,000	$1,250
1948-1955	1111, natural	$1,000	$1,250

Model 1120 New Yorker

1954-1958. Renamed from New Yorker Spanish, 16.25" electric archtop, 1 pickup on floating 'guard, dot markers, blond.

1954-1958		$1,000	$1,250

Model 1122 Cosmopolitan

1954-1957. Small wood non-cutaway solidbody, dot markers, 1 pickup, 2 knobs on mounted 'guard.

1954-1957		$950	$1,250

Model 1122 Val-Trol Junior

1959-1960. Single-cut solidbody, 1 pickup and 1piezo, dot inlays, ivory.

1959-1960		$1,000	$1,250

Model 1123 Bolero

1954-1957. Les Paul-shape, control knobs mounted on 'guard, single pickup, trapeze tailpiece, sunburst.

1954-1957		$900	$1,125

Model 1124/1124B/1134 Avalon

1954-1957. Small wood solidbody, 2 pickups, 4 control knobs and switch on top-mounted 'guard, block markers, short trapeze bridge, sunburst (1124) or blond (1124B).

1954-1957	1124, sunburst	$1,000	$1,250
1954-1957	1124B/1134, blond	$1,250	$1,500

Model 1125 Dynamic

1951-1959. Full body 15.5" acoustic-electric archtop, sunburst version of New Yorker 1120 with some appointments slightly below the New Yorker, dot markers, 1 pickup, sunburst.

1951-1959		$850	$1,125

Model 1135 Acoustic Archtop

1948-1954. 17.25" full body acoustic archtop, carved top, split pearl markers.

1948-1954		$1,250	$1,500

Model 1140 Acoustic Archtop

1948-1957. 15.5" full body acoustic archtop, carved top, dot markers.

1948-1957		$850	$1,125

Model 1150 Flat-Top Auditorium

1951-1958. Auditorium-size flat-top, 14.25" narrow-waist, dot markers.

1951-1958		$850	$1,125

Model 1155/1155E /N-66 Jumbo

1948-1961. Flat-top acoustic with Gibson Jumbo body, mahogany back and sides, bolt-on neck.

1947	N-66	$2,500	$3,250
1948-1961	1155/1155E	$2,500	$3,250

Model 1170 Club Combo

1952-1955, 1959-1961. Electric hollowbody archtop, 2 pickups, rounded cutaway.

1952-1961		$1,250	$1,500

N600 Series

1968. Offset double-cut solidbody, 1, 2, and 3 pickup models, with and without vibrato.

1968	N624, 1 pickup	$500	$650
1968	N634, 2 pus, vibrato	$600	$750
1968	N644, 3 pus, vibrato	$800	$1,000
1968	N654, 12-string	$600	$750

N700 Series

1968. Flat-top, 700/710 dreadnoughts, 720/730 jumbos.

1968	N700 Western	$600	$750
1968	N710	$350	$450
1968	N720 Western	$400	$500
1968	N730 Deluxe	$550	$750

N800 Series

1968. Double-cut semi-hollow body, various models with or without Bigsby.

1968	No Bigsby	$600	$750
1968	With Bigsby	$700	$875

New Yorker Spanish

1939-1953. Electric archtop, 15.5" body until '47 then 16.25", 1 neck pickup, dot-diamond markers, sunburst or natural. Renamed New Yorker 1120 in '54.

1939-1946	155"	$2,000	$2,500

MODEL YEAR	FEATURES	EXC. COND. LOW	HIGH
1947-1949	1625"	$1,750	$2,250
1950-1953	1625"	$1,500	$1,875

Newport 82

1963-1965. Renamed from Val-Pro 82, USA map-shaped Res-O-Glas, 1 pickup, Pepper Red finish.

1963-1965		$2,250	$3,000

Newport 84

1963-1965. Renamed from Val-Pro 84, USA map-shaped Res-O-Glas, 1 regular and 1 bridge pickup, Sea Foam Green finish.

1963-1965		$3,500	$4,500

Newport 88

1963-1965. Renamed from Val-Pro 88, USA map-shaped Res-O-Glas, 2 regular and 1 bridge pickup, Raven Black finish.

1963-1965		$2,500	$3,500

Reso-phonic

1956-1964. Pearloid-covered, single-cut semi-solidbody acoustic, single resonator, maroon or white, also a non-cut, square neck version was offered, which is included in these values.

1956-1964	Round neck, common finish	$1,500	$1,875
1956-1964	Round neck, rare finish	$1,750	$2,250
1956-1964	Square neck	$1,250	$1,500

Rosita

1933-1939. Plywood body by Harmony, plain metal resonator, plain appointments.

1933-1939		$1,125	$1,500

Silvo (Electric Hawaiian)

1937-1941. Nickel-plated metal body flat-top, small upper bout, f-holes, square neck, multiple straight line body art over dark background, Roman numeral parallelogram markers, National badge headstock logo, Silvo name on coverplate.

1937-1941	Silver	$3,250	$4,000

Studio 66

1961-1964. Electric solidbody of Res-O-Glas, single-cut, 1 pickup, renamed Varsity 66 in '65.

1961-1962	Sand Buff, bridge pu	$1,250	$1,500
1963-1964	Jet Black, neck pu	$1,250	$1,500

Style 0

1930-1942. Acoustic single-cone brass body (early models had a steel body), Hawaiian scene etching, 12-fret neck '30-'34, 14-fret neck '35 on, round (all years) or square ('33 on) neck.

1930-1934	Round neck, 12-fret, common etching	$3,500	$4,500
1930-1934	Round neck, 12-fret, rare etching	$4,500	$8,000
1933-1942	Square neck, common etching	$1,500	$2,000
1933-1942	Square neck, rare etching	$3,000	$3,750
1935-1942	Round, 14-fret (Knopfler assoc)	$7,000	$9,000
1935-1942	Round, 14-fret, common etching	$3,000	$3,750
1935-1942	Round, 14-fret, rare etching	$4,500	$7,500

Style 0 Tenor

1929-1930. Tenor, 4 strings, single-cone brass body, Hawaiian scene etching.

1929-1930		$950	$1,250

Style 1 Tricone

1927-1943. German silver body tricone resonator, ebony 'board, mahogany square (Hawaiian) or round (Spanish) neck, plain body, 12-fret neck until '34, 14-fret after.

1927-1943	Round neck	$5,500	$7,500
1928-1943	Square neck	$4,000	$5,000

Style 1 Tricone Plectrum

1928-1935. 26" scale versus the 23" scale of the tenor.

1928-1935		$2,000	$2,500

Style 1 Tricone Tenor

1928-1935. Tenor, 4 strings, 23" scale, square neck is Hawaiian, round neck is Spanish.

1928-1935		$2,000	$2,500

Style 1.5 Tricone

1930s. A "1/2" style like the 1.5 represents a different engraving pattern.

1930s	Round neck	$9,000	$11,500
1930s	Square neck	$3,000	$4,000

Style 2 Tricone

1927-1942. German silver body tricone resonator, wild rose engraving, square (Hawaiian) or round (Spanish) neck, 12-fret neck until '34, 14-fret after.

1927-1942	Round neck	$11,500	$14,500
1927-1942	Square neck	$3,500	$4,500

Style 2 Tricone Plectrum

1928-1935. 26" scale versus the 23" scale of the tenor.

1928-1935		$1,500	$2,000

Style 2 Tricone Tenor

1928-1935. Tenor.

1928-1935		$1,750	$2,250

Style 2.5 Tricone

1927-1928. Collector term for Style 2 with additional rose engravings on coverplate, bound ebony fretboard.

1927-1928		$8,500	$11,500

Style 3 Tricone

1928-1941. German silver body tricone resonator, lily-of-the-valley engraving, square (Hawaiian) or round (Spanish) neck, 12-fret neck until '34, 14-fret after, reintroduced with a nickel-plated brass body in '94.

1928-1939	Round neck	$14,000	$18,000
1928-1941	Square neck	$5,000	$6,500

Style 3 Tricone Plectrum

1928-1935. 26" scale versus the 23" scale of the tenor.

1928-1935		$3,000	$4,000

Style 3 Tricone Tenor

1928-1939. Tenor version.

1928-1939		$2,750	$3,500

Style 4 Tricone

1928-1940. German silver body tricone resonator, chrysanthemum etching, 12-fret neck until '34, 14-fret after, reissued in '95 with same specs.

1928-1940	Round neck	$18,000	$22,500
1928-1940	Square neck	$5,000	$7,000

1968 National N634

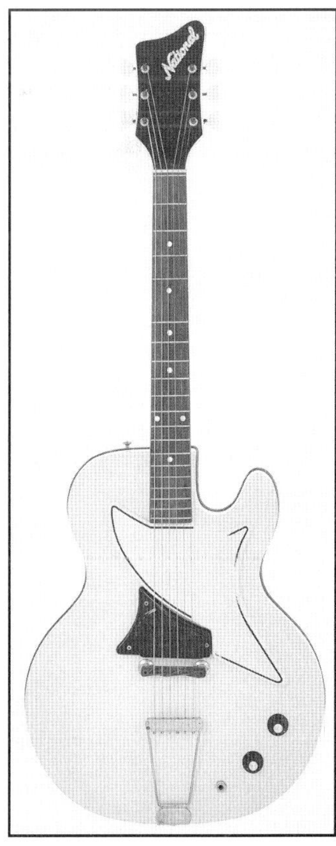

1962 National Studio 66

Imaged by Heritage Auctions, HA.com

GUITARS

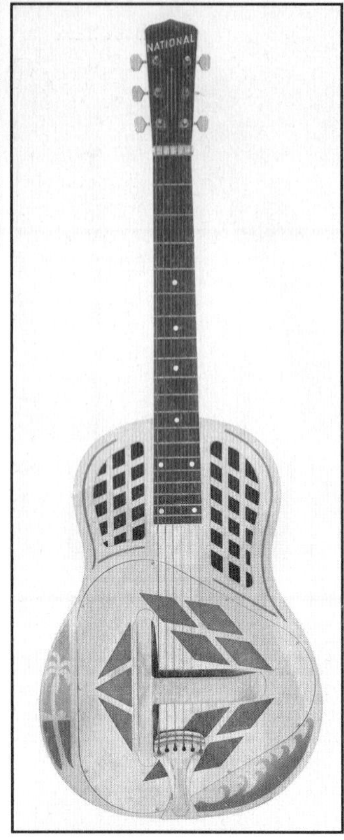
1936 National Style 97
Imaged by Heritage Auctions, HA.com

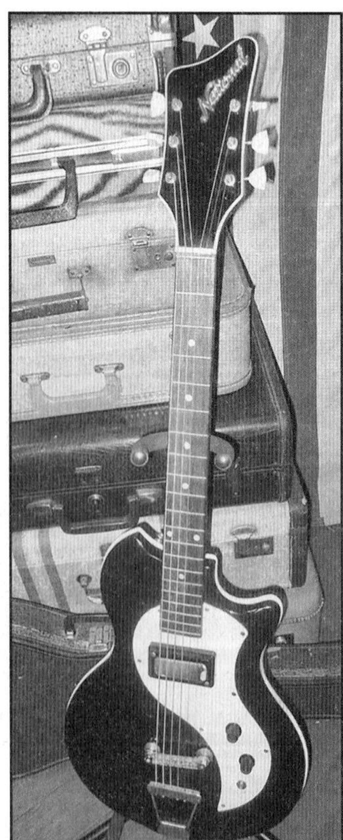
1964 National Varsity 66
Rivington Guitars

MODEL YEAR	FEATURES	EXC. COND. LOW	HIGH

Style 35

1936-1942. Brass body tricone resonator, sandblasted minstrel and trees scene, 12 frets, square (Hawaiian) or round (Spanish) neck.

1936-1942	Round neck	$31,500	$40,000
1936-1942	Square neck	$10,500	$13,500

Style 97

1936-1940. Nickel-plated brass body tricone resonator, sandblasted scene of female surf rider and palm trees, 12 frets, slotted peghead.

1936	Early '36, square neck	$10,500	$13,500
1936	Late '36, square neck, different 'board	$7,000	$9,000
1936-1940	Round neck	$28,000	$35,000

Style N

1930-1931. Nickel-plated brass body single-cone resonator, plain finish, 12 frets.

1930-1931		$5,000	$7,000

Triolian

1928-1941. Single-cone resonator, wood body replaced by metal body in '29, 12-fret neck and slotted headstock '28-'34, changed to 14-fret neck in '35 and solid headstock in '36, round or square ('33 on) neck available.

1928-1936	Various colors	$3,000	$3,750
1936-1937	Fake rosewood grain	$2,750	$3,500

Triolian Tenor

1928-1936. Tenor, metal body.

1928-1936		$1,125	$1,500

Trojan

1934-1942. Single-cone resonator wood body, f-holes, bound top, 14-fret round neck.

1934-1942		$1,250	$1,750

Val-Pro 82

1962-1963. USA map-shaped Res-O-Glas, 1 pickup, Vermillion Red finish, renamed Newport 82 in '63.

1962-1963		$1,500	$1,875

Val-Pro 84

1962-1963. USA map-shaped Res-O-Glas, 1 regular and 1 bridge pickup, snow white finish, renamed Newport 84 in '63.

1962-1963		$1,750	$2,250

Val-Pro 88

1962-1963. USA map-shaped Res-O-Glas, 2 regular and 1 bridge pickup, black finish, renamed Newport 88 in '63.

1962-1963		$2,500	$3,000

Varsity 66

1964-1965. Renamed from Studio 66 in '64, molded Res-O-Glas, 1 pickup, 2 knobs, beige finish.

1964-1965		$1,250	$1,500

Westwood 72

1962-1964. USA map-shaped solid hardwood body (not fiberglass), 1 pickup, Cherry Red.

1962-1964		$2,000	$2,500

Westwood 75

1962-1964. USA map-shaped solid hardwood body (not fiberglass), 1 regular and 1 bridge pickup, cherry-to-black sunburst finish.

1962-1964		$2,000	$2,500

MODEL YEAR	FEATURES	EXC. COND. LOW	HIGH

Westwood 77

1962-1965. USA map-shaped solid hardwood body (not fiberglass), 2 regular and 1 bridge pickup.

1962-1965	Blond-Ivory	$2,000	$2,500

National Reso-Phonic

1989-present. Professional and premium grade, production/custom, single cone, acoustic-electric, and tricone guitars (all with resonators), built in San Luis Obispo, California. They also build basses, mandolins, and ukuleles. McGregor Gaines and Don Young formed the National Reso-Phonic Guitar Company with the objective of building instruments based upon the original National designs. Replicon is the aging process to capture the appearance and sound of a vintage National.

Collegian

2010-2020. Thin gauge steel body, 9.5" cone, biscuit bridge, aged ivory finish.

2010-2020		$1,250	$1,750

Delphi

1993-2010. Single cone, steel body.

1993-2010		$1,500	$2,000

Dueco

2012-2020. Gold or Silver crystalline finish.

2012-2020		$1,875	$2,250

El Trovador

2010-present. Wood body Dobro-style, single cone, biscuit bridge.

2010-2024		$2,000	$2,500

Estralita Deluxe

2006-2021. Single cone, walnut body, figured maple top, Koa offered in '03.

2006-2021	Maple or Koa	$2,000	$2,500

Estralita Harlem Slim

2010. Laminate maple.

2010		$1,250	$1,500

Model 97

2002-2009. Nickel-plated tricone resonator, female surf rider and palm trees scene.

2002-2009		$2,500	$3,250

Model D

2003-2010. Laminate wood body, spruce top, walnut back and sides, spun cone and spider bridge. Replaced by Smith and Young Model 1 (metal body) and Model 11 (wood body).

2003-2010		$1,375	$1,750

NRP Steel

2009-present. Steel body with rubbed nickel finish, Honduran mahogany neck, slotted headstock.

2009-2024		$2,000	$2,500

Resoelectric Jr./Jr. II

2005-2010. Basic model of ResoLectric with painted body, Jr. with P-90, Jr. II with Lollar lipstick-tube. Replaced by the ResoTone.

2005-2010		$775	$1,000

Resolectric

1992-present. Single-cut electric resonator, maple (flamed maple since '96), single biscuit, 1 regular pickup (lipstick-tube up to '95, P-90 since) and 1 under-saddle.

1992-1995	Lipstick pickup	$1,500	$1,875
1996-2024	P-90 pickup	$1,500	$1,875

GUITARS

MODEL YEAR	FEATURES	EXC. COND. LOW	HIGH

ResoRocket

2005-2024. Single-cut steel body, Tricone style grill.

2005-2024		$2,250	$3,000

ResoRocket N

2009-present. Highly polished nickel-plated finish.

2009-2024		$2,250	$3,000

Style M-1/M-2

1990-1994, 2003-2010. Bound mahogany body single-cone, M-1 with ebony 'board, M-2 with bound rosewood 'board.

1990-2010		$1,500	$1,875

Style N

1993-2005. Nickel-plated brass body single-cone resonator, plain mirror finish, 12 fret neck.

1993-2005		$2,250	$3,000

Style O/O Deluxe/O Replicon 14-Fret

1992-present. Nickel-plated brass body, Hawaiian palm tree etched. Deluxe has upgrades like figured-maple neck and mother-of-pearl diamond inlays. Replicon 14-Fret is a replica of Mark Knopfler model.

1992-2024	O	$2,250	$3,000
1992-2024	O Deluxe	$2,750	$3,500
1992-2024	O Replicon	$2,500	$3,250

Tricone

1994-present. Nickel-plated brass body, bound ebony 'board.

1994-2024	Style 1	$2,000	$2,500
1994-2024	Style 15	$2,500	$3,250
1995-2004	Style 3, Lily of the Valley	$4,250	$5,500

Triolian

2009-present. Steel body with f-holes, sieve-hole coverplate, maple neck, 12 or 14 fret neck, ivoroid-bound rosewood 'board, mother-of-pearl markers, hand painted walnut-burst.

2009-2024	12 fret	$1,500	$1,875
2009-2024	14 fret	$1,500	$1,875

Navarro Custom

1986-present. Professional and premium grade, production/custom, electric guitars and basses built in San Juan, Puerto Rico by luthier Mike Navarro.

Neubauer

1966-1990s. Luthier Helmut Neubauer built his acoustic and electric archtop guitars in Bubenreuth, Germany.

New Era Guitars

See listing under ARK - New Era Guitars.

New Orleans Guitar Company

1992-present. Luthier Vincent Guidroz builds his premium grade, production/custom, solid and semi-hollow body guitars in New Orleans, Louisiana.

Nickerson Guitars

1983-present. Luthier Brad Nickerson builds his professional and premium grade, production/custom, archtop and flat-top guitars in Northampton, Massachusetts.

Nielsen

2004-present. Premium grade, custom/production, archtop guitars built by luthier Dale Nielsen in Duluth, Minnesota.

Nik Huber Guitars

1997-present. Premium grade, production/custom, electric guitars built in Rodgau, Germany by luthier Nik Huber.

Nioma

1932-1952. NIOMA, the National Institute of Music and Arts, was founded in Seattle but soon had schools across the western U.S. and Canada. By '35 they added guitar instruction, offering their own branded Spanish, resonator and lap steel (with matching amps) guitars, made by Regal, Harmony, Dickerson.

Noble

Ca. 1950-ca. 1969. Instruments made by others and distributed by Don Noble and Company of Chicago. Plastic-covered guitars made by EKO debuted in '62. Aluminum-necked Wandré guitars were added to the line in early-'63. By ca. '65-'66 the brand is owned by Chicago-area importer and distributor Strum 'N Drum and used mainly on Japanese-made solidbodies. Strum 'N Drum bought the National brand name in '69 and imported Japanese copies of American designs under the National brand and Japanese original designs under Norma through the early '70s.

The Noble brand disappears at least by the advent of the Japanese National brand, if not before. They also offered amps.

NoName Guitars

1999-present. Luthier Dan Kugler builds his production/custom, professional and premium grade, acoustic guitars and basses in Conifer, Colorado.

Nordy (Nordstrand Guitars)

2003-present. Professional and premium grade, production/custom, electric guitars and basses built by luthier Carey Nordstrand in Yucaipa, California.

Norma

Ca.1965-1970. Imported from Japan by Strum 'N Drum, Inc. of Chicago (see Noble brand info). Early examples were built by Tombo, most notably sparkle plastic covered guitars and basses.

Electric Solidbody

1965-1970. Type of finish has effect on value. Various models include; EG-350 (student double-cut, 1 pickup), EG-403 (unique pointy cutaway, 2 pickups), EG-400 (double-cut, 2 pickups), EG-450 (double-cut, 2 split-coil pickups), EG-421 (double-cut, 4 pickups), EG-412-12 (double-cut, 12-string).

1965-1968	Blue, red, gold sparkle	$325	$700
1965-1970	Non-sparkle	$225	$400

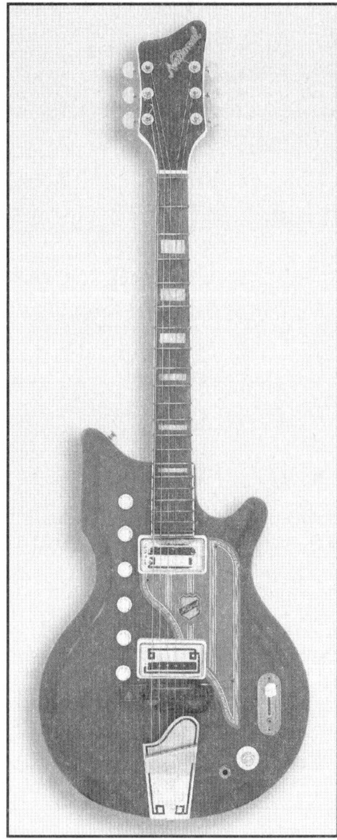

National Westwood 77

Nik Huber Dolphin II

Novax Charlie Hunter 8-String

1954 Old Kraftsman Model K1

John Neff

MODEL YEAR	FEATURES	EXC. COND. LOW	HIGH

Norman

1972-present. Intermediate grade, production, acoustic and acoustic/electric guitars built in LaPatrie, Quebec. Norman was the first guitar production venture luthier Robert Godin was involved with. He has since added the Seagull, Godin, and Patrick & Simon brands of instruments.

Normandy Guitars

2008-present. Jim Normandy builds professional grade, production, aluminum archtop and electric guitars and basses, first in Salem and currently in Portland, Oregon.

North American Instrument Company, Inc.

1961-present. Corporation founded by several people including Dr. Hal Hammer, Jr., Ronald Stewart Armstrong (deceased) and Jimmy C. Bennett (deceased). Professional and premium grade, production/custom, electric guitars and basses built by luthier J. Baxter Goode, in Dayton, Tennessee, with some modifications done in Inverness, Florida.

Northworthy Guitars

Professional and premium grade, production/custom, flat-top and electric guitars and basses built by luthier Alan Marshall in Ashbourne, Derbyshire, U.K., starting in 1987. He also builds mandolins.

Norwood

1960s. Budget guitars imported most likely from Japan.

Electric Solidbody

1960s. Offset double-cut body, 3 soapbar-style pickups, Norwood label on headstock.

1960s		$180	$300

Novax Guitars

1989-present. Luthier Ralph Novak builds his fanned-fret professional and premium grade, production/custom, solidbody and acoustic guitars and basses, originally in San Leandro, California, and since May '06, in Eugene, Oregon.

Noyce

Luthier Ian Noyce, started in 1974, builds production/custom, professional and premium grade, acoustic and electric guitars and basses in Ballarat, Victoria, Australia.

Nyberg Instruments

1993-present. Professional grade, custom, flat-top and Maccaferri-style guitars built by luthier Lawrence Nyberg in Hornby Island, British Columbia. He also builds mandolins, mandolas, bouzoukis and citterns.

Oahu

1926-1985, present. The Oahu Publishing Company and Honolulu Conservatory, based in Cleveland, Ohio was active in the sheet music and student instrument business in the '30s. An instrument, set of instructional sheet music, and lessons were offered as a complete package. Lessons were often given to large groups of students. Instruments, lessons, and sheet music could also be purchased by mail order. The Oahu Publishing Co. advertised itself as The World's Largest Guitar Dealer. Most '30s Oahu guitars were made by Kay with smaller numbers from the Oscar Schmidt Company.

Guitar Models from the Mid-'30s include: 71K (jumbo square neck), 72K (jumbo roundneck), 68B (jumbo, vine body decoration), 68K (deluxe jumbo square neck), 69K (deluxe jumbo roundneck), 65K and 66K (mahogany, square neck), 64K and 67K (mahogany, roundneck), 65M (standard-size, checker binding, mahogany), 53K (roundneck, mahogany), 51 (black, Hawaiian scene, pearlette 'board), 51K (black, pond scene decoration), 52K (black, Hawaiian scene decoration), 50 and 50K (student guitar, brown).

The brand has been revived on a line of tube amps.

Graphic Body

1930s. 13" painted artwork bodies, includes Styles 51 and 52 Hawaiian scene.

1930s	Floral, etc	$400	$600
1930s	Hawaiian scenes	$400	$600

Round Neck 14" Flat-Top

1930s. Spruce top, figured maple back and sides, thin logo.

1932		$1,000	$1,500

Style 50K Student

1930s. Student-size guitar, brown finish.

1935		$150	$300

Style 52K

1930s. 13" with fancy Hawaiian stencil, slotted headstock.

1930s		$350	$600

Style 65M

1933-1935. Standard-size mahogany body, checker binding, natural brown.

1933-1935		$600	$900

Style 68K De Luxe Jumbo

1930s. Hawaiian, 15.5" wide, square neck, Brazilian back and sides, spruce top, fancy pearl vine inlay, abalone trim on top and soundhole, rosewood pyramid bridge, fancy pearl headstock inlay, butterbean tuners, ladder-braced, natural. High-end model made for Oahu by Kay.

1934-1935		$4,000	$6,000

Style 71K Hawaiian

1930s.Hawaiian, gold vine pattern on bound sunburst top, dot inlays.

1930s		$1,200	$1,800

Ochoteco Guitars

1979-present. Production/custom steel- and nylon-stringed guitars built by luthier Gabriel Ochoteco in Germany until '84 and in Brisbane, Australia since.

GUITARS

MODEL YEAR	FEATURES	EXC. COND. LOW	HIGH

Odessa

1981-1990s. Budget guitars imported by Davitt & Hanser (BC Rich). Mainly acoustics in the '90s, but some electrics early on.

O'Hagan

1979-1983. Designed by clarinetist and importer Jerol O'Hagan in St. Louis Park, Minnesota. Primarily neck-thru construction, most with German-carved bodies. In '81 became Jemar Corporation and in '83 it was closed by the I.R.S., a victim of recession.

SN=YYM(M)NN (e.g., 80905, September '80, 5th guitar); or MYMNNN (e.g., A34006, April 1983, 6th guitar). Approximately 3000 total instruments were made with the majority being NightWatches (approx. 200 Twenty Twos, 100-150 Sharks, 100 Lasers; about 25 with birdseye maple

Shark

1979-1983. Explorer-looking solidbody, maple body, 2 Shaller humbucker pickups, 3-piece maple/walnut laminate neck, natural.

1979-1983		$900	$1,400

Ohio

1959-ca. 1965. Line of electric solidbodies and basses made by France's Jacobacci company, which also built under its own brand. Sparkle finish, bolt-on aluminum necks, strings-thru-body design.

Old Kraftsman

Ca. 1930s-ca. 1960s. Brand name used by the Spiegel catalog company for instruments made by other American manufacturers, including Regal, Kay and even Gibson. The instruments were of mixed quality, but some better grade instruments were comparable to those offered by Wards.

Archtop

1930s-1960s. Various models.

1930s-40s		$400	$600
1950s-60s		$325	$500

Flat-Top

1930s-1960s. Various models.

1950s	Prairie Ramblers (stencil)	$325	$500

Jazz II K775

1960-1963. Kay 775 with Old Kraftsman logo on large headstock, small double-cut thinline, 2 pickups, Bigsby, natural.

1960-1963		$1,100	$1,600

Sizzler K4140

1959. Single-cut, single neck pickup, Sizzler logo on body with other art images.

1959		$500	$800

Thin Twin Jimmy Reed

1952-1958		$1,100	$1,600

Value Leader

1961-1965. Electric single-cut semi-solid, 1 pickup, Kay Value Leader series.

1961-1965		$400	$600

MODEL YEAR	FEATURES	EXC. COND. LOW	HIGH

OLP (Officially Licensed Product)

2001-2009. Intermediate grade, production, imported guitars and basses based on higher dollar guitar models officially licensed from the original manufacturer. OLP logo on headstock.

Olson Guitars

1977-present. Luthier James A. Olson builds his presentation grade, custom, flat-tops in Circle Pines, Minnesota.

Olympia by Tacoma

1997-2006. Import acoustic guitars and mandolins from Tacoma Guitars.

OD Series

1997-2006	Various models	$115	$350

Omega

1996-2010. Luthier Kevin Gallagher built his premium grade, custom/production acoustic guitars in East Saylorsburg, Pennsylvania. He died in '10.

Oncor Sound

1980-ca. 1981. This Salt Lake City, Utah-based company made both a guitar and a bass synthesizer.

Optek

1980s-present. Intermediate grade, production, imported Fretlight acoustic/electric and electric guitars. Located in Reno, Nevada.

Fretlight

1989-present. Double-cut, 126 LED lights in fretboard controlled by a scale/chord selector.

1989-2024		$350	$600

Opus

1972-Mid 1970s. Acoustic and classical guitars, imported from Japan by Ampeg/Selmer. In '75-'76, Harmony made a line of acoustics with the Opus model name.

Original Senn

2004-present. Luthier Jeff Senn builds his professional and premium grade, production/custom, solidbody electric guitars and basses in Nashville, Tennessee.

Ormsby Guitars

2003-present. Luthier Perry Ormsby builds his custom, professional and premium grade, solid and chambered electric guitars in Perth, Western Australia.

Orpheum

1897-1942, 1944-late 1960s, 2001-2006. Intermediate grade, production, acoustic and resonator guitars. They also offered mandolins. Orpheum originally was a brand of Rettberg and Lange, who made instruments for other companies as well. William Rettberg and William Lange bought the

Olson James Taylor Signature

Optek Fretlight

1993 Orville by Gibson ES-335

Steve Soest

2001 Ovation Adamas 1598-MEII Melissa Etheridge

Imaged by Heritage Auctions, HA.com

MODEL YEAR	FEATURES	EXC. COND. LOW	HIGH

facilities of New York banjo maker James H. Buckbee in 1897. Lange went out on his own in '21 to start the Paramount brand. He apparently continued using the Orpheum brand as well. He went out of business in '42. In '44 the brand was acquired by New York's Maurice Lipsky Music Co. who used it primarily on beginner to medium grade instruments, which were manufactured by Regal, Kay, and United Guitar (and maybe others). In the early '60s Lipsky applied the brand to Japanese and European (by Egmond) imports. Lipsky dropped the name in the early '70s. The brand was revived from '01 to '06 by Tacoma Guitars.

Auditorium Archtop 835/837

1950s. Acoustic archtop, auditorium size, dot markers, Orpheum shell headpiece, white celluloid 'guard, model 835 with spruce top/back/sides, 837 with mahogany.

1950s		$350	$600

Orpheum Special

1930s. Made by Regal, slot head, Dobro-style wood body, metal resonator, sunburst.

1930s		$900	$1,400

President

1940s. 18" pro-level acoustic archtop, Orpheum block logo and President script logo on headstock, large split-block markers, sunburst.

1940s		$1,600	$2,500

Style B

1940s. Acoustic archtop, Style B logo on headstock, block markers, sunburst.

1940s		$700	$1,000

Thin Twin Jimmy Reed 865E

1950s. Model 865E is the Orpheum version of the generically named Thin Twin Jimmy Reed style electric Spanish cutaway thin solidbody, hand engraved shell celluloid Orpheum headpiece, described as #865E Cutaway Thin Electric Guitar in catalog.

1950s		$1,000	$1,500

Ultra Deluxe Professional 899

1950s. 17" cutaway, 2 pickups, 2 knobs, maple back and sides, top material varies, dot markers, finishes as follows: E-C copper, E-G gold, E-G-B gold-black sunburst, E-B blond curly maple, E-S golden orange sunburst.

1950s		$1,300	$2,000

Orville

1984-1993. Orville by Gibson and Orville guitars were made by Japan's Fuji Gen Gakki for Gibson. See following listing for details. Guitars listed here state only Orville (no By Gibson) on the headstock.

Electric

1984-1993	CE Atkins	$1,000	$1,500
1984-1993	ES-335	$1,300	$2,000
1984-1993	LP Custom	$1,100	$1,600
1984-1993	LP Standard	$1,100	$1,600

Orville by Gibson

1984-1993. Orville by Gibson and Orville guitars were made by Japan's Fuji Gen Gakki for Gibson.

MODEL YEAR	FEATURES	EXC. COND. LOW	HIGH

Basically, the same models except the Orville by Gibson guitars had real Gibson USA PAF '57 Classic pickups and a true nitrocellulose lacquer finish. The Orville models used Japanese electronics and a poly finish. Prices here are for the Orville by Gibson models.

Acoustic-Electric

1984-1993. On-board electronics.

1984-1993	Dove	$1,500	$2,200
1984-1993	J-160E	$1,500	$2,200
1984-1993	J-200NE	$1,500	$2,200

Electric

1984-1993. Various models.

1984-1993	ES-175	$1,500	$2,200
1984-1993	ES-335	$1,500	$2,200
1984-1993	Explorer	$1,500	$2,200
1984-1993	Firebird V	$1,300	$2,000
1984-1993	Firebird VII	$1,300	$2,000
1984-1993	Flying V	$1,500	$2,200
1984-1993	Les Paul Custom	$1,500	$2,200
1984-1993	Les Paul Jr	$800	$1,200
1984-1993	LP Standard	$1,500	$2,200
1984-1993	LP Studio JP	$1,100	$1,600
1984-1993	MM/Les Paul Jr	$700	$1,000
1984-1993	SG LP Custom	$1,100	$1,600
1984-1993	SG LP Standard	$1,100	$1,600

Osborne Sound Laboratories

Late 1970s. Founded by Ralph Scaffidi and wife guitarist Mary Osborne; originally building guitar amps, they did also offer solidbody guitars.

Oscar Schmidt

1879-1938, 1979-present. Budget and intermediate grade, production, acoustic, acoustic/electric, and electric guitars and basses distributed by U.S. Music Corp. (Washburn, Randall, etc.). They also offer mandolins, banjos, ukuleles and the famous Oscar Schmidt autoharp.

The original Oscar Schmidt Company, Jersey City, New Jersey, offered banjo mandolins, tenor banjos, guitar banjos, ukuleles, mandolins and guitars under their own brand and others (including Sovereign and Stella). By the early 1900s, the company had factories in the U.S. and Europe producing instruments producing instruments under their own brand as well as other brands for mail-order and other distributors. Oscar Schmidt was also an early contributor to innovative mandolin designs and the company participated in the '00-'30 mandolin boom. The company hit hard times during the Depression and was sold to Harmony by the end of the '30s. In '79, Washburn acquired the brand and it is now part of U.S. Music.

Oskar Graf Guitars

1970-present. Premium and presentation grade, custom, archtop, acoustic and classical guitars and basses built in Clarendon, Ontario, by luthier Oskar Graf. He also builds lutes.

GUITARS

MODEL YEAR	FEATURES	EXC. COND. LOW	HIGH

Otwin

1950s-1960s. A brand used on electric guitars made by the Musima company of East Germany. Musima also produced guitars under their own brand.

Outbound Instruments

1990-2002. Intermediate grade, production, travel-size acoustics from the Boulder, Colorado-based company.

Ovation

1966-present. Intermediate and professional grade, production, acoustic and acoustic/electric guitars. They also build basses and mandolins. Until 2014, they also had U.S. production.

Helicopter manufacturer Kaman Corporation, founded in 1945 by jazz guitarist and aeronautical engineer Charles Huron Kaman in Bloomfield, Connecticut, decided to use their helicopter expertise (working with synthetic materials, spruce, high tolerances) and designed, with the help of employee and violin restorer John Ringso, the first fiberglass-backed (Lyracord) acoustic guitars in '65. Production began in '66 and the music factory moved to New Hartford, Connecticut, in '67. Early input was provided by fingerstyle jazz guitarist Charlie Byrd, who gave Kaman the idea for the name Ovation. Kaman Music purchased Hamer Guitars in '88, and Trace Elliot amplifiers (U.K.) in '90. In '08, Fender acquired Kaman Music Corporation and the Ovation brand; in '14 U.S. production ceased, and the brand was sold to Drum Workshop, Inc., who re-opened the Hartford, CT plant in late '15.

Adamas 1581-KK Kaki King

2011-2014. Deep bowl cutaway, rosewood 'board, 12th-fret crown inlay, OP-Pro preamp, Kaki personally signs the label on each guitar.

2011-2014 | | $2,500 | $3,500

Adamas 1587

1979-1998. Carbon top, walnut, single-cut, bowl back, binding, mini-soundholes.

1979-1998 | Black Sparkle | $2,000 | $3,500

Adamas 1597

1998-2003. Carbon birch composite top, on-board electronics.

1998-2003 | Black | $1,200 | $1,800

Adamas 1598-MEII Melissa Etheridge

2001-2014. Mid-depth cutaway, ebony 'board, 'ME' maple symbol at 12th fret, OP-Pro preamp, Melissa personally signs the label on each guitar.

2001-2014 | 12-string | $1,500 | $2,500

Adamas 1687

1977-1998. Acoustic/electric, carbon top, non-cut, bowl back, mini-sound holes.

1977-1998 | Sunburst | $2,000 | $3,500

Adamas CVT W591

2000. Crossweave fiber top, mid-depth body, on-board electronics.

2000 | | $1,000 | $1,500

Adamas II 1881 NB-2

1993-1998. Acoustic/electric, single-cut, shallow bowl, brown.

1993-1998 | | $1,800 | $3,000

Adamas Millenium

2000. Limited edition, 75 made, planet inlays, Cobalt Blue.

2000 | | $2,500 | $4,500

Anniversary Electric 1657

1978. Deep bowl, abalone inlays, gold-plated parts, for Ovation's 10th anniversary. They also offered an acoustic Anniversary.

1978 | | $1,000 | $1,500

Balladeer 1111

1968-1983, 1993-2000. Acoustic, non-cut with deep bowl, bound body, natural top, later called the Standard Balladeer.

1976-1983 | | $500 | $1,200

Balladeer Artist 1121

1968-1990. Acoustic, non-cut with shallow bowl, bound body.

1968-1969 | Early production | $800 | $1,500

1970-1990 | | $600 | $1,200

Balladeer Classic 1122

1970s. Classical shallow-bowl version of Concert Classic, nylon strings, slotted headstock.

1970s | | $500 | $1,000

Balladeer Custom 1112

1976-1990. Acoustic, deep bowl, diamond inlays.

1976-1990 | | $600 | $1,300

Balladeer Custom Electric 12-String 1655/1755

1982-1994. 12-string version of Balladeer Custom Electric.

1982-1994 | | $800 | $1,500

Balladeer Custom Electric 1612/1712

1976-1990. Acoustic/electric version of Balladeer Custom, deep bowl.

1976-1990 | | $700 | $1,400

Balladeer Standard 1561/1661/1761/1861

1982-2000. Acoustic/electric, deep bowl, rounded cutaway.

1982-2000 | | $400 | $1,000

Balladeer Standard 1771 LX

2008-2010. Acoustic/electric, mid-depth bowl, rosewood, Sitka spruce top.

2008-2010 | | $500 | $1,200

Balladeer Standard 12-String 6751 LX

2008-2010. Acoustic/electric, 12 strings, rosewood, spruce top.

2008-2010 | | $600 | $1,400

Breadwinner 1251

1971-1983. Axe-like shaped single-cut solidbody, 2 pickups, textured finish, black, blue, tan or white.

1971-1983 | | $1,000 | $2,500

Celebrity CC-48

2007-2013. Acoustic/electric, super shallow, laminated spruce top, white bound rosewood 'board with abalone dot inlays.

2007-2013 | | $300 | $600

1976 Ovation Adamas
Sam Stathakis

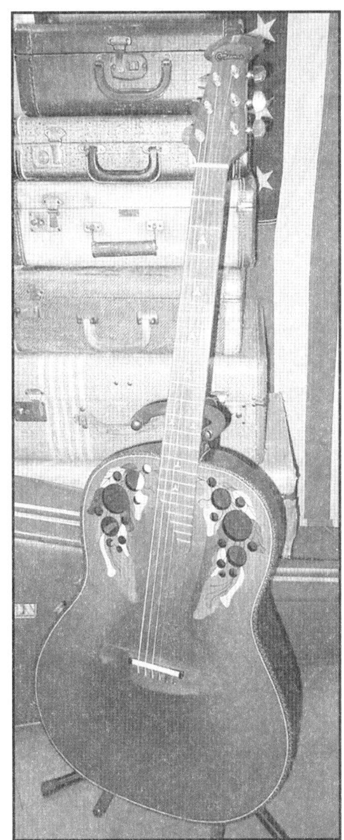

1981 Ovation Adamas II
Rivington Guitars

GUITARS

Ovation Concert Classic 1116
Sam Stathakis

Ovation Custom Legend 1619
Imaged by Heritage Auctions, HA.com

MODEL YEAR	FEATURES	EXC. COND. LOW	HIGH

Celebrity CC-57

1990-1996. Laminated spruce top, shallow bowl, mahogany neck.

1990-1996		$250	$500

Celebrity CC-63

1984-1996. Classical, deep bowl, piezo bridge pickup.

1984-1996		$300	$600

Celebrity CK-057

2002-2004. Acoustic/electric rounded cutaway, shallow back.

2002-2004		$350	$650

Celebrity CS-257

1992-2005, 2010. Made in Korea, super shallow bowl back body, single-cut, Adamas sound holes, alternating dot and diamond markers.

1992-2005	Celebrity	$300	$600
2010	Celebrity Deluxe	$400	$700

Classic 1613/1713

1971-1993. Acoustic/electric, non-cut, deep bowl, no inlay, slotted headstock, gold tuners, natural.

1971-1993		$600	$1,500

Classic 1663/1763

1982-1998. Acoustic/electric, single-cut, deep bowl, cedar top, EQ, no inlay, slotted headstock, gold tuners.

1982-1998		$500	$1,200

Classic 1863

1989-1998. Acoustic/electric, single-cut, shallow bowl, no inlay, cedar top, EQ, slotted headstock, gold tuners.

1989-1998		$600	$1,400

Collectors Series

1982-2008. Limited edition, different model featured each year and production limited to that year only, the year designation is marked at the 12th fret, various colors (each year different).

1982-2008	Common models	$1,000	$1,500
1982-2008	Rare models	$2,500	$5,000

Concert Classic 1116

1974-1990. Deep-bowl nylon string classical, slotted headstock.

1974-1990		$400	$1,000

Contemporary Folk Classic Electric 1616

1974-1990. Acoustic/electric, no inlay, slotted headstock, natural or sunburst.

1974-1990		$500	$1,200

Country Artist Classic Electric 6773

1995-2011. Classic electric, soft-cut, solid spruce top, slotted headstock, Ovation pickup system.

1995-2011		$800	$1,800

Country Artist Electric 1624

1971-1990. Nylon strings, slotted headstock, standard steel-string sized neck to simulate a folk guitar, on-board electronics.

1971-1990		$700	$1,500

Custom Ballader 1762

1992. Rounded cutaway, higher-end specs.

1992		$600	$1,200

Custom Elite Guitar Center 30th Anniversary

1994	50 made	$2,000	$4,000

Custom Legend 1117

1970s. non-electric 2nd generation Ovation, higher-end with abalone inlays and gold hardware, open V-bracing pattern. Model 1117-4, natural.

1970s		$800	$1,800

Custom Legend 1569

1980s. Rounded cutaway acoustic/electric, super shallow bowl, gloss black finish.

1980s		$900	$2,000

Custom Legend 1619/1719

1970s. Acoustic/electric 2nd generation Ovation, electric version of model 1117, higher-end with abalone inlays and gold hardware, open V-bracing pattern.

1970s		$800	$1,800

Custom Legend 1759

1984-2004. Single-cut acoustic/electric, 12-string.

1984-2004		$1,200	$2,500

Custom Legend 1769

1982, 1993, 1996-1999. Single-cut acoustic/electric.

1982-1999		$900	$2,000

Custom Legend 1869

1994, 2003. Acoustic/electric, cutaway, super shallow bowl.

1994, 2003		$1,000	$2,200

Custom Legend 6759

2003		$1,200	$2,500

Deacon 1252

1973-1980. Axe-shaped solidbody electric, active electronics, diamond fret markers.

1973-1980		$1,500	$3,000

Deacon 12-String 1253

1975. Axe-shaped solidbody, diamond inlay, 2 pickups. only a few made.

1975		$2,000	$4,000

Eclipse

1971-1973. Thinline double cut acoustic-electric archtop, 2 pickups.

1971-1973		$1,200	$1,500

Elite 1718

1982-1997. Acoustic/electric, non-cut, deep bowl, solid spruce top, Adamas-type sound hole, volume and tone controls, stereo output.

1982-1997		$800	$1,800

Elite 1758

1990-1998. Acoustic/electric, non-cut, deep bowl.

1990-1998		$900	$2,000

Elite 1768

1990-1998. Acoustic/electric, cutaway, deep bowl.

1990-1998		$800	$1,800

Elite 1858 12-String

1993-2004. 12-string acoustic/electric, ebony 'board and bridge.

1993-2004		$1,000	$2,200

Elite 1868

1983-2004. Acoustic/electric, cutaway, shallow bowl.

1983-2004		$900	$2,000

Elite 5858

1991. Super shallow bowl, single cutaway, Adamas-style sound hole, gold hardware, on-board factory OP24 pickup.

1991		$1,000	$2,500

MODEL YEAR	FEATURES	EXC. COND. LOW	HIGH

Elite Doubleneck

1989-1990s. Six- and 12-string necks, can be ordered with a variety of custom options.

1989		$3,000	$6,000

Elite Standard 6868

1994-1999. Elite Standard with cutaway shallow bowl.

1994-1999		$800	$1,800

Elite T/TX 1778

2002-2018. Acoustic/electric, cutaway, U.S. T replaced by import TX in '08.

2002-2008	T, original version	$1,000	$2,200
2008-2018	TX, Import	$600	$1,500

Folklore 1614

1972-1983. Acoustic/electric, 12-fret neck on full-size body, wide neck, on-board electronics.

1972-1983		$600	$1,500

GCXT

2008. Acoustic-electric made for Guitar Center, single-cut, flamed paint graphic.

2008		$800	$1,800

Glen Campbell 12-String 1118 (K-1118)

1968-1982. Acoustic, 12 strings, shallow bowl version of Legend, gold tuners, diamond inlay.

1968-1982		$1,000	$2,500

Glen Campbell Artist 1627

2006. Glen Campbell 40th Anniversary model, diamond inlay, gold tuners.

2006		$1,500	$3,000

Glen Campbell Artist Balladeer 1127

1968-1990. Acoustic, shallow bowl, diamond inlay, gold tuners, natural.

1968-1990		$800	$2,000

Hurricane 12-String K-1120

1968-1969. ES-335-style electric semi-hollowbody, double-cut, 12 strings, f-holes, 2 pickups.

1968-1969		$1,500	$3,500

Josh White 1114

1967-1970, 1972-1983. Wide 12-fret neck, dot markers, classical-style tuners.

1967-1970		$1,200	$3,000
1972-1983		$700	$1,800

Legend 1117

1972-1999. Deep bowl acoustic, 5-ply top binding, gold tuners, various colors (most natural).

1972-1999		$800	$2,000

Legend 1567/1867

1984-2004. Acoustic/electric, shallow bowl, single-cut, gold tuners.

1984-2004		$900	$2,200

Legend 12-String 1866

1989-2007. Acoustic/electric, cutaway, 12 strings, shallow bowl, 5-ply top binding, black.

1989-2007		$1,200	$2,500

Legend 1717

1990-2008. Acoustic/electric, 5-ply top binding, various colors.

1990-2008		$900	$2,200

Legend 1767

1990s. Acoustic/electric, deep bowl, single-cut, black.

1990s		$800	$2,000

Legend Cutaway 1667

1982-1996. Acoustic/electric, cutaway, deep bowl, abalone, gold tuners.

1982-1996		$900	$2,200

Legend Electric 1617

1972-1998. Acoustic/electric, deep bowl, abalone, gold tuners, various colors.

1972-1998		$800	$2,000

Pacemaker 12-String 1115/1615

1968-1982. Originally called the K-1115 12-string, Renamed Pacemaker in '72.

1968-1982		$800	$2,000

Patriot Bicentennial

*1976. Limited run of 1776 guitars, Legend Custom model with drum and flag decal and 1776*1976 decal on lower bout.*

1976		$2,000	$5,000

Pinnacle

1990-1992. Spruce or sycamore top, broad leaf pattern rosette, mahogany neck, piezo bridge pickup, sunburst.

1990-1992		$400	$1,000

Pinnacle Shallow Cutaway

1990-1994. Pinnacle with shallow bowl body and single-cut, sunburst.

1990-1994		$500	$1,200

Preacher 1281

1975-1982. Solidbody, mahogany body, double-cut, 2 pickups.

1975-1982		$1,000	$2,500

Preacher Deluxe 1282

1975-1982. Double-cut solidbody, 2 pickups with series/parallel pickup switch and mid-range control.

1975-1982		$1,200	$3,000

Preacher 12-String 1285

1975-1983. Double-cut solidbody, 12 strings, 2 pickups.

1975-1983		$1,500	$3,500

Thunderhead 1460

1968-1972. Double-cut, 2 pickups, gold hardware, phase switch, master volume, separate tone controls, pickup balance/blend control, vibrato.

1968-1972	Natural or rare color	$1,500	$3,500
1968-1972	Sunburst	$1,200	$3,000

Tornado 1260

1968-1973. Same as Thunderhead without phase switch, with chrome hardware.

1968-1973		$1,200	$3,000

UK II 1291

1980-1982. Single-cut solidbody, 2 pickups, body made of Urelite on aluminum frame, bolt-on neck, gold hardware.

1980-1982		$800	$2,000

Ultra GS/GP Series

1984. Korean solidbodies and necks assembled in U.S., DiMarzio pickups, offset double-cut (GS) with 1 hum, or hum/single/single or LP style (GP) with 2 humbuckers. There was also a bass.

1984		$500	$1,500

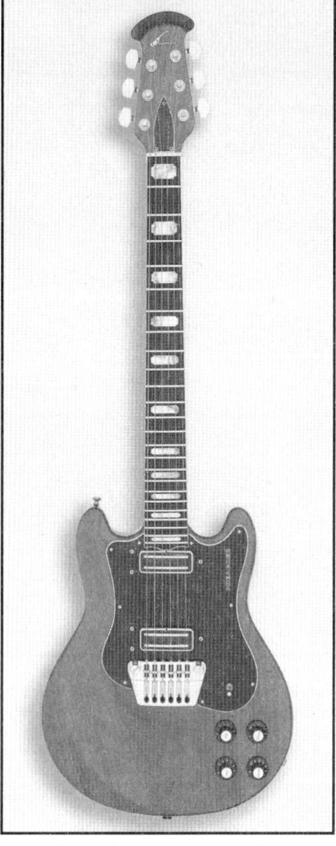

1977 Ovation Preacher

1970 Ovation Thunderhead 1460

Cream City Music

GUITARS

Ovation Viper 1271
Rivington Guitars

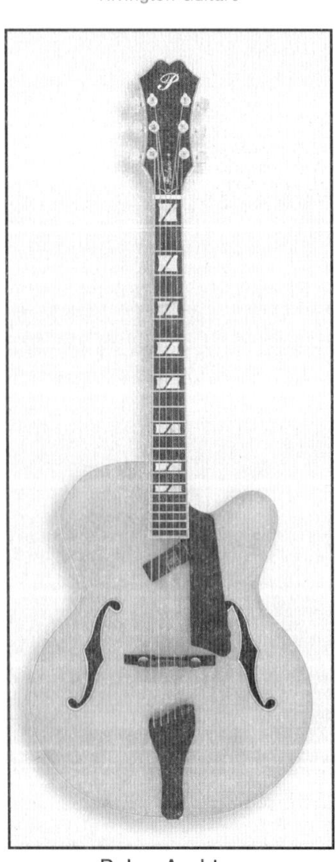
Palen Archtop

MODEL YEAR	FEATURES	EXC. COND. LOW	HIGH

Ultra Series

1970s-2000s. Various Ultra model acoustic/electrics.

1970-2000s		$400	$2,000

Viper 1271

1975-1982. Single-cut, 2 single-coil pickups.

1975-1982		$1,000	$2,500

Viper EA 68

1994-2008. Thin acoustic/electric, single-cut mahogany body, spruce top over sound chamber with multiple upper bout sound holes, black.

1994-2008		$800	$2,000

Viper III 1273

1975-1982. Single-cut, 3 single-coil pickups.

1975-1982		$1,200	$3,000

VXT Hybrid

2007-2009. Single-cut solidbody, 2 Seymour Duncan '59 humbuckers, Fishman Power Bridge.

2007-2009		$1,000	$2,500

Overture Guitars

Luthier Justin Hoffman began building in the year 2008, professional to presentation grade, custom/production, solidbody guitars and basses in Morton, Illinois.

P. W. Crump Company

1975-present. Luthier Phil Crump builds his custom flat-top guitars in Arcata, California. He also builds mandolin-family instruments.

Palen

1998-present. Premium grade, production/custom, archtop guitars built by luthier Nelson Palen in Beloit, Kansas.

Palmer

Budget and intermediate grade, production acoustic, acoustic/electric and classical guitars imported from Europe and Asia, starting in the early 1970s. They also have offered electrics.

Panache

2004-2008. Budget grade, production, solidbody electric and acoustic guitars imported from China.

PANaramic

1961-1963. Guitars and basses made in Italy by the Crucianelli accordion company and imported by PANaramic accordion. They also offered amps made by Magnatone.

Acoustic-Electric Archtop

1961-1963. Full body cutaway, 2 pickups.

1961-1963		$1,000	$1,500

Paolo Soprani

Early 1960s. Italian plastic covered guitars with pushbutton controls made by the Polverini Brothers.

Paramount

1921-1942, Late 1940s. The William L. Lange Company began selling Paramount banjos, guitar banjos and mandolin banjos in the early 1920s, and added archtop guitars in '34. The guitars were made by Martin and possibly others. Lange went out of business by '42; Gretsch picked up the Paramount name and used it on acoustics and electrics for a time in the late '40s.

MODEL YEAR	FEATURES	EXC. COND. LOW	HIGH

GB

1920s-1930s. Guitar banjo.

1920s-30s		$1,200	$1,800

Style C

1930s. 16" acoustic archtop, maple back and sides.

1930s		$600	$900

Style L

1930s. Made by Martin, limited to about 36 instruments, small body with resonator, Brazilian rosewood.

1930s	Spanish 6-string	$7,500	$10,000
1930s	Tenor 4-string	$5,500	$7,500

Parker

1992-2016. U.S.-made and imported intermediate, professional, and premium grade, production/custom, solidbody guitars featuring a thin skin of carbon and glass fibers bonded to a wooden guitar body. In '05, they added wood body acoustic/electrics. They also build basses. Originally located northwest of Boston, Parker was founded by Ken Parker and Larry Fishman (Fishman Transducers). Korg USA committed money to get the Fly Deluxe model into production in July '93. Parker added a Custom Shop in '03 to produce special build instruments and non-core higher-end models that were no longer available as a standard product offering. In early '04, Parker was acquired by U.S. Music Corp. and moved USA production from the Boston area to Chicago. U.S. Music was acquired by Jam Industries in '09 and production of Parker Guitars was ceased in '16.

Concert

1997 only. Solid Sitka spruce top, only piezo system pickup, no magnetic pickups, transparent butterscotch.

1997		$2,000	$3,500

Fly

1993-1994. There are many Parker Fly models, the model simply called Fly is similar to the more common Fly Deluxe, except it does not have the Fishman piezo pickup system.

1993-1994		$2,500	$5,000

Fly Artist

1998-1999. Solid Sitka spruce top, vibrato, Deluxe-style electronics, transparent blond finish.

1998-1999		$2,500	$4,500

Fly Classic

1996-1998, 2000-2011. One-piece Honduras mahogany body, basswood neck, electronics same as Fly Deluxe.

1996-2011		$2,000	$4,000

Fly Classic Maple

2000. Classic with maple body (vs. mahogany), transparent butterscotch.

2000		$2,200	$4,200

MODEL YEAR	FEATURES	EXC. COND. LOW	HIGH

Fly Deluxe

1993-2016. Poplar body, basswood neck, 2 pickups, Fishman bridge transducer, '93-'96 models were offered with or without vibrato, then non-vibrato discontinued. The Deluxe normally came with a gig bag, but also offered with a hardshell case, which would add about $50 to the values listed.

1993-2016		$2,500	$5,500

Fly Supreme

1996-1999. One-piece flame maple body, electronics same as the Fly Deluxe, highly flamed butterscotch, includes hard molded case.

1996-1999		$3,000	$6,000

MaxxFly PDF Series

2013-2016. PDF is import line of more traditionally-shaped Maxx solidbodies, various models.

2013-2016	PDF30	$800	$1,500
2013-2016	PDF60	$900	$1,800
2013-2016	PDF70	$1,000	$2,000

Mojo

2003-2010. Fly either single-cut or double-cut.

2003-2007	Single-cut	$1,800	$3,500
2003-2010	Double-cut	$1,500	$3,000

NiteFly Series

1996-2009. Two single-coil and 1 humbucker pickup NiteFly, Fishman piezo system, bolt neck, maple body for '96-'98, ash for '99-present. Called the NiteFly in '96, NiteFly NFV2 ('97-'98), NiteFly NFV4 ('98), NiteFly NFV6 ('99), NiteFly SA ('00-present).

1996-2009	Various models	$1,000	$2,500

P Series

2000-2009. Various acoustic and solidbody electric models.

2000-2009		$400	$1,200

Tulipwood Limited Edition

1998. Limited build of 35, standard Deluxe features with tulipwood body.

1998		$3,500	$7,000

Parkwood

2007-present. Intermediate grade, acoustic and acoustic-electric guitars, Parkwood logo on headstock.

Patrick Eggle Guitars

1991-present. Founded by Patrick Eggle and others in Birmingham, England, building solid and semi-solidbody electric guitars and basses. In '95, Eggle left the company to build acoustics.

Patrick James Eggle

2001-present. Eggle co-founded the Patrick Eggle Guitar company in '91 building solidbodies. In '95, he left to do repairs and custom work. In '01 he opened a new workshop in Bedforshire, England, building professional and premium grade, production/custom, archtop and flatop guitars. For a short time he relocated to Hendersonville, North Carolina, but in '05 returned to England and opened a shop in Oswestry.

MODEL YEAR	FEATURES	EXC. COND. LOW	HIGH

Paul Berger

1972-2015. Acoustic guitars built by luthier Paul Berger in St. Augustine, Florida. He died in '15.

Paul H. Jacobson

1974-present. Premium grade, production/custom, classical guitars built by luthier Paul H. Jacobson in Cleveland, Missouri.

Paul Reed Smith

1985-present. Intermediate, professional, and premium grade, production/custom, solid, semi-hollow body, and acoustic guitars made in the U.S. and imported. They also build basses. Paul Reed Smith built his first guitar in '75 as an independent study project in college and refined his design over the next 10 years building custom guitars. After building two prototypes and getting several orders from East Coast guitar dealers, Smith was able to secure the support necessary to start PRS in a factory on Virginia Avenue in Annapolis, Maryland. In '95, they moved to their current location on Kent Island in Stevensville. In 2001 PRS introduced the Korean-made SE Series. Acoustics were added in '08.

10th Anniversary

1995. 200 made, mother-of-pearl inlays, abalone purfling, gold pickups, either wide-fat or wide-thin neck, 10th Anniversary logo, price includes certificate of authenticity.

1995	With certificate	$5,500	$7,500

305

2010-2013. Alder body, maple neck and 'board, birds, 3 single-coils.

2010-2013		$1,300	$2,100

305 25th Anniversary

2010. 305 made, 3 single-coils, wide-fat or wide-thin, 25th Anniversary logo.

2010		$1,500	$2,000

513 Rosewood

Dec.2003-2006. Brazilian rosewood neck, newly developed PRS pickup system with 13 sound settings, hum-single-hum pickups.

2003-2006		$3,500	$5,000

513 Swamp Ash

2010. Figured ash, natural.

2010		$2,000	$2,500

513 25th Anniversary

2010. Carved figured maple top, 25th Anniversary shadow birds inlay.

2010		$2,000	$2,500

Al Di Meola Prism

2008-2014. Curly maple 10 top, 22-fret, prism multicolor finish.

2008-2014		$3,000	$4,000

Angelus Cutaway

2009-2015. Flat-top, on-board electronics, European spruce top, figured mahogany back and sides, flamed maple binding. Listed under Private Stock in '20, with select wood options.

2009-2015		$2,500	$3,500

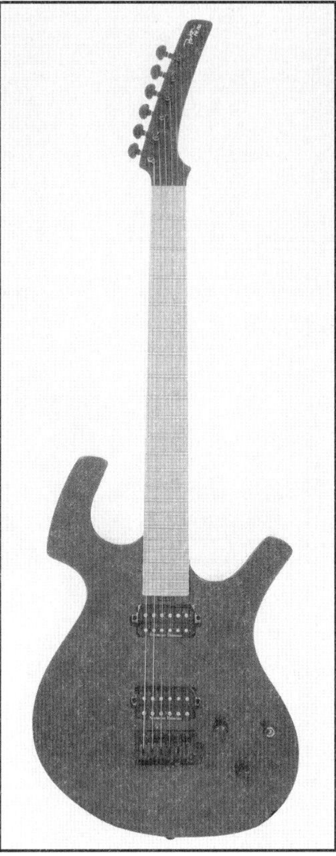

2008 Parker Fly P-42 Pro

PRS Angelus Cutaway

GUITARS

2003 PRS Custom 22
Cream City Music

1991 PRS Custom 24
Eric Van Gansen

MODEL YEAR	FEATURES	EXC. COND. LOW	HIGH

Artist/Artist I/Artist 24

1991-1994. Carved maple top, offset double-cut, 24-fret neck, bird markers, less than 500 made. A different Custom 24 Artist package was subsequently offered in the 2000s.

1991-1994		$3,500	$5,000

Artist II/Artist 22

1993-1995. Curly maple top, maple purfling on rosewood 'board, inlaid maple bound headstock, abalone birds, 22 frets, gold hardware, short run of less than 500.

1993-1995		$3,800	$5,500

Artist III

1996-1997. Continuation of the 22-fret neck with some changes in materials and specs, figured maple tops, short run of less than 500 instruments.

1996-1997		$3,500	$5,000

Artist IV

1996. Continuation of the 22-fret neck with some upgrades in materials and specs, short run of less than 70 instruments.

1996		$4,000	$5,500

Artist Limited

1994-1995. Like the Artist II with 14-carat gold bird inlays, abalone purfling on neck, headstock and truss rod cover, Brazilian rosewood 'board, 165 made.

1994-1995		$5,000	$7,000

Black Gold

2010. Limited Edition, celebrating PRS 25th Anniversary and the 4th Experience PRS event, 200 made, 50 each in Black Gold, Slate, Orange Tiger Burst and Sunset Burst finishes.

2010		$3,500	$5,000

CE 22

1994-2000, 2005-2008. Double-cut carved alder body (1995), mahogany '96-'00 and '05-'07, back to alder in '08, bolt-on maple neck with rosewood 'board, dot inlays, 2 humbuckers, chrome hardware, translucent colors, options include vibrato and gold hardware and custom colors.

1994-1995	Alder	$1,000	$1,500
1996-2000	Mahogany	$1,000	$1,500
2005-2008	Reintroduced	$1,000	$1,500

CE 22 Maple Top

1994-2008. CE 22 with figured maple top, upgrade options included gold hardware, custom colors or 10 top.

1994-2008		$1,800	$2,600
2003	Brazilian 'board	$2,500	$3,500

CE 24 (Classic Electric, CE)

1988-2000, 2005-2008. Double-cut, alder body to '95, mahogany '96-'00 and '05-'07, back to alder in '08, carved top, 24-fret bolt-on maple neck, 2 humbuckers, dot inlays, upgrade options included gold hardware, custom colors or 10 top.

1988-1991	Rosewood 'board	$1,500	$2,200
1992-2008		$1,500	$2,200

CE 24 Maple Top (CE Maple Top)

1989-2008. CE 24 with figured maple top, upgrade options may include any or all the following: gold hardware, custom colors or 10 top.

1989-2008		$1,600	$2,300

Chris Henderson Signature

2007-2012. Single-cut, 3 exposed humbucker pickups, carved flame maple top on mahogany body, wide flat neck profile, 22 frets.

2007-2012		$1,800	$2,500

Corvette

2005-2006. Custom 22 with Velcity Yellow finish, Standard 22 red finish, Z06 inlays, Corvette logo on body.

2005	Custom 22, yellow	$2,000	$2,500
2006	Standard 22, red	$2,000	$2,500

Custom (Custom 24/PRS Custom)

1985-present. Double-cut solidbody, curly maple top, mahogany back and neck, pearl and abalone moon inlays, 24 frets, 2 humbuckers, tremolo, options include quilted or 10 Top, bird inlays, and gold hardware. 1985 Customs should be evaluated on a case-by-case basis.

1985		$10,000	$18,000
1986		$6,500	$11,000
1987		$5,000	$7,500
1988		$4,000	$6,000
1989		$3,000	$5,000
1990-1995	Wood Library adds $1,000	$3,200	$4,500
1996-2005		$2,800	$3,800
2006-2025		$2,000	$3,000

Custom 22

1990-2009, 2013-2023. Custom 22 with flamed or quilted maple top on mahogany body, 22-fret set-neck, upgrade option is gold hardware, normally the quilt top is higher than flamed top. Listed under Private Stock in '21, with select wood options.

1990-1995		$1,800	$3,200
1996-2005		$1,600	$3,000
2006-2023		$1,500	$2,500

Custom 22 (Brazilian)

2003-2004. Limited run of 500 with Brazilian rosewood 'board, figured 10 top, pearl bird inlays.

2003-2004		$3,500	$4,500

Custom 22 20th Anniversary

2005. Abalone 20th Anniversary birds inlay, 20th engraved on truss rod cover.

2005		$2,000	$3,500

Custom 22 30th Anniversary "Vine"

2015. Limited run of 100, Mother of Pearl 30th Anniversary vine with Paua/Paua heart vine inlay.

2015		$3,500	$5,000

Custom 22 Soapbar

1998-2002. 3 Seymour Duncan soapbar single-coils.

1998-2002		$2,500	$3,500

Custom 22 Special

2009. 3 Limited Edition, classic Custom 22 with enhanced features, carved figured maple 10-top, abalone bird inlays, Teal Black finish.

2009		$2,500	$3,000

Custom 22/12

December 2003-2009. 12-string version, flame or quilt maple top, hum/single/hum pickups.

2003-2009		$2,800	$4,000

MODEL YEAR	FEATURES	EXC. COND. LOW	HIGH

Custom 24 (Brazilian)

2003-2004. Limited run with Brazilian rosewood 'board, figured 10 top, pearl bird inlays.

2003-2004		$3,500	$5,500

Custom 24 (Walnut)

1992. Seamless matched walnut over mahogany, 3 made.

1992		$2,500	$3,500

Custom 24 20th Anniversary

2005. Abalone 20th Anniversary birds inlay, 20th engraved on truss rod cover.

2005		$3,000	$4,000

Custom 24 25th Anniversary

2010. Carved figured maple top, 25th Anniversary shadow birds inlay.

2010		$3,000	$4,000

Custom 24 Experience 2010

2010. Limited model created for PRS 2010 Experience event, run of 200, 50 each in Black Gold, Slate, Orange Tiger Burst and Sunset Burst.

2010		$3,000	$4,000

Custom 24 Rasta

1992. Rare, custom-order or small-batch model, unique "Rasta" finish with green/yellow/red stripes.

1992		$4,000	$7,000

Custom 24 Rosewood

2008. Limited run, mahogany body, carved figured maple 10-top, East Indian rosewood neck, abalone bird inlays, various finishes.

2008		$3,000	$4,000

Dave Navarro Signature

2005-2014. Carved maple top, bird inlays, tremolo, white.

2005-2014		$2,500	$3,500

DC3

2010-2013. Double-cut contoured body, bolt-on neck, 3 special single-coils.

2010-2013		$1,800	$2,500

DC245 Double-Cut

2007-2009. Double-cut mahogany body, carved figured maple top, rosewood 'board, abalone bird inlays, various finishes.

2007-2009		$2,500	$3,500

DC245 McCarty

2010. Limited Edition, mahogany body and neck, carved figured maple 10-top, rosewood 'board, mother-of-pearl bird inlays, various finishes.

2010		$2,500	$3,500

DGT David Grissom Trem

2007-present. Based on the McCarty Tremolo model with an added volume control, a nitro topcoat, vintage colors, large frets designed for .011-gauge strings.

2007-2024		$2,500	$3,500

Dragon I

1992. Fingerboard inlay of a dragon made of 201 pieces of abalone, turquoise and mother-of-pearl, gold hardware, 50 made. The Dragon model collector requires an instrument to be truly mint and pristine with no play wear. The values shown here are for pristine instruments. Any issue whatsoever may dramatically reduce the high-side price shown. Price includes the certificate of authenticity.

MODEL YEAR	FEATURES	EXC. COND. LOW	HIGH
1992	Amber quilt, amber flame	$25,000	$35,000
1992	Teal black	$20,000	$25,000

Dragon II

1993. Fingerboard inlay of a dragon made of 218 pieces of gold, coral, abalone, malachite, onyx and mother-of-pearl, 100 made.

1993		$12,000	$18,000

Dragon III

1994. Fingerboard inlay of a dragon made of 438 pieces of gold, red and green abalone, mother-of-pearl, mammoth ivory, and stone, 100 made.

1994		$12,000	$18,000

Dragon 2002

2002. Limited edition of 100 guitars, ultra-inlay work depicting dragon head on the guitar body.

2002		$18,000	$25,000

Dragon 25th Anniversary

2009-2010. Multi-material dragon fingerboard inlay, green ripple abalone Modern Eagle headstock, body shape and electronics are modeled after an early company PRS guitar, 60 made.

2009-2010		$18,000	$25,000

Dragon Doubleneck

2005. Limited edition 20th Anniversary model, about 50 made.

2005		$35,000	$50,000

Dragon Millenium/Dragon 2000

1999-2000. Three-D dragon inlay in body versus neck inlay of previous models, limited production of 50 guitars.

1999-2000	Black cherry	$20,000	$25,000
1999-2000	Rare color	$25,000	$30,000

EG II

1991-1995. Double-cut solidbody, bolt-on neck, 3 single-coils, single-single-hum, or hum-single-hum pickup options, opaque finish.

1991-1995		$1,200	$1,800

EG II Maple Top

1991-1995. EG II with flamed maple top, chrome hardware.

1991-1995		$1,200	$1,800

EG 3

1990-1991. Double-cut solidbody, bolt-on 22-fret neck, 3 single-coil pickups.

1990-1991	Flamed 10 top	$1,500	$2,500
1990-1991	Opaque finish	$1,200	$2,200
1990-1991	Plain top, sunburst	$1,200	$2,200

EG 4

1990-1991. Similar to EG 3 with single-single-hum pickup configuration, opaque finish.

1990-1991		$1,200	$2,200

Golden Eagle

1997-1998. Very limited production, eagle head and shoulders carved into lower bouts, varied high-end appointments.

1997-1998		$8,000	$12,000

John Mayer Silver Sky

2018-present. Alder body, maple neck, rosewood or maple 'board, 3 single-coil pickups, various colors available.

2018-2024		$2,000	$2,800

PRS Dragon 2000

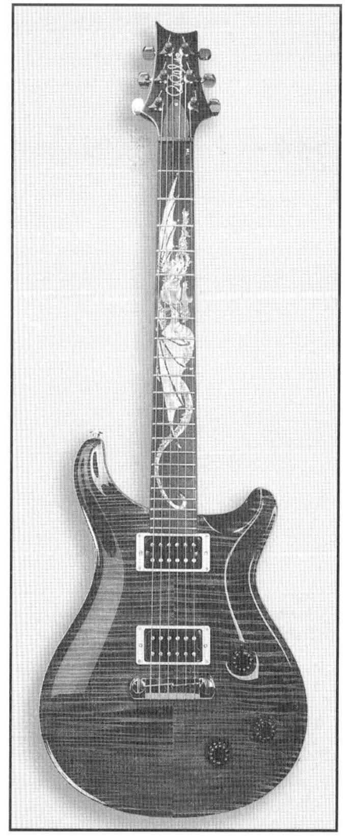

1993 PRS Dragon II

PRS Mark Tremonti Signature

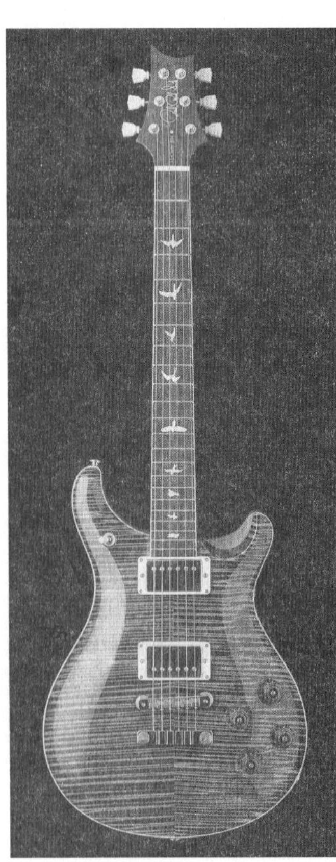

PRS McCarty 594

MODEL YEAR	FEATURES	EXC. COND. LOW	HIGH

John Mayer Silver Sky Limited Edition

2020-2021. Lunar Ice color with unique polychromatic finish.

2020-2021		$3,500	$5,000

Johnny Hiland

2006-2009. Maple fretboard.

2006-2009		$1,500	$2,000

KL-33 Korina

2008. Double-cut solid korina body, rosewood 'board, PRS Mira pickups, limited run of 100.

2008		$1,500	$2,000

KQ-24 Custom 24 (Killer Quilt)

2009. Limited Edition of 120, quilted maple top over korina body, 24 frets.

2009		$3,500	$4,500

Limited Edition

1989-1991, 2000. Double-cut, semi-hollow mahogany body, figured cedar top, gold hardware, less than 300 made. In '00, single-cut, short run of 5 antique white and 5 black offered via Garrett Park Guitars.

1989-1991	Less than 300 made	$6,000	$9,000
2000	Garrett Park	$4,000	$5,500

Limited Edition Howard Leese Golden Eagle

2009. Private Stock, curly maple top, old style mother of pearl birds, 100 made.

2009		$7,000	$10,000

LTD Experience (Limited Experience)

2007. 200 built to commemorate PRS 2007 Experience Open House, 24 frets, matching headstock, maple top with mahogany body.

2007		$3,500	$5,000

Mark Tremonti Model

2001-2007. Single-cut, 2 humbuckers, black or platinum finish.

2001-2007		$2,500	$3,500

Mark Tremonti Signature

2007-present. Single-cut, 2 humbuckers, figured maple top (10 top upgrade offered), various finishes.

2007-2024	10 top upgrade	$2,500	$3,500
2007-2024	Figured maple top	$3,000	$4,000

Mark Tremonti Tribal

2004-2006. With Tribal artwork, 100 made.

2004-2006		$6,000	$9,000

McCarty Model

1994-2007. Mahogany body with figured maple top, upgrade options may include a 10 top, gold hardware, bird inlays. Replaced by McCarty II.

1994-2007		$2,500	$3,500

McCarty II

2008-2009. Replaced the McCarty, featured new MVC (Mastering Voice Control) circuitry for switching between a single-coil voice to a heavy-metal voice, opaque finish.

2008-2009		$1,800	$3,000

McCarty 1957/2008 Limited

2008. "1957/2008" logo on truss rod cover, 08 serial number series, 150 made.

2008		$3,000	$4,500

McCarty 58/MC-58

2009-2011. "MC-58" logo on truss rod cover, similar to other McCarty models except for new neck shape, 57/08 humbucker pickups and V12 finish.

2009-2011		$2,500	$3,500

McCarty 594

2016-present. Figured maple top, mahogany back, bird inlays, various colors.

2016-2024		$2,800	$4,000

McCarty Archtop (Spruce)

1998-2000. Deep mahogany body, archtop, spruce top, 22-fret set-neck.

1998-2000		$3,500	$5,000

McCarty Archtop Artist

1998-2002. Highest grade figured maple top and highest appointments, gold hardware.

1998-2002		$4,500	$7,000

McCarty Archtop II (Maple)

1998-2000. Like Archtop but with figured maple top.

1998-2000	Flamed or quilt	$3,800	$5,500

McCarty Hollowbody I/Hollowbody I

1998-2009. Medium deep mahogany hollowbody, maple top, 22-fret set-neck, chrome hardware. McCarty dropped from name in '06.

1998-2009		$2,800	$4,200

McCarty Hollowbody II/Hollowbody II

1998-2017. Like Hollowbody I but with figured maple top and back. McCarty dropped from name in '06.

1998-2017		$3,500	$5,000

McCarty Hollowbody/Hollowbody Spruce

2000-2009. Similar to Hollowbody I with less appointments, spruce top. McCarty dropped from name in '06.

2000-2009		$3,000	$4,000

McCarty Model/McCarty Brazilian

2003-2004. Limited run of 250, Brazilian rosewood 'board, Brazilian is printed on headstock just below the PRS script logo.

1999		$5,000	$7,500
2003-2004		$5,500	$8,000

McCarty Rosewood

2004-2005. PRS-22 fret with Indian rosewood neck.

2004-2005		$6,000	$9,000

McCarty Soapbar (Korina)

2008-2009. Korina body, 2 Duncan soapbar pickups.

2008-2009		$2,800	$4,000

McCarty Soapbar (Maple)

1998-2007. Soapbar with figured maple top option, nickel hardware.

1998-2007		$2,300	$3,000

McCarty Soapbar Standard

1998-2009. Solid mahogany body, P-90-style soapbar pickups, 22-fret set-neck, nickel-plated hardware, upgrade options may include gold hardware and bird inlays.

1998-2009		$2,000	$3,000

McCarty Standard

1994-2006. McCarty Model with carved mahogany body but without maple top, nickel-plated hardware, upgrade options may include gold hardware and bird inlays.

1994-2006		$2,000	$3,000

GUITARS

MODEL YEAR	FEATURES	EXC. COND. LOW	HIGH

Metal Bud Davis

1985-1986. Solid mahogany body with custom 2-color striped body finish and graphics, 24-fret set-neck, nickel hardware, 2 humbuckers.

1985-1986		$8,000	$12,000

Metal '85 Reissue (Private Stock)

2008. With certificate of authenticity.

2008		$5,000	$7,500

Mira

2007-2013. 2 exposed-coil humbuckers, abalone moon inlays, various opaque finishes. Replaced by S2 Mira in '14.

2007-2013		$1,300	$2,000

Mira 25th Anniversary

2010. 2 soapbar single-coils, shadow bird inlays.

2010		$1,500	$2,200

Mira Korina

2007-2009. Korina body and neck version, natural.

2007-2009		$1,500	$2,500

Mira Maple Top (MT)

2008-2009. Figured maple, moon or bird inlays.

2008-2009		$1,700	$2,200

Modern Eagle

2004-2007. Higher-end model based on Private Stock innovations, satin nitrocellulose finish, Brazilian rosewood neck.

2004-2007		$5,500	$7,500

Modern Eagle II/MEII

2008-2009. Curly maple top, black rosewood neck and 'board.

2008-2009		$5,500	$7,500

Modern Eagle Quatro/ME Quatro

2010-2012. Updated version of Modern Eagle, 53/10 humbucker pickups, select upgraded woods.

2010-2012		$5,000	$7,000

NF3

2010-2013. 3 Narrowfield pickups on top-mounted 1-piece assembly, double-cut contoured body, bolt-on neck.

2010-2013		$1,800	$2,500

P22

2012-2016. Carved figured maple top, birds, rosewood 'board, 10-top flame optional.

2012-2016		$3,500	$5,000

P245

2015. Semi-hollow electric, single-cut, 2 humbuckers and a piezo.

2015		$2,500	$3,500

Paul's Dirty 100

2010. Private Stock run of 100, highly figured curly maple top, moon inlays, 'Paul's Dirty 100' logo on back of headstock, black gold finish, paisley hard case.

2010		$5,000	$7,500

Paul's Guitar

2013-2024. Carved figured maple top, mahogany back and neck, Honduran rosewood 'board with brushstroke birds, various colors. Artist package and other options offered.

2013-2024		$3,000	$4,200

Private Stock Program

April 1996-present. Custom instruments based around existing PRS models. Values may be somewhat near regular production equivalent models or higher. The Private Stock option was reintroduced by 2003. That year a standard production offering might retail at about $7,500, but a '03 Santana I Private Stock might retail at over $15,000, so each guitar should be evaluated on a case-by-case basis.

1996-2024	Various models	$5,000	$18,000

PRS Guitar

1975-1985. About 75 to 100 guitars were built by Paul Smith himself or with a team of others, from '75 to '85, before he formed the current PRS company. Each guitar from this era should be evaluated on a case-by-case basis and the values shown are for guidance only. Authentication is highly recommended; these guitars do not have a PRS serial number. Some of these went to celebrity players and, as such, may command values higher than shown here because of that connection.

1975-1983	Mahogany	$9,000	$50,000
1975-1983	Maple	$15,000	$45,000
1984-1985	Preproduction with provenance	$10,000	$25,000
1985-1986	Team-built	$6,000	$10,000

Rosewood Limited

1996. Mahogany body with figured maple top, 1-piece rosewood neck with ultra-deluxe tree-of-life neck inlay, gold hardware.

1996		$7,000	$9,500

Santana

1995-1998, 2011-present. Limited production special order, figured maple top, 24-fret, symmetric Santana headstock, unique body purfling, chrome and nickel-plated hardware, yellow is the most popular color, followed by orange, quality of top will affect price.

1995	1st 100 signed	$6,500	$8,500
1995-1998		$4,000	$6,000

Santana II

1998-2007. Three-way toggle replaces former dual mini-switches, special order, Brazilian 'board.

1998-2007		$5,500	$8,000

Santana III

2001-2006. Less ornate version of Santana II.

2001-2006		$3,500	$5,000

Santana (Brazilian)

2003. Quilted or flamed maple top, Brazilian rosewood neck and fretboard, eagle inlay on headstock, Santana Brazilian logo on back cover plate, 200 made.

2003-2004		$6,000	$8,500

Santana 25th Anniversary Santana II

2010. Figured maple top, rosewood 'board, eagle inlay on headstock, 25th Anniversary shadow birds.

2010		$4,000	$6,000

SC 58 Artist

2011-2012. Artist grade figured maple top, rosewood 'board, MOP/Paua birds.

2011-2012		$3,500	$4,500

SC 245

2007-2010. Single-cut 22-fret, 2 humbuckers, bird markers, SC 245 logo on truss rod cover.

2007	Flamed top, Brazilian 'board	$5,500	$8,000
2007-2010	Solid color top	$2,500	$3,500

PRS Paul's Guitar

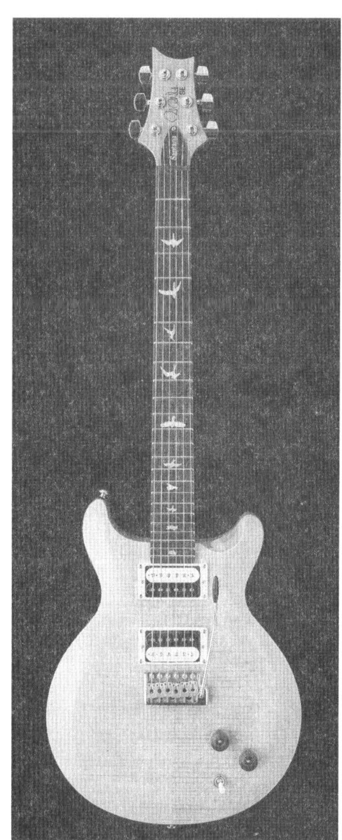

PRS SE Santana

GUITARS

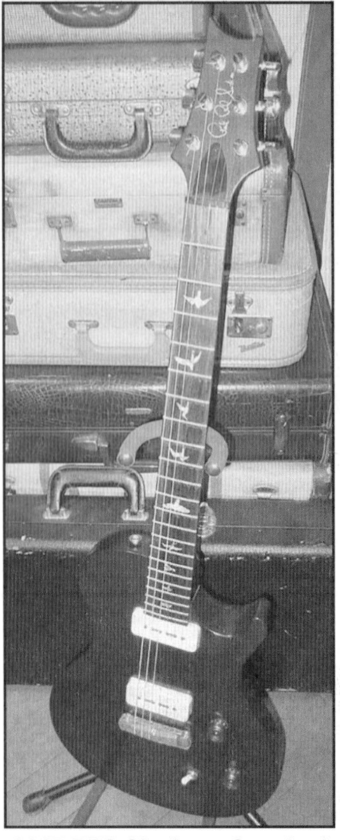
2007 PRS Singlecut Standard
Rivington Guitars

PRS Swamp Ash Special
Imaged by Heritage Auctions, HA.com

MODEL YEAR	FEATURES	EXC. COND. LOW	HIGH

SC 250

2007-2010. Figured maple top, 2 humbuckers, 25" scale and locking tuners.

2007-2010		$2,800	$3,800

SC-J Thinline

2008. Large full-scale single-cut hollowbody, originally part of Private Stock program until made in limited run of 300, select grade maple top and back over a mahogany middle body section, SC-J logo on truss rod cover.

2008		$4,500	$5,500

SE Series

2001-present. PRS import line, solidbody and semi-hollow.

2001-2024	Higher-end models	$800	$1,500
2001-2024	Most models	$500	$1,200

Signature/PRS Signature

1987-1991. 1,000 made, solid mahogany body, figured maple top, hand-signed signature on headstock, Vintage Yellow is most valuable color and will fetch more, orange is second, quilt top is more valuable than flametop. Each guitar should be evaluated on a case-by-case basis.

1987	Various colors	$5,000	$7,500
1988-1991	Various colors	$4,500	$7,000

Signature (Private Stock)

2011. Limited run by Private Stock, 100 made, 408 humbucker pickups (8 tonal configurations), special signature headstock and fretboard inlays.

2011		$6,000	$9,000

Singlecut

2000-2004, 2005-early 2008. Single-cut mahogany body, maple top, 22-fret 'board, upgrade options include 10 top flamed maple, gold hardware, bird inlays. Replaced by SC 245 and SC 250.

2000-2007	Various specs	$2,300	$3,200
2001	Brazilian neck/'board	$5,000	$7,000
2006-2007	Artist 20th Anniv, Brazilian	$5,000	$7,500
2006-2007	Standard 20th Anniv, Indian	$3,000	$4,000
2007-2008	Ltd Ed, Indian	$4,000	$6,000

Singlecut Hollowbody I

Introduced 2008. Carved figured maple top, mahogany back, sides and neck, Indian rosewood 'board.

2008		$3,500	$5,000

Singlecut Hollowbody II CB 25th Anniversary

2010. Semi-hollow (CB means center block), f-holes, 10 maple top, bird inlays.

2010		$4,500	$6,500

Singlecut Hollowbody Standard

2008-2009. Mahogany body.

2008-2009		$3,000	$4,500

Singlecut Soap Bar

2006-2007. Post law-suit, mahogany body and neck, carved maple top, Indian rosewood 'board.

2006-2007		$2,800	$4,000

Singlecut Standard Satin

2006-2007. Thinner solid mahogany body, thin nitro cellulose finish, humbuckers or soapbars.

2006-2007		$2,200	$3,200

Singlecut Tremolo 20th Anniversary

2005-2006. Limited run with Artist package, mahogany body and neck, figured maple 10-top, Indian rosewood 'board, abalone bird inlays, various finishes.

2005-2006		$4,000	$5,500

Smokeburst McCarty

2009. Limited Edition, classic 22-fret PRS design, 1957/2008 humbuckers, PRS Smokeburst nitro finish.

2009		$3,500	$5,000

Special

1987-1990, 1991-1993. Similar to Standard with upgrades, wide-thin neck, 2 HFS humbuckers. From '91-'93, a special option package was offered featuring a wide-thin neck and high output humbuckers.

1987-1990	Solid color finish	$5,000	$7,500
1991-1993	Special order only	$4,000	$6,000

Standard

1987-1998. Set-neck, solid mahogany body, 24-fret 'board, 2 humbuckers, chrome hardware. Originally called the PRS Guitar from '85-'86 (see that listing), renamed Standard 24 from '98.

1987-1989	Sunburst & optional colors	$4,500	$7,500
1990-1991	Last Brazilian 'board	$4,000	$6,500
1992-1995		$2,500	$3,500
1995-1998	Stevensville	$2,200	$3,200

Standard 22

1994-2009. 22-fret Standard.

1994-1995		$2,500	$3,500
1995-1999	Stevensville	$2,200	$3,200
2000-2009		$1,800	$2,800

Standard 24

1998-2009. Renamed from Standard, solid mahogany body, 24-fret set-neck.

1998-2009		$1,800	$2,800

Starla

2008-2013. Single-cut solidbody with retro-vibe, glued neck, 2 chrome humbuckers. Replaced by S2 Starla in '14.

2008-2013		$1,200	$1,800

Studio

1988-1991, 2011-2013. Standard model variant, 24-fret set-neck, chrome and nickel hardware, single-single-hum pickups. The Studio package of pickups was offered until '96 on other models. Reissued in '11 with 22 frets, flamed maple top.

1988-1991		$2,000	$3,000
2011-2013	Reintroduced	$2,000	$3,000

Studio Maple Top

1990-1991. Mahogany solidbody, bird inlays, 2 single-coils and 1 humbucker, tremolo, transparent finish.

1990-1991		$2,500	$3,500

Super Eagle

2016. Private Stock collaboration with John Mayer (Dead & Company), 100 made.

2016		$25,000	$40,000

MODEL YEAR	FEATURES	EXC. COND. LOW	HIGH

Super Eagle II

2016-2017. Private Stock collaboration with John Mayer, 120 made.

2016-2017		$18,000	$36,000

Swamp Ash Special

1996-2009. Solid swamp ash body, 22-fret bolt-on maple neck, 3 pickups, upgrade options available.

1996-2009		$1,500	$2,500

Swamp Ash Special 25th Anniversary

2010. Swamp ash body, bolt-on neck, 25th Anniversary shadow bird inlays.

2010		$2,200	$3,500

Tonare Grand

2009-2016. Full-body flat-top, European/German spruce top, rosewood back and sides, optional Adirondack red spruce top or AAAA grade top, onboard Acoustic Pickup System.

2009-2016		$4,000	$5,500

West Street/1980 West Street Limited

2008. 180 made for the US market, 120 made for export market, faithful replica of the model made in the original West Street shop, Sapele top.

2008		$3,500	$6,000

Pawar

1999-2010. Founded by Jay Pawar, Jeff Johnston and Kevin Johnston in Willoughby Hills, Ohio, Pawar built professional and premium grade, production/custom, solidbody guitars.

PBC Guitar Technology

See Bunker Guitars for more info.

Pearl

1971-ca.1974. Acoustic and electric guitars sold by Pearl Musical Instrument Co. (Pearl drums), and built by other Japanese builders.

Peavey

1965-present. Headquartered in Meridan, Mississippi, Peavey builds budget, intermediate, professional, and premium grade, production/custom, acoustic and electric guitars. They also build basses, amps, PA gear, effects, and drums. Hartley Peavey's first products were guitar amps. He added guitars to the mix in '78.

Axcelerator/AX

1994-1998. Offset double-cut swamp ash or poplar body, bolt-on maple neck, dot markers, AX with locking vibrato, various colors.

1994-1998		$500	$650

Cropper Classic

1995-2005. Single-cut solidbody, 1 humbucker and 1 single coil, figured maple top over thin mahogany body, transparent Onion Green.

1995-2005		$500	$750

Defender

1994-1995. Double-cut, solid poplar body, 2 humbuckers and 1 single-coil pickup, locking Floyd Rose tremolo, metallic or pearl finish.

1994-1995		$200	$250

Destiny

1989-1992. Double-cut, mahogany body, maple top, neck-thru-bridge, maple neck, 3 integrated pickups, double locking tremolo.

1989-1992		$400	$550

Destiny Custom

1989-1992. Destiny with figured wood and higher-end appointments, various colors.

1989-1992		$750	$1,000

Detonator AX

1995-1998. Double-cut, maple neck, rosewood 'board, dot markers, hum/single/hum pickups, black.

1995-1998		$350	$500

EVH Wolfgang

1996-2004. Offset double-cut, arched top, bolt neck, stop tailpiece or Floyd Rose vibrato, quilted or flamed maple top upgrade option.

1996	Pat pending early production	$3,500	$4,500
1997-1998	Pat pending	$2,500	$3,500
1999-2004	Flamed maple top	$2,375	$3,000
1999-2004	Standard top	$1,750	$2,250

EVH Wolfgang Special

1997-2004. Offset double-cut lower-end Wolfgang model, various opaque finishes, flamed top optional.

1996-2004	Standard top, D-Tuna	$950	$1,500
1997-2004	Flamed maple top	$1,000	$1,750
1997-2004	Standard basswood	$900	$1,250

EVH Wolfgang Special EXP

2002-2004. Made in Korea.

2002-2004		$800	$1,000

Falcon/Falcon Active/Falcon Custom

1987-1992. Double-cut, 3 pickups, passive or active electronics, Kahler locking vibrato.

1987-1992	Custom color	$350	$450
1987-1992	Standard color	$275	$350

Firenza

1994-1999. Offset double-cut, bolt-on neck, single-coil pickups.

1994-1999		$400	$575

Firenza AX

1994-1999. Upscale Firenza Impact with humbucking pickups.

1994-1999		$500	$650

Generation Custom EX

2006-2008. Single-cut solidbody, 2 humbuckers, 5-way switch.

2006-2008		$200	$250

Generation S-1/S-2/S-3

1988-1994. Single-cut, maple cap on mahogany body, bolt-on maple neck, six-on-a-side tuners, active single/hum pickups, S-2 with locking vibrato system.

1988-1994		$450	$550

Horizon/Horizon II

1983-1985. Extended pointy horns, angled lower bout, maple body, rear routing for electronics, 2 humbucking pickups. Horizon II has added blade pickup.

1983-1985		$400	$500

HP Special USA

2008-2011. Offset cutaway, 2 humbuckers.

2008-2011		$750	$1,250

2000 Peavey EVH Wolfgang Special

Willie Moseley

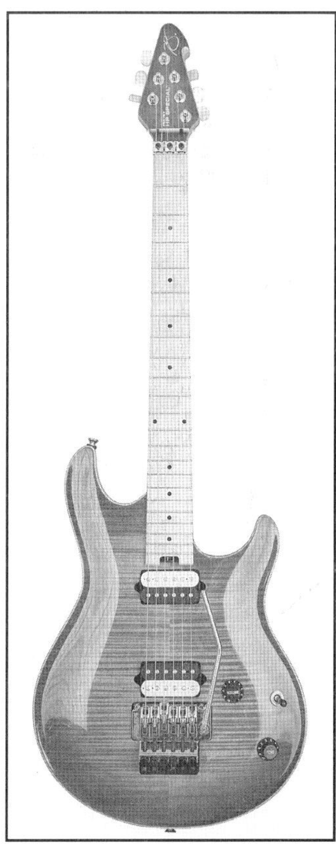

Peavey HP Special USA

GUITARS

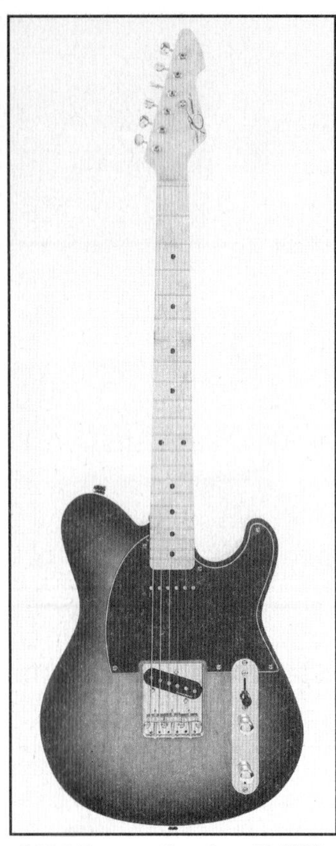
2008 Peavey Omniac JD USA
Imaged by Heritage Auctions, HA.com

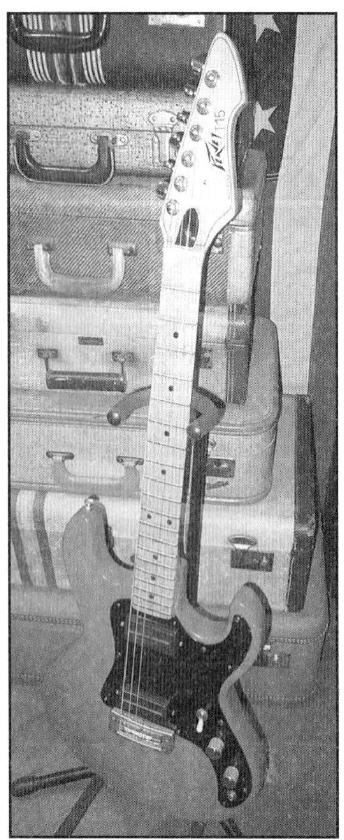
1983 Peavey T-15 Red
Rivington Guitars

MODEL YEAR	FEATURES	EXC. COND. LOW	HIGH

Hydra Doubleneck
1985-1989. Available as a custom order, 6/12-string necks each with 2 humbuckers, 3-way pickup select.

1985-1989		$800	$1,000

Impact 1/Impact 2
1985-1987. Offset double-cut, Impact 1 has higher-end synthetic 'board, Impact 2 with conventional rosewood 'board.

1985-1987		$350	$500

Liberator JT-85 A435 John Taylor
2007. Models by John Taylor and Juicy Couture, basswood body, maple neck, 1 humbucker and 2 single-coils, black with graphics, certificate of authenticity.

2007	100 made	$700	$900

Mantis
1984-1989. Hybrid X-shaped solidbody, 1 humbucking pickup, tremolo, laminated maple neck.

1984-1989		$350	$500

Milestone 12-String
1985-1986. Offset double-cut, 12 strings.

1985-1986		$250	$325

Milestone/Milestone Custom
1983-1986. Offset double-cut solidbody.

1983-1986		$225	$300

Mystic
1983-1989. Double-cut, 2 pickups, stop tailpiece initially, later Power Bend vibrato, maple body and neck.

1983-1989		$400	$500

Nitro I Active
1988-1990. Active electronics.

1988-1990		$350	$450

Nitro I/II/III
1986-1989. Offset double-cut, banana-style headstock, 1 humbucker (I), 2 humbuckers (II), or single/single/hum pickups (III).

1986-1989	Nitro I	$250	$350
1986-1989	Nitro II	$350	$500
1986-1989	Nitro III	$400	$550

Odyssey
1990-1994. Single-cut, figured carved maple top on mahogany body, humbuckers.

1990-1994		$600	$750

Odyssey 25th Anniversary
1990. Single-cut body, limited production.

1990		$750	$950

Omniac JD USA
2005-2010. Designed by Jerry Donahue, single-cut solidbody, 2 single-coils.

2005-2010		$825	$1,125

Patriot
1983-1987. Double-cut, single bridge humbucker.

1983-1987		$300	$400

Patriot Plus
1983-1987. Double-cut, 2 humbucker pickups, bi-laminated maple neck.

1983-1987		$400	$500

Patriot Tremolo
1986-1990. Double-cut, single bridge humbucker, tremolo, replaced the standard Patriot.

1986-1990		$400	$500

Predator Plus 7ST
2008-2010. 7-string.

2008-2010		$400	$500

Predator Series
1985-1988, 1990-2016. Double-cut poplar body, 2 pickups until '87, 3 after, vibrato.

1985-2016		$250	$350

Raptor Series
1997-present. Offset double-cut solidbody, 3 pickups.

1997-2024	Various models	$100	$125

Razer
1983-1989. Double-cut with arrowhead point for lower bout, 2 pickups, 1 volume and 2 tone controls, stop tailpiece or vibrato.

1983-1989		$400	$550

Reactor
1993-1999. Classic single-cut style, 2 single-coils.

1993-1999		$300	$400

Rockmaster II Stage Pack
2000s. Student solidbody Rockmaster electric guitar and GT-5 amp pack.

2000		$100	$125

Rotor Series
2004-2010. Classic futuristic body, elongated upper treble bout/lower bass bout, 2 humbuckers.

2004-2008	Rotor EXP	$300	$400
2004-2010	Rotor EX	$275	$375

T-15
1981-1983. Offset double-cut, bolt-on neck, dual ferrite blade single-coil pickups, natural. Amp-in-case available.

1981-1983	Amp-in-case	$500	$700
1981-1983	Guitar only	$400	$550

T-25
1979-1985. Synthetic polymer body, 2 pickups, cream 'guard, sunburst finish.

1979-1985		$500	$600

T-25 Special
1979-1985. Same as T-25, but with super high output pickups, phenolic 'board, black/white/black 'guard, ebony black finish.

1979-1985		$500	$600

T-26
1982-1986. Same as T-25, but with 3 single-coil pickups and 5-way switch.

1982-1986		$450	$550

T-27
1981-1983. Offset double-cut, bolt-on neck, dual ferrite blade single-coil pickups.

1981-1983		$500	$600

T-30
1982-1985. Short-scale, 3 single-coil pickups, 5-way select, by '83 amp-in-case available.

1982-1985	Guitar only	$500	$650
1983-1985	Amp-in-case	$600	$750

T-60
1978-1988. Contoured offset double-cut, ash body, six-in-line tuners, 2 humbuckers, thru-body strings, by '87 maple bodies, various finishes.

1978-1988		$700	$1,000

MODEL YEAR	FEATURES	EXC. COND. LOW	HIGH

T-1000 LT

1992-1994. Double-cut, 2 single-coils and humbucker with coil-tap.

1992-1994		$350	$450

Tracer Custom

1989-1990. Tracer with 2 single humbuckers and extras.

1989-1990		$350	$450

Tracer/Tracer II

1987-1994. Offset scooped double-cut with extended pointy horns, poplar body, 1 pickup, Floyd Rose.

1987-1994		$350	$450

Vandenberg Quilt Top

1989-1992. Vandenberg Custom with quilted maple top, 2 humbuckers, glued-in neck, mahogany body and neck.

1989-1992		$2,000	$2,500

Vandenberg Signature/Signature 2

1988-1992. Double-cut, reverse headstock, bolt-on neck, locking vibrato, various colors. Signature 2 has jigsaw puzzle finish.

1988-1992		$2,000	$2,500
1989-1990	Signature 2	$2,500	$5,000

Vortex I/Vortex II

1986. Streamlined Mantis with 2 pickups, 3-way, Kahler locking vibrato. Vortex II has Randy Rhoads Sharkfin V.

1986		$550	$700

V-Type Series

2004-2007. Offset double-cut solidbody, pointed reverse 6-on-a-side headstock, 2 humbuckers.

2004-2007		$450	$600

Wolfgang Special

1996 1997. Peavy logo on headstock (not EVH), curly maple quilt top, various colors.

1996-1997		$2,000	$3,000

Pederson Custom Guitars

2009-present. Luthier Kevin Pederson builds his premium grade, production/custom, hollowbody and solidbody guitars in Forest City, Iowa. From 1997-2009 he produced guitars under the Abyss brand name.

Pedro de Miguel

1991-present. Luthiers Pedro Pérez and Miguel Rodriguez build their professional and premium grade, custom/production, classical guitars in Madrid, Spain. They also offer factory-made instruments built to their specifications.

Pedulla

1975-2019. Known for basses, Pedulla did offer a few solidbody guitar models into the early 1980s.

MVP

1981-1984. Double-cut solidbody, 2 humbuckers, dot markers, 4 knobs with main toggle and 3 mini-toggle switches, stencil Pedulla logo, MVP serial number series.

1981-1984		$2,200	$3,300

Peekamoose

1983-present. Production/custom, premium grade, solidbody, chambered, and archtop electric guitars built in New York City, New York by luthier Paul Schwartz.

Pegasus Guitars and Ukuleles

1977-present. Premium grade, custom steel-string guitars built by luthier Bob Gleason in Kurtistown, Hawaii, who also builds ukulele family instruments.

Penco

Ca. 1974-1978. Generally high-quality Japanese-made copies of classic American acoustic, electric and bass guitars. Imported by Philadelphia Music Company of Limerick, Pennsylvania during the copy era. Includes dreadnought acoustics with laminated woods, bolt-neck solidbody electric guitars and basses, mandolins, and banjos.

Acoustic Flat-Top

1974-1978	Various models	$125	$400

Electric

1974-1978	Solidbody	$325	$500
1974-1978	Thinline Archtop	$325	$500
1977	E-72 Howard Roberts	$900	$1,400

Penn

1950s. Archtop and acoustic guitars built by made by United Guitar Corporation in Jersey City, New Jersey, which also made Premier acoustics. Penn was located in L.A.

Pensa (Pensa-Suhr)

1982-present. Premium grade, production/custom, solidbody guitars and basses built in the U.S. Rudy Pensa, of Rudy's Music Stop, New York City, New York, started building Pensa guitars in '82. In '85 he teamed up with John Suhr to build Pensa-Suhr instruments. Name changed back to Pensa in '96.

Classic

1992-Ca. 1998. Offset double-cut, 3 single-coils, gold hardware.

1992-1998	Various models	$4,000	$8,000

MK 1 (Mark Knopfler)

1985-2018. Offset double-cut solidbody, carved flamed maple bound top, 3 pickups, gold hardware, dot markers, bolt-on neck.

1985-2018		$8,000	$12,000

Suhr Custom

1985-1989. Two-piece maple body, bolt-on maple neck with rosewood 'board, custom order basis with a variety of woods and options available.

1985-1989	Various options	$5,000	$7,500

Suhr Pro S1

1980s-1990s. Solidbody electric, alder body, maple neck, rosewood 'board, various colors.

1980s-90s		$4,000	$10,000

1978 Peavey T-60

Tom Pfeifer

1976 Penco

Reese Shellman

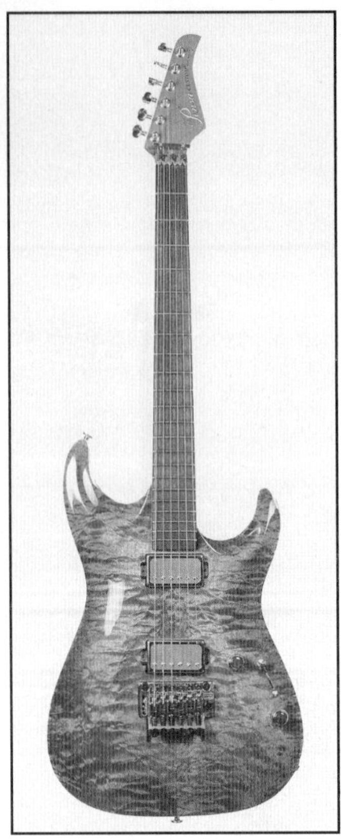

Pensa MK1

Petillo Archtop

MODEL YEAR	FEATURES	EXC. COND. LOW	HIGH

Suhr Standard

1985-1991. Double-cut, single/single/hum pickup configuration, opaque solid finish normally, dot markers.

1985-1991		$4,500	$9,000

Vandenberg Quilt Top

1989-1992. As Suhr Custom with quilted top, various colors.

1989-1992		$6,000	$15,000

Vortex I/Vortex II

1986. Various woods and colors.

1986		$7,000	$12,000

Perlman Guitars

1976-present. Luthier Alan Perlman builds his premium grade, custom, steel-string and classical guitars in San Francisco, California.

Perri Ink.

Custom, professional grade, solidbody electric guitars built by luthier Nick Perri in Los Angeles, California, starting in 2009.

Perry Guitars

1982-present. Premium grade, production/custom, classical guitars built by luthier Daryl Perry in Winnipeg, Manitoba. He also builds lutes.

Petillo Masterpiece Guitars

1965-present. Intermediate, professional and premium grade, custom, steel-string, nylon-string, 12-string, resonator, archtop, and Hawaiian guitars in Ocean, New Jersey, originally by father and son luthiers Phillip J. "Doc" and David Petillo. Doc died in August 2010.

Petros Guitars

1992-present. Premium grade, production/custom, flat-top, 12-string, and nylon-string guitars built by father and son luthiers Bruce and Matthew Petros in Kaukauna, Wisconsin.

PH Guitars

2006-present. Luthier Paul A. Hartmann builds professional and premium grade, custom, acoustic archtop and electric guitars in Hyde Park, New York.

Phantom Guitar Works

1992-present. Intermediate grade, production/custom, classic Phantom, and Teardrop shaped solid and hollowbody guitars and basses assembled in Clatskanie, Oregon. They also offer the Mando-Guitar. Phantom was established by Jack Charles, former lead guitarist of the band Quarterflash. Some earlier guitars were built overseas.

Pheo

Luthier Phil Sylvester, began building in 1996, unique premium grade, production/custom, electric and acoustic guitars in Portland, Oregon.

MODEL YEAR	FEATURES	EXC. COND. LOW	HIGH

Phoenix Guitar Company

1994-present. Luthiers George Leach and Diana Huber build their premium grade, production/custom, archtop and classical guitars in Scottsdale, Arizona.

Pieper

Premium grade, custom, solidbody guitars and basses built by luthier Robert Pieper in New Haven, Connecticut starting in 2005.

Pignose

1972-present. The original portable amp company also offers intermediate grade, production, dreadnaught and amplified electric guitars. They also offer effects. Refer to Amps section for more company info.

Pilgrim

1970's-late-1980s, 2010-present. Built in the U.K., luthier Paul Tebbutt introduced the brand back in the '70s and his guitars were available until late '80s. His designs are now used on intermediate grade, production, electric acoustic guitars, built in the Far East and distributed by John Hornby Skewes & Co. Ltd. They also offer mandolins, ukuleles and banjos.

Pimentel and Sons

1951-present. Luthiers Lorenzo Pimentel and sons build their professional, premium and presentation grade, flat-top, jazz, cutaway electric, and classical guitars in Albuquerque, New Mexico.

Player

1984-1985. Player guitars featured interchangeable pickup modules that mounted through the back of the guitar. They offered a double-cut solidbody with various options and the pickup modules were sold separately. The company was located in Scarsdale, New York.

Pleasant

Late 1940s-ca.1966. Solidbody electric guitars, obviously others, Japanese manufacturer, probably not imported into the U.S.

Electric Solidbody

1940s-1966. Various models.

1940s-1966		$225	$400

Potvin

2003-present. Production/custom, professional and premium grade, chambered, hollowbody and solidbody electric guitars built by luthier Mike Potvin in Ontario.

Prairie State

1927-ca. 1940. A Larson Brothers brand, basically a derivative of Maurer & Company. The Prairie State models were slightly more expensive than the equivalent Maurer models. They featured a patented steel rod mechanism to strengthen the body, which ran from the end block to the neck block. The model

GUITARS

usually had Brazilian rosewood back and sides, laminated necks and X-bracing. Some later models were built with figured maple.

Prairiewood

Luthier Robert Dixon of Fargo, North Dakota, began in 2005, builds professional grade, production/custom, hollowbody archtop and solidbody guitars.

Premier

Ca.1938-ca.1975, 1990s-2010. Brands originally offered by Premier include Premier, Multivox, Marvel, Belltone and Strad-O-Lin. Produced by Peter Sorkin Music Company in Manhattan, New York City, New York, who began in Philadelphia, relocating to NYC in '35. First radio-sized amplifiers and stick-on pickups for acoustic archtops were introduced by '38. After WWII, they set up the Multivox subsidiary to manufacture amplifiers ca. '46. The first flat-top with pickup appeared in '46.

Most acoustic instruments were made by United Guitar Corporation in Jersey City, New Jersey. Ca. '57 Multivox acquires Strad-O-Lin. Ca.'64-'65 their Custom line guitars are assembled with probably Italian bodies and hardware, Japanese electronics, possibly Egmond necks from Holland. By ca. '74-'75, there were a few Japanese-made guitars, then Premier brand goes into hiatus. The brand reappears on Asian-made budget and intermediate grade, production, solidbody guitars and basses beginning in the '90s.

MODEL YEAR	FEATURES	EXC. COND. LOW	HIGH
Bantam Custom			
1950s-1960s. Single-cut archtop, dots, earlier with white potted pickups, then metal-covered pickups, and finally Japanese-made pickups (least valued).			
1950s-60s		$900	$1,400
Bantam Deluxe			
1950s-1960s. Single-cut archtop, fully bound, sparkle knobs, earlier with white potted pickups, then metal-covered pickups, and finally Japanese-made pickups (least valued), block markers, 1 or 2 pickups (deduct $100 for 1 pickup).			
1950s-60s	Blond, sunburst	$1,800	$2,800
Bantam Special			
1950s-1960s. Single-cut archtop, dots, early models with white potted pickups, then metal-covered pickups, and finally Japanese-made pickups (least valued), 1 or 2 pickups (deduct $100 for 1 pickup).			
1950s-60s		$900	$1,400
Custom Solidbody			
1958-1970. Notable solidbody bass scroll cutaway, various models with various components used, finally import components only.			
1958-1970	1 pickup	$600	$900
1958-1970	2 pickups	$700	$1,000
1958-1970	3 pickups	$900	$1,400
Deluxe Archtop			
1950s-1960s. Full body 17 1/4" archtop, square block markers, single-cut, early models with white potted pickups, later '60s models with metal pickups.			
1950s-60s		$1,500	$2,200
E-727			
1958-1962. E-scroll style solidbody with scroll bass bout, 3 single-coil pickups, Premier headstock logo, made by the Multivox factory in New York.			
1958-1962		$1,200	$1,800
Semi-Pro 16" Archtop			
1950s-early-1960s. Thinline electric 16" archtop with 2 1/4" deep body, acoustic or electric.			
1950s-60s	Acoustic	$800	$1,200
1950s-60s	Electric	$900	$1,400
Semi-Pro Bantam Series			
1960s. Thinline electric archtop with 2 3/4" deep body, offered in cutaway and non-cut models.			
1960s		$400	$600
Special Archtop			
1950s-1960s. Full body 17 1/4" archtop, less fancy than Deluxe, single-cut, early models with white potted pickups, '60s models with metal pickups.			
1950s-60s		$1,000	$1,500
Studio Six Archtop			
1950s-early-1960s. 16" wide archtop, single pickup, early pickups white potted, changed later to metal top.			
1950s-60s		$600	$900

Prenkert Guitars

1980-present. Premium and presentation grade, production/custom, classical and flamenco guitars built in Sebastopol, California by luthier Richard Prenkert.

Prenkert

Prestige

2003-present. Intermediate, professional, and premium grade, production/custom, acoustic, solidbody and hollowbody guitars and basses from Vancouver, British Columbia.

PST Guitars

Ca. 2000-present. Professional and premium grade, custom, electric guitars and basses, built by luthier P. Scott Tucker, in King George, Virginia. He has also built acoustic guitars.

Queen Shoals Stringed Instruments

1972-ca. 2010. Luthier Larry Cadle builds his production/custom, flat-top, 12-string, and nylon-string guitars in Clendenin, West Virginia.

Queguiner, Alain

1982-present. Custom flat-tops, 12 strings, and nylon strings built by luthier Alain Queguiner in Paris, France.

Quest

1982-ca. 1986. Originally labeled Quest by Vantage, these solidbody guitars and basses were built in Japan, mostly by Chushin Gakki.

R.C. Allen

1951-2014. Luthier R. C. "Dick" Allen built professional and premium grade, custom hollow-

Prestige Heritage Elite Spalt Maple

1996 R.C. Allen Leader
Imaged by Heritage Auctions, HA.com

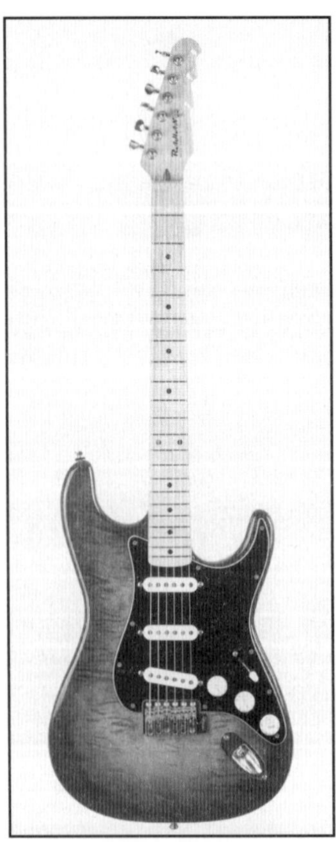
Rahan S-Style
Cream City Music

body and semi-hollowbody guitars in El Monte, California. He has also built solidbody guitars. He passed away in '14.

Rahan

1999-present. Professional grade, production/custom, solidbody guitars built by luthiers Mike Curd and Rick Cantu in Houston, Texas.

Rahbek Guitars

2000-present. Professional and premium grade, production/custom, solidbody electrics built by luthier Peter Rahbek in Copenhagen, Denmark.

Raimundo

1970s-present. Intermediate, professional and premium grade flamenco and classical guitars made in Valencia, Spain, by luthiers Antonio Aparicio and Manual Raimundo.

RainSong

1991-2023. Professional grade, production, all-graphite and graphite and wood acoustic guitars built originally in Maui, and currently in Woodinville, Washington. Developed by luthier engineer John Decker with help from luthier Lorenzo Pimentel, engineer Chris Halford, and sailboard builder George Clayton.

RAM Guitars

2007-present. Luthier Ron Mielzynski builds his professional grade, production/custom, solidbody, chambered and archtop electric guitars in Fox River Grove, Illinois.

Rambler

See Strobel Guitars listing.

Ramirez, Jose

1882-present. Professional, premium, and presentation grade, custom/production, classical guitars built in Madrid, Spain. Founded by Jose Ramirez (1858-1923) who was an apprentice at the shop of Francisco Gonzales. Jose opened his own workshop in 1882 working with his younger brother, Manuel. Manuel split with Jose and opened his own, competing workshop. Jose's business was continued by Jose's son Jose Ramirez II (1885-1957), grandson Jose III (1922-1995), and great grandchildren Jose IV (1953-2000) and Amalia Ramirez. In the 1930's a larger body instrument with improved fan bracing was developed to meet the need for more power and volume. Other refinements were developed and the Ramirez 1A Tradicional was soon introduced which found favor with Andres Segovia. The Ramirez company has produced both student and professional instruments, but in the classical guitar field, like the old-master violin business, a student model is often a very fine instrument that is now valued at $2,000 or more. In the 1980s Ramirez offered the E Series student guitar line that was built for, but not by, Ramirez. In 1991 the company offered the even more affordable R Series which was offered for about $1,300. As is typically the case, Ramirez classical guitars do not have a name-logo on the headstock. The brand is identified by a Ramirez label on the inside back which also may have the model number listed.

MODEL YEAR	FEATURES	EXC. COND. LOW	HIGH
A/1A			
1960s-2000s. Classical, Brazilian or Indian rosewood.			
1960s-70s	Brazilian, cedar	$8,000	$12,000
1970s-80s	Indian	$4,000	$6,000
1980s	Brazilian	$6,000	$8,000
1990-2000s	Indian	$4,500	$6,500
A/2A			
1970s-80s	Indian	$2,500	$3,500
AE Estudio			
2004		$1,800	$2,500
De Camera			
1980s. Classical, cedar top, Brazilian rosewood back and sides.			
1980s		$5,000	$7,000
E/1E/Estudio			
1988-1990s. Intermediate level.			
1988-1990s		$1,200	$2,000
E/2E			
1990s-2000s. Red cedar top, Indian rosewood back and sides, Spanish cedar neck, ebony 'board.			
1990-2000s		$1,800	$2,500
E/3E/Estudio			
1990s. Cedar, rosewood.			
1990s		$2,000	$3,000
E/4E/Estudio			
1980s-2000s. Top of the E Series line, solid red cedar top, solid Indian rosewood back and sides.			
1980-2000s		$2,500	$3,500
Flamenco			
1920s-1979. European spruce top, cypress back and sides.			
1920s-50s		$6,000	$8,000
1960-1969		$4,500	$6,500
1970-1979		$4,000	$6,000
R1			
1991-2014. Red cedar top, mahogany sides and back, Spanish cedar neck, ebony 'board. Replaced by RA series in '14.			
1991-2014		$600	$900
R2			
1991-2014. Red cedar top, Indian rosewood back and sides, cedar neck, ebony 'board. Replaced by RA series in '14.			
1991-2014		$1,200	$1,800
R3			
1998. Cedar, rosewood.			
1998		$1,200	$1,800
R4 Classical			
1995-2014. All solid wood, Western red cedar top, rosewood back and sides. Replaced by RB series in '14.			
1995-2014		$1,800	$2,800
S/S1			
2005-2007. Solid German spruce top, African mahogany sides and back, most affordable in Estudio line.			
2005-2007		$1,000	$1,500

MODEL YEAR	FEATURES	EXC. COND. LOW	HIGH

Segovia

Cedar, Indian rosewood.

1966		$8,000	$12,000
1974-1978		$5,000	$7,000

SP Series

2002-2018. Semi-professional level designed to be between the company's 'concert/professional' series and 'student' series.

2002-2018		$4,000	$6,000

Ramirez, Manuel

1890-1916. Brother of Jose Ramirez, and a respected professional classical guitar builder from Madrid, Spain. His small shop left no heirs, so the business was not continued after Manuel's death in 1916. Manuel was generally considered to be more famous during his lifetime than his brother Jose, and while his business did not continue, Manuel trained many well-known Spanish classical guitar luthiers who prospered with their own businesses. During Manuel's era his shop produced at least 48 different models, with prices ranging from 10 to 1,000 pesetas, therefore vintage prices can vary widely. Guitars made prior to 1912 have a label with a street address of Arlaban 10, in 1912 the shop moved to Arlaban 11.

Randy Reynolds Guitars

1996-2018. Luthier Randy Reynolds builds his premium grade, production/custom classical and flamenco guitars in Colorado Springs, Colorado. Reynolds announced his retirement on January 1, 2019.

Randy Wood Guitars

1968-present. Premium grade, custom/production, archtop, flat-top, and resonator guitars built by luthier Randy Wood in Bloomingdale, Georgia. He also builds mandolins.

Rarebird Guitars

1978-present. Luthier Bruce Clay builds his professional and premium grade, production/custom, guitars and basses, originally in Arvada, Colorado, and currently in Hoehne, Colorado.

Rat Fink

2002-2005. Lace Music Products, the makers of the Lace Sensor pickup, offered the intermediate grade, production, guitars and basses, featuring the artwork of Ed "Big Daddy" Roth until '05.

Rayco

2002-present. Professional and premium grade, custom, resonator and Hawaiian-style acoustic guitars built in British Columbia, by luthiers Mark Thibeault and Jason Friesen.

MODEL YEAR	FEATURES	EXC. COND. LOW	HIGH

Recco

1960s. Electric guitar imports made by Teisco, pricing similar to Teisco models, Recco logo on headstock, upscale solidbodies can have four pickups with several knobs and four switches.

Electric Solidbody

1960s	4 pickups	$700	$1,200

Recording King

1929-1943. Brand name used by Montgomery Ward for instruments made by various American manufacturers, including Kay, Gibson and Gretsch. Generally mid-grade instruments. M Series are Gibson-made archtops.

Carson Robison/Model 1052

1938-1939. Made by Gibson, flat-top, 16", sunburst.

1938-1939		$2,500	$3,800

Kay 17" Flat-Top

1940-1941		$1,000	$1,500

M-2

1936-1941. Gibson-made archtop with carved top and f-holes, maple back and sides.

1936-1941		$800	$1,200

M-3

1936-1941. Gibson-made archtop, f-holes, maple back and sides, carved top.

1936-1941		$900	$1,400

M-4

1937-1940. Gibson-made archtop, f-holes, maple back and sides, rope-checkered binding, flying bat wing markers.

1937-1940		$1,000	$1,500

M-5

1936-1941. Gibson-made archtop with f-holes, maple back and sides, trapeze tailpiece, checkered top binding.

1936-1938	16" body	$1,500	$2,200
1939-1941	17" body	$1,500	$2,200

M-6

1938-1939. M-5 with upgraded gold hardware.

1938-1939		$1,500	$2,200

Model 681

Mid-1930s. Small flat top by Gibson, ladder braced.

1930s		$1,500	$2,200

Model 1124

1937. 16" acoustic archtop, body by Gibson, attractive higher-end appointments, block-dot markers, sunburst.

1937		$2,000	$3,000

Ray Whitley

1939-1940. High-quality model made by Gibson, round shoulder flat-top, mahogany (Model 1028) or Brazilian rosewood (Model 1027) back and sides, 5-piece maple neck, Ray Whitley stencil script peghead logo, pearl crown inlay on peghead, fancy inlaid markers.

1939-1940	Brazilian	$25,000	$30,000
1939-1940	Mahogany	$12,000	$15,000

Roy Smeck

1938-1940. 16.25" electric archtop, large Recording King badge logo, Roy Smeck stencil logo, bar pickup, 2 control knobs on upper bass bout, dot markers.

1938-1940		$1,300	$2,000

Rahbek Cos-T

1939 Recording King Carson Robinson/Model 1052
Jet City Guitars

Redentore Psalmist

2004 Reverend Wolfman
Thomas Whitty

MODEL YEAR	FEATURES	EXC. COND. LOW	HIGH

Recording King (TML)

2005-present. Budget grade, production, acoustic cowboy stenciled guitars designed by Greg Rich for The Music Link, which also offers Johnson and other brand instruments. They also have banjos and ukes.

Redentore

2007-present. Luthier Mark Piper builds professional and premium grade, production/custom, archtop jazz, acoustic flat-top, carve-top and semi-hollow electric guitars in Columbia, Tennessee.

RedLine Acoustics and RedLine Resophonics

2007-present. Professional and premium grade, production, acoustic and resophonic guitars built in Hendersonville, Tennessee by luthiers Steve Smith, Jason Denton, Christian McAdams and Ryan Futch. They also build mandolins and plan to add lap steels.

Regal

Ca. 1895-1966, 1987-present. Intermediate and professional grade, production, acoustic and wood and metal body resonator guitars and basses. Originally a mass manufacturer founded in Indianapolis, Indiana, the Regal brand was first used by Emil Wulschner & Son. After 1900, new owners changed the company name to The Regal Manufacturing Company. The company was moved to Chicago in '08 and renamed the Regal Musical Instrument Company. Regal made brands for distributors and mass merchandisers as well as marketing its own Regal brand. Regal purchased the Lyon & Healy factory in '28. Regal was licensed to co-manufacture Dobros in '32 and became the sole manufacturer of them in '37 (see Dobro for those instruments). Most Regal instruments were beginner-grade; however, some very fancy archtops were made during the '30s. The company was purchased by Harmony in '54 and absorbed. From '59 to '66, Harmony made acoustics under the Regal name for Fender. In '87 the Regal name was revived on a line of resonator instruments by Saga.

Acoustic Hawaiian

1930s. Student model, small 13" body, square neck, glued or trapeze bridge.

1930s	Faux grain painted finish	$450	$700
1930s	Plain sunburst, birch, trapeze	$250	$400

Concert Folk H6382

1960s. Regal by Harmony, solid spruce top, mahogany back and sides, dot markers, natural.

1960s		$325	$500

Deluxe Dreadnought H6600

1960s. Regal by Harmony, solid spruce top, mahogany back and sides, bound top and back, rosewood 'board, dot markers, natural.

1960s		$325	$500

MODEL YEAR	FEATURES	EXC. COND. LOW	HIGH

Dreadnought 12-String H1269

1960s. Regal by Harmony, solid spruce top, 12-string version of Deluxe, natural.

1960s		$325	$500

Esquire

1940s. 15 1/2" acoustic archtop, higher-end appointments, fancy logo art and script pearl Esquire headstock logo and Regal logo, natural.

1940s		$1,200	$1,800

Meteor

1960s. Single-cut acoustic-electric archtop, 2 pickups.

1960s		$1,200	$1,800

Model 27

1933-1942. Birch wood body, mahogany or maple, 2-tone walnut finish, single-bound top, round or square neck.

1933-1942		$1,000	$1,500

Model 45

1933-1937. Spruce top and mahogany back and sides, bound body, square neck.

1933-1937		$1,600	$2,500

Model 46

1933-1937. Round neck.

1933-1937		$1,600	$2,500

Model 55 Standard

1933-1934. Regal's version of Dobro Model 55 which was discontinued in '33.

1933-1934		$1,000	$1,500

Model 75

1939-1940. Metal body, square neck.

1939-1940		$2,000	$3,000

Model TG 60 Resonator Tenor

1930s. Wood body, large single cone biscuit bridge resonator, 2 upper bout metal ports, 4-string tenor.

1930s		$1,500	$2,200

Parlor

1920s. Small body, slotted headstock, birch sides and back, spruce top.

1920s		$325	$500

Prince

1930s. High-end 18" acoustic archtop, fancy appointments, Prince name inlaid in headstock along with Regal script logo and strolling guitarist art.

1930s		$1,800	$2,800

Spirit Of '76

1976. Red-white-blue, flat-top.

1976		$450	$700

Reliance

1920s. Instruments built by the Oscar Schmidt Co. and possibly others. Most likely a brand made for a distributor.

Relixx

2001-2013. Intermediate and professional grade, production/custom, aged vintage-style solidbody guitars built in Sanborn, New York by luthier Nick Hazlett. He discontinued complete guitars in '13 and now offers only vintage parts.

MODEL YEAR	FEATURES	EXC. COND. LOW	HIGH

Renaissance

1978-1980. Plexiglass solidbody electric guitars and basses. Founded in Malvern, Pennsylvania, by John Marshall (designer), Phil Goldberg and Daniel Lamb. Original partners gradually leave, and John Dragonetti takes over by late-'79. The line is redesigned with passive electronics on guitars, exotic shapes, but when deal with Sunn amplifiers falls through, company closes. Brand name currently used on a line of guitars and basses made by Rick Turner in Santa Cruz, California.

Fewer than 300 of first series made, plus a few prototypes and several wooden versions; six or so prototypes of second series made. SN=M(M) YYXXXX: month, year, consecutive number.

Electric Plexiglas Solidbody

1978-1980. Models include the SPG ('78-'79, DiMarzio pickups, active electronics), T-200G ('80, Bich-style with 2 passive DiMarzio pickups), and the S-200G ('80, double-cut, 2 DiMarzio pickups, passive electronics).

1978-1980		$1,200	$1,800

Renaissance Guitars

1994-present. Professional grade, custom, semi-acoustic flat-top, nylon-string and solidbody guitars and basses built by luthier Rick Turner in Santa Cruz, California. He also builds ukes.

Repiso

Late-1950s-early-1970s. Spanish-born luthier Sergio Repiso Villarruel made professional and premium grade, Gypsy-style jazz and solidbody electric guitars, mostly in Argentina. It is estimated that throughout his life he produced about 1,000 instruments.

Republic Guitars

2006-present. Intermediate grade, production, reso-phonic and Weissenborn-style guitars imported by American Folklore, Inc. of Austin, Texas. They also offer mandolins and ukes.

Retronix

2013-present. Korean-made solidbody guitars designed and imported by J. Backlund. They also build J. Backlund guitars.

Reuter Guitars

1984-present. Professional and premium grade, custom, flat-top, 12-string, resonator, and Hawaiian guitars built by luthier John Reuter, the Director of Training at the Roberto-Venn School of Luthiery, in Tempe, Arizona.

Reverend

1996-present. Intermediate grade, production, guitars and basses, designed by luthier and founder Joe Naylor, manufactured in South Korea, and setup by Reverend originally in Warren, Livonia, Michigan, and currently in Toledo, Ohio. There were also earlier U.S. production guitars built in Warren. Reverend has built amps and effects in the past. In 2010, Ken and Penny Haas purchased the company with Naylor continuing with design. Naylor also founded Naylor Amps, Armor Gold Cables, Stringdog, and Railhammer Pickups.

Electric

1996-present. Solid and semi-solid bodies, bolt or set-neck, various pickups.

1996-2024	Various models	$400	$2,000

Rex

1920s-1940s, 1950s-1960s. Generally, beginner-grade guitars made by Kay and sold through Fred Gretsch distributors. In the '50s and '60s, the Lamberti Brothers Company in Melbourne, Australia built electrics bearing the Rex brand that were not distributed by Gretsch. They also had built amps.

Ribbecke Guitars

Premium and presentation grade, custom thinline, flat-top, and archtop guitars built by luthier Tom Ribbecke, starting in 1973, in Healdsburg, California.

Rice Custom Guitars

1998-present. Father and son luthiers, Richard Rice and Christopher Rice, build professional and premium grade, custom, solidbody, semi-hollow and hollowbody electric guitars and basses in Arlington Heights, Illinois.

Rich and Taylor

1993-1996. Custom acoustic and electric guitars, mandolins and banjos from luthiers Greg Rich and Mark Taylor (Crafters of Tennessee).

Richard Schneider

1960s-1997. Luthier Richard Schneider built his acoustic guitars in Washington state. Over the years, he collaborated with Dr. Michael A. Kasha on many guitar designs and innovations. Originally from Michigan, he also was involved in designing guitars for Gretsch and Gibson. He died in early '97.

Richie's Guitar Shop

Intermediate and professional grade, custom, electric guitars and basses, built by luthier Richard 'Richie' Baxt, in New York City, New York. He began in 1983 and also does repairs and modifications.

Richmond

Luthiers Robert Godin (Godin Guitars) and Daniel Fiocco build intermediate and professional grade, production, chambered and solidbody electric guitars in Richmond, Quebec. Richmond is one of several brands used by Godin.

Richter Mfg.

1930s. One of many Chicago makers of the era, the company allegedly bought already-made guitars from other manufacturers, painted and decorated them to their liking and resold them.

Reverend Rick Vito Soulshaker

Rick Vito

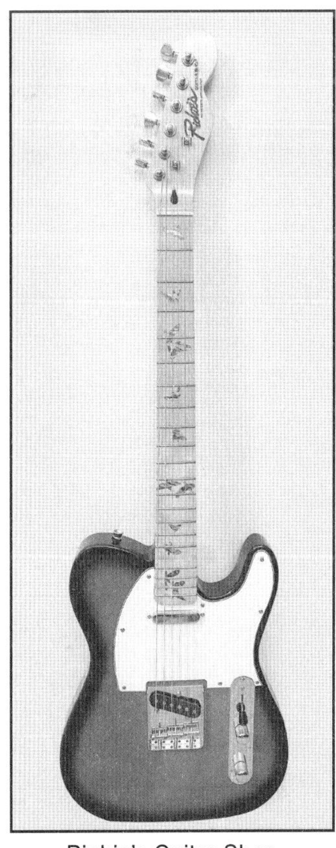

Richie's Guitar Shop

Rick Hayes

Rick Turner Model 1

Rick Hayes Instruments

2006-present. Owned by Rick and Lyn Hayes and offering professional and premium grade, production/custom, dreadnought acoustic and electric guitars, and mandolins built by Rick and Steve Hogsed in Goshen, Ohio.

Rick Turner

1979-1981, 1990-present. Rick Turner has a long career as a luthier, electronics designer and innovator. He also makes the Renaissance line of guitars in his shop in Santa Cruz, California. The guitars and basses built in 1979-'81 were numbered sequentially in the order they were completed and shipped with the second part of the serial number indicating the year the instrument was built. Turner estimates that approximately 200 instruments were made during that period.

Rickenbacker

1931-present. Professional and premium grade, production/custom, acoustic and electric guitars built in California. They also build basses. Founded in Los Angeles as Ro-Pat-In by ex-National executives George Beauchamp, Paul Barth and National's resonator cone supplier Adolph Rickenbacher. Rickenbacher was born in Basel, Switzerland in 1886, emigrated to the U.S. and moved to Los Angeles in 1918, opening a tool and die business in '20.

In the mid-'20s, Rickenbacher began providing resonator cones and other metal parts to George Beauchamp and Louis Dopyera of National String Instrument Corporation and became a shareholder in National. Beauchamp, Barth and Harry Watson came up with wooden "frying pan" electric Hawaiian lap steel for National in '31; National was not interested, so Beauchamp and Barth joined with Rickenbacher as Ro-Pat-In (probably for ElectRO-PATent-INstruments) to produce Electro guitars. Cast aluminum frying pans were introduced in '32. Some Spanish guitars (flat-top, F-holes) with Electro pickups were produced beginning in '32. Ro-Pat-In changes their name to Electro String Instrument Corporation in '34, and brand becomes Rickenbacher Electro, soon changed to Rickenbacker, with a "k." Beauchamp retires in '40. There was a production hiatus during World War II.

In '53, Electro was purchased by Francis Cary Hall (born 1908), owner of Radio and Television Equipment Company (Radio-Tel) in Santa Ana, California (founded in '20s as Hall's Radio Service, which began distributing Fender instruments in '46). The factory was relocated to Santa Ana in '62 and the sales/distribution company's name changed from Radio-Tel to Rickenbacker Inc. in '65.

1950s serial numbers have from 4 to 7 letters and numbers, with the number following the letter indicating the '50s year (e.g., NNL8NN would be from '58). From '61 to '86 serial numbers indicate month and year of production with initial letter A-Z for the year A=1961, Z=1986) followed by letter for the month A-M (A=January) plus numbers as before followed by a number 0-9 for the year (0=1987; 9=1996). To avoid confusion, we have listed all instruments by model number. For example, the Combo 400 is listed as Model 400/Combo 400. OS and NS stands for Old Style and New Style. On the 360, for example, Ric changed the design in 1964 to their New Style with more rounded body horns and rounded top edges and other changes. But they still offered the Old Style with more pointed horns and top binding until the late 1960s. Ric still sometimes uses the two designations on some of their vintage reissues.

Electro ES-16

1964-1971. Double-cut, set neck, solidbody, 3/4 size, 1 pickup. The Electro line was manufactured by Rickenbacker and distributed by Radio-Tel. The Electro logo appears on the headstock.

1964-1971		$1,250	$1,750

Electro ES-17

1964-1975. Cutaway, set neck, solidbody, 1 pickup.

1964-1975		$1,500	$2,000

Electro Spanish (Model B Spanish)

1935-1943. Small guitar with a lap steel appearance played Spanish-style, hollow black bakelite body augmented with 5 chrome plates (white enamel in '40), 1 octagon knob (2 round-ridged in '38), called the Model B ca. '40.

1935-1937	Chrome, 1 knob	$4,000	$5,000
1935-1937	Tenor 4-string, 1 knob	$4,000	$5,000
1938-1939	Chrome, 2 knobs	$4,000	$5,000
1940-1943	White, 2 knobs	$3,500	$4,500

Electro-Spanish Ken Roberts

1935-1939. Mahogany body, f-holes in lower bout, horseshoe pickup, Kauffman vibrato.

1935-1939		$5,000	$6,500

Model 220 Hamburg

1992-1997. Solidbody.

1992-1997		$1,500	$2,500

Model 230 GF Glenn Frey

1992-1997. Glenn Frey Limited Edition, solidbody, 2 high output humbuckers, black hardware, chrome 'guard.

1992-1997		$3,000	$4,000

Model 230 Hamburg

1983-1991. Solidbody, offset double-cut, 2 pickups, dot inlay, rosewood 'board, chrome-plated hardware.

1983-1991		$1,000	$1,500

Model 250 El Dorado

1983-1991. Deluxe version of Hamburg, gold hardware, white binding.

1983-1991		$1,250	$2,000

Model 260 El Dorado

1992-1995. Replaces 250.

1992-1995		$1,750	$3,000

Model 310

1959-1969, 1981-1985. Two-pickup version of Model 320.

1959-1960	Capri, thick body	$15,000	$20,000
1964-1969	Thinner body	$6,500	$8,500
1981-1985	Reintroduced	$2,000	$2,500

Model 315
1959-1974. Two-pickup version of Model 325.

MODEL YEAR	FEATURES	EXC. COND. LOW	HIGH
1959-1960	Capri, thick body	$15,000	$20,000
1964-1969	Thinner body	$8,000	$10,000
1974		$3,500	$4,500

Model 320
1964-1992. Short-scale hollowbody, 3 pickups, f-holes optional in '61 and standard in '64 and optional again in '79.

MODEL YEAR	FEATURES	EXC. COND. LOW	HIGH
1964-1969	Fireglo	$6,500	$8,500
1966-1969	Mapleglo	$6,000	$7,500
1974-1979		$3,500	$4,500
1980-1992		$2,750	$3,500

Model 320/12V63
1986. Short run for Japanese market.

MODEL YEAR	FEATURES	EXC. COND. LOW	HIGH
1986		$2,500	$3,500

Model 325
1958-1979, 1985-1992. This was a low production model, with some years having no production. In the mid-'60s, the 325 was unofficially known as the John Lennon Model due to his guitar's high exposure on the Ed Sullivan Show and in the Saturday Evening Post.

MODEL YEAR	FEATURES	EXC. COND. LOW	HIGH
1958	Early, solid top, John Lennon, 6 made	$100,000	$250,000
1958	Late, Capri, thick body, F-hole	$40,000	$50,000
1959-1960		$30,000	$38,000
1964-1970	Fireglo or Jetglo	$6,500	$8,500
1966-1970	Mapleglo	$6,000	$7,500
1974-1979		$3,500	$4,500

Model 325/12
1985-1986, 1999. Based on John Lennon's one-of-a-kind '64 325/12.

MODEL YEAR	FEATURES	EXC. COND. LOW	HIGH
1985-1986		$3,000	$4,500
1999		$3,000	$4,500

Model 325B
1983-1984. Reissue of early '60s model.

MODEL YEAR	FEATURES	EXC. COND. LOW	HIGH
1983-1984		$3,500	$5,000

Model 325C58
2002-2014. Copy of the '58 model that John Lennon saw in Germany.

MODEL YEAR	FEATURES	EXC. COND. LOW	HIGH
2002-2014		$2,750	$3,500

Model 325C64
2002-present. Copy of the famous '64 model.

MODEL YEAR	FEATURES	EXC. COND. LOW	HIGH
2002-2019		$2,500	$3,500

Model 325JL (John Lennon)
1989-1993. John Lennon Limited Edition, 3 vintage Ric pickups, vintage vibrato, maple body; 3/4-size rosewood neck, a 12-string and a full-scale version are also available.

MODEL YEAR	FEATURES	EXC. COND. LOW	HIGH
1989-1993		$4,000	$6,000

Model 325S
1964-1967. F-holes.

MODEL YEAR	FEATURES	EXC. COND. LOW	HIGH
1964-1967		$8,000	$12,000

Model 325V59
1984-2001. Reissue of John Lennon's modified '59 325, 3 pickups, short-scale.

MODEL YEAR	FEATURES	EXC. COND. LOW	HIGH
1984-2001		$3,000	$4,500

Model 325V63
1984-2001. Reissue of John Lennon's '63 325.

MODEL YEAR	FEATURES	EXC. COND. LOW	HIGH
1984-2001		$2,750	$4,000

Model 330
1958-present. Thinline hollowbody, 2 pickups, slash soundhole, natural or sunburst.

MODEL YEAR	FEATURES	EXC. COND. LOW	HIGH
1958-1960	Capri, thick body	$9,000	$12,000
1965-1969	Thinner body	$4,000	$6,500
1970-1976	21 frets	$2,500	$4,000
1977-1983	Small hdstk, Jetglo or Burgundyglo	$2,500	$4,000
1984-2024		$2,000	$3,000

Model 330/12
1965-present. Thinline, 2 pickups, 12-string version of Model 300.

MODEL YEAR	FEATURES	EXC. COND. LOW	HIGH
1965-1969	330-style body	$4,500	$6,500
1970-1976	21 frets	$3,000	$4,500
1980-1989		$2,500	$3,500
1990-1999		$2,250	$3,000
2000-2024		$2,000	$2,500

Model 330F
1958-1973. F-style.

MODEL YEAR	FEATURES	EXC. COND. LOW	HIGH
1958-1960	Thick version	$12,500	$15,000
1968-1973	Thin version	$8,000	$12,000

Model 330S/12
1964 (1 made)-1965 (2 made). Rare, total of 3 made.

MODEL YEAR	FEATURES	EXC. COND. LOW	HIGH
1964-1965		$25,000	$35,000

Model 331 Light Show
1970-1975. Model 330 with translucent top with lights in body that lit up when played, needed external transformer. The first offering's design, noted as Type 1, had heat problems and a fully original one is difficult to find. The 2nd offering's design, noted as Type 2, was a more stable design and is more highly valued in the market.

MODEL YEAR	FEATURES	EXC. COND. LOW	HIGH
1970-1971	Type 1 1st edition	$10,000	$15,000
1971-1975	Type 2 2nd edition	$12,000	$16,000

Model 335
1958-1976. Thinline, 330-style body, 2 pickups, vibrato, Fireglo. Called the 330VB from '85-'97.

MODEL YEAR	FEATURES	EXC. COND. LOW	HIGH
1958-1960	Capri, thick body	$9,000	$12,000
1965-1969	Thinner body	$4,000	$6,500
1970-1976	21 frets	$2,500	$4,000

Model 335F
1958-1969. F-style.

MODEL YEAR	FEATURES	EXC. COND. LOW	HIGH
1958-1961	Thick version	$12,500	$15,000
1961-1969	Thin version	$8,000	$12,000

Model 335S
1964-1967. Rose Morris model, 2 or 3 pickups.

MODEL YEAR	FEATURES	EXC. COND. LOW	HIGH
1964-1967		$6,500	$9,000

Model 336/12
1966-1969. Like 300-12, but with 6-12 converter comb, 330-style body.

MODEL YEAR	FEATURES	EXC. COND. LOW	HIGH
1966-1969		$5,500	$7,000

Model 340
1958-2014. Thin semi-hollowbody, thru-body maple neck, 2 single-coil pickups, sharp point horns, very limited production '58-'65, with first notable volume of 45 units starting in '66.

MODEL YEAR	FEATURES	EXC. COND. LOW	HIGH
1958-1960	Capri, thick body	$9,000	$12,000
1965-1969	Thinner body	$4,000	$6,500
1970-1976	21 frets	$3,500	$5,500
1974-1979	24 frets	$2,500	$3,500
1980-2014		$2,000	$3,000

Rickenbacker Model 330 75th

Ron O'Keefe

1966 Rickenbacker Model 335

Jeffrey Phelps

GUITARS

1960 Rickenbacker 360F

Rickenbacker Model 365 Capri

Ron O'Keefe

MODEL YEAR	FEATURES	EXC. COND. LOW	HIGH

Model 340/12

1980-2014. 12-string version, 330-style body.

1980-2014 $2,500 $3,500

Model 340F

1958-1960. F-style.

1958-1960 Thick version $12,500 $15,000

Model 345

1958-1979. Thinline 330-345 series, version with 3 pickups and vibrato tailpiece.

1958-1960	Capri, thick body	$9,000	$12,500
1965-1969	Thinner body	$4,000	$7,500
1970-1976	21 frets	$3,500	$5,500
1974-1979	24 frets	$2,500	$3,500

Model 345 Reissue

2002. Low production, 3 pickups.

2002 $2,250 $3,000

Model 345F

1958-1960. F-style.

1958-1960 Thick version $12,500 $15,000

Model 350 Liverpool

1983-1997. Thinline, 3 pickups, vibrato, no sound hole.

1983-1997 $2,000 $3,000

Model 350/12V63 Liverpool

1994-2014. Vintage Series, 12-string 350V63.

1994-2014 $2,750 $3,750

Model 350SH (Susanna Hoffs)

1988-1990. Susanna Hoffs Limited Edition.

1988-1990 $4,000 $6,000

Model 350V59

1988. Very low production.

1988 $2,500 $3,500

Model 350V63 Liverpool

1994-present. Vintage Series, like 355 JL, but without signature.

1994-2024 $2,500 $3,500

Model 355/12JL (John Lennon)

1989-1993. 12-string 355 JL, limited production.

1989-1993 $6,000 $8,500

Model 355JL (John Lennon)

1989-1993. John Lennon model, signature and drawing on 'guard.

1989-1993 $5,000 $7,000

Model 360

1958-1991, 2000-present. Deluxe thinline, 2 pickups, slash sound hole, bound body until '64.

1958-1960	Capri, thick body	$12,000	$15,000
1961-1963	New Capri, bound body	$8,000	$12,000
1964-1969	New style body	$5,500	$7,000
1965-1970	OS body	$7,500	$9,500
1970-1973	360, no vibrato, 21 frets	$4,000	$5,000
1974-1984	360VB, vibrato, 24 frets	$3,000	$4,000
1985-2024	360VB, vibrato	$2,000	$3,500

Model 360/12

1964-present. Deluxe double-cut thinline, 2 pickups, triangle inlays. The 360/12 was offered in both the Old Style (OS) body with double-bound body and pointed horns, and the New Style (NS) body with rounded top edges and rounder horns. George Harrison's original 360/12 had the OS body in a Fireglo finish. Production of the OS and NS bodies overlapped.

1964-1969	NS, Fireglo, rounded horns	$6,500	$8,500
1964-1969	NS, Mapleglo, rounded horns	$6,500	$8,500
1964-1969	OS, Mapleglo, pointed horns	$20,000	$25,000
1965-1969	OS, Fireglo, pointed horns	$25,000	$35,000
1970-1973	21 frets, '60s features	$4,500	$6,500
1974-1979	24 frets	$3,500	$5,000
1980-2009		$3,000	$4,000
2010-2024		$2,500	$3,500

Model 360/12 RCA

1992. Limited edition made for RCA Nashville as gifts for their artists, has RCA dog-and-gramophone logo on pickguard.

1992 $10,000 $15,000

Model 360/12 Tuxedo

1987 only. 12-string version of 360 Tuxedo.

1987 $6,000 $9,000

Model 360/12C63

2004-present. More exact replica of the Harrison model.

2004-2024 $2,500 $3,500

Model 360/12CW (Carl Wilson)

2000. Carl Wilson, 12-string version of 360 CW.

2000 $4,000 $6,000

Model 360/12V64

1985-2003. Deluxe thinline with '64 features, 2 pickups, 12 strings, slanted plate tailpiece.

1985-2003 $2,750 $4,000

Model 360/12VP

2004. VP is vintage pickup.

2004 $2,750 $4,000

Model 360/12WB

1984-1998. 12-string version of 360WB.

1984-1998 $2,750 $4,000

Model 360CW (Carl Wilson)

2000. Carl Wilson Limited Edition, 6-string, includes certificate, 500 made.

2000 $3,500 $5,000

Model 360DCM 75th Anniversary

2006. 360 with 75th Anniversary dark cherry metallic finish, 75 made.

2006 $4,000 $6,000

Model 360F

1959-1969. F-style.

1959-1960	Thick version	$12,000	$15,000
1968-1969	Thin version	$8,000	$12,000

Model 360F/12

1968-1969. F-style, 12-string.

1968-1969 $11,500 $14,000

Model 360SF

1968-ca. 1972. Slanted frets (SF), standard on some models, an option on others.

1968-1972 $7,500 $9,000

GUITARS

MODEL YEAR	FEATURES	EXC. COND. LOW	HIGH

Model 360 Tuxedo

1987 only. Tuxedo option included white body, white painted fretboard, and black hardware.

1987		$5,000	$7,500

Model 360V64

1991-2003. Reissue of '64 Model 360 old style body without vibrola, has binding with full length inlays.

1991-2003		$2,500	$3,500

Model 360WB

1984-1998. Double bound body, 2 pickups, vibrato optional (VB).

1984-1990		$3,000	$4,500
1991-1998	WB no vibrato	$2,750	$4,000
1991-1998	WBVB, vibrato	$3,000	$4,500

Model 362/12

1975-1992. Doubleneck 6 & 12, 360 features.

1975-1992		$5,000	$7,500

Model 365

1958-1973. Deluxe thinline, 2 pickups, vibrato, called Model 360 WBVB from '84-'98.

1958-1960	Capri, thick body	$12,000	$15,000
1961-1963	New Capri, bound body	$8,000	$12,000
1964-1970	New style body, 21 frets	$5,500	$7,000
1965-1970	OS body	$7,500	$9,500
1970-1973		$5,500	$7,000

Model 365F

1959-1969. Thin full-body (F designation), 2 pickups, Deluxe features.

1959-1960	Capri, thick body	$12,000	$15,000
1968-1969	Thin version	$10,000	$12,000

Model 366/12 Convertible

1967-1970. Two pickups, 12 strings, comb-like device that converts it to a 6-string, production only noted in '68, perhaps available on custom order basis.

1967-1970	New style body	$5,500	$7,500
1967-1970	OS, double bound	$10,000	$12,500

Model 370

1958-1990, 1994-2007. Deluxe thinline, 3 pickups. Could be considered a dealer special order item from '58-'67 with limited production.

1958-1960	Capri, thick body	$12,000	$15,000
1961-1963	New Capri, bound body	$8,000	$12,000
1964-1970	New style body, 21 frets	$5,500	$7,000
1965-1970	OS body	$7,500	$9,500
1974-1979	24 frets	$3,000	$3,750
1980-1989		$2,500	$3,000
2000-2007		$2,500	$3,000

Model 370/12

1964-1972, 1974-2023. Not regular production until '80, deluxe thinline, 3 pickups, 12 strings. Could be considered a dealer special order item in the '60s and '70s with limited production.

1964-1972		$7,000	$10,000
1974-2023	24 frets	$3,000	$4,000

Model 370/12RM (Roger McGuinn)

1988-1990. Limited Edition Roger McGuinn, 1000 made, higher-quality appointments.

1988-1990		$5,000	$7,500

Model 370F

1959-1969. F-style, 3 pickups, Deluxe features.

1959-1961	Thick version	$12,000	$15,000
1968-1969	Thin version	$10,000	$12,000

Model 370VP

2006-2007. Limited run with special specs including vintage toaster pickups (VP).

2006-2007		$2,750	$4,000

Model 370WB

1984-1998. Double bound body, 3 pickups, vibrato optional (VB).

1984-1998		$3,500	$5,000

Model 375

1958-1974. Deluxe thinline, 3 pickups, vibrato, called Model 370 WBVB from '84-'98.

1958-1960	Capri, thick body	$12,000	$15,000
1961-1963	New Capri, bound body	$8,000	$12,000
1961-1969	New style body, 21 frets	$5,500	$7,000
1965-1970	OS body	$7,500	$9,500
1970-1974	21 frets	$5,500	$7,000

Model 375F

1959-1969. F-style, 2 pickups.

1959-1960	Thick version	$12,000	$15,000
1968-1969	Thin version	$10,000	$12,000

Model 380L Laguna

1996-2005. Semi-hollow, oil-finished walnut body, Maple neck and 'board, 2 humbuckers, PZ saddle pickups optional.

1996-2005		$2,500	$3,500
1996-2005	PZ option	$2,500	$3,500

Model 381

1969-1974. Double-cut archtop, 2 pickups, slash sound hole.

1969-1974	Various colors, some rare	$7,000	$9,500

Model 381/12V69

1987-2023. Reissue of 381/12, deep double-cut body, sound body cavity, catseye sound hole, triangle inlays, bridge with 12 individual saddles. Finishes include Fireglo, Mapleglo and Jetglo.

1987-2023	Figured top	$4,500	$6,500

Model 381JK (John Kay)

1988-1997. Limited Edition, 250 made, 2 humbucking pickups, active electronics, stereo and mono outputs, Jetglo black.

1988-1997		$5,000	$7,500

Model 381V69

1991-2023. Reissue of vintage 381.

1987-2023		$4,000	$5,500

Model 400/Combo 400

1956-1958. Double-cut tulip body, neck-thru, 1 pickup, gold anodized 'guard, 21 frets, replaced by Model 425 in '58. Available in black (216 made), blue turquoise (53), Cloverfield Green (53), Montezuma Brown (41), and 4 in other custom colors.

1956-1958		$6,000	$8,000

Rickenbacker Model 375 Capri

Ron O'Keefe

1968 Rickenbacker Model 366-12

Ron O'Keefe

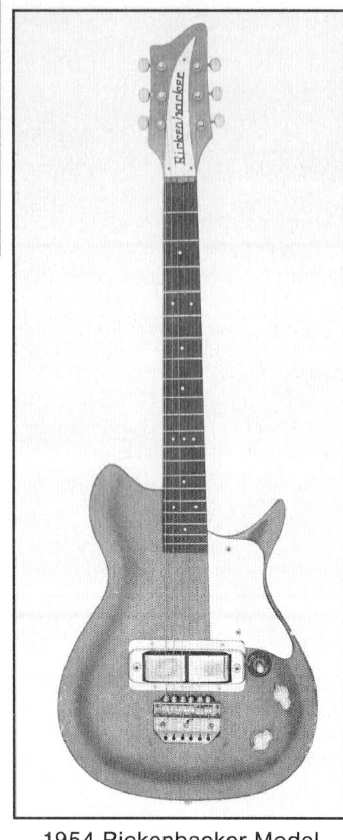

1954 Rickenbacker Model 600/Combo 600

Imaged by Heritage Auctions, HA.com

Rickenbacker 660

Ron O'Keefe

MODEL YEAR	FEATURES	EXC. COND. LOW	HIGH

Model 420

1965-1983. Non-vibrato version of Model 425, single pickup.

1965-1968		$2,250	$2,875
1969-1983		$1,750	$2,250

Model 425/Combo 425

1958-1973. Double-cut solidbody, 1 pickup, sunburst.

1958-1959	425 Cresting Wave	$4,000	$5,000
1960		$3,000	$3,750
1961-1964		$2,250	$2,750
1965-1968		$2,000	$2,500
1969-1973		$1,750	$2,250

Model 425/12V63

1999-2000. 136 made.

1999-2000		$3,500	$5,000

Model 425V63

1999-2000. Beatles associated model, 145 JG black made, 116 BG burgundy transparent made, originally custom ordered by Rickenbacker collectors and they were not part of Rickenbacker's sales literature in the late '90s.

1999-2000		$2,750	$3,500

Model 430

1971-1982. Style 200 body, natural.

1971-1982		$2,000	$3,500

Model 450/Combo 450

1957-1984. Replaces Combo 450, 2 pickups (3 optional '62-'77), tulip body shape '57-'59, cresting wave body shape after.

1957-1958	450 Tulip body (Combo)	$5,500	$7,000
1958-1959	450 Cresting Wave	$4,000	$5,000
1960	Cresting Wave, flat body	$3,000	$3,750
1961-1966	Cresting Wave, super slim	$2,500	$3,250
1970-1979	Includes rare color	$2,250	$3,000
1980-1984		$1,500	$2,000

Model 450/12

1964-1985. Double-cut solidbody, 12-string version of Model 450, 2 pickups.

1964-1966		$3,000	$3,750
1967-1969		$2,750	$3,500
1970-1979	Includes rare color	$2,250	$2,750
1980-1985		$1,875	$2,375

Model 450V63

1999-2001. Reissue of '63 450.

1999-2001		$2,500	$3,500

Model 456/12 Convertible

1968-1978. Double-cut solidbody, 2 pickups, comb-like device to convert it to 6-string.

1968-1969		$3,500	$4,500
1970-1978		$3,000	$4,000

Model 460

1961-1985. Double-cut solidbody, 2 pickups, neck-thru-body, deluxe trim.

1961-1965		$3,500	$4,500
1966-1969		$3,000	$3,750
1970-1979	Includes rare color	$2,500	$3,250
1980-1985		$1,750	$2,250

Model 480

1973-1984. Double-cut solidbody with long thin bass horn in 4001 bass series style, 2 pickups, cresting wave body and headstock, bolt-on neck.

1973-1979		$2,500	$3,500
1980-1984		$2,250	$3,250

Model 481

1973-1983. Cresting wave body with longer bass horn, 2 humbuckers (3 optional), angled frets.

1973-1979		$2,750	$4,000
1980-1983		$2,500	$3,750

Model 483

1973-1983. Cresting wave body with longer bass horn, 3 humbuckers.

1973-1979		$3,000	$4,500
1980-1983		$2,500	$3,500

Model 600/Combo 600

1954-1958. Modified double-cut, horseshoe pickup.

1954-1957	Blond/white	$6,000	$8,000
1956-1958	OT/Blue Turquoise	$6,000	$8,000

Model 610

1985-1991. Cresting-wave cutaway solidbody, 2 pickups, trapeze R-tailpiece, Jetglo.

1985-1991		$2,500	$3,500

Model 610/12

1988-1997. 12-string version of Model 610.

1988-1997		$2,250	$3,000

Model 615

1962-1966, 1969-1977. Double-cut solidbody, 2 pickups, vibrato.

1962-1965		$2,750	$3,500
1966-1977		$2,500	$3,125

Model 620

1974-present. Double-cut solidbody, deluxe binding, 2 pickups, neck-thru-body.

1974-1979		$2,500	$3,500
1980-2024		$2,000	$3,000

Model 620/12

1981-2023. Double-cut solidbody, 2 pickups, 12 strings, standard trim.

1981-2023		$2,500	$3,500

Model 625

1962-1977. Double-cut solidbody, deluxe trim, 2 pickups, vibrato.

1962-1963		$4,500	$6,000
1965-1969		$4,500	$5,500
1970-1977		$3,000	$4,000

Model 650/Combo 650

1957-1959. Standard color, 1 pickup.

1957-1959		$5,000	$6,500

Model 650A Atlantis

1992-2003. Double cut cresting wave solidbody, maple body wings, neck-thru, 2 pickups, chrome hardware, turquoise.

1992-2003		$2,000	$3,000

Model 650C Colorado

1993-2017. Like Atlantis but with black finish.

1993-2017		$1,750	$2,500

MODEL YEAR	FEATURES	EXC. COND. LOW	HIGH

Model 650D Dakota

1993-2017. Like Atlantis but with walnut body wings and oil-satin finish.

1993-2017		$1,750	$2,500

Model 650E Excalibur/F Frisco

1991-2003. Like Atlantis but with brown vermilion body wings and gold hardware. Name changed to Frisco in '95.

1991-2003		$1,750	$2,500

Model 650S Sierra

1993-2017. Like Dakota but with gold hardware.

1993-2017		$1,750	$2,500

Model 660

1998-present. Cresting wave maple body, triangle inlays, 2 pickups.

1998-2024		$2,250	$3,000

Model 660/12

1998-present. 12-string 660.

1998-2024		$2,500	$3,500

Model 660/12TP (Tom Petty)

1991-1998. Tom Petty model, 12 strings, cresting wave body, 2 pickups, deluxe trim, limited run of 1000, certificate of authenticity.

1991-1998	With certificate	$6,000	$8,500

Model 660DCM 75th Anniversary

2006-2007. 75th 1931-2006 Anniversary pickguard logo.

2006-2007		$4,000	$6,000

Model 800/Combo 800

1954-1959. Offset double-cut, 1 horseshoe pickup until late-'57, second bar type after.

1954-1957	Blond/white, 1 pickup	$7,500	$9,500
1954-1957	Blue or green, 1 pickup	$7,500	$9,500
1957-1959	Blond/white, 2 pickups	$7,500	$9,500
1957-1959	Blue or green, 2 pickups	$7,500	$9,500

Model 850/Combo 850

1957-1959. Extreme double-cut, 1 pickup until '58, 2 after, various colors, called Model 850 in the '60s.

1957-1959	Various colors	$7,500	$9,500

Model 900/Combo 900

1957-1980. Double-cut tulip body shape, 3/4 size, 1 pickup. Body changes to cresting wave shape in '69.

1957-1966		$2,500	$3,500

Model 950/Combo 950

1957-1980. Like Model 900, but with 2 pickups, 21 frets. Body changes to cresting wave shape in '69.

1957-1964		$3,000	$4,000
1965-1980		$2,250	$2,750

Model 1000

1956-1970. Like Model 900, but with 18 frets, 1 pickup, black and white. Body does not change to cresting wave shape.

1956-1966		$2,000	$2,500
1967-1970		$2,000	$2,500

Model 1993/12RM (Rose-Morris)

1964-1967. Export 'slim-line' 12-string model made for English distributor Rose-Morris of London, built along the lines of the U.S. Model 360/12 but with small differences that are considered important in the vintage guitar market.

July 1964	Flat tailpiece (stubby), 25 made	$25,000	$35,000
1964-1967	R tailpiece, 75 made	$22,000	$30,000

Model 1995RM (Rose-Morris)

1964-1967. Rose-Morris import.

1964-1967		$3,500	$5,000

Model 1996RM (Rose-Morris)

1964-1967. Rose-Morris import, 3/4 size built similiarly to the U.S. Model 325.

1964-1967		$8,000	$12,000

Model 1996RM Reissue

2006. Reissue of the Rose-Morris version of Model 325, this reissue available on special order in 2006.

2006		$4,500	$6,500

Model 1997PT (Pete Townshend)

1987-1988. Pete Townshend Signature Model, semi-hollowbody, single f-hole, maple neck, 21-fret rosewood 'board, 3 pickups, Firemist finish, limited to 250 total production.

1987-1988		$5,500	$7,500

Model 1997RM (Rose-Morris)

1964-1967. Export 'slim-line' model made for English distributor Rose-Morris of London, built along the lines of the U.S. Model 335, but with small differences that are considered important in the vintage guitar market, 2 pickups, vibrola tailpiece. Rose-Morris export models sent to the USA generally had a red-lined guitar case vs. the USA domestic blue-lined guitar case.

1964-1967		$6,500	$9,000

Model 1997RM Reissue

1987-1995. Reissue of '60s Rose-Morris model, but with vibrola (VB) or without.

1987-1995		$2,500	$3,500

Model 1997SPC

1993-2002. 3 pickup version of reissue.

1993-2002		$2,750	$4,000

Model 1998RM (Rose-Morris)

1964-1967. Export 'slim-line' model made for English distributor Rose-Morris of London, built along the lines of a U.S. Model 345 but with small differences that are considered important in the vintage guitar market, 3 pickups, vibrola tailpiece.

1964-1967		$6,500	$9,000

Rickenbacker Spanish/Spanish/SP

1946-1949. Block markers.

1946-1949		$2,250	$2,875

S-59

1940-1942. Arch top body built by Kay, horseshoe magnet pickup.

1940-1942		$2,000	$2,500

Rigaud Guitars

1978-present. Luthier Robert Rigaud builds his premium grade, custom, parlor to jumbo acoustic guitars in Greensboro, North Carolina. He also builds ukuleles under the New Moon brand.

1964 Rickenbacker Model 950
Rivington Guitars

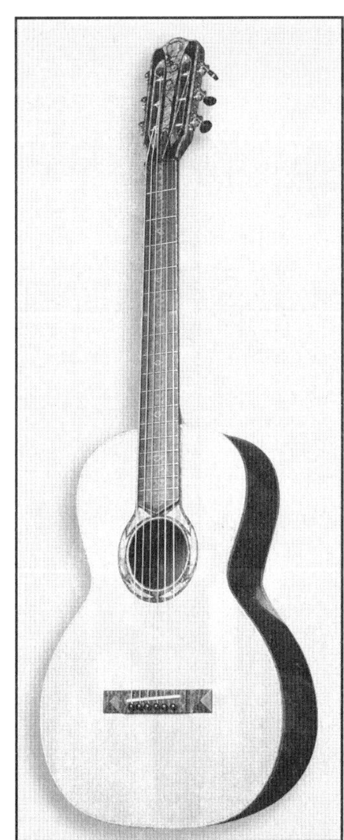

Rigaud Acoustics Parlor

GUITARS

Robin Octave

Allen Eagles

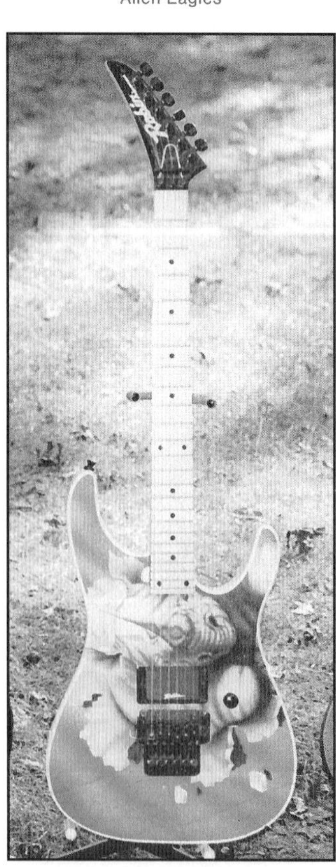

1989 Robin Medley Standard

Bob Reina

MODEL YEAR	FEATURES	EXC. COND. LOW	HIGH

Ritz

1989. Solidbody electric guitars and basses produced in Calimesa, California, by Wayne Charvel, Eric Galletta and Brad Becnel, many of which featured cracked shell mosiac finishes.

RKS

Professional and premium grade, production/custom, electric hollowbody and solidbody guitars and basses designed by Ravi Sawhney and guitarist Dave Mason and built in Thousand Oaks, California. They began in 2003.

Robert Cefalu

Luthier Robert Cefalu built his professional grade, production/custom, acoustic guitars in Buffalo, New York. The guitars have an RC on the headstock.

Robert Guitars

1981-present. Luthier Mikhail Robert builds his premium grade, production/custom, classical guitars in Summerland, British Columbia.

Robertson Guitars

1995-present. Luthier Jeff Robertson builds his premium grade, production/custom flat-top guitars in South New Berlin, New York.

Robin

1982-2010. Professional and premium grade, production/custom, guitars from luthier David Wintz and built in Houston, Texas. Most guitars were Japanese made until '87; American production began in '88. Most Japanese Robins were pretty consistent in features, but the American ones were often custom-made, so many variations in models exist. They also made Metropolitan ('96-'08) and Alamo ('00-'08) brand guitars.

Avalon Classic

1994-2010. Single-cut, figured maple top, 2 humbuckers.

1994-2010	Various options	$1,500	$3,500

Fleetwood Standard

2007. Reverse-body with large treble horn, 4/2 split headstock shape, set neck.

2007		$1,800	$3,500

Medley Pro

1990s. Solidbody with 2 extreme cutaway horns, hum-single-single.

1990s	US-made	$2,000	$4,500

Medley Special

1992-1995. Ash body, maple neck, rosewood 'board, 24 frets, various pickup options.

1992-1995		$1,800	$4,000

Medley Standard

1985-2010. Offset double-cut swamp ash solidbody, bolt neck, originally with hum-single-single pickups, but now also available with 2 humbuckers.

1985-1987	Japan-made	$1,000	$2,500
1988-2010	US-made	$1,500	$3,500

MODEL YEAR	FEATURES	EXC. COND. LOW	HIGH

Octave

1982-1990s. Tuned an octave above standard tuning, full body size with 15 1/2" short-scale bolt maple neck. Japanese-made production model until '87, U.S.-made custom shop after.

1990s	With original case	$2,500	$5,000

Raider I/Raider II/Raider III

1985-1991. Double-cut solidbody, 1 humbucker pickup (Raider I), 2 humbuckers (Raider II), or 3 single-coils (Raider III), maple neck, either maple or rosewood 'board, sunburst.

1985-1991	1 pickup	$1,000	$2,500
1985-1991	2 pickups	$1,200	$3,000
1985-1991	3 pickups	$1,500	$3,500

Ranger

1982. First production model with 2 single-coil pickups in middle and neck position, reverse headstock, dot markers.

1982		$1,500	$3,500

Ranger Custom

1982-1986, 1988-2010. Swamp ash bound body, bolt-on maple neck, rosewood or maple 'board, 2 single coils and 1 humbucker, orange, made in Japan until '86, U.S.-made after.

1982-1986	Japan-made	$1,800	$4,000
1988-2010	US-made	$2,000	$5,000

RDN-Doubleneck Octave/Six

1982-1985. Six-string standard neck with 3 pickups, 6-string octave neck with 1 pickup, double-cut solidbody.

1982-1985	With original case	$5,000	$10,000

Savoy Deluxe/Standard

1995-2010. Semi-hollow thinline single cut archtop, 2 pickups, set neck.

1996-2010		$1,500	$3,500

Soloist/Artisan

1982-1986. Mahogany double-cut solidbody, carved bound maple top, set neck, 2 humbuckers. Renamed Artisan in '85. Only about 125 made in Japan.

1982-1986		$1,500	$3,500

Wedge

1985-ca. 1988. Triangle-shaped body, 2 humbuckers, Custom with set neck and triangle inlays, Standard with bolt neck and dots, about 200 made.

1980s		$2,500	$6,000

Wrangler

1995-2002. Classic '50s single-cut slab body, 3 Rio Grande pickups, opaque finish.

1995-2002		$1,200	$3,000

Robinson Guitars

2002-present. Premium and presentation grade, custom/production, steel string guitars built by luthier Jake Robinson first in Kalamazoo, and since '08 in Hoxeyville, Michigan.

RockBeach Guitars

2005-present. Luthier Greg Bogoshian builds his custom, professional grade, chambered electric guitars and basses in Rochester, New York.

MODEL YEAR	FEATURES	EXC. COND. LOW	HIGH

Rockinbetter

2011-2014. Intermediate grade, production electric guitars and basses, copies of Rickenbacker models, made in China.

Rocking F

See listing under Fox.

Rockit Guitar

Luthier Rod MacKenzie builds his premium grade, custom, electric guitars and basses in Everett, Washington, starting in 2006.

Rogands

Late 1960s. Produced by France's Jacobacci company and named after brothers Roger and Andre. Short-lived brand; the brothers made instruments under several other brands as well.

Roger

Guitars built in Germany by luthier Wenzel Rossmeisl and named for his son Roger. Roger Rossmeisl would go on to work at Rickenbacker and Fender.

Rogue

2001-present. Budget and intermediate grade, production, acoustic, resonator, electric and sitar guitars and basses. They also offer mandolins, banjos, ukuleles, and lap steels. They previously offered effects and amps. Fender offered instruments branded Rogue by Squire for a short period starting in '99.

Roland

Best known for keyboards, effects, and amps, Roland offered synthesizer-based guitars and basses from 1977 to '97.

Rolando

1916-ca. 1919. Private branded instruments made for the Southern California Music Company of Los Angeles, by Martin. There were three models.

00-28K/1500

1916-1919		$9,000	$11,500

Rolf Spuler

1981-2014. Presentation grade, custom, hybrid electric-acoustic guitars, built by luthier Rolf Spuler in Gebenstorf, Switzerland. He also built basses. He passed away in '14.

Roman & Lipman Guitars

1989-2000. Production/custom, solidbody guitars and basses made in Danbury, Connecticut by Ed Roman Guitars.

Roman Abstract Guitars

1989-present. Professional and premium grade, production/custom, solidbody guitars made by Roman Guitars.

MODEL YEAR	FEATURES	EXC. COND. LOW	HIGH

Roman Centurion Guitars

2001-present. Premium and presentation grade, custom guitars made by Ed Roman Guitars.

Roman Pearlcaster Guitars

1999-present. Professional and premium grade, production/custom, solidbody guitars made by Ed Roman Guitars.

Roman Quicksilver Guitars

1997-present. Professional and premium grade, production/custom, solid and hollow-body guitars made by Ed Roman Guitars.

Roman RVC Guitars

1999-present. Professional and premium grade, production/custom, solidbody guitars made by Ed Roman Guitars.

Roman Vampire Guitars

2004-2020. Professional and premium grade, production/custom, solidbody guitars made by Ed Roman Guitars. Special orders only about '13-'20.

Rono

In 1967 luthier Ron Oates began building professional and premium grade, production/custom, flat-top, jazz, Wiesenborn-style, and resonator guitars and basses in Boulder, Colorado. He also built mandolins.

Ro-Pat-In

See Rickenbacker.

Rosetti

1950s-1960s. Guitars imported into England by distributor Rosetti, made by Holland's Egmond, and maybe others.

Solid 7

1960s. Symmetrical cutaway electric semi-hollow, large 'guard with top-mounted dual pickups, 4 control knobs, value is associated with Paul McCartney's use in '60, value dependent on completely original McCartney specs.

1960s	McCartney model	$2,500	$3,500
1960s	Various other	$800	$1,200

Roudhloff

1810s-1840s. Luthier Francois Roudhloff built his instruments in France. Labels could state F. Roudhloff-Mauchand or Roudhloff Brothers. Valuation depends strongly on condition and repair. His sons built guitars under the D & A Roudhloff label.

Rowan

Professional and premium grade, production/custom, solidbody and acoustic/electric guitars built by luthier Michael Rowan in Garland, Texas.

Royal

Ca. 1954-ca. 1965. Line of jazz style guitars made by France's Jacobacci company, which also built under its own brand.

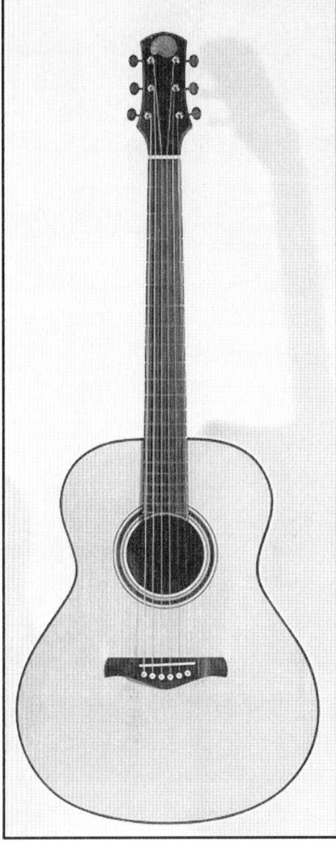

Robinson Small Jumbo

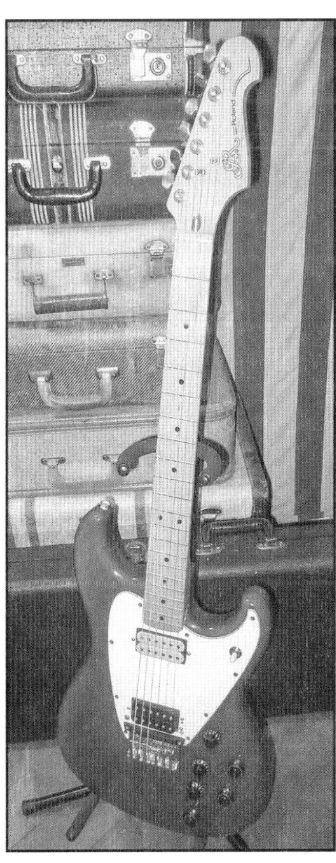

1985 Roland G-202 GR Synth

Rivington Guitars

RS Guitarworks Slab Blackguard

S. Walker Custom The Revelator

Royal (Japan)

1957-1960s. Early budget level instruments made by Tokyo Sound Company and Gakki and exported by Japan's Hoshino (Ibanez).

Royden Guitars

Professional grade, production/custom, flat-tops and solidbody electrics built by luthier Royden Moran in Peterborough, Ontario, starting in 1996.

RS Guitarworks

1994-present. Professional grade, production/custom, solid and hollowbody guitars built by luthier Roy Bowen in Winchester, Kentucky.

Rubio, German Vasquez

1993-present. Luthier German Vasquez Rubio builds his professional and premium grade, production/custom classical and flamenco guitars in Los Angeles, California.

Ruck, Robert

1966-2018. Premium grade, custom classical and flamenco guitars built by luthier Robert Ruck originally in Kalaheo, Hawaii, then in Eugene, Oregon. Ruck died in '18.

Running Dog Guitars

Luthier Rick Davis, started in 1994, builds professional and premium grade, custom flat-tops in Seattle, Washington. He was originally located in Richmond, Vermont.

Ruokangas

1995-present. Luthier Juha Ruokangas builds his premium and presentation grade, production/custom, solidbody and semi-acoustic electric guitars in Hyvinkaa, Finland.

Rustler

1993-ca. 1998. Solidbody electrics with hand-tooled leather bound and studded sides and R branded into the top, built by luthier Charles Caponi in Mason City, Iowa.

RWK

1991-present. Luthier Bob Karger builds his intermediate grade, production/custom, solidbody electrics and travel guitars in Highland Park, Illinois.

Ryder

1963. Made by Rickenbacker, the one model with this brand was the same as their solidbody Model 425.

S. Walker Custom Guitars

2002-present. Luthier Scott Walker builds his premium grade, production/custom, solid and semi hollow body electric guitars in Santa Cruz, California.

MODEL YEAR	FEATURES	EXC. COND. LOW	HIGH

S. Yairi

Ca. 1960-1980s. Steel string folk guitars and classical nylon string guitars by master Japanese luthier Sadao Yairi, imported by Philadelphia Music Company of Limerick, Pennsylvania. Early sales literature called the brand Syairi. Most steel string models have dreadnought bodies and nylon-string classical guitars are mostly standard grand concert size. All models are handmade. Steel string Jumbos and dreadnoughts have Syairi logo on the headstock, nylon-classical models have no logo. The Model 900 has a solid wood body, others assumed to have laminate bodies.

S.B. Brown Guitars

Custom flat-tops made by luthier Steve Brown in Fullerton, California.

S.B. MacDonald Custom Instruments

1988-present. Professional and premium grade, custom/production, flat-top, resonator, and solidbody guitars built by luthier Scott B. MacDonald in Huntington, New York.

S.D. Curlee

1975-1982. Founded in Matteson, Illinois by music store owner Randy Curlee, after an unsuccessful attempt to recruit builder Dan Armstrong. S.D. Curlee guitars were made in Illinois, while S.D. Curlee International instruments were made by Matsumoku in Japan. The guitars featured mostly Watco oil finishes, often with exotic hardwoods, and unique neck-thru-bridge construction on American and Japanese instruments. These were the first production guitars to use a single-coil pickup at the bridge with a humbucker at the neck, and a square brass nut. DiMarzio pickups. Offered in a variety of shapes, later some copies. Approximately 12,000 American-made basses and 3,000 guitars were made, most of which were sold overseas. Two hundred were made in '75-'76; the first production guitar numbered 518.

Electric Solidbody

1975-1982. Models include the '75-'81 Standard I, II and III, '76-'81 International C-10 and C-11, '80-'81 Yankee, Liberty, Butcher, Curbeck, Summit, Special, and the '81-'82 Destroyer, Flying V.

1975-1982		$400	$1,200

S.L. Smith Guitars

Professional grade, production/custom, acoustic guitars built by Steven Smith in Brant Lake, New York beginning in 2007.

S.S. Stewart

The original S.S. Stewart Company (1878-1904), of Philadelphia, Pennsylvania is considered to be one of the most important banjo manufacturers of the late 19th century. Samuel Swaim Stewart died in 1888 and his family was out of the company by the early 1900s, and the brand was soon acquired

MODEL YEAR	FEATURES	EXC. COND. LOW	HIGH

by Bugellsein & Jacobsen of New York. The brand name was used on guitars into the 1960s.

Flat-Top

1930s. Gibson L-2 style body.

1932		$8,500	$12,000

S101

Budget and intermediate grade, production, classical, acoustic, resonator, solid and semi-hollow body guitars and basses imported from China by America Sejung Corp. They also offer mandolins, and banjos.

Sadowsky

1980-present. Professional and premium grade, production/custom, solidbody, semi-hollowbody, archtop, and electric nylon-string guitars built by luthier Roger Sadowsky in Brooklyn, New York. He also builds basses and amps. In '96, luthier Yoshi Kikuchi started building Sadowsky Tokyo instruments in Japan.

Saga

Saga Musical Instruments, of San Francisco, California distributes a wide variety of instruments and brands, occasionally including their own line of solidbody guitars called the Saga Gladiator Series (1987-'88, '94-'95). In the 2000s, Saga also offered component kits ($90-$130) that allowed for complete assembly in white wood.

Sahlin Guitars

Luthier Eric Sahlin hs built his premium grade, custom, classical and flamenco guitars in Spokane, Washington since 1975.

Samick

1958-2001, 2002-present. Budget, intermediate and professional grade, production, imported acoustic and electric guitars and basses. They also offer mandolins, ukes and banjos and distribute Abilene and Silvertone brand instruments.

Samick started out producing pianos, adding guitars in '65 under other brands. In '88 Samick greatly increased their guitar production. The Samick line of 350 models was totally closed out in 2001. A new line of 250 models was introduced January 2002 at NAMM. All 2002 models have the new compact smaller headstock and highly styled S logo.

Sammo

1920s. Labels on these instruments state they were made by the Osborne Mfg. Co. with an address of Masonic Temple, Chicago, Illinois. High quality and often with a high degree of ornamentation. They also made ukes and mandolins.

Sand Guitars

Luthier Kirk Sand opened the Guitar Shoppe in Laguna Beach, California in 1972 with James Matthews. By '79, he started producing his own line of premium grade, production/custom-made flat-tops.

Sandoval Engineering

1979-present. Luthier Karl Sandoval builds his premium grade, custom, solidbody guitars in Santa Fe Springs, California.

Sano

1944-ca. 1970. Sano was a New Jersey-based accordion company that imported Italian-made solid and semi-hollow body guitars for a few years, starting in 1966; some, if not all, made by Zero Sette. They also built their own amps and reverb units.

Santa Cruz

1976-present. Professional, premium and presentation grade, production/custom, flat-top, 12-string, and archtop guitars from luthier Richard Hoover in Santa Cruz, California. They also build a mandocello and ukuleles. Founded by Hoover, Bruce Ross and William Davis. Hoover became sole owner in '89. Custom ordered instruments with special upgrades may have higher values than the ranges listed here. Other models offer "build-your-own" options on woods and features and this means larger value ranges on those instruments.

00 12-Fret

1997-present. Indian rosewood, Brazilian offered in 2006.

1997-2024	Indian rosewood	$3,500	$5,500
2006	Brazilian rosewood	$6,000	$9,000

000 12-Fret

1994-present. 000 size, 12-fret body, Indian rosewood back and sides, ebony 'board, ivoroid binding.

1994-2024	Indian rosewood	$4,000	$6,500
2011	Brazilian rosewood	$7,000	$10,000

35th Anniversary Clementine

2018. Only 10 made, Italian spruce top, Cocobolo back and sides, cowgirl inlay on headstock, rope purfling on body and neck.

2018		$10,000	$15,000

Archtop

Early 1980s-2010. Originally the FJZ, by mid-'90s, called the Archtop, offering 16", 17" and 18" cutaway acoustic/electric models, often special order. Curly maple body, ebony 'board, floating pickup, f-holes, sunburst or natural. Many custom options are available.

1980s-90s		$5,000	$8,000

Bob Brozman Baritone

1998-2019. Flat-top acoustic, mahogany body, spruce top.

1998-2019		$5,500	$8,000

D 12-Fret

1994-present. 12-fret neck, slotted headstock, round shoulders, mahogany back and sides, notch diamond markers, herringbone trim. Special orders vary in value and could exceed the posted range.

1994-2024		$3,500	$5,500

D Koa

1980s-1990s. Style D with Koa back and sides.

1980s-90s		$4,500	$7,000

Sadowsky SS-15

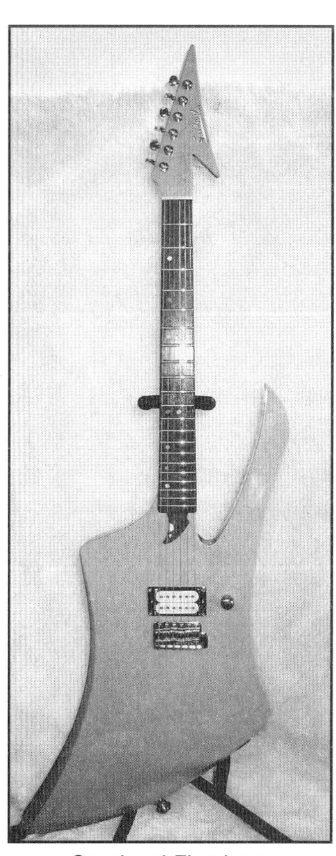

Sandoval Flamingo

Santa Cruz Vintage Southerner

Schechter Blackjack SLS Avenger
Michael Mitchell

MODEL YEAR	FEATURES	EXC. COND. LOW	HIGH

D/HR

Style D with Indian rosewood back and sides, Brazilian rosewood headstock overlay.

2000		$4,000	$6,000

D/PW Pre-War

2001-present. Pre-war D-style. "Build-your-own" options cause a wide value range.

2001-2024	Various models	$5,000	$8,000

Eric Skye 00

Signature model, Cocobolo/Adirondack.

2020		$8,000	$12,000

F

1979-present. 15 7/8" scale with narrow waist, Sitka spruce top, Indian rosewood back and sides, natural.

1979-2024		$4,000	$6,500

F46R

1980s. Brazilian rosewood, single-cut.

1980s		$5,000	$7,500

Firefly

2009-present. Premium quality travel/parlor guitar, cedar top, flamed maple sides and back.

2009-2024		$6,000	$9,000

FS (Finger Style)

1988-present. Single-cut, cedar top, Indian rosewood back and sides, mahogany neck, modified X-bracing.

1988-2024		$4,500	$7,000

H

1977-present. Parlor size, originally a 13-fret neck, but soon changed to 14, Indian rosewood back and sides. The H A/E ('92-'04) added electronics and cutaway.

1977-2024	Indian rosewood	$3,500	$5,500
1994	Flamed Koa	$4,500	$6,500
2005	Brazilian rosewood	$6,500	$9,000

H/13

2004-present. Like H, but with 13-fret neck, mahogany back and sides and slotted headstock.

2004-2024	Mahogany	$4,000	$6,000
2005	Flamed Koa	$5,000	$7,500

H91

1990s. 14 5/8", flamed Koa.

1990s		$5,000	$7,500

Model 1929 00

2010-present. 00-size, all mahogany, 12-fret neck.

2010-2024		$5,000	$7,500

OM (Orchestra Model)

1987-present. Orchestra model acoustic, Sitka spruce top, Indian rosewood (Brazilian optional) back and sides, herringbone rosette, scalloped braces.

1987-2024	Brazilian rosewood	$7,000	$12,000
1987-2024	Indian rosewood	$4,500	$7,500
1995	Koa	$5,000	$8,000
2002	German spruce	$5,500	$8,500
2010	Italian spruce	$6,000	$9,000
2012	Figured mahogany	$6,500	$9,500

OM/PW Pre-War

1999-present. Indian rosewood, advanced X and scalloped top bracing.

1999-2024		$4,500	$7,000

MODEL YEAR	FEATURES	EXC. COND. LOW	HIGH

PJ

1990s-present. Parlor-size, Indian rosewood back and sides, 24" scale, 12-fret neck.

1990s-2024		$4,000	$6,500

Style 1

Indian rosewood standard, various other woods optional.

2014	Brazilian, Adirondack	$8,000	$12,000

Tony Rice

1976-present. Dreadnought, Indian rosewood body (Brazilian optional until Tony Rice Professional model available), Sitka spruce top, solid peghead, zigzag back stripe, pickup optional.

1976-2024		$5,000	$8,000

Tony Rice Professional

1997-present. Brazilian rosewood back and sides, carved German spruce top, zigzag back stripe, solid peghead.

1997-2024		$8,000	$12,000

Vintage Artist (VA)

1992-present. Mahogany body, Sitka spruce top, zigzag back stripe, solid peghead, scalloped X-bracing, pickup optional.

1992-2024		$4,000	$6,500

Vintage Artist Custom

1992-2004. Martin D-42 style, mahogany body, Indian rosewood back and sides, Sitka spruce top, zigzag back stripe, solid peghead, scalloped X-bracing, pickup optional.

1992-2004		$5,000	$8,000

Vintage Jumbo (VJ)

2000-present. 16" scale, round shouldered body, Sitka spruce, figured mahogany back and sides, natural.

2000-2024		$4,500	$7,000

Vintage Southerner (VS)

2007-present. Sitka spruce top standard, various other woods optional.

2007-2024		$4,500	$7,000

Santos Martinez

Ca. 1997-present. Intermediate grade, production, acoustic and electro-acoustic classical guitars, imported from China by John Hornby Skewes & Co. in the U.K.

Sardonyx

1978-1979. Guitars and basses built by luthier Jeff Levin in the back of Matt Umanov's New York City guitar shop, industrial looking design with 2 aluminum outrigger-style tubes extended from the rectangle body. Very limited production.

Saturn

1960s-1970s. Imported, most likely from Japan, solid and semi-hollow body electric guitars and basses. Large S logo with Saturn name inside the S. Many sold through Eaton's in Canada.

Saturn

1960s-1970s. Solidbody, 4 pickups.

1960s		$500	$800
1970s		$450	$600

MODEL YEAR	FEATURES	EXC. COND. LOW	HIGH

Sawchyn Guitars

1972-2023. Professional and premium grade, production/custom, flat-top and flamenco guitars and mandolins built by luthier Peter Sawchyn in Regina, Saskatchewan.

Schaefer

1997-2014. Premium grade, production/custom, flat-top acoustic guitars built by luthier Edward A. Schaefer in Austin, Texas. He previously built archtops, basses and mandolins. He retired in '14.

Schecter

1976-present. Intermediate, professional and premium grade, production/custom, acoustic and electric guitars and basses. Guitar component manufacturer founded in California by four partners (David Schecter's name sounded the best), started offering complete instruments in '79. The company was bought out and moved to Dallas, Texas in the early '80s. By '88 the company was back in California and in '89 was purchased by Hisatake Shibuya. Schecter Custom Shop guitars are made in Burbank, California and their intermediate grade Diamond Series is made in South Korea.

Scheerhorn

1989-present. Professional and premium grade, custom, resonator and Hawaiian guitars built by luthier Tim Scheerhorn in Kentwood, Michigan. Around 2010, Scheerhorn becomes a division of National Reso-Phonic.

Schoenberg

1986-present. Premium grade, production/custom, flat-tops offered by Eric Schoenberg of Tiburon, California. From '86-'94 guitars were made to Schoenberg's specifications by Martin. From '86-'90 constructed by Schoenberg's luthier and from '90-'94 assembled by Martin but voiced and inlaid in the Schoenberg shop. Current models made to Schoenberg specs by various smaller shops.

Schon

1986-1991. Designed by guitarist Neal Schon, early production by Charvel/Jackson building about 200 in the San Dimas factory. The final 500 were built by Larrivee in Canada. Leo Knapp also built custom Schon guitars from '85-'87, and '90s custom-made Schon guitars were also available.

Standard (Canada)

1987-1991. Made in Canada on headstock.

1987-1991		$2,500	$5,500

Standard (U.S.A.)

1986 only. Made in U.S.A. on headstock, San Dimas/Jackson model, single-cut, pointy headstock shape.

1986		$5,000	$12,000

Schramm Guitars

1990-present. Premium grade, production/custom, classical and flamenco guitars built by luthier David Schramm in Clovis, California.

Schroder Guitars

Luthier Timothy Schroeder (he drops the first e in his name on the guitars) builds premium grade, production/custom, archtops in Northbrook, Illinois. He began in 1993.

Schulte

1950s-2000. Luthier C. Eric Schulte made solidbody, semi-hollow body, hollowbody and acoustic guitars, both original designs and copies, covering a range of prices, in the Philadelphia area.

Custom Copy

1982. Single-cut solidbody, figured maple top.

1982		$1,000	$1,500

Schulz

Ca. 1903-1917. Luthier August Schulz built harp guitars and lute-guitars in Nuremberg, Germany.

Harp Guitar

1906		$1,500	$2,500

Schwartz Guitars

1992-present. Premium grade, custom, flat-top guitars built by luthier Sheldon Schwartz in Concord, Ontario.

ScoGo

Professional and premium grade, production/custom, solidbody guitars built by luthier Scott Gordon in Parkesburg, Pennsylvania starting in 2001.

Scorpion Guitars

1998-2014. Professional and premium grade, custom, solidbody guitars made by Ed Roman Guitars.

Scott French

2004-present. Professional grade, production/custom, electric guitars and basses built by luthier Scott French in Auburn, California. In '12 he discontinued offering custom built.

Scott Walker Custom Guitars

Refer to S. Walker Custom Guitars.

SeaGlass Guitars USA

2011-present. Professional grade, production/custom, electric guitars, built by luthier Roger Mello in Groton, Massachusetts.

Seagull

1982-present. Intermediate grade, production, acoustic and acoustic/electric guitars built in Canada. Seagull was founded by luthier Robert Godin, who also has the Norman, Godin, and Patrick & Simon brands of instruments.

Sebring

1980s-mid-1990s. Entry level Korean imports distributed by V.M.I. Industries.

Schoenberg Standard

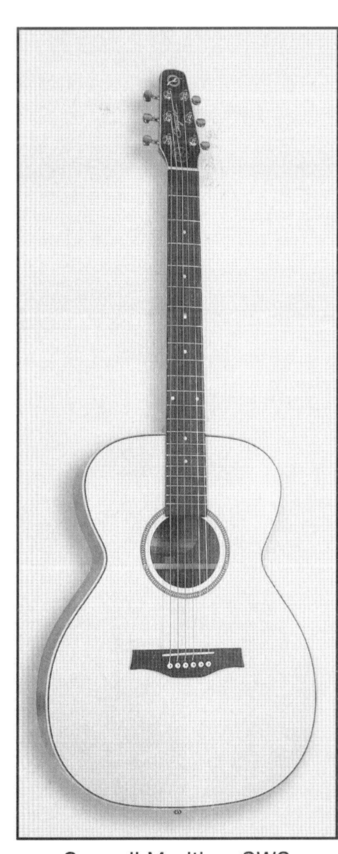

Seagull Maritime SWS Concert Hall SG

GUITARS

1937 Selmer Orchestra

Sheppard Guitars

MODEL YEAR	FEATURES	EXC. COND. LOW	HIGH

Seiwa

Early 1980s. Entry-level to mid-level Japanese electric guitars and basses, logo may indicate Since 1956.

Sekova

Mid-1960s-mid-1970s. Entry level instruments imported by the U.S. Musical Merchandise Corporation of New York.

Selmer

1932-1952. France-based Selmer & Cie was primarily a maker of wind instruments when they asked Mario Maccaferri to design a line of guitars for them. The guitars, with an internal sound chamber for increased volume, were built in Mantes-la-Ville. Both gut and steel string models were offered. Maccaferri left Selmer in '33, but guitar production continued, and the original models are gradually phased out. In '36, only the 14 fret oval model was built. Production stopped for WWII and resumed in '46, finally stopping in '52. Less than 900 guitars are built in total.

Classique

1942. Solid Rosewood back and sides, no cutaway, solid spruce top, round sound hole, classical guitar size, possibly only 2 built.

1942	$6,000	$8,000

Concert

1932-1933. For gut strings, cutaway, laminated Indian rosewood back and sides, internal resonator, spruce top with D hole, wide walnut neck, ebony 'board, only a few dozen built.

1932	$12,500	$18,000
1933	$17,000	$25,000

Eddie Freeman Special

1933. For steel strings, 4 strings, laminated Indian rosewood back and sides, cutaway, no internal resonator, solid spruce top, D hole, black and white rosette inlays, walnut 12 fret neck, ebony 'board, 640mm scale, approx. 100 made.

1933	$6,500	$10,000

Espagnol

1932. For gut strings, laminated Indian rosewood back and sides, no cutaway, internal resonator, solid spruce top, round soundhole, wide walnut neck, ebony 'board, only a few made.

1932	$9,000	$13,500

Grand Modele 4 Cordes

1932-1933. For steel strings, 4 string model, laminated back and sides, cutaway, internal resonator, solid spruce top, D hole, walnut neck, ebony 'board, 12 fret, 640mm scale, 2 or 3 dozen made.

1932-1933	$12,500	$20,000

Harp Guitar

1933. For gut strings, solid mahogany body, extended horn holding 3 sub bass strings, 3 screw adjustable neck, wide walnut neck, ebony 'board, only about 12 built.

1933	$12,500	$20,000

Hawaienne

1932-1934. For steel strings, 6 or 7 strings, laminated back and sides, no cutaway, internal resonator, solid spruce top, D hole, wide walnut neck, ebony 'board, 2 or 3 dozen built.

1932-1934	$25,000	$35,000

Modele Jazz

1936-1942, 1946-1952. For steel strings, laminated Indian rosewood back and sides (some laminated or solid mahogany), cutaway, solid spruce top, small oval soundhole, walnut neck, ebony 'board (latest ones with rosewood necks), 14 fret to the body, 670mm scale. Production interrupted for WWII.

1936-1952	$33,000	$50,000

Modeles de Transition

1934-1936. Transition models appearing before 14 fret oval hole model, some in solid maple with solid headstock, some with round soundhole and cutaway, some 12 fret models with oval hole.

1934-1936	$20,000	$30,000

Orchestre

1932-1934. For steel strings, laminated back and sides, cutaway, internal resonator, solid spruce top, D hole, walnut neck, ebony 'board, about 100 made.

1932-1934	$35,000	$50,000

Tenor

1932-1933. For steel strings, 4 strings, laminated back and sides, internal resonator, solid spruce top, D hole, walnut neck, ebony 'board, 12 fret, 570mm scale, 2 or 3 dozen built.

1932-1933	$5,500	$8,500

Serenghetti

2007-present. Luthier Ray Patterson builds professional and premium grade, production/custom, 1-piece and neck-thru guitars and basses in Ocala, Florida.

Serge Guitars

Luthier Serge Michaud builds his production/custom, classical, steel-string, resophonic and archtop guitars in Breakeyville, Quebec. He started in 1995.

Series 10

1980s. Budget grade electric guitars, Series 10 by Bently on headstock.

Sexauer Guitars

1967-present. Premium and presentation grade, custom, steel-string, 12-string, nylon-string, and archtop guitars built by luthier Bruce Sexauer in Petaluma, California.

Shadow

1990s. Made in Europe, copy models such as the classic offset double cutaway solidbody, large Shadow logo on headstock, Shadow logo on pickup cover, student to intermediate grade.

MODEL YEAR	FEATURES	EXC. COND. LOW	HIGH

Shanti Guitars

1985-2019. Premium and presentation grade, custom, steel-string, 12-string, nylon-string and archtop guitars built by luthier Michael Hornick in Avery, California. He made a few more guitars after retiring in '19.

Shelley D. Park Guitars

1991-present. Luthier Shelley D. Park builds her professional grade, custom, nylon- and steel-string guitars in Vancouver, British Columbia.

Shelton-Farretta

1967-present. Premium grade, production/custom, flamenco, and classical guitars built by luthiers John Shelton and Susan Farretta originally in Portland, Oregon, and since '05 in Alsea, Oregon.

Sheppard Guitars

1993-2019. Luthier Gerald Sheppard builds his premium grade, production/custom, steel-string guitars in Kingsport, Tennessee. He retired in '19.

Shergold

1968-1992. Founded by Jack Golder and Norman Houlder, Shergold originally made guitars for other brands like Hayman and Barnes and Mullins. In '75, they started building guitars and basses under their own name. By '82, general guitar production was halted but custom orders were filled through '90. In '91, general production was again started but ended in '92 when Golder died.

Sherwood

Late 1940s-early 1950s. Archtop and lap steel guitars made for Montgomery Ward by Chicago manufacturers such as Kay. There were also Sherwood amps made by Danelectro. Value ranges are about the same as Kay model equivalent.

Shifflett

Luthier Charles Shifflett built his premium grade, production/custom, flat-top, classical, flamenco, resophonic, and harp guitars, basses and banjos in High River, Alberta. He began in 1990.

Sho-Bro

1969-1978. Spanish and Hawaiian style resonator guitars made by Sho-Bud in Nashville, Tennessee and distributed by Gretsch. Designed by Shot Jackson and Buddy Emmons.

7-String Dobro

1972-1978		$2,000	$3,000

Grand Slam

1978. Acoustic, spruce top, mahogany neck, jacaranda sides and back, and mother-of-pearl inlays, abalone sound hole purfling.

1970s		$80	$1,200

Resonator

1972-1978. Flat-top style guitar with metal resonator with 2 small circular grilled sound holes.

1972-1978		$1,200	$1,800

MODEL YEAR	FEATURES	EXC. COND. LOW	HIGH

Siegmund Guitars & Amplifiers

Luthier Chris Siegmund builds his professional, premium, and presentation grade, custom/production, archtop, solidbody, and resonator guitars in Los Angeles, California. He founded the company in Seattle in 1993, moving to Austin, Texas for '95-'97. He also builds amps and effects pedals.

Sierra

Budget level imports by Musicorp, starting in 2006. There is an unrelated brand of Sierra steels and lap steels.

Sigma

1970-2007. Budget and intermediate grade, production, import acoustic and electric guitars and basses distributed by C.F. Martin Company. They also offered mandolins and banjos. Japanese-made for 1970-'72; lower-end model production moved to Korea in '73; most of remaining Japanese production moved to Korea in '83; most production moved to Taiwan and Indonesia in '96.

Acoustic/Acoustic Electric/Electric

1970-2007	Various models	$150	$1,000

Signature

2005-ca. 2013. See listing under Gibson Baldwin.

Signature Guitar Company (Canada)

1987-1990. Intermediate/professional grade, electric guitars and basses built in Ontario, Canada. Mother of pearl inlaid on 21st fret with model name and, as an option, you could custom order any model with your name inlaid on the 12th fret.

Odyssey

1987-1990. Flat-top, figured maple top, 3 pickups.

1987-1990		$1,800	$2,800

Oracle

1987-1990. Flat-top, figured maple top, 3 pickups.

1987-1990		$1,800	$2,800

Signet

1972-Mid 1970s. Acoustic flat-top guitars, imported from Japan by Ampeg/Selmer.

Silber

1992-1998. Solid wood, steel-string guitars designed by Marc Silber, made in Paracho, Mexico, and distributed by K & S Music. Silber continues to offer the same models under the Marc Silber Music brand.

Silver Street

1979-1986. Founded by brothers Bruce and Craig Hardy, production of solidbody electric guitars built in Elkhart, Indiana and later in Shelby, Michigan. Original TAXI model prototypes built by luthier Richard Schneider. Later models included Spitfire, Cobra, MX, Nightwing, Tommy Shaw and Elite, all offered with

Sherwood Deluxe
Donald DiLoreto

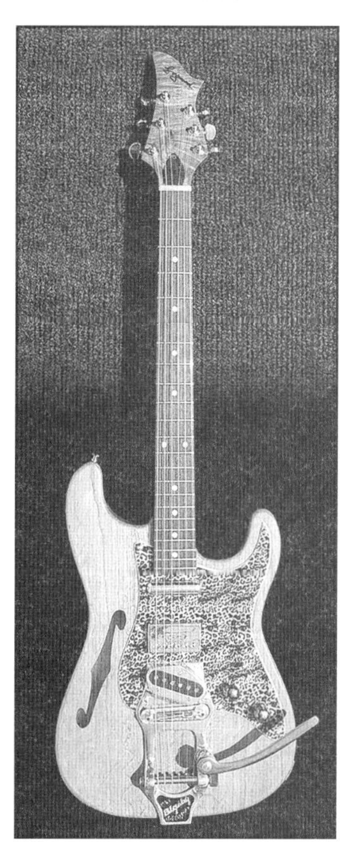

Siegmund Outcaster

GUITARS

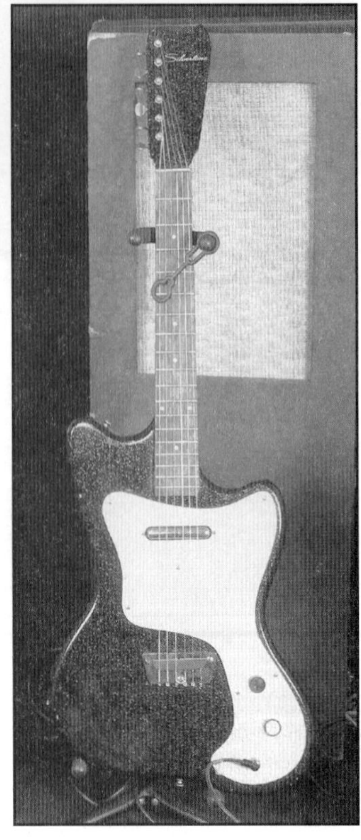

1967 Silvertone Amp-In-Case 1451
Ted Barham

Silvertone Espanada
Mercedes Girard

MODEL YEAR	FEATURES	EXC. COND. LOW	HIGH

various pickups, custom paint and optional hardware. Total production is estimated to be 550 units.

Various Models

1979-1986	Early small models	$600	$900
1979-1986	Larger models	$1,000	$1,500

Silvertone

1941-ca. 1970, present. Brand of Sears instruments which replaced their Supertone brand in '41. The Silvertone name was used on Sears phonographs, records and radios as early as the 'teens, and on occasional guitar models. When Sears divested itself of the Harmony guitar subsidiary in '40 it turned to other suppliers including Kay. In '40 Kay-made archtops and Hawaiian electric lap steels appeared in the catalog bearing the Silvertone brand, and after '41-'42, all guitars, regardless of manufacturer, were called Silvertone.

Sears offered Danelectro-made solidbodies in the fall of '54. Danelectro hollowbodies appeared in '56. By '65, the Silvertones were Teisco-made guitars from W.M.I., but never sold through the catalog. The first imports shown in the catalog were in '69. By '70, most guitars sold by Sears were imports and did not carry the Silvertone name.

Currently, Samick offers a line of acoustic and electric guitars, basses and amps under the Silvertone name.

Amp-In-Case

1962-1968. The black, sharp double cutaway, 1-pickup 1448, introduced in '62, came with a smaller wattage amp without tremolo. The black, 2-pickup 1449, introduced in '63, came with a higher-watt amp with tremolo and better-quality Jensen speaker and was replaced by the red burst 1457 in '64. Gray tolex covered the guitar-amp case. In '66 they were replaced with the black 1451 and 1452 with soft, rounded cutaway horns.

1962-1966	1448, 1 pu, black	$675	$850
1963-1966	1449, 2 pus, black	$850	$1,125
1964-1966	1457, 2 pus, red burst	$850	$1,125
1966-1968	1451, 1 pu, round cut	$675	$850
1966-1968	1452, 2 pus, round cut	$850	$1,125

Belmont

1958. Single-cut solidbody, 2 pickups, black.

1958		$950	$1,250

Black Beauty 1384L

1956-1958. Called 'The Black Beauty' in Sears catalog, large body acoustic-electric archtop, cutaway, 2 pickups, block markers, white binding, spruce top, mahogany sides and back, black lacquer finish.

1956-1958		$1,125	$1,500

Black Beauty 1385

1957. Basically the same as model 1384L.

1957		$1,125	$1,500

Espanada

1960s. Bigsby, 2 pickups, black.

1960s		$1,375	$1,750

Estrelita

1960s. Semi-hollowbody archtop, 2 pickups, black, Harmony-made.

1960s		$1,250	$1,750

F-66

1964. Similar to Harmony Rocket III, single-cut, thinline electric, 3 pickups, Bigsby.

1964		$950	$1,250

Gene Autry Melody Ranch

1941-1955. 13" Harmony-made acoustic, Gene Autry signature on belly, cowboy roundup stencil, same as earlier Supertone Gene Autry Roundup.

1941-1955		$350	$450

H1214

1951. Full-size acoustic archtop, script Silvertone headstock logo, dot markers, blond with simulated grain finish.

1951		$550	$700

H1260 Sovereign Jumbo

1968. Silvertone's version of Harmony's Sovereign jumbo flat-top, dot markers, sunburst.

1968		$700	$875

H1434 Rocket

1965. Similar to Harmony Rocket H59, sold by Sears, 3 pickups, Bigsby vibrato.

1965		$950	$1,250

Meteor

1955. Single-cut, 1 pickup, sunburst.

1955		$475	$600

Model 623

Late-1950s. Large-body acoustic archtop, dot markers, white 'guard, black finish, painted white binding to give a black and white attractive appearance.

1950s		$225	$300

Model 1300/Model 1302

1958-1959. Single-cut, 1 lipstick pickup, dot markers, 3-on-a-side symmetric headstock, bronze (1300) or black (1302).

1958-1959	1300	$700	$900
1958-1959	1302	$700	$900

Model 1301/Model 1303

1958-1959. 1300 with 2 lipstick pickups, bronze (1301) or black (1303).

1958-1959	1301	$925	$1,125
1958-1959	1303	$925	$1,125

Model 1305

1958-1959. Single-cut, 3 lipstick pickups, dot markers, 3-on-a-side symmetric headstock, white and black finish.

1958-1959		$1,375	$1,750

Model 1317

1957. Single-cut solidbody, 1 lipstick pickup, dot markers, 3-on-a-side symmetric headstock, bronze finish.

1957		$550	$700

Model 1381/Model 1382

1954-1957. Kay-made (many '50s Silvertones were made by Danelectro), slim-style electric similar to Thin Twin/Jimmy Reed, 2 lipstick pickups, 4 knobs, crown-crest logo on 'guard under strings, bolt neck, block markers, sunburst, sold without (Model 1381) and with a case (1382).

1954-1957	1381	$600	$725
1954-1957	1382	$950	$1,250

MODEL YEAR	FEATURES	EXC. COND. LOW	HIGH

Model 1413

1962-1964. Double-cut slab body, single pickup, 2 control knobs, dot markers.

1962-1964		$225	$300

Model 1415/Model 1417

1960-1962. Single-cut, 1 lipstick pickup, 6-on-a-side dolphin headstock, dot markers, bronze (1415) or black (1417).

1960	1417	$550	$700
1961-1962	1415	$550	$700

Model 1420

1959-1963. Single-cut extra thin solidbody, bolt neck, 2 pickups, natural shaded or black finish.

1959-1963		$550	$700

Model 1423L

1960. Single-cut solidbody, 2 pickups, 5 control knobs with rotator switch, block markers, gleaming gold-color splatter-effect over black finish.

1960		$575	$725

Model 1429L

1962-1963. Harmony-made and similar to Harmony's H-75, single-cut thinline electric, 3 pickups, trapeze tailpiece, 3 toggles, 6 knobs, block marker, sunburst.

1962-1963		$950	$1,250

Model 1445L

1960s. Teisco-made solidbody, 3 pickups.

1960s		$775	$1,000

Model 1446

1962-1966. Single-cut thin acoustic archtop, 2 pickups, original factory Bigsby tailpiece, black lacquer finish with white 'guard.

1962-1966		$1,375	$1,750

Model 1454

1962-1966. Single-cut thin acoustic archtop, 3 pick ups, original factory Bigsby tailpiece, red lacquer finish.

1962-1966		$1,375	$1,750

Model 1476/Model 1477

1964-1966. Offset double-cut solidbody, 2 pickups, dot markers. 4 control knobs, tremolo, black (1476) or sunburst (1477).

1964-1966	1476	$550	$700
1964-1966	1477	$550	$700

Model 1478/Model 1488 Silhouette

1964-1967. Offset double-cut, rectangular pickups, tremolo, bound 'board, block markers.

1964-1967	1478, 1 pickup	$375	$550
1964-1967	1478, 2 pickups	$450	$600
1964-1967	1488, 3 pickups	$700	$900

Model S1352

1955		$700	$875

Model S1453 Rebel

1968. Two sharp cutaway, single f-hole, 2 pickups, vibrato.

1968		$550	$700

Student-level 13" Flat-Top

1960s. Harmony-made, 13" lower bout.

1960s		$40	$60

Student-level 15.5" Flat-Top

1960s. Harmony-made, 15.5" lower bout.

1960s	Model S621	$175	$250

Simon & Patrick

1985-present. Intermediate and professional grade, production, acoustic and acoustic/electric guitars built in Canada. Founded by luthier Robert Godin and named after his sons. He also produces the Seagull, Godin, and Norman brands of instruments.

Sims Custom Shop

2007-present. Custom, professional and premium grade, electric guitars built in Chattanooga, Tennessee by luthier Patrick Sims.

Singletouch

Luthier Mark Singleton builds his professional and premium grade, custom/production, solid and semi-hollow body guitars and basses in Phillips Ranch, California.

Skylark

1981. Solidbody guitars made in Japan and distributed by JC Penney. Two set-neck models and one bolt-neck model were offered. Most likely a one-time deal as brand quickly disappeared.

Slammer

1998-2009. Budget and intermediate grade, production, guitars and basses imported from Indonesia by Hamer. Not to be confused with Hamer's Korean-made series of guitars from 1990-'97 called Hamer Slammer.

Slammer Series (Import)

1998-2009	Various models	$200	$300

Slingerland

Ca. 1914-2019. Henry Slingerland opened a music school in Chicago, Illinois, in 1914 where he supplied instruments made by others to students who took his course. That grew into the Slingerland Manufacturing Company, then Slingerland Banjo and Drum Company in '28, selling banjos, guitars and ukes, built by them and others into the '40s. They also marketed the May Bell brand. Many of the guitars were made by other companies, including Regal. Slingerland ownership changed multiple times in the 1970s-80s until it was acquired by Gibson (from Gretsch) in 1994. The current owner, Drum Workshop (DW), acquired Slingerland in 2019.

Nitehawk

1930s. 16" archtop, Nitehawk logo on headstock, fancy position neck markers.

1930s		$1,200	$1,800

Songster Archtop/Flat-Top

1930s	Archtop	$900	$1,300
1930s	Flat-Top	$1,200	$1,800

Songster Tenor

1930s. Archtop.

1930s		$600	$900

1960 Silvertone Model 1423L Jupiter

Tom Pfeifer

1965 Silvertone Model 1476 Bobkat

Ray Hammond

SMK Music Works

Spalt Instruments Purpleheart Special

MODEL YEAR	FEATURES	EXC. COND. LOW	HIGH

Smart Fine Instruments

1986-present. Luthier A. Lawrence Smart builds his professional and premium grade, custom, flat-top guitars first in McCall and now Hailey, Idaho. He also builds mandolin-family instruments.

Smith, George

1959-2020. Custom classical and flamenco guitars built by luthier George Smith in Portland, Oregon.

Smith, Lawrence K.

1989-present. Luthier Lawrence Smith builds his professional and premium grade, production/custom, flat-top, nylon-string, and archtop guitars in Thirrow, New South Wales, Australia. He also builds mandolins.

SMK Music Works

2002-present. Luthier Scott Kenerson builds production/custom, professional grade, solidbody electric guitars and basses in Waterford, Michigan.

Smooth Stone Guitar

Luthier R. Dale Humphries builds his professional and premium grade, production/custom, acoustic and electric guitars and basses in Pocatello, Idaho. He began in 2007.

Solomon Guitars

1995-present. Luthier Erich Solomon builds his premium and presentation grade, production/custom, archtop, flat-top, classical and electric guitars in Epping, New Hampshire. Prior to '99 he was in Anchorage, Alaska.

Somervell

Luthier Douglas P. Somervell built premium and presentation grade, production/custom, classical and flamenco guitars in Brasstown, North Carolina.

Somogyi, Ervin

1971-present. Luthier Ervin Somogyi builds his presentation grade, production/custom, flat-top, flamenco, and classical guitars in Oakland, California.

Sonata

1960s. Private brand Harmony-made, Sonata brand logo on headstock and pickguard.

Superior

1965. Grand Auditorium acoustic archtop, block markers, celluloid bound edges, similar to Harmony 1456, Superior logo on headstock.

1965		$450	$700

SonFather Guitars

1994-2016. Luthier David A. Cassotta built his production/custom, flat-top, 12-string, nylon-string and electric guitars in Rocklin, California.

Sorrentino

1930s. Private brand made by Epiphone and distributed by C.M.I. Quality close to similar Epiphone models.

Arcadia

1930s. Lower-end f-hole acoustic archtop similar to Epiphone Blackstone.

1930s		$600	$900

Sorrento

1960s. Electric guitar imports made by Teisco, pricing similar to Teisco models, Sorrento logo on headstock, upscale solidbodies can have four pickups with five knobs and four switches.

Electric Solidbody

1960s	4 pickups	$400	$600

Southwell Guitars

1983-present. Premium grade, custom, nylon-string guitars built by luthier Gary Southwell in Nottingham, U.K.

Sovereign

Ca. 1899-1938. Sovereign was originally a brand of The Oscar Schmidt Company of Jersey City, New Jersey, and used on guitars, banjos and mandolins starting in the very late 1800s. In the late '30s, Harmony purchased several trade names from the Schmidt Company, including Sovereign and Stella. Sovereign then ceased as a brand, but Harmony continued using it on a model line of Harmony guitars.

Spalt Instruments

2002-present. Professional and premium grade, production/custom, electric solidbody and hollowbody guitars and basses built by luthier Michael Spalt, originally in Los Angeles, California and since '11 in Vienna, Austria.

Sparrow Guitars

Guitars manufactured in China are dismantled and "overhauled" in Vancouver, British Columbia, starting in '04. From these imports, luthier Billy Bones builds his intermediate and professional grade, production/custom solidbody and hollowbody electric guitars.

Specht Guitars

1991-present. Premium grade, production/custom, acoustic, baritone, parlor, jazz and classical guitars and basses built by luthier Oliver Specht in Vancouver, British Columbia.

Specimen Products

1984-present. Luthier Ian Schneller builds his professional and premium grade, production/custom, aluminum and wood body guitars and basses in Chicago, Illinois. He also builds ukes and amps.

Spector/Stuart Spector Design

1975-1990 (Spector), 1991-1998 (SSD), 1998-present (Spector SSD). Known mainly for basses, Spector

MODEL YEAR	FEATURES	EXC. COND. LOW	HIGH

offered U.S.-made guitars during '75-'90 and '96-'99, and imports for '87-'90 and '96-'99. Since 2003, they again offer U.S.-professional grade, production, solidbody guitars. See Bass Section for more company info.

SPG

2006-2009. Originally professional grade, custom, solidbody and chambered guitars built by luthier Rick Welch in Farmingdale, Maine and Hanson, Massachusetts. He also built lapsteels. Currently brand is used on imported line.

Squier

See models listed under Squier in Fender section.

St. Blues

1980-1989, 2005-2023. Intermediate and professional grade, production/custom, solidbody guitars and basses imported and built in Memphis, Tennessee. The original '80s line was designed by Tom Keckler and Charles Lawing at Memphis' Strings & Things.

St. George

Mid to late 1960s. Early Japanese brand imported possibly by Buegeleisen & Jacobson of New York, New York.

Electric Solidbody

1960s. Early Japanese import duplicate of Zim Gar model, top mounted controls, 3 pickups, bolt-on neck.

1960s	Sunburst	$600	$900

St. Moritz

1960s. Guitars and basses imported from Japan by the Manhattan Novelty Corp. Manufacturer unknown, but some appear to be Fuji Gen Gakki products. Generally shorter scale beginner guitars, some with interesting pickup configurations.

Stahl

1900-1941. William C. Stahl, of Milwaukee, Wisconsin, ran a publishing company, taught stringed instrument classes and sold instruments to his students as well as by mail order across America. His label claimed that he was the maker but most of his products were built by the Larson brothers of Maurer & Co. of Chicago, with the balance mostly from Washburn. The most commonly found Larson-built models are the Style 6 and 7 as seen in the ca. 1912 Stahl catalog. Jimi Hendrix was the proud owner of a Style 8. The Style 6 is a moderately trimmed 15" Brazilian rosewood beauty that is much like the highly sought Maurer Style 551. The Style 7 and 8 are pearl trimmed 13 ½" concert size Brazilians comparable to the Maurer Style 562 ½. The 1912 Stahl catalog Styles 4, 5 and 9 were built by Washburn.

Stambaugh

1995-present. Luthier Chris Stambaugh builds his professional grade, custom/production, solidbody guitars basses in Stratham, New Hampshire.

Standel

1952-1974, 1997-present. Amp builder Bob Crooks offered instruments under his Standel brand 3 different times during the '60s. In '61 Semie Moseley, later of Mosrite fame, made 2 guitar models and 1 bass for Standel, in limited numbers. Also, in '61, Standel began distributing Sierra steels and Dobro resonators, sometimes under the Standel name. In '65 and '66 Standel offered a guitar and a bass made by Joe Hall, who also made the Hallmark guitars. In '66 Standel connected with Sam Koontz, who designed and produced the most numerous Standel models (but still in relatively small numbers) in Newark, New Jersey. These models hit the market in '67 and were handled by Harptone, which was associated with Koontz. By '70 Standel was out of the guitar biz. See Amp section for more company info.

Custom Deluxe 101/101X

1967-1968. Custom solidbody with better electronics, 101X has no vibrato, sunburst, black, pearl white and metallic red.

1967-1968		$1,500	$2,200

Custom Deluxe 102/102X

1967-1968. Custom thin body with better electronics, 102X has no vibrato, offered in sunburst and 5 solid color options.

1967-1968		$1,500	$2,200

Custom 201/201X

1967-1968. Solidbody, 2 pickups, vibrola, 2 pointed cutaways, headstock similar to that on Fender XII, 201X has no vibrato, sunburst, black, pearl white and metallic red.

1967-1968		$1,200	$1,800

Custom 202/202X

1967-1968. Thin body, headstock similar to that on Fender XII, 202X has no vibrato, offered in sunburst and 5 solid color options.

1967-1968		$1,200	$1,800

Custom 420S

1967-1968. Custom thin body with 2 pickups.

1967-1968		$1,500	$2,200

Star

1957-1960s. Early budget level instruments made by Tokyo Sound Company and Gakki and exported by Japan's Hoshino (translates to Star) company which also has Ibanez.

Starcaster

2000s. Budget brand from Fender that has been used on acoustic, electric and bass guitars, effects, amps and drums and sold through mass retailers such as Costco, Target and others. See Fender listing for guitar values.

Starfield

1992-1993. Solidbody guitars from Hoshino (Ibanez) made in the U.S. and Japan. U.S. guitars are identified as American models; Japanese ones as SJ models. Hoshino also used the Star Field name on a line of Japanese guitars in the late '70s. These Star Fields had nothing to do with the '90s versions and were not sold in the U.S.

Steinegger D-45
Carter Vintage Guitars

1969 Standel
Jerry Amend

GUITARS

1968 Stella
Edward Sparks

Stonebridge Bridgeport 200 Series AC-CM

MODEL YEAR	FEATURES	EXC. COND. LOW	HIGH

Starforce

Ca. 1989. Import copies from Starforce Music/Starforce USA.

Stars

Intermediate grade, production, solidbody guitars made in Korea.

Status Graphite

1981-present. Professional grade, production/custom, solidbody guitars and basses built in Colchester, Essex, U.K. Status was the first English company to produce a carbon fiber instrument.

Stauffer

1800s. Old World violin and guitar maker, Georg Stauffer. Valid attributions include signed or labeled by the maker indicating the guitar was actually made by Stauffer, as opposed to attributed to Stauffer or one of his contemporaries. See Martin for listing.

Stefan Sobell Musical Instruments

1982-present. Premium grade, production/custom, flat-top, 12-string, and archtop guitars built by luthier Stefan Sobell in Hetham, Northumberland, England. He also builds mandolins, citterns and bouzoukis.

Steinberger

1979-present. Currently Steinberger offers budget, intermediate, and professional grade, production, electric guitars. They also offer basses. Founded by Ned Steinberger, who started designing NS Models for Stuart Spector in '76. In '79, he designed the L-2 headless bass. In '80, the Steinberger Sound Corp. was founded. Steinberger Sound was purchased by the Gibson Guitar Corp. in '87, and in '92, Steinberger relocated to Nashville, Tennessee.

Headless model codes for '85-'93 are:
First letter is X for bass or G for guitar.
Second letter is for body shape:
M is regular offset double-cut guitar body; L is rectangle body; P is mini V shaped body.
Number is pickup designation:
2 = 2 humbuckers, 3 = 3 single coils, 4 = single/single/humbucker.
Last letter is type of tremolo:
S = S-Trem tremolo; T = Trans-Trem which cost more on original retail.

GL

1979-1984. Headless, rectangle body, 2 pickups.

1979-1984		$5,000	$8,500

Steinegger

1976-2021. Premium grade, custom steel-string flat-top guitars built by luthier Robert Steinegger in Portland, Oregon. He retired in March, 2021.

MODEL YEAR	FEATURES	EXC. COND. LOW	HIGH

Stella

Ca. 1899-1974, 2000s. Stella was a brand of the Oscar Schmidt Company which started using the brand on low-mid to mid-level instruments in the very late 1800s. Oscar Schmidt produced all types of stringed instruments and was very successful in the 1920s. Company salesmen reached many rural areas and Stella instruments were available in general stores, furniture stores, and dry goods stores, ending up in the hands of musicians such as Leadbelly and Charlie Patton. Harmony acquired the Stella brand in '39 and built thousands of instruments with that name in the '50s and '60s. Harmony dissolved in '74. The Stella brand was reintroduced in the 2000s by MBT International.

00 Style

1900-1930. Oak body flat-top.

1900-1930		$500	$800

Flat-Top 15" 12-String

1920s-1930s. Associated with early blues and folk musicians, top of the line for Stella.

1920s-30s		$8,000	$10,000

Flat-Top by Harmony

1950s-1960s. The low end of the Harmony-built models, US-made until the end of the '60s, student level, Stella logo on headstock, playing action can often be very high which makes them difficult to play.

1950s-60s	13", student	$75	$200
1950s-60s	14", 12-string	$100	$200
1950s-60s	Sundale (colors)	$400	$600
1950s-60s	Tenor 4-string	$75	$200

Harp Guitar

Early-1900s.

1900s		$2,200	$3,300

Singing Cowboy

2000s. Copy of Supertone (black background)/Silvertone/Harmony Singing Cowboy, import with laminated wood construction and ladder bracing.

2000s	Stencil over black	$50	$100

Stetson

1884-ca. 1924. Stetson was a house brand of William John Dyer's St. Paul, Minnesota, music store. They started advertising this brand as early as 1894, but those built by the Larson brothers of Maurer & Co. date from ca. 1904-c. 1924. Most Stetsons were made by the Larsons. Others were built by Harmony (early ones), Washburn and three are credited to the Martin Co.

Stevenson

1999-present. Professional grade, production/custom, solidbody electric guitars and basses built by luthier Ted Stevenson in Lachine, Quebec. He also builds amps.

Stiehler

Production/custom, professional and premium grade, acoustic electric and electric solidbody guitars and basses, built by luthier Bob Stiehler, first in Wellington and since '11 in Carson City, Nevada. He started in 2005.

MODEL YEAR	FEATURES	EXC. COND. LOW	HIGH

Stonebridge

1981-present. Czech Republic luthier Frantisek Furch builds professional and premium grade, production/custom, acoustic guitars. He also builds mandolins.

Stonetree Custom Guitars

1996-present. Luthier Scott Platts builds his professional and premium grade, custom/production, solidbody and chambered electric guitars and basses first in Saratoga, Wyoming and currently in Colville, Washington.

Strad-O-Lin/Stradolin

Ca.1920s-ca.1960s. The Strad-O-Lin company was operated by the Hominic brothers in New York, primarily making mandolins for wholesalers. Around '57 Multivox/Premier bought the company and also used the name on electric and acoustic guitars, basses and amps. Premier also marketed student level guitars under the U.S. Strad brand.

Electric

1960s	Various models	$400	$600

Stratosphere

1954-1958. Solidbody electrics made in Springfield, Missouri by brothers Claude and Russ Deaver, some featuring fanned frets. They also made an odd double neck called the Stratosphere Twin with a regular 6-string neck and a 12-string tuned in minor and major thirds. The brothers likely made less than 200 instruments.

Electric

1954-1958		$900	$1,400

Strobel Guitars

2003-present. Luthier Russ Strobel builds custom, professional grade, electric travel guitars and basses in Boca Raton, Florida. He also offers a production, intermediate grade, travel guitar built in Asia.

Stromberg

1906-1955, 2001-2024. Intermediate and professional grade, production, archtop guitars imported by Larry Davis.

Founded in Boston by master luthier Charles Stromberg, a Swedish immigrant, building banjos and drums. Son Harry joined the company in 1907and stayed until '27. Son Elmer started in 1910 at age 15. The shop was well known for tenor banjos, but when the banjo's popularity declined, they began building archtop orchestra model guitars. The shop moved to Hanover Street in Boston in '27 and began producing custom order archtop guitars, in particular the 16" G-series and the Deluxe. As styles changed the G-series was increased to 17 3/8" and the 19" Master 400 model was introduced in '37. Stromberg designs radically changed around '40, most likely when Elmer took over guitar production. Both Charles and Elmer died within a few months of each other in '55. Most of the interest in vintage Strombergs comes out of the Boston area.

Larry Davis of WD Music Products revived the Stromberg name and introduced a series of moderately priced jazz guitars in June 2001. The models are crafted by a small Korean shop with component parts supplied by WD.

Deluxe

1927-1955. Non-cut, 16" body to '34, 17 3/8" body after '35, also sometimes labeled Delux.

1927-1939	2 parallel 3 ladder	$3,000	$4,500
1940-1947	2 braces	$4,000	$6,000
1948-1955	1 brace	$12,000	$20,000

G-1

1927-1955. Non-cut, 16" body to '35, 17 3/8" body after '35, sunburst.

1927-1935	2 parallel 3 ladder	$3,000	$5,000
1936-1947	2 braces	$4,000	$6,000
1948-1955	1 brace	$12,000	$20,000

G-3

Early 1930s. Archtop, 16 3/8", 3 segment F-holes, ladder bracing, gold hardware, engraved tailpiece, 8-ply 'guard, 5-ply body binding, laminate maple back, fancy engraved headstock with Stromberg name, less total refinement than higher-end Stromberg models.

1927-1935	2 parallel 3 ladder	$3,000	$5,000

G-5

1952-1955. 17" cutaway.

1952-1955	1 brace	$20,000	$30,000

Master 300

1937-1955. 19" non-cut.

1937-1947	2 braces, natural	$5,000	$6,500
1937-1947	2 braces, sunburst	$5,500	$6,500
1948-1955	1 brace, natural	$10,000	$20,000
1948-1955	1 brace, sunburst	$10,000	$20,000

Master 400

1937-1955. 19" top-of-the-line non-cut, the most common of Stromberg's models.

1937-1947	2 braces, natural	$10,000	$15,000
1937-1947	2 braces, sunburst	$10,000	$15,000
1948-1955	1 brace, natural	$20,000	$50,000
1948-1955	1 brace, sunburst	$20,000	$50,000

Master 400 Cutaway

1949, 1953. Only 7 cutaway Strombergs are known to exist.

1949, 1953	1 brace, natural	$40,000	$60,000

Stromberg-Voisinet

1921-ca.1932. Marketed Stromberg (not to be confused with Charles Stromberg of Boston) and Kay Kraft brands, plus guitars of other distributors and retailers. Stromberg was the successor to the Groehsl Company (or Groehsel) founded in Chicago, Illinois in 1890; and the predecessor to the Kay Musical Instrument Company. In 1921, the name was changed to Stromberg-Voisinet Company. Henry Kay "Hank" Kuhrmeyer joined the company in '23 and was secretary by '25. By the mid-'20s, the company was making many better Montgomery Ward guitars, banjos and mandolins, often with lots of pearloid.

Stonetree Roscoecaster

1950 Stromberg DeLuxe

Ranger Doug

Stromberg-Voisinet Hawaiian Parlor
David Stone

Supertone Lone Ranger
Imaged by Heritage Auctions, HA.com

MODEL YEAR	FEATURES	EXC. COND. LOW	HIGH

Joseph Zorzi, Philip Gabriel and John Abbott left Lyon & Healy for S-V in '26 or '27, developing a 2-point Venetian shape, which was offered in '27. The first production of electric guitars and amps was introduced with big fanfare in '28; perhaps only 200 or so were made. The last Stromberg acoustic instruments were seen in '32. The Kay Kraft brand was introduced by Kuhrmeyer in '31 as the company made its transition to Kay (see Kay).

Acoustic

1921-1932. Various art and colors.

1921-1932	Various models	$350	$2,500

Stroup

Luthier Gary D. Stroup builds his intermediate and professional grade, production/custom, archtop and flat-top guitars in Eckley, Colorado, starting in 2003.

Stuart Custom Guitars

Professional and premium grade, production/custom, solid and semi-hollow body guitars built by luthier Fred Stuart, starting the year 2004, in Riverside, California. Stuart was a Senior Master Builder at Fender. He also builds pickups.

Suhr Guitars

1997-present. Luthier John Suhr builds his professional and premium grade, production/custom, solidbody electrics guitars and basses in Lake Elsinore, California. He also builds amps. He previously built Pensa-Suhr guitars with Rudy Pensa in New York.

Electric Solidbody

1997-2024	Various models	$2,500	$5,000

Sunset

2010-present. Luthier Leon White builds professional and premium grade, production/custom, electric solidbody, chambered and hollowbody guitars in Los Angeles, California.

Superior Guitars

1987-present. Intermediate grade, production/custom Hawaiian, flamenco, and classical guitars made in Mexico for George Katechis Montalvo of Berkeley Musical Instrument Exchange. They also offer lap steels and mandolin-family instruments.

Supersound

1952-1974. Founded by England's Alan Wootton, building custom amps and radios. In 1958-'59 he worked with Jim Burns to produce about 20 short scale, single-cut solidbodies bearing this name. They also built a bass model. The firm continued to build amps and effects into the early '60s.

Supertone

1914-1941. Brand used by Sears, Roebuck and Company for instruments made by various American manufacturers, including especially its own subsidiary Harmony (which it purchased in 1916). When Sears divested itself of Harmony in '40, instruments began making a transition to the Silvertone brand. By '41 the Supertone name was gone.

Acoustic Flat-Top (High-End Appointments)

1920s	Pearl trim 00-42 likeness	$1,500	$2,200
1920s	Pearl trim, Lindbergh model	$1,500	$2,200

Acoustic Flat-Top 13"

1920s-30s	Non-stencil, plain top	$200	$300
1920s-30s	Stencil top	$300	$500

Gene Autry Roundup

1932-1939. Harmony made acoustic, Gene Autry signature on belly, cowboy roundup stencil, 13" body until '35, then 14".

1932-1939		$400	$600

Lone Ranger

1936-1941. Black with red and silver Lone Ranger and Tonto stencil, silver-painted fretboard, 13 1/2" wide. "Hi-Yo Silver" added in '37, changed to "Hi-Ho Silver" in '38.

1936-1941		$400	$600

Robin Hood

1930s. 13" flat-top similar to Singing Cowboys, but with green and white art showing Robin Hood and his men against a black background.

1933		$400	$600

Singing Cowboys

1938-1943. Stencil of guitar strumming cowboys around chuck wagon and campfire, branded Silvertone after '41.

1938-1943		$400	$600

Supertone Wedge

1930s. Triangle-shaped wedge body, laminate construction, blue-silver Supertone label inside sound chamber, art decals on body.

1930s		$300	$500

Supro

1935-1968, 2004-present. Budget brand of National Dobro Company and Valco. Some Supro models also sold under the Airline brand for Montgomery Ward. In '42 Victor Smith, Al Frost and Louis Dopyera bought National and changed the name to Valco Manufacturing Company. Valco Manufacturing Company name changed to Valco Guitars, Inc., in '62. Company treasurer Robert Engelhardt bought Valco in '64. In '67 Valco bought Kay and in '68 Valco/Kay went out of business. In the summer of '69, Valco/Kay brands and assets were sold at auction and the Supro and National names purchased by Chicago-area importer and distributor Strum N' Drum (Norma, Noble). In the early-'80s, ownership of the Supro name was transferred to Archer's Music, Fresno, California. Some Supros assembled from new-old-stock parts.

Amp builder Bruce Zinky revived the Supro name for a line of guitars built in the U.S. by luthier John Bolin and others. He also offers amps. In 2013,

MODEL YEAR	FEATURES	EXC. COND. LOW	HIGH

Absara Audio, LLC acquired the Supro trademark and started releasing amps and guitars in July 2014.

Arlington

1967-1967. Jazzmaster-style, wood body, 6 buttons, 4 knobs, vibrato, 2 pickups.

1966-1967	Various colors	$1,250	$1,500

Atlas

1958. Rare model, Atlas logo, semi-single cutaway, 2 pickups plus bridge-tailpiece pickup, blond finish.

1958		$1,750	$2,500

Belmont

1955-1964. For '55-'60, 12" wide, single-cut, 1 neck pickup, 2 knobs treble side in 'guard, reverse-stairs tailpiece, No-Mar plastic maroon-colored covering. For '60, size increased to 13 1/2" wide. For '62-'64, Res-o-glas fiberglass was used for the body, a slight cutaway on bass side, 1 bridge pickup, 2 knobs on opposite sides, Polar White.

1955-1962	Black or white No-Mar	$1,125	$1,500
1961-1964	Polar White Res-o-glas	$1,250	$1,750

Bermuda

1962 only. Slab body (not beveled), double pickups, dot markers, cherry glass-fiber finish.

1962		$1,375	$1,750

Collegian Spanish

1939-1942. Metal body, 12 frets. Moved to National line in '42.

1939-1942		$1,125	$1,500

Coronado/Coronado II

1961-1967, 2017-2021. Listed as II in '62 15 1/2" scale, single-cut thinline, 2 pickups, natural blond spruce top. Changed to slight cutaway on bass side in '62 when renamed II. Reintroduced 2017, Americana series.

1961-1962	Blond, spruce top	$1,625	$2,000
1963-1967	Black fiberglass	$1,750	$2,250
2017-2021	II, Americana Series	$550	$750

Dual-Tone

1954-1966, 2004-2014. The Dual Tone had several body style changes, all instruments had dual pickups. '54, 11 1/4" body, No Mar Arctic White plastic body ('54-'62). '55, 12" body. '58, 13" body. '60, 13 1/2" body. '62, Res-o-glas Ermine White body, light cutaway on bass side.

1954-1961	Arctic White No-Mar	$1,375	$1,750
1962-1964	Ermine White Res-o-glas	$1,500	$1,875

El Capitan

1948-1955. Archtop, 1 single-coil pickup.

1948-1955		$650	$900

Folk Star/Vagabond

1964-1967. Molded Res-o-glas body, single-cone resonator, dot inlays, Fire Engine Red. Name changed to Vagabond in '66.

1964-1967		$950	$1,375

Jamesport

2017-2021. Island Series, electric solidbody, '60s-era design, alder body, maple neck, rosewood 'board, Gold Foil pickup, antique white or jet black.

2017-2021		$350	$500

MODEL YEAR	FEATURES	EXC. COND. LOW	HIGH

Kingston

1962-1963. Double-cut slab body, bridge pickup, glass-fiber sand finish, similar to same vintage Ozark.

1962-1963		$950	$1,250

Lexington

1967. Double-cut, wood body.

1967		$750	$950

Martinique (Val-Trol)

1962-1967. Single-cut, 13 1/2" wide, 2 standard and 1 bridge pickups, block markers, Val-Trol script on 'guard, Bigsby, blue or Ermine White Polyester Glas. Collectors sometimes call this Val-Trol, referring to the 6 mini tone and volume controls. Not to be confused with Silverwood model which also has 6 mini-knobs.

1962-1967		$2,000	$3,000

N800 Thinline Electric

1967-1968. Thin body, symmetrical double-cut, 2 pickups, copy model, similar to National N800 series models.

1967-1968		$600	$750

Ozark

1952-1954, 1958-1967, 2004-2013. Non-cut, 1 pickup, dot inlay, white pearloid body, name reintroduced in '58 as a continuation of model Sixty with single-cut, Dobro tailpiece.

1952-1954	White pearloid	$950	$1,250
1958-1961	Red	$950	$1,250
1962-1967	Jet Black or Fire Bronze	$950	$1,250

Ranchero

1948-1960. Full body electric archtop, neck pickup, dot markers, bound body, sunburst.

1948-1960		$725	$950

Rhythm Master (Val-Trol)

1959. Val-Trol 'guard.

1959		$1,500	$1,875

S710 Flat-Top

1967-1968. Jumbo-style 15.5" flat-top, block markers, asymmetrical headstock, natural.

1967-1968		$425	$550

Sahara/Sahara 70

1960-1967. 13 1/2" body-style similar to Dual-Tone, single pickup, 2 knobs, Sand-Buff or Wedgewood Blue, Sahara until '63, Sahara 70 after.

1960-1967		$1,125	$1,500

Silverwood (Val-Trol)

1960-1962, 2019-2021. Single-cut, 13 1/2" wide, 2 standard and 1 bridge pickups, block markers, natural blond, Val-Trol script on 'guard, renamed Martinique in '62. Collectors sometimes call this Val-Trol, referring to the guitar's 6 mini tone and volume controls. The Martinique also has the Val-Trol system but the knobs are not in a straight line like on the Silverwood. Reintroduced 2019, mahogany or ash body, maple neck, 2 Gold Foil pickups, Daphne Blue, Ash Natural, British Racing Green and Transparent Red.

1960-1962		$1,750	$2,250
2019-2021		$750	$950

Sixty

1955-1958. Single-cut, single pickup, white No-Mar, became Ozark in '58.

1955-1958		$750	$1,000

1960s Supro Bermuda

Bernunzio Uptown Music

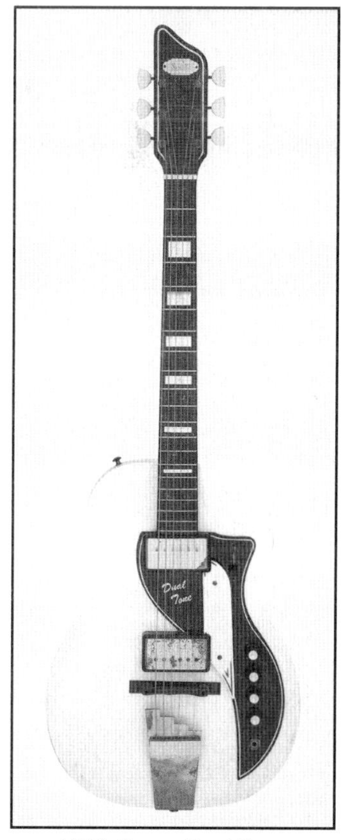

1960 Supro Dual Tone

Imaged by Heritage Auctions, HA.com

Szlag

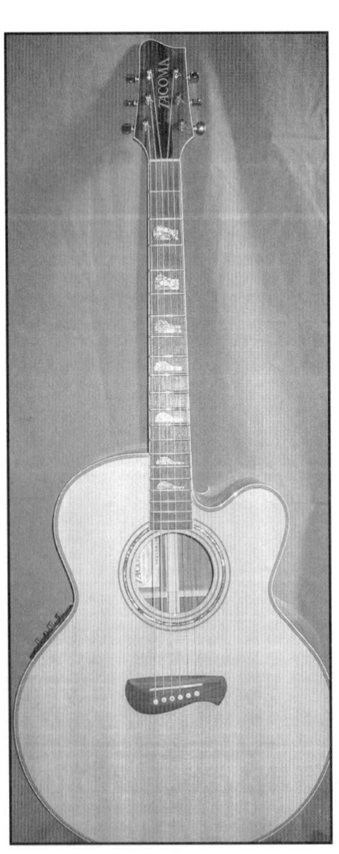

Tacoma JK50-CE
Vic Hines

MODEL YEAR	FEATURES	EXC. COND. LOW	HIGH

Special 12
1958-1960. Single-cut, replaces Supro Sixty, neck pickup 'guard mounted.

1958-1960		$750	$1,000

Stratford
1968. ES-335-style double-cut, 3 pickups, 3 switches, 6 knobs, vibrato.

1968		$725	$950

Strum 'N Drum Solidbody
1970s. Student-level import, 1 pickup, large Supro logo on headstock.

1970s	Higher-end	$450	$575
1970s	Lower-end	$350	$450

Super
1958-1964. 12" wide single-cut body style like mid-'50s models, single bridge pickup, short-scale, ivory.

1958-1964		$625	$900

Super Seven
1965-1967. Offset double-cut solidbody, short scale, middle pickup, Calypso Blue.

1965-1967		$625	$900

Suprosonic 30
1963-1967. Introduced as Suprosonic, renamed Suprosonic 30 in '64, double-cut, single neck pickup, vibrato tailpiece, more of a student model, Holly Red.

1963-1967		$600	$750

Tremo-Lectric
1965. Fiberglas hollowbody, 2 pickups, unique built-in electric tremolo (not mechanical), Wedgewood Blue finish, multiple controls associated with electric tremolo.

1965		$1,375	$1,750

Tri Tone
Reintroduced 2019-2021. Single-cut mahogany body, maple neck, 3 pickups, black.

2019-2021		$950	$1,125

Westbury
Reintroduced 2017-2021. Island Series, alder body, maple neck, 2 Gold Foil pickups, black, white, turquoise, or tobacco burst.

2017-2021		$400	$500

Westwood 1580A
1955-1958. Single-cut archtop solidbody, 1 pickup.

1955-1958		$950	$1,250

White Holiday/Holiday
1963-1967, 2018-2021. Introduced as Holiday, renamed White Holiday in '64, fiberglas double-cut, vibrato tailpiece, single bridge pickup, Dawn White. Reintroduced 2018, Americana Series, mahogany body and neck, 2 pickups.

1963-1967		$1,000	$1,500
2018-2021		$500	$650

Suzuki Takeharu

See listing for Takeharu.

SX

See listing for Essex.

Szlag

2000-present. Luthier John J. Slog builds his professional and premium grade, custom carved, guitars and basses in Bethlehem, Pennsylvania.

T.D. Hibbs

Production/custom, professional grade, steel string and classical guitars built in Cambridge, Ontario by luthier Trevor Hibbs.

T.H. Davis

1976-2008. Professional and premium grade, custom, steel string and classical guitars built by luthier Ted Davis in Loudon, Tennessee. He also built mandolins. Davis died in '08.

T.J. Thompson

Luthier T.J. Thompson began in the 1980's building presentation grade, custom, steel string guitars in West Concord, Massachusetts.

Tacoma

1995-2009. Intermediate, and professional grade, production, acoustic guitars produced in Tacoma, Washington and New Hartford, Connecticut. They also built acoustic basses and mandolins. In October, '04, Fender acquired Tacoma and in '09 ceased production.

BM6C Thunderhawk Baritone
2004-2009. Single-cut acoustic baritone.

2004-2009		$1,500	$2,200

C-1C/C-1CE Chief
1997-2009. Cutaway flat-top with upper bass bout sound hole, solid cedar top, mahogany back and sides, rosewood 'board. Sides laminated until 2000, solid after, CE is acoustic/electric.

1997-2009		$500	$800
1997-2009	Fishman electronics	$550	$900

DM Series
1997-2006. Dreadnought, solid spruce top, mahogany back and sides, satin finish, natural, C suffix indicates cutaway.

1997-2006	Various models	$300	$500

DR Series
1997-2006. Dreadnought, solid Sitka spruce top, rosewood back and sides, natural. Models include DR-20 (non-cut, herringbone trim, abalone rosette), DR-20E (with on-board electronics), DR-8C (cutaway), and DR-38.

1997-2006	Various models	$400	$600

EM Series
1999-2008. Little Jumbo series, spruce top, mahogany back and sides, C suffix indicates cutaway.

1999-2008	Various models	$600	$900

JM Series
1997-2006. Jumbo series, spruce top, mahogany back and sides.

1997-2006		$900	$1,400

JR-14C Jumbo Rosewood
Late-1990s. Jumbo cutaway, 16 5/8" lower bout, gloss spruce top, satin rosewood body.

1990s		$1,000	$1,500

MODEL YEAR	FEATURES	EXC. COND. LOW	HIGH

JR-50CE4 Jumbo Koa

1997-2003. Jumbo cutaway, 17" lower bout, Sitka spruce top, figured Koa back and sides.

1997-2003		$1,000	$1,500

P-1/P-2 Papoose

1995-2009. Travel-size mini-flat-top, all solid wood, mahogany back and sides (P-1), with on-board electronics (P-1E) or solid rosewood (P-2), cedar top, natural satin finish.

1995-2000	P-2	$400	$600
1995-2009	P-1	$300	$500
1995-2009	P-1E	$500	$800

Parlor Series

1997-2003. Smaller 14 3/4" body, solid spruce top, various woods for back and sides.

1997-2003	PK-30 Koa	$800	$1,200
1997-2003	PK-40 Rosewood	$800	$1,200

PM Series

1997-2003. Full-size, standard sound hole.

1997-2003	Various models	$400	$600

Takamine

1962-present. Intermediate and professional grade, production, steel- and nylon-string, acoustic and acoustic/electric guitars and basses. Takamine is named after a mountain near its factory in Sakashita, Japan. Mass Hirade joined Takamine in '68 and revamped the brand's designs and improved quality. In '75, Takamine began exporting to other countries, including U.S. distribution by Kaman Music (Ovation). In '78, Takamine introduced acoustic/electric guitars. They offered solidbody electrics and some archtops for '83-'84.

Takeharu (by Suzuki)

Mid-1970s. Classical guitars offered by Suzuki as part of their internationally known teaching method (e.g., Violin Suzuki method), various sized instruments designed to eliminate the confusion of size that has been a problem for classroom guitar programs.

Taku Sakashta Guitars

1994-2010. Premium and presentation grade, production/custom, archtop, flat-top, 12-sting, and nylon-string guitars, built by luthier Taku Sakashta in Sebastopol, California. He died in February 2010.

Tama

Ca. 1959-1967, 1974-1979. Hoshino's (Ibanez) brand of higher-end acoustic flat-tops made in Japan. Many of the brand's features would be transferred to Ibanez's Artwood acoustics.

Tamura

1970s. Made in Japan by Mitsura Tamura, the line includes intermediate grade solid wood classical guitars.

Tanglewood Guitar Company UK

1991-present. Owners Dirk Kommer and Tony Flatt in Biggin Hill, U.K. import intermediate and professional grade, production, acoustic, classical, resonator and electric guitars and basses from China. They also offer mandolins, banjos, ukuleles and amps.

Taylor

1974-present. Intermediate, professional, premium, and presentation grade, production/custom, steel- and nylon-string, acoustic, acoustic/electric, semi-hollow, and solidbody guitars built in El Cajon, California and Tecate, Mexico. They have also built basses. Founded by Bob Taylor, Steve Schemmer and Kurt Listug in Lemon Grove, California, the company was originally named the Westland Music Company, but was soon changed to Taylor (Bob designed the guitars and it fit on the logo). Taylor and Listug bought out Schemmer in '83. Bob Taylor was the first commercially successful guitar maker to harness CAD/CAM CNC technology for acoustic guitars and in '91 introduced the 410 Model, the first all-solid wood American-made guitar with a list price under $1,000. The plain-appointment model using CNC technology was a major innovation combining quality and price. They added semi-hollowbodies in '05 and solidbodies in '07. In '08, they added the Build To Order custom shop. In '18, they added their new V-Class bracing to most every steel-string model in the 300 Series and above. V-Class braced Taylors have a black graphite nut vs the white one on standard braced models.

Understanding Taylor's Model Numbering System:

The first digit or letter identifies the series (100 Series to 900 Series, PS-Presentation and K-Koa Series) and most models within each series share the same back and side woods and appointment package.

The second digit: 1=6-string with softwood (spruce) top; 2=6-string with hardwood top; 5=12-string with softwood top; 2=12-string with hardwood top.

The third digit is body shape: 0=Dreadnought; 2=Grand Concert; 4=Grand Auditorium; 6=Grand Symphony; 7=Grand Pacific; 8=Grand Orchestra.

A "c" at the end of the number indicates cutaway, an "e" onboard electronics, and a "N" nylon-string.

110 Series

2003-present. Dreadnought, sapele back and sides, Sitka spruce top, e and ce begin '08.

2003-2016	110	$475	$600
2008-2024	110ce	$600	$750
2008-2023	110e	$525	$675

114 Series

2007-present. Grand Auditorium, sapele back and sides, Sitka spruce top.

2007-2016	114	$475	$600
2008-2024	114ce	$600	$750
2008-2023	114e	$525	$675

2012 Takamine Ef508Kc 50th Anniversary Koa

Cream City Music

Taylor 110e

GUITARS

2016 Taylor 150e
Cream City Music

Taylor 324e

MODEL YEAR	FEATURES	EXC. COND. LOW	HIGH

150 Series

2016-present. Dreadnought 12-string, Sitka spruce top, walnut back and sides.

2016-2024	150ce	$575	$725

210 Series

2005-present. Dreadnought, sapele or Indian rosewood back and sides, Sitka spruce top.

2005-2016	210	$575	$725
2005-2016	210e	$625	$800
2008-2024	210ce	$700	$875

214 Series

2004-present. Grand Auditorium, sapele or Indian rosewood back and sides, Sitka spruce top.

2004-2016	214	$525	$675
2004-2016	214c	$575	$725
2005-2016	214e	$575	$725
2008-2024	214ce	$650	$825
2012-2024	214ce-N Classic	$775	$975
2014-2024	214ce-K DLX (Koa)	$800	$1,000
2020	214ce DLX	$925	$1,125
2020	214ce-SB DLX	$1,000	$1,250

224ce-K DLX

2016-present. Grand Auditorium, solid Koa top, laminated Koa back and sides.

2016-2024		$1,125	$1,500

254ce

2018-present. Venetian cutaway, Sitka spruce top, rosewood back and sides.

2018-2024		$650	$825

310 Series

1998-2018. Dreadnought, mahogany or sapele back and sides, Sitka spruce top. The non-cut 310 discontinued '07-'12, then reappeared in '13 along with 310e version.

1998-2006	310	$750	$950
1998-2018	310ce	$900	$1,125

310ce-L30

2004. Limited Edition 30th Anniversary, myrtlewood leaf inlays, Koa rosette, 30th Anniversary headstock logo.

2004		$950	$1,250

312 Series

1998-present. Grand Concert, Venetian cutaway, mahogany or sapele back and sides, Sitka spruce top. Non-cut 312 and 312e versions were offered in 2013. V-Class introduced '20.

1998-2019	312ce	$1,375	$1,750
2019-2024	312ce V-Class	$1,500	$1,875

314 Series

1998-2006, 2013-present. Mid-size Grand Auditorium, mahogany or sapele back and sides, Sitka spruce top. Non-cut offered again in '13 along with 314e version. V-Class introduced '20.

1998-2006	314	$1,125	$1,500
1998-2019	314ce	$1,250	$1,625
2000	314ce-K (Koa)	$1,500	$1,875
2019-2024	314ce V-Class	$1,500	$1,875

314ce-LTD

2012-2018. Hawaiian Koa back and sides, Indian rosewood headstock. Also offered with nylon strings (N).

2012-2018		$1,375	$1,750

315 Series

1998-2011. Jumbo, mahogany or sapele back and sides, Sitka spruce top.

1998-2011	315ce	$1,000	$1,250

316 Series

2012-2019. Grand Symphony, Sitka spruce top, sapele back and sides.

2012-2019	316ce	$1,125	$1,500
2013-2016	316	$950	$1,250
2013-2016	316e	$1,125	$1,500
2018	316e Baritone-8 LTD	$1,500	$1,875

320e Baritone SLTD

2014. Limited Edition Dreadnought, mahogany top and body, Expression electronics.

2014		$1,375	$1,750

322 Series

2019-present. Grand Concert, non-cut, blackwood/mahogany top.

2019-2024	322ce V-Class	$1,375	$1,750
2020	322e	$1,375	$1,750

324 Series

2015-present. Grand Auditorium, mahogany top, African sapele back and sides.

2015-2020	324e	$1,125	$1,500
2019-2024	324ce V-Class	$1,500	$1,875
2020-2023	324	$1,000	$1,250

326ce Baritone

2015-present. Grand Symphony, special edition, 6- or 8-string, mahogany top.

2015-2024		$1,375	$1,750

352 Series

2019-present. Grand Concert 12-string, Sitka spruce top, sapele back and sides, natural.

2019-2024	352ce V-Class	$1,375	$1,750

354ce

2004-2011. Grand Auditorium 12-string, cutaway, mahogany back and sides, Expression system.

2004-2011		$1,375	$1,750

355 Series

1998-2011. Jumbo 12-string, mahogany or sapele back and sides, Sitka spruce top.

1998-2006	355	$1,000	$1,250
1998-2011	355ce	$1,250	$1,500

356 Series

2014-2019. Grand Symphony 12-string, Sitka spruce top, sapele back and sides, non-cut, cutaway, or ce cutaway electric.

2014-2019	356ce	$1,250	$1,500

362 Series

2019-present. Grand Concert 12-string, mahogany top, blackwood back and sides.

2019-2024	362ce V-Class	$1,375	$1,750

363 Series

2020	363ce V-Class	$1,375	$1,750

410 Series

1991-2018. Dreadnought, mahogany back and sides until '98, ovangkol after '98, Sitka spruce top. Non-cut offered again in '13 along with 410e version.

1991-2006	410	$950	$1,250
1991-2018	410ce	$1,250	$1,500
2000	410-MA, maple	$1,125	$1,500

MODEL YEAR	FEATURES	EXC. COND. LOW	HIGH

412 Series

1991-present. Grand Concert, mahogany back and sides until '98, ovangkol after, Sitka spruce top. Cutaway electric version replaced the 412 in '98. Non-cut offered again in '13 along with 412e version.

1991-1998	412	$1,375	$1,750
1996	412-K (Koa)	$1,500	$1,875
1998-2024	412ce	$1,625	$2,000
1998-2023	412ce-R	$1,625	$2,000

414 Series

1998-present. Grand Auditorium, ovangkol back and sides, Sitka spruce top. Non-cut offered again in '13 along with 414e version.

1998	414-K (Koa)	$1,500	$1,875
1998-2006	414	$1,375	$1,750
1998-2024	414ce	$1,625	$2,000
2019-2023	414ce-R V-Class	$1,625	$2,000

414ce-LTD

2013. Limited Edition, Sitka spruce top, tropical mahogany neck.

2013		$1,250	$1,500

414-L10

2005. Limited Edition, rosewood sides and back, gloss spruce top, satin finish.

2005		$1,125	$1,500

414-L30

2004. Limited Edition 30th Anniversary, Hawaiian Koa back and sides, Engelmann spruce top, pearl and gold 30th Anniversary inlay.

2004		$1,125	$1,500

415 Series

1998-2006. Jumbo, ovangkol back and sides, Sitka spruce top.

1998-2006	415ce	$1,250	$1,500

416 Series

2011-2019. Grand Symphony, ovangkol back and sides, Sitka spruce top.

2011-2019	416ce	$1,250	$1,500

418 Series

2015-2019. Grand Orchestra, ovangkol back and sides, Sitka spruce top.

2015-2019	418e	$1,250	$1,500

420

1990-1997. Dreadnought, Indian rosewood back and sides, Sitka spruce top.

1990-1997		$1,125	$1,500

422 Series

1991-1998. Grand Concert, solid maple construction.

1991-1998	422-K (Koa)	$1,375	$1,750
1997	422-R (Rosewood)	$1,375	$1,750

426ce-LTD

2008. Limited Edition, Tasmanian blackwood top, back and sides.

2008		$1,500	$1,875

450

1996-1997. Dreadnought 12-string, mahogany back and sides, spruce top.

1996-1997		$1,000	$1,250

454ce

2004-2011. Grand Auditorium 12-string, Ovangkol back and sides, Sitka spruce top.

2004-2011		$1,250	$1,500

455 Series

2001-2011. Jumbo 12-string, Ovangkol back and sides, Sitka spruce top.

2001-2006	455	$1,125	$1,500
2001-2011	455ce	$1,250	$1,500

455ce-LTD

2001-2003. Limited Edition, imbuia back and sides.

2001-2003		$1,500	$1,875

456 Series

2012-2016. Grand Symphony 12-string.

2012-2016	456e and 456ce	$1,625	$2,000

458e

2016-2019. Grand Orchestra 12-string.

2016-2019		$1,500	$1,875

510 Series

1978-2017. Dreadnought, mahogany back and sides, spruce top. Non-cut offered again in '13 along with 510e version.

1978-2006	510	$1,125	$1,500
1978-2017	510ce	$1,375	$1,750

510ce-AB 25th Anniversary

1999. Limited Edition, 25th Anniversary on headstock, spruce top, mahogany back, sides and neck.

1999		$1,875	$2,500

510-LTD

2002. Limited Edition, mahogany back and sides, Sitka spruce top.

2002		$1,250	$1,500

512 Series

1978-present. Grand Concert, mahogany back and sides, red cedar top. Non-cut offered again in '13-'16 along with 512e version.

1978-2000	512	$1,125	$1,500
1978-2000	512c	$1,250	$1,500
1978-2024	512ce	$1,500	$1,875
2012-2016	512ce-N	$1,500	$1,875

512ce-L10

2005. Limited Edition, American mahogany body and neck, abalone sound hole rosette, pearl diamond inlays, gold tuners.

2005		$1,375	$1,750

512-NG Nanci Griffith

1996-1997. 512ce with sunburst finish.

1996-1997		$1,875	$2,500

514 Series

1990-present. Grand Auditorium, mahogany back and sides, Engelmann or Sitka spruce top. Western red cedar top on 514c and ce. Non-cut offered again in '13-'16 along with 514e version. V-Class introduced '20.

1990-1998	514	$1,500	$1,875
1996-1998	514c	$1,625	$2,000
1998-2024	514ce	$1,750	$2,250

515-LTD

1981. Limited Edition, mahogany back and sides, black binding, tortoise 'guard.

1981		$1,500	$1,875

Taylor 414ce

Taylor 514ce

GUITARS

Taylor 552ce

Taylor 618e

MODEL YEAR	FEATURES	EXC. COND. LOW	HIGH

516 Series

2008-2019. Grand Symphony, mahogany back and sides, Engelmann spruce top. Non-cut 516 offered in '13 along with 516e version.

2008-2019	516ce	$1,625	$2,000

516ce-LTD

2010. Spring Limited Editions, Tasmanian blackwood back and sides, Sitka spruce top.

2010		$2,250	$3,000

518 Series

2012-2014. Grand Orchestra, tropical mahogany back and sides, Sitka spruce top, tortoise 'guard.

2012-2014	518/518e	$1,500	$1,875

522 Series

2013-2023. Grand Concert, all tropical mahogany. V-Class introduced '20.

2013-2018	522	$1,500	$1,875
2013-2019	522e	$1,500	$1,875
2013-2023	522ce	$1,625	$2,000

524ce-LTD

2018. Grand Auditorium, all walnut.

2018		$2,125	$2,750

554 Series

2004-2005. Grand Auditorium 12-string, mahogany.

2004-2005	554	$1,875	$2,500

555 Series

1978-2006. Jumbo 12-string, mahogany back and sides, Sitka spruce top, higher-end appointments.

1994-2006	555	$1,500	$1,875
1994-2006	555ce	$1,750	$2,250

562 Series

2019-2022. Grand Concert 12-strings, V-Class bracing, mahogany top.

2019-2022	562ce	$1,750	$2,250

610 Series

1978-2017. Dreadnought, big leaf maple back and sides, Sitka spruce top. Non-cut offered again in '13 along with 610e version.

1978-1998	610	$1,750	$2,250
1998-2017	610ce	$2,000	$2,500
2013-2017	610e	$1,875	$2,500

612 Series

1984-present. Grand Concert, big leaf maple back and sides, Sitka spruce top. Non-cut offered again in '13 along with 612e version. V-Class introduced '20.

1984-1998	612	$1,750	$2,250
1998-2024	612ce	$2,000	$2,500
2013-2016	612e	$1,875	$2,500

614 Series

1978-present. Grand Auditorium, big leaf maple back and sides, Sitka spruce top. Non-cut offered again in '13 along with 614e version. V-Class introduced '20.

1978-1998	614	$1,750	$2,250
1998-2024	614ce	$2,000	$2,500
2013-2016	614e	$1,875	$2,500

615 Series

1981-2011. Jumbo, big leaf maple back and sides, Sitka spruce top.

1981-1998	615	$1,750	$2,250
1981-1998	615e	$1,875	$2,500
1998-2011	615ce	$2,000	$2,500

MODEL YEAR	FEATURES	EXC. COND. LOW	HIGH

616 Series

2008-2019. Grand Symphony, big leaf maple back and sides, Sitka spruce top. Non-cut 616 offered in '13-'16 along with 616e version.

2008-2019	616ce	$2,250	$3,000
2013-2016	616e	$1,875	$2,500

618 Series

2013-present. Grand Orchestra, Sitka spruce top, big leaf maple back and sides.

2013-2024	618e	$2,000	$2,500

654 Series

2004-2011. Grand Auditorium 12-string, big leaf maple back and sides, Sitka spruce top.

2004-2011	654ce	$2,000	$2,500

655 Series

1978-1991, 1996-2011. Jumbo 12-string, big leaf maple back and sides, Sitka spruce top.

1978-2006	655	$1,750	$2,250
1998-2011	655ce	$2,125	$2,750

656 Series

2008-2019. Grand Symphony 12-string, big leaf maple back and sides.

2018-2019	656ce	$2,000	$2,500

710 Series

1977-2017. Dreadnought, Indian rosewood back and sides, Englemann or Sitka spruce top. Non-cut offered again in '13 along with 710e version.

1977-2006	710 (Spruce)	$1,625	$2,000
1990s	710-BR (Brazilian)	$2,625	$3,500
1998-2006	710 (Cedar)	$1,625	$2,000
1998-2017	710ce (Cedar)	$2,125	$2,750

710-B 25th Anniversary

1999. Limited Edition, 25th Anniversary on headstock, spruce top, abalone rosette, Brazilian rosewood sides and back, mahogany neck.

1999		$2,625	$3,250

710ce-L30

2004. Limited Edition 30th Anniversary, Englemann top, Indian rosewood body, 30th Anniversary inlay.

2004		$1,500	$1,875

712 Series

1984-2023. Grand Concert, Indian rosewood back and sides, Englemann or Sitka spruce top. Non-cut offered again in '13 along with 712e version. V-Class introduced '20.

1984-2006	712	$1,750	$2,250
2000-2023	712ce	$2,000	$2,500
2013-2019	712e	$1,875	$2,500

714 Series

1996-2023. Grand Auditorium, Indian rosewood back and sides, red cedar top. Non-cut offered again in '13-'16 along with 714e version. V-Class introduced '20.

1996-2006	714	$1,750	$2,250
1998-2019	714ce	$2,000	$2,500
2020-2023	714ce, V-Class	$2,125	$2,750

714-BRZ

1997. Brazilian rosewood, cedar, fancy.

1997		$4,000	$5,000

GUITARS

MODEL YEAR	FEATURES	EXC. COND. LOW	HIGH

714ce-L1

2003-2004. Limited Edition, Western red cedar top, grafted walnut sides and back, pearl inlay, Hawaiian Koa rosette.

2003-2004		$2,000	$2,500

714ce-S-LTD

2015. Limited Edition Grand Auditorium, Sitka spruce top, blackheart sassafras back and sides.

2015		$2,000	$2,500

716ce

2007-2019. Grand Symphony, lutz spruce, Indian rosewood.

2007-2019		$2,000	$2,500

716ce-LTD

2009. Limited Edition, Sitka spruce top, Madagascar rosewood back and sides.

2009		$2,000	$2,500

750

1990-2000s. Dreadnought 12-string, spruce top.

1990-2000s		$1,875	$2,500

755

1990-1998. Jumbo 12-string, rosewood back and sides.

1990-1998		$1,875	$2,500

810 Series

1975-2017. Classic Dreadnought, Indian rosewood back and sides, Sitka spruce top. Non-cut offered again in '13 along with 810e version.

1975-2006	810	$1,750	$2,250
1975-2006	810e	$1,875	$2,500
1993-1998	810c	$1,875	$2,500
1996-2016	810ce-BR (Brazilian)	$3,000	$3,750
1996-2017	810ce	$2,000	$2,500

810-L30

2004. Limited Edition 30th Anniversary, maple leaf inlays, sound hole rosette, 30th Anniversary logo.

2004		$2,125	$2,750

810ce-LTD

2010. Limited Edition, Venetian cutaway, Madagascar rosewood back and sides, solid Sitka spruce top.

2010		$2,375	$3,000

812 Series

1985, 1993-present. Grand Concert, Indian rosewood back and sides, Sitka spruce top. Non-cut offered again in '13-'16 along with 812e version. V-Class introduced '20.

1985	812	$1,750	$2,250
1993-1998	812c	$1,875	$2,500
1998-2019	812ce	$2,000	$2,500
2013-2016	812e	$1,875	$2,500
2019-2024	812ce V-Class	$2,500	$3,250

814 Series

1993-present. Grand Auditorium, Indian rosewood back and sides, Sitka spruce top. Non-cut offered again in '13 along with 814e version. V-Class introduced '20.

1993-1998	814	$2,250	$3,000
1996-1998	814c	$2,375	$3,000
1998-2019	814ce	$2,375	$3,000
2000	814-BE (Brazilian /Englemann)	$3,000	$3,750
2020-2024	814ce V-Class	$2,500	$3,250

814ce-LTD

2012. Spring Limited Edition, cocobolo back and sides, Sitka spruce top.

2012		$2,375	$3,000

815 Series

1970s-2011. Jumbo, Indian rosewood back and sides, Sitka spruce top.

1970s-2006	815	$2,125	$2,750
1993-1998	815c	$2,375	$3,000
1997	815c-BR (Brazilian)	$3,000	$3,750
1998-2011	815ce	$2,500	$3,250

816 Series

2008-2019. Grand Symphony, Sitka spruce top, Indian rosewood back and sides.

2008-2014	816e	$2,375	$3,000
2008-2019	816ce	$2,500	$3,250
2013-2016	816	$2,125	$2,750

818 Series

2014-present. Grand Orchestra, Sitka spruce, Indian rosewood. V-Class introduced '20.

2014-2019	818e	$2,375	$3,000

854ce-LTD

2002. Grand Auditorium 12-string, Indian rosewood back and sides, Sitka spruce top.

2002		$2,375	$3,000

855 Series

1981-2011. Jumbo 12-string, Indian rosewood back and sides, Sitka spruce top.

1981-2011	855	$1,875	$2,500
2004-2011	855ce	$2,125	$2,750

856 Series

2012-2019. Grand Symphony 12-string, Sitka spruce, Indian rosewood.

2012-2018	856e	$1,875	$2,500
2013-2019	856ce	$2,000	$2,500

910 Series

1977-2017. Dreadnought, maple back and sides, changed to Brazilian rosewood in '86, wide abalone-style rosette. Non-cut offered again in '13 along with 910e version, Indian rosewood back and sides, Sitka spruce top.

1977-1985	910 Maple	$2,750	$3,500
1986-2006	910 Brazilian	$5,250	$6,500
1998-2016	910ce	$3,125	$4,000

912 Series

1993-2024. Grand Concert, Indian rosewood back and sides, Engelmann spruce top, abalone. Non-cut offered in '13 along with 912e version. V-Class introduced '20.

1993-2002	912c	$2,875	$3,750
1993-2019	912ce	$3,000	$3,750
2020-2024	912ce V-Class	$3,250	$4,000

914 Series

1990s-2024. Grand Concert, Indian rosewood back and sides, Engelmann spruce top. Non-cut offered in '13 along with 914e version. V-Class introduced '20.

2002-2019	914ce	$3,000	$3,750
2020-2024	914ce V-Class	$3,250	$4,000

914ce-L1

2003. Fall Limited Edition, Indian rosewood back and sides, Engelmann spruce top, abalone leaf and vine inlays.

2003		$2,875	$3,750

2000 Taylor 814ce
Cream City Music

2003 Taylor 910
Cream City Music

GUITARS

Taylor AD27e

Taylor Builder's Edition 652ce

MODEL YEAR	FEATURES	EXC. COND. LOW	HIGH

914ce-L7

2004. Sitka spruce top, Brazilian rosewood back and sides, abalone rosette.

2004		$4,750	$6,000

916 Series

2010-2019. Grand Symphony, Florentine cutaway, Indian rosewood back and sides.

2010-2019	916ce	$2,875	$3,750

918 Series

2013-2014. Grand Orchestra, Sitka spruce top, Indian rosewood back and sides.

2013-2014	918e	$2,875	$3,750

955

1996-2000. Jumbo 12 string, rosewood back and sides, spruce top.

1996-2000		$2,875	$3,750

Academy Series

2017-present. Designed for beginner guitar players, 10 is D-size and 12 is 000-size, e indicates on-board electronics.

2017-2024	10	$375	$500
2017-2024	10e	$400	$500
2017-2024	12e	$400	$500
2017-2024	12e-N	$400	$500

American Dream Series (AD)

2020-present. Grand Pacific body style, wood pairings include sapele/mahogany and ovangkol/spruce, V-Class bracing, e indicates on-board electronics.

2020-2024	AD17	$850	$1,125
2020-2024	AD17e	$1,000	$1,250
2020-2024	AD27e	$1,000	$1,250
2020-2023	AD28e	$1,000	$1,250

Baby Taylor

1996-present. 3/4-size Dreadnought, mahogany laminated back and sides until '99, sapele laminate after, various tops.

1996-2024	BT1, Sitka spruce	$225	$300
1998-2024	BT2, mahogany	$225	$300
2000-2003	BT3, maple	$225	$300
2010-2024	TSBT Taylor Swift	$225	$300
2016-2024	BTe-Koa	$275	$350

Baby Rosewood

2000-2003. Laminated Indian rosewood back and sides Baby.

2000-2003		$225	$300

Baritone 6

2010-2013. Grand Symphony 6-string baritone, Indian rosewood or mahogany back and sides.

2010-2013		$2,125	$2,750

Baritone 8/GT-8 Baritone

2010-2013. Grand Symphony 8-string baritone, Indian rosewood or mahogany back and sides.

2010-2013		$2,500	$3,250

Big Baby BBT

2000-present. 15/16-size Dreadnought, sapele laminate back and sides, Sitka spruce top.

2000-2024		$300	$375

Builder's Edition

2018-present. New designs from master builders, premium features. All models have 'Builder's Edition' in the model name.

MODEL YEAR	FEATURES	EXC. COND. LOW	HIGH
2019-2024	517	$2,125	$2,750
2019-2024	717	$2,125	$2,750
2020-2024	324ce	$2,000	$2,500
2020-2024	614ce	$2,750	$3,500
2020-2024	652ce	$2,750	$3,500
2020-2024	816ce	$2,625	$3,250
2020-2024	K-14ce Koa, vine inlay	$3,500	$4,500
2020-2024	K-24ce Koa	$3,500	$4,500

Builder's Reserve (BR)

A series of special limited guitars built using Taylor's private wood reserves accumulated 30-plus years.

2008	BR VII	$2,125	$2,750

CPSM Chris Proctor Signature

2000-2001. Limited edition, 100 made, Indian rosewood body, Engelmann spruce top.

2000-2001		$1,875	$2,500

CUJO-10/CUJO-14

1997. Dreadnought (CUJO-10) or Grand Auditorium (CUJO-14), made from 100+ year old black walnut tree appearing in famous Stephen King movie "Cujo" (1983). Robert Taylor purchased the tree when it was dying of old age. The DN has spruce top, GA has cedar, both have elaborate appointments and are signed by Taylor and King. Only 125 made of each.

1997		$1,625	$2,000

Custom Shop

2008-present. Custom shop models - some are one-offs, others are series ordered by specific dealers. Previously called Taylor's Build To Order program.

Custom Dreadnought/Custom DN

2008-2017	AA+ Indian/ Adirondack	$2,625	$3,250

Custom Grand Auditorium

2008-2017	Adirondack/ mahogany	$3,000	$3,750
2008-2024	Figured Koa	$4,000	$5,000
2008-2024	Spruce/maple	$3,250	$4,000

Custom Grand Concert

2008-2017	Various woods	$3,250	$4,000

Custom TF

2011. Acoustic-electric, slotted headstock, rosewood, Taylor Build To Order program.

2011		$2,625	$3,500

DCSM Dan Crary Signature

1986-2000. Dreadnought, Venetian cutaway, thin spruce top, Indian rosewood back and sides, Crary signature on headstock.

1986-2000		$1,750	$2,250

DDAD Doyle Dykes Signature Anniversary

2005. Indian rosewood back and sides, soft cutaway, on-board transducer.

2005		$2,875	$4,000

DDSM Doyle Dykes Signature

2000-2012. Grand auditorium cutaway acoustic/ electric, figured maple body.

2000-2012		$2,875	$4,000

MODEL YEAR	FEATURES	EXC. COND. LOW	HIGH

DDSM-LTD Doyle Dykes Desert Rose Edition

2000-2003. Grand Auditorium, Limited Edition, 72 offered, Sitka spruce, flamed maple, on-board electronics.

2000-2003		$3,000	$3,750

DMSM Dave Matthews Signature

2010-2012. Limited Edition based on 914ce, Taylor Expression pickup system.

2010-2012		$4,000	$5,000

DN Series

2007-2012. Dreadnought Series, various woods.

2007-2011	DNK (Koa)	$1,875	$2,500
2007-2012	DN3	$850	$1,125
2007-2012	DN5	$1,375	$1,750
2007-2012	DN8	$1,375	$1,750

E14ce Limited Edition

2018-2019. Grand Auditorium, Venetian cutaway, V-Class bracing, spruce top, African ebony back and sides, natural finish.

2018-2019		$2,125	$2,750

GA Limited Editions

1995. Grand Auditorium Limited Editions. GA-BE has Brazilian rosewood back and sides with Engelmann spruce top, KC has Koa/cedar, KS Koa/spruce, MC mahogany/cedar, RS Indian rosewood/spruce, and WS walnut/spruce.

1995	GABE (Brazilian)	$4,250	$5,250
1995	GAKC (Koa)	$2,875	$3,500
1995	GAMC (Cedar)	$2,250	$3,000
1995	GARS (Indian)	$2,250	$3,000
1995	GAWS (Walnut)	$2,500	$3,250

GA Series

2007-2012. Grand Auditorium Series, various woods.

2007-2012	GA3, Sitka/sapele	$850	$1,125
2007-2012	GA3-12	$850	$1,125
2007-2012	GA4, Sitka/ovangkol	$950	$1,250
2007-2012	GA5, cedar/ mahogany	$1,375	$1,750
2007-2012	GA6, Sitka/ flamed maple	$1,375	$1,750
2007-2012	GA6-12	$1,375	$1,750
2007-2012	GA7, cedar/ rosewood	$1,375	$1,750
2007-2012	GA8, Sitka/ rosewood	$1,375	$1,750
2008-2012	GA-K-12, cedar/Koa	$2,125	$2,750
2012	GACE (Fall LE)	$2,000	$2,500
2013	GAMC (Fall LE)	$2,000	$2,500

GC Series

2007-2012. Grand Concert Series, various woods.

2007-2012	GC3, Sitka/sapele	$850	$1,125
2007-2012	GC4, Sitka/ovangkol	$950	$1,250
2007-2012	GC5, cedar/ mahogany	$1,375	$1,750
2007-2012	GC6, Sitka/maple	$1,375	$1,750
2007-2012	GC7, cedar/ rosewood	$1,375	$1,750
2007-2012	GC8, Sitka/ rosewood	$1,375	$1,750
2011	GC-LTD, all mahogany	$1,375	$1,750

MODEL YEAR	FEATURES	EXC. COND. LOW	HIGH

GS Series

2006-present. Grand Symphony Series, various woods.

2007	GS4E-LTD	$1,500	$1,875
2007-2012	GS3, Sitka/sapele	$900	$1,125
2007-2012	GS5, cedar/ mahogany	$1,500	$1,875
2007-2012	GS5-12, cedar/ mahogany	$1,500	$1,875
2007-2012	GS6, Sitka/maple	$1,500	$1,875
2007-2012	GS7, cedar/ rosewood	$1,500	$1,875
2007-2012	GS8, Sitka/ rosewood	$1,500	$1,875
2007-2012	GS8-12, Sitka/ rosewood	$1,500	$1,875
2011-2024	GS Mini	$375	$475
2019-2024	GS Mini-e Koa	$550	$700
2019-2024	GS Mini-e Mahogany	$475	$600
2019-2024	GS Mini-e Plus	$650	$825

GT Series

2020-2024. Grand Theater Series, various woods, e indicates on-board electronics.

2020-2024	GT, Sitka/ash	$875	$1,125
2020-2022	GT811e, Sitka/ Indian	$2,125	$2,625
2020-2024	GTe, Sitka/ash	$1,125	$1,500
2020-2022	GTK21e, all Koa	$3,125	$4,000

Hot Rod Limited Edition HR14-LTD/HR15-LTD

2003. Grand Auditorium (HR14) or Jumbo (HR15), 32 of each made, natural finish with red-stained back and sides or gloss black with transparent black.

2003		$2,250	$3,000

K Series

1983-present. Koa Series, various models with Hawaiian Koa. V-Class introduced '20.

1983-1992	K20	$2,000	$2,500
1983-2006	K10	$1,875	$2,500
1992-2002	K20c	$2,125	$2,750
1995-1998	K65, 12-string	$2,750	$3,500
1998-2000	K22	$2,125	$2,750
1998-2002	K14c	$1,875	$2,500
1998-2012	K14ce	$1,875	$2,500
2001-2006	K55, 12-string	$2,375	$3,000
2001-2016	K20ce	$2,375	$3,000
2003-2024	K22ce	$2,375	$3,000
2007-2011	K54ce	$2,750	$3,500
2007-2012	K10ce	$1,875	$2,500
2007-2023	K24ce	$2,500	$3,250
2008-2022	K26ce	$2,500	$3,250
2020-2024	K24ce V-Class	$2,625	$3,250

LKSM-6/12 Leo Kottke Signature

1981-2012. Jumbo 17" body, 6- or 12-string, rounded cutaway, Sitka spruce top, mahogany back and sides, gloss finish, Leo Kottke signature.

1981-2012	12-string	$2,375	$3,000
1981-2012	6-string	$2,375	$3,000

Taylor GT K21e

Taylor K24ce

Taylor T-5
Charlie Brown

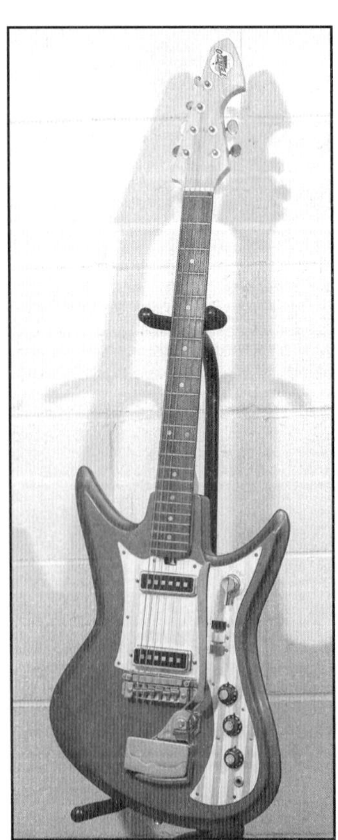

Teisco Del Rey ET-230
Tom Pfeifer

MODEL YEAR	FEATURES	EXC. COND. LOW	HIGH

LTG Liberty Tree L.E.

2002. Limited Edition includes DVD and certificate which are important to instrument's value, solid wood grand concert body, high-end art and appointments. Around 400 made.

2002		$5,250	$6,500

NS Series

2002-2011. Nylon Strung series, various models and woods, models include NS24e/NS24ce (Indian rosewood/spruce), NS32ce/NS34ce (mahogany/spruce), NS42ce/NS44ce (ovangkol), NS52ce/NS54ce (mahogany), NS62ce/NS64ce (maple/Engelmann) and NS72ce/NS74ce (Indian rosewood/cedar). All models were cutaway electric (ce) by '04, until '10 when NS24e was offered.

2002-2006	NS42ce	$850	$1,125
2002-2006	NS44/NS44ce	$1,000	$1,375
2002-2006	NS52ce	$1,000	$1,375
2002-2006	NS54ce	$1,125	$1,500
2002-2011	NS32ce	$850	$1,125
2002-2011	NS62ce	$1,500	$1,875
2002-2011	NS64ce	$1,500	$1,875
2002-2011	NS72ce	$1,625	$2,000
2002-2011	NS74/NS74ce	$1,875	$2,500
2004-2011	NS34ce	$850	$1,125
2010-2011	NS24e/NS24ce	$600	$800

PS Series

1996-present. Presentation Series, various models, Hawaiian Koa with Engelmann spruce used early on, followed by Brazilian rosewood, by '07 a variety of woods were offered, values vary depending on specs and appointments.

1996-2024	Various options	$4,500	$10,000

Solidbody Classic

2008-2014. Single- or double-cut, ash body, 2 humbuckers or single-coils, pearl 'guard.

2008-2014		$850	$1,000

Solidbody Custom

2008-2010. Single- or double-cut, Koa top with Tasmanian blackwood body in '08 and mahogany after or walnut top with sapele body, 2 humbuckers, diamond inlays, ivoroid binding.

2008-2010		$1,375	$1,750

Solidbody Standard

2008-2014. Single- or double-cut, Tamo ash top ('08-'09) and maple after, sapele body (08-'10) and mahogany after, 2 exposed coil humbuckers, ivoroid binding.

2008-2014		$750	$950

T3 Series

2009-2020. Semi-hollow thinline, single-cut, figured maple. T3/B with Bigsby.

2009-2020	T3, T3/B	$1,875	$2,500

T5/T5z Series

2005-present. T5 '05-'19 and T5z introduced '20, semi-hollow thinline body, sapele back and sides, spruce, maple, or Koa tops, Custom models have gold hardware and Artist inlays, Standard is chrome with micro-dots. Prices will vary depending on type of figured-wood used, figured maple and Koa will be more than plain tops.

2005-2020	12-string	$1,875	$2,500
2005-2024	6-string	$1,875	$2,500

MODEL YEAR	FEATURES	EXC. COND. LOW	HIGH

Walnut/W Series

1998-2006. Highly figured claro walnut backs and sides with spruce, cedar, or walnut tops. Ivoroid, ebony, gold and abalone accents.

1998-2000	W12c	$1,875	$2,500
1998-2006	W10	$1,875	$2,500
2000-2006	W14ce	$1,875	$2,500

WHCM Windham Hill

2003. Commemorative Model, D-size, spruce top, rosewood sides and back, fancy appointments with Windham Hill logo inlay.

2003		$1,875	$2,500

XX 20th Anniversary Series

1994. Limited Edition, grand auditorium, "XX" solid 18 karat gold inlay, mother-of-pearl inlay, abalone rosette, available either mahogany back and sides with cedar top (XX-MC) or Indian rosewood with spruce (XX-RS).

1994	XX-MC	$2,500	$3,500
1994	XX-RS	$2,500	$3,500

XXV 25th Anniversary

1999-2000. Dreadnought (XXV-DR) and grand auditorium (XXV-GA) models, various woods.

1999-2000	Both models	$1,875	$2,500

XXX 30th Anniversary Series

2004-2005. Limited Edition, grand concert, "XXX" solid 18 karat gold inlay, fancy appointments, XXX-BE has Brazilian rosewood back and sides with Engelmann spruce top, KE has Koa/Engelmann spruce, MS maple/spruce and RS Indian rosewood/spruce.

2004-2005	XXX-BE	$4,000	$5,000
2004-2005	XXX-KE	$2,500	$3,250
2004-2005	XXX-MS	$2,375	$3,000
2004-2005	XXX-RS	$2,375	$3,000

XXXV 35th Anniversary Series

2009. Limited Edition, various models and woods, "35" between the 11th and 12th frets. Models include DN (Dreadnought), GC (Grand Concert), GS (Grand Symphony), P (Parlor), TF (12-Fret), 9-string, plus more.

2009	All models	$2,375	$3,000

Taylor/R. Taylor Guitars

2006-2011. Bob Taylor set up the R. Taylor studio with a small group of elite luthiers to handcraft a limited amount of guitars each year, using higher grade materials and offered in a few body styles - essentially custom made models. Each style has a number of options.

Style 1

2006-2009	Various options	$2,500	$3,500

Teisco

Founded in 1946 in Tokyo, Japan by Hawaiian and Spanish guitarist Atswo Kaneko and electrical engineer Doryu Matsuda, the original company name was Aoi Onpa Kenkyujo; Teisco was the instrument name. Most imported into U.S. by Jack Westheimer beginning ca. '60 and Chicago's W.M.I. Corporation beginning around '64, some early ones for New York's Bugeleisen and Jacobson. Brands made by the company include Teisco, Teisco Del Rey, Kingston, World Teisco, Silvertone, Kent, Kimberly and Heit Deluxe.

In '56, the company's name was changed to Nippon Onpa Kogyo Co., Ltd., and in '64 the name changed again to Teisco Co., Ltd. In January '67, the company was purchased by Kawai. After '73, the brand was converted to Kay in U.S.; Teisco went into hiatus in Japan until being beifly revived in the early-'90s with plexiglas reproductions of the Spectrum 5 (not available in U.S.). Some older Teisco Del Rey stock continued to be sold in U.S. through the '70s.

Electric

MODEL YEAR	FEATURES	EXC. COND. LOW	HIGH
1966-1969	1 pickup	$300	$800
1966-1969	2 pickups	$400	$1,200
1966-1969	3 pickups	$600	$1,800
1966-1969	4 pus or sparkle	$800	$3,000
1966-1969	Spectrum V	$1,500	$3,500
1968-1969	May Queen, black	$1,200	$3,000
1968-1969	May Queen, red	$1,200	$3,000
1968-1969	Phantom	$800	$2,000

Tele-Star

1965-ca.1972. Imported from Japan by Tele-Star Musical Instrument Corporation of New York, New York. Primarily made by Kawai, many inspired by Burns designs, some in cool sparkle finishes. They also built basses.

Electric

MODEL YEAR	FEATURES	EXC. COND. LOW	HIGH
1966-1969	1, 2, 3 pickups	$300	$800
1966-1969	4 pus or sparkle	$800	$3,000
1966-1969	Amp-in-case	$500	$1,500
1969-1970	Double neck 6/4	$1,500	$4,000

Tempo

1950s-1970s. Solid and semi-hollow body electric and acoustic guitars, most likely imported by Merson Musical Products from Japan. They also offered basses and amps.

Terada

Japanese guitar manufacturer began producing semi-acoustic and acoustic guitars in the year 1912. They have made guitars for Ibanez, Orville by Gibson, Epiphone Japan, Gretsch, and other well-known brands. At their peak (late '70s to early '90s), they were producing around 10,000 guitars a month using 3 factories.

Teuffel

1988-present. Luthier Ulrich Teuffel builds his production/custom, premium and presentation grade electric solidbody guitars in Neu-Ulm, Bavaria, Germany.

Texas

1959-ca. 1965. Line of aluminum neck electric solidbodies and basses made by France's Jacobacci company, which also built under its own brand. One, two, or three pickups.

Teye

2006-present. Luthier Teye Wijterp builds his premium and presentation grade, production/custom, solid and chambered body guitars in Austin, Texas. Some instruments are branded as Electric Gypsy guitars.

Thomas

1960s-1970s. Single, double and triple-neck electrics made by luthier Harvey Thomas in Midway, Washington. Best known for his Maltese cross shaped models, he also offered several other unique shaped designs and one-offs.

Thomas Rein

1972-present. Luthier Thomas Rein builds his premium grade, production/custom, classical guitars in St. Louis, Missouri.

Thompson Guitars

1980-2023. Luthier Ted Thompson built his professional and premium grade, production/custom, flat-top, 12-string, and nylon-string guitars in Vernon, British Columbia. He died in '23.

Thorell Fine Guitars

1994-present. Premium grade, custom/production, archtop, flattop and classical guitars built by luthier Ryan Thorell in Logan, Utah.

Thorn Custom Guitars

2000-present. Professional and premium grade, custom/production, solid and hollowbody electrics built by luthiers Bill Thorn and his sons Bill, Jr. and Ron in Glendale, California. They started Thorn Custom Inlay in the early '90s to do custom inlay work for other builders. In '00, they added their own line of guitars.

Thornward

Ca. 1901-ca. 1910. Line of guitars sold by the Montgomery Ward company and built by others including Lyon & Healy. The name is from a combination of the last names of company founder Aaron Montgomery Ward and company manager George Thorne.

Threet Guitars

1990-present. Premium grade, production/custom, flat-tops built by luthier Judy Threet in Calgary, Alberta.

Tilton

1850s-late 1800s. Built by William B. Tilton, of New York City, New York. He was quite an innovator and held several guitar-related patents. He also built banjos.

Parlor

1850s-1890s. Parlor guitar with various woods.

MODEL YEAR	FEATURES	EXC. COND. LOW	HIGH
1850s-80s	Brazilian, fancy binding	$2,000	$3,000

Ca. 1970s Teisco ET-110
Jim Edwards

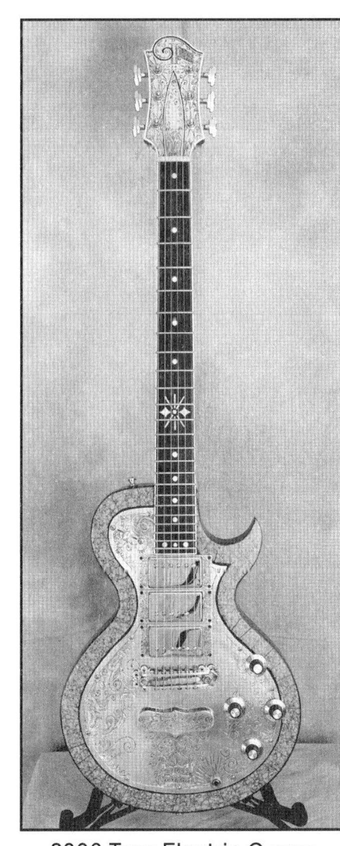

2006 Teye Electric Gypsy

GUITARS

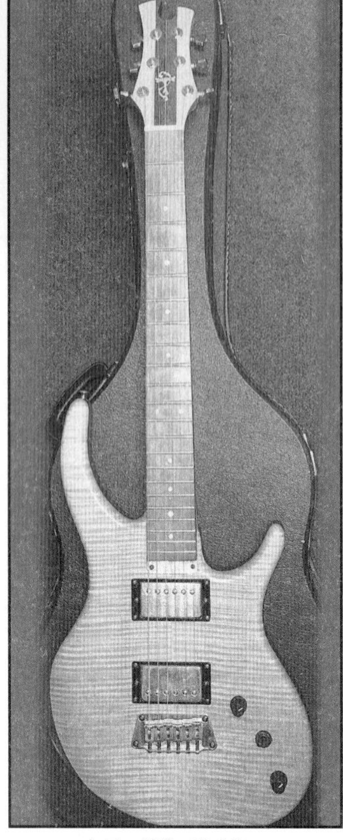

Late-'90s Tobias
Greg Perrine

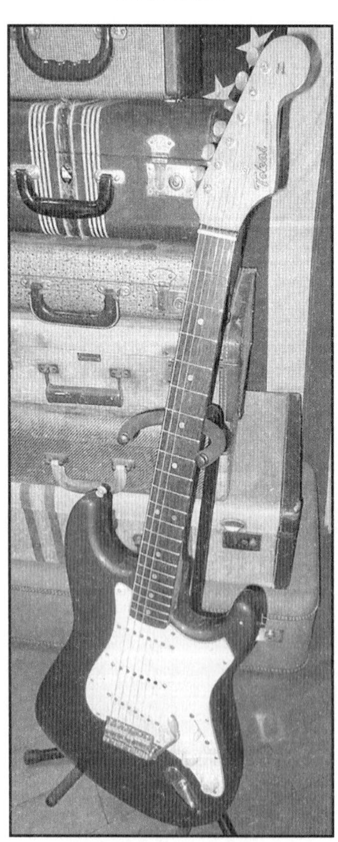

1983 Tokai Goldstar
Rivington Guitars

MODEL YEAR	FEATURES	EXC. COND. LOW	HIGH
1890s	Diagonal grain spruce, Brazilian	$1,800	$2,800
1890s	Pearl trim, Brazilian	$3,000	$4,500
1890s	Standard grain spruce, Brazilian	$850	$1,200

Tim Reede Custom Guitars

2004-present. Luthier Tim Reede builds his professional and premium grade, production/custom, archtop, flat-top and electric guitars in Minneapolis, Minnesota.

Timeless Instruments

1980-present. Luthier David Freeman builds his professional, premium and presentation grade, custom, flattop, 12-string, nylon-string, and resonator guitars in Tugaske, Saskatchewan. He also builds mandolins and dulcimers.

Timm Guitars

Professional grade, custom, flat-top, resonator and travel guitars built by luthier Jerry Timm in Auburn, Washington. He started in 1997.

Timtone Custom Guitars

1993-2006. Luthier Tim Diebert built his premium grade, custom, solidbody, chambered-body and acoustic guitars and basses in Grand Forks, British Columbia. He also built lap steels.

Tippin Guitar Co.

1978-present. Professional, premium and presentation grade, production/custom, flat-top guitars built by luthier Bill Tippin in Marblehead, Massachusetts.

Tobias

1977-2019. Known mainly for basses, Tobias did offer guitar models in the '80s. See Bass Section for more company info.

TogaMan GuitarViol

2003-present. Premium grade, production/custom, bow-playable solidbody guitars built by luthier Jonathan Wilson in Sylmar, California.

Tokai

1947-present. Japan's Tokai Company started out making a keyboard harmonica that was widely used in Japanese schools. In '65, they started producing acoustic guitars, followed shortly by electrics. In the late '60s, Tokai hooked up with Tommy Moore, a successful instrument merchandiser from Fort Worth, Texas, and by '70 they were producing private label and OEM guitars, sold in the U.S. under the brands of various importers. By the '70s, the Tokai name was being used on the instruments. In 2021, Tokai was acquired by Grace Company, LTD and continues to offer electrics, acoustics, and electric basses made in Japan and Korea.

MODEL YEAR	FEATURES	EXC. COND. LOW	HIGH

ASD-403 Custom Edition

1980s. Strat copy, single-single-hum pickups, locking tremolo.

1980s		$1,000	$2,500

AST Series

Early 1980s. Strat copies, maple board (AST-56) or slab rosewood (AST-62), 3 single-coils.

1980s	AST-56	$800	$1,800
1980s	AST-62	$900	$2,000

ATE Series

Early 1980s. Tele copies, blond (ATE-52) and pink paisley (ATE-67), 2 single-coils.

1980s	ATE-52	$600	$1,200
1980s	ATE-67	$700	$1,500

Blazing Fire

1982-1984. Hybrid-shaped solidbody with 2 medium-short pointy horns, cast aluminum body.

1982-1984		$800	$2,000

Breezy Sound

1977-1984. Copy of '60s rosewood board Tele.

1977-1984		$500	$1,500

CE-180W Cat's Eyes

Late-1970s-Early-1980s. D-style flat-top, made by Tokai Gakki, Nyatoh sides and back.

1979-1980s		$300	$600

CE-250 Cat's Eyes

Late-1970s-Early-1980s. D-style flat-top.

1979-1980s		$400	$800

CE-300 Cat's Eyes

Late-1970s-Early-1980s. D-style flat-top, made by Tokai Gakki, rosewood sides and back.

1979-1980s		$500	$1,000

CE-400 Cat's Eyes

Late-1970s-Early-1980s. D-style flat-top, made by Tokai Gakki, rosewood sides and back.

1979-1980s		$600	$1,200

CE-600 Cat's Eyes

1979-1980. D-style flat-top, rosewood sides and back.

1979-1980		$800	$1,500

FV48

1980s. Flying V copy.

1980s		$1,000	$2,500

Goldstar Sound

1984. Replica that replaced the Springy Sound, new less pointy headstock shape.

1984		$800	$2,000

J-200N

1979-1980. Gibson J-200 natural copy.

1979-1980		$600	$1,200

Les Paul Reborn

1976-1985. LP copy with Gibson-style Tokai headstock logo and Les Paul Reborn script logo instead of Les Paul Model, renamed Reborn Old in '82, becomes Love Rock in mid-'80s.

1976-1982	Les Paul Reborn	$1,000	$3,000
1982-1985	Reborn Old	$1,200	$3,500

Love Rock/LS Series

1980s-2000s. Various LP Std copy models (LC are LP Custom copies), 2 humbuckers, sunburst, gold top, black, figured tops at the high end, Love Rock in script logo on headstock.

MODEL YEAR	FEATURES	EXC. COND. LOW	HIGH
1980s		$800	$2,500
2003	LS 75 Love Rock	$600	$1,200
2003	LS 80 Love Rock	$700	$1,500

SC Series

Tele copies.

MODEL YEAR	FEATURES	LOW	HIGH
2000s	SC-1	$300	$700

Silver Star

1977-1984. Copy of post-CBS large headstock Strat.

MODEL YEAR	FEATURES	LOW	HIGH
1977-1984		$500	$1,200

Springy Sound/ST-60

1977-1984. Strat copy, original high-end nitro-finish.

MODEL YEAR	FEATURES	LOW	HIGH
1977-1979	With skunk stripe	$1,000	$2,500
1979-1984	No skunk stripe	$900	$2,000

Vintage Series EX-55

1980s. Vintage Series, Explorer copies, bolt neck, 1 or 2 humbuckers.

MODEL YEAR	FEATURES	LOW	HIGH
1980s	1 pickup	$500	$1,000
1980s	2 pickups	$600	$1,200

Vintage Series TST

Early-1980s. Copy of maple neck (TST-56) and rosewood slab board (TST-62) Strats, 4-bolt neck plate with serial number.

MODEL YEAR	FEATURES	LOW	HIGH
1980s	TST-56	$800	$1,800
1980s	TST-62	$900	$2,000

Tom Anderson Guitarworks

1984-present. Professional and premium grade, production/custom, solidbody, semi-solidbody and acoustic guitars built by luthier Tom Anderson in Newbury Park, California.

Solidbody Electric

1984-present. Various models.

MODEL YEAR	FEATURES	LOW	HIGH
1984-2024	Most models	$2,000	$3,000

TommyHawk

1993-2005. Acoustic travel guitars built by luthier Tom Barth in Succasunna, New Jersey. They also offered a full-scale acoustic/electric model. Barth died in '05.

Toneline

1950s. Student-level private brand built by Chicago builders (Kay, Harmony). Typical '50s Stella brand specs like birch body with painted binding and rosette, pointed Toneline script logo on headstock.

Tonemaster

1960s. Guitars and basses, made in Italy by the Crucianelli Company, with typical '60s Italian sparkle plastic finish and push-button controls, bolt-on neck. Imported into the U.S. by The Imperial Accordion Company. They also offered guitar amps.

Rhythm Tone

1960-1963. Tonemaster headstock logo, Rhythm Tone logo on 'guard, single neck pickup, 3-in-line control knobs, bolt-on neck, black finish.

MODEL YEAR	FEATURES	LOW	HIGH
1960-1963		$900	$1,200

ToneSmith

1997-present. Luthier Kevin Smith builds his professional and premium grade, production/custom, semi-hollow body guitars and basses in Rogers, Minnesota. He previously built GLF brand guitars and built the line of Vox USA guitars from '98-'01.

Tony Nobles

Professional and premium grade, custom, acoustic and electric guitars built by luthier Tony Nobles in Wimberley, Texas starting in 1990.

Tony Vines Guitars

Luthier Tony Vines began in 1989, builds premium and presentation grade, custom/production, steel string guitars in Kingsport, Tennessee.

Torres (Antonio de Torres Jurado)

19th Century luthier most often associated with the initial development of the Classical Spanish guitar.

Tosca

1950s. Private economy brand made by Valco, possibly for a jobber, mail-order catalog or local department store.

Bolero 1123

1954-1957. Small three-quarter size electric similar to National (Valco) model 1123, single-cut, 1 neck pickup, guard mounted controls.

MODEL YEAR	FEATURES	LOW	HIGH
1954-1957		$900	$1,400

Toyota

1972-1970s. Imported from Japan by Hershman of New York, New York. At least 1 high-end acoustic designed by T. Kurosawa was ambitiously priced at $650.

Traphagen, Dake

1972-present. Luthier Dake Traphagen builds his premium grade, custom, classical and steel-string guitars in Bellingham, Washington.

Traugott Guitars

1991-present. Premium grade, production/custom, flat-top and acoustic/electric guitars built by luthier Jeff Traugott in Santa Cruz, California.

Traveler Guitar

1992-present. Intermediate grade, production, travel size electric, acoustic, classical, and acoustic/electric guitars and basses made in Redlands, California.

Travis Bean

1974-1979, 1999. Aluminum-necked solidbody electric guitars and basses. The company was founded by motorcycle and metal-sculpture enthusiast Travis Bean and guitar repairman Marc McElwee in Southern California; soon joined by Gary Kramer (see Kramer guitars). Kramer left Travis Bean in '75 and founded Kramer guitars with other partners. Guitar production began in

Tom Anderson Hollow T

Curtis Hill

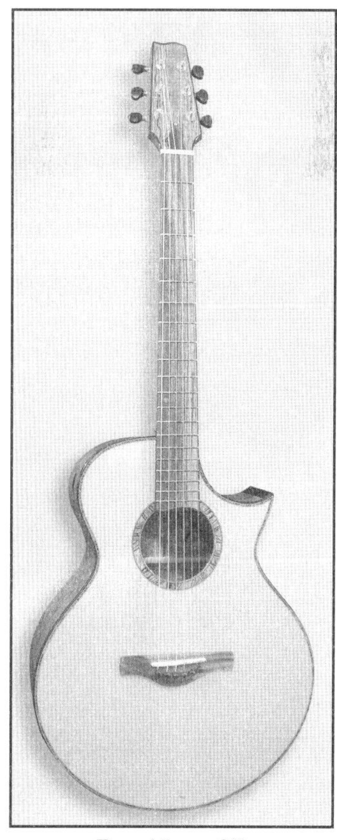

Tony Vines CX

Triggs Custom

TV Jones Spectra Sonic Supreme

MODEL YEAR	FEATURES	EXC. COND. LOW	HIGH

mid-'76. The guitars featured carved aluminum necks with three-and-three heads with a T cutout in the center and wooden 'boards. Some necks had bare aluminum backs; some were painted black. A total of about 3,650 instruments were produced. Travis Bean guitar production was stopped in the summer of '79.

Serial numbers were stamped on headstock and were more-or-less consecutive. Original retail prices were $895 to $1195.

The company announced renewed production in '99 with updated versions of original designs and new models, but it evidently never got going.

TB-500

1975-1976. Aluminum neck, T-slotted headstock, double-cut, 2 single coils mounted in 'guard, 2 controls, dot markers, white.

1975-1976		$7,000	$10,000

TB-1000 Artist

1974-1979. Aluminum neck, T-slotted headstock, double-cut archtop, 2 humbuckers, 4 controls, block inlays.

1974-1979		$7,500	$12,000
1974-1979	Rare colors	$9,000	$13,500

TB-1000 Standard

1974-1979. Similar to TB-1000 Artist, but with dot inlays.

1974-1979		$8,500	$12,500

TB-3000 Wedge

1976-1979. Aluminum neck with T-slotted headstock, triangle-shaped body, 2 humbucking pickups, 4 controls, block markers on 'board.

1976-1979		$11,500	$15,000

Tregan Guitars

2007-present. Solidbody electrics including Bison-style sharp curved horns body style, plus other less traditional styles, student and intermediate grade.

Tremblett Archtops

Luthier Mark Tremblett started in the year 2006, he builds professional grade, custom, archtop guitars in Pouch Cove, Newfoundland.

Tremcaster

Luthier John Mosconi, along with Robert Gelley and Jeff Russell, started in 2008, build professional grade, production/custom, electric and acoustic guitars in Akron, Ohio.

Trenier

1998-present. Premium grade, production/custom, archtop guitars built by luthier Bryant Trenier in Seattle, Washington. From '02 to '04 he was located in Prague, Czech Republic.

Triggs

1992-present. Luthiers Jim Triggs and his son Ryan build their professional and premium grade, production/custom, archtop, flat-top, and solidbody guitars originally in Nashville Tennessee, and, since '98, in Kansas City, Kansas. They also build mandolins.

Acoustic/Electric Archtop

1992-present. Various archtop cutaway models.

1992-2009	Byrdland 17"	$4,000	$8,000
1992-2009	Excel 17"	$3,500	$7,500
1992-2009	Jazzmaster	$4,000	$8,500
1992-2009	New Yorker 18"	$5,000	$10,000
1992-2010	Stromberg Master 400	$6,000	$12,000
1997	Trinity 18"	$5,500	$11,000
2006	San Salvador	$3,500	$7,500

Trinity River

Located in Fort Worth, Texas, luthiers Marcus Lawyer and Ross McLeod import their production/custom, budget and intermediate grade, acoustic and resonator guitars and basses from Asia. They started in 2004 and also import mandolins and banjos.

True North Guitars

1994-present. Luthier Dennis Scannell builds his premium grade, custom, flat-tops in Waterbury, Vermont.

True Tone

1960s. Guitars, basses and amps retailed by Western Auto, manufactured by Chicago guitar makers like Kay. The brand was most likely gone by '68.

Double Cutaway (K300 Kay)

1962-1966. Made by Kay and similar to their K300, double-cut solidbody, dual pickups and vibrola arm, red.

1962-1966		$500	$800

Double Cutaway Electric Archtop (K592 Kay)

1960s. Made by Kay and similar to their K592 double-cut thinline acoustic, 2 pickups, Bigsby tailpiece, burgundy red.

1960s		$550	$900

Fun Time

Early- to mid-1960s. Student 13" flat-top, painted 5-point 'guard, red sunburst finish.

1960s		$95	$200

Imperial Deluxe

Mid-1960s. Harmony-made (Rocket), 3 pickups, trapeze tailpiece, 6 control knobs, block markers, sunburst.

1960s		$650	$1,000

Jazz King (K573 Kay)

1960s. Kay's K573 Speed Demon, 3 pickups, thinline archtop electric with f-hole, eighth note art on 'guard, sunburst.

1960s		$500	$800

Rock 'n Roll Electric (K100 Kay)

1960s. Kay's K100, slab body, single pickup, but with a bright red multiple lacquer finish.

1960s		$400	$600

MODEL YEAR	FEATURES	EXC. COND. LOW	HIGH

Speed Master (K6533 Kay)

1960s. Made by Kay and similar to their K6533 full-body electric archtop Value Leader line, eighth note art 'guard, sunburst.

1960s		$400	$600

Western Spanish Auditorium

Early- to mid-1960s. 15" flat-top, laminate construction, celluloid 'guard, sunburst.

1960s		$150	$250

Tsunami

Custom, intermediate grade, one-off solidbody electric guitars built by luthier Paul Brzozowski, starting in 2009, in Cleveland, Tennessee.

Tucker

Founded by John N. "Jack" Tucker, John Morrall, and David Killingsworth in 2000, Tucker builds professional and premium grade, production/custom, albizzia wood solidbody guitars and basses in Hanalei, Hawaii.

Tuscany Guitars

2008-2013. Intermediate grade, production, classic model electric guitars imported from Asia and finished by luthier Galeazzo Frudua in San Lazzaro di Savena, Italy.

Tut Taylor

Line of professional and premium grade, production/custom, resophonic guitars built by luthier Mark Taylor of Crafters of Tennessee in Old Hickory, Tennessee. Brand named for his father, dobro artist Tut Taylor. Taylor also builds the Tennessee line of guitars, mandolins and banjos and was part of Rich and Taylor guitars for '93-'96.

TV Jones

1993-present. Professional and premium grade, production/custom, hollow, chambered, and solid body guitars built by luthier Thomas Vincent Jones originally in California, now in Poulsbo, Washington. The instruments have either Jones or TV Jones inlaid on the headstock. He also builds pickups.

U. A. C.

1920s. Instruments built by the Oscar Schmidt Co. and possibly others. Most likely a brand made for a distributor.

Unique Guitars

2003-ca. 2007. Professional and premium grade, production/custom, solidbody guitars and basses built by luthier Joey Rico in California. Joey is the son of Bernie Rico, the founder of BC Rich guitars.

Univox

1964-1978. Univox started out as an amp line and added guitars around '68. Guitars were imported from Japan by the Merson Musical Supply Company, later Unicord, Westbury, New York. Many if not all supplied by Arai and Company (Aria, Aria Pro II), some made by Matsumoku. Univox Lucy ('69) first copy of lucite Ampeg Dan Armstrong. Generally mid-level copies of American designs.

MODEL YEAR	FEATURES	EXC. COND. LOW	HIGH

Acoustic Flat-Top

1969-1978. Various models.

1970s		$200	$300

Bicentennial

1976. Offset double-cut, heavily carved body, brown stain, 3 humbucker-style pickups.

1976		$1,000	$1,500

Deep Body Electric

1960s-70s	ES-175 style	$600	$900

GuitOrgan FSB C-3000

1970s. Double-cut semi-hollow body, multiple controls, GuitOrgan logo on headstock, foot pedal.

1970s	Fully functional	$1,200	$1,800

Solid Body Electric

1960s-1970s. Includes Flying V, Mosrite and Hofner violin-guitar copies.

1960s-70s	Hi Flier	$800	$1,200
1960s-70s	Various models	$700	$1,000
1970s	Effector	$600	$900

Thin Line (Coily)

1960s-70s	12-string	$500	$800
1960s-70s	6-string	$500	$800

USA Custom Guitars

1999-2020. Professional and premium grade, custom/production, solidbody electric guitars built in Tacoma, Washington. They also did work for other luthiers. In late '20, USA was acquired by MJT Aged Guitar Finishes in Carthage, Missouri.

Vaccaro

1997-2002. Founded by Henry Vaccaro, Sr., one of the founders of Kramer Guitars. They offered intermediate and professional grade, production/custom, aluminum-necked guitars and basses designed by Vaccaro, former Kramer designer Phil Petillo, and Henry Vaccaro, Jr., which were made in Asbury Park, New Jersey.

Val Dez

Early-1960s-early-1970s. Less expensive guitars built by Landola in Sweden or Finland; they also made the Espana brand.

Valco

1942-1968. Valco, of Chicago, was a big player in the guitar and amplifier business. Their products were private branded for other companies like National, Supro, Airline, Oahu, and Gretsch. In '42, National Dobro ceased operations and Victor Smith, Al Frost and Louis Dopyera bought the company and changed the name to Valco Manufacturing Company. Post-war production resumed in '46. Valco was purchased by treasurer Robert Engelhardt in '64. In '67, Valco bought Kay, but in '68 the new Valco/Kay company went out of business.

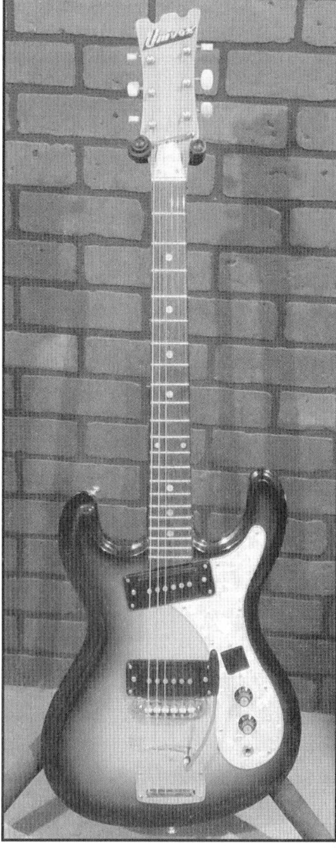

Univox Hi Flier

Charlie Brown

1958 Valco Supro Thunderstick

Rivington Guitars

GUITARS

1938 Vega C-75 Vegaphone
Michael J. Scanlon

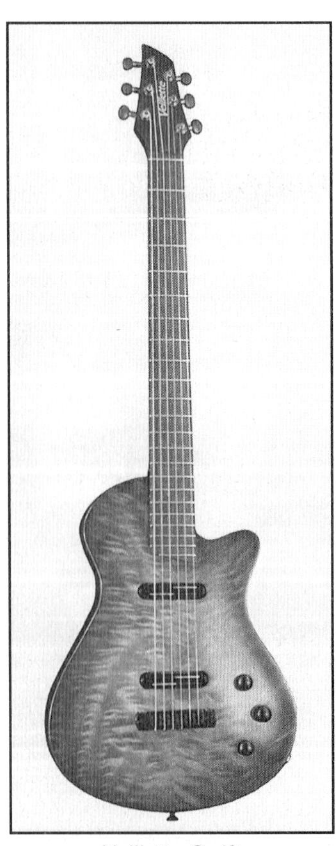
Veillette Swift

MODEL YEAR	FEATURES	EXC. COND. LOW	HIGH

Valencia

1985-present. Budget grade, production, classical guitars imported first by Rondo Music of Union, New Jersey and presently distributed by others.

Valley Arts

Ca. 1977-2010. Professional and premium grade, production/custom, semi-hollow and solidbody guitars and basses built in Nashville, Tennessee. Valley Arts originally was a Southern California music store owned by partners Al Carness and Mike McGuire where McGuire taught and did most of the repairs. Around '77, McGuire and Valley Arts started making custom instruments on a large scale. By '83, they opened a separate manufacturing facility to build the guitars. In '92 Samick acquired half of the company with McGuire staying on for a year as a consultant. Samick offered made-in-the-U.S. production and custom models under the Valley Arts name. In '02, Valley Arts became a division of Gibson Guitar Corp., which built the guitars in Nashville. Founders Carness and McGuire were once again involved with the company. They reintroduced the line in January, '03. The brand has been inactive since '10.

Vantage

1977-1998. Budget and intermediate grade, production, acoustic and electric guitars and basses from Japan '77-'90 and from Korea '90-'98.

Vega

1889-1980s, 1989-present. Founded in Boston by the Nelson family, Vega was big in the banjo market into the 1930s, before adding guitars to their line. The company was purchased by C.F. Martin in '70 who built Vega banjos and starting in '76 they also used the brand on imported guitars, first from the Netherlands and later from Japan, with the Japanese Vegas being of higher quality. In '79, Martin sold the Vega trademark to Korea's Galaxy Trading Company. The Deering Banjo Company, in Spring Valley, California acquired the brand in '89 and uses it (and the star logo) on a line of banjos.

C Series (Archtop)

1933-1950s. Carved-top archtops, '30's models are the 14 5/8" mahogany body C-20 and C-40, 16 1/8" maple body C-60, and the C-70/C75 Vehaphone with rosewood body and gold parts, and the figured-maple body C-80 with deluxe appointments. By '40 the line was the 14-16" C-19, -26, -46, and -56, and the 17" Professional Series C-66 Professional, C-71 Soloist, C-76 Artist, and C-86 Deluxe. Optional blond finish available by '40.

1933-1939	C-20	$1,000	$1,500
1933-1939	C-40	$1,000	$1,500
1933-1939	C-60	$1,500	$2,200
1933-1939	C-70	$1,800	$2,800
1933-1939	C-80	$2,000	$3,000
1938	C-75	$3,000	$4,500
1940-1949	C-19, C-26, C-46	$900	$1,400
1940-1949	C-56	$1,800	$2,800
1940-1949	C-66 Professional	$1,800	$2,800
1940-1949	C-71 Soloist	$1,800	$2,800
1940-1949	C-76 Artist	$2,000	$3,000
1940-1949	C-86 Deluxe	$2,000	$3,000

Duo-Tron Series (Electric Archtop)

1947-late 1950s. Various mid-level large body cutaway and non-cut carved-top archtops, 1, 2 or 3 (rare) floating pickups, dot or block markers, natural or sunburst.

1947-50s	High-end models	$2,500	$4,000
1947-50s	Low-end models	$750	$1,200
1947-50s	Mid-range models	$1,000	$1,500

E-201 Electric Archtop

1959. One pickup, sunburst.

1959		$1,800	$2,800

FT-90 Flat-Top

1960s. 15" body with narrow waist, dot markers, Vega logo, natural.

1960s		$400	$600

G-30

1968-ca. 1970. D-style with solid spruce top and solid mahogany sides and back, Vega logo with star on headstock, dot markers, natural finish.

1968-1970		$300	$500

O'Dell

1950s. Full body, single cut, acoustic-electric, 1 pickup, tailpiece controls.

1950s	Sunburst	$1,000	$1,500

Parlor

Early-1900s-1920s. Small parlor-sized instrument, styles and appointment levels, including binding, purfling and inlays, vary.

1900s	Mahogany	$450	$700
1910s	Brazilian	$1,000	$1,500
1910s-20s	Brazilian, fancy	$3,500	$5,500

Profundo Flat-Top

1930s-1950s. Flat-top D-style body, spruce top, mahogany or rosewood back and sides.

1930s-50s	Mahogany	$1,500	$2,200
1940s-50s	Rosewood	$2,200	$3,300

Solidbody Electric (Import)

1970s-1980s. Solidbody copies of classic designs, Vega script logo on headstock, bolt-on necks.

1970s		$300	$500

Vega Electric Archtop

1939. Full-body electric archtop, figured maple, 1 pickup, 2 control knobs, trapeze bridge, diamond markers, large Vega and star headstock logo, blond.

1939		$1,200	$1,800

Vega, Charles

1993-2010. Luthier Charles Vega built his premium, production/custom, nylon-string guitars in Baltimore, Maryland.

Veillette

1991-present. Luthiers Joe Veillette (of Veillette-Citron fame) and Martin Keith build their professional grade, production/custom, acoustic, acoustic/electric, electric 6- and 12-string and baritone guitars and basses in Woodstock, New York. They also build mandolins.

MODEL YEAR	FEATURES	EXC. COND. LOW	HIGH

Veillette-Citron

1975-1983. Founded by Joe Veillette and Harvey Citron who met at the New York College School of Architecture in the late '60s. Joe took a guitar building course from Michael Gurian and by the Summer of '76, he and Harvey started producing neck-thru solidbody guitars and basses. Veillette and Citron both are back building instruments.

Velázquez

1948-1972. Manuel Velázquez, New York, New York, gained a reputation as a fine repairman in the late 1940s. He opened his 3rd Avenue guitar building shop in the early 1950s. By the mid-1950s he was considered by some as being the finest American builder of classical guitars. Velázquez left New York in 1972 and moved to Puerto Rico. He continued building guitars for the Japanese market. He returned to the United States in 1982. By the 2000s he built instruments with his son and daughter.

Veleno

1967, 1970-1977, 2003-2018. Premium and presentation grade, production/custom, all-aluminum electric solidbody guitars built by luthier John Veleno in St. Petersburg, Florida. First prototype in '67. Later production begins in the late '70s and lasts until '75 or '76. The guitars were chrome or gold-plated, with various anodized colors. The Traveler Guitar was the idea of B.B. King; only 10 were made. Two Ankh guitars were made for Todd Rundgren in '77. Only one bass was made. Approximately 185 instruments were made up to '77 and are sequentially numbered. In 2003, John Veleno reintroduced his brand, he died in '18.

Original (Aluminum Solidbody)

1973-1976. V-headstock, chrome and aluminum.

1973-1976	Rare color	$20,000	$25,000
1973-1976	Standard	$15,000	$20,000

Traveler

1973-1976. Limited production of about a dozen instruments, drop-anchor-style metal body.

1973-1976		$12,000	$15,000

Vengeance Guitars & Graphix

2002-present. Luthier Rick Stewart builds his professional and premium grade, custom/production, solidbody guitars and basses in Arden, North Carolina.

Ventura

1970s. Acoustic and electric guitars imported by C. Bruno Company, mainly copies of classic American models. They also offered basses.

Acoustic Flat-Top

1970s		$450	$700

Guitorgan

1970s. Based on MCI Guitorgan, converts standard electric guitar into a Guitorgan through the addition of electronic organ components, multiple switches, large Barney Kessel sharp-horned acoustic-electric style body.

1970s		$1,000	$1,500

Hollowbody Electric

1970s		$700	$1,000

Solidbody Electric

1970s		$700	$1,000

Verri

Premium grade, production/custom, archtop guitars built by luthier Henry Verri in Little Falls, New York starting in 1992.

Versoul, LTD

1989-present. Premium grade, production/custom steel-string flat-top, acoustic/electric, nylon-string, resonator, solidbody, and baritone guitars, basses and sitars built by luthier Kari Nieminen in Helsinki, Finland.

VibraWood

2012-present. Luthier John J. Slog builds custom, professional and premium grade, vintage-style guitars and basses in Bethlehem, Pennsylvania.

Vicente Tatay

1894-late 1930s. Classical guitars built by luthier Vicente Tatay and his sons in Valencia, Spain.

Victor Baker Guitars

1998-present. Professional and premium grade, custom, carved archtop, flat-top and solidbody electric guitars built by luthier Victor Baker in Philadelphia, Pennsylvania. In '10 he relocated to Brooklyn, New York and is currently in Astoria.

Victor Guitars

2002-2008. Luthiers Edward Victor Dick and Greg German built their premium grade, production/custom, flat-top guitars in Denver, Colorado.

Victoria

Ca. 1902-1920s. Brand name for New York distributor Buegeleisen & Jacobson. Instruments built by the Oscar Schmidt Co. and possibly others. Most likely a brand made for a distributor.

Vigier

1980-present. Luthier Patrice Vigier builds high-end electric guitars and basses near Paris, France.

Electric Solidbody

1980-present. Various models.

1980	Arpege	$1,500	$3,500
1983	Passion	$1,800	$4,000
2000-2006	Expert	$1,500	$3,500
2005-2024	Excalibur Shawn Lane	$3,000	$6,500
2009	GV Wood	$2,000	$4,500
2012-2013	Excalibur Special 7	$2,500	$5,000
2020-2024	Excalibur Special	$2,500	$5,500
2020-2024	Excalibur Supra 7	$3,000	$6,000

Ventura Bruno VS III

W. H. Stephens

VibraWood

GUITARS

Vintage V100 M
Thomas Booth

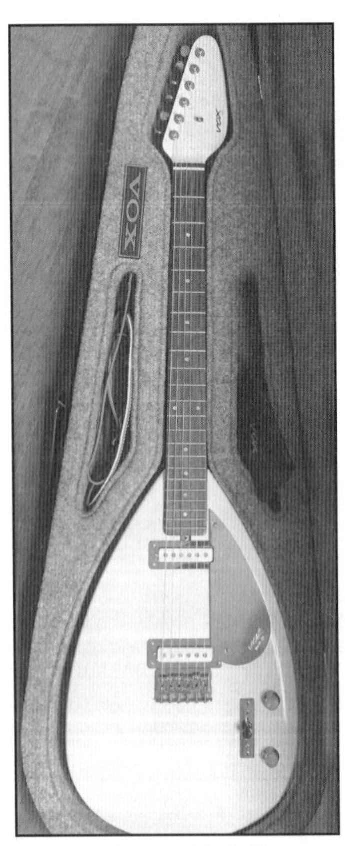
1998 Vox Mark III
Frank Quarracino

MODEL YEAR	FEATURES	EXC. COND. LOW	HIGH
2020-2024	Excalibur Thirteen	$3,500	$7,000
2020-2024	Excalibur Nautilus II	$3,000	$6,500
2020-2024	Excalibur Ultra Blues	$2,500	$5,000
2021-2024	Texas Blues	$2,000	$4,500

Viking Guitars

2003-present. Premium grade, solidbody guitars made by Ed Roman Guitars. Production was '03-'04, custom only since.

Vinetto

2003-present. Luthier Vince Cunetto builds his professional grade, production/custom, solid, chambered and semi-hollow body guitars in St. Louis, Missouri.

Vintage

Ca. 1993-present. Intermediate grade, production, solidbody and semi-hollow acoustic, electro-acoustic and resonator guitars and basses, imported from China, Korea and Vietnam by John Hornby Skewes & Co. in the U.K. They also offer folk instruments.

Vintique

Luthier Jay Monterose built premium grade, custom/production, electric guitars in Suffern, New York. Vintique also manufactured guitar hardware.

Vivi-Tone

1932-1938. Founded in Kalamazoo, Michigan, by former Gibson designer Lloyd Loar, Walter Moon and Lewis Williams, Vivi-Tone built acoustic archtop guitars as well as some of the earliest electric solidbodies. They also built basses and mandolins and offered amps built by Webster Electric. A Vivi-Tone instrument must be all original. Any missing part makes this instrument practically unsellable in the vintage-market.

Various Models

MODEL YEAR	FEATURES	EXC. COND. LOW	HIGH
1932-1938	Rare models	$4,000	$6,000
1932-1938	Standard models	$2,800	$4,000
1932-1938	Tenor, 4-string	$2,200	$3,300

Vox

1954-present. Name introduced by Jennings Musical Instruments (JMI) of England. First Vox products was a volume pedal, amplifiers were brought to the market in late '57 by Tom Jennings and Dick Denny. Guitars were introduced in '61, with an Echo Unit starting the Vox line of effects in '63.

Guitars and basses bearing the Vox name were offered from '61-'69 (made in England and Italy), '82-'85 (Japan), '85-'88 (Korea), '98-2001 (U.S.), and they introduced a limited-edition U.S.-made teardrop guitar in '07 and the semi-hollow Virage guitars in '08.

Ace/Super Ace

1963-1968. Offset double cut solidbody, 2 single-coils. Super Ace has 3 pickups.

MODEL YEAR	FEATURES	EXC. COND. LOW	HIGH
1963-1968	Ace	$700	$1,000
1963-1968	Super Ace	$900	$1,400

Apache

1960s. Modified teardrop body, 3 pickups, vibrato.

MODEL YEAR	FEATURES	EXC. COND. LOW	HIGH
1966		$850	$1,200

Apollo

1967-1968. Single sharp cutaway, 1 pickup, distortion, treble and bass booster, available in sunburst or cherry.

MODEL YEAR	FEATURES	EXC. COND. LOW	HIGH
1967-1968		$850	$1,200

Bobcat

1963-1968. Double-cut semi-hollowbody style, block markers, 3 pickups, vibrato, 2 volume and 2 tone controls.

MODEL YEAR	FEATURES	EXC. COND. LOW	HIGH
1963-1965	England	$1,200	$1,800
1966-1968	Italy	$900	$1,400

Bossman

1967-1968. Single rounded cutaway, 1 pickup, distortion, treble and bass booster, available in sunburst or cherry.

MODEL YEAR	FEATURES	EXC. COND. LOW	HIGH
1967-1968		$750	$1,200

Bulldog

1966. Solidbody double-cut, 3 pickups.

MODEL YEAR	FEATURES	EXC. COND. LOW	HIGH
1966		$1,200	$1,800

Delta

1967-1968. 5-sided Phantom shaped solidbody, 2 pickups, distortion, treble and bass boosters, vibrato, 1 volume and 2 tone controls, available in white only.

MODEL YEAR	FEATURES	EXC. COND. LOW	HIGH
1967-1968		$1,500	$2,200

Folk XII

1966-1969. Dreadnought 12-string flat-top, large 3-point 'guard, block markers, natural.

MODEL YEAR	FEATURES	EXC. COND. LOW	HIGH
1966-1969		$450	$700

Guitar-Organ

1966. Standard Phantom with oscillators from a Continental organ installed inside. Plays either organ sounds, guitar sounds, or both. Weighs over 20 pounds. Prices vary widely due to operating issues with this model.

MODEL YEAR	FEATURES	EXC. COND. LOW	HIGH
1966	Fully functional	$2,500	$3,800
1966	Functional 'board	$1,500	$2,200
1966	Partial function	$800	$1,200

Harlem

1965-1967. Offset double-cut solidbody, 2 extended range pickups, sunburst or color option. Values vary widely due to operating issues with this model.

MODEL YEAR	FEATURES	EXC. COND. LOW	HIGH
1965-1967		$850	$1,200

Hurricane

1965-1967. Double-cut solidbody, 2 pickups, spring action vibrato, sunburst or color option.

MODEL YEAR	FEATURES	EXC. COND. LOW	HIGH
1965-1967		$750	$1,200

Invader (V262)

1966-1967. Solidbody double-cut, 2 pickups, on-board effects, sunburst. Must have fully functional electronics.

MODEL YEAR	FEATURES	EXC. COND. LOW	HIGH
1966-1967		$2,000	$3,000

Mando Guitar

1966. Made in Italy, 12-string mandolin thing.

MODEL YEAR	FEATURES	EXC. COND. LOW	HIGH
1966		$1,200	$1,800

Mark III (U.S.A)

1998-2001. Teardrop reissue, made in U.S.A., 2 single-coils, fixed bridge or Bigsby. A limited model was introduced in '08.

MODEL YEAR	FEATURES	EXC. COND. LOW	HIGH
1998-2001		$900	$1,400

MODEL YEAR	FEATURES	EXC. COND. LOW	HIGH

Mark III 50th Anniversary

2007. Only 100 made, teardrop body, 2 pickups, white finish.

Year	Features	Low	High
2007		$1,200	$1,800

Mark III Limited Edition

2008. Custom Shop USA model, white hardwood body, maple neck, rosewood 'board.

Year	Features	Low	High
2008		$1,800	$2,800

Mark III/Phantom Mark III

1963-1964. Made in England, teardrop body, 2 pickups, 2 controls, Marvin Bigsby, guitar version of Mark IV bass, while it is called a Phantom Mark III it does not have a Phantom shape.

Year	Features	Low	High
1963-1964		$3,000	$4,500

Mark IX

1965-1966. Solidbody teardrop-shaped, 9 strings, 3 pickups, vibrato, 1 volume and 2 tone controls.

Year	Features	Low	High
1965-1966		$1,500	$2,200

Mark VI

1965-1967. Teardrop-shaped solidbody, 3 pickups, vibrato, 1 volume and 2 tone controls.

Year	Features	Low	High
1964-1965	England, white, Brian Jones	$3,500	$5,500
1965-1967	Italy, sunburst	$2,000	$3,000

Mark VI Reissue

1998-2001. Actually, this is a reissue of the original Phantom VI (Vox couldn't use that name due to trademark reasons), made in U.S.A.

Year	Features	Low	High
1998-2001		$900	$1,400

Mark XII

1965-1967. Teardrop-shaped solidbody, 12 strings, 3 pickups, vibrato, 1 volume and 2 tone controls, sunburst. Reissued for '98-'01.

Year	Features	Low	High
1965-1967		$1,800	$2,800

Meteor/Super Meteor

1965-1967. Solidbody double-cut, 1 pickup, Super Meteor with vibrato.

Year	Features	Low	High
1965-1967	Meteor	$500	$800
1965-1967	Super Meteor	$550	$900

New Orleans

1966. Thin double-cut acoustic electric similar to ES-330, 2 pickups, a scaled down version of the 3-pickup Bobcat model.

Year	Features	Low	High
1966		$850	$1,200

Phantom VI

1962-1967. Five-sided body, 6 strings, 3 pickups, vibrato, 1 volume and 2 tone controls.

Year	Features	Low	High
1962-1964	English-made	$3,500	$5,500
1965-1967	Italian-made	$2,200	$3,300

Phantom XII

1964-1967. 12 string version of VI.

Year	Features	Low	High
1964	English-made	$3,500	$5,500
1965-1967	Italian-made	$2,200	$3,300

Phantom XII Stereo

1966. Phantom XII with 3 special offset stereo pickups making 6 pickup combinations, 3 separate pickup mode selectors, color option.

Year	Features	Low	High
1966		$2,500	$3,800

Shadow

1965. Solidbody double-cut, 3 pickups, tremolo tailpiece, sunburst.

Year	Features	Low	High
1965	English-made	$1,000	$1,500

Spitfire

1965-1967. Solidbody double-cut, 3 pickups, vibrato.

Year	Features	Low	High
1965-1967		$900	$1,400

Starstream

1967-1968. Teardrop-shaped hollowbody, 2 pickups, distortion, treble and bass boosters, wah-wah, vibrato, 1 volume and 2 tone controls, 3-way pickup selector, available in cherry or sandburst.

Year	Features	Low	High
1967-1968		$1,800	$2,800

Starstream XII

1967-1968. 12 string version.

Year	Features	Low	High
1967-1968		$1,800	$2,800

Stroller

1961-1966. Made in England, solidbody, single bridge pickup, Hurricane-style contoured body, dot markers, red.

Year	Features	Low	High
1961-1966		$550	$900

Student Prince

1965-1967. Made in Italy, mahogany body thinline archtop electric, 2 knobs, dot markers.

Year	Features	Low	High
1965-1967		$500	$800

Super Lynx

1965-1967. Similar to Bobcat but with 2 pickups and no vibrola, double-cut, 2 pickups, adjustable truss rod, 2 bass and 2 volume controls.

Year	Features	Low	High
1965-1967		$900	$1,400

Super Lynx Deluxe

1965-1967. Super Lynx with added vibrato tailpiece.

Year	Features	Low	High
1965-1967		$900	$1,400

Tempest XII

1965-1967. Solidbody double-cut, 12 strings, 3 pickups.

Year	Features	Low	High
1965-1967		$900	$1,400

Thunder Jet

1960s-style with single pickup and vibrato arm.

Year	Features	Low	High
1960s		$650	$1,000

Tornado

1965-1967. Thinline archtop, single pickup, dot markers, sunburst.

Year	Features	Low	High
1965-1967		$450	$700

Typhoon

1965-1967. Hollowbody single-cut, 2 pickups, 3-piece laminated neck.

Year	Features	Low	High
1965-1967		$550	$900

Ultrasonic

1967-1968. Hollowbody double-cut, 2 pickups, distortion, treble and bass boosters, wah-wah, vibrato, 1 volume and 2 tone controls, 3-way pickup selector, available in sunburst or cherry.

Year	Features	Low	High
1967-1968	12-string	$2,200	$3,300
1967-1968	6-string	$2,200	$3,300

Viper

1968. Double-cut, thinline archtop electric, built-in distortion.

Year	Features	Low	High
1968		$1,200	$1,800

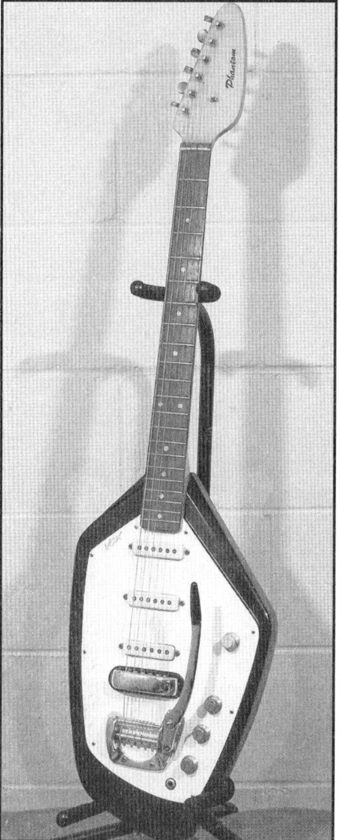

1965 Vox Phantom VI

Tom Pfeifer

Vox Ultrasonic

Imaged by Heritage Auctions, HA.com

GUITARS

Walden Madera

1960s Wandre Orpheum Spazial

MODEL YEAR	FEATURES	EXC. COND. LOW	HIGH

Virage/Virage II

2008-2014. Semi-hollowbody made in Japan, single-cut or double (II), 2 triple-coil pickups.

2008-2014		$1,800	$2,800

Wildcat

1965-1967. Single-cut acoustic-electric archtop, 1 pickup, Wildcat and Vox logos on 'guard, dot markers.

1965-1967		$500	$800

W. J. Dyer

See listing under Dyer.

Wabash

1950s. Acoustic and electric guitars distributed by the David Wexler company and made by others, most likely Kay. They also offered lap steels and amps.

Walden Guitars

Luthier Jonathan Lee of Portland, Oregon imports production, budget to professional grade, acoustic, acoustic-electric and classical guitars from Lilan, China. He began in 1996.

Walker

1994-present. Premium and presentation grade, production/custom, flat-top and archtop guitars built by luthier Kim Walker in North Stonington, Connecticut.

Walker (Kramer)

1981. Kramer came up with idea to offer this brand to produce wood-neck guitars and basses; they didn't want to dilute the Kramer aluminum-neck market they had built up. The idea didn't last long, and few, if any, of these instruments were produced, but prototypes exist.

Wandre (Davoli)

Ca. 1956/57-1969. Solidbody and thinline hollowbody electric guitars and basses created by German-descended Italian motorcycle and guitar enthusiast, artist, and sculptor from Milan, Italy, Wandre Pioli. Brands include Wandre (pronounced Vahn-dray), Davoli, Framez, JMI, Noble, Dallas, Avalon, Avanti I and others. Until '60, they were built by Pioli himself; from '60-'63 built in Milan by Framez; '63-'65 built by Davoli; '66-'69 built in Pioli's own factory.

The guitars originally used Framez pickups, but from '63 on (or earlier) they used Davoli pickups. Mostly strange shapes characterized by neck-thru-tailpiece aluminum neck with plastic back and rosewood 'board. Often multi-color and sparkle finishes, using unusual materials like linoleum, fiberglass and laminates, metal bindings. Often the instruments will have numerous identifying names but usually somewhere there is a Wandre blob logo.

Distributed early on in the U.K. by Jennings Musical Industries, Ltd. (JMI) and in the U.S. by Don Noble and Company. Model B.B. dedicated to Brigitte Bardot. Among more exotic instruments were the minimalist Krundaal Bikini guitar with a built-in amplifier and attached speaker, and the pogo stick Swedenbass. These guitars are relatively rare and highly collectible. In '05, the brand was revived on a line of imported intermediate grade, production, solidbodies from Eastwood guitars.

Electric

1956-1969	Common models	$5,000	$10,000
1956-1969	Rare models	$10,000	$20,000

Warren

2005-present. Luthier Don Warren builds his professional and premium grade, custom/production, solidbody electric guitars in Latham, New York.

Warrior

1995-present. Professional, premium, and presentation grade, production/custom, acoustic and solidbody electric guitars and basses built by luthier J.D. Lewis in Rossville, Georgia.

Washburn

1962-present. Budget, intermediate, professional, and premium grade, production/custom, acoustic and electric guitars and basses made in the U.S., Japan, and Korea. They also make amps, banjos and mandolins.

Originally a Lyon & Healy brand, the Washburn line was revived on a line of imports in '62 by Roland who sold it to Beckman Musical Instruments in '74/'75. Beckman sold the rights to the Washburn name to Fretted Instruments, Inc. in '76. Guitars originally made in Japan and Korea, but production moved back to U.S. in '91. Currently Washburn is part of U.S. Music.

Washburn (Lyon & Healy)

1880s-ca.1949. Washburn was founded in Chicago as one of the lines for Lyon & Healy to promote high quality stringed instruments, ca. 1880s. The rights to manufacture Washburns were sold to J.R. Stewart Co. in '28, but rights to Washburn name were sold to Tonk Brothers of Chicago. In the Great Depression (about 1930), J.R. Stewart Co. was hit hard and declared bankruptcy. Tonk Brothers bought at auction all Stewart trade names, then sold them to Regal Musical Instrument Co. Regal built Washburns by the mid-'30s. The Tonk Brothers still licensed the name. These Washburn models lasted until ca. '49. In '62 the brand resurfaced on a line of imports from Roland.

Washington

Washington was a brand manufactured by Kansas City, Missouri instrument wholesalers J.W. Jenkins & Sons. First introduced in 1895, the brand also offered mandolins.

MODEL YEAR	FEATURES	EXC. COND. LOW	HIGH

Waterloo

2014-present. Professional grade, production, acoustic guitars based on Depression-era models, built by Bill Collings in Austin, Texas. Waterloo was the original city name of Austin.

WL-12

2014-present. Parlor size, vintage-style sunburst finish.

2014-2024		$1,200	$2,200

WL-14 Scissortail

2014-present. Solid spruce top, maple back and sides, X-bracing.

2014-2024		$1,500	$2,500

WL-14LTR

2014-2024. Acoustic 14.75", solid headstock, ladder bracing (L).

2014-2024		$1,200	$2,200

WL-14MH

2014-2024. Parlor size, all mahogany.

2014-2024		$1,300	$2,300

WL-14X

2014-2024. Acoustic 14.75", solid headstock, X bracing (X).

2014-2024		$1,200	$2,200

WL-JK

2014-2024. Nick-named 'Jumbo King', 15.75" body, X-bracing. Optional East Indian rosewood back and sides.

2014-2024		$1,500	$3,000

WL-JK Deluxe

2014-2024. Ornate appointments.

2014-2024		$1,800	$3,500

WL-K

2014-present. Lightweight 14.75", '30s Kel Kroyden inspired, optional hand-painted "Southwest" scene.

2014-2024		$1,400	$2,500

WL-S

2014-present. Slotted headstock 14", '30s Stella inspired, solid cherry wood back and sides, iced tea sunburst.

2014-2024		$1,300	$2,300

WL-S Deluxe

2014-present. Ornate appointments.

2014-2024		$1,600	$2,800

Waterstone

2003-present. Intermediate and professional grade, production/custom, electric solid and semi-hollowbody and acoustic guitars and basses imported from Korea by Waterstone Musical Instruments, LLC of Nashville, Tennessee.

Watkins/WEM

1957-present. Watkins Electric Music (WEM) was founded by Charlie Watkins. Their first commercial product was the Watkins Dominator (wedge Gibson stereo amp shape) in '57. They made the Rapier line of guitars and basses from the beginning. Watkins offered guitars and basses up to '82. They currently build accordion amps.

MODEL YEAR	FEATURES	EXC. COND. LOW	HIGH

Wayne

1998-present. Professional and premium grade, production/custom, solidbody guitars built by luthiers Wayne and Michael (son) Charvel in Paradise, California. They also build lap steels.

Webber

1988-2020. Professional grade, production/custom flat-top guitars built by luthier David Webber in North Vancouver, British Columbia. Webber retired in '20.

Weber

1996-present. Premium grade, production/custom, carved-top acoustic and resonator guitars built by luthier Bruce Weber and his Sound To Earth, Ltd. company, originally in Belgrade, Montana, in '04 moving to Logan, Montana. They also build mandolins. In '12, Two Old Hippies (Breedlove, Bedell) acquired the brand, moving production in '13 to Oregon where Bruce Weber oversees development.

Webster

1940s. Archtop and acoustic guitars, most likely built by Kay or other mass builder.

Model 16C Acoustic Archtop

1940s		$650	$1,000

Wechter

1984-present. Intermediate, professional and premium grade, production/custom, flat-top, 12-string, resonator and nylon-string guitars and basses from luthier Abe Wechter in Paw Paw, Michigan. The Elite line is built in Paw Paw, the others in Asia. Until '94 he built guitars on a custom basis. In '95, he set up a manufacturing facility in Paw Paw to produce his new line and in '00 he added the Asian guitars. In '04, he added resonators designed by Tim Scheerhorn. Wechter was associated with Gibson Kalamazoo from the mid-'70s to '84. He also offers the Maple Lake brand of acoustics. In '08 he moved his shop to Fort Wayne, Indiana. Then in '13 he moved to Guangzhou China where he offers custom guitars only.

Weissenborn

1910s-1937, present. Hermann Weissenborn was well-established as a violin and piano builder in Los Angeles by the early 1910s. Around '20, he added guitars, ukes and steels to his line. Most of his production was in the '20s and '30s until his death in '37. He made tenor, plectrum, parlor, and Spanish guitars, ukuleles, and mandolins, but is best remembered for his Koa Hawaiian guitars that caught the popular wave of Hawaiian music. That music captivated America after being introduced to the masses at San Francisco's Panama Pacific International Exposition which was thrown in '15 to celebrate the opening of the Panama Canal and attended by more than 13 million people. He also made instruments for Kona and other brands. Most

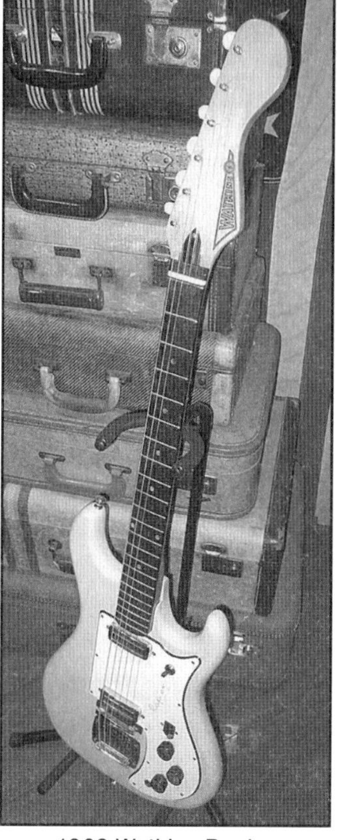

1962 Watkins Rapier
Rivington Guitars

Wechter
Benjamin E. Rios

1960s Welson 7731
Tom Pfeifer

Westminster Archtop
W. H. Stephens

of his instruments were most likely sold before the late 1920s. The Weissenborn brand has been revived on a line of reissue style guitars.

MODEL YEAR	FEATURES	EXC. COND. LOW	HIGH
Spanish Acoustic			
1920s. High-end Spanish set-up, rope binding, Koa top, sides and back, limited production.			
1920s		$2,200	$3,300
Style #1 Hawaiian			
1920-1930s. Koa, no binding, 3 wood circle sound hole inlays.			
1920s-30s		$3,200	$4,800
Style #2 Hawaiian			
1920-1930s. Koa, black celluloid body binding, white wood 'board binding, rope sound hole binding.			
1920s-30s		$3,500	$5,500
Style #2 Spanish			
1920s. Spanish set-up, Style 2 features.			
1920s		$2,500	$3,800
Style #3 Hawaiian			
1920-1930s. Koa, rope binding on top, 'board, and sound hole.			
1920s-30s		$4,500	$7,000
Style #4 Hawaiian			
1920-1930s. Koa, rope binding on body, 'board, headstock and sound hole.			
1920s-30s		$5,500	$8,500
Teardrop			
Late 1920s-1930s. Teardrop/spoon shaped, Style 1 features.			
1930s		$900	$1,400
Tenor			
1920-1927		$1,200	$1,800

Welker Custom

Professional and premium grade, production/custom, archtop and flat-top guitars built by luthier Fred Welker in Nashville, Tennessee.

Welson

1960s-1970s. Models made by Quagliardi, an accordion maker in Italy, ranging from acoustics to solidbodies, thinlines, archtops and basses. Some acoustic Welsons were sold in the U.S. by Wurlitzer. By the '70s, they had jumped on the copy-guitar bandwagon.

MODEL YEAR	FEATURES	EXC. COND. LOW	HIGH
Electric			
1960s	Various models	$325	$1,200

Wendler

1999-present. Intermediate and professional grade, production/custom, solidbody, electro-acoustic guitars and basses from luthier Dave Wendler of Ozark Instrument Building in Branson, Missouri. He also builds amps. In '91, Wendler patented a pickup system that became the Taylor ES system.

Westbury-Unicord

1978-ca. 1983. Imported from Japan by Unicord of Westbury, New York. High quality original designs, generally with 2 humbuckers, some with varitone and glued-in necks. They also had basses.

Westminster

One of the many guitar brands built by Japan's Matsumoku company.

Westone

1970s-1990, 1996-2001. Made by Matsumoku in Japan and imported by St. Louis Music. Around '81, St. Louis Music purchased an interest in Matsumoku and began to make a transition from its own Electra brand to the Westone brand previously used by Matsumoku. In the beginning of '84, the brand became Electra-Westone with a phoenix bird head surrounded by circular wings and flames. By the end of '84 the Electra name was dropped, leaving only Westone and a squared-off bird with W-shaped wings logo. Electra, Electra-Westone and Westone instruments from this period are virtually identical except for the brand and logo treatment. Many of these guitars and basses were made in very limited runs and are relatively rare.

From '96 to '01, England's FCN Music offered Westone branded electric and acoustic guitars. The electrics were built in England and the acoustics in Korea. Matsumoku-made guitars feature a serial number in which the first 1 or 2 digits represent the year of manufacture. Electra-Westone guitars should begin with either a 4 or 84.

Weymann

1864-1933. H.A. Weymann & Sons was a musical instrument distributor located in Philadelphia that marketed various stringed instruments, but mainly known for banjos. Some guitar models were made by Regal and Vega, but they also built their own instruments.

MODEL YEAR	FEATURES	EXC. COND. LOW	HIGH
Large Models			
1890-1928	Most w/Brazilian	$4,000	$6,000
1928-1932	Most w/Brazilian	$5,000	$7,500
Small Models/Standard			
1890-1928	Brazilian	$3,000	$4,500
1890-1928	Mahogany	$800	$1,200
1928-1932	Brazilian	$4,000	$6,000
1928-1932	Mahogany	$900	$1,400
Jimmie Rodgers Signature Edition			
1929-1932		$8,000	$10,000

White Guitars and Woodley White Luthier

1992-present. Premium grade, custom, classical, acoustic and electric guitars, built by luthier Woodley White, first in Portland, Oregon and since 2008 in Naalehu, Hawaii.

Wicked

2004-present. Production/custom, intermediate and professional grade, semi-hollow and electric solidbody guitars and basses built by luthier Nicholas Dijkman in Montreal, Quebec.

Widman Custom Electrics

2008-present. Professional and premium grade, custom, electric guitars built in Arden, North Carolina by luthier John Widman.

Wilkanowski

Early-1930s-mid-1940s. W. Wilkanowski primarily built violins. He did make a few dozen guitars which were heavily influenced by violin design concepts and in fact look very similar to a large violin with a guitar neck.

Wilkat Guitars

1998-2013. Professional grade, custom, electric guitars and basses built by luthier Bill Wilkat in Montreal, Quebec. He retired in '13.

Wilkins

1984-present. Custom guitars built by luthier Pat Wilkins in Van Nuys, California. Wilkins also does finish work for individuals and a variety of other builders.

William C. Stahl

See listing under Stahl.

William Hall and Son

William Hall and Son was a New York City based distributor offering guitars built by other luthiers in the mid to late 1800s.

William Jeffrey Jones

2006-present. Luthier William Jeffrey Jones builds his ornately carved, professional and premium grade, production/custom, solidbody and semi-hollow electric guitars in Neosho, Missouri.

Wilson

1960s-1970s. One of the brand names of guitars built in the 1960s for others by Egmond in Holland. Also, a brand name used by the U.K.'s Watkins WEM in the 1960s and '70s.

Wilson Brothers Guitars

2004-present. Intermediate and professional grade, production, imported electric and acoustic guitars and basses. Founded by Ventures guitarist Don Wilson. VCM and VSP models made in Japan; VM electrics in Korea; VM acoustic in China.

Windsor

Ca. 1890s-ca. 1914. Brand used by Montgomery Ward for flat-top guitars and mandolins made by various American manufacturers, including Lyon & Healy and, possibly, Harmony. Generally, beginner-grade instruments.

Winston

Ca. 1963-1967. Imported from Japan by Buegeleisen and Jacobson of New York. Manufacturers unknown, but some are by Guyatone. Generally shorter scale beginner guitars and basses.

MODEL YEAR	FEATURES	EXC. COND. LOW	HIGH

Worland

1997-present. Luthier Jim Worland builds professional through presentation grade, production/custom, acoustic flat-top guitars and harp guitars in Rockford, Illinois. He also builds under the Worlatron brand.

Worlatron

2010-present. Professional grade, production/custom, hollowbody electric-acoustic guitars and basses built by luthier Jim Worland in Rockford, Illinois.

WRC Music International

1989-mid-1990s. Guitars by Wayne Richard Charvel, who was the original founder of Charvel Guitars. He now builds Wayne guitars with his son Michael.

Wright Guitar Technology

1993-present. Luthier Rossco Wright builds his unique intermediate and professional grade, production, travel/practice steel-string and nylon-string guitars in The Dalles, Oregon. Basses were added in 2009.

Wurlitzer

Wurlitzer had full-line music stores in several major cities and marketed a line of American-made guitars in the 1920s. They also offered American- and foreign-made guitars starting in '65. The American ones were built from '65-'66 by the Holman-Woodell guitar factory in Neodesha, Kansas. In '67, Wurlitzer switched to Italian-made Welson guitars.

00-18

1920s		$6,000	$12,000

Model 2077 (Martin 0-K)

1920s. Made by Martin, size 0 with Koa top, back and sides, limited production of about 28 instruments.

1920s	Natural	$8,000	$20,000

Model 2090 (Martin 0-28)

1920s. Made by Martin, size 0 with appointments similar to a Martin 0-28 of that era, limited production of about 11 instruments, Wurlitzer branded on the back of the headstock and on the inside back seam, Martin name also branded on inside seam.

1920s	Natural	$7,500	$15,000

Wild One Stereo

1960s. Two pickups, various colors.

1960s		$500	$1,500

Xaviere

Budget and intermediate grade, production, solid and semi-hollow body guitars from Guitar Fetish, which also has GFS pickups and effects.

Xotic Guitars

1996-present. Luthier Hiro Miura builds his professional grade, production/custom guitars and basses in San Fernando, California. The Xotic brand is also used on a line of guitar effects.

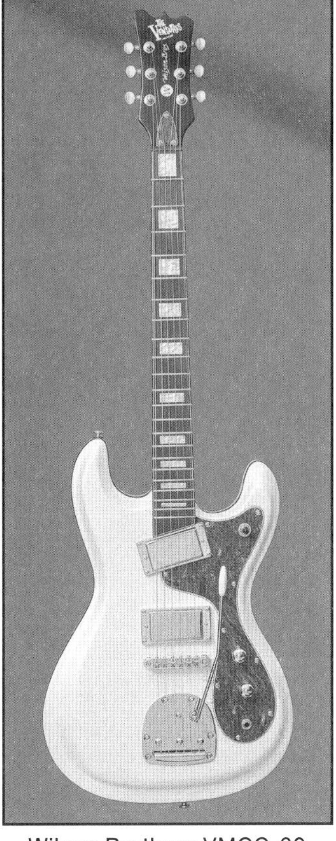

Wilson Brothers VMCC-60 Ventures Custom Classic PW

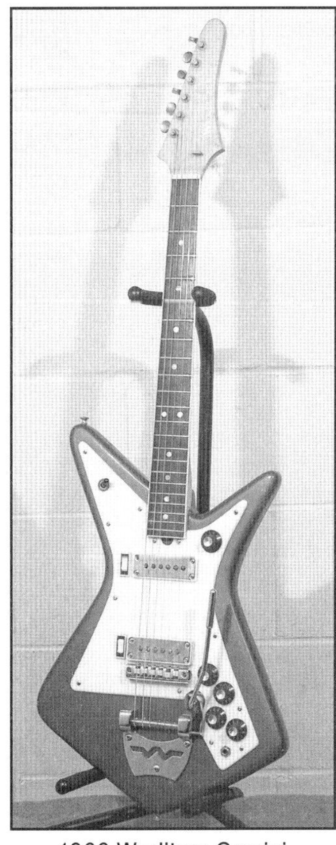
1966 Wurlitzer Gemini
Tom Pfeifer

Yamaha FG-180
Kris Nocula

Yamaha LS6M

MODEL YEAR	FEATURES	EXC. COND. LOW	HIGH

XOX Audio Tools

2007-present. U.S. debut in '08 of premium grade, production/custom, carbon fiber electric guitars built by luthier Peter Solomon in Europe.

Xtone

2003-2014. Semi-hollow body electric, acoustic and acoustic/electric guitars from ESP. Originally branded Xtone on headstock, in '10 the instruments were marketed as a model series under LTD (ESP's other brand) and stated as such on the headstock.

XXL Guitars

2003-present. Luthier Marc Lupien builds his production/custom, professional grade, chambered electric guitars in Montreal, Quebec.

Yamaha

1946-present. Budget, intermediate, professional, and presentation grade, production/custom, acoustic, acoustic/electric, and electric guitars. They also build basses, amps, and effects. The Japanese instrument maker was founded in 1887. Began classical guitar production around 1946. Solidbody electric production began in '66; steel string acoustics debuted sometime after that. They began to export guitars into the U.S. in '69. Production shifted from Japan to Taiwan (Yamaha's special-built plant) in the '80s, though some high-end guitars still made in Japan. Some Korean production began in '90s.

Serialization patterns:

Serial numbers are coded as follows:

H = 1, I = 2, J = 3, etc., Z = 12

To use this pattern, you need to know the decade of production.

Serial numbers are ordered as follows:

Year/Month/Day/Factory Order

Example: NL 29159 represents a N=1987 year, L=5th month or May, 29=29th day (of May), 159=159th guitar made that day (the factory order). This guitar was the 159 guitar made on May 29, 1987.

AE Series (Archtop)

1966-2011. Various archtop models.

1966-2011	Higher-end	$1,500	$3,500
1966-2011	Lower-end	$300	$800
1966-2011	Mid-level	$800	$2,000

AES Series (Semi-Hollowbody)

1990-2011. Various semi-hollowbody models.

1990-2011	Higher-end	$1,500	$3,500
1990-2011	Lower-end	$300	$600
1990-2011	Mid-level	$600	$1,500

AEX-1500

1995-2011. Full-body archtop electric, set neck, humbucker and piezo, EQ, multi-bound.

1995-2011		$1,500	$3,500

APX Series (Acoustic-Electric)

1987-present. Acoustic-electric, various features.

1987-2024	Higher-end	$800	$2,000
1987-2024	Lower-end	$150	$400
1987-2024	Mid-level	$300	$800

CG Series (Classical)

1984-present. Various classical models.

1984-2024	Higher-end	$500	$1,500
1984-2024	Lower-end	$100	$300
1984-2024	Mid-level	$200	$600

DW Series (Dreadnought)

1999-2002. Dreadnought flat-top models, sunburst, solid spruce top, higher-end appointments like abalone rosette and top purfling.

1999-2002	Higher-end	$400	$800
1999-2002	Lower-end	$100	$250
1999-2002	Mid-level	$200	$500

EG Series (Electric Solidbody)

2000-2009. Various electric solidbody models.

2000-2009		$300	$1,200

Eterna Series (Folk Acoustic)

1983-1994. Folk-style acoustics, there were 4 models.

1983-1994		$200	$800

FG Series (Flat-Top)

1970s-present. Economy market flat-top models, laminated sides and back, a 12 suffix indicates 12-string, CE indicates on-board electronics, many models are D-style bodies.

1970-2024	Higher-end	$600	$1,500
1970-2024	Highest-end	$1,500	$3,500
1970-2024	Lower-end	$100	$300
1970-2024	Mid-level	$200	$600

G Series (Classical)

1981-2000. Various Classical models.

1981-2000		$150	$600

GC Series (Classical)

1970s-present. Classical models, '70s made in Japan, '80s made in Taiwan.

1970s-2024	Higher-end	$1,500	$10,000
1970s-2024	Lower-end	$150	$400
1970s-2024	Mid-level	$400	$1,500

Image Custom

1988-1992. Electric double-cut, Brazilian rosewood 'board, maple top, 2 humbuckers, active circuitry, LED position markers, script Image logo on truss rod cover. The Image was called the MSG in the U.K.

1988-1992		$400	$1,000

L Series (Flat-Top)

1984-present. Custom hand-built flat-top models, solid wood.

1984-2024	Higher-end	$1,500	$5,000
1984-2024	Lower-end	$200	$500
1984-2024	Mid-level	$400	$1,200

PAC Pacifica Series

1989-present. Offset double-cut with longer horns, dot markers, large script Pacifica logo and small block Yamaha logo on headstock, various models.

1989-2024		$200	$2,500

RGX Series

1988-2011. Bolt-on neck for the 600 series and neck-thru body designs for 1200 series, various models include 110 (1 hum), 211 (hum-single), 220 (2 hums), 312 (hum-single-single), 603 (3 singles), 612 (hum-single-single), 620 (2 hums), 1203S (3 singles), 1212S (hum-single-single), 1220S (2 hums).

1988-2011	Higher-end	$800	$2,500

MODEL YEAR	FEATURES	EXC. COND. LOW	HIGH
1988-2011	Lower-end	$200	$500
1988-2011	Mid-level	$400	$1,000

RGZ Series

1989-1994. Double-cut solidbodies, various pickups.

1989-1994	Higher-end	$700	$2,000
1989-1994	Lower-end	$200	$500
1989-1994	Mid-level	$400	$900

SA (Super Axe) Series

1966-1994. Super Axe series, full-size and thinline archtop models.

1966-1994	Higher-end	$1,500	$3,500
1966-1994	Highest-end	$2,000	$5,000
1966-1994	Lower-end	$300	$800
1966-1994	Mid-level	$800	$1,800

SBG Series (Solidbody)

1983-1992. Solidbody models, set necks, model name logo on truss rod cover.

1983-1992	Higher-end	$1,500	$3,500
1983-1992	Highest-end	$2,500	$5,000
1983-1992	Lower-end	$400	$1,000
1983-1992	Mid-level	$800	$1,800

SE Series (Solidbody Electric)

1986-1992. Solidbody electric models.

1986-1992	Higher-end	$800	$2,000
1986-1992	Lower-end	$200	$500
1986-1992	Mid-level	$400	$1,000

SF (Super Flighter) Series

1977-early 1980s. Super Flighter series, double-cut solidbody electrics, 2 humbuckers.

1977-80s	Various models	$500	$2,000

SG-3

1965-1966. Early double-cut solidbody with sharp horns, bolt neck, 3 hum-single pickup layout, large white guard, rotor controls, tremolo.

1965-1966		$800	$2,000

SG-5/SG-5A

1966-1971. Asymmetrical double-cut solidbody with extended lower horn, bolt neck, 2 pickups, chrome hardware.

1966-1971		$700	$1,800

SG-7/SG-7A

1966-1971. Like SG-5, but with gold hardware.

1966-1971		$800	$2,500
1993-1996	7A	$600	$1,500

SG-7A 20th Anniversary

1986		$1,000	$2,500

SG-12

1966-1972. Made in Japan, 12-string.

1966-1972		$1,000	$2,500

SG-20

1972-1973. Bolt-on neck, slab body, single-cut, 1 pickup.

1972-1973		$600	$1,500

SG-30/SG-30A

1973-1976. Slab katsura wood (30) or slab maple (30A) solidbody, bolt-on neck, 2 humbuckers, dot inlays.

1973-1976		$500	$1,200

SG-35/SG-35A

1973-1976. Slab mahogany (35) or slab maple (35A) solidbody, bolt-on neck, 2 humbuckers, parallelogram inlays.

1973-1976		$600	$1,500

SG-40

1972-1973. Bolt-on neck, carved body, single-cut.

1972-1973		$600	$1,500

SG-45

1972-1976. Glued neck, single-cut, bound flat-top.

1972-1976		$700	$1,800

SG-50

1974-1976. Slab katsura wood solidbody, glued neck, 2 humbuckers, dot inlays, large 'guard.

1974-1976		$800	$2,000

SG-60

1972 only. Bolt-on neck, carved body, single-cut.

1972		$700	$1,800

SG-60T

1973 only. SG-60 with large cast vibrato system.

1973		$800	$2,000

SG-65

1972-1976. Glued neck, single-cut, bound flat-top.

1972-1976		$700	$1,800

SG-70

1974-1976. Slab maple solidbody, glued neck, 2 humbuckers, dot inlays, large 'guard.

1974-1976		$900	$2,200

SG-80

1972 only. Bolt-on neck, carved body, single-cut.

1972		$800	$2,000

SG-80T

1973. SG-60 with large cast vibrato system.

1973		$900	$2,200

SG-85

1972-1976. Glued neck, single-cut, bound flat-top.

1972-1976		$700	$1,800

SG-90

1974-1976. Carved top mahogany solidbody, glued neck, elevated 'guard, bound top, dot inlays, chrome hardware.

1974-1976		$1,000	$2,500

SG-175

1974-1976. Carved top mahogany solidbody, glued neck, elevated 'guard, abalone bound top, abalone split wing or pyramid inlays, gold hardware.

1974-1976		$1,500	$3,500

SG-500

1976-1978. Carved unbound maple top, double pointed cutaways, glued neck, 2 exposed humbuckers, 3-ply bound headstock, bound neck with clay split wing inlays, chrome hardware. Reissued as the SBG-500 (800S in Japan) in '81.

1976-1978		$600	$1,500

SG-700

1976-1978. Carved unbound maple top, double pointed cutaways, glued neck, 2 humbuckers, 3-ply bound headstock, bound neck with clay split wing inlays, chrome hardware.

1976-1978		$800	$2,000

SG-700S

1999-2001. Set neck, mahogany body, 2 humbuckers with coil tap.

1999-2001		$700	$1,800

1966 Yamaha SA-15

Brian Goff

1985 Yamaha SA2100

Craig Brody

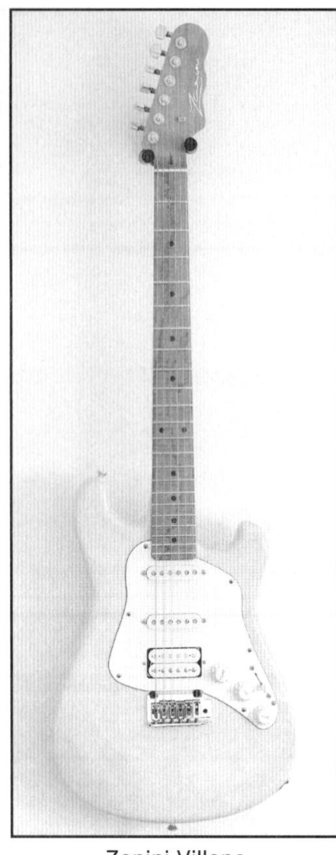

Zanini Villano

1994 Zemaitis Pearl Front

Phil Winfield

MODEL YEAR	FEATURES	EXC. COND. LOW	HIGH

SG-800S

1981-1984. Eastern mahogany with maple top, set neck, 2 pickups, blue, tobacco burst or cherry sunburst.

1981-1984		$800	$2,000

SG-1000/SBG-1000

1976-1983 ('84 in Japan), 2007-2013. Carved maple top, double pointed cutaways, glued neck, 2 humbuckers, 3-ply bound headstock, unbound body, bound neck with clay split wing inlays, gold hardware. Export model name changed to SBG-1000 in '80. SBG-1000 reissued in '07.

1976-1979	SG-1000	$1,200	$3,000
1980-1983	SBG-1000	$1,000	$2,500

SG-1500

1976-1979. Carved maple top, double pointed cutaways, laminated neck-thru-body neck, laminated mahogany body wings, 2 humbuckers, 5-ply bound headstock and body, bound neck with dot inlays, chrome hardware. Name used on Japan-only model in the '80s.

1976-1979		$1,500	$3,500

SG-2000/SG-2000S

1976-1980 (1988 in Japan). Maple top, double pointed cutaways, neck-thru-body, mahogany body wings, 2 humbuckers, 5-ply bound headstock and body, bound neck with abalone split wing inlays, gold hardware. In '80, the model was changed to the SBG-2000 in the U.S., and the SG-2000S everywhere else except Japan (where it remained the SG-2000). Export model renamed SBG-2100 in '84.

1976-1980		$2,000	$5,000

SG-2100S

1983. Similar to SG-2000 with upgrades such as the pickups.

1983		$2,500	$5,500

SG-3000/SBG-3000/Custom Professional

1982-1992. SG-2000 upgrade with higher output pickups and abalone purfling on top.

1982-1992		$3,000	$10,000

SGV-300

2000-2006. 1960s SG model features.

2000-2006		$400	$1,000

SHB-400

1981-1985. Solidbody electric, set-in neck, 2 pickups.

1981-1985		$300	$800

SJ-180

1983-1994. Student Jumbo, entry level Folk Series model, laminated top.

1983-1994		$150	$400

SJ-400S

1983-1994. Student Jumbo Folk Series model, solid wood top.

1983-1994		$200	$500

SL (Studio Lord) Series

1977-1981. LP-style copy models.

1977-1981	Various models	$600	$2,000

SR (Super Rock'n Roller) Series

1977-1981. Strat copy models.

1977-1981	Various models	$500	$1,500

SSC Series (Solidbody Electric)

1983-1992. Solidbody electric models.

1983-1992	SSC-400/SC-400	$400	$900
1983-1992	SSC-500	$500	$1,200
1983-1992	SSC-600/SC-600	$600	$1,500

Weddington Classic

1989-1992. Electric solidbody, redesigned set-in neck/body joint for increased access to the higher frets.

1989-1992		$1,000	$2,500

Yanuziello Stringed Instruments

1980-present. Production/custom resonator and Hawaiian guitars built by luthier Joseph Yanuziello, in Toronto, Ontario.

Yosco

1900-1930s. Lawrence L. Yosco was a New York City luthier building guitars, round back mandolins and banjos under his own brand and for others.

Zachary

1996-present. Luthier Alex Csiky builds his professional grade, production, solidbody electric guitars and basses in Windsor, Ontario.

Zanini

2007-2020. Premium grade, production, electric guitars designed by Luca Zanini of Italy and built in the U.S.

Zaukus Guitars

Luthier Joseph Zaukus started in 2011, builds premium grade, production/custom, solidbody electric guitars in Antioch, Tennessee.

Zeiler Guitars

1992-present. Custom flat-top, 12-string, and nylon-string guitars built by luthier Jamonn Zeiler in Aurora, Indiana.

MODEL YEAR	FEATURES	EXC. COND. LOW	HIGH

Zemaitis

1960-1999, 2004-present. Professional, premium, and presentation grade, custom/production, electric and acoustic guitars. Tony Zemaitis (born Antanus Casimere Zemaitis) began selling his guitars in 1960. He emphasized simple light-weight construction and was known for hand engraved metal front guitars. The metal front designs were originally engineered to reduce hum, but they became popular as functional art. Each hand-built guitar and bass was a unique instrument. Ron Wood was an early customer and his use created a demand for them. Approximately 6 to 10 instruments were built each year. Tony retired in '99 and passed away in '02 at the age of 67. In '04, Japan's Kanda Shokai Corporation, with the endorsement of Tony Zemaitis, Jr., started building the guitars again. KSC builds the higher priced ones and licenses the lower priced guitars to Greco.

Celebrity association with Zemaitis is not uncommon. Validated celebrity provenance may add 25% to 100% (or more) to a guitar's value. Tony Zemaitis also made so-called student model instruments for customers with average incomes. These had wood tops instead of metal or pearl. Some wood top instruments have been converted to non-Zemaitis metal tops, which are therefore not fully original Zemaitis instruments.

Acoustic instruments are valued more as collectibles and less so for their acoustic sound. Originality and verifiable, documented provenance are required in the Zemaitis market as fake instruments can be a problem.

Zen-On

1946-ca.1968. Japanese manufacturer. By '67 using the Morales brand name. Not heavily imported into the U.S., if at all (see Morales).

Acoustic Hollowbody

1946-1968	Various models	$200	$800

Electric Solidbody

1946-1968	Various models	$150	$600

Zerberus

2002-present. Professional and premium grade, production/custom, electric guitars built in Speyer, Germany by luthier Frank Scheucher.

MODEL YEAR	FEATURES	EXC. COND. LOW	HIGH

Zeta

1982-2010. Zeta made solid, semi-hollow and resonator guitars, many with electronic and MIDI options, and mandolins in Oakland, California over the years, but mainly offered upright basses, amps and violins.

Ziegenfuss Guitars

2006-present. Luthier Stephen Ziegenfuss builds his professional and premium grade, custom, acoustic and solidbody electric guitars and basses in Jackson, Michigan.

Zim-Gar

1960s. Imported from Japan by Gar-Zim Musical Instrument Corporation of Brooklyn, New York. Manufacturers unknown. Generally shorter scale beginner guitars.

Electric Solidbody

1960s		$100	$400

Zimnicki, Gary

1980-present. Luthier Gary Zimnicki builds his professional and premium grade, custom, flat-top, 12-string, nylon-string, and archtop guitars in Allen Park, Michigan.

Zion

1980-present. Professional and premium grade, production/custom, semi-hollow and solidbody guitars built by luthier Ken Hoover, originally in Greensboro, North Carolina, currently in Raleigh.

Zolla

Professional grade, production/custom, electric guitars and basses built by luthier Bill Zolla in San Diego, California starting in 1979.

Zon

1981-present. Currently luthier Joe Zon only offers basses, but he also built guitars from '85-'91. See Bass Section for more company info.

Zuni

1993-present. Premium grade, custom, solidbody electric guitars built by luthier Michael Blank in Alto Pass, Illinois and Amasa, Michigan.

ZZ Ryder

Solidbody electric guitars and basses from Stenzler Musical Instruments of Ft. Worth, Texas.

Zen-On W100
Bruce Hughes

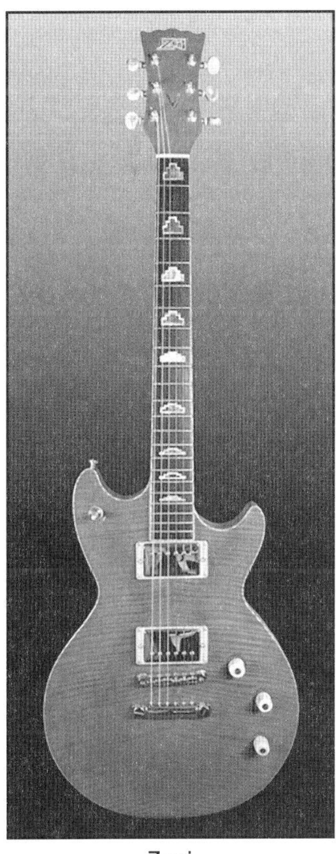

Zuni

GUITARS

BASSES

1962 Gibson EB-0 in Cherry Red and a 1959 EB-2 in sunburst: The Vault at Chicago Music Exchange.

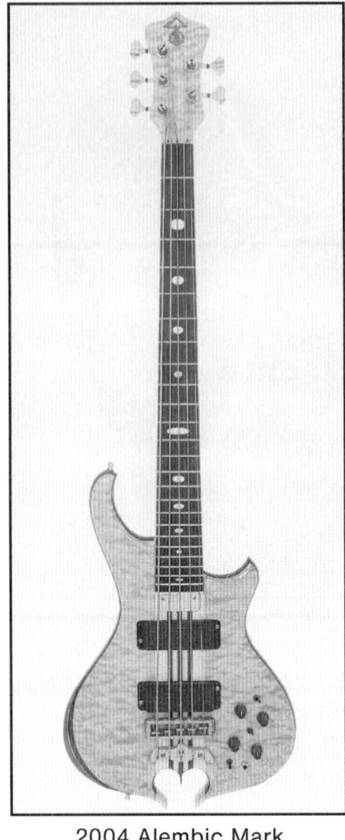
2004 Alembic Mark King Signature
Imaged by Heritage Auctions, HA.com

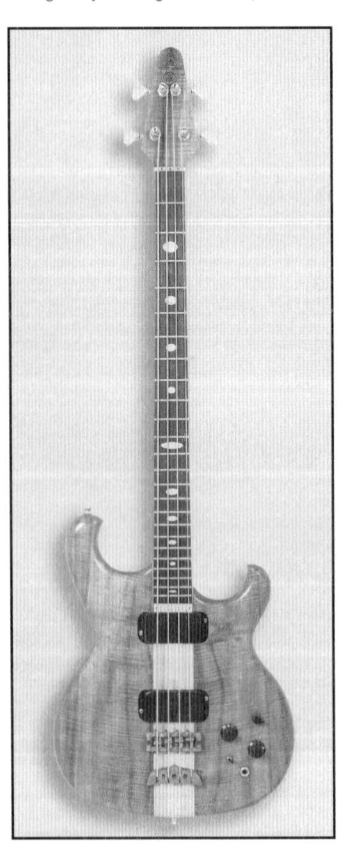
1984 Alembic Spoiler

MODEL YEAR	FEATURES	EXC. COND. LOW	HIGH

A Basses

1976-2002. Luthier Albey Balgochian built his professional grade, solidbody basses in Waltham, Massachusetts. Sports the A logo on headstock.

Solidbody

1976-2002		$1,125	$1,500

Acoustic

Ca. 1965-ca. 1987, 2001-2005, 2008-present. Mainly known for solidstate amps, the Acoustic Control Corp. of Los Angeles, did offer guitars and basses from around '69 to late '74. The brand was revived in '01 by Samick for a line of amps.

Black Widow AC600/AC650

1969-1970, 1972-1974. The AC600 featured a black double-cut body, German carve, Ebonite 'board, 2 pickups, and a protective "spider design" pad on back. The AC650 is short-scale. The '72-'74 versions had a rosewood 'board and 1 pickup. Acoustic outsourced the production of the basses, possibly to Japan, but at least part of the final production was by Semie Moseley.

1969-1970		$1,125	$1,500
1972-1974		$1,000	$1,375

Airline

1958-1968, 2004-present. Brand for Montgomery Ward. Built by Kay, Harmony and Valco. In '04, the brand was revived on a line of reissues from Eastwood guitars.

Electric Solidbody

1958-1968	Various models	$650	$850

Pocket 3/4 (Valco/National)

1962-1968. Airline brand of double-cut Pocket Bass, short-scale, 2 pickups, 1 acoustic bridge and 1 neck humbucker, sunburst and other colors.

1962-1968		$750	$950

Alamo

1947-1982. Founded by Charles Eilenberg, Milton Fink, and Southern Music, San Antonio, Texas. Distributed by Bruno & Sons.

Eldorado (Model 2600)

1965-1966. Solidbody, 1 pickup, angular offset shape, double cut.

1965-1966		$450	$575

Titan

1963-1970. Hollowbody, 1 pickup, angular offset shape.

1963-1970		$450	$575

Alembic

1969-present. Professional, premium, and presentation grade, production/custom, 4-, 5-, and 6-string basses built in Santa Rosa, California. They also build guitars. Established in San Francisco as one of the first handmade bass builders. Alembic basses come with many options concerning woods (examples are maple, bubinga, walnut, vermilion, wenge, zebrawood), finishes, inlays, etc., all of which affect the values listed here. These dollar amounts should be used as a baseline guide to values for Alembic.

MODEL YEAR	FEATURES	EXC. COND. LOW	HIGH

Distillate

1981-1991. One of Alembic's early lower-cost models, early ones with 1 pickup, 2 pickups by '82, exotic woods, active electronics.

1981-1991	Distillate 4	$3,500	$4,875
1981-1991	Distillate 5	$3,500	$4,875

Elan

1985-1996. Available in 4-, 5-, 6- and 8-string models, 3-piece thru-body laminated maple neck, solid maple body, active electronics, solid brass hardware, offered in a variety of hardwood tops and custom finishes.

1985-1996	Elan 4	$3,500	$5,000
1985-1996	Elan 5	$3,625	$5,250
1985-1996	Elan 6	$4,000	$5,500

Epic

1993-2015. Mahogany body with various tops, extra-large pointed bass horn, maple/walnut veneer set-neck, available in 4-, 5-, and 6-string versions.

1993-2015	4-string	$2,250	$3,000
1993-2015	5-string	$2,250	$3,000
1993-2015	6-string	$2,500	$3,500

Essence

1991-present. Mahogany body with various tops, extra-large pointed bass horn, walnut/maple laminate neck-thru.

1991-2024	Essence 4	$2,500	$3,250
1991-2024	Essence 5	$2,625	$3,500
1991-2024	Essence 6	$2,875	$3,750

Europa

1992-present. Mahogany body with various tops, ebony 'board, available as 4-, 5-, and 6-string.

1992-2024		$3,500	$5,000

Excel

1999-present. Solidbody 5-string, set neck, several wood options.

1998-2024		$2,500	$4,000

Exploiter

1980s. Figured maple solidbody 4-string, neck-thru, transparent finish.

1984-1988		$3,500	$7,500

Mark King Signature

1989-2019. Standard or Deluxe models.

1989-2008		$6,000	$9,500

Orion

1996-present. Offset double cut solidbody, various figured-wood top, 4, 5, or 6 strings.

1996-2024		$3,500	$4,875

Persuader

1983-1991. Offset double-cut solidbody, 4-string, neck-thru.

1983-1991		$3,000	$4,250

Rogue

1996-present. Double-cut solidbody, extreme long pointed bass horn.

1996-2024		$3,000	$4,250

Series I

1971-present. Mahogany body with various tops, maple/purpleheart laminate neck-thru, active electronics, available in 3 scale lengths and with 4, 5 or 6 strings.

1971-1979	All scales	$6,000	$8,000
1980-1989	All scales	$6,000	$8,000
1990-2024	Highly figured	$6,500	$8,500

MODEL YEAR	FEATURES	EXC. COND. LOW	HIGH

Series II

1971-present. Generally custom-made option, each instrument valued on a case-by-case basis, guidance pricing only.

1971-1979		$8,500	$12,000
1980-2024		$8,500	$16,000

Spoiler

1981-1999. Solid mahogany body, maple neck-thru, 4, 5 or 6 strings, active electronics, various high-end wood options.

1981-1986	6-string	$3,875	$4,875
1981-1989	5-string	$3,500	$4,500
1981-1999	4-string	$3,500	$4,500

Stanley Clarke Signature Deluxe

1990-present. Neck-thru-body, active electronics, 24-fret ebony 'board, mahogany body with various wood and laminate tops, 4-, 5-, and 6-string versions.

1990-2024	All scales	$6,500	$9,500

Stanley Clarke Signature Standard

1990-present. Neck-thru-body, active electronics, 24-fret ebony 'board, mahogany body with various wood and laminate tops, 4-, 5-, and 6-string versions.

1990-2024	All scales	$6,000	$8,500

Alleva-Coppolo Basses and Guitars

1995-present. Professional and premium grade, custom/production, solidbody electric guitars and basses built by luthier Jimmy Coppolo in Dallas, TX for '95-'97, in New York City for '98-2008, Upland, CA for '99-'21 and in Gadsden, AL '21-present.

Alvarez

1965-present. Imported by St. Louis Music, they offered electric basses from '90 to '02 and acoustic basses in the mid-'90s.

American Showster

1986-2004, 2010-2011. Established by Bill Meeker and David Haines, Bayville, New Jersey. They also made guitars.

AS-57-B Classic

1987-1997. Bass version of AS-57 with body styled like a '57 Chevy tail fin.

1987-1997		$3,500	$4,500

Ampeg

1949-present. Ampeg was founded on a vision of an amplified bass peg, which evolved into the Baby Bass. Ampeg has sold basses on and off throughout its history. In '08 they got back into basses with the reissue of the Dan Armstrong Plexi Bass.

AEB-1

1966-1967. F-holes through the body, fretted, scroll headstock, pickup in body, sunburst. Reissued as the AEB-2 for '97-'99.

1966-1967		$4,500	$7,000

ASB-1 Devil/AUSB-1 Devil

1966-1967. Long-horn body, fretted (ASB-1) or fretless (AUSB-1), triangular f-holes through the body, fireburst.

1966-1967		$4,500	$7,000

AUB-1

1966-1967. Same as AEB-1, but fretless, sunburst. Reissued as the AUB-2 for '97-'99.

1966-1967		$4,000	$5,000

BB-4 Baby (4-string)

1962-1971. Electric upright slim-looking bass that is smaller than a cello, 4-string, available in sunburst, white, red, black, and a few turquoise. Reissued as the ABB-1 Baby Bass for '97-'99.

1962-1971	Solid color	$2,750	$4,000
1962-1971	Sunburst	$2,500	$3,250

BB-5 Baby (5-string)

1964-1971. Five-string version.

1964-1971	Solid color	$3,000	$3,750
1964-1971	Sunburst	$2,500	$3,250

Dan Armstrong Lucite

1969-1971. Clear solid lucite body, did not have switchable pickups like the Lucite guitar.

1969-1971	Clear	$2,000	$3,000
1969-1971	Smoke	$2,500	$4,000

Dan Armstrong Lucite Reissue/ADA4

1998-2001, 2008-2009. Lucite body, Dan Armstrong Ampeg block lettering on 'guard. Reissue in '08 as the ADA4.

1998-2001		$1,125	$1,750
2008-2009	Reintroduced	$1,125	$1,500

EB-1 Wild Dog

1963-1964. Made by Burns of London, along with the Wild Dog Guitar, offset double cut solidbody, 3 pickups.

1963-1964		$1,000	$1,250

GEB-101 Little Stud

1973-1975. Import from Japan, offset double-cut solidbody, two-on-a-side tuners, 1 pickup.

1973-1975		$500	$750

GEB-750 Big Stud

1973-1975. Import from Japan, similar to Little Stud, but with 2 pickups.

1973-1975		$600	$800

SSB

1967-1968. Short scale, fretted, 4-string.

1967-1968		$3,500	$5,000

SSUB

1967-1968. Short scale, fretless, 4-string.

1967-1968		$3,500	$5,000

Andreas

1995-2004. Aluminium-necked, solidbody guitars and basses built by luthier Andreas Pichler in Dollach, Austria.

Angelica

1967-1975. Student and entry-level basses and guitars imported from Japan.

Electric Solid Body

1970s. Japanese imports.

1970s	Various models	$175	$400

Apollo

Ca. 1967-1972. Entry-level basses imported from Japan by St. Louis Music. They also had guitars and effects.

1966 Ampeg AEB-1

Imaged by Heritage Auctions, HA.com

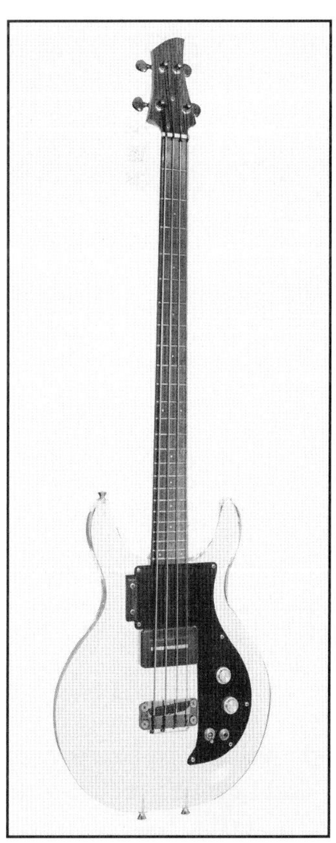

Ampeg Dan Armstrong Lucite

Imaged by Heritage Auctions, HA.com

BASSES

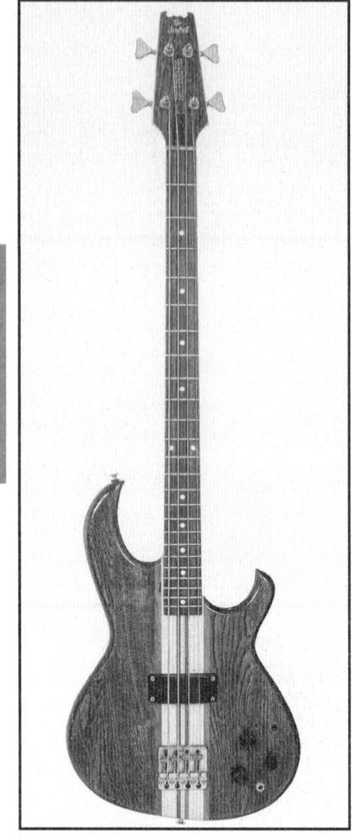

1980 Aria Pro II
Imaged by Heritage Auctions, HA.com

1995 B.C. Rich Mockingbird
Imaged by Heritage Auctions, HA.com

Electric Hollow Body

1967-1972. Japanese imports.

MODEL YEAR	FEATURES	EXC. COND. LOW	HIGH
1967-1972		$500	$700

Arbor

1983-ca. 2013. Budget grade, production, solid body basses imported by Musicorp (MBT). They also offered guitars.

Electric

MODEL YEAR	FEATURES	EXC. COND. LOW	HIGH
1983-2013	Various models	$250	$550

Aria/Aria Pro II

1956-present. Budget and intermediate grade, production, acoustic, acoustic/electric, solidbody, hollowbody and upright basses. They also make guitars, mandolins, and banjos. Originally branded as Aria; renamed Aria Pro II in '75; both names used over the next several years; in '01, the Pro II part of the name was dropped altogether.

Electric

MODEL YEAR	FEATURES	EXC. COND. LOW	HIGH
1980s	Various models	$300	$2,000

Austin Hatchet

Mid-1970s-mid-1980s. Trademark of distributor Targ and Dinner, Chicago, Illinois.

Hatchet

MODEL YEAR	FEATURES	EXC. COND. LOW	HIGH
1981	Travel bass	$500	$950

B.C. Rich

1966-present. Budget, intermediate, and premium grade, production/custom, import and U.S.-made basses. They also offer guitars. Many B.C. Rich models came in a variety of colors. For example, in '88 they offered black, Competition Red, metallic red, GlitteRock White, Ultra Violet, and Thunder Blue. Also in '88, other custom colors, graphic features, paint-to-match headstocks, and special inlays were offered.

Bich

1978-1998. Solidbody, neck-thru, 2 pickups.

MODEL YEAR	FEATURES	EXC. COND. LOW	HIGH
1978-1979	USA	$8,000	$10,000
1980-1985		$3,750	$6,000
1986-1989		$3,750	$6,000
1989-1993	Class Axe era	$2,000	$2,500
1994-1998	2nd Rico-era	$2,000	$2,500

Bich Supreme 8-String

Late-1970s-early-1980s.

MODEL YEAR	FEATURES	EXC. COND. LOW	HIGH
1978-1982	Painted wood	$8,000	$9,500
1978-1982	Translucent wood	$8,500	$10,000

Eagle (U.S.A.)

1977-1996. Curved double-cut, solidbody, natural.

MODEL YEAR	FEATURES	EXC. COND. LOW	HIGH
1977-1979	Translucent wood	$4,500	$5,500
1977-1996	Painted wood	$4,250	$5,500
1980-1996	Translucent wood	$4,000	$5,000

Gunslinger

1987-1999. Inverted headstock, 1 humbucker.

MODEL YEAR	FEATURES	EXC. COND. LOW	HIGH
1987-1989		$1,750	$2,250
1989-1993	Class Axe era	$1,750	$2,250
1994-1999		$1,500	$1,875

Ironbird

1984-1998. Kind of star-shaped, neck-thru, solidbody, 2 pickups, active electronics, diamond inlays.

MODEL YEAR	FEATURES	EXC. COND. LOW	HIGH
1984-1989		$1,750	$2,250
1989-1993	Class Axe era	$1,750	$2,250
1994-1998	2nd Rico era	$1,500	$1,875

Mockingbird

1976-2009. US-made, short horn until '78, long horn after.

MODEL YEAR	FEATURES	EXC. COND. LOW	HIGH
1976	Painted	$4,500	$6,000
1976	Translucent	$5,000	$6,500
1977-1978	Painted	$4,000	$5,000
1977-1978	Translucent	$4,500	$6,000
1979-1983	Painted	$4,500	$6,000
1979-1983	Translucent	$4,500	$6,000
1984-1985	End 1st Rico-era	$4,000	$5,000
1986-1989	End 1st Rico era	$3,500	$4,500
1994-2009	New Rico-era	$2,500	$3,500

Mockingbird Heritage Classic

2007-2015. 4-string, neck-thru, quilted maple top, cloud inlay.

MODEL YEAR	FEATURES	EXC. COND. LOW	HIGH
2007-2015		$500	$750

Nighthawk

1980-1982. Bolt-neck.

MODEL YEAR	FEATURES	EXC. COND. LOW	HIGH
1980-1982		$2,500	$3,500

NJ Series

1983-2006. Various mid-level import models include Beast, Eagle, Innovator, Mockingbird, Virgin and Warlock. Replaced by NT Series.

MODEL YEAR	FEATURES	EXC. COND. LOW	HIGH
1983-1984	Early, Japan	$600	$2,000
1985-1986	Japan	$600	$2,000
1987-2006		$600	$2,000

Platinum Series

1986-2006. Lower-priced import versions including Eagle, Mockingbird, Beast, Warlock.

MODEL YEAR	FEATURES	EXC. COND. LOW	HIGH
1986-1999	Various models	$450	$650

Seagull

1973-1975. Solidbody, single cut, changed to Seagull II in '76.

MODEL YEAR	FEATURES	EXC. COND. LOW	HIGH
1973		$4,250	$5,500
1974-1975		$3,750	$4,500

Seagull II

1976-1977. Double-cut version.

MODEL YEAR	FEATURES	EXC. COND. LOW	HIGH
1976-1977		$3,250	$4,000

Son Of A Rich

1980-1981. Double-cut, 4-string.

MODEL YEAR	FEATURES	EXC. COND. LOW	HIGH
1980-1981		$1,750	$2,250

ST-III

1987-1998. Bolt or set neck, black hardware, P-Bass/J-Bass pickup configuration, ebony 'board.

MODEL YEAR	FEATURES	EXC. COND. LOW	HIGH
1987-1989	Bolt-on	$850	$1,125
1987-1989	Neck-thru	$925	$1,250
1989-1993	Class Axe-era	$850	$1,125
1994-1998	New Rico-era	$925	$1,250

Warlock (U.S.A.)

1981-2015. Bolt neck, maple body, rosewood 'board, Badass II low profile bridge by '88.

MODEL YEAR	FEATURES	EXC. COND. LOW	HIGH
1981-1985		$2,750	$3,500
1986-1989		$2,250	$3,000

MODEL YEAR	FEATURES	EXC. COND. LOW	HIGH

Wave

Early 1980s. Double-cut, cresting wave, neck-thru, solid body, 2 pickups, active electronics.

1983		$5,000	$6,500

B.C. Rico

1978-1982. B.C. Rich's first Japan-made guitars and basses were labeled B.C. Rico.

Eagle

1978-1982		$3,000	$4,000

Baldwin

1965-1970. The giant organ company got into guitars and basses in '65 when it bought Burns Guitars of England and sold those models in the U.S. under the Baldwin name.

Baby Bison

1965-1970. Scroll head, 2 pickups, black, red or white finishes.

1965-1966		$1,000	$1,375
1966-1970	Model 560	$1,000	$1,375

Bison

1965-1970. Scroll headstock, 3 pickups, black or white finishes.

1965-1966		$1,500	$2,000
1966-1970	Model 516	$1,000	$1,375

G.B. 66

1965-1966. Bass equivalent of G.B. 66 guitar, covered bridge tailpiece.

1965-1966		$1,000	$1,375

Jazz Split Sound

1965-1970. Offset double-cut solidbody, 2 pickups, red sunburst.

1965-1966	Long-scale	$1,125	$1,500
1966-1970	Short-scale	$1,000	$1,375

Nu-Sonic

1965-1966. Bass version of Nu-Sonic.

1965-1966		$950	$1,375

Shadows/Shadows Signature

1965-1970. Named after Hank Marvin's backup band, solidbody, 3 slanted pickups, white finish.

1965-1966	Shadows	$2,000	$2,500
1966-1970	Shadows Signature	$1,875	$2,375

Vibraslim

1965-1970. Thin body, scroll head, 2 pickups, sunburst.

1965-1966		$1,750	$2,250
1966-1970	Model 549	$1,500	$2,000

Barclay

1960s. Generally shorter-scale, student-level imports from Japan. They also made guitars.

Bass Collection

1985-1992. Mid-level imports from Japan, distributed by Meisel Music of Springfield, New Jersey. Sam Ash Music, New York, sold the remaining inventory from '92 to '94.

Black Jack

1960s. Entry-level and mid-level imports from Japan. They also offered guitars.

Bradford

1960s. House brand of W.T. Grant department store, often imported. They also offered guitars.

Brian Moore

1992-present. Brian Moore added basses in '97. Currently they offer professional grade, production, solidbody basses. They also build guitars and mandolins.

i2000 Series

2000-present. Offset double-cut solidbody with extended bass horn, 2 pickups, 4- (i4) or 5-string (i5), options include piezo (p), fretless (-f), Bartolini pickups (B), and 13-pin mid (.13).

2000-2024		$950	$1,250

Brice

1985-present. Budget grade, production, electric and acoustic basses imported by Rondo Music of Union, New Jersey.

BSX Bass

1990-present. Luthier Dino Fiumara builds his professional and premium grade, production/custom, acoustic, solidbody, semi-solid upright basses in Aliquippa, Pennsylvania.

Burns

1960-1970, 1974-1983, 1992-present. Intermediate and professional grade, production, basses built in England and Korea. They also build guitars.

Baby Bison

1965-1968. Early version had "V" headstock and long Rez-O-Tube vibrato. Later short Rezo-Tube tailpiece.

1965-1968		$1,000	$1,375

Bison

1965-1968. Double-cut, long scale, 4-string.

1965-1968		$1,750	$2,250

Nu-Sonic

1964-1965, 2011-2020. Offset double-cut solidbody, 2 pickups.

1964-1965		$1,125	$1,500

Scorpion

Introduced 1979, 2003-2009. Double-cut scorpion-like solidbody.

2003-2009		$550	$725

Cameo

1960s-1970s. Japanese- and Korean-made electric basses. They also offered guitars.

Electric

1960s-70s		$400	$550

Charvel

1976-present. U.S.-made from '78 to '85 and a combination of imports and U.S.-made post-'85. They also build guitars.

Pre-Pro

1980-1981. Pre-mass production basses made Nov. '80 to '81. Refer to Charvel guitar section for details.

1980-1981	All models	$3,500	$4,500

1965 Baldwin Baby Bison

Rivington Guitars

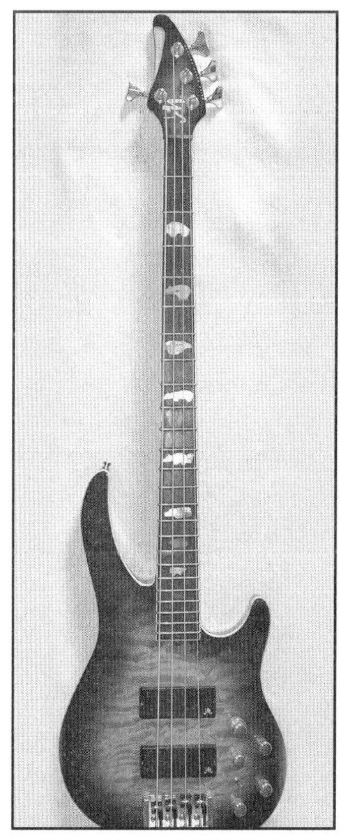

Brian Moore i2000 Series

Richard Memmel

BASSES

BASSES

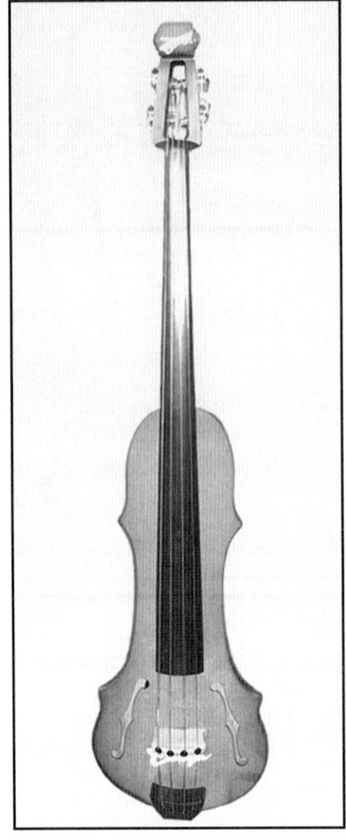
Clevinger Concerto Grande

1968 Coral Firefly
Imaged by Heritage Auctions, HA.com

MODEL YEAR	FEATURES	EXC. COND. LOW	HIGH

850 XL

1988-1991. Four-string, neck-thru, active.

1988-1991		$925	$1,250

CX-490

1991-1994. Double-cut, 4-string, bolt neck, red or white.

1991-1994		$325	$425

Eliminator

1990-1991. Offset double-cut, active electronics, bolt neck.

1990-1991		$500	$650

Fusion

1989-1991. Active circuitry, 4- and 5-string models.

1989-1991	IV	$650	$850
1989-1991	V	$725	$950

Model 1

1986-1988. Double-cut, bolt neck, 1 pickup.

1986-1988		$525	$675

Model 2

1986-1988. Double-cut, bolt neck, 2 pickups.

1986-1988		$550	$725

Model 3

1986-1988. Neck-thru, 2 single-coils, active, master volume, bass and treble knobs.

1986-1988		$650	$850

Model 4

1986-1988. Like Model 3, but with bolt neck.

1986-1988		$750	$975

Model 5

1986-1989. Double-cut, P/J pickups.

1986-1989		$750	$975

San Dimas Serialized Plated

1981-1982. Soft headstock early models.

1981-1982		$3,500	$4,500

SB-4

1990s. Offset double cut solid, long bass horn, 2 pickups.

1990s		$550	$725

Star

1980-1981. Unique 4-point solidbody, 1 pickup, considered by Charvel collectors to be Charvel's only original early design.

1980-1981		$4,500	$6,000

Surfcaster

1991-1994. Semi-hollow, lipstick tube pickups.

1991-1994		$1,375	$1,750

Cipher

1960s. Student market basses imported from Japan. They also made guitars.

Electric Solid Body

1960s. Japanese imports.

1960s		$400	$525

Clevinger

Established in 1982 by Martin Clevinger, Oakland, California. Mainly specializing in electric upright basses but has offered bass guitars as well.

College Line

One of many Lyon & Healy brands, made during the era of extreme design experimentation.

Monster (Style 2089)

Early-1900s. 22" lower bout, flat-top guitar/bass, natural.

1915		$3,000	$4,000

Conrad

Ca.1968-1978. Student and mid-level copy basses imported by David Wexler, Chicago, Illinois. They also offered guitars, mandolins and banjos.

Electric

1970s	Various models	$425	$550

Professional Bison

1970s. Solidbody, 2 pickups.

1970s		$500	$650

Coral

1967-1969. In '66 MCA bought Danelectro and in '67 introduced the Coral brand of guitars, basses and amps. The line included several solid and semi-solidbody basses.

Deluxe D2N4

1967-1969. Offset double-cut, 2 pickups.

1967-1969	Black	$1,375	$1,875
1967-1969	Sunburst	$1,375	$1,875

Fiddle FB2B4

1967-1969. Violin bass hollow body, 2 pickups.

1967-1969		$1,375	$1,875

Firefly F2B4

1968-1969. 335-style semi-hollow, 2 pickups.

1968-1969	Red	$1,125	$1,375
1968-1969	Sunburst	$1,125	$1,375

Long Horn

1968-1969. Standard neck (L2B4) or extended neck (L2LB4), 4 strings.

1968	L2LB4	$2,375	$2,875
1968-1969	L2B4	$1,875	$2,375

Wasp

1967-1969. 4-string (2B4) or 6-string (2B6), black, red or sunburst.

1967-1969	2B4, black or red	$1,375	$1,875
1967-1969	2B4, sunburst	$1,375	$1,875
1967-1969	2B6, black or red	$1,375	$1,875
1967-1969	2B6, sunburst	$1,375	$1,875

Crestwood

1970s. Imported by La Playa Distributing Company of Detroit. Product line includes copies of the popular classical guitars, flat-tops, electric solidbodies and basses of the era.

Electric

1970s. Includes models 2048, 2049, 2079, 2090, 2092, 2093, and 2098.

1970s		$325	$450

Crown

1960s. Violin-shaped hollowbody electrics, solidbody electric guitars and basses, possibly others. Imported from Japan.

Electric Solidbody

1960s	Import	$325	$450

MODEL YEAR	FEATURES	EXC. COND. LOW	HIGH

Custom Kraft

Late-1950s-1968. A house brand of St. Louis Music Supply, instruments built by Valco and others. They also offered guitars and amps.

Bone Buzzer Model 12178

Late 1960s. Symmetrical double-cut thin hollow body, lightning bolt f-holes, 4-on-a-side tuners, 2 pickups, sunburst or emerald sunburst.

1960s		$675	$900

D'Agostino

1976-early 1990s. Import company established by Pat D'Agostino. Solidbodies imported from EKO Italy '77-'82, Japan '82-'84, and in Korea for '84 on. Overall, about 60% of guitars and basses were Japanese, 40% Korean.

Electric Solidbody

1970s	Various models	$850	$1,125

Daion

1978-1984. Higher quality copy basses imported from Japan. Original designs were introduced in '80s. They also had guitars.

Electric

1978-1984	Higher-end	$1,125	$1,500
1978-1984	Lower-end	$650	$850

Danelectro

1946-1969, 1997-present. Danelectro offered basses throughout most of its early history. In '96, the Evets Corporation, of San Clemente, California, introduced a line of Danelectro effects; amps, basses and guitars, many reissues of earlier instruments, soon followed. In early '03, Evets discontinued the guitar, bass and amp lines, but revived the guitar and bass line in '05. Danelectro also built Coral brand instruments (see Coral).

Dane A Series

1967. Solidbody, 2 pickups, 4-string.

1967		$950	$1,125

Dane C Series

1967. Semi-solidbody 4- or 6-string, 2 pickups.

1967	4-string	$1,125	$1,375
1967	6-string	$1,250	$1,875

Dane D Series

1967. Solidbody, 2 pickups, 4- or 6-string.

1967	4-string	$1,125	$1,375
1967	6-string	$1,375	$1,875

Dane E Series

1967. Solidbody, 2 pickups, 4-string.

1967		$1,375	$1,875

Hawk

1967. Solidbody, 4-string, 1 pickup.

1967		$1,375	$1,875

Model 1444L

Ca.1958-ca.1964. Masonite body, single-cut, 2 pickups, copper finish.

1958-1964		$1,375	$1,875

Model 3412 Standard (Shorthorn)

1959-1966. Coke bottle headstock, 4- or 6-string, 1 pickup, kidney 'guard through '60, seal 'guard after, copper finish.

1959-1960	Kidney 'guard, 4-string	$950	$1,375
1959-1960	Kidney 'guard, 6-string	$1,375	$1,875
1961-1966	Seal 'guard, 4-string	$950	$1,375
1961-1966	Seal 'guard, 6-string	$1,375	$1,875

Model 3612 Standard (Shorthorn)

1959-1966. 6-string version.

1959-1962	Kidney 'guard	$1,125	$1,375
1961-1966	Seal 'guard	$1,125	$1,375

'58 Shorthorn Reissue

1997-2003. Reissues of classic Shorthorn bass.

1997-2003		$350	$500

Model 4423 Longhorn 4-String

1959-1966. Coke bottle headstock, 4-string, 2 pickups, tweed case '59, gray tolex after.

1959	Tweed case	$2,375	$2,875
1960-1966	Gray tolex case	$2,375	$2,875

Model 4623 Longhorn 6-String

1959-1966, 1969-1970. 6-string version.

1959	Tweed case	$3,000	$3,500
1960-1966	Gray tolex case	$3,000	$3,500
1969-1970		$2,000	$2,500

'58 Longhorn Reissue/Longhorn Pro

1997-2010. Reissues of classic Longhorn bass.

1997-2010		$300	$400

UB-2 6-String

1956-1958. Single-cut, 2 pickups, black, bronze or ivory.

1956-1958		$2,000	$2,500

David J King

1987-present. Production/custom, professional and premium grade, electric basses built by luthier David King first in Amherst, Massachusetts and since '92 in Portland, Oregon.

Dean

1976-present. Intermediate and professional grade, production, solidbody, hollowbody, acoustic, and acoustic/electric, basses made overseas. They also offer guitars, banjos, mandolins, and amps.

Baby ML

1982-1986. Downsized version of ML.

1982-1986	Import	$550	$750

Mach V

1985-1986. U.S.-made pointed solidbody, 2 pickups, rosewood 'board.

1985-1986		$2,000	$2,500

ML

1977-1986, 2001-2010. Futuristic body style, fork headstock.

1977-1983	US-made	$2,500	$4,250
1984-1986	Korean import	$1,250	$1,625

Rhapsody Series (USA)

2001-2004. Scroll shaped offset double-cut, various models.

2001-2004	12-string	$1,000	$1,500
2001-2004	8-string	$1,000	$1,500
2001-2004	HFB fretless	$650	$850

1959 Danelectro Model 3412 Shorthorn

Thomas J. Pervanje

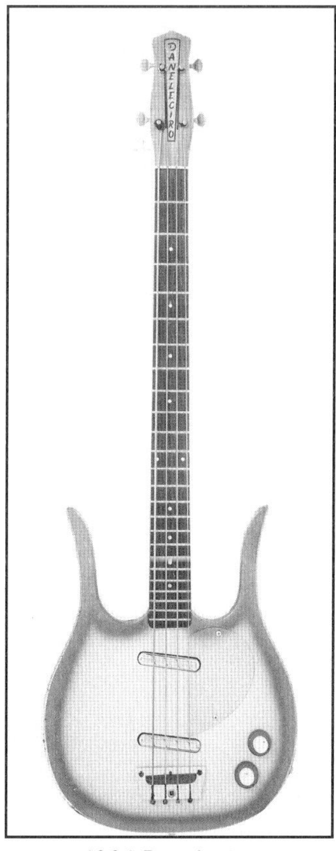

1964 Danelectro 4423 Longhorn

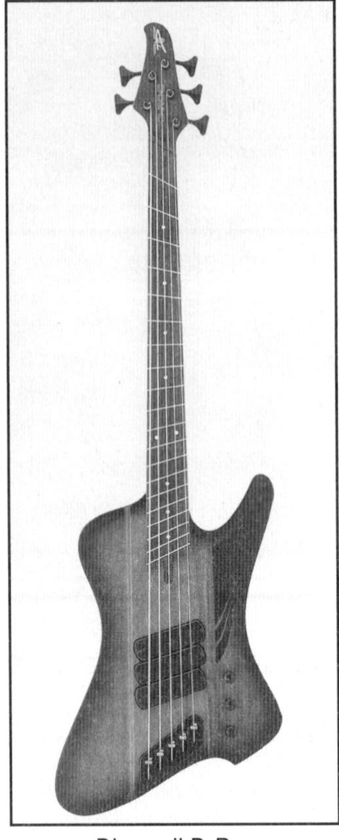

Dingwall D-Roc

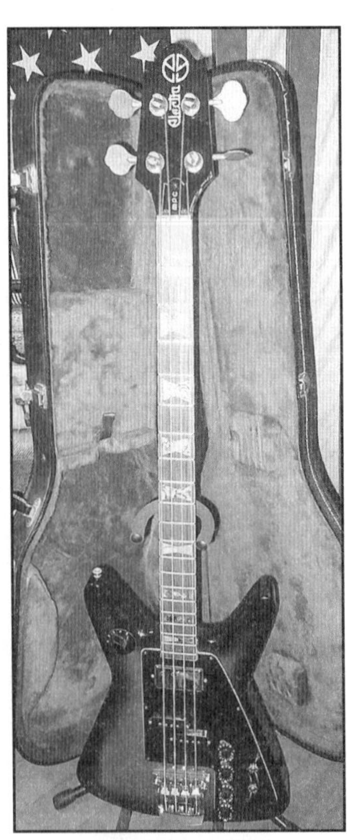

1978 Electra MPC X-620 Outlaw

Rivington Guitars

MODEL YEAR	FEATURES	EXC. COND. LOW	HIGH

DeArmond

1999-2004. Electric basses based on Guild models and imported from Korea by Fender. They also offered guitars.

Electric

1999-2004. Various imported models.

1999-2004		$550	$725

Dingwall

1988-present. Luthier Sheldon Dingwall, Saskatoon, Saskatchewan, started producing guitar bodies and necks, eventually offering complete guitars and basses. Currently, Dingwall offers professional to premium grade, production/custom 4-, 5-, and 6-string basses featuring the Novax Fanned-Fret System.

Domino

Ca. 1967-1968. Imported from Japan by Maurice Lipsky Music of New York, mainly copies, but some original designs. They also offered guitars.

Electric

1967-1968. Includes the Beatle Bass and Fireball Bass, a Vox Phantom IV copy.

1967-1968		$450	$650

Dorado

Ca. 1972-1973. Name used briefly by Baldwin/Gretsch on a line of Japanese guitar and bass imports.

Electric Solidbody

1970s	Import	$350	$450

Earthwood

1972-1985. Acoustic designs by Ernie Ball with input from George Fullerton and made in Newport Beach, California. One of the first to offer acoustic basses.

Acoustic

1972-1985. Big bodied acoustic bass alternative between Kay double bass and solidbody Fender bass.

1972-1985		$3,000	$4,000

EKO

1959-1985, 2000-present. Built by the Oliviero Pigini Company, Italy. Original importers included LoDuca Brothers, Milwaukee, Wisconsin. Since about 2000, production, acoustic and electric EKO basses are again available and made in Italy and China. They also make guitars and amps.

Barracuda

1967-1978. Offset double-cut semi-hollow, 2 pickups.

1967-1978		$625	$800

Cobra II

1967-ca.1969. Offset double-cut solidbody, 2 pickups.

1967-1969		$500	$650

Kadett

1967-1978. Red or sunburst.

1967-1978		$500	$650

Model 995/2 Violin

1966-ca.1969.

1966-1969		$800	$1,000

Model 1100/2

1961-1966. Jaguar-style plastic covered solidbody, 2 pickups, sparkle finish.

1961-1966		$700	$875

Rocket IV/Rokes

1967-early-1970s. Rocket-shape design, solidbody, says Rokes on the headstock, the Rokes were a popular English band that endorsed EKO guitars. Marketed as the Rocket IV in the U.S. and as the Rokes in Europe. Often called the Rok. Sunburst, 1 pickup.

1967-1971		$1,125	$1,500

Electra

1970-1984, 2013-present. Originally basses imported from Japan by St. Louis Music. They also offered guitars. Currently U.S.-made in Tampa, Florida.

Electric Solidbody

1970s. Japanese imports, various models.

1970s		$650	$850

MPC Outlaw

1970s. Symmetric solidbody with large straight horns, 2 separate plug-in modules for different effects, MPC headstock logo, bowtie markers, sunburst.

1970s		$950	$1,250

Emperador

1966-1992. Student-level basses imported by Westheimer Musical Instruments. Early models appear to be made by either Teisco or Kawai; later models were made by Cort. They also had guitars.

Electric Solidbody

1960s. Japanese imports, various models.

1960s	Beatle Violin Bass	$350	$550
1960s	Various models	$200	$300

Engelhardt

Engelhardt specializes in student acoustic basses and cellos and is located in Elk Grove Village, Illinois.

Epiphone

1928-present. Epiphone didn't add basses until 1959, after Gibson acquired the brand. The Gibson Epiphones were American made until '69, then all imports until into the '80s, when some models were again made in the U.S. Currently Epiphone offers intermediate and professional grade, production, acoustic and electric basses.

B-1 Acoustic Viol

1940-1949. Maple back and sides, cherry sunburst.

1940-1949		$2,000	$2,500

B-2 Acoustic Viol

1940-1949. Mid-level maple back and sides.

1940-1949		$2,250	$3,000

B-3 Acoustic Viol

1940-1949. Higher-level maple back and sides.

1940-1949		$2,250	$3,000

B-4 Acoustic Viol

1940-1964. Highly figured maple back and sides.

1940-1964		$3,000	$4,000

MODEL YEAR	FEATURES	EXC. COND. LOW	HIGH

B-5 Artist Acoustic Viol

1941-1964. Highly figured maple back and sides.

1941-1964		$3,500	$4,500

EA/ET/ES Series (Japan)

1970-1979. Production of the Epiphone brand was moved to Japan in '70. Models included the EA (electric thinline) and ET (electric solidbody).

1970-1975	Various models	$650	$850

EB-0/EB-1/EB-3/EBM-4

1991-2019. EB-0 ('98-'19), EB-1 ('98-'00), EB-3 ('99-'19) and EBM-4 ('91-'98).

1991-2019	Various models	$250	$600

Elitist Series

2003-2005. Higher-end appointments such as set-necks and USA pickups.

2003-2005	Various models	$850	$1,250

Embassy Deluxe

1963-1969. Solidbody, double-cut, 2 pickups, tune-o-matic bridge, cherry finish.

1963-1964		$5,500	$7,000
1965		$5,500	$7,000
1966-1969		$5,000	$6,500

Explorer Korina

2000-2001. Made in Korea, Gibson Explorer body style, genuine korina body, set neck, gold hardware.

2000-2001		$650	$850

Genesis

1979-1980. Double-cut solidbody, 2 humbuckers, Made in Taiwan.

1979-1980		$1,125	$1,500

Jack Cassady Signature

1997-present. Maple body, mahogany neck, rosewood 'board, 1 pickup, metallic gold or ebony finish.

1997-2024		$700	$875

Les Paul Special

1997-2013. LP Jr.-style slab body, single-cut, bolt neck, 2 humbuckers.

1997-2013		$325	$400

Newport EB-6

1962-1964	6-String	$6,500	$8,500

Newport EBD

1960-1970. Double-cut solidbody, 1 pickup (2 pickups optional until '63), 2-on-a-side tuners until '63, 4-on-a-side after that, cherry.

1960-1964		$3,000	$3,750
1965		$2,500	$3,250
1966		$2,000	$2,500
1967-1970		$2,000	$2,500

Newport EB-SF

1962-1963. Newport with added built-in fuzz, cherry.

1962-1963		$3,000	$4,000

Ripper

1998-2000, 2006-2008. Offset double-cut, 1 humbucker pickup, black or natural.

1998-2000		$700	$875

Rivoli (1 Pickup)

1959-1961, 1964-1970, 1994-2000. ES-335-style semi-hollowbody bass, 2-on-a-side tuners, 1 pickup (2 in '70).

1959-1960	Banjo tuners, natural	$4,500	$6,000
1959-1960	Banjo tuners, sunburst	$4,500	$6,000
1961	Standard tuners, natural	$4,250	$5,500
1961	Standard tuners, sunburst	$4,000	$5,000
1964		$3,000	$4,000
1965		$2,500	$3,500
1966-1969		$2,500	$3,250
1967	Sparkling Burgundy	$3,500	$4,250
1970		$2,500	$3,250

Rivoli (2 Pickups)

1970 only. Double pickup Epiphone version of Gibson EB-2D.

1970		$2,500	$3,250

Rivoli II Reissue

1995-2000. Made in Korea, set neck, blond.

1995-2000		$800	$1,000

Thunderbird IV

1997-2019. Reverse-style mahogany body, 2 pickups, sunburst.

1997-2019		$500	$650

Thunderbird IV (Non-Reverse)

1995-1998. Non-reverse-style mahogany body, 2 pickups, 5-string optional.

1995-1998		$525	$675

Viola

1995-present. Beatle Bass 500/1 copy, sunburst.

1995-2024		$450	$600

ESP

1975-present. Intermediate, professional, and premium grade, production/custom, electric basses. Japan's ESP (Electric Sound Products) made inroads in the U.S. market with mainly copy styles in the early '80s, mixing in original designs over the years. In the '90s, ESP opened a California-based Custom Shop. They also build guitars.

Electric

1980s-1990s. Various factory production models.

1980s-90s		$800	$1,500

Essex (SX)

1985-present. Budget grade, production, electric basses imported by Rondo Music of Union, New Jersey. They also offer guitars.

Estrada

1960s-1970s. Line of classical, acoustic and electric guitars and basses imported from Japan.

Violin

1960s	Import	$500	$650

Fender

1946-present. Intermediate, professional, and premium grade, production/custom, electric and acoustic basses made in the U.S. and overseas. Leo Fender is the father of the electric bass. The introduction of his Precision Bass in late '51 changed forever how music was performed, recorded and heard. Leo followed with other popular models

1997 Epiphone Rivoli 1 Pickup

Angelo Guarini

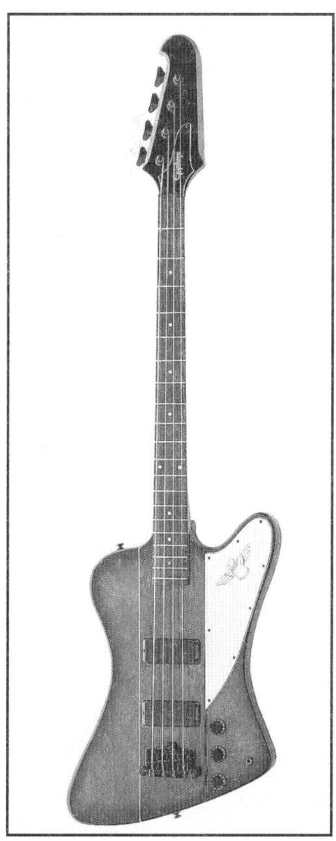
Epiphone Thunderbird IV Bass

1966 Fender Bass V
Izzy Miller

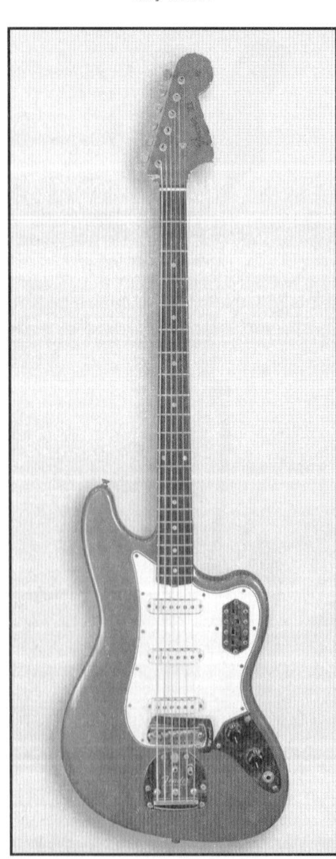
1964 Fender Bass VI
David Swartz

of basses that continue to make up a large part of Fender's production. Please note that all the variations of the Jazz and Precision Basses are grouped under those general headings.

The Precision Bass first left the Fender factory painted blond (same color as the Telecaster). It changed to a 2-color sunburst in mid-1955 (same color as Stratocaster). Some blond Precision basses were shipped after 1955. They are typically worth 50% more. The Jazz Bass standard color is sunburst. All Fender basses could be shipped in a custom DuPont Duco or DuPont Lucite color. Some custom colors are rarer than others. Below is a list of the custom colors offered in 1960 by Fender. They are sorted in ascending order with the most valuable color, Shell Pink, listed last. In the 1960 list, Black and Blond are the least valuable and Shell Pink is the most valuable. A Fiesta Red is typically worth 12% more than a Black or Blond. In the rare color group, a Foam Green is normally worth 8% more than a Shoreline Gold. The two very rare colors are often worth 30% more than a Shoreline Gold. In our pricing information we will list the standard color, then the relative value of a common custom color, and then the value of a rare custom color. Remember that the amount of fade also affects the price. These prices are for factory original custom colors with slight or no fade. Fade implies a lighter color, but with custom colors a faded example can also be much darker in color due to the yellowing of the nitrocellulose clearcoat. Blue can fade to dark green. White can fade to deep yellow.

The Price Guide lists the standard color, plus the value of a Common Color and the value of a Rare Color. The list below defines which group a color falls into for 1960, and it is in ascending order so, for example, a Daphne Blue should be considered more valuable than a Lake Placid Blue, assuming they are in equal condition.

Common Colors: Black, Blond, Candy Apple Red, Olympic White, Lake Placid Blue, Dakota Red, Daphne Blue, Fiesta Red

Rare Colors: Shoreline Gold, Inca Silver, Burgundy Mist, Sherwood Green, Sonic Blue, Foam Green

Rare (Very Rare) Pastel Colors: Surf Green, Shell Pink

Ashbory

2003-2006. Unique-shaped travel bass, Ashbory logo on body, Fender logo on back of headstock, previously sold under Fender's DeArmond brand.

MODEL YEAR	FEATURES	EXC. COND. LOW	HIGH
2003-2006		$250	$350

Bass V

1965-1970. Five strings, double-cut, 1 pickup, dot inlay '65-'66, block inlay '66-'70. Please refer to the beginning of the Fender Bass Section for details on Fender color options.

MODEL YEAR	FEATURES	EXC. COND. LOW	HIGH
1965	Common color	$5,250	$8,000
1965	Rare color	$6,750	$10,000
1965	Sunburst	$4,000	$5,000
1966-1970	Common color	$4,750	$8,500
1966-1970	Rare color	$6,250	$10,000
1966-1970	Sunburst	$4,250	$5,000

Bass VI

1961-1975. Six strings, Jazzmaster-like body, 3 pickups, dot inlay until '66, block inlay '66-'75. Reintroduced as Japanese-made Collectable model '95-'98. Please refer to the beginning of the Fender Bass Section for details on Fender color options.

MODEL YEAR	FEATURES	EXC. COND. LOW	HIGH
1961-1962	Common color	$15,500	$25,000
1961-1962	Rare color	$20,000	$30,000
1961-1962	Sunburst	$8,500	$12,500
1963-1964	Common color	$14,500	$25,000
1963-1964	Rare color	$20,000	$30,000
1963-1964	Sunburst	$8,000	$11,500
1965	Common color	$13,000	$20,000
1965	Rare color	$18,500	$25,000
1965	Sunburst	$7,000	$9,500
1966-1969	Common color	$10,000	$15,000
1966-1969	Rare color	$12,500	$20,000
1966-1969	Sunburst	$6,500	$8,500
1970-1971	Custom color	$9,000	$12,000
1970-1971	Sunburst	$5,500	$7,500
1972-1974	Custom color	$8,500	$11,500
1972-1974	Natural	$5,250	$7,000
1972-1974	Sunburst	$5,250	$7,000
1972-1974	Walnut	$5,250	$7,000
1975	Black, blond, white	$5,250	$7,000
1975	Natural	$4,750	$6,500
1975	Sunburst	$4,750	$6,500
1975	Walnut	$4,750	$6,500

Bass VI Reissue (CS)

2006. Custom Shop, 3-tone sunburst, certificate of authenticity.

MODEL YEAR	FEATURES	EXC. COND. LOW	HIGH
2006		$2,250	$3,000

Bass VI Reissue (Import)

1995-1998. Import, sunburst.

MODEL YEAR	FEATURES	EXC. COND. LOW	HIGH
1995-1998		$1,125	$1,500

Bass VI Reissue (Japan)

Japanese market only, JD serial number.

MODEL YEAR	FEATURES	EXC. COND. LOW	HIGH
2014		$1,125	$1,500

Bass VI Pawn Shop

2013-2014. Alder body, maple neck, rosewood 'board, 3-color sunburst.

MODEL YEAR	FEATURES	EXC. COND. LOW	HIGH
2013-2014		$700	$900

BG Series

1995-2012. Acoustic flat-top basses, single-cut, two-on-a-side tuners, Fishman on-board controls.

MODEL YEAR	FEATURES	EXC. COND. LOW	HIGH
1995-2012	Various models	$175	$250

Bullet (B30, B34, B40)

1982-1983. Alder body, 1 pickup, offered in short- and long-scale, red or walnut. U.S.-made, replaced by Japanese-made Squire Bullet Bass.

MODEL YEAR	FEATURES	EXC. COND. LOW	HIGH
1982-1983		$800	$1,000

Bullet Deluxe

1982-1983. Fender logo with Bullet Bass Deluxe on headstock, E-series serial number, small Telecaster-style headstock shape.

MODEL YEAR	FEATURES	EXC. COND. LOW	HIGH
1982-1983		$950	$1,250

Coronado I

1966-1970. Thinline, double-cut, 1 pickup, dot inlay, sunburst and cherry red were the standard colors, but custom colors could be ordered.

MODEL YEAR	FEATURES	EXC. COND. LOW	HIGH
1966-1970	Various colors	$1,625	$2,250

MODEL YEAR	FEATURES	EXC. COND. LOW	HIGH

Coronado II

1966-1972. Two pickups, block inlay, sunburst and cherry red standard colors, but custom colors could be ordered. Only Antigua finish offered from '70 on.

1966-1969	Various colors	$2,125	$2,875
1966-1969	Wildwood option	$3,000	$4,500
1970-1972	Antigua only	$2,500	$3,500

Coronado Reissue

2014-2016. Reissue of the 2 pickup (Coronado II), block inlay.

2014-2016		$600	$800

Dimension

2004-2006. Made in Mexico, 4- or 5-string, P and J pickups.

2004-2006		$650	$850

HM

1989-1991. Japanese-made, 4 strings (IV) or 5 strings (V), basswood body, no 'guard, 3 Jazz Bass pickups, 5-way switch, master volume, master TBX, sunburst.

1989-1991	IV, 4-string	$800	$1,000
1989-1991	V, 5-string	$900	$1,125

Jaguar

1995, 2006-2010. Crafted in Japan, Jaguar Bass logo on headstock.

1995		$950	$1,250
2006-2010		$900	$1,125

Jaguar (Modern Player)

2012-2016. Made in China, koto body, maple neck and 'board, black.

2012-2016		$325	$425

Jaguar Baritone Custom

2007. Fender Jaguar Baritone Custom logo on headstock, 6-string.

2007		$1,000	$1,250

Deluxe Jaguar

2012-2014. Maple neck, rosewood 'board, 2 pickups, 3-color sunburst, Candy Apple Red, Cobalt Blue.

2012-2014		$550	$750

Troy Sanders Jaguar

2014-2023. Artist series, alder body, bolt-on maple neck, 2 pickups, silverburst.

2014-2023		$800	$1,000

Jazz Bass

The following are variations of the Jazz Bass. The first seven listings are for the main U.S.-made models. All others are listed alphabetically after that in the following order:

Jazz
Standard Jazz
American Standard Jazz
American Standard Jazz V
American Series Jazz
American Series Jazz V
American Professional/Professional II Jazz
50th Anniversary American Standard Jazz
50th Anniversary Jazz Limited Edition
'60 Custom Shop Limited Jazz
'60s Jazz (Custom Shop)
'60s Jazz (Import)
Road Worn '60s Jazz
Vintera '60s Jazz
60th Anniversary American Jazz
60th Anniversary Road Worn Jazz
'61 Journeyman Jazz
'62 Jazz (U.S.A.)
'64 Jazz (Custom Shop)
'64 Jazz (American Vintage)
'66 Jazz Special Limited Edition
'66 Journeyman Jazz
'74 Jazz (American Vintage)
'75 Jazz (American Vintage)
75th Anniversary Commemorative Jazz
75th Anniversary Jazz (Diamond Anniversary)
Aerodyne Jazz
American Deluxe Jazz/Jazz V
American Deluxe FMT Jazz
American Elite Jazz/Jazz V
American Ultra Jazz
Contemporary Jazz
Custom Classic Jazz/Jazz V
Deluxe Jazz/Jazz V (Active)
Deluxe Power Jazz
Flea Signature Jazz
Foto Flame Jazz
FSR Standard Special Edition Jazz
Geddy Lee Signature Jazz
Gold Jazz
Highway One Jazz
Jaco Pastorius Jazz
Jazz Plus IV/Jazz Plus V
Jazz Special (Import)
Marcus Miller Signature Jazz
Masterbuilt Custom Shop Jazz
Noel Redding Signature Jazz
Rarities Flame Ash Top Jazz
Reggie Hamilton Jazz
Roscoe Beck Jazz IV/Jazz V
Select Jazz
Standard Jazz (Import)
Standard Jazz Fretless (Import)
Steve Bailey Jazz VI
Ventures Limited Edition Jazz
Victor Baily Jazz

Jazz

1960-1981. Two stack knobs '60-'62, 3 regular controls '62 on. Dot markers '60-'66, block markers from '66 on. Rosewood 'board standard, but maple available from '68 on. With the introduction of vintage reissue models in '81, Fender started calling the American-made version the Standard Jazz Bass. That became the American Standard Jazz Bass in '88, the American Series Jazz Bass in '00, back to the American Standard Jazz Bass in '08, and currently the American Professional Jazz Bass. Post '71 Jazz Bass values are affected more by condition than color or neck option. The Jazz Bass was fitted with a 3-bolt neck or bullet rod in late-'74. Prices assume a 3-bolt neck starting in '75. Please refer to the beginning of the Fender Bass Section for details on Fender color options. Post '71 Jazz Bass values are affected more by condition than color or neck option. The Jazz Bass was

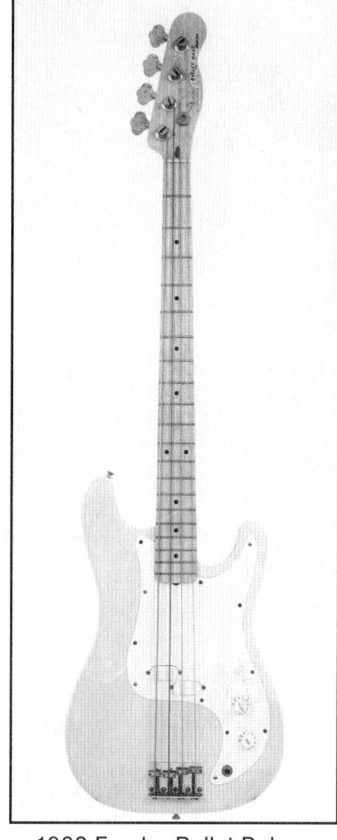

1982 Fender Bullet Deluxe
Imaged by Heritage Auctions, HA.com

Fender Troy Sanders Jaguar

1964 Fender Jazz
Ron Cascisa

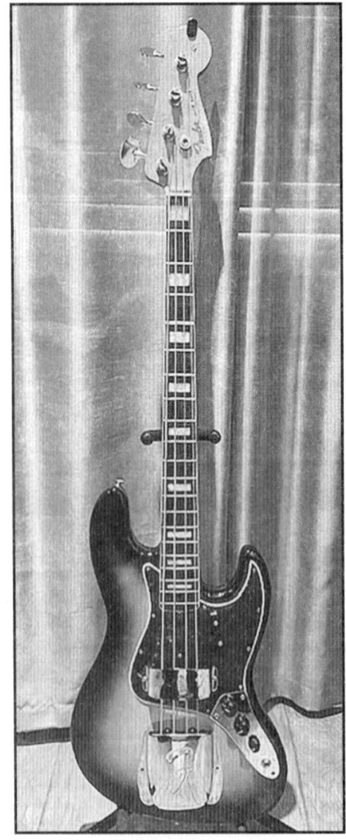
1966 Fender Jazz
David Carlino

fitted with a 3-bolt neck or bullet rod in late-'74. Prices assume a 3-bolt neck starting in '75. Please refer to the beginning of the Fender Bass Section for details on Fender color options.

MODEL YEAR	FEATURES	EXC. COND. LOW	HIGH
1960	Common color	$37,000	$45,000
1960	Rare color	$47,500	$150,000
1960	Sunburst	$25,000	$35,000
1961-1962	Common color, stack knob	$37,000	$45,000
1961-1962	Rare color, stack knob	$47,500	$150,000
1961-1962	Sunburst, stack knob	$25,000	$35,000
1962	Common color, 3 knob, curved	$22,000	$35,000
1962	Common color, 3 knob, slab	$27,000	$45,000
1962	Rare color, 3 knob, curved	$27,000	$40,000
1962	Rare color, 3 knob, slab	$30,000	$45,000
1962	Sunburst, 3 knob, curved	$18,000	$22,500
1962	Sunburst, 3 knob, slab	$20,000	$25,000
1963	Common color	$20,000	$30,000
1963	Rare color	$22,000	$35,000
1963	Sunburst	$15,500	$20,000
1964	Common color	$20,000	$25,000
1964	Rare color	$22,000	$30,000
1964	Sunburst, early '64	$15,500	$20,000
1964	Sunburst, late '64	$13,500	$17,500
1965	Common color	$13,000	$18,000
1965	Rare color	$18,000	$25,000
1965	Sunburst	$10,000	$15,000
1966	Common color	$10,000	$18,000
1966	Rare color	$15,000	$25,000
1966	Sunburst, blocks	$7,500	$11,000
1966	Sunburst, dots	$8,000	$11,000
1967-1969	Custom color	$9,000	$15,000
1967-1969	Sunburst	$6,000	$8,500
1970	Common color	$5,500	$8,000
1970	Rare color	$8,500	$12,000
1970	Sunburst	$5,000	$6,500
1971	Common color	$5,500	$8,000
1971	Rare color	$8,500	$12,000
1971	Sunburst	$4,500	$5,500
1972	Custom color	$5,500	$7,000
1972	Natural, black block option	$4,000	$5,000
1972	Natural, standard markers	$4,250	$5,500
1972	Sunburst	$4,000	$5,375
1973	Custom color	$5,000	$6,500
1973	Natural	$3,750	$4,750
1973	Sunburst	$3,750	$4,500
1973	Walnut	$3,500	$4,500
1974	Black, blond, white, 3-bolt	$3,000	$4,000
1974	Black, blond, white, 4-bolt	$3,250	$4,500
1974	Natural, 3-bolt	$2,750	$3,500
1974	Natural, 4-bolt	$2,750	$3,500
1974	Sunburst, 3-bolt, late-'74	$2,750	$4,000
1974	Sunburst, 4-bolt	$2,750	$4,500
1974	Walnut, 3-bolt	$2,750	$4,000
1974	Walnut, 4-bolt	$3,000	$4,000
1975-1977	All colors	$2,750	$4,000
1978-1980	All Colors	$2,250	$4,000
1981	Black & Gold	$2,500	$3,250
1981	Black, white, wine	$2,250	$3,000
1981	International colors	$2,500	$4,250
1981	Sunburst	$2,125	$2,875

Standard Jazz

1981-1984. Replaced Jazz Bass ('60-'81) and replaced by the American Standard Jazz Bass in '88. Name now used on import version. Please refer to the beginning of the Fender Bass Section for details on Fender color options.

1981-1984		$1,250	$2,000

American Standard Jazz

1988-2000, 2008-2016. Replaced Standard Jazz Bass ('81-'88) and replaced by the American Series Jazz Bass in '00, back to American Standard in Jan. '08.

1988-2016		$1,000	$1,500

American Standard Jazz V

1998-2000, 2008-2016. 5-string version.

1998-2016		$1,000	$1,250

American Series Jazz

2000-2007. Replaces American Standard Jazz Bass. Renamed American Standard in '08.

2000-2007		$1,000	$1,250

American Series Jazz V

2000-2007. 5-string version.

2000-2007		$1,000	$1,250

American Professional/ Professional II Jazz

2017-present. Redesign includes V-Mod pickups, narrow-tall frets, 'deep C' neck profile, various colors. Also available left-hand model. Renamed American Professional II in '20.

2017-2024		$1,250	$1,500

50th Anniversary American Standard Jazz

1996. Regular American Standard with gold hardware, 4- or 5-string, gold Fender's 50th Anniversary commemorative neck plate, rosewood 'board, sunburst.

1996	IV	$1,500	$2,000
1996	V	$1,500	$2,000

50th Anniversary Jazz Limited Edition

2010. 50th anniversary of the Jazz Bass, nitro Candy Apple Red with matching headstock, mix of vintage and modern specs, rosewood 'board, block markers, 50th Anniversary neck plate.

2010		$1,750	$2,500

'60 Custom Shop Limited Jazz

2020. Limited Edition, heavy relic.

2020		$3,000	$4,000

'60s Jazz (Custom Shop)

1994-1998. Early '60s specs, relic for 1996-1998. Replaced by the CS '64 Jazz Bass. Early Relic work was

MODEL YEAR	FEATURES	EXC. COND. LOW	HIGH

done outside of Fender by Vince Cunetto or his staff.

1994-1995		$3,000	$4,000
1996	Relic (Cunetto)	$3,000	$4,000
1997-1998	Relic (Cunetto staff)	$3,000	$4,000

'60s Jazz (Import)

1991-1994, 2001-2019. Classic series, '60s features, rosewood 'board, Japan-made for first years, Mexico after.

1991-1994	Japan	$600	$750
2001-2019	Mexico	$525	$675

Road Worn '60s Jazz

2009-2019. Rosewood 'board, aged finish.

2009-2019 $575 $725

Vintera '60s Jazz

2020-present. Vintage style appointments, 3-Color Sunburst, Daphne Blue or Firemist Gold.

2020-2024 $625 $800

60th Anniversary American Jazz

2006. Rosewood 'board, 3-tone sunburst.

2006 $1,250 $1,750

60th Anniversary Road Worn Jazz

2020-2021. Road Worn lacquer finish, 3-color sunburst, Firemist Silver or Olympic White.

2020-2021 $825 $1,000

'61 Journeyman Jazz

2020. Heavy relic.

2020 $3,000 $4,000

'62 Jazz (U.S.A.)

1982-1984, 1986-2012. U.S.A.-made, American Vintage series, reissue of '62 Jazz Bass. Please refer to the beginning of the Fender Bass Section for details on Fender color options.

1982-1984		$3,500	$4,500
1986-1999		$2,000	$3,000
2000-2012		$1,500	$2,000

'64 Jazz (Custom Shop)

1998-2009. Alder body, rosewood 'board, tortoise shell 'guard. From June '95 to June '99 Relic work was done outside of Fender by Vince Cunetto and included a certificate noting model and year built, a bass without the certificate is valued less than shown.

1998-1999	Relic (Cunetto)	$3,000	$4,000
2000-2009	Closet Classic option	$3,000	$4,000
2000-2009	NOS option	$3,000	$4,000
2000-2009	Relic option	$3,000	$4,000

'64 Jazz (American Vintage)

2013-2017. American Vintage series, dot inlays.

2013-2017 $1,375 $1,750

'66 Jazz Special Limited Edition

2013. Japan, made for retailer Sweetwater, aged Oly White, 132 made for North American distribution.

2013 $1,000 $1,375

'66 Journeyman Jazz

2020. Relic.

2020 $3,000 $4,000

'74 Jazz (American Vintage)

2013-2017. American Vintage series, block inlays.

2013-2017 $1,375 $1,750

'75 Jazz (American Vintage)

1994-2012. American Vintage series, maple neck with black block markers.

1994-2012 $1,375 $1,750

75th Anniversary Commemorative Jazz

2021. Limited Edition, gold 75th ingot back of headstock and 75th anniversary neck plate, gold hardware, 2-color Bourbon Burst.

2021 $1,000 $1,250

75th Anniversary Jazz (Diamond Anniversary)

2021. Diamond Anniversary metallic finish with matching painted headstock, 75th engraved silver neck plate.

2021 $525 $675

Aerodyne Jazz

2003-present. Bound basswood body, P/J pickups, Deluxe Series.

2003-2024 $800 $1,000

American Deluxe Jazz/Jazz V

1998-2016. U.S., 4 (IV) or 5-string (V), active electronics, alder or ash body. Alder body colors - sunburst or transparent red, ash body colors - white, blond, transparent teal green or transparent purple.

1998-2016 IV or V $1,125 $1,500

American Deluxe FMT Jazz

2001-2006. Flame maple top version (FMT), active EQ, dual J pickups.

2001-2006 $1,375 $1,750

American Elite Jazz/Jazz V

2016-2019. Compound radius 'board, 4 (IV) or 5-string (V), Noiseless pickups, onboard preamp, various colors.

2016-2019 IV or V $1,125 $1,500

American Ultra Jazz

2019-present. Alder or ash body, 2 Noiseless Vintage pickups, redesigned active/passive preamp, 4- (IV) or 5-string (V), various colors with satin finish.

2019-2024 IV or V $1,250 $1,750

Contemporary Jazz

1987. Made in Japan.

1987 $550 $700

Custom Classic Jazz/Jazz V

2001-2009. Custom Shop, slightly slimmer waist, deeper cutaways, maple or rosewood 'board, block inlays, 4 (IV) or 5-string (V).

2001-2009 IV or V $2,000 $2,500

Deluxe Jazz/Jazz V (Active)

1995-2021. Made in Mexico, active electronics, 4 (IV) or 5-string (V), various colors.

1995-2021 IV or V $425 $550

Deluxe Power Jazz

2006. Part of Deluxe Series with Fishman piezo power bridge.

2006 $725 $950

Flea Signature Jazz

2019-present. Flea logo neck plate, Road Worn Faded Shell Pink lacquer finish.

2019-2024 $875 $1,125

Foto Flame Jazz

1994-1996. Japanese import, alder and basswood body with Foto Flame figured wood image.

1994-1996 $725 $950

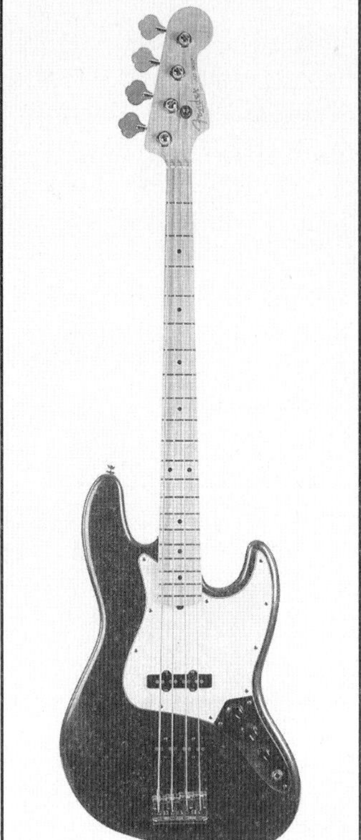

2012 Fender American Standard Jazz

Cream City Music

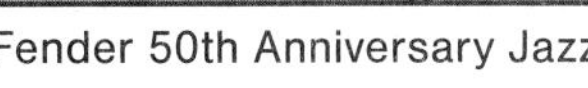

Fender 50th Anniversary Jazz

Rivington Guitars

BASSES

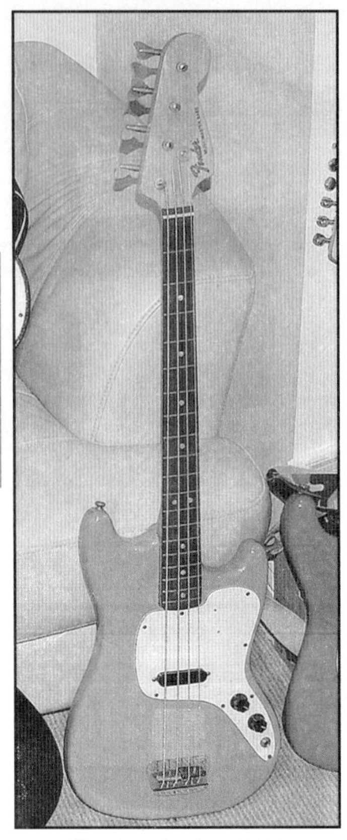
Fender Musicmaster
John Lento

Fender Parallel Universe '51 Telecaster PJ

MODEL YEAR	FEATURES	EXC. COND. LOW	HIGH

FSR Standard Special Edition Jazz
2007-2009. Made in Mexico, Fender Special Edition logo on back of headstock, ash body with natural finish.
2007-2009 $500 $650

Geddy Lee Signature Jazz
1998-present. Limited run import in '98, now part of Artist Series, black.
1998-2024 $775 $1,000

Gold Jazz
1981-1984. Gold finish and gold-plated hardware.
1981-1984 $2,500 $3,500

Highway One Jazz
2003-2011. U.S.-made, alder body, satin lacquer finish.
2003-2011 $725 $925

Jaco Pastorius Jazz
1999-present. Artist Series, standard production model made in Corona, '62 3-color sunburst body without pickup covers.
1999-2000 Fretted $2,250 $3,500
1999-2024 Fretless $2,250 $3,500

Jazz Plus IV/Jazz Plus V
1990-1994. Alder body, 4-string (IV) or 5-string (V), 2 Lace Sensors, active electronics, rotary circuit selector, master volume, balance, bass boost, bass cut, treble boost, treble cut, various colors.
1990-1994 Various colors $950 $1,250

Jazz Special (Import)
1984-1991. Japanese-made, Jazz/Precision hybrid, Precision-shaped basswood body, Jazz neck (fretless available), 2 P/J pickups, offered with active (Power) or passive electronics.
1984-1991 $625 $800

Marcus Miller Signature Jazz
1998-2014. Artist series.
1998-2004 Import $950 $1,250
2005-2014 US Custom Shop $2,000 $2,500

Masterbuilt Custom Shop Jazz
2003-2024. Various models and builders.
2003-2024 $4,000 $10,000

Noel Redding Signature Jazz
1997. Limited Edition import, artist signature on 'guard, sunburst, rosewood 'board.
1997 $1,125 $1,500

Rarities Flame Ash Top Jazz
2019-2021. Two-piece alder body with flame ash top, Plasma Red Burst finish.
2019-2021 $1,625 $2,250

Reggie Hamilton Jazz
2002-2016. Custom Artist series, alder body, passive/active switch and pan control.
2002-2016 $550 $700

Roscoe Beck Jazz IV/Jazz V
1997-2009. 5-string version offered '97-'06, 4-string '04-'09.
1997-2006 V, 5-string $1,500 $1,875
2004-2009 IV, 4-string $1,500 $1,875

Select Jazz
2012-2013. US-made, figured top, rear-headstock 'Fender Select' medallion.
2012-2013 $1,875 $2,500

Standard Jazz (Import)
1985-2018. Standard series, Japan-made into '90, Mexico after. Not to be confused with '81-'84 American-made model with the same name. Replaced by Player Series.
1985-1990 Japan $950 $1,250
1991-2018 Mexico $400 $500

Standard Jazz Fretless (Import)
1994-2018. Standard series, fretless version. Replaced by Player Series.
1994-2018 IV or V $400 $500

Steve Bailey Jazz VI
2009-2011. USA, 6-string, fretless or fretted, sunburst or black.
2009-2011 $1,625 $2,000

Ventures Limited Edition Jazz
1996. Made in Japan, part of Ventures guitar and bass set, dark purple.
1996 $1,125 $1,500

Victor Baily Jazz
2002-2011. Artist series, koa, rosewood and mahogany body, fretless with white fret markers.
2002-2011 $1,250 $1,625

JP-90
1990-1994. Two P/J pickups, rosewood fretboard, poplar body, black or red.
1990-1994 $600 $750

Kingman
2011-present. Acoustic, solid spruce top, mahogany back and sides.
2011-2024 $550 $700

MB IV/MB V
1994-1995. Made in Japan, offset double-cut, 1 P- and 1 J-style pickup, 4-string (IV) or 5-string (V).
1994-1995 IV or V $500 $650

Musicmaster
1970-1983. Shorter scale, solidbody, 1 pickup. various colors.
1970-1983 $1,000 $1,250

Mustang
1966-1982. Shorter scale, solidbody, 1 pickup, offered in standard colors and, for '69-'73, Competition Red, Blue and Orange with racing stripes on the body (with matching headstock for '69-'70).
1966-1969 $4,250 $5,000
1969-1970 Competition $3,250 $4,000
1970-1979 $2,000 $4,000
1978-1980 Antigua finish $2,875 $3,500
1980-1982 $2,000 $2,500

Mustang (Import)
2002-2018. First made in Japan, later Mexico (ca. 2015), alder body, '60s features.
2002-2018 $700 $875

Parallel Universe '51 Telecaster PJ
2018. Limited edition, authentic '51 style, mixes elements from both Jazz and Precision Basses.
2018 $1,250 $1,750

Performer
1985-1986. Swinger-like body style, active electronics, various colors.
1985-1986 $1,250 $1,750

MODEL YEAR	FEATURES	EXC. COND. LOW	HIGH

Postmodern

2015-2019. Custom Shop, P-Bass body, Jazz Bass neck, at times offered in Relic, Journeyman Relic, NOS, and Lush Closet Classic finishes.

2015-2019	Various options	$2,250	$3,000

Precision Bass

The following are variations of the Precision Bass. The first six listings are for the main U.S.-made models. All others are listed alphabetically after that in the following order:

- Precision
- Standard Precision
- American Standard Precision
- American Series Precision
- American Series Precision V
- American Professional/Professional II Precision
- 40th Anniversary Precision (Custom Shop)
- 50th Anniversary American Standard Precision
- 50th Anniversary Precision
- '50s Precision
- Road Worn '50s Precision
- '51 Precision
- '55 Precision (Custom Shop)
- '57 Precision
- '57 Precision (Custom Shop)
- '57 Precision (Import)
- '59 Precision (Custom Shop)
- 60th Anniversary Precision (Mexico)
- 60th Anniversary Precision (USA)
- '61 Precision (Custom Shop)
- '62 Precision
- '62 Precision (Import)
- '63 Precision (U.S.A.)
- 75th Anniversary Commemorative Precision
- 75th Anniversary Precision (Diamond Anniversary)
- Adam Clayton Signature Precision
- Aerodyne Classic Precision Special
- American Deluxe Precision
- American Ultra Precision
- Big Block Precision
- Cabronita Precision
- California Precision Special
- Deluxe Active Precision Special
- Elite/Gold Elite Precision Series
- Foto Flame Precision
- Highway One Precision
- Magnificent Seven LE American Standard PJ
- Mark Hoppus Signature Precision
- Mike Dirnt Road Worn Precision
- Nate Mendel Precision
- Pino Palladino Signature Precision
- Precision Jr.
- Precision Lyte
- Precision Special (Mexico)
- Precision Special (U.S.A.)
- Precision U.S. Plus/Plus
- Precision U.S. Deluxe/Plus Deluxe
- Roger Waters Precision
- Select Precision
- Standard/Player Precision (Import)
- Sting Precision
- Tony Franklin Precision
- Walnut Elite Precision
- Walnut Precision Special

Precision

1951-1981. Slab body until '54, 1-piece maple neck standard until '59, optional after '69, rosewood 'board standard '59 on (slab until mid-'62, curved after), blond finish standard until '54, sunburst standard after that (2-tone '54-'58, 3-tone after '58). Became the Standard Precision Bass in '81-'85, the American Standard Precision for '88-'00, the American Series Precision Bass in '00-'08, and the American Standard Precision again for '08-'16. Currently called the American Professional Precision Bass. Unlike the Jazz and Telecaster Basses, the Precision was never fitted with a 3-bolt neck or bullet rod. Please refer to the beginning of the Fender Bass Section for details on Fender color options.

MODEL YEAR	FEATURES	EXC. COND. LOW	HIGH
1951	Blond, slab	$25,000	$35,000
1952-1954	Blond, slab	$18,000	$25,000
1955	Blond, contour	$15,000	$20,000
1956	Blond, contour	$15,000	$20,000
1956	Sunburst, contour	$12,000	$16,000
1957	Blond	$14,000	$18,000
1957	Blond, anodized guard	$32,000	$40,000
1957	Sunburst, anodized guard	$22,000	$28,000
1958	Blond	$32,000	$40,000
1958	Sunburst, anodized guard	$20,000	$28,000
1959	Blond	$32,000	$40,000
1959	Sunburst, anodized guard	$20,000	$28,000
1959	Sunburst, tortoise guard	$15,000	$20,000
1960	Blond	$18,500	$23,500
1960	Custom color	$18,500	$50,000
1960	Sunburst	$15,000	$20,000
1961	Custom color	$16,000	$45,000
1961	Sunburst	$15,000	$20,000
1962	Custom color, curved	$15,500	$45,000
1962	Custom color, slab	$19,000	$50,000
1962	Sunburst, curved	$14,000	$16,500
1962	Sunburst, slab	$14,000	$17,500
1963	Custom color	$14,000	$36,000
1963	Sunburst	$13,000	$17,000
1964	Custom color	$12,000	$35,000
1964	Sunburst, early '64, spaghetti logo, green guard	$11,500	$14,000
1964	Sunburst, late '64	$10,750	$14,000
1965	Custom color	$12,000	$23,000
1965	Sunburst	$9,000	$11,500
1966	Custom color	$9,000	$20,000
1966	Sunburst	$6,500	$9,500
1967-1969	Custom color	$8,500	$15,000
1967-1969	Sunburst	$6,500	$9,500
1970	Custom color	$7,500	$10,000
1970	Sunburst	$4,000	$5,500

1990 Fender JP-90
Rivington Guitars

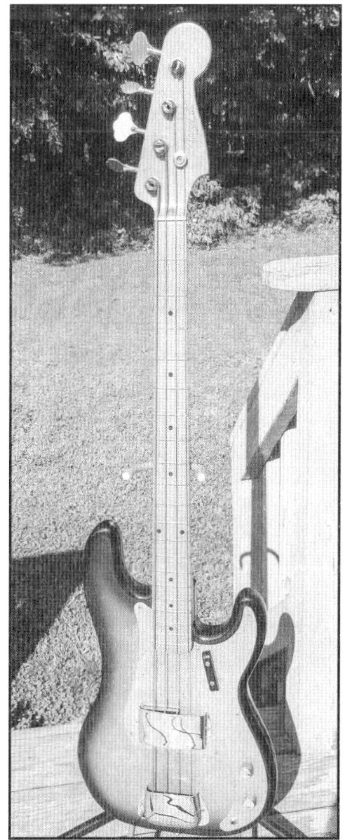
1958 Fender Precision
Phil Avelli

BASSES

BASSES

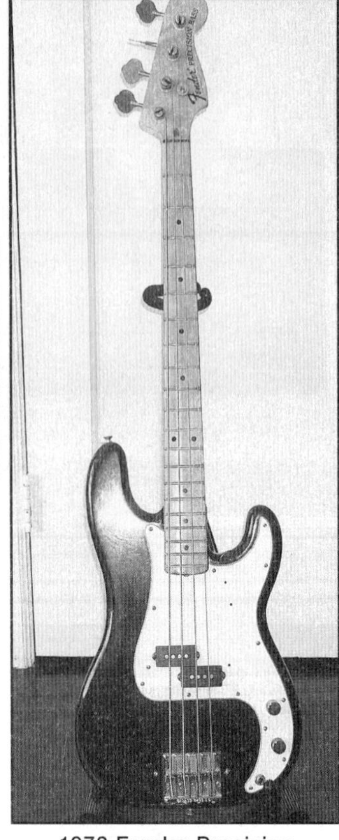
1973 Fender Precision
KC Cormack

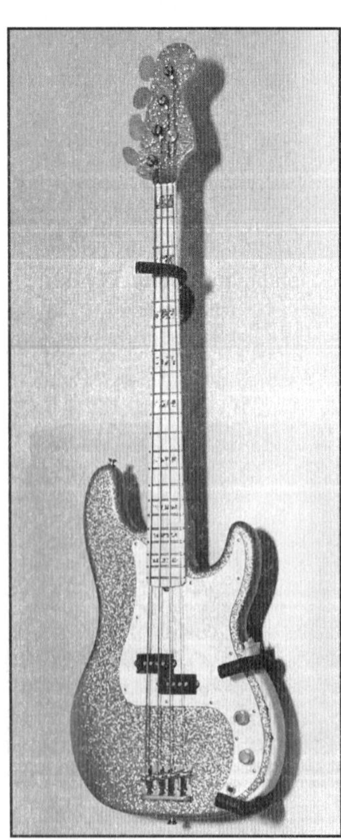
2017 Fender Adam Clayton Precision
Randy Weddle

MODEL YEAR	FEATURES	EXC. COND. LOW	HIGH
1971	Custom color	$6,000	$7,500
1971	Sunburst	$4,000	$5,000
1972	Custom color	$4,500	$6,000
1972	Sunburst	$3,500	$5,000
1973	Custom color	$4,000	$5,500
1973	Natural, sunburst, walnut	$3,250	$4,500
1974	All colors	$2,500	$4,000
1975-1977	All colors	$2,000	$4,000
1978-1979	All colors	$2,000	$4,000
1980	Color with matching hdstk, gold hw	$2,000	$3,000
1980	International colors	$2,000	$3,750
1980	Other colors	$2,000	$2,500
1981	Black & gold	$2,250	$3,000
1981	International colors	$2,000	$3,750
1981	Other colors	$1,500	$2,250

Standard Precision

1981-1984. Replaces Precision Bass, various colors. Replaced by American Standard Precision '88-'00. The Standard name is used on import Precision model for '88-present.

1981-1984		$1,250	$2,000

American Standard Precision

1988-2000, 2008-2016. Replaces Standard Precision Bass, replaced by American Series Precision in '00, back to American Standard in Jan. '08.

1988-1989	Blond, gold hw	$1,500	$2,250
1988-2016	Various colors	$1,000	$1,250

American Series Precision

2000-2007. Replaces American Standard Precision Bass, various colors. Renamed American Standard in '08.

2000-2007		$1,125	$1,500

American Series Precision V

2000-2007. 5-string version.

2000-2007		$1,125	$1,500

American Professional/ Professional II Precision

2017-present. Redesign includes V-Mod pickups, '63 P Bass neck profile, narrow-tall frets, various colors. Also available left-hand model. Renamed American Professional II in '20.

2017-2024		$1,125	$1,500

40th Anniversary Precision (Custom Shop)

1991. 400 made, quilted amber maple top, gold hardware.

1991		$3,000	$4,000

50th Anniversary American Standard Precision

1996. Regular American Standard with gold hardware, 4- or 5-string, gold 50th Anniversary commemorative neck plate, rosewood 'board, sunburst.

1996		$1,250	$1,500

50th Anniversary Precision

2001. Commemorative certificate with date and serial number, butterscotch finish, ash body, maple neck, black 'guard.

2001	With certificate	$1,250	$1,500

'50s Precision

1992-1996, 2006-2019. First run made in Japan, currently in Mexico, 1 split-coil, maple neck.

1992-1996	Japan	$750	$1,000
2006-2019	Mexico	$525	$675

Road Worn '50s Precision

2009-2019. Mexico, 1 split-coil, maple neck, aged finish.

2009-2019		$550	$700

'51 Precision

1994-1997, 2003-2010. Import from Japan, no pickup or bridge covers, blond or sunburst. Offered in Japan in the '90s.

1994-1997	Japan only	$1,000	$1,250
2003-2010		$1,000	$1,250

'55 Precision (Custom Shop)

2003-2011. 1955 specs, including oversized 'guard, 1-piece maple neck/fretboard, preproduction bridge and pickup covers, single-coil pickup. Offered in N.O.S., Closet Classic or highest-end Relic.

2003-2006	NOS	$3,000	$4,000
2003-2006	Relic	$3,000	$4,000
2003-2011	Closet Classic	$3,000	$4,000

'57 Precision

1982-1984, 1986-2012. U.S.-made reissue, American Vintage series, various colors.

1982-1984		$3,500	$4,500
1986-1999		$1,750	$2,500
2000-2012		$1,625	$2,250

'57 Precision (Custom Shop)

2013	Heavy relic	$3,000	$4,000

'57 Precision (Import)

1984-1986	Black	$2,000	$2,500

'59 Precision (Custom Shop)

2003-2010. Custom Shop built with late-'59 specs, rosewood 'board.

2003-2008	Closet Classic	$3,000	$4,000
2003-2010	NOS	$3,000	$4,000
2003-2010	Relic	$3,000	$4,000

60th Anniversary Precision (Mexico)

2011. Made in Mexico, with 60th Anniversary gig bag.

2011		$450	$575

60th Anniversary Precision (USA)

2011. 1951-2011 Anniversary date label.

2011		$1,250	$1,750

'61 Precision (Custom Shop)

2010-2013. Made for Musician's Friend and Guitar Center.

2010-2013	Closet Classic	$3,000	$4,000
2010-2013	NOS	$3,000	$4,000
2010-2013	Relic	$3,000	$4,000

'62 Precision

1982-1984, 1986-2012. American Vintage series, alder body. No production in '85. Limited run Mary Kaye Blond (gold hardware) in '90.

1982-1984		$2,750	$3,500
1986-1999		$1,750	$2,250
1990	Mary Kaye Blond	$1,250	$2,000
2000-2012		$1,125	$1,500

MODEL YEAR	FEATURES	EXC. COND. LOW	HIGH

'62 Precision (Import)

1984-1986. Foreign-made, black.

1984-1986 $1,000 $1,250

'63 Precision (U.S.A.)

2013-2017. American Vintage series.

2013-2017 $1,250 $1,750

75th Anniversary Commemorative Precision

2021. Limited Edition, gold 75th ingot back of headstock and 75th anniversary neck plate, gold hardware, 2-color Bourbon Burst.

2021 $1,250 $1,750

75th Anniversary Precision (Diamond Anniversary)

2021. Diamond Anniversary metallic finish with matching painted headstock, 75th engraved silver neck plate.

2021 $600 $750

Adam Clayton Signature Precision

2011. Custom Shop Limited Edition.

2011 $3,000 $4,000

Aerodyne Classic Precision Special

2006. Made in Japan, labeled Precision and Aerodyne P Bass, figured maple top, matching headstock, P-J pickup.

2006 $800 $1,000

American Deluxe Precision

1998-2016. U.S., active electronics, 4 (IV) or 5-string (V), alder or ash body. Alder body colors - sunburst or transparent red. Ash body colors - white blond, transparent teal green or transparent purple.

1998-2016 IV or V $1,125 $1,500

American Ultra Precision

2019-present. Alder or ash body, 2 Noiseless Vintage pickups, 4-string, various colors with gloss finish.

2019-2024 $1,250 $1,750

Big Block Precision

2005-2009. Made in Mexico, pearloid block markers, black finish with matching headstock, 1 double Jazz Bass humbucker, bass and treble boost and cut controls.

2005-2009 $700 $875

Cabronita Precision

2014-2015. One Fideli'Tron pickup, 2 knobs.

2014-2015 $325 $450

California Precision Special

1997. California Series, assembled and finished in Mexico and California, P/J pickup configuration.

1997 $650 $850

Deluxe Active Precision Special

1995-2021. Made in Mexico, P/J pickups, Jazz Bass neck.

1995-2021 $450 $575

Elite/Gold Elite Precision Series

1983-1985. Active electronics, noise-cancelling pickups, Elite I (ash body, 1 pickup), Elite II (2 pickups), Gold Elite I (gold-plated hardware, 1 pickup), Gold Elite II (2 pickups), various colors.

1983-1985 Various models $2,000 $2,500

Foto Flame Precision

1994-1996. Made in Japan, simulated woodgrain finish, natural or sunburst.

1994-1996 $725 $950

MODEL YEAR	FEATURES	EXC. COND. LOW	HIGH

Highway One Precision

2003-2011. U.S.-made, alder body, satin lacquer finish.

2003-2011 $725 $950

Magnificent Seven LE American Standard PJ

2016. U.S., Limited Edition, P-bass body with Jazz neck, 500 made.

2016 $950 $1,250

Mark Hoppus Signature Precision

2002-2016. Mark Hoppus engraved on neck plate.

2002-2016 Mexico serial no $550 $700

Mike Dirnt Road Worn Precision

2014-present. '51 era P-Bass style, ash body, maple or rosewood 'board.

2014-2024 $825 $1,125

Nate Mendel Precision

2013-present. Ash body, rosewood 'board.

2013-2024 $650 $850

Pino Palladino Signature Precision

2006-present. Custom Shop Artist series, based on '62 used by Palladino, certificate of authenticity, Fiesta Red.

2006-2024 $3,000 $4,000

Precision Jr.

2004-2006. 3/4 size.

2004-2006 $550 $700

Precision Lyte

1992-2001. Japanese-made, smaller, lighter basswood body, 2 pickups, sunburst.

1992-2001 $850 $1,125

Precision Special (Mexico)

1997-1998. Chrome hardware, 1 P- and 1 J-pickup.

1997-1998 $600 $750

Precision Special (U.S.A.)

1980-1982. Gold hardware, matching headstock, active electronics, CA Red, LP Blue, Oly White or walnut (see separate listing).

1980-1982 Rare color $2,000 $3,000

1980-1982 Standard color $1,500 $2,500

Precision U.S. Plus/Plus

1989-1992. P-style bass with P- and J-bass pickups.

1989-1992 Rare color $1,125 $1,500

1989-1992 Standard color $950 $1,250

Precision U.S. Deluxe/Plus Deluxe

1991-1994. P-style bass with P- and J-bass pickups, active electronics, no 'guard models available.

1991-1994 Rare color $1,125 $1,500

1991-1994 Standard color $950 $1,250

Roger Waters Precision

2010-2019. Alder body, maple neck, black.

2010-2019 $750 $950

Select Precision

2012. Alder body, flamed maple top, rear headstock 'Fender Select' medallion.

2012 $1,750 $2,500

Standard/Player Precision (Import)

1985-present. Made in Japan into '90, and Mexico after. Not to be confused with '81-'84 American-made model with the same name. Also available left-handed. Replaced by Player Series in 18.

1985-1990 Japan $950 $1,250

Fender Nate Mendel Precision

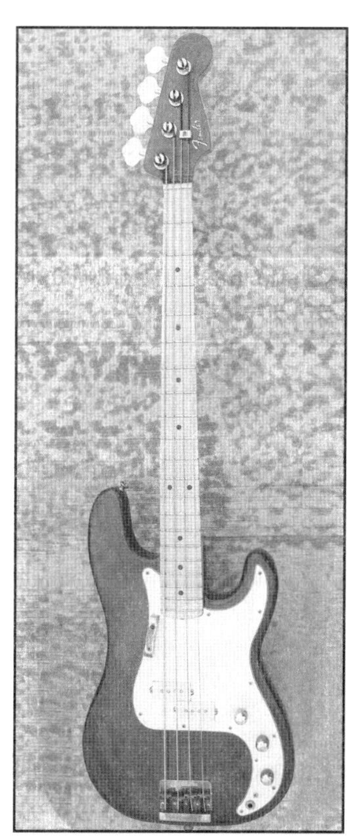

1981 Fender Precision Special (U.S.A.)

Willie Moseley

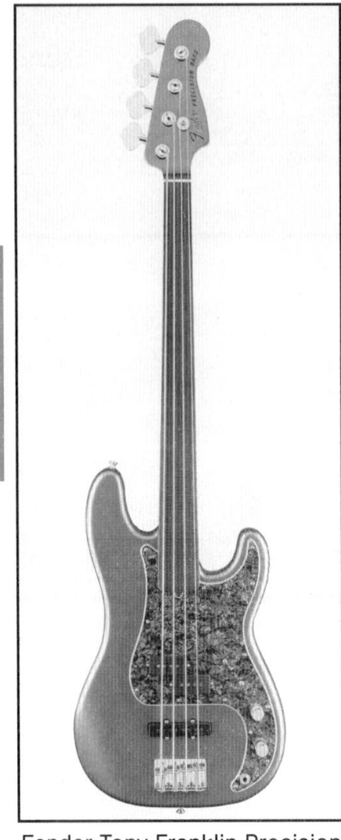

Fender Tony Franklin Precision

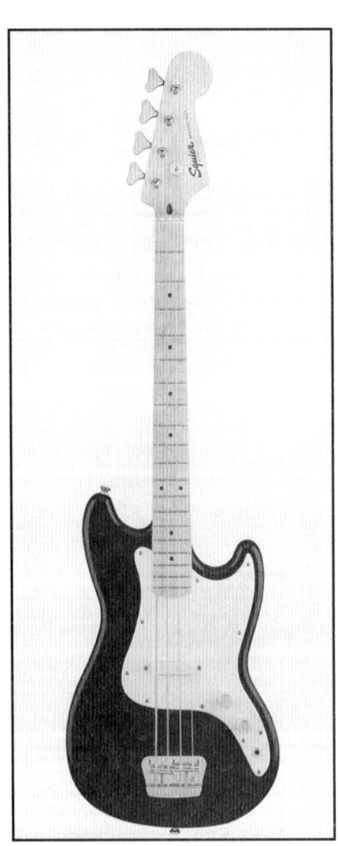

Fender Squier Bronco

MODEL YEAR	FEATURES	EXC. COND. LOW	HIGH
1991-2024	Mexico	$400	$500
2016	Mexico, Custom Art Series	$400	$500

Sting Precision

2001-2013. Made in Japan, 2-tone sunburst, 1 single-coil, Sting's signature.

2001-2013		$950	$1,250

Tony Franklin Precision

2007-present. Fretless, P and J pickups, 3-way selector, lacquer finish.

2007-2024		$1,250	$1,500

Walnut Elite Precision

1983-1985. The Elite Series features active electronics and noise-cancelling pickups, walnut body, 1 pickup (Elite I) or 2 (Elite II), rosewood 'board, natural.

1983-1985	Elite I	$1,875	$2,250
1983-1985	Elite II	$1,875	$2,250

Walnut Precision Special

1980-1982. Precision Bass Special with a walnut body, natural.

1980-1982		$1,875	$2,250

Prodigy Active

1992-1995. U.S.-made, poplar body, 1 J- and 1 P-style pickup, active.

1992-1995		$950	$1,250

Rhodes Piano

1962. Electric keyboard in bass register, Fender-Rhodes sticker, Piano Bass logo, various colors.

1962		$2,125	$2,750

Squier Affinity Jazz

1997-present. Affinity is the lower priced series made in China.

1997-2024		$115	$150

Squier Bronco

1998-present. The lowest priced Squier bass, single coil plastic cover pickup, 3/4 body.

1998-2024		$125	$175

Squier Bullet

1983-1990. Japanese-made, Squier-branded, replaces Bullet Bass, black.

1983-1990		$600	$800

Squier Classic Vibe Series

2009-present. Various models.

2009-2024		$265	$350

Squier HM/HM V

1989-1993. Korean-made, 5-string also offered.

1989-1993		$265	$350

Squier Jazz Standard

1983-2010. Jazz bass import, without cover plates, various colors.

1983-1984	1st logo	$650	$900
1985-1989	2nd logo	$500	$650
1990-1999		$185	$250
2000-2010		$175	$225

Squier Katana

1985-1986. Made in Japan, wedge-shaped, arrow headstock.

1985-1986		$950	$1,250

Squier Precision Special

1998-2010. Agathis body, P/J pickups, 4-string (IV) or 5-string (V).

1998-2010	IV or V	$115	$150

Squier Precision Standard

1983-1984	1st logo	$650	$900
1985-1989	2nd logo	$500	$650
1990-1999	Some from Mexico	$185	$250
2000-2006	Indonesia	$135	$175

Squier Vintage Modified Series

2007-2019. Includes Jaguar, Jazz and Precision models.

2007-2019	Various models	$175	$230

Stu Hamm Urge (U.S.A.)

1992-1999. Contoured Precision-style body with smaller wide treble cutaway, J and P pickups, 32" scale.

1992-1999		$1,250	$1,750

Stu Hamm Urge II (U.S.A.)

1999-2009. J and P pickups, 34" scale.

1999-2009		$1,250	$1,750

Telecaster

1968-1979. Slab solidbody, 1 pickup, fretless option '70, blond and custom colors available (Pink Paisley or Blue Floral '68-'69). Please refer to the beginning of the Fender Bass Section for details on Fender color options.

1968	Black, nitro	$5,500	$8,500
1968	Black, poly	$5,500	$8,500
1968	Blond, nitro	$4,000	$5,000
1968	Blond, poly	$4,000	$5,000
1968	Blue Floral Paisley	$18,000	$25,000
1968	Lake Placid Blue	$5,500	$8,500
1968	Pink Paisley	$17,000	$20,500
1969-1972	4-bolt, single-coil	$4,000	$5,000
1973-1974	3-bolt, hum, rare color	$3,500	$6,000
1973-1974	3-bolt, humbucker	$2,500	$3,500
1975-1979	3-bolt, humbucker	$2,500	$3,500

Zone (American Deluxe)

2001-2006. Smaller lightweight offset double-cut, active humbuckers, exotic tone woods, U.S.-made.

2001-2006		$1,500	$2,000

Fodera

1983-present. Luthiers Vinnie Fodera and Joseph Lauricella build their professional and premium grade, production/custom, solidbody basses in Brooklyn, New York.

High-level

1983-2024	4, 5, 6 strings	$7,500	$8,500

Mid-level

1983-2024	4, 5, 6 strings	$4,500	$6,000

Low-level

1983-2024	4, 5, 6 strings	$3,500	$4,500

Framus

1946-1975, 1996-present. Professional and premium grade, production/custom, basses made in Germany. They also build guitars and amps.

Atlantic Model 5/140

1960s. Single-cut thinline with f-holes, 2 pickups, sunburst or blackrose.

1960s		$675	$850

MODEL YEAR	FEATURES	EXC. COND. LOW	HIGH

Atlantic Model 5/143

1960s. Offset double-cut thinbody with f-holes, 2 pickups, 4-on-a-side keys.

1960s		$675	$850

Atlantic Model 5/144

1960s. Double-cut thinbody with f-holes, ES-335 body style, 2 pickups. Becomes Model J/144 in the '70s.

1960s		$675	$850

Charavelle 4 Model 5/153

1960s. Double-cut thinline with f-holes, 335-style body, 2 pickups, sunburst, cherry red or Sunset.

1960s		$725	$925

De Luxe 4 Model 5/154

1960s. Double-cut thinline, sharp horns and f-holes, 2 pickups, mute, sunburst or natural/blond.

1960s		$725	$925

Electric Upright

1950s. Full-scale neck, triangular body, black.

1958		$2,000	$2,500

Star Series (Bill Wyman)

1959-1968. Early flyer says, Bill Wyman of the Rolling Stones prefers the Star Bass. The model's name was later changed to Framus Stone Bass. Single-cut semi-hollow body, 5/149 (1 pickup) and 5/150 (2 pickups), sunburst.

1959-1965	Model 5/150	$1,000	$1,375
1960s	Model 5/149	$1,000	$1,375

Strato De Luxe Star Model 5/165

Ca. 1964-ca. 1972. Offset double-cut solidbody, 2 pickups, sunburst. There was also a gold hardware version (5/165 gl) and a 6-string (5/166).

1960s		$775	$1,000

Strato Star Series

Ca. 1963-ca. 1972. Double-cut solidbody, 5/156/50 (1 pickup) or 5/156/52 (2 pickups), beige, cherry or sunburst.

1960s	Model 5/156/50	$775	$1,000
1960s	Model 5/156/52	$775	$1,000

T.V. Star

1960s. Offset double-cut thinbody with f-holes, 2 pickups, short-scale, sunburst or cherry red. Most expensive of the '60s Framus basses, although not as popular as the Bill Wyman 5/150 model.

1960s		$775	$1,000

Triumph Electric Upright

1956-1960. Solidbody bean pole electric bass, small body, long neck, slotted viol peghead, gold or black.

1956-1960		$2,000	$2,750

Fresher

1973-1985. Japanese-made, mainly copies of popular brands and not imported into the U.S., but they do show up at guitar shows. They also made guitars.

Solidbody Electric

1970s		$500	$650

G&L

1980-present. Intermediate and professional grade, production/custom, electric basses made in the U.S. In '03, G&L introduced the Korean-made G&L Tribute Series. A Tribute logo is clearly identified on the headstock. They also build guitars.

ASAT

1989-2020. Single-cut, solidbody, active and passive modes, 2 humbuckers, various colors.

1989-1991	About 400 made	$1,500	$2,000
1992-2020		$1,375	$1,750

ASAT Commemorative

1991-1992. About 150 made, 4-string ASAT commemorating Leo Fender's life.

1991-1992		$1,750	$2,250

ASAT Semi-Hollow

2001-2020. Semi-hollowbody style on ASAT bass.

2001-2020		$1,375	$1,750

Climax

1992-1996. Single active humbucker MFD.

1992-1996		$1,000	$1,375

El Toro

1983-1989. Double-cut, solidbody, 2 active, smaller, humbuckers, sunburst.

1983-1987		$1,250	$1,625
1988-1989		$1,125	$1,500

Interceptor

1984-1991. Sharp pointed double-cut, solidbody, 2 active, smaller humbuckers, sunburst.

1984-1986		$2,750	$3,500
1988-1991	Body signature	$1,500	$2,000

JB-2

2001-2018. Alder body, 2 Alnico V pickups.

2001-2018		$1,000	$1,375

Kiloton

2016-present. Single MFD humbucker pickup, custom options and finishes.

2016-2024	Standard top	$1,125	$1,500
2020-2024	Premium figured	$1,250	$1,625

L-1000

1980-1994, 2008. Offset double-cut, solidbody, 1 pickup, various colors. Limited run in '08.

1980-1985	Ash	$1,250	$1,750
1980-1985	Mahogany	$1,250	$1,750
1980-1985	Maple	$1,250	$1,750
1986-1991		$1,250	$1,500
1992-1999	3-bolt	$1,250	$1,500
2008	4-bolt	$1,250	$1,500

L-1500

1997-2018. Offset double-cut solidbody, 1 MFD humbucker.

1997-2018		$900	$1,250

L-1500 Custom

1997	Only year made	$1,125	$1,500

L-1505

1998-2018. Five-string version, single MFD humbucker.

1998-2018		$1,125	$1,500

L-2000

1980-present. Offset double-cut solidbody, 2 pickups, active electronics. Originally, the L-2000 was available with active (L-2000E) or passive (L-2000) electronics.

1980-1985	Ash	$1,625	$2,250
1986		$1,375	$1,750
1987-1991	Leo signature	$1,250	$1,750
1992-2024		$1,375	$1,750

1968 Fender Telecaster Bass

Robbie Keene

1965 Framus Strato Star

BASSES

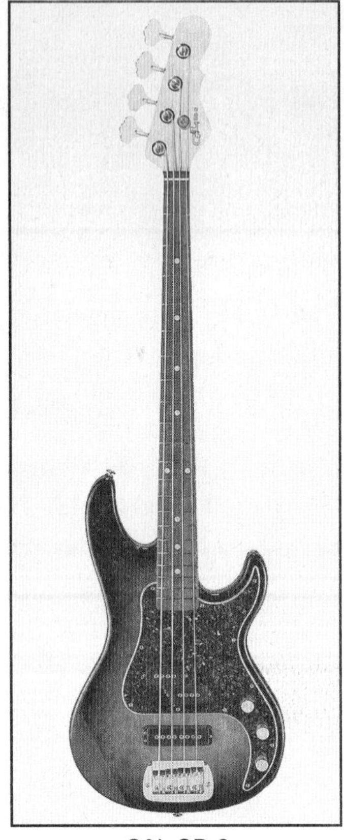

G&L SB-2

1969 Gibson EB-0

Cream City Music

MODEL YEAR	FEATURES	EXC. COND. LOW	HIGH

L-2000 30th Anniversary

2010. Pearl Frost with matching headstock.

2010		$1,500	$2,000

L-2000 40th Anniversary

2020. Ruby Red finish.

2020		$2,125	$2,750

L-2000 C.L.F. Centennial

2009-2010. Swamp ash body, blonde, black hardware, planned run of 50. Certificate of Authenticity.

2009-2010	COA, CD	$1,625	$2,250

L-2000 Custom

1997. Ash top, wood-grain binding upgrade.

1997		$1,375	$1,750

L-2000 Fretless

1980-1998. Fretless version.

1980-1982		$1,625	$2,250

L-2000E

1980-1982. Offset double-cut, solidbody, 2 pickups, active electronics. Originally, the L-2000 was available with active (L-2000E) or passive (L-2000) electronics.

1980-1982		$1,625	$2,250

L-2500

1997-present. Dual MFD humbuckers, 5-string, figured tops can vary.

1997-2024		$1,375	$1,750

L-2500 Custom

1997. Ash top, wood-grain binding upgrade.

1997		$1,375	$1,750

L-5000

1988-1993. Offset double-cut, solidbody, G&L Z-shaped split-humbucker, 5 strings, approximately 400 made.

1988-1992		$1,000	$1,375

L-5500

1993-1997		$1,000	$1,375

L-5500 Custom

1997. Ash top, wood-grain binding upgrade.

1997		$1,000	$1,375

LB-100

1993-present. Follow-up to earlier Legacy Bass.

1993-2024		$1,000	$1,375

Legacy

1992-1993. Offset double-cut solidbody, 1 split-coil, renamed LB-100 in '93.

1992-1993		$1,000	$1,375

Lynx

1984-1991. Offset double-cut, solidbody, 2 single-coils, black.

1984-1991		$1,000	$1,375

M-2500

2012-2022. Dual MFD humbuckers, 5-string, options and finishes.

2012-2022		$1,000	$1,375

SB-1

1982-2000, 2014-present. Solidbody, maple neck, body and 'board, split-humbucker, 1 tone and 1 volume control. Reappears in '14 as Fullerton Deluxe SB-1.

1982-2000		$950	$1,250

SB-2

1982-present. Maple neck with tilt adjustment, 1 split-coil humbucker and 1 single-coil.

1982-2024		$1,000	$1,500

Tribute Series

2003-present. Various models, options and finishes.

2003-2024	Various models	$400	$1,000

Garage by Wicked

2004-2010. A line of basses imported from China by luthier Nicholas Dijkman (Wicked) of Montreal, Quebec.

Gibson

1890s (1902)-present. Professional grade, production, U.S.-made electric basses. Gibson got into the electric bass market with the introduction of their Gibson Electric Bass in '53 (that model was renamed the EB-1 in '58 and reintroduced under that name in '69). Many more bass models followed. Gibson's custom colors can greatly increase the value of older instruments. Custom colors offered from '63 to '69 are Cardinal Red, Ember Red, Frost Blue, Golden Mist Metallic, Heather Metallic, Inverness Green, Kerry Green, Pelham Blue Metallic, Polaris White, Silver Mist Metallic.

20/20

1987-1988. Designed by Ned Steinberger, slim-wedge Steinberger style solidbody, 2 humbucker pickups, 20/20 logo on headstock, Luna Silver or Ferrari Red finish.

1987-1988		$1,125	$1,375

Electric (EB-1)

1953-1958. Introduced as Gibson Electric Bass in '53 but was called the EB-1 by Gibson in its last year of '58, thus, the whole line is commonly called the EB-1 by collectors, reissued in '69 as the EB-1 (see EB-1 listing), brown.

1953-1958		$5,500	$8,000

EB

1970, 2013-2019. Renamed from Melody Maker Bass, SG body, 1 humbucker pickup. Reintroduced in '13, 4- or 5-string, 2 pickups.

1970		$3,500	$4,500
2013-2019	Reintroduced	$700	$1,250

EB-0

1959-1979. Double-cut slab body with banjo-type tuners in '59 and '60, double-cut SG-type body with conventional tuners from '61 on, 1 pickup. Faded custom colors are of less value.

1959-1960	Cherry, slab body	$3,500	$6,000
1961	Cherry, SG body	$2,500	$3,500
1962	Cherry	$2,500	$3,500
1963	Cherry	$2,500	$3,500
1964	Cherry, late '64 truss rod	$2,250	$3,250
1964	Cherry, raised truss rod	$2,750	$3,250
1965-1966	Cherry	$2,500	$3,000
1965-1966	Pelham Blue	$3,500	$4,500
1967-1968	Cherry	$2,000	$2,500
1967-1968	Pelham Blue	$4,000	$5,500
1968	Black	$4,000	$5,000
1968	Burgundy Metallic	$3,000	$4,500
1969	Cherry, solid head	$1,750	$2,250
1969	Pelham Blue	$2,500	$3,500

MODEL YEAR	FEATURES	EXC. COND. LOW	HIGH
1969-1974	Slotted head	$1,250	$1,750
1975-1979		$1,250	$1,750

EB-0 F

1962-1965. EB-0 with added built-in fuzz, cherry.

MODEL YEAR	FEATURES	LOW	HIGH
1962-1965		$3,250	$4,500

EB-0 L

1969-1979. 34.5-inch scale version of the EB-0, various colors.

MODEL YEAR	FEATURES	LOW	HIGH
1969-1979		$1,750	$2,500

EB-1

1969-1972. The Gibson Electric Bass ('53-'58) is often also called the EB-1 (see Electric Bass). Violin-shaped mahogany body, 1 pickup, standard tuners.

MODEL YEAR	FEATURES	LOW	HIGH
1969-1972		$3,500	$4,500

EB-2

1958-1961, 1964-1972. ES-335-type semi-hollowbody, double-cut, 1 pickup, banjo tuners '58-'60 and conventional tuners '60 on.

MODEL YEAR	FEATURES	LOW	HIGH
1958	Sunburst	$5,000	$7,000
1959	Natural	$6,000	$9,500
1959	Sunburst	$4,500	$6,500
1960	Natural	$6,000	$8,000
1960	Sunburst	$4,250	$5,500
1961	Sunburst, black pu	$4,000	$5,000
1961	Sunburst, brown pu	$4,250	$5,000
1964	Sunburst	$2,750	$3,500
1965	Sunburst	$2,750	$3,500
1966-1969	Cherry, sunburst	$2,500	$3,250
1967-1969	Sparkling Burgundy	$3,000	$4,000
1967-1969	Walnut	$3,000	$3,500
1970-1972	Sunburst	$2,500	$3,000

EB-2 D

1966-1972. Two-pickup version of EB-2, cherry, sunburst, or walnut.

MODEL YEAR	FEATURES	LOW	HIGH
1966-1969	Cherry, sunburst	$3,000	$5,000
1967-1969	Sparkling Burgundy	$2,750	$3,500
1967-1969	Walnut	$3,500	$4,500
1970-1972	Cherry, sunburst	$2,500	$3,500

EB-3

1961-1979. SG-style solidbody, 2 humbuckers, solid peghead '61-'68 and '72-'79, slotted peghead '69-'71, cherry to '71, various colors after.

MODEL YEAR	FEATURES	LOW	HIGH
1961-1964		$4,500	$6,500
1965	Early '65 version	$4,000	$6,000
1965	Late '65 version	$3,500	$4,500
1965	White (rare)	$5,000	$10,000
1966		$3,000	$4,000
1967-1968		$2,500	$3,250
1969	Early '69	$2,250	$3,000
1969	Late '69	$2,250	$2,750
1970		$2,000	$2,500
1971		$2,000	$2,500
1972-1979		$1,750	$2,250

EB-3 L

1969-1972. 34.5" scale version of EB-3, slotted headstock, EB-3L logo on truss rod cover, cherry, natural, or walnut.

MODEL YEAR	FEATURES	LOW	HIGH
1969-1972		$2,250	$3,000

EB-4 L

1972-1979. SG-style, 1 humbucker, 34.5" scale, cherry or walnut.

MODEL YEAR	FEATURES	LOW	HIGH
1972-1979		$1,500	$2,000

EB-6

1960-1966. Introduced as semi-hollowbody 335-style 6-string with 1 humbucker, changed to SG-style with 2 pickups in '62.

MODEL YEAR	FEATURES	LOW	HIGH
1960	Natural, 335-style	$8,000	$12,500
1960-1961	Sunburst, 335-style	$6,000	$8,750
1962-1964	Cherry, SG-style	$10,000	$15,000
1965-1966	Cherry, SG-style	$10,000	$15,000

EB-650

1991-1993. Semi-acoustic single cut, maple neck, laminated maple body with center block, 2 TB Plus pickups.

MODEL YEAR	FEATURES	LOW	HIGH
1991-1993	Blond	$4,500	$6,000
1991-1993	Blue	$4,250	$5,500
1991-1993	Other colors	$4,000	$5,250

EB-750

1991-1993. Like EB-650, but with Bartolini pickups and TCT active EQ.

MODEL YEAR	FEATURES	LOW	HIGH
1991-1993	Blond	$4,500	$6,000
1991-1993	Blue	$4,250	$5,500
1991-1993	Other colors	$4,000	$5,250

ES-335

2013. Sunburst or ebony.

MODEL YEAR	FEATURES	LOW	HIGH
2013		$1,375	$2,000

ES-Les Paul

2015-2018. Semi-solid, 3-ply maple/poplar/maple top, back and sides, rosewood 'board, mother-of-pearl inlay, faded darkburst or gold top finish.

MODEL YEAR	FEATURES	LOW	HIGH
2015-2018		$2,250	$3,000

Explorer

1984-1987, 2011-2012. Alder body, ebony 'board, dot inlays, 2 humbuckers, various colors. Limited run in '11 in sunburst or silverburst.

MODEL YEAR	FEATURES	LOW	HIGH
1984-1987	Various finishes	$1,750	$2,750
1985	Designer graphics	$1,750	$2,750
2011-2012	Silverburst	$2,000	$3,000
2011-2012	Sunburst	$1,500	$2,500

Flying V

1981-1982, 2011-2012, 2020-2021. Solidbody, Flying V body. Offered again in '20 with 2 Burstbucker pickups and Antique Natural finish.

MODEL YEAR	FEATURES	LOW	HIGH
1981-1982	Blue stain, ebony	$3,750	$5,000
1981-1982	Silverburst	$5,000	$8,000
2011-2012		$2,000	$2,500
2020-2021		$1,500	$2,000

Flying V B-2

2019-2020. Dirty Fingers humbucker pickups, satin ebony finish.

MODEL YEAR	FEATURES	LOW	HIGH
2019-2020		$1,000	$1,375

Grabber

1973-1982. Double-cut solidbody, 1 pickup, bolt maple neck, maple 'board, various colors.

MODEL YEAR	FEATURES	LOW	HIGH
1973-1982		$2,000	$2,500

Grabber II

2009-2011. Limited Run series, 350 offered, based on '73-'75 model, certificate of authenticity, black.

MODEL YEAR	FEATURES	LOW	HIGH
2009-2011		$1,500	$2,000

Grabber III (G-3)

1975-1982. Double-cut solidbody, 3 pickups, bolt maple neck, maple 'board, nickel-plated hardware, various colors.

MODEL YEAR	FEATURES	LOW	HIGH
1975-1982		$1,750	$2,250

1982 Gibson Flying V

Russell Sutherland

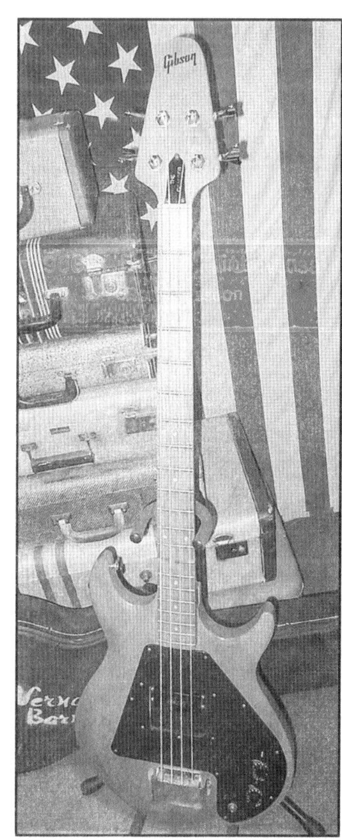

1974 Gibson Grabber

Rivington Guitars

BASSES

1970 Gibson Les Paul
Jim Mathis

1970s Gibson Melody Maker
The Vault at Chicago Music Exchange

MODEL YEAR	FEATURES	EXC. COND. LOW	HIGH

Gibson IV

1986-1988. Mahogany body and neck, double-cut, 2 pickups, black chrome hardware, various colors.

1986-1988		$1,500	$2,000

Gibson V

1986-1988. Double-cut, 5 strings, 2 pickups.

1986-1988		$1,250	$1,750

L9-S

1973. Natural maple or cherry, renamed Ripper Bass in '74.

1973		$2,000	$2,500

Les Paul

1970-1971. Single-cut solidbody, 2 pickups, walnut finish, renamed Les Paul Triumph Bass '71-'79.

1970-1971		$2,000	$2,750

Les Paul Money

2007-2008. Solidbody offset double-cut, 2 humbuckers, dot markers, figured maple top over mahogany body, 400 made.

2007-2008		$1,500	$2,000

Les Paul Signature

1973-1979. Double-cut, semi-hollowbody, 1 pickup, sunburst or gold (gold only by '76). Name also used on LPB-3 bass in '90s.

1973-1979	Sunburst or gold	$4,000	$5,500

Les Paul Special LPB-1

1991-1998. 2 TB-Plus pickups, ebony 'board, dots, slab mahogany body, active electronics, also available as 5-string.

1991-1998		$1,500	$2,000

Les Paul Deluxe Plus LPB-2

1991-1998. Upgraded LPB-1, carved maple top, trapezoid inlays, active eq and Bartolini pickups. Flame maple top Premium version offered '93-'98.

1991-1998		$1,500	$2,000

Les Paul Smartwood

1998. 2 TB pickups, active electronics, trapezoid inlays.

1998		$1,500	$2,000

Les Paul Special V

1993-1996. Single-cut slab body, 5-string, 2 pickups, dot markers, black/ebony.

1993-1996		$900	$1,250

Les Paul Standard

1999-2018. Maple top, chambered mahogany body, trapezoid inlays, 2 pickups.

1999-2018	Various colors	$2,000	$2,750

Les Paul Standard LPB-3

1991-1995. Like Les Paul Deluxe LPB-2 Bass, but with TB Plus pickups. Flame maple top Premium version offered '93-'95.

1993-1995	Flamed top	$2,000	$2,750

Les Paul Triumph

1971-1979. Renamed from Les Paul Bass.

1971-1979	Various colors	$2,500	$3,250
1973-1974	Optional white	$3,500	$5,500

Melody Maker

1967-1970. SG body, 1 humbucker pickup.

1967-1970		$1,750	$3,000

Midtown Standard

2012-2018. Semi-hollow body, double-cut, baked maple or rosewood board, 2 pickups.

2012-2018		$1,625	$2,250

Nikki Sixx Blackbird/Thunderbird

2000-2003, 2009-2010. Blackbird has black hardware and finish, iron cross inlays. '09 Thunderbird was flamed maple.

2000-2003		$2,125	$2,750

Q-80

1986-1988. Victory Series body shape, 2 pickups, bolt neck, black chrome hardware, renamed Q-90 in '88.

1986-1988		$750	$1,250

Q-90

1988-1992. Renamed from Q-80, mahogany body, 2 active humbuckers, maple neck, ebony 'board.

1988-1992		$750	$1,250

RD Artist

1977-1982. Double-cut solid maple body, laminated neck, 2 pickups, active electronics, string-thru-body, block inlays, various colors.

1977-1982		$2,500	$3,125

RD Artist CMT

1982. Flamed maple top.

1982		$3,250	$4,000

RD Artist VI

1980. Only 6 made, 6-string.

1980		$4,500	$6,000

RD Standard

1977-1979. Double-cut, solid maple body, laminated neck, 2 pickups, regular electronics, string-thru-body, dot inlays, various colors.

1977-1979		$2,500	$3,250

Ripper

1974-1982. Introduced as L-9 S Bass in '73, double-cut solidbody, glued neck, 2 pickups, string-thru-body, sunburst or natural maple until '76, sunburst only after. Black option '78-'79 and silverburst '80.

1974-1976	Natural maple	$2,250	$2,750
1974-1982	Sunburst	$2,250	$2,750
1978-1979	Black option	$2,250	$2,750
1980	Silverburst option	$3,500	$5,000

Ripper II

2009-2011. Solid maple body, 34" scale, 2 pickups, natural nitro lacquer.

2009-2011		$1,000	$1,375

SB Series

1971-1978. In '71, oval pickups, replaced mid-model with rectangular pickups. Includes 300 and 350 (30" scale, 1 and 2 pickups), 350 (30", 2 pickups), 400 (34", 1 pickup), 450 (34", 2 pickups). The 450 was special order only.

1971-1973	SB-300, 400	$725	$1,000
1972-1974	SB-350, 450	$725	$1,000
1975-1978	SB-450 special order	$725	$1,000

SG Reissue/SG Standard

2005-present. Similar to '60s EB-3, 2 pickups, mahogany body, cherry or white. Renamed SG Standard in '08, various colors.

2005-2024	Various colors	$1,000	$1,375

BASSES

MODEL YEAR	FEATURES	EXC. COND. LOW	HIGH

SG Standard Faded

2013-2018. Solid mahogany body, baked maple 'board, worn cherry or ebony finish.

2013-2018		$625	$825

SG Supreme

2007-2008. Made in Nashville, SG body with AAA maple top, 2 pickups.

2007-2008		$1,250	$1,625

Thunderbird II

1963-1969. Reverse solidbody until '65, non-reverse solidbody '65-'69, 1 pickup, custom colors available, reintroduced with reverse body for '83-'84.

1963	Sunburst, reverse	$10,000	$14,000
1964	Pelham Blue, reverse	$15,000	$24,500
1964	Sunburst, reverse	$10,000	$14,000
1965	Cardinal Red, non-reverse	$10,000	$13,000
1965	Inverness Green, non-reverse	$10,000	$13,000
1965	Sunburst, non-reverse	$7,000	$9,500
1965	Sunburst, reverse	$10,000	$14,000
1966	Cardinal Red, non-reverse	$14,000	$18,000
1966	Pelham Blue	$14,000	$18,000
1966	Sunburst, non-reverse	$7,000	$10,000
1967	Cardinal Red, non-reverse	$12,000	$15,500
1967	Sunburst, non-reverse	$7,000	$9,500
1968	Cardinal Red, non-reverse	$12,000	$15,500
1968-1969	Sunburst, non-reverse	$7,000	$9,500

Thunderbird III

1979-1982. Reverse body, 2 pickups, Thunderbird logo on 'guard.

1979-1982		$3,500	$4,250

Thunderbird IV

1963-1969. Reverse solidbody until '64, non-reverse solidbody '65-'69, 2 pickups, custom colors available, reintroduced with reverse body for '86-present (see Thunderbird IV Bass Reissue).

1963	Sunburst, reverse	$11,500	$14,500
1964	Frost Blue, reverse	$23,500	$30,000
1964	Pelham Blue, reverse	$23,500	$30,000
1964	Sunburst, reverse	$11,500	$15,000
1965	Cardinal Red, non-reverse	$11,000	$22,000
1965	Inverness Green, non-reverse	$11,000	$22,000
1965	Sunburst, reverse	$11,500	$14,500
1965-1966	Sunburst, non-reverse	$8,500	$11,500
1966	White, non-reverse	$14,000	$22,500
1967-1969	Sunburst, non-reverse	$8,500	$11,500

MODEL YEAR	FEATURES	EXC. COND. LOW	HIGH

Thunderbird IV (Reissue)

1987-2016. Has reverse body and 2 pickups, various colors.

1987-2016	Various colors	$1,750	$2,250

Thunderbird IV Zebra Wood

2007. Guitar of the Week (week 11 of '07), limited run of 400, Zebrawood body.

2007		$1,875	$2,500

Thunderbird 50th Anniversary

2013-2018. Mahogany body and neck, rosewood 'board, Bullion Gold finish.

2013-2018		$2,250	$3,000

Thunderbird 76

1976 only. Reverse solidbody, 2 pickups, rosewood 'board, various colors.

1976		$3,500	$6,000

Thunderbird 79

1979 only. Reverse solidbody, 2 pickups, sunburst.

1979		$3,500	$6,000

Thunderbird Short Scale

2011-2013. 30.5" scale, 2 pickups, nitro satin ebony finish.

2011-2013		$1,125	$1,500

Thunderbird Studio/IV Studio

2005-2007. 4- or 5-string versions.

2005-2007		$1,250	$1,625

Victory Artist

1981-1985. Double-cut, solidbody, 2 humbuckers and active electronics, various colors.

1981-1985		$1,625	$2,125

Victory Custom

1982-1984. Double-cut, solidbody, 2 humbuckers, passive electronics, limited production.

1982-1984		$1,625	$2,125

Victory Standard

1981-1986. Double-cut, solidbody, 1 humbucker, active electronics, various colors.

1981-1986		$1,250	$1,625

Godin

1987-present. Intermediate and professional grade, production, solidbody electric and acoustic/electric basses from luthier Robert Godin. They also build guitars and mandolins.

A Series

1990s-present. Various acoustic/electric, 4- or 5-string.

1990s-2024	A-4, A-5	$475	$650

Freeway A Series

2005-2012. Double-cut solidbodies, 4- or 5-string, passive or active.

2005-2012	Freeway A-4	$475	$650
2005-2012	Freeway A-5	$525	$700

Godlyke

2006-present. Professional and premium grade, production, solidbody basses from effects distributor Godlyke.

1982 Gibson The Ripper
Rivington Guitars

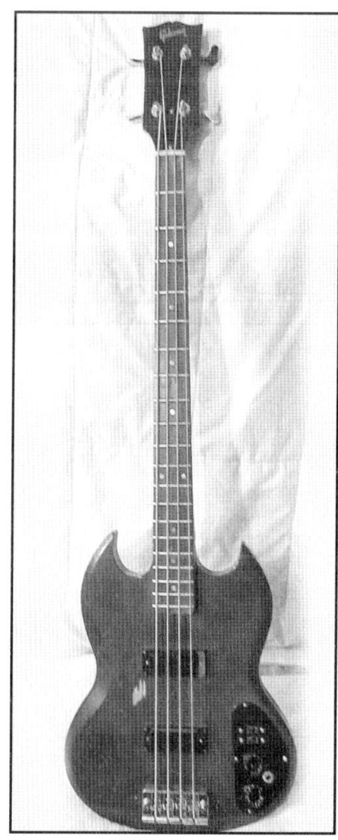

1972 Gibson SB-450
Richard Memmel

BASSES

Gretsch G2220 Electromatic Jr. Jet II

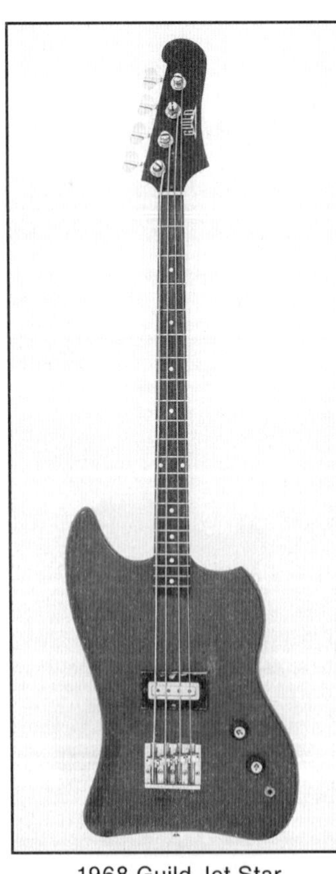
1968 Guild Jet Star
Imaged by Heritage Auctions, HA.com

MODEL YEAR	FEATURES	EXC. COND. LOW	HIGH

Goya

1955-1996. Originally imports from Sweden, brand later used on Japanese and Korean imports. They also offered guitars, mandolins, and banjos.

Electric Solidbody

1960s	Various models	$575	$850

Gretsch

1883-present. Intermediate and professional grade, production, solidbody, hollow body, and acoustic/electric basses. Gretsch came late to the electric bass game, introducing their first models in the early '60s. They also build guitars, amps and steels. In 2012 they again offered mandolins, ukes and banjos.

Broadkaster (6119-B)

1991-2013. Single-cut hollowbody, maple top, back and sides.

1991-2013		$1,500	$2,000

Broadkaster (7605/7606)

1975-1979. Double-cut solidbody, 1 pickup, bolt-on maple neck, natural (7605) or sunburst (7606).

1975-1979		$800	$1,000

Committee (7629)

1977-1980. Double-cut walnut and maple soldibody, neck-thru, 1 pickup, natural.

1977-1980		$800	$1,000

G2220 Electromatic Jr. Jet II

2012-present. Short scale, 2 pickups, various colors.

2012-2024		$275	$375

G5440LS Electromatic Long Scale Hollow Body

2012-2020. Single-cut, 2 pickups, "G" tailpiece, various colors.

2012-2020		$700	$950

G6072 Long Scale Hollow Body

1998-2006. Reissue of the '68 double-cut hollowbody, 2 pickups, sunburst, gold hardware.

1998-2006		$1,000	$1,375

G6136 White Falcon

2008. Single-cut hollowbody, 2 pickups, gold hardware.

2008		$2,250	$3,000

G6199 Billy-Bo Jupiter Thunderbird

2011. Double-cut solidbody, 2 pickups, gold hardware, black.

2011		$1,750	$2,250

Model 6070/6072

1963-1971 (1972 for 6070). Originally listed as the PX6070 Cello Bass, large thinline hollowbody double-cut archtop, fake f-holes, 1 pickup (6070) or 2 (6072), gold hardware.

1963-1964	6070, with endpin	$2,000	$2,750
1965-1972	6070, no endpin	$1,625	$2,000
1968-1971	6072, 2 pickups	$1,625	$2,000

Model 6071/6073

1968-1971 (1972 for 6071). Single-cut hollowbody, fake f-holes, 1 pickup (6071) or 2 (6073), padded back, red mahogany.

1968-1971	6073, 2 pickups	$2,000	$2,750
1968-1972	6071, 1 pickup	$1,500	$2,000

MODEL YEAR	FEATURES	EXC. COND. LOW	HIGH

Model 7615

1972-1975. Offset double-cut solidbody, slotted bass horn (monkey grip), large, polished rosewood 'guard covering most of the body, 2 pickups, dot markers, brown mahogany finish. Only bass offered in Gretsch catalog for this era.

1972-1975		$1,000	$1,375

TK 300 (7626/7627)

1976-1981. Double-cut solidbody, 1 pickup, Autumn Red Stain or natural.

1976-1981		$700	$950

Guild

1952-present. Guild added electric basses in the mid-'60s and offered them until '02. New owner, Cordoba Music, reintroduced acoustic and electric basses to the line in '15.

Ashbory

1986-1988, 2009. 18" scale, total length 30", fretless, silicone rubber strings, active electronics, low-impedance circuitry.

1986-1988		$525	$675
2009	Fender Guild reissue	$225	$300

B-4 E

1993-2000. Acoustic/electric single-cut flat-top, mahogany sides with arched mahogany back, multi-bound, gold hardware until '95, chrome after.

1993-2000		$550	$750

B-30 E

1987-1999. Single-cut flat-top acoustic/electric, mahogany sides, arched mahogany back, multi-bound, fretless optional.

1987-1999		$1,125	$1,500

B-50 Acoustic

1975-1987. Acoustic flat-top, mahogany sides with arched mahogany back, spruce top, multi-bound, renamed B-30 in '87.

1975-1987		$1,125	$1,500

B-301/B-302

1976-1981. Double-cut solidbody, chrome-plated hardware. Models include B-301 (mahogany, 1 pickup), B-301A (ash, 1 pickup), B-302 (mahogany, 2 pickups), B-302A (ash, 2 pickups), and B-302AF (ash, fretless).

1976-1981	B-301, B-301A	$950	$1,250
1976-1981	B-302, B-302A	$950	$1,250
1977-1981	B-302AF	$950	$1,250

B-401/B-402

1980-1983. Model 401 with active circuit, 1 pickup. Model 402 passive and active, 2 pickups. A for ash body.

1980-1981	B-401, B-401A	$950	$1,250
1980-1983	B-402, B402A	$950	$1,250

B-500 C Acoustic

1992-1993. Acoustic/electric flat-top, round soundhole, single-cut, solid spruce top, maple back and sides, dark stain, limited production.

1992-1993		$1,250	$1,500

FS-46

1983. Acoustic-electric flat-top, single-cut, sharp horn fretless.

1983		$750	$950

MODEL YEAR	FEATURES	EXC. COND. LOW	HIGH

Jet Star

1964-1970 (limited production '68-'70). Offset double-cut solidbody, short treble horn, 1 pickup, 2-on-a-side tuners '64-'66 and 4 in-line tuners '66-'70.

1964-1966	2-on-side tuners	$1,500	$2,000
1966-1970	4-in-line tuners	$1,500	$2,000

JS I/JS II

1970-1977. Double-cut solidbody, 30" scale, 1 pickup (JS I or 1) or 2 (JS II or 2), carved-top oak leaf design available for '72-'76. 34" long scale (LS) versions offered fretted and fretless for '74-'75.

1970-1977	JS I	$1,500	$2,000
1970-1977	JS II	$1,500	$2,000
1974-1976	JS I, carved	$1,500	$2,000
1974-1976	JS II, carved	$1,500	$2,000

M-85 I/M-85 II

1967-1972. Single-cut semi-hollowbody, 1 pickup (M-85 I) or 2 (M-85 II).

1967-1972	M-85 I	$1,500	$2,000
1967-1972	M-85 II	$1,500	$2,000

M-85 I/M-85 II BluesBird

1972-1976. Single-cut soldibody archtop, Chesterfield headstock inlay, cherry mahogany, 1 humbucker pickup (I) or 2 (II).

1972-1973	M-85 I	$1,750	$2,250
1972-1976	M-85 II	$1,750	$2,250

MB-801

1981-1982. Double-cut solidbody, 1 pickup, dot inlays.

1981-1982		$750	$950

SB-201/SB-202/SB-203

1982-1983. Double-cut solidbody, 1 split coil pickup (201), 1 split coil and 1 single coil (202), or 1 split coil and 2 single coils (203).

1982-1983	SB-201	$850	$1,000
1982-1983	SB-202	$900	$1,125
1983	SB-203	$950	$1,250

SB-502 E

1984-1985. Double-cut solidbody, 2 pickups, active electronics.

1984-1985		$950	$1,250

SB-600/Pilot Series

1983-1993. Offset double-cut solidbody, bolt-on neck, poplar body. Models include SB-601 (1 pickup), SB-602 (2 pickups or fretless), SB-602 V (2 pickups, 5-string), SB-604 (2 pickups, offset peghead) and SB-605 (5-string, hipshot low D tuner). Models 604 and 605 are replaced in '93 with Pro4 and Pro5 Pilot.

1983-1989	SB-601	$625	$800
1983-1989	SB-602	$725	$900
1983-1989	SB-602, fretless	$725	$900
1983-1989	SB-602V	$725	$900
1986-1988	SB-604 Pilot	$725	$900
1986-1993	SB-605	$725	$900

SB-608 Flying Star Motley Crue

1984-1985. Pointy 4-point star body, 2 pickups, E version had EMG pickups.

1984-1985		$1,125	$1,500

Starfire

1965-1975. Double-cut semi-hollow thinbody, 1 pickup, mahogany neck, chrome-plated hardware, cherry or sunburst.

1965-1969	Single-coil	$2,250	$3,250
1970-1975	Humbucker	$2,250	$3,250

Starfire II

1967-1978. Two-pickup version of Starfire Bass. Single-coils until '69, humbuckers after, sunburst, cherry or very rare black. Starfire II Bass Special had gold hardware.

1967-1969	2 single-coils	$2,250	$3,250
1967-1969	Black	$2,750	$3,500
1970-1978	2 humbuckers	$2,250	$3,250

Starfire II Reissue

1997-present. Reissue of 2 humbucker version.

1997-2024		$950	$1,250

X-100 Blade Runner

1985-1986. Poplar body and neck, ebony 'board, 1 pickup.

1985-1986		$2,750	$3,500

X-701/X-702

1982-1984. Body with 4 sharp horns with extra-long bass horn, 1 pickup (X-701) or 2 (X-702), various metallic finishes.

1982-1984	X-701	$1,125	$1,500
1982-1984	X-702	$1,125	$1,500

GW Basses & Luthiery

2004-present. Professional and premium grade, production/custom, basses built by luthier Grandon Westlund in West Lafayette, Indiana.

Hagstrom

1921-1983, 2004-present. This Swedish guitar company first offered electric basses in '61.

Concord II Deluxe

1967-1970. Bass version of V-IN guitar, 335-style body, 2 pickups, sunburst.

1967-1970		$1,500	$2,000

Coronado IV

1963-1970. Offset double cut, Bi-Sonic pickups.

1963-1970		$1,000	$1,375

H-8

1967-1969. Double-cut solidbody, 8 strings, 2 pickups, various colors.

1967-1969		$2,125	$2,750

Kent

1963-1964. 2 single-coils, 4 sliders.

1962-1966		$700	$925

Model I B/F-100 B

1965-1973. Offset double-cut solidbody, 2 single-coils, 5 sliders, 30" scale, red, black, white or blue.

1965-1973		$750	$975

Model II B/F-400

1965-1970. Like Model I, but with 30.75" scale, red, black, white or blue. Called F-400 in U.S., II B elsewhere.

1965-1970		$750	$975

Swede 2000 (With Synth)

1977. Circuitry on this Swede bass connected to the Ampeg Patch 2000 pedal so bass would work with various synths.

1977		$650	$1,250

1968 Hagstrom H-8
Willie Moseley

1970 Hagstrom Model II
Robbie Keene

BASSES

To get the most from this book, be sure to read "Using *The Guide*" in the introduction.

BASSES

Hamer Chaparral 12-String
Imaged by Heritage Auctions, HA.com

Harmony H-25
Tom Pfeifer

MODEL YEAR	FEATURES	EXC. COND. LOW	HIGH

Swede

1971-1976, 2004-present. Single-cut solidbody, block inlays, bolt neck, 2 humbuckers, 30.75" scale, cherry or black

1971-1976		$950	$1,250

Super Swede

1979-1983, 2004-present. Like Swede, but with neck-thru body, 32" scale, sunburst, mahogany or black.

1979-1983		$950	$1,250

Hamer

1975-2012, 2017-present. Founded in Arlington Heights, Illinois, by Paul Hamer and Jol Dantzig, Hamer was purchased by Kaman in '88. They also built guitars. Fender acquired Hamer in '08 and suspended production in '12. The brand was reintroduced in '17 by Jam Industries.

8-String Short-Scale

1978-1993. Double cut solidbody, 1 or 2 pickups, 30.5" scale.

1978-1993		$2,250	$3,000

12-String Acoustic

1985-2010. Semi-hollow, long scale, single cut, sound hole, 2 pickups. Import XT model added in the 2000s.

1985-2010		$2,750	$3,500

12-String Short-Scale

1978-1996. Four sets of 3 strings - a fundamental and 2 tuned an octave higher, double cut maple and mahogany solidbody, 30.5" scale.

1978-1996		$2,250	$3,000

Blitz

1982-1990. Explorer-style solidbody, 2 pickups, bolt-on neck.

1982-1990		$1,750	$2,500

Chaparral

1986-1995, 2000-2008. Solidbody, 2 pickups, glued-in neck, later basses have bolt-on neck.

1986-1987	Set-neck	$1,750	$2,500
1987-1995	Bolt-on neck	$1,750	$2,500

Chaparral 5-String

1987-1995. Five strings, solidbody, 2 pickups, glued-in neck, later basses have 5-on-a-side reverse peghead.

1987-1995		$1,750	$2,500

Chaparral 12-String

1992-2012. Long 34" scale 12-string, offset double cut. Import XT model added in '01.

1992-2012	USA	$2,250	$3,000
2000-2012	Import	$500	$650

Chaparral Max

1986-1995. Chaparral Bass with figured maple body, glued-in neck and boomerang inlays.

1986-1995		$1,000	$1,500

Cruise

1982-1990, 1995-1999. J-style solidbody, 2 pickups, glued neck ('82-'90) or bolt-on neck ('95-'99), also available as a 5-string.

1982-1990	Set-neck	$1,000	$1,500
1995-1999	Bolt-on neck	$1,000	$1,500

Cruise 5

1982-1989 Five-string version, various colors

1982-1989		$1,250	$1,625

FBIV

1985-1987. Reverse Firebird shape, 1 P-Bass Slammer and 1 J-Bass Slammer pickup, mahogany body, rosewood 'board, dots.

1985-1987		$1,250	$1,625

Monaco 4

2002-2012. Flamed maple top, rosewood 'board, Tobacco Burst or '59 Burst finish.

2002-2012		$2,500	$3,250

Standard

1975-1984, 2001. US-made, Explorer-style headstock, 2 humbuckers. Imported in '01.

1975-1979	Flamed top, bound	$7,500	$10,000
1975-1984	Plain top, unbound	$4,500	$6,000
1980-1984	Flamed top, bound	$6,000	$8,000
2001	Import	$500	$650

Velocity 5

2002-2012. Offset double-cut, long bass horn, active, 1 humbucker.

2002-2012		$500	$650

Harmony

1892-1976, late 1970s-present. Harmony once was one of the biggest instrument makers in the world, making guitars and basses under their own brand and for others.

H Series

Late-1980s-early-1990s. F-style solidbody copies, 1 or 2 pickups, all models begin H.

1980s-90s		$200	$250

H-22

1959-1972. Single-cut hollowbody, 2-on-a-side, 1 pickup.

1959-1969		$1,375	$1,750
1970-1972		$1,125	$1,500

H-22 Reissue

2000s. Imported reissue, 1 pickup.

2000s		$400	$550

H-25/Silhouette

1963-1967. Offset double-cut solidbody, 1 pickup (H-25) or 2 (Silhouette).

1963-1967	H-25	$825	$1,125
1963-1967	Silhouette	$825	$1,125

H-27

1968-1972. Double-cut hollowbody, 4-on-a-side, 2 pickups.

1968-1972		$825	$1,125

Hartke

Hartke offered a line of wood and aluminum-necked basses from 2000 to '03.

Heartfield

1989-1994. Distributed by Fender, imported from Japan. They also offered guitars.

Electric

1989-1994. Double-cut solidbody, graphite reinforced neck, 2 single-coils, available in 4-, 5- and 6-string models.

1989-1994		$300	$400

BASSES

Heritage

1985-present. Mainly a builder of guitars, Kalamazoo, Michigan's Heritage has offered a few basses in the past.

HB-1

1987. P-style body, limited production, single-split pickup, 4-on-a-side tuners, figured maple body, bolt-on neck.

MODEL YEAR	FEATURES	EXC. COND. LOW	HIGH
1987		$700	$925

Höfner

1887-present. Professional grade, production, basses. They also offer guitars and bowed instruments. Höfner basses, made famous in the U.S. by one Paul McCartney, are made in Germany.

G5000/1 Super Beatle (G500/1)

1968-2011. Bound ebony 'board, gold-plated hardware, natural finish, the version with active circuit is called G500/1 Super Beatle, reissued in '94.

MODEL YEAR	FEATURES	EXC. COND. LOW	HIGH
1968-1979	LH	$2,500	$3,000
1968-1979	RH	$2,125	$2,750

Icon Series

2007-2011. Chinese versions of classic Höfners, often sold without a case or gig bag.

MODEL YEAR	FEATURES	EXC. COND. LOW	HIGH
2007-2011		$225	$300

Model 172 Series

1968-1970. Offset double-cut, 6-on-a-side tuners, 2 pickups, 2 slide switches, dot markers, 172/S shaded sunburst, 172/R red vinyl covered body, 172/I vinyl covered with white top and black back.

MODEL YEAR	FEATURES	EXC. COND. LOW	HIGH
1968-1970	172/I, white	$1,000	$1,375
1968-1970	172/R, red	$1,000	$1,375
1968-1970	172/S, sunburst	$1,000	$1,375

Model 182 Solid

1962-1985. Offset double-cut solidbody, 2 pickups.

MODEL YEAR	FEATURES	EXC. COND. LOW	HIGH
1962-1965		$1,000	$1,375

Model 185 Solid

1962-ca. 1970. Classic offset double-cut solidbody, 2 double-coil pickups.

MODEL YEAR	FEATURES	EXC. COND. LOW	HIGH
1962-1970		$1,000	$1,375

Model 500/1 Beatle

1956-present. Semi-acoustic, bound body in violin shape, glued-in neck, 2 pickups, right- or left-handed, sunburst. Listed as 500/1 Vintage '58, '59, '62 and '63 in '90s through 2014. Currently named 500/1 Violin Bass.

MODEL YEAR	FEATURES	EXC. COND. LOW	HIGH
1956-1959	LH or RH	$7,500	$10,000
1960	LH, McCartney	$7,000	$9,500
1960	RH	$5,750	$7,500
1961	LH	$7,000	$9,000
1961	LH, McCartney	$11,500	$15,000
1961	RH	$6,000	$8,000
1962-1963	LH	$6,000	$8,000
1962-1963	RH	$6,000	$8,000
1964	LH	$6,000	$8,000
1964	LH, McCartney	$9,000	$12,000
1964	RH	$4,000	$6,500
1964	RH, McCartney	$5,500	$6,500
1965	LH	$3,500	$5,000
1965	RH	$3,500	$5,000
1966	LH	$3,500	$4,500
1966	RH	$3,500	$4,250
1967	LH	$2,750	$3,000
1967	RH	$2,500	$3,000
1968-1973	LH	$2,250	$2,875
1968-1973	RH	$2,125	$2,750
1974-1979	LH or RH	$1,875	$2,500

'58 Model 500/1 Beatle Reissue

2008-2013. Right- or left-handed.

MODEL YEAR	FEATURES	EXC. COND. LOW	HIGH
2008-2013		$1,750	$2,250

'62 Model 500/1 Beatle Reissue

1990s-2014. Right- or left-handed.

MODEL YEAR	FEATURES	EXC. COND. LOW	HIGH
1990s-2014		$1,750	$2,250

'63 Model 500/1 Beatle Reissue

1994-2010. Right- or left-handed.

MODEL YEAR	FEATURES	EXC. COND. LOW	HIGH
1994-2010		$1,750	$2,250

'64 Model 500/1 Beatle Reissue

2015-2016. Right- or left-handed.

MODEL YEAR	FEATURES	EXC. COND. LOW	HIGH
2015-2016		$1,750	$2,250

Model 500/1 1964-1984 Reissue

1984. '1964-1984' neckplate notation.

MODEL YEAR	FEATURES	EXC. COND. LOW	HIGH
1984		$1,750	$2,250

Model 500/1 40th Anniversary

1995-1996. Only 300 made.

MODEL YEAR	FEATURES	EXC. COND. LOW	HIGH
1995-1996		$2,750	$3,500

Model 500/1 50th Anniversary

2006. Pickguard logo states '50th Anniversary Höfner Violin Bass 1956-2006', large red Höfner logo also on 'guard, 150 made.

MODEL YEAR	FEATURES	EXC. COND. LOW	HIGH
2006		$2,750	$3,500

Model 500/1 Cavern

2005. Limited run of 12, includes certificate.

MODEL YEAR	FEATURES	EXC. COND. LOW	HIGH
2005		$1,750	$2,250

Model 500/1 Cavern Music Ground

1993. UK commissioned by Music Ground, said to be one of the first accurate reissues, 40 made.

MODEL YEAR	FEATURES	EXC. COND. LOW	HIGH
1993		$1,750	$2,250

Model 500/1 Contemporary

2007-2008. Contemporary Series.

MODEL YEAR	FEATURES	EXC. COND. LOW	HIGH
2007-2008		$700	$950

Model 500/2 and Club

1965-1970, 2015-present. Similar to the 500/1, but with 'club' body Höfner made for England's Selmer, sunburst. Club Bass has been reissued in various colors.

MODEL YEAR	FEATURES	EXC. COND. LOW	HIGH
1965-1970		$2,000	$2,500
2015-2024		$2,000	$2,500

Model 500/3 Senator

1962-1964. Single-cut thin body, f-holes, 1 511b pickup, sunburst.

MODEL YEAR	FEATURES	EXC. COND. LOW	HIGH
1962-1964		$1,750	$2,250

Model 500/5

1959-1963. Single-cut body with Beatle Bass-style pickups, sunburst. Becomes President Bass in '63.

MODEL YEAR	FEATURES	EXC. COND. LOW	HIGH
1959-1963		$3,500	$5,000

Model 500/6

Late-1960s. Introduced in '67, semi-acoustic, thinline, soft double-cut, 2 pickups, 4 control knobs, dot markers, sunburst.

MODEL YEAR	FEATURES	EXC. COND. LOW	HIGH
1967		$2,000	$2,500

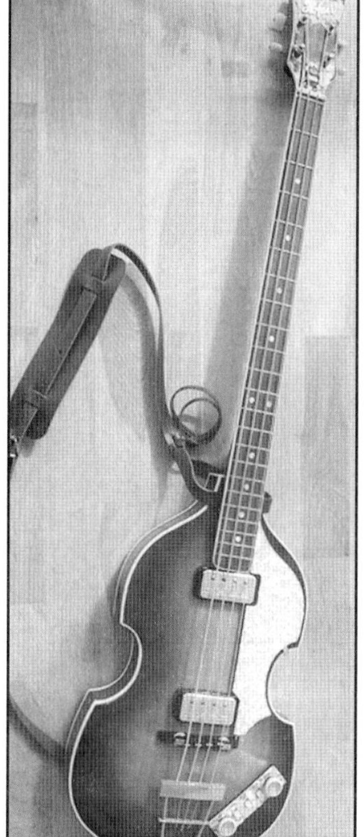

1964 Höfner 500/1 Beatle

Steve Lee

1963 Höfner 500/1 Club

Larry Wassgren

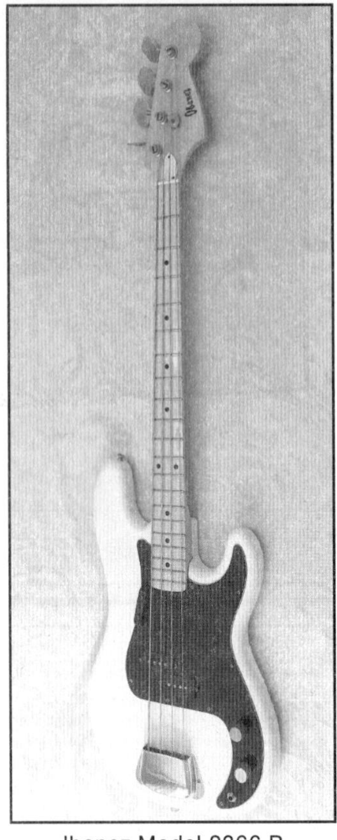

Ibanez Model 2366 B
Michael Burns

1984 Ibanez RS Roadstar II
Brian Chambers

MODEL YEAR	FEATURES	EXC. COND. LOW	HIGH

Model 500/8BZ/B500/8BZ

Late-1960s. Semi-acoustic, thinline, sharp double-cut, multiple-line position markers, built in flip-fuzz and bass boost, sunburst or natural.

1967	500/8BZ, sunburst	$2,000	$2,500
1967	B500/8BZ, natural	$2,000	$2,500

President

1963-1972. Made for England's Selmer, single-cut archtop, 2 Beatle Bass-style pickups, sunburst.

1963-1965		$2,500	$3,250
1966-1969		$2,000	$2,500
1970-1972		$2,000	$2,500

Hondo/Hondo II

1969-1987, 1991-2005. Budget grade, production, imported acoustic and electric solidbody basses. They also offered guitars, banjos and mandolins.

Electric Solidbody

1969-1987, 1991-2005. Various models.

1969-1999	Rare models	$425	$1,125
1969-1999	Standard models	$150	$300

Hoyer

1874-1987. Intermediate grade, production, electric basses. They also build guitars.

Electric

1960s	Various models	$600	$850

Ibanez

1932-present. Intermediate and professional grade, production, solidbody basses. They also have guitars, amps, and effects.

AXB Axstar Series

1986-1987. Various headless solidbody models.

1986-1987		$450	$600

BTB Series

1999-present. Various models.

1999-2024		$325	$450

Challenger

1977-1978. Offered as P-bass or J-bass style, and with ash body option.

1977-1978		$550	$750

DB Destroyer II X Series

1984-1986. Futuristic-style body, P- and J-style pickups, dot markers, bolt neck.

1984-1986	Various models	$550	$750

DT Destroyer II Series

1980-1985. Futuristic-style body.

1983-1986	Various models	$700	$950

ICB Iceman

1994-1996, 2011. Iceman body, basswood (300) or mahogany (500) body. 300 reissued in '11.

1994	ICB500, black	$600	$850
1994-1996	ICB300, white	$600	$850

Jet King

2009-2010. Retro offset double-cut solidbody, bolt neck.

2009-2010		$300	$400

MC Musician Series

1978-1988. Various models, solidbody, neck-thru.

1978-1988		$1,125	$1,500

MODEL YEAR	FEATURES	EXC. COND. LOW	HIGH

Model 2030

1970-1973. First copy era bass, offset double-cut, sunburst.

1970-1973		$850	$1,125

Model 2353

1974-1976. Copy model, offset double-cut, 1 pickup, black.

1974-1976		$750	$975

Model 2364B

1971-1973. Dan Armstrong see-thru Lucite copy with 2 mounted humbucker pickups, clear finish.

1971-1973		$1,000	$1,375

Model 2365

1974-1975. Copy model, Offset double-cut, rosewood 'board, pearloid block markers, sunburst.

1974-1975		$850	$1,125

Model 2366B/2366FLB

1974-1975. Copy model, offset double-cut, 1 split-coil pickup, sunburst, FLB fretless model.

1974-1975		$800	$1,125

Model 2385

1974-1975. Copy model, offset double-cut, 1 pickup, ash natural finish.

1974-1975		$800	$1,125

Model 2388B

1974-1976. Ric 4001 copy.

1974-1976		$800	$1,125

Model 2452

1975. Ripper copy.

1975		$800	$1,125

Model 2459B Destroyer

1974-1977. Laminated ash body, copy of Korina Explorer-style.

1974-1977		$3,000	$4,000

Model 2537 DX

1974-1975. Hofner Beatle copy.

1974-1975		$800	$1,125

Model 2609B Black Eagle

1974-1976. Burns-like bass, offset double-cut solidbody, sharp curving horns.

1974-1976		$1,500	$2,000

PL Pro Line Series

1986-1987. Offset double cut solidbody.

1986-1987	Various models	$550	$750

RB/RS Roadstar Series

1983-1987. Solidbody basses, various models and colors.

1983-1987		$400	$650

Rocket Roll

1974-1976. Korina solidbody, V-shape, natural.

1974-1976		$2,250	$3,000

S/SB Solidbody Series

1990-1992. Various ultra slim solidbody basses.

1990-1992		$350	$450

SR Sound Gear Series

1987-present. Sleek, lightweight designs, active electronics, bolt necks. Model numbers higher than 1000 are usually arched-top, lower usually flat body.

1987-2024	Various models	$300	$400

ST-980 Studio

1979-1980. Double cut, 8-string, bolt-on neck, walnut-maple-mahogany body.

1979-1980		$750	$1,000

MODEL YEAR	FEATURES	EXC. COND. LOW	HIGH

Imperial

Ca.1963-ca.1970. Imported by the Imperial Accordion Company of Chicago, Illinois. Early guitars and basses made in Italy, but by ca. '66 Japanese-made.

Electric Hollowbody

1960s	Various models	$250	$350

Electric Solidbody

1960s	Various models	$250	$350

Jackson

1980-present. Intermediate, professional, and premium grade, production, solidbody basses. They also offer guitars. Founded by Grover Jackson, who owned Charvel.

Concert C5P 5-String (Import)

1998-2000. Bolt neck, dot inlay, chrome hardware.

1998-2000		$200	$250

Concert Custom (U.S.A.)

1984-1995. Neck-thru Custom Shop bass.

1984-1989		$1,500	$3,000
1990-1995		$1,000	$1,375

Concert EX 4-String (Import)

1992-1995. Bolt neck, dot inlay, black hardware.

1992-1995		$300	$400

Concert V 5-String (Import)

1992-1995. Bound neck, shark tooth inlay.

1992-1995		$400	$550

Concert XL 4-String (Import)

1992-1995. Bound neck, shark tooth inlay.

1992-1995		$350	$450

Kelly Pro

1994-1995. Pointy-cut bouts, neck-thru solidbody, shark fin marker inlays, includes Standard and Custom models.

1994-1995		$800	$1,125

Piezo

1986. Piezo bridge pickup, neck-thru, shark tooth inlays. The Student model has rosewood 'board, no binding. Custom Model has ebony 'board and binding.

1986		$1,500	$2,000

Soloist

1996. Pointy headstock, 4-string.

1996		$800	$1,125

Surfcaster SC1

1998-2001. Tube and humbucker pickups.

1998-2001		$1,125	$1,500

Jerry Jones

1981-2011. Intermediate grade, production, semi-hollow body electric basses from luthier Jerry Jones, and built in Nashville, Tennessee. They also build guitars and sitars. Jones retired in 2011.

Neptune Longhorn 4

1988-2011. Based on Danelectro longhorn models, 4-string, 2 lipstick-tube pickups, 30" scale.

1988-2011		$1,875	$2,500

Neptune Longhorn 6

1988-2011. 6-string version.

1988-2011		$2,250	$3,000

Neptune Shorthorn 4

1988-2011. Danelectro Coke bottle headstock, short horns double cut, 2 pickups.

1988-2011		$1,875	$2,500

Juzek

Violin maker John Juzek was originally located in Prague, Czeckoslovakia, but moved to West Germany due to World War II. Prague instruments are considered by most to be more valuable. Many German instruments were mass produced with laminate construction and some equate these German basses with the Kay laminate basses of the same era. Juzek still makes instruments.

Kalamazoo

1933-1942, 1965-1970. Kalamazoo was a brand Gibson used on one of their budget lines. They also used the name on electric basses, guitars and amps from '65 to '67.

Electric

1965-1970	Various models	$500	$650

Kapa

Ca. 1962-1970. Kapa was founded by Koob Veneman in Maryland and offered basses and guitars.

Electric

1962-1970	Various models	$250	$750

Kawai

1927-present. Japanese instrument manufacturer Kawai started offering guitars under other brand names around '56. There were few imports carrying the Kawai brand until the late-'70s; best known for high quality basses. Kawai quit offering guitars and basses around 2002.

Electric

1960s-80s	Various models	$275	$800

Kay

Ca. 1931-present. Currently, budget and intermediate grade, production, imported solidbody basses. They also make amps, guitars, banjos, mandolins, ukes, and violins. Kay introduced upright acoustic laminate basses and 3/4 viols in '38 and electric basses in '54.

C1 Concert String

1938-1967. Standard (3/4) size student bass, laminated construction, spruce top, figured maple back and sides, shaded light brown.

1938-1949		$1,875	$2,250
1950-1959		$1,875	$2,250
1960-1967		$1,875	$2,250

K-160 Electronic

1955-1956. Same as K-162, but with plain white plastic trim.

1955-1956		$950	$1,250

K-162 Electronic

1955-1956. Bass version of K-161Thin Twin "Jimmy Reed," single-cut, 1 tube-style pickup.

1955-1956		$950	$1,250

Ibanez SR605 Bass
Richard Memmel

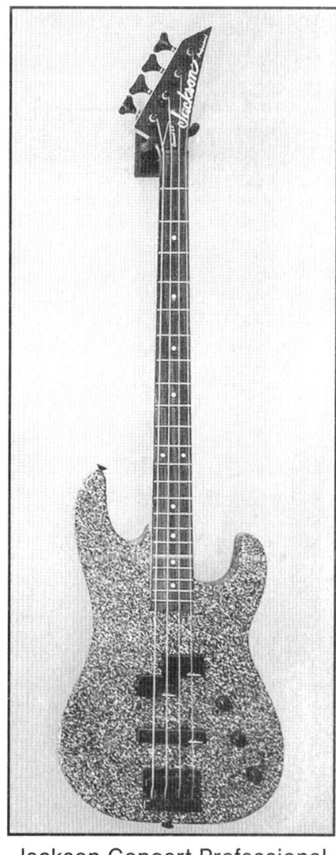

Jackson Concert Professional
Ken Kraynak

BASSES

BASSES

Kay Solidbody
Imaged by Heritage Auctions, HA.com

1977 Kramer 450-B Deluxe

MODEL YEAR	FEATURES	EXC. COND. LOW	HIGH

K-5965 Pro

1954-1965. Single-cut, 1 pickup. named K-5965 Pro by 1961.

1954-1965		$950	$1,250

K-5970 Jazz Special

1960-1964. Double-cut, pickup, Kelvinator headstock, black or blond.

1960-1964		$2,250	$3,000

M-1 (Maestro) String

1952-late-1960s. Standard (3/4) size bass, laminated construction, spruce top and curly maple back and sides. Model M-3 is the Junior (1/4) size bass, Model M-1 B has a blond finish, other models include the S-51 B Chubby Jackson Five-String Bass and the S-9 Swingmaster.

1952-1967		$2,250	$3,000

M-5 (Maestro) String

1957-late-1960s. Five strings.

1957-1967		$2,500	$3,500

Semi-hollowbody

1954-1966. Various models, single or double cut, 1 or 2 pickups.

1954-1966	1 pickup	$350	$450
1954-1966	2 pickups	$400	$500

Solidbody

1965-1968. Various models, single or double cut, 1 or 2 pickups.

1965-1968	1 pickup	$350	$450
1965-1968	2 pickups	$400	$500

Ken Smith

See listing under Smith.

Kent

1961-1969. Guitars and basses imported from Japan by Buegeleisen and Jacobson of New York, New York. Manufacturers unknown but many early instruments by Guyatone and Teisco.

Electric

1962-1969. Import models include 628 Newport, 634 Basin Street, 629, and 635.

1961-1969	Common model	$250	$350
1961-1969	Rare model	$550	$700

Kimberly

Late-1960s-early-1970s. Private branded import made in the same Japanese factory as Teisco. They also made guitars.

Violin

1960s		$425	$550

Kingston

Ca. 1958-1967. Imported from Japan by Westheimer Importing Corp. of Chicago. Early examples made by Guyatone and Teisco. They also offered guitars, mandolins and banjos.

Electric

1960s	Common model	$150	$400
1960s	Rare model	$400	$650

Klira

Founded 1887 in Schoenbach, Germany, mainly making violins, but added guitars and basses in the 1950s. The instruments of the '50s and '60s were aimed at the budget market, but workmanship improved with the '70s models.

Electric

1960s	Common model	$400	$800
1960s	Rare model	$800	$1,500

Kramer

1976-1990, 1995-present. Budget grade, production, imported solidbody basses. They also offer guitars. Kramer's first guitars and basses featured aluminum necks with wooden inserts on the back. Around '80 they started to switch to more economical wood necks and aluminum necks were last produced in '85. Gibson acquired the brand in '97.

250-B Special

1977-1979. Offset double-cut, aluminum neck, Ebonol 'board, zero fret, 1 single-coil, natural.

1977-1979		$775	$975

350-B Standard

1976-1979. Offset double-cut, aluminum neck, Ebonol 'board, tropical woods, 1 single-coil, dots. The 350 and 450 were Kramer's first basses.

1976-1979		$950	$1,250

450-B Deluxe

1976-1980. As 350-B, but with 2 single-coils and blocks.

1976-1980		$950	$1,250

650-B Artist

1977-1980. Double-cut, birdseye maple/burled walnut, aluminum neck, zero fret, mother-of-pearl crowns, 2 humbuckers.

1977-1980		$1,625	$2,250

Deluxe 8

1980. Multi-piece body, aluminum neck.

1980		$1,375	$1,875

DMB 2000

1979. Bolt-on aluminum neck, slot headstock.

1979		$1,000	$1,500

DMZ 4000

1978-1982. Bolt-on aluminum neck, slot headstock, double-cut solidbody, active EQ and dual-coil humbucking pickup, dot inlay.

1978-1981		$800	$1,000
1982	Bill Wyman-type	$800	$1,000

DMZ 4001

1979-1980. Aluminum neck, slot headstock, double-cut solidbody, 1 dual-coil humbucker pickup, dot inlay.

1979-1980		$1,125	$1,500

DMZ 5000

1979-1980. Double-cut solidbody, aluminum neck, slotted headstock, 2 pickups, crown inlays.

1979-1980		$1,000	$1,250

DMZ 6000B

1979-1980. Double-cut, aluminum neck, slotted headstock, 2 pickups, crown inlays.

1979-1980		$1,125	$1,500

MODEL YEAR	FEATURES	EXC. COND. LOW	HIGH

Duke Custom/Standard

1981-1983. Headless, aluminum neck, 1 humbucker.

1981-1983		$425	$550

Duke Special

1982-1985. Headless, aluminum neck, 2 pickups, with frets or fretless.

1982-1985		$450	$600

Ferrington KFB-1/KFB-2 Acoustic

1987-1990. Acoustic/electric, bridge-mounted active pickup, tone and volume control, various colors. KFB-1 has binding and diamond dot inlays; the KFB-2 has no binding and dot inlays. Danny Ferrington continued to offer the KFB-1 after Kramer closed in '90.

1987-1990		$325	$450

Focus Series

1984-1987. Made in Japan, double-cut solidbody, 1 or 2 pickups, various models.

1984-1987		$250	$800

Forum Series

1987-1990. Made in Japan, double-cut solidbody, 2 pickups, neck-thru (I & III) or bolt-neck (II & IV).

1987-1990		$350	$550

Gene Simmons Axe

1980-1981. Axe-shaped body, aluminum neck.

1980-1981		$3,500	$7,000

Hundred Series

1988-1990. Import budget line, 7/8th solidbody, various models.

1988-1990		$200	$350

Pacer Series

1982-1984. Offset double-cut solidbody, various models.

1982-1984		$600	$1,500

Pioneer Series

1981-1986. Various models, first wood neck basses, offset double-cut, JBX or PBX pickups, dots, '81-'84 models with soft headstocks, later '84 on with banana headstocks.

1981-1986		$450	$1,000

Ripley

1984-1987. Offset double-cut, 4 (IV) or 5 (V) strings, stereo, pan pots for each string, front and back pickups for each string, active circuitry.

1984-1987	IV and V	$700	$950

Stagemaster Custom (Import)

1982-1985, 1987-1990. First version had an aluminum neck (wood optional). Later version was neck-thru-body, bound neck, either active or passive pickups.

1982-1985	Imperial	$950	$1,250
1982-1985	Special	$950	$1,250
1982-1985	Standard	$950	$1,250

Stagemaster Deluxe (U.S.A.)

1981. Made in USA, 8-string, metal neck.

1981		$1,125	$1,500

Striker 700

1985-1989. Korean import, offset double-cut, 1 pickup until '87, 2 after. Striker name was again used on a bass in '99.

1985-1989		$200	$300

Vanguard

1981-1983. V-shaped body, Special (aluminum neck) or Standard (wood neck).

1981-1982	Special	$900	$1,250
1983-1984	Standard	$900	$1,250

Voyager

1982-1983. X-body, headless.

1982-1983		$900	$1,250

XKB-10 (Wedge)

1980-1981. Wedge-shaped body, aluminum neck.

1980-1981		$900	$1,250

XKB-20

1981. 2nd version, more traditional double cut body.

1981		$950	$1,125

XL Series

1980-1981. Odd shaped double-cut solidbody, aluminum neck, various models.

1980-1981	XL-24, 4-string	$1,125	$1,875
1980-1981	XL-8, 8-string	$1,125	$1,875
1980-1981	XL-9, 4-string	$1,125	$1,875

ZX Aero Star Series (Import)

1986-1989. Various models include ZX-70 (offset double-cut solidbody, 1 pickup).

1986-1989		$150	$300

KSD

2003-present. Intermediate grade, production, imported bass line designed by Ken Smith (see Smith listing).

Kubicki

1973-present. Professional and premium grade, production/custom, solidbody basses built by luthier Phil Kubicki in Santa Barbara, California. Kubicki began building acoustic guitars when he was 15. In '64 at age 19, he went to work with Roger Rossmeisl at Fender Musical Instrument's research and development department for acoustic guitars. Nine years later he moved to Santa Barbara, California, and established Philip Kubicki Technology, which is best known for its line of Factor basses and also builds acoustic guitars, custom electric guitars, bodies and necks, and mini-guitars and does custom work, repairs and restorations. Phil Kubicki died in '13.

Kustom

1968-present. Founded by Bud Ross in Chanute, Kansas, and best known for the tuck-and-roll amps, Kustom also offered guitars and basses from '68 to '69.

Electric Hollowbody

1968-1969	Various models	$1,500	$2,000

La Baye

1967. Short-lived brand out of Green Bay, Wisconsin and built by the Holman-Woodell factory in Neodesha, Kansas. There was also a guitar model.

Model 2x4 II

1967. Very low production, dual pickups, long-scale, small rectangle solidbody, sometimes referred to as the Bass II.

1967		$2,000	$3,000

Model 2x4 Mini

1967. Short-scale, 1 pickup, small rectangle solidbody.

1967		$2,000	$3,000

1981 Kramer DMZ 6000B

Imaged by Heritage Auctions, HA.com

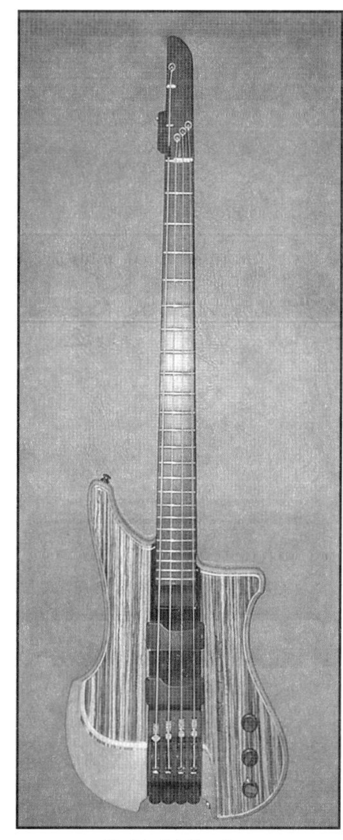

Kubicki Factor

BASSES

BASSES

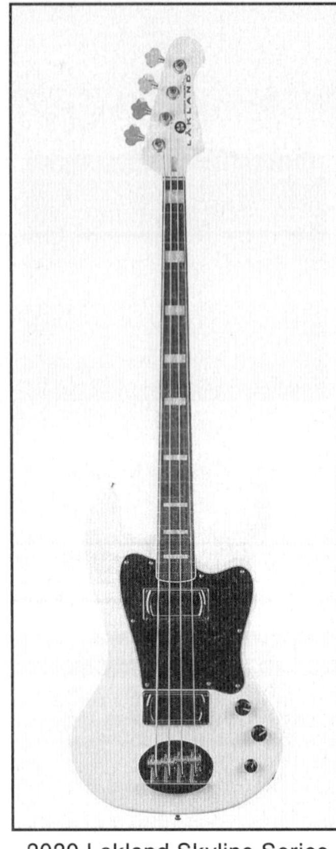
2020 Lakland Skyline Series
Cream City Music

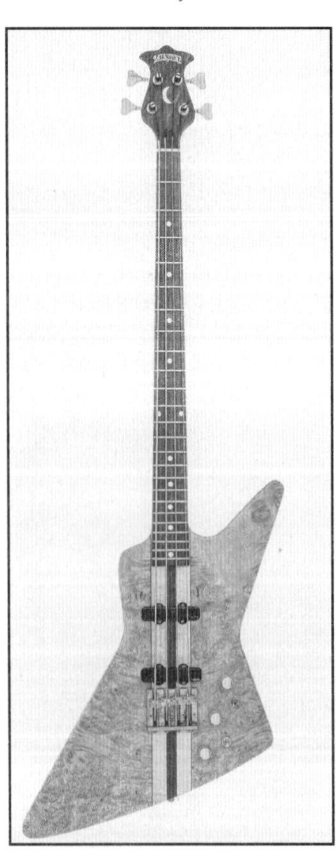
1982 Moonstone Exploder
Imaged by Heritage Auctions, HA.com

MODEL YEAR	FEATURES	EXC. COND. LOW	HIGH

Lakland

1994-present. Professional and premium grade, production/custom, solid and hollowbody basses from luthier Dan Lakin in Chicago, Illinois. Lakland basses are built in the U.S. and overseas (Skyline series).

Electric

1994-present. Various models.

1994-2002	4-63 Classic	$2,500	$3,500
1994-2002	4-63 Deluxe	$2,750	$3,750
1994-2002	4-63 Standard	$2,500	$3,500
1994-2002	4-94 / 44-94 Classic	$2,500	$3,500
1994-2024	4-94 / 44-94 Deluxe	$2,750	$3,750
1994-2024	4-94 / 44-94 Standard	$2,500	$3,500
1998-2003	Joe Osborn	$2,750	$3,750
2012-2024	Skyline 44-60	$1,250	$1,750

Lowrider Basses

2003-2018. Professional grade, production/custom, solidbody basses made by Ed Roman Guitars.

M Basses or Maghini

1998-present. Production/custom, professional and premium grade, solidbody electric basses built in Terryville, Connecticut by luthier Jon Maghini.

Magnatone

Ca. 1937-1971, 2013-present. Founded as Dickerson Brothers, known as Magna Electronics from '47. Produced instruments under own brand and for many others.

Mark VI/Artist Mark VI

1959. Designed by luthier Paul Barth for Magnatone, double-cut, 4-string, 1 pickup.

1959		$1,250	$1,750

X-10 Hurricane

1965-1966. Offset double cut solidbody, 1 single-coil, 4-on-a-side tuners, Magnatone logo on guard and headstock, Hurricane logo on headstock.

1965-1966		$1,000	$1,500

Mako

1985-1989. Line of solidbody basses from Kaman (Ovation, Hamer). They also offered guitars and amps.

Electric Solidbody

1985-1989	Various models	$150	$500

Marco Polo

1960-ca.1964. One of the first inexpensive Japanese brands to be imported into the U.S., they also offered guitars.

Solidbody

1960s	Various models	$100	$300

Marleaux

1990-present. Luthier Gerald Marleaux builds his custom, premium grade, electric basses in Clausthal-Zellerfeld, Germany.

MODEL YEAR	FEATURES	EXC. COND. LOW	HIGH

Marling

Ca. 1975. Budget line instruments marketed by EKO of Recanati, Italy; probably made by them, although possibly imported. They also had guitars.

Electric Solidbody

Models include the E.495 (copy of LP), E.485 (copy of Tele), and the E.465 (Manta-style).

1970s	Various models	$100	$300

Martin

1833-present. Professional grade, production, acoustic basses made in the U.S. In 1978, Martin re-entered the electric market and introduced their solidbody EB-18 and EB-28 Basses. In the '80s they offered Stinger brand electric basses. By the late '80s, they started offering acoustic basses.

00C-16GTAE

2006-2011. Mahogany back and sides, Fishman electronics.

2006-2011		$1,000	$1,500

B-1/B-1E Acoustic

2002-2006. Mahogany back and sides, E has Fishman electronics.

2002-2006		$1,000	$1,500

B-40/B-40B Acoustic

1989-1996. Jumbo, rosewood back and sides, built-in pickup and volume and tone controls. The B-40B had a pickup.

1989-1996	B-40B	$1,500	$2,000
1989-1996	No pickup	$1,500	$2,000

B-65 Acoustic

1989-1993. Like B-40 but with maple back and sides, built-in pickup and volume and tone controls.

1989-1993		$1,500	$2,000

BC-15E Acoustic

2000-2006. Single-cut, all mahogany, on-board electronics.

2000-2006		$1,250	$1,750

BC-16E Acoustic-Electric

2020-2022. Solid sitka spruce top, East Indian rosewood back and sides, built-in Fishman electronics.

2020-2022		$1,750	$2,250

BC-16GTE Acoustic

2009-2013. Jumbo, cutaway, mahogany back and sides.

2009-2013		$1,500	$2,000

BCPA4 Acoustic-Electric

2013-2020. Performing Artist series, single-cut, sitka spruce top, sapele back and sides.

2013-2020		$1,500	$2,000

EB-18

1979-1982. Electric solidbody, neck-thru, 1 pickup, natural.

1979-1982		$1,250	$1,750

EB-28

1980-1982. Electric solidbody.

1980-1982		$1,500	$2,000

SBL-10

1980s. Stinger brand solidbody, maple neck, 1 split and 1 bar pickup.

1980s		$200	$275

MODEL YEAR	FEATURES	EXC. COND. LOW	HIGH

Marvel

1950s-mid 1960s. Budget guitars and basses marketed by Peter Sorkin Company in New York, New York.

Electric Solidbody

1950s-60s	Various models	$250	$550

Messenger

1967-1968. Built by Musicraft, Inc., Messengers featured a neck-thru metal alloy neck. They also made guitars.

Metal Neck

1967-1968. Metal alloy neck. Messenger mainly made guitars - they offered a bass, but it is unlikely many were built.

1967-1968		$2,000	$2,500

Messenger Upright

Made by Knutson Luthiery, see that listing.

Microfrets

1967-1975, 2004-2005. Professional grade, production, electric basses built in Myersville, Maryland. They also built guitars.

Husky

1971-1974/75. Double-cut, 2 pickups, 2-on-a-side tuners.

1971-1975		$1,125	$1,500

Rendezvous

1970. One pickup, orange sunburst.

1970		$1,125	$1,500

Signature

1969-1975. Double-cut, 2 pickups, 2-on-a-side tuners.

1969-1975		$1,750	$2,250

Stage II

1969-1975. Double-cut, 2 pickups, 2-on-a-side tuners.

1969-1975		$1,750	$2,250

Thundermaster

1967-1975. Double-cut, 2 pickups, 2-on-a-side tuners.

1967-1975		$1,750	$2,250

Modulus

1978-2013. Founded by aerospace engineer Geoff Gould, Modulus offered professional and premium grade, production/custom, solidbody basses built in California. They also built guitars.

Electric

1978-2013. Various standard models.

1978-2013		$1,500	$3,500

Mollerup Basses

In 1984 luthier Laurence Mollerup began building professional grade, custom/production, electric basses and electric double basses in Vancouver, British Columbia. He has also built guitars.

Moonstone

1972-2020. Luthier Steve Helgeson built his premium grade, production/custom, acoustic and electric basses in Eureka, California. He also built guitars.

MODEL YEAR	FEATURES	EXC. COND. LOW	HIGH

Eclipse Deluxe

1980-1984. Double-cut solidbody.

1980-1984		$2,000	$3,500

Exploder

1980-1983. Figured wood body, Explorer-style neck-thru-body.

1980-1983		$2,000	$3,500

Vulcan

1982-1984. Solidbody, flat-top (Vulcan) or carved top (Vulcan II), maple body, gold hardware.

1982-1984		$2,000	$3,500

Morales

Ca.1967-1968. Guitars and basses made in Japan by Zen-On and not heavily imported into the U.S.

Electric Solidbody

1967-1968	Various models	$150	$400

Mosrite

Semie Moseley's Mosrite offered various bass models throughout the many versions of the Mosrite company.

Brut

Late-1960s. Assymetrical body with small cutaway on upper treble bout.

1960s		$675	$850

Celebrity

1965-1969. ES-335-style semi-thick double-cut body with f-holes, 2 pickups.

1965-1966	Custom color	$900	$1,125
1965-1967	Sunburst	$800	$1,000
1968-1969	Red	$750	$950
1969	Sunburst	$775	$975

Combo

1966-1968. Hollowbody, 2 pickups.

1966-1968		$1,375	$1,875

Joe Maphis

1966-1969. Ventures-style body, hollow without f-holes, 2 pickups, natural.

1966-1969		$1,625	$2,000

Ventures

1965-1972. Various colors, 1 or 2 pickups.

1965	1 pickup	$1,875	$2,375
1965	2 pickups	$2,125	$2,750
1966	1 pickup	$1,500	$1,875
1966	2 pickups	$1,875	$2,375
1967-1968	1 pickup	$1,375	$1,750
1967-1968	2 pickups	$1,500	$1,875
1969	1 pickup	$1,250	$1,625
1969	2 pickups	$1,500	$1,875
1970-1972	1 pickup	$1,375	$1,750
1970-1972	2 pickups	$1,375	$1,750

V-II

1973-1974. Ventures-style, 2 humbuckers, sunburst.

1973-1974		$1,625	$2,000

MTD

1994-present. Intermediate, professional, and premium grade, production/custom, electric basses built by luthier Michael Tobias (who founded Tobias Basses in '77) in Kingston, New York. Since '00, he also imports basses built in Korea to his specifications.

1966 Mosrite Celebrity

Rivington Guitars

1965 Mosrite Ventures

Cream City Music

BASSES

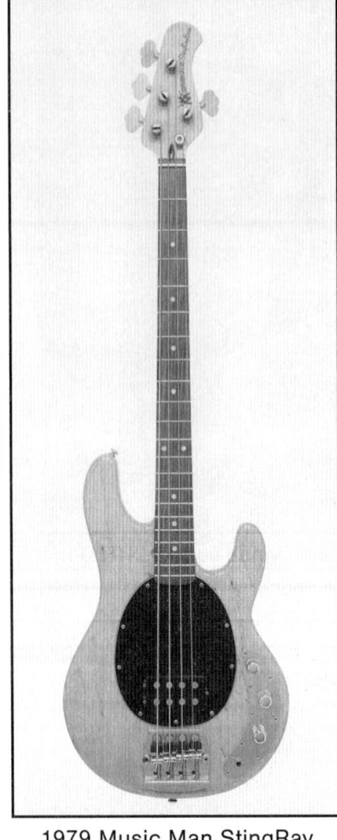
1979 Music Man StingRay
Imaged by Heritage Auctions, HA.com

1962 National Valpro 85
Imaged by Heritage Auctions, HA.com

MODEL YEAR	FEATURES	EXC. COND. LOW	HIGH

Murph

1965-1967. Mid-level electric solidbody basses built by Pat Murphy in San Fernado, California. Murph logo on headstock. They also offered guitars and amps.

Solidbody

1965-1967		$875	$1,125

Music Man

1972-present. Intermediate and professional grade, production, electric basses. They also build guitars.

Bongo

2003-present. Double cut solidbody, squared-off horns, 2 pickups, 4-, 5- and 6-string.

2003-2024	Bongo 4	$1,375	$1,750
2003-2024	Bongo 5	$1,500	$1,875
2003-2024	Bongo 6	$1,625	$2,125

Cutlass I/Cutlass II

1982-1987. Ash body, graphite neck, string-thru-body.

1982-1984	I, CLF era	$3,000	$5,000
1982-1984	II, CLF era	$2,500	$4,000
1984-1987	I, Ernie Ball era	$2,000	$2,500
1984-1987	II, Ernie Ball era	$2,000	$2,500

S.U.B. Series

2003-2007. Offset double-cut, 4- or 5-string, 1 humbucker.

2003-2007	IV Bass	$600	$800
2003-2007	V Bass	$700	$900

Sabre

1978-ca.1991. Double-cut solidbody bass, 3-and-1 tuning keys, 2 humbucking pickups, on-board preamp, natural.

1978-1984	CLF era	$3,000	$4,000
1984-1991	Ernie Ball era	$2,500	$3,250

Sterling

1993-present. Rosewood, 1 pickup, EQ, pearl blue. In '05, additional pickup options available. 5-string introduced in '08.

1993-2024	4-string	$1,500	$2,000
2008-2024	5-string	$1,500	$2,000

StingRay

1976-present. Offset double-cut solidbody, 1 pickup, 3-and-1 tuners, string-thru until '80, various colors. 5-string introduced in '87. In '05, additional pickup options are available.

1976-1979	CLF era	$4,000	$6,000
1980-1984	CLF era	$3,000	$4,000
1984-1989	Ernie Ball era	$2,000	$3,000
1987-2024	5-string	$1,750	$2,500
1990-2024	4-string	$1,500	$2,250

StingRay 20th Anniversary

1996. 1400 made, flamed maple body.

1996		$2,000	$2,750

StingRay 30th Anniversary

2003. 800 made.

2003		$1,875	$2,500

StingRay Classic

2010-2019. Ash body, birds-eye or flame maple neck, 4- or 5-string.

2010-2019		$1,500	$2,500

National

Ca. 1927-present. National offered electric basses in the '60s when Valco owned the brand.

Beatle (Violin)

1970s. Strum & Drum era import, National script logo on headstock, 2 pickups, shaded brown finish.

1970s		$550	$750

EG 700V-2HB German Style

1970s. Strum & Drum era import, Beatle-style violin body, 2 humbuckers, bolt neck.

1970s		$550	$750

N-850

1967-1968. Semi-hollow double-cut, art deco f-holes, 2 pickups, block markers, bout control knobs, sunburst.

1967-1968		$800	$1,000

Val-Pro 85

1961-1962. Res-O-Glas body shaped like the U.S. map, 2 pickups, snow white, renamed National 85 in '63.

1961-1962		$1,000	$1,375

National Reso-Phonic

1988-present. Professional grade, production/custom, acoustic and acoustic/electric resonator basses built in San Luis Obispo, California. They also build guitars, mandolins and ukuleles.

New York Bass Works

1989-present. Luthier David Segal builds his professional and premium grade, production/custom, electric basses in New York.

Norma

Ca.1965-1970. Guitars and basses imported from Japan by Chicago's Strum and Drum.

Electric Solidbody

1960s	Various models	$165	$600

O'Hagan

1979-1983. Designed by Jerol O'Hagan in St. Louis Park, Minnesota. He also offered guitars.

Electric Solidbody

1979-1983. Models include the Shark Bass, Night-Watch Bass, NightWatch Regular Bass, and the Twenty Two Bass.

1979-1983		$625	$800

Old Kraftsman

1930s-1960s. Brand used by the Spiegel Company. Guitars and basses made by other American manufacturers.

Electric Solidbody

1950s	Various models	$400	$550

Orville by Gibson

1984-1993. Orville by Gibson and Orville guitars were made by Japan's Fuji Gen Gakki for Gibson. Basically the same models except the Orville by Gibson guitars had Gibson USA pickups and nitrocellulose lacquer finish. The Orville models used Japanese electronics and a poly finish. Prices here are for the Orville by Gibson models.

MODEL YEAR | FEATURES | EXC. COND. LOW | HIGH

Thunderbird

1984-1993 $1,125 $1,500

Ovation

1966-present. Intermediate and professional grade, production, acoustic/electric basses. Ovation offered electric solidbody basses early on and added acoustic basses in the '90s. They also offer guitars and mandolins.

B768/Elite B768

1990. Single-cut acoustic-electric bass, Elite body style with upper bout soundholes.

1990 $900 $1,250

Celebrity Series

1990s-2013. Deep bowl back, cutaway, acoustic/electric.

1990s-2013 Various models $400 $550

Magnum Series

1974-1980. Magnum I is an odd-shaped mahogany solidbody, 2 pickups, mono/stereo, mute, sunburst, red or natural. Magnum II has battery-powered preamp and 3-band EQ. Magnum III and IV had a new offset double-cut body.

1974-1980 Various models $1,500 $2,000

NSB778 Elite T Nikki Sixx Limited Edition

2005-2013. Made in USA, acoustic-electric 4-string, 1 pickup, solid spruce top, ebony 'board, custom iron cross inlays, red or gray flame finish.

2005-2013 $1,500 $2,000

Typhoon II/Typhoon III

1968-1971. Ovation necks, but bodies and hardware were German imports. Semi-hollowbody, 2 pickups, red or sunburst. Typhoon II is 335-style and III is fretless.

1968-1971 Typhoon II $900 $1,250

1968-1971 Typhoon III $900 $1,250

Ultra

1984. Korean solidbodies and necks assembled in U.S., offset double-cut with 1 pickup.

1984 $850 $1,125

PANaramic

1961-1963. Guitars and basses made in Italy by the Crucianelli accordion company and imported by PANaramic accordion. They also offered amps made by Magnatone.

Electric Hollowbody

1961-1963. Double-cut hollowbody, 2 pickups, dot markers, sunburst.

1961-1963 $1,000 $1,500

Parker

1992-2016. Premium grade, production/custom, solidbody electric basses. They also built guitars.

Fly

2002-2011. Offered in 4- and 5-string models.

2002-2011 $1,750 $2,500

Paul Reed Smith

1985-present. PRS added basses in '86, but by '92 had dropped the models. In 2000 PRS started again offering professional and premium grade, production, solidbody electric basses. Bird inlays can add $100 or more to the values of PRS basses listed here.

MODEL YEAR | FEATURES | EXC. COND. LOW | HIGH

Bass-4

1987-1991, 2007. Mahogany, set neck, 3 single-coil pickups, hum-cancelling coil, active circuitry, 22-fret Brazilian rosewood 'board. Reintroduced (OEB Series) in 2000s.

1987 $2,250 $3,000

1988-1991 $2,000 $2,750

2007 $2,000 $2,750

Bass-5

1987-1991. Mahogany, 5-string, set-neck, rosewood 'board, 3 single-coil pickups, active electronics. Options include custom colors, bird inlays, fretless 'board.

1987 $2,500 $3,500

1988-1991 $2,000 $3,000

CE Bass-4

1990-1991. Solidbody, 4-string, alder or maple body, bolt-on neck, rosewood 'board.

1990-1991 Alder $1,125 $1,500

1990-1991 Maple $1,125 $1,500

CE Bass-5

1990-1991. Solidbody, 5-string, alder or maple body, bolt-on neck, rosewood 'board.

1990-1991 Alder $1,250 $1,750

1990-1991 Maple $1,500 $2,000

Curly Bass-4

1987-1991. Double-cut solidbody, curly maple top, set maple neck, Brazilian rosewood 'board (ebony on fretless), 3 single-coil and 1 hum-cancelling pickups, various grades of maple tops, moon inlays.

1987 $3,000 $5,000

1988-1991 $2,000 $3,000

Curly Bass-5

1987-1991. Five-string version of Curly Bass-4.

1987 $3,000 $4,500

1988-1991 $2,000 $3,000

Electric

2000-2007. Bolt neck 4-string, offered in regular and maple top versions.

2000-2007 Maple $1,500 $2,000

2000-2007 Plain $1,000 $1,500

Private Stock Program

2010-present. Custom instruments based around existing PRS models.

2010-2024 $4,000 $8,000

SE Series

2014-present. Various models, i.e., SE Kestrel and Kingfisher.

2014-2024 Higher models $550 $750

2014-2024 Most models $450 $600

Peavey

1965-present. Intermediate and professional grade, production/custom, electric basses. They also build guitars and amps. Hartley Peavey's first products were guitar amps and he added guitars and basses to the mix in '78.

Axcelerator

1994-1998. Offset double-cut, long thin horns, 2 humbuckers, stacked control knobs, bolt neck, dot markers.

1994-1998 $400 $650

1969 Ovation Typhoon II

Rivington Guitars

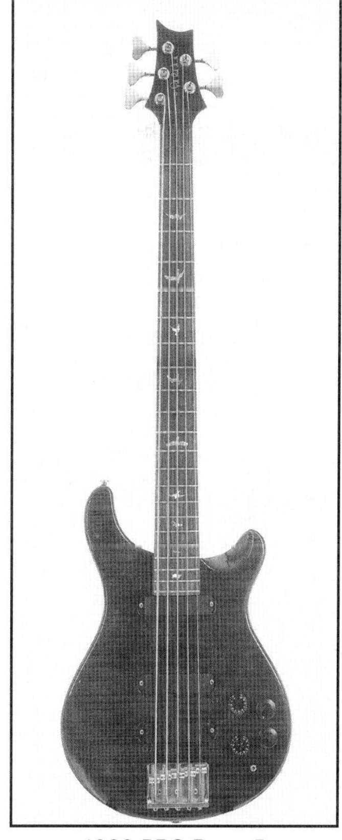

1988 PRS Bass-5

Imaged by Heritage Auctions, HA.com

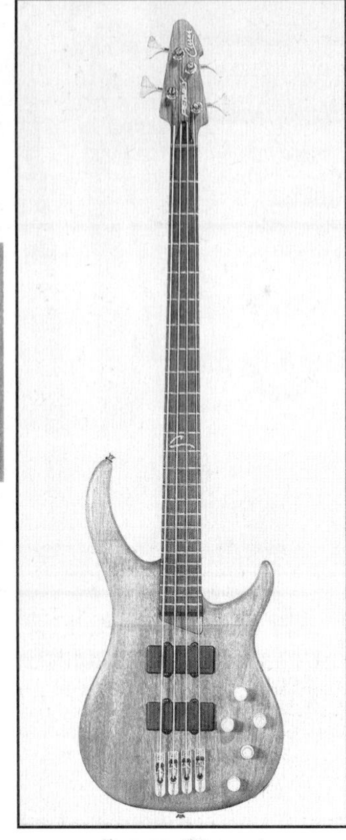
Peavey Cirrus 4

Peavey Milestone 4

MODEL YEAR	FEATURES	EXC. COND. LOW	HIGH

Cirrus Series

1998-2012. Offset double-cut, active electronics, in 4-, 5-, 6-string, and custom shop versions.

1998-2009	Cirrus 5	$800	$1,500
1998-2012	Cirrus 4	$750	$1,250
1998-2012	Cirrus 6	$850	$1,750

Dyna-Bass

1987-1993. Double-cut solidbody, active electronics, 3-band EQ, rosewood 'board, opaque finish.

1987-1993 $425 $650

Dyna-Bass Limited

1987-1990. Neck-thru-body, ebony 'board, flamed maple neck/body construction, purple heart strips, mother-of-pearl inlays.

1987-1990 $600 $775

Forum

1994-1995. Double-cut solidbody, rosewood 'board, dot inlays, 2 humbuckers.

1994-1995 $300 $400

Forum Plus

1994. Forum Bass with added active electronics.

1994 $300 $400

Foundation

1984-2002. Double-cut solidbody, 2 pickups, maple neck.

1984-2002 $450 $600

Foundation S

1986-1991. Two split-coil pickups, maple body, rosewood 'board, black hardware, black painted headstock.

1986-1991 $450 $600

Foundation S Active

1987-1991. Similar to Foundation S Bass with added active circuitry, provides low-impedance output, 2 pickups.

1987-1991 $450 $600

Fury

1983-1999. Double-cut solidbody, rosewood 'board, 1 split-coil humbucker.

1983-1999 $300 $400

Fury Custom

1986-1993. Fury Bass with black hardware and narrow neck.

1986-1993 $300 $400

Fury VI

2001-2003. 6-string, active electronics, quilt top.

2001-2003 $375 $500

G-Bass V

1999-2002. Offset double-cut 5-string, humbucker, 3-band EQ.

1999-2002 $750 $1,000

Grind Series

2001-2020. Offset double-cut, neck-thru, long bass horn, 2 pickups, 4, 5, or 6 strings.

2001-2020 Various models $225 $300

Liberator JT-84 John Taylor

2007. 2 humbuckers, black with graphics.

2007 $1,250 $1,625

Milestone Series

1994-present. Import offset double cut, Milestone I ('94) replaced by 1 P-style pickup II ('95-'01), split humbucker IV ('99-'04); 2 single-coil III ('99-present) now just called Milestone.

1994-2024 $125 $350

Millenium Series

2001-2020 Various models $150 $1,000

Patriot

1984-1988. General J-Bass styling with larger thinner horns, 1 single-coil, maple neck.

1984-1988 $200 $450

Patriot Custom

1986-1988. Patriot with rosewood neck, matching headstock.

1986-1988 $200 $450

RJ-IV Randy Jackson

1990-1993. Randy Jackson Signature model, neck-thru-body, 2 split-coil active pickups, ebony 'board, mother-of-pearl position markers.

1990-1993 $550 $850

Rudy Sarzo Signature

1989-1993. Double-cut solidbody, active EQ, ebony 'board, 2 pickups.

1989-1993 $500 $750

T-20FL

1980s. Fretless double-cut solidbody, 1 pickup, also available as the fretted T-20 ('82-'83).

1980s $250 $350

T-40/T-40FL

1978-1987. Double-cut solidbody, 2 pickups. T-40FL is fretless.

1978-1987	T-40	$550	$950
1978-1987	T-40FL	$550	$950

T-45

1982-1986. T-40 with 1 humbucking pickup, and a mid-frequency roll off knob.

1982-1986 $550 $950

TL Series

1988-1998. Neck-thru-body, gold hardware, active humbuckers, EQ, flamed maple neck and body, 5-string (TL-Five) or 6 (TL-Six).

1988-1998	TL-Five	$625	$850
1989-1998	TL-Six	$675	$900

Void IV

2012. Maple neck, 2 pickups, gloss finish in red, white or black.

2012 $250 $350

Zodiac

2006-2012. Solid alder body, maple neck, 2 pickups.

2006-2012 $250 $350

Pedulla

1975-2019. Professional and premium grade, production/custom, electric basses made in Rockland, Massachusetts. Founded by Michael Pedulla, and which offered various upscale options that affect valuation, so each instrument should be evaluated on a case-by-case basis. Unless specifically noted, the following listings have standard to mid-level features. High-end options are specifically noted; if not, these options will have a relatively higher value than those shown here. Peduallа announced his retirement in '19.

MODEL YEAR	FEATURES	EXC. COND. LOW	HIGH

Buzz-4/Buzz-5

1980-2008. Double-cut neck-thru solidbody, fretless, long-scale, maple neck and body wings, 2 pickups, preamp, some with other active electronics, various colors, 4-, 5-, 6-, 8-string versions.

1980-1999		$2,250	$3,000

Interceptor

1980s. Double-cut, maple/walnut laminated neck-thru.

1980s		$2,000	$2,500

MVP Series

1984-2019. Fretted version of Buzz Bass, standard or flame top, 4-, 5-, 6-, 8-string versions, MVP II is bolt-on neck version.

1980s	MVP-6	$3,000	$3,750
1984-1990s	MVP-4, flame top	$2,500	$3,500
1984-1990s	MVP-4, standard top	$2,250	$3,000
1984-1990s	MVP-5	$2,500	$3,500
1990s	MVP II	$1,500	$2,000

Orsini Wurlitzer 4-String

Mid-1970s. Body style similar to late-'50s Gibson double-cut slab body SG Special, neck-thru, 2 pickups, natural. Sold by Boston's Wurlitzer music store chain.

1970s		$2,000	$2,500

Quilt Limited

Neck-thru-body with curly maple center strip, quilted maple body wings, 2 Bartolini pickups, available in fretted or fretless 4- and 5-string models.

1987		$2,250	$3,000

Rapture Series

1995-2019. Solidbody with extra-long thin bass horn and extra short treble horn, 4- or 5-string, various colors.

1995-2019	Rapture 4	$2,000	$2,500
1995 2019	Rapture 5	$2,250	$3,000

Series II

1987-1992. Bolt neck, rosewood 'board, mother-of-pearl dot inlays, Bartolini pickups.

1987-1992		$1,750	$2,500

Thunderbass Series

1993-2019. Solidbody with extra-long thin bass horn and extra short treble horn, 4-, 5- or 6-string, standard features or triple A top.

1993-1999	4, AAA top	$2,750	$3,500
1993-1999	4, Standard	$2,250	$3,000
1993-1999	5, AAA top	$3,000	$3,750
1993-1999	5, Standard	$2,250	$3,000
1993-1999	6, AAA top	$3,000	$3,750
1993-1999	6, Standard	$2,500	$3,250
2000-2019	4, AAA top	$2,500	$3,250
2000-2019	5, AAA top	$3,000	$3,750
2000-2019	6, AAA top	$3,000	$3,750

Thunderbolt Series

1994-2019. Similar to Thunderbass Series but with bolt necks, 4-, 5- or 6-string, standard AA or AAA maple or optional 5A or exotic wood (ET) tops.

1994-2019	Various models	$2,000	$3,000

Penco

Ca. 1974-1978. Generally high-quality Japanese-made copies of classic American bass guitars. They also made guitars, mandolins and banjos.

Electric

1974-1978	Various models	$150	$400

Premier

Ca.1938-ca.1975, 1990s-2010. Originally American-made instruments, but by the '60s imported parts were being used. 1990s instruments were Asian imports.

Bantam

1950-1970. Small body, single-cut short-scale archtop electric, torch headstock inlay, sparkle 'guard, sunburst.

1950-1970		$800	$1,500

Electric Solidbody

1960s	Various models	$400	$1,250

Renaissance

1978-1980. Plexiglass solidbody electric guitars and basses made in Malvern, Pennsylvania.

Plexiglas

1978-1980. Plexiglas bodies and active electronics, models include the DPB bass (double-cut, 1 pickup, '78-'79), SPB (single-cut, 2 pickups, '78-'79), T-100B (Bich-style, 1 pickup, '80), S-100B (double-cut, 1 pickup, '80), and the S-200B (double-cut, 2 pickups, '80).

1978-1980	Various models	$750	$1,500

Rickenbacker

1931-present. Professional grade, production/custom, electric basses. They also build guitars. Rickenbacker introduced their first electric bass in '57 and has always been a strong player in the bass market.

Electric Upright

1936. Cast aluminum neck and body, horseshoe pickup, extension pole.

1936		$4,000	$5,500

Model 1999 (Rose-Morris)

1964-1966. Export made for English distributor Rose-Morris of London, built along the lines of the U.S. Model 4000 Bass but with small differences that are considered important in the vintage guitar market.

1964-1966		$18,000	$25,000

Model 2030 Hamburg

1984-1997. Rounded double-cut, 2 pickups, active electronics.

1984-1997		$2,000	$2,625

Model 2030GF (Glenn Frey)

1992-1995. Limited Edition, double-cut, 2 humbuckers, Jetglo finish.

1992-1995		$2,000	$3,000

Model 2050 El Dorado

1984-1992. Gold hardware, 2 pickups, active.

1984-1992		$2,000	$2,500

Model 2060 El Dorado

1992-1997. Gold hardware, 2 pickups, active, double-bound body.

1992-1997		$2,000	$2,500

Model 3000

1975-1984. Rounded double-cut, 30" scale, 1 pickup, brown sunburst.

1975-1984		$1,875	$2,500

Peavey T-40

1987 Pedulla Buzz-4

Imaged by Heritage Auctions, HA.com

BASSES

BASSES

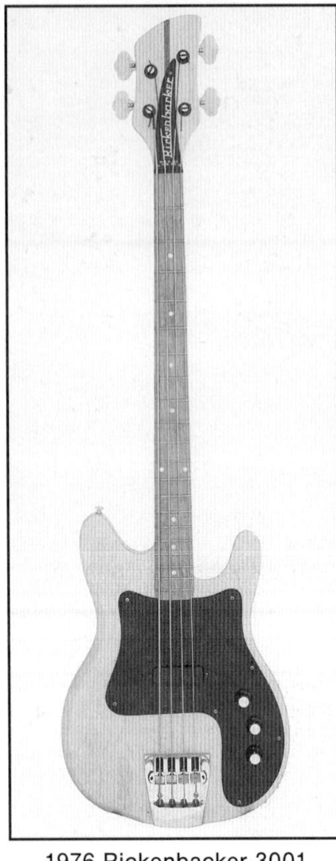
1976 Rickenbacker 3001
Imaged by Heritage Auctions, HA.com

1969 Rickenbacker Model 4000
Rivington Guitars

MODEL YEAR	FEATURES	EXC. COND. LOW	HIGH

Model 3001

1975-1984. Same as Model 3000 but with longer 33-1/2" scale, Wine Red.

1975-1984		$1,875	$2,500

Model 3261 (Rose-Morris Slim-Line)

1967. Export model made for English distributor Rose-Morris, built along the lines of a U.S. equivalent Model 4005 Bass.

1967		$10,500	$14,500

Model 4000

1958-1985. Cresting wave body and headstock, 1 horseshoe pickup (changed to regular pickup in '64), neck-thru-body.

1958-1962	Plank style	$14,500	$19,500
1963-1966		$12,500	$16,500
1967-1969		$9,500	$12,500
1970-1972		$3,500	$4,500
1973-1985		$2,875	$3,750

Model 4001

1961-1986. Fancy version of 4000, 1 horseshoe magnet pickup (changed to regular pickup in '64) and 1 bar magnet pickup, triangle inlays, bound neck.

1961-1963	Fireglo	$20,000	$25,000
1963-1966	Mapleglo	$18,000	$25,000
1964-1966	Fireglo	$20,000	$25,000
1967-1969	Various colors	$9,000	$12,000
1970-1972	Various colors	$6,750	$8,250
1973	Early '73 features	$3,500	$5,500
1973	Late '73 features	$3,500	$5,250
1974-1979	Various colors	$2,875	$4,500
1980-1986	Various colors	$2,750	$3,500

Model 4001C64S

2001-2014. Recreation of Paul McCartney's 4001 featuring changes he made like a reshaped body and zero-fret 'board.

2001-2014		$2,875	$3,750

Model 4001CS (Chris Squire)

1991-1997. Chris Squire signature model, with certificate.

1991-1997		$5,000	$7,500

Model 4001FL

1968-1986. Fretless version of 4001 Bass, special order in '60s, various colors.

1968-1986		$2,750	$5,000

Model 4001S

1964-1985. Same as Model 4000, but with 2 pickups, export model.

1980-1985		$2,000	$2,500

Model 4001V63

1984-2000. Vintage '63 reissue of Model 4001S, horseshoe-magnet pickup, Mapleglo.

1984-2000		$3,000	$3,750

Model 4002

1977-1984. Cresting wave body and headstock, 2 humbuckers, black 'guard, checkerboard binding.

1977-1984		$11,500	$13,500

Model 4003

1979-present. Similar to Model 4001, split 'guard, deluxe features.

1979-2024		$1,875	$2,750

Model 4003FL

1979-2017. Fretless version.

1979-2017		$1,750	$2,500

Model 4003 Shadow

1986. About 60 made for Guitar Center, all black 'board, inlays and hardware, Jetglo finish.

1986		$3,500	$5,500

Model 4003S

1986-2003, 2012-present. Standard feature version of 4003, 4 strings. Reissued in '12.

1986-2003		$1,750	$2,500
2012-2024	Reissue	$1,500	$2,000

Model 4003S Redneck

1988. Red body, 'board and headstock, black hardware.

1988		$3,500	$5,500

Model 4003S Tuxedo

1987. White body with black 'guard and hardware. 100 made.

1987		$3,500	$5,500

Model 4003S/5

1986-2003. Model 4003S with 5 strings.

1986-2003		$3,750	$4,500

Model 4003S/8

1986-2003. Model 4003S with 8 strings.

1986-2003		$3,500	$5,000

Model 4003S/SPC Blackstar

1989. Back finish, board, knobs, and hardware. Also offered as 5-string.

1989		$4,500	$5,500

Model 4003SW

2014-present. Solid walnut body, dot markers, satin natural finish.

2014-2024		$1,750	$2,375

Model 4003W

2013-present. Solid walnut body, deluxe triangle markers, satin natural finish.

2013-2024		$1,500	$2,000

Model 4004C Cheyenne/4004Cii Cheyenne II

1993-2019. Cresting wave, maple neck-thru-body with walnut body and head wings, gold hardware, dot inlay. Replaced by maple top 4004Cii Cheyenne II in '00.

1993-1999	Cheyenne	$2,250	$2,750
2000-2019	Cheyenne II	$2,250	$2,750

Model 4004L Laredo

1993-2022. Like Cheyenne but without walnut wings.

1993-2022		$2,250	$2,750

Model 4005

1965-1984. New style double-cut semi-hollowbody, 2 pickups, R tailpiece, cresting wave headstock.

1965-1966	Fireglo	$10,500	$14,000
1965-1966	Jetglo	$10,000	$13,000
1965-1966	Mapleglo	$10,500	$13,000
1967-1969	Fireglo	$10,000	$12,500
1967-1969	Jetglo	$8,000	$10,500
1967-1969	Mapleglo	$9,500	$12,500
1970-1979	Various colors	$7,000	$9,000
1980-1984	Various colors	$6,000	$8,000

MODEL YEAR	FEATURES	EXC. COND. LOW	HIGH

Model 4005-6

1965-1977. Model 4005 with 6 strings.

1965-1969		$10,500	$13,500
1970-1977		$7,000	$9,500

Model 4005-8

Late-1960s. Eight-string Model 4005, Fireglo or Mapleglo.

1968-1969		$10,000	$13,000

Model 4005L (Lightshow)

1970-1975. Model 4005 with translucent top with lights in body that lit up when played, needed external transformer.

1970-1971	1st edition	$17,000	$30,000
1972-1975	2nd edition	$20,000	$25,000

Model 4005WB

1966-1983. Old style Model 4005 with white-bound body, Fireglo.

1966		$11,000	$14,000
1967-1969		$10,000	$12,500
1970-1979		$6,500	$8,500
1980-1983		$6,000	$7,500

Model 4008

1975-1983. Eight-string, cresting wave body and headstock.

1975-1979		$4,500	$5,500
1980-1983		$4,500	$5,500

Model 4080 Doubleneck

1975-1992. Bolt-on 6- and 4-string necks, Jetglo or Mapleglo.

1975-1979		$10,000	$15,000
1980-1992		$8,000	$12,000

Ritter Royal Instruments

Production/custom, solidbody basses built by luthier Jens Ritter in Wachenheim, Germany.

Rob Allen

1997-present. Professional grade, production/custom, lightweight basses made by luthier Robert Allen in Santa Barbara, California.

Robin

1982-2010. Founded by David Wintz and located in Houston, Texas, Robin built basses until 1997. Most basses were Japanese made until '87; American production began in '88. They also built guitars and also made Metropolitan ('96-'08) and Alamo ('00-'08) brand guitars.

Freedom I

1984-1986. Offset double-cut, active treble and bass EQ controls, 1 pickup.

1984-1986		$750	$1,000

Freedom I Passive

1986-1989. Non-active version of Freedom Bass, 1 humbucker. Passive dropped from name in '87.

1986-1989		$750	$1,000

Medley

1984-1997. Offset deep cutaways, 2 pickups, reverse headstock until '89, then split headstock, back to reverse by '94. Japanese-made until '87, U.S. after.

1984-1987	Japan	$550	$750
1988-1997	USA	$1,250	$1,750

Ranger

1984-1997. Vintage style body, dot markers, medium scale and 1 pickup from '84 to '88 and long scale with P-style and J-style pickup configuration from '89 to '97.

1984-1987	Japan	$550	$750
1988-1997	USA	$1,000	$1,375

Rock Bass

2002-2015. Chinese-made, intermediate and professional grade, production, bolt neck solidbody basses from the makers of Warwick basses.

Roland

Best known for keyboards, effects, and amps, Roland offered synthesizer-based guitars and basses from 1977 to '86.

GR-33B (G-88) Bass Guitar Synthesizer

Early-mid 1980s. Solidbody bass with synthesizer in the guitar case, G-88 deluxe bass.

1983-1985		$2,000	$3,000

Roman & Blake Basses

1977-2003. Professional grade, production/custom, solidbody bass guitars made by Ed Roman Guitars.

Roman USA Basses

Professional grade, production/custom, solidbody basses made by Ed Roman Guitars starting in 2000.

Roscoe Guitars

Early 1980s-present. Luthier Keith Roscoe builds his production/custom, professional and premium grade, solidbody electric basses in Greensboro, North Carolina.

S.D. Curlee

1975-1982. S.D. Curlee guitars and basses were made in Illinois; S.D. Curlee International instruments were made in Japan.

Electric Solidbody

1970s	Various models	$500	$1,500

Sadowsky

1980-present. Professional and premium grade, production/custom, solidbody basses built by luthier Roger Sadowsky in Brooklyn, New York. He also builds guitars and amps.

Serenader

Mainly known for lap steels this Seattle, Washington brand also built a solidbody bass.

Silvertone

1941-ca.1970, present. Brand used by Sears. Instruments were U.S.-made and imported. Currently, Samick offers a line of acoustic and electric guitars, basses and amps under the Silvertone name.

Model 1373L/1376L

1956-1959		$1,375	$1,750

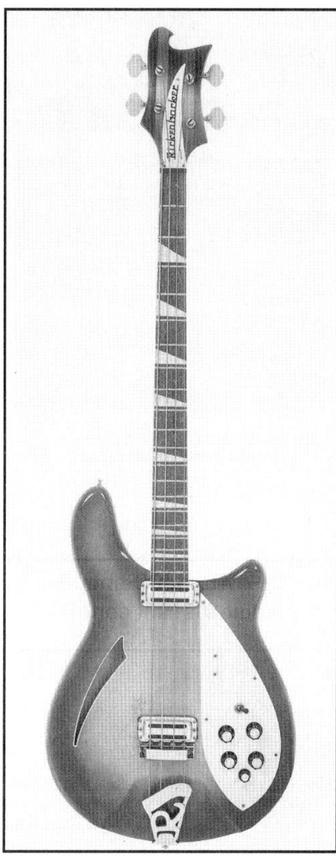

1966 Rickenbacker 4005

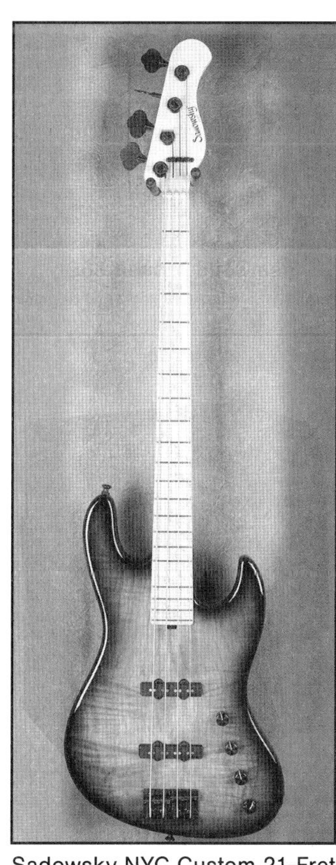
Sadowsky NYC Custom 21-Fret

1960 Silvertone 1442
Rivington Guitars

1965 Silvertone Model 1444
Erick Warner

MODEL YEAR	FEATURES	EXC. COND. LOW	HIGH

Model 1442 Standard

1966-1968. Solidbody 30" standard size, 1 pickup, dot markers, shaded brown.

1966-1968		$725	$1,000

Model 1443 Extra Long

1966-1968. Solidbody 34" size, 2 pickups, dot markers, red sunburst.

1966-1968		$725	$1,000

Model 1443 Hornet

1950s-1960s. Made by Danelectro, 34" scale, red/black sunburst.

1950s-60s		$950	$1,250

Model 1444 Electric

1959-1965. Bass version of 6-string electric guitar Model 1415 (bronze) and 1416 (black), 4-on-a-side replaces the prior year coke-bottle headstock, 1 pickup on single-cut U-1 style body, black finish.

1959-1965		$950	$1,250

Model 1452

1966-1967. Made by Danelectro, 2 lipstick pickups, red/black sunburst.

1966-1967		$425	$550

Simmons

Luthier David L. Simmons, began in 2002, builds professional grade, production/custom, 4- and 5-string basses in Hendersonville, North Carolina.

Sinister

2003. A short run of intermediate grade, solidbody basses built for Sinister Guitars by luthier Jon Kammerer.

Smith

1978-present. Professional and premium grade, production/custom, electric basses built by luthier Ken Smith in Perkasie, Pennsylvania. Earlier models had Ken Smith on the headstock, recent models have a large S logo. He also designs the imported KSD line of basses.

American-Made

1978-2024	Various models	$3,500	$4,500

Imported

1990s	Various models	$700	$1,000

Soundgear by Ibanez

SDGR Soundgear by Ibanez headstock logo, intermediate grade, production, solidbody electric basses, made in Japan, Korea and Indonesia, starting in 1987.

Spector/Stuart Spector Design

1975-1990 (Spector), 1991-1998 (SSD), 1998-present (Spector SSD). Imtermediate, professional, and premium grade, production/custom, basses made in the U.S., the Czech Republic, Korea, and China. Stuart Spector's first bass was the NS and the company quickly grew to the point where Kramer acquired it in '85. After Kramer went out of business in '90, Spector started building basses with the SSD logo (Stuart Spector Design). In '98 he recovered the Spector trademark.

MODEL YEAR	FEATURES	EXC. COND. LOW	HIGH

Squier

See models listed under Squier in Fender section.

Standel

1952-1974, 1997-present. Amp builder Bob Crooks offered instruments under his Standel brand name three different times during the '60s. See Guitar section for production details. See Amp section for more company information.

Custom Deluxe Solidbody 401

1967-1968. Custom with higher appointments, various colors.

1967-1968		$1,250	$1,750

Custom Deluxe Thinbody 402

1967-1968. Custom with higher appointments, various colors.

1967-1968		$1,250	$1,750

Custom Solidbody 501

1967-1968. Solidbody, 1 pickup, various colors.

1967-1968		$1,000	$1,500

Custom Thinbody 502

1967-1968. Thin solidbody, 2 pickups, various colors.

1967-1968		$1,000	$1,500

Steinberger

1979-present. Steinberger offers budget and intermediate grade, production, electric basses. They also offer guitars.

H Series

1979-1982. Reinforced molded plastic wedge-shaped body, headless neck, 1 (H1) or 2 (H2) high impedence pickups, black, red or white.

1979-1982	H1, black	$3,500	$5,000
1979-1982	H1, red or white	$5,000	$6,500
1979-1982	H2, black	$3,500	$5,000
1979-1982	H2, red or white	$5,000	$6,500

L Series

1979-1984. Reinforced molded plastic wedge-shaped body, headless neck, 1 (L1) or 2 (L2) low impedence active pickups, black, red or white. Evolved into XL series.

1979-1984	L1, black	$3,000	$4,000
1979-1984	L1, black, fretless	$3,000	$4,000
1979-1984	L1, red or white	$4,500	$6,000
1979-1984	L2, black	$3,000	$4,000
1979-1984	L2, black, fretless	$3,000	$4,000
1979-1984	L2, red or white	$4,500	$6,000

Q-4

1990-1991. Composite neck, Double Bass system, headless with traditional-style maple body, low-impedance pickups.

1990-1991		$2,500	$3,000

Q-5

1990-1991. Five-string version of Q Bass.

1990-1991		$2,500	$3,000

XL-2

1984-1993. Rectangular composite body, 4-string, headless, 2 pickups.

1984-1989		$3,000	$4,000
1990-1993		$3,000	$4,000

BASSES

MODEL YEAR	FEATURES	EXC. COND. LOW	HIGH

XL-2GR

1985-1990. Headless, Roland GR synthesizer controller.

1985-1990		$3,000	$4,000

XM-2

1986-1992. Headless, double-cut maple body, 4-string, 2 low-impedance pickups, optional fretted, lined fretless or unlined fretless, black, red or white.

1986-1992		$3,000	$4,000

XT-2/XZ-2 Spirit

1995-present. Headless, rectangular XL body, import.

1995-2024		$400	$600

Stewart Basses

2000-ca. 2009. Luthier Fred Stewart built his premium grade, custom/production, solidbody basses in Charlton, Maryland. He also built guitars starting in '94.

Stinger

See Martin listing.

Supro

1935-1968, 2004-present. Supro was a budget brand for the National Dobro Company. Supro offered only two bass models in the '60s. The brand name was revived in '04.

Pocket

1960-1968. Double-cut, neck pickup and bridge mounted pickup, semi-hollow, short-scale, black.

1960-1968		$850	$1,250

Taurus

1967-1968. Asymmetrical double-cut, neck pickup and bridge mounted pickup.

1967-1968		$750	$1,000

SX

See listing for Essex.

Tacoma

1995-2009. Professional grade, production, acoustic basses produced in Tacoma, Washington. They also built acoustic guitars and mandolins.

Thunderchief

1998-2009. 17 3/4 flat-top, solid spruce top, solid mahogany back, laminated mahogany sides, rounded cutaway, bolt-on neck, dot markers, natural satin finish.

1998-2009	Various models	$900	$1,750

Taylor

1974-present. Professional and premium grade, production, acoustic basses built in El Cajon, California. They are currently building guitars.

AB1

1996-2003. Acoustic/electric, sitka spruce top, imbuia walnut back and sides, designed for 'loose' woody sound.

1996-2003		$1,500	$2,000

AB2

1996-2003. Acoustic/electric, all imbuia walnut body.

1996-2003		$1,750	$2,500

AB3

1998-2003. Acoustic/electric, sitka spruce top, maple back and sides.

1998-2003		$2,000	$2,500

GS Series

2006-present. Grand Symphony, the GS Mini is scaled-down version.

2006-2024	Various models	$600	$800

Teisco

The Japanese Teisco line started offering basses in the '60s.

Electric

1968-1969. EB-100 (1 pickup, white 'guard), EB-200 (solidbody), EB-200B (semi-hollowbody) and Violin bass.

1968-1969	EB-100	$250	$350
1968-1969	EB-200	$650	$950
1968-1969	EB-200 B	$650	$950
1968-1969	Violin	$650	$950

Tele-Star

1965-ca.1972. Guitars and basses imported from Japan by Tele-Star Musical Instrument Corporation of New York. Primarily made by Kawai, many inspired by Burns designs, some in cool sparkle finishes.

Electric Solidbody

1960s	Various models	$200	$450

Tobias

1977-2019. Founded by Mike Tobias in Orlando, Florida. Moved to San Francisco for '80-'81, then to Costa Mesa, eventually ending up in Hollywood. In '90, he sold the company to Gibson which moved it to Burbank. The first Tobias made under Gibson ownership was serial number 1094. The instruments continued to be made by the pre-Gibson crew until '92, when the company was moved to Nashville. The last LA Tobias/Gibson serial number is 2044. Mike left the company in '92 and started a new business in '94 called MTD where he continues to make electric and acoustic basses. In '99, production of Tobias basses was moved overseas. In late '03, Gibson started again offering U.S.-made Tobias instruments; they are made in Conway, Arkansas, in the former Baldwin grand piano facility. Currently Tobias offers imported and U.S.-made, intermediate and professional grade, production, acoustic and electric basses.

Basic Series

1984-1999. 30", 32", or 34" scale, neck-thru-body in alder, koa or walnut, 5-piece laminated neck.

1984-1999	Basic B-4	$2,000	$2,500
1984-1999	Basic B-5	$2,000	$2,500

Classic C-4

1978-1999. One or 2 pickups, active or passive electronics, 2-octave rosewood 'board, available in short-, medium-, and long-scale models.

1978-1999		$2,000	$2,500

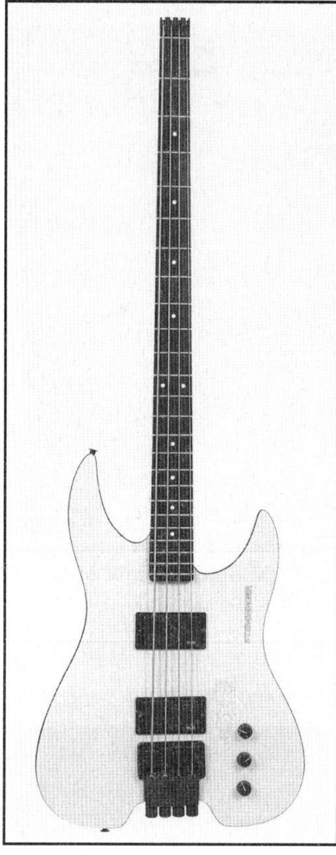

1988 Steinberger XM-2

Imaged by Heritage Auctions, HA.com

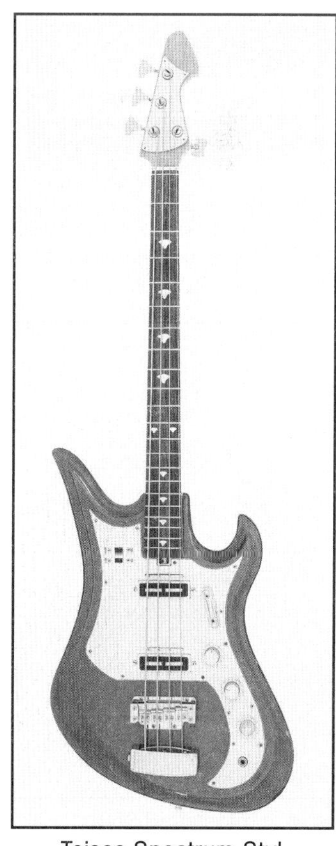

Teisco Spectrum-Styl

BASSES

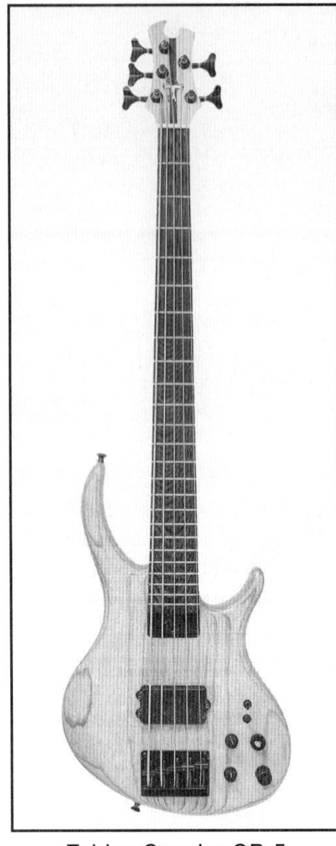
Tobias Growler GR-5
Imaged by Heritage Auctions, HA.com

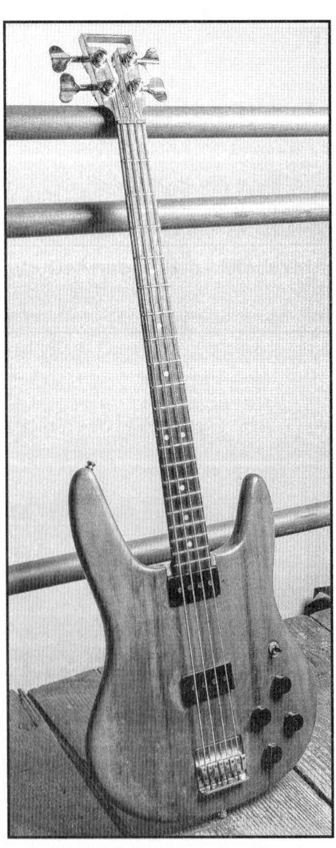
1976 Travis Bean TB-2000
The Vault at Chicago Music Exchange

MODEL YEAR	FEATURES	EXC. COND. LOW	HIGH

Classic C-5

1985-1999. 30", 32" or 34" scale, alder, koa or walnut body, book matched top, ebony or phenolic 'board, hardwood neck.

1985-1999		$2,000	$2,500

Classic C-6

Ca. 1986-1999. Flamed maple and padauk neck, alder body, padauk top, ebony 'board, active electronics, 32" or 34" scale.

1986-1999		$2,250	$3,000

Growler GR-5

1996-1999. 5-string, offset double-cut, bolt neck, various colors.

1996-1999		$750	$1,000

Growler Limited

2009. Limited run, natural finish swamp ash body, set neck.

2009		$850	$1,250

Killer Bee

1991-1999. Offset double-cut, swamp ash or lacewood body, various colors.

1991-1999	KB-4	$1,750	$2,250
1991-1999	KB-5	$2,000	$2,500
1991-1999	KB-6	$2,000	$2,500

Model T

1989-1991. Line of 4- and 5-string basses, 3-piece maple neck-thru-body, maple body halves, active treble and bass controls. Fretless available.

1989-1991		$1,500	$2,000

Renegade

1998-2001. Offset double-cut, 1 single-coil and 1 humbucker.

1998-2001		$1,750	$2,250

Signature S-4

1978-1999. Available in 4-, 5-, and 6-string models, chrome-plated milled brass bridge.

1978-1990	Tobias-Burbank	$3,000	$4,000
1990-1992	Gibson-Burbank	$2,750	$3,500

Standard ST-4

1992-1995. Japanese-made, 5-piece maple neck-thru, swamp ash body wings.

1992-1995		$1,250	$1,500

Toby Deluxe TD-4

1994-1996. Offset double-cut, bolt neck.

1994-1996		$600	$775

Toby Deluxe TD-5

1994-1996. 5-string version.

1994-1996		$650	$850

Toby Pro 5

1994-1996. Solidbody 5-string, Toby Pro logo on truss rod cover, neck-thru body.

1994-1996		$600	$800

Toby Pro 6

1994-1996. Solidbody 6-string, Toby Pro logo on truss rod cover, neck-thru body.

1994-1996		$700	$900

Tokai

1947-present. Tokai started making guitars and basses around '70 and by the end of that decade they were being imported into the U.S. Today Tokai offers electrics, acoustics, and electric basses made in Japan and Korea.

Vintage

1970s-1980s. Tokai offered near copies of classic U.S. basses.

1970s-80s	Copy models	$550	$1,500

Tonemaster

1960s. Guitars and basses, imported from Italy, with typical '60s Italian sparkle plastic finish and push-button controls, bolt-on neck.

Electric

1960s	Various models	$550	$1,000

Traben

Intermediate grade, production, solidbody basses imported by Elite Music Brands of Clearwater, Florida, starting in 2004.

Travis Bean

1974-1979, 1999. The unique Travis Bean line included a couple of bass models. Travis Bean announced some new instruments in '99, but general production was not resumed.

TB-2000

1974-1979. Aluminum neck, T-slotted headstock, longer horned, double-cut body, 2 pickups, 4 controls, dot markers, various colors.

1974-1979		$7,000	$9,000

TB-4000 (Wedge Vee)

1974-1979. Bass version of Bean's Wedge guitar, few made.

1974-1979		$9,000	$11,000

True Tone

1960s. Western Auto retailed this line of basses, guitars and amps which were manufactured by Chicago builders like Kay. The brand was most likely gone by '68.

Electric

1960s	Various models	$250	$500

Univox

1964-1978. Univox started out as an amp line and added guitars and basses around '69. Guitars were imported from Japan by the Merson Musical Supply Company, later Unicord, Westbury, New York. Generally mid-level copies of American designs.

Badazz

1971-ca. 1975. Based on the Guild S-100.

1971-1975		$450	$650

Bicentennial

1976. Carved eagle in body, matches Bicentennial guitar (see that listing), brown stain, maple 'board.

1976		$850	$1,125

Hi Flier

1969-1977. Mosrite Ventures Bass copy, 2 pickups, rosewood 'board.

1969-1977		$550	$750

MODEL YEAR	FEATURES	EXC. COND. LOW	HIGH

Model 1970F 'Lectra

1969-ca. 1973. Violin bass, walnut.

1969-1973		$700	$950

Model 3340 Semi-Hollow

1970-1971. Copy of Gibson EB-0 semi-hollow bass.

1970-1971		$550	$750

Precisely

1971-ca. 1975. Copy of Fender P-Bass.

1971-1975		$550	$750

Stereo

1976-1977. Rickenbacker 4001 Bass copy, model U1975B.

1976-1977		$550	$750

Thin Line

1960s. EB-2 style, f-holes, 2 pickups.

1960s		$550	$750

Ventura

1970s. Import classic bass copies distributed by C. Bruno (Kaman). They also had guitars.

Vintage Electric

1970s	Copy models	$550	$750

Vox

1954-present. Guitars and basses bearing the Vox name were offered from 1961-'69 (made in England, Italy), '82-'85 (Japan), '85-'88 (Korea), '98-2001 (U.S.), with a limited-edition teardrop bass offered in late '07. Special thanks to Jim Rhoads of Rhoads Music in Elizabethtown, Pennsylvania, for help on production years of these models.

Apollo IV

1967-1969. Single-cut hollowbody, bolt maple neck, 1 pickup, on-board fuzz, booster, sunburst.

1967-1969		$850	$1,125

Astro IV

1967-1969. Violin-copy bass, 2 pickups.

1967-1969		$950	$1,250

Bassmaster

1961-1965. Offset double-cut, 2 pickups, 2 knobs.

1961-1965		$750	$950

Clubman

1961-1966. Double-cut 2-pickup solidbody, red.

1961-1966		$500	$700

Constellation IV

1967-1968. Teardrop-shaped body, 2 pickups, 1 f-hole, 1 set of controls, treble, bass and distortion boosters.

1967-1968		$1,250	$1,750

Cougar

1963-1967. Double-cut semi-hollow body, 2 f-holes, 2 pickups, 2 sets of controls, sunburst.

1963-1967		$950	$1,250

Delta IV

1967-1968. Five-sided body, 2 pickups, 1 volume and 2 tone controls, distortion, treble and bass boosters.

1967-1968		$2,750	$3,500

Guitar-Organ

1966. The 4-string bass version of the Guitar-Organ, Phantom-style body, white.

1966	Excellent cond	$2,500	$3,500
1966	Functional	$1,750	$2,250

Mark IV

1963-1969. Made in England first (white), then Italy (sunburst), teardrop-shaped body, 2 pickups, 1 set of controls.

1963-1965	England	$2,500	$3,500
1965-1969	Italy	$1,750	$2,250

Panther

1967-1968. Double-cut solidbody, 1 slanted pickup, rosewood 'board, sunburst.

1967-1968		$700	$950

Phantom IV

1963-1969. Made in England first, then Italy, 5-sided body, 2 pickups, 1 set of controls.

1963-1964	England	$2,750	$3,500
1965-1969	Italy	$1,750	$2,250

Saturn IV

1967-1968. Single-cut, 2 f-holes, 1 set of controls, 1 pickup.

1967-1968		$700	$950

Sidewinder IV (V272)

1967-1968. Double-cut semi-hollow body, 2 f-holes, 2 pickups, 1 set of controls, treble, bass, and distortion boosters.

1967-1968		$1,125	$1,500

Stinger

1968. Teardrop-shaped, boat oar headstock.

1968		$850	$1,125

Violin

1966. Electro-acoustic bass with violin shaped body, 2 extended range pickups, sunburst.

1966		$1,125	$1,500

Wyman

1966. Teardrop-shaped body, 2 pickups, 1 f-hole, 1 set of controls, sunburst.

1966		$1,250	$2,000

Wal

1976-present. Founded in England by luthier Ian Waller and his partner Peter Stevens, forming the company under the name Electric Wood in '78. Waller died in '88, Stevens enlists help of luthier Paul Herman, and in 2000s Stevens retires and Herman takes over. In the early years, the Mark designation was used generically. Newer contemporary models are named Mk1, Mk2 and Mk3. Prices shown will increase 5% with LED option, or 10% with rare top, but no value difference between fretted and fretless. MIDI electronics does not increase the value.

Custom (IV)

1980s-1990s. 4-string, active, no guard, generally highly figured front and back.

1980s-90s	Mark I	$8,500	$12,000
1980s-90s	Mark II	$8,500	$12,000
1980s-90s	Mark III	$8,500	$12,000

Custom (V)

1980s-1990s. 5-string, active, no guard, generally highly figured front and back.

1980s-90s	Mark II	$10,500	$15,000
1980s-90s	Mark III	$10,500	$15,000

1965 Vox Phantom IV

Craig Brody

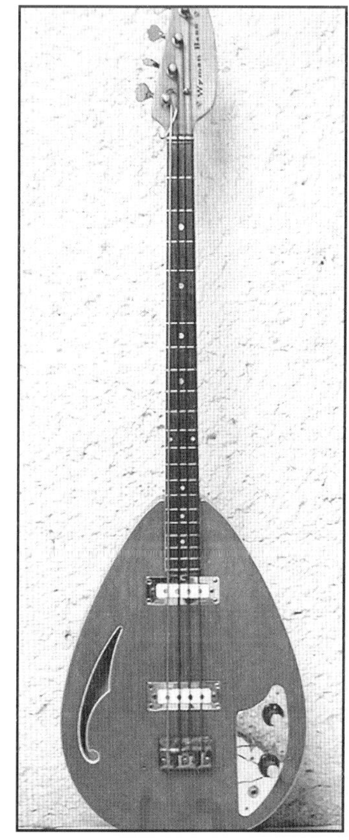

1966 Vox Wyman

Jorge Franco Avila

BASSES

BASSES

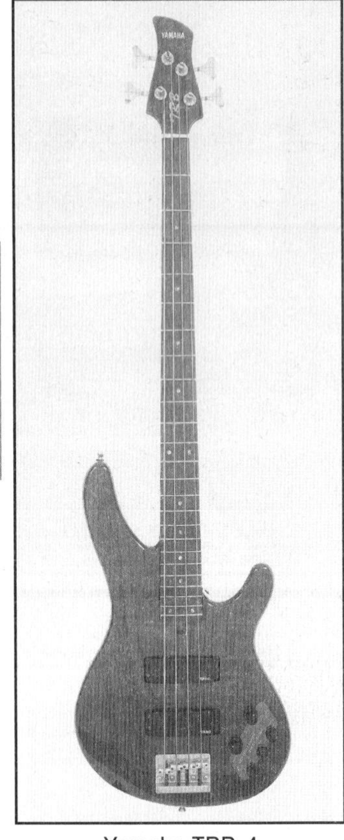

Yamaha TRB-4

Imaged by Heritage Auctions, HA.com

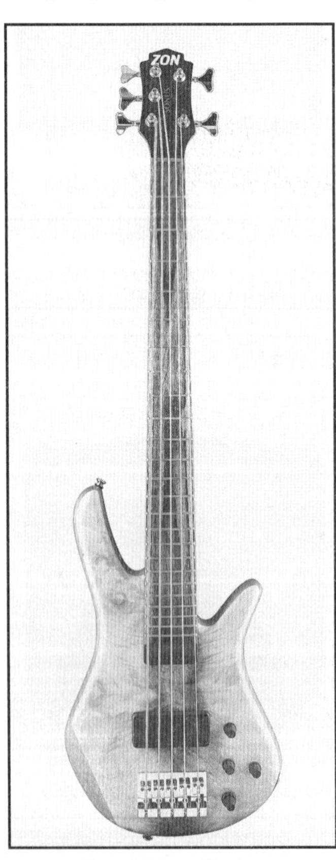

Zon Sonus Series

MODEL YEAR	FEATURES	EXC. COND. LOW	HIGH

Custom (VI)

1990s. 6-string, active, no guard, generally highly figured front and back.

1990s	Mark III	$12,500	$16,000

JG

1976-1978. 4-string, passive with either tooled leather (34 made), or leather guard.

1976-1978	Non-tooled	$8,500	$12,000
1976-1978	Tooled	$9,500	$13,000

Pro

Late-1970s. Passive, black guard.

1970s	Pro I	$5,500	$7,500
1970s	Pro II	$5,500	$7,500

Wandre (Davoli)

Ca. 1956/57-1969. Italian-made guitars and basses.

Electric

1956-1969	Common models	$3,000	$5,000
1956-1969	Rare models	$7,500	$10,000

Warwick

1982-present. Professional and premium grade, production/custom, electric and acoustic basses made in Markneukirchen, Germany; founded by Hans Peter Wilfer, whose father started Framus guitars. They also build amps.

Welson

1960s. Italian-made copy model guitars and basses.

Electric

1960s	Copy models	$150	$400

Wurlitzer

Large music retailer Wurlitzer marketed a line of American-made guitars in the 1920s. They also offered American- and foreign-made guitars starting in '65. In '67, Wurlitzer switched to Italian-made Welson guitars.

Hollowbody Electric

1960s	Italian-made	$500	$750

Yamaha

1946-present. Budget, intermediate, professional and premium grade, production, electric basses. They also build guitars. Yamaha began producing solidbody instruments in '66.

Electric

1960-present. Wide variety of models.

1960-2024	Various models	$200	$1,500

MODEL YEAR	FEATURES	EXC. COND. LOW	HIGH

Zemaitis

1960-1999, 2004-present. Tony Zemaitis began selling his guitars in '60 and he retired in '99. He emphasized simple lightweight construction, and his instruments are known for hand engraved metal fronts. Each hand-built custom guitar or bass was a unique instrument. Approximately 10 custom guitars were built each year. In '04, Japan's Kanda Shokai, with the endorsement of Tony Zemaitis, Jr., started building a new generation of instruments.

Zen-On

1946-ca.1968. Japanese-made. By '67 using the Morales brand name. Not heavily imported into the U.S., if at all (see Morales).

Electric Solidbody

1950s	Various models	$150	$400

Zim-Gar

1960s. Japanese guitars and basses imported by Gar-Zim Musical Instrument Corporation of Brooklyn, New York.

Electric Solidbody

1960s	Various models	$150	$400

Zon

1981-present. Luthier Joe Zon builds his professional and premium grade, production/custom, solidbody basses in Redwood City, California. Zon started the brand in Buffalo, New York and relocated to Redwood City in '87. He has also built guitars.

Legacy Elite

1989-present. 34" scale carbon-fiber neck, Bartolini pickups, ZP-2 active electronics.

1989-2024	V, 5-string	$2,500	$3,500
1989-2024	VI, 6-string	$2,500	$3,500

Scepter

1984-1993. Offset body shape, 24 frets, 1 pickup, tremolo.

1984-1993		$2,500	$3,500

Sonus Custom

1990s-present. Offset swamp ash body, 2 pickups.

1990s-2024		$3,000	$4,000

Zorko

Late-1950s-early-1962. Original maker of the Ampeg Baby Bass (see that listing), sold to Ampeg in 1962, Zorko logo on scroll.

Baby

1950s-1962		$2,500	$3,500

AMPS

1960 Gibson Les Paul Junior and '74 Marshal Model 1987 paired with a Model 1990 8x10" cabinet. Gregg Poe.

3 Monkeys Sock Monkey 18

3rd Power Dragon 45 Combo

Acoustic 115
Rivington Guitars

MODEL YEAR	FEATURES	LOW	HIGH

The price of a vintage amp is affected by three things: the rarity of the amp, the historical significance of the amp, and the "wow" factor. The latter is the most important because the amp is responsible for shaping and coloring most of a purist's vintage tone.

Unlike a guitar, which generates a tiny signal and is usually pampered, the amplifier operates in a high-voltage, high-temperate environment. It was also likely manhandled most of its life. Thus, it's almost impossible to find rare and historically significant amps in excellent cosmetic condition. The only thing that matters to the tone purist is that these amps still function perfectly.

Two prices are shown in the guide. The first is the median value of an all-original amplifier that still functions perfectly. The vast majority of these amps will show signs of wear and tear. The marketplace accepts that these amps need to be regularly maintained. They will likely have grounded electrical plugs and non-original electrolytic capacitors. All other passive components in the electrical circuit should be original.

The second price shown is the premium paid for an all-original amp that functions perfectly and is in excellent cosmetic condition.

The prices shown do not include an original cloth cover. Having the original cover is highly desired.

Traditionally, recovering an amp will result in it losing half its value. A replaced output transformer will also result in lowering the value 40- to 50-percent. Non-original speakers will significantly reduce an amp's value. Alnico speaker replacement is more significant than ceramic speaker replacement. The marketplace no longer shuns re-coned speakers since the original paper cones have continuously deteriorated over time. Multi-speaker amps generally have matching speaker codes. Different speaker codes require explanation. Leather handles are often broken and replaced. A replacement handle drops the value of an amp. Grille cloths should have no tears or stains and a single tear can also drop the value of an amp.

3 Monkeys Amps

2007-present. Intermediate and professional grade, production/custom, amps and cabinets built by Greg Howard in Raleigh, North Carolina.

3rd Power

Mid-2009-present. Professional grade, production/custom, guitar amps built in Franklin, Tennessee by Jamie Scott.

65amps

Founded by Peter Stroud and Dan Boul in 2004, 65amps builds tube guitar head and combo amps and speaker cabs in Valley Village, California.

MODEL YEAR	FEATURES	LOW	HIGH

Ace Tone

Late-1960-1970s. Made by Sakata Shokai Limited of Osaka, Japan, early importer of amps and effects pedals. Later became Roland/Boss.

B-9

Late-1960s-early-1970s. Solid-state bass amp head.

1960s-70s		$135	$175

Mighty-5

Late-1960s-early-1970s. Tubes, 50-watt head.

1960s-70s		$100	$125

Solid A-5

Late-1960s-early-1970s. Solidstate 2x12 combo with vertical cab, reverb and tremolo, black tolex, silver grille.

1960s-70s		$150	$195

Acoustic

Ca.1965-ca.1987, 2001-2005, 2008-present. The Acoustic Control Corp., of Los Angeles, California, was mostly known for solidstate amplifiers. Heads and cabinets were sold separately with their own model numbers but were also combined (amp sets) and marketed under a different model number (for example, the 153 amp set was the 150b head with a 2x15" cabinet). The brand was revived by Samick in '01 for a line of amps. In '08 brand back again online of amps sold through Guitar Center and Musician's Friend.

104

1970s. 6x10".

1970s		$325	$400

114

Ca.1977-mid-1980s. Solidstate, 50 watts, 2x10", reverb, master volume.

1977-1984		$275	$350

115

1977-1978. Solidstate, 1x12", 50 watts, reverb, master volume.

1977-1978		$275	$350

116 Bass

1978-mid-1980s. Solidstate, 75 watts, 1x15", power boost switch.

1978-1984		$275	$350

120 Head

1977-mid-1980s. Solidstate head, 125 watts.

1977-1984		$225	$285

123

1977-1984. 1x12" combo.

1977-1984		$225	$285

124

1977-mid-1980s. Solidstate, 4x10", 5-band EQ, 100 watts, master volume.

1977-1984		$325	$400

125

1977-mid-1980s. Solidstate, 2x12", 5-band EQ, 100 watts, master volume.

1977-1984		$325	$400

126 Bass

1977-mid-1980s. Solidstate, 100 watts, 1x15", 5-band EQ.

1977-1984		$325	$400

MODEL YEAR	FEATURES	LOW	HIGH

134

1972-1976. Solidstate, 100-125 watts, 4x10" combo.

1972-1976 $325 $400

135

1972-1976. Solidstate, 125 watts, 2x12" combo, reverb, tremolo.

1972-1976 $325 $400

136

1972-1976. Solidstate, 125 watts, 1x15" combo.

1972-1976 $325 $400

140 Bass Head

1972-1976. Solidstate, 125 watts, 2 channels.

1972-1976 $225 $285

150 Head

1960s-1976. Popular selling model, generally many available in the used market. Solidstate, 110 watts until '72, 125 watts after.

1968-1976 $275 $350

150b Bass Head

1960s-1971. Bass amp version of 150 head.

1968-1971 $225 $300

153 Bass Set

1960s-1971. 150b head (bass version of 150) with 2x15" 466 cabinet, 110 watts.

1968-1971 $500 $625

165

1979-mid-1980s. All tube combo, switchable to 60 or 100 watts, brown tolex.

1979-1984 $400 $500

220 Bass Head

1977-1980s. Solidstate, 5-band EQ, either 125 or 160 watts, later models 170 or 200 watts, black tolex.

1977-1984 $275 $350

230 Head

1977-1980s. Solidstate head, 125/160 watts, 5-band EQ.

1977-1984 $275 $350

260 Head

1960s-1971. Solidstate, 275 watts, stereo/mono.

1968-1971 $575 $725

261 Head and Cabinet Set

1960s-1971. 275 watts with 2x15" cab.

1969-1971 $1,750 $2,500

270 Head

1970s. 400 watts.

1970s $375 $475

320 Bass Head

1977-1980s. Solidstate, 5-band EQ, 160/300 watts, 2 switchable channels, black tolex.

1977-1984 $375 $475

360 Bass Head

1960s-1971. One of Acoustic's most popular models, 200 watts. By '72, the 360 is listed as a "preamp only".

1968-1971 $850 $1,000

360/361 Head and Cabinet Set

1968-1971. Must match, 200 watts.

1968-1971 $1,750 $2,500

370 Bass Head

1972-1977. Solidstate bass head, 365 watts early on, 275 later, Jaco Pastorius associated.

1972-1977 275 or 365 watt $575 $850

402 Cabinet

1977-1980s. 2x15" bass cab, black tolex, black grille.

1977-1984 $250 $325

404 Cabinet

1970s. 6x10", Jaco Pastorius associated.

1970s $425 $550

450 Head

1974-1976. 170 watts, 5-band EQ, normal and bright inputs.

1974-1976 $325 $400

455 Set

1974-1977. 170 watts, 450 head with 4x12" cabinet, black.

1974-1977 $650 $825

470 Head

1974-1977. 170 watts, dual channel.

1974-1977 $375 $475

AG15

2008-2016. Small combo, 15 watts.

2008-2016 $35 $45

B100 (MK II)

2008-2016. Classic style bass combo, 100 watts, 1x15.

2008-2016 $125 $175

B200 (MK II)

2009-2019. Bass combo, 200 watts, 1x15.

2009-2019 $175 $250

G20-110

1981-mid-1980s. Solidstate, 20 watts, 1x10". The G series was a lower-priced combo line.

1981-1985 $85 $125

G20-120

1981-mid-1980s. Solidstate, 20 watts, 1x12".

1981 1985 $85 $125

G60-112

1981-mid-1980s. Solidstate, 60 watts, 1x12".

1981-1985 $125 $175

G60-212

1981-mid-1980s. Solidstate, 60 watts, 2x12".

1981-1985 $150 $200

G60T-112

1981-1987. Tube, 60 watts, 1x12".

1981-1985 $275 $350

Tube 60

1986-1987. Combo, 60 watts, 1x12", spring reverb, bright switch, master volume control, effects loop.

1986-1987 $275 $350

ADA

1977-2002. ADA (Analog/Digital Associates) was located in Berkeley, California, and introduced its Flanger and Final Phase in '77. The company later moved to Oakland and made amplifiers, high-tech signal processors, and a reissue of its original Flanger.

Aguilar

1995-present. U.S.-made tube and solidstate amp heads, cabinets, and pre-amps from New York City, New York. They also made effect pedals.

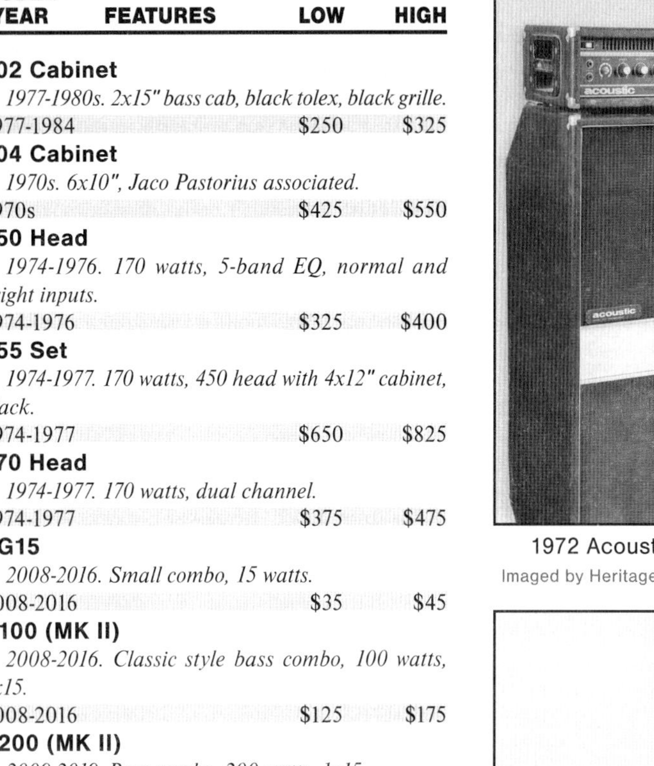

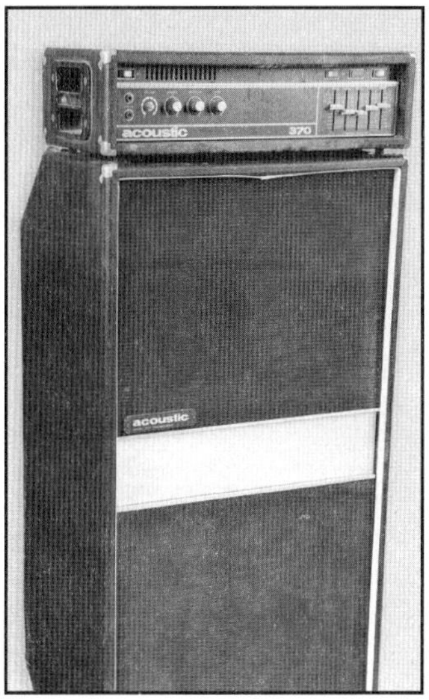

1972 Acoustic 370 Bass

Imaged by Heritage Auctions, HA.com

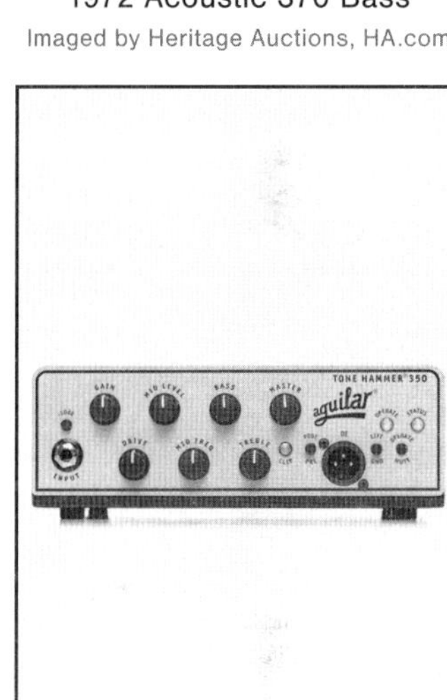

Aguilar Tone Hammer 350

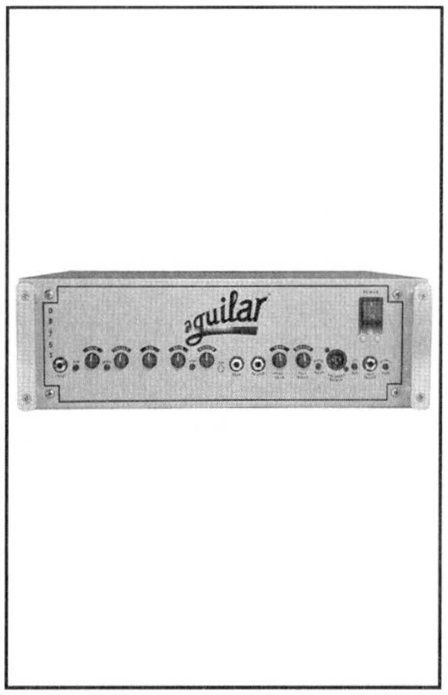

Aguilar DB 751

AMPS

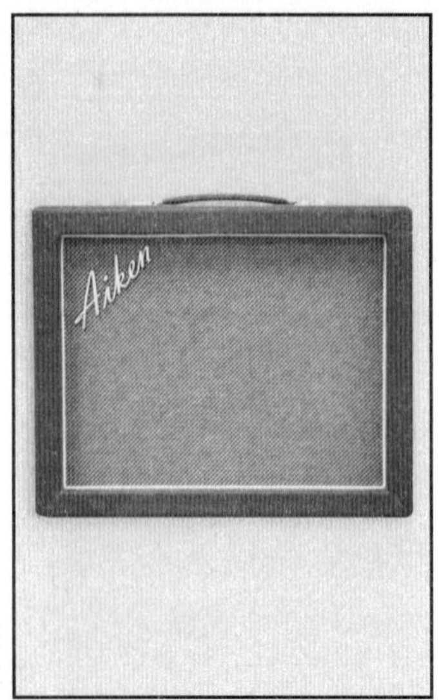

Aiken

1965 Airline 62-9020A Thunderbolt
Rivington Guitars

1967 Alamo Fury
Tom Pfeifer

MODEL YEAR	FEATURES	LOW	HIGH

Aiken Amplification

2000-present. Tube amps, combos, and cabinets built by Randall Aiken originally in Buford, Georgia, and since '05 in Pensacola, Florida.

Airline

Ca.1958-1968, 2004-present. Brand for Montgomery Ward, built by Danelectro, Valco and others. In '04, the brand was revived on a line of reissues from Eastwood guitars.

Tube Amp 1x6" Speaker
1958-1960s $250 $400

Tube Amp 1x8" Speaker
1958-1960s $350 $500

Tube Amp 1x10" Speaker
1958-1960s $450 $650

Tube Amp 1x12" Speaker
1958-1960s $650 $850

Tube Amp Higher-End
1958-1960s $700 $875

Tube Amp Highest-End
1958-1960s $1,000 $1,500

Alamo

1947-1982. Founded by Charles Eilenberg, Milton Fink, and Southern Music, San Antonio, Texas, and distributed by Bruno and Sons. Alamo started producing amps in '49 and the amps were all-tube until '73; solidstate preamp and tube output from '73 to ca. '80; all solidstate for ca. '80 to '82.

Bass Solidstate Preamp-Tube Output
1973-ca.1979. Solidstate preamp section with tube output section, 35 or 40 watts, 15" speakers, combo or piggyback. Models include the Paragon Bass, Paragon Bass Piggyback, Paragon Country Western Bass, Paragon Super Bass, and the Fury Bass.
1973-1979 $165 $200

Bass Tube
1960-1972. Leatherette covered, all tube, 20 to 35 watts, 15" speakers, combo or piggyback, some with Lansing speaker option. Models include the Paragon Special, Paragon Bass, Piggyback Band, Piggyback Bass, Fury Bass, and Paragon Bass (piggyback).
1960-1972 $400 $500

Birch "A" Combo
1949-1962. Birch wood cabinets with A-shaped grill cutout, 2 to 5 tubes. Models include the Embassy Amp 3, Jet Amp 4, Challenger Amp 2, Amp 5, and the Montclair.
1949-1962 $750 $1,250

Mid-Power Solidstate Preamp-Tube Output
1973-ca.1979. Solidstate preamp section with tube output section, 25 watts, 12" speaker, with reverb and tremolo. Models include the Montclair.
1973-1979 $165 $200

Mid-Power Tube
1960-1970. Leatherette covered, all tube, 15 to 30 watts, 12" or 15" speakers, some with tremolo and reverb, some with Lansing speaker option. Models include Montclair, Paragon, Paragon Band, Titan, and Futura.
1960-1970 $500 $650

Small Solidstate Preamp-Tube Output
1973-ca.1979. Solidstate preamp section with tube output section, 3 to 12 watts, 5" to 12" speaker, some with reverb. Models include the Challenger, Capri, Special, Embassy, Dart, and Jet.
1973-1979 $165 $200

Small Tube
1960-1972. Leatherette covered, all tube, 3 to 10 watts, 6" to 10" speakers, some with tremolo. Models include the Jet, Embassy, Challenger, Capri, Fiesta, Dart, and Special.
1960-1972 $275 $350

Solidstate
Ca.1980-1982. All solidstate.
1980-1982 $45 $65

Twin Speaker Combo (Tube/Hybrid)
1973-ca.1979. Solidstate preamp section with tube output section, 20 or 70 watts, 10", 12" and 15" speaker configurations, some with reverb and tremolo. Models include the 70-watt Paragon Super Reverb Piggybacks, the 45-watt Futura 2x12, and the 20-watt Twin-Ten.
1973-1979 $275 $400

Twin Speaker Tube
1962-1972. Leatherette covered, all tube, up to 45 watts, 8", 10", 12" or 15" speaker configurations, some with tremolo and reverb, some with Lansing speaker option. Models include the Electra Twin Ten, Century Twin Ten, Futuramic Twin Eight, Galaxie Twin Twelve, Galaxie Twin Twelve Piggyback, Piggyback Super Band, Alamo Pro Reverb Piggyback, Futura, Galaxie Twin Ten, Twin-Ten, and Band Piggyback.
1962-1972 $525 $750

Alden

Small budget grade solidstate guitar and bass amps from Muse, Inc. of China.

Alesis

1992-present. Alesis has a wide range of products for the music industry, including digital modeling guitar amps. They also offer guitar effects.

Alessandro

1998-present. Tube amps built by George Alessandro in Huntingdon Valley, Pennsylvania. Founded in '94 as the Hound Dog Corporation, in '98 the company name was changed to Alessandro. The Redbone ('94) and the Bloodhound ('96) were the only models bearing the Hound Dog mark. Serial numbers are consecutive regardless of model (the earliest 20-30 did not have serial numbers). In '98 the company converted to exotic/high-end components and the name changed to Alessandro High-End Products. In '01, he added the Working Dog brand line of amps.

Allen Amplification

1998-present. Tube combo amps, heads and cabinets built by David Allen in Walton, Kentucky. He also offers the amps in kit form and produces replacement and upgrade transformers and a tube overdrive pedal.

MODEL YEAR	FEATURES	LOW	HIGH

Allston Amplifiers

Professional and premium grade, custom, amps and cabinets built, starting in 2005, by Rob Lohr in Allston, Massachusetts.

Aloha

Late-1940s. Electric lap steel and amp Hawaiian outfits made for the Dallas-based Aloha.

Ampeg

1949-present. Ampeg was originally primarily known for their bass amps. In the eastern U.S., Ampeg was Fender's greatest challenger in the '60s and '70s bass amplifier market. Currently offering tube and solidstate heads, combos, and speaker cabinets. They have also built guitars.

Amp Covering Dates: Wood veneer 1946-1949, Smooth brown 1949-1952, Dot tweed 1952-1954, Tweed 1954-1955, Rough gray 1957-1958, Rough tan 1957-1958, Cream 1957-1958, Light blue 1958, Navy blue 1958-1962, Blue check 1962-1967, Black pebble 1967, Smooth black 1967-1980, Rough black 1967-1985.

AC-12

1970. 20 watts, 1x12", accordion amp that was a market failure and dropped after 1 year.

1970 $550 $850

AX-44 C

1990-1992. AX hybrid amp with solidstate power section and 1 preamp tube, 22 watts, 2x8 combo.

1990-1992 $150 $200

B-2 Bass

1994-2000. Solidstate, 200 watts, 1x15" combo or 4x8" combo, black vinyl, black grille, large A logo.

1994-2000 1x15" $325 $400

B-2 R Bass Head

1994-2005. 200 watts, rackmount, replaced by 450-watt B2RE.

1994-2005 $225 $300

B-3

1995-2001. Solidstate head, 150 watts, 1x15".

1995-2001 $325 $425

B-4 Bass Head

1998-2008. Solidstate 1000-watt head, early models made in USA, then outsourced.

1998-2008 $250 $325

B-5 R Bass Head

2000-2005. 500 watts, 2-channel.

2000s $250 $325

B-12 N Portaflex

1961-1965. 25 watts, 2x12", 2 6L6 power tubes.

1961-1965 $1,875 $2,375

B-12 X/B-12 XT Portaflex

1961-1969. Tube, 50 watts, 2x12", reverb, vibrato, 2x7027A power tubes.

1961-1969 $1,875 $2,375

B-15 N (NB, NC, NF) Portaflex

1960-1970. Introduced as B-15 using 2 6L6 power tubes, B-15 N in '61, B-15 NB in '62, B-15 NC with rectifier tube in '64, B-15 NF with fixed-bias 2 6L6 power tubes and 30 watts in '67, 1x15".

1960-1965 $1,875 $2,375

1966-1970 1x15 $1,875 $2,375

1967-1968 2x15 $1,875 $2,375

B-15 R Portaflex (Reissue)

1997-2007. Reissue of '65 Portaflex 1x15", blue check, 60/100 watts.

1997-2007 $1,125 $1,500

B-15 S Portaflex

1971-1977. 60 watts, 2x7027A power tubes, 1x12".

1971-1977 $1,500 $1,875

B-18 N Portaflex

1964-1969. Bass, 50 watts, 1x18".

1964-1969 $1,625 $2,125

B-25

1969 only. 55 watts, 2 7027A power tubes, 2x15", no reverb, guitar amp.

1969 $1,125 $1,500

B-25 B Bass

1969-1980. Bass amp, 55 watts, 2 7027A power tubes, 2x15".

1969-1980 $1,125 $1,500

B-50 R Rocket Bass (Reissue)

1996-2005. 50 watts, 1x12" combo, vintage-style blue check cover.

1996-2005 $225 $300

B-100 R Rocket Bass (Reissue)

1996-2005. Solidstate, 100 watts, 1x15" combo bass amp, vintage-style blue check cover.

1996-2005 $225 $300

B-115

1973-1980. 120 watts, solidstate, 1x15" combo.

1973-1980 $400 $750

B-115 E Cabinet

2006-2017. Bass cab, 1x15".

2006-2017 $175 $225

B-410 Bass

1973-1980. Solidstate, 120 watts, 4x10", black vinyl, black grille.

1973-1980 $375 $475

BA Series

1999-2023. Solidstate bass combo amps, model number is speaker configuration.

1999-2023 Various models $115 $350

BT-15

1966-1968. Ampeg introduced solidstate amps in '66, the same year as Fender. Solidstate, 50 watts, 1x15", generally used as a bass amp. The BT-15D has 2 1x15" cabinets. The BT-15C is a 2x15" column portaflex cabinet.

1966-1968 $400 $700

BT-18

1966-1968. Solidstate, 50 watts, 1x18", generally used as a bass amp. The BT-18D has dual 1x18" cabinets. The BT-18C is a 2x18" column portaflex cabinet.

1966-1968 $400 $700

Continental I

1956-1959. Single-channel version of Duette, 30 watts, 1x15".

1956-1959 $750 $950

1974 Alamo Montclair Reverb 2565
Tom Pfeifer

1965 Ampeg B-12 X Portaflex
Tom Pfeifer

1969 Ampeg B-15 N
Imaged by Heritage Auctions, HA.com

AMPS

Ampeg ET-2 Super Echo Twin
Imaged by Heritage Auctions, HA.com

1965 Ampeg GS-12-R Reverberocket 2
Tom Pfeifer

1965 Ampeg J-12 D Jet
Ron Tedesco

MODEL YEAR	FEATURES	LOW	HIGH

Dolphin

1956-1960. Smallest combo offered during this era, 15 watts, 1x12", single-channel (I) and dual-channel (II) options.

1956-1959	Dolphin I	$500	$650
1956-1960	Dolphin II	$550	$700

Duette

1956-1958. Dual-channel, 3 combo models offered: Zephyr (20w, 1x15"), Continental (30w, 1x15") and Duette 50 D-50 (50w, 2x12", tremolo).

1956-1958	Continental Duette	$600	$750
1956-1958	Zephyr Duette	$600	$750
1957-1958	Duette 50 D-50	$850	$1,125

ET-1 Echo Twin

1961-1964. Tube, 30 watts, 1x12", stereo reverb.

1961-1964		$950	$1,250

ET-2 Super Echo Twin

1962-1964. Tube, 2x12", 30 watts, stereo reverb.

1962-1964		$1,000	$1,500

G-12 Gemini I

1964-1971. Tube, 1x12", 22 watts, reverb.

1964-1971		$700	$875

G-15 Gemini II

1965-1968. Tube, 30 watts, 1x15", reverb.

1965-1968		$700	$875

G-18

1977-1980. Solidstate, 1 channel, 10 watts, 1x8", volume, treble, and bass controls.

1977-1980		$80	$125

G-20 Gemini 20

1969-1970. Tubes, 35 watts, 2x10".

1968-1969		$700	$875

G-110

1978-1980. Solidstate, 20 watts, 1x10", reverb, tremolo.

1978-1980		$115	$150

G-115

1979-1980. Solidstate, 175 watts, 1x15" JBL, reverb and tremolo, designed for steel guitar.

1979-1980		$135	$200

G-212

1973-1980. Solidstate, 120 watts, 2x12".

1973-1980		$200	$250

GS-12 Rocket 2

1965-1968. This name replaced the Reverberocket 2 (II), 15 watts, 1x12".

1965-1968		$650	$825

GS-12-R Reverberocket 2

1965-1969. Tube, 1x12", 18 watts, reverb. Called the Reverberocket II in '68 and '69, then Rocket II in '69.

1965-1969		$650	$825

GS-15-R Gemini VI

1966-1967. 30 watts, 1x15", single channel, considered to be "the accordion version" of the Gemini II.

1966-1967		$650	$825

GT-10

1971-1980. Solidstate, 15 watts, 1x10", basic practice amp with reverb.

1971-1980		$135	$175

GV-15 Gemini V

1968-1971. Unimusic-era tube amp, 30 watts, 1x15" combo, reverb and tremolo.

1968-1971		$650	$825

GV-22 Gemini 22

Tube, 1x12", reverb, vibrato.

1969-1972		$725	$925

J-12 Jet

1958-1964, 1967-1972. 20 watts, 1x12", 6V6GT power tubes. The second addition, also known as the Jet II, was like the J-12 D Jet but with 12AX7s.

1958	Rough tan	$550	$700
1959	Blue	$525	$675
1960-1964	Blue	$425	$550
1967-1972	Model reappears	$350	$450

J-12 A Jet

1964. Jet Amp with 7591A power tubes.

1964		$425	$550

J-12 D Jet

1966. Jet Amp with new solidstate rectifier.

1966		$400	$525

J-12 R Reverbojet

1967-1970. Part of Golden Glo Series, nicknamed 'copper front', 18 watts, 1x12" combo, single channel, tremolo and reverb, printed circuit replaces point-to-point wiring.

1967-1970		$500	$650

J-12 T Jet

1965, 2006-2008. J-12 A with revised preamp.

1965		$425	$550

J-20 Jet

2007-2008. Tubes, 20 watts, 1x12.

2007-2008		$375	$500

Jet II/J-12 T

2007-2008. 15 watts, 1x12".

2007-2008		$250	$350

Jupiter

1956-1958. Part of Accordiamp Series, similar to Dolphin except preamp voiced for accordion, 15 watts, 1x12".

1956-1958		$450	$600

M-12 Mercury

1957-1965. 15 watts, 2 channels, Rocket 1x12".

1957-1965		$575	$750

M-15 Big M

1959-1965. 20 watts, 2x6L6 power, 1x15".

1959-1965		$650	$825

Model 815 Bassamp

1955. 15-watt combo, 1 channel. Ampeg Bassamp logo on control panel.

1955		$700	$2,500

Model 820 Bassamp

1956-1958. 20-watt combo, 1 channel.

1956-1958		$750	$950

Model 822 Bassamp

1957-1958. 2 channel 820.

1957-1958		$775	$975

Model 830 Bassamp

1956-1958. 30-watt combo.

1956-1958		$750	$950

MODEL YEAR	FEATURES	LOW	HIGH

Model 835 Bassamp

1959-1961. 35-watt 1x15" combo, 2 channels.

1959-1961		$750	$950

New Yorker

1956-1958. Part of Accordiamp Series, similar to Continental except preamp voiced for accordion, 30 watts, 1x15".

1956-1958		$550	$675

Portabass (PB) Series

2002-2008. Portabass (PB) amps and speaker cabs.

2002-2004	PB-122H Cab	$225	$300
2002-2008	PB-250 Head	$225	$300

Portaflex (PF) Series

2011-present. Portaflex (PF) ultra-compact amp heads offered with flip-top cabs, 350 watt or 500 watt head and 115, 210 or 410 cab options.

2011-2022	PF350 Head	$225	$275
2011-2022	PF500 Head	$225	$275

R-12 Rocket

1957-1963. 12 watts, 1x12", 1 channel.

1957-1963		$550	$725

R-12 B Rocket

1964. 12 watts, 1x12", follow-up to the R-12 Rocket.

1964		$550	$725

R-12 R Reverberocket

1961-1963. Rocket with added on-board reverb.

1961-1963		$725	$925

R-12 R Reverberocket (Reissue)

1996-2007. 50 watts, 2xEL34 power tubes, 1x12" (R-212R is 2x12").

1996-2007		$425	$550

R-12 R-B Reverberocket

1964. 7591A power tubes replace R-12-R 6V6 power tubes.

1964		$650	$825

R-12 R-T Reverberocket

1965. 7591A or 7868 power tubes, revised preamp.

1965		$650	$825

R-15 R Superbreverb (Supereverb)

1963-1964. 1x15 combo, originally called Super-everb, but Fender had a problem with that name.

1963-1964		$800	$1,000

R-50 H Reverberocket

1997-2003. 50-watt head usually sold with a 4x12" bottom, blue check covering.

1997-2003	Head and cab	$450	$575

R-212 R Reverberocket Combo 50 (Reissue)

1996-2007. 50 watts, 2x12", all tube reissue, vintage-style blue check cover, vintage-style grille.

1996-2007		$450	$575

Rhapsody

1956-1958. Part of Accordiamp Series, similar to Zephyr except preamp voiced for accordion, 20 watts, 1x15".

1956-1958		$550	$700

SB-12 Portaflex

1965-1971. 22 watts, 1x12", designed for use with Ampeg's Baby Bass, black.

1965-1971		$1,000	$1,250

SBT

1969-1971. 120 watts, 1x15", bass version of SST Amp.

1969-1971		$800	$1,125

SE-412 Cabinet

1996-1999. 4x12" speakers.

1996-1999		$225	$300

SJ-12 R/RT Super Jet

1996-2007. 50 watts, tube, 1x12", SJ-12 RT has tremolo added.

1996-2007		$325	$400

SS-35

1987-1992. Solidstate, 35 watts, 1x12", black vinyl, black grille, large A logo.

1987-1992		$135	$200

SS-70

1987-1990. Solidstate, 70 watts, 1x12".

1987-1990		$150	$200

SS-70 C

1987-1992. Solidstate, 70 watts, 2x10", chorus, black vinyl.

1987-1992		$200	$250

SS-140 C

1987-1992. Solidstate, 2x12 combo, chorus and reverb.

1987-1992		$225	$300

SS-150 Head

1987-1992. Solidstate, 150 watts.

1987-1992		$475	$600

SS-412 Cabinet

1987-1992. Matching 4x12 cab for SS series heads.

1987-1992		$275	$350

Super Combo/Model 833 Combo/ Model 950C Super Combo

1956-1960. 30 watts, 3 channels. 950C is 50 watts with 2 15" speakers (very few made).

1956-1957	Super Combo	$750	$950
1958	Model 833	$750	$950
1959-1960	Model 950C	$750	$950

SVT Bass Cabinets

1969-1985. Two 8x10" cabs only.

1969		$1,500	$1,750
1970-1985		$1,500	$1,750

SVT Bass Head

1969-1985. 300-watt head only.

1969	Stones World-Tour Assoc	$3,000	$4,000
1970-1973		$2,225	$2,750
1974-1979		$2,000	$2,500
1980-1985		$1,500	$1,750

SVT-II Bass Head

1989-1994. Rackmount, 300 watts, tube.

1989-1994		$800	$1,000

SVT-2 Pro Bass Head

1993-2014. 300 watts, rackmount, tube preamp and power section, black metal.

1993-2014		$850	$1,125

SVT-III Bass Head

1991-1994. Mosfet, 275/450 watts.

1991-1994		$500	$700

Ampeg J-12 R Reverbojet
Tom Pfeifer

1955 Ampeg 815 Bassamp
Imaged by Heritage Auctions, HA.com

1968 Ampeg SB-12 Portaflex
Tom Pfeifer

AMPS

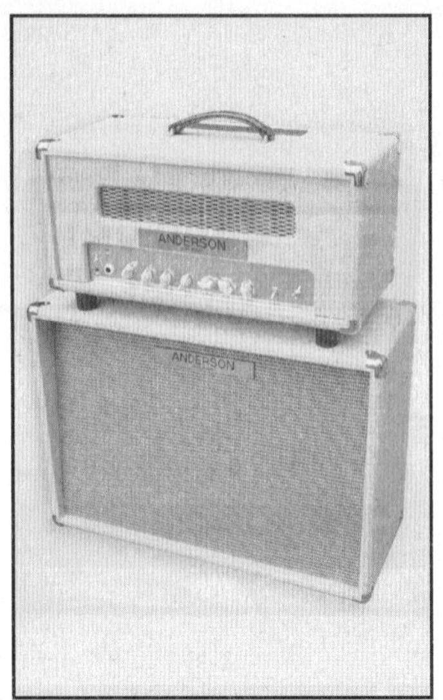
Anderson 45 RT

Andrews Para-Dyne 25

Aria Pro II Revolution II

MODEL YEAR	FEATURES	LOW	HIGH

SVT-3 Pro Bass Head
1993-present. Tube preamp and MOS-FET power section, 450 watts, rackmount, black metal.
1993-2024 $450 $700

SVT-4 Pro Bass Head
1997-present. Rackmount, all tube preamp, MOS-FET power section yielding 1600 watts.
1997-2024 $550 $700

SVT-5 Pro Bass Head
2002-2005. Rackmount, all tube preamp, MOS-FET power section yielding 1350 watts.
2002-2005 $550 $700

SVT-6 Pro Bass Head
2005-2009. Rackmount, all tube preamp, MOS-FET power section yielding 1100 watts.
2005-2009 $450 $700

SVT-7 Pro Bass Head
2005-present. Rackmount, all tube preamp, MOS-FET power section yielding 1000 watts.
2005-2024 $425 $550

SVT-15 E Bass Cabinet
1994-2017. Compact 1x15.
1994-2017 $300 $375

SVT-100 T Bass Combo
1990-1992. Solidstate, ultra-compact bass combo, 100 watts, 2x8".
1990-1992 $325 $425

SVT-120 Combo
1990s. Solidstate, compact, 120 watts, 2x8".
1990s $200 $250

SVT-200 T Head
1987 only. Solidstate, 200 watts to 8 ohms or 320 watts to 4 ohms.
1987 $300 $375

SVT-210 AV Cabinet
2010. Bass enclosure 2x10, 200 watts.
2010 $225 $300

SVT-350 Head
1995-2005. Solidstate head, 350 watts, graphic EQ.
1995-2005 $350 $450

SVT-400 Head
1987-1997. Solidstate, 2 200 watt stereo amps, rack-mountable head with advanced (in '87) technology.
1987-1997 $350 $450

SVT-410 HE/HSVT-410 Bass Cabinet
1994-present. 4x10, horn/driver. H added to model name in '24.
1994-2024 $375 $500

SVT-450 H Head
2007-2017. Solidstate head, 275/450 watts.
2007-2017 $375 $500

SVT-610 HLF Cabinet
2003-2023. 6x10, horn/driver.
2003-2023 $375 $500

SVT-810 E/HSVT-810 Cabinet
1994-present. 8x10, H added to model name in '24..
1994-2024 $500 $650

SVT-AV Anniversary Edition
300-watt head.
2001 $800 $1,000

SVT-CL/HSVT-CL Classic Bass Head
1994-present. Tube, 300 watts. H added to name in '24.
1994-2024 $1,000 $1,500

SVT-GS Gene Simmons Punisher Head
1999. SVT-GS logo on front panel, Punisher logo and Simmon's signature also on front panel.
1999 $1,000 $1,500

SVT-VR Head
2007. All tube, 300 watts.
2007 $1,000 $1,375

V-2 Cabinet
1971-1980. 4x12" cab, black tolex.
1971-1980 $550 $700

V-2 Head
1971-1980. 60-watt tube head.
1971-1980 $650 $850

V-3 Head
1971-1972. 55-watt tube head.
1971-1972 $700 $875

V-4 B Bass Head
1972-1980. Bass version of V-4 without reverb.
1972-1980 Head only $975 $1,250

V-4 BH Bass Head
2007. Reissue.
2007 Head only $800 $1,250

V-4 Cabinet
1970s. Single 4x12" cabinet only.
1970-1980 $550 $700

V-7 SC
1981-1985. Tube, 100 watts, 1x12", master volume, channel switching, reverb.
1981-1985 $600 $750

VH-70
1991-1992. Varying Harmonics, 70 watts, 1x12" combo with channel switching.
1991-1992 $275 $350

VH-140 C
1992-1995. Varying Harmonics (VH) with Chorus (C), two 70-watt channel stereo, 2x12".
1992-1995 $350 $450

VH-150 Head
1991-1992. 150 watts, channel-switchable, reverb.
1991-1992 $350 $450

VL-502
1991-1995. 50 watts, channel-switchable, all tube.
1991-1995 $425 $550

VL-1001 Head
1991-1993. 100 watts, non-switchable channels, all tube.
1991-1993 $350 $450

VL-1002 Head
1991-1995. 100 watts, channel-switchable, all tube.
1991-1995 $375 $500

VT-22
1970-1980. 100-watt combo version of V-4, 2x12".
1970-1980 $650 $850

VT-40
1971-1980. 60-watt combo, 4x10".
1971-1980 $650 $850

MODEL YEAR	FEATURES	LOW	HIGH

VT-60 Combo

1989-1991. Tube, 6L6 power, 60 watts, 1x12".

1989-1991	$300	$400

VT-60 Head

1989-1991. Tube head only, 6L6 power, 60 watts.

1989-1991	$350	$450

VT-120 Combo

1989-1992. Tube, 6L6 power, 120 watts, 1x12", also offered as head only.

1989-1992	$350	$450

VT-120 Head

1989-1992. 120 watts, 6L6 tube head.

1989-1992	$350	$450

Zephyr I

1956-1959. Single-channel, 20 watts, 1x15".

1956-1959	$550	$700

Anderson Amplifiers

1993-present. Tube amps and combos built by Jack Anderson in Gig Harbor, Washington.

Andrews

2006-2022. Professional grade, production/custom, amps and cabinets built by Jeff Andrews first in Dunwoody, then Atlanta, Georgia.

ARACOM Amplifiers

1997-present. Jeff Aragaki builds his tube amp heads, combos, and cabinets in Morgan Hill, California.

Area 51

2003-present. Guitar amps made in Newaygo, Michigan (made in Texas until early '06), by Dan Albrecht. They also build effects.

Aria/Aria Pro II

1956-present. The Japanese instrument builder offered a range of amps from around '79 to '89.

Ariatone

1962. Another private brand made by Magnatone, sold by private music and accordion studios.

Model 810

1962. 12 watts, 1x8, tremolo, brown cover.

1962	$525	$750

Ark

Owners Matt Schellenberg and Bill Compeau, started in 2005, build professional and premium grade, production/custom amps in Farmington Hills, Michigan (cabinet shop), with all wiring done in Windsor, Ontario.

Ashdown Amplification

1999-present. Founded in England by Mark Gooday after he spent several years with Trace Elliot, Ashdown offers amps, combos, and cabinets.

MODEL YEAR	FEATURES	LOW	HIGH

Audio Guild

1960s-1974. Audio Guild was already making amps under such brands as Universal and Versatone and others when they launched their own brand in the '60s.

Grand Prix

1969-1974. Tube combo 1x12, reverb and tremolo, dual channel.

1969-1974	$575	$725

Ultraflex

1969-1974. All-tube, higher power combo, 2 speakers, reverb and tremolo.

1969-1974	$900	$1,250

Universal

1960s-1974. Universal was a brand of Audio Guild. Tube combo amp, reverb, tremolo.

1960s-1974	$700	$1,125

Versatone Pan-O-Flex

1960s-1974. Versatone was a brand of Audio Guild, Carol Kaye and Jack Casady association. Mid-power tube amp, 1x12" and 1x8" combo, high and low gain input, volume, bass, treble and pan-o-flex balance control knobs, black cover.

1960s-1974	$3,500	$4,500

Audiovox

Ca.1935-ca.1950. Paul Tutmarc's Audiovox Manufacturing, of Seattle, Washington, was a pioneer in electric lap steels, basses, guitars, and amps.

Auralux

2000-2011. Founded by Mitchell Omori and David Salzmann, Auralux built effects and tube amps in Highland Park, Illinois.

Austin

1999-present. Budget and intermediate grade, production, guitar and bass amps imported by St. Louis Music. They also offer guitars, basses, mandolins, ukes and banjos.

Bacino

Tube combo amps, heads and cabinets built by Mike Bacino in Arlington Heights, Illinois starting in 2002.

Backline Engineering

Gary Lee builds his tube amp heads, starting 2004, in Camarillo, California. He also builds guitar effects.

Bad Cat Amplifier Company

1999-present. Originally located in Corona, California, and now in Santa Ana, Bad Cat offers class A combo amps, heads, cabinets and effects.

Baer Amplification

2009-present. Professional grade, production, bass amps built in Palmdale, California by Roger Baer.

Ashdown RM-C210T-500 EVO II Combo

1960s Audio Guild Universal

Ron Tedesco

Bad Cat Cub IV 15R Handwired Series

AMPS

BC Audio Amplifier No. 9

Behringer VT100FX

Bogner Mephisto

AMPS

MODEL YEAR	FEATURES	LOW	HIGH

Baldwin

Piano maker Baldwin offered amplifiers from 1965 to '70. The amps were solidstate with organ-like pastel-colored pushbutton switches.

Exterminator

1965-1970. Solidstate, 100 watts, 2x15"/2x12"/2x7", 4' vertical combo cabinet, reverb and tremolo, Supersound switch and slide controls.

1965-1970		$600	$750

Model B1 Bass

1965-1970. Solidstate, 45 watts, 1x15"/1x12", 2 channels.

1965-1970		$400	$500

Model B2 Bass

1965-1970. Solidstate, 35 watts, 1x15", 2 channels.

1965-1970		$325	$450

Model C1 Custom (Professional)

1965-1970. Solidstate, 45 watts, 2x12", reverb and tremolo, Supersound switch and slide controls.

1965-1970		$500	$850

Model C2 Custom

1965-1970. Solidstate, 40 watts, 2x12", reverb and tremolo.

1965-1970		$450	$575

Model D1 Deluxe (Professional)

1965-1970. Solidstate, 30 watts, 1x12", reverb and tremolo, Supersound switch and slide controls.

1965-1970		$550	$750

Barcus-Berry

1964-present. Pickup maker Barcus-Berry offered a line of amps from '75 to '79.

Barth

1950s-1960s. Products of Paul Barth's Barth Musical Instrument Company. Barth was also a co-founder of Rickenbacker. He also produced guitars and lap steels.

Studio Deluxe 958

1950s-1960s. Small practice combo amp.

1950s-60s		$850	$1,125

Basson

Speaker cabinets for guitar, bass and PA made by Victor Basson in Carlsbad, California, starting in 2001.

BC Audio

2009-present. Bruce Clement builds his production/custom, professional grade, tube amps in San Francisco, California.

Bedrock

1984-1997. Tube amp company founded by Brad Jeter and Ron Pinto in Nashua, New Hampshire. They produced 50 amps carrying the brand name Fred before changing the company name to Bedrock in '86. Around '88, Jay Abend joined the company. In '90, Jeter left and, shortly after, Pinto and Abend moved the company to Framingham, Massachusetts. The company closed in '97.

Behringer

1989-present. Founded in Germany by Uli Behringer, offering a full line of professional audio products. In '98 they added tube, solidstate, and modeling amps. They also offer effects and guitars.

Beltone

1950s-1960s. Japan's Teisco made a variety of brands for others, including the Beltone line of amps. There were also guitars sold under this name made by a variety of builders.

Benson

1967-1974. Ron Benson designed and built amps in conjunction with jazz ace Howard Roberts who needed a more versatile amp for recording sessions. Some featured built-in fuzz and plug-in equalizer modules. Originally built in California, later in Seattle. Some 2,000 amps total production.

Big M

1966-1967, 1975-1976. The Marshall name in Germany was owned by a trumpet maker, so Jim Marshall marketed his amps and cabs there under the Big M Made in England brand name until the issue was resolved. A decade later, in a failed attempt to lower speaker cabinets prices in the U.S., Marshall's American distributor-built cabs, with Marshall's permission, on Long Island, mainly for sales with Marshall solidstate lead and bass heads of the time, and labeled them Big M. They were loaded with cheaper Eminence speakers, instead of the usual Celestions.

Cabinet

1975-1976. The M2412 with 4x12 for lead and the M2212F 2x12 bass cabs.

1975-1976	2x12	$850	$1,500
1975-1976	4x12	$1,500	$2,000

JTM-45 Head

1966-1967. Branded Big M.

1966-1967		$9,500	$12,000

BigDog Amps

2005-2007. Tube head and combo guitar and bass amps and speaker cabinets built in Galveston, Texas, by Steve Gaines.

Bird

Ca. 1959-1965. Bird built electronic organs in the U.K. and offered tubes amps from around '59 to '65.

Blackstar Amplification

2007-present. Intermediate and professional grade guitar amps and cabinets from Joel Richardson of Northampton, U.K. He also offers effects pedals.

Blackwing

2016-2018. Professional and premium grade head and combo amps, and cabinets built in Corona, California by James Heidrich. He died in '18.

MODEL YEAR | FEATURES | LOW | HIGH

Blankenship Amplification

2005-present. Roy Blankenship builds his tube head and combo amps and cabinets in Northridge, California. He also built amps under the Point Blank brand.

Bluetone Amplifiers

2002-present. Founded by Alex Cooper in Worcestershire, England, Bluetone offers professional grade, production amps employing their virtual valve technology.

Bogen

1932-present. Founded in New York City by David Bogen, this company has made a wide range of electronic products for consumers and industry including a few small guitar combo tube amps such as the GA-5 and GA-20 and tube PA equipment. The company name (David Bogen, New York) and model number are on the lower back panel. The '50s Bogen tube amps are well respected as tone-generating workhorses. In '56 he sold the company, and it was moved to New Jersey, and they continue to offer pro audio PA gear.

Bogner

Tube combos, amp heads, and speaker cabinets from builder Reinhold Bogner of North Hollywood, California, starting in 1988.

Bolt

Professional grade, production, tube amps and cabinets built in Salt Lake City, Utah starting in 2009. They also built the Morpheus brand effects.

Brand X

2004-2007. Small solidstate combo amps from Fender Musical Instruments Corporation.

Bronson

1930s-1950s. Private brand utilized by Detroit lap steel instructor George Bronson. These amps were often sold with a matching lap steel and were made by other companies.

Lap Steel

MODEL YEAR	FEATURES	LOW	HIGH
1930s-50s	Melody King	$450	$575
1930s-50s	Pearloid	$300	$375
1947	Supreme	$525	$675

Bruno (Tony)

1995-present. Tube combos, amp heads, and speaker cabinets from builder Tony Bruno of Cairo, New York.

Budda

1995-present. Amps, combos, and cabinets originally built by Jeff Bober and Scott Sier in San Francisco, California. In '09, Budda was acquired by Peavey, and they started building Budda products in their Meridian, Mississippi Custom Shop. They also produce effects pedals.

MODEL YEAR | FEATURES | LOW | HIGH

Bugera

2008-present. Uli Behringer builds his budget and intermediate grade, production, tube amps in China. He also offers the Behringer brand.

Burriss

2001-present. Bob Burriss builds custom and production guitar and bass tube amps, bass preamps and speaker cabinets in Lexington, Kentucky. He also builds effects.

Byers

2001-2010. Tube combo amps built by Trevor Byers, in Corona, California. His initial focus was on small early-Fender era and K&F era models.

Cage

1998-present. Production/custom, professional grade, amp heads and cabinets built in Damascus, Maryland by Pete Cage.

California

2004-present. Student/budget level amps and guitar/amp packs, imported by Eleca International.

Callaham

1989-present. Custom tube amp heads built by Bill Callaham in Winchester, Virginia. He also builds solidbody electric guitars.

Campbell Sound

Intermediate and professional grade, production/custom, guitar amps built by Walt Campbell in Roseville, California, starting in 1999.

Carl Martin

1993-present. In '05, the Denmark-based guitar effects company added tube combo amps.

Carlsbro

1959-present. Guitar, bass, and keyboard combo amps, heads and cabinets from Carlsbro Electronics Limited of Nottingham, U.K. They also offer PA amps and speaker cabinets.

Carol-Ann Custom Amplifiers

2003-2022. Premium grade, production/custom, tube guitar amps built by Alan Phillips in North Andover, Massachusetts.

Carr Amplifiers

1998-present. Steve Carr started producing amps in his Chapel Hill, North Carolina amp repair business in '98. The company is now located in Pittsboro, North Carolina, and makes tube combo amps, heads, and cabinets.

Artemus

2010-2015. Combo 1x12", 15/30 watts.

MODEL YEAR	FEATURES	LOW	HIGH
2010-2015		$1,500	$2,000

Budda Superdrive 30 Series II 212 Combo

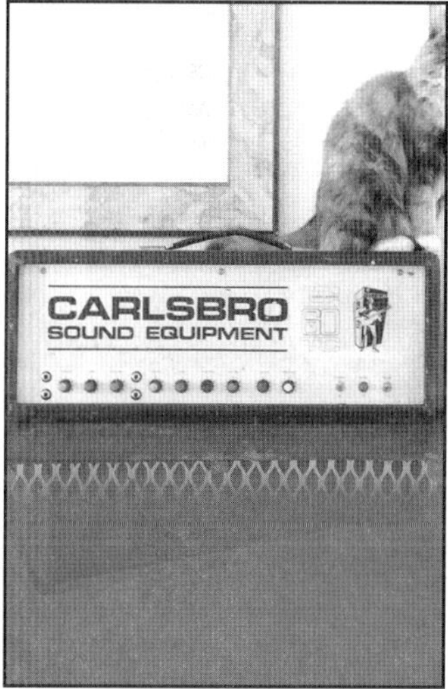

Carlsbro 60TC
Alex Drinkall

Carr Artemus

AMPS

Carr Impala

Carr Mercury V

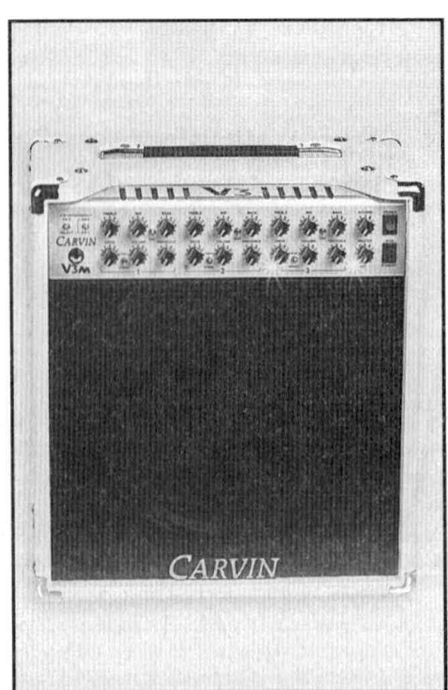

Carvin V3MC

Bloke

2012-2015. 48 watts, 1x12".

MODEL YEAR	FEATURES	LOW	HIGH
2012-2015	1x12"	$1,250	$1,750

Hammerhead MK 1/MK 2

2000-2004 (MK 1), 2004-2008 (MK 2). 25 watts (28 for MK 2), head or combo, 1x12", 2x10" or 2x12".

MODEL YEAR	FEATURES	LOW	HIGH
2000-2004	2x12" combo	$1,000	$1,500

Impala

2013-present. Combo 1x12", 44 watts - max 55 watts, reverb.

MODEL YEAR	FEATURES	LOW	HIGH
2013-2024		$1,750	$2,250

Imperial Combo

2000-2004. 60 watts, with 1x15", 2x12" or 4x10".

MODEL YEAR	FEATURES	LOW	HIGH
2000-2004	4x10"	$1,750	$2,500

Lincoln

2016-2018. Combo 1x12", 6 watts - max 18 watts, 2 channels.

MODEL YEAR	FEATURES	LOW	HIGH
2016-2018		$1,500	$2,000

Mercury Combo

2002-2014. 1x12", tube, 8 watts, reverb, built-in attenuator.

MODEL YEAR	FEATURES	LOW	HIGH
2002-2014		$1,625	$2,250

Mercury V

2017-present. Combo 1x12", 16 watts, built in attenuator.

MODEL YEAR	FEATURES	LOW	HIGH
2017-2024		$1,625	$2,250

Raleigh

2008-present. Practice/studio amp, 1x10", 3 watts.

MODEL YEAR	FEATURES	LOW	HIGH
2008-2024		$1,000	$1,500

Rambler

1999-present. Class A, tubes, 28 watts pentode/14 watts triode, with 1x12", 2x10", 2x12" or 1x15" speakers.

MODEL YEAR	FEATURES	LOW	HIGH
1999-2019	1x12"	$1,625	$2,000
1999-2024	2x12"	$1,875	$2,500

Skylark

2014-present. 12 watts, 1x12" with built in attenuator.

MODEL YEAR	FEATURES	LOW	HIGH
2014-2024		$1,875	$2,500

Slant 6V (Dual 6V6)

1998-2023. 40 watts, 2 channel, combo amp, 2x12" or 1x15", also available as a head.

MODEL YEAR	FEATURES	LOW	HIGH
1998-2023		$1,875	$2,500

Sportsman

2011-present. Available in 1x12 and 1x10 combos and head, 16-19 watts.

MODEL YEAR	FEATURES	LOW	HIGH
2011-2024	1x12"	$1,375	$2,000

Telstar

2018-present. Combo 17-watt with built in attenuator.

MODEL YEAR	FEATURES	LOW	HIGH
2018-2024		$1,625	$2,250

Viceroy

2006-2018. Class A, tubes, 33 or 7 watts, 1x12" or 1x15".

MODEL YEAR	FEATURES	LOW	HIGH
2006-2018		$1,625	$2,250

Carvin

1946-present. Founded in Los Angeles by Lowell C. Kiesel who sold guitars and amps under the Kiesel name until late-'49, when the Carvin brand was introduced. They added small tube amps to their product line in '47 and today offer a variety of models. They also build guitars, basses and mandolins.

Caswell Amplification

2006-present. Programmable tube amp heads built by Tim Caswell in California.

Chicago Blues Box/ Butler Custom Sound

Tube combo amps built by Dan Butler of Butler Custom Sound originally in Elmhurst, then Lombard, Illinois. He began in 2001.

Clark Amplification

1995-present. Tweed-era replica tube amplifiers from builder Mike Clark, of Cayce, South Carolina. He also makes effects.

Club Amplifiers

2005-present. Don Anderson builds intermediate to premium grade, custom, vacuum tube guitar amps and cabinets in Felton, California.

CMI

1976-1977. Amps made by Marshall for Cleartone Musical Instruments of Birmingham, U.K. Mainly PA amps, but two tube heads and one combo amp were offered.

CMI Electronics

Late-1960s-1970s. CMI branded amplifiers designed to replace the Gibson Kalamazoo-made amps that ceased production in '67 when Gibson moved the electronics lab to Chicago, Illinois.

Sabre Reverb 1

Late-1960s-early-1970s. Keyboard amp, 1x15" and side-mounted horn, utilized mid- to late-'60s cabinets and grilles, look similar to mid-late '60s Gibson black tolex and Epiphone gray amp series, black or gray tolex and silver grille.

MODEL YEAR	FEATURES	LOW	HIGH
1960s-70s		$350	$450

CMW Amps

2002-present. Chris Winsemius builds his premium grade, production/custom, guitar amps in The Netherlands.

Colby

2012-present. Professional and premium grade, production/custom, tube amp heads, combos and cabinets built by Mitch Colby in City Island, New York. He also builds Park amps.

Comins

1992-present. Archtop luthier Bill Comins, of Willow Grove, Pennsylvania, introduced a Comins combo amp, built in collaboration with George Alessandro, in '03.

MODEL YEAR	FEATURES	LOW	HIGH

Coral

1967-1969. In '66 MCA bought Danelectro and in '67 introduced the Coral brand of guitars, basses and amps. The amp line included tube, solidstate, and hybrid models ranging from small combo amps to the Kilowatt (1000 Watts of Peak Power!), a hybrid head available with two 8x12" cabinets.

Cornell/Plexi

Amps based on the '67 Marshall plexi chassis built by Denis Cornell in the U.K. Large Plexi logo on front.

Cosmosound

Italy's Cosmosound made small amps with Leslie rotating drums in the late '60s and '70s. They also made effects pedals.

Crafter USA

1986-present. Giant Korean guitar and bass manufacturer Crafter also builds an acoustic guitar amp.

Crate

Solidstate and tube amplifiers originally distributed by St. Louis Music, beginning in 1979. In '05 LOUD Technologies acquired SLM and the Crate brand.

CA Series

1995-2005. Crate Acoustic series.

1995-2005		$195	$350

Solidstate

1979-1990s. Various student to mid-level amps, up to 150 watts.

1979-90s		$75	$125

Vintage Club Series

1994-2001. Tube amps.

1994-2001	Various models	$300	$550

XT Series

2000s. Solid State series.

2000s	XT-120R	$80	$125

Cruise Audio Systems

1999-2003. Founded by Mark Altekruse, Cruise offered amps, combos, and cabinets built in Cuyahoga Falls, Ohio. It appears the company was out of business by '03.

Cruzer

Solidstate guitar amps built by Korea's Crafter Guitars. They also build guitars, basses and effects under that brand.

Custom Kraft

Late-1950s-1968. A house brand of St. Louis Music Supply, instruments built by others. They also offered basses and guitars.

Import Student

1960s	1x6 or 1x8	$100	$125

Valco-Made

1960s	1x12 or 1x15	$550	$750

Da Vinci

Late-1950s-early-1960s. Another one of several private brands (for example, Unique, Twilighter, Titano, etc.) that Magnatone made for teaching studios and accordion companies.

D60 Custom

1965. 2x12", reverb, vibrato.

1965		$1,375	$1,750

Model 250

1958-1962. Similar to Magnatone Model 250 with about 20 watts and 1x12".

1958-1962		$1,250	$1,500

Model 440A/D40 Custom

1964-1966. 1x12", reverb, vibrato.

1964-1966		$1,375	$1,750

Danelectro

1946-1969, 1997-present. Founded in Red Bank, New Jersey, by Nathan I. "Nate" or "Nat" Daniel. His first amps were made for Montgomery Ward in '47, and in '48 he began supplying Silvertone Amps for Sears. His own amps were distributed by Targ and Dinner as Danelectro and S.S. Maxwell brands. In '96, the Evets Corporation, of San Clemente, California, reintroduced the Danelectro brand on effects, amps, basses, and guitars. In early '03, Evets discontinued the amp line, but still offers guitars, basses, and effects.

DM-10

1965-1967. Combo 'large knobs' cabinet, 10 watts, 1x8", 2 control vibrato, 2 inputs, 1 volume, 1 tone, dark vinyl with light grille, DM-10 logo next to script Danelectro logo right upper front.

1965-1967		$250	$350

DM-25

1965-1967. Stow-away piggyback, 25 watts, 1x12", reverb, vibrato, 4 inputs, 9 control knobs, dark vinyl cabinet with light grille, DM-25 logo next to script Danelectro logo below control knobs.

1965-1967		$650	$1,250

DS-50

1965-1969. 75 watts, 3x10" stow-away piggyback cabinet, reverb and tremolo, suitable for bass accordion.

1965-1969		$725	$950

DS-100

1967-1969. 150 watts, stow-away piggyback cabinet, 6x10" Jensens, reverb, tremolo, suitable for bass accordion, 36x22x12" cabinet weighs 79 lbs.

1965-1969		$1,125	$1,500

DTR-40

1965. Solidstate combo, 40 watts, 2x10", vibrato, DTR-40 logo under control knobs.

1965		$375	$475

Model 68 Special

1954-1957. 20 watts, 1x12", light tweed-fabric cover, light grille, leather handle, script Danelectro plexi-plate logo.

1954-1957		$500	$625

Model 72 Centurion

1954-1957. Series D 1x12" combo, blond tweed, rounded front D cabinet.

1954-1957		$500	$625

Crate Vintage Club 5212
Imaged by Heritage Auctions, HA.com

Danelectro Cadet
Erick Warner

1952 Danelectro Model 68 Special
Tom Pfeifer

AMPS

1961 Danelectro 142 Viscount
Rivington Guitars

DeArmond R-5T Studio
Imaged by Heritage Auctions, HA.com

Devilcat Gussie Combo

MODEL YEAR	FEATURES	LOW	HIGH

Model 78A Artist

1954-1957. Artist Series D, 115 watts,

1954-1957		$500	$625

Model 88 Commando

1954-1957. Series D, 25 watts with 4x6V6 power, suitcase-style amp with 8x8" speaker, light beige cover.

1954-1957		$2,000	$3,500

Model 89 Challenger

1954-1957. Series D 1x15" combo, blond tweed, rounded front D cabinet.

1954-1957		$400	$500

Model 98 Twin 12

1954-ca.1957. Rounded front Series D 2x12", blond tweed-style cover, brown control panel, vibrato speed and strength.

1954-1957		$800	$1,000

Model 122 Cadet

1955-1969. A longstanding model name, offered in different era cabinets and coverings but all using the standard 3-tube 1x6" format. Models 122 and 123 had 6 watts. 1x6", 3 tubes, 1 volume, 1 control, 2 inputs, 16x15x6" 'picture frame' cabinet with light-colored cover, dark grille.

1955-1969	Various models	$200	$250

Model 132 Corporal

1962-1964. 2x8", 4 tubes, 3 inputs, 4 control knobs, 19x15x7" picture frame cabinet in light-colored material with dark grille.

1962-1964		$325	$425

Model 142 Viscount

Late-1950s. Combo amp, lower watts, 1x12", light cover, brown grille, vibrato.

1959		$550	$625

Model 143 Viscount

1962-1964. 12 watts, 1x12", 6 tubes, 2 control vibrato, 1 volume, 1 tone, 'picture frame' narrow panel cabinet, light-colored cover with dark grille.

1962-1964		$450	$650

Model 217 Twin-Fifteen

1962-1964. Combo amp, 60 watts, 2x15" Jensen C15P speakers, black cover, white-silver grille, 2 channels with tremolo.

1962-1964		$950	$1,500

Model 274 Centurion

1961-1962. 15 watts, 1x12", 6 tubes, 2 channels with separate volume, treble, bass controls, Vibravox electronic vibrato, 4 inputs, 20x20x9 weighing 25 lbs., 'picture frame' cabinet with black cover and light grille.

1961-1962		$450	$625

Model 275 Centurion

1963-1964. Reverb added in '63, 15 watts, 1x12", 7 tubes, Vibravox vibrato, 2 channels with separate volume, bass, treble, picture frame cabinet with black cover and light grille.

1963-1964		$550	$675

Model 291 Explorer

1961-1964. 30 watts, 1x15", 7 tubes, 2 channels each with volume, bass, and treble controls, Vibravox vibrato, square picture frame cabinet, black cover and light grille.

1961-1964		$525	$675

MODEL YEAR	FEATURES	LOW	HIGH

Model 300 Twin-Twelve

1962-1964. 30 watts, 2x12", reverb, 8 tubes, 2 channels with separate volume, bass, and treble, Vibravox vibrato, picture frame cabinet with black cover and light grille.

1962-1964		$800	$1,125

Model 354 Twin-Twelve

Early 1950s. Series C twin 12" combo with diagonal speaker baffle holes, brown cover with light gold grille, Twin Twelve script logo on front as well as script Danelectro logo, diagonally mounted amp chassis, leather handle.

1950s		$1,125	$1,500

Dean

1976-present. Acoustic, electric, and bass amps made overseas. They also offer guitars, banjos, mandolins, and basses.

Dean Markley

The string and pickup manufacturer added a line of amps in 1983. Distributed by Kaman, they now offer combo guitar and bass amps and PA systems.

K Series

1980s. All solidstate, various models include K-15 (10 watts, 1x6"), K-20/K-20X (10 to 20 watts, 1x8", master volume, overdrive switch), K-50 (25 watts, 1x10", master volume, reverb), K-75 (35 watts, 1x12", master volume, reverb), K-200B (compact 1x12 combo).

1980s	K-15, K20, K20X	$45	$60
1980s	K-200B	$135	$185
1980s	K-50	$45	$65
1980s	K-75	$75	$100

DeArmond

Pickup manufacturer DeArmond started building tube guitar amps in 1950s. By '63, they were out of the amp business. They also made effects. Fender revived the name for a line of guitars in the late '90s.

R-5T Studio

1959-1960. 1x10", low power, 1-channel, brown.

1959-1960		$3,000	$4,000

R-15

1959-1961. 1x12", 15 watts, 2 channels, no tremolo, tan.

1959-1961		$3,500	$4,500

R-15T/Model 112

1959-1961. 1x12", 15 watts, 2 channels, tremolo, tan.

1959-1961		$4,000	$5,000

Decca

Mid-1960s. Small student-level amps made in Japan by Teisco and imported by Decca Records. They also offered guitars and a bass.

Demeter

1980-present. James Demeter founded the company as Innovative Audio and renamed it Demeter Amplification in '90. Originally located in Van Nuys, in '08 they moved to Templeton, California. The first products were direct boxes and by '85,

MODEL YEAR	FEATURES	LOW	HIGH

amps were added. Currently they build amp heads, combos, and cabinets. They also have pro audio gear and guitar effects.

Devilcat

2012-present. Professional grade, production/custom, tube amps built in Statesboro, Georgia by Chris Mitchell.

Diaz

Cesar Diaz restored amps for many of rock's biggest names, often working with them to develop desired tones. By the early '80s he was producing his own line of professional and premium grade, high-end custom amps and effects. Diaz died in '02; his widow Maggie and longtime friend Peter McMahon resumed production in '04 under Diaz Musical Products.

Dickerson

1937-1947. Dickerson was founded by the Dickerson brothers in 1937, primarily for electric lap steels and small amps. Instruments were also private branded for Cleveland's Oahu company, and for the Gourley brand. By '47, the company changed ownership and was renamed Magna Electronics (Magnatone). Amps were usually sold with a matching lap steel.

Oasis

1940s. Blue pearloid cover, 1x10", low wattage, Dickerson silk-screen logo on grille with Hawaiian background.

1940s		$350	$475

Dime Amplification

2011-ca. 2014. Solidstate combo and head amps and cabinets from Dean Guitars, designed by Gary Sunda and Grady Champion.

Dinosaur

2004-2015. Student/budget level amps and guitar/amp packs, imported by Eleca International. They also offered effects.

Divided By Thirteen

Mid-1990s-present. Fred Taccone builds his tube amp heads and cabinets in the Los Angeles, California area. He also builds effects.

Dr. Z

1988-present. Mike Zaite started building Dr. Z amps in the basement of the Music Manor in Maple Heights, Ohio. The company is now located in its own larger facility in the same city. Dr. Z offers combo amps, heads and cabinets.

Drive

Ca. 2001-ca. 2011. Budget grade, production, import solidstate amps. They also offered guitars.

DST Engineering

2002-2014. Jeff Swanson and Bob Dettorre built their tube amp combos, heads and cabinets in Beverly, Massachusetts. They also built reverb units.

Duca Tone

The Duca Tone brand was distributed by Lo Duca Brothers, Milwaukee, Wisconsin, which also distributed EKO guitars in the U.S.

Tube

1950s. 12 watts, 1x12".

1950s		$750	$950

Dumble

1963-2022. Made by Howard Alexander Dumble, an early custom-order amp maker from California. Initial efforts were a few Mosrite amps for Semie Moseley. The first shop was in '68 in Santa Cruz, California. Early on, Dumble also modified other brands such as Fender and those Dumble-modified amps are also valuable, based on authenticated provenance. Top dollar goes for combos or heads with the cab. A head alone would be 10-20% lower. Higher values are considered for an amp that has not been modified in any way, unless the mod is certified as being done by Dumble. The used/vintage Dumble market is a sophisticated luxury-market for those musicians and collectors that are wealthy enough to afford these amps. Each amplifier's value should be considered on a case-by-case basis. Dealers have reported that some Dumble amplifiers will sell upwards from $150,000 to $250,000. Mr. Dumble died January 2022.

Dynamic Amps

2008-present. David Carambula builds production/custom, professional grade, combo amps, heads and cabinets in Kalamazoo, Michigan.

Dynamo

2010-present. Professional and premium grade, production/custom, amps and cabinets built by Ervin Williams in Lake Dallas, Texas.

Earth Sound Research

1970s. Earth Sound was a product of ISC Audio of Farmingdale, New York, and offered a range of amps, cabinets and PA gear starting in the '70s. They also made Plush amps.

2000 G Half-Stack

1970s. 100 watts plus cab.

1970s		$575	$750

Model G-1000 Head

1970s	Reverb	$300	$500

Original 2000 Model 340

1970s. Black Tolex, 400-watt head and matching 2x15" cab.

1970s		$575	$750

Producer Model 440

1970s. 700-watt head and matching 2x15" cab.

1970s		$575	$750

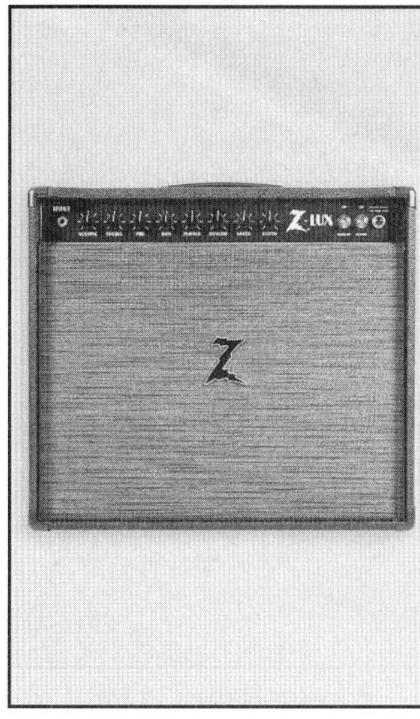
Dr. Z Z-Lux

Dumble Overdrive Special

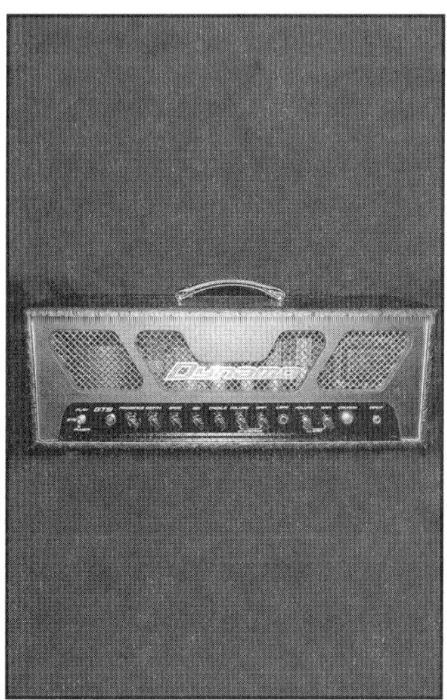
Dynamo GTS

AMPS

Egnater Rebel 30 MK2

Eleca California

Electro-Harmonix Dirt Road Special

Revival

1970s. 2x12" tweed twin copy, with similar back mounted control panel, tweed covering, but with solid-state preamp section and 4x6L6 power.

MODEL YEAR	FEATURES	LOW	HIGH
1970		$575	$750

Super Bass/B-2000

1970s. Tuck & roll black cover, 2 channels - super and normal, volume, bass, mid range, and treble tone controls, no reverb or tremolo.

MODEL YEAR	FEATURES	LOW	HIGH
1970s	Cabinet	$275	$375
1970s	Head only	$300	$500

Traveler

1970s. Vertical cab solidstate combo amp, 50 watts, 2x12 offset, black tolex.

MODEL YEAR	FEATURES	LOW	HIGH
1977		$550	$750

EBS

1988-present. The EBS Sweden AB company builds professional grade, production bass amps and cabinets in Stockholm, Sweden. They also build effects.

EchoSonic

1950s. Tube combo amps with built-in tape echo built by Ray Butts in Cairo, Illinois, with the first in '53. Used by greats such as Chet Atkins, Scotty Moore and Carl Perkins, probably less than 70 were made. Butts also developed the hum bucking Filter'Tron pickup for Gretsch.

Eden

1976-2011. Founded by David Nordschow in Minnesota as a custom builder, Eden offered a full line of amps, combos, and cabinets for the bassist, built in Mundelein, Illinois. In '02, the brand became a division of U.S. Music Corp (Washburn, Randall), they also produce the Nemesis brand of amps. In '11 Eden was sold to Marshall.

Egnater

1980-present. Production/custom, intermediate and professional grade, tube amps, combos, preamps and cabinets built in Berkley, Michigan by Bruce Egnater. He also imports some models.

Rebel

2008-2024. 20-watt head, 1x12" cabinet.

MODEL YEAR	FEATURES	LOW	HIGH
2008-2024		$550	$700

Renegade Head

2009-2024. 65 watts, 2 channel head.

MODEL YEAR	FEATURES	LOW	HIGH
2009-2024		$550	$700

Tourmaster Series

2009-2024. 100-watt, all-tube amp and combo.

MODEL YEAR	FEATURES	LOW	HIGH
2009-2024	Various models	$550	$700

Tweaker

2013-2024. 15 to 88-watt tube heads and cabinets.

MODEL YEAR	FEATURES	LOW	HIGH
2013-2024	1x12 combo	$500	$650
2013-2024	40-watt head/1x12 cab	$550	$700

EKO

1959-1985, 2000-present. In '67 EKO added amps to their product line, offering three piggyback and four combo amps, all with dark covering, dark grille, and the EKO logo. The amp line may have lasted into the early '70s. Since about 2000, EKO Asian-made, solidstate guitar and bass amps are again available. They also make basses and guitars.

El Grande

1951-1953. Built by Chicago's Valco Manufacturing Co. and sold together with lap steels. El Grande logo on front, Valco logo on back chassis, all have burgundy and white covering.

Valco Spectator

1951-1953. Same as Supro Spectator, 1x8", 5 watts, volume and tone.

MODEL YEAR	FEATURES	LOW	HIGH
1951-1953		$400	$575

Eleca

2004-present. Student level imported combo amps, Eleca logo on bottom of grille. They also offer guitars, effects and mandolins.

Electar

1996-2008. The Gibson owned Electar brand offered tube and solidstate amps, PA gear and wireless systems. Though branded separately, Electar amps were often marketed with other Epiphone products, so see them listed there. Epiphone also had amp models named Electar in the 1930s.

Electro-Harmonix

1968-1981, 1996-present. Electro-Harmonix has offered a few amps to go with its line of effects.

Freedom Brothers

Introduced in 1977. Small AC/DC amp with 2x5 1/2" speakers. E-H has reissued the similar Freedom amp.

MODEL YEAR	FEATURES	LOW	HIGH
1977		$300	$375

Mike Matthews Dirt Road Special

1970s. 25 watts, 1x12" Celestion, built-in Small Stone phase shifter. A 40-watt version was released in 2019.

MODEL YEAR	FEATURES	LOW	HIGH
1977		$300	$375

Electromuse

1940s-1950s. Tube amps made by others, like Valco, and usually sold as a package with a lap steel. They also offered guitars.

Various Models

Late-1940s. Vertical cabinet with metal handle, Electromuse stencil logo on front of cab.

MODEL YEAR	FEATURES	LOW	HIGH
1948-1949	Lower power	$450	$650

Electrosonic Amplifiers

2002-2009. Intermediate and professional grade, production/custom, tube amps built by Josh Corn in Boonville, Indiana. He also builds effects.

Elk

Late-1960s. Japanese-made by Elk Gakki Co., Ltd. Many were copies of American designs. They also offered guitars and effects.

MODEL YEAR	FEATURES	LOW	HIGH

Custom EL 150L

Late-1960s. Piggyback set, all-tube with head styled after very early Marshall and cab styled after large vertical Fender cab.

1968 $400 $500

Guitar Man EB 105 (Super Reverb)

Late-1960s. All-tube, reverb, copy of blackface Super Reverb.

1968 $450 $575

Twin 60/Twin 50 EB202

Late-1960s. All-tube, reverb, copy of blackface Dual Showman set (head plus horizontal cab).

1968 $400 $500

Viking 100 VK 100

Late-1960s. Piggyback set, head styled after very early Marshall and cab styled after very large vertical Fender cab.

1968 $950 $1,125

Elmwood Amps

1998-2015. Jan Alm builds his production/custom, professional and premium grade, guitar tube amps and cabinets in Tanumshede, Sweden.

Elpico

1960s. Made in Europe, PA tube amp heads are sometimes used for guitar.

PA Power Tube

1960s. Tubes, 20-watt, metal case, 3 channels, treble and bass control, 2 speaker outs on front panel, Elpico logo on front, small Mexican characterization logo on front.

1960s $550 $750

Emery Sound

1997-2024. Founded by Curt Emery in El Cerrito, California, Emery Sound specializes in custom-made low wattage tube amps. Curt died in 2024.

Emmons

1970s-present. Owned by Lashley, Inc. of Burlington, North Carolina. Amps sold in conjunction with their steel guitars.

Epiphone

1928-present. Epiphone offered amps into the mid-'70s and reintroduced them in '91 with the EP series. Currently they offer tube and solidstate amps.

Century

1939. Lap steel companion amp, 1x12" combo, lattice wood front with Electar insignia "E" logo.

1939 $525 $750

Cornet

1939. Lap steel companion amp, square shaped wood box, Electar insignia "E" logo.

1939 $425 $600

E-30B

1972-1975. Solidstate model offered similarly to Gibson G-Series (not GA-Series), 30 watts, 2x10", 4 knobs.

1972-1975 $175 $250

MODEL YEAR	FEATURES	LOW	HIGH

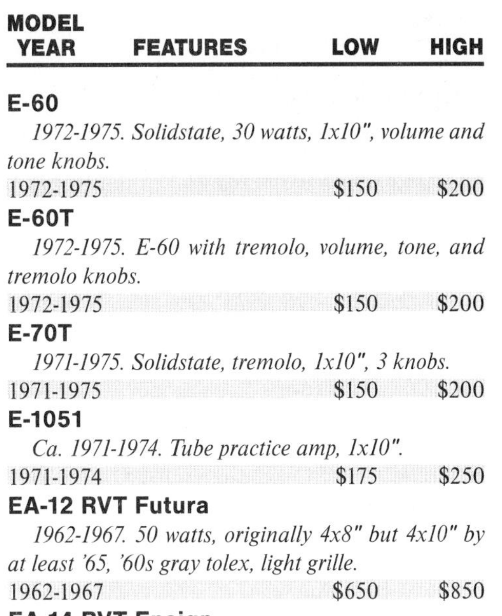

E-60

1972-1975. Solidstate, 30 watts, 1x10", volume and tone knobs.

1972-1975 $150 $200

E-60T

1972-1975. E-60 with tremolo, volume, tone, and tremolo knobs.

1972-1975 $150 $200

E-70T

1971-1975. Solidstate, tremolo, 1x10", 3 knobs.

1971-1975 $150 $200

E-1051

Ca. 1971-1974. Tube practice amp, 1x10".

1971-1974 $175 $250

EA-12 RVT Futura

1962-1967. 50 watts, originally 4x8" but 4x10" by at least '65, '60s gray tolex, light grille.

1962-1967 $650 $850

EA-14 RVT Ensign

1965-1969. Gray tolex, silver-gray grille, 50 watts, 2x10", split C logo.

1965-1969 $600 $850

EA-15 RVT Zephyr

1961-1965. 14 or 20 watts, 1x15", gray tolex, light grille, split C logo on panel, tremolo and reverb, script Epiphone logo lower right grille.

1961-1965 $600 $850

EA-16 RVT Regent

1965-1969. 25 watts, 1x12", gray vinyl, gray grille, tremolo, reverb. Called the Lancer in first year.

1965-1969 $500 $700

EA-22 RVT Mighty Mite

1964-1967. 1x12", mid-level power, stereo, reverb, vibrato, old style rear mounted control panel.

1964-1967 $1,000 $1,500

EA-26 RVT Electra

1965-1969. Gray tolex, reverb, tremolo, footswitch, 1x12".

1965-1969 $500 $700

EA-28 RVT Pathfinder

Mid-1960s. Similar to Gibson's GA-19 RVT, medium power, 1x12, reverb and tremolo.

1964-1966 $500 $700

EA-30 Triumph

1959-1961. Low-power, limited production, 1x12, light colored cover, 3 knobs.

1959-1961 $950 $1,250

EA-32 RVT Comet

1965-1967. 1x10", tremolo, reverb.

1965-1967 $500 $700

EA-33 RVT Galaxie

1963-1964. Gray tolex, gray grille, 1x10".

1963-1964 $500 $700

EA-35 Devon

1961-1963. 1x10" until '62, 1x12" with tremolo in '63.

1961-1963 $500 $700

EA-35T Devon

1963. Tremolo, 6 knobs.

1963 $500 $700

Elmwood Bonneville 50

1961 Epiphone EA-15 RVT Zephyr
Tom Pfeifer

Epiphone EA-30 Triumph
Imaged by Heritage Auctions, HA.com

AMPS

Epiphone EA-50 Pacemaker
Imaged by Heritage Auctions, HA.com

Epiphone Electar
Imaged by Heritage Auctions, HA.com

Evans Custom Amplifiers AE200

MODEL YEAR	FEATURES	LOW	HIGH

EA-50 Pacemaker

1961-1969. 1x8" until '62, 1x10" after. EA-50T with tremolo added in '63. Non-tremolo version dropped around '67.

1961-1965	1x8	$450	$650
1966-1969	1x10	$500	$700

EA-300 RVT Embassy

1965-1969. 90 watts, 2x12", gray vinyl, gray grille, tremolo, reverb.

1965-1969		$700	$950

EA-500T Panorama

1963-1967. 65 watts, head and large cabinet, tremolo, 1x15" and 1x10" until '64, 1x15" and 2x10" after.

1964-1967		$550	$750

EA-600 RVT Maxima

1966-1969. Solidstate Epiphone version of Gibson GSS-100, gray vinyl, gray grille, two 2x10" cabs and hi-fi stereo-style amp head.

1966-1969		$400	$550

Electar

1935-1939. All models have large "E" insignia logo on front, first model Electar in rectangular box with 1x8" speaker, 3 models introduced in '36 (Model C, Model M, and Super AC-DC), the Special AC-DC was introduced in '37, later models were 1x12" combos. Old Electar amps are rarely found in excellent working condition and the prices shown are for those rare examples.

1935	Electar	$550	$750
1936-1939	Model C	$750	$1,125
1936-1939	Model M	$750	$1,125
1936-1939	Super AC-DC	$875	$1,250
1937-1939	Special AC-DC	$875	$1,250

Electar Tube 10

1997-2004. These modern Electar amps were branded as Electar, not Epiphone, but since they were often marketed with other Epi products, they are included here. 10-watt combo, all tube, 8" speaker.

1997-2004		$125	$175

Electar Tube 30

1997-2004. 30-watt combo, all tube, 10" speaker, reverb added in 2002.

1997-2004		$125	$175

Model 100

1965-1967. Made in Kalamazoo, label with serial number, Model 100 logo on small 10" speaker, blue cover, 3 tubes, 3 knobs.

1965-1967		$500	$700

Zephyr

1939-1957. Maple veneer cabinet, 30 watts with 2x6L6 power, 1x12" until '54, 1x15" after, made by Danelectro using their typical designs, Dano D-style blond covering, large split "E" logo on front, brown grille cloth, large block Zephyr logo on back panel.

1939-1953	1x12	$850	$1,250
1953-1957	1x15	$850	$1,250

Zephyr Dreadnaught

1939. Similar to Zephyr amp but higher power and added microphone input.

1939		$850	$1,250

Esteban

2005-2007. Imported brand from China, student budget level compact amps.

Compact

2005-2007		$30	$50

Estey

Late-1960s. In 1959, Magnatone merged with the Estey Organ Company and in late '66/early '67 they introduced models branded Estey and based on their budget Magnatone Starlite series.

Model T12

Late-1960s. Based on Magnatone Starlite model 412.

1960s		$350	$700

Model T22

Late-1960s. Based on Magnatone Starlite model 422 but with larger 12" speaker.

1960s		$475	$600

Model T32

Late-1960s. Based on Magnatone Starlite model 432 with reverb and vibrato.

1960s		$550	$700

Model T42

Late-1960s. Based on Magnatone Starlite model 442 bass amp.

1960s		$550	$700

Evans Custom Amplifiers

1994-present. Professional grade, production, solidstate head and combo amps built by Scot Buffington in Burlington, North Carolina.

EVH

2007-present. Eddie Van Halen's line of professional and premium grade, production, tube amp heads and cabinets built by Fender. They also build guitars.

5150 III 50-Watt

2011-present. 50-watt head with 2x12 cab.

2011-2024		$1,125	$1,500

5150 III 100-Watt

2007-present. 100-watt head.

2007-2024		$1,250	$1,750

Evil Robot

2010-2014. Produced by David Brass and Fretted Americana, made in the U.S.A., initial product produced in limited quantities is based on the '59 Tonemaster (Magnatone) Troubadour amp. Production ceased in '14.

E-Wave Amplifiers

Built by Hangzhou Shengbei Sound Co. Ltd. in China, starting in 2004.

Excelsior

The Excelsior Company started offering accordions in 1924 and had a large factory in Italy by the late '40s. They started offering guitars and amps, uaually built by others including Valco and possibly Sano, around '62. By the early '70s they were out of the guitar business.

MODEL YEAR	FEATURES	LOW	HIGH

Americana Stereophonic High Fidelity

Late 1960s. 50 watts, 1x15", 2x8", 2x3x9" ovals, 2xEL34 power, tube rectifier, large Excelsior logo and small Excelsior The House of Music logo, guitar and accordion inputs, stereo reverb and vibrato.

1968-1969		$1,000	$1,250

Citation C-15

1962. Made by Sano, mid power with 2x6V6 power tubes, single speaker combo amp, large Citation by Excelsior logo on front panel.

1962		$650	$850

Fargen

1999-present. Benjamin Fargen builds his professional and premium grade, production/custom, guitar and bass tube amps in Sacramento, California. He also builds guitar effects.

Fender

1946-present. Leo Fender developed many ground-breaking instruments, but Leo's primary passion was amplifiers, and of all his important contributions to musicians, none exceeded those he made to the electric tube amplifier.

Tweed Fender amp circuits are highly valued because they define the tones of rock and roll. Blackface models remained basically the same until mid-'67. Some silverface circuits remained the same as the blackface circuits, while others were changed in the name of reliability.

Fender heads that are sold separately from their original cabinet are 75% of total value. Cabinets sold separately are 40% of the total value.

From 1953 to '67, Fender stamped a two-letter date code on the paper tube chart glued inside the cabinet. The first letter was the year (C='53, D='54, etc.) with the second the month (A=January, etc.).

The speaker code found on the frame of an original speaker will identify the manufacturer, and the week and year that the speaker was assembled. The speaker code is typically six (sometimes seven) digits. The first three digits represent the Electronics Industries Association (E.I.A.) source code which identifies the manufacturer. For example, a speaker code 220402 indicates a Jensen speaker (220), made in '54 (4) during the second week (02) of that year. This sample speaker also has another code stamped on the frame. ST654 P15N C4964 indicates the model of the speaker, in this case it is a P15N 15" speaker. The sample speaker also had a code stamped on the speaker cone, 4965 1, which indicates the cone number. All of these codes help identify the originality of the speaker.

Most Fender speakers from the '50s will be Jensens (code 220). By the late-'50s other suppliers were used. The supplier codes are Oxford (465), C.T.S. (137), Utah (328). JBL speakers were first used in the late-'50s Vibrasonic, and then in the Showman series, but JBL did not normally have a E.I.A. source code. An amp's speaker code should be reconciled with other dating info when the amp's original status is being verified.

General Production Eras: Diagonal tweed era, Brown tolex era, Blackface era, Silverface era with raised Fender logo with underlining tail, Silverface era with raised Fender logo without underlining tail, Silverface era with raised Fender logo with small MADE IN USA designation.

Nameplate and Logo Attribution: Fender nameplate with city but without model name (tweed era), Fender nameplate without city or model name (tweed era), Fender nameplate with model name noted (tweed era), Fender flat logo (brown era), Fender script raised logo (blackface era).

30

1980-1981. Tube combo amp, 30 watts, 2x10" or 1x12".

1980-1981	1x12	$500	$700
1980-1981	2x10	$550	$750

75

1980-1982. Tube, 75 watts, offered as a 1x15" or 1x12" combo, or as head and 4x10" or 2x12" cab.

1980-1982	1x15	$500	$675
1980-1982	2x12	$550	$700
1980-1982	4x10	$600	$800

85

1988-1992. Solidstate, 85-watt 1x12" combo, black cover, silver grille.

1988-1992		$250	$325

800 Pro Bass Head

2004-2008. Rackmount, 800 watts, 5-band EQ.

2004-2008		$350	$450

Acoustasonic 15

2013-present. Student 1x6" amp, 15 watts.

2013-2024		$70	$90

Acoustasonic 30/30 DSP

2000-2011. Small combo, brown tolex, wheat grille. Upgrade model includes DSP (Digital Signal Processor) effects.

2000-2005	30	$225	$300
2000-2011	30 DSP	$250	$325

Acoustasonic 100 Combo

2012-2013. 100 watts, 1x8", horn.

2012-2013		$300	$375

Acoustasonic 150 Combo

2012-2017. 150 (2x75 stereo) watts, 2x8", piezo horn.

2012-2017		$300	$375

Acoustasonic Junior/Junior DSP

1998-2011. 2x40 watts, 2x8", Piezo horn.

1998-2011		$250	$325

Acoustasonic SFX/SFX II

1998-2011. SFX technology, 32 stereo digital presents, 2x80 watts, SFX is taller combo with one 10", a sideways mounted 8", and a horn. SFX II is a shorter cab with 8", sideways 6".

1998-2003	SFX, tall cab	$300	$375
2003-2011	SFX II, short cab	$325	$400

Acoustasonic Ultralight

2006-2009. Small 2x125-watt 2 channel head with 2x8 w/tweeters stereo cab.

2006-2009		$500	$700

EVH 5150 III 50-Watt

E-Wave G-158R

Fargen MPMKIII

Fender Acoustic Pro

1964 Fender Bandmaster
Tom Pfeifer

Fender Bassbreaker 45 Combo

MODEL YEAR	FEATURES	LOW	HIGH

Acoustic Pro

2016-2019. 200-watt digital combo, 12" and tweeter, natural blonde cab.

2016-2019		$525	$700

Acoustic SFX

2016-2019. 160-watt digital combo, 8" and 6.5" and tweeter, natural blonde cab.

2016-2019		$525	$700

AmpCan

1997-2008. Cylindrical can-shaped battery powered portable amp.

1997-2008		$150	$175

Automatic SE

1998-2000. Solidstate 25-watt, 1x10" (12" in 2000) combo, blackface cosmetics.

1998-2000		$85	$125

Bandmaster

1953-1975. Wide-panel 1x15" combo '53-'54, narrow-panel 3x10" combo '55-'60, tolex '60, brownface with 1x12" piggyback speaker cabinet '61, 2x12" '62, blackface '62-'67, silverface '68-'74.

1953-1954	Tweed, 1x15	$4,000	$5,000
1955-1958	Tweed, 3x10	$8,500	$11,000
1959-1960	Old style cab, pink brown tolex	$8,500	$11,000
1959-1960	Tweed, 3x10	$8,500	$11,000
1960	Brown tolex, 3x10	$4,500	$6,000
1960	Brown tolex, 3x10, reverse controls	$8,500	$11,000
1961	Rough white/ oxblood, 1x12	$3,000	$4,000
1961-1962	Rough white/ oxblood, 2x12	$2,500	$3,250
1963-1964	Smooth white/ gold, 2x12	$2,125	$2,750
1963-1964	Smooth white/ gold, head only	$1,250	$1,750
1964-1967	Black tolex, 2x12	$1,250	$1,750
1964-1967	Black tolex, head only	$850	$1,125
1967-1968	Black, 2x12	$1,125	$1,500
1967-1969	Black, head only	$850	$1,125
1967-1969	Silverface, 2x12	$950	$1,250
1967-1970	Silverface, head only	$650	$850
1970-1974	Silverface, 2x12	$850	$1,125
1970-1975	Silverface, head only	$500	$650

Bandmaster Reverb

1968-1980. 45-watt silverface head with 2x12" cabinet.

1968-1972		$1,000	$1,250
1973-1980		$950	$1,125

Band-Master VM Set

2009-2012. Vintage Modified, 40 watts, piggyback, DSP reverb and effects.

2009-2012		$600	$750

Bantam Bass

1969-1971. 50 watts, large unusual 1x10" Yamaha speaker.

1969-1971	Original speaker	$650	$850

Bassbreaker 15

2015-2024. Tube, 15 watts, 1x12" combo, master volume, gray tweed standard. Also offered in FSR limited editions.

2015-2021	Combo, gray tweed	$350	$450
2015-2024	Head, gray tweed	$300	$400
2017	Combo, LE Blonde Nubtex	$375	$525
2017	Combo, LE British Green	$375	$525

Bassbreaker 45

2015-2022. Head (until '18) or 2x12" combo, 45 watts, gray tweed.

2015-2018	Head	$500	$650
2016-2022	Combo	$575	$725

Bassman

1952-1971. Tweed TV front combo, 1x15" in '52, wide-panel '53-'54, narrow-panel and 4x10" '54-'60, tolex brownface with 1x12" in piggyback cabinet '61, 2x12" cabinet '61-'62, blackface '63-'67, silverface '67-'71, 2x15" cabinet '68-'71. Renamed the Bassman 50 in '72.

1952	TV front, 1x15	$3,000	$4,000
1953-1954	Wide panel, 1x15	$3,000	$4,000
1955-1957	Tweed, 4x10, 2 inputs	$7,000	$9,000
1957-1958	Tweed, 4x10, 4 inputs	$8,500	$11,000
1959-1960	Old style cab, pink brown tolex	$8,500	$11,000
1959-1960	Tweed, 4x10, 4 inputs	$8,500	$11,000
1961	White 1x12, 6G6, tube rectifier	$3,500	$4,500
1962	Late '62, white 2x12	$2,125	$2,750
1962	White 1x12, 6G6A, ss rectifier	$3,000	$4,000
1963-1964	Smooth white 2x12, 6G6A/B	$2,500	$3,500
1963-1964	Smooth white 2x12, 6G6A/B, head only	$1,500	$2,000
1964	Transition, black, white knobs	$1,750	$2,250
1965-1966	AA165/AB165, black knobs	$1,500	$2,000
1965-1966	AA165/AB165, head only	$1,125	$1,500
1967-1969	Silverface, vertical 2x15	$800	$1,000
1967-1969	Silverface, head only	$700	$950
1970-1971	Silverface, 2x15	$700	$950
1970-1971	Silverface, head only	$500	$650

'59 Bassman

1990-2003. Tube, 45 watts, 4x10", birch ply cab, solidstate rectifier.

1990-2003		$850	$1,125

'59 Bassman LTD

2004-present. Lacquered Tweed (LTD), tube, 45 watts, 4x10", solid pine cab, tube rectifier.

2004-2024		$1,000	$1,500

MODEL YEAR	FEATURES	LOW	HIGH

Bassman 10

1972-1982. 4x10" combo, silverface and 50 watts for '72-'80, blackface and 70 watts after.

1972-1980	50w	$725	$1,000
1981-1982	70w	$725	$1,000

Bassman 20

1982-1985. Tubes, 20 watts, 1x15".

1982-1985		$450	$550

Bassman 25

2000-2005. Wedge shape, 1x10", 25 watts, 3-band EQ.

2000-2005		$95	$125

Bassman 50

1972-1977. 50 watts, with 2x12" cab.

1972-1977		$650	$950

Bassman 60

1972-1976. 60 watts, 1x12".

1972-1976		$650	$950

Bassman 60 (later version)

2000-2005. Solidstate, 60 watts, 1x12".

2000-2005	Combo	$95	$125

Bassman 70

1977-1979. 70 watts, 2x15" cab.

1977-1979		$650	$950

Bassman 100

1972-1977, 2000-2009. Tube, 100 watts, 4x12", name reused on solidstate combo amp.

1972-1977	4x12	$650	$950
2000-2009	1x15 combo	$200	$275

Bassman 100 T

2012-2020. 100-watt head, master volume, '65 blackface cosmetics. Usually paired with Bassman NEO cabs.

2012-2020	Head only	$850	$1,250

Bassman 135

1978-1983. Tube, 135 watts, 4x10".

1978-1983		$825	$1,125

Bassman 150 Combo

2005-2009. Solidstate 1x12" combo, 150 watts.

2005-2009		$200	$250

Bassman 250 Combo

2005-2006. Import from Indonesia, 250 watts, 2x10".

2005-2006		$200	$250

Bassman 300 Pro Head

2002-2012. All tube, 300 watts, 6x6550, black cover, black metal grille.

2002-2012		$850	$1,125

Bassman 400

2000-2004. Solidstate, 350 watts with 2x10" plus horn, combo, black cover, black metal grille.

2000-2004	Combo	$250	$350
2000-2004	Head	$225	$300

Bassman Bassbreaker (Custom Shop)

1998-2003. Classic Bassman 4x10" configuration. Not offered by 2004 when the '59 Bassman LTD was introduced.

1998-2003	2x12	$1,000	$1,250
1998-2003	4x10	$1,000	$1,250

MODEL YEAR	FEATURES	LOW	HIGH

Bassman NEO Cabinet

2012-present. Cabinets used with Bassman 100 T head and Super Bassman head, standard '65 blackface cosmetics.

2012-2024	115	$400	$500
2012-2024	410	$525	$650
2012-2024	610	$575	$725
2012-2024	810	$650	$850

Bassman Solidstate

1968-1971. Small head, piggyback cab. The whole late 1960s Solidstate series was unreliable and prone to overheating, more of a historical novelty than a musical instrument.

1968-1971		$525	$675

B-Dec 30

2006-2009. Bass version of the G-Dec, 30 watts, 1x10.

2006-2009		$150	$200

Blues Deluxe

1993-2005. All tube, 40 watts, reverb, 1x12", tweed covering (blond tolex optional '95 only).

1993-2005	Tweed	$500	$650
1995	Blond tolex	$500	$650

Blues Deluxe Reissue

2006-present. All tube, tweed, 40 watts, reverb, 1x12".

2006-2024		$425	$550

Blues DeVille

1993-1996. All tube Tweed Series, 60 watts, 4x10" (optional 2x12" in '94), reverb, high-gain channel, tweed cover (blond tolex optional '95 only).

1993-1996	Tweed	$575	$750
1995	Blond tolex	$575	$750

Blues DeVille Reissue

2006-2015. 60 watts, 4x10, tweed.

2006-2015		$550	$700

Blues Junior (III) (IV)/LE

1995-present. Tube, 15 watts, 1x12", spring reverb, tweed in '95, black tolex with silver grille '96 on, blond '00-'09, brown '08, surf green '09. Woody Custom Shop (hardwood) in '02-'03. III update in '10, IV in '18. Limited Edition After the Gold Rush, Surf-Tone Green, Red Nova Two-Tone, Creamy Wine Two-Tone, Navy Blues, Silver Noir Two-Tone, and Chocolate Tweed offered in '12.

1995-2024	Black	$425	$550
2000-2009	Blond	$500	$650
2002-2003	Woody, Custom Shop	$700	$900
2008	Brown	$500	$650
2009	Green	$500	$650
2010-2012	LE Colors	$500	$650
2015-2024	Lacquer tweed	$475	$625

Bronco

1967-1972, 1993-2001. 1x 8" speaker, all tube, 5 watts until '72, 6 watts for '72-'74, ('90s issue is 15 watts), solidstate, tweed covering (blond tolex was optional for '95 only).

1967-1972	Tubes, 5w	$950	$1,250
1993-2001	Solidstate, 15w	$135	$175

Bronco 40 Bass

2012-2018. 40 watts, 1x10", 12 effects.

2012-2018		$150	$200

1963 Fender Bassman

Brett Alexander

1975 Fender Bassman 100

Johnny Zapp

2020 Fender Blues Junior IV

Cream City Music

AMPS

1957 Fender Champ
JC Tepper

1953 Fender Champion 600
Jeffrey Smith

1962 Fender Concert
KC Cormack

MODEL YEAR	FEATURES	LOW	HIGH

Bullet/Bullet Reverb
1994-2005. Solidstate, 15 watts, 1x8", with or without reverb.

1994-2005		$80	$100

BXR Series Bass

1987-2000	Various models	$85	$500

Capricorn
1970-1972. Solidstate, 105 watts, 3x12".

1970-1972		$625	$800

Champ
1953-1982. Renamed from the Champion 600. Tweed until '64, black tolex after, 3 watts in '53, 4 watts '54-'64, 5 watts '65-'71, 6 watts '72-'82, 1x6" until '57, 1x8" after.

1953-1954	Wide panel, 1x6, 5C1	$2,250	$3,000
1955-1956	Narrow panel, 1x6, 5E1	$2,250	$3,000
1956-1964	Narrow panel, 1x8, 5F1	$3,000	$4,000
1964	New cab, black, AA764	$1,750	$2,250
1964	Old cab, black 1x8, F51	$2,125	$2,750
1965-1967	New cab, black, AA764	$1,250	$1,750
1968-1972	Silverface, 1x8	$725	$950
1973-1980	Silverface, 1x8	$650	$850
1981-1982	Blackface	$650	$850

Champ II
1982-1985. 18 watts, 1x10".

1982-1985		$800	$1,125

'57 Champ/'57 Custom Champ
2009-2011, 2016-present. Custom Series reissue, tweed, leather handle, 5 watts, 1x8". Custom added to model name in '16.

2009-2024		$750	$975

Champ 12
1986-1992. Tube, 12 watts, overdrive, reverb, 1x12".

1986-1992	Black	$400	$500
1986-1992	Other colors	$550	$700

Champ 25 SE
1992-1993. Hybrid solidstate and tube combo, 25 watts, 1x12".

1992-1993		$250	$325

Champion 20
2014-present. Solidstate, 20 watts, 1x8", black and silver.

2014-2024		$75	$100

Champion 30/30 DSP
1999-2003. Small solidstate combo, 30 watts, 1x8", reverb.

1999-2003		$95	$125

Champion 40
2014-present. Solidstate, 40 watts, 1x12".

2014-2024		$135	$175

Champion 100
2014-present. Solidstate, 100 watts, 2x12", 2 channels.

2014-2024		$200	$275

Champion 100XL
2019-2021. 100 watts, 2x12", 16 on-board effects, black.

2019-2021		$325	$450

Champion 110
1993-2000. Solidstate, 25 watts, 1x10", 2 channels.

1993-2000		$135	$175

Champion 300
2004-2007. 30-watt solidstate combo, Dyna-Touch Series, DSP effects.

2004-2007		$160	$200

Champion 600
1949-1953. Replaced the Champion 800, 3 watts, 1x6", 2-tone tolex, TV front. Replaced by the Champ.

1949-1953		$1,750	$2,750

Champion 600 (later version)
2007-2012. Small 5-watt combo.

2007-2012		$225	$300

Champion 800
1948. About 100 made, TV front, luggage tweed cover, 1x8, 3 tubes, becomes Champion 600 in '49.

1948		$2,750	$3,500

Concert
1960-1965. Introduced with 40 watts and 4x10", brown tolex until '63, blackface '63-'65. In '62 white tolex was ordered by Webbs Music (CA) instead of the standard brown tolex. A wide range is noted for the rare white tolex, and each amp should be valued on a case-by-case basis. In '60, the very first brown tolex had a pink tint but only on the first-year amps.

1960	Brown (pink) tolex	$2,500	$3,500
1960	Brown (pink) tweed	$2,500	$3,500
1961-1963	Brown tolex	$2,500	$3,500
1962	White tolex (Webbs Music)	$2,500	$3,500
1963-1965	Blackface	$2,500	$3,500

Concert (Pro Tube Series)
1993-1995. Tube combo, 60 watts, 1x12, blackface.

1993-1995		$650	$850

Concert Reverb (Pro Tube Series)
2002-2005. 4x10" combo, reverb, tremolo, overdrive.

2002-2005		$725	$925

Concert 112
1982-1985. Tube, 60 watts, 1x12", smaller Concert logo (not similar to '60s style logo).

1982-1985		$950	$1,250

Concert 210
1982-1985. Tube, 60 watts, 2x10".

1982-1985		$750	$950

Concert 410
1982-1985. Tube, 60 watts, 4x10".

1982-1985		$800	$1,000

Concert II Head
1982-1987. 60 watts, 2 channels.

1982-1987		$650	$850

Cyber Champ
2004-2005. 65 watts, 1x12", Cyber features, 21 presets.

2004-2005		$200	$275

AMPS

MODEL YEAR	FEATURES	LOW	HIGH

Cyber Deluxe

2002-2005. 65 watts, 1x12", Cyber features, 64 presets.

2002-2005		$225	$325

Cyber-Twin (SE)

2001-2011. Hybrid tube/solidstate modeling amp, 2x65 watts, head or 2x12" combo, became the SE in '05.

2001-2003	Head only	$400	$500
2001-2004	Combo	$450	$575
2005-2011	SE, 2nd Edition	$450	$575

Deco-Tone (Custom Shop)

2000. Art-deco styling, 165 made, all tube, 15 watts, 1x12", round speaker baffle opening, uses 6BQ5/ES84 power tubes.

2000		$775	$975

Deluxe

1948-1966. Name changed from Model 26 ('46-'48). 10 watts (15 by '54 and 20 by '63), 1x12", TV front with tweed '48-'53, wide-panel '53-'55, narrow-panel '55-'60, brown tolex with brownface '61-'63, black tolex with blackface '63-'66.

1948-1952	Tweed, TV front	$4,250	$5,500
1953-1954	Wide panel	$4,250	$5,500
1955	Narrow panel, small cab	$7,250	$9,000
1956-1960	Narrow panel, large cab	$7,250	$9,000
1961-1963	Brown tolex	$4,000	$5,000
1964-1966	Black tolex	$4,000	$5,000

Deluxe Reverb

1963-1981. 1x12", 20 watts, blackface '63-'67, silverface '68-'80, blackface with silver grille option introduced in mid-'80. Replaced by Deluxe Reverb II. Reissued as Deluxe Reverb '65 Reissue.

1963-1967	Blackface	$4,000	$5,000
1967-1968	Silverface	$2,125	$2,500
1969-1970	Silverface	$1,750	$2,250
1971-1980	Silverface	$1,250	$1,750
1980-1981	Blackface	$1,125	$1,500

Deluxe Reverb Solidstate

1966-1969. Part of Fender's early solidstate series.

1966-1969		$600	$750

'57 Deluxe/'57 Custom Deluxe

2007-2011, 2016-present. Custom Series reissue, hand-wired, 12 watts, 1x12" combo, tweed. Custom added to model name in '17. A '57 Deluxe head version was offered '16-'17 and Limited Editions in '18-'19.

2007-2011		$1,375	$1,750
2016-2017	Head only	$1,250	$1,500
2016-2024		$1,375	$1,750
2018	LE Blond	$1,375	$1,750

'57 Custom Deluxe Front Row

2019. Limited Edition, 5 offered, exotic wood cab made of century-old Alaskan yellow cedar, from Hollywood Bowl bench seats.

2019	LE Exotic Wood	$5,250	$6,500

'65 Deluxe Reverb

1993-present. Blackface reissue, 22 watts, 1x12".

1993-2024		$950	$1,125

'68 Custom Deluxe Reverb

2014-present. Vintage Modified silverface reissue with modified circuit, 1x12".

2014-2024		$950	$1,125

Deluxe Reverb II

1982-1986. Updated Deluxe Reverb with 2 6V6 power tubes, all tube preamp section, black tolex, blackface, 20 watts, 1x12".

1982-1986		$950	$1,250

Deluxe 85

1988-1993. Solidstate, 65 watts, 1x12", black tolex, silver grille, Red Knob Series.

1988-1993		$275	$350

Deluxe 90

1999-2003. Solidstate, 90 watts, 1x12" combo, DSP added in '02.

1999-2002		$175	$225
2002-2003	DSP option	$200	$250

Deluxe 112

1992-1995. Solidstate, 65 watts, 1x12", black tolex with silver grille.

1992-1995		$200	$250

Deluxe 112 Plus

1995-2000. 90 watts, 1x12", channel switching.

1995-2000		$200	$250

Deluxe 900

2004-2006. Solidstate, 90 watts, 1x12" combo, DSP effects.

2004-2006		$250	$325

Deluxe VM

2009-2013. Vintage Modified Series, 40 watts, 1x12", black.

2009-2013		$575	$725

MD20 Mini Deluxe

2007-present. One-watt, dual 2" speakers, headphone jack, 9V adapter jack.

2007-2024		$20	$25

The Edge Deluxe

2016-2019. 12-watts, 1x12" combo, tube, tweed. The Edge front panel badge.

2016-2019		$1,750	$2,250

Dual Professional

1994-2002. Custom Shop amp, all tube, point-to-point wiring, 100 watts, 2x12" Celestion Vintage 30s, fat switch, reverb, tremolo, white tolex, oxblood grille.

1994-2002		$1,250	$1,750

Dual Professional/Super

1947. V-front, early-'47 small metal name tag "Fender/Dual Professional/Fullerton California" tacked on front of cab, 2x10 Jensen PM10-C each with transformer attached to speaker frame, tube chart on inside of cab, late-'47 renamed Super and new metal badge "Fender/Fullerton"

1947		$7,250	$10,000

Dual Showman

1962-1969. Called the Double Showman for the first year. White tolex (black available from '64), 2x15", 85 watts. Reintroduced '87-'94 as solidstate, 100 watts, optional speaker cabs.

1962	Rough blond/ oxblood	$3,000	$3,750

1955 Fender Deluxe
Jerome Pinkham

1962 Fender Deluxe
David Gant

1980 Fender Deluxe Reverb
Tom Pfeifer

AMPS

Fender Frontman
Rick Reilly

Fender G-DEC

Fender Mustang GTX50

MODEL YEAR	FEATURES	LOW	HIGH
1963	Smooth blond/wheat	$2,500	$3,250
1964-1967	Black tolex, horizontal cab	$1,750	$2,250
1964-1967	Black tolex, head only	$1,000	$1,250
1968	Blackface, large vertical cab	$1,000	$1,250
1968	Blackface, head only	$850	$1,125
1968-1969	Silverface	$950	$1,250
1968-1969	Silverface, head only	$750	$950

Dual Showman Reverb

1968-1981. Black tolex with silver grille, silverface, 100 watts, 2x15".

1968-1972		$1,000	$1,375
1973-1981		$975	$1,250

Fender '57

2007. Only 300 made, limited edition combo, hand-wired, 1x12", retro styling.

2007		$1,375	$1,750

FM Series

2003-2010. Lower-priced solidstate amps, heads and combos.

2003-2006	FM-212R, 2x12	$200	$250
2003-2010	FM-100 Head/Cab	$215	$275

Frontman Series

1997-present. Student combo amps, models include 10G (10 watts, 1x6"), 15/15B/15G/15R (15 watts, 1x8"), 25R (25 watts, 1x10", reverb), 212R (100 watts, 2x12", reverb).

1997-2004	15DSP, 15 FX selections	$50	$65
1997-2004	25DSP	$65	$90
1997-2006	65DSP	$125	$175
1997-2011	15/15B/15G/15R	$45	$60
1997-2011	65R	$85	$110
1997-2013	25R	$50	$65
2007-2013	212R	$170	$225

G-Dec

2005-2012. Digital, amp and effects presets.

2005-2009	G-Dec, small cab	$80	$100
2006-2009	G-Dec 30, larger cab	$125	$165
2007-2008	G-Dec Exec, maple cab	$225	$300
2011-2012	G-Dec Jr, Champ cab	$65	$85

GE-112 Cabinet

2003-2007. Extension cab, 1x12.

2003-2007		$110	$150

H.O.T.

1990-1996. Solidstate, 25 watts, 1x10", gray carpet cover (black by '92), black grille.

1990-1996		$80	$100

Harvard Solidstate

1980-1983. Reintroduced from tube model, black tolex with blackface, 20 watts, 1x10".

1980-1983		$200	$250

Harvard Tube

1956-1961. Tweed, 10 watts, 1x10", 2 knobs volume and roll-off tone, some were issued with 1x8". Reintroduced as a solidstate model in '80.

1956-1961		$6,500	$9,000

Harvard Reverb

1981-1982. Solidstate, 20 watts, 1x10", reverb, replaced by Harvard Reverb II in '83.

1981-1982		$200	$250

Harvard Reverb II

1983-1985. Solidstate, black tolex with blackface, 20 watts, 1x10", reverb.

1983-1985		$200	$250

Hot Rod Blues Junior Limited

2000s. Compact tube combo, rough blond tolex, dark tolex sides, wheat grille.

2000s		$450	$600

Hot Rod Deluxe/Deluxe III/Deluxe IV

1996-present. Updated Blues Deluxe, tube, 40 watts, 1x12", black tolex. Various covering optional by '98, also a wood cab in 2003. III added to name in '11 with various limited-edition colors. Renamed Deluxe IV in '20, offered in black.

1996-2024	Various colors	$450	$750

Hot Rod DeVille 212

1996-2011. Updated Blues DeVille, tube, 60 watts, black tolex, 2x12".

1996-2011	Various colors	$550	$750

Hot Rod DeVille 410/DeVille 410 III

1996-2018. Tube, 60 watts, black tolex, 4x10". III added to name in '11.

1996-2018	Various colors	$550	$750

Hot Rod DeVille IV

2018-present. Tube, 60 watts, black vinyl, 2x12".

2018-2024		$525	$675

Hot Rod Pro Junior III

2010-2018. Tube, 15 watts, black, 1x10".

2010-2018		$500	$650
2011-2013	Red October LE	$325	$425

Hot Rod Pro Junior IV

2018-present. Tube, 15 watts, lacquered tweed, 1x10". Hot Rod removed from name in '20.

2018-2024		$325	$450

J.A.M.

1990-1996. Solidstate, 25 watts, 1x12", 4 preprogrammed sounds, gray carpet cover (black by '92).

1990-1996		$85	$125

Jazz King

2005-2008. 140-watt solidstate 1x15" combo.

2005-2008		$650	$850

Jazzmaster Ultralight

2006-2011. 250-watt solidstate 1x12".

2006-2011		$450	$600

KXR Series

1995-2002. Keyboard combo amps, 50 to 200 watts, solidstate, 1x12" or 15".

1995-2002	Various models	$200	$275

Libra

1970-1972. Solidstate, 105 watts, 4x12" JBL speakers, black tolex.

1970-1972		$550	$750

London 185

1988-1992. Solidstate, 160 watts, black tolex.

1988-1992	Head only	$250	$350

MODEL YEAR | FEATURES | LOW | HIGH

London Reverb

1983-1985. Solidstate, 100 watts, 1x12" or 2x10", black tolex.

1983-1985 1x12 $350 $450
1983-1985 2x10 $375 $500
1983-1985 Head $250 $350

M-80 Series

1989-1994. Solidstate, 90 watts, 1x12", also offered as head only, Bass (160w, 1x15"), Chorus (90w, 2x12") and Pro (90w, rackmount).

1989-1993 M-80 Pro $175 $225
1989-1994 M-80 $175 $225
1990-1994 M-80 Bass $175 $225
1990-1994 M-80 Chorus $175 $225

Machette

2012-2013. 50 watts, 1x12" tube combo, inlaid white piping and gray vinyl accents on black tolex.

2012-2013 $1,875 $2,375

Model 26

1946-1947. Tube, 10 watts, 1x10", hardwood cabinet. Sometimes called Deluxe Model 26, renamed Deluxe in '48.

1946-1947 $4,500 $6,500

Montreux

1983-1985. Solidstate, 100 watts, 1x12", black tolex with silver grille.

1983-1985 $350 $450

Musicmaster Bass

1970-1983. Tube, 12 watts, 1x12", black tolex.

1970-1980 Silverface $550 $750
1981-1983 Blackface $550 $750

Mustang Series

2010-present. Mustang I through V, modeling amp effects, small combo up to a half-stack. Mustang GTX and LT added in '20.

2010-2016 II, 40w, 1x12 $135 $175
2010-2019 I, 20w, 1x8 $75 $100
2011-2016 III, 100w, 1x12 $200 $275
2011-2016 IV, 150w, 2x12 $325 $425
2011-2016 V, 150w, 4x12 $375 $500

PA-100 Head

Early to mid-1970s. All tube head, 100 watts, 4 channels with standard guitar inputs, master volume.

1970s $450 $575

PA-135 Head

Later 1970s. All tube head, 135 watts, 4 channels, master volume.

1970s $550 $700

Pawn Shop Special Excelsior/ Excelsior Pro

2012-2013. Retro late-'40s vertical combo slate-grille cab, 13-watt 1x15" combo tube amp, tremolo, brown textured vinyl covering.

2012-2013 $350 $450

Pawn Shop Special Greta

2012-2013. Mini tube tabletop amp, 2 watts, 1x4" vintage radio-style cab, red.

2012-2013 $175 $225

Pawn Shop Special Ramparte

2014. Tube amp, 9 watts, 1x12", 2-tone chocolate and copper grille cloth with wheat.

2014 $275 $375

Pawn Shop Special Vaporizer

2014. Tube amp, 12 watts, 2x10", Rocket Red, Slate Blue or Surf Green dimpled vinyl covering with silver grille cloth.

2014 $350 $450

Performer 650

1993-1995. Solidstate hybrid amp with single tube, 70 watts, 1x12".

1993-1995 $200 $250

Performer 1000

1993-1995. Solidstate hybrid amp with a single tube, 100 watts, 1x12".

1993-1995 $250 $300

Princeton

1948-1979. Tube, 4.5 watts (12 watts by '61), 1x8" (1x10" by '61), tweed '48-'61, brown '61-'63, black with blackface '63-'69, silverface '69-'79.

1948 Tweed, TV front $3,125 $4,000
1949-1953 Tweed, TV front $2,750 $3,500
1953-1954 Wide panel $2,750 $3,500
1955-1956 Narrow panel, small cab $5,000 $6,250
1956-1961 Narrow panel, large cab $5,000 $6,250
1961-1963 Brown, 6G2 $3,125 $4,000
1963-1964 Black, 6G2 $2,500 $3,250
1964-1966 Black, AA964, no grille logo $2,250 $2,750
1966-1967 Black, AA964, raised grille logo $1,750 $2,250
1968-1969 Silverface, alum grille trim $1,250 $1,500
1969-1970 Silverface, no grille trim $950 $1,250
1971-1979 Silverface, AB1270 $950 $1,250
1973-1975 Fender logo-tail $950 $1,250
1975-1978 No Fender logo-tail $950 $1,250
1978-1979 With boost pull-knob $950 $1,250

Princeton Reverb

1964-1981. Tube, black tolex, blackface until '67, silverface after until blackface again in '80.

1964-1967 Blackface $3,000 $4,000
1968-1972 Silverface, Fender logo-tail $2,250 $3,000
1973-1979 Silverface, no Fender logo-tail $1,750 $2,250
1980-1981 Blackface $900 $1,250

Princeton Reverb II

1982-1985. Tube amp, 20 watts, 1x12", black tolex, silver grille, distortion feature.

1982-1985 $850 $1,125

'65 Princeton Reverb

2009-present. Vintage Reissue series, includes various Limited-Edition colors.

2009-2024 Various colors $750 $1,125

'68 Custom Princeton Reverb

2014-present. 12 watts, silver-and-turquoise front panel, aluminum grille cloth trim, black.

2014-2024 $650 $850

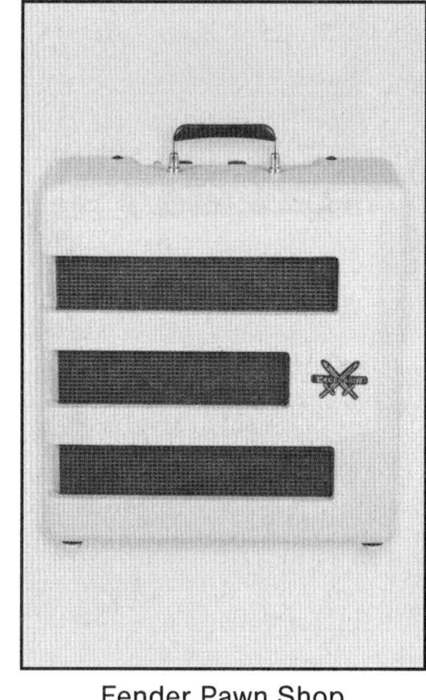

Fender Pawn Shop Special Excelsior

1964 Fender Princeton
Scott Anderson

1964 Fender Princeton Reverb
Vern Juran

AMPS

AMPS

1961 Fender Pro
Thomas Pervanje

1979 Fender Pro Reverb Silverface
Rivington Guitars

2015 Fender Pro Junior III
Rivington Guitars

MODEL YEAR	FEATURES	LOW	HIGH

Princeton Chorus

1988-1996. Solidstate, 2x10", 2 channels at 25 watts each, black tolex. Replaced by Princeton Stereo Chorus in '96.

1988-1996		$225	$300

Princeton 65

1999-2003. Combo 1x2", reverb, blackface, DSP added in '02.

1999-2001		$150	$200

Princeton 112/112 Plus

1993-1997. Solidstate, 40 watts (112) or 60 watts (112 Plus), 1x12", black tolex.

1993-1994	40 watts	$200	$250
1995-1997	60 watts	$200	$250

Princeton 650

2004-2006. Solidstate 65-watt 1x12" combo, DSP effects, black tolex.

2004-2006		$175	$225

Princeton Recording

2007-2009. Based on classic '65 Princeton Reverb, 15 watts, 1x10" combo, 2 on-board effects (overdrive/compression), 4-button footswitch, blackface cosmetics.

2007-2009		$600	$850

Pro

1946-1965. Called Professional '46-'48. 15 watts (26 by '54 and 25 by '60), 1x15", tweed TV front '48-'53, wide-panel '53-'54, narrow-panel '55-'60, brown tolex and brownface '60-'63, black and blackface '63-'65.

1946-1953	Tweed, TV front	$3,500	$4,500
1953-1954	Wide panel	$3,750	$4,750
1955	Narrow panel, old chassis	$4,250	$5,500
1955-1959	Narrow panel, new chassis	$4,750	$6,000
1960	Pink/brown, tweed	$2,500	$3,500
1961-1962	Brown tolex	$2,250	$3,000
1963-1965	Black tolex	$2,250	$3,000

'57 Custom Pro

2016-2019. Hand-wired, 26 watts, 1x15", lacquered tweed.

2016-2019		$1,500	$1,875

Pro Reverb

1965-1982. Tube, black tolex, 40 watts (45 watts by '72, 70 watts by '81), 2x12", blackface '65-'69 and '81-'83, silverface '69-'81.

1965-1967	Blackface	$2,250	$3,000
1968	Silverface	$1,500	$2,000
1969-1970	Silverface	$1,250	$1,500
1971-1980	Silverface	$1,000	$1,250
1981-1982	Blackface	$1,000	$1,250

Pro Reverb Solidstate

1967-1969. Fender's first attempt at solidstate design, the attempt was unsuccessful and many of these models will overheat and are known to be unreliable. 50 watts, 2x12", upright vertical combo cabinet.

1967-1969		$600	$750

Pro Reverb Reissue (Pro Series)

2002-2005. 50 watts, 1x12", 2 modern designed channels - clean and high gain.

2002-2005		$750	$1,000

Pro 185

1989-1991. Solidstate, 160 watts, 2x12", black tolex.

1989-1991		$300	$400

Pro Junior (III/IV)

1994-present. All tube, 2xEL84 tubes, 15 watts, 1x10" Alnico Blue speaker, tweed '94-'96, blonde in '95, black tolex '96-'17. Lacquered Tweed '18-present. III update in '10, IV in '18.

1994-1996	Tweed	$400	$550
1995	Blonde	$325	$450
1996-2017	Black tolex	$275	$350
2018-2024	Lacquered Tweed	$350	$450

Pro Junior 60th Anniversary Woody

2006. Recreation of original Fender model (1946-2006), 15 watts, 1x10, lacquered wood cab.

2006		$750	$950

Pro Junior Masterbuilt (Custom Shop)

Late-1990s. Transparent white-blond wood finish.

1990s		$775	$975

Prosonic

1996-2001. Custom Shop 2x10" combo or head/4x12" cab, 60 watts, 2 channels, 3-way rectifier switch, tube reverb, black, red or green.

1996-2001	Cab	$375	$500
1996-2001	Combo	$825	$1,125
1996-2001	Head	$675	$925

Quad Reverb

1971-1978. Black tolex, silverface, 4x12", tube, 100 watts.

1971-1978		$1,000	$1,500

R.A.D.

1990-1996. Solidstate, 20 watts, 1x8", gray carpet cover until '92, black after.

1990-1996		$90	$125

R.A.D. Bass

1992-1994. Solidstate, 25 watts, 1x10", renamed BXR 25.

1992-1994		$90	$125

Roc-Pro 1000

1997-2001. Hybrid tube combo or head, 100 watts, 1x12", spring reverb, 1000 logo on front panel.

1997-2001	Combo	$250	$325
1997-2001	Half stack, head & cab	$350	$450

Rumble Bass

1994-1998. Custom Shop tube amp, 300 watts, 4x10" cabs, blond tolex, oxblood grille. Not to be confused with later budget Rumble series.

1994-1998	Cab	$725	$950
1994-1998	Head	$1,250	$1,500
1994-1998	Head & 2 cabs	$2,750	$3,750

Rumble Series

2003-present. Solidstate bass amps, model number indicates watts, models include Rumble 15 (1x8"), 25 (1x10"), 30 (1x10"), 40 (1x10"), 60 (1x12"), 75 (1x12"), 100 (1x15" or 2x10"), 150 (1x15") and 350 (2x10"). Some models discontinued in '09 then restarted in '14.

2003-2009	Rumble 60	$150	$200
2003-2013	Rumble 150	$175	$250
2003-2013	Rumble 150 Head	$135	$175
2003-2013	Rumble 30	$125	$175
2003-2013	Rumble 350 Combo	$280	$375
2003-2013	Rumble 350 Head	$175	$250

MODEL YEAR	FEATURES	LOW	HIGH
2003-2013	Rumble 75	$160	$200
2003-2024	Rumble 100	$175	$225
2003-2025	Rumble 15	$60	$75
2003-2025	Rumble 25	$75	$100
2003-2025	Rumble 40	$140	$175

Scorpio

1970-1972. Solidstate, 56 watts, 2x12", black tolex.

1970-1972		$550	$700

SFX Keyboard 200

1998-1999. 2 stereo channels generate 80 watts per channel (160w).

1998-1999		$150	$200

SFX Satellite

1998-2000. 80 watts, 12" speaker.

1998-2000		$125	$150

Showman 12

1960-1966. Piggyback cabinet with 1x12", 85 watts, blond tolex (changed to black in '64), maroon grille '61-'63, gold grille '63-'64, silver grille '64-'67.

1960-1962	Rough blonde/oxblood	$4,000	$6,000
1963-1964	Smooth blonde/gold	$3,125	$4,000
1964-1966	Black	$2,250	$3,000

Showman 15

1960-1968. Piggyback cabinet with 1x15", 85 watts, blonde tolex (changed to black in '64), maroon grille '61-'63, gold grille '63-'64, silver grille '64-'67.

1960-1962	Rough blonde/oxblood	$3,500	$5,000
1963-1964	Smooth blonde/gold	$3,125	$4,000
1964-1967	Blackface	$1,750	$2,500
1964-1967	Blackface, head only	$1,000	$1,500
1967-1968	Silverface	$1,250	$1,750
1967-1968	Silverface, head only	$850	$1,000

Showman Solidstate

1983-1987. Solidstate, 200 watts, 2 channels, reverb, EQ, effects loop, model number indicates size, models include; 112, 115, 210 and 212.

1983-1987	Various models	$350	$450

Sidekick 10

1983-1985. Small solidstate Japanese or Mexican import, 10 watts, 1x8".

1983-1985		$60	$80

Sidekick Bass 30

1983-1985. Combo, 30 watts, 1x12".

1983-1985		$75	$100

Sidekick Reverb 15

1983-1985. Small solidstate import, reverb, 15 watts.

1983-1985		$85	$110

Sidekick Reverb 20

1983-1985. Small solidstate Japanese or Mexican import, 20 watts, reverb, 1x10".

1983-1985		$95	$125

Sidekick Reverb 30

1983-1985. Small solidstate Japanese or Mexican import, 30 watts, 1x12", reverb.

1983-1985		$100	$125

Sidekick Reverb 65

1986-1988. Small solidstate Japanese or Mexican import, 65 watts, 1x12".

1986-1988		$115	$150

Sidekick 100 Bass Head

1986-1993. 100-watt bass head.

1986-1993		$100	$125

Squier Champ 15

1990s-2000s. 1x8, 15 watts, solidstate.

1990s-00s		$50	$65

Squier SKX Series

1990-1992. Solidstate, 15 watts, 1x8", model SKX15R with reverb. Model SKX25R is 25 watts, 1x10, reverb.

1990-1992	15, no reverb	$50	$65
1990-1992	15R, reverb	$55	$75
1990-1992	25R, reverb	$60	$80

Squier SP10

2003-2012. 10-watt solidstate, usually sold as part of a Guitar Pack.

2003-2012		$50	$65

Stage 100/Stage 1000

1999-2006. Solidstate, 1x12", combo or head only options, 100 watts, blackface. Head available until 2004.

1999-2004	Head only	$250	$325
1999-2006	Combo	$325	$425
1999-2006	Combo stack, 2 cabs	$425	$550

Stage 112 SE

2000s. Solidstate, 160 watts, 1x12" combo.

2000s		$165	$225

Stage 185

2000s. Solidstate, 150 watts, 1x12" combo.

2000s		$180	$250

Stage 1000 Dyna-Touch III

2000s. Solidstate, 100 watts, 1x12" combo.

2000s		$325	$425

Stage 1600 DSP

2004-2006. Solidstate, 160 watts, 2x12" combo, 16 digital effects (DSP).

2004-2006		$350	$450

Stage Lead/Lead II

1983-1985. Solidstate, 100 watts, 1x12", reverb, channel switching, black tolex. Stage Lead II has 2x12".

1983-1985	1x12	$225	$300
1983-1985	2x12	$225	$300

Starcaster 15G by Fender

2000s. Student economy pac amp, sold with a guitar, strap and stand, Starcaster by Fender logo. Sold in Costco and other discounters.

2000s		$35	$45

Steel-King

2004-2009. Designed for pedal steel, 200 watts, solidstate, 1x15".

2004-2009		$625	$825

Studio 85

1988. Studio 85 logo on upper right front of grille, solidstate, 1x12" combo, 65 watts, red knobs.

1988		$225	$300

Studio Bass

1977-1980. Uses Super Twin design, tube, 200-watt combo, 5-band eq, 1x15".

1977-1980		$675	$900

Fender Rumble 100

AMPS

1963 Fender Showman

Imaged by Heritage Auctions, HA.com

Fender Sidekick Bass 30

1956 Fender Super
Rivington Guitars

1978 Fender Super Reverb
Tom Pfeifer

1958 Fender Tremolux
Scott Chapin

AMPS

MODEL YEAR	FEATURES	LOW	HIGH

Studio Lead

1983-1986. Solidstate, 50 watts, 1x12", black tolex.

1983-1986		$250	$350

Super

1947-1963, 1992-1997. Introduced as Dual Professional in 1946, renamed Super '47, 2x10" speakers, 20 watts (30 watts by '60 with 45 watts in '62), tweed TV front '47-'53, wide-panel '53-'54, narrow-panel '55-'60, brown tolex '60-'64. Reintroduced '92-'97 with 4x10", 60 watts, black tolex.

1947-1952	V-front	$6,500	$8,500
1953-1954	Tweed, wide panel	$4,250	$5,500
1955	Tweed, narrow panel, 6L6	$6,500	$8,500
1956-1957	Tweed, narrow panel, 5E4, 6V6	$6,000	$8,000
1957-1960	Tweed, narrow panel, 6L6	$8,000	$10,500
1960	Pink, tweed-era grille	$3,000	$4,000
1960	Pink/brown, metal knobs	$3,000	$4,000
1960	Pink/brown, reverse knobs	$3,000	$4,000
1960-1962	Brown, oxblood grille, 6G4	$2,500	$3,500
1962-1963	Brown, tan/wheat grille, 6G4	$2,500	$3,500

Super 60

1989-1993. Red Knob series, 1x12", 60 watts, earlier versions with red knobs, later models with black knobs, offered in optional covers such as red, white, gray or snakeskin.

1989-1993	Combo	$350	$450
1989-1993	Head	$350	$450

Super 112

1990-1993. Red Knob series, 1x12", 60 watts, earlier versions with red knobs, later models with black knobs, originally designed to replace the Super60 but the Super60 remained until '93.

1990-1993		$350	$450

Super 210

1990-1993. Red Knob series, 2x10", 60 watts, earlier versions with red knobs, later models with black knobs.

1990-1993		$400	$550

Super 410

1992-1997. 60 watts, 4x10", black tolex, silver grille, blackface control panel.

1992-1997		$650	$900

Super Bassman Head

2012-present. 300-watt head, 6x6550 power tubes, master volume, standard '65 blackface cosmetics.

2012-2024		$1,000	$1,500

Super Champ

1982-1986. Black tolex, 18 watts, blackface, 1x10".

1982-1986		$1,000	$1,500

Super Champ Deluxe

1982-1986. Solid oak cabinet, 18 watts, upgrade 10" Electro-Voice speaker, see-thru brown grille cloth.

1982-1986		$1,000	$1,500

Super Champ XD

2008-2011. Tube amp with extra preamp voicing, 1x10" combo, blackface cosmetics. Replaced by X2 version.

2008-2011		$250	$350

Super Reverb

1963-1982. 4x10" speakers, blackface until '67 and '80-'82, silverface '68-'80.

1963-1964	Blackface, Fender Elec	$2,250	$4,000
1965-1967	Blackface, FMI	$2,000	$3,500
1968	Silverface, AB763	$1,250	$1,750
1969-1970	Silverface	$1,000	$1,500
1970-1972	Silverface, AA270	$1,000	$1,250
1972-1975	Int Master	$850	$1,125
1975-1980	MV with pull	$850	$1,125
1981-1982	Blackface	$850	$1,125

Super Reverb Solidstate

1967-1970. 50 watts, 4x10".

1967-1970		$600	$750

'65 Super Reverb

2001-present. 45 watts, all tube, 4x10", blackface cosmetics.

2001-2024		$950	$1,125

Super Showman XFL-1000/XFL-2000

1969-1971. Solidstate Super Showman head controlled 1 or more powered speaker cabs. The XFL-1000 was a 4x12" cab with 2 70-watt power amps, the 8x10" XFL-2000 had the same power amps.

1969-1971		$750	$950

Super Six Reverb

1970-1979. Large combo amp based on the Twin Reverb chassis, 100 watts, 6x10", black tolex.

1970-1979		$1,125	$1,500

Super Twin

1975-1980. 180 watts (6 6L6 power tubes), 2x12", distinctive dark grille.

1975-1976	Non-reverb	$825	$1,250
1976-1980	Reverb	$850	$1,125

Super-Sonic/60

2006-present. All tube, 60 watts, various options, 1x12" combo or 2x12" piggyback, blonde/oxblood or blackface. Straight and slant 4x12" cab added '11.

2006-2013	1x12, blonde/oxblood	$750	$950
2006-2014	1x12, blackface	$700	$900
2006-2015	2x12 piggy-back, blonde	$975	$1,250

Super-Sonic 22 Combo Limited Edition "Black Gold" FSR

2012. 150 made, 1x12, 2-tone gold and black vinyl with white piping, black grille.

2012		$800	$1,000

Taurus

1970-1972. Solidstate, 42 watts, 2x10" JBL, black tolex, silver grille, JBL badge.

1970-1972		$450	$600

TB 600 Bass

2008-2019. Combo, 600 watts (4 ohms), 400 watts (8 ohms).

2008-2019		$325	$425

MODEL YEAR	FEATURES	LOW	HIGH

TB 1200 Bass Head

2013. Hybrid, 1200 watts (2 ohms), 800 watts (4 ohms), 550 watts (8 ohms), 4-button footswitch.

2013		$550	$750

Tone Master Set

1993-2002. Custom Shop, hand-wired head with Tonemaster 2x12" or 4x12" cabinet, blonde or oxblood.

1993-2002		$1,375	$1,875

Tone Master Deluxe Reverb

2019-present. 100-watt digital, reverb and tremolo, black or blonde.

2019-2024	Black	$725	$950
2019-2024	Blonde	$775	$1,000

Tone Master Twin Reverb

2019-present. 200-watt digital, reverb and tremolo, black or blonde.

2019-2024	Black	$700	$925
2019-2024	Blonde	$725	$950

Tremolux

1955-1966. Tube, tweed, 1x12" '55-'60, white tolex with piggyback 1x10" cabinet '61-'62, 2x10" '62-'64, black tolex '64-'66.

1955-1960	Tweed, 1x12, narrow panel	$5,500	$7,000
1961	Rare 6G9 Ckt, EL84s	$4,000	$5,250
1961	Rough white/ oxblood, 1x10	$5,000	$6,500
1961-1962	Rough white/ oxblood, 2x10	$3,000	$4,000
1962-1963	Rough white/ wheat, 2x10	$2,500	$3,500
1963-1964	Smooth white/ gold, 2x10	$2,500	$3,500
1964-1966	Black tolex, 2x10	$2,250	$3,000
1964-1966	Black tolex, head only	$1,250	$1,750

EC Tremolux

2011-2016. Eric Clapton's variation on a '57, hand-wired, 12 watts, 1x12".

2011-2016		$1,500	$2,000

Twin

1952-1963, 1996-2010. Tube, 2x12"; 15 watts, tweed wide-panel '52-'55; narrow-panel '55-'60; 50 watts '55-'57; 80 watts '58; brown tolex '60; white tolex '61-'63. Reintroduced in '96 with black tolex, spring reverb and output control for 100 watts or 25 watts.

1952-1954	Tweed, wide panel	$8,500	$11,000
1955-1957	Tweed, 50w	$12,500	$17,000
1958-1959	Tweed, 80w	$18,000	$25,000
1960	Brown tolex, 80w	$13,500	$18,000
1960-1962	Rough white/ oxblood	$7,500	$9,500
1963	Smooth white/gold	$6,500	$8,500

'57 Twin/'57 Custom Twin

2004-2011, 2016-present. Custom Series reissue, tweed, 40 watts, 2x12". Custom added to model name in '16.

2004-2011		$1,875	$2,500
2016-2024		$2,125	$3,000

MODEL YEAR	FEATURES	LOW	HIGH

'59 Twin JB Edition Joe Bonamassa

2018-2019. Joe Bonamassa's specs, 80 watts, 2x12", aged tweed.

2018-2019		$2,750	$3,500

Twin Reverb

1963-1982. Black tolex, 85 watts (changed to 135 watts in '81), 2x12", blackface '63-'67 and '81-'82, silverface '68-'81, blackface optional in '80-'81 and standard in '82.

1963-1967	Blackface	$2,500	$3,500
1968	Silverface, no master vol	$1,250	$1,750
1969-1970	Silverface, no master vol	$1,125	$1,500
1971-1972	Silverface, no master vol	$900	$1,250
1973-1975	Silverface, master vol	$850	$1,125
1976-1980	Silverface, push/pull	$850	$1,125
1980-1982	Blackface	$850	$1,125

Twin Reverb Solidstate

1966-1969. 100 watts, 2x12", black tolex.

1966-1969		$500	$650

'65 Twin Reverb

1991-present. Black tolex, 2x12", 85 watts.

1991-2024		$850	$1,125

'65 Twin Custom 15

2009-2017. 85-watt Twin Reverb with 1x15".

2009-2017		$850	$1,125

'68 Custom Twin Reverb

2014-present. Vintage Modified silverface reissue, 1x12", 85 watts, modified all-tube circuitry.

2014-2024		$850	$1,125

Twin Reverb II

1983 1985. Black tolex, 2x12", 105 watts, channel switching, effects loop, blackface panel, silver grille.

1983-1985		$875	$1,125

Twin "The Twin"/"Evil Twin"

1987-1992. 100 watts, 2x12", red knobs, mostly black tolex, but white, red and snakeskin covers offered.

1987-1992		$675	$850

EC Twinolux

2011-2016. Eric Clapton's variation on a '57, hand-wired, 40 watts, 2x12".

2011-2016		$2,500	$3,250

Two Tone (Custom Shop)

2001-2003. Limited production, modern styling, slanted grille, 15 watts, 1x10" and 1x12", 2-tone blonde cab, based on modified Blues Deluxe circuit, Two Tone on name plate.

2001-2003		$1,000	$1,500

Ultimate Chorus DSP

1995-2001. Solidstate, 2x65 watts, 2x12", 32 built-in effect variations, blackface cosmetics.

1995-2001		$225	$325

Ultra Chorus

1992-1994. Solidstate, 2x65 watts, 2x12", standard control panel with chorus.

1992-1994		$225	$300

Vibrasonic

1959-1963. First amp to receive the new brown tolex and JBL, 1x15", 25 watts.

1959-1963		$2,250	$3,000

1962 Fender Twin
Jim Sheehan

1969 Fender Twin Reverb
Tom Pfeifer

1960s Fender Vibrasonic
David Gant

AMPS

1970 Fender Vibro Champ Silverface
Rivington Guitars

1965 Fender Vibrolux Reverb
Scott Chapin

1964 Fender Vibroverb
David Gant

AMPS

MODEL YEAR	FEATURES	LOW	HIGH

Vibrasonic Custom

1995-1997. Custom Shop designed for steel guitar and guitar, blackface, 1x15", 100 watts.

1995-1997		$850	$1,250

Vibrasonic Reverb

1972-1981. Black tolex, 100 watts, 1x15", silverface.

1972-1981		$950	$1,250

Vibro-Champ

1964-1982. Black tolex, 4 watts, (5 watts '69-'71, 6 watts '72-'80), 1x8", blackface '64-'68 and '82, silverface '69-'81.

1964-1967	Blackface, AA764	$1,250	$1,750
1968-1972	Silverface	$850	$1,125
1973-1981	Silverface	$800	$1,000
1982	Blackface	$750	$975

EC Vibro Champ

2011-2016. Eric Clapton's variation on a '57 Champ, hand-wired, 5 watts, 1x8".

2011-2016		$1,250	$1,750

Vibro-Champ XD

2008-2011. Made in China, 5 watts, 1x8.

2008-2011		$150	$200

Vibro-King Custom

1993-2012. Custom Shop combo, 60 watts, 3x10", vintage reverb, tremolo, single channel, all tube, blond or black.

1993-2012		$1,625	$2,250

Vibro-King 212 Cabinet

1993-2012. Custom Shop extension cab, blond tolex, 2x12" Celestion GK80.

1993-2012		$450	$700

Vibro-King Custom Limited Edition

2012-2013. Limited Edition production of unique colors, Chocolate Crème Two-Tone, wheat grille (25 made) and Tequila Sunrise, 3-color sunburst on figured birdseye maple cab, oxblood grille.

2012	Chocolate Crème	$2,000	$2,500
2013	Tequila Sunrise	$2,500	$3,500

Vibrolux

1956-1964. Narrow-panel, 10 watts, tweed with 1x10" '56-'61, brown tolex and brownface with 1x12" and 30 watts '61-'62, black tolex and blackface '63-'64.

1956-1961	Tweed, 1x10	$6,000	$7,500
1961-1962	Brown tolex, 1x12	$4,000	$5,000
1963-1964	Black tolex, 1x12	$3,500	$4,500

Vibrolux Reverb

1964-1982. Black tolex, 2x10", blackface '64-'67 and '81-'82, silverface '70-'80. Reissued in '96 with blackface and 40 watts.

1964-1967	Blackface	$3,500	$5,000
1968	Silverface	$2,250	$3,000
1969-1970	Silverface	$1,750	$2,500
1971-1980	Silverface	$1,500	$2,000
1981-1982	Blackface	$1,250	$1,750

Vibrolux Reverb Solidstate

1967-1969. Fender CBS solidstate, 35 watts, 2x10", black tolex.

1967-1969		$500	$675

Vibrolux Custom Reverb

1995-2013. Part of Professional Series, Custom Shop designed, standard factory built, 40 watts, 2x10", tube, white knobs, blond tolex and tan grill for '95 only, black tolex, silver grille after. Does not say Custom on face plate.

1995-2013	Various colors	$850	$1,125

'68 Custom Vibrolux Reverb

2014-2020. Silverface-style, 35 watts, 2x10", black vinyl with silver-turquoise grille.

2014-2020		$850	$1,125

Vibroverb

1963-1964. Brown tolex with 35 watts, 2x10" and brownface '63, black tolex with 1x15" and blackface late '63-'64.

1963	Brown tolex, 2x10	$7,500	$10,000
1963-1964	Black tolex, 1x15	$5,000	$7,500

'63 Vibroverb Reissue

1990-1995. Reissue of 1963 Vibroverb, 40 watts, 2x10", reverb, vibrato, brown tolex.

1990-1995		$1,500	$1,750

'64 Vibroverb (Custom Shop)

2003-2008. Reissue of 1964 Vibroverb with 1x15" blackface specs.

2003-2008		$1,500	$1,875

Yale Reverb

1983-1985. Solidstate, black tolex, 50 watts, 1x12", silverface.

1983-1985		$375	$500

FireBelly Amps

2008-present. Production/custom, professional and premium grade, vintage tube amps built by father/son, Steven and Scott Cohen, in Santa Monica, California.

Fishman

2003-present. Larry Fishman offers professional grade, production, amps that are designed and engineered in Andover, Massachusetts and assembled in China. They also build effects.

Loudbox 100

2006-2013. 100 watts, 1x8" with dome.

2006-2013		$275	$425

Loudbox Artist Pro-LBX-600

2006-present. 120 watts,

2006-2024		$300	$450

Loudbox Mini Pro-LBX-500

2006-present. 60 watts.

2006-2024		$200	$300

Loudbox Performer Pro-LBX-700

2006-present. 180 watts.

2006-2024		$400	$575

Flot-A-Tone

Ca.1946-early 1960s. Flot-A-Tone was in Milwaukee, Wisconsin, and made a variety of tube guitar and accordion amps. Most were distributed by the Lo Duca Brothers.

Large Models

1960s. Four speakers.

1946-60s		$775	$1,500

Smaller Models

1960s. 1x8" speaker.

1946-60s		$450	$850

Fortune

1978-1979. Created by Jim Kelley just prior to branding Jim Kelley Amplifiers in 1980, Fortune Amplifiers logo on front panel, specifications and performance similar to early Jim Kelley amplifiers, difficult to find in original condition, professional grade, designed and manufactured by Active Guitar Electronics company.

Fox Amps

Marc Vos builds professional grade, production/custom, guitar amps and cabinets, starting 2007, in Budel, Netherlands.

Framus

1946-1977, 1996-present. Tube guitar amp heads, combos and cabinets made in Markneukirchen, Germany. They also build guitars, basses, mandolins and banjos. Begun as an acoustic instrument manufacturer, Framus added electrics in the mid-'50s. In the '60s, Framus instruments were imported into the U.S. by Philadelphia Music Company. The brand was revived in '96 by Hans Peter Wilfer, the president of Warwick, with production in Warwick's factory in Germany. Distributed in the U.S. by Dana B. Goods.

Fred

1984-1986. Before settling on the name Bedrock, company founders Brad Jeter and Ron Pinto produced 50 amps carrying the brand name Fred in Nashua, New Hampshire.

Frenzel

1952-present. Jim Frenzel built his first amp in '52 and began using his brand in '01. He offers intermediate and professional grade, production/custom, hand-wired, vintage tube, guitar and bass amps built in Mabank, Texas.

Frudua Guitar Works

1988-present. Intermediate grade, production, guitar and bass amps built by guitar luthier Galeazzo Frudua in Calusco d'Adda, Italy. He also builds guitars and basses.

Fryette

2009-present. Professional and premium grade amps, combos, and cabinets built by Steven M. Fryette, who also founded VHT amps. At the beginning of '09 AXL guitars acquired the VHT name to build their own product. Fryette continues to manufacture the VHT amp models under the Fryette brand in Burbank, California.

Fuchs Audio Technology

2000-present. Andy Fuchs started the company in '99 to rebuild and modify tube amps. In 2000 he started production of his own brand of amps, offering combos and heads from 10 to 150 watts. They also custom build audiophile and studio tube electronics. Originally located in Bloomfield, New Jersey, since '07 in Clifton, New Jersey.

MODEL YEAR	FEATURES	LOW	HIGH

Fulton-Webb

Steve Fulton and Bill Webb started in 1997, build tube amp heads, combos and cabinets in Austin, Texas, beginning.

Gabriel Sound Garage

2004-2014. Gabriel Bucataru built his tube amp heads and combos in Arlington Heights, Illinois.

Gallien-Krueger

1969-present. Gallien-Krueger has offered a variety of bass and guitar amps, combos and cabinets and is located in San Jose, California.

Garcia

Tube amp heads and speaker cabinets built by Matthew Garcia in Myrtle Beach, South Carolina, starting in 2004. He also built effects.

Garnet

Mid 1960s-1989. In the mid '60s, "Gar" Gillies started the Garnet Amplifier Company with his two sons, Russell and Garnet, after he started making PA systems in his Canadian radio and TV repair shop. The first PA from the new company was for Chad Allen & the Expressions (later known as The Guess Who). A wide variety of tube amps were offered, and all were designed by Gar, Sr. The company also produced the all-tube effects The Herzog, H-zog, and two stand-alone reverb units designed by Gar in the late '60s and early '70s. The company closed in '89, due to financial reasons caused largely by a too rapid expansion. Gar repaired and designed custom amps up to his death in early 2007.

GDS Amplification

1998-present. Tube amps, combos and speaker cabinets from builder Graydon D. Stuckey of Fenton, Michigan. GDS also offers amp kits. In January, '09, GDS bought the assets of Guytron Amplification.

Genesis

Genesis was a 1980s line of student amps from Gibson.

B40

1984-late-1980s. Bass combo with 40 watts.

1984-1989		$110	$175

G Series

1984-late-1980s. Small combo amps.

1984-1989	G10, 10w	$70	$100
1984-1989	G25, 25w	$90	$150
1984-1989	G40R, 40w, reverb	$140	$200

Genz Benz

Founded by Jeff and Cathy Genzler in 1984 and located in Scottsdale, Arizona, the company offers guitar, bass, and PA amps and speaker cabinets. In late 2003, Genz Benz was acquired by Kaman (Ovation, Hamer, Takamine). On January 1, '08, Fender acquired Kaman Music Corporation and the Genz Benz brand.

Fryette Aether

Fuchs Lucky 7

Cream City Music

Garnet Gnome Reverb

John Maysenhoelder

Gerhart Gilmore

1963 Gibson Atlas IV
Imaged by Heritage Auctions, HA.com

1953 Gibson BR-6

MODEL YEAR	FEATURES	LOW	HIGH

George Dennis

1991-present. Founded by George Burgerstein, the original products were a line of effects pedals. In '96 they added a line of tube amps. The company is in Prague, Czech Republic.

Gerhart

2000-present. Production/custom, intermediate and professional grade, amps and cabinets from builder Gary Gerhart of West Hills, California. He also offers an amp in kit form.

Germino

2002-present. Intermediate to professional grade tube amps, combos and cabinets built by Greg Germino in Graham, North Carolina.

Gibson

1890s (1902)-present. Gibson has offered a variety of amps since the mid-'30s to the present under the Gibson brandname and others. Many Gibson amps have missing or broken logos. The prices listed are for amps with fully intact logos. A broken or missing logo can diminish the value of the amp. Amps with a changed handle, power cord, and especially a broken logo should be taken on a case-by-case basis.

Atlas IV

1963-1967. Piggyback head and cab, introduced with trapezoid shape, changed to rectangular cabs in '65-'66 with black cover, simple circuit with 4 knobs, no reverb or tremolo, mid-power with 2 6L6, 1x15".

1963-1965	Brown	$600	$950
1966-1967	Black	$600	$950

Atlas Medalist

1964-1967. Combo version with 1x15".

1964-1967		$525	$750

B-40

1972-1975. Solidstate, 40 watts, 1x12".

1972-1975		$225	$350

BR-1

1946-1948. 15 watts, 1x12" field-coil speaker, brown leatherette cover, rectangular metal grille with large G.

1946-1948		$950	$1,250

BR-3

1946-1947. 12 watts, 1x12" Utah field-coil speaker (most BR models used Jensen speakers).

1946-1947		$950	$1,250

BR-4

1946-1948. 14 watts, 1x12" Utah field-coil speaker (most BR models used Jensen speakers).

1946-1948		$850	$1,250

BR-6

1946-1954. 10 to 12 watts, 1x10", brown leatherette, speaker opening split by cross panel with G logo, bottom mounted chassis with single on-off volume pointer knob.

1946-1947	Verticle cab	$750	$1,000
1948-1954	Horizontal cab	$750	$1,000

MODEL YEAR	FEATURES	LOW	HIGH

BR-9

1948-1954. Cream leatherette, 10 watts, 1x8". Originally sold with the BR-9 lap steel. Renamed GA-9 in '54.

1948-1954		$650	$850

Duo Metalist

1968-early 1970s. Upright vertical combo cab, tubes, faux wood grain panel, mid-power, 1x12".

1968-1970s		$450	$650

EH-100

1936-1942. Electric-Hawaiian companion amp, 1x10". AC/DC version called EH-110.

1936-1942		$1,000	$1,500

EH-125

1941-1942. 1x12", rounded shoulder cab, brown cover in '41 and dark green in '42, leather handle.

1941-1942		$1,125	$1,500

EH-126

1941. Experimental model, 6-volt variant of EH-125, about 5 made.

1941		$1,500	$2,500

EH-135

1941. Experimental model, alternating and direct current switchable, about 7 made.

1941		$1,500	$2,500

EH-150

1935-1942. Electric-Hawaiian companion amp, 1x12" ('35-'37) or 1x10" ('38-'42). AC/DC version called EH-160.

1935	13 3/4" square cab	$1,500	$2,500
1936-1937	14 3/4" square cab	$1,500	$2,500
1937-1942	15 3/8" round cab	$1,500	$2,500

EH-185

1939-1942. 1x12", tweed cover, black and orange vertical stripes, marketed as companion amp to the EH-185 Lap Steel. AC/DC version called EH-195.

1939-1942		$2,500	$3,500

EH-195

1939-1942. EH-185 variant with vibrato.

1939-1942		$2,250	$3,500

EH-250

1940. Upgraded natural maple cabinet using EH-185 chassis, only 2 made, evolved into EH-275.

1940		$2,500	$4,000

EH-275

1940-1942. Similar to EH-185 but with maple cab and celluloid binding, about 30 made.

1940-1942		$2,500	$4,000

Epoch Series

2000s. Solidstate student practice amps.

2000s	Various models	$35	$45

Falcon III F-3

Early 1970s. Solidstate, 1x12" combo, 65 watts, made in Chicago by CMI after Gibson ceased amp production in Kalamazoo ('67), black tolex, dark grille.

1970		$250	$350

Falcon Medalist (Hybrid)

1967. Transitional tube 1x12" combo amp from GA-19 tube Falcon to the solidstate Falcon, Falcon logo and Gibson logo on front panel, brown control panel, dark cover and dark grille, vertical combo cabinet.

1967		$400	$500

MODEL YEAR	FEATURES	LOW	HIGH

Falcon Medalist (Solidstate)

1968-1969. Solidstate combo, 15 watts, 1x12".

1968-1969		$350	$450

G-10

1972-1975. Solidstate, 10 watts, 1x10", no tremolo or reverb.

1972-1975		$150	$200

G-20

1972-1975. Solidstate with tremolo, 1x10", 10 watts.

1972-1975		$150	$200

G-25

1972-1975. 25 watts, 1x10".

1972-1975		$200	$300

G-35

1975. Solidstate, 30 watts, 1x12".

1975		$250	$350

G-40/G-40R

1972-1974. Solidstate with tremolo and reverb, 40 watts, 1x12" (G-40) and 2x10" (G-40 R).

1972-1974		$325	$450

G-50/G-50A/G-50B

1972, 1975. Solidstate with tremolo and reverb, models G-50 and 50 A are 1x12", 40 watts, model 50 B is a bass 1x15", 50 watts.

1972-1975		$350	$500

G-55

1975. 50 watts, 1x12".

1975		$325	$450

G-60

1972-1973. Solidstate with tremolo and reverb, 1x15", 60 watts.

1972-1973		$350	$450

G-70

1972-1973. Solidstate with tremolo and reverb, 2x12", 60 watts.

1972-1973		$400	$550

G-80

1972-1973. Solidstate with tremolo and reverb, 4x10", 60 watts.

1972-1973		$450	$600

G-100A/G-100B

1975. 100 watts, model 100 A is 2x12" and 100 B is 2x15".

1975		$450	$600

G-105

1974-1975. Solidstate, 100 watts, 2x12", reverb.

1974-1975		$450	$600

G-115

1975. 100 watts, 4x10".

1974-1975		$500	$650

GA-5 Les Paul Junior

1954-1957. Tan fabric cover (Mottled Brown by '57), 7" oval speaker, 4 watts. Renamed Skylark in '58.

1954-1957		$800	$1,000

GA-5 Les Paul Junior (Reissue)

2004-2008. Goldtone Series, class A, 5 watts, 1x8".

2004-2008		$375	$500

GA-5 Skylark

1958-1968. Gold cover (brown by '63 and black by '66), 1x8" (1x10" from '64 on), 4.5 watts (10 watts from '64 on), tremolo. Often sold with the Skylark Lap Steel.

1958-1959	Gold, 45w, 1x8	$650	$850
1960-1962	Gold, 45w, 1x8	$525	$800
1963	Brown, 45w, 1x8	$500	$750
1964	Brown, 10w, 1x10	$450	$700
1965-1967	Black, 10w, 1x10	$425	$650
1968	Skylark, last version	$300	$500

GA-5T Skylark

1960-1968. Tremolo, 4.5 watts early, 10 later, gold covering and 1x8" until '63, brown '63-'64, black and 1x10" after.

1960-1962	Gold, 45w, 1x8	$525	$750
1963	Brown, 45w, 1x8	$500	$725
1964	Brown, 10w, 1x10	$500	$725
1965-1967	Kalamazoo, black	$425	$575
1968	Norlin, vertical cab	$425	$575

GA-5W

Late-1960s. Norlin-era, post-Kalamazoo production, 15 watts, small speaker, volume and tone controls.

1969		$125	$175

GA-6

1956-1959. Replaced the BR-6, 8 to 12 watts, 1x12", has Gibson 6 above the grille. Renamed GA-6 Lancer in '60.

1956-1959		$1,000	$1,250

GA-6 Lancer

1960-1961. Renamed from GA-6, 1x12", tweed cover, 3 knobs, 14 watts.

1960-1961		$1,000	$1,500

GA-7 Les Paul TV Model

1954-1956. Basic old-style GA-5 with different graphics, 4 watts, small speaker.

1954-1956		$950	$1,375

GA-8 Discoverer

1962-1964. Renamed from GA-8 Gibsonette, gold fabric cover, 1x12", 10 watts.

1962-1964		$650	$950

GA-8 Gibsonette

1955-1962. Tan fabric cover (gold by '58), 1x10", 8 watts (9 watts by '58). See Gibsonette for 1952-'54. Name changed to GA-8 Discoverer in '62.

1955-1957	Gibsonette logo	$750	$975
1958-1959	Gibson logo	$650	$850
1960-1962	Gibson logo, tweed	$575	$800

GA-8T Discoverer

1960-1966. Tweed, 1x10", 9-watt, tremolo. Tan cover, 1x12", 15-watt '63-'64, black after.

1960-1962	Tweed, 9w, 1x10	$950	$1,375
1963-1964	Tan, 15w, 1x12	$750	$950
1965-1966	Black	$750	$950

GA-9

1954-1959. Renamed from BR-9, tan fabric cover, 8 watts, 1x10". Often sold with the BR-9 Lap Steel.

1954-1959	Gibson 9 logo	$750	$1,000

GA-14 Titan

1959-1961. About 15 watts using 2x6V6 power tubes, 1x10", tweed cover.

1959-1961		$1,000	$1,500

GA-15 RV Goldtone

1999-2004. 15 watts, Class A, 1x12", spring reverb.

1999-2004		$550	$850

1936 Gibson EH-150
Tom Pfeifer

1964 Gibeon GA-5 T Skylark
Tom Pfeifer

1958 Gibson GA-9
Imaged by Heritage Auctions, HA.com

AMPS

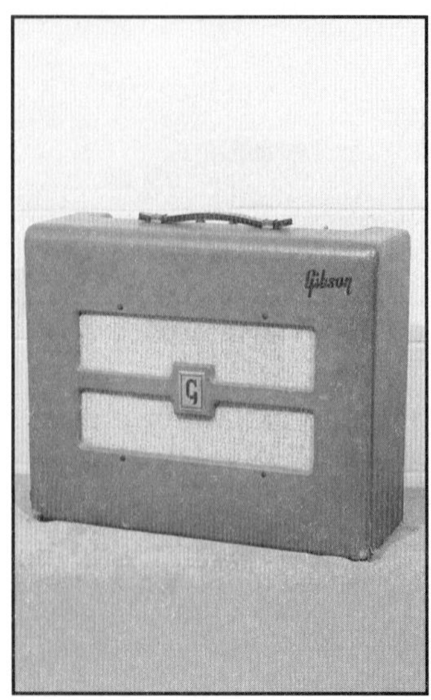

1953 Gibson GA-20

Tom Pfeifer

1950 Gibson GA-30

Imaged by Heritage Auctions, HA.com

1961 Gibson GA-40 Les Paul

Tom Pfeifer

MODEL YEAR	FEATURES	LOW	HIGH
GA-15 RVT Explorer			
1965-1967. Tube, 1x10", tremolo, reverb, black vinyl.			
1965-1967		$450	$700
GA-17 RVT Scout			
1963-1967. Low power, 1x10", reverb and tremolo.			
1963	Smooth brown	$500	$650
1964-1965	Textured brown	$500	$650
1966-1967	Black	$375	$500
GA-18 Explorer			
1959. Tweed, tube, 14 watts, 1x10". Replaced in '60 by the GA-18 T Explorer.			
1959		$1,250	$1,500
GA-18T Explorer			
1960-1963. Tweed, 14 watts, 1x10", tremolo.			
1960-1962	Tweed	$1,000	$1,500
1963	Brown	$750	$1,000
GA-19 RVT Falcon			
1961-1967. One of Gibson's best-selling amps. Initially tweed covered, followed by smooth brown, textured brown, and black. Each amp has a different tone. One 12" Jensen with deep-sounding reverb and tremolo.			
1961-1962	Tweed	$1,000	$1,500
1962-1963	Smooth brown	$800	$1,250
1964	Textured brown	$725	$1,125
1965-1967	Black	$550	$850
GA-20			
1950-1962. Brown leatherette (2-tone by '55 and tweed by '60), tube, 12 watts early, 14 watts later, 1x12". Renamed Crest in '60.			
1950-1954	Brown, single G logo	$1,250	$1,500
1955-1958	2-tone salt/maroon	$1,500	$2,000
1959	2-tone blue/blond	$1,500	$2,000
GA-20 Crest			
1960-1961. Tweed, tube, 14 watts, 1x12".			
1960-1961		$1,125	$1,500
GA-20 RVT			
2004-2007. 15 watts, 1x12", reverb, tremolo.			
2004-2007		$600	$750
GA-20 RVT Minuteman			
1965-1967. Black, 14 watts, 1x12", tube, reverb, tremolo.			
1965-1967		$450	$650
GA-20T			
1956-1959. Tube, 16 watts, tremolo, 1x12", 2-tone. Renamed Ranger in '60.			
1956-1958	2-tone	$1,500	$2,000
1959	New 2-tone	$1,500	$2,000
GA-20T Ranger			
1960-1961. Tube, 16 watts, tremolo, 1x12", tweed.			
1960-1962		$1,500	$2,000
GA-25			
1947-1948. Brown, 1x12" and 1x8", 15 watts. Replaced by GA-30 in '48.			
1947-1948		$1,250	$1,750
GA-25 RVT Hawk			
1963-1968. Reverb, tremolo, 1x15".			
1963	Smooth brown	$750	$950
1964	Rough brown	$550	$700
1965-1967	Black	$550	$700
1968	Last version	$550	$700
GA-30/Invader			
1948-1961. Brown until '54, 2-tone after, tweed in '60, 1x12" and 1x8", 14 watts. Renamed GA-30 Invader in '60.			
1948-1954	Brown	$1,750	$2,500
1955-1959	2-tone salt/maroon	$1,750	$2,500
1960-1961	Invader, tweed	$1,750	$2,500
GA-30 RV Invader			
1961. Tweed, 1x12" and 1x8", 14-16 watts, reverb but no tremolo.			
1961		$1,250	$1,750
GA-30 RVH Goldtone Head			
1999-2004. 30 watts, Class A head, reverb.			
1999-2004		$1,000	$1,500
GA-30 RVS (Stereo) Goldtone			
1999-2004. 15 watts per channel, Class A stereo, 2x12", reverb.			
1999-2004		$1,125	$1,750
GA-30 RVT Invader			
1962-1967. Updated model with reverb and tremolo, 25 watts, 1x12" and 1x10" speakers, first issue in tweed.			
1962	Tweed	$1,500	$2,000
1963	Smooth brown	$950	$1,500
1964	Rough brown	$725	$1,250
1965-1967	Black	$650	$1,000
GA-35 RVT Lancer			
1966-1967. Black, 1x12", tremolo, reverb.			
1966-1967		$650	$850
GA-40 Les Paul			
1952-1960. Introduced with the Les Paul Model guitar, 1x12" Jensen speaker, 14 watts earlier and 16 later, recessed leather handle using spring mounting (the handle is easily broken and replacement handle is more common than not). Two-tone leatherette covering, '50s checkerboard grille ('52-early-'55), Les Paul script logo on front of the amp ('52-'55), plastic grille insert with LP monogram, gold Gibson logo above grille. Cosmetics changed dramatically in early/mid-'55. Renamed GA-40 T Les Paul in '60.			
1952-1955	Brown 2-tone, LP grille	$3,000	$4,000
1955-1957	2-tone salt/maroon	$3,000	$4,500
1958-1959	2-tone blue/blond	$3,000	$4,500
GA-40 RVT Limited Edition			
2008-2011. GA-40RVT Limited Edition logo, 200 made, 2-tone brown/tan, front control panel, 30/15 switchable watts.			
2008-2011		$750	$950
GA-40T Les Paul			
1960-1962. Renamed from GA-40 Les Paul, 1x12", 16 watts, tremolo. Renamed Mariner in '62-'67.			
1960-1961	Tweed	$2,500	$3,500
1962	Smooth brown	$650	$850
GA-40T Mariner			
1962-1967. 1x12" combo, 25 watts, tremolo.			
1962-1963	Smooth brown	$750	$950
1964	Rough brown	$600	$750
1965-1967	Black	$550	$700
GA-45 RVT Saturn			
1965-1967. 2x10", mid power, tremolo, reverb.			
1965-1967		$600	$750

MODEL YEAR	FEATURES	LOW	HIGH

GA-50/GA-50T

1948-1955. Brown leatherette, 25 watts, 1x12" and 1x8", T had tremolo.

1948-1955	GA-50	$2,500	$3,500
1948-1955	GA-50T	$2,250	$3,500

GA-55 RVT Ranger

1965-1967. Black cover, 4x10", tremolo, reverb.

1965-1967		$650	$850

GA-55/GA-55V

1954-1958. 2x12", 20 watts, GA-55V with vibrato.

1954-1958	GA-55	$3,000	$4,000
1954-1958	GA-55 V	$3,000	$4,000

GA-60 Hercules

1962-1963. 25 watts, 1x15, no-frills 1-channel amp, no reverb, no tremolo.

1962-1963		$650	$850

GA-60 RV Goldtone

1999-2004. 60 watts, A/B circuit, 2x12", spring reverb, earliest production in England.

1999-2004		$1,000	$1,500

GA-70 Country and Western

1955-1958. 25 watts, 1x15", 2-tone, longhorn cattle western logo on front, advertised to have extra bright sound.

1955-1958		$3,000	$4,000

GA-75

1950-1955. Mottled Brown leatherette, 1x15", 25 watts.

1950-1955		$2,500	$3,250

GA-75 Recording

1964-1967. 2x10" speakers, no reverb or tremolo, 2 channels, dark cover, gray grille.

1964-1967		$750	$1,250

GA-75L Recording

1964-1967. 1x15" Lansing speaker, no reverb or tremolo, 2 channels, dark cover, gray grille.

1964-1967		$700	$1,125

GA-77

1954-1959. 1x15" JBL, 25-30 watts, 2x6L6 power tubes, 2-tone covering, near top-of-the-line for the mid-'50s.

1954-1958	2-tone salt/maroon, leather handle	$2,500	$3,000
1958-1959	2-tone blue/blond, metal handle	$2,500	$3,000

GA-77 RET Vanguard

1964-1967. Mid-power, 2x10", tremolo, reverb, echo.

1964	Rough brown	$1,125	$1,500
1965-1967	Black	$950	$1,250

GA-77 RETL Vanguard

1964-1967. GA-77 RET with 1x15" Lansing speaker option (L).

1964-1967		$850	$1,125

GA-77 RVTL Vanguard

1962-1967		$850	$1,125

GA-77 Vanguard

1960-1961. 1x15" JBL, 25-30 watts, 2 6L6 power tubes, tweed cover, first use of Vanguard model name.

1960-1961		$1,625	$2,250

GA-78 Bell Stereo

1960. Gibson-branded amp made by Bell, same as GA-79 series, Bell 30 logo on front, 30 watts, 2x10" wedge cab.

1960		$2,250	$3,500

GA-79 RV

1960-1962. Stereo-reverb, 2x10", 30 watts.

1960-1961	Tweed	$2,500	$4,000
1962	Textured brown	$2,500	$3,500

GA-79 RVT Multi-Stereo

1961-1967. Introduced as GA-79 RVT, Multi-Stereo was added to name in '61. Stereo-reverb and tremolo, 2x10", tweed (black and brown also available), 30 watts.

1961	Tweed	$2,500	$4,000
1961-1962	Gray sparkle	$2,250	$3,500
1963-1965	Textured brown	$2,250	$3,500
1965-1967	Black	$2,250	$3,500

GA-80/GA-80T/Vari-Tone

1959-1961. 25 watts, 1x15", 2 channels, described as "6-in-1 amplifier with improved tremolo," 6 Vari-Tone push buttons which give "six distinctively separate sounds," 7 tubes, tweed cover.

1959-1961		$2,500	$3,500

GA-83S Stereo-Vibe

1959-1961. Interesting stereo amp with front baffle mounted 1x12" and 4x8" side-mounted speakers (2 on each side), 35 watts, Gibson logo on upper right corner of the grille, tweed cover, brown grille (late '50s Fender-style), 3 pointer knobs and 3 round knobs, 4 inputs.

1959-1961		$2,750	$3,750

GA-85 Bass Reflex

1957-1958. Removable head, 25 watts, 1x12", very limited production.

1957-1958		$1,375	$2,000

GA-86 Ensemble

1960. 25-watt head plus 1x12" cab, tweed.

1960		$1,875	$2,500

GA-88S Stereo Twin

1960. Control panel and 2 separate 1x12" speaker cabs, 35 watts, 8 tubes, tweed.

1960		$4,250	$5,500

GA-90 High Fidelity

1953-1960. 25 watts, 6x8", 2 channels, advertised for guitar, bass, accordion, or hi-fi.

1953-1960		$1,750	$2,500

GA-95 RVT Apollo

1965-1967. 90 watts, 2x12", black vinyl, black grille, tremolo, reverb.

1965-1967		$750	$975

GA-100 Bass

1960-1963. 35 watts, 1x12" cabinet, for '60-'61 tweed and tripod included for separate head, for '62-'63 brown covering and Crestline Tuck-A-Way head.

1960-1961	Tweed	$1,500	$2,250
1962-1963	Smooth brown	$925	$1,375

GA-200 Rhythm King

1957-1961. Introduced as GA-200, renamed Rhythm King in '60, 2-channel version of GA-400. Bass amp, 60 watts, 2x12".

1957-1959	2-tone	$2,500	$3,500
1959-1961	Tweed	$2,500	$3,500
1961	Smooth brown	$2,250	$3,000

GA-300 RVT Super 300

1962-1963. 60 watts, 2x12" combo, reverb, tremolo, smooth brown.

1962-1963		$2,250	$3,000

1954 Gibson GA-50 T

Imaged by Heritage Auctions, HA.com

AMPS

1958 Gibson GA-70 Country and Western

RT Jackson

1964 Gibson GA-77 RET Vanguard

Rick Buckendahl

1963 Gibson Titan III
Imaged by Heritage Auctions, HA.com

Goodsell Super 17 MkIV

1965 Gregory Mercury 600
Vern Juran

MODEL YEAR	FEATURES	LOW	HIGH

GA-400 Super 400

1956-1961. 60 watts, 2x12", 3 channels, same size as GA-200 cab, 1 more tube than GA-200.

1956-1959	2-tone	$2,500	$3,500
1959-1961	Tweed	$2,500	$3,500
1961	Smooth brown	$2,500	$3,500

GA-CB Custom-Built

1949-1953. 25-30 watts, 1x15", the top model in Gibson's '51 line of amps, described as having sound quality found only in the finest public address broadcasting systems, about 47 made, this high-end amp was replaced by the GA-77 and a completely different GA-90.

1949-1953 $2,250 $3,500

Gibsonette

1952-1954. Gibsonette logo on front, round hole. See GA-8 Gibsonette for later models.

1952-1954 $625 $950

GM05

2009-2012. Small 5-watt solidstate amp usually sold with Maestro guitar pack.

2009-2012 $30 $40

GSS-50

1966-1967. Solidstate, 50 watts, 2x10" combo, reverb and tremolo, black vinyl cover, silver grille, no grille logo.

1966-1967 $450 $650

GSS-100

1966-1967, 1970. Solidstate, 100 watts, two 24"x12" 2x10" sealed cabs, black vinyl cover, silver grille, 8 black knobs and 3 red knobs, slanted raised Gibson logo. Speakers are prone to distortion. Reissued in '70 in 3 variations.

1966-1967 $450 $650

Lancer

1968-1969. CMI-Chicago produced, small combo, black upright cab, dark grille, post-McCarty era Gibson logo.

1968-1969 $95 $150

LP-1/LP-2 Set

1970. Les Paul model, piggyback amp and cab set, LP-1 head and LP-2 4x12" plus 2 horns cab, large vertical speaker cabinet, rather small compact 190-watt solidstate amp head.

1970 $450 $600

Medalist 2/12

1968-1970. Vertical cabinet, 2x12", reverb and temolo.

1968-1970 $550 $750

Medalist 4/10

1968-1970. Vertical cabinet, 4x10", reverb and tremolo.

1968-1970 $550 $750

Mercury I

1963-1965. Piggyback trapezoid-shaped head with 2x12" trapezoid cabinet, tremolo, brown.

1963-1965 $650 $950

Mercury II

1963-1967. Mercury I with 1x15" and 1x10", initially brown trapezoid cabinets, then changed to black rectangular.

1963-1964	Trapezoid cabs	$750	$1,125
1965-1967	Rectangular cabs	$775	$1,250

Plus-50

1966-1967. 50 watts, powered extension amplifier. Similar to GSS-100 cabinet of the same era, 2x10" cab, black vinyl cover, silver grille, slant Gibson logo.

1966-1967 $600 $800

Super Thor Bass

1970-1974. Solidstate, part of the new G-Series (not GA-Series), 65 watts, 2x15", black tolex, black grille, upright vertical cab with front control, single channel.

1970-1974 $500 $750

Thor Bass

1970-1974. Solidstate, smaller 2x10" 50-watt version of Super Thor.

1970-1974 $450 $600

Titan I

1963-1965. Piggyback trapezoid-shaped head and 2x12" trapezoid-shaped cabinet, tremolo.

1963-1965 $625 $900

Titan III

1963-1967. Piggyback trapezoid-shaped head and 1x15" + 2x10" trapezoid-shaped cabinet, tremolo.

1963-1964	Brown	$650	$975
1965-1967	Black	$650	$975

Titan Medalist

1964-1967. Combo version of Titan Series with 1x15" and 1x10", tremolo only, no reverb, black.

1964-1967 $650 $975

Titan V

1963-1967. Piggyback trapezoid-shaped tube head and 2x15" trapezoid-shaped cabinet, tremolo.

1963-1964	Brown	$650	$975
1965-1967	Black	$650	$975

TR-1000 T/TR-1000 RVT Starfire

1962-1967. Solidstate, 1x12" combo, 40 watts, tremolo, RVT with reverb.

1962-1967 $350 $500

Ginelle

Rick Emery builds his tube combo amps in Ardmore, Pennsylvania starting in 1996.

Giulietti

1962-1965. The Giulietti Accordion Company, New York, offered guitars and amps in the '60s. The amps were made by Magnatone and the models and model numbers are often similar to the Magnatone model.

Pearloid Lap Steel

1962-1965. Small student level, 1x12", 2-channel, tremolo.

1962-1965 $250 $400

S 1x12" Combo

1962-1965. Tremolo, 2-channel.

1962-1965 $1,125 $1,500

S-9 (Magnatone 460)

1962-1965. 35 watts, 2x12 plus 2 tweeters, true vibrato combo, black sparkle.

1962-1965 $1,500 $1,875

MODEL YEAR	FEATURES	LOW	HIGH

Gjika Amplification

1980-present. Premium and presentation grade tube amp heads and cabinets built by Robert Gjika in Escondido, California.

Gnome Amplifiers

Dan Munro builds professional grade, production, guitar amps and cabinets, starting in 2008, in Olympia, Washington. He also builds effects.

Gomez Amplification

2005-2015. Tube combo amps built by Dario G. Gomez in Rancho Santa Margarita, California.

Goodsell

2004-present. Tube head and combo amps built by Richard Goodsell in Atlanta, Georgia.

Gorilla

1980s-2009. Small solidstate entry-level amps, distributed by Pignose, Las Vegas, Nevada.

Compact Practice Student

1980s-2009. Solidstate, 10 to 30 watts, compact design.

1980s-2009		$25	$50

Goya

1955-1996. Goya was mainly known for acoustics but offered a few amps in the '60s. The brand was purchased by Avnet/Guild in '66 and by Martin in the late '70s.

Grammatico Amps

2009-present. Production/custom, professional and premium grade, hand-wired, guitar and bass amps built by John Grammatico in Austin, Texas.

Green

1993-present. Amp model line made in England by Matamp (see that brand for listing), bright green covering, large Green logo on the front.

Greer Amplification

1999-present. Tube guitar amps and speaker cabinets built by Nick Greer in Athens, Georgia. He also builds effects.

Gregory

1950s-1960s. Private branded amps sold via music wholesalers, by late '60s solidstate models made by Harmony including the 007, C.I.A., Mark Six, Mark Eight, Saturn 80, most models were combo amps with Gregory logo.

Solidstate

1950s-60s	Various models	$350	$525

Gretsch

1883-present. In '05, Gretsch again started offering amps after previously selling them from the 1950s to '73. Initially private branded for them by Valco (look for the Valco oval or rectangular serialized label on the back). Early-'50s amps were covered in the requisite tweed but evolved into the Gretsch charcoal gray covering. The mid-'50s to early-'60s amps were part of the Electromatic group of amps. The mid-'50s to '62 amps often sported wrap-around and slanted grilles. In '62, the more traditional box style was introduced. In '66, the large amps went piggyback. Baldwin-Gretsch began to phase out amps effective '65, but solidstate amps continued being offered for a period. The '73 Gretsch product line only offered Sonax amps, made in Canada and Sho-Bud amps made in the U.S. In '05, they introduced a line of tube combo amps made in U.S. by Victoria Amp Company.

Artist

1946. Early post-war Gretsch amp made before Valco began to make their amps. Appears to be made by Operadio Mfg. Co., St. Charles, Illinois. Low power small combo amp, Gretsch Artist script logo on grille, round speaker baffle hole.

1946		$300	$450

Broadkaster Mini Lead 50

Late-1960s. Solidstate compact verticle combo amp.

1969		$250	$350

Carousel

Early-1960s. Solidstate,1x10" and 1x3" speakers, tremolo speed and depth knobs, brown cover.

1960s		$550	$775

Electromatic (5222)

1947-1949. Valco-made with era-typical styling, 3 slat speaker baffle openings, leather handle, two-tone leatherette, 3 tubes with small speaker, single volume knob.

1947-1949		$700	$1,125

Electromatic Artist (6155)

1950s. Small amp, 2x6V6 power, 1x10", volume and tone knobs.

1950s		$700	$875

Electromatic Deluxe (6163)

1950s. 1x12", 2x6L6, brown tweed grille. Also offered in Western Finish.

1950s		$1,000	$1,500

Model 6150 Compact

Late-1950s-1960s. Early amps in tweed, '60s amps in gray covering, no tremolo, single volume knob, no treble or bass knob, 1x8".

1950s	Brown tweed	$600	$750
1960s	Gray	$600	$750

Model 6151 Electromatic Standard/Compact Tremolo

Late-1940s-late-1960s. 1x8", various covers.

1940s-60s		$500	$650

Model 6152 Compact Tremolo Reverb

Ca.1964-late-1960s. Five watts, 11"x6" elliptical speaker early on, 1x12" later.

1964-1969		$850	$1,500

Model 6153T White Princess

1962. Compact combo, 6x9" oval speaker, higher priced than the typical small amp because it is relatively rare and associated with the White Princess guitar - making it valuable in a set, condition is very important, an amp with any issues will be worth much less.

1962		$1,000	$1,250

Green Electric

Greer Mini Chief

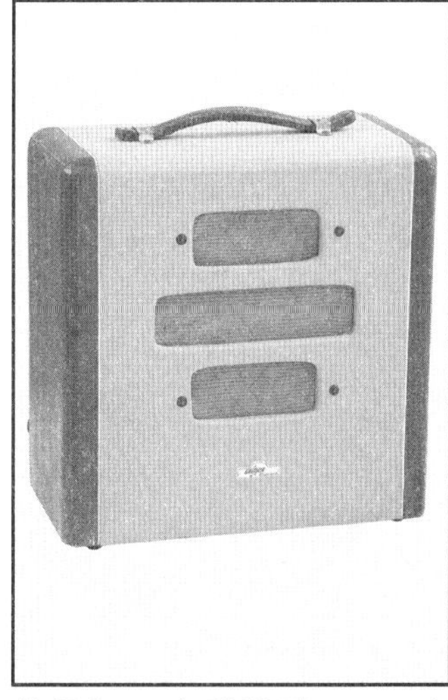
1947 Gretsch 5222 Electromatic
Imaged by Heritage Auctions, HA.com

AMPS

1969 Gretsch 6162 Dual Twin
Rivington Guitars

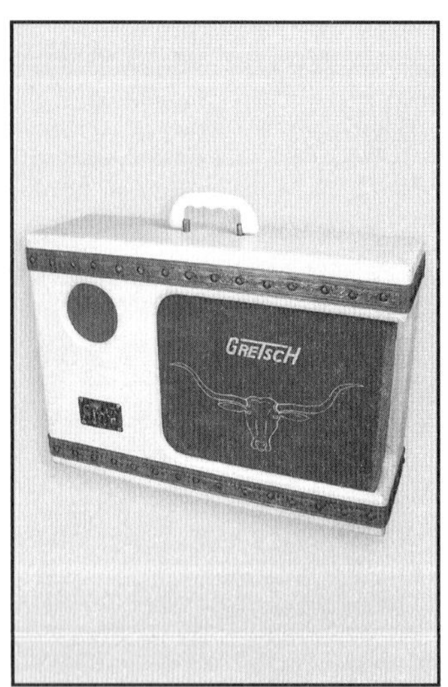

1955 Gretsch Model 6169 Electromatic Twin Western

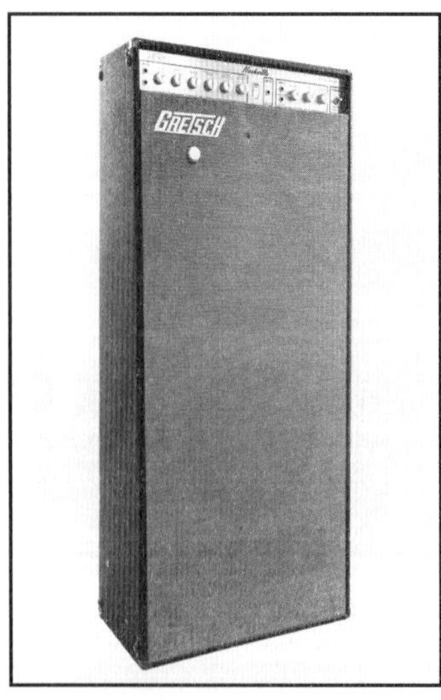

Gretsch 7154 Nashville
Imaged by Heritage Auctions, HA.com

MODEL YEAR	FEATURES	LOW	HIGH

Model 6154 Super-Bass

Early-1960s-mid-1960s. Gray covering, 2x12", 70 watts, tube.

MODEL YEAR	FEATURES	LOW	HIGH
1960s		$950	$1,250

Model 6156 Playboy

Early-1950s-1966. Tube amp, 17 watts, 1x10" until '61 when converted to 1x12", tweed, then gray, then finally black covered.

MODEL YEAR	FEATURES	LOW	HIGH
1950s-1960	Tweed, 1x10"	$900	$1,125
1961-1962	Tweed, 1x12"	$900	$1,125
1963-1966	Black or gray, 1x12"	$900	$1,125

Model 6156 Playboy (Reissue)

2005-2007. Model G6156, made by Victoria, 15 watts, 1x12" combo amp with retro Gretsch styling.

MODEL YEAR	FEATURES	LOW	HIGH
2005-2007		$1,125	$1,500

Model 6157 Super-Bass (Piggyback)

Mid-late-1960s. 35 watts, 2x15" cabinet, single channel.

MODEL YEAR	FEATURES	LOW	HIGH
1960s		$750	$1,125

Model 6159 Dual Bass

Mid-late-1960s. 35 watts, tube, 2x12" cabinet, dual channel, black covering. Replaced by 6163 Chet Atkins Piggyback Amp.

MODEL YEAR	FEATURES	LOW	HIGH
1960s		$850	$1,125

Model 6160 Chet Atkins Country Gentleman

Early-late-1960s. Combo tube amp, 35 watts, 2x12" cabinet, 2 channels. Replaced by 6163 Chet Atkins Piggyback amp with tremolo but no reverb.

MODEL YEAR	FEATURES	LOW	HIGH
1960s		$950	$1,125

Model 6161 Dual Twin Tremolo

Ca.1962-late-1960s. 19 watts (later 17 watts), 2x10" with 5" tweeter, tremolo.

MODEL YEAR	FEATURES	LOW	HIGH
1962-1967		$850	$1,125

Model 6161 Electromatic Twin

Ca.1953-ca.1960. Gray Silverflake covering, two 11x6" speakers, 14 watts, tremolo, wraparound grille '55 and after.

MODEL YEAR	FEATURES	LOW	HIGH
1953-1960		$1,375	$1,750

Model 6162 Dual Twin Tremolo/Reverb

Ca.1964-late-1960s. 17 watts, 2x10", reverb, tremolo. Vertical combo amp style introduced in '68.

MODEL YEAR	FEATURES	LOW	HIGH
1964-1967	Horizontal	$1,000	$1,250
1968-1969	Vertical	$875	$1,000

Model 6163 Chet Atkins (Piggyback)

Mid-late-1960s. 70 watts, 1x12" and 1x15", black covering, tremolo, reverb.

MODEL YEAR	FEATURES	LOW	HIGH
1960s		$800	$1,250

Model 6163 Executive

1959. 1x15, gray cover.

MODEL YEAR	FEATURES	LOW	HIGH
1959		$1,750	$2,125

Model 6163 Executive (Reissue)

2005-2007. Model G6163, boutique quality made by Victoria for FMIC Gretsch, 20 watts, 1x15", cabinet Uses to the modern retro early '60s Supro Supreme modified-triangle front grille pattern, maroon baffle with white grille, tremolo and reverb.

MODEL YEAR	FEATURES	LOW	HIGH
2005-2007		$1,250	$1,875

Model 6164 Variety

Early-mid-1960s. 35 watts, tube, 2x12".

MODEL YEAR	FEATURES	LOW	HIGH
1960s		$800	$1,000

Model 6164 Variety 125th Anniversary

2008. Limited edition by Victoria Amps, 3x10" combo, 40 watts, white sparkle.

MODEL YEAR	FEATURES	LOW	HIGH
2008		$3,000	$3,500

Model 6165 Variety Plus

Early-mid-1960s. Tube amp, 35 watts, 2x12", reverb and tremolo, separate controls for both channels.

MODEL YEAR	FEATURES	LOW	HIGH
1960s		$850	$1,250

Model 6166 Fury (Combo)

Mid-1960s. Tube combo stereo amp, 70 watts, 2x12", separate controls for both channels, large metal handle, reverb.

MODEL YEAR	FEATURES	LOW	HIGH
1960s		$850	$1,250

Model 6169 Electromatic Twin Western

Ca.1953-ca.1960. Western finish, 14 watts, 2-11x6" speakers, tremolo, wraparound grill '55 and after.

MODEL YEAR	FEATURES	LOW	HIGH
1953-1960		$7,500	$9,500

Model 6169 Fury (Piggyback)

Late-1960s. Tube amp, 70 watts, 2x12", separate controls for both channels.

MODEL YEAR	FEATURES	LOW	HIGH
1960s		$1,000	$1,250

Model 6170 Pro Bass

1966-late-1960s. 25 or 35 watts, depending on model, 1x15", vertical cabinet style (vs. box cabinet).

MODEL YEAR	FEATURES	LOW	HIGH
1966-1969		$750	$950

Model 7154 Nashville

Introduced in 1969. Solidstate combo amp, 4' tall, 75 watts, 2x15", reverb, tremolo, magic echo.

MODEL YEAR	FEATURES	LOW	HIGH
1969-1970s		$475	$600

Model 7155 Tornado PA System

Introduced in 1969. Solidstate piggyback head and cab, 150 watts, 2 column speaker cabs, reverb, tremolo, magic echo.

MODEL YEAR	FEATURES	LOW	HIGH
1969-1970s	2x2x15"	$525	$650
1969-1970s	2x4x15"	$600	$750

Model 7517 Rogue

1970s. Solidstate, 40 watts, 2x12", tall vertical cabinet, front control panel.

MODEL YEAR	FEATURES	LOW	HIGH
1970s		$225	$550

Rex Royal Model M-197-3V

1950s. Small student compact amp, low power, 1x8", Rex Royal logo on grille, Fred Gretsch logo on back panel, single on-off volume knob.

MODEL YEAR	FEATURES	LOW	HIGH
1951		$400	$500

Gries

2004-present. Dave Gries builds his intermediate and professional grade, production/custom, amps and cabinets in Mattapoisett, Massachusetts.

Groove Tubes

1979-2008. Started by Aspen Pittman in his garage in Sylmar, California, Groove Tubes is now located in San Fernando. GT manufactures and distributes a full line of tubes. In '86 they added amp production and in '91 tube microphones. Aspen is also the author of the Tube Amp Book. The Groove Tubes brand was purchased by Fender in June, '08.

MODEL YEAR	FEATURES	LOW	HIGH

Guild

1952-present. Guild offered amps from the '60s into the '80s. Some of the early models were built by Hagstrom.

Double Twin

1953-1955. 35 watts, 2x12" plus 2 tweeters, 2-tone leatherette covered cab.

1953-1955		$1,000	$1,500

G-1000 Stereo

1992-1994. Stereo acoustic combo amp with cushioned seat on top, 4x6 and 1x10 speakers.

1992-1994		$650	$850

Master

Ca. 1957- Ca. 1959. Combo 2x6L6 power, tremolo, 2-tone tweed and leatherette.

1957-1959		$550	$700

Maverick

Late-1960s-early-1970s. Dual speaker combo, 6 tubes, verticle cab, tremolo, reverb, red/pink control panel, 2-tone black and silver grille.

1960s-70s		$450	$575

Model One

Mid-1970s-1977. Solidstate 1x12" vertical cab combo, 30 watts, reverb and tremolo.

1970s		$175	$275

Model Two

Mid-1970s-1977. Solidstate 2x10" vertical cab combo, 50 watts, reverb and tremolo.

1977-1978		$250	$375

Model Three

Mid-1970s-1977. Solidstate 1x15" vertical cab bass combo, 60 watts, organ and guitar.

1977-1978		$200	$300

Model Four

Early-1980s. Solidstate, 6 watts.

1980s		$125	$175

Model Five

Early-1980s. Solidstate, 10 watts, 6.25" speaker.

1980s		$175	$275

Model Six

Early-1980s. Same as Model Five but with reverb.

1980s		$200	$300

Model Seven

Early-1980s. Solidstate, 12 watts, small amp for guitar, bass and keyboard.

1980s		$200	$300

Model 50-J

Early-1960s. 14 watts, 1x12", tremolo, blue/gray vinyl.

1962-1963		$600	$800

Model 66

1953-1955. 15 watts, 1x12", tremolo, 2-tone leatherette.

1953-1955		$650	$1,125

Model 66-J

1962-1963. 20 watts, 1x12", tremolo, blue/gray vinyl.

1962-1963		$650	$1,125

Model 98-RT

1962-1963. The only stand-alone reverb amp from Guild in the early '60s, 30 watts, 1x12", blue/gray vinyl.

1962-1963		$800	$1,125

Model 99

1953-1955. 30 watts, 1x12", tremolo, 2-tone leatherette.

1953-1955		$700	$1,125

Model 99-J

Early-1960s. 30 watts, 1x12", tremolo, blue/gray vinyl.

1962-1963		$550	$750

Model 99-U Ultra

Early-1960s. Piggyback 30-watt head with optional 1x12" or 1x15" cab, cab and head lock together, tremolo, blue/gray vinyl.

1962-1963		$700	$950

Model 100-J

1958-1959, 1962-1963. Masteramp series, 35 watts, 1x15", blue/gray vinyl.

1958-1959		$2,500	$4,500
1962-1963		$750	$1,125

Model 200-S Stereo Combo

Early-1960s. 25 watts per channel, total 50 watts stereo, 2x12", tremolo, blue/gray vinyl, wheat grille.

1962-1963		$1,000	$1,250

Model RC-30 Reverb Converter

Early-1960s. Similar to Gibson GA-1 converter, attaches with 2 wires clipped to originating amp's speaker, 8 watts, 1x10", blue/gray vinyl.

1962-1963		$700	$1,000

Superbird

1968. Piggyback tube amp with 2x12 cab.

1968		$800	$1,125

SuperStar

Ca.1972-ca.1974. 50 watts, all tubes, 1x15" Jensen speakers, vertical combo, reverb, tremolo, black vinyl cover, 2-tone black/silver grille.

1972-1974		$550	$750

Thunder 1

1965-1972. Combo with single speaker, no reverb, light tan cover, 2-tone tan grille.

1965-1972	1x10"	$450	$650
1965-1972	1x12"	$450	$650

Thunder 1 (Model T1-RVT)/T1

1965-1972. Combo with dual speakers and reverb, light tan cover, 2-tone tan grille.

1965-1972		$650	$1,125

ThunderBass

1965-1972. Piggyback combo, 2x15".

1965-1972	100-watt	$650	$1,125
1965-1972	200-watt	$650	$1,125

ThunderBird

1965-1972. 50 watts, tube, 2x12", reverb, tremolo, with or without TD-1 dolly, black vinyl, black/silver grille.

1965-1972		$600	$800

ThunderStar Bass

1965-1972. Piggyback bass tube head or combo, 50 watts.

1965-1972	Full stack, 2x1x15"	$675	$850
1965-1972	Half stack, 1x1x15"	$600	$800

ThunderStar Guitar

1965-1972. Combo, 50 watts, 1x12".

1965-1972		$600	$800

Guild Master
Imaged by Heritage Auctions, HA.com

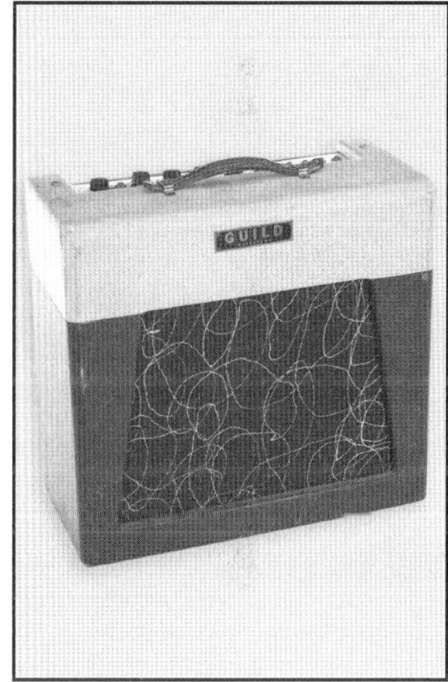

Ca. 1958 Guild Model 66-J
Imaged by Heritage Auctions, HA.com

1970 Guild ThunderBass

1963 Harmony H-303A
Rivington Guitars

1965 Harmony H400A
Imaged by Heritage Auctions, HA.com

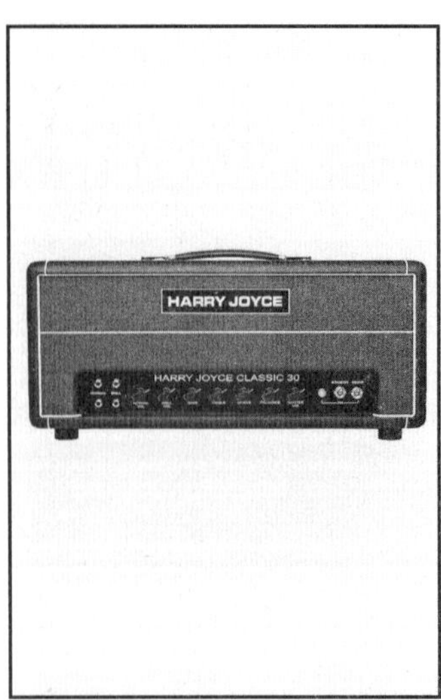

Harry Joyce Classic 30 Watt

MODEL YEAR	FEATURES	LOW	HIGH

Guyatone

1933-present. Started offering amps by at least the late '40s with their Guya lap steels. In '51 the Guyatone brand is first used on guitars and most likely amps. Guyatone also made the Marco Polo, Winston, Kingston, Kent, LaFayette and Bradford brands.

Guytron

1995-present. Tube amp heads and speaker cabinets built by Guy Hedrick in Columbiaville, Michigan. In January, '09, GDS Amplification bought the assets of Guytron Amplification.

Hagstrom

1921-1983, 2004-present. The Swedish guitar maker built a variety of tube and solidstate amps from ca. 1961 into the '70s. They also supplied amps to Guild.

Hanburt

1940-ca. 1950. Harvey M. Hansen built electric Hawaiian guitars in Seattle, Washington, some sold as a set with a small amp. The wooden amps have a large HB in the speaker cutout. He also built at least one mandolin.

Harmony

1892-1976, late-1970s-present. Harmony was one of the biggest producers of guitars and offered amps as well. MBT International offered Harmony amps for 2000-'02.

H Series

1940s-1960s. Harmony model numbers begin with H, such as H-304, all H series models shown are tube amps unless otherwise noted as solidstate.

MODEL YEAR	FEATURES	LOW	HIGH
1940s-50s	H-190/H-191	$425	$550
1940s-50s	H-200	$425	$550
1950s	H-204, 18w, 1x12	$425	$550
1960s	H-303A, 8w, 1x8	$225	$300
1960s	H-304, low power	$225	$300
1960s	H-305A, low power	$225	$300
1960s	H-306A, 1x12	$350	$450
1960s	H-306C, 2x12	$400	$500
1960s	H-400, vol	$200	$250
1960s	H-400A, vol/tone	$225	$300
1960s	H-410A, 10w, 1x10	$400	$500
1960s	H-415, 18w, 2x12	$650	$850
1960s	H-420, 20w, 1x15	$425	$550
1960s	H-430, 30w, 2x10	$525	$675
1960s	H-440, 2x12, trem/verb	$600	$750
1960s	H-512, solidstate	$625	$800
1960s	H-530, solidstate	$525	$675

Solidstate

1970s. Various models, dark covering, dark grille.

MODEL YEAR	FEATURES	LOW	HIGH
1970s	Large models	$200	$300
1970s	Small models	$30	$40

Harry Joyce

1993-2011, 2015-present. Hand-wired British tube amps, combos, and cabinets from builder/designer Harry Joyce. Joyce was contracted to build Hiwatt amps in England during the '70s. Joyce died in 2002, and the brand was carried on by Charles Bertonazzi and George Scholz until 2011. Brand brought back by Kevin Wood and Scholz through Harry Joyce USA with new versions of the classic models.

Hartke

1984-present. Guitar and bass amps, combos and cabinets made in the U.S. Founded by Larry Hartke, since the mid-'80s, Hartke has been distributed by Samson Technologies. Hartke also offered basses in the past.

Haynes

Haynes guitar amps were built by the Amplifier Corporation of America (ACA) of Westbury, New York. ACA also made an early distortion device powered by batteries. Unicord purchased the company in around 1964 and used the factory to produce its Univox line of amps, most likely discontinuing the Haynes brand at the same time.

Jazz King II

1960s. Solidstate, stereo console-style, 2x12", Haynes logo upper left side.

MODEL YEAR	FEATURES	LOW	HIGH
1960s		$325	$450

Headstrong

2003-present. Tube combo amps and cabinets built by Wayne Jones in Asheville, North Carolina.

Henriksen JazzAmp

2006-present. Professional grade, production, solidstate amps voiced for jazz guitar built by Peter Henriksen in Golden, Colorado.

Heritage

Founded in 2004 by Malcolm MacDonald and Lane Zastrow who was formerly involved with Holland amps. Located in the former Holland facility in Brentwood, Tennessee, they built tube combo and piggyback amps.

Hilgen

1960s. Mid-level amplifiers from Hilgen Manufacturing, Hillside, New Jersey. Dark tolex covering and swiggle-lined light color grille cloth. Examples have been found with original Jensen speakers.

Basso B-2501

1960s. 25 watts, 1x15" combo, swirl grille, Hilgen crest logo, compact size.

MODEL YEAR	FEATURES	LOW	HIGH
1965		$350	$450

Basso B-2502

1960s. 25 watts, 1x15" combo, swirl grille, Hilgen crest logo, large cab.

MODEL YEAR	FEATURES	LOW	HIGH
1965		$400	$525

Basso Grande B-2503

1960s. Brown sparkle cover, piggyback, 2x12".

MODEL YEAR	FEATURES	LOW	HIGH
1965		$500	$650

Basso Profondo B-2502

1965. Combo 1x15".

MODEL YEAR	FEATURES	LOW	HIGH
1965		$400	$525

MODEL YEAR	FEATURES	LOW	HIGH

Champion R-2523
Mid-1960s. Highest offering in their amp line, piggyback with 2x12" cab, tremolo, reverb, swirl grille cloth.

1965		$500	$650

Galaxie T-2513
1960s. 25 watts, 2x12" piggyback cab, tremolo.

1965		$500	$650

Metero T-2511
Mid-1960s. Compact 1x12" combo, tremolo.

1965		$400	$550

Pacesetter R-2521
Mid-1960s. 1x12" combo, tremolo, reverb, swirl grille cloth.

1965		$400	$550

Star T-2512
1960s. 25 watts, 1x12" combo, tremolo.

1965		$400	$550

Troubadour T-1506
Mid-1960s. Small practice amp.

1965		$300	$400

Victor R-2522
Mid-1960s. 1x12" combo, larger cab, reverb, tremolo.

1965		$500	$650

HiWatt

1963-1984, ca.1990-present. Amp builder Dave Reeves started his Hylight Electronics in a garage in England in the early 1960s, doing amp and other electronic repairs. By 1964 he had produced the first amps bearing the Hiwatt brand. By the early '70s, Hiwatt's reputation was growing, and production was moved to a factory in Kingston-upon-Thames, expanding the amp line and adding PA gear. In '81, Reeves suffered a fatal fall, and ownership of Hiwatt was taken over by Biacrown Ltd, a company made up of Hiwatt employees. Biacrown struggled and closed in '84. From ca.1990 to ca.1994, a line of American-made Hiwatts, designed by Frank Levi, were available. By the mid-'90s, amps with the Hiwatt brand were again being built in England and, separately, imported from Asia by Fernandes.

Bass 100 Head

1980s	100 watts, England	$1,500	$2,000

Bulldog SA112
1980s, 1994-2019. 50 watts, combo, 1x12".

1980s		$1,750	$2,250
1994-2019		$1,750	$2,250

Bulldog SA112FL
1980s-1990s. 100 watts, combo, 1x12".

1980s		$1,750	$2,250
1990s		$1,750	$2,250

Custom 100 Head

2007	100 watts	$1,750	$2,500

DR-103 Custom 100 Head
1970-late-1980s, 2005-present. Tube head, 100 watts, custom Hiwatt 100 logo on front.

1970s		$3,500	$5,000
1980s		$2,500	$3,500

DR-201 Hiwatt 200 Head
1970s. 200-watt amp head, Hiwatt 200 logo on front.

1970s		$3,000	$4,000

DR-405 Hiwatt 400 Head
1970s. 400-watt amp head.

1970s		$3,500	$5,000

DR-504 Custom 50 Head
1970-late-1980s, 1995-1999. Tube head, 50 watts.

1970-1980s		$3,000	$4,000

DR-508 50-Watt Head
1966. Tube head, 50 watts, gold script logo.

1966		$8,000	$10,000

Harry Joyce 50-Watt Head
1997. Custom Harry Joyce 50 gold script logo.

1997		$3,250	$4,250

Lead 20 (SG-20) Head
1980s. Tube amp head, 30 watts, black cover, rectangular HiWatt plate logo.

1980s		$850	$1,125

Lead 30 Combo
1980s. Combo tube amp, 30 watts, 1x12".

1980s		$1,000	$1,250

Lead 50R Combo
1980s. Combo tube amp, 50 watts, 1x12", reverb, dark cover, dark grille, HiWatt rectangular plate logo.

1980s		$1,000	$1,250

OL-103 Lead 100 Head

1982	100 watts, England	$1,625	$2,250

PW-50 Tube
1989-1993. Stereo tube amp, 50 watts per channel.

1989-1993		$1,000	$1,250

S50L Head
1989-1993. Lead guitar head, 50 watts, gain, master volume, EQ.

1989-1993		$925	$1,250

S100L Head
1989-1993. 100 watts.

1989-1993		$2,750	$3,500

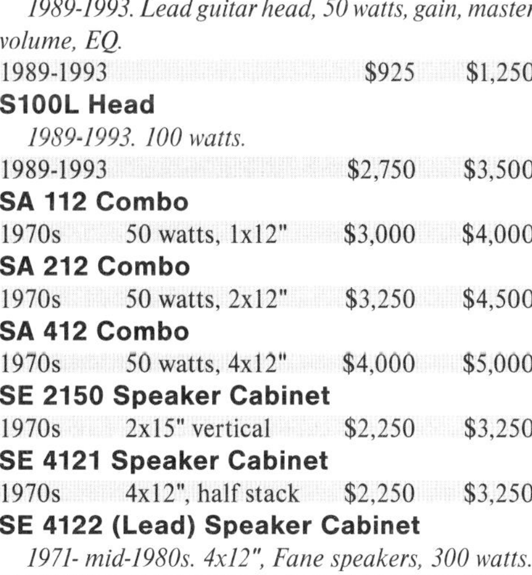

SA 112 Combo

1970s	50 watts, 1x12"	$3,000	$4,000

SA 212 Combo

1970s	50 watts, 2x12"	$3,250	$4,500

SA 412 Combo

1970s	50 watts, 4x12"	$4,000	$5,000

SE 2150 Speaker Cabinet

1970s	2x15" vertical	$2,250	$3,250

SE 4121 Speaker Cabinet

1970s	4x12", half stack	$2,250	$3,250

SE 4122 (Lead) Speaker Cabinet
1971- mid-1980s. 4x12", Fane speakers, 300 watts.

1971-1980s	4x12", half stack	$2,250	$3,250

SE 4123 (Bass) Speaker Cabinet
1970s. Bass version of SE, often used with DR103 head, straight-front cab and stackable, black tolex with gray grille, Hiwatt logo plate in center of grille.

1970s	4x12", half stack	$2,250	$3,250

SE 4129 (Bass) Speaker Cabinet
1970s. SE series for bass, 4x12", often used with DR 201 head.

1970s		$2,250	$3,250

SE 4151 Speaker Cabinet
1970s. SE series with 4x15".

1970s		$2,250	$3,250

Headstrong Lil' King

Henriksen Bud

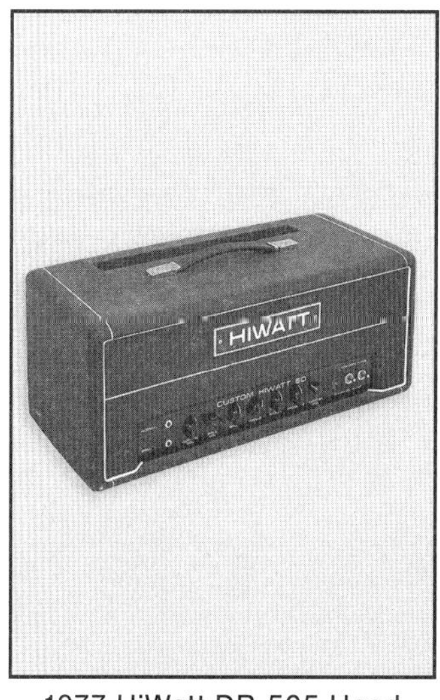

1977 HiWatt DR-505 Head
Imaged by Heritage Auctions, HA.com

AMPS

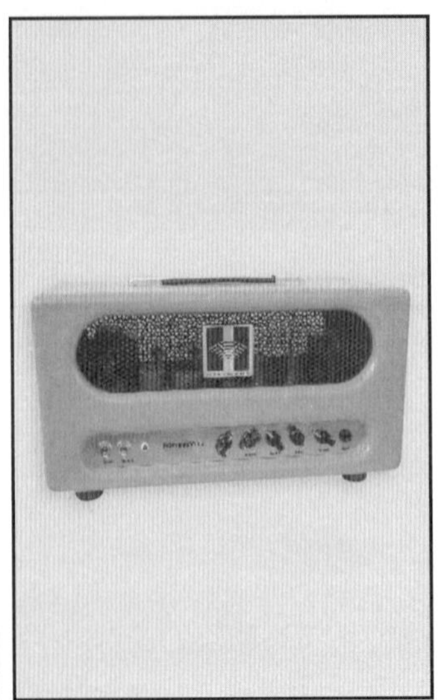
Hoffmann 15

Humphrey

Jet City 800 Hand-wired Custom 50 Sable

MODEL YEAR	FEATURES	LOW	HIGH

Hoagland

Professional grade, production, guitar amps built by Dan Hoagland in Land O Lakes, Florida starting in 2008.

Hoffman

1993-present. Tube amps, combos, reverb units, and cabinets built by Doug Hoffman from 1993 to '99, in Sarasota, Florida. Hoffman no longer builds amps, concentrating on selling tube amp building supplies, and since 2001 has been located in Pisgah Forest, North Carolina.

Hoffmann

1983-present. Tube amp heads for guitar and other musical instruments built by Kim Hoffmann in Hawthorne, California.

Hohner

1857-present. Matthias Hohner, a clockmaker in Trossingen, Germany, founded Hohner in 1857, making harmonicas. Hohner has been offering guitars and amps at least since the early '70s.

Panther Series

1980s. Smaller combo amps, master volume, gain, EQ.

1980s	Various models	$75	$125

Sound Producer Series

1980s. Master volume, normal and overdrive, reverb, headphone jack.

1980s	Various models	$75	$125

Holland

1992-2004. Tube combo amps from builder Mike Holland, originally in Virginia Beach, Virginia, and since 2000 in Brentwood, Tennessee. In 2000, Holland took Lane Zastrow as a partner, forming L&M Amplifiers to build the Holland line. The company closed in '04.

Holmes

1970-late 1980s. Founded by Harrison Holmes. Holmes amplifiers were manufactured in Mississippi and their product line included guitar and bass amps, PA systems, and mixing boards. In the early '80s, Harrison Holmes sold the company to On-Site Music which called the firm The Holmes Corp. Products manufactured by Harrison have an all-caps HOLMES logo and the serial number plate says The Holmes Company.

Mississippi Blues Master

Solid state, head only.

1980s		$450	$600

Performer PB-115 Bass

60 watts, 1x15", black tolex.

1980s		$125	$195

Pro Compact 210S

60 watts, 2x10", 2 channels, active EQ, black tolex.

1980s		$125	$195

Pro Compact 212S

2x12" version of Pro.

1980s		$150	$225

Rebel RB-112 Bass

35 watts, 1x12", black tolex.

1980s		$125	$225

Hondo

1969-1987, 1991-2005. Hondo has offered imported amps over the years. 1990s models ranged from the H20 Practice Amp to the H160SRC with 160 watts (peak) and 2x10" speakers.

Various Models

1970s-90s	Mid-size	$65	$100
1970s-90s	Small	$35	$50

Hottie

Jean-Claude Escudie and Mike Bernards started in 2005, build budget and intermediate grade, production/custom, solid state "toaster" amps in Portland, Oregon. They also offered guitars in '09.

Hound Dog

1994-1998. Founded by George Alessandro as the Hound Dog Corporation. Name was changed to Alessandro in 1998 (see that brand for more information).

Hughes & Kettner

1985-present. Hughes & Kettner offers a line of solidstate and tube guitar and bass amps, combos, cabinets and effects, all made in Germany.

Humphrey

2010-present. Custom, professional and premium grade, tube amps built in Chanhassen, Minnesota by Gerry Humphrey. He also builds preamps and reverb units.

Hurricane

Tube guitar and harmonica combo amps built by Gary Drouin in Sarasota, Florida. Drouin started the company in 1998 with harp master Rock Bottom, who died in September 2001.

Hy Lo

1960s-1970s. Budget grade, small compact amps made in Japan, Hy Lo logo on grille.

Ibanez

1932-present. Ibanez added solidstate amps to their product line in '98. They also build guitars, basses and effects.

Idol

Late-1960s. Made in Japan. Dark tolex cover, dark grille, Hobby Series with large Idol logo on front.

Hobby Series

1968	Hobby 10	$100	$150
1968	Hobby 100	$200	$300
1968	Hobby 20	$110	$175
1968	Hobby 45	$175	$275

Impact

1963-early 1970s. Based in London, England, tube amps made by Don Mackrill and Laurie Naiff for Pan Musical Instrument Company and their music stores. About a dozen different models of combos, piggyback half-stacks and PAs were offered.

Imperial

Ca.1963-ca.1970. The Imperial Accordion Company of Chicago, Illinois offered one or two imported small amps in the '60s.

Jack Daniel's

2004-2017. Tube guitar amp built by Peavey for the Jack Daniel Distillery, offered until about '10. They offered guitars until '17.

Jackson

1980-present. The Jackson-Charvel Company offered budget to intermediate grade amps and cabinets in the late '80s and the '90s.

Jackson Ampworks

2001-present. Brad Jackson builds his tube amp heads and speaker cabinets in Bedford, Texas.

Jackson-Guldan

1920s-1960s. The Jackson-Guldan Violin Company, of Columbus, Ohio, offered lap steels and small tube amps early on. They also built acoustic guitars.

Jay Turser

1997-present. Smaller, inexpensive imported solidstate guitar and bass amps. They also offer basses and guitars.

JCA Circuits

Premium and presentation grade tube guitar combo amps built by Jason C. Arthur in Pottstown, Pennsylvania, starting in 1995.

Jennings

Late 1960s. Tom Jennings formed another company after resigning from Vox. Large block letter Jennings logo on front panel, Jennings Amplifier logo on back control plate with model number and serial number.

Jet City Amplification

2009-present. Budget to professional grade, production/custom, guitar amps and cabinets designed in Seattle, Washington by Doug White, Dan Gallagher, Michael Soldano and built in Asia.

Jim Kelley

1979-1985. Channel-switching tube amps, compact combos and heads, hardwood cabinets available, made by Jim Kelley at his Active Guitar Electronics in Tustin, California. He produced about 100 amps a year. In 1978 and early '79 he produced a few amps under the Fortune brand name for Fortune Guitars.

MODEL YEAR	FEATURES	LOW	HIGH

JMI (Jennings Musical Industries)

Tom Jennings built the Vox amps of the 1960s. In 2004, he began building tube amp heads and cabinets based on some of their classic models. Large block letter Jennings logo on front panel, Jennings Amplifier logo on back control plate with model number and serial number. They also offer effects.

Johnson

Mid-1990s-2024. Line of solidstate amps imported by Music Link, Brisbane, California. Johnson also offers guitars, basses, mandolins and effects.

Johnson Amplification

Intermediate and professional grade, production, modeling amps and effects designed by John Johnson, starting 1997 in Sandy, Utah. The company is part of Harman International. In 2002, they quit building amps, but continue the effects line.

JoMama

1994-present. Tube amps and combos under the JoMama and Kelemen brands built by Joe Kelemen in Santa Fe, New Mexico.

Jordan

1966-early 1970s. Jordan Electronics, of Alhambra, California, built a range of electronics, including, starting around 1966, solid state guitar amps and effects.

Juke

Tube guitar and harmonica amps built by G.R. Croteau, starting 1989, in Troy, New Hampshire. He also built the Warbler line of amps.

Kafel

Jack Kafel built his tube amp heads in Chicago, Illinois, starting in 2004.

Kalamazoo

1933-1942, 1965-1970. Kalamazoo was a brand Gibson used on one of their budget lines. They used the name on amps from '65 to '67.

Bass

1965-1967. Enclosed back, 2x10", flip-out control panel, not a commonly found model as compared to numerous Model 1 and 2 student amps.

1965-1967		$600	$850

Bass 30

Late 1960s-early 1970s. Tube combo, vertical cabinet, 2x10".

1970		$450	$650

KEA

1948-1952. Small compact amp, round speaker baffle grille, slant Kalamazoo logo on front, oxblood leatherette.

1948-1952		$450	$700

Jordan Entertainer J 110

Rivington Guitars

Juke Warbler Muse

Carter Vintage guitars

Kalamazoo Bass 30

Rivington Guitars

AMPS

AMPS

1964 Kay Model 703C
Tom Pfeifer

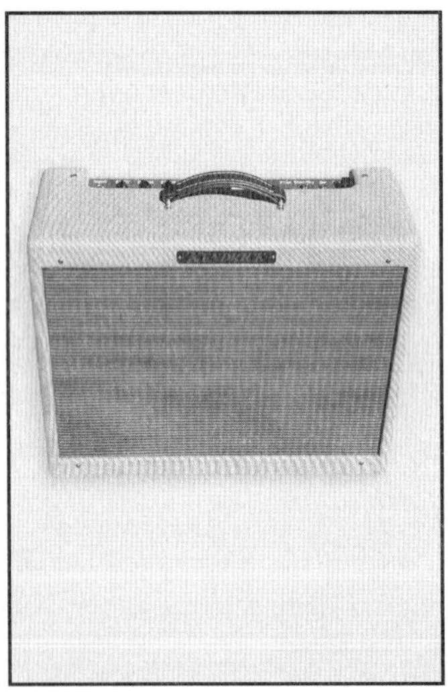
Kendrick Double Trouble

1967 Kingston
Rivington Guitars

MODEL YEAR	FEATURES	LOW	HIGH

Lap Steel

1940s. Kalamazoo logo on front lower right, low power with 1-6V6, round speaker grille opening, red/brown leatherette.

1940s		$400	$550

Model 1

1965-1967. No tremolo, 1x10", front control panel, black.

1965-1967		$275	$400

Model 2

1965-1967. Same as Model 1 with tremolo, black.

1965-1967	Black panel	$400	$825
1967	Silver panel	$225	$375

Model 3

Late 1960s-early 1970s. Made by CMI Electronics in Chicago, post Gibson Kalamazoo era, student compact solidstate combo, Kalamazoo 3 logo on front panel, Kalamazoo Model 3 logo on label on speaker magnet.

1960s-70s		$115	$150

Model 4

Late 1960s-early 1970s. Made by CMI Electronics in Chicago, post Gibson Kalamazoo era, student compact solidstate combo, 3 control knobs, tone, tremolo, volume, Kalamazoo 4 logo on front panel, Kalamazoo Model 4 logo on label on speaker magnet.

1960s-70s		$115	$150

Reverb 12

1965-1967. Black vinyl cover, 1x12", reverb, tremolo.

1965-1967		$600	$900

Kay

Ca.1931-present. Kay originally offered amps up to around '68 when the brand changed hands. Currently they offer a couple of small solidstate imported amps. They also make basses, guitars, banjos, mandolins, ukes, and violins.

K506 Vibrato 12

1960s. 12 watts, 1x12", swirl grille, metal handle.

1960s		$500	$650

K507 Twin Ten Special

1960s. 20 watts, 2x10", swirl grille, metal handle.

1960s		$750	$1,000

K700 Series

Introduced in 1965. Value Leader/Vanguard/Galaxie models, transistorized amps promoted as eliminates tube-changing annoyance and reliable performance, combo amps with tapered cabinets, rear slant control panel, rich brown and tan vinyl cover, brown grille cloth.

1965-1966	Various models	$200	$500

Model 703

1962-1964. Tube student amp, small speaker, 3 tubes, 1 volume, 1 tone, 2-tone white front with brown back cabinet, metal handle, model number noted on back panel, Kay logo and model number badge lower front right.

1962-1964		$225	$350

Model 803

1962-1964. Student amp, 1x8", 3 tubes, 1 volume, 1 tone, metal handle, 14.75x11.75x6.75" cabinet with dark gray cover.

1962-1964		$225	$350

Model 805

1965. Solidstate, 35 watts, 1x10", 4 control knobs, 2-tone cabinet.

1965		$125	$175

Small Tube

1940s	Wood cabinet	$350	$500
1950s	Various models	$350	$500
1960s	Models K503, K504, K505	$425	$650

Kelemen

1994-present. Tube amps and combos under the JoMama and Kelemen brands built by Joe Kelemen in Santa Fe, New Mexico.

Kendrick

1989-present. Founded by Gerald Weber in Austin, Texas and currently located in Kempner, Texas. Mainly known for their intermediate to professional grade, tube amps, Kendrick also offers guitars, speakers, and effects. Weber died in 2024, wife Jill and daughter Helen plan to continue his Kendrick amps.

Kent

Ca.1962-1969. Imported budget line of guitars and amps.

Guitar and Bass

1960s. Various models.

1960s	1475	$80	$130
1960s	2198	$80	$130
1960s	5999	$115	$150
1960s	6104	$160	$225
1960s	6610	$55	$100

Kiesel

See Guitar section.

King Amplification

Tube combo amps, head and cabinets built by Val King in San Jose, California starting in 2005.

Kingsley

1998-present. Production/custom, professional grade, tube amps and cabinets built by Simon Jarrett in Vancouver, British Columbia.

Kingston

1958-1967. Economy solidstate amps imported by Westheimer Importing, Chicago, Illinois.

Cat Series

Mid-1960s. Solidstate Cat Series amps have dark vinyl and dark grilles.

1960s	P-1 3w	$90	$125
1960s	P-2, 5w	$90	$125
1960s	P-3, 8w	$90	$125
1960s	P-8T, 20w	$90	$125

Cougar BA-21 Bass Piggyback

Mid-1960s. Solidstate, 60 watts, 2x12" cab, dark vinyl, light silver grille.

1960s		$175	$250

MODEL YEAR	FEATURES	LOW	HIGH

Cougar PB-5 Bass Combo

Mid-1960s. Solidstate, 15 watts, 1x8".

1960s		$100	$150

Lion 2000 Piggyback

Mid-1960s. Solidstate, 90 watts, 2x12" cab.

1960s		$225	$325

Lion 3000 Piggyback

Mid-1960s. Solidstate, 250 watts, 4x12" cab.

1960s		$275	$400

Lion AP-281 R Piggyback

Mid-1960s. Solidstate, 30 watts, 2x8" cab, dark vinyl cover, light silver grille.

1960s		$175	$275

Lion AP-281 R10 Piggyback

Mid-1960s. Solidstate, 30 watts, 2x10" cab.

1960s		$200	$300

Kinsman

2012-present. Budget and intermediate grade, production, guitar amps and cabinets built in China and distributed worldwide by John Hornby Skewes & Co. Ltd. in England. They also use the brand on a line of guitar effects.

Kitchen-Marshall

1965-1966. Private branded for Kitchen Music by Marshall, primarily PA units with block logos. Limited production.

JTM 45 MKII 45-Watt Head

1965-1966. Private branded for Kitchen Music, JTM 45 Marshall with Kitchen logo plate, 45 watts.

1965-1966		$7,000	$11,000

Slant 4x12 1960 Cabinet

1965-1966. Slant front 4x12" 1960 style cab with gray bluesbreaker grille, black on green vinyl, very limited production.

1965-1966		$4,000	$6,000

KJL

Founded in 1995 by Kenny Lannes, MSEE, a professor of Electrical Engineering at the University of New Orleans. KJL makes budget to intermediate grade, tube combo amps, heads and an ABY box.

KMD (Kaman)

1986-ca.1990. Distributed by Kaman (Ovation, Hamer, etc.) in the late '80s, KMD offered a variety of amps and effects.

Koch

1988-present. Koch Guitar Electronics produces all-tube combo amps, heads, effects and cabinets built in The Netherlands.

Komet

1999-present. Intermediate to professional grade, tube amp heads built in Baton Rouge, Louisiana, by Holger Notzel and Michael Kennedy with circuits designed by Ken Fischer of Trainwreck fame. They also build a power attenuator.

Kona Guitar Company

2001-present. Budget solidstate amps made in Asia. They also offer guitars, basses, mandolins, ukes and banjos.

Krank

1996-2013, 2015-2020. Founded by Tony Krank and offering tube amp heads, combos and speaker cabinets built in Tempe, Arizona. They also built effects.

Kustom

1965-present. Kustom, a division of Hanser Holdings, offers guitar and bass combo amps and PA equipment. Founded by Bud Ross in Chanute, Kansas, who offered tuck-and-roll amps as early as '58 but began using the Kustom brand name in '65. From '69 to '75 Ross gradually sold interest in the company (in the late '70s, Ross introduced the line of Ross effects stomp boxes). The brand changed hands a few times, and by the mid-'80s it was no longer in use. In '89 Kustom was in bankruptcy court and was purchased by Hanser Holdings Incorporated of Cincinnati, Ohio (Davitt & Hanser) and by '94, they had a new line of amps available.

Prices are for amps with no tears in the tuck-and-roll cover and no grille tears. A tear in the tuck-and-roll will reduce the value, sometimes significantly.

Kustom model identification can be frustrating as they used series numbers, catalog numbers (the numbers in the catalogs and price lists), and model numbers (the number often found next to the serial number on the amp's back panel). Most of the discussion that follows is by series number (100, 200, 300, etc.) and catalog number. Unfortunately, vintage amp dealers use the serial number and model number, so the best way is to cross-check speaker and amplifier attributes. Model numbers were used primarily for repair purposes and were found in the repair manuals. In many, but not all cases, the model number is the last digit of the catalog number; for example, the catalog lists a 100 series Model 1-15J-1, where the last digit 1 signifies a Model 1 amplifier chassis which is a basic amp without reverb or tremolo. A Model 1-15J-2 signifies a Model 2 amp chassis that has reverb and tremolo. In this example, Kustom uses a different model number on the back of the amp head. For the 1-15J-2, the model number on the back panel of the amp head would be K100-2, indicating a series 100 (50 watts) amp with reverb and tremolo (amp chassis Model 2).

Model numbers relate to the amplifier's schematic and electronics, while catalog numbers describe the amp's relative power rating and speaker configuration.

Amp Chassis Model Numbers ('68-'72)

Model 1 Amp (basic)
Model 2 Amp with reverb
Model 3 Amp with Harmonic Clip and Boost
Model 4 Amp with reverb, tremolo, vibrato, Harmonic Clip and Selective Boost
Model 5 PA with reverb
Model 6 Amp (basic) with Selectone

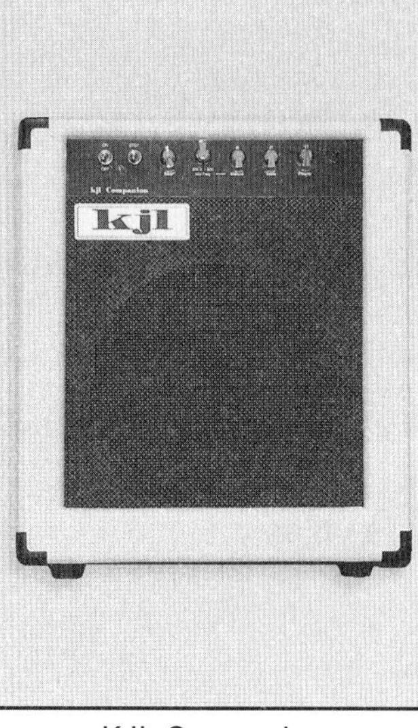

KJL Companion

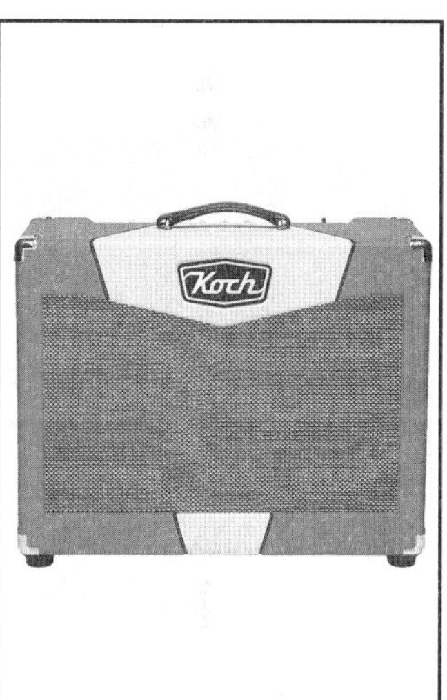

Koch Ventura

Komet Songwriter 30

Kustom Hustler
Imaged by Heritage Auctions, HA.com

1971 Kustom K150-8
Tom Pfeifer

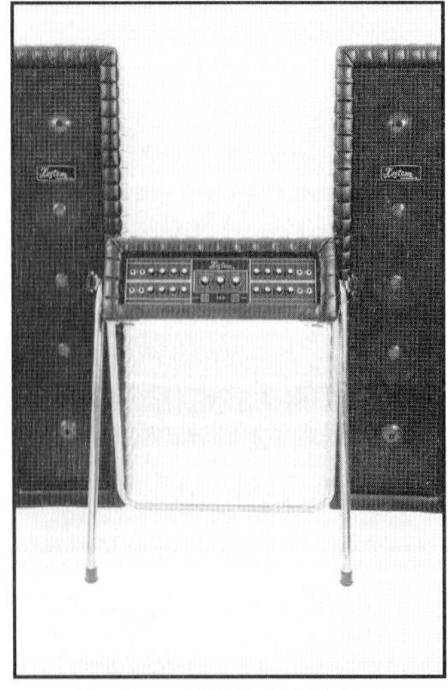
Kustom K150-5 PA Set
Imaged by Heritage Auctions, HA.com

Model 7 Amp with reverb, tremolo, vibrato, boost (different parts)
Model 8 Amp with reverb, tremolo, vibrato, boost (different parts)

Naugahyde Tuck-&-Roll 200 ('65-'67)

The very first Kustoms did not have the model series on the front control panel. The early logo stipulated Kustom by Ross, Inc. The name was then updated to Kustom Electronics, Inc. 1965-'67 amp heads have a high profile/tall "forehead" area (the area on top of the controls) and these have been nicknamed "Frankenstein models." The '65-'67 catalog numbers were often 4 or 5 digits, for example J695. The first digit represents the speaker type (J = Jensen, etc.), other examples are L995, L1195, L795RV, etc. Some '67 catalog numbers changed to 2 digits followed by 3 digits, like 4-D 140f, or 3-15C (3 CTS speakers), etc. Others sported 5 characters like 4-15J-1, where 4 = 4 speakers, 15 = 15" speakers, J = Jensen, and 1 = basic amp chassis with no effects. The fifth digit indicated amp chassis model number as described above.

Naugahyde Tuck-&-Roll 100/200/400 ('68-'71)

Starting in '68, the Kustom logo also included the model series. A K100, for example, would have 100 displayed below the Kustom name. The model series generally is twice the relative output wattage, for example, the 100 Series is a 50-watt amp. Keep in mind, solidstate ratings are often higher than tube-amp ratings, so use the ratings as relative measurements. Most '68-'70 Kustom catalog numbers are x-xxx-x, for example 1-15L-1. The first digit represents the number of speakers, the 2nd and 3rd represent the speaker size, the fourth represents the speaker type (A = Altec Lansing, L = J.B.L., J = Jensen, C = C.T.S. Bass), the fifth digit represents the amp chassis number. The power units were interchangeable in production, so amps could have similar front-ends but different power units (more power and different effect options) and vice versa. Some '68 bass amp catalog numbers were 4 digits, for example 2-12C, meaning two 12" CTS speakers. Again, there were several different numbers used. Kustom also introduced the 200 and 400 amp series and the logo included the series number. The catalog numbers were similar to the 100 series, but they had a higher power rating of 100 equivalent watts (200 series), or 200 equivalent watts (400 series). Kustom U.S. Naugahyde (tuck-&-roll) covers came in 7 colors: black (the most common), Cascade (blue/green), silver (white-silver), gold (light gold), red, blue, and Charcoal (gray). The market historically shows color options fetching more. The market has not noticeably distinguished power and features options. Condition and color seem to be the most important. Gold and Cascade may be the rarest seen colors.

Naugahyde Tuck-&-Roll 150/250/300/500/600 (c.'71-c.'75)

The amp heads changed with a slightly slanted control panel and the Kustom logo moved to the right/upper-right portion of the front panel. They continued to be tuck-&-roll offered in the same variety of colors. The sales literature indicated a 150 series had 150 watts, 250 had 250 watts, etc.

Naugahyde Tuck-&-Roll SC (Self Contained) Series

Most SC combo amps were rated at 150 watts, with the 1-12SC listed at 50 watts. They were offered in 7 colors of tuck-and-roll. Again, the model numbers indicate the features as follows: 4-10 SC is a 4 x 10", 2-10 SC is a 2x10", etc.

Super Sound Tuck-and-Roll Combo Series

The last tuck-and-roll combo amps with slightly smaller tucks. The Amp control panel is noticeably smaller and the Kustom logo is in the right side of the control panel.

Black Vinyl ('75-c.'78)

By '75 ownership changes were complete, and the colorful tuck-and-roll was dropped in favor of more traditional black vinyl. The products had a slant Kustom logo spelled-out and placed in a position on the grille similar to a Fender blackface baffle. Models included the I, II, III, and IV Lead amps. Heads with half- and full stacks were available. Bass amps included the Kustom 1, Bass I, II, III, IV, and IV SRO.

Black Vinyl K logo ('78-'83)

This era is easily recognized by the prominent capital K logo.

MODEL YEAR	FEATURES	LOW	HIGH

Bass V

1990s. Large Kustom Bass V logo upper right side of amp, 35 watts, 1x12", black vinyl.

1990s		$85	$130

Challenger Combo

1973-1975. 1x12" speaker.

1973-1975	Black	$300	$375
1973-1975	Color option	$425	$550

Hustler Combo

1973-1975. Solidstate, 4x10", tremolo, tuck-and-roll.

1973-1975	Black	$325	$425
1973-1975	Color option	$450	$575

K25/K25 C-2 SC

1960s. SC (self-contained) Series, small combo tuck-and-roll, 1x12", solidstate, reverb, black control panel.

1971-1973	Black	$300	$375
1971-1973	Color option	$450	$575

K50-2 SC

1971-1973. Self-contained (SC) small combo tuck-and-roll, 1x12", reverb and tremolo.

1971-1973	Black	$300	$375
1971-1973	Color option	$450	$575

K100-1 1-15C Bass Set

1968-1972. The K100-1 with 1-15C speaker option with matching 1x15" cab, black tuck-and-roll standard, but several sparkle colors offered, C.T.S. bass reflex speaker.

1968-1972	Black	$350	$450
1968-1972	Color option	$500	$625

K100-1 1-15L-1/1-15A-1/1-15J-1 Set

1968-1972. K100-1 with matching 1x15" cab, black tuck-and-roll standard, but several colors offered, speaker options are JBL, Altec Lansing or Jensen.

1968-1972	Black	$350	$450
1968-1972	Color option	$500	$625

MODEL YEAR	FEATURES	LOW	HIGH

K100-1 1-D140F Bass Set

1968-1972. K100-1 with matching 1x15" JBL D-140F cab, black tuck-and-roll standard, but several sparkle colors offered.

1968-1972	Black	$350	$450
1968-1972	Color option	$500	$625

K100-1 2-12C Bass Set

1968-1972. K100-1 with matching 2x12" cab, black tuck-and-roll standard, but several sparkle colors offered, C.T.S. bass reflex speakers.

1968-1972	Black	$400	$500
1968-1972	Color option	$800	$1,000

K100-2 1-15L-2/1-15A-2/1-15J-2 Set

1968-1972. K100-2 head and matching 1x15" cab, black tuck-and-roll standard, but several sparkle colors offered.

1968-1972	Black	$350	$450
1968-1972	Color option	$500	$625

K100-2 2-12A-2/2-12J-2 Set

1968-1972. K100-2 head with matching 2x12" cab, black tuck-and-roll standard, but several sparkle colors offered.

1968-1972	Black	$400	$500
1968-1972	Color option	$800	$1,000

K100-5 PA Head

1968-1972. 50 watts, 2 channels with 8 control knobs per channel, reverb.

1968-1972	Black	$450	$575

K100-6 SC

1970-1972. Basic combo amp with selectone, no reverb.

1970-1972	Black	$250	$325

K100-7 SC

1970-1972. Combo amp with reverb, tremolo, vibrato and boost.

1970-1972	Black	$300	$375
1970-1972	Color option	$450	$575

K100-8 SC

1970-1972. Combo amp with reverb, tremolo, vibrato and boost.

1970-1972	Black	$300	$375
1970-1972	Color option	$450	$575

K100C-6 Combo

1968-1970. Kustom 100 logo middle of the front control panel, 1x15" combo, selectone option.

1968-1970	Black	$300	$375
1968-1970	Color option	$450	$575

K100C-8 Combo

1968-1970. Kustom 100 logo middle of the front control panel, 4x10" combo, reverb, tremolo, vibrato.

1968-1970	Black	$400	$500

K150-1 Set

1972-1975. Piggyback, 150 watts, 2x12", no reverb, logo in upper right corner of amp head, tuck-and-roll, black or color option.

1972-1975	Color option	$450	$575

K150-2 Set

1972-1975. K150 with added reverb and tremolo, piggyback, 2x12", tuck-and-roll, black or color option.

1972-1975	Color option	$450	$575

MODEL YEAR	FEATURES	LOW	HIGH

K150-5 PA Set

1972-1975. PA head plus 2 PA cabs.

1972-1975		$400	$500

K150/150C Combo

1972-1975. Combo, 2x10".

1972-1975	Black	$300	$375

K200-1/K200B Bass Set

1966-1972. K200 head with 2x15" cab.

1966-1972	Black	$450	$575
1966-1972	Color option	$700	$875

K200-2 Reverb/Tremolo Set

1966-1972. K200-2 head with 2x15" or 3x12" cab, available with JBL D-140F speakers, Altec Lansing (A) speakers, C.T.S. (C), or Jensen (J).

1966-1972	Black	$450	$575
1966-1972	Color option	$750	$950

K250 Set

1971-1975. K250 head with 2x15" cab, tuck-and-roll cover.

1971-1975	Black	$400	$500
1971-1975	Color option	$750	$950

K300 PA Amp and Speaker Set

1971-1975. Includes 302 PA, 303 PA, 304 PA, 305 PA, head and 2 cabs.

1971-1975	Color option	$725	$900

K400-2 Reverb/Tremolo Set

1968-1972. 200 relative watts, reverb, tremolo, with 6x12" or 8x12" cab, available with JBL D-140F speakers, Altec Lansing (A), C.T.S. (C), or Jensen (J). The K400 was offered with no effects (suffix 1), with reverb and tremolo (suffix 2), with Harmonic Clipper & Boost (suffix 3), and Reverb/Trem/Clipper/Boost (suffix 4). The 400 heads came with a separate chrome amp head stand.

1968-1972	Black	$400	$500
1968-1972	Color option	$750	$950

KBA-10 Combo

Late-1980s-1990s. Compact solidstate bass amp, 10 watts, 1x8".

1990s		$40	$60

KBA-20 Combo

Late-1980s-early-1990s. KBA series were compact solidstate bass amps with built-in limiter, 20 watts, 1x8".

1989-1990		$40	$60

KBA-30 Combo

Late-1980s-early-1990s. 30 watts, 1x10".

1989-1990		$40	$60

KBA-40 Combo

Late-1980s-early-1990s. 40 watts, 1x12".

1989-1990		$65	$100

KBA-80 Combo

Late-1980s-early-1990s. 80 watts, 1x15".

1989-1990		$100	$125

KBA-160 Combo

Late-1980s-early-1990s. Solidstate bass amp with built-in limiter, 160 watts, 1x15".

1989-1990		$130	$175

KGA-10 VC

1999-2006. 10 watts, 1x6.5" speaker, switchable overdrive.

1999-2006		$40	$60

1968 Kustom K200-2

Imaged by Heritage Auctions, HA.com

Kustom K250

Tom Pfeifer

Kustom K400-2 Reverb

Lab Series L3 Combo

Laboga AD5200 SA

Carter Vintage Guitars

Landry LS30

MODEL YEAR	FEATURES	LOW	HIGH

KLA-15 Combo

Late-1980s-early-1990s. Solidstate, overdrive, 15 watts, 1x8".

1989-1990		$65	$100

KLA-20

Mid-1980s-late-1980s. 1x10", MOS-FET, gain, EQ, reverb, headphone jack.

1986		$65	$100

KLA-25 Combo

Late-1980s-early-1990s. Solidstate, overdrive, reverb, 25 watts, 1x10".

1989-1990		$65	$100

KLA-50 Combo

Late-1980s-early-1990s. Solidstate, overdrive, reverb, 50 watts, 1x12".

1989-1990		$100	$125

KLA-75

Mid-1980s-late-1980s. 75 watts, reverb, footswitching.

1987		$125	$175

KLA-100 Combo

Late-1980s-early-1990s. Solidstate, reverb, 100-watt dual channel, 1x12".

1989-1990		$125	$175

KLA-185 Combo

Late-1980s-early-1990s. Solidstate, reverb, 185-watt dual channel, 1x12".

1989-1990		$150	$200

KPB-200 Bass Combo

1994-1997. 200 watts, 1x15".

1994-1997		$250	$325

SC 1-12 SC

1971-1973. 50 watts, 1x12" Jensen speaker.

1971-1973	Black	$325	$425
1971-1973	Color option	$450	$575

SC 1-15 SC

1971-1973. 150 watts, 1x15" C.T.S. speaker.

1971-1973	Black	$325	$425
1971-1973	Color option	$450	$575

SC 1-15AB SC

1971-1973. 150 watts, 1x15" Altec Lansing speaker.

1971-1973	Black	$325	$425
1971-1973	Color option	$450	$575

SC 2-12A SC

1971-1973. 150 watts, 2x12" Altec Lansing speakers.

1971-1973	Black	$350	$450
1971-1973	Color option	$450	$575

SC 2-12J SC

1971-1973. 150 watts, 2x12" Jensen speakers.

1971-1973	Black	$350	$450
1971-1973	Color option	$450	$575

SC 4-10 SC

1971-1973. 150 watts, 4x10" Jensen speakers.

1971-1973	Black	$350	$450
1971-1973	Color option	$450	$575

Lab Series

1977-1980s. Five models of Lab Series amps, ranging in price from $600 to $3,700, were introduced at the '77 NAMM show by Norlin (then owner of Gibson). Two more were added later. The '80s models were Lab Series 2 amps and had a Gibson logo on the upper-left front.

B120 Bass Combo

Ca.1984. 120 watts, 2 channels, 1x15".

1984		$350	$450

G120 R-10 Combo

Ca.1984. 120 watts, 3-band EQ, channel switching, reverb, 4x10".

1984		$400	$500

G120 R-12 Combo

Ca.1984. 120 watts, 3-band EQ, channel switching, reverb, 2x12".

1984		$400	$600

L2 Head

1977-ca.1983. 100 watts, black covering.

1977-1983		$300	$375

L3 Combo

1977-ca.1983. 60-watt 1x12".

1977-1983		$350	$450

L4 Head

1977-ca.1983. Solidstate, 200 watts, black cover, dark grille, large L4 logo on front panel.

1977-1983		$275	$350

L5 Combo

1977-ca.1983. Solidstate, 100 watts, 2x12" combo.

1977-1983		$400	$500

L5 Set

1977-ca.1983. Solidstate, 100 watts, 2x12" piggyback.

1977-1983		$400	$500

L7 Set

1977-ca.1983. Solidstate, 100 watts, 4x10" piggyback.

1977-1983		$450	$575

L9 Combo

1977-ca.1983. Solidstate, 100 watts, 1x15".

1977-1983		$350	$450

L11 Set

1977-ca.1983. 200 watts, 8x12" piggyback.

1977-1983		$475	$600

Laboga

1973-present. Adam Laboga builds intermediate and professional grade, production, tube guitar amps and cabinets in Wroclaw, Poland.

Lace Music Products

1979-present. Lace Music Products, founded by pickup innovator Don Lace Sr., offered amplifiers for a while starting in '96. They also offered amps under the Rat Fink and Mooneyes brands.

Lafayette

Ca.1963-1967. Japanese-made guitars and amps sold through the Lafayette Electronics catalogs.

Tube

1960s. Japanese-made tube, gray speckle 1x12" with art deco design or black 2x12".

1960s	Larger, 2 speakers	$275	$375
1960s	Small, 1 speaker	$225	$300

MODEL YEAR	FEATURES	LOW	HIGH

Landry

2008-present. Production, professional grade, amps and cabinets built by Bill Landry in St. Louis, Missouri.

Laney

1968-present. Founded by Lyndon Laney and Bob Thomas in Birmingham, U.K. Laney offered tube amps exclusively into the '80s. Currently they offer intermediate and professional grade, tube and solidstate amp heads and combos and cabinets.

L60 60-Watt Head

1968-1969		$1,500	$2,000

L100 100-Watt Head

1968-1969. Similar to short head Plexi Marshall amp cab, 100 watts, large Laney with underlined "y" logo plate on front upper left corner, black vinyl cover, grayish grille.

1968-1969		$1,500	$2,000

Lectrolab

1950s-1960s. Budget house brand for music stores, made by Sound Projects Company of Cicero, Illinois. Similar to Valco, Oahu, and Danelectro student amps of the '50s, cabinets were generally made from inexpensive material. The Lectrolab logo can generally be found somewhere on the amp.

Tube

1950s-60s	Larger	$425	$650
1950s-60s	Small	$350	$500

Legend

1978-1984. From Legend Musical Instruments of East Syracuse, New York, these amps featured cool wood cabinets. They offered heads, combos with a 1x12" or 2x12" configuration, and cabinets with 1x12", 1x15", 2x12" or 4x12".

A-30

1978-1984. Natural wood cabinet, 30 watts, 1x12".

1978-1984		$450	$575

A-60

1978-1984. Natural wood cabinet, transtube design dual tube preamp with solidstate power section.

1978-1984		$575	$725

Rock & Roll 50

1978-1983. Mesa-Boogie-style wood compact amp, head/half stack or 1x12", 1x15" or 2x12" combo, tube preamp section and solidstate power supply.

1978-1983	1x12" combo	$425	$550
1978-1983	1x15" combo	$425	$550
1978-1983	2x12" combo	$575	$725
1978-1983	Half stack set	$825	$1,125

Super Lead 50

1978-1983. Rock & Roll 50-watt model with added bass boost and reverb, 1x12", hybrid tube and solidstate.

1978-1983		$425	$550

Super Lead 100

1978-1983. 100-watt version, 2x12".

1978-1983		$550	$700

Lenahan

Professional grade, production/custom, vintage-style amps and cabinets built by James T. Lenahan - presently in Fort Smith, Arkansas and prior to '91 in Hollywood, California - starting in 1983. He also built guitar effects.

Leslie

Most often seen with Hammond organs, the cool Leslie rotating speakers have been adopted by many guitarists. Many guitar effects have tried to duplicate their sound. And they are still making them.

16 Rotating Speaker Cabinet

1960s-1970s. 1 cab.

1960s-70s		$750	$1,000

60M Rotating Speaker Cabinets

1960s-1970s. 2 cabs.

1960s-70s		$625	$800

103

1960s. Maximum power 22 watts.

1960s		$625	$800

118

1960s. 1x12".

1960s		$750	$1,000

122A

1960s. Hammond-only model, considered the official Hammond B-3 Leslie. RV indicates reverb.

1960s		$1,250	$2,000

125

Late-1960s. All tube amp with 2-speed rotating 1x12" speaker, bottom rotor only, less features.

1960s		$950	$1,500

142

1960s. Hammond-only model, smaller cabinet than 122 amp.

1960s		$1,250	$2,000

145

1960s. Similar to 147 amp, but smaller and easier to move.

1960s		$1,250	$2,000

147A

1960s. Universal-use model, "7" denotes "universal" usage. RV has added reverb.

1960s		$1,250	$2,000

Lickliter Amplification

In 2009, Michael Lickliter began building professional and premium grade, custom, guitar amps in Punta Gorda, Florida.

Line 6

1996-present. Founded by Marcus Ryle and Michel Doidic and specializing in digital signal processing in both effects and amps. They also produce tube amps. Purchased by Yamaha in 2014.

Little Lanilei

1997-present. Small hand-made, intermediate grade, production/custom, amps made by Mahaffay Amplifiers (formerly Songworks Systems & Products) of Aliso Viejo, California. They also build a reverb unit and a rotary effect.

1980 Legend Rock & Roll 50
Alex Xenos

1967 Leslie 330
Imaged by Heritage Auctions, HA.com

Little Lanilei

AMPS

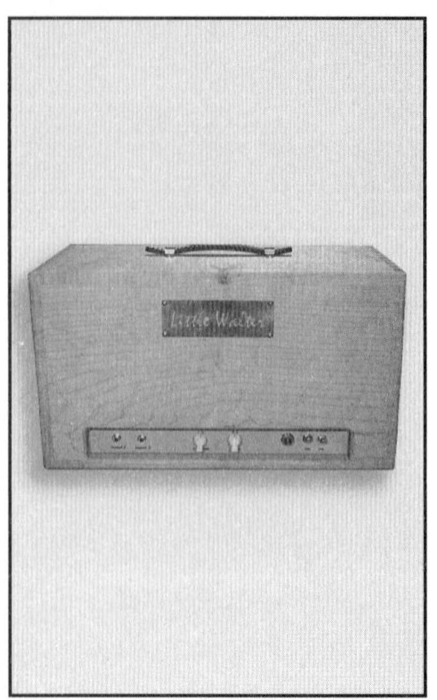

Little Walter 30W

Louis Electric Deltone

1960 Gibson Maestro GA-16T Viscount
Rivington Guitars

MODEL YEAR	FEATURES	LOW	HIGH

Little Walter

2008-present. Phil Bradbury builds his professional grade, production, amp heads and cabinets in West End, North Carolina.

London City

Late 1960s-early 1970s. Intermediate to professional grade amps and cabinets made in Netherlands, London City logo.

Louis Electric Amplifier Co.

1993-present. Founded by Louis Rosano in Bergenfield, New Jersey. Louis produces custom-built tweeds and various combo amps from 35 to 80 watts.

Luker

Professional grade, production/custom, guitar and bass amps and cabinets built in Eugene, Oregon by Ken Luker, starting in 2006.

Luna Guitars

2005-present. Located in Tampa, Florida, Yvonne de Villiers imports her budget to professional grade, production, acoustic and electric guitars from Japan, Korea, and China. She also imports guitars, basses and ukes.

Lyric

Late 1950s-ca. 1965. One of several private brands that Magnatone made for others, these were built for Lyric Electronics, located in Lomita, California.

Model 660 Custom

Ca. 1959-ca. 1965. 2x12" combo amp, 35 watts.

1959-1965		$1,750	$2,250

Mack

2005-2019. Made in Toronto, Ontario by builder Don Mackrill, the company offered intermediate and professional grade, production, tube amps.

Mad Professor

2002-present. Bjorn Juhl and Jukka Monkkonen built their premium grade, production/custom, tube amps in Tampere, Finland. In '24 they sold the company to Mikko Karikko and Jusa Palve. They also offer effects pedals.

Maestro

Maestro amps are associated with Gibson and were included in the Gibson catalogs. For example, in the '62-'63 orange cover Gibson catalog, tweed Maestro amps were displayed in their own section. Tweed Maestro amps are very similar to Gibson tweed amps. Maestro amps were often associated with accordions in the early-'60s but the amps featured standard guitar inputs. Gibson also used the Maestro name on effects in the '60s and '70s and in 01, Gibson revived the name for a line of effects, banjos, and mandolins and added guitars and amps in '09.

MODEL YEAR	FEATURES	LOW	HIGH

The prices listed are for amps with fully intact logos. A broken or missing logo may diminish the value of the amp. Amps with a changed handle, power cord, and especially a broken logo, should be taken on a case-by-case basis.

Amp models in '58 include the Super Maestro and Maestro, in '60 the Stereo Maestro Accordion GA-87, Super Maestro Accordion GA-46 T, Standard Accordion GA-45 T, Viscount Accordion GA-16 T, in '62 the Reverb-Echo GA-1 RT, Reverb-Echo GA-2 RT, 30 Stereo Accordion Amp, Stereo Accordion GA-78 RV.

GA-1 RT Reverb-Echo

1961. Tweed, 1x8".

1961		$750	$950

GA-2 RT Deluxe Reverb-Echo

1961. Deluxe more powerful version of GA-1 RT, 1x12", tweed.

1961		$1,625	$2,250

GA-15 RV/Bell 15 RV

1961. 15 watts, 1x12", gray sparkle.

1961		$950	$1,250

GA-16T Viscount

1959-1961. 14 watts, 1x10", white cab with brown grille.

1959-1961		$750	$950

GA-45 Maestro

1955-1961. 14-16 watts, 4x8", 2-tone.

1955-1961		$1,500	$2,000

GA-45 RV Standard

1961. 16 watts, 4x8", reverb.

1961		$1,500	$2,000

GA-45T Standard Accordion

1961. 16 watts, 4x8", tremolo.

1961		$1,500	$2,000

GA-46T Super Maestro Accordion and Bass

1957-1961. Based on the Gibson GA-200 and advertised to be designed especially for amplified accordions, 60 watts, 2x12", vibrato, 2-tone cover, large Maestro Super logo on top center of grille.

1957-1961		$2,250	$2,750

GA-78 Maestro Series

1960-1961. Wedge stereo cab, 2x10", reverb and tremolo.

1960-1961	GA-78 RV Maestro 30	$2,500	$3,250
1960-1961	GA-78 RVS	$2,250	$3,000
1960-1961	GA-78 RVT	$2,250	$3,000

Magnatone

Ca.1937-1971, 2013-present. Magnatone made a huge variety of amps sold under their own name and under brands like Dickerson, Oahu, Bronson, and Estey (see separate listings). They also private branded amps for several accordion companies or accordion teaching studios like Ariatone, Audio Guild, Da Vinci, Excelsior, Giulietti, Lyric, Noble, PAC-AMP, PANaramic, Titano, Tonemaster, Twilighter, and Unique (see separate listings). In 2013, Ted Kornblum revived the Magnatone name on a

MODEL YEAR	FEATURES	LOW	HIGH

line of tube amps based on the earlier models and built in St. Louis, Missouri.

Model 108 Varsity/Varsity Deluxe

1948-1954. Gray pearloid cover, small student amp or lap steel companion amp.

1948-1954		$525	$700

Model 109 Melodier Deluxe

1950s. 10 watts, 2 speakers.

1950s		$775	$975

Model 110 Melodier

1953-1954. 12 watts, 1x10", brown leatherette cover, light grille.

1953-1954		$700	$875

Model 111 Student

1955-1959. 1x8", 2-3 watts, brown leatherette, brown grille.

1955-1959		$450	$575

Model 112/113 Troubadour

1955-1959. 18 watts, 1x12", brown leatherette, brown grille, slant back rear control panel.

1955-1959		$900	$1,125

Model 118

1960. Compact, tubes, low power, volume and tone knobs, brown tolex era, Model 118 logo on rear-mounted control panel.

1960		$500	$625

Model 120B Cougar Bass

1967-1968. Initial Magnatone entry into the solid-state market, superseded by Brute Series in '68, 120 watts, 2x12" solidstate bass piggyback amp, naugahyde vinyl cover with polyester rosewood side panels.

1967-1968		$425	$550

Model 120R Sting Ray Reverb Bass

1967-1968. Initial Magnatone entry into the solid-state market, superseded by Brute Series in '68, 150 watts, 4x10" solidstate combo amp, naugahyde vinyl cover with polyester rosewood side panels.

1967-1968		$475	$600

Model 130V Custom

1969-1971. Solidstate 1x12" combo amp.

1969-1971		$300	$375

Model 150R Firestar Reverb

1967-1968. Initial Magnatone entry into the solid-state market, superseded by Brute Series in '68, 120 watts, 2x12" solidstate combo amp, naugahyde vinyl cover with polyester rosewood side panels.

1967-1968		$325	$425

Model 180 Triplex

Mid-to-late-1950s. Mid-level power using 2 6L6 power tubes, 1x15" and 1x8" speakers.

1950s		$1,125	$1,500

Model 192-5-S Troubadour

Early-1950s. 18 watts, 1x12" Jensen Concert speaker, brown alligator covering, lower back control panel, 3 chicken-head knobs, Magnatone script logo on front, Troubadour script logo on back control panel.

1950s		$700	$875

Model 194 Lyric

1947-mid-1950s. 1x12" speaker, old-style tweed vertical cab typical of '40s.

1940s		$600	$750

Model 195 Melodier

1951-1954. Vertical cab with 1x10" speaker, pearloid with flowing grille slats.

1951-1954		$600	$750

Model 196

1947-mid-1950s. 1x12", 5-10 watts, scroll grille design, snakeskin leatherette cover.

1940s		$600	$750

Model 197 V Varsity

1948-1952. Small compact student amp, 1x8", tubes, Varsity model logo and model number on back panel, old style layout with back bottom-mounted chassis, curved crossbars on front baffle, brown lizard leatherette, leather handle.

1948-1952		$550	$700

Model 198 Varsity

1948-1954. 1x8", tubes.

1948-1954		$600	$750

Model 199 Student

1950s. About 6 to 10 watts, 1x8", snakeskin leatherette cover, metal handle, slant grille design.

1950s		$600	$750

Model 210 Deluxe Student

1958-1960. 5 watts, 1x8", vibrato, brown leatherette, V logo lower right front on grille.

1958-1960		$600	$750

Model 213 Troubadour

1957-1958. 10 watts, 1x12", vibrato, brown leatherette cover, V logo lower right of grille.

1957-1958		$1,375	$1,750

Model 240 SV Magna-Chordion

1967-1968. Initial Magnatone entry into the solid-state market, superseded by Brute Series in '68, 240 watts, 2x12" solidstate stereo accordion or organ amp, naugahyde vinyl cover, polyester rosewood side panels, input jacks suitable for guitar, reverb and vibrato, lateral combo cab, rear mounted controls.

1967-1968		$425	$550

Model 250 Professional

1958-1960. 20 watts, 1x12", vibrato, brown leatherette with V logo lower right front of grille.

1958-1960		$1,125	$1,500

Model 260

1957-1958. 35 watts, 2x12", brown leatherette, vibrato, V logo lower right front corner of grille.

1957-1958		$1,625	$2,000

Model 262 Jupiter/Custom Pro

1961-1963. 35 watts, 2x12", vibrato, brown leatherette.

1961-1963		$1,250	$1,500

Model 280/Custom 280

1957-1958. 50 watts, brown leatherette covering, brown-yellow tweed grille, 2x12" plus 2x5" speakers, double V logo.

1957-1958		$1,625	$2,000

Model 280A

1958-1960. 50 watts, brown leatherette covering, brown-yellow tweed grille, 2x12" plus 2x5" speakers, V logo lower right front.

1958-1960		$1,625	$2,000
1958-1960	With matching cab	$2,250	$3,000

1950s Magnatone Model 192-5 Troubadour

Tom Pfeifer

Magnatone 195 Melodier

Tom Pfeifer

1958 Magnatone Model 210

tednugentlives

AMPS

1961 Magnatone Model 410

Magnatone 480 Venus

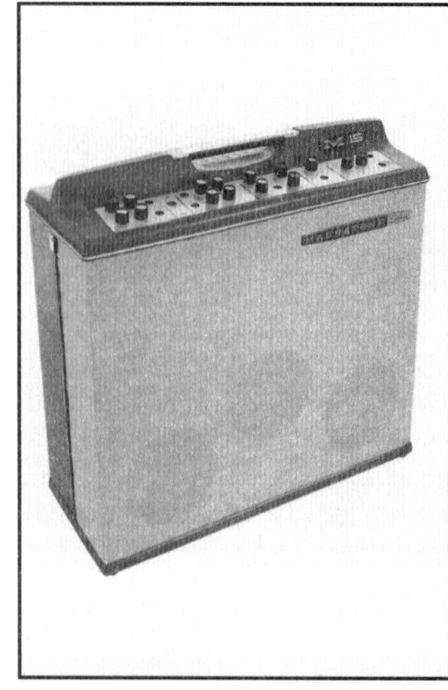
Ca.1969 Magnatone Model M15
Rivington Guitars

MODEL YEAR	FEATURES	LOW	HIGH

Model 410 Diana
1961-1963. Five watts, 1x12", advertised as a 'studio' low power professional amp, brown leatherette cover, vibrato.

1961-1963		$750	$950

Model 411 Estey
1960s. Tubes, 15 watts, 1x8".

1960s		$1,375	$1,750

Model 412
1960s. Estey era compact student amp, low power, 1x8", tubes.

1960s		$325	$425

Model 413 Centaur
1961-1963. 18 watts, 1x12", brown leatherette cover, vibrato.

1961-1963		$1,125	$1,500

Model 415 Clio Bass
1961-1963. 25 watts, 4x8", bass or accordion amp, brown leatherette cover.

1961-1963		$1,125	$1,500

Model 422
1966-1967. Low power 1x12", 3 inputs, black vinyl, light swirl grille.

1966-1967		$625	$800

Model 425
1961. Tube, 55 watts, 4x12".

1961		$1,500	$1,875

Model 432
Mid-1960s. Compact student model, wavey-squiggle art deco-style grille, black cover, vibrato and reverb.

1960s		$700	$875

Model 435 Athene Bass
1961-1963. 55 watts, 4x10", piggyback head and cab, brown leatherette.

1961-1963		$1,375	$1,750

Model 440 Mercury
1961-1963. 18 watts, 1x12", vibrato, brown leatherette.

1961-1963		$1,250	$1,500

Model 450 Juno/Twin Hi-Fi
1961-1963. 25 watts, 1x12" and 1 oval 5"x7" speakers, reverb, vibrato, brown leatherette.

1961-1963		$1,375	$1,750
1961-1963	Extension cab only	$700	$875

Model 460 Victory
1961-1963. 35 watts, 2x12" and 2 oval 5"x7" speakers, early-'60s next to the top-of-the-line, reverb and vibrato, brown leatherette.

1961-1963		$1,500	$1,875

Model 480 Venus
1961-1963. 50 watts, 2x12" and 2 oval 5"x7" speakers, early-'60s top-of-the-line, reverb and stereo vibrato, brown leatherette.

1961-1963		$1,375	$1,750

Model M2
1963-1964. 1x8", 12-15 watts, 1 channel.

1963-1964		$425	$550

Model M6
1964 (not seen in '65 catalog). 25 watts, 1x12", black molded plastic suitcase amp.

1964		$600	$750

Model M7 Bass
1964-1966. 38 watts, 1x15" bass amp, black molded plastic suitcase amp.

1964-1966		$625	$800

Model M8
1964-1966. 27 watts, 1x12", reverb and tremolo, black molded plastic suitcase amp.

1964-1966		$675	$850

Model M9
1964-1966. 38 watts, 1x15", tremolo, no reverb, black molded plastic suitcase amp.

1964-1966		$675	$850

Model M10/M10A
1964-1966. 38 watts, 1x15", tone boost, tremolo, transistorized reverb section, black molded plastic suitcase amp.

1964-1966		$650	$825

Model M12 Bass
1964-1966. 80 watts, 1x15" or 2x12", mid-'60s top-of-the-line bass amp, black molded plastic suitcase amp.

1964-1966		$675	$850

Model M13 Imperial
Mid-1963-1964. 1x15", 45 watts, 3 channels.

1963-1964		$675	$850

Model M14
1964-1966. Stereo, 75 watts, 2x12" plus 2 tweeters, stereo vibrato, no reverb, black molded plastic suitcase amp.

1964-1966		$875	$1,125

Model M15
1964-1966. Stereo 75 watts, 2x12" plus 2 tweeters, stereo vibrato, transistorized reverb, black molded plastic suitcase amp.

1964-1966		$900	$1,125

Model M27 Bad Boy Bass
1968-1971. 150 watts, 2x15" (1 passive), reverb, vibrato, solidstate, vertical profile bass amp, part of Brute Series.

1968-1971		$375	$500

Model M30 Fang
1968-1971. 150 watts, 2x15" (1 passive), 1 exponential horn, solidstate, vibrato, reverb, vertical profile amp.

1968-1971		$375	$500

Model M32 Big Henry Bass
1968-1971. 300 watts, 2x15" solidstate vertical profile bass amp.

1968-1971		$375	$500

Model M35 The Killer
1968-1971. 300 watts, 2x15" and 2 horns, solidstate, vibrato, vertical profile amp.

1968-1971		$375	$500

Model MP-1 (Magna Power I)
1966-1967. 30 watts, 1x12", dark vinyl, light grille, Magnatone-Estey logo on upper right of grille.

1966-1967		$675	$850

Model MP-3 (Magna Power 3)
1966-1967. Mid-power, 2x12", reverb, dark vinyl, light grille, Magnatone-Estey logo on upper right of grille.

1966-1967		$775	$975

MODEL YEAR	FEATURES	LOW	HIGH

Model MP-5 (Magna Power)

1966-1967. Mid-power, piggyback 2x12", Magnatone-Estey logo on upper right of grille.

1966-1967		$825	$1,125

Model PS150

1968-1971. Powered slave speaker cabinets, 150 watts, 2x15" linkable cabinets.

1968-1971		$225	$300

Model PS300

1968-1971. Powered slave speaker cabinets, 300 watts, 2x15" (1 passive) linkable cabinets.

1968-1971		$225	$300

Small Pearloid

1947-1955. Pearloid (MOTS) covered low- and mid-power amps generally associated with pearloid lap steel sets.

1947-1955	Fancy grille	$425	$550
1947-1955	Plain grille	$300	$375

Starlet Model 107

1951-1952. Student model, 1x8", pearloid cover early, leatherette later, low power, single on-off volume control, Starlet logo on back panel, Magnatone logo plate upper left front of grille.

1951-1954	Pearloid	$425	$550
1955-1959	Leatherette	$375	$500

Starlite Model 401

1964-1966. Magnatone produced the mid-'60s Starlite amplifier line for the budget minded musician. Each Starlite model prominently notes the Magnatone name. The grilles show art deco wavy circles. Magnatone 1960-'63 standard amps offer models starting with 12" speakers. Starlite models offer 10" and below. Model 401 has 15 watts, 1x8" and 3 tubes.

1964-1966		$375	$500

Starlite Model 411

1964-1966. 15 watts, 1x8", 5 tubes, tremolo (not advertised as vibrato), art deco wavy grille.

1964-1966		$425	$550

Starlite Model 441A Bass

1964-1966. Lower power with less than 25 watts, 1x15", tube amp.

1964-1966		$625	$800

Starlite Model Custom 421

1964-1966. Tube amp, 25 watts, 1x10".

1964-1966		$625	$800

Starlite Model Custom 431

1964-1966. Tube amp, 30 watts, 1x10", vibrato and reverb.

1964-1966		$650	$825

Mahaffay Amplifiers

2009-present. See Little Lanilei.

Mako

1985-1989. Line of solidstate amps from Kaman (Ovation, Hamer). They also offered guitars and basses.

Marlboro Sound Works

1970-1980s. Economy solidstate amps imported by Musical Instruments Corp., Syosset, New York. Initially, Marlboro targeted the economy compact amp market, but quickly added larger amps and PAs.

Solid State

1970-1980s	Various models	$45	$65

Marshall

1962-present. Drummer Jim Marshall (1923-2012) started building bass speaker and PA cabinets in his garage in 1960. He opened a retail drum shop for his students and others and soon added guitars and amps. When Ken Bran joined the business as service manager in '62, the two decided to build their own amps. By '63 they had expanded the shop to house a small manufacturing space and by late that year they were offering the amps to other retailers. Marshall also made amps under the Park, CMI, Narb, Big M, and Kitchen-Marshall brands.

Mark I, II, III and IVs are generally '60s and '70s and also are generally part of a larger series (for example JTM) or have a model number that is a more specific identifier. Describing an amp only as Mark II can be misleading. The most important identifier is the Model Number, which Marshall often called the Stock Number. To help avoid confusion we have added the Model number as often as possible. In addition, when appropriate, we have included the wattage, number of channels, master or no-master info in the title. This should help the reader more quickly find a specific amp. Check the model's description for such things as two inputs or four inputs, because this will help with identification. Vintage Marshall amps do not always have the Model/Stock number on the front or back panel, so the additional identifiers should help. The JMP logo on the front is common and really does not help with specific identification. For example, a JMP Mark II Super Lead 100-Watt description is less helpful than the actual model/stock number. Unfortunately, many people are not familiar with specific model/stock numbers. VG has tried to include as much information in the title as space will allow.

Marshall amps are sorted as follows:

- AVT Series - Advanced Valvestate Technology
- Club and Country Series (Rose-Morris)-introduced in '78
- JCM 800 Series - basically the '80s
- JCM 900 Series - basically the '90s
- JCM 2000 Series - basically the '00s
- JTM Series
- Micro Stack Group
- Model Number/Stock Number (no specific series, basically the '60s, '70s) - including Artist and Valvestate models (Valvestate refers to specific Model numbers in 8000 Series)
- Silver Jubilee Series

Acoustic Soloist (AS) Series

1994-present. Acoustic guitar amps, models include AS50R and D (50 watts, 2 channels, 2x8"), AS80R (40-watt x2 stereo, 3 channels, 2x8"), AS100D (50-watt x2 stereo, 4 channels, 2x8").

1994-2024	Various models	$225	$300

1966 Magnatone MP-1

Imaged by Heritage Auctions, HA.com

1950 Magnatone Small Pearloid

Marshall AS100D

Marshall Code 25

1986 Marshall JCM 800 2204
Scott Davis

Marshall JCM 900 Model 4100 Dual Reverb
Imaged by Heritage Auctions, HA.com

MODEL YEAR	FEATURES	LOW	HIGH

AVT 20
2001-2011. Solidstate, 20 watts, 12AX7 preamp tube, 1x10", Advanced Valvestate Technology (AVT) models have black covering and grille, and gold panel.
2001-2011 Combo $150 $200

AVT 50
2001-2011. Solidstate, 50 watts, 4x12".
2001-2011 Combo $200 $275
2001-2011 Head & cab $425 $575

AVT 100
2001-2011. Solidstate, 100 watts, tube preamp, 1x12".
2001-2011 $250 $350

AVT 150
2001-2011. Solidstate, additional features over AVT 100. Combo (100 watts, 1x12"), Half-Stack (150 watts, 4x12") and Head only (150 watts).
2001-2011 Combo $250 $350
2001-2011 Half-stack $325 $450

AVT 275
2001-2007. Solidstate DFX stereo, 75 watts per side, 2x12".
2001-2007 Combo $300 $400

Capri
1966-1967. Only about 100 made, 5 watts, 1x8, 2x8 or 1x10 combo, red cover.
1966-1967 $2,000 $2,500

Class 5
2009-2014. 5 watts, 1x10" tube combo.
2009-2014 Head $250 $375
2009-2014 Head & cab $350 $450

Club and Country Model 4140
1978-1982. Tubes, 100 watts, 2x12" combo, Rose-Morris era, designed for the country music market, hence the name, brown vinyl cover, straw grille.
1978-1982 $1,000 $1,250

Club and Country Model 4145
1978-1982. Tubes, 100 watts, 4x10" combo, Rose-Morris era, designed for the country music market, hence the name, brown vinyl, straw grille.
1978-1982 $1,000 $1,250

Club and Country Model 4150 Bass
1978-1982. Tubes, 100 watts, 4x10" bass combo, Rose-Morris era, designed for the country music market, hence the name, brown vinyl cover, straw grille.
1978-1982 $1,000 $1,250

Code Series
2016-present. Marshall-Softube (MST) modelling, digital capabilities, series includes CODE25, 50, 100 and 100H. Number indicates watts.
2016-2024 $120 $165

Haze (MHZ) Series
2009-2014. All tube, multi-functional amps, MHZ15 (15w, head, 2 cabs), 40C (40w, 1x12 combo) 215 (15w, 2x1x12).
2009-2014 MHZ15 $550 $700
2009-2014 MHZ40C $350 $450

JCM 600 Series
1997-2000. All tube, 60-watt models with modern features, includes the JCM600 head, JCM601 1x12" combo and JCM602 2x12" combo.
1997-2000 JCM600 $450 $600
1997-2000 JCM601 $500 $650
1997-2000 JCM602 $600 $750

JCM 800 Model 1959 Head
1981-1991. 100 watts.
1981-1991 $2,000 $2,500

JCM 800 Model 1987 Head
1981-1991. 50 watts.
1981-1991 $2,000 $2,500

JCM 800 Model 1992 Bass Head
1981-1986. Active tone circuit.
1981-1986 $2,000 $2,500

JCM 800 Model 2000 Head
1981-1982. 200 watts.
1981-1982 $2,000 $2,500

JCM 800 Model 2001 Head
1981-1982. Bass head, 300 watts.
1981-1982 $2,000 $2,500

JCM 800 Model 2004 Head
1981-1990. 50 watts, master.
1981-1990 $2,000 $2,500

JCM 800 Model 2004S Head
1986-1987. 50 watts, short head.
1986-1987 $2,000 $2,500

JCM 800 Model 2005 Full Stack
1983-1990. Limited Edition, 2005 head with 2 2x12 cabs.
1983-1990 $2,500 $3,500

JCM 800 Model 2005 Head
1983-1990. 50 watts, split channel.
1983-1990 $2,000 $2,500

JCM 800 Model 2203 20th Anniversary Half Stack
1982. 20th Anniversary plate in lower right corner of matching 1960A cab, matching white tolex cover.
1982 $4,500 $5,500

JCM 800 Model 2203 Head
1981-1990, 2002-2020. 100 watts, master volume, reissued '02 in Vintage Series.
1981-1990 Full stack $4,500 $6,000
1981-1990 Head only $2,250 $2,875
2002-2020 Reissue $1,500 $1,875

JCM 800 Model 2203KK Kerry King Signature
2008-2012. King Signature logo, 100 watts, 3-band EQ.
2008-2012 $1,500 $1,875

JCM 800 Model 2203ZW Zack Wylde Signature
2002. About 600 amp heads and 60 half-stacks made.
2002 Half-stack $3,500 $4,500
2002 Head only $2,250 $2,875

JCM 800 Model 2204 Head
1981-1990. 50 watts, 1 channel, 2 inputs, master volume, front panel says JCM 800 Lead Series, back panel says Master Model 50w Mk 2.
1981-1990 Full stack $3,000 $4,000
1981-1990 Head only $2,000 $2,500

JCM 800 Model 2204S Head
1986-1987. Short head, 50 watts.
1986-1987 $2,000 $2,500

MODEL YEAR	FEATURES	LOW	HIGH

JCM 800 Model 2205

1983-1990. 50 watts, split channel (1 clean and 1 distortion), switchable, both channels with reverb, 4x12" cabinet, front panel reads JCM 800 Lead Series.

1983-1990	Cab	$650	$850
1983-1990	Head only	$1,625	$2,000

JCM 800 Model 2210 Head

1983-1990. 100 watts.

1983-1990		$2,000	$2,500

JCM 800 Model 4010 Combo

1980-1990. 50 watts, 1x12", non-reverb ('80), reverb begins '81, single channel master volume.

1980-1990		$1,625	$2,000

JCM 800 Model 4103 Combo

1981-1990. Lead combo amp, 100 watts, 2x12".

1981-1990		$1,625	$2,000

JCM 800 Model 4104 Combo

1980-1990. Tube lead amp, 50 watts, 2x12".

1980-1990	Black	$1,625	$2,000
1980-1990	Head only	$1,500	$1,875
1980-1990	White option	$1,625	$2,000

JCM 800 Model 4210 Combo

1982-1990. 50 watts, 1x12" tube combo, split-channel, single input, master volume.

1982-1990		$1,625	$2,000

JCM 800 Model 4211 Combo

1983-1990. Lead combo amp, 100 watts, 2x12".

1983-1990		$1,625	$2,000

JCM 800 Model 4212 Combo

1983-1990. 50-watt, 2x12" combo.

1983-1990		$1,250	$1,500

JCM 800 Model 5010 Combo

1983-1991. Solidstate, 30 watts, master volume, 1x12".

1983-1991		$350	$500

JCM 800 Model 5150 Combo

1987-1991. Solidstate, 150 watts, 12" Celestion, 2 channels, presence and effects-mix master controls.

1987-1991		$400	$600

JCM 800 Model 5210 Combo

1986-1991. Solidstate, 50 watts, channel switching, 1x12".

1986-1991		$350	$500

JCM 800 Model 5212 Combo

1986-1991. Solidstate, 50 watts, 2x12" split channel reverb combo.

1986-1991		$450	$650

JCM 800 Model 5213 Combo

1986-1991. Solidstate, 2x12", channel-switching, effects loop.

1986-1991		$350	$500

JCM 800 Model 5215 Combo

1986-1991. Solidstate, 1x15", Accutronics reverb, effects loop.

1986-1991		$350	$500

JCM 900 Model 2100 Mark III Head

1990-1993. FX loop, 100/50-watt selectable lead head.

1990-1993		$850	$1,125

JCM 900 Model 2100 SL-X Head

1992-1998. Hi-gain 100-watt head amp, additional 12AX7 preamp tube.

1992-1998		$850	$1,125

JCM 900 Model 2500 SL-X Head

1990-2000. 50-watt version of SL-X.

1992-1998		$850	$1,125

JCM 900 Model 4100 Dual Reverb

1990-2017. Vintage Series, 100/50 switchable head, JCM 900 on front panel, 4x10 or 2x12 matching cab, black with black front.

1990-2017	4x10 or 2x12	$550	$700
1990-2017	Head only	$625	$950

JCM 900 Model 4101 Combo

1990-2000. All tube, 100 watts, 1x12" combo.

1990-2000		$850	$1,125

JCM 900 Model 4102 Combo

1990-2000. Combo amp, 100/50 watts switchable, 2x12".

1990-2000		$850	$1,125

JCM 900 Model 4500 Head

1990-2000. All tube, 2 channels, 50/25 watts, EL34 powered, reverb, effects loop, compensated recording out, master volume, black.

1990-2000		$750	$975

JCM 900 Model 4501 Dual Reverb Combo

1990-2000. 50/25 switchable, 1x12".

1990-2000		$800	$1,125

JCM 900 Model 4502 Combo

1990-2000. 50/25 switchable, 2x12".

1990-2000		$800	$1,125

JCM 2000 DSL Series

1998-2015. DSL is Dual Super Lead, 2 independent channels labelled classic and ultra, JCM 2000 and DSL logos both on front panel.

1998-2015	Half-stacks/combos	$300	$850

JCM 2000 TSL Series

1998-2013. TSL is Triple Super Lead, 3 independent channels labelled clean, crunch and lead, 8 tubes, JCM 2000 and TSL logos both on front panel.

1998-2013	Full-stacks	$1,500	$1,875
1998-2013	Half-stacks/combos	$750	$950

JCM Slash Signature Model 2555SL Set

1996. Based on JCM 800 with higher gain, matching amp and cab set, JCM Slash Signature logo on front panel, single channel, Slash Signature 1960AV 4x12" slant cab, black.

1996	4x12 cab	$750	$1,125
1996	Head only	$2,000	$2,500

JMD Series

2010-2013. JMD is Jim Marshall Digital. Models include JMD50 & 100 heads and JMD 102 (100w, 2x12) & 501 (50w, 1x12) combos.

2010-2013	501	$500	$675

JTM 30 Series

1995-1997. Tube combo, reverb, 30 watts, effects loops, 5881 output sections, foot switchable high-gain modes. Available as 1x15", 1x12", 2x12" or 3x10" combo or as 4x10" half-stack.

1995-1997	Combo 1x12	$425	$575
1995-1997	Combo 2x10	$450	$575
1995-1997	Combo 2x12	$475	$625
1995-1997	Combo 3x10	$475	$625

2003 Marshall JCM 2000 DSL

Imaged by Heritage Auctions, HA.com

Marshall JCM 2000 TSL

Imaged by Heritage Auctions, HA.com

Marshall JTM 45 1961 MK IV

Pang Leo

AMPS

Marshall JTM 50 Model 1962 Bluesbreaker Reissue

Marshall JVM210C

Marshall MG10

AMPS

MODEL YEAR	FEATURES	LOW	HIGH

JTM 45 Head

1962-1964. Amp head, 45 watts. The original Marshall amp. Became the Model 1987 45-watt for '65-'66.

1962	Coffin logo	$18,000	$25,000
1963-1964	Block logo	$9,000	$15,000

JTM 45 Model 1961 MK IV 4x10 Combo

1965-1966. 45 watts, 4x10", tremolo, JTM 45 MK IV on panel, Bluesbreaker association.

1965-1966		$7,500	$10,000

JTM 45 Model 1962 MK IV 2x12 Combo

1965-1966. 45 watts, 2x12", tremolo, JTM 45 MK IV on panel, Bluesbreaker association.

1965-1966		$8,000	$10,500

JTM 45 Model 1987 Head Reissue

1988-1999. Black/green tolex.

1988-1999		$1,750	$2,250

JTM 45 Model 1987 Mark II Lead Head

1965-1966. Replaced JTM 45 Amp ('62-'64) but was subsequently replaced by the Model 1987 50-watt Head during '66.

1965-1966		$6,500	$8,500

JTM 45 Offset Limited Edition Set Reissue

Introduced in 2000. Limited run of 300 units, old style cosmetics, 45-watt head and offset 2x12" cab, dark vinyl cover, light gray grille, rectangular logo plate on front of amp and cab, Limited Edition plate on rear of cab, serial number xxx of 300.

2000		$3,500	$4,500

JTM 50 Head

1966-1967. Script logo, JTM 50 panel logo, EL34 power tubes.

1966-1967		$7,500	$10,000

JTM 50 Model 1961 MK IV 4x10 Combo

1965-1972. 50 watts, "Bluesbreaker," 4x10", tremolo, JTM 50 MK IV on front panel to '68, plain front panel without model description '68-'72.

1966-1967		$8,000	$10,500
1968		$7,000	$9,500
1969		$6,000	$8,000
1970		$5,000	$6,500
1971-1972		$4,500	$6,000

JTM 50 Model 1962 Bluesbreaker Reissue

1989-1999. 50 watts, 2x12", Model 1962 reissue Bluesbreaker.

1989-1999		$1,500	$2,000

JTM 50 Model 1962 MK IV 2x12 Combo

1966-1972. 50 watts, "Bluesbreaker," 2x12", tremolo, JTM 50 MK IV on front panel to '68, plain front panel without model description '68-'72.

1966-1967	"Bluesbreaker"	$13,500	$18,000
1968		$7,500	$10,000
1969		$6,500	$8,500
1970		$6,000	$8,000
1971-1972		$5,000	$6,500

JTM 50 Model 1963 PA Head

1965-1966. MK II PA head, block logo.

1965-1966		$2,500	$3,500

JTM 60 Series

1995-1997. Tube, 60 watts, 1x12", 1x15", 2x12" or 3x10" combo or as 4x10" half-stack.

1995-1997	1x12 Combo	$500	$650
1995-1997	2x12 Combo	$525	$700
1995-1997	3x10 Combo	$550	$725
1995-1997	4x10 Mini half-stack	$550	$725

JTM 310

1995-1997. JTM 30 with 2x10".

1995-1997		$500	$675

JTM 612 Combo

1995-1997. Tube combo amp, 60 watts, 1x12", EQ, reverb, effects loop.

1995-1997		$500	$650

JVM Series

2007-present. Models (H for Head, C Combo) include 205H/205C (50-watt head/combo 2x12), 210H/210C (100-watt head/combo 2x12), 215C (50-watt 1x12 combo), 410H/410C (100-watt head/combo 2x12, 4-channel), 410HJS (100-watt, Joe Satriani).

2007-2017	JVM410C	$1,250	$1,500
2008-2024	JVM205H	$950	$1,250
2008-2024	JVM210C	$1,250	$1,625
2008-2024	JVM210H	$1,000	$1,250
2013-2018	JVM410HJS	$2,500	$3,250

MA Series

2009-2013. Models include 50C (50 watts, 1x12"), 50H (50-watt head), 100C (100 watts, 2x12"), 100H (100-watt head) and 412 (4x12" slant cabinet).

2009-2013	Half-stacks/combos	$400	$550

MB Series

2006-2012. Bass Combo Series, models include 30C (30watts, 1x10").

2006-2012	MB30C	$125	$175

MG Series

1999-present. Models include 10KK (10 watts, 1x6"), 15CD, 15RCD or CDR (15 watts, 1x8"), 15MS (15 watts, micro stack, 1x8" slant and straight cabs), 15MSII, (in '02, 10" speakers), 15MSZW (15 watts, 2x1x10"), 50DFX (50 watts, 1x12"), 100DFX (100 watts, combo), 100HDFX (100-watt head), 100RCD (Valvestate Series, 100-watt), 102FX (100 watts, 2x12"), 250DFX (250 watts, combo), 412A (4x12" cabinet).

1999-2024	Various models	$50	$450

MGP Series

1980s-1990s. Solidstate rackmount preamps.

1980s-90s	Various models	$175	$225

Micro Stack 3005

1986-1991. Solidstate head, 12 watts, 2 1x10" stackable cabs (one slant, one straight). The standard model is black, but was also offered in white, green, red, or the silver Silver Jubilee version with Jubilee 25/50 logo.

1986-1991	Black	$450	$575
1986-1991	Green or red	$575	$725
1986-1991	White	$575	$725
1987-1989	Silver Jubilee/silver	$750	$1,125

Mini-Stack 3210 MOS-FET Head

1984-1991. Model 3210 MOS-FET head with 2 4x10" cabs, designed as affordable stack.

1984-1991		$500	$750

MODEL YEAR	FEATURES	LOW	HIGH

Model 1710 Bass Cabinet

1990s. 1x15" speaker.

1990s		$325	$450

Model 1912 Cabinet

1989-1998, 2013-2017. 1x12", 150 watts.

2013-2017		$325	$450

Model 1917 PA-20 Head

1967-1973. PA head with 20 watts, but often used for guitar, matching cabinet.

1967-1968	Matching cab	$2,750	$3,500
1967-1968	Plexi head	$4,500	$6,000
1969-1973	Aluminum head	$3,750	$5,000
1969-1973	Matching cab	$2,250	$3,000

Model 1922 Cabinet

1989-present. 2x12" extension cab for JCM 800 Series amps.

1989-2024		$325	$450

Model 1923 85th Anniversary

2008. Based on Jim Marshall's 85th birthday amp, limited edition, 50 watts.

2008		$1,250	$1,500

Model 1930 Popular Combo

1969-1973. 10 watts, 1x12", tremolo.

1969-1972		$3,500	$5,000
1973		$3,750	$6,000

Model 1933 Amp Cabinet

1981-1991. 1x12" extension cab for JCM 800 Series amps.

1981-1991		$325	$450

Model 1935/1935A/1935B Bass Cabinet

1967-1990s. Models 1935, 4x12", black, A slant front, B straight front.

1967-1970	75w	$5,000	$6,000
1971-1972	Black, weave	$2,500	$3,500
1973-1975	Black, checkerboard	$2,500	$3,500
1976-1979	Black	$2,000	$2,500
1979-1983	260w	$1,250	$1,500
1983-1986	280w	$1,250	$1,500
1990s		$1,000	$1,250

Model 1936 Cabinet

1981-2011. Extension straight-front cab for JCM 800/900 Series amps, 2x12" speakers, black.

1981-2011		$425	$550

Model 1937 Bass Cabinet

1981-1986. 4x12", 140 watts.

1981-1986		$525	$675

Model 1958 18-Watt Lead Combo

1965-1972. 18 watts, 2x10", Bluesbreaker cosmetics, black.

1965-1968		$10,000	$15,000
1968		$5,500	$7,500
1969		$5,000	$6,500
1970		$4,500	$6,000
1971-1972		$4,000	$5,500

Model 1959 Super Lead 100-Watt Head

1966-1981. Two channels, 100 watts, 4 inputs, no master volume. Plexiglas control panels until mid-'69, aluminum after. See Model T1959 for tremolo version. Early custom color versions are rare and more valuable. Becomes JCM 800 1959 in '81.

1966-1969	Black, plexi	$6,000	$8,000
1966-1969	Custom color, plexi	$8,000	$12,000
1969-1970	Black, aluminum	$3,000	$4,000
1969-1970	Custom color, aluminum	$5,500	$7,500
1971-1972	Black, hand-wired, small box	$3,000	$4,000
1971-1972	Custom color, hand-wired	$3,500	$4,500
1973-1975	Black, printed CB, large box	$2,000	$3,000
1973-1975	Custom color, printed CB	$2,500	$3,500
1976-1979	Black	$1,500	$2,000
1976-1979	Custom color	$2,000	$2,500
1980-1981	Black	$1,500	$2,000
1980-1981	Custom color	$1,750	$2,250

Model T1959 Super Lead (Tremolo) Head

1966-1973. 100 watts, plexi until mid-'69, aluminum after. Tremolo version of the Model 1959 Amp.

1966-1969	Black, plexi	$6,000	$8,000
1966-1969	Custom color, plexi	$8,000	$12,000
1969-1970	Black, aluminum	$2,500	$3,500
1969-1970	Custom color, aluminum	$5,500	$7,500
1971-1973	Black, hand-wired, small box	$3,000	$4,000
1971-1973	Custom color, hand-wired	$3,500	$4,500

35th Anniversary Marshall Limited Edition Set

1997. Limited Edition 1997 logo, includes matching Super Lead MKII 100-watt head, PB100 power brake and MKII 1960A slant cab, all in white covering.

1997		$2,500	$3,750

Model 1959 SLP Reissue Head

1992-2017. Vintage Series, Super Lead Plexi (SLP), vinyl covering, black, purple or white.

1992-1999	Black	$1,750	$2,250
1992-1999	Purple or white	$2,125	$2,625
2000-2017	Black	$2,125	$2,625

Model 1959 SLP Reissue Set

1992-2013. Vintage Series, 100-watt Super Lead head and matching 4x12" slant cab.

1992-2013	4x12 Cab	$2,500	$3,500

Model 1959HW

2005-present. Hand-wired, 100 watts, 4x12" slant front cab.

2005-2014	Cab	$550	$750
2005-2024	Head only	$2,000	$2,500

Model 1959RR Randy Rhoads Limited Edition

2008-2013. Randy Rhoads Tribute, full stack, 100 watts.

2008-2013		$5,500	$7,500

Model 1960 4x12 Speaker Cabinet

1965-1979. Both straight and slant front. The original Marshall 4x12" cab designed for compact size with 4x12" speakers. First issue in '64/'65 is 60-watt cab, from '65-'70 75 watts, from '70-'79 100 watts. After '79, model numbers contained an alpha suffix: A for slant front, B straight.

1965-1970	Black, weave	$5,000	$6,500
1965-1970	Custom color, weave	$6,500	$8,500
1971-1972	Black, weave	$3,000	$4,000

1988 Marshall Micro Stack 3005

Tom Pfeifer

Marshall Model 1958 18-Watt Lead

Kris Blakely

Marshall Model 1959HW

AMPS

1991 Marshall Model 1960A 4x12 Speaker Cabinet
Rivington Guitars

Marshall Model 1962 Bluesbreaker Combo

Marshall Model 1974X

AMPS

MODEL YEAR	FEATURES	LOW	HIGH
1971-1972	Custom color, weave	$4,500	$5,500
1973-1975	Black, checkerboard	$2,000	$2,500
1973-1975	Custom color, checkerboard	$2,500	$3,500
1976-1979	Black	$1,500	$2,000
1976-1979	Custom color	$2,000	$2,500

Model 1960A/1960B 4x12 Speaker Cabinet

1980-1983 (260 watts), '84-'86 (280 watts, JCM 800 era), '86-'90 (300 watts, JCM 800 era), '90-present (300 watts, JCM 900 era, stereo-mono switching). A slant or B straight front.

1980-1983	Black	$850	$1,500
1980-1983	Custom color	$1,250	$1,750
1984-1986	Black	$675	$950
1984-1986	Custom color	$1,000	$1,250
1984-1986	Rare color	$1,500	$2,000
1987-1990	Black	$675	$950
1987-1990	Custom color	$900	$1,250
1987-1990	Rare color	$1,250	$1,750
2000-2007	A, Black	$600	$850
2000-2007	B, Black	$675	$950

Model 1960AC/1960BC Classic Speaker Cabinet

2005-2013. 100 watts, 4x12" Celestion G-12M-25 greenback speakers, black, AC slant front, BC straight front.

2005-2013	AC	$950	$1,250
2005-2013	BC	$875	$1,125

Model 1960AHW/1960BHW 4x12 Cabinet

2005-present. Half stack cab for HW series, AHW slant or BHW straight front.

2005-2024	A or B	$950	$1,250

Model 1960AV/1960BV 4x12 Cabinet

1990-present. JCM 900 updated, stereo/mono switching, AV slant, BV straight front.

1990-1999	Red vinyl, tan grille	$750	$950
1990-2012	Black vinyl, black grille	$750	$950
1990-2024	Various colors	$650	$850

Model 1960AX/1960BX 4x12 Cabinet

1990-present. Cab for Model 1987X and 1959X reissue heads, AX slant, BX straight.

1990-2024	AX	$750	$950
1990-2024	BX	$750	$950

Model 1960TV 4x12 Slant Cabinet

1990-2012. Extra tall for JTM 45, mono, 100 watts.

1990-2012	Various colors	$600	$750

Model 1962 Bluesbreaker Combo

1997-2017. Vintage Series, similar to JTM 45 but with 2 reissue 'Greenback' 25-watt 2x12" speakers and addition of footswitchable tremolo effect. Limited Edition 35th Anniversary model was produced in '97 with white tolex, only 250 made.

1997	35th Anniv	$3,500	$4,500
1997-2017		$1,500	$2,000

Model 1964 Lead/Bass 50-Watt Head

1973-1976. Head with 50 watts, designed for lead or bass.

1973-1976		$3,000	$3,500

Model 1965A/1965B Cabinet

1984-1991. 140-watt 4x10" slant front (A) or straight front (B) cab.

1984-1991		$400	$550

Model 1966 Cabinet

1985-1991. 150-watt 2x12" cab.

1985-1991		$400	$550

Model 1967 Major 200-Watt Head

1968-1974. 200 watts, the original Marshall 200 Pig was not popular and revised into the 200 'Major'. The new Major 200 was similar to the other large amps and included 2 channels, 4 inputs, but a larger amp cab.

1968	Plexi	$3,500	$5,000
1969-1970	Aluminum	$2,500	$3,500
1971-1972	Small box	$1,250	$2,000
1973-1974	Large box	$1,250	$2,000

Model 1967 Pig 200-Watt Head

1967-early-1968 only. Head with 200 watts. The control panel was short and stubby and nicknamed the Pig, the 200-watt circuit was dissimilar (and unpopular) to the 50-watt and 100-watt circuits.

1967-1968		$3,500	$5,000

Model 1968 100-Watt Super PA Head

1966-1975. PA head with 100 watts, 2 sets of 4 inputs (identifies PA configuration), often used for guitar, matching cabinet.

1966-1969	Matching cab	$2,000	$3,000
1966-1969	Plexi	$4,000	$5,500
1969-1972	Aluminum	$2,500	$3,500
1969-1975	Matching cab	$1,000	$1,500

Model 1973 Combo

1965-1968. Tube combo, 18 watts, 2x12".

1965		$13,500	$20,000
1966		$10,500	$15,000
1967		$6,500	$8,500
1968		$6,000	$8,000

Model 1973 JMP Lead/Bass 20

1973 only. Front panel: JMP, back panel: Lead & Bass 20, 20 watts, 1x12" straight front checkered grille cab, head and cab black vinyl.

1973		$2,500	$4,000

Model 1974 Combo

1965-1968. Tube combo, 18 watts, 1x12".

1965		$12,500	$18,000
1966		$10,500	$15,000
1967		$6,000	$8,000
1968		$6,500	$10,000

Model 1974X/1974CX

2004-present. Handwired Series, reissue of 18-watt, 1x12" combo, extension cabinet available (CX).

2004-2024	1974CX cab	$600	$800
2004-2024	Combo	$1,375	$1,750

Model 1982/1982A/1982B Cabinet

1967-1987. Bass and lead 4x12", 100-watt 1982/1982B, upped to 120 watts in '70. Becomes higher powered 320 and 400 watts Model 1982A/B in '81 and '82.

1967-1970		$2,500	$3,500
1971-1980		$1,250	$1,750
1981-1982		$850	$1,250
1983-1987		$850	$1,250

MODEL YEAR	FEATURES	LOW	HIGH

Model 1986 50-Watt Bass Head

1966-1981. Bass version of 1987, 50-watt, black.

1966-1969	Plexi	$3,500	$5,000
1969-1970	Aluminum	$2,500	$3,500
1971-1972	Hand-wired, small box	$2,000	$3,000
1973-1975	Printed CB, large box	$1,750	$2,500
1976-1979		$1,500	$2,000
1980-1981		$1,375	$1,750

Model 1987 50-Watt Head

1966-1981. Head amp, 50 watts, plexiglas panel until mid-'69, aluminum panel after.

1966-1969	Black, plexi	$6,000	$8,000
1966-1969	Custom color, plexi	$8,500	$12,000
1969-1970	Black, aluminum	$3,000	$4,000
1969-1970	Custom color, aluminum	$5,000	$6,500
1971-1972	Black, hand-wired, small box	$2,250	$3,000
1971-1972	Custom color, hand-wired	$3,250	$4,500
1973-1975	Black, printed CB, large box	$2,000	$3,000
1973-1975	Custom color, printed CB	$2,500	$3,500
1976-1979	Black	$1,500	$2,000
1976-1979	Custom color	$2,000	$3,000
1980-1981	Black	$1,500	$2,000
1980-1981	Custom color	$2,000	$3,000

Model 1987X Head

1992-present. Vintage Series amp, all tube, 50 watts, 4 inputs, plexi.

1992-2024		$1,250	$1,625

Model 1992 Super Bass 100-Watt Head

1966-1981. 100 watts, plexi panel until mid-'69 when replaced by aluminum front panel, 2 channels, 4 inputs.

1966-1969	Black, plexi	$5,500	$7,500
1966-1969	Custom color, plexi	$8,000	$10,500
1969-1970	Black, aluminum	$3,125	$4,000
1969-1970	Custom color, aluminum	$6,000	$10,000
1971-1972	Black, hand-wired, small box	$3,250	$4,500
1971-1972	Custom color, hand-wired	$3,500	$5,500
1973-1975	Black, printed CB, large box	$2,250	$3,000
1973-1975	Custom color, printed CB	$2,750	$4,500
1976-1979	Black	$2,000	$2,500
1976-1979	Custom color	$2,250	$3,500
1980-1981	Black	$1,500	$2,000
1980-1981	Custom color	$2,000	$3,000

Model 1992LEM Lemmy Signature Super Bass

2008-2013. Lemmy Kilmister specs, matching 100-watt head with 4x12" and 4x15" stacked cabinets.

2008-2013	Full-stack	$3,500	$5,000

MODEL YEAR	FEATURES	LOW	HIGH

Model 2040 Artist 50-Watt Combo

1971-1978. 50 watts, 2x12" Artist/Artiste combo model with a different (less popular?) circuit.

1971-1978		$1,750	$2,500

Model 2041 Artist Head/Cabinet Set

1971-1978. 50 watts, 2x12" half stack Artist/Artiste cab with a different (less popular?) circuit.

1971-1978		$2,250	$3,000

Model 2046 Specialist 25-Watt Combo

1972-1973. 25 watts, 1x15" speaker, limited production due to design flaw (amp overheats).

1972-1973		$650	$975

Model 2060 Mercury Combo

1972-1973. Combo amp, 5 watts, 1x12", available in red or orange covering.

1972-1973		$750	$975

Model 2061 20-Watt Lead/Bass Head

1968-1973. Lead/bass head, 20 watts, plexi until '69, aluminum after, black. Reissued in '04 as the Model 2061X.

1968-1969	Plexi	$3,500	$4,500
1969-1970	Aluminum	$2,500	$3,500
1971-1972	Aluminum	$2,000	$2,500
1973	Aluminum	$1,750	$2,250

Model 2061X 20-Watt Lead/ Bass Head Reissue

2004-2017. Handwired Series, reissue of 2061 amp head, 20 watts.

2004-2014	1x12 cab	$450	$600
2004-2015	2x12 cab	$450	$600
2004-2017	Head only	$1,000	$1,375

Model 2068 Artist (JMP) Set

1971-1978. 100-watt head with matching Artist cab, reverb, small logo.

1971-1978		$2,500	$3,250

Model 2078 Combo

1973-1978. Solidstate, 100 watts, 4x12" combo, gold front panel, dark cover, gray grille.

1973-1978		$1,250	$1,500

Model 2103 100-Watt 1-Channel Master Combo

1975-1981. One channel, 2 inputs, 100 watts, 2x12", first master volume design, combo version of 2203 head.

1975-1981		$1,875	$2,500

Model 2104 50-Watt 1-Channel Master Combo

1975-1981. One channel, 2 inputs, 50 watts, 2x12", first master volume design, combo version of 2204 head.

1975-1981		$1,875	$2,500

Model 2144 Master Reverb Combo

1978 only. Master volume similar to 2104 but with reverb and boost, 50 watts, 2x12".

1978		$2,000	$2,250

Model 2150 100-Watt 1x12 Combo

1978. Tubes.

1978		$1,250	$1,500

Model 2159 100-Watt 2-Channel Combo

1977-1981. 100 watts, 2 channels, 4 inputs, 2x12" combo version of Model 1959 Super Lead head.

1977-1981		$1,875	$2,500

Marshall Model 1987X
Ted Wulfers

AMPS

1968 Marshall Model 1992 Super Bass Head

1972 Marshall Model 2040 Artist
Mark K

Marshall Model 2203X JCM800 Head Reissue

Marshall Model 4001 Studio 15
Imaged by Heritage Auctions, HA.com

Marshall Model 6100 30th Anniversary
Imaged by Heritage Auctions, HA.com

MODEL YEAR	FEATURES	LOW	HIGH

Model 2199
1979. Solidstate 2x12" combo.

1979		$900	$1,125

Model 2200 100-Watt Lead Combo
1977-1981. 100 watts, 2x12" combo, early solidstate, includes boost section, no reverb.

1977-1981		$1,000	$1,500

Model 2203 Lead Head
1975-1981. Head amp, 100 watts, 2 inputs, first master volume model design, often seen with Mark II logo.

1975-1981	Black	$2,250	$3,000
1975-1981	Fawn Beige	$2,500	$3,250

Model 2203X JCM800 Head Reissue
2002-2010. 100 watts.

2002-2010		$1,750	$2,250

Model 2204 50-Watt Head
1975-1981. Head only, 50 watts with master volume.

1975-1981		$2,000	$2,500

Model 2266 50-Watt Combo
2007-2013. Vintage Modern series, 2x12".

2007-2013		$850	$1,125

Model 2466 100-Watt Head
2007-2013. Vintage Modern series.

2007-2013		$850	$1,125

Model 3203 Artist Head
1986-1991. Tube head version of earlier '84 Model 3210 MOS-FET, designed as affordable alternative, 30 watts, standard short cab, 2 inputs separated by 3 control knobs, Artist 3203 logo on front panel, black.

1986-1991		$550	$750

Model 3210 MOS-FET Head
1984-1991. MOS-FET solidstate head, refer Mini-Stack listing for 3210 with 4x10" stacked cabinets. Early-'80s front panel: Lead 100 MOS-FET.

1984-1991		$450	$575

Model 3310 100-Watt Lead
1988-1991. Solidstate, 100 watts, lead head with channel switching and reverb.

1988-1991		$500	$650

Model 4001 Studio 15
1985-1992. 15 watts using 6V6 (only model to do this up to this time), 1x12" Celestion Vintage 30 speakers.

1985-1992		$850	$1,125

Model 4104 50-Watt Combo
1981-1990. Combo version of 2204 head, 50 watts, 2x12", master volume.

1981-1990		$1,250	$1,750

Model 4203 Artist 30-Watt Combo

1986-1991		$400	$500

Model 5002 Combo
1984-1991. Solidstate combo amp, 20 watts, 1x10", master volume.

1984-1991		$200	$300

Model 5005 Lead 12
1983-1991. Solidstate student amp, 12 watts, master volume, 1x10".

1983-1991		$250	$325

Model 5205 Reverb 12
1986. Solidstate, 12 watts, 1x10", Reverb 12 logo on front panel.

1986		$250	$325

Model 5302 Keyboard
1984-1988. Solidstate, 20 watts, 1x10", marketed for keyboard application.

1984-1988		$200	$275

Model 5502 Bass
1984-ca.1992. Solidstate bass combo amp, 20 watts, 1x10" Celestion.

1984-1992		$200	$275

Model 6100 30th Anniversary
1992-1998. Head with 100/50/25 switchable watts and 4x12" cabinet (matching colors), first year and into early '93 was blue tolex, black afterwards.

1992-1998	4x12 cab	$450	$600
1992-1998	Head only	$850	$1,125

Model 6101 30th Anniversary Combo
1992-1998. 1x12" combo version of 6100 amp, first year and into early '93 was blue tolex, black afterwards.

1992-1998		$1,125	$1,500

Model 8008 Valvestate Rackmount
1991-2001. Valvestate solidstate rack mount power amp with dual 40-watt channels.

1991-2001		$175	$225

Model 8010 Valvestate VS15 Combo
1991-1997. Valvestate solidstate, 10 watts, 1x8", compact size, black vinyl, black grille.

1991-1997		$150	$200

Model 8040 Valvestate 40V Combo
1991-1997. Valvestate solidstate with tube preamp, 40 watts, 1x12", compact size, black vinyl, black grille.

1991-1997		$175	$250

Model 8080 Valvestate 80V Combo
1991-1997. Valvestate solidstate with tube 12AX7 preamp, 80 watts, 1x12", compact size, black vinyl, black grille.

1991-1997		$175	$250

Model 8100 100-Watt Valvestate VS100H Head
1991-2001. Valvestate solidstate head, 100 watts.

1991-2001		$200	$275

Model 8200 200-Watt Valvestate Head
1993-1998. Valvestate solidstate reverb head, 2x100-watt channels.

1993-1998		$225	$300

Model 8222 Valvestate Cabinet
1993-1998. 200 watts, 2x12 extention cab, designed for 8200 head.

1993-1998		$175	$250

Model 8240 Valvestate Stereo Chorus
1992-1996. Valvestate, 80 watts (2x40 watts stereo), 2x12" combo, reverb, chorus.

1992-1996		$250	$350

Model 8280 2x80-Watt Valvestate Combo
1993-1996. Valvestate solidstate, 2x80 watts, 2x12".

1993-1996		$275	$375

Model 8412 Valvestate Cabinet
1991-2001. 140 watts, 4x12 extention cab, designed for 8100 head.

1991-2001		$225	$300

MODEL YEAR	FEATURES	LOW	HIGH

MS-2/R/C

1990-present. Microamp series, 1 watt, battery operated, miniature black half-stack amp and cab. Red MS-2R and checkered speaker grille and gold logo MS-2C added in '93.

1990-2024		$40	$55

MS-4

1998-present. Full-stack version of MS-2, black.

1998-2024		$45	$60

Origin (OR) Series

2018-present. Various tube models include ORIGIN5, 20C, 20H and 50C. Number indicates watts, C is combo, H is head only.

2018-2024		$275	$350

Silver Jubilee Model 2550 50/25 (Tall) Head

1987-1989. 50/25 switchable tall box head for full Jubilee stack, silver vinyl and chrome control panel.

1987-1989		$2,750	$3,750

Silver Jubilee Model 2551 4x12 Cabinet

1987-1989. Matching silver 4x12" cabs for Jubilee 2550 head, various models, silver vinyl.

1987-1989	2551A, slant	$1,250	$1,500
1987-1989	2551AV, Vintage 30	$1,250	$1,500
1987-1989	2551B, straight	$1,250	$1,500
1987-1989	2551BV, Vintage 30	$1,250	$1,500

Silver Jubilee Model 2553 50/25 (Short) Head

1987-1988. 50/25 switchable small box head for mini-short stack, silver vinyl and chrome control panel.

1987-1988		$2,500	$3,500

Silver Jubilee Model 2554 1x12 Combo

1987-1989. 50/25 watts, 1x12" combo using 2550 chassis, silver vinyl and chrome control panel.

1987-1989		$2,750	$3,750

Silver Jubilee Model 2555 Head

1987-1989. 100/50 version of 2550 head, silver vinyl and chrome control panel.

1987-1989		$2,500	$3,500

Silver Jubilee Model 2556 2x12 Cabinet

1987-1989. Matching silver 2x12" cabs for Jubilee heads, various models, silver vinyl.

1987-1989	2556A, slant	$1,250	$1,500
1987-1989	2556AV, Vintage 30	$1,250	$1,500
1987-1989	2556B, straight	$1,250	$1,500
1987-1989	2556BV, Vintage 30	$1,250	$1,500

Silver Jubilee Model 2558 2x12 Combo

1987-1989. 50/25 watts, 2x12" combo using 2550 chassis, silver vinyl and chrome control panel.

1987-1989		$2,250	$3,500

Silver Jubilee Model 3560 600 Head

1987. Rackmount 2x300 watts.

1987		$500	$750

SL-5

2013-2015. Tube combo, 5 watts, 1x12", script logo signature on front panel.

2013-2015		$750	$975

Super 100 40th Anniversary JTM45 MK II Full Stack

2005. 100 watts, 2 4x12 cabs, 250 made.

2005		$4,000	$6,000

MODEL YEAR	FEATURES	LOW	HIGH

Martin

Martin has dabbled in amps a few times, under both the Martin and Stinger brand names. The first batch were amps made by others introduced with their electric acoustics in 1959.

Model 110

1959-1961. Tube, 1x10" combo.

1959-1961		$4,500	$5,500

Model 112T

1959-1961. Branded C.F. Martin inside label, made by Rowe-DeArmond, 1x12 combo, limited production, 2x6V6 power tubes, 2x12AX7 preamp tubes, with tube rectifier, 4 inputs, 3 control knobs.

1959-1961		$4,500	$5,500

SS140

1965-1966. Large amp.

1965-1966		$950	$1,250

Stinger FX-1

1988-1990. 10 watts, EQ, switchable solidstate tube-synth circuit, line out and footswitch jacks.

1988-1990		$165	$225

Stinger FX-1R

1988-1990. Mini-stack amp, 2x10", 15 watts, dual-stage circuitry.

1988-1990		$175	$250

Stinger FX-6B

1989-1990. Combo bass amp, 60 watts, 1x15".

1988-1990		$175	$250

Masco

1940s-1950s. The Mark Alan Sampson Company, Long Island, New York, produced a variety of electronic products including tube PA amps and small combo instrument amps. The PA heads are also popular with harp players.

Massie

1940s. Ray Massie worked in Leo Fender's repair shop in the 1940s and built tube amps. He later worked at the Fender company.

Matamp

1966-present. Tube amps, combos and cabinets built in Huddersfield, England, bearing names like Red, Green, White, Black, and Blue. German-born Mat Mathias started building amps in England in '58 and designed his first Matamp in '66. From '69 to '73, Mathias also made Orange amps. In '89, Mathias died at age 66 and his family later sold the factory to Jeff Lewis.

1x15" Cabinet

1970s		$950	$1,250

GT-120 Green Stack

1990s. 120-watt GT head with 4x12" straight front cab.

1993-1999		$1,875	$2,500

GT-120 Head

1971		$2,500	$3,250

Marshall Origin 20

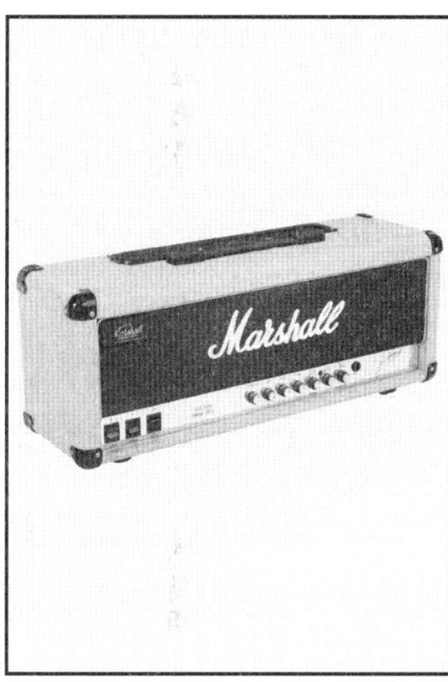

1987 Marshall Silver Jubilee Model 2555 Head

Imaged by Heritage Auctions, HA.com

Matamp GT2 MK II

AMPS

1995 Matchless Chieftan 212

Imaged by Heritage Auctions, HA.com

Matchless Nighthawk

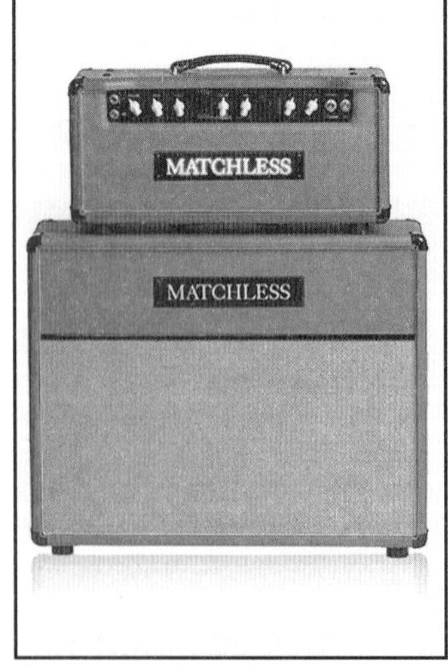

Matchless Phoenix 35 (PH-35) Head

MODEL YEAR	FEATURES	LOW	HIGH

Matchless

1989-1999, 2001-present. Founded by Mark Sampson and Rick Perrotta in California. Circuits based on Vox AC-30 with special attention to transformers. A new Matchless company was reorganized in 2001 by Phil Jamison, former head of production for the original company.

Avalon 35 Head

2009-2010. 35 watts head, reverb.

2009-2010		$1,625	$2,500

Brave 40 112

1997-1999. 40 watts class A, 1x12", foot switchable between high and low inputs.

1997-1999		$1,875	$2,500

Brave 40 212

1997-1999. 2x12" version of Brave.

1997-1999		$1,875	$2,500

Chief Head

1995-1999. 100 watts class A, head.

1995-1999		$3,000	$4,000

Chief 212

1995-1999. 100 watts class A, 2x12", reverb.

1995-1999		$3,000	$4,000

Chief 410

1995-1999. 100 watts class A, 4x10", reverb.

1995-1999		$3,000	$4,000

Chieftan Head

1995-1999. 40 watts class A head, reverb, chicken-head knobs.

1995-1999		$2,000	$2,500

Chieftan 112

1995-1999, 2001-present. 40 watts class A, 1x12", reverb.

1995-1999		$2,500	$3,500
2001-2024	Jamison era	$2,500	$3,500

Chieftan 210

1995-1999. 40 watts class A, 2x10", reverb.

1995-1999		$3,000	$4,000

Chieftan 212

1995-1999, 2001-present. 40 watts class A, 2x12", reverb.

1995-1999		$3,000	$4,000
2001-2019	Jamison era	$3,000	$3,500

Chieftan 410

1995-1999. 40 watts class A, 4x10", reverb.

1995-1999		$3,000	$4,000

Clipper 15 112

1998-1999. 15 watts, single channel, 1x12".

1998-1999		$1,500	$1,875

Clipper 15 210

1998-1999. 15 watts, single channel, 2x10".

1998-1999		$1,500	$1,875

Clubman 35 Head

1993-1999. 35 watts class A head.

1993-1999		$2,250	$3,000

DC-30 Standard Cabinet

1991-1999. 30 watts, 2x12", with or without reverb.

1991-1999		$3,250	$4,500

DC-30 Exotic Wood Cabinet (Option)

1995-1999. 30 watts, 2x12", gold plating, limited production.

1995-1999		$5,250	$8,000

ES/EB Cabinet

ES = speaker cabinets and EB = bass speaker cabinets.

1991-1999	1x12	$475	$650
1993-1999	2x10	$575	$825
1993-1999	2x10+2x12	$725	$1,000
1993-1999	2x12	$600	$850
1993-1999	4x12	$800	$1,125
1997-1999	1x15	$475	$675
1997-1999	4x10	$675	$975

HC-30 Head

1991-1999, 2003. The first model offered by Matchless, 30 watts class A head.

1991-1999		$3,000	$4,000
2003	Jamison era	$2,500	$3,500

HC-85 Head

1992. Only 25 made, similar to HC-30 but more flexible using various tube substitutions.

1992		$3,000	$3,750

Hurricane Head

1997. 15 watts class A head.

1997		$1,500	$2,000

Hurricane 112

1994-1997. 15 watts class A, 1x12".

1994-1997		$1,500	$2,000

Hurricane 210

1996-1997. 15 watts class A, 2x10".

1996-1997		$1,875	$2,500

Independence 35 Head

2005-2017. 35 watts, with or without reverb.

2005-2017		$2,000	$3,000

JJ-30 112 John Jorgensen

1997-1999. 30 watts, DC-30 chassis with reverb and tremolo, 1x12" Celestion 30, offered in white, blue, gray sparkle tolex or black.

1997-1999		$4,500	$5,750

Lightning 15 Head

1994-1997, 2005-present. 15 watts class A head.

1994-1997		$1,750	$2,125

Lightning 15 112

1994-1999, 2001-present. 15 watts class A, 1x12".

1994-1999		$2,500	$3,500
2001-2024	Jamison era	$2,000	$3,000

Lightning 15 210

1996-1997, 2001-2006. 15 watts class A, 2x10".

1996-1997		$2,500	$3,500
2001-2006	Jamison era	$2,250	$3,000

Lightning 15 212

1998, 2001-2022. 15 watts class A, 2x12".

1998-2022		$2,500	$3,500

Little Monster/The Little Monster

2007-2009. 9 watts, offered as head, and 1x12" or 2x12" combo.

2007-2009		$2,000	$2,500

Nighthawk

2003-present. 15 watts, offered as head, and 1x12", 2x10" or 2x12" combo.

2003-2014	2x10	$1,375	$2,000
2003-2024	1x12	$1,250	$1,750
2003-2024	2x12	$1,500	$2,250

MODEL YEAR	FEATURES	LOW	HIGH

Phoenix 35 (PH-35) Head

2003-present. 35-watt head, black or red.

2003-2024		$2,125	$3,000

SC-30 Standard Cabinet

1991-1999. 30 watts class A, 1x12".

1991-1999		$3,500	$4,500
2001-2006	Jamison era	$2,750	$4,000

SC-30 Exotic Wood Cabinet

1995-1999. 30 watts class A, 1x12", gold plating, limited production.

1995-1999		$5,500	$8,000

Skyliner Reverb 15 112

1998-1999. 15 watts, 2 channels, 1x12".

1998-1999		$1,125	$1,500

Skyliner Reverb 15 210

1998-1999. 15 watts, 2 channels, 2x10".

1998-1999		$1,250	$1,625

Spitfire 15 Head

1997. 15 watts, head.

1997		$1,500	$2,000

Spitfire 15 112

1994-1997. 15 watts, 1x12".

1994-1997		$1,750	$2,125

Spitfire 15 210

1996-1997. 15 watts, 2x10".

1996-1997		$1,875	$2,500

Starliner 40 212

1999. 40 watts, 2x12".

1999		$2,000	$2,500

Superchief 120 Head

1994-1999. 120 watts, class A head.

1994-1999		$3,000	$4,000

TC-30 Standard Cabinet

1991-1999. 30 watts, 2x10" class A, low production numbers make value approximate with DC-30.

1991-1999		$3,500	$4,500

TC-30 Exotic Wood Cabinet

1991-1999. 30 watts, 2x10" class A, limited production.

1991-1999		$5,500	$8,000

Thunderchief Bass Head

1994-1999. 200 watts, class A bass head.

1994-1999		$2,500	$3,500

Thunderman 100 Bass Combo

1997-1998. 100 watts, 1x15" in portaflex-style flip-top cab.

1997-1998		$3,500	$4,500

Tornado 15 112

1994-1995. Compact, 15 watts, 1x12", 2-tone covering, simple controls - volume, tone, tremolo speed, tremolo depth.

1994-1995		$1,125	$1,500

Maven Peal

Amps, combos and cabinets built by David Zimmerman in Plainfield, Vermont, beginning in 1999. Serial number format is by amp wattage and sequential build; for example, 15-watt amp 15-001.

Mega Amplifiers

Budget and intermediate grade, production, solidstate and tube amps from Guitar Jones, Inc. of Pomona, California.

Merlin

Rack mount bass heads built in Germany by Musician Sound Design. They also offer MSD guitar effects.

Mesa-Boogie

1971-present. Founded by Randall Smith in San Francisco, California. Circuits styled on high-gain Fender-based chassis designs, ushering in the compact high-gain amp market. Mesa was acquired by Gibson in early 2021.

The following serial number information and specs courtesy of Mesa Engineering.

.50 Caliber/.50 Caliber+ Head

Jan. 1987-Dec. 1988, 1992-1993. Serial numbers: SS3100 - SS11,499. Mesa Engineering calls it Caliber .50. Tube head amp, 50 watts, 5-band EQ, effects loop. Called the .50 Caliber Plus in '92 and '93.

1987-1988	Caliber	$1,250	$1,750
1992-1993	Caliber+	$1,250	$1,750

.50 Caliber+ Combo

Dec. 1988-Oct. 1993. Serial numbers FP11,550 - FP29,080. 50 watts, 1x12" combo amp.

1988-1993		$1,000	$1,500

20/20

Jun. 1995-2010. Serial numbers: TT-01. 20-22 watts per channel.

1995-2010		$850	$1,125

50/50 (Fifty/Fifty)

May 1989-2001. Serial numbers: FF001-. 100 watts total power, 50 watts per channel, front panel reads Fifty/Fifty, contains 4 6L6 power tubes.

1989-2001		$850	$1,125

395

Feb. 1991-Apr. 1992. Serial numbers: S2572 - S3237.

1991-1992		$1,125	$1,500

Bass 400/Bass 400+ Head

Aug. 1989-Aug. 1990. Serial numbers: B001-B1200. About 500 watts using 12 5881 power tubes. Replaced by 400+ Aug.1990-present, serial numbers: B1200- . Update change to 7-band EQ at serial number B1677.

1989-1990	Bass 400	$1,250	$1,750
1990-1999	Bass 400+	$1,375	$1,875

Big Block Series

2004-2014. Rackmount bass amps, models 750 (750w head) and Titan V-12 (650/1200w).

2004-2014	750	$1,375	$1,875
2006-2010	Titan V-12	$1,375	$1,875

Blue Angel Series

Jun. 1994-2004. Serial numbers BA01-. Switchable between 15, 33 or 38 watts, offered as head, 1x12" combo or 4x10" combo, blue cover.

1994-2004	Combo 1x12	$1,125	$1,375
1994-2004	Combo 4x10	$1,250	$1,500

Buster Bass Combo

1999-2001. 200 watts, 2x10", wedge cabinet, black vinyl, metal grille.

1999-2001		$825	$1,125

Buster Bass Head

Dec. 1997-Jan. 2001. Serial numbers: BS-1-999. 200 watts via 6 6L6 power tubes.

1997-2001		$850	$1,125

Matchless Spitfire 15 112

AMPS

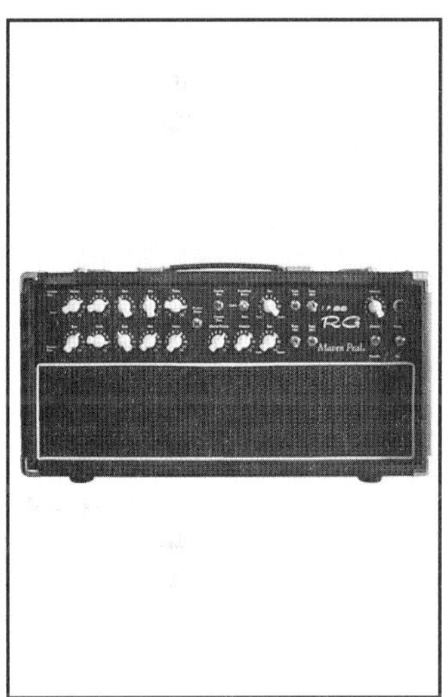

Maven Peal RG88

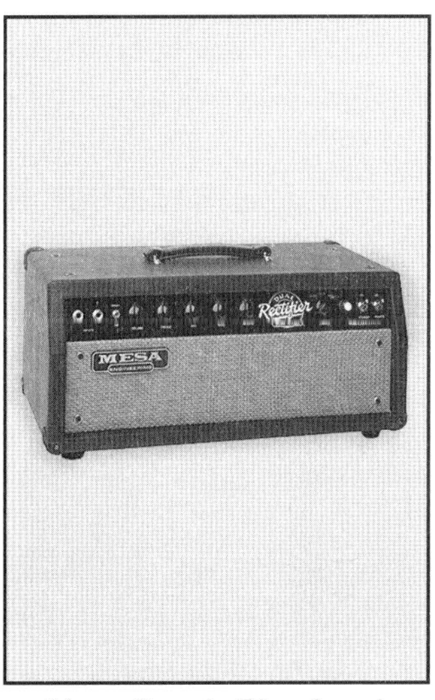

Mesa-Boogie Blue Angel

Mesa-Boogie Express 5:50

Mesa-Boogie Fillmore 100 Combo

1970s Mesa-Boogie Mark I Combo

Tom Allen

MODEL YEAR	FEATURES	LOW	HIGH

Coliseum 300

Oct. 1997-2000. Serial numbers: COL-01 - COL-132. 200 watts/channel, 12 6L6 power tubes, rack mount.

1997-2000		$1,250	$1,625

D-180 Head

Jul. 1982-Dec. 1985. Serial numbers: D001-D681. All tube head amp, 200 watts, preamp, switchable.

1982-1985		$1,125	$1,500

DC-3

Sep. 1994-Jan. 1999. Serial numbers: DC3-001 - DC3-4523. 35 watts, 1x12".

1994-1999	Combo 1x12	$750	$1,000
1994-1999	Head only	$600	$850

DC-5

Oct. 1993-Jan. 1999. Serial numbers: DC1024 - DC31,941. 50-watt head, 1x12" combo.

1993-1999	Combo 1x12	$900	$1,125
1993-1999	Head only	$650	$850

DC-10

May 1996-Jan. 1999. Serial numbers: DCX-001 - DCX-999. Dirty/Clean (DC), 100 watts (6L6s), 2x12".

1993-1996	Combo 2x12	$950	$1,250
1996-1999	Head only	$800	$1,000

Electra Dyne Head

2009-2013. 45/90 watts, Black Taurus/black grille or British Tan Bronco/tan grille.

2009-2013		$1,125	$1,500

Express Series

2007-2017. Compact combo tube amps with power switching.

2007-2016	5:50, 2x12, 5-50w	$1,000	$1,250
2007-2017	5:25, 1x10, 5-25w	$875	$1,125
2007-2017	5:50, 1x12, 5-50w	$1,000	$1,250
2008	5:25, short head, 25w	$850	$1,125

Extension Cabinet

1980s-present. Mesa-Boogie offered 'extension cabinets' which could be mixed and matched with amp heads, using different configurations with correct impedance. Other manufacturers often consider an extension cab as an extra cab, but Mesa Engineering considers it to be the main cab (not an extra). The company has generic cabs as well as cabs associated with specific models, but both generic and model-specific fall into similar price ranges. Some other variances include vertical or horizontal, open back or closed, slant or straight front, grille could be metal or cloth, and some cabs are designated for bass guitar. Specialized cabinets may be more than values shown.

1980-2024	Various sizes	$450	$550

F-30

2002-Feb. 2007. Combo, 30 watts, 1x12".

2002-2007		$650	$800

F-50

2002-Feb. 2007. Combo, 50 watts, 1x12", AB 2 6L6 power.

2002-2007		$750	$950
2002-2007	Head only	$700	$900

F-100

2002-Feb. 2007. Combo, 100 watts, 2x12".

2002-2007	Combo 2x12	$950	$1,250
2002-2007	Head only	$850	$1,125

Fillmore 100 Combo

2019-present. 100 watts, 1x12" or 2x12", 2 foot-switchable channels.

2019-2024		$1,500	$2,000

Formula Preamp

Jul. 1998-2002. Serial numbers: F-01. Used 5 12AX7 tubes, 3 channels.

1998-2002		$500	$700

Heartbreaker Combo

Jun. 1996-2001. Serial numbers: HRT-01. 60 to 100 watts switchable, 2x12" combo, designed to switch-out 6L6s, EL34s or the lower powered 6V6s in the power section, switchable solidstate or tube rectifier.

1996-2001		$1,250	$1,875

Heartbreaker Head

1996-2001. Head only, 100 watts.

1996-2001		$1,500	$2,250

Lone Star Series

2004-2020. Designed by founder Randall Smith and Doug West with focus on boutique-type amp. Class A (EL84) or AB (4 6L6) circuits, long or short head, 1x12" combo, 2x12" combo, and short head 4x10" cab, and long head 4x12" cab.

2004-2016	Combo 1x12, hardwood	$2,500	$3,750
2004-2016	Combo 4x10, blue	$2,000	$2,625
2004-2020	Combo 1x12	$1,750	$2,500
2004-2020	Combo 2x12	$2,000	$2,750
2004-2020	Head, class A or AB	$1,625	$2,250

Lone Star Special

2005-2020. Smaller lighter version using EL84 power tubes, 5/15/30 watts, long or short head amp or 1x12", 2x12" or 4x10" combo.

2005-2020	Combo 1x12	$1,750	$2,250

M-180

Apr. 1982-Jan. 1986. Serial numbers: M001-M275. Rack mount tube power amp.

1982-1986		$800	$1,000

M-190

1980s. Rack mount tube power amp.

1980s		$550	$750

M-2000/Bass-2000 Head

Jun. 1995-2003. Serial numbers: B2K-01.

1995-2003		$850	$1,125

M6 Carbine Bass Head

2011-2017. 600-watt head, also offered in 2x12 combo.

2011-2017		$650	$850

Mark I Combo (Model A)

1971-1978. The original Boogie amp, not called the Mark I until the Mark II was issued, 60 or 100 watts, 1x12", Model A serial numbers: 1-2999, very early serial numbers 1-299 had 1x15".

1971-1978	1x12 or 1x15	$3,000	$4,000

Mark I Head

1990. 60/100 watts, tweed cover.

1990		$3,000	$4,000

Mark I Reissue

Nov. 1989-Sept. 2007. Serial numbers: H001-. 100

MODEL YEAR	FEATURES	LOW	HIGH

watts, 1x12", reissue features include figured maple cab and wicker grille.

2000-2007	Hardwood cab	$1,500	$2,000
2000-2007	Standard cab	$1,250	$1,750

Mark II B Combo

1980-1983. Effective Aug. '80 1x12" models, serial numbers 5575-110000. May '83 1x15" models, serial numbers 560-11000. The 300 series serial numbers K1-K336.

1981-1983	1x12 or 1x15	$2,000	$2,750
1981-1983	Hardwood cab	$2,500	$3,500

Mark II B Head

1981-1983. Head only.

1981-1983		$1,500	$2,000

Mark II C/Mark II C+ Combo

May 1983-Mar. 1985. Serial numbers 11001-14999 for 60 watts, 1x15", offered with optional white tolex cover. 300 series serial numbers after C+ are in the series K337-K422.

1983-1985		$4,500	$7,500
1985	Hardwood cab	$5,500	$10,000

Mark II C+ Head

1983-1985. 60-watt head.

1983-1985	Hardwood cab	$6,000	$10,000
1983-1985	Standard cab	$5,000	$8,000

Mark II Combo

1978-1980. Late-'78 1x12", serial numbers: 3000-5574. Effective Aug.'80 1x15", serial numbers: 300-559 until Mark II B replaced.

1978-1980	1x12 or 1x15	$1,750	$2,500

Mark III Combo

Mar. 1985-Feb. 1999. Serial numbers: 15000-28384. 300 series serialization K500-. Graphic equalizer only Mark III since Aug.'90, 100 watts, 1x12" combo. Custom cover or exotic hardwood cab will bring more than standard vinyl cover cab. There is also a Simul-Class Mark III which can run in 25, 60 or 85 watts.

1985-1990	Black	$2,000	$3,000
1985-1990	Custom color	$2,500	$3,500
1985-1999	Custom hardwood	$3,500	$4,500
1990-1999	Graphic EQ, standard cab	$2,500	$3,500

Mark III Head

1985-1999. 100 watts, black vinyl.

1985-1990		$3,000	$4,000
1985-1990	Custom hardwood	$4,250	$6,000
1990-1999	Graphic EQ	$3,500	$5,000

Mark IV (Rack Mount) Head

1990-May 2008. Rack mount version.

1990-2008		$1,500	$1,875

Mark IV Head

1990-May 2008. Clean rhythm, crunch rhythm and lead modes, 85 watts, EQ, 3-spring reverb, dual effects loops, digital foot switching. Also available in custom hardwood cab with wicker grille.

1990-2008	Custom hardwood	$3,000	$4,500
1990-2008	Short head, tolex	$2,000	$3,000

Mark IV/Mark IV B Combo

May 1990-May 2008. Changed to Model IV B Feb.'95, serial numbers: IV001. Clean rhythm, crunch rhythm and lead modes, 40 watts, EQ, 3-spring reverb, dual effects loops, digital foot switching.

1991-1999		$2,500	$3,500
1991-1999	Custom hardwood	$3,500	$5,500
2000-2008		$2,500	$3,500
2000-2008	Custom hardwood	$3,500	$5,500

Mark V Private Reserve

2011-2016. Special order, 1x12" combo.

2011-2016		$4,500	$6,500

Mark V Private Reserve 40th Anniversary

2009-2010. Limited production, 1x12 combo, 40th Anniversary logo.

2009-2010		$5,000	$7,500

Mark V/Mark Five

2010-present. 3 channels, 10/45/90 watts, also in 1x12" combo.

2010-2024	Combo 1x12	$2,250	$3,500
2010-2024	Head	$2,000	$3,000

Mark V:35/Mark Five:35

2015-present. 35/25/10 watts, also 1x12 combo, black.

2015-2024	Combo 1x12	$2,000	$2,500
2015-2024	Head	$2,000	$2,500

Maverick Dual Rectifier Combo

1997-Feb. 2005. Dual channels, 4 EL84s, 35 watts, 1x12", 2x12" or 4x10" combo amp, 5AR4 tube rectifier, cream vinyl covering. Serial number: MAV. Also available as head.

1997-2005	1x12	$1,500	$2,000
1997-2005	2x12	$1,250	$1,750
2005	4x10	$1,250	$1,750

Maverick Dual Rectifier Head

1994-Feb. 2005. 35 watts, Dual Rectifier head, white/blond vinyl cover.

1994-2005		$1,000	$1,500

Mini Rectifier Twenty-Five Head

2012-present. Ultra compact design, 10/25 watts, 2 channels.

2012-2024		$1,000	$1,250

M-Pulse 360

Jul. 2001-2005. Serial numbers: MP3-01-. Rack mount, silver panel.

2001-2003		$1,000	$1,250

M-Pulse 600

Apr. 2001-2011. Serial numbers: MP6-01- . Rack mount bass with 600 watts, tube preamp.

2001-2011		$1,000	$1,250

Nomad 45 Combo

Jul. 1999-Feb. 2005. Serial numbers: NM45-01. 45 watts, 1x12, 2x12" or 4x10" combo, dark vinyl cover, dark grille.

1999-2005	1x12	$650	$950
1999-2005	2x12	$700	$1,000
1999-2005	4x10	$850	$1,250

Nomad 45 Head

1999-Feb. 2005. 45 watts, dark vinyl cover, dark grille.

1999-2005		$575	$850

Nomad 55 Combo

Jul. 1999-2004. Serial numbers: NM55-01. 55 watts, 1x12", 2x12" or 4x10" combo.

1999-2004	1x12	$650	$1,000
1999-2004	2x12	$700	$1,125

Mesa-Boogie Mark II C+

1980s Mesa-Boogie Mark III Combo
Imaged by Heritage Auctions, HA.com

Mesa-Boogie Mark V

AMPS

Mesa-Boogie Rect-O-Verb I
Imaged by Heritage Auctions, HA.com

1984 Mesa-Boogie Son Of Boogie
Tom Pfeifer

1988 Mesa-Boogie Studio .22
Rivington Guitars

MODEL YEAR	FEATURES	LOW	HIGH

Nomad 55 Head

1999-2004. 55 watts.

1999-2004		$575	$850

Nomad 100 Combo

Jul. 1999-Feb. 2005. 100 watts, 1x12" or 2x12" combo, black cover, black grille.

1999-2005	1x12	$700	$1,000
1999-2005	2x12	$725	$1,125

Nomad 100 Head

Jul. 1999-Feb. 2005. 100 watts, black cover, black grille.

1999-2005		$650	$950

Princeton Boost Fender Conversion

1970. Fender Princeton modified by Randall Smith, Boogie badge logo instead of the Fender blackface logo on upper left corner of the grille. About 300 amps were modified and were one of the early mods that became Mesa-Boogie.

1970		$3,500	$5,000

Quad Preamp

Sep. 1987-1992. Serial numbers: Q001-Q2857. Optional Quad with FU2-A footswitch Aug.'90-Jan.'92, serial numbers: Q2022-Q2857.

1990-1992	With footswitch	$775	$1,250

Recto Recording Preamp

2004-2018. Rack mount preamp.

2004-2018		$1,125	$1,500

Rect-O-Verb Combo

Dec. 1998-2001. Serial numbers R50-. 50 watts, 1x12", black vinyl cover, black grille.

1998-2001		$1,125	$1,500

Rect-O-Verb I Head

Dec. 1998-2001. Serial numbers: R50-. 50 watts, head with 2 6L6 power tubes, upgraded Apr.'01 to II Series.

1998-2001		$1,000	$1,500

Rect-O-Verb II Combo

April 2001-2010. Upgrade R5H-750, 50 watts, AB, 2 6L6, spring reverb.

2001-2010		$1,125	$1,625

Rect-O-Verb II Head

Apr. 2001-2010. Upgrade, serial number R5H-750.

2001-2010		$1,000	$1,500

Road King Dual Rectifier Combo

2002-2015. 2x12" combo version, Series II upgrades start in '06.

2002-2005	Select watts	$3,000	$4,000
2006-2015	Series II	$3,000	$4,000

Road King Dual Rectifier Head

2002-May 2017. Tube head, various power tube selections based upon a chassis which uses 2 EL34s and 4 6L6, 2 5U4 dual rectifier tubes or silicon diode rectifiers, 50, 100 or 120 watts. Series II upgrades start in '06.

2002-2011		$2,750	$4,000
2006-2017	Series II	$2,750	$4,000

Roadster Dual Rectifier

2006-May 2017. 50/100 watts, head only, 1x12" or 2x12" combo.

2006-2014	Combo 1x12	$2,500	$3,500
2006-2017	Combo 2x12	$2,250	$3,500
2006-2017	Head	$2,000	$3,000

Rocket 44

2011. 45 watts, 1x12" combo, spring reverb, FX loop.

2011		$600	$800

Rocket 440

Mar. 1999-Aug. 2000. Serial numbers: R440-R44-1159. 45 watts, 4x10".

1999-2000		$775	$1,125

Satellite/Satellite 60

Aug. 1990-1999. Serial numbers: ST001-ST841. Uses either 6L6s for 100 watts or EL34s for 60 watts, dark vinyl, dark grille.

1990-1999		$725	$1,000

Solo 50 Rectifier Series I Head

Nov. 1998-Apr. 2001. Serial numbers: R50. 50-watt head.

1998-2001		$850	$1,125

Solo 50 Rectifier Series II Head

Apr. 2001-2011. Upgrade, serial numbers: S50-S1709. Upgrades preamp section, head with 50 watts.

2001-2011		$850	$1,125

Solo Dual Rectifier Head

1997-2011. Dual Rectifier Solo logo on front panel, 3x5U4, 150 watts.

1997-2011		$3,000	$4,000

Solo Triple Rectifier Head

1997-2011. Triple Rectifier Solo logo on front panel, 3x5U4, 150 watts.

1997-2011		$3,000	$4,000

Son Of Boogie

May 1982-Dec. 1985. Serial numbers: S100-S2390. 60 watts, 1x12", considered the first reissue of the original Mark I.

1982-1985		$750	$1,250

Stereo 290 (Simul 2-Ninety)

Jun. 1992-2021. Serial numbers: R0001-. Dual 90-watt stereo channels, rack mount.

1992-2021		$1,000	$1,250

Stereo 295

Mar. 1987-May 1991. Serial numbers: S001-S2673. Dual 95-watt class A/B stereo channels, rack mount. Selectable 30 watts Class A (EL34 power tubes) power.

1987-1991		$675	$950

Stiletto Ace

2007-2011. 50 watts, 2 channels, head or combo.

2007-2011	Combo 1x12	$1,250	$1,625
2007-2011	Combo 2x12	$1,250	$1,625
2007-2011	Head only	$1,250	$1,625

Stiletto Series

2004-2011. Series includes the Deuce (50 or 100 watts, 4 EL-34s) and Trident (50 or 150 watts, 6 EL-34s).

2004-2011	Deuce	$1,375	$2,000
2004-2011	Trident	$1,500	$2,250

Strategy 400

Mar. 1987-May 1991. Serial numbers: S001-S2627. 400 to 500 watts, power amplifier with 12 6L6 power tubes.

1987-1991		$1,125	$1,500

Strategy 500

Jun. 1991-Apr. 1992. S2,552- . Rack mount, 500 watts, 4 6550 power tubes.

1991-1992		$1,250	$1,750

MODEL YEAR	FEATURES	LOW	HIGH

Studio .22/Studio .22+

Nov. 1985-1988. Serial numbers: SS000-SS11499, black vinyl, black grille, 22 watts, 1x12". Replaced by .22+ Dec. '88-Aug. '93. Serial numbers: FP11,500-FP28,582. 22 watts.

1985-1988	22	$700	$1,000
1988-1993	22+	$700	$1,000

Studio Caliber DC-2

Apr. 1994-Jan. 1999. Serial numbers: DC2-01 - DC2-4247 (formerly called DC-2). 20 watts, 1x12" combo, dark vinyl, dark grille.

1994-1999		$575	$850

Studio Preamp

Aug. 1988-Dec. 1993. Serial numbers: SP000-SP7890. Tube preamp, EQ, reverb, effects loop.

1988-1993		$575	$850

Subway Reverb Rocket

Jun. 1998-Aug. 2001. Serial numbers: RR1000-RR2461. 20 watts, 1x10".

1998-2001		$700	$1,000

Subway Rocket (Non-Reverb)

Jan. 1996-Jul. 1998. Serial numbers: SR001-SR2825. No reverb, 20 watts, 1x10".

1996-1998		$700	$1,000

Subway/Subway Blues

Sep. 1994-Aug. 2000. Serial numbers: SB001-SB2515. 20 watts, 1x10".

1994-2000		$700	$1,000

TA-15 Head

2010-2015. TransAtlantic series, lunchbox-sized tube head, 2 channels, 5/15/25 watts.

2010-2015		$700	$1,000

TA-30 Combo

2012-2015. TransAtlantic series, 15/30/40 watts, 1x12" or 2x12" combo, 2 channels.

2012-2015		$1,125	$1,750

Trem-O-Verb Dual Rectifier Combo

Jun.1993-Jan.2001. Serial numbers: R- to about R-21210. 100 watts, 2x12" Celestion Vintage 30.

1993-2001		$1,250	$2,000

Trem-O-Verb Dual Rectifier Head

Jun. 1993-Jan. 2001. 100-watt head version.

1993-2001		$1,250	$2,000
1993-2001	Rackmount version	$1,250	$2,000

Triaxis Programmable Preamp

Oct. 1991-2016. Serial numbers: T0001-. 5 12AX7 tube preamp, rack mount.

1991-2016		$1,250	$2,000

Venture Bass (M-Pulse)

2007-2009		$1,125	$1,500

V-Twin Rackmount

May 1995-Jun. 1998. Serial numbers: V2R-001 to V2R-2258.

1995-1998		$600	$850

WalkAbout M-Pulse Bass Head

Sep. 2001-May 2017. Serial numbers: WK-01-. Lightweight 13 pounds, 2 12AX7s + 300 MOS-FET.

2001-2017		$750	$1,125

WalkAbout Scout Convertible Combo

2001-May 2017. Head and 1x12 combo.

2001-2017		$1,125	$1,625

Meteoro

1986-present. Guitar, bass, harp and keyboard combo amps, heads, and cabinets built in Brazil. They also build effects.

Metropoulos Amplification

2004-present. George Metropoulos builds his professional and premium grade amps in Flint, Michigan.

MG

2004-present. Tube combo guitar amps built by Marcelo Giangrande in São Paulo, Brazil. He also builds effects.

Mighty Moe Ampstraps

Peter Bellak built his guitar amp straps in Sacramento, California, starting in 2007. He also offered an amp strap for ukulele.

Milbert Amplifiers

2009-present. Professional and premium grade, production/custom, amps for guitars and cars, built in Gaithersburg, Maryland by Michael Milbert.

Mission Amps

1996-present. Bruce Collins' Mission Amps, located in Arvada, Colorado, produces a line of custom-made combo amps, heads, and cabinets.

Mojave Amp Works

2002-present. Tube amp heads and speaker cabinets by Victor Mason in Apple Valley, California.

Montgomery Ward

Amps for this large retailer were sometimes branded as Montgomery Ward, but usually as Airline (see that listing).

1x12" Combo

1950s. 1x12", about 2 6L6 power tubes, includes Model 8439 and brown covered Maestro C Series with cloverleaf grille.

1950s		$450	$575

Model 55 JDR 8437

1950s. 4x8" speakers in 'suitcase' amp cabinet, brown control panel.

1950s		$750	$950

Mooneyes

Budget solid state amp line from Lace Music Products. They also offered amps under the Rat Fink and Lace brands. Lace had a Mooneyes guitar model line.

Morley

Late-1960s-present. The effects company offered an amp in the late '70s. See Effects section for more company information.

Bigfoot

1979-ca.1981. Looks like Morley's '70s effects pedals, produced 25 watts and pedal controlled volume. Amp only, speakers were sold separately.

1979-1981		$300	$375

Mesa-Boogie Road King II Dual Rectifier Combo

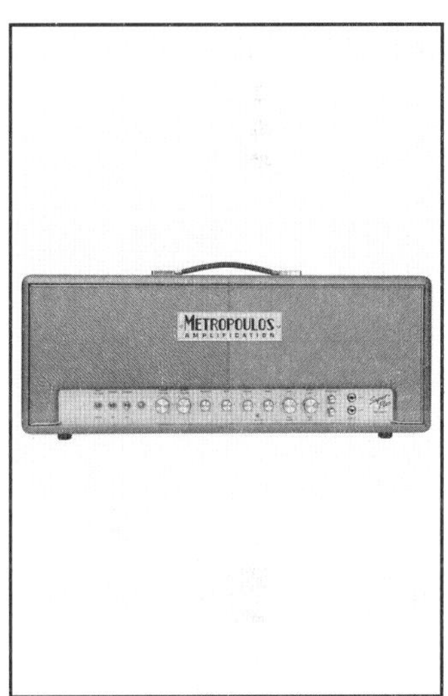

Metropoulos Super-Plex

Mission Amps

AMPS

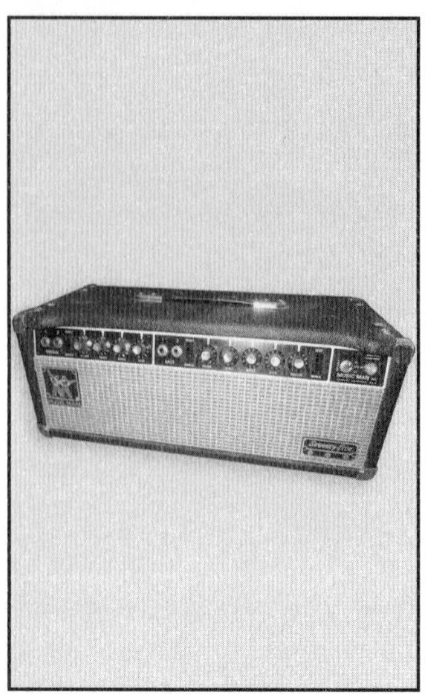
1979 Music Man Seventy Five
Rivington Guitars

1982 Music Man 110 RD Fifty
Richard Potter

1980 Music Man 212 Sixty-Five
Imaged by Heritage Auctions, HA.com

MODEL YEAR	FEATURES	LOW	HIGH

Mosrite

1968-1969. Mosrite jumped into the amp business during the last stages of the company history, the company was founded as a guitar company in 1954 and attained national fame in the '60s but by the time the company entered the amp business, the guitar boom began to fade, forcing the original Mosrite out of business in '69.

Model 400 Fuzzrite

1968-1969. Solidstate, 1x15 combo, black tolex with silver grille, reverb and tremolo.

1968-1969 $750 $950

Model SS-550 The Gospel

1968. Solidstate, 1 speaker combo, 2 channels normal and tremolo, reverb, black tolex.

1968 $725 $975

Mountain

Mountain builds a 9-volt amp in a wood cabinet. Originally built in California, then Nevada; currently being made in Vancouver, British Columbia.

Multivox

Ca.1946-ca.1984. Multivox was started as a subsidiary of Premier to manufacture amps, and later, effects. Generally student grade to low intermediate grade amps.

Murph

1965-1967. Amps marketed by Murph Guitars of San Fernado, California. At first they were custom-made tube amps, but most were later solidstate production models made by another manufacturer.

Music Man

1972-present. Music Man made amps from '73 to '83. The number preceding the amp model indicates the speaker configuration. The last number in model name usually refers to the watts. RD indicated Reverb Distortion. RP indicated Reverb Phase. Many models were available in head-only versions and as combos with various speaker combinations.

Sixty Five Head

1973-1981 65-watt $550 $700

Seventy Five Reverb/75 Reverb

1973-1981. Head, 75 watts, reverb.

1973-1981 $450 $550

110 RD Fifty

1980-1983. 50 watts, 1x10", reverb, distortion.

1980-1983 $550 $850

112 B Bass

1983. 50 watts, 1x12".

1983 $550 $850

112 RD Fifty

1980-1983. 50 watts, 1x12", reverb, distortion.

1980-1983 $550 $850

112 RD Sixty Five

1978-1983. 65 watts, 1x12", reverb, distortion.

1978-1983 $550 $850

MODEL YEAR	FEATURES	LOW	HIGH

112 RD One Hundred

1978-1983. 100 watts, 1x12", reverb, distortion, EVM option for heavy duty 12" Electro-Voice speakers.

1978-1983 $650 $825

1978-1983 EVM option $650 $825

112 RP Sixty Five

1978-1983. 65 watts, 1x12", reverb, built-in phaser.

1978-1983 $550 $700

112 RP One Hundred

1978-1983. Combo amp, 100 watts, 1x12", reverb, built-in phaser.

1978-1983 $575 $850

112 Sixty Five

1973-1981. Combo amp, 65 watts, 1x12", reverb, tremolo.

1973-1981 $575 $850

115 Sixty Five

1973-1981. Combo amp, 65 watts, 1x15", reverb, tremolo.

1973-1981 $575 $850

210 HD130

1973-1981. 130 watts, 2x10", reverb, tremolo.

1973-1981 $675 $950

210 Sixty Five

1973-1981. 65 watts, 2x10", reverb, tremolo.

1973-1981 $675 $950

212 HD130

1973-1981. 130 watts, 2x12", reverb, tremolo.

1973-1981 $675 $950

212 Sixty Five

1973-1981. 65 watts, 2x12", reverb, tremolo.

1973-1981 $675 $950

410 Sixty Five

1973-1981. 65 watts, 4x10", reverb, tremolo.

1973-1981 $675 $950

410 Seventy Five

1982-1983. 75 watts, 4x10", reverb, tremolo.

1982-1983 $675 $950

HD-130 Head

1973-1981. 130 watts, reverb, tremolo.

1973-1981 $550 $850

HD-150 Head

1973-1981. 75/100 watts.

1973-1981 $500 $750

RD Fifty Head

1980-1983. 50 watts, reverb, distortion.

1980-1983 $500 $750

Nady

1976-present. Wireless sound company Nady Systems started offering tube combo and amp heads in '06.

NARB

1973. Briefly made by Ken Bran and Jim Marshall, about 24 made, all were Marshall 100-watt tremolo half-stack, NARB logo on amp and cabinet.

100 Watt Half-Stack

1973. 100 watts, 4x12".

1973 $4,000 $6,000

MODEL YEAR	FEATURES	LOW	HIGH

National

Ca.1927-present. National/Valco amps date back to the late-'30s. National introduced a modern group of amps about the same time they introduced their new Res-O-Glas space-age guitar models in '62. In '64, the amp line was partially redesigned and renamed. By '68, the Res-O-Glas models were gone and National introduced many large vertical and horizontal piggyback models which lasted until National's assets were assigned during bankruptcy in '69. The National name went to Chicago importer Strum N' Drum. Initially, Strum N' Drum had one amp, the National GA 950 P Tremolo/Reverb piggyback.

Aztec

1948-1950s. Combo, early '50s version with 3 Rola 7x11" speakers using 3 speaker baffle openings, about 20 watts using 2x6L6 power tubes, 2-tone brown leatherette and tweed cover. By '56, amp has one 15" speaker and does not have segmented grill.

1948-1950s	3 Rola 7x11	$900	$1,250
1950s	1x15	$875	$1,125

Bass 70/Bass 75

1962-1967. 35 watts (per channel), 2x12" (often Jensen) speakers, large knobs, Raven Black tolex with silver and white grille, designed for bass. New model name in '64 with nearly identical features but listed as total of 70 watts, in '62 called Bass 70 but renamed Bass 75 in '64.

1962-1963	Bass 70	$750	$950
1964-1967	Bass 75 N6475B	$750	$950

Chicagoan Model 1220

1940s-1950s 17 watts, 1x10", tube, says "Valco Chicago 51" on control panel

1940s-50s		$800	$1,000

Dynamic 20

1962-1963. 17 watts, 2x8" (often Jensen) speakers, 2 large knobs, Raven Black tolex with silver and white grille, compact student-intermediate amp.

1962-1963		$850	$1,125

Glenwood 90

1962-1967. 35 watts, 2x12" (often Jensen) speakers, large knobs, reverb, tremolo, Raven Black tolex with silver and white grille, top of the line, becomes the nearly identical N6490TR in '64.

1962-1963		$1,250	$1,625
1964-1967	Model N6490TR	$1,125	$1,500

Glenwood Vibrato

Two 12" speakers, reverb, tremolo.

1964-1967	Model N6499VR	$1,250	$1,625

Model 75

1940s. Vertical tweed combo cabinet, volume and tone knobs, 3 inputs.

1940s		$550	$700

Model 100

1940s. Tube amp, 40 watts, 1x12".

1940s		$625	$800

Model 1202 Twin

1954. 18 watts, 2x8" Jensen speaker, 2 channels (Instrument and microphone), horizontal flying bird logo on grille.

1954		$850	$1,125

Model 1210 High Fidelity

1954. 20 watts, 1x15" Jensen speaker, 4 input jacks, 2 channels (instrument and microphone), 20x24x10" combo, metal handle.

1954		$850	$1,125

Model 1212

1954. 12 watts, 1x12", 5 tubes, 3 inputs, 15x18x8" combo, divingflying bird logo on grille, plastic handle.

1954		$800	$1,000

Model 1215

1952. 1x12", 2 channels.

1952		$800	$1,000

Model 1275

1953. Combo 1x10", 12 watts, 5 tubes, light tan weave cover, deep brown grille cloth.

1953		$800	$1,000

Model GA 950-P Tremolo/ Reverb Piggyback

1970s. Strum N' Drum/National model, solidstate, 50 watts, 2-channel 2x12" and 1x7" in 32" tall vertical cabinet, black.

1970s		$325	$450

Model N6800 - N6899 Piggyback

1968-1969. National introduced a new line of tube amps in '68 and most of them were piggybacks. The N6895 was sized like a Fender piggyback Tremolux, the N6875 and N6878 bass amps were sized like a '68 Fender large cab piggyback with a 26" tall vertical cab, the N6898 and N6899 were the large piggyback guitar amps. These amps feature the standard Jensen speakers or the upgrade JBL speakers, the largest model was the N6800 for PA or guitar, which sported 3x70-watt channels and 2 column speakers using a bass 2x12" + 1x3" horn cab and a voice guitar 4x10" + 1x3" horn cab.

1968-1969		$625	$800

Model N6816 (Model 16)

1968-1969. Valco-made tube amp, 6 watts, 1x10" Jensen speaker, 17" vertical cab, tremolo, no reverb, black vinyl cover and Coppertone grille.

1968-1969		$425	$550

Model N6820 Thunderball Bass

1968-1969. Valco-made tube amp, about 35 watts, 1x15" Jensen speaker, 19" vertical cab, black vinyl cover and Coppertone grille.

1968-1969		$500	$650

Model N6822 (Model 22)

1968-1969. Valco-made, 6 watts tube (4 tubes) amp, 1x12" Jensen speaker, 19" vertical cab, tremolo and reverb, black vinyl cover and Coppertone grille.

1968-1969		$450	$600

National Dobro

1930s. Sold by the National Dobro Corp. when the company was still in Los Angeles (they later moved to Chicago). National Dobro plate on rear back panel, suitcase style case that flips open to reveal the speaker and amp, National logo on outside of suitcase.

1930s	Early metal baffle	$650	$850
1930s	Later standard baffle	$500	$650
1930s	Suitcase style	$600	$750

1967 National Bass 75
Tom Pfeifer

1964 National Glenwood Vibrato
Imaged by Heritage Auctions, HA.com

1930s National Dobro Model 5960 Brown
Imaged by Heritage Auctions, HA.com

AMPS

1964 National Studio 10
Vic Albright

Naylor Dual 38

Nobles Streetman 15

MODEL YEAR	FEATURES	LOW	HIGH

Newport 40

1964-1967. 17 watts, 2x10", tremolo only.

1964-1967	Model N6440T	$800	$1,000

Newport 50

1964-1967. 17 watts, 2x10", tremolo and reverb.

1964-1967	Model N6450TR	$800	$1,000

Newport 97

1964-1967. 35 watts, 1x15", rear mounted chassis, tremolo.

1964-1967	Model N6497T	$800	$1,000

Sportsman

1950s. Tweed combo with brown leatherette speaker surround, 1x10".

1950s		$800	$1,000

Student Practice

1970s. Strum N' Drum era, small solidstate, single control.

1970s		$45	$60

Studio 10

1962-1967. Five watts, 1x8", 3 tubes, 1 channel, 1 volume control, no tone control, no reverb or tremolo.

1962-1963		$525	$700
1964-1967	Model N6410	$525	$700

Tremo-Tone Model 1224

1956-1959. Small combo, tremolo, dual Rola oval 6x11" speakers, tweed, by Valco, flying bird pattern on lower front grille.

1956-1959		$1,000	$1,375

Val-Pro 80

1962-1963. 35 watts, 2x12" (often Jensen) speakers, 8 tubes, large control knobs, tremolo, black cover with white and silver trim, replaced by Glenwood 90 in '64 with added reverb.

1962-1963		$1,125	$1,500

Val-Trem 40

1962-1963. 17 watts, 2x10" (often Jensen) speakers, large knobs, Val-Trem logo on back panel, Clear-Wave tremolo, Raven Black tolex with silver and white grille, open back combo amp, became Newport 40 in '64.

1962-1963		$975	$1,250

Val-Verb 60

1962-1963. 17 watts, 2x10" (often Jensen) speakers, large knobs, Val-Verb logo on back panel, reverb, no tremolo, Raven Black tolex with silver and white grille, open back combo amp.

1962-1963		$1,125	$1,500

Westwood 16

1964-1967. Five watts using 1 6V6 power, 2 12AX7 preamp, 1 5Y3GT rectifier, tremolo, 2x8", dark vinyl cover, silver grille.

1964-1967	Model N6416T	$800	$1,000

Westwood 22

1964-1967. 5 watts, 2x8", reverb and tremolo, 1 channel, 6 tubes.

1964-1967	Model N6422TR	$900	$1,125

Naylor Engineering

1994-present. Joe Naylor and Kyle Kurtz founded the company in East Pointe, Michigan, in the early '90s, selling J.F. Naylor speakers. In '94 they started producing amps. In '96, Naylor sold his interest in the business to Kurtz and left to form Reverend Guitars. In '99 David King bought the company and moved it to Los Angeles, California, then to Dallas, Texas. Currently Naylor builds tube amps, combos, speakers, and cabinets.

Nemesis

From the makers of Eden amps, Nemesis is a line of made-in-the-U.S., FET powered bass combos and extension cabinets. The brand is a division of U.S. Music Corp.

Newcomb

1950s. Newcomb Audio Products, Hollywood, California, Newcomb script logo on back panel along with model number, they offered instrument amplifiers that could also be used as small PA.

Model G 12

1953. 1x12" (Rolla) combo amp, 2 controls (volume and tone), large metal handle, oxblood-brown leatherette.

1953		$450	$600

Nobels

1997-present. Effects manufacturer Nobels Electronics of Hamburg, Germany also offers a line of small practice and portable amps.

Noble

Ca. 1950-ca. 1969. From Don Noble and Company, of Chicago, Illinois, owned by Strum N' Drum by mid-'60s. They also offered guitars and amps.

Model 381/Custom 381

1950s. 2x12" and 2x5".

1958-1960		$1,500	$2,000

Norma

1965-1970. Economy line imported and distributed by Strum N' Drum, Wheeling (Chicago), Illinois. As noted in the National section, Strum N' Drum acquired the National brand in the '70s. Some early amps were tube, but the majority were solidstate.

Solid State

1969-1970	Various models	$80	$125

Oahu

The Oahu Publishing Company and Honolulu Conservatory, based in Cleveland, Ohio, started with acoustic Hawaiian and Spanish guitars, selling large quantities in the 1930s. As electric models became popular, Oahu responded with guitar/amp sets. The brand has been revived on a line of U.S.-made tube amps.

Mid-Size Combo

1940s-50s	1x10	$500	$750

Small Combo

1965. Small 1x10" combo, 1 6V6, 4 12AX7. 15Y3GT, white cover, light grille, Oahu script logo upper left grille.

1965		$750	$1,125

MODEL YEAR	FEATURES	LOW	HIGH

Small Guitar/Lap Steel

1940s-1950s. 1x8", various colors.

1940s-50s		$400	$600

Thunderbolt

1965. 1x12", 6 tubes.

1965		$1,750	$2,500

Oliver

Ca.1966-ca. 1978. The Oliver Sound Company, Westbury, New York, was founded by former Ampeg engineer, Jess Oliver, after he left Ampeg in '65. Tube amp designs were based upon Oliver's work at Ampeg. The Oliver Powerflex Amp is the best-known design, and featured an elevator platform that would lift the amp head out of the speaker cabinet.

Model B-120 Head

1970s. B-120 logo on front panel, 35 watts, all tube head.

1970s		$550	$950

Model G-150R Combo

1970s. Reverb, tremolo, 2 6L6 power tubes, 40 watts, 1x15", black tolex with black grille, silver control panel.

1970s		$650	$1,125

Model P-500 Combo

1960s. All tube combo with 15" motorized amp chassis that rises out of tall lateral speaker cabinet as amp warms up.

1960s		$1,000	$2,000

Orbital Power Projector

Late-1960s-early-1970s. Rotating speaker cabinet with horn, Leslie-like voice.

1960s-70s		$1,250	$1,750

Sam Ash Oliver Head

Late-1960s-early-1970s. Private branded for Sam Ash Music, about 30 watts using the extinct 7027A power tubes, Sam Ash script logo on front grille.

1960s-70s		$450	$650

Omega

2009-present. James Price builds his premium grade, production/custom, amps in Moravian Falls, North Carolina.

Orange

1968-1981, 1995-present. Orange amps and PAs were made in the U.K. by Cliff Cooper and Matthew Mathias. The Orange-colored amps were well-built and were used by many notable guitarists. Since '95, Cliff Cooper is once again making Orange amplifiers in the U.K., with the exception of the small Crush Practice Combo amps, which are made in Korea. '68-'70 amps made by Matamp in Huddersfield; classic designs started in '71 at Bexleyheath/London plant.

Model GRO-100 Graphic Overdrive Head

1969-1971. Four EL34 power, only 2 pre-amp tubes, short-style head, model number on back panel.

1969-1971		$3,500	$5,000

Model OR-50 Limited Edition Head

2008. Switches between 30 and 50 watts.

2008		$1,250	$1,750

Model OR-50H Head (Reissue)

2012. Single channel, 50 watts, footswitch master volume.

2012		$1,000	$1,500

Model OR-80

1971-1981. Half-stack head and cab, 80 watts, 4x12" straight-front cab with Orange crest on grille, orange vinyl and light orange grille.

1971-1975		$3,000	$4,500
1976-1981		$2,750	$3,500

Model OR-80 Combo

1971-1981. About 80 watts, 2x12" combo.

1971-1975		$3,000	$3,750
1976-1981		$2,250	$3,000

Model OR-120 Graphic

1972-1981. Half-stack head and cab, 120 watts, 4x12" straight front cab with Orange crest on grille, orange vinyl and light orange grille.

1972-1975		$3,250	$5,000
1976-1981		$3,000	$4,000

Model OR-200 212 Twin

1970s. 120 watts, 2x12" combo, orange vinyl, dark grille, Orange crest on grille, reverb and vibrato, master volume.

1971-1975		$3,500	$5,500
1976-1981		$3,000	$4,500

Orepheus

Early 1960s. Private branded for Coast Wholesale Music Co., Orepheus logo on control panel along with model number.

Student Compact

1960s. Small student compact tube amps, some with 2 knobs, volume and tone.

1960s		$375	$500

Orpheum

Late-1950s-1960s. Student to medium level amps from New York's Maurice Lipsky Music.

Mid-Size/Small

Late-1950s-1960s. U.S.-made, 2 6V6 power tubes, Jensen P12R 12" speaker, light cover with gray swirl grille.

1950s-60s	Mid-Size	$625	$800
1950s-60s	Small	$425	$550

Osborne Sound Laboratories

Late 1970s. Guitar amps built by Ralph Scaffidi and wife guitarist Mary Osborne in Bakersfield, California. They also offered guitars.

Ovation

1966-present. Kaman made few amps under the Ovation name. They offered a variety of amps under the KMD brand from '85 to around '94.

Little Dude

1969-ca.1971. Solidstate combo, 100 watts, 1x15" and horn, matching slave unit also available.

1970s		$200	$300

The Kat (Model 6012)

1970s. Solidstate, 2x12" combo.

1970s		$200	$300

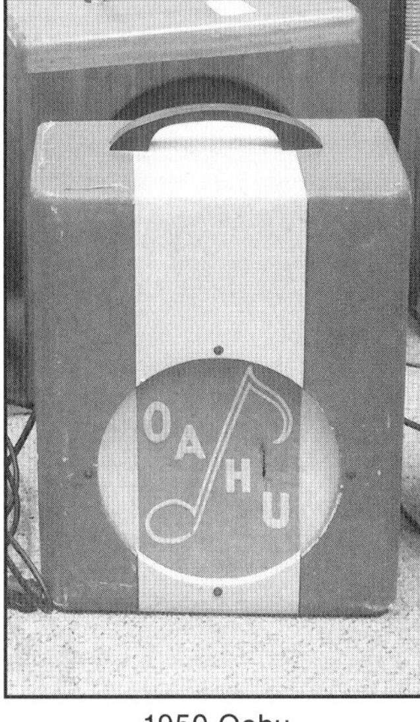

1950 Oahu

Bill Parsons

Omega

Ovation 6012 The Kat

Imaged by Heritage Auctions, HA.com

AMPS

1966 PANaramic Model 1210
Rivington Guitars

PRS Archon

Paul Ruby Amplifiers

MODEL YEAR	FEATURES	LOW	HIGH

Overbuilt Amps

1999-2007. Tube amps and combos built by Richard Seccombe in West Hills, California. He nows works at Fender R&D.

PAC-AMP (Magnatone)

Late-1950s-early-1960s. Private branded by Magnatone, often for accordion studios.

Model 213 Troubadour

1957-1958. 10 watts, 1x12".

1957-1958		$1,125	$1,500

Model 280-A

1961-1963. About 50 watts, 2x12" + 2x5", brown leatherette, light brown grille, stereo vibrato, PAC-AMP nameplate logo.

1961-1963		$1,625	$2,250

Palette Amps

Robert Wakeling began building his tube amp heads and combos and speaker cabinets in Stillwater, Oklahoma in 2003.

PANaramic (Magnatone)

1961-1963. Private branded equivalent of '61-'63 Magnatone brown leatherette series, large PANaramic logo. Many Magnatone private brands were associated with accordion companies or accordian teaching studios. PANaramic was a brand name of PANaramic accordion. They also made guitars.

Model 260/262-Style

1961-1963. 35 watts, 2x12", gray vinyl and light grille, vibrato, large PANaramic logo.

1961-1963		$1,625	$2,000

Model 413-Style

1961-1963. 18 watts, 1x12", black leatherette cover, light silver grille, vibrato, large PANaramic logo.

1961-1963		$1,000	$1,500

Model 450-Style

1961-1963. 20 watts, 1x12", reverb and vibrato, reverb not generally included in an early-'60s 1x12" Magnatone amp, dark vinyl, dark cross-threaded grille, large PANaramic logo.

1961-1963		$1,375	$2,000

Model 1210 (250-Style)

1961-1963. 1x12" combo, 20 watts, 2.5 channels, true vibrato.

1961-1963		$1,125	$1,875

Paris

1960s. Brand name used on a line of solidstate amps distributed by a music wholesaler. Possibly built by Kay.

Master Series

1960s. Compact combo, 1x12", black tolex-style cover, silver grille, rear mounted slanted control panel.

1960s		$95	$150

Park

1965-1982, 1993-1998, 2013-present. Park amps were made by Marshall from '65 to '82. Park logo on front with elongated P. In the '90s, Marshall revived the name for use on small solidstate amps imported from Asia. Brand name acquired by Mitch Colby (Colby Amps) in '13 and used on tube head amps and cabs built in New York City.

G Series

1992-2000. Student compact amps, models include G-10 (10 watts, 1x8"), G-25R (25w, reverb), G-215R (15w, 2x8") and GB-25 (25w, 1x12" bass).

1990s	G-10	$60	$125
1990s	G-15R	$65	$125
1990s	G-215R	$75	$125
1990s	G-25R	$70	$125
1990s	GB-25	$70	$125

Model 50 Head

1967-1969. Plexi, 50 watts.

1967-1969		$4,500	$5,500

Model 1001L Lead Head

1967-1969	Plexi	$5,000	$8,000
1969-1971	Aluminum	$3,000	$4,500

Model 1008A 4x12 Slant Cabinet

Late-1960s-early-1970s. Similar to Marshall 1960 4x12" cab.

1960s-70s		$2,250	$3,500

Model 1206 50W Master Volume Head

Late-1970s-1982. 50 watts, similar to JCM 800 50-watt made during same era.

1970s-1982		$2,250	$3,500

Model 1212 50W Reverb Combo

Late-1960s-early-1970s. 50 watts, 2x12", reverb, tube.

1960s-70s		$2,875	$4,000

Model 1213 100W Reverb Combo

Late-1960s-early-1970s. 100 watts, 2x12", reverb, tube.

1960s-70s		$2,875	$4,000

Model 1228 50W Lead Head

Late-1970s-1982. 50 watts, based upon Marshall 50-watt made during same era.

1970s-1982		$2,250	$3,500

Model 1229 100W Lead Head

Late-1970s-1982. 100 watts, tube.

1970s-1982		$2,250	$3,500

Model 1231 Vintage 20 LE Combo

Late-1970s-1982. 20 watts, 1x12".

1970s-1982		$2,500	$3,750

Model 1239 50W Master Volume Reverb Combo

Late-1970s-1982. 50 watts, 1x12".

1970s-1982		$2,500	$3,750

Paul Reed Smith

1985-present. In the late '80s, PRS offered two amp models. Only 350 amp units shipped. Includes HG-70 Head and HG-212 Combo. HG stands for Harmonic Generator, effectively a non-tube, solidstate amp. In '09, PRS introduced tube combo and head amps and cabinets designed by Doug Sewell.

Paul Ruby Amplifiers

2000-present. Professional grade, custom, tube amps built by Paul Ruby in Folsom, California.

MODEL YEAR	FEATURES	LOW	HIGH

Peavey

1965-present. Hartley Peavey's first products were guitar amps. He added guitars to the mix in '78. Headquartered in Meridan, Mississippi, Peavey continues to offer a huge variety of guitars, amps, and PAs. TransTube redesign of amps occurs in '95.

3120 Head

2009-2016. Tubes, 120 watts, 3 foot-switchable channels.

2009-2016 $375 $550

5150 212 Combo

1995-2004. Combo version of 5150 head, 60 watts, 2x12", large 5150 logo on front panel, small Peavey logo on lower right of grille.

1995-2004 $550 $925

5150 EVH Head/Cabinet Set

1995-2008. Half stack 5150 head and 4x12" cab, large 5150 logo on front of amp.

1995-2008 Half-stack $1,125 $1,500

5150 II

1999-2004. Has 5051 II logo on front, look for 'II' designation.

1999-2004 Half-stack $1,000 $1,375

6505 Series

2008-present. Promoted for modern "heavy'" metal sound.

2008-2019 6505, combo 2x12, 60w $450 $700

2008-2019 6505+, combo 1x12 $450 $700

2008-2024 6505+ head, 120w $450 $700

Alphabass

1988-1990. Rack mount all tube, 160 watts, EQ, includes 2x15" Black Widow or 2x12" Scorpion cabinet.

1988-1990 $250 $375

Artist

Introduced in 1975 as 120 watts, 1x12", bright and normal channels, EQ, reverb, master volume.

1970s $250 $400

Artist 110

1990s. TransTubes, 10 watts.

1990s $125 $175

Artist 240

1975-1980s. 120-watt combo, 1x12".

1975-1980s $200 $275

Artist 250

1990s. 100 watts, 1x12", solidstate preamp, 4 6L6 power tubes.

1990s $200 $275

Artist VT

1990s. Combo amp, 120 watts, 1x12".

1990s $275 $375

Audition 20

1980s-1990s. 20 watts, single speaker combo.

1980-90s $55 $75

Audition 30

1980s-1990s. 30 watts, 1x12" combo amp, channel switching.

1980-90s $55 $75

Audition 110

1990s. 25 watts, 1x10" combo, 2 channels.

1990s $60 $95

Audition Chorus

1980s. 2x10-watt channels, 2x6", channel switching, post gain and normal gain controls.

1980s $100 $125

Audition Plus

1980s. Solidstate, 20 watts, 1x10".

1980s $65 $100

Backstage 30/Plus/50/110

1977-1991. 1x10 combo, Backstage 30 (15 then 18 watts) '77-'83, Backstage Plus (35w) '84-'87, Backstage 50 (50w) '88-'89, Backstage 110 (65w) '89-'91. Name reused in 2000s on small 10-watt amp.

1977-1991 $60 $125

Backstage Chorus 208

1990-1996. 150 watts, 2x8", reverb, channel switching.

1990-1996 $125 $175

Bandit/65/75

1981-1989. 1x12" combo, originally 50 watts, upped to 65 watts in '85 and 75 in '87, renamed Bandit 112 in '90.

1981-1984 Bandit $125 $200

1985-1986 Bandit 65 $125 $200

1987-1989 Bandit 75 $125 $200

Bandit 112/Bandit II 112

1990-present. 80 watts (II is 100), 1x12", active EQ circuit for lead channel, active controls. TransTube series in '95.

1990-1994 $150 $225

1995-2024 TransTube $200 $250

Basic 40

1980s. 40 watts, 1x12".

1980s $90 $130

Basic 60

1988-1995. Solidstate combo amp, 50-60 watts, 1x12", 4-band EQ, gain controls, black.

1988-1995 $125 $175

Basic 112 Bass

1996-2006. 75 watts, 1x12" bass combo, 2000-era red border control panel.

1996-2006 $125 $175

Blazer 158

1995-2005. 15 watts, 1x8", clean and distortion, later called the TransTube Blazer III.

1995-2005 $75 $100

Bluesman

1992. Tweed, 1x12" or 1x15".

1992 $250 $350

Bravo 112

1988-1994. All tube reverb, 25 watts, 1x12", 3-band EQ, 2 independent input channels.

1988-1994 $225 $300

Butcher Head

1985-1987, 2010-2017. All tube head, 120 watts. Current version is all tube, 100 watts with half power switch.

1985-1987 $350 $500

Century 200H Head

2000s. 100 watts.

2000s $225 $300

Peavey 5150 212 Combo

Imaged by Heritage Auctions, HA.com

Peavey 6505

Peavey Classic 30/112

Peavey Delta Blues
Imaged by Heritage Auctions, HA.com

Ca.1980s Peavey Deuce
Imaged by Heritage Auctions, HA.com

Peavey Ecoustic E110

MODEL YEAR	FEATURES	LOW	HIGH

Classic 20

1990s. Small tube amp with 2xEL84 power tubes, 1x10" narrow panel combo, tweed cover.

1990s $325 $450

Classic 30/112

1994-present. Tweed combo, 30 watts, 1x12", EL84 tubes.

1994-2024 Narrow panel $375 $550
2008-2014 Badge front $375 $550
2008-2014 Head $325 $500

Classic 50/212

1990-2023. Combo, 50 watts, 2x12", 4 EL84s, 3 12AX7s, reverb, high-gain section.

1990-2023 $400 $600

Classic 50/410

1990-2023. Combo amp, 4x10", EL84 power, reverb, foot switchable high-gain mode.

1990-2023 $500 $600

Classic 120 Head

1988-ca.1990. Tube, 120 watts.

1988-1990 $300 $450

Combo 300

1982-1993. 1x15" bass combo, 300 watts.

1982-1993 $150 $250

DECA/750

1989-ca.1990. Digital, 2 channels, 350 watts per channel, distortion, reverb, exciter, pitch shift, multi-EQ.

1989-1990 $200 $300

Decade

1970s. Practice amp, 10 watts, 1x8", runs on 12 volt or AC.

1970s $100 $150

Delta Blues

1995-2014. 30 watts, tube combo, 4 EL84 tubes, 1x15" or 2x10", tremolo, large-panel-style cab, blond tweed.

1995-2014 $450 $600

Deuce

1972-1980s. 120 watts, tube amp, 2x12" or 4x10".

1972-1980s $225 $325

Deuce Head

1972-1980s. Tube head, 120 watts.

1972-1980s $175 $250

Ecoustic Series

1996-2022. Acoustic combo amps, 110 (1x10) and 112 (1x12, offered until '10) at 100 watts, digital effects (EFX, later E) added in '03. E20 and E208 added in '11.

1996-2010 112 $150 $250
2003-2022 E110 $150 $250

Encore 65

1983. Tube combo, 65 watts.

1983 $250 $350

Envoy 110

1988-2020. Solidstate, 40 watts, 1x10", TransTubes.

1988-2020 $115 $150

Heritage VTX

1980s. 130 watts, 4 6L6s, solidstate preamp, 2x12" combo.

1980s $175 $300

Jazz Classic

1980s. Solidstate, 210 watts, 1x15", electronic channel switching, 6-spring reverb.

1980s $175 $300

JSX (Joe Satriani)

2004-2010. Joe Satriani signature, 120-watt tube head. Also offered were JSX 50 (50 watts, '09-'10), JSX 212 Combo ('05-'10) and 5-watt JSX Mini Colossal ('07-'10).

2004-2010 120w head $575 $875
2004-2010 Combo 2x12 $575 $875

KB Series

1980s. Keyboard amp, models include KB-60 (60 watts, 1x12", reverb), KB-100 (100w, 1x15"), and KB-300 (300w, 1x15" with horn).

1980s KB-100 $150 $200
1980s KB-300 $200 $250
1980s KB-60 $125 $150

LTD

1975-1980s. Solidstate, 200 watts, 1x12" Altec or 1x15" JBL.

1975-1982 $175 $250

Mace Head

1976-1980s. Tube, 180 watts.

1976-1980s $275 $400

Mark III Bass Head

1978-1983. 300 watts, 2 channels, graphic EQ.

1978-1983 $200 $275

MegaBass

1986-ca. 1992. Rack mount preamp/power amp, 200 watts per 2 channels, solidstate, EQ, effects loop, chorus.

1986-1992 $180 $250

Microbass

1988-2005. 20 watts, 1x8" practice amp, made in China.

1988-2005 $45 $65

Minx 110 Bass

1987-2005. Solidstate, 35 watts RMS, 1x10" heavy-duty speaker.

1987-2005 $95 $135

Musician Head

Introduced in 1965 as 120-watt head, upped to 210 watts in '72.

1965-1970s $150 $200

Nashville 112 Steel Guitar

2008-present. Compact size, 1x12", 80 watts.

2008-2024 $400 $550

Nashville 400 Steel Guitar

1982-2000. 210 watts, 1x15" solidstate steel guitar combo amp.

1982-2000 $400 $550

Nashville 1000 Steel Guitar

1998-2008. 1x15" speaker, solidstate steel guitar combo amp.

1998-2008 $400 $550

Pacer

1974-1985. Master volume, 45 watts, 1x12", 3-band EQ.

1974-1985 $75 $100

MODEL YEAR	FEATURES	LOW	HIGH

Penta Head/Gary Rossington Signature Penta

2005-2015. Tubes, 140 watts, 4x12", 5 selectable preamp settings. Becomes the Gary Rossington Signature Penta in 2009.

2005-2015	Cab	$275	$375
2005-2015	Head	$300	$400

ProBass 1000

1980s. Rack mount, effects loops, preamp, EQ, crossover, headphone output.

1980s		$175	$250

Rage/Rage 158

1988-2008. Compact practice amp, 15 watts, 1x8". 158 starts '95. Replaced by 25-watt Rage 258.

1988-2008		$50	$65

Reno 400

1984-late 1980s. Solidstate, 200 watts, 1x15" with horn, 4-band EQ.

1980s		$150	$200

Renown 112

1989-1994. Crunch and lead SuperSat, 160 watts, 1x12", master volume, digital reverb, EQ.

1989-1994		$150	$200

Renown 212

1989-1994. Crunch and lead SuperSat, 160 watts, 2x12", master volume, digital reverb, EQ.

1989-1994		$150	$250

Renown 400

1981-late 1980s. Combo, 200 watts, 2x12", channel switching, Hammond reverb, pre- and post-gain controls.

1980s		$200	$300

Revolution 112

1992-2002. 100 watts, 1x12" combo, black vinyl, black grille.

1992-2002		$175	$250

Session 400

1974-ca. 1999. 200 watts, 1x15 or early on as 2x12, steel amp, available in the smaller box LTD, offered as a head in '76, available in wedge-shaped enclosure in '88.

1974-1999		$400	$550

Session 500

1979-1980s. 250 watts, 1x15", steel amp.

1979-1985		$400	$550

Special 112

1981-1994. 160 watts, 1x12". In 1988, available in wedge-shaped enclosure.

1981-1994		$150	$250

Special 130

1980s. 1x12", 130 watts.

1980s		$200	$300

Special 212

1995-2005. 160 watts, 2x12", transtube, solidstate series.

1995-2005		$200	$300

Stereo Chorus 212

1990s. 2x12" combo.

1990s		$275	$375

Studio Pro 50

1986-late 1980s. 50 watts, 1x12".

1980s		$110	$150

Studio Pro 112

1980s. Repackaged and revoiced in 1988. Solidstate, 65 watts, 1x12", Peavey SuperSat preamp circuitry, new power sections.

1980s		$125	$200

TKO Series Bass

1978-2011. Solidstate, 1x15, original TKO was 40 watts, followed by TKO 65 (65 watts) for '82-'87, TKO 75 for '88-'90, and TKO 80 for '91-'92. Renamed TKO 115 in '93 with 75, 80 or 100 watts until '09 when jumping to 400 watts.

1982-1987	TKO 65	$110	$150
1988-1990	TKO 75	$150	$200
1991-1992	TKO 80	$185	$250

TNT Series Bass

1974-2009. Solidstate, 1x15, original TNT was 45 watts, upped to 50 for '79-'81, followed by TNT 130 (130 watts) for '82-'87, TNT 150 for '88-'90, and TNT 160 for '91-'92. Renamed TNT 115 in '93 with 150, 160 or 200 watts until '09 when jumping to 600 watts (Tour TNT 115 - see Tour Series).

1982-1987	TNT 130	$250	$350
1988-1990	TNT 150	$250	$350
1991-1992	TNT 160	$250	$350

Tour Series

2004-2019. Imported bass heads and cabinets, various models.

2004-2019	Various models	$275	$400

Transchorus 210

1999-2000. 50 watts, 2x10 combo, stereo chorus, channel switching, reverb.

1999-2000		$250	$350

Triple XXX Series

2001-2009. Made in the USA.

2001-2009	Head, 120 watts	$650	$850
2001-2009	Super 40, 40w, 1x12	$500	$700

Triumph 60 Combo

1980s. Tube head, effects loop, reverb, 60 watts, 1x12", multi-stage gain.

1980s		$175	$250

Triumph 120

1989-1990. Tube, 120 watts, 1x12", 3 gain blocks in preamp, low-level post-effects loop, built-in reverb.

1989-1990		$200	$275

Ultra 60 Head

1991-1994. 60 watts, all tube, 2 6L6 power, black, black grille.

1991-1994		$350	$500

Ultra Series

1998-2002. All tube combos and cabs.

1998-2002	Ulta 112, 60 watts	$275	$350
1998-2002	Ulta 212, 60 watts	$325	$450
1998-2002	Ulta 410, 60 watts	$325	$450
1998-2002	Ulta Plus, 120 watts	$350	$475

ValveKing Series

2005-2018. Tube head, combos and cabs.

2005-2016	VK212, 100w, 2x12	$325	$450
2005-2018	VK100, 100w head	$275	$350
2005-2018	VK112, 50w, 1x12	$300	$400

Peavey Nashville 400
Imaged by Heritage Auctions, HA.com

Peavey TKO 80

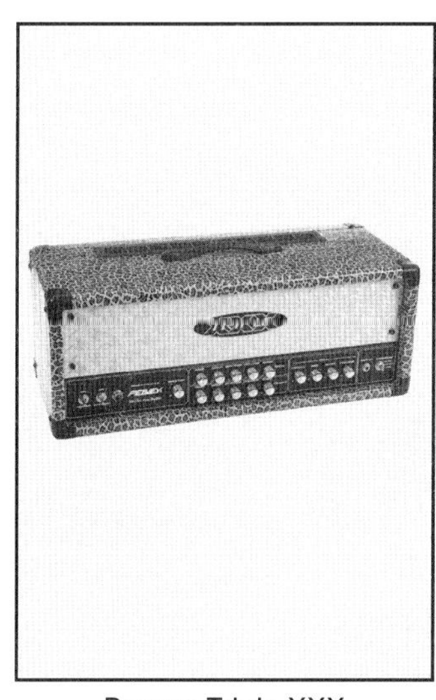

Peavey Triple XXX
Imaged by Heritage Auctions, HA.com

AMPS

Penn The Pennalizer 35

Plush PRB 1000S
Imaged by Heritage Auctions, HA.com

Port City Merino Combo

MODEL YEAR	FEATURES	LOW	HIGH

Vegas 400

1984-late 1980s. 210 watts, 1x15, some prefer as a steel guitar amp.

1980s		$350	$450

VTM Series

1987-1993. Vintage Tube Modified series, tube heads, 60 or 120 watts.

1987-1993	VTM120, 120w	$450	$800
1987-1993	VTM60, 60w	$450	$800

Vypyr Series

2008-2014. Modeling amp heads and combos, 60 and 120-watt tube and 15, 30, 75 and 100-watt solidstate models. Changes to Vypyr VIP in late '14.

2008-2014	15w, combo	$65	$100
2008-2014	30w, combo 1x12	$135	$200
2010	75w, combo	$200	$300

Wiggy 212

2001-2008. 100-watt head in mono (2x75-watt in stereo) with matching 2x12" cab, 2 EQ, 5-band sliders, rounded amp head.

2001-2008		$450	$650

Windsor Head

Introduced 2006 summer NAMM. All tube, 100- or 300-watt head.

2000s	100w	$275	$400
2000s	300w	$275	$400

Penn

Tube amps, combos, and cabinets built by Billy Penn, starting in 1994, originally in Colts Neck, then in Long Branch, New Jersey.

Pignose

1972-present. Pignose was started by people associated with the band Chicago, including guitarist Terry Kath, with help from designers Wayne Kimball and Richard Erlund. In 2023, Aria Guitars assumed ownership. They also offer guitars and have offered effects in the past.

7-100 Practice

1972-present. The original Pignose, 7"x5"x3" battery-powered portable amplifier, 1x5".

1972-2024		$55	$100

30/60

1978-ca.1987. Solidstate, 30 watts, 1x10", master volume.

1978-1987		$75	$125

60R Studio Reverb

Solidstate, 30 watts.

1980		$100	$150

G40V

1997-2009. Tubes, 1x10", 40 watts.

1997-2009		$215	$350

G60VR

1998-2009. Tubes, 1x12", 60 watts.

1998-2009		$225	$350

Hog Rechargeable Portable

1995-2023. Small rechargeable solidstate, models include Hog 20 (20W, 6.5" speaker) and Hog 30 (30W, 8").

1995-2023		$120	$175

Plush

Late 1960s-early 1970s. Tuck and roll covered tube amps made by the same company that made Earth Sound Research amps in Farmingdale, New York.

Tube

Early-1970s. All tube heads and combos including the 450 Super 2x12" combo, 1000/P1000S head, and 1060S Royal Bass combo.

1971-1972	Various models	$875	$1,125

Point Blank

2002-2004. Tube amps built by Roy Blankenship in Orlando, Florida before he started his Blankenship brand.

Polytone

Beginning in the 1960s and made in North Hollywood, California, Polytone offers compact combo amps, heads, and cabinets and a pickup system for acoustic bass.

Guitar or Bass

1980-2000s	Various models	$365	$500

Port City

2005-present. Daniel Klein builds his amp heads, combos, and cabinets in Rocky Point, North Carolina.

Premier

Ca.1938-ca.1975, 1990s-2010. Produced by Peter Sorkin Music Company in Manhattan. First radio-sized amplifiers introduced by '38. After World War II, established Multivox subsidiary to manufacture amplifiers ca.'46. By the mid-'50s at least, the amps featured lyre grilles. Dark brown/light tan amp covering by '60. By '64 amps covered in brown woodgrain and light tan. Multivox amps were made until around '84.

B-160 Club Bass

1963-1968. 15 to 20 watts, 1x12" Jensen speaker, '60s 2-tone brown styling, 6V6 tubes.

1963-1968		$700	$875

Model 50

1940s-1960s. In '62 this was their entry-level amp, 4 to 5 watts, 1x8" similar to Fender Champ circuit with more of a vertical suitcase-style cab.

1940s-60s		$475	$600

Model 71

1961-1962. Combo with 1x12" (woofer) and 2 small tweeters, 24 watts. '61 styling with circular speaker baffle protected with metal X frame, 2 tweeter ports on upper baffle, 2-tone light tan and brown, 8 tubes, tremolo. The '62 styling changed to baffle with a slight V at the top, and 2-tone cover.

1961	Round baffle	$1,000	$1,500
1962	V-baffle	$1,000	$1,500

Model 76

1950s-1960s Suitcase latchable cabinet that opens out into 2 wedges, 2-tone brown, lyre grille, 1x12"

1950s-60s		$875	$1,125

MODEL YEAR	FEATURES	LOW	HIGH

Model 88 Multivox

1962. Multi-purpose combo amp, organ-stop control panel, 1x15" woofer with 2 tweeters, vertical suitcase cab, 2-tone cover, classic circular speaker baffle with X brace, 10 tubes, top-of-the-line in '62 catalog.

1962		$1,000	$1,500

Model 88N

1950s-1961. Rectangular suitcase cabinet, 2-tone tan and brown, Premier and lyre logo, 25 watts, 1x12".

1950s-1961		$1,000	$1,500

Model 100R

1960s. Combo amp, 1x12", reverb and tremolo.

1960s		$1,000	$1,500

Model 110

1962. 12-watt 1x10 student combo, lyre grille logo, 2-tone cab.

1962		$675	$900

Model 120/120R

1958-1963. 12-watt 1x12" combo, tremolo, reverb ('62), 2-tone brown cab.

1958-1963		$775	$1,000
1962	With reverb	$875	$1,125

Model 200 Rhythm Bass

1962. 1x15" combo bass amp.

1962		$825	$1,125

T-8 Twin-8

1950s, 1964-1966. 20 watts, 2x8", tremolo, reverb.

1950s		$1,500	$1,875
1964-1966		$1,375	$1,750

T-12 Twin-12

1958-1962. Early reverb amp with tremolo, 2x12", rectangular cabinet typical of twin 12 amps (Dano and Fender), brown cover.

1958-1959		$1,625	$2,250
1960-1962		$1,500	$1,875

Pritchard Amps

Professional grade, production/custom, single and two-channel amps and cabinets built, beginning in 2004, by Eric Pritchard in Berkeley Springs, West Virginia.

Pyramid Car Audio

Inexpensive student models, imported.

Quantum

1980s. Economy amps distributed by DME, Indianapolis, Indiana.

Q Terminator Economy

1980s. Economy solidstate amps ranging from 12 to 25 watts and 1x6" to 1x12".

1980s	Various models	$50	$100

Quidley Guitar Amplifiers

Intermediate and professional grade, production/custom, tube guitar amp heads, combos and cabinets built by Ed Quidley in Wilmington, North Carolina, starting in 2006.

MODEL YEAR	FEATURES	LOW	HIGH

Quilter

2011-present. Patrick Quilter builds his intermediate and professional grade, production guitar amps in Costa Mesa, California.

Quinn

Professional and premium grade, production/custom, amps and cabinets built by Shadwell J. Damron III, starting 2005, in Vancouver, Washington.

Randall

1960s-present. Randall Instruments was originally out of California and is now a division of U.S. Music Corp. They have offered a range of tube and solidstate combo amps, heads and cabinets over the years.

Rastop Designs

2002-present. Professional grade, custom amps built by Alexander Rastopchin in Long Island City, New York. He also builds effects.

Rat Fink

Early 2000s. Solidstate amp line from Lace Music Products. They also sold guitars and basses under this brand and offered amps under the Mooneyes and Lace brands.

Realistic

Radio Shack offered a couple made-in-the-U.S. combo tube amps in the '60s, including the Entertainer 34 with a flip down record turntable in the back! Their radio and stereo gear were also branded Realistic.

Reason

2007-2016. Professional grade, production/custom, amps and cabinets built by Obeid Khan and Anthony Bonadio in St. Louis, Missouri.

Red Bear

1994-1997. Tube amps designed by Sergei Novikov and built in St. Petersburg, Russia. Red Bear amps were distributed in the U.S. under a joint project between Gibson and Novik, Ltd. Novik stills builds amps under other brands.

MK 60 Lead Tube

1994-1997. Head with 4x12" half stack, Red Bear logo on amp and cab.

1994-1997		$600	$750

MK 100 Full Stack

1994-1997. 100 watts, 2x4x12".

1994-1997		$1,000	$1,375

Red Iron Amps

2001-present. Paul Sanchez builds his tube amp heads in Lockhart, Texas.

RedPlate Amps

2006-present. Professional and premium grade, production/custom, guitar amplifiers built in Phoenix, Arizona by Henry Heistand.

1964 Premier B-160 Club Bass
Imaged by Heritage Auctions, HA.com

Quilter OverDrive 202

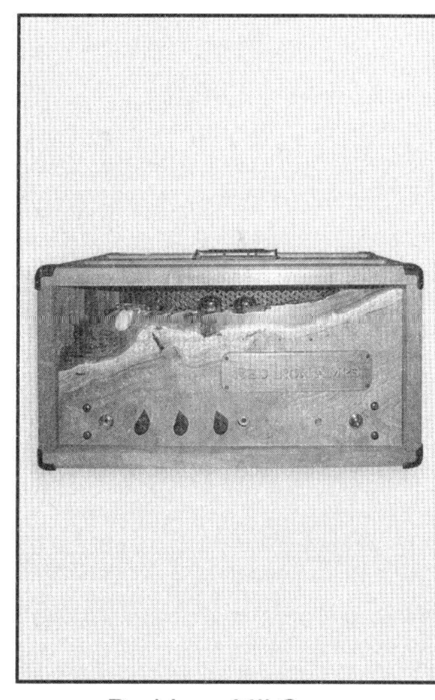

Red Iron Mil Spec

Reeves Custom 12

Retro-King Catalina Reverb

Reverend Kingsnake

MODEL YEAR	FEATURES	LOW	HIGH

Reeves Amplification

2002-present. Started by Bill Jansen, Reeves builds tube amps, combos, and cabinets in Cincinnati, Ohio, based on the classic British designs of Dan Reeves.

Regal

Ca.1895-1966, 1987-present. The original Regal company distributed instruments built by them and others.

Gibson EH

1936. Rare private-branded Gibson EH amp, 1x10", single control, alligator tweed.

1936	$850	$1,500

Reinhardt

2004-2012. Bob Reinhardt builds his professional grade, production/custom, guitar and bass amps and cabinets in Lynchburg, Virginia. He also builds effects pedals.

Resonant Amplifiers

Owners Wes Kuhnley and Peter Bregman build their professional grade, vacuum tube guitar and hi-fi amps in Minneapolis, Minnesota, starting in 2007. They also build the Field Effects.

Retro-King Amplifier Company

2004-present. Tube combo and head amps built by Chuck Dean in Marcellus, New York.

Revenge Amps

Greg Perrine began building in 1996, intermediate grade, production/custom, guitar amplifiers and attenuators in Conway, Arkansas. He also imports a line of amps.

Reverend

1996-present. Joe Naylor started building amps under the Naylor brand in '94. In '96 he left Naylor to build guitars under the Reverend brand. From '01 to '05, Reverend offered tube amps, combos, and cabinets built in Warren, Michigan, that Naylor co-designed with Dennis Kager.

Rex

1950s-1960s. Tube amps built by the Lamberti Bros. Co. in Melbourne, Australia. They also built guitars. In the 1920s-1940s, Gretsch has an unrelated line of guitars with that brand.

Reynolds Valveart

1997-present. Professional and premium grade, production/custom, amps and cabinets built by Peter Reynolds in Windsor, Australia.

Rickenbacker

1931-present. Rickenbacker made amps from the beginning of the company up to the late '80s. Rickenbacker had many different models, from the small early models that were usually sold as a guitar/amp set, to the large, very cool, Transonic.

E-12

1963. 1x12" combo with tremolo depth and speed, volume, and on-off tone knobs.

1963	$625	$800

Electro-Student

Late-1940s. Typical late-'40s vertical combo cabinet, 1x12" speaker, lower power using 5 tubes, bottom mounted chassis, dark gray leatherette cover.

1948-1949	$600	$750

Hi Fi Model 98

1956. Tube amp, long horizontal cab with 3 speakers, Rickenbacker Hi Fi and Model 98 logo on back panel, blond cover, wheat grille cloth.

1956	$1,250	$1,750

Model B-9E

1960s. 1x12" combo, 4 knobs, gray.

1960s	$800	$1,000

Model M-8

1950s-1960s. Gray, 1x8".

1950s-60s	$525	$750

Model M-9

1960s. Green, 1x12".

1960s	$675	$850

Model M-10

1930s. Silver metal, 1x10".

1935	$550	$700

Model M-11

1950s. 12-15 watts, 1x12", 2x6V6 power. There was a different M-11 offered in the 1930s.

1950s	$850	$1,125

Model M-12

1950s. 12-15 watts, 1x12", M-12 logo on back panel, brown leatherette. There was a different M-12 offered in the 1930s.

1950s	$850	$1,125

Model M-14A

Late 1950s-early 1960s. 1x12 combo, mid-power 2x6V6, dual channel with vibrato, rough-brown tolex cover.

1950s-60s	$850	$1,125

Model M-15

1950s-Early 1960s. 1x15" combo, 35 watts, 2 x 6L6 power tubes, model name on top panel.

1950s-60s	$850	$1,125

Model M-16

1950s-Early 1960s. 1x15", 35 watts, model name on top panel.

1950s-60s	$850	$1,125

Model M-30 EK-O-Sound

1961. Recording echo chamber and amp in 1x12 combo format, 11 tubes, gray grille and cover, very limited production.

1961	$4,000	$5,000

Model M-59

1930s. Small lap steel amp.

1935	$450	$600

Professional Model 200-A

1938. 15 watts, was sold with the Vibrola Spanish guitar.

1938	$600	$750

MODEL YEAR	FEATURES	LOW	HIGH

RB and RG Series

1987-1989. Various bass (RB) and guitar (RG) amp models.

1987-1989 $150 $250

Supersonic Model B-16

1960s. 4x10" speakers, gray cover.

1960s $925 $1,125

Supersonic Model B-22 Head

1960s. Tube head, gray cover.

1960s $725 $1,000

TR7

1978-1982. Solidstate, 7 watts, 1x10", tremolo.

1978-1982 $150 $200

TR14

1978-ca.1982. Solidstate, 1x10", reverb, distortion.

1978-1982 $145 $200

TR25

1979-1982. Solidstate, 1x12" combo, reverb, tremolo, distortion.

1979-1982 $225 $325

TR35B Bass

1978-ca.1982. Solidstate, mid-power, 1x15".

1978-1982 $225 $325

TR50

1977-ca. 1982. Solid state with Rick-o-Sound stereo inputs.

1977-1982 $175 $250

TR75G

1978-ca.1982. 75 watts, 2x12", 2 channels.

1978-1982 $225 $350

TR75SG

1978-ca.1983. 1x10" and 1x15" speakers.

1978-1982 $225 $350

TR100G

1978-ca.1982. Solidstate, 100 watts with 4x12", 2 channels.

1978-1982 $225 $350

Transonic TS100/TS200

1967-1973. Trapezoid shaped combo, solidstate, 100-watt (2x12") or 200-watt (2x15"), Rick-O-Select.

1967-1973 100w $7,500 $10,000

1967-1973 200w $8,500 $12,000

Risson

1970-1984, 2012-present. Bob Rissi builds his intermediate, professional and premium grade, production/custom, guitar and bass amplifiers in Placentia, California. From 1970-84 they were built in Santa Ana.

Rivera

1985-present. Amp designer and builder Paul Rivera modded and designed amps for other companies before starting his own line in California. He offers heads, combos, and cabinets. He also builds guitar pedals.

Chubster 40

2000-present. 40 watts, 1x12" combo, burgundy tolex, light grille.

2000-2024 $800 $1,125

MODEL YEAR	FEATURES	LOW	HIGH

Clubster 25

2005-2016. 25 watts, 1x10", 6V6.

2005-2016 $650 $950

Clubster 45

2005-2015. 45 watts, 1x12" combo.

2005-2015 $800 $1,125

Fandango 112 Combo

2001-present. 55 watts, 2xEL34, 1x12".

2001-2024 $1,000 $1,500

Fandango 212 Combo

2001-2015. 55 or 100 watts, 2x12" tube amp.

2001-2015 $1,125 $1,500

Jake Studio Combo

1997. 55 watts, 1x12", reverb and effects loop.

1997 $800 $1,125

Knucklehead 55

1994-2002. 55-watt amp head, replaced by reverb model.

1994-2002 $650 $950

Knucklehead 100

1994-2002. 100-watt amp head, replaced by reverb model.

1994-2002 $700 $1,125

Knucklehead Reverb 112

2003-2007. 55 watts, 1x12" amp combo, reverb.

2003-2007 $1,000 $1,500

Los Lobottom/Sub 1

1999-2004. 1x12" cabinet with 300-watt powered 12" subwoofer.

1999-2004 $450 $700

M-60 Head

1990-2009. 60 watts.

1990-2009 $575 $850

M-60 112 Combo

1989-2009. 60 watts, 1x12".

1989-2009 $675 $950

M-100 Head

1990-2009. 100 watts.

1990-2009 $625 $900

M-100 212 Combo

1990-2009. 100 watts, 2x12" combo.

1990-2009 $750 $1,125

Pubster 25

2005-2017. 25 watts, 1x10".

2015-2017 $450 $700

Pubster 45

2005-2014. 45 watts, 1x12".

2005-2014 $475 $750

Quiana Combo

2000-present. Combo, 55 watts.

2000-2014 2x12 $900 $1,250

2000-2014 4x10 $1,000 $1,375

2000-2024 1x12 $800 $1,125

R-30 112 Combo

1993-2007. 30 watts, 1x12", compact cab, black tolex cover, gray-black grille.

1993-2007 $825 $1,250

R-100 212 Combo

1993-2007. 100 watts, 2x12".

1993-2007 $900 $1,250

Rickenbacker Model M-8
Rivington Guitars

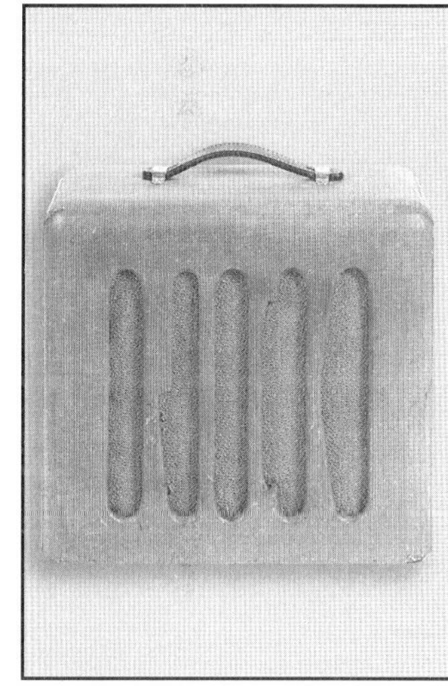

1937 Rickenbacher Model M-11

1980 Rickenbacker TR-100GT
Imaged by Heritage Auctions, HA.com

Rivera Suprema R-55

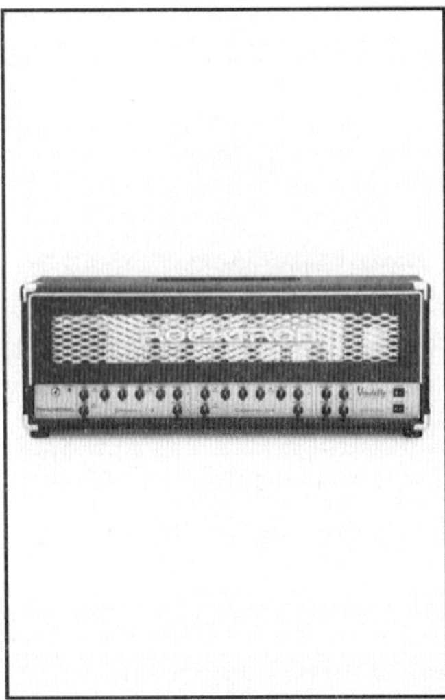
Rocktron Vendetta

1979 Roland Cube 60B
Imaged by Heritage Auctions, HA.com

MODEL YEAR	FEATURES	LOW	HIGH

Sedona 112

2008-2020. 55 watts, 1x12".

2008-2020		$1,125	$1,500

Sedona Lite 55

2005-present. For electric and acoustic guitars, 55 watts, 1x12".

2005-2024		$1,000	$1,500

Suprema R-55 112/115 Combo

2000-present. Tube amp, 55 watts, 1x12" (still available) or 1x15" ('00-'01).

2000-2024	1x12 or 1x15	$950	$1,500

TBR-1

1985-1999. First Rivera production model, rack mount, 60 watts.

1985-1999		$750	$1,125

Venus Series

2007-present. Series includes the 7/15-watt 3 combo (1x10 or 1x12), and the 15-watt 5 and 35-watt 6, both as combos (1x12, 2x12) and heads with cabs (1x12, 2x12).

2007-2024	Venus 6, 1x12	$950	$1,375
2007-2024	Venus 6, 2x12	$1,000	$1,500
2007-2024	Venus 6, head	$925	$1,375
2009-2024	Venus 3, 1x10	$875	$1,250
2009-2024	Venus 5, 1x12	$875	$1,250

Roccaforte Amps

1993-present. Tube amps, combos, and cabinets built by Doug Roccaforte in San Clemente, California.

Rocktron

1980s-present. Tube and solidstate amp heads, combos and cabinets. Rocktron is a division of GHS Strings and also offers stomp boxes and preamps.

Rogue

2001-present. They offered student-level solidstate import (Korea) compact amps up to around '06. They also offer guitars, basses, lap steels, mandolins, banjos, ukuleles and effects.

Small Solidstate

2001-2006. Various models.

2001-2006		$45	$100

Roland

Japan's Roland Corporation's products include amplifiers and keyboards and, under the Boss brand, effects.

Acoustic Chorus (AC) Series

1995-present. Number in model indicates wattage.

1995-2009	AC-100, 1x12, 2x5	$375	$525
1995-2020	AC-90, 2x8	$375	$525
1995-2024	AC-60, 2x6	$300	$425

Blues Cube

1996-present.

1996	BC60, 3x10	$275	$400
1996-2024	BC30, 1x12	$225	$300
1996-2024	BC60, 1x12	$250	$325

Bolt 60

Early 1980s. Solidstate/tube, 1x12".

1980s		$200	$300

Cube Series

1978-present. Number in model indicates wattage..

1978-1982	Cube 100, 1x12	$200	$275
1978-1982	Cube 20, 1x8	$115	$150
1978-1983	Cube 40, 1x10	$200	$275
1978-1983	Cube 60, 1x12	$200	$275
1978-1983	Cube 60B, 1x12	$200	$275
2000-2009	Cube 30 Bass, 1x10	$130	$175
2000s	Cube 80GX, 1x12	$200	$275
2000s	Cube 80XL, 1x12	$200	$275
2006-2010	Cube 30X, 1x10	$130	$175
2006-2013	Cube 15X, 1x8	$115	$150
2006-2013	Cube 20X, 1x8	$115	$150
2008-2013	Cube 80X, 1x12	$200	$275

Jazz Chorus (JC) Series

1975-present. Includes the JC-50 (50 watts, 1x12"), JC-55 (50 watts, 2x8"), JC-77 (80 watts, 2x10"), JC-90 (90 watts, 2x10") and JC-120 (120 watts, 2x12" and 4x12").

1975-2024	JC-120, 2x12	$650	$1,250
1980s	JC-50, 1x12	$350	$550
1987-1994	JC-55, 2x8	$350	$550
1987-1994	JC-77, 2x10	$400	$550
1990s	JC-120, 4x12	$500	$750
1990s	JC-90, 2x10	$400	$550

Micro Cube

2000-2024. Compact AC power or battery, 2 watts, 1x5".

2000-2024	Various models	$90	$125

Spirit Series

1982-1989. Compact, model number indicates wattage.

1982-1989	Spirit 30, 1x12	$90	$150
1982-1989	Spirit 40A, combo	$90	$150
1982-1989	Spirit 50, combo	$90	$150

Studio Bass

1979		$250	$325

VGA3 V-Guitar

2003-2009. GK digital modeling amp, 50 watts, 1x12" combo.

2003-2009		$225	$300

VGA5 V-Guitar

2001-2004		$225	$300

VGA7 V-Guitar

2000-2009		$250	$350

S.S. Maxwell

See info under Danelectro.

Sadowsky

1980-present. From '05 to '07, luthier Roger Sadowsky built a bass tube amp head in Brooklyn, New York. He also builds basses and guitars.

Sam Ash

1960s-1970s. Sam Ash Music was founded by Sam Ash (formerly Ashkynase) in Brooklyn, New York, in 1924, and by '66 there were about four Ash stores. During the '60s they private branded their own amp line, was built by Jess Oliver of Oliver Amps and based upon Oliver's Ampeg designs.

MODEL YEAR	FEATURES	LOW	HIGH

Sam Ash Mark II Pro Combo

1960s. 2x12" with reverb combo amp.

1960s		$650	$850

SamAmp

2004-present. Intermediate and professional grade, boutique amps built by Sam Timberlake in Vestavia Hills, Alabama.

Sano

1951-ca. 1980. Combos, heads and cabinets were made in three factories around New Jersey. Founded by Joseph Zonfrilli, Louis Iorio, and Nick Sano, initially offering accordion pickups, amplifiers, and all-electric accordions. Sano patented his accordion pickup in '44 and also developed a highly acclaimed stereophonic pickup accordion and matching amp. By '66 the Sano augmented their all-tube accordion amps with new solidstate circuitry models. In the mid-'60s they offered a new line of amps specifically designed for the guitar and bass market. Sano amps are generally low-gain, low power amplifiers. They also marketed reverb units and guitars.

Compact Combo

1960s	160R, 15w, 1x12	$500	$650
1960s	Sano-ette	$400	$500

Satellite Amplifiers

2004-present. Professional and premium grade, production/custom, tube amps, preamps and cabinets built by Adam Grimm in San Diego, California. He also builds effects.

Savage

1994-present. Tube combos, amp heads and cabinets built by Jeff Krumm at Savage Audio, in Savage, Minnesota.

Sceptre

1960s. Canadian-made. Sceptre script logo on upper left side of grille ('60s Fender-style and placement).

Signet

1960s. Low power, 1x10", Class-A 6V6 power.

1960s		$325	$450

Schaller

The German guitar accessory company began in 1945, main products in the late '50s were tube amps and they had solid-state amps in the '60s.

Schertler

Made in Switzerland, model logo on front, intermediate to professional grade, modern designs for modern applications.

SDG Vintage

2003-present. Intermediate and professional grade, production/custom, tube amps, combos and heads built by Steven Gupta in Bristow, Virginia.

MODEL YEAR	FEATURES	LOW	HIGH

Selmer

1930s-late 1970s. The Selmer UK distributor offered mid- to high-level amps starting as early as 1935 and by the '50s was one of the strongest European brands of amps.

Bassmaster 50

1960s. Amp and cabinet set.

1960s		$2,000	$2,500

Constellation 14

1962-1965. Single speaker combo, 14 watts, gray snakeskin tolex-type cover.

1962-1965		$2,500	$3,500

Futurama Caravelle

1960s. Mid-size 1x12" combo.

1960s		$1,000	$1,375

Futurama Corvette

1960s. Class A low power 1x8", 4 tubes, volume and tone controls, plus amplitude and speed tremolo controls, large script Futurama logo on front of amp, Futurama Corvette and Selmer logo on top panel.

1960s		$850	$1,125

Goliath Bass Set

1960s. 50 watts, 1x18".

1960s		$1,250	$1,625

Little Giant

1960s. Small combo, red.

1963		$1,125	$1,500

Mark 2 Treble and Bass Head

1960s. About 30 watts (2xEL34s), requires power line transformer for U.S. use, large Selmer logo on grille.

1960s		$1,125	$1,500

Thunderbird Twin 30

1960s. 30 watts, 2x12".

1962-1965		$4,000	$5,000

Thunderbird Twin 50

1960s. 50 watts, 2x12".

1964		$4,000	$5,000
1968		$2,500	$3,500

Truvoice

1960s. Truvoice and Selectortone logo on top-mounted chassis, 30-watt combo, 1x15 or 2x12 Goodmans speaker, 2xEL34 power tubes, tremolo, 6 push button Selectortone Automatic.

1961	1x15 combo	$2,250	$3,000
1965	2x12 combo	$2,750	$4,000

Zodiac Twin 30

1964-1971. Combo amp, gray snakeskin tolex cover.

1964-1971		$3,250	$4,500

Sewell

1998-2008. Doug Sewell built his tube combo and head amps in Texas. He currently is the senior amp designer for Paul Reed Smith.

Seymour Duncan

Pickup maker Seymour Duncan, located in Santa Barbara, California, offered a line of amps from around 1984 to '95.

1975 Sano Supernova
Tom Pfeifer

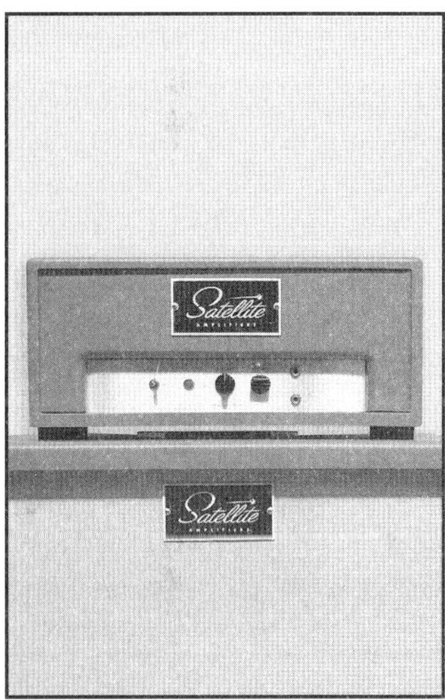

Satellite Amplifiers Barracuda

Selmer Zodiac Twin 30
Ron Cascisa

AMPS

Shaw Tonerod MG

Sherlock Fat Head

1972 Sho-Bud Twin Tube

Imaged by Heritage Auctions, HA.com

MODEL YEAR	FEATURES	LOW	HIGH

84-40/84-50

1989-1995. Tube combo, 2 switchable channels, 1x12", includes the 84-40 ('89-'91, 40 watts) and the 84-50 ('91-'95, 50 watts).

1989-1995	84-40 or 84-50	$350	$450

Bass 300 x 2

1986-1987. Solidstate, 2 channels (300 or 600 watts), EQ, contour boost switches, effects loop.

1986-1987		$350	$450

Bass 400

1986-1987. Solidstate, 400 watts, EQ, contour boost, balanced line output, effects loop.

1986-1987		$350	$450

Convertible

1986-1995. 60-watt; dual-channel; effects loop; Accutronics spring reverb; 3-band EQ.

1986-1987	Head only	$525	$675
1988-1995	Combo	$525	$675

KTG-2075 Stereo

1989-1993. Part of the King Tone Generator Series, 2 channels with 75 watts per channel.

1989-1993		$250	$350

SG Systems

1970s. A Division of the Chicago Musical Instrument Company (CMI), who also owned Gibson Guitars. Gibson outsourced amplifier production from Kalamazoo to CMI in '67 and CMI (Chicago) continued for a year or two with Gibson-branded amplifiers. In the early '70s CMI introduced the SG Systems brand of hybrid amplifiers, which had a tube power section and a solidstate preamp section. CMI was trying to stay modern with SG Systems by introducing futuristic features like the Notch Shift which would quickly switch between popular rock sounds and mellow jazz delivery. SG amps have a large SG logo on the front baffle and were built with metal corners. Amplifiers have similar power specs; for example, the models issued in '73 all were rated with 100-watt RMS with 200-watts peak music power, so models were based on different speaker configurations.

SG Series

1970s	SG115, 1x15	$500	$650
1970s	SG212, 2x12	$500	$650
1970s	SG215 Bass, 2x15	$500	$650
1970s	SG410, 4x10	$500	$650
1970s	SG610, 6x10	$550	$700
1970s	SG812 PA	$350	$450

Shaw

2008-present. Custom/production, intermediate and professional grade, guitar amp heads and cabinets built by Kevin Shaw in Lebanon, Tennessee.

Sherlock Amplifiers

1990-present. Dale Sherlock builds his intermediate to premium grade, production/custom, tube guitar amps and cabinets in Melbourne Victoria, Australia.

MODEL YEAR	FEATURES	LOW	HIGH

Sherwood

Late 1940s-early 1950s. Amps made by Danelectro for Montgomery Ward. There are also Sherwood guitars and lap steels made by Kay.

Sho-Bud

Introduced and manufactured by the Baldwin/Gretsch factory in 1970. Distributed by Kustom/Gretsch in the '80s. Models include D-15 Model 7838, S-15 Model 7836, Twin Tube Model 7834, and Twin Trans Model 7832.

Compactra 100

1960s. Hybrid tube, 45 watts, 1x12", model name logo on lower left control panel.

1960s		$600	$850

D15 Double

Introduced in 1970. Solidstate, 100 watts. 2 channels 1x15" JBL speaker.

1970s		$575	$850

S15 Single

Introduced in 1972. Like D15, but with single channel.

1970s		$400	$550

Sho-Bass

Introduced in 1972. 100 watts, 1x15", solidstate combo, black grille, black vinyl cover.

1970s		$400	$550

Twin Trans

Introduced in 1972. 100 watts, solidstate combo, 2x12", reverb, black vinyl cover, dark grille, Sho-Bud script logo front upper right.

1970s		$650	$850

Twin Tube

Introduced in 1972. 100-watt tube combo, 4 6L6s, 2x12", reverb, black vinyl cover, dark grille.

1970s		$750	$1,125

Siegmund Guitars & Amplifiers

Chris Siegmund builds his tube amp heads, combos and cabinets in Los Angeles, California. He founded the company in Seattle in 1993, moving it to Austin, Texas for '95-'97. He also builds effects pedals and guitars.

Silvertone

1941-ca.1970, present. Brand used by Sears. All Silvertone amps were supplied by American companies up to around '66.

Model 1300

1948. Vertical combo cab, treble-clef logo on grille, 2-tone, 3 inputs, 2 controls.

1948		$450	$600

Model 1304

1949-1951. 18 watts, 1x12, 2x6L6 power tubes, 2-tone leatherette cover, round speaker baffle hole, volume, treble, bass and tremolo control knobs, becomes Model 1344.

1949-1951		$450	$600

MODEL YEAR	FEATURES	LOW	HIGH

Model 1330

1954-1957. Introduced in Sears Fall '54 catalog, 3 tubes (with rectifier), 1x6", wide-panel 13x13.75x7.5" cab in tan artificial leather, 9 lbs., replaced Model 1339 at the same price but with new wide-panel style, small Silvertone logo above the grille, replaced in '58 by Model 1390 Silvertone Meteor.

1954-1957		$250	$300

Model 1331

1954-1957. Made by Danelectro, 14 lbs., 1x8" student combo, 3 tubes (with rectifier), 1 volume, 1 tone, 2 inputs, tan tweed-effect cover with brown alligator trim, large-thread wheat-gold grille, brown metal control panel.

1954-1957		$325	$400

Model 1333

1954-1957. Made by Danelectro, 23 lbs., 1x12" combo, 2x6V6 power, 5 tubes (with rectifier), 2 volumes, 1 tone, 3 inputs, 2-control vibrato, tan tweed-effect cover with brown alligator trim, large-thread wheat-gold grille, brown metal control panel.

1954-1957		$500	$650

Model 1334

1954-1957. Made by Danelectro, 29 lbs., heavy-duty 1x12" combo, 6 tubes (with rectifier), 2 volumes, 2 tones, 3 inputs, 2-control vibrato, tan tweed-effect cover with brown alligator trim, large-thread wheat-gold grille, brown metal control panel.

1954-1957		$500	$650

Model 1335

1954-1957. Made by Danelectro, 99 lbs., heavy-duty 1x15" combo, 6 tubes (with rectifier), 2 volumes, 2 tones, 4 inputs, 2-control vibrato, tan tweed-effect cover with brown alligator trim, large-thread wheat-gold grille, brown metal control panel.

1954-1957		$550	$700

Model 1336 (Twin Twelve)

1954-1957. Made by Danelectro, 26.75x17.5x9.25" cab, 45 lbs., 2x12" combo, 4x6L6 power tubes, 3 volumes, 2 tones, 4 inputs, 2-control vibrato, tan tweed-effect cover with brown alligator trim, large-thread wheat-gold grille, brown metal control panel.

1954-1957		$850	$1,125

Model 1337 "Wide Range Eight Speaker"

1956. Odd-looking suitcase cab that opens into 2 separate speaker baffles each containing 4x8" speakers, 2 preamps, 2 channels with separate controls for volume, bass and treble, 2-control vibrato, 42 lbs.

1956		$850	$1,125

Model 1339

Ca.1952-1954. Sears lowest-priced amp, 3 tubes (with rectifier), 1x6", 1 input, 1 knob, maroon artificial leather cover over 10.5x8x5" vertical cab, script Silvertone logo on low right grille, 7 lbs.

1952-1954		$325	$350

Model 1340

Ca.1952-1954. Sears second lowest-priced amp, 3 tubes (with rectifier), 1x6", 2 inputs, 1 knob, brown and white imitation leather cover over 15x12x8.5" vertical cab, script Silvertone logo on low right grille, 14 lbs.

1952-1954		$325	$350

Model 1342 Streamlined

Ca.1952-1954. Sears third lowest-priced amp, 4 tubes (with rectifier), 1x12", 3 inputs, 2 knobs, green and beige imitation leather cover over 16x19x7.25" slanted-side cab, script Silvertone logo on low right grille, 23 lbs.

1952-1954		$500	$650

Model 1344

1950-1954. Retro-styled vertical 22.5x15.5x9.5" cab with round speaker baffle hole, 1x12" combo, first Silvertone built-in vibrato, 6 tubes (with rectifier), 3 inputs, 3 controls (treble, bass, volume) plus vibrato control, maroon imitation leather cover with sports-stripe around the bottom, 33 lbs., script Silvertone logo low right side of cab.

1952-1954		$500	$650

Model 1346 Twin Twelve

Ca.1952-1954. Danelectro-made, brown control panel, 2x12", 4 6L6s, vibrato, leather handle, tan smooth leatherette cover, 2 speaker baffle openings.

1952-1954		$850	$1,125

Model 1390 Meteor

1958-1959. Renamed from Model 1330, Meteor logo on front panel, 1x6" practice amp, 3 tubes (with rectifier), tan simulated leather cover, in '60 renamed Model 1430 (but no longer a Meteor).

1958-1959		$325	$350

Model 1391

1958-1959. Modern-style cab, 3 tubes (with rectifier), 5 watts, 1x8".

1958-1959		$325	$350

Model 1392

1958-1959. Modern-style cab, 6 tubes (with rectifier), 10 watts, 1x12", vibrato.

1958-1959		$500	$650

Model 1393

1958-1959. Modern-style cab, 7 tubes (with rectifier), 15 watts, heavy-duty 1x12", vibrato.

1958-1959		$500	$650

Model 1396 Two-Twelve

1958-1959. Script Two-Twelve logo on lower left front and Silvertone logo on lower right front, 50 watts, 2x12", 4x6L6 power tubes, 9 tubes (with rectifier), vibrato, 26.75x17.5x9.25" with gray and metallic fleck cover, white grille, 45 lbs.

1958-1959		$850	$1,125

Model 1420

1968. Tube-powered, 5 watts, 1x8" student combo.

1968		$350	$450

Model 1421

1968. Tube-powered, 10 watts, 1x8" combo, covered in dark olive vinyl.

1968		$350	$450

Model 1422

1968. Tube-powered, 40 watts, 1x12" combo, covered in dark olive vinyl.

1968		$500	$650

Model 1423

1968. Solidstate, 125 watts, 2x12" cab, 55 lbs., dark olive.

1968		$400	$500

1948 Silvertone Model 1300
Vic Albright

Silvertone Model 1331
Tom Pfeifer

1953 Silverton Model 1346 Twin Twelve
Rivington Guitars

AMPS

1960 Silvertone Model 1471
Ron Tedesco

1961 Silvertone Model 1474 Twin Twelve
Imaged by Heritage Auctions, HA.com

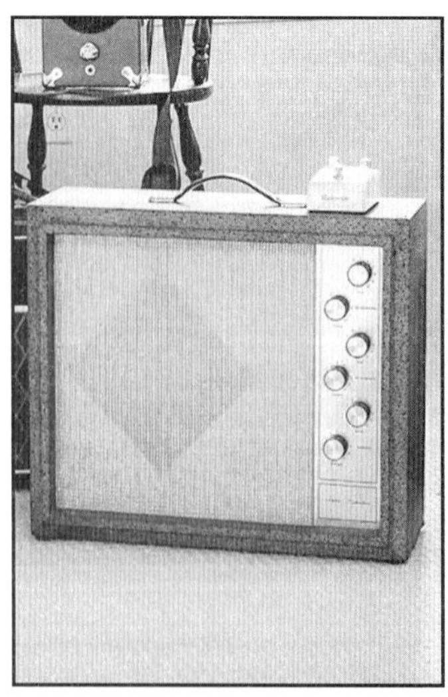
1966 Silvertone Model 1482
Larry Niven

MODEL YEAR	FEATURES	LOW	HIGH

Model 1425

1968. Solidstate, 200 watts, 6x10" cab, 86 lbs., dark olive.

1968		$975	$1,375

Model 1426

1968. Solidstate, 250 watts, 6x15" cab, slide switches instead of control knobs, automatic E-tone for tuning, casters for 149 lb. head and cab.

1968		$975	$1,375

Model 1428

1968. Solidstate, 60 watts, 1x15" cab, 36 lbs., dark olive.

1968		$400	$500

Model 1430

1959-1966. Silvertone's lowest-price model, 3 tubes, 1x6", previously called Model 1390 Meteor, and prior to that named Model 1330, retro cab basically unchanged since first introduced in '54.

1959-1966		$325	$450

Model 1431

1959-1961. 5 watts, 1x8", overhanging-top wrap-around grille cab, 3 tubes (with rectifier), light gray cover with white grille.

1959-1961		$325	$450

Model 1431 Bass

1968. Solidstate, 200 watts, 6x12" cab, 91 lbs., dark olive.

1968		$975	$1,375

Model 1432

1959-1961. 10 watts, 1x12", vibrato, overhanging-top wrap-around grille cab, 6 tubes (with rectifier), dark gray tweed-effect cover with white grille.

1959-1961		$500	$650

Model 1433

1959-1961. 15 watts, 1x15", vibrato, overhanging-top wrap-around grille cab, 7 tubes (with rectifier), gray with metallic fleck cover with white grille.

1959-1961		$650	$850

Model 1434 Twin Twelve

1959-1961. 50 watts using 4x6L6 power, 2x12" combo, vibrato, 2 channels each with volume, bass and treble controls, black cover with gold-colored trim.

1959-1961		$975	$1,375

Model 1459

1960s. Student tube amp, 3 watts, 1x8", black vinyl, square cab, 1 tone, 1 volume, 1 channel, 2 inputs.

1967-1968		$350	$450

Model 1463 Bass

1967-1968. Solidstate, 1x15", piggyback, 60 lbs., reverb, tremolo.

1967-1968		$400	$500

Model 1464

1967-1968. Solidstate, 100 watts, 2x12", piggyback, 60 lbs., reverb, tremolo, gray vinyl cover.

1967-1968		$450	$600

Model 1465

1966-1968. Solidstate, piggyback, 150 watts, 6x10", reverb, tremolo, gray vinyl cover, replaces Model 1485.

1966-1968		$850	$1,125

Model 1466 Bass

1966-1968. Solidstate, 150 watts, 6x10", gray vinyl cover.

1966-1968		$700	$900

MODEL YEAR	FEATURES	LOW	HIGH

Model 1471

1961-1963. 5 watts, 1x8", 3 tubes, 1 volume, 1 tone, 2 inputs, black leathette cover with white grille.

1961-1963		$350	$450

Model 1472

1960s. 10 watts, 2 6V6s provide mid-level power, 1x12", front controls mounted vertically on front right side, black cover with silver grille, large stationary handle, tremolo.

1961-1963		$500	$650

Model 1473 Bass

1961-1963. Designed for bass or accordion, 25 watts, 1x15" combo, 6 tubes (with rectifier), 2 channels, 4 inputs, 19x29x9" cab, 43 lbs., black leatherette with white grille.

1961-1963		$650	$975

Model 1474 Twin Twelve

1961-1963. Silvertone's first reverb amp, 50 watts, 4x6L6 power, 10 tubes (with rectifier), 2x12" combo, 2 control vibrato with dual remote footswitch, 2 channels each with bass, treble, and volume, 4 inputs, ground switch, standby switch, 19x29x9" combo cab, 54 lbs., black leatherette with silver grille.

1961-1963		$850	$1,250

Model 1481

1963-1968. Compact student amp, 5 watts, 1x8", 3 tubes (with rectifier), volume and tone controls, gray leatherette cover with white grille, replaces Model 1471.

1963-1968		$350	$450

Model 1482

1960s. 15 watts, 1x12", 6 tubes, control panel mounted on right side vertically, tremolo, gray leatherette.

1963-1968		$500	$750

Model 1483 Bass

1963-1966. 23 watts, 1x15" piggyback tube amp, gray tolex and gray grille.

1963-1966		$650	$850

Model 1484 Twin Twelve

1963-1966. 60 watts, 2x12" piggyback tube amp, tremolo and reverb, gray cover with light grille.

1963-1966		$850	$1,250

Model 1485

1963-1965. 120 watts, 6x10" (Jensen C-10Q) piggyback, 10 tubes with 5 silicon rectifiers, 2 channels, reverb, tremolo, charcoal-gray tolex-style cover, white grille, replaced in '66 by solidstate Model 1465.

1963-1965		$1,125	$1,625

Model 4707 Organ

1960s. Interesting '60s family room style cabinet with legs, 45-watt tube amp with vibrato, 1x12", front controls, could be used for organ, stereo, or record player turntable.

1960s		$450	$600

Simms-Watts

Late 1960s-1970s. Tube amp heads, combos, PA heads and cabinets made in London, England. Similar to Marshall and HiWatt offerings of the era.

MODEL YEAR	FEATURES	LOW	HIGH

Skip Simmons

1990-present. Custom and production tube combo amps built by Skip Simmons in Loma Rica, California.

Skrydstrup R&D

1997-present. Production/custom, premium grade, amps and cabinets built by Steen Skrydstrup in Denmark. He also builds effects.

Sligo Amps

Intermediate and professional grade, production/custom, amps built starting in 2004, by Steven Clark in Leesburg, Virginia.

SMF

Mid-1970s. Amp head and cabinets from Dallas Music Industries, Ltd., of Mahwah, New Jersey. Offered the Tour Series which featured a 150-watt head and 4x12" bottoms with metal speaker grilles and metal corners.

Tour MK 2 Head

Mid-1970s. 150-watt head, high- and low-gain inputs, master volume, 8xEL34 power tubes, black.

1970s		$1,250	$1,750

SMF (Sonic Machine Factory)

2002-2009. Tube amps and cabinets designed by Mark Sampson (Matchless, Bad Cat, Star) and Rick Hamel (SIB effects) and built in California.

Smicz Amplification

Tube combos and extension cabinets built by Bob Smicz in Bristol, Connecticut.

Smith Custom Amplifiers

All tube combo amps, heads and speaker cabinets built by Sam Smith in Montgomery, Alabama starting in 2002.

Smokey

1997-present. Mini amps often packaged in cigarette packs made by Bruce Zinky in Flagstaff, Arizona. He also builds Zinky amps and effects and has revived the Supro brand on a guitar and amp.

Snider

Jeff Snider has been building various combo tube amps in San Diego, California, since '95. In 1999 he started branding them with his last name.

Soldano

1987-present. Made in Seattle, Washington by amp builder Mike Soldano, the company offers a range of all-tube combo amps, heads and cabinets. They also offer a reverb unit.

Astroverb 16 Combo

1997-2020. Atomic with added reverb.

1997-2020		$875	$1,500

Atomic 16 Combo

1996-2001. Combo, 20 watts, 1x12".

1996-2001		$725	$1,125

Avenger Head

2004-2020. Single channel, 4 preamp tubes, 100-watt with 4 power tubes, or 50-watt with 2.

2004-2020		$1,500	$2,000

Decatone Combo

1998-2020. 2x12" 100-watt combo, rear mounted controls, still available as a head.

1998-2008	Combo 2x12	$2,000	$2,500
2009-2020	Head only	$1,500	$2,000

HR 50/Hot Rod 50/50+ Head

1992-2012. 50-watt single channel head.

1992-2012		$1,125	$1,500

HR 100/Hot Rod 100/100+ Head

1994-2001. 100-watt single channel head.

1994-2001		$1,250	$1,750

Lucky 13 Combo

2000-2020. 100 watts (50 also available), 2x12" combo.

2000-2020		$1,750	$2,500

Reverb-O-Sonic Combo

1990s-2020. 50 watts, 2 channels, 2x12" combo, reverb.

1990s-2020		$1,250	$1,750

SLO-100 Super Cabinet

1988-2019. 4x12" slant-front or straight-front cabinet, prices shown are for slant, deduct $100 for straight.

1988-1989		$1,000	$1,250
1990-2019		$850	$1,125

SLO-100 Super Lead Overdrive

1988-2020. First production model, 100-watt amp head, snakeskin cover, 4x12" cabinet. Replaced by SLO-100 Classic in '21.

1988-1989		$3,000	$4,500
1990-2009		$2,500	$4,000
2010-2020		$2,500	$4,000

Sommatone

1998-present. Jim Somma builds his tube combo and head amps and cabinets in Somerville, New Jersey.

Sonax

Introduced in 1972. Budget line of solidstate amps offered by Gretsch/Baldwin, made by Yorkville Sound (Traynor) in Toronto. Introduced with dark grille and dark cover.

530-B Bass

1970s. Solidstate, 30 watts, 1x12".

1970s		$150	$200

550-B Bass

1970s. Solidstate, 50 watts, 1x15".

1970s		$175	$250

720-G

1970s. Solidstate student amp, 20 watts, 2x8", reverb.

1970s		$175	$250

730-G

1970s. Solidstate, 30 watts, 2x10", reverb and tremolo.

1970s		$250	$350

1967 Silvertone Model 1484 Twin Twelve

Tom Pfeifer

Smokey

Soldano SLO-100

Imaged by Heritage Auctions, HA.com

AMPS

Sound City 120 and L-412
Imaged by Heritage Auctions, HA.com

Sovtek Mig 100

Speedster 25 Watt Deluxe

MODEL YEAR	FEATURES	LOW	HIGH

750-G

1970s. Solidstate, 50 watts, 2x12", reverb and tremolo.

1970s		$275	$350

770-G

1970s. Solidstate, 75 watts, 4x10", reverb and tremolo.

1970s		$275	$350

Songworks Systems

See the listing under Little Lanilei.

Sonny Jr.

Harmonica amplifiers built by harmonica player Sonny Jr. in conjunction with Cotton Amps in Tolland, Connecticut. Was started in 1996.

Sonola

Tube combo amps made for the Sonola Accordian company of Chicago in the 1950s and '60s, possibly built by Guild or Ampeg. There are also Sonola tube amp heads from the '70s made by MHB Amplifiers in Adelaide, South Australia.

Sound City

Made in England from 1966-'67 to the late-'70s, the tube Sound City amps were Marshall-looking heads and separate cabinets. They were imported, for a time, into the U.S. by Gretsch.

50 PA Plus

Late-1960s-late-1970s. Similar to 50 Plus but with 4 channels.

1970s		$850	$1,125

50 Plus/50R Head

Late-1960s-late-1970s. Amp head, labeled 50 Plus or 50 R.

1960s-70s		$1,125	$1,625

120 Energizer Slave Unit

1970s. 120-watt power amp only, no preamp, Energizer Slave Unit logo on front panel.

1970s		$700	$950

120/120R Head

Early-late-1970s. The 120-watt head replaced the late-1960s 100-watt model.

1970s	120, no reverb	$1,000	$1,500
1970s	120R, reverb	$1,250	$1,750

200 Plus Head

1970s		$1,500	$1,750

Concord Combo

80 watts, 2x12" Fane speakers, cream, basketweave grille.

1968		$1,250	$1,625

L-80 Cabinet

1970s. 4x10" speaker cabinet.

1970s		$750	$1,500

L-412 Cabinet

1970s. 4x12" speaker cabinet.

1970s		$850	$1,500

X-60 Cabinet

1970s. 2x12" speaker cabinet.

1970s		$800	$1,500

MODEL YEAR	FEATURES	LOW	HIGH

Sound Electronics

Sound Electronics Corporation introduced a line of amplifiers in 1965 that were manufactured in Long Island. Six models were initially offered, with solidstate rectifiers and tube preamp and power sections. Their catalog did not list power wattages but did list features and speaker configurations. The initial models had dark vinyl-style covers and sparkling silver grille cloth. The amps were combos with the large models having vertical cabinets, silver script Sound logo on upper left of grille. The larger models used JBL D120F and D130F speakers. Standalone extension speakers were also available.

Various Models

Mid-1960s. Made in U.S.A., models include X-101, X-101R, X-202 Bass/Organ, X-404 Bass and Organ, X-505R amps, hi-fi chassis often using 7868 power tubes.

1960s		$600	$850

Southbay Ampworks/ Scumback Amps

2002-present. Tube combo amps and speaker cabinets built by Jim Seavall in Whittier, California. He also builds Scumback Speakers. In '14, name changed to Scumback Amps.

Sovtek

1992-1996. Sovtek amps were products of Mike Matthews of Electro-Harmonix fame and his New Sensor Corporation. The guitar and bass amps and cabinets were made in Russia.

Mig Cabinet

1992-1996	2x12"	$350	$450

Mig Series Head

1992-1996. Tube amp heads, model number indicates watts, point-to-point wiring, models include Mig 30, 50, 60, 100, 100B (bass).

1992-1996	Various models	$500	$850

Space Tone

See Swart Amplifiers.

Specimen Products

1984-present. Luthier Ian Schneller added tube amps and speaker cabinets in '93. He also builds guitars, basses and ukes in Chicago, Illinois.

Speedster

1995-2000, 2003-2007. Founded by Lynn Ellsworth, offering tube amps and combos designed by Bishop Cochran with looks inspired by dashboards of classic autos. In '03, Joe Valosay and Jevco International purchased the company and revived the brand with help from former owner Cory Wilds. Amps were originally built by Soldono, but later ones were built by Speedster in Gig Harbor, Washington. They also built effects pedals.

Splawn

2004-present. Production, professional grade, tube amps and cabinets built by Scott Splawn in Dallas, North Carolina.

MODEL YEAR	FEATURES	LOW	HIGH

St. George

1960s. There were Japanese guitars bearing this brand, but these amps may have been built in California.

Mid-Size Tube

1965. Low power, 1x10" Jensen, 2 5065 and 2 12AX7 tubes.

1960s		$225	$300

Standel

1952-1974, 1997-present. Bob Crooks started custom building amps part time in '52, going into full time standard model production in '58 in Temple City, California. In '61 Standel started distributing guitars under their own brand and others. By late '63 or '64, Standel had introduced solidstate amps, two years before Fender and Ampeg introduced their solidstate models. In '67 Standel moved to a new, larger facility in El Monte, California. In '73 Chicago Musical Instruments (CMI), which owned Gibson at the time, bought the company and built amps in El Monte until '74. In '97 the Standel name was revived by Danny McKinney who, with the help of original Standel founder Bob Crooks and Frank Garlock (PR man for first Standel), set about building reissues of some of the early models in Ventura, California.

A-30 B Artist 30 Bass

1964-early-1970s. Artist Series, the original Standel solidstate series, 80 watts, 2x15".

1964-1969		$450	$625

A-30 G Artist 30 Guitar

1964-early-1970s. Solidstate, 80 watts, 2x15".

1964-1974		$500	$650

A-48 G Artist 48 Guitar

1964-early-1970s. Solidstate, 80 watts, 4x12".

1964-1974		$550	$750

A-60 B Artist 60 Bass

1964-early-1970s. Solidstate, 160 watts, 4x15".

1964-1974		$550	$750

A-60 G Artist 60 Guitar

1964-early-1970s. Solidstate, 160 watts, 4x15".

1964-1974		$550	$750

A-96 G Artist 96 Guitar

1964-early-1970s. Solidstate, 160 watts, 8x12".

1964-1974		$600	$850

Artist XV

1960s. Piggyback, hybrid solidstate preamp with power tubes.

1962		$450	$575

C-24 Custom 24

Late-1960s-1970s. Custom Slim Line Series, solidstate, 100 watts, 2x12", dark vinyl, dark grille.

1960s-70s		$550	$750

I-30 B Imperial 30 Bass

1964-early-1970s. Imperial Series, the original Standel solidstate series, 100 watts, 2x15".

1964-1974		$550	$750

I-30 G Imperial 30 Guitar

1964-early-1970s. Imperial Series, the original Standel solidstate series, 100 watts, 2x15".

1964-1974		$550	$750

S-10 Studio 10

Late-1960s-1970s. Studio Slim Line Series, solidstate, 30 watts, 1x10", dark vinyl, dark grille.

1960s-70s		$350	$475

S-24 G

1970s. Solidstate, 2x12".

1970s		$425	$550

S-50 Studio 50

Early-late-1960s. Not listed in '69 Standel catalog, 60 watts, gray tolex, gray grille, piggyback.

1960s		$475	$650

SM-60 Power Magnifier

1970s. Tall, verticle combo solidstate amp, 100 watts, 6x10".

1970		$425	$550

Tube

1953-1958. Early custom-made tube amps made by Bob Crooks in his garage, padded Naugahyde cabinet with varying options and colors. There are a limited number of these amps, and brand knowledge is also limited, therefore there is a wide value range. Legend has it that the early Standel amps made Leo Fender re-think and introduce even more powerful amps.

1953-1958	Various models	$3,500	$5,000

Star

Tube amps, combos and speaker cabinets built by Mark Sampson in the Los Angeles, California area, starting 2004. Sampson has also been involved with Matchless, Bad Cat, and SMF amps.

Starcaster

See listing under Fender.

Starlite

Starlite was a budget brand made and sold by Magnatone. See Magnatone for listings.

Stella Vee

1999-2005. Jason Lockwood built his combo amps, heads, and cabinets in Lexington, Kentucky.

Stephenson

1997-present. Mark Stephenson builds his intermediate to premium grade, production/custom, tube amps and cabinets in Regina, Saskatchewan 1997-'99, in Hope, British Columbia 2000-'06, and since in Parksville, British Columbia. He also offers effects.

Stevenson

1999-present. Luthier Ted Stevenson, of Lachine, Quebec, added amps to his product line in '05. He also builds basses and guitars.

Stimer

Brothers Yves and Jean Guen started building guitar pickups in France in 1946. By the late '40s they had added their Stimer line of amps to sell with the pickups. Early amp models were the M.6, M.10 and M.12 (6, 10 and 12 watts, respectively). An early user of Guen products was Django Reinhardt.

Splawn Supersport

Standel 25L15

Imaged by Heritage Auctions, HA.com

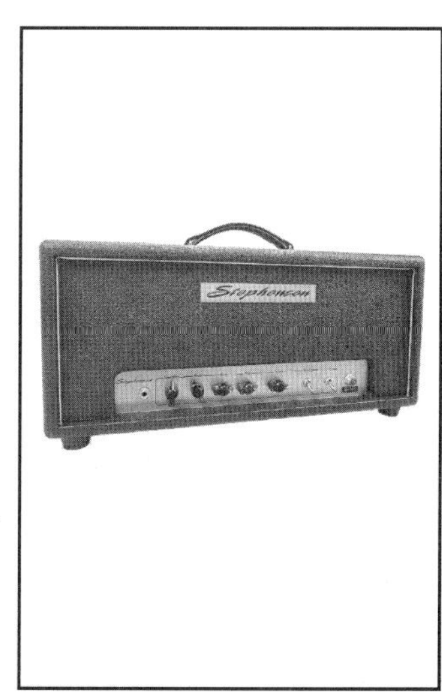

Stephenson B-100

AMPS

AMPS

Straub Twisted Triode 12 Watt

Suhr Badger
Rob Bernstein

1970 Sunn Sceptre
Imaged by Heritage Auctions, HA.com

MODEL YEAR	FEATURES	LOW	HIGH

Stinger

1980s-1990s. Stinger was a budget line of guitars and solidstate amps imported by Martin.

Strad-O-Lin/Stradolin

Ca.1920s-ca.1960s. The Strad-O-Lin company primarily made mandolins for wholesalers but around '57 Multivox/Premier bought the company and used the name on guitars and amps.

Compact Solidstate

1960s. Made in U.S.A., logo on control panel and grille, black grille and cover.

1960s		$125	$175

Stramp

1970s. Stramp, of Hamburg, Germany, offered audio mixers, amps and compact powered speaker units, all in aluminum flight cases.

Solidstate

1970s. Solidstate amp head in metal suitcase with separate Stramp logo cabinet.

1970s		$350	$500

Straub Amps

2003-present. Harry Straub builds his professional grade, production/custom, amps in St. Paul, Minnesota.

Suhr

1997-present. John Suhr builds his production/custom amps in Lake Elsinore, California. He also builds guitars and basses.

Sundown

1983-1988. Combo amps, heads and cabinets designed and built by Dennis Kager. By '88, he had sold his interest in the company.

Sunn

1965-2002, 2023-present. Started in Oregon by brothers Conrad and Norm Sundhold (Norm was the bass player for the Kingsman), Sunn introduced powerful amps and extra heavy-duty bottoms and was soon popular with many major rock acts. Norm sold his interest to Conrad in '69. Conrad sold the company to the Hartzell Corporation of Minnesota around '72. Fender Musical Instruments acquired the brand in '85 shortly after parting ways with CBS and used the brand until '89. They resurrected the brand again in '98 but quit offering the name in '02. In '23, the Sunn brand was relaunched by a team of music industry veterans with product made in the U.S.

100S Amp and Cabinet Set

1965-1970s. 60 watts, 1x15" JBL D130F and 1 LE 100S JBL Driver and Horn, piggyback, 5 tubes (with rectifier).

1965-1969		$1,750	$2,500

190L Amp and Cabinet Set

1970s. Solidstate, 80 watts, 2 speakers.

1970s		$850	$1,375

200S/215B Amp and Cabinet Set

1966-1970s. 60 watts, 2x6550s, large vertical cab with 1x15" or 2x15" speakers.

1966-1969	1x15	$1,500	$2,250
1966-1969	2x15	$1,500	$2,250
1966-1969	Head only	$900	$1,375

601-L Cabinet

1980s. 6x10" plus 2 tweeters cab.

1980s		$500	$650

2000S

1968-1970s. 4x6550 power tubes, 120 watts.

1968-1970s	Head & cab	$2,000	$2,500
1968-1970s	Head only	$1,500	$2,000

Alpha 112

1980s. Solidstate, MOS-FET preamp section, 1x12" combo, reverb, overdrive, black.

1980s		$200	$300

Alpha 115

1980s. Solidstate, MOS-FET preamp section, 1x15", clean and overdrive.

1980s		$200	$300

Alpha 212 R

1980s. Solidstate, MOS-FET preamp section, 2x12", reverb.

1980s		$250	$350

Beta Bass

1978-1980s. Solidstate 100-watt head and combos, large Beta Bass logo on front panel.

1978-1980s	4x12	$725	$1,250
1978-1980s	6x10	$725	$1,250
1978-1980s	Combo 1x15	$725	$1,250
1978-1980s	Combo 2x12	$725	$1,250
1978-1980s	Combo 4x10	$725	$1,250

Coliseum 300 Bass

1970s. Solidstate, Coliseum-300 logo on front.

1970s	Head & cab	$950	$1,250
1970s	Head only	$500	$750

Coliseum Lead

1970s. Solidstate, Coliseum Lead logo on front.

1970s	Head & cab	$950	$1,250
1970s	Head only	$650	$950

Coliseum Lead Full Stack

1970s. Coliseum Lead logo on amp head, two 4x12" cabs.

1970s		$1,500	$2,125

Concert 215S Bass Set

1970s. Solidstate head, 200 watts, Model 215S tall vertical cabinet with 2x12" Sunn label speakers, dark vinyl cover, silver sparkle grille.

1970s		$875	$1,250

Concert Lead 610S Set

1970s. Solidstate, 200 watts, 6x10" piggyback, reverb and built-in distortion.

1970s		$1,125	$1,500

Enforcer

1980s. Tube, 60/100-watt 2x12" or 100 watt head.

1980s	Combo	$850	$1,250
1980s	Head & cab	$900	$1,375

Fuse 200S

1970s. Sunn Fuse logo and model number on front panel, 140 watts.

1970s		$1,375	$2,000

MODEL YEAR	FEATURES	LOW	HIGH

Model T Head

Early-1970s. 100 watts.

1970s	Head only	$3,500	$5,500

Model T (Reissue)

1998-2002. Reissue of '70s Model T, 100-watt head, with 4x12" cab.

1998-2002	Head & cab	$1,250	$1,875

SB-160 Bass

1985. Combo, 60 watts.

1985		$375	$550

SB-200

1985. 200 watts, 1x15", 4-band EQ, master volume, compressor.

1985		$400	$600

Sceptre

1968-1972. 60 watts, 6550 power tubes, tremolo, reverb.

1968-1972	Head only	$1,250	$1,750

Sentura

1967-1970s. Rectifier and power tubes, I and II versions.

1967-1969	I, 1x15 set	$1,250	$1,750
1967-1969	II, 2x15 set	$1,375	$2,000

SL 250

1980s. 60 watts, 2x12" combo, SL 250 logo.

1980s		$500	$750

SL 260

1982-ca.1985. 60 watts, 2x12" combo with reverb, SL 260 logo.

1982-1985		$550	$800

Solarus

1967-1970s. Tube amp (EL34s), reverb, tremolo, 2x12" 40-watt combo to '68; 60 watt head with 2x12" cab for '69 on.

1967-1968	Combo	$775	$1,250
1969-1970s	Head and cab	$950	$1,375

Solo II

Early-1970s. Solo II logo on front panel, 120 watts, 2x12" combo, black tolex.

1970s		$700	$975

Sonaro

Early-1970s. Head and 1x15" cab, 60 watts.

1970s	Head and cab	$700	$975

Sonic 1-40

1967-1969. Tube head, 1x15" bass amp, 40 watts.

1967-1969	Head and cab	$1,250	$1,750

Sonic I

1967-1969. 125 watts, 1x15" JBL D130F in short cabinet, 5 tubes (with rectifier), piggyback, dark tolex.

1967-1969	Head and cab	$1,000	$1,500

Sonic II

1967-1969. 250 watts, 2x15" JBL D130F in folding horn large cabinet, 5 tubes (with rectifier), piggyback, dark tolex.

1967-1969	Head and cab	$1,000	$1,500

Sorado

1970s. 50 watts, tubes, 2x15" matching cab.

1970s	Head and cab	$1,000	$1,500

Spectrum I

1967-1969. 125 watts, 1x15" JBL D130F large cabinet, 5 tubes (with rectifier), piggyback, dark tolex cover.

1967-1969	Head and cab	$1,000	$1,500

Spectrum II

1967-1969. 250 watts, 2x12", piggyback, 5 tubes (with rectifier), Spectrum II logo on front panel.

1967-1969	Head and cab	$1,000	$1,500

SPL 7250

Dual channels, 250 watts per channel, forced air cooling, switch-selectable peak compressor with LEDs.

1989	Head and cab	$525	$750

Stagemaster

1980s. 120 watts, 2x12".

1980s	Combo	$425	$600
1980s	Head and cab	$525	$750

T50C

1998-2002. Fender era, combo 1x12", 50 watts.

1998-2002		$600	$950

Supersound

1952-1974. Founded in the U.K. by Alan Wootton, building custom amps and radios, the firm continued to build amps and effects into the early '60s. They also built guitars and basses.

Supertone

1914-1941. Supertone was a brand used by Sears for their musical instruments. In the '40s Sears started using the Silvertone name on those products. Amps were made by other companies.

Various Models

1930s		$325	$500

Supro

1935-1968, 2004-present. Supro was a budget brand of the National Dobro Company, made by Valco in Chicago, Illinois. Amp builder Bruce Zinky revived the Supro name in '04 for a line of guitars and amps. In '13, Absara Audio, LLC acquired the Supro trademark and started releasing amps in July '14.

'64 Reverb/'64 Super

2020-present. 5 watts, 1x8", reverb, Jensen speaker, blue. Renamed Super in '22.

2020-2024	1605RJ	$500	$650

Accordion 1615T

1957-1959. Compact combo, 1x15", 24 watts, 2x6L6 power, 5V4, 3x12AX7, 2 channels, tremolo, 3 control knobs, Accordion (model) logo upper left corner of grille, Supro logo lower right, Rhino-Hide gray with white sides.

1957-1959		$900	$1,125

Bantam

1961-1966. Petite, 4 watts, 3 tubes, 1x 8" Jensen, gold weave Saran Wrap grille, Spanish Ivory fabric cover, red in '64, gray in '66. Also sold as matching set, for example in '64 with student-level red and white lap steel, add 65% to price for matching guitar and amp set.

1961-1963	1611S, Spanish ivory	$450	$575
1964-1965	S6411, red cover	$450	$575
1966	Gray cover	$450	$575

Bass Combo

Early 1960s. 35 watts, 2x12", 2 channels (bass and standard), 7 tubes, tremolo, woven embossed black and

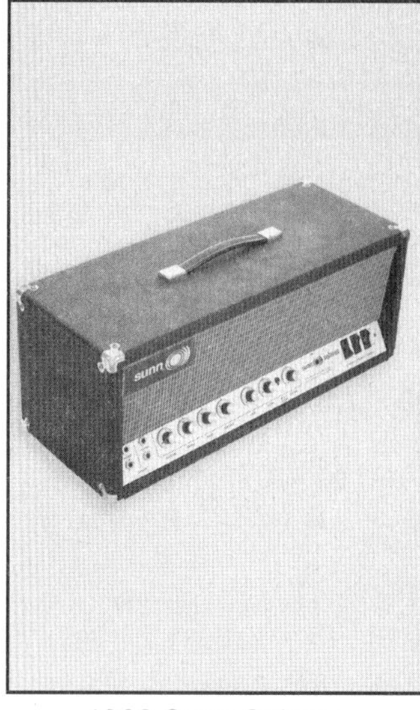

1968 Sunn Solarus

Imaged by Heritage Auctions, HA.com

Sunn Solo

Imaged by Heritage Auctions, HA.com

Sunn Stagemaster

Robert Curd

AMPS

Supro 1688T
Carter Vintage Guitars

Supro Combo Model 1696 TN
Rivington Guitars

Supro Model 24
Michael Wright

MODEL YEAR	FEATURES	LOW	HIGH

white tolex that appears grey. The '61 model 1688T has a narrow panel body style somewhat similar to the Fender narrow panel cab style of the late '50s, in '62 the cab panel was removed, and the 'no panel' style became the 1688TA model, the new cab was less expensive to build and Supro offered a price reduction on applicable models in '62.

1961	1688T, narrow panel	$875	$1,125
1962-1963	1688TA, no panel	$875	$1,125

Big Star Reverb S6451TR

1964. 35 watts, 2x12", reverb and tremolo, 'no panel' cab.

1964		$1,125	$1,500

Black Magick

2017-present. 25 watts, 1x12", head (1695TH), tremolo combo (1695TJ), reverb and tremolo combo (1696RT). Extention cabinets also offered.

2017-2024	1695TH, head	$675	$850
2017-2024	1x12 cab	$300	$375
2017-2024	2x12 cab	$400	$500
2018-2024	1696RT	$900	$1,125
2020-2024	1695TJ	$800	$1,000

Blues King

2019-2020. 5 watts, 1x10".

2019-2020		$250	$325

Blues King 8

2020. 1 watt, 1x8".

2020	1808	$225	$300

Brentwood 1650T

Mid-1950s. Advertised as Supro's "finest amplifier", model 1650T described as the "professional twin speaker luxury amplifier", 2 channels including high-gain, tremolo with speed control.

1956		$1,125	$1,500

Combo

1961-1964. 24 watts, 6 tubes, 1x15" Jensen, Rhino-Hide covering in black and white, light grille, tremolo.

1961	1696T, narrow panel	$850	$1,125
1962-1963	1696TA, no panel	$850	$1,125

Combo Tremolo S6497T

1964. 35 watts, 1x15", standard 'no panel' cab, tremolo.

1964		$900	$1,125

Comet 1610B

1957-1959. Gray Rhino-Hide, 1x10".

1957-1959		$800	$1,000

Comet 1610E

Mid-1950s. Supro's only 1x10" amp from the mid-'50s, 3 input jacks, 2 control knobs, woven tweed and leatherette 2-tone covering.

1956		$800	$1,000

Coronado

1960-1963. 24 watts, 2x10", tremolo, 2 channels, 6 tubes, Supro logo upper right above grille, black and white mixed tolex appears gray, described as tremolo twin-speaker pro amp, '61 has 'narrow panel' body style, new body style in '62 becomes 1690TA model with grille only and no panel.

1960-1961	1690T, narrow panel	$1,125	$1,500
1962-1963	1690TA, no panel	$1,125	$1,500

MODEL YEAR	FEATURES	LOW	HIGH

Corsica

Mid-1960s. Redesigned vertical combo amp, reverb, tremolo, blue control panel, black tolex, silver grille.

1965-1967		$675	$850

Delta King 8

2020-2021. 1 watt, 1x8", tweed/black (1818TB) or black/cream (1818BC).

2020-2021		$250	$325

Delta King 10

2020-present. 5 watts, 1x10", reverb, tweed/black (1820RTB) or black/cream (1820RBC).

2020-2024		$325	$425

Delta King 12

2020-present. 15 watts, 1x12", reverb, tweed/black (1822RTB) or black/cream (1822RBC).

2020-2024		$375	$575

Dual-Tone

1961-1965, 2014-2020. 17 watts, 6 tubes, 1x12" Jensen, organ tone tremolo, restyled in '64, Trinidad Blue vinyl fabric cover, light color grille. Reintroduced in '14, 24 watts.

1961	1624T, narrow panel	$900	$1,125
1962-1963	1624TA, no panel	$900	$1,125
1964-1965	S6424T, no panel	$900	$1,125
2014-2020	1624T, no panel	$525	$675

Galaxy

2019-2020. 50 watts, 1x12".

2019-2020	1697R	$775	$975

Galaxy Tremolo S6488

1965. 35 watts, 2x12" (often Jensen), 7 tubes, tremolo, multi-purpose for guitar, bass and accordion.

1965		$900	$1,125

Galaxy Tremolo S6688

1966-1967. 35 watts, 2x12" (often Jensen), turquoise front control panel with Supro logo (not on grille), model name/number also on front control panel.

1966-1967		$900	$1,125

Golden Holiday 1665T

Mid-1950s. Supro's model for the 'semi-professional', 2 oval 11x6" speakers, 14 watts, 6 tubes, tremolo, 2 control knobs, black and tweed cover.

1956		$1,125	$1,500

Keeley Custom

2020-2021. Designed with Robert Keeley (Keeley Electronics), 25 watts, 1x10" (Custom 10) or 1x12" (Custom 12).

2020-2021	Custom 10	$550	$700
2020-2021	Custom 12	$675	$850

Model 24

1965. 18 watts, 1x12 combo, 2 channels each with bass and treble inputs, tremolo, Model 24 logo on top panel, Calypso Blue vinyl cover.

1965		$900	$1,125

Reverb 1650R

1963. 17 watts, 1x10", 'no panel' grille front style cab, reverb.

1963		$900	$1,125

Royal Reverb 1650TR

1963-1965. 17 watts, 15 tubes, 2x10" Jensens, catalog says "authentic tremolo and magic-reverberation."

1963-1965		$1,250	$1,750

MODEL YEAR	FEATURES	LOW	HIGH

Royal Reverb S6650

1965-1967. Updated cabinet with turquoise-blue front control panel, 2x10" combo, 2 channels (standard and reverb-tremolo).

1965-1967		$725	$950

Special 1633E

Mid-1950s. Supro's entry level student amp, 1x8", 3 tubes, large Supro stencil logo on grille, 2-tone red and white fabric cover, leather handle, available with matching Special Lap Steel covered in wine-maroon plastic.

1956		$550	$700

Spectator 1614E

Mid-1950s. 1x8", 3 tubes, 2 control knobs, white front with red and black body.

1956		$625	$800

Sportsman S6689

1966. Piggyback, twin speakers.

1966		$875	$1,125

Statesman S6699

1966-1967, 2017-2020. Piggyback with blue-green control panel, 4x6L6 power, horizontal 2x12" cab, reverb, tremolo, script Statesman logo with model number on upper left front of chassis. Reintroduced in '17, 50 watts, 1x12" combo.

1966-1967	Piggyback	$825	$1,125
2017-2020	Combo	$900	$1,125

Studio 1644E

Mid-1950s. Supro's student model for teaching studios, 2 input jacks for student and instructor or guitar and lap steel guitar, 3 tubes, advertised for "true Hawaiian tone reproduction", covered in royal blue leatherette (in '56), available with a matching Studio Lap Steel covered in blue plastic.

1956-1957	Blue leatherette	$575	$725

Super

1961-1963, 2017-2020. 4.5 watts, 3 tubes, 1x8", 1606S has contrasting black and white covering with old narrow panel cab, in '63 new 1606B has 'no panel' style cab with lighter (gray) covering. Reintroduced in '17, 5 watts, 1x8".

1961-1962	1606S	$575	$725
1963	1606B	$575	$725
2017-2020	1606	$450	$575

Super 1606E

Mid-1950s. Supro advertising states, "with features important to women", oval 11x6" Rola speaker, 3 tubes, 1 control knob, 2 inputs, white (front) and grey sides, elliptical baffle soundhole with Supro logo, model number with E suffix common for '50s Supro's.

1956	White and grey	$625	$800

Super Six S6406

1964-1965. Student practice amp, 4.5 watts, 1x8", blue vinyl cover.

1964-1965		$575	$725

Super Six S6606

1966. Updated version of student compact amp.

1966		$625	$800

Supreme

1961-1963. 17 watts, 1x10", designed for use with Model 600 Reverb Accessory Unit, value shown does not include the Model 600 (see Effects Section for reverb unit). The initial 1600R model was designed with a triangle-like shaped sound hole, in '62 the more typical Supro no panel cab was introduced which Supro called the new slope front design.

1961	1600R	$1,125	$1,500
1962-1963	1600S, no panel	$1,125	$1,500

Supreme 17 S6400

1964-1965. 17 watts, 1x10", cab larger than prior models of this type.

1964-1965		$900	$1,125

Supreme Twin Speaker 1600E

Mid-1950s. 2 oval 11x6" speakers, 5 tubes, 3 input jacks, 2 control knobs, grille logo states "Twin Speaker" but unlike most Supro amps of this era the Supro logo does not appear on the front.

1956		$825	$1,125

Thunderbolt S6420(B) Bass

1964-1967. 35 watts, 1x15" Jensen, introduced in the '64 catalog as a no frills - no fancy extra circuits amp. Sometimes referred to as the "Jimmy Page" based on his use of this amp in his early career.

1964-1967		$1,625	$2,250

Thunderbolt S6920

1967-1968. Redesign circuit replaced S6420B, 35 watts, 1x12".

1967-1968		$800	$1,000

Tremo-Verb S6422TR

1964-1965. Lower power using 4 12AX7s, 1 5Y3GT, and 1 6V6, 1x10", tremolo and reverb, Persian Red vinyl cover.

1964-1965		$1,125	$1,500

Trojan Tremolo

1961-1966. 5 watts, 4 tubes, 1 11"x6" oval (generally Rolla) speaker, '61-'64 black and white fabric cover and Saran Wrap grille, '64-'66 new larger cab with vinyl cover and light grille.

1961	1616T, narrow panel	$550	$700
1962-1963	1616TA, no panel	$550	$700
1964-1966	S6461, blue cover	$550	$700

Vibra-Verb S6498VR

1964-1965. Billed as Supro's finest amplifier, 2x35-watt channels, 1x15" and 1x10" Jensens, vibrato and reverb.

1964-1965		$1,625	$2,250

Surreal Amplification

2007-present. Production/custom, professional grade amp heads, combos and cabinets built in Westminster, California by Jerry Dyer.

Swampdonkey

2006-present. Professional and premium grade, production/custom, guitar amp heads, combos and speaker cabinets built in Rural Rocky View, Alberta by Chris Czech.

Swanpro Amps

Robert Swanson started building tube combo and head amps and cabinets in Denver, Colorado in 2004.

1965 Supro Thunderbolt S6420(B)
Imaged by Heritage Auctions, HA.com

Surreal Cult 45

Swampdonkey Gypsy

AMPS

Swart AST Head Mk II

SWR California Blonde
Imaged by Heritage Auctions, HA.com

Tanglewood T3

MODEL YEAR	FEATURES	LOW	HIGH

Swart Amplifier Co. (Space Tone)

2003-present. Michael J. Swart builds tube combo and head amps and cabinets under the Swart and Space Tone brand names in Wilmington, North Carolina. He also builds effects.

SWR Sound

1984-2013. Founded by Steve W. Rabe in '84, with an initial product focus on bass amplifiers. Fender Musical Instruments Corp. acquired SWR in June 2003.

Baby Blue Studio Bass System

1990-2003. Combo, all tube preamp, 150 watts solidstate power amp, 2x8", 1x5" cone tweeter, gain, master volume, EQ, effects-blend.

1990-2003		$400	$550

Basic Black

1992-1999. Solidstate, 100 watts, 1x12", basic black block logo on front, black tolex, black metal grille.

1992-1999		$325	$450

California Blonde

2000s. Vertical upright combo, 100 watts, 1x12" plus high-end tweeters, blond cover, thin black metal grille.

2003		$325	$700

Goliath III Cabinet

1996-2008. Black tolex, black metal grille, includes the Goliath III Jr. (2x10") and the Goliath III (4x10").

1996-2008	2x10"	$275	$400
1996-2008	4x10"	$325	$450

Strawberry Blonde

1998-2011. 80 watts, 1x10" acoustic instrument amp.

1998-2011		$325	$450

Strawberry Blonde II

2007-2011. 90 watts, 1x10" acoustic instrument amp.

2007-2011		$325	$450

Studio 220 Bass Head

1988-1995. 220-watt solidstate head, tube preamp

1988-1995		$200	$275

Workingman's Series

1995-2004. Includes 10 (200w, 2x10), 12 (100w, 1x12), 15 (bass, 1x15), replaced by WorkingPro in '05.

1995-2004	Various models	$225	$350

Symphony

1950s. Probably a brand from a teaching studio, large Symphony script red letter logo on front.

Small Tube

1950s. Two guitar inputs, 1x6" speaker, alligator tweed suitcase.

1950s		$325	$450

Synaptic Amplification

Intermediate to premium grade, production/custom, amps built in Brunswick, Maine by Steven O'Connor, starting in 2007.

Takt

Late-1960s. Made in Japan, tube and solidstate models.

GA Series

1968. GA-9 (2 inputs and 5 controls, 3 tubes), GA-10, GA-11, GA-12, GA-14, GA-15.

1968	GA-14/GA-15	$75	$100
1968	GA-9 thru GA-12	$50	$75

Talos

Doug Weisbrod and Bill Thalmann build their tube amp heads, combo amps, and speaker cabinets in Springfield, Virginia. They started building and testing prototypes in '01.

Tanglewood Guitar Company UK

1991-present. Intermediate and professional grade, production, acoustic amps imported from China by Dirk Kommer and Tony Flatt in the U.K. They also import guitars, basses, mandolins, banjos and ukes.

Tech 21

1989-present. Long known for their SansAmp tube amplifier emulator, Tech 21 added solidstate combo amps, heads and cabinets in '96.

Teisco

1946-1974. Japanese brand first imported into the U.S. around '63. Teisco offered both tube and solidstate amps.

Checkmate CM-10

1960s. Tubes or solidstate, 10 watts.

1960s	Solidstate	$100	$275
1960s	Tubes	$400	$800

Checkmate CM-15

Late-1960s. Tubes, 15 watts.

1960s		$400	$800

Checkmate CM-16

1960s. Tubes or solidstate, 15 watts.

1960s	Solidstate	$125	$375
1960s	Tubes	$400	$800

Checkmate CM-17

1960s. Tubes, 1x10", reverb, tremolo.

1960s		$475	$800

Checkmate CM-20

Late-1960s. Tubes, 20 watts.

1960s		$475	$800

Checkmate CM-25

Late-1960s. Tubes, 25 watts.

1960s		$475	$800

Checkmate CM-50

Late-1950s-early-1960s. Tubes, 2 6L6s, 50 watts, 2x12" open back, reverb, tremolo, piggyback, gray tolex cover, light gray grille.

1960s		$650	$850

Checkmate CM-60

Late-1960s. Tubes, 60 watts, piggyback amp and cab with wheels.

1960s		$375	$500

Checkmate CM-66

Late-1960s. Solidstate, dual speaker combo, Check Mate 66 logo on front panel.

1960s		$100	$150

MODEL YEAR	FEATURES	LOW	HIGH

Checkmate CM-88

1960s. Solidstate, 10 watts, 2x8".

1960s $100 $150

Checkmate CM-100

Late-1960s. Tubes, 4x6L6 power, 100 watts, piggyback with Vox-style trolley stand.

1960s $400 $500

King 1800

Late-1960s. Tubes, 180 watts, piggyback with 2 cabinets, large Teisco logo on cabinets, King logo on lower right side of one cabinet.

1960s $700 $950

Teisco 8

Late-1960s. Solidstate, 5 watts.

1960s $100 $150

Teisco 10

Late-1960s. Solidstate, 5 watts.

1960s $100 $150

Teisco 88

Late-1960s. Solidstate, 8 watts.

1960s $150 $250

Tempo

1950s-1970s. Tube (early on) and solidstate amps, most likely imported from Japan by Merson Musical Products. They also offered basses and guitars.

Model 39

1950s. Compact amp, vertical cab, tweed, 3 tubes, single control knob for on-off volume.

1953 $300 $400

Teneyck

1960s. Solidstate amp heads and speaker cabinets built by Bob Teneyck, who had previously done design work for Ampeg.

THD

1987-present. Tube amps and cabinets built in Seattle, Washington, founded by Andy Marshall.

The Valve

Guitar luthier Galeazzo Frudua also builds a line of professional grade, production/custom, amps in San Lazzaro di Savena, Italy.

ThroBak Electronics

2004-present. Jonathan Gundry builds his tube combo guitar amps in Grand Rapids, Michigan. He also builds guitar effects and pickups.

Titano (Magnatone)

1961-1963. Private branded by Magnatone, often for an accordion company or accordion studio, uses standard guitar input jacks.

Model 262 R Custom

1961-1963. 35 watts, 2x12" + 2x5", reverb and vibrato make this one of the top-of-the-line models, black vinyl, light silver grille.

1961-1963 $1,250 $1,750

MODEL YEAR	FEATURES	LOW	HIGH

Model 313

1961-1963. Like Magnatone 213 Troubadour, 10 watts, 1x12" combo, vibrato, brown tolex, brownish grille.

1961-1963 $1,125 $1,500

Model 415 Bass

1961-1963. 25 watts, 4x8", bass or accordion amp, black cover, darkish grille.

1961-1963 $1,125 $1,750

TomasZewicZ Amplifiers

2008-present. Intermediate and professional grade, production/custom, tube guitar amp heads and combos built by John Tomaszewicz in Coral Springs, Florida. He also builds effects.

Tombo

This Japanese harmonica manufacturer introduced a solidbody electric ukulele and a Silvertone-esque case with onboard amplifier in the mid-1960s.

Tone Americana

2011-2014. David and Caroline Brass built intermediate and professional grade, production/custom, amp heads, combos and cabinets in Calabasas, California. They also offered an amp combo built in Asia.

Tone King

1993-present. Tube amps, combos, and cabinets built by Mark Bartel in Baltimore, Maryland. The company started in New York and moved to Baltimore in '94.

Tonemaster (Magnatone)

Late-1950s-early-1960s. Magnatone amps private branded for Imperial Accordion Company. Prominent block-style capital TONEMASTER logo on front panel, generally something nearly equal to Magnatone equivalent. This is just one of many private branded Magnatones. Covers range from brown to black leatherette and brown to light silver grilles. They also offered guitars.

Model 214

1959-1960. Ten watts, 1x12", vibrato, brown leatherette, V logo front lower right corner, large TONEMASTER logo.

1959-1960 $1,125 $1,750

Model 260

1961-1963. About 30 watts, 2x12", vibrato, brown leatherette and brown grille, large TONEMASTER logo on front.

1961-1963 $1,750 $2,250

Model 261 Custom

1961-1963. Tonemaster Custom 261 High Fidelity logo on back chassis panel, Tonemaster logo on front panel, 35 watts, 2x12" combo, 2 channels, vibrato.

1961-1963 $1,750 $2,250

Model 380

1961-1963. 50 watts, 2x12" and 2 oval 5"x7" speakers, vibrato, no reverb.

1961-1963 $1,750 $2,250

Tech 21 Trademark 60

1960s Teisco Checkmate Model 18

Tom Pfeifer

Tone King Royalist 15

Carter Vintage Guitars

ToneTron Hall Rocker

Tonic Torpedo

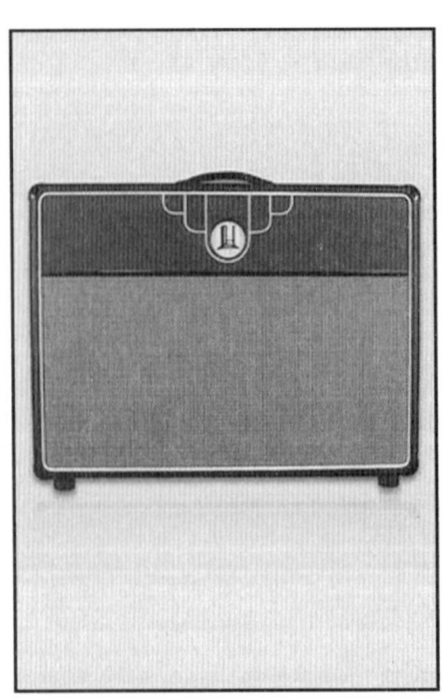
Top Hat King Royal

MODEL YEAR	FEATURES	LOW	HIGH

Model 381 Custom

1961-1963. Tonemaster Custom 381 High Fidelity logo on back chassis panel, Tonemaster logo on front panel, 2x12", 1x5".

1961-1963		$1,750	$2,250

Small Combo

1950s-1960s. 1x8", tremolo, light tan.

1950s-60s		$650	$850

ToneTron Amps

2006-present. Professional grade, custom, guitar and bass tube amps and cabinets built in Minneapolis, Minnesota by Jeffrey Falla.

ToneVille Amps

Matthew Lucci and Phil Jung began in 2013, building professional grade, production, amps and cabinets in Colorado Springs, Colorado.

Tonic Amps

2003-present. Darin Ellingson builds professional and premium grade, production/custom, amps and cabinets in Redwood City, California.

Top Hat Amplification

1994-present. Mostly Class A guitar amps built by Brian Gerhard, previously in La Habra, California, and Apex, North Carolina, and currently in Fuquay-Varina, North Carolina. He also makes effects.

Ambassador 100 TH-A100 Head

Jan.1999-2013. 100 watts, Class AB, 4 6L6s, reverb, dark green vinyl cover, white chicken-head knobs.

1999-2013		$1,125	$1,500

Ambassador T-35C 212

1999-2013. 35 watts, 2x12" combo, reverb, master volume, blond cover, tweed-style fabric grille.

1999-2013		$1,250	$1,625

Club Deluxe

1998-2009. 20 watts, 6V6 power tubes, 1x12".

1998-2009		$1,250	$1,625

Club Royale TC-R1

Jan.1998-2020. Class A using EL84s, 20 watts, 1x12". Replaced by Club Royal 20 in '21.

1998-2020		$775	$1,000

Club Royale TC-R2

Jan.1999-2014. Class A using EL84s, 20 watts, 2x12".

1999-2014		$1,125	$1,500

Emplexador 50 TH-E50 Head

Jan.1997-2020. 50 watts, Class AB vint/high-gain head. Replaced by Emplexador E-50 in '21.

1997-2020		$1,125	$1,500

King Royale/Royal

1996-present. 35 watts, Class A using 4 EL84s, 2x12". Name changed to King Royal in '21.

1996-2024		$1,250	$1,500

Portly Cadet TC-PC

Jan.1999-2004. Five watts, 6V6 power, 1x8", dark gray, light gray grille.

1999-2004		$525	$675

Prince Royale TC-PR

Jan.2000-2002. Five watts using EL84 power, 1x8", deep red, light grille.

2000-2002		$525	$675

Super Deluxe TC-SD2

Jan.2000-2012. 30 watts, Class A, 7591 power tubes, 2x12".

2000-2012		$1,250	$1,500

Torres Engineering

Founded by Dan Torres, the company builds tube amps, combos, cabinets and amp kits originally in San Mateo, California, then San Carlos and since '11 in Milton, Washington. Dan wrote monthly columns for Vintage Guitar magazine for many years and authored the book Inside Tube Amps.

Trace Elliot

1978-present. Founded in Essex, U.K. The U.S. distribution picked up by Kaman (Ovation) in '88 which bought Trace Elliot in '92. In '98 Gibson acquired the brand and in early '02 closed the factory and moved what production was left to the U.S. In '05 Peavey bought the brand name, hiring back many of the old key people, and currently offers professional grade, production, tube and solidstate, acoustic guitar and bass amp heads, combos, and cabinets, with product built in the U.K. and U.S.

Trainwreck

1983-2006. Limited production, custom-made, high-end tube guitar amp heads built by Ken Fischer in Colonia, New Jersey. Models include the Rocket, Liverpool and Express, plus variations. Instead of using serial numbers, he gave each amp a woman's name. Due to illness, Fischer didn't build many amps after the mid '90s, but he continued to design amps for other builders. His total production is estimated at less than 100. Each amp's value should be evaluated on a case-by-case basis. Ken wrote many amp articles for Vintage Guitar. He died in late 2006.

Ken Fisher Custom Built

1983-1998		$35,000	$75,000

Traynor

1963-present. Started by Pete Traynor and Jack Long in the back of Long & McQuade Music in Toronto, Canada where Traynor was a repairman. Currently offering tube and solidstate amp heads, combos and cabinets made by parent company Yorkville Sound, in Pickering, Ontario.

YBA1 Bass Master Head

1963-1979. 45 watts, called Dynabass for 1963-'64, this was Pete Traynor's first amp design.

1963-1979		$550	$850

YBA1A Mark II Bass Master Head

1968-1976. Like YBA1, but with 90 watts and cooling fan.

1968-1976		$550	$850

MODEL YEAR	FEATURES	LOW	HIGH

YBA3 Custom Special Bass Set

1967-1972. Tube head with 130 watts and 8x10" large vertical matching cab, dark vinyl cover, light grille.

1967-1972		$1,000	$1,250

YBA4 Bass Master

1967-1972. 45-watt 1x15" combo.

1967-1972		$850	$1,125

YCV80 Custom Valve

2003-2009. Tube, 80 watts, 4x10" combo.

2003-2009		$350	$500

YGA1 Head

1966-1967. 45 watts guitar amp, tremolo.

1966-1967		$550	$750

YGL3 Mark III

1971-1979. All tube, 80 watts, 2x12" combo, reverb, tremolo.

1971-1979		$725	$950

YGM3 Guitar Mate Reverb

1969-1979. Tubes, 25 watts, 1x12", black tolex, gray grille until '74, black after.

1969-1979		$725	$950

YGM3 Guitar Mate Reverb Reissue

2011-2013. 1x12" combo, 'flying wing' Traynor badge.

2011-2013		$400	$550

YRM1 Reverb Master Head

1973-1979. 45-watt tube amp, reverb, tremolo.

1973-1979		$525	$700

YRM1SC Reverb Master

1973-1979. YRM1 as a 4x10" combo.

1973-1979		$750	$1,000

YSR1 Custom Reverb Head

1968-1973. 45-watt tube amp, reverb, tremolo.

1968-1973		$525	$700

YVM Series PA Head

1967-1980. Public address heads, models include tube YVM-1 Voice Master, and solidstate YVM-2 and 3 Voice Mate and YVM-4, all with 4 inputs.

1967-1972	1, tubes	$450	$600
1969-1975	2, solidstate	$195	$275
1970-1980	3, solidstate, reverb	$250	$350
1972-1977	4, solidstate, reverb	$250	$350

Trillium Amplifier Company

Brothers Stephen and Scott Campbell built professional and premium grade, production/custom tube amps in Indianapolis, Indiana, starting in 2007.

Trinity Amps

2003-present. Stephen Cohrs builds his production/custom, professional grade, tube amps and cabinets in Toronto, Ontario.

True Tone

1960s. Guitars and amps retailed by Western Auto, manufactured by Chicago guitar makers like Kay.

Hi-Fi 4 (K503 Hot-Line Special)

1960s. Similar to K503, 4 watts from 3 tubes, gray cabinet, gray grille, metal handle.

1960s		$275	$400

Model 5 (K503A)

1960s. 4 tubes, 1x8".

1960s		$275	$400

Vibrato 704

1960s. Solidstate, 10 watts, 1x8", white sides and gray back, gray grille.

1960s		$135	$175

Vibrato 706

1960s. Solidstate, 15 watts, 1x15", white sides and gray back, brown grille.

1960s		$145	$200

Tube Works

1987-2004. Founded by B.K. Butler in Denver, Tube Works became a division of Genz Benz Enclosures of Scottsdale, Arizona in 1997. Tube Works' first products were tube guitar effects and in '91 they added tube/solidstate amps, cabinets, and DI boxes to the product mix. In '04, Genz Benz dropped the brand.

Twilighter (Magnatone)

Late-1950s-early-1960s. Magnatone amps private branded for LoDuca Brothers. Prominent block-style capital TWILIGHTER logo on front panel, generally something nearly equal to Magnatone equivalent. This is just one of many private branded Magnatones. Covers range from brown to black leatherette, and brown to light silver grilles.

Model 213

1961-1963. About 20 watts, 1x12", vibrato, brown leatherette and brown grille.

1961-1963		$1,125	$1,500

Model 260R

1961-1963. About 18 to 25 watts, 1x12", vibrato, brown leatherette cover.

1961-1963		$1,250	$1,750

Model 280A

Late-1950s-early-1960s. About 35 watts, 2x12", vibrato, brown leatherette cover.

1961-1963		$1,250	$1,750

Two-Rock

1999-present. Tube guitar amp heads, combos and cabinets built by Joe Mloganoski and Bill Krinard (K&M Analog Designs) originally in Cotati, California, currently in Rohnert Park. They also build speakers.

Ugly Amps

2003-present. Steve O'Boyle builds his tube head and combo amps and cabinets in Burbank, California and Reading, Pennsylvania.

UltraSound

A division of UJC Electronics, UltraSound builds acoustically transparent amps, designed by Greg Farres for the acoustic guitarist, in Adel, Iowa.

Unique (Magnatone)

1961-1963. Private branded, typically for an accordion company or accordion studio, uses standard guitar input jacks.

1969 Traynor YSR1 Custom Reverb
Scott Anderson

Trinity Tweed

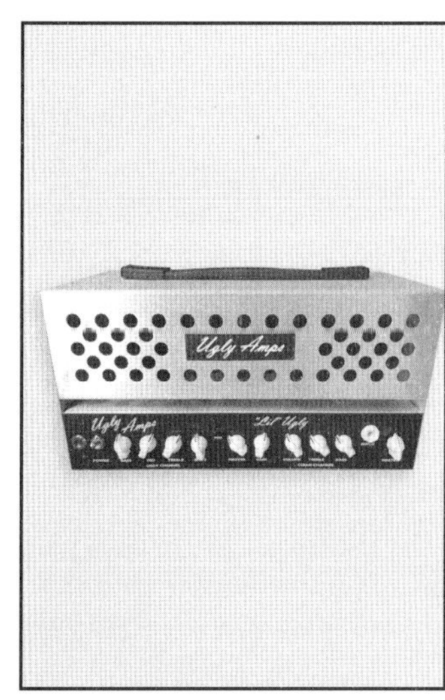

Ugly Lil' Ugly

AMPS

Univox Model U202R
Imaged by Heritage Auctions, HA.com

1971 Univox Model U1226
Carter Vintage Guitars

Ca. 1951 Valco Chicago 51
Rivington Guitars

MODEL YEAR	FEATURES	LOW	HIGH

Model 260R

1961-1963. Based on Magnatone 260 Series amp, 35 watts, 2x12" but with reverb, black vinyl-style cover with distinctive black diamond-check pattern running through the top and sides.

1961-1963		$1,500	$1,875

Model 460

1961-1963. 35 watts, 2x12" and oval 5"x7" speakers, reverb and vibrato make it one of the top models, black vinyl, black grille.

1961-1963		$1,250	$1,750

Universal (Audio Guild)

See Audio Guild amps.

Univox

1964-ca.1978. From '64 to early-'68, these were American-made tube amps with Jensen speakers. By '68, they were using Japanese components in American cabinets, still with Jensen speakers. Electronics were a combination of tube and transistors during this time; this type lasted until the mid-'70s. Around '71, Univox introduced a line of all solidstate amps, as well.

Lead Model Tube

1960s. Tube amp, 2x10" or 2x12".

1965-1969		$675	$875

Model U45B Bass

1965-1968. 1x12" combo tube bass amp, 10 watts.

1965-1968		$325	$450

Model U60A

1965-1968. 1x12" tube combo.

1965-1968		$375	$500

Model U65R

1965-1968. 20 watts, 1x12" tube combo.

1965-1968		$425	$550

Model U65RD Lead 65

1976-1978. Solidstate, 65 watts, reverb, 1x12" or 2x12" in a vertical cab.

1976-1978		$50	$75

Model U102

1965-1968. 1x12" tube combo.

1965-1968		$425	$550

Model U130B Bass

1976-1978. Solidstate, 130 watts, 1x15".

1976-1978		$135	$175

Model U130L Lead

1976-1978. Solidstate, 130 watts.

1976-1978		$135	$175

Model U155R

1965-1968. 20 watts, 1x12" tube combo.

1965-1968		$550	$750

Model U202R

1965-1968. 1x12" tube combo.

1965-1968		$550	$750

Model U305R

1965-1968. 30 watts, 1x15" tube combo.

1965-1968		$650	$850

Model U1011 Lead Head

1976-1978. Solidstate, 100 watts, reverb, tremolo. Name also used on earlier tube head.

1976-1978		$200	$250

Model U1061 Bass Head

1976-1978. Solidstate.

1976-1978		$200	$250

Model U1220

1968-1971. Tubes or tube-hybrid, piggyback, 2x12".

1968-1971		$325	$450

Model U1226 Head

1971-1972. 60-watt tube amp head.

1971-1972		$550	$750

Model U1246B Bass Head

1976-1978. Solidstate, 60 watts.

1976-1978		$200	$275

Model U1246L Lead Head

1976-1978. Solidstate.

1976-1978		$200	$275

Valco

Valco, from Chicago, Illinois, was a big player in the guitar and amplifier business. Their products were private branded for other companies like National, Supro, Airline, Oahu, El Grande and Gretsch.

Valvetech

Production/custom, professional grade, amps built by Rob Pierce, starting in 1997, in Ossian, Indiana.

Valvetrain Amplification

2005-present. Tube combos, amp heads, and speaker cabinets built by Rick Gessner in Sorrento, Florida. He also builds reverb units.

Vamp

1970s. Tube and solidstate amps and speaker cabinets built at Triumph Electronics in England.

Bass Master Head

1970s	100 watts	$1,250	$1,625

VanAmps

Tim Van Tassel, started in 1999, builds professional, production/custom, amps and cabinets in Golden Valley, Minnesota. He also builds effects.

Vega

The original Boston-based company (1903) was purchased by C.F. Martin in '70. In '80, the Vega trademark was sold to a Korean company.

A-49

1960s. Tubes, 6 watts, 1x8", tan cover.

1960s		$325	$450

Director Combo

1950s. Small to mid-size tube amp, 2-tone cover, 2 volume and 1 tone controls, rear mounted control chassis similar to Fender or Gibson from the '50s.

1950s		$500	$650

Lap Steel

1930s-1940s. Various models.

1930s	1x12, dark cover	$500	$650
1940s	1x10, tweed	$500	$650

MODEL YEAR	FEATURES	LOW	HIGH

Super

Early 1950s. 1 6L6, 1x10", vertical combo amp typical of the era.

1950s		$500	$650

Triumphal

Late-1940s. Vega Triumphal logo on back control pane, 6L6 power, 1x12".

1940s		$500	$650

Versatone (Audio Guild)

See Audio Guild amps.

Vesta Fire

1980s. Japanese imports by Shiino Musical Instruments Corp.; later by Midco International. Mainly known for effects pedals.

VHT

Founded by Steven M. Fryette in 1989, VHT built amps, combos, and cabinets in Burbank, California. At the beginning of '09 AXL guitars acquired the VHT name and manufactures their own product under that brand. Fryette continues to build the VHT amp models under Fryette Amplification.

Vibe Amplification

2008-2013. Intermediate grade, production, tube amps, imported from Asia by Lorenzo Brogi in Bologna, Italy.

Victor

Late-1960s. Made in Japan.

Victoria

1994-present. Tube amps, combos, and reverb units built by Mark Baier in Naperville, Illinois. In '08, they changed the logo from the original script Victoria Amp Co. to the current stylized lightning bolt Victoria logo.

Cherry Bomb

2011-present. Tube tremolo, 40 watts, 1x15", alligator/cream tolex.

2011-2024		$1,500	$2,000

Double Deluxe

1994-present. 35 watts, 2x12".

1994-2024		$1,500	$2,000

Electro King

2008-present. 1957 GA-40 type circuit, tubes, 15 watts, 1x12".

2008-2024		$1,375	$1,875

Golden Melody

2008-present. Tubes, reverb, 50 watts, 2x12", alligator/brown tolex.

2008-2024		$1,500	$2,000

Ivy League

2010-present. Tweed Harvard specs, 14 watts, 1x10".

2011-2024		$1,125	$1,500

Model 518

1994-present. Tweed, 1x8".

1994-2024		$850	$1,125

Model 5112-T

2001-present. Tweed, 5 watts, 5F1 circuit, 1x12".

2001-2024		$875	$1,125

Model 20112

1994-present. Tweed, 20 watts, 1x12", tweed.

1994-2024		$1,125	$1,500

Model 35115

1994-present. Tweed combo, 28 watts, 1x15".

1994-2024		$1,375	$1,875

Model 35210

1994-present. Tweed, 28 watts, 2x10", tweed.

1994-2024		$1,500	$2,000

Model 35212-T

1990s. Tweed, 35 watts, 2x12".

1990s		$1,500	$2,000

Model 35310-T

1994-present. Tweed, 28 watts, 3x10".

1994-2024		$1,625	$2,125

Model 45115-T

2008-2009. Tweed, 45 watts, 1x15".

2008-2009		$1,375	$1,875

Model 45410-T

1994-present. Tweed, 45 watts, 4x10" combo, tweed.

1994-2024		$1,500	$2,000

Model 50212-T

2002-present. Tweed, 50 watts, 2x12" combo.

2002-2024		$1,500	$2,000

Model 80212

1994-present. Tweed, 80 watts, 2x12", tweed.

1994-2024		$1,625	$2,125

Regal

2004-2006. Class A with 1 x 6L6, 15 watts, 1x15", brown tolex cover, rear mount controls.

2004-2006		$1,375	$1,875

Regal II/Regal

2006-present. Class A, 35 watts, 1x15", tweed or vanilla tolex, rear mount controls. The II removed from name about '13.

2006-2024		$1,375	$1,875

Reverberato

1996-2016. Tube reverb unit with vibrato, tweed or color options.

1996-2016		$1,125	$1,500

Silver Sonic

2011-present. Tube reverb, 20 watts, 1x12", 2-tone black/cream cab with Sonic Blue or black tolex.

2011-2024		$1,500	$2,000

Trem d'La Trem

2007-present. Tweed design,14 watts, 1x15".

2007-2024		$1,375	$1,875

Victoriette

2001-present. 20 watts, 1x12" or 2x10", reverb, tremolo in '01.

2001-2024	2x10	$1,500	$2,000

Victorilux

2001-present. 45 watts, 2x12", 3x10" or 1x15", EL84s, reverb, tremolo.

2001-2024	3x10	$1,625	$2,250

Vega Commander

Imaged by Heritage Auctions, HA.com

Victoria 35115

Carter Vintage Guitars

Victoria Silver Sonic

AMPS

Vintage47 VA-20

1961 Vox AC4
Frank Silvestry

Vox AC10C1

MODEL YEAR	FEATURES	LOW	HIGH

Vintage47

2010-present. Founder/builder David Barnes, of California, builds retro-inspired compact amps that reflect old-school Valco values, handwired, intermediate and professional grade.

Vivi-Tone

1933-1938. Founded in Kalamazoo, Michigan, by former Gibson designer Lloyd Loar and others, Vivi-Tone sold small amps built by Webster Electric to accompany their early electric solidbody guitars.

V-M (Voice of Music) Corp.

1944-1977. Started building record changers in Benton Harbor, Michigan. By the early '50s had added amplified phonographs, consoles, and tape recorders as well as OEM products for others. Their portable PA systems can be used for musical instruments. Products sport the VM logo.

Small Portable

1950s. Standard phono input for instrument, phono and microphone controls, wood combo cabinet, 1x10" or 1x12" Jensen.

1950s		$350	$500

Voltmaster

Trapezoid-shaped combo amps and reverb units made in Plano, Texas, in the late 1990s.

Voodoo

1998-present. Tube amp heads and speaker cabinets built in Lansing, New York by Trace Davis, Anthony Cacciotti, and Mike Foster.

Vox

1954-present. Tom Jennings and Dick Denney combined forces in '57 to produce the first Vox amp, the 15-watt AC-15. The period between '57-'68 is considered to be the Vox heyday. Vox produced tube amps in England and also the U.S. from '64 to '65. English-made tube amps were standardized between '60 and '65. U.S.-made Vox amps in '66 were solidstate. In the mid-'60s, similar model names were sometimes used for tube and solidstate amps. In '93 Korg bought the Vox name and current products are built by Marshall. Those amps that originally came with a trolley or stand are priced including the original trolley or stand, and an amp without one will be worth less than the amount shown. Smaller amps were not originally equipped with a trolley or stand (if a speaker cabinet mounts to it and it tilts, it is called a trolley; otherwise referred to as a stand).

4120 Bass

1966-1967. Hybrid solidstate and tube bass amp.

1966-1967		$450	$650

7120 Guitar

1966-1967. Hybrid solidstate and tube amp, 120 watts.

1966-1967		$450	$650

MODEL YEAR	FEATURES	LOW	HIGH

AC4

1961-1965. Made in England, early Vox tube design, 3.5 watts, 1x8", tremolo.

1961-1965		$1,250	$2,000

AC4TV

2009-2019. Tube, 4 watts, in 1x10 (AC4TV8 is 1x8) combo or amp head with 1x12 cab, EL84 power tube, 12AX7 powered preamp. AC4TVmini combo has 6.5-inch speaker.

2009-2013	1x12	$120	$200
2009-2013	1x8	$125	$200
2009-2013	Head only	$140	$200
2009-2019	1x10	$140	$200

AC10

1958-1965. Made in England, 12 watts, 1x10", tremolo, this tube version not made in U.S. ('64-'65).

1958-1965		$3,500	$5,500

AC10 Twin

1962-1965. Made in England, also made in U.S. '64-'65, 12 watts (2xEL84s), 2x10".

1962-1965		$4,000	$6,500

AC10C1

2015-present. Custom series, 10 watts, 1x10", black and maroon 2-tone.

2015-2024		$350	$500

AC15

1958-1965. 15 watts, 1x12", TV front changed to split front in fall '60.

1958	TV front	$4,250	$6,500
1958-1965	Split front	$3,500	$5,000

AC15 Twin

1961-1965. Tube, 2x12", 18 watts.

1961-1965	Standard colors	$4,000	$6,000
1962-1965	Custom colors	$7,500	$11,000

AC15 50th Anniversary

2007. 50th Anniversary 1957-2007 plaque on lower left front of grille, hand wired, white tolex.

2007		$750	$1,125

AC15C1

2010-2020. Custom Series, made in China, 15 watts, 1x12", tube, reverb and tremolo.

2010-2020		$400	$600

AC15CC (Custom Classic)

2006-2012. Made in China, 15 watts, 1x12" tube combo, master volume, reverb, tremolo, 2-button footswitch.

2006-2012		$400	$600

AC15H1TV

2008-2009. Part of Heritage Collection, limited edition, 200 made, hand wired, oiled mahogany cabinet.

2008-2009		$1,000	$1,500

AC15HW1

2015-2021. Hand-wired, 15 watts, 1x12".

2015-2021		$925	$1,250

AC15TB/TBX

1996-2004. 15 watts, top boost, 1x12" Celestion (lower cost Eminence available).

1996-2004	TB	$825	$1,250
1996-2004	TBX	$1,000	$1,500

AMPS

MODEL YEAR	FEATURES	LOW	HIGH

AC30 Reissue Model

1980s-1990s-2000s. Standard reissue and limited edition models with identification plate on back of amp. Models include the AC30 Reissue and Reissue custom color (1980s-1990s), AC30 25th Anniv. (1985-1986), AC30 30th Anniv. (1991), AC30 Collector Model (1990s, mahogany cabinet), AC30HW Hand Wired (1990s) and HW Limited (2000s).

1980s	Rose Morris era	$1,500	$2,500
1985-1986	25th Anniv	$1,500	$2,500
1990s	Collector model	$2,000	$3,000
1990s	Custom colors	$1,500	$2,000
1990s	Hand wired	$2,250	$3,000
1990s	Reissue	$1,250	$2,000
1991	30th Anniv	$1,750	$2,500
1995	TBT, LE, tan	$1,625	$2,250
2000s	Hand wired LE	$2,250	$3,000
2000s	Reissue	$1,375	$2,000

AC30 Super Twin Set

1960-1965. Piggyback head and 2x12" pressure cabinet with amp trolley.

1960-1965		$4,000	$6,500

AC30 Twin/AC-30 Twin Top Boost

1960-1973. Made in England, tube, 30-watt head, 36 watts 2x12", Top Boost includes additional treble and bass, custom colors available in '60-'63.

1960-1963	Custom colors	$6,000	$9,000
1960-1965	Black	$4,000	$6,000
1966	Black	$2,500	$4,500
1967-1973	Black	$2,000	$3,500

AC30BM Brian May Limited Edition

2006-2007. Limited run of 500, 30 watts, 2x12" combo.

2006-2007		$1,250	$1,750

AC30C2X Custom

2004-2018. 30 watts, 2x12" Celestion Alnico Blue speakers.

2004-2018		$550	$800

AC30CC (Custom Classic)

2004-2012. 30 watts, 2x12", tubes, 2-button foot-switch.

2004-2012		$550	$800

AC30VR Valve Reactor

2010-2019. 2x12" combo, digital reverb, 30 watts.

2010-2019		$350	$500

AC50 Cabinet

1963-1975	Black	$850	$1,250

AC50 Head

1963-1975. Made in England, 50-watt head, U.S. production '64-'65 tube version is Westminster Bass, U.S. post-'66 is solidstate.

1963-1975		$2,750	$3,750

AC100 MK I

1963-1965. All tube 100-watt with 4x12 cab, due to reliability concerns it was transitioned to AC100 Super De Luxe MK II in '65.

1963-1965		$4,250	$6,500

AC100 Super De Luxe/MK II

1965. Solidstate 100-watt head with 4x12 cab on speaker trolley.

1965		$2,500	$4,000

AD Series

2004-2008. Import small to large modeling amps with single 12AXT preamp tube, chrome grills, includes applicable footswitch, some available with amp trolley (i.e. AD60VT).

2004-2006	AD120VT	$400	$550
2004-2006	AD60VT	$250	$350
2004-2008	AD100VTH	$200	$275
2004-2008	AD15VT	$110	$150
2004-2008	AD30VT	$120	$150
2004-2008	AD50VT	$155	$200
2006-2008	AD100VT	$275	$350

Berkeley II V108 (Tube)

1964-1966. U.S.-made tube amp revised '66-'69 to U.S.-made solidstate model V1081, 18 watts, 2x10" piggyback.

1964-1966		$1,500	$1,750

Berkeley II V1081 (Solidstate)

1966-1967. U.S.-made solidstate, 35 watts, 2x10" piggyback, includes trolley stand.

1966-1969		$650	$850

Berkeley III (Solidstate)

1968. Berkeley III logo on top panel of amp.

1968-1969		$850	$1,125

Buckingham

1966-1968. Solidstate, 35 watts, 2x12" piggyback, includes trolley stand.

1966-1968		$750	$950

Cambridge 15

1999-2001. 15 watts, 1x8", tremolo.

1999-2001		$150	$200

Cambridge 30 Reverb

1999-2002. 30 watts, 1x10", tremolo and reverb.

1999-2002		$175	$250

Cambridge 30 Reverb Twin 210

1999-2002. 30 watts hybrid circuit, 2x10", reverb.

1999-2002		$225	$300

Cambridge Reverb V1031/ V1032 (Solidstate)

1966-1968. Solidstate, 35 watts, 1x10", model V1031 replaced tube version V103.

1966-1968		$750	$950

Cambridge Reverb V3/V103 (Tube)

1965-1966. U.S-made tube version, 18 watts, 1x10", a Pacemaker with reverb, superseded by solidstate Model V1031 by '67.

1965-1966		$1,500	$1,750

Churchill PAV119 Head and V1091 Cabinet Set

Late-1960s. PA head with multiple inputs and 2 column speakers.

1960s	PA head only	$450	$600
1960s	Set	$800	$1,000

Climax V125/VO125 Lead Combo

1970-1991. Solidstate, 125 watts, 2x12" combo, 5-band EQ, master volume.

1970-1991	Combo	$650	$850
1970-1991	Half-Stack	$825	$1,125

1963 Vox AC30 Twin
KC Cormack

2018 Vox AC30C2
Ted Wulfers

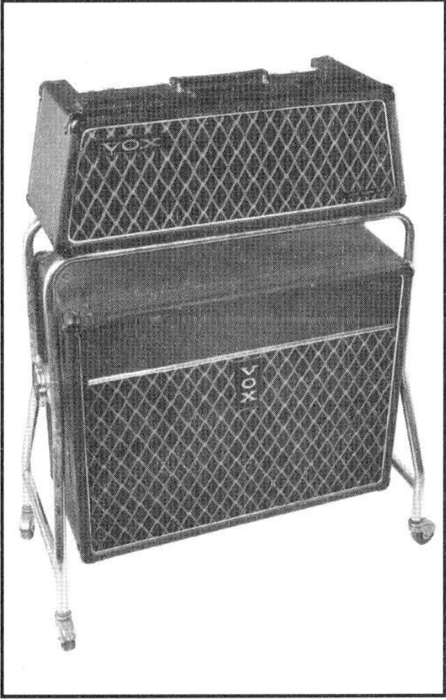

Vox Buckingham
Imaged by Heritage Auctions, HA.com

AMPS

1967 Vox Royal Guardsman
Imaged by Heritage Auctions, HA.com

Vox VT20+

Warwick LWA 1000

MODEL YEAR	FEATURES	LOW	HIGH

DA Series

2006-2013. Small digital modeling amps, AC/DC power, solidstate.

2006-2013	DA5, 5w, 1x65	$95	$150
2007-2009	DA10, 10w, 2x6	$125	$175
2007-2009	DA20, 20w, 2x8	$125	$175
2010	DA15, 15w, 1x8	$100	$150

Defiant

1966-1970. Made in England, 50 watts, 2x12" + Midax horn cabinet.

1966-1970		$1,500	$2,250

Escort

Late 1960s-1983. 2.5 watt battery-powered portable amp.

1968-1986		$350	$500

Essex V1042 Bass

1966-1968. U.S.-made solidstate, 35 watts, 2x12". Also called Essex Bass Deluxe.

1966-1968		$550	$750

Foundation Bass

1966-1970. Tube in '66, solidstate after, 50 watts, 1x18", made in England only.

1966	Tubes	$1,625	$2,250
1967-1970	Solidstate	$650	$850

Kensington V1241 Bass

1966-1968. U.S.-made solidstate bass amp, 22 watts, 1x15", G-tuner, called Kensington Bass Deluxe in '67.

1966-1968		$650	$950

Night Train Series

2009-2016. Small tube head and combo, 2 channels, Celestion speaker, models available; NT15C1 (15w, 1x12 combo), NT15H-G2 (15w, 1x12 head/cab), NT50H-G2 (50w, 2x12 head/cab).

2009-2016	NT, 2x12 cab	$250	$350
2009-2016	NT15H-G2, cab	$200	$300
2009-2016	NT15H-G2, head	$325	$450
2015-2016	NT15C1, combo	$475	$650

Pacemaker V1021 (Solidstate)

1966-1968. U.S.-made solidstate amp, 35 watts, 1x10", replaced Pacemaker model V102.

1966-1968		$400	$550

Pacemaker V2/V102 (Tube)

1965-1966. U.S.-made tube amp, 18 watts, 1x10", replaced by solidstate Pacemaker model V1021.

1965-1966		$1,000	$1,500

Pathfinder (Import)

1998-present. Compact amps with 1960s cosmetics.

1998-2013	15, 15w, 1x8	$75	$100
2002-2024	10, 10w, 1x65	$60	$85

Pathfinder V1/V101 (Tube)

1965-1966. U.S.-made tube amp, 4 watts, 1x8", '66-'69 became U.S.-made solidstate V1011.

1965-1966		$925	$1,250

Pathfinder V1011 (Solidstate)

1966-1968. U.S.-made solidstate, 25 watts peak power, 1x8".

1966-1968		$400	$550

Royal Guardsman V1131/V1132

1966-1968. U.S.-made solidstate, 50 watts piggyback, 2x12" + 1 horn, the model below the Super Beatle V1141/V1142.

1966-1968		$1,000	$1,500

Scorpion (Solidstate)

1968. Solidstate, 120 watts, 4x10" Vox Oxford speaker.

1968		$500	$650

Super Beatle Reissue Cabinet

2011-2012. 2x15" cab only.

2011-2012		$350	$500

Super Beatle V1141/V1142

1965-1966. U.S.-made 120-watt solidstate, 4x12" + 2 horns, with distortion pedal (V1141), or without (V1142).

1965-1966		$3,000	$4,500

T60

1962-1966. Solidstate bass head, around 40 watts, sold with 2x15" or 1x12" and 1x15" cabinet.

1962-1966		$725	$1,000

VBM1 Brian May Special

2010. Compact 10-watt, 1x6" speaker, also called VBM1 Brian May Recording Amp, white cover, includes headphone/recording line out, Brian May logo on lower right grille.

2010		$125	$200

Viscount V1151/V1152

1966-1968. U.S.-made solidstate, 70 watts, 2x12" combo, 1151, 1153, and 1154 with distortion.

1966-1968		$750	$950

VT Valvetronix/Valvetronix + Series

2008-present. Line of digital modeling combo amps, ranging from the 15-watt, 1x8" VT15 ('08-'11) to the Valvetronix+ 120-watt, 2x12" VT120+.

2008-2011	VT15	$100	$150
2012-2024	VT20+	$100	$150
2015-2016	VT80	$165	$250
2015-2024	VT40+	$150	$225

Westminster V118 Bass

1966-1969. Solidstate, 120 watts, 1x18".

1966-1969		$600	$850

V-Series

See Crate.

Wabash

1950s. Private branded amps, made by others, distributed by the David Wexler company. They also offered lap steels and guitars.

Model 1158

1950s. Danelectro-made, 1x15", 2x6L6 power tubes, tweed.

1950s		$600	$850

Small Tube

1950s	3 tubes	$225	$350

Wallace Amplification

2000-present. Production/custom, professional grade, amps built by Brian Wallace in Livonia, Michigan. (Not affiliated with a 1970's amp com-

MODEL YEAR	FEATURES	LOW	HIGH

pany from the United Kingdom also called Wallace that has since gone out of business.)

Warbler

See listing under Juke amps.

Warwick

1982-present. Combos, amp heads and cabinets from Warwick Basses of Markneukirchen, Germany.

Washburn

1962-present. Imported guitar and bass amps. Washburn also offers guitars, banjos, mandolins, and basses.

Watkins

1957-present. England's Watkins Electric Music (WEM) was founded by Charlie Watkins. Their first commercial product was the Watkins Dominator (wedge Gibson stereo amp shape) in '57, followed by the Copicat Echo in '58. They currently build accordion amps.

Clubman

1960s. Small combo amp with typical Watkins styling, blue cover, white grille.

1960s		$750	$1,000

Dominator MK Series

1970s. Similar circuit to '50s tube amps except solidstate rectifier, 25 watts, different speaker used for different applications.

1970s	MK I, bass, 1x15	$550	$750
1970s	MK II, organ, 1x12	$550	$750
1970s	MK III, guitar, 1x12	$550	$750

Dominator V-Front

Late-1950s-1960s, 2004. 18 watts, 2x10", wedge cabinet similar to Gibson GA-79 stereo amp, tortoise and light beige cab, light grille, requires 220V step-up transformer. Was again offered in '04.

1959-1962		$2,500	$4,500

Joker

1960-1962. Watkins logo on front, 25-watt 1x12, tubes, 2-tone red and grey covering.

1960-1962		$2,500	$4,500

Scout

1960s. Watkins and Scout logo on top control panel, 17 watts, 1x10 combo, 6 tubes.

1960s		$1,000	$1,500

Westminster Tremolo

1959-1962. 10-watt 1x10" combo, Westminster Tremolo logo on top panel, 3 control knobs, blue and white cover.

1959-1962		$1,000	$1,500

Webcor

1940s-1950s. The Webster-Chicago Company built recording and audio equipment including portable amplifiers suitable for record turntables, PAs, or general utility. Low power with one or two small speakers.

Small

1950s	1 or 2 speakers	$325	$500

MODEL YEAR	FEATURES	LOW	HIGH

West Laboratories

1965-1970s, 2005-2015. Founded by David W. West in Flint, Michigan, moved to Lansing in '68. The '71 catalog included three tube and two solidstate amps, speaker cabinets, as well as Vocal Units and Mini Series combo amps. Amps were available as heads, piggyback half-stacks and full stacks, with the exception of the combo Mini Series. The Fillmore tube amp head was the most popular model. West equipment has a West logo on the front and the cabinets also have a model number logo on the grille. David West reestablished his company in 2005, located in Okemos, Michigan, with models offered on a custom order basis, concentrating on lower power EL84 designs. West died November, '15.

Avalon Head

1965-1970s. 50 watts, 2 6CA7 output tubes.

1965-1970s		$850	$1,250

Fillmore Head

1970s. 200 watts, 4 KT88 output tubes.

1965-1970s		$1,500	$2,500

Grande Head

1970s. 100 watts, 2 KT88 output tubes.

1965-1970s		$1,000	$1,500

Mini IR

1970s. 50 watts, 1x12 tube combo with reverb, black tolex, large West logo and model name Mini IR on front panel.

1965-1970s		$1,000	$1,500

White

1955-1960. The White brand, named after plant manager Forrest White, was established by Fender to provide steel and small amp sets to teaching studios that were not Fender-authorized dealers. The amps were sold with the matching steel guitar. See Steel section for pricing.

White (Matamp)

See Matamp listing.

Winfield Amplification

2001-present. Intermediate and professional grade, production, vacuum tube amps built by Winfield N. Thomas first in Greensboro, Vermont and presently in Cochise, Arizona.

Wizard

1988-present. Professional and premium grade, production/custom, guitar and bass, amps and cabinets built by Rick St Pierre in Cornwall, Ontario.

Woodson

Early 1970s. Obscure builder from Bolivar, Missouri. Woodson logo on front panel and Woodson Model and Serial Number plate on back panel, solidstate circuit, student level pricing.

1970s Watkins Dominator MK III

Jeffrey Phelps

Wallace Amplification Sophia

West Laboratories Mini I

Mark Harvey

AMPS

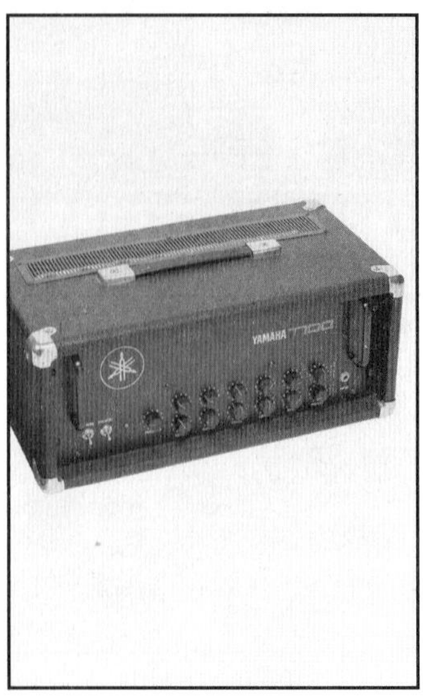
Yamaha T100

1968 Yamaha TA-60
Tom Pfeifer

Yamaha YTA-95

MODEL YEAR	FEATURES	LOW	HIGH

Working Dog

2001-2014. Lower cost tube amps and combos built by Alessandro High-End Products (Alessandro, Hound Dog) in Huntingdon Valley, Pennsylvania.

Wright Amplification

Aaron C. Wright builds his professional grade, production/custom, amps and cabinets in Lincoln, Nebraska starting in 2004.

Yamaha

1946-present. Yamaha started building amps in the '60s and offered a variety of guitar and bass amps over the years. The current models are solidstate bass amps. They also build guitars, basses, effects, sound gear and other instruments.

Budokan HY-10G II

1987-1992. Portable, 10 watts, distortion control, EQ.

1987-1992 $55 $75

Budokan HY-20G

1988-1992. Portable, 20 watts, distortion, EQ.

1988-1992 $65 $85

G30-112

1983-1992. Solidstate combo, 30 watts, 1x12".

1983-1992 $130 $175

G50-112

1983-1992. 50 watts, 1x12".

1983-1992 $175 $250

G100-112

1983-1992. 100 watts, 1x12" combo, black cover, striped grille.

1983-1992 $175 $250

G100-212

1983-1992. 100, 2x12" combo, black cover, striped grille.

1983-1992 $200 $275

JX30B

1983-1992. Bass amp, 30 watts.

1983-1992 $125 $175

T50

1988-1992. Made by Soldano, 50-watt head, 2 channels.

1988-1992 $500 $750

T100

1988-1992. Made by Soldano, 100-watt head, 2 channels.

1988-1992 $850 $1,250

TA-20

1968-1972. Upright wedge shape with controls facing upwards, solidstate.

1968-1972 $100 $150

TA-25

1968-1972. Upright wedge shape with controls facing upwards, 40 watts, 1x12", solidstate, black or red cover.

1968-1972 $125 $175

TA-30

1968-1972. Upright wedge shape, solidstate.

1968-1972 $150 $200

TA-50

1971-1972. Solidstate combo, 80 watts, 2x12", includes built-in cart with wheels, black cover.

1971-1972 $150 $200

TA-60

1968-1972. Upright wedge shape, solidstate, most expensive of wedge-shape amps.

1968-1972 $450 $650

VR3000

1988-1992. Combo 1x12", 2 channels, identical control sections for each channel, settings are completely independent.

1988-1992 $125 $175

VR4000

1988-1992. 50-watt stereo, 2 channels, EQ, stereo chorus, reverb and dual effects loops.

1988-1992 $200 $275

MODEL YEAR	FEATURES	LOW	HIGH

VR6000

1988-1992. 100-watt stereo, 2 channels which can also be combined, EQ, chorus, reverb and dual effects loops.

1988-1992	$500	$700

VX-15

1988-1992. 15 watts.

1988-1992	$100	$150

VX-65D Bass

1984-1992. 80 watts, 2 speakers.

1984-1992	$125	$175

YBA-65 Bass

1972-1976. Solidstate combo, 60 watts, 1x15".

1972-1976	$125	$175

YTA-25

1972-1976. Solidstate combo, 25 watts, 1x12".

1972-1976	$125	$175

YTA-45

1972-1976. Solidstate combo, 45 watts, 1x12".

1972-1976	$125	$175

YTA-95

1972-1976. Solidstate combo, 90 watts, 2x12".

1972-1976	$125	$175

YTA-100

1972-1976. Solidstate piggyback, 100 watts, 2x12".

1972-1976	$150	$200

YTA-110

1972-1976. Solidstate piggyback, 100 watts, 2x12" in extra-large cab.

1972-1976	$150	$200

YTA-200

1972-1976. Solidstate piggyback, 200 watts, 4x12".

1972-1976	$175	$250

YTA-300

1972-1976. Solidstate piggyback, 200 watts, dual cabs with 2x12" and 4x12".

1972-1976	$275	$375

YTA-400

1972-1976. Solidstate piggyback, 200 watts, dual 4x12".

1972-1976	$275	$375

MODEL YEAR	FEATURES	LOW	HIGH

Z.Vex Amps

2002-present. Intermediate grade, production amps built by Zachary Vex in Minneapolis, Minnesota, with some subassembly work done in Michigan. He also builds effects.

Zapp

Ca.1978-early-1980s. Zapp amps were distributed by Red Tree Music, Inc., of Mamaroneck, New York.

Z-10

1978-1980s. Small student amp, 8 watts.

1979-1982	$25	$40

Z-50

1978-1980s. Small student amp, 10 watts, reverb, tremelo.

1978-1982	$30	$50

Zeppelin Design Labs

2014-present. Brach Siemens and Glen van Alkemade build budget and intermediate grade amps and cabinets in Chicago, Illinois. They also offer their products as DIY kits.

Zeta

1982-2010. Solid state amps with MIDI options, made in Oakland, California. They also made upright basses and violins.

Zinky

Tube head and combo amps and cabinets built by Bruce Zinky, starting in 1999, in Flagstaff, Arizona. He also builds the mini Smokey amps (since '97), effects, and has revived the Supro brand on a guitar and amp.

ZT Amplifiers

2009-present. Ken Kantor of Berkeley, California imports intermediate grade, production, solid state compact amps from China. He also offers effects.

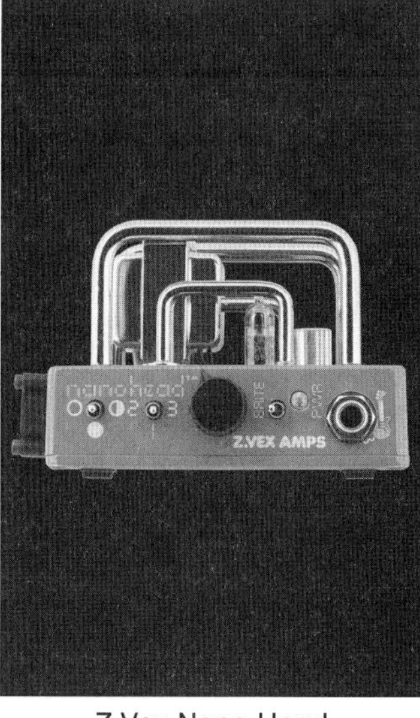

Z.Vex Nano Head

Zeppelin Design Labs The Percolator

ZT Jazz Club

AMPS

EFFECTS

Wampler Ego and Diaz Texas Tremodillo: Will Snodgrass.

Ace Tone Fuzz Master FM-2
Antonio Rebolledo Ferrari

ADA MP-1

Ca. 1970s ADA Flanger

MODEL YEAR | FEATURES | LOW | HIGH

Vintage pedals and effects are the most volatile segment in the vintage guitar marketplace. Their values can change rapidly. This is because there are many "influencers" on YouTube that demonstrate and compare effects. Some pedals become very popular after being featured.

Two prices are shown for the effects. The first is the median price of an all-original pedal that functions perfectly. The vast majority of these vintage pedals will show signs of wear and tear. The second is the "exceptional condition price." This is for an all-original excellent condition pedal that still functions perfectly. Pedals that come in their original box, have associated "box candy" (instructions, warranty cards, stickers, etc.), and no Velcro or tape marks on bottom are highly desired. Collectors will often pay 10- to 20-percent more for these pedals.

Able Electronics

1990s. Started by John Rogers and based in Pwllheli, Wales.

Bassmaker

1990s. Octave pedal.

1990s $250 $350

Ace Tone

1968-1972. Effects from Ace Electronic Industry, which was a part of Sakata Shokai Limited of Osaka, Japan, which also made organs, amps, pioneering Rhythm Ace FR-1 and FR-2 drum machines, etc. Their Ace Tone effects line was the predecessor to Roland and Boss.

Echo Chamber EC-10

1968-1972. Solidstate tape echo.

1968-1972 $850 $1,250

Expander EXP-4

1968-1972. "Expander" effect.

1968-1972 $200 $350

Fuzz Master FM-1

1968-1972. Distortion and overdrive.

1968-1972 $650 $850

Fuzz Master FM-2

1968-1972. Fuzz. Black housing. 2 Control knobs.

1968-1972 $350 $450

Fuzz Master FM-3

1968-1972. Distortion and clean boost.

1968-1972 $450 $700

Stereo Phasor LH-100

1968-1972. Phaser.

1968-1972 $500 $650

Wah Master WM-1

1968-1972. Filter wah.

1968-1972 $125 $200

Acoustyx

1977-1982. Made by the Highland Corporation of North Springfield, Vermont.

Image Synthesizer IS-1

1977-ca.1982. Synthesizer effects.

1977-1982 $150 $200

MODEL YEAR | FEATURES | LOW | HIGH

Phase Five

1977-ca.1982. Used 6 C cell batteries!

1977-1982 $150 $200

ADA

1975-2002. Analog/Digital Associates was located in Berkeley, California, and introduced its Flanger and Final Phase in '77. The company later moved to Oakland and made amplifiers, high-tech signal processors, and a reissue of its original Flanger.

Final Phase

1977-1979. Reissued in '97.

1977-1979 $400 $500

Flanger

1977-1983, 1996-2002. Reissued in '96.

1977-1979 No control pedal $400 $500
1977-1979 With control pedal $450 $575
1980-1983 $100 $150
1996-2002 $275 $350

MP-1

1987-1995. Tube preamp with chorus and effects loop, MIDI.

1987-1995 No foot controller $400 $650
1987-1995 With optional foot controller $550
$875

MP-2

Ca.1988-1995. Tube preamp with chorus, 9-band EQ and effects loop, MIDI.

1988-1995 $600 $950

Pitchtraq

1987. Programmable pitch transposer including octave shifts.

1987 $250 $350

Stereo Tapped Delay STD-1

Introduced in 1981.

1980s $250 $450

TFX4 Time Effects

Introduced in 1982, includes flanger, chorus, doubler, echo.

1980s $250 $350

Aguilar

1995-present. The New York, New York amp builder also offers a line of tube and solidstate pre-amps.

Akai (Akai Electric Company Ltd.)

1984-present. In '99, Akai added guitar effects to their line of electronic samplers and sequencers for musicians.

UniBass UB1

2000s. Bass octave pedal.

2000s $225 $450

Alamo

1947-1982. Founded by Charles Eilenberg, Milton Fink, and Southern Music, San Antonio, Texas. Distributed by Bruno & Sons. Mainly known for guitars and amps, Alamo did offer a reverb unit.

MODEL YEAR	FEATURES	LOW	HIGH

Reverb Unit
1965-ca.1979. Has a Hammond reverb system, balance and intensity controls. By '73 the unit had 3 controls - mixer, contour, and intensity.
1965-1970 $375 $550

Alesis
1992-present. Alesis has a wide range of products for the music industry, including digital processors and amps for guitars.

Allen Amplification
1998-present. David Allen's company, located in Richwood, Kentucky, mainly produces amps, but they also offer a tube overdrive pedal.

Altair Corp.
1977-1980s. The company was in Ann Arbor, Michigan.

Power Attenuator PW-5
1977-1980. Goes between amp and speaker to dampen volume.
1977-1980 $85 $200

Amdek
Mid-1980s. Amdek offered many electronic products over the years, including drum machines and guitar effects. Most of these were sold in kit form so the quality of construction can vary.

Delay Machine DMK-200
1983. Variable delay times.
1983 $225 $350

Octaver OCK-100
1983. Produces tone 1 or 2 octaves below the note played.
1983 $125 $200

Phaser PHK-100
1983 $85 $135

Phlanger
1983 $85 $135

Ampeg
Ampeg entered the effects market in the late-1960s. Their offerings in the early-'60s were really amplifier-outboard reverb units similar to the ones offered by Gibson (GA-1). Ampeg offered a line of imported effects in '82-'83, known as the A-series (A-1 through A-9), and reintroduced effects to their product line in '05.

Analog Delay A-8
1982-1983. Made in Japan.
1982-1983 $250 $450

Chorus A-6
1982-1983. Made in Japan.
1982-1983 $150 $300

Compressor A-2
1982-1983. Made in Japan.
1982-1983 $150 $200

Distortion A-1
1982-1983. Made in Japan.
1982-1983 $150 $200

Echo Jet Reverb EJ-12
1963-1965. Outboard, alligator clip reverb unit with 12" speaker, 12 watts, technically a reverb unit. When used as a stand-alone amp, the reverb is off. Named EJ-12A in '65.
1963-1965 $650 $850

Echo Satellite ES-1
1961-1963. Outboard reverb unit with amplifier and speaker alligator clip.
1961-1963 $770 $1,000

Flanger A-5
1982-1983. Made in Japan.
1982-1983 $150 $200

Multi-Octaver A-7
1982-1983. Made in Japan.
1982-1983 $150 $200

Over Drive A-3
1982-1983. Made in Japan.
1982-1983 $150 $200

Parametric Equalizer A-9
1982-1983. Made in Japan.
1982-1983 $150 $200

Phaser A-4
1982-1983. Made in Japan.
1982-1983 $150 $200

Phazzer
1975-1979. Phase shifter, single speed knob.
1975-1979 $250 $350

Scrambler Fuzz
1969-1970. Distortion pedal, black housing. 2 Control knobs. Reissued in '05.
1969-1970 $1,250 $1,500

Sub Blaster SCP-OCT
2005-2007. Bass octave pedal.
2005-2007 $350 $450

Amplifier Corporation of America
Late '60s company that made amps for Univox and marketed effects under their own name.

Amptweaker
2010-present. James Brown, an amp design engineer previously employed by Peavey, then for Kustom amps, now designs and builds effects in Batavia, Ohio.

amukaT Gadgets
Guitar effects built by Takuma Kanaiwa, starting 2006, in New York, New York.

Analog Man
1994-present. Founded by Mike Piera in '94 with full-time production by 2000. Located in Danbury, Connecticut (until '07 in Bethel), producing chorus, compressor, fuzz, and boost pedals by '03.

Astro Tone
2000s-present. Fuzz.
2000s-2024 $160 $350

Bad Bob
2000s-present. Boost.
2000s-2024 $160 $250

Akai E2 Headrush

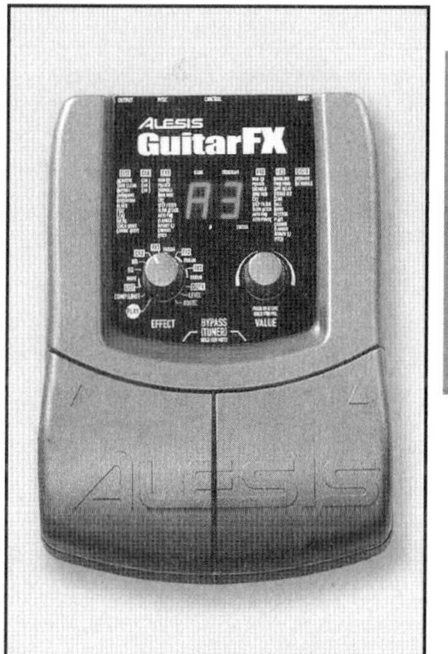

Alesis GuitarFX

Amptweaker Big Rock Pro II

Analog.Man King of Tone

Analog.Man Sun Face

1967 Applied Big Bass Boost
Rivington Guitars

MODEL YEAR	FEATURES	LOW	HIGH

Beano Boost

2000s-present. Boost.

2000s-2024		$185	$275

Dual Analog Delay

2000s-present. Delay.

2000s-2024		$350	$525

Envelope Filter

2000s-present. Envelope 'auto-wah'.

2000s-2024		$175	$250

Juicer

2000s-present. Compressor.

2000s-2024		$150	$200

King of Tone

2000s-present. Overdrive pedal, 4 generations, numerous options available.

2000s-2024		$700	$1,000

Peppermint Fuzz

2000s-present. Fuzz.

2000s-2024		$145	$250

Prince of Tone

2000s-present. Overdrive.

2000s-2024		$185	$200

Sun Bender

2000s-present. Fuzz.

2000s-2024		$250	$350

Sun Face

2000s-present. Fuzz.

2000s-2024		$275	$400
2010s-2015	White Dot NKT 275	$1,500	$2,000

Aphex Systems

1975-present. Founded in Massachusetts by Marvin Caesar and Curt Knoppel, to build their Aural Exciter and other pro sound gear. Currently located in Sun Valley, California, and building a variety of gear for the pro audio broadcast, pro music and home-recording markets.

Apollo

Ca.1967-1972. Imported from Japan by St. Louis Music, includes Fuzz Treble Boost Box, Crier Wa-Wa, Deluxe Fuzz. They also offered basses and guitars.

Crier Wa-Wa

Ca.1967-1972.

1967-1972		$250	$350

Fuzz/Deluxe Fuzz

Ca.1967-1972. Includes the Fuzz Treble Boost Box and the Deluxe Fuzz.

1967-1972		$500	$850

Surf Tornado Wah Wah

Ca.1967-1972.

1967-1972		$250	$350

Applied

1960s. Effects brand of the Goya Music Company. Some models may have been sold under the Nomad brand.

Banshee Fuzz

1960s. Also sold as the Nomad Banshee Fuzz.

1960s		$400	$500

Arbiter

Ivor Arbiter and Arbiter Music, London, began making the circular Fuzz Face stompbox in 1966. Other products included the Fuzz Wah and Fuzz Wah Face. In '68 the company went public as Arbiter and Western, later transitioning to Dallas-Arbiter. Refer to Dallas-Arbiter for listings.

Area 51

2003-present. Guitar effects made in Newaygo, Michigan (made in Texas until early '06), by Dan Albrecht. They also build amps.

Aria/Aria Pro II

1956-present. Aria provided a line of effects, made by Maxon, in the mid-'80s.

Analog Delay AD-10

1983-1985. Dual-stage stereo.

1983-1985		$100	$150

Chorus ACH-1

1986-1987. Stereo.

1986-1987		$75	$100

Chorus CH-10

1983-1985. Dual-stage stereo.

1983-1985		$75	$100

Chorus CH-5

1985-1987		$75	$100

Compressor CO-10

1983-1985		$75	$100

Digital Delay ADD-100

1984-1986. Delay, flanging, chorus, doubling, hold.

1984-1986		$125	$175

Digital Delay DD-X10

1985-1987		$125	$175

Distortion DT-10

1983-1985. Dual stage.

1983-1985		$75	$100

Distortion DT-5

1985-1987		$75	$100

Flanger AFL-1

1986. Stereo.

1986		$75	$100

Flanger FL-10

1983-1985. Dual-stage stereo.

1983-1985		$75	$100

Flanger FL-5

1985-1987		$75	$100

Metal Pedal MP-5

1985-1987		$75	$100

Noise Gate NG-10

1983-1985		$50	$75

Over Drive OD-10

1983-1985. Dual stage.

1983-1985		$75	$100

Parametric Equalizer EQ-10

1983-1985		$75	$100

Phase Shifter PS-10

1983-1984. Dual stage.

1983-1984		$75	$100

MODEL YEAR	FEATURES	LOW	HIGH

Programmable Effects Pedal APE-1

1984-1986. Compression, distortion, delay, chorus.

1984-1986		$175	$250

Arion

1984-2014. Arion offers a wide variety of budget imported effects.

Guitar and Bass Effects

1984-2014		$25	$100

Arteffect

Tom Kochawi and Dan Orr started building analog effects in 2006, in Haifa and Natanya, Israel.

Artesania Sonora Lab

2010s-present. Based in Fortaleza, Brazil.

Fabrica del Fuzz

2016-2024		$100	$150

Asama

1970s-1980s. This Japanese company offered solidbody guitars with built-in effects as well as stand-alone units. They also offered basses, drum machines and other music products.

Astro Amp

Late 1960s. Universal Amplifier Corporation of New York City made and sold Astro Amps as well as Astro effects. The company also made the Sam Ash Fuzzz Boxx.

Astrotone

1966		$1,500	$2,000

ATD

Mid-1960s-early 1980s. Made by the All-Test Devices corporation of Long Beach, New York. In the mid-'60s, Richard Minz and an associate started making effects part-time, selling them through Manny's Music in New York. They formed All-Test and started making Maestro effects and transducer pickups for CMI, which owned Gibson at the time. By '75, All-Test was marketing effects under their own brand. All-Test is still making products for other industries, but by the early to mid-'80s they were no longer making products for the guitar.

PB-1 Power Booster

1976-ca.1980.

1979-1980		$100	$150

Volume Pedal EV-1

1979-ca.1980.

1979-1980		$100	$150

Wah-Wah/Volume Pedal WV-1

1979-ca.1981.

1979-1981		$100	$150

Audio Disruption Devices

2010s. Based in Mooresville, Indiana.

Optical Ring V2

2010s. Ring modulator.

2010s		$150	$200

MODEL YEAR	FEATURES	LOW	HIGH

Audio Matrix

1979-1984. Effects built by B.K Butler in Escondido, California. He later designed the Tube Driver and founded Tube Works in 1987. He now operates Butler Audio, making home and auto hybrid tube stereo amps.

Mini Boogee B81

1981. Four-stage, all-tube preamp, overdrive, distortion.

1981		$250	$500

Audio-Phonic

1970s. Effects built in Argentina.

Mu-Tron III

1970s. Musitronics Mu-Tron III copy.

1970s		$800	$1,500

Audioworks

1980s. The company was located in Niles, Illinois.

F.E.T. Distortion

1980s		$75	$100

Auralux

2000-2011. Founded by Mitchell Omori and David Salzmann, Auralux built effects and tube amps in Highland Park, Illinois.

Austone Electronics

1997-2009. Founded by Jon Bessent and Randy Larkin, Austone offered a range of stomp boxes, all made in Austin, Texas. Bessent passed away in '09.

Overdrive and Fuzz Pedals

1997-2009. Various overdrive and fuzz boxes.

1997-2009		$200	$250

Automagic

Wah pedals and distortion boxes made in Germany by Musician Sound Design, starting in 1998.

Avalanche

Late 1980s. Effects built by Brian Langer in Toronto, Ontario.

Brianizer

Late-1980s. Leslie effect, dual rotor, adjustable speed and rate.

1980s		$150	$200

Axe

1980s. Early '80s line of Japanese effects, possibly made by Maxon.

B&M

1970s. A private brand made by Sola/Colorsound for Barns and Mullens, a U.K. distributor.

Fuzz Unit

1970s. Long thin orange case, volume, sustain, tone knobs, on-off stomp switch.

1970s		$1,000	$1,500

Area 51 The Alienist

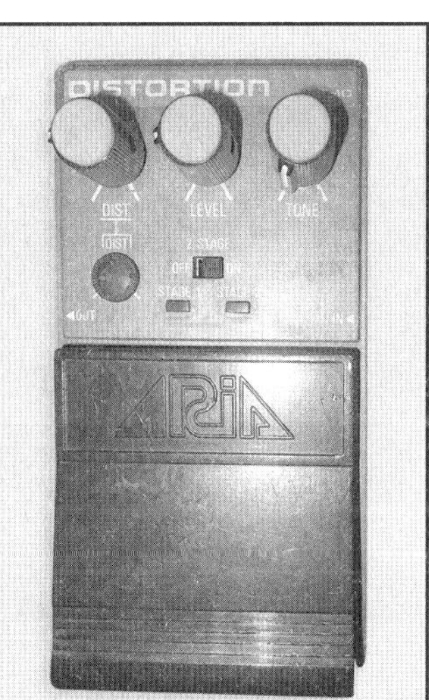

1985 Aria Distortion DT-10

Rivington Guitars

Arion Delay SAD-1

Niclas Löfgren

Bad Cat Double Drive

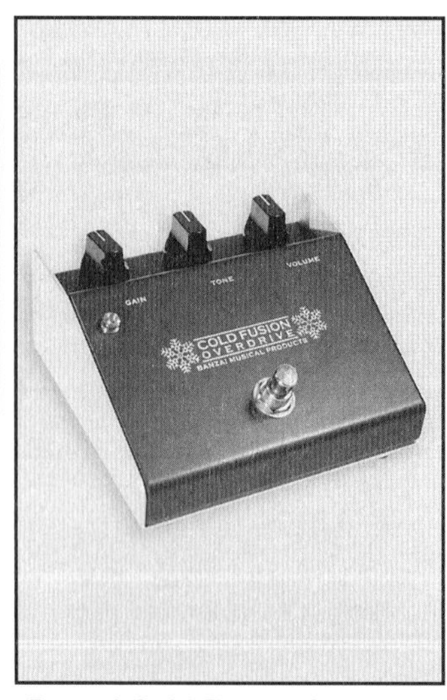

Banzai Cold Fusion Overdrive

BBE Sonic Stomp

MODEL YEAR	FEATURES	LOW	HIGH

Backline Engineering

Guitar multi-effects built by Gary Lee, starting 2004 in Camarillo, California. In '07, they added tube amps.

Bad Cat Amplifier Company

2000-present. Amp company Bad Cat, originally of Corona, California, also offers guitar effects. In '09 the company was moved to Anaheim.

Baldwin

1965-1970. The piano maker got into the guitar market when it acquired Burns of London in '65 and sold the guitars in the U.S. under the Baldwin name. They also marketed a couple of effects at the same time.

Banzai

2000-present. Effects built by Olaf Nobis in Berlin, Germany.

Bartolini

The pickup manufacturer offered a few effects from around 1982 to '87.

Tube-It

1982-ca.1987. Marshall tube amplification simulator with bass, treble, sustain controls.

1982-1987	Red case	$350	$500

Basic Systems' Side Effects

1980s. This company was in Tulsa, Oklahoma.

Audio Delay

1986-ca.1987. Variable delay speeds.

1986-1987		$150	$200

Triple Fuzz

1986-ca.1987. Selectable distortion types.

1986-1987		$100	$150

BBE

1985-present. BBE, owner of G&L Guitars and located in California, manufactures rack-mount effects and added a new line of stomp boxes in '05.

Behringer

1989-present. The German professional audio products company added modeling effects in '01 and guitar stomp boxes in '05. They also offer guitars and amps.

Beigel Sound Lab

Music product designer Mike Beigel helped form Musitronics Corp, where he made the Mu-Tron III. In 1978 he started Beigel Sound Lab to provide product design in Warwick, New York, where in '80 he made 50 rackmount Enveloped Controlled Filters under this brand name. In 2013, Mike Beigel's Beigel Sound Lab started making a Mu-FX Tru-Tron 3X and Octave Divider.

Boostron 3

2016-2017. Combines preamp boost, compression, and distortion in one pedal.

2016-2017		$350	$475

Octave Divider

2015. Updated and expanded version of original Musitronics Mu-Tron Octave Divider.

2015		$400	$900

Tru-Tron 3X

2015-2019. Updated and expanded version of original Musitronics Mu-Tron III envelope filter.

2015-2019		$400	$900

Bell Electrolabs

1970s. This English company offered a line of effects in the '70s.

Vibrato

1970s		$150	$200

Bennett Music Labs

Effects built in Chatanooga, Tennessee by Bruce Bennett.

Bigsby

1948-1966. Paul Bigsby made steel guitars, pedal steels, and electric guitars and mandolins, as well as developing the Bigsby vibrato tailpiece and other components.

Foot Volume and Tone Control

1950s-1960s. Beautifully crafted pedal in a cast-aluminum housing featuring a side-to-side tone sweep.

1950s-60s		$500	$650

Binson

Late 1950s-1982. Binson, of Milan, Italy, made several models of the Echorec, using tubes or transistors. They also made units for Guild, Sound City and EKO.

Echorec

Ca.1960-1979. Four knob models with 12 echo selections, 1 head, complex multitap effects, settings for record level, playback and regeneration. Includes B1, B2, Echomaster1, T5 (has 6 knobs), T5E, and Baby. Used a magnetic disk instead of tape. Guild later offered the Guild Echorec by Binson which is a different stripped-down version.

1960s	Tube	$4,500	$8,000
1970s	Solidstate	$1,500	$2,000

Bixonic

1995-2007. The round silver distortion pedals were originally distributed by SoundBarrier Music, later by Godlyke, Inc.

Expandora EXP-2000

1995-2000. Analog distortion, round silver case, internal DIP switches.

1995-2000		$250	$350

Expandora EXP-2000R

2005-2007. Reissue, round silver case with red print.

2005-2007		$250	$350

Black Arts Toneworks

2010s. Founded by Mark Wentz of Chattanooga, Tennessee.

Pharaoh

2010s		$150	$175

MODEL YEAR	FEATURES	LOW	HIGH

Ritual Fuzz

2010s. Inspired by the Colorsound Fuzz Box.

2010s		$150	$175

Black Cat Pedals

1993-2007, 2009-2022. Founded by Fred Bonte and located in Texas until late 2007 when production was discontinued. In '09, using Bonte's same designs, new owner Tom Hughes restarted production in Foxon, Connecticut.

Black Cat OD-1

2010-2022. Overdrive.

2010-2022		$150	$200

Blackbox Music Electronics

2000-2009. Founded by Loren Stafford and located in Minneapolis, Minnesota, Blackbox offered a line of effects for guitar and bass. The Blackbox models are now made under the Ooh La La brand.

Blackout Effectors

Kyle Tompkins began building effects pedals in 2007, in Vancouver, British Columbia and now builds them in Asheville, North Carolina.

Blackstar Amplification

2007-present. Guitar effects pedals built by Joel Richardson in Northampton, U.K. He also builds amps.

Blackstone Appliances

1999-present. Distortion effects crafted by Jon Blackstone in New York City.

Mosfet Overdrive

1999-present. Though the designation doesn't appear on the housing, the original was subsequently called 2Sv1 after later versions were issued.

1999	2Sv1, no controls on top	$200	$300
2000	2Sv2	$200	$300
2006-2024	2Sv3, 2Sv31, 2Sv32, 2Sv33	$200	$300
2012	Billybox Limited Edition	$200	$300

Bon, Mfg

Bon was in Escondido, California.

Tube Driver 204

1979-ca.1981.

1979-1981		$1,000	$1,500

Boomerang

1995-present. Effects pedals built in Grapevine, Texas by Boomerang Musical Products, Ltd.

Boss

1976-present. Japan's Roland Corporation first launched effect pedals in '74. A year or two later the subsidiary company, Boss, debuted its own line. They were marketed concurrently at first but gradually Boss became reserved for effects and drum machines while the Roland name was used on amplifiers and keyboards. Boss still offers a wide line of pedals.

Acoustic Simulator AC-2

1997-2007. Four modes that emulate various acoustic tones.

1997-2007		$60	$85

Acoustic Simulator AC-3

2007-present. Four modes that emulate various acoustic tones.

2007-2024		$60	$125

Auto Wah AW-2

1991-1999. Becomes Dynamic Wah (AW-3) in 2000.

1991-1999		$70	$125

Bass Chorus CE-2B

1987-1995		$85	$135

Bass Equalizer GE-7B

1987-1995. Seven-band, name changed to GEB-7 in '95.

1987-1995		$70	$125

Bass Flanger BF-2B

1987-1994		$90	$150

Bass Limiter LM-2B

1990-1994		$60	$85

Bass Limiter/Enhancer LMB-3

1990s		$60	$125

Bass Overdrive ODB-3

1994-present. Yellow case.

1994-2024		$60	$125

Blues Driver BD-2

1995-present. Blue case.

1995-2024		$75	$90
1995-2024	Keeley modded	$225	$300

Chorus Ensemble CE-1

1976-1978. Vibrato and chorus.

1976-1978		$650	$900

Chorus Ensemble CE-2

1979-1982		$250	$350

Chorus Ensemble CE-3

1982-1992		$70	$175

Chorus Ensemble CE-5

1991-present. Pale blue case.

1991-2020		$60	$125

Compressor Sustainer CS-1

1978-1982		$90	$175

Compressor Sustainer CS-2

1981-1986		$130	$185

Compressor Sustainer CS-3

1986-present. Blue case.

1986-2024		$65	$85
1986-2024	JHS modded	$125	$175

Delay DM-2

1979-1985. Analog, hot pink case.

1979-1980	MN3025 Chip	$350	$400
1981-1985	MN3005 Chip	$200	$250

Delay DM-3

1984-1988		$150	$200

Digital Delay DD-2

1983-1986		$150	$250

Black Arts Toneworks Pharaoh Supreme

Rivington Guitars

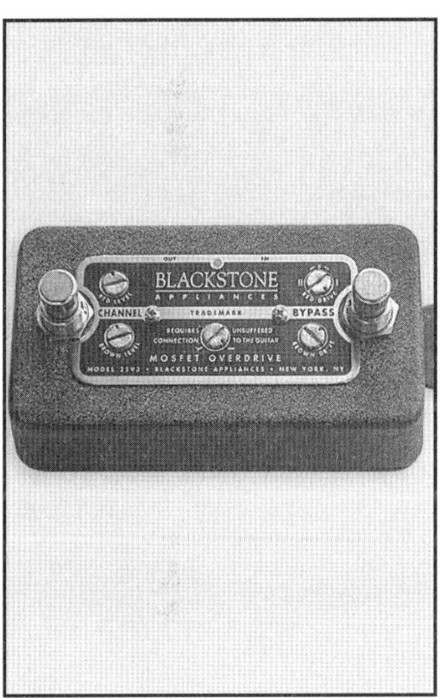

Blackstone Mosfet Overdrive

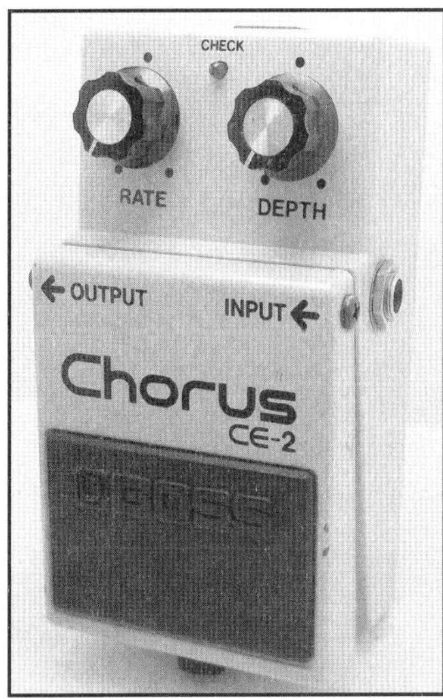

Boss Chorus Ensemble CE-2

Keith Myers

EFFECTS

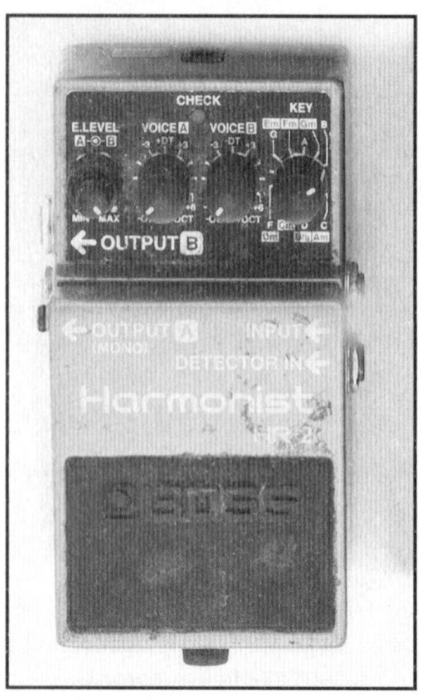
Boss Harmonist HR-2
Imaged by Heritage Auctions, HA.com

1984 Boss Heavy Metal HM-2
Rivington Guitars

Boss Metal Zone MT-2

EFFECTS

MODEL YEAR	FEATURES	LOW	HIGH
Digital Delay DD-3			
1986-present. Up to 800 ms of delay, white case.			
1986-1989		$90	$150
1986-2024	Keeley modded	$150	$250
1990-2024		$75	$125
Digital Delay DD-5			
1995-2005. Up to 2 seconds of delay.			
1995-2005		$90	$150
Digital Delay DD-6			
2003-2007. Up to 5 seconds of delay.			
2003-2007		$75	$125
Digital Delay DD-7			
2008-2022. Up to 6.4 seconds of delay, crème case.			
2008-2022		$90	$135
Digital Dimension C DC-2			
1985-1989. Two chorus effects and tremolo.			
1985-1989		$250	$350
Digital Metalizer MZ-2			
1987-1992		$150	$250
Digital Reverb RV-2			
1987-1990		$120	$200
Digital Reverb RV-5			
2003-2019. Dual input and dual output, four control knobs, silver case.			
2003-2019		$90	$125
Digital Reverb/Delay RV-3			
1994-2004		$120	$175
Digital Sampler/Delay DSD-2			
1985-1986		$120	$175
Digital Space-D DC-3/ Digital Dimension DC-3			
1988-1993. Originally called the Digital Space-D, later changed to Digital Dimension. Chorus with EQ.			
1988-1993		$175	$275
Digital Stereo Reverb RV-70			
1994-1995. Rack mount, MIDI control, reverb/delay, 199 presets.			
1994-1995		$175	$225
Distortion DS-1			
1978-1989, 1990s-present. Orange case.			
1978-1989		$125	$225
1978-2024	Keeley modded	$175	$250
1990-1999		$60	$80
2000-2024		$30	$40
Dr. Rhythm DR-55			
1979-1989. Drum machine.			
1979-1989		$200	$400
Dual Over Drive SD-2			
1993-1998		$125	$165
Dynamic Filter FT-2			
1986-1988. Auto wah.			
1986-1988		$225	$350
Dynamic Wah AW-3			
2000-present. Auto wah with humanizer, for guitar or bass.			
2000-2024		$85	$125
Enhancer EH-2			
1990-1998		$60	$100
Flanger BF-1			
1977-1980		$225	$400
Flanger BF-2			
1980-1989		$125	$175
1990-2005		$90	$125
Foot Wah FW-3			
1992-1996		$90	$125
Graphic Equalizer GE-6			
1978-1981. Six bands.			
1978-1981		$120	$175
Graphic Equalizer GE-7			
1981-present. Seven bands, white case.			
1982-1989		$90	$150
1990-2024		$60	$80
1990-2024	Analogman modded	$250	$300
Graphic Equalizer GE-10			
1976-1985. 10-band EQ for guitar or bass.			
1976-1985		$150	$300
Harmonist HR-2			
1994-1999. Pitch shifter.			
1994-1999		$100	$125
Heavy Metal HM-2			
1983-1991. Distortion.			
1983-1991		$150	$225
Hyper Fuzz FZ-2			
1993-1997		$225	$350
Hyper Metal HM-3			
1993-1998		$90	$150
Limiter LM-2			
1987-1992		$90	$125
Line Selector LS-2			
1991-2021. Select between 2 effects loops, white case.			
1991-2021	With adapter	$60	$95
Mega Distortion MD-2			
2003-present. Red case.			
2003-2024		$60	$80
Metal Zone MT-2			
1991-present. Distortion and 3-band EQ, grey case.			
1991-2024		$125	$200
1991-2024	Keeley modded	$175	$225
Multi Effects ME-5			
1988-1991. Floor unit.			
1988-1991		$120	$225
Multi Effects ME-6			
1992-1997		$70	$100
Multi Effects ME-8			
1996-1997		$125	$175
Multi Effects ME-20			
1990-2000s		$115	$150
Multi Effects ME-25			
1990-2000s		$120	$150
Multi Effects ME-30			
1998-2002		$90	$125
Multi Effects ME-50			
2003-2009. Floor unit.			
2003-2009		$150	$195
Multi Effects ME-70			
2000s		$150	$200
Multi Effects ME-80			
2000s-present.			
2000s-2024		$150	$200
Noise Gate NF-1			
1979-1988		$75	$95

MODEL YEAR	FEATURES	LOW	HIGH

Noise Suppressor NS-2
1987-present. White case.
1987-2024 $60 $150

Octaver OC-2/Octave OC-2
1982-2003. Originally called the Octaver.
1982 $200 $275
1983-2003 $125 $175

Overdrive OD-1
1977-1979 $350 $500
1980-1985 $300 $350

Overdrive OD-2
1990s $80 $125

Overdrive OD-3
1997-present. Yellow case.
1997-2024 $95 $125

Parametric Equalizer PQ-4
1991-1997 $175 $300

Phase Shifter PH-3
2000-present. Added effects, light green case.
2000-2024 $85 $125

Phaser PH-1
1977-1981. Green box, 2 knobs.
1977-1981 $225 $300

Phaser PH-1R
1982-1985. Resonance control added to PH-1.
1982-1985 $175 $225

Phaser PH-2
1984-2001. 12 levels of phase shift, 4 knobs.
1984-2001 $80 $125

Pitch Sifter/Delay PS-2
1987-1993 $135 $175

Reverb Box RX-100
1981-mid-1980s.
1981-1985 $135 $325

Rocker Distortion PD-1
1980-mid-1980s. Variable pedal using magnetic field.
1980-1985 $185 $250

Rocker Volume PV-1
1981-mid-1980s.
1980-1985 $60 $125

Rocker Wah PW-1
1980-mid-1980s. Magnetic field variable pedal.
1980-1985 $65 $125

Slow Gear SG-1
1979-1982. Violin swell effect, automatically adjusts volume.
1979-1982 $375 $500

Spectrum SP-1
1977-1981. Single-band parametric EQ.
1977-1981 $350 $650

Super Chorus CH-1
1989-present. Blue case.
1989-2024 $70 $95

Super Distortion & Feedbacker DF-2
1984-1994. Also labeled as the Super Feedbacker & Distortion.
1984-1994 $175 $250

Super Octave OC-3
2004-2021. Brown case.
2004-2021 $125 $175

Super Over Drive SD-1
1981-present. Yellow case.
1981-1989 $125 $225
1990-2024 $60 $85

Super Phaser PH-2
1984-1989 $125 $175
1990-2001 $60 $80

Super Shifter PS-5
1999-2013. Pitch shifter/harmonizer, aqua case.
1999-2013 $125 $150

Touch Wah TW-1/T Wah TW-1
1978-1987. Auto wah, early models were labeled as Touch Wah.
1978-1987 $125 $175

Tremolo TR-2
1997-present. Aqua case.
1997-2024 $75 $95
1997-2024 Analogman modded $200 $250
1997-2024 Keeley modded $130 $175

Tremolo/Pan PN-2
1990-1995 $275 $350

Turbo Distortion DS-2
1987-present. Orange case.
1987-2024 $75 $95

Turbo Over Drive OD-2
1985-1994. Called OD-2R after '94, due to added remote on/off jack.
1985-1994 $90 $125

Vibrato VB-2
1982-1986. True pitch-changing vibrato, warm analog tone, 'rise time' control allows for slow attach, 4 knobs, aqua-blue case.
1982-1986 $500 $600

Volume FV-50H
1987-1997. High impedance, stereo volume pedal with inputs and outputs.
1987-1997 $60 $85

Volume FV-50L
1987-1997. Low impedance version of FV-50.
1987-1997 $55 $75

Volume Pedal FV-100
Late-1980s-1991. Guitar volume pedal.
1987-1991 $45 $75

Brimstone Audio

Shad Sundberg builds his guitar effects in California, starting in 2011.

Browntone Electronics

2006-2012. Guitar effects built in Lincolnton, North Carolina by Tim Brown.

Bruno

Music distributor Bruno and Sons had a line of Japanese-made effects in the early '70s.

Fuzz Machine
1970s. Rebranded version of the Ibanez No. 59 Standard Fuzz.
1970s $300 $400

Boss Super Over Drive SD-1
Rivington Guitars

1995 Boss Super Phaser PH-2
Rivington Guitars

Boss Rocker Wah PW-1
Marco Antonio Rebolledo Ferrari

EFFECTS

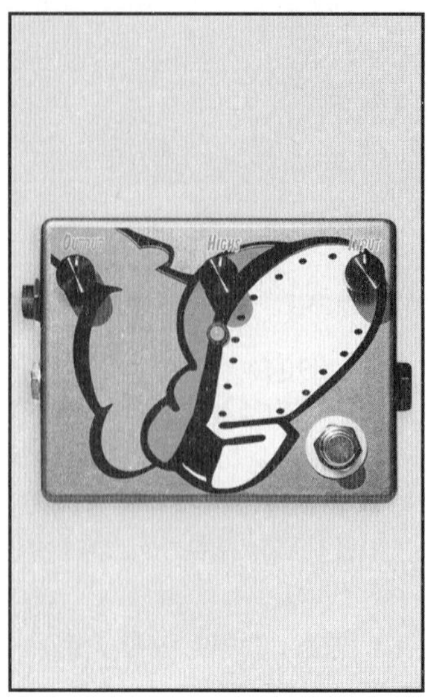

Burriss Boostier

Carl Martin Bass Drive

Catalinbread Sabbra Cadabra

Rivington Guitars

MODEL YEAR | FEATURES | LOW | HIGH

Budda

1995-present. Wahs and distortion pedals originally built by Jeff Bober and Scott Sier in San Francisco, California. In '09, Budda was acquired by Peavey Electronics. They also build amps.

Bud Wah

1997-2018. Wah pedal.

1990s-2018 $135 $275

Phat Bass

2000s $175 $275

Build Your Own Clone

2005-2024. Build it yourself kits based on vintage effects produced by Keith Vonderhulls in Othello, Washington. Assembled kits are offered by their Canadian distributor. They closed in '24.

Burriss

2001-present. Guitar effects from Bob Burriss of Lexington, Kentucky. He also builds amps.

Carl Martin

1993-present. Line of effects from Søren Jongberg and East Sound Research of Denmark. In '06 they added their Chinese-made Vintage Series. They also build amps.

Carlsbro

1959-present. English amp company Carlsbro Electronics Limited offered a line of effects from '77 to '81.

Fuzz

1970s. Tone Bender MkIII fuzz built by Sola Sound.

1970s $1,000 $1,500

Suzz

1970s. Built by Sola Sound.

1970s $650 $850

Suzz Wah Wah

1970s. Built by Sola Sound.

1970s $300 $375

Carrotron

Late-1970s-mid-1980s. Carrotron was out of California and offered a line of effects.

Noise Fader C900B1

1981-ca.1982.

1981-1982 $75 $125

Preamp C821B

1981-ca.1982.

1981-1982 $75 $125

Carvin

1946-present. Carvin introduced its line of Ground Effects in '02 and discontinued them in '03.

Castle Instruments

Early 1980s. Castle was located in Madison, New Jersey, and made rackmount and floor phaser units.

Phaser III

1980-1982. Offered mode switching for various levels of phase.

1980-1982 $350 $500

MODEL YEAR | FEATURES | LOW | HIGH

Catalinbread

2003-present. Nicholas Harris founded Catalinbread Specialized Mechanisms of Music in Seattle, Washington, in '02 to do mods and in '03 added his own line of guitar effects.

Adineko

2000s $130 $180

Belle Epoch

2000s $130 $180

Callisto

2000s $130 $180

Echorec

2000s $140 $195

Formula No. 5

2000s $150 $230

Naga Viper

2000s $100 $150

Perseus

2000s $130 $160

Rah

2000s $150 $180

Sabbra Cadabra

2000s $130 $150

Semaphore

2000s $130 $150

Super Chili Picoso

2000s $100 $150

Topanga

2000s $110 $175

Cat's Eye

Dean Solorzano and Lisa Kroeker began building their analog guitar effects in Oceanside, California in 2001.

Cause & Effect Pedals

Guitar effects pedals built in Ontario by Mark Roberts and Brian Alexson, starting in 2009.

Celmo

The Celmo Sardine Can Compressor is made by Kezako Productions in Montcaret, France, starting in 2008.

Chandler

Located in California, Chandler Musical Instruments offers instruments, pickups, and pickguards, as well as effects.

Digital Echo

1992-2000. Rackmount, 1 second delay, stereo.

1992-2000 $250 $500

Tube Driver

1984-1991. Uses a 12AX7 tube. Not to be confused with the Tube Works Tube Driver.

1984-1987 Made by BK Butler $600 $700

1988-1991 $250 $300

Chapman

1970-present. From Emmett Chapman, maker of the Stick.

MODEL YEAR	FEATURES	LOW	HIGH

Patch of Shades

1981, 1989. Wah, with pressure sensitive pad instead of pedal. 2 production runs.

1980s	$500	$650

Chicago Iron

1998-present. Faithful reproductions of classic effects built by Kurt Steir in Chicago, Illinois.

Chunk Systems

1996-present. Guitar and bass effects pedals built by Richard Cartwright in Sydney, Australia.

Clark

1960s. Built in Clark, New Jersey, same unit as the Orpheum Fuzz and the Mannys Music Fuzz.

SS-600 Fuzz

1960s. Chrome-plated, volume and tone knobs, toggle switch.

1960s	$350	$850

Clark Amplification

1995-present. Amplifier builder Mike Clark, of Cayce, South Carolina, offers a reverb unit and started building guitar effects as well, in '98.

ClinchFX

2006-present. Handmade pedals by Peter Clinch in Brisbane, Queensland, Australia.

CMI

1970s. English music company.

Fuzz Unit

1970s. Built by Colorsound based on its Jumbo Tone Bender.

1970s	$750	$1,250

Coffin

Case manufacturer Coffin Case added U.S.-made guitar effects pedals to their product line in 2006.

Cohrane

2010s. Effects built by Paul Cohrane.

Tim

2010s. Overdrive pedal.

2010s	$600	$700

Timmy

2010s. Upgraded from Tim pedal.

2010s	$250	$400

Timmy V3

2019. Overdrive pedal.

2019	$200	$250

Colorsound

1967-2010. Colorsound effects were produced by England's Sola Sound, beginning with fuzz pedals. In the late-'60s, wah and fuzz-wah pedals were added, and by the end of the '70s, Colorsound offered 18 different effects, an amp, and accessories. Few early Colorsound products were imported into the U.S., so today they're scarce. Except for the Wah-Wah pedal, Colorsound's production stopped by the early '80s, but in '96 most of their early line was reissued by Dick Denny of Vox fame. Denny died in 2001. Since then, Anthony and Steve Macari have built Colorsound effects in London. Mutronics offered a licensed rack mount combination of 4 classic Colorsound effects for a short time in the early 2000s.

Chuck-a-Wah

1975-1977. Auto wah pedal.

1975-1977	$500	$650

Dipthonizer

1970s. "Talking" pedal with foot control.

1970s	$500	$650

Dopplatone Phase Unit

1970s. Large phase and vibrato effect with Bubble control.

1970s	$500	$650

Electro Echo

1979-1980s. Analog delay pedal.

1979-1980s	$500	$650

Flanger

1970s	$375	$500

FuzzPhaze

Introduced in 1973.

1970s	$500	$650

Jumbo Tone-Bender

1974-early 1980s. Replaced the Tone-Bender fuzz, with wider case and light blue lettering.

1974-1980s	$750	$1,750

Octivider

Introduced in 1973.

1970s	$600	$800

Overdriver

Introduced in 1972. Controls for drive, treble and bass.

1970s	$1,000	$2,000

Phazer

Introduced in 1973. Magenta/purple-pink case, slanted block Phazer logo on front.

1970s	$375	$500

Power Boost

1970s	$750	$975

Ring Modulator

Introduced in 1973. Purple case, Ring Modulator name with atom orbit slanted block logo on case.

1970s	$600	$800

Supa Tone Bender

1977-early 1980s. Sustain and volume knobs, tone control and toggle. Same white case as Jumbo Tone-Bender, but with new circuit.

1970s	$600	$800

Supa Wah-Swell

1970s. Supa Wah-Swell in slanted block letters on the end of the pedal, silver case.

1970s	$500	$650

Supaphase

1970s	$600	$800

Supasustain

1960s	$375	$500

Swell

1970s	$175	$300

2000 Chicago Iron Octavian
Rivington Guitars

Clark Amplification Gainster

Colorsound Power Boost

EFFECTS

Coopersonic Germaniac

Crazy Tube Circuits Ziggy
Rivington Guitars

Crowther Audio
Double Hotcake

MODEL YEAR	FEATURES	LOW	HIGH

Tremolo

1970s		$200	$300

Tremolo Reissue

1996-2009. Purple case.

1996-2009		$200	$300

Vocalizer

1979-1980s. "Talking" pedal with foot control.

1979-1980s		$1,000	$2,500

Wah Fuzz Straight

Introduced in 1973. Aqua-blue case, Wah-Fuzz-Straight in capital block letters on end of wah pedal.

1970s		$375	$500

Wah Fuzz Swell

Introduced in 1973. Yellow case, block letter Wah Fuzz Swell logo on front, three control knobs and toggle.

1970s		$500	$650

Wah Swell

1970s. Light purple case, block letter Wah-Swell logo on front.

1970s		$500	$650

Wah Wah

1970s. Dark gray case, Wah-Wah in capital block letters on end of wah pedal.

1975		$750	$975

Wah Wah Reissue

1996-2005. Red case, large Colorsound letter logo and small Wah Wah lettering on end of pedal.

1996-2005		$200	$275

Wah Wah Supremo

1970s. Silver/chrome metal case, Wah-Wah Supremo in block letters on end of wah pedal.

1975		$2,000	$2,500

Companion

1970s. Private branded by Shin-ei of Japan, which made effects for others as well.

Tape Echo

1960-1970		$600	$800

Wah Pedal

1970s		$250	$300

Conn

Ca.1968-ca.1978. Band instrument manufacturer and distributor Conn/Continental Music Company, of Elkhart, Indiana, imported guitars and effects from Japan.

Strobe Tuner

Brown or later, grey, case.

1960s	ST-4	$200	$350
1960s	ST-6	$200	$350
1960s	ST-8	$200	$350
1968	ST-2	$200	$350
1970s	Strobotuner ST-11	$200	$350
1970s	Strobotuner ST-12	$200	$350

Coopersonic

2006-present. Martin Cooper builds his guitar effects in Nottingham, UK.

Coron

1970s-1980s. Japanese-made effects, early ones are close copies of MXR pedals.

Cosmosound

Italy's Cosmosound made small amps with Leslie drums and effects pedals in the late '60s and '70s. Cosmosound logo is on top of pedals.

Wah Fuzz CSE-3

1970s. Volume and distortion knobs, wah and distortion on-off buttons, silver case.

1970s		$300	$400

Wild Sound

1970s		$250	$300

Crazy Tube Circuits

2004-present. Guitar effects designed and built by Chris Ntaifotis in Athens, Greece.

Creation Audio Labs

2005-present. Guitar and bass boost pedal and re-amplifying gear built in Nashville, Tennessee.

Crowther Audio

1976-present. Guitar effects built by Paul Crowther, who was the original drummer of the band Split Enz, in Auckland, New Zealand. His first effect was the Hot Cake.

Crucial Audio

2005-present. Effects by Steve Kollander engineered and assembled in Sussex County, Delaware, with chassis manufactured by machine shops within the U.S. They also provide OEM products and design engineering services to companies including Matchless, Requisite Audio & West Coast Pedal Boards.

Apollo-18 Vacuum Tube Leslie Interface

2015-present. High-voltage vacuum tube interface module for Leslie 122 or 147 type rotary speaker systems; can be used with a tube preamp and/or two channel vacuum tube direct box.

2015-2024		$1,000	$1,250

Das Götterdämmerung - Germanium Fuzz/Ring Modulator

2017-2023. Provides full function controls combined with germanium fuzz generated from matched NOS 2N404.

2017-2023		$325	$400

Echo-Nugget Vacuum Tube Analog Delay

2008-present. Tube-driven analog delay with selectable boost/tone preamp.

2008-2024		$500	$600

Time Warp Vacuum Tube Analog Delay

2008-present. Tube-driven analog delay with selectable modulation/warp function.

2008-2024		$500	$600

Vacuum Tube Direct Box Recording Interface (DUB-5)

2016-present. Interface for recording studios or live sound to sweeten the tone of instruments.

2016-2024		$400	$500

Cruzer

Effects made by Korea's Crafter Guitars. They also build guitars, basses and amps under that brand.

MODEL YEAR	FEATURES	LOW	HIGH

Crybaby

See listing under Vox for early models, and Dunlop for recent versions.

CSL

1970s. Charles Summerfield Ltd., was an English music company with a line of effects made by Sola Sound.

Power Boost

1970s		$1,000	$1,500

Super Fuzz

1970s		$1,000	$1,500

Cusack Music

2003-present. Effects built in Holland, Michigan by Jon Cusack.

Dallas/Dallas Arbiter

Dallas Arbiter, Ltd. was based in London, and it appeared in the late-1960s as a division of a Dallas group of companies headed by Ivor Arbiter. Early products identified with Dallas logo with the company noted as John E. Dallas & Sons Ltd., Dallas Building, Clifton Street, London, E.C.2. They also manufactured Sound City amplifiers and made Vox amps from '72 to '78. The Fuzz Face is still available from Jim Dunlop.

Fuzz Face

1966-1975, 1977-1981, 1986-1987. Late '70s and '80s version was built for Dallas Arbiter by Crest Audio of New Jersey. The current reissue is built by Jim Dunlop USA (see that listing).

1966-1967	Grey, Black or Red, NKT275	$4,500	$6,000
1968-1969	Red, BC108	$2,500	$3,500
1970-1980	Blue	$1,000	$1,500
1981	Grey, reissue	$650	$1,000

Fuzz Wah Face

1970s	Black	$300	$400
1990s	Reissue copy	$85	$150

Rangemaster Fuzzbug

1966. Tone Bender Mk1.5 effect built by Sola Sound.

1966		$2,500	$3,000

Rangemaster Treble Booster

1966. 2000s. Grey housing. 1 Control knob. On-off slider switch. Old-style round-barrel 9-volt battery powered; many converted to later rectangular battery. Various current reissues built by JMI and other firms.

1966		$3,000	$4,000
2000s	JMI reissue	$350	$500

Sustain

1970s		$650	$900

Treble and Bass Face

1960s		$850	$1,250

Trem Face

Ca.1970-ca.1975. Reissued in '80s, round red case, depth and speed control knobs, Dallas-Arbiter England logo plate.

1970-1975		$850	$1,250

MODEL YEAR	FEATURES	LOW	HIGH

Wah Baby

1970s. Gray speckle case, Wah Baby logo caps and small letters on end of pedal.

1970s		$850	$1,250

Damage Control

2004-2009. Guitar effects pedals and digital multi-effects built in Moorpark, California. The company was founded with the release of a line of tube-driven effects pedals. In '09, it began developing products under the Strymon brand name.

Demonizer

2004-2009. Class A distortion preamp pedal powered by dual vacuum tubes.

2004-2009		$200	$275

Liquid Blues

2004-2009. Class A overdrive pedal powered by dual vacuum tubes.

2004-2009		$200	$275

Solid Metal

2004-2009. Class A distortion pedal powered by dual vacuum tubes.

2004-2009		$200	$275

TimeLine

2004-2009. Delay pedal powered by dual vacuum tubes.

2004-2009		$450	$600

Womanizer

2004-2009. Class A overdrive preamp pedal powered by dual vacuum tubes.

2004-2009		$250	$350

Dan Armstrong

1976-1981. In '76, Musitronics, based in Rosemont, New Jersey, introduced 6 inexpensive plug-in effects designed by Dan Armstrong. Perhaps under the influence of John D. MacDonald's Travis McGee novels, each effect name incorporated a color, like Purple Peaker. Shipping box labeled Dan Armstrong by Musitronics. They disappeared a few years later but were reissued by WD Products from '91 to '02 (See WD for those models). From '03 to '06, Vintage Tone Project offered the Dan Armstrong Orange Crusher. Since '06, a licensed line of Dan Armstrong effects that plug directly into the output of a guitar or bass (since '07 some also as stomp boxes) has been offered by Grafton Electronics of Grafton, Vermont. Dan Armstrong died in '04.

Blue Clipper

1976-1981. Fuzz, blue-green case.

1976-1981		$200	$300

Green Ringer

1976-1981. Ring Modulator/Fuzz, green case.

1976-1981		$300	$400

Orange Squeezer

1976-1981. Compressor, orange case.

1976-1981		$400	$500

Purple Peaker

1976-1981. Frequency Booster, light purple case.

1976-1981		$200	$300

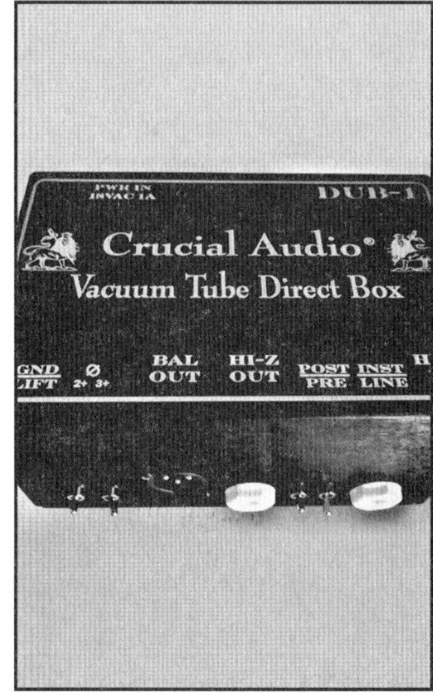

Crucial Audio Vacuum Tube Direct Box Recording Interface

Cusack Effects Tap-A-Delay
Rivington Guitars

1969 Dallas Arbiter Fuzz Face
Dean Nissen

Danelectro Daddy-O
Jim Schreck

Daredevil Silver Solo

DDyna Music Thinman OD

MODEL YEAR	FEATURES	LOW	HIGH

Red Ranger

1976-1981. Bass/Treble Booster, light red case.

1976-1981		$150	$250

Yellow Humper

1976-1981. Yellow case.

1976-1981		$150	$250

Danelectro

1946-1969, 1996-present. The Danelectro brand was revived in '96 with a line of effects pedals. They have also offered the Wasabi line of effects. Prices do not include AC adapter, add $10 for the Zero-Hum adapter.

Chicken Salad Vibrato

2000-2009. Orange case.

2000-2009		$85	$110

Cool Cat

1996-2018		$35	$60

Cool Cat Chorus

1996-2018. Blue case.

1996-2018		$75	$110

Corned Beef Reverb

2000-2009. Blue-black case.

2000-2009		$50	$65

Daddy-O Overdrive

1996-2009. White case.

1996-2009		$50	$65

Dan Echo

1998-2009. Lavender case.

1998-2009		$50	$75

Echo Box

1953-ca. 1958. Reverb unit, metal housing with black endplates.

1953-1958		$225	$450

Fab Tone Distortion

1996-2014. Red case.

1996-2014		$85	$110

Reel Echo

2000s. Light green case.

2000s		$125	$250

Reverb Unit Model 9100

1962-ca. 1967. Tube-driven spring reverb, long grey housing.

1962-1967		$600	$750

Daredevil

2012-present. Guitar effects pedals built in Chicago, Illinois by Johnny Wator.

Davoli

1960s-1970. Davoli was an Italian pickup and guitar builder and is often associated with Wandre guitars.

TRD

1970s. Solidstate tremolo, reverb, distortion unit.

1970s		$200	$275

DDyna Music

2008-present. Dan Simon builds his guitar effects pedals in Bothell, Washington.

MODEL YEAR	FEATURES	LOW	HIGH

Dean Markley

The string and pickup manufacturer offered a line of effects from 1976 to the early-'90s.

Overlord Classic Overdrive Model III

1990-1991. Battery-powered version of Overlord pedal. Black case with red letters.

1990-1991		$125	$200

Overlord Classic Tube Overdrive

1988-1991. Uses a 12AX7A tube, AC powered.

1988-1991		$125	$200

Voice Box 50 (Watt Model)

1976-1979		$125	$150

Voice Box 100 (Watt Model)

1976-1979, 1982-ca.1985.

1976-1979		$125	$150

Voice Box 200 (Watt Model)

1976-1979		$125	$150

DeArmond

In 1946, DeArmond may have introduced the first actual signal-processing effect pedal, the Tremolo Control. They made a variety of effects into the '70s, but only one caught on - their classic volume pedal. DeArmond is primarily noted for pickups.

Pedal Phaser Model 1900

1974-ca.1979.

1974-1979		$200	$275

Square Wave Distortion Generator

1977-ca.1979.

1977-1979		$300	$400

Thunderbolt B166

1977-ca.1979. Five octave wah.

1977-1979		$250	$300

Tone/Volume Pedal 610

1978-ca.1979.

1978-1979		$200	$250

Tornado Phase Shifter

1977-ca.1979.

1977-1979		$150	$200

Tremolo Control Model 60A/60B

The Model 60 Tremolo Control dates from ca. 1946 to the early-1950s. Model 60A dates from mid- to late-'50s. Model 60B (plastic housing), early-'60s. Also labeled as the Trem-Trol or 601.

1950s	60A	$950	$1,250
1960s	60B	$325	$425
1960s	800 Trem-Trol	$325	$425

Twister 1930

1980. Phase shifter.

1980		$200	$300

Volume Pedal Model 602

1960s		$75	$150

Volume Pedal Model 1602

1978-ca. 1980s.

1970s		$75	$150

Volume Pedal Model 1630

1978-1980s. Optoelectric.

1970s		$75	$150

Weeper Wah Model 1802

1970s. Weeper logo on foot pedal.

1970s		$125	$175

MODEL YEAR	FEATURES	LOW	HIGH

Death By Audio

2001-present. Oliver Ackermann builds production and custom guitar effects in Brooklyn, New York.

Absolute Destruction

2000s-2024		$125	$200

Apocalyse

2000s-2024		$165	$325

Armageddon

2006		$175	$300

Crash Modulator

2005		$175	$300

Deep Animation

2000s-2023		$175	$225

Echo Dream 2

2000s-2024		$175	$250

Echo Master

2000s-2024		$175	$250

Evil Filter

2000s-2024		$125	$225

Fuzz Fuzz Fuzz

2006		$175	$300

Fuzz War

2000s-2024		$125	$300

Interstellar Overdriver

2000s-2023		$110	$150

Interstellar Overdriver 2

2000s-2021		$175	$225

Interstellar Overdriver Deluxe

2000s-2023		$180	$250

Micro Dream

2000s-2024		$125	$165

Micro Harmonic Transformer

2000s-2023		$125	$165

Reverberation Machine

2000s-2024		$180	$300

Robot

2000s-2024		$150	$250

Rooms

"Stereo Reverberator" pedal.

2000s-2024		$180	$350

Soundwave Breakdown

2000s-2024		$100	$150

Space Galaxy

Prototype pedal.

2009		$375	$800

Sunshine Reverberation

Designed in collaboration with Ty Seagall, limited edition of 100 pedals.

2013		$375	$800

Supersonic Fuzz Gun

2000s-2024		$125	$225

Time Shadows

Collaboration with EarthQuaker Devices, limited edition of 1,000 pedals.

2020		$250	$350

Total Sonic Annihilation

2000s-2021		$125	$165

Total Sonic Annihilation 2

2000s-2024		$125	$200

Waveformer Destroyer

2000s-2023		$175	$350

DeltaLab Research

Late 1970s-early 1980s. DeltaLab, which was in Chelmsford, Massachusetts, was an early builder of rackmount gear.

DL-2 Acousticomputer

1980s. Delay.

1980s		$750	$1,250

DL-4 Time Line

1980s. Delay.

1980s		$750	$1,250

DL-5

1980s. Various digital processing effects, blue case, rackmount.

1980s		$750	$1,250

DLB-1 Delay Control Pedal

1980s. Controls other DeltaLab pedals, chrome, Morley-looking pedal.

1980s		$50	$95

Electron I ADM/II ADM

1980s. Blue case, rackmount effects. Models include the Electron I ADM, and the Electron II ADM.

1980s	Electron I ADM	$300	$600
1980s	Electron II ADM	$300	$600

Demeter

1980-present. Amp builder James Demeter and company, located in Van Nuys, California, also build guitar effects.

Denio

Line of Japanese-made Boss lookalikes sold in Asia and Australia.

Devi Ever : Fx

2009-present. Devi Ever builds his guitar effects in Portland, Oregon. Prior to '09 he built the Effector 13 effects.

Diamond Pedals

2004-present. Designed by Michael Knappe and Tim Fifield, these effects are built in Bedford, Nova Scotia.

Diaz

Early-1980s-2002, 2004-2022. Line of effects from the amp doctor Cesar Diaz. Diaz died in '02; in '04, his family granted Diaz's friend Peter McMahon the license to resume production. Helping to differentiate the builder, Diaz and McMahon pedals are often signed inside.

Texas Ranger

1980s-2002, 2004-2022. Treble booster. 2 control knobs. Variety of colorful housings.

1980s-2002	Signed by Diaz	$1,000	$1,250
2004-2022		$800	$1,000

Texas Square Face

1980s-2002, 2004-2022. Fuzz pedal. 2 control knobs. Variety of colorful housings.

1980s-2002	Signed by Diaz	$1,500	$2,000
2004-2022		$1,000	$1,500

Death By Audio Interstellar Overdriver

Diamond Pedals Boost-EQ BEQ1

Diaz Texas Ranger

EFFECTS

Diaz Texas Tremodillo
Will Snodgrass

DLS Reckless Driver

1981 DOD AB Box 270
Rivington Guitars

MODEL YEAR	FEATURES	LOW	HIGH

Tremodillo

1980s-2002, 2004-2022. Tremolo pedal. 2 control knobs. Variety of colorful housings.

1980s-2002		$800	$1,000
2004-2022		$600	$800

DigiTech

The DigiTech/DOD company is in Utah and the effects are made in the U.S.A. The DigiTech name started as a line under the DOD brand in the early 1980s; later spinning off into its own brand. They also produce vocal products and studio processors and are now part of Harman International Industries.

Digital Delay and Sampler PDS 2000

1985-1991. 2 second delay.

1985-1991		$100	$200

Digital Delay PDS 1000

1985-ca.1989. One second delay.

1985-1989		$100	$150

Digital Delay PDS 2700 Double Play

1989-1991. Delay and chorus

1989-1991		$100	$250

Digital Stereo Chorus/Flanger PDS 1700

1986-1991		$100	$150

Echo Plus 8 Second Delay PDS 8000

1985-1991		$200	$400

Guitar Effects Processor RP 1

1992-1996. Floor unit, 150 presets.

1992-1996		$100	$150

Guitar Effects Processor RP 3

1998-2003. Floor unit.

1998-2003		$100	$150

Guitar Effects Processor RP 5

1994-1996. Floor unit, 80 presets.

1994-1996		$100	$150

Guitar Effects Processor RP 6

1996-1997. Floor unit.

1996-1997		$100	$150

Guitar Effects Processor RP 7

1996-1997. Floor unit.

1996-1997		$100	$150

Guitar Effects Processor RP 10

1994-1996. Floor unit, 200 presets.

1994-1996		$150	$200

Guitar Effects Processor RP 14D

1999. Floor unit with expression pedal, 1x12AX7 tube, 100 presets.

1999		$150	$200

Guitar Effects Processor RP 100

2000-2006		$100	$150

Guitar Effects Processor RP 200

2001-2006. 140 presets, drum machine, Expression pedal.

2001-2006		$100	$150

Hot Box PDS 2730

1989-1991. Delay and distortion

1989-1991		$100	$150

Modulator Pedal XP 200

1996-2002. Floor unit, 61 presets.

1996-2002		$100	$150

MODEL YEAR	FEATURES	LOW	HIGH

Multi Play PDS 20/20

1987-1991. Multi-function digital delay.

1987-1991		$125	$250

Pedalverb Digital Reverb Pedal PDS 3000

1987-1991		$125	$250

Programmable Distortion PDS 1550

1986-1991	Yellow case	$75	$175

Programmable Distortion PDS 1650

1989-1991	Red case	$75	$175

Rock Box PDS 2715

1989-1991. Chorus and distortion.

1989-1991		$75	$175

Two Second Digital Delay PDS 1002

1987-1991		$100	$200

Whammy Pedal Reissue

2000-present. Reissue version of classic WP-1 with added dive bomb and MIDI features.

2000-2020		$125	$140

Whammy Pedal WP I

1990-1993. Original Whammy Pedal, red case, reissued as WP IV in '00.

1990-1993		$300	$650

Whammy Pedal WP II

1994-1997. Can switch between 2 presets, black case.

1994-1997		$225	$450

DiMarzio

The pickup maker offered a couple of effects in the late-1980s to the mid-'90s.

Metal Pedal

1987-1989		$250	$425

Very Metal Fuzz

Ca.1989-1995. Distortion/overdrive pedal.

1989-1995		$200	$350

Dino's

A social co-op founded by Alessio Casati and Andy Bagnasco, in Albisola, Italy. It builds a line of boutique analog pedals as well as guitars.

Dinosaur

2004-2015. Guitar effects pedals imported by Eleca International. They also offered amps.

Divided By Thirteen

Mid-1990s-present. Fred Taccone builds his stomp box guitar effects in the Los Angeles, California area. He also builds amps.

DLS Effects

1999-present. Guitar effects pedals built by Dave Sestito in Fairport, New York.

DNA Analogic

Line of Japanese-built guitar effects distributed first by Godlyke, then Pedals Plus+ Effects Warehouse.

DOD

DOD Electronics started in Salt Lake City, Utah in 1974. Today, they're a major effects manufacturer

MODEL YEAR	FEATURES	LOW	HIGH

with dozens of pedals made in the U.S. They also market effects under the name DigiTech and are now part of Harman International Industries.

6 Band Equalizer EQ601
1977-1982 $65 $80

AB Box 270
1978-1982 $40 $45

American Metal FX56
1985-1991 $75 $125

Analog Delay 680
1979-ca. 1982.
1979-1982 $150 $350

Attacker FX54
1992-1994. Distortion and compressor.
1992-1994 $65 $100

Bass Compressor FX82
1987-ca.1989.
1987-1989 $65 $100

Bass EQ FX42B
1987-1996 $65 $100

Bass Grunge FX92
1995-1996 $120 $300

Bass Overdrive FX91
1998-2012. Yellow case.
1998-2012 $75 $125

Bass Stereo Chorus Flanger FX72
1987-1997 $65 $100

Bass Stereo Chorus FX62
1987-1996 $65 $100

Bi-FET Preamp FX10
1982-1996 $100 $150

Buzz Box FX33
1994-1996. Grunge distortion.
1994-1996 $200 $400

Chorus 690
1980-ca.1982. Dual speed chorus.
1980-1982 $200 $400

Classic Fuzz FX52
1990-1997 $65 $100

Classic Tube FX53
1990-1997 $65 $100

Compressor 280
1978-ca.1982.
1978-1982 $65 $100

Compressor FX80
1982-1985 $85 $125

Compressor Sustainer FX80B
1986-1996 $65 $85

Death Metal FX86
1994-2009. Distortion.
1994-2009 $75 $125

Delay FX90
1984-ca.1987.
1984-1987 $85 $150

Digital Delay DFX9
1989-ca.1990.
1989-1990 $75 $100

Digital Delay Sampler DFX94
1995-1997 $85 $150

Distortion FX55
1982-1986. Red case.
1982-1986 $65 $125

MODEL YEAR	FEATURES	LOW	HIGH

Edge Pedal FX87
1988-1989 $100 $150

Envelope Filter 440
1981-1982 $200 $300

Envelope Filter FX25
1982-1997. Replaced by FX25B.
1982-1997 $100 $150

Envelope Filter FX25B
1981-2013. Light aqua case.
1998-2013 $95 $125

Equalizer FX40
1982-1986 $65 $100

Equalizer FX40B
1987-2010. Eight bands for bass.
1987-2010 $65 $100

Fet Preamp 210
1981-ca.1982.
1981-1982 $100 $225

Flanger 670
1981-1982 $125 $250

Gate Loop FX30
1980s $65 $85

Gonkulator
1980s $100 $175

Graphic Equalizer EQ-610
1980-ca.1982. Ten bands.
1980-1982 $65 $85

Graphic Equalizer EQ-660
1980-ca.1982. Six bands.
1980-1982 $65 $75

Grunge FX69
1993-2009. Distortion.
1993-2009 $100 $175

Hard Rock Distortion FX57
1987-1994. With built-in delay.
1987-1994 $100 $165

Harmonic Enhancer FX85
1986-ca.1989.
1986-1989 $65 $85

I. T. FX100
1997. Intergrated Tube distortion, produces harmonics.
1997 $85 $165

IceBox FX64
1996-2008. Chorus, high EQ.
1996-2008 $65 $100

Juice Box FX51
1996-1997 $125 $250

Master Switch 225
1988-ca.1989. A/B switch and loop selector.
1988-1989 $40 $50

Meat Box FX32
1994-1996 $150 $300

Metal Maniac FX58
1990-1996 $100 $150

Metal Triple Play Guitar Effects System TR3M
1994 $90 $125

Metal X FX70
1993-1996 $100 $200

DOD Compressor Sustainer FX80B

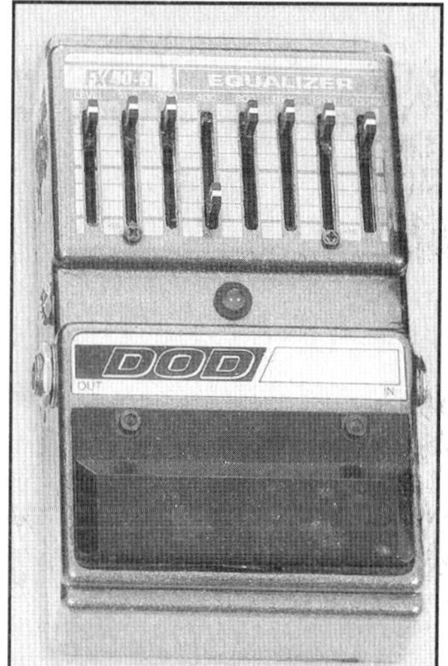

DOD Equalizer FX40B

DOD Gonkulator FX 13
Vinny Roth

EFFECTS

1979 DOD Mini-Chorus 460
Rivington Guitars

1981 DOD Phasor 201
Rivington Guitars

Dunlop Cry Baby EVH Wah

MODEL YEAR	FEATURES	LOW	HIGH
Milk Box FX84			
1994-2012. Compressor/expander, white case.			
1994-2012		$100	$175
Mini-Chorus 460			
1981-ca.1982.			
1981-1982		$90	$175
Mixer 240			
1978-ca.1982.			
1978-1982		$25	$35
Momentary Footswitch			
Introduced in 1987. Temporally engages other boxes.			
1980s		$25	$35
Mystic Blues Overdrive FX102			
1998-2012. Medium gain overdrive, purple case.			
1998-2012		$100	$150
Noise Gate 230			
1978-1982		$100	$150
Noise Gate FX30			
1982-ca.1987.			
1982-1987		$65	$75
Octoplus FX35			
1987-1996. Octaves.			
1987-1996		$65	$85
Overdrive Plus FX50B			
1986-1997		$65	$100
Overdrive Preamp 250			
1978-1982, 1995-2020. Reissued in '95, yellow case.			
1978-1981	Gray box	$400	$600
1981-1984	Yellow box	$200	$250
1995-2020		$100	$150
Overdrive Preamp FX50			
1982-1985		$75	$150
Performer Compressor Limiter 525			
1981-1984		$75	$150
Performer Delay 585			
1982-1985		$75	$175
Performer Distortion 555			
1981-1984		$75	$165
Performer Flanger 575			
1981-1985		$75	$165
Performer Phasor 595			
1981-1984		$75	$165
Performer Stereo Chorus 565			
1981-1985. FET switching.			
1981-1985		$75	$150
Performer Wah Filter 545			
1981-1984		$75	$150
Phasor 201			
1981-ca.1982. Reissued in '95.			
1981-1982		$175	$300
Phasor 401			
1978-1981		$100	$250
Phasor 490			
1980-ca.1982.			
1980-1982		$100	$200
Phasor FX20			
1982-1985		$100	$150
Psychoacoustic Processor FX87			
1988-1989		$100	$135
Punkifier FX76			
1997		$200	$300
Resistance Mixer 240			
1978-ca.1982.			
1978-1982		$30	$40
Silencer FX27			
1988-ca.1989. Noise reducer.			
1988-1989		$35	$45
Stereo Chorus FX60			
1982-1986		$100	$150
Stereo Chorus FX65			
1986-1996. Light blue case.			
1986-1996		$100	$150
Stereo Flanger FX70			
1982-ca.1985.			
1982-1985		$65	$125
Stereo Flanger FX75			
1986-1987. Silver case with blue trim.			
1986-1987		$65	$125
Stereo Flanger FX75B			
1987-1997		$100	$150
Stereo Phasor FX20B			
1986-1999		$85	$100
Stereo Turbo Chorus FX67			
1988-1991		$100	$125
Super American Metal FX56B			
1992-1996		$100	$200
Super Stereo Chorus FX68			
1992-1996		$65	$100
Supra Distortion FX55			
1986-2012. Red case.			
1986-2012		$40	$65
Thrash Master FX59			
1990-1996		$100	$175
Vibrothang FX22			
1990s		$100	$135
Votec Vocal Effects Processor and Mic Preamp			
1998-2001		$75	$100
Wah-Volume FX-17 (pedal)			
1987-2000		$75	$100

Dredge-Tone

Located in Berkeley, California, Dredge-Tone offers effects and electronic kits.

DST Engineering

2001-2014. Jeff Swanson and Bob Dettorre built reverb units in Beverly, Massachusetts. They also built amps.

Dunlop

Jim Dunlop, USA offers the Crybaby, MXR (see MXR), Rockman, High Gain, Heil Sound (see Heil), Tremolo, Jimi Hendrix, Rotovibe, Uni-Vibe and Way Huge brand effects.

MODEL YEAR	FEATURES	LOW	HIGH
Cry Baby Bass			
1985-present. Bass wah.			
1985-2024		$80	$110
Cry Baby EVH Wah			
1990's-present.			
1990s-2024		$100	$150

MODEL YEAR	FEATURES	LOW	HIGH

Cry Baby Multi-Wah 535/535Q

1995-present. Multi-range pedal with an external boost control.

1995-2024		$75	$110

Cry Baby Wah-Wah GCB-95

1982-present. Dunlop began manufacturing the Cry Baby in '82.

1982-1989		$55	$85
1990-1999		$50	$80
2000-2024		$45	$75

Fuzz Face Distortion JDF2

1993-present. Reissue of the classic Dallas Arbiter effect (see that listing for earlier versions).

1993-2024	Red, reissue	$100	$150

High Gain Volume + Boost Pedal

1983-1996		$45	$75

High Gain Volume Pedal GCB-80

1983-2010		$45	$75

Jimi Hendrix Fuzz JH-2 (Round)

1987-1993. Round face fuzz, JH-2S is the square box version.

1987-1993		$100	$200

Rotovibe JH-4S Standard

1989-1998. Standard is finished in bright red enamel with chrome top.

1989-1998		$150	$275

Tremolo Volume Plus TVP-1

1995-1998. Pedal.

1995-1998		$115	$300

Uni-Vibe UV-1

1995-2012. Rotating speaker effect.

1995-1999		$350	$500
2000-2012		$250	$325

Durham Electronics

2001-present. Alan Durham builds his line of guitar effects in Austin, Texas.

Dutch Kazoo

2013-present. Guitar effects pedals built in Parker Ford, Pennsylvania by Corinne Mandell.

Dynacord

1950-present. Dynacord is a German company that makes audio and pro sound amps, as well as other electronic equipment and is now owned by TELEX/EVI Audio (an U.S. company), which also owns the Electro-Voice brand. In the '60s they offered tape echo machines and guitars. In '94 a line of multi-effects processors was introduced under the Electro-Voice/Dynacord name, but by the following year they were just listed as Electro-Voice.

EchoCord

Introduced in 1959. Tape echo unit.

1959-1960s		$400	$800

Dyno

See Dytronics.

MODEL YEAR	FEATURES	LOW	HIGH

Dytronics

Mid-1970s-early 1980s. The Japanese Dytronics company made a chorus rackmount unit for electric piano called the Dyno My Piano with flying piano keys or a lightning bolt on the front. Another version was called the Tri-Stereo Chorus and a third, called the Songbird, had a bird's head on the front.

E Bow

See Heet Sound Products.

E.W.S. (Engineering Work Store)

2007-present. Guitar effects pedals built in Tokyo, Japan for Prosound Communications in Van Nuys, California.

EarthQuaker Devices

2005-present. Jamie Stillman started building Fuzz Face and Rangemaster clones for friends and in '07, he built a modified Big Muff for Dan Auerbach of the Black Keys, who he tour-managed at the time. After extensive revisions, this became the Hoof Fuzz and he began retailing his pedals.

Acapulco Gold

2015-present. Power amp distortion. Grandma Cyclops limited-edition version was made '16 in collaboration with visual artist and Devo co-founder Mark Mothersbaugh and the Akron Art Museum.

2015-2024		$85	$115
2016	Grandma Cyclops	$90	$120

Afterneath

2014-present. Ambient reverb.

2014-2024		$110	$150

Amp Hammer II

2009		$65	$110

Arpanoid

2013-2023. Polyphonic arpeggiator.

2013-2023		$165	$220

Arrows

2014-present. Preamp boost.

2014-2024		$55	$90

Avalanche Run

2016-present. Stereo reverb and delay.

2016-2024		$200	$250

Bellows

2016-2019. Fuzz driver.

2016-2019		$85	$120

Bit Commander

2011-present. Guitar synthesizer.

2011-2024		$100	$145

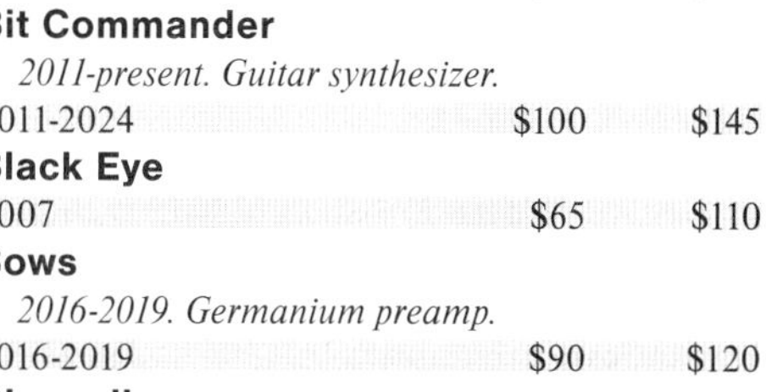

Black Eye

2007		$65	$110

Bows

2016-2019. Germanium preamp.

2016-2019		$90	$120

Chrysalis

2010		$65	$110

Cloven Hoof

2014-2020. Fuzz grinder.

2014-2020		$90	$120

E.W.S. Stormy Bass Drive

EarthQuaker Devices Bellows

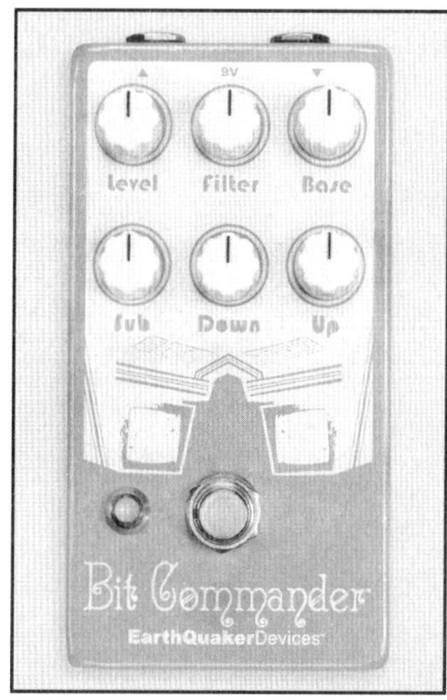

EarthQuaker Devices Bit Commander

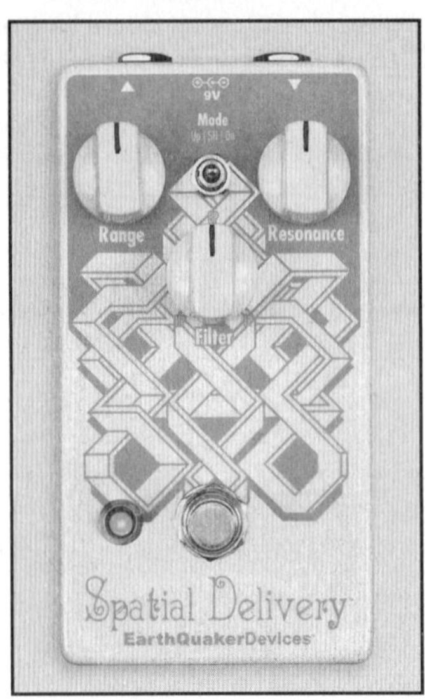

Earthquaker Devices Spatial Delivery

EarthQuaker Devices The Warden

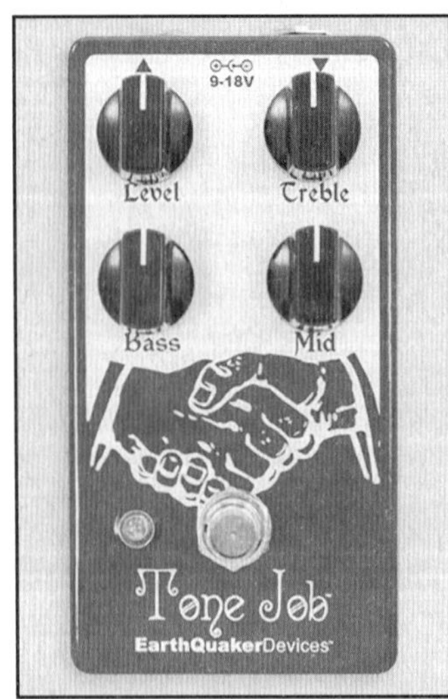

EarthQuaker Devices Tone Job

MODEL YEAR	FEATURES	LOW	HIGH
Cloven Hoof Reaper			
2015-2017. Fuzz.			
2015-2017		$110	$150
Crimson Drive			
2007		$65	$110
Dirt Transmitter			
2008-2019. Fuzz driver.			
2008-2019		$100	$130
Disaster Transport			
2007. Delay pedal.			
2007		$65	$150
Disaster Transport Jr.			
2010		$65	$100
Disaster Transport Sr.			
2013-2021. Advanced modulation delay and reverb.			
2013-2021		$200	$250
Dispatch Master			
2011-present. Hi-fi digital delay and reverb.			
2011-2024		$110	$150
Dream Crusher			
2009		$65	$110
Dunes			
2015-2020. Mini mega overdrive.			
2015-2020		$100	$170
Erupter			
2017-2022. Fuzz.			
2017-2022		$100	$120
Fuzz Master General			
2015-2019. Octave fuzz pedal.			
2015-2019		$100	$140
Ghost Disaster			
2010		$65	$110
Ghost Echo			
2009-present. Vintage-voiced reverb.			
2009-2024		$110	$150
Grand Orbiter			
2009-present. Phaser/vibrato.			
2009-2024		$110	$150
Gray Channel			
2016-2020. Dynamic dirt doubler.			
2016-2020		$110	$150
Hoof			
2007-present. Germanium/silicon hybrid fuzz.			
2007-2024		$110	$140
Hoof Reaper			
2012-2024. Dual fuzz octave.			
2012-2024		$175	$250
Hummingbird			
2007-present. Repeat percussion/tremolo.			
2007-2024		$110	$150
Interstellar Orbiter			
2015-2020. Dual resonant filter built in collaboration with turntablist Kid Koala for his "Turntable Orchestra" tour. Features original artwork by Koala.			
2015-2020		$135	$200
Levitation			
2008-2021. Psychedlic reverb.			
2008-2021		$100	$130
Monarch			
2010		$65	$110
Night Wire			
2016-2024. Harmonic tremolo.			
2016-2024		$125	$170
Organizer			
2012-present. Polyphonic organ emulator.			
2012-2024		$110	$150
Palisades			
2014-2022. Mega ultimate overdrive.			
2014-2022		$135	$185
Park Fuzz Sound			
2015-present. Reissue of the Park Amplification fuzz pedal built in cooperation with Park.			
2015-2024		$110	$150
Pitch Bay			
2014-2017. Dirty polyphonic harmonizer.			
2014-2017		$110	$180
Pulse Machine Tremolo			
2007		$65	$110
Rainbow Machine			
2011-present. Polyphonic pitch-shifting modulator.			
2011-2024		$135	$200
Royal Drive			
2007		$65	$110
Sea Machine			
2010-present. Chorus.			
2010-2024		$90	$150
Sound Shank			
2009		$65	$110
Space Spiral			
2017-2021. Modulation delay.			
2017-2021		$110	$150
Spatial Delivery			
2016-present. Envelope filter with sample and hold functions.			
2016-2024		$110	$150
Spires			
2016-2019. Nü-Face double fuzz.			
2016-2019		$110	$150
Stealth Fuzz			
2007		$65	$110
Talons			
2012-2017. Hi-gain overdrive.			
2012-2017		$110	$150
Tentacle			
2015-present. Analog octave up. Grandpa Cyclops limited-edition version was made '16 in collaboration with visual artist and Devo co-founder Mark Mothersbaugh and the Akron Art Museum.			
2015-2024		$110	$150
2016	Grandpa Cyclops	$110	$150
Terminal			
2014-2019. Fuzz.			
2014-2019		$110	$150
The Depths			
2013-2017. Optical vibrato.			
2013-2017		$100	$140
The Grim Reefer			
2014-2017. Fuzz pedal.			
2014-2017		$110	$150

MODEL YEAR	FEATURES	LOW	HIGH

The Warden

2013-present. Optical compression.

2013-2024		$110	$150

Time Shadows

2020-present. Collaboration with EarthQuaker Devices, limited edition of 1,000 pedals.

2020-2024		$225	$350

Tone Job

2012-present. EQ and boost.

2012-2024		$110	$150

Tone Reaper

2009		$110	$150

Transmisser

2016-2019. Reverb.

2016-2019		$140	$200

White Light

2008		$150	$250

Zap Machine

2010		$65	$110

Z-Drive

2015-2017. Overdrive built in collaboration with Dr. Z Amplification.

2015-2017		$190	$230

EBS

1992-present. Bass and guitar effects built in Stockholm, Sweden by the EBS Sweden AB company. They also build bass amps.

Ecco-Fonic

1959-1968. The Ecco-Fonic was designed by Ray Stolle and sold from his radio and TV repair shop in Los Angeles. Theis first Ecco Ecco-Fonic was distributed by Fender in 1958-'59. Stolle sold the company to E.S. "Eddie" Tubin in late 1959-'60, who sold the company in 1961 to Milton Brucker. Starting in 1963, Fender offered a solidstate Ecco-Fonic designed by new-owner Bob Marks and Russ Allee and labeled as the Fender Echo.

Model 109

1959-1960. Tube-driven tape-echo unit, 2 control knobs, revised to 3 knobs, 1-piece top, gold housing.

1959	Brown case	$1,500	$2,000

Model 109-B

1960-1962. Tube-driven tape echo unit, 4 Control knobs, 2-piece top, gold housing.

1960-1962	Brown or black case	$1,000	$1,500

Model 109-C

1961-1962. Tube-driven tape echo unit, multiple playback heads, black housing.

1961-1962	Black case	$1,500	$2,500

Echoplex

The Echoplex tape echo unit was invented around 1959 in Akron, Ohio, by Don Dixon and Mike Battle, who originally produced it in small numbers. Production was soon moved to Market Electronics in Cleveland, and those units were sold under the Maestro brand (see listings under Maestro). After Maestro dropped the Echoplex, it was marketed under the Market Electronics name from the late-'70s to the late-'80s (see listing under Market Electronics for '80s models). In '94, Gibson's Oberheim division introduced a rackmount unit called the Echoplex. In '01, it was relabeled as Gibson.

Echoplex

1959. Dixon- and Battle-built pre-Maestro production tube-driven tape echo. Black case.

1959		$1,750	$2,500

EchoSonic

2010s. Ray Butts of EchoSonic amp fame crafted a pioneering fuzz circuit that never went into production. Tim Masters of Florida built a limited run of stompboxes with the circuitry.

Ray-O-Fuzz

2010s. Metal housings in various colors with the logo surrounded by lightning bolts. Attack and Volume controls plus footswitch.

2010s		$275	$500

Eden Analog

Guitar effects pedals built by Chris Sheppard and Robert Hafley in Pelham, Alabama, starting in 2004.

Effector 13

2002-2008. Guitar effects built by Devi Ever in Minneapolis, Minnesota. Located in Austin, Texas until mid-'04. Name changed to Devi Ever : Fx in '09.

Effectrode

1996-present. Effects pedals built in Corvallis, Oregon by Phil Taylor.

EFX

1980s. Brand name of the Los Angeles-based EFX Center; they also offered a direct box and a powered pedal box/board.

Switch Box B287

1984. Dual effects loop selector.

1984		$35	$45

EKO

1959-1985, 2000-present. In the '60s and '70s EKO offered effects made by EME and JEN Elettronica, which also made Vox effects.

Eleca

2004-present. Guitar effects pedals imported by Eleca International. They also offer guitars, mandolins, and amps.

Electra

1970-1984, 2013-present. Guitar importer St. Louis Music offered Electra effects in the late '70s.

Chorus 504CH

Ca.1975-ca.1980.

1975-1980		$100	$150

Compressor 502C/602C

Ca.1975-ca.1980.

1975-1980		$75	$95

EBS ValveDrive DI

Effectrode Blue Bottle Booster

Eleca EBB-1

EFFECTS

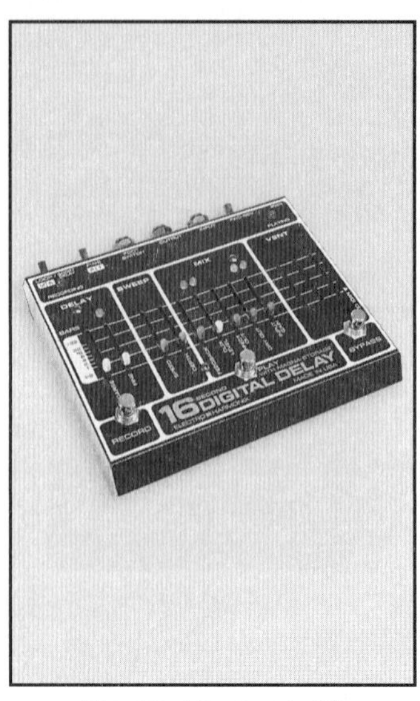

Electro-Harmonix 16 Second Digital Delay

1974 E-H Big Muff PI
Suzie Williams

E-H Deluxe Memory Man

Distortion 500D

Ca.1976-ca.1980.

MODEL YEAR	FEATURES	LOW	HIGH
1976-1980		$150	$225

Flanger (stereo) 605F

Ca.1975-ca.1980.

MODEL YEAR	FEATURES	LOW	HIGH
1975-1980		$90	$150

Fuzz Wah

Ca.1975-ca.1980.

MODEL YEAR	FEATURES	LOW	HIGH
1975-1980		$135	$300

Pedal Drive 515AC

Ca.1976-ca.1980. Overdrive.

MODEL YEAR	FEATURES	LOW	HIGH
1976-1980		$50	$65

Phaser Model 501P

Ca.1976-ca.1980.

MODEL YEAR	FEATURES	LOW	HIGH
1976-1980		$110	$200

Phaser Model 875

Ca.1975-ca.1980.

MODEL YEAR	FEATURES	LOW	HIGH
1975-1980		$110	$200

Roto Phase I

1975-ca.1980. Small pocket phaser.

MODEL YEAR	FEATURES	LOW	HIGH
1975-1980		$80	$100

Roto Phase II

1975-ca.1980. Pedal phasor.

MODEL YEAR	FEATURES	LOW	HIGH
1975-1980		$90	$115

Electro-Harmonix

1968-1984, 1996-present. Founded by Mike Matthews in New York City, the company initially produced small plug-in boosters such as the LPB-1. In '71, they unveiled the awe-inspiring Big Muff Pi fuzz and dozens of innovative pedals followed. After closing in '84, Matthews again began producing reissues of many of his classic effects as well as new designs in '96.

10 Band Graphic Equalizer

1977-1981. Includes footswitch.

MODEL YEAR	FEATURES	LOW	HIGH
1977-1981		$90	$115

16-Second Digital Delay

Early-1980s, 2004-2008. An updated version was reissued in '04.

MODEL YEAR	FEATURES	LOW	HIGH
1980s	No foot controller	$600	$750
1980s	With foot controller	$850	$1,125
1990s		$400	$550
2004-2008		$350	$500

3 Phase Liner

MODEL YEAR	FEATURES	LOW	HIGH
1981		$55	$75

5X Junction Mixer

MODEL YEAR	FEATURES	LOW	HIGH
1977-1981		$30	$75

Attack Equalizer

1975-1981. Active EQ, a.k.a. "Knock Out."

MODEL YEAR	FEATURES	LOW	HIGH
1975-1981		$150	$200

Attack/Decay

1980-1981. Tape reverse simulator.

MODEL YEAR	FEATURES	LOW	HIGH
1980-1981		$1,250	$1,500

Axis

1969-1970s. Modified Mosrite Fuzzrite circuit.

MODEL YEAR	FEATURES	LOW	HIGH
1969-1970s		$775	$1,000

Bad Stone Phase Shifter

1975-1981.

MODEL YEAR	FEATURES	LOW	HIGH
1975-1981	Three knobs	$350	$500
1975-1981	Two knobs, color switch	$300	$400

Bass Micro-Synthesizer

1981-1984, 1999-present. Analog synthesizer sounds.

MODEL YEAR	FEATURES	LOW	HIGH
1981-1984		$250	$350
1999-2024		$200	$300

Bassballs

1978-1984, 1998-present. Bass envelope filter/distortion.

MODEL YEAR	FEATURES	LOW	HIGH
1978-1984		$150	$200

Big Muff Pi

1971-1984. Sustain, floor unit, issued in 3 different looks, as described below.

MODEL YEAR	FEATURES	LOW	HIGH
1970s	V1, Black graphics, knobs in triangle pattern	$1,000	$1,250
1970s	V2, "Rams Head"	$1,250	$1,500
1970s	V2, "Violet Rams Head"	$2,500	$4,000
1976	V3, GE transitor, no LED, red/black graphics	$500	$600
1977	V4, Integrated op amp ckt	$400	$500
1978-1980	V5, Tone bypass	$300	$400
1980s	RV6, GE transitor	$250	$350

Big Muff Pi (Reissue)

1996-present. Originally made in Russia, but currently both Russian- and U.S.-made versions are available.

MODEL YEAR	FEATURES	LOW	HIGH
1996-2024	Russian-made	$150	$300

Big Muff Sovtek

2000s. Big Muff Pi, Electro Harmonix, and Sovtek logos on an olive-green case. Sold in a wooden box.

MODEL YEAR	FEATURES	LOW	HIGH
2000s	With wooden box	$400	$500

Black Finger Compressor Sustainer

1977, 2003-2019. The original has 3 knobs in triangle pattern.

MODEL YEAR	FEATURES	LOW	HIGH
1977		$350	$450
2003-2019		$175	$225

Clap Track

1980-1984. Drum effect.

MODEL YEAR	FEATURES	LOW	HIGH
1980-1984		$350	$500

Clone Theory

1977-1981. Chorus effect, The Clone Theory logo.

MODEL YEAR	FEATURES	LOW	HIGH
1977-1981		$500	$750

Crash Pad

1980-1984. Percussion synth.

MODEL YEAR	FEATURES	LOW	HIGH
1980-1984		$100	$300

Crying Tone Pedal

1976-1978. Wah-wah.

MODEL YEAR	FEATURES	LOW	HIGH
1976-1978		$200	$250

Deluxe Big Muff Pi

1978-1981. Sustain, AC version of Big Muff Pi, includes a complete Soul Preacher unit.

MODEL YEAR	FEATURES	LOW	HIGH
1978-1981	Red graphics	$250	$400

Deluxe Electric Mistress Flanger

1977-1983, 1996-present. AC.

MODEL YEAR	FEATURES	LOW	HIGH
1977-1979		$500	$650
1980-1983		$225	$400

MODEL YEAR	FEATURES	LOW	HIGH

Deluxe Memory Man

1977-1983, 1996-present. Echo and delay, featured 4 knobs '77-'78, from '79-'83 it has 5 knobs and added vibrato and chorus.

1977-1978	4 knobs	$700	$900
1979-1983	5 knobs	$700	$900
1996-2024	3-prong power cord	$1,000	$1,250

Deluxe Octave Multiplexer

1977-1981 $350 $400

Digital Delay/Chorus

1981-1984. With digital chorus.

1981-1984 $350 $400

Digital Rhythm Matrix DRM-15

1981-1984 $350 $500

Digital Rhythm Matrix DRM-16

1979-1983 $150 $400

Digital Rhythm Matrix DRM-32

1981-1984 $600 $1,250

Doctor Q Envelope Follower

1976-1983, 2001-2020. For bass or guitar.

1976-1983 $100 $150
2001-2020 $50 $75

Domino Theory

1981. Sound sensitive light tube.

1981 $65 $100

Echo 600

1981 $200 $250

Echoflanger

1977-1982. Flange, slapback, chorus, filter.

1977-1982 $875 $1,250

Electric Mistress Flanger

1976-1979 $750 $1,500
1980-1984 $350 $450

Electronic Metronome

1978-1980 $100 $125

Frequency Analyzer

1977-1984, 2001-2022. Ring modulator.

1977-1984 $350 $500

Full Double Tracking Effect

1978-1981. Doubling, slapback.

1978-1981 $150 $200

Fuzz Wah

Introduced around 1974.

1970s $250 $300

Golden Throat

1977-1984 $400 $550

Golden Throat Deluxe

1977-1979. Deluxe has a built-in monitor amp.

1977-1979 $500 $650

Golden Throat II

1978-1981 $150 $300

Guitar Synthesizer

1981. Sold for $1,495 in May '81.

1981 $200 $250

Hog's Foot Bass Booster

1977-1980 $100 $150

Holy Grail

2002-present. Digital reverb.

2002-2024 $75 $150

Hot Foot

1977-1978. Rocker pedal turns knob of other E-H effects, gold case, red graphics.

1977-1978 $150 $250

Hot Tubes

1978-1984, 2001-2007. Tube distortion.

1978-1984 $250 $400

Linear Power Booster LPB-1

1968-1983.

1976-1979 $125 $200
1980-1983 $50 $75

Linear Power Booster LPB-2

Ca.1968-1983.

1968-1983 $125 $200

Little Big Muff Pi

1976-1980, 2006-present. Sustain, 1-knob floor unit.

1976-1980 $150 $300
2006-2024 $50 $75

Little Muff Pi

1971-1975. Sustain, 1-knob floor unit, issued in 2 styles: blue or red graphics.

1971-1975 $250 $350

Memory Man/Stereo Memory Man

1976-1984, 1999-present. Analog delay, newer version in stereo.

1976-1979 $500 $800
1980-1984 $250 $350

Micro Synthesizer

1978-1984, 1998-present. Mini keyboard phaser.

1978-1984 $400 $500
1998-2024 $150 $200

Mini Q-Tron/Micro Q-Tron

2002-present. Battery-operated smaller version of Q-Tron envelope follower, changed to identical effect in smaller box Micro in '06.

2002-2024 $65 $100

Mini-Mixer

1978-1981. Mini mic mixer, reissued in '01.

1978-1981 $100 $150

MiniSynthesizer

1981-1983. Mini keyboard with phaser.

1981-1983 $350 $450

MiniSynthesizer With Echo

1981 $450 $600

Mole Bass Booster

1968-1978.

1968-1969 $95 $125
1970-1978 $50 $75

Muff Fuzz

1976-1983. Fuzz and line boost, silver case with orange lettering.

1976-1983 $125 $250

Muff Fuzz Crying Tone

1977-1978. Fuzz, wah.

1977-1978 $175 $300

Octave Multiplexer Floor Unit

1976-1980 $175 $300

Octave Multiplexer Pedal

1976-1977, 2001-2022.

1976-1977 $500 $650
2001-2022 $50 $65

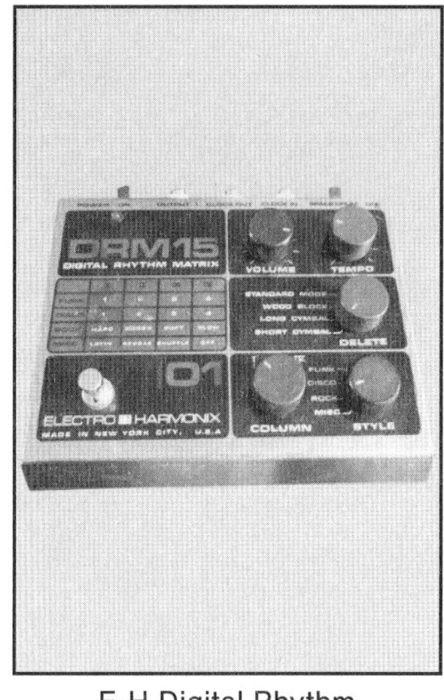

E-H Digital Rhythm Matrix DRM-15
Jim Schreck

1978 E-H Linear Power Booster LPB-2
Rivington Guitars

1976 E-H Memory Man
Jim Schreck

EFFECTS

1981 E-H Poly Chorus
Jim Schreck

E-H Small Clone

E-H Soul Food

MODEL YEAR	FEATURES	LOW	HIGH

Panic Button

1981. Siren sounds for drums.

1981		$100	$200

Poly Chorus/Stereo Polychorus

1981, 1999-2021. Same as Echoflanger.

1981		$550	$800
1999-2021		$150	$200

Polyphase

1979-1981. With envelope.

1979-1981		$300	$550

Pulsar/Stereo Pulsar

2004-present. Variable wave form tremolo.

2004-2024		$50	$65

Pulse Modulator

Ca.1968 -ca.1972. Triple tremolo.

1968-1969		$300	$400
1970-1972		$250	$300

Q-Tron

1997-2017. Envelope controlled filter.

1997-2017		$200	$250

Q-Tron +

1999-present. With added effects loop and Attack Response switch.

1999-2024		$115	$150

Queen Triggered Wah

1976-1978. Wah/Envelope Filter.

1976-1978		$500	$750

Random Tone Generator RTG

1981		$60	$75

Rhythm 12 (Rhythm Machine)

1978		$150	$200

Rolling Thunder

1980-1981. Percussion synth.

1980-1981		$50	$65

Screaming Bird Treble Booster

Ca.1968-1980. In-line unit.

1968-1980		$150	$200

Screaming Tree Treble Booster

1977-1981. Floor unit.

1977-1981		$150	$200

Sequencer Drum

1981. Drum effect.

1981		$450	$800

Slapback Echo

1977-1978. Stereo.

1977-1978		$150	$200

Small Clone

1983-1984, 1999-present. Analog chorus, depth and rate controls, purple face plate, white logo.

1983-1984		$500	$700
1999-2024		$60	$100

Small Stone Phase Shifter

1975-1984, 1996-present. Both Russian and U.S. reissues were made.

1975-1979		$300	$400
1980-1984		$150	$200

Solid State Reverb

1980s. Input, output, blend, and feedback controls.

1980s		$250	$500

Soul Food

2000s		$50	$65
2000s	JHS modded	$125	$175

Soul Preacher

1977-1983, 2007-present. Compressor sustainer. Nano version for present.

1977-1983		$125	$250

Space Drum/Super Space Drum

1980-1981. Percussion synthesizer.

1980-1981		$150	$200

Switch Blade

1977-1983. A-B Box.

1977-1983		$50	$75

Talking Pedal

1977-1978. Creates vowel sounds.

1977-1978		$350	$550

The Silencer

1976-1981. Noise elimination.

1976-1981		$75	$150

Tube Zipper

2001-2018. Tube (2x12AX7) envelope follower.

2001-2018		$125	$150

Vocoder

1978-1981. Modulates voice with instrument.

1978-1981	Rackmount	$450	$550

Volume Pedal

1978-1981		$50	$65

Wiggler

2002-2019. All-tube modulator including pitch vibrato and volume tremolo.

2002-2019		$150	$300

Worm/The Worm

2002-present. Wah/Phaser.

2002-2024		$60	$75

Y-Triggered Filter

1976-1977		$150	$200

Zipper Envelope Follower

1976-1978. The Tube Zipper was introduced in '01.

1976-1978		$200	$300

Electrosonic Amplifiers

2002-2010. Amp builder Josh Corn also offers a preamp pedal, built in Boonville, Indiana.

Elektronika

1980s-1990s. Russian effects pedals by the Soviet Ministry of Electronic Industry.

Compressor-Sustainer

1980s		$200	$250

Equalizer E-02

1980s		$200	$250

Fazer-2

1980s		$200	$250

Flanger FL-01

1980s		$200	$300

Flanger PE-05

1980s		$200	$250

Jet-Phaser

1980s		$200	$250

Synchro-Wah

1980s		$200	$250

EFFECTS

MODEL YEAR	FEATURES	LOW	HIGH

Volna

1980s. Auto wah.

1980s		$200	$250

Elk Gakki

Late-1960s. Japanese company Elk Gakki Co., Ltd. mainly made guitars and amps, but did offer effects as well.

Big Muff Sustainer

1970s. Electro-Harmonix Big Muff Pi copy.

1970s		$800	$950

Elka

In the late '60s or early '70s, Italian organ and synthesizer company Elka-Orla (later just Elka) offered a few effects, likely made by JEN Elettronica (Vox, others).

EMMA Electronic

Line of guitar effects built in Denmark and distributed by Godlyke.

ReezaFRATzitz RF-1/ReezaFRATzitz II

2004-present. Overdrive and distortion, red case.

2004-2024		$100	$150

Empress Effects

2005-present. Guitar effects pedals built by Steve Bragg and Jason Fee in Ottawa, Ontario.

EMS

1969-1979. Peter Zinnovieff's English synth company (Electronic Music Studios) also offered a guitar synthesizer. The company has reopened to work on original EMS gear.

Synthi Hi-Fli

Early-1970s. Analog guitar synthesizer, rare, only around 350 were made.

1972		$8,000	$50,000

Eowave

2002-present. Effects built first in Paris and now in Burgundy, France by Marc Sirguy.

Epiphone

Over the years, Epiphone offered a variety of different effect lines. Epiphone pedals which are labeled G.A.S Guitar Audio System were offered from around 1988 to '91.

Pedals

Various models with years available.

1988-1989	Chorus EP-CH-70	$45	$60
1988-1989	Delay EP-DE-80	$55	$75
1988-1991	Compressor EP-CO-20	$45	$60
1988-1991	Distortion EP-DI-10	$45	$60
1988-1991	Flanger EP-FL-60	$55	$75
1988-1991	Overdrive EP-OD-30	$45	$60

Rocco Tonexpressor

1937. Designed by steel-guitar ace Anthony Rocco, this pedal allows steel guitarists to adjust volume and tone with their foot.

1937		$250	$500

MODEL YEAR	FEATURES	LOW	HIGH

Ernie Ball

1972-present. The Ernie Ball company also builds Music Man instruments.

Volume Pedals

1977-present. Aluminum housing.

1977-2024		$35	$75

Euthymia Electronics

Line of guitar effects built by Erik Miller in Alameda, California.

Eventide

1971-present. This New Jersey electronics manufacturer has offered studio and rackmount effects since the late '70s. In '08 they added guitar effects pedals.

EXR

The EXR Corporation was in Brighton, Michigan.

Projector

1983-ca.1984. Psychoacoustic enhancer pedal.

1983-1984		$100	$125

Projector SP III

1983-ca.1984. Psychoacoustic enhancer pedal, volume pedal/sound boost.

1983-1984		$100	$125

Farfisa

The organ company offered effects pedals in the 1960s. Their products were manufactured in Italy by the Italian Accordion Company and distributed by Chicago Musical Instruments.

Model VIP 345 Organ

Mid-1960s. Portable organ with Syntheslalom used in the rock and roll venue.

1960s		$550	$650

Repeater

1969		$165	$300

Sferasound

1960s. Vibrato pedal for a Farfisa Organ but it works well with the guitar, gray case.

1960s		$300	$400

Wah/Volume

1969		$110	$150

Fargen

1999-present. Guitar effects built in Sacramento, California by Benjamin Fargen. He also builds amps.

Fender

1946-present. Although Fender has flirted with effects since the 1950s (the volume/volume-tone pedal and the Ecco-Fonic), the company concentrated mainly on guitars and amps. Fender effects ranged from the sublime to the ridiculous, from the tube Reverb to the Dimension IV. In 2013 Fender added a line of pedals.

E-H Soul Preacher
Jim Schreck

E-H Switch Blade
Jim Schreck

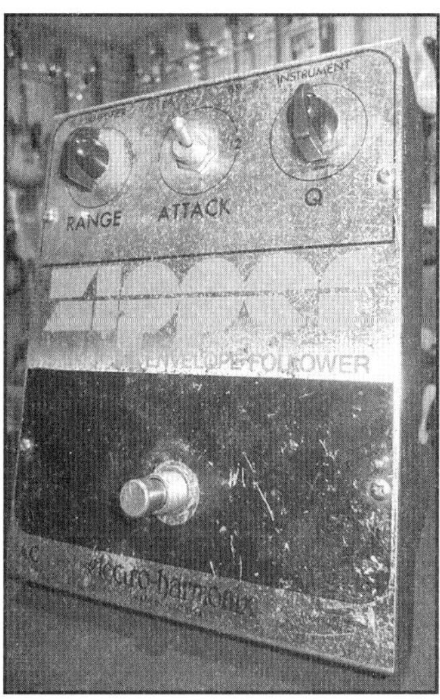

1977 E-H Zipper
Rivington Guitars

EFFECTS

Fender '63 Tube Reverb

1971 Fender Fuzz Wah
Rivington Guitars

1962 Fender Reverb Unit
Michael Alonz

MODEL YEAR	FEATURES	LOW	HIGH

'63 Tube Reverb

1994-2017. Reissue spring/tube Reverb Units with various era cosmetics as listed below. Currently offered in brown or, since '09, in lacquered tweed.

1994	White (limited run)	$800	$1,125
1994-1997	Black	$800	$1,125
1994-1997	Blond	$800	$1,125
1994-1997	Tweed	$800	$1,125
1994-2008	Brown	$800	$1,125
2009-2017	Lacquered Tweed	$1,000	$1,250

Blender

1968-1977, 2005-2010. Battery-operated unit with fuzz, sustain, and octave controls.

1968-1969		$475	$650
1970-1977		$375	$600
2005-2010	Reissue	$200	$300

Contempo Organ

1967-1968. Portable organ, all solidstate, 61 keys including a 17-key bass section, catalog shows with red cover material.

1967-1968		$650	$1,250

Dimension IV

1968-1970. Multi-effects unit using an oil-filled drum.

1968-1970		$325	$425

Echo and Electronic Echo Chamber

1963-1968. Solidstate tape echo built by Ecco-Fonic, up to 400 ms of delay, rectangle box with 2 controls '63-'67, slanted front '67-'68.

1963-1967		$450	$800
1967-1968		$325	$600

Echo-Reverb

1966-1970. Solidstate, echo-reverb effect produced by rotating metal disk, black tolex, silver grille.

1966-1970		$500	$650

Fuzz-Wah

1968-1984, 2007-2011. Has Fuzz and Wah switches on sides of pedal '68-'73, has 3 switches above the pedal '74-'84. The newer version ('07-'11) has switches on sides.

1968-1973	Switches on side	$250	$325
1974-1984	Switches above	$175	$225
2007-2011	Switches on side	$110	$150

Phaser

1975-1977, 2007-2011. AC powered, reissued in '07.

1975-1977		$225	$300
2007-2011		$65	$130

Reverb Unit

1961-1966, 1975-1978. Fender used a wide variety of tolex coverings in the early-'60s as the coverings matched those on the amps. Initially, Fender used rough blond tolex, then rough brown tolex, followed by smooth white or black tolex.

1961	Blond tolex, Oxblood grille	$2,500	$3,750
1961	Brown tolex	$1,750	$3,500
1962	Blond tolex, Oxblood grille	$1,750	$3,500
1962	Brown tolex, Wheat grille	$1,500	$2,500
1963	Brown tolex	$1,500	$2,500
1963	Rough blond tolex	$1,500	$2,500
1963	Smooth white tolex	$1,500	$2,500
1964	Black tolex	$1,250	$2,000
1964	Brown tolex, gold grille	$1,250	$2,000
1964	Smooth white tolex	$1,250	$2,000
1965-1966	Black tolex	$1,250	$2,000
1966	Solidstate, flat cabinet	$350	$450
1975-1978	Tube reverb reinstated	$975	$1,500

Vibratone

1967-1972. Fender's parent company at the time, CBS, bought Leslie in 1965, and Fender began offering a Leslie-type rotating-speaker-emulator as the Vibratone in 1967. Based on the Leslie Model 16 cabinet and made specifically for the guitar, it featured a single fixed 4-ohm 10-inch speaker fronted by a rotating drum. Designed to be powered by an external amp. 2-speed motor. Black tolex.

1967-1968	Fender cast logo in upper left corner	$850	$2,000
1968-1972	Fender logo plate through center	$700	$1,500

Volume-Tone Pedal

1954-1984, 2007-2018. Swivel foot controller.

1954-1984		$400	$525
2007-2018		$45	$60

Fernandes

1970s. Japanese guitar and effects maker.

Funky-Filter FR-3F

1970s. Built by Univox for Fernandes.

1970s		$250	$325

Field Effects by Resonant Electronic Design

Guitar effects pedals, starting in 2010, built in Minneapolis, Minnesota by Wes Kuhnley and Peter Bregman. They also build the Resonant brand amps.

Fishman

2003-present. Larry Fishman of Andover, Massachusetts offers a line of acoustic guitar effects pedals. He also builds amps.

FJA Mods

Jerry Pinnelli began building guitar effects in 2002, in Central Square, New York. He added professional grade, production, guitar amps in '07, then relocates to Charlotte, North Carolina in '18 and takes a hiatus from building.

FlexiSound

FlexiSound products were made in Lancaster, Pennsylvania.

F. S. Clipper

1975-ca.1976. Distortion, plugged directly into guitar jack.

1975-1976		$60	$75

MODEL YEAR	FEATURES	LOW	HIGH

The Beefer

1975. Power booster, plugged directly into guitar jack.

1975		$45	$60

Flip

Line of tube effects by Guyatone and distributed in the U.S. by Godlyke Distributing.

Tube Echo (TD-X)

2004-2017. Hybrid tube power delay pedal.

2004-2017		$150	$175

FM Acoustics

FM Acoustics pedals were made in Switzerland.

E-1 Pedal

1975. Volume, distortion, filter pedal.

1975		$75	$100

Foxx

Foxx pedals are readily identifiable by their fur-like covering. They slunk onto the scene in 1971 and were extinct by '78. Made by Hollywood's Ridinger Associates, their most notable product was the Tone Machine fuzz. Foxx-made pedals also have appeared under various brands such as G & G, Guild, Yamaha, and Sears Roebuck, generally without fur. Since 2005, reissues of some of the classic Foxx pedals are being built in Provo, Utah.

Clean Machine

1974-1978		$250	$350

Down Machine

1971-1977. Bass wah.

1971-1977	Blue case	$250	$350

Foot Phaser

1975-1977, 2006.

1975-1977		$800	$1,250

Fuzz and Wa and Volume

1974-1978, 2006. Currently called the Fuzz Wah Volume.

1974-1978		$300	$500

Guitar Synthesizer I

1975		$625	$1,750

Loud Machine

1970s. Volume pedal.

1970s		$65	$150

O.D. Machine

1972-ca.1975.

1972-1975		$250	$325

Phase III

1975-1978		$200	$250

Tone Machine

1971-1978, 2005. Fuzz with Octave, blue or black housing.

1971-1978		$500	$650

Wa and Volume

1971-1978		$375	$500

Wa Machine

1971-ca.1978.

1971-1978		$250	$325

Framptone

Founded by Peter Frampton in the year 2000, Framptone offers hand-made guitar effects.

3 Banger

2000-2021. Three-way amp switch box, white housing.

2000-2021		$250	$500

Amp Switcher

2000-2021. A-B switch box, white housing.

2000-2021		$200	$250

Talk Box

2000-2021. Talk box, white housing, no control knobs, on-off footswitch.

2000-2021		$250	$500

Frantone

1994-present. Effects and accessories hand built in New York City.

Fulltone

1991-present. Effects based on some of the classics of the past and built in Los Angeles, California, by Michael Fuller.

Choralflange

2000s. Dark green and silver case.

2000s		$250	$400

DejàVibe

1991-2004. Uni-Vibe-type pedal, later models have a Vintage/Modern switch. A stereo version also available.

1991-1993	Mono, gold housing	$350	$550
1993-2004	Mono, black housing	$275	$350

DejàVibe 2

1997-2018. Like DejàVibe but with built-in speed control. A stereo version also available.

1997-2018	Mono	$350	$550

Distortion Pro

2002-2008. Red case, volume, and distortion knobs with four voicing controls.

2002-2008		$125	$175

Fat Boost

2001-2007. Clean boost, silver-sparkle case, volume, and drive knobs.

2001-2007		$150	$200

Full-Drive 2

1995-present. Blue case, four control knobs.

1995-2024		$150	$400

Mini-DejàVibe

2004-2018. Uni-Vibe-type pedal, white housing, 3 Control knobs, stereo version also available.

2004-2018	Mono	$200	$400

OCD

1990-present. Obsessive compulsive drive.

1990-2012	V11 to V13	$250	$300
2013-2024	V14 to V17	$80	$140

Octafuzz

1996-2019. Copy of the Tycobrahe Octavia.

1996-2019		$150	$400

Soul Bender

1994-present. Volume, tone, and dirt knobs.

1994-2024		$200	$550

Fishman Fission Bass Powerchord

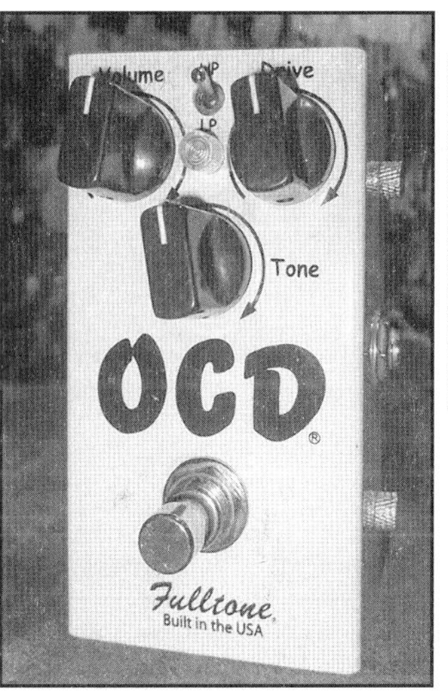

1999 Fulltone OCD
Rivington Guitars

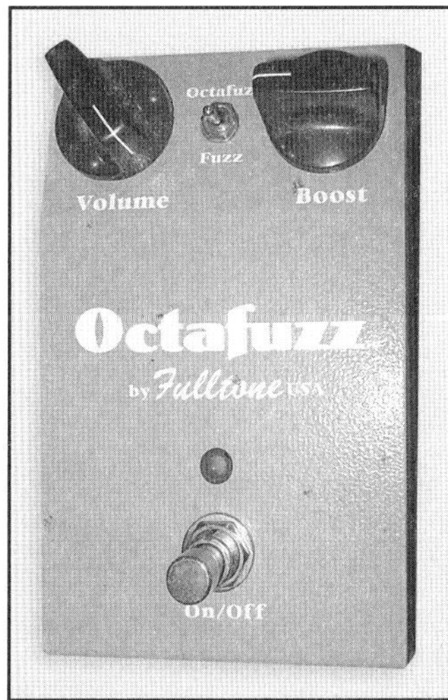

2006 Fulltone Octafuzz
Rivington Guitars

EFFECTS

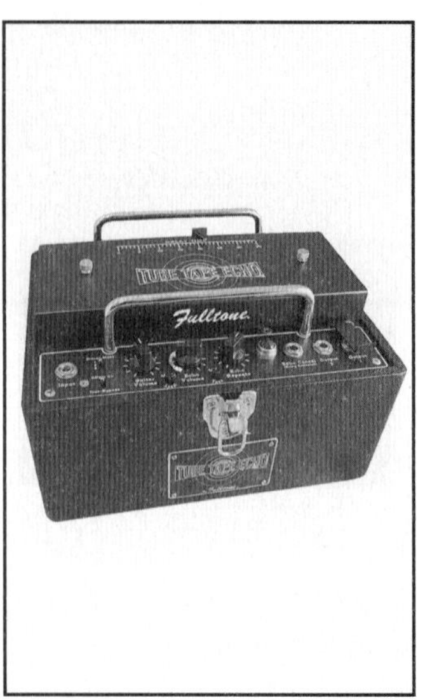

Fulltone Tube Tape Echo TTE

George Dennis Elite Wah

Gizmoaudio Sawmill

MODEL YEAR	FEATURES	LOW	HIGH

Supa-Trem
1996-2019. Black case, white Supa-Trem logo, rate, and mix controls.
1996-2019 $150 $200

Supa-Trem2
2000s. Yellow housing, 3 control knobs.
2000s $200 $450

Tube Tape Echo
2000s. Echo-Plex-style echo unit, white case.
2000s $1,500 $2,000

Tube Tape Echo TTE
2004-2022. Echoplex-style tube-powered tape unit, different colored housings.
2004-2022 $1,500 $2,000

Furman Sound

1993-present. Located in Petaluma, California, Furman makes audio and video signal processors and AC power conditioning products for music and other markets.

LC-2 Limiter Compressor
1990s. Rackmount unit with a black suitcase and red knobs.
1990s $65 $85

PQ3 Parametric EQ
1990s. Rackmount preamp and equalizer.
1998-1999 $225 $400

PQ6 Parametric Stereo
1990s $225 $400

RV1 Reverb Rackmount
1990s $225 $400

Fxdoctor

2003-present. Joshua Zalegowski originally built his effects in Amherst, Massachusetts, and in 2005 moved to Boston.

Fxengineering

2002-present. Production and custom guitar effects built by Montez Aldridge in Raleigh, North Carolina.

G.M. Electronics

1960s. Based in Detroit, Michigan.

Dual Range Fuzz Up FD3-A
1960s. Fuzz pedal combining 2 Gibson Maestro FZ-1 Fuzz Tone circuits.
1960s $350 $450

Fuzz Up FM3-B
1960s. Clone of the Gibson Maestro FZ-1 Fuzz Tone.
1960s $350 $450

G.S. Wyllie

2000s. Glenn Wyllie built effects in North Carolina.

Moonrock
2000s. Octave fuzz.
2000s $450 $1,000

NewMoon
2000s. Updated version of Moonrock octave fuzz.
2000s $450 $1,000

MODEL YEAR	FEATURES	LOW	HIGH

Ozo
2000s. Ring modulator.
2000s $450 $1,000

X-Fuzz
2000s. High-gain fuzz.
2000s $450 $1,000

G2D

1999-present. David Manning and Grant Wills build their guitar effects pedals in Auckland, New Zealand.

Garcia

Guitar effects built by Matthew Garcia in Myrtle Beach, South Carolina, starting in 2004. He also built amps.

Geek MacDaddy

See listing under The Original Geek.

George Dennis

1991-present. Founded by George Burgerstein, the original products were a line of effects pedals. In '96 they added a line of tube amps. The company is in Prague, Czech Republic.

Gibson

Gibson did offer a few effects bearing their own name, but most were sold under the Maestro name (see that listing).

Echoplex Digital Pro Plus
1994-2010. Rackmount unit with digital recording, sampling, and digital delay. Labeled as just Echoplex until '01 when Gibson name added.
1994-2010 $425 $550

GA-3RV Reverb Unit
1964-1967. Small, compact, spring reverb unit, black tolex, gray grille.
1964-1967 $400 $550

GA-4RE Reverb-Echo Unit
1964-1967. Small, compact, lightweight accessory reverb-echo unit that produces complete reverberation and authentic echo, utilizes Gibson's "electronic memory" system for both reverb and echo, black tolex, gray grille.
1964-1967 $400 $550

Gig-FX

2004-present. Founder Jeff Purchon of Waltham, Massachusetts, imports guitar effects pedals built at his company-owned factory in Shenzhen, China.

Gizmo, Inc.

Ca.1980. Short-lived company that grew out of the ashes of Musitronics' attempt to make the Gizomotron. See Mu-Tron.

Gizmoaudio

2009-present. Guitar effects built by Charles Luke in Cumming, Georgia.

MODEL YEAR | FEATURES | LOW | HIGH

Gnome Amplifiers

Guitar effects pedals built by Dan Munro in Olympia, Washington. He started in 2008 and builds amps.

Godbout

Godbout sold a variety of effects do-it-yourself kits in the 1970s, which are difficult to value because quality depends on skills of builder.

Effects Kits

1970s $25 $35

Godley Crème

1978-1980. Kevin Godley and Lol Crème, members of the band 10cc, developed the Gizmotron, which mounted on the face of a bass or guitar and continously strummed the strings to give a bowed-string effect. The device was built by Musitronics of New Jersey, which built the MuTron III and other effects.

Gizmotron

1978-1980. A "ultimate sustain" mechanical add-on to guitar or bass bridges with rotating plectrums.

1978-1980 $350 $500

Goodrich Sound

1970s-present. Originally located in Michigan, and currently in Dublin, Georgia, Goodrich currently offers volume pedals and a line boost.

Match Box Line Boost

Early-1980s-2011. Small rectangular line buffer/driver.

1980s-2011 $125 $175

Volume Pedal 6122

Late-1970s-1980s. Uses a potentiometer.

1970s $125 $175

Volume Pedal 6400ST

Late-1970s-1980s. Stereo pedal, using photocells.

1970s $125 $175

Volume Pedal 6402

Late-1970s-1980s. Uses photocell.

1970s $125 $175

Goran Custom Guitars

1998-present. Luthier Goran Djuric from Belgrade, Serbia also offers guitar pedals.

Goya

1960s. Goya Music sold effects under the brands Goya, Applied, Nomad, Conrad and maybe more.

Fury Box

1960s $200 $250

Greer Amplification

1999-present. Guitar stomp box effects built by Nick Greer in Athens, Georgia. He also builds amps.

Gretsch

Gretsch has offered a limited line of effects from time to time.

MODEL YEAR | FEATURES | LOW | HIGH

Controfuzz

Mid-1970s. Distortion.

1970s $250 $350

Deluxe Reverb Unit Model 6149

1963-1969. Similar to Gibson's GA-1 introduced around the same time.

1963-1969 $650 $850

Expandafuzz

Mid-1970s. Distortion.

1970s $300 $400

Reverb Unit Model 6144 Preamp Reverb

1963-1967. Approximately 17 watts, preamp functionality, no speaker.

1963-1967 $650 $1,000

Tremofect

Mid-1970s. Tremolo effect, 3-band EQ, speed, effect, bass, total, and treble knobs.

1970s $400 $550

Guild

Guild marketed effects made by Binson, Electro-Harmonix, Foxx, WEM and Applied in the 1960s and '70s.

Copicat

1960s-1979. Echo.

1970s $750 $1,500

DE-20 Auto-Rhythm Unit

1971-1974. 50-watt rhythm accompaniment unit. Included 20 rhythms and a separate instrument channel with its own volume control. 1x12" plus tweeter.

1971-1974 $300 $400

Echorec (by Binson)

Ca.1960-1979. Stripped-down version of the Binson Echorec.

1960s $5,500 $7,500

Foxey Lady Fuzz

1968-1977. Distortion, sustain.

1968-1975 2 knobs, made by E-H $750 $1,000

1976-1977 3 knobs in row, same as Big Muff $850 $1,250

Fuzz Wah FW-3

1975-ca.1979. Distortion, volume, wah, made by Foxx.

1970s $150 $300

HH Echo Unit

1976-ca.1979.

1970s $350 $550

VW-1

1975-ca.1979. Volume, wah, made by Foxx.

1970s $200 $250

Guyatone (Tokyo Sound Company)

1930s-present. Founded by Mitsuo Matsuki, maker of guitars, amps, and effects. Imported stomp boxes, tape echo units and outboard reverb units distributed by Godlyke Distributing. In 2013 they merged with DeMont Guitars of Oswego, Illinois and effects are made in the US and Japan.

Bazz Box FS-1

1960s. Vox V828 Tone Bender copy.

1960s $200 $300

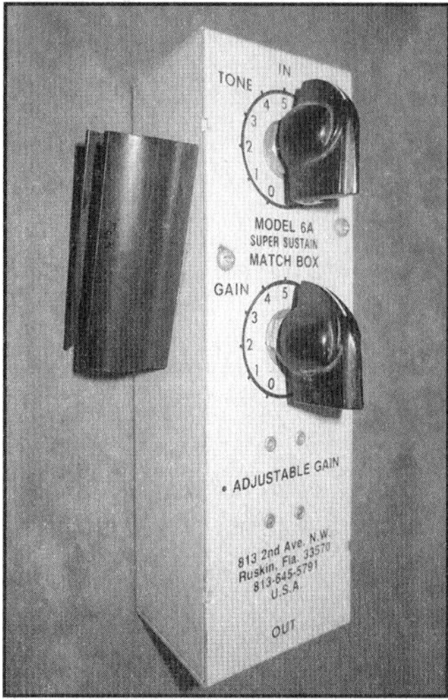

1990 Goodrich Sound Match Box Line Boost

Rivington Guitars

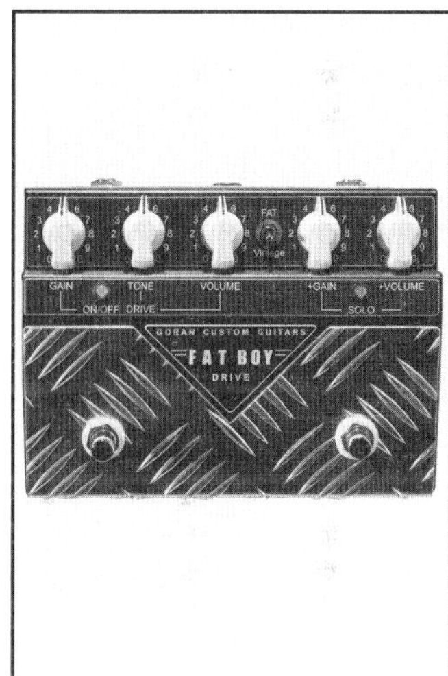

Goran Fat Boy

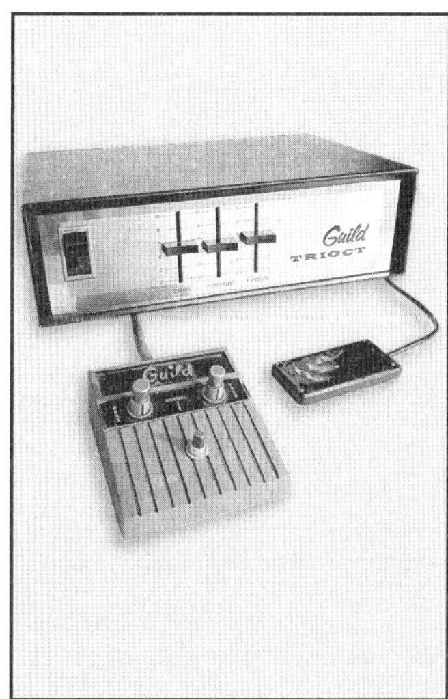

Guild Tri-Oct

Mary-Anne Hammer

HAO Rust Driver

Henretta Engineering
The Valley Reverb

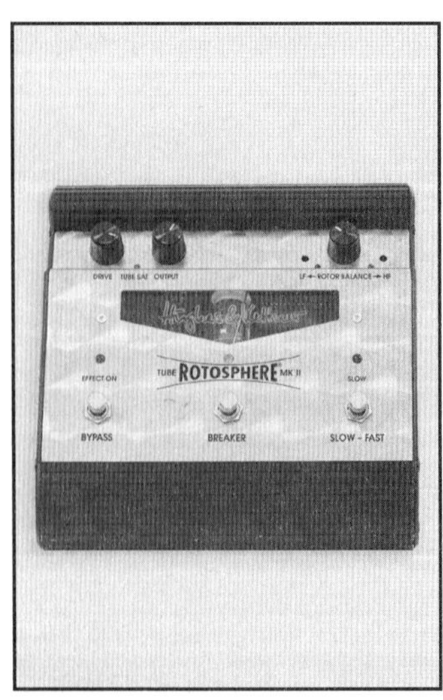

Hughes & Kettner Rotosphere
Imaged by Heritage Auctions, HA.com

MODEL YEAR	FEATURES	LOW	HIGH

Bazz Box FS-2

1960s. Univox Super-Fuzz copy.

1960s		$200	$300

Crazy-Face

1970s. Dallas-Arbiter Fuzz Face copy.

1970s		$300	$600

Sustainer FS-6

1970s. Circular Fuzz Face-like housing.

1970s		$500	$800

Wah-Fuzz FS-5

1970s		$200	$450

HAO

Line of guitar effects built in Japan by J.E.S. International, distributed in the U.S. by Godlyke.

Harden Engineering

2006-present. Distortion/boost guitar effects pedals built by William Harden in Chicago, Illinois. He also builds guitars.

Heathkit

1960s. These were sold as do-it-yourself kits and are difficult to value because quality depends on the skills of builder.

TA-28 Distortion Booster

1960s. Fuzz assembly kit, heavy '60s super fuzz, case-by-case quality depending on the builder.

1960s		$250	$350

Heavy Metal Products

Mid-1970s. From Alto Loma, California, products for the heavy metal guitarist.

Raunchbox Fuzz

1975-1976		$150	$200

Switchbox

1975-1976. A/B box.

1975-1976		$30	$40

Heet Sound Products

1974-present. The E Bow concept goes back to '67, but a hand-held model wasn't available until '74. Made in Los Angeles, California.

E Bow

1974-1979, 1985-1987, 1994-present. The Energy Bow, hand-held electro-magnetic string driver.

1974-1979		$75	$100

E Bow for Pedal Steels

1979. Hand-held electro-magnetic string driver.

1979		$55	$75

Heil Sound

1960-present. Founded by Bob Heil, Marissa, Illinois. Created the talk box technology as popularized by Joe Walsh and Peter Frampton. In the '60s and '70s Heil was dedicated to innovative products for the music industry. In the late-'70s, innovative creations were more in the amateur radio market, and by the '90s Heil's focus was on the home theater market. The Heil Sound Talkbox was reissued by Jim Dunlop USA in '89.

MODEL YEAR	FEATURES	LOW	HIGH

Talk Box

1976-ca.1980, 1989-present. Reissued by Dunlop.

1976-1980		$200	$250
1989-1999		$100	$125
2000-2024		$80	$110

Henretta Engineering

2009-present. Analog guitar effects built by Kevin Henretta first in Chicago, Illinois and presently Saint Paul, Minnesota.

Hermida Audio

2003-2013. Alfonso Hermida built his guitar effects in Miramar, Florida. Hermida was acquired by Lovepedal in '13.

High Gain

See the listing under Dunlop.

Hohner

Hohner offered effects in the late-1970s.

Dirty Booster

1977-ca.1978. Distortion.

1977-1978		$550	$775

Dirty Wah Wah'er

1977-ca.1978. Adds distortion.

1977-1978		$225	$300

Fuzz Wah

1970s. Morley-like volume pedal with volume knob and fuzz knob, switch for soft or hard fuzz, gray box with black foot pedal.

1970s		$225	$350

Multi-Exciter

1977-ca.1978. Volume, wah, surf, tornado, siren.

1977-1978		$250	$350

Tape Echo/Echo Plus

1970s. Black alligator suitcase.

1970s		$300	$550

Tri-Booster

1977-ca.1978. Distortion, sustain.

1977-1978		$550	$775

Vari-Phaser

1977-ca.1978.

1977-1978		$300	$400

Vol-Kicker Volume Pedal

1977-ca.1978.

1977-1978		$225	$350

Wah-Wah'er

1977-ca.1978. Wah, volume.

1977-1978		$225	$350

HomeBrew Electronics

2001-2014. Stomp box effects hand made by Joel and Andrea Weaver in Glendale, Arizona.

Honey

1967-1969. Honey Company Ltd. Was formed by ex-Teisco workers after that firm was acquired by Kawai. Honey launched several effects designed by engineer Fumio Mieda, before going bankrupt in March, '69. The company was reborn as Shin-ei

MODEL YEAR	FEATURES	LOW	HIGH

and many of its designs continued production in various forms; see Shin-ei for more.

Baby Crying

1960s. Univox Super-Fuzz copy.

1960s		$650	$950

Psychedelic Machine

1967-1969. Amp head-sized effect with numerous controls.

1967-1969		$3,000	$5,000

Special Fuzz

1967-1970s		$550	$850

Vibra Chorus

1967-1969. Original version of the Uni-Vibe, which Shin-ei would produce after Honey went bankrupt.

1967-1969		$2,000	$3,000

Hughes & Kettner

1985-present. Hughes & Kettner builds a line of tube-driven guitar effects made in Germany. They also build amps and cabinets.

Ibanez

1932-present. Ibanez effects were introduced ca. 1974 and were manufactured by Japan's Maxon Electronics. Although results were mixed at first, a more uniform and modern product line, including the now legendary Tube Screamer, built Ibanez's reputation for quality. They continue to produce a wide range of effects.

60s Fuzz FZ5 (SoundTank)

1991-1992, 1996-1998. Fuzz with level, tone and distortion controls, black plastic case, green label.

1990s		$55	$75

7th Heaven SH7 (Tone-Lok)

2000-2004. Lo, high, drive and level controls, gray-silver case, blue-green label.

2000-2004		$50	$75

Acoustic Effects PT4

1993-1998. Acoustic guitar multi-effect with compressor/limiter, tone shaper, stereo chorus, digital reverb, with power supply.

1993-1998		$200	$500

Analog Delay 202 (Rack Mount)

1981-1983. Rack mount with delay, doubling, flanger, stereo chorus, dual inputs with tone and level.

1981-1983		$300	$400

Analog Delay AD9

1982-1984, 2000s. 3 control analog delay, Hot Pink metal case, reissued in the 2000s.

1982-1984		$150	$350
2000s	Reissue	$85	$150

Analog Delay AD80

1980-1981. Pink case.

1980-1981		$200	$300

Analog Delay AD99

1996-1998. Reissue, 3 control knobs and on/off switch, winged-hand logo, black case.

1996-1998		$100	$150

Analog Delay AD100 (Table Unit)

1981-1983. Stand-alone table/studio unit (not rack mount) with power cord.

1981-1983		$200	$250

Analog Delay ADL

1985-1986		$100	$130

Auto Filter AF9

1982-1984. Replaces AF201 model.

1982-1984		$200	$300

Auto Filter AF201

1981. Two min-max sliders, 3 mode toggle switches, orange metal case.

1981		$200	$350

Auto Wah AW5 (SoundTank)

1994-1999. Plastic case SoundTank series.

1994-1999		$50	$90

Auto Wah AW7 (Tone-Lok)

2000-2010. Silver case.

2000-2010		$50	$100

Bass Compressor BP10

1986-1991		$80	$125

Bass Stack BS10

1987-1988		$450	$600

Bi-Mode Chorus BC9

1984. Dual channel for 2 independent speed and width settings.

1984		$150	$225

Chorus CS-505

1980-1981. Speed and depth controls, gray-blue case, stereo or mono input, battery or external power option.

1980-1981		$200	$250

Chorus Flanger CF7 (Tone-Lok)

1999-2010. Speed, depth, delay, regeneration controls, mode, and crazy switches.

1999-2010		$75	$125

Chorus Flanger DCF-10

1986-1989		$175	$225

Classic Flange FL99

1997-1999. Analog reissue, silver metal case, winged-hand artwork, 4 controls, 2 footswitch buttons.

1997-1999		$275	$350

Classic Phase PH99

1995-1999. Analog reissue, silver metal case, winged-hand artwork, speed, depth, feedback, effect level controls, intense and bypass footswitches.

1995-1999		$125	$150

Compressor CP5 (SoundTank)

1991-1998		$30	$45

Compressor CP10

1986-1992		$85	$125

Compressor CP830

1975-1979		$100	$150

Compressor II CP835

1980-1981		$125	$150

Compressor Limiter CP9

1982-1984		$75	$100

DCP Distortion PDS1

1980s		$75	$100

DCP Parametric EQ PPE1

1980s		$110	$200

Delay Champ CD10

1986-1989. Red case, 3 knobs.

1986-1989		$120	$160

Ibanez Analog Delay AD9
Rivington Guitars

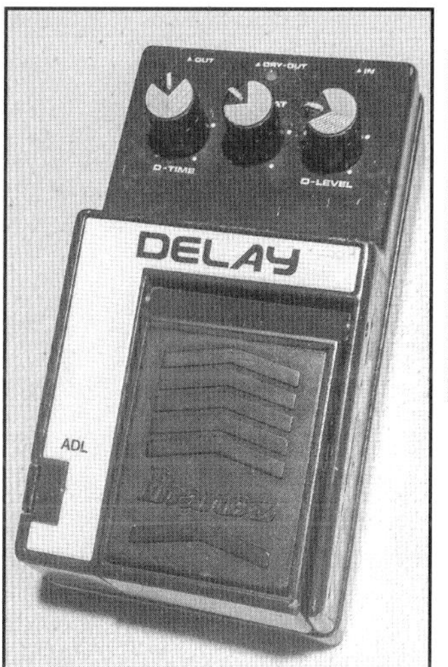

Ibanez Analog Delay ADL
Keith Myers

1983 Ibanez Compressor Limiter CP9
Mark Mondahl

EFFECTS

1993 Ibanez Fat Cat Distortion FC10
Rivington Guitars

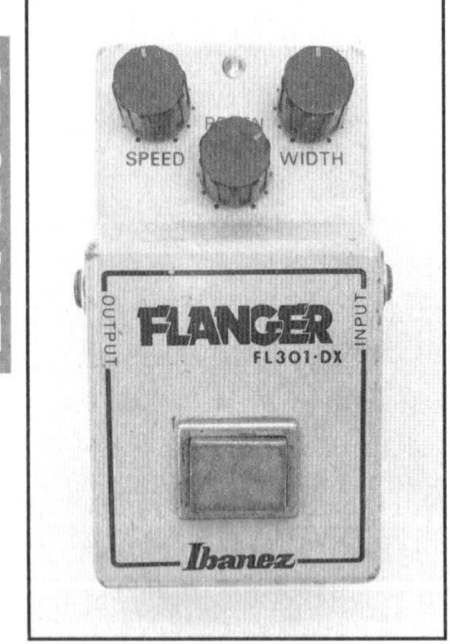

1982 Ibanez Flanger FL301-DX
Bernunzio Uptown Music

1975 Ibanez Overdrive OD850
Rivington Guitars

MODEL YEAR	FEATURES	LOW	HIGH

Delay Echo DE7 (Tone-Lok)
1999-2010. Stereo delay/echo.
1999-2010 $100 $125

Delay Harmonizer DM1000
1983-1984. Rack mount, with chorus, 9 control knobs.
1983-1984 $175 $225

Delay II DDL10
1986-1988 $125 $175

Delay III DDL20 Digital Delay
1988-1989. Filtering, doubling, slap back, echo S, echo M, echo L, Seafoam Green coloring on pedal.
1988-1989 $130 $150

Delay PDD1 (DPC Series)
1988-1989. Programmable Digital Delay (PDD) with display screen.
1988-1989 $125 $150

Digital Chorus DSC10
1990-1992. 3 control knobs and slider selection toggle.
1990-1992 $100 $125

Digital Delay DL5 (SoundTank)
1991-1998 $40 $80

Digital Delay DL10
1989-1992. Digital Delay made in Japan, blue case, 3 green control knobs, stompbox.
1989-1992 $100 $130

Distortion Charger DS10
1986-1989 $110 $150

Distortion DS7 (Tone-Lok)
2000-2010. Drive, tone, and level controls.
2000-2010 $45 $65

Dual Chorus CCL
1990s $100 $150

Echo Machine EM5 (SoundTank)
1996-1998. Simulates tape echo.
1996-1998 $200 $300

Fat Cat Distortion FC10
1987-1989. 3-knob pedal with distortion, tone, and level controls.
1987-1989 $150 $300

Flanger FFL5 (Master Series)
1984-1985. Speed, regeneration, width, D-time controls, battery or adapter option.
1984-1985 $75 $100

Flanger FL5 (SoundTank)
1991-1998 $40 $60

Flanger FL9
1982-1984. Yellow case.
1982-1984 $100 $200

Flanger FL301
1979-1982. Mini flanger, 3 knobs, called the FL-301 DX in late '81-'82.
1979-1982 $120 $150

Flanger FL305
1976-1979. Five knobs.
1976-1979 $300 $400

Flying Pan FP777
1976-1979. Auto pan/phase shifter, 4 control knobs, phase on/off button, pan on/off button, silver metal case with blue trim and Flying Pan winged-hand logo.
1976-1979 $350 $450

MODEL YEAR	FEATURES	LOW	HIGH

Flying Pan FP777 Reissue
2007 777 made $250 $350

Fuzz FZ7 (Tone-Lok)
2000-2010. Drive, tone and level controls, gray-silver case, blue green FZ7 label.
2000-2010 $60 $80

Graphic Bass EQ BE10
1986-1992. Later labeled as the BEQ10.
1986-1992 $70 $100

Graphic EQ GE9
1982-1984. Six EQ sliders, 1 overall volume slider, turquoise blue case.
1982-1984 $100 $200

Graphic EQ GE10
1986-1992. Eight sliders.
1986-1992 $75 $130

Graphic Equalizer GE601 (808 Series)
1980-1981. 7-slider EQ, aqua blue metal case.
1980-1981 $75 $100

Guitar Multi-Processor PT5
1993-1997. Floor unit, programmable with 25 presets and 25 user presets, effects include distortion, chorus, flanger, etc, green case.
1993-1997 $100 $150

Jetlyzer JL70
1975-1977. Phase shifter and jet plane effect, orange and black case.
1975-1977 $350 $550

LA Metal LM7
1988-1989. Silver case.
1988-1989 $100 $135

LoFi LF7 (Tone-Lok)
2000-2010. Filter, 4 knobs.
2000-2010 $100 $175

Metal Charger MS10
1986-1992. Distortion, level, attack, punch and edge control knobs, green case.
1986-1992 $100 $125

Metal Screamer MSL
1985. 3 control knobs.
1985 $150 $200

Modern Fusion MF5 (SoundTank)
1990-1991. Level, tone and distortion controls.
1990-1991 $80 $160

Modulation Delay DM500
1983-1984. Rack mount.
1983-1984 $100 $200

Modulation Delay DM1000
1983-1984. Rack mount with delay, reverb, modulation.
1983-1984 $100 $200

Modulation Delay PDM1
1988-1989. Programmable Digital Modulation pedal.
1988-1989 $100 $200

Mostortion MT10
1990-1992. Mos-FET circuit distortion pedal, 5 control knobs, green case.
1990-1992 $450 $650

Multi-Effect PUE5/PUE5 Tube (Floor Unit)
1990-1993. Yellow version has tube, blue one does not. Also available in PUE5B bass version.
1990-1993 Tube $300 $400

MODEL YEAR	FEATURES	LOW	HIGH

Multi-Effect UE300 (Floor Unit)

1983-1984. Floor unit, 4 footswitches for super metal, digital delay, digital stereo chorus, and master power, 3 delay modes.

1983-1984 $250 $350

Multi-Effect UE300B (Floor Unit)

1983-1984. Floor unit for bass.

1983-1984 $250 $350

Multi-Effect UE305 (Floor Unit)

1983-1984 $200 $300

Multi-Effect UE400 (Rackmount)

1980-1984. Rack mount with foot switch.

1980-1984 $300 $375

Multi-Effect UE405 (Rackmount)

1981-1984. Rack mount with analog delay, parametric EQ, compressor/limiter, stereo chorus and loop.

1981-1984 $300 $375

Noise Buster NB10

1988-1989. Eliminates 60-cycle hum and other outside signals, metal case.

1988-1989 $70 $100

Overdrive OD850

1975-1979 $300 $400

Overdrive II OD855

1977-1979. Distortion, tone, and level controls, yellow/green case, large Overdrive II logo.

1977-1979 $300 $400

Pan Delay DPL10

1990-1992. Royal Blue case, 3 green control knobs.

1990-1992 $100 $125

Parametric EQ PQ9

1982-1984 $125 $200

Parametric EQ PQ401

1981. 3 sliders, dial-in knob, light aqua blue case.

1981 $200 $275

Phase Tone II PT707

1976-1979. Blue box, script logo for first 2 years.

1976-1979 $100 $130

Phase Tone PT909

1979-1982. Blue box, 3 knobs, early models with flat case (logo at bottom or later in the middle) or later wedge case.

1979-1982 $140 $200

Phase Tone PT999

1975-1979. Script logo, 1 knob, round footswitch, becomes PT-909.

1975-1979 $125 $150

Phase Tone PT1000

1974-1975. Morley-style pedal phase, light blue case, early model of Phase Tone.

1974-1975 $200 $300

Phaser PH5 (SoundTank)

1991-1998 $40 $70

Phaser PH7 (Tone-Lok)

1999-2010. Speed, depth, feedback, and level controls.

1999-2010 $60 $75

Phaser PT9

1982-1984. Three control knobs, red case.

1982-1984 $125 $220

MODEL YEAR	FEATURES	LOW	HIGH

Powerlead PL5 (SoundTank)

1991-1998. Metal case '91, plastic case '91-'98.

1991 Metal $25 $35

1991-1998 Plastic $30 $50

Renometer

1976-1979. 5-band equalizer with preamp.

1976-1979 $150 $200

Rotary Chorus RC99

1996-1999. Black or silver cases available, requires a power pack and does not use a battery.

1996-1999 Black case $125 $175

Session Man SS10

1988-1989. Distortion, chorus.

1988-1989 $300 $450

Session Man II SS20

1988-1989. 4 controls plus toggle, light pink-purple case.

1988-1989 $200 $300

Slam Punk SP5 (SoundTank)

1996-1999 $50 $70

Smash Box SM7 (Tone-Lok)

2000-2010 $70 $85

Sonic Distortion SD9

1982-1984 $150 $200

Standard Fuzz (No. 59)

1974-1979. Two buttons (fuzz on/off and tone change).

1974-1979 $400 $600

Stereo Bass Chorus BC10

1986-1993. Purple case.

1986-1993 $100 $125

Stereo Box ST800

1975-1979. One input, 2 outputs for panning, small yellow case.

1975-1979 $125 $250

Stereo Chorus CS9

1982-1984 $125 $250

Stereo Chorus CSL (Master Series)

1985-1986 $100 $125

Super Chorus CS5 (SoundTank)

1991-1998 $25 $40

Super Metal SM9

1984. Distortion.

1984 $150 $220

Super Stereo Chorus SC10

1986-1992 $100 $150

Super Tube Screamer ST9

1984-1985. 4 knobs, light green metal case.

1984-1985 $450 $600

Super Tube STL

1985 $150 $275

Swell Flanger SF10

1986-1992. Speed, regeneration, width and time controls, yellow case.

1986-1992 $130 $250

Time Machine AD190 Delay

1978-1980. Analog delay and flanger.

1978-1980 $400 $500

Trashmetal TM5 (SoundTank)

1990-1998. Tone and distortion pedal, 3 editions (1st edition, 2nd edition metal case, 2nd edition plastic case).

1990-1998 $50 $70

1977 Ibanez Phase Tone II PT707

Keith Myers,

1984 Ibanez Phaser PT9

Rivington Guitars

1984 Ibanez Super Metal SM9

Mark Mondahl

Ibanez Tube Screamer TS5

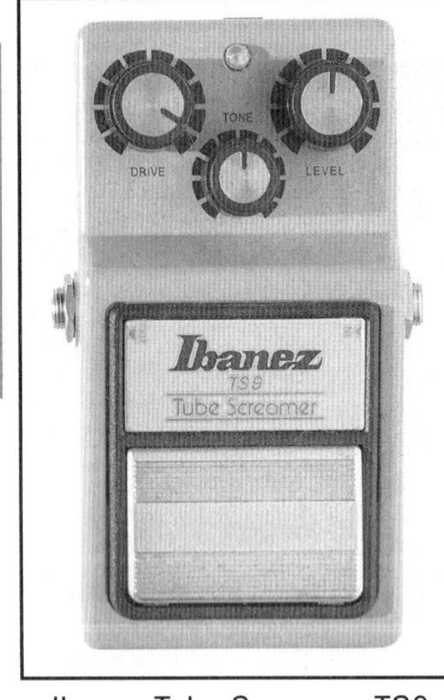

Ibanez Tube Screamer TS9

JAM Pedals Delay Llama

MODEL YEAR	FEATURES	LOW	HIGH

Tremolo Pedal TL5 (SoundTank)

1995-1998 $40 $70

Tube King TK999

1994-1995. Has a 12AX7 tube and 3-band equalizer.

1994-1995 Includes power pack $150 $200

Tube King TK999US

1996-1998. Has a 12AX7 tube and 3-band equalizer, does not have the noise switch of the original TK999. Made in the U.S.

1996-1998 Includes power pack $150 $200

Tube Screamer TS5 (SoundTank)

1991-1998 $25 $100

Tube Screamer TS7 (Tone-Lok)

1999-2010. 3 control knobs.

1999-2010 $60 $100

Tube Screamer TS9

1982-1984, 1993-present. Reissued in '93.

1982-1984 $400 $500

1993-2024 $125 $175

1993-2024 AnalogMan modded $175 $225

1993-2024 Keeley modded $225 $300

Tube Screamer Classic TS10

1986-1993 $350 $500

Tube Screamer TS808

1980-1982, 2004-present. Reissued in '04.

1980-1982 Original $1,250 $1,500

2004-2024 Reissue $100 $130

Turbo Tube Screamer TS9DX

1998-present. Tube Screamer circuit with added 3 settings for low-end.

1998-2024 $100 $150

Twin Cam Chorus TC10

1986-1989. Four control knobs, light blue case.

1986-1989 $75 $180

Virtual Amp VA3 (floor unit)

1995-1998. Digital effects processor.

1995-1998 $75 $125

Visual Super Product SK-10

1986. Very rare, limited run for small shop in Japan.

1986 $3,000 $3,500

VL10

1987-1997. Stereo volume pedal.

1987-1997 $50 $75

Wah Fuzz Standard (Model 58)

1974-1981. Fuzz tone change toggle, fuzz on toggle, fuzz depth control, balance control, wah volume pedal with circular friction pads on footpedal.

1974-1981 $125 $275

Wah WH10

1987-1996 $100 $300

Wau Wau Fuzz

1970s. Volume plus fuzz control.

1970s $150 $250

Ilitch Electronics

2003-present. Ilitch Chiliachki builds his effects in Camarillo, California.

Indy Guitarist

See listing under Wampler Pedals.

InterFax Electronics

Mid-1970s-1980s. Started by Ed Giese, located in Milwaukee, Wisconsin.

HP-1 Harmonic Percolator

Mid-1970s. Distortion/fuzz unit, harmonics and balance sliders.

1970s $175 $300

Intersound

1970s-1980s. Intersound, Inc. was in Boulder, Colorado and was a division of Electro-Voice.

Reverb-Equalizer R100F

1977-1979. Reverb and 4-band EQ, fader.

1977-1979 $75 $100

J. Everman

Analog guitar effects built by Justin J. Everman in Richardson, Texas, starting in 2000.

Jack Deville Electronics

2008-present. Production/custom, guitar effects built in Portland, Oregon by Jack Deville.

Jacques

One-of-a-kind handmade stomp boxes and production models made in France.

JAM Pedals

2007-present. Pedals built by Jannis Anastasakis Marinos of Athens, Greece.

Black Muck

2017-2018. Fuzz distortion.

2017-2018 $200 $250

Boomster

2007-present. Silicon clean boost.

2007-2024 $80 $100

Boomster Mini

2017-2022. Silicon clean boost.

2017-2022 $55 $100

DanComp

2007-2015. Compressor based on the Dan Armstrong Orange Squeezer compressor circuit.

2007-2015 $200 $250

Delay Llama

2007-present. Analog delay.

2007-2024 $150 $200

Delay Llama Supreme

2014-2019. Analog delay with tap tempo modulation.

2014-2019 $300 $350

Delay Llama+

2009-2019. Analog delay with hold function.

2009-2019 $175 $225

Dyna-ssoR

2007-present. Compression/sustainer.

2007-2024 $150 $200

Fuzz Phase

2007-2018. Germanium fuzz.

2007-2018 $200 $250

LucyDreamer Supreme

2017-present. Overdrive/boost.

2017-2024 $200 $250

MODEL YEAR	FEATURES	LOW	HIGH

Rattler

2008-present. Distortion.

2008-2024 $150 $200

Rattler+

2008-2018. Distortion with low-gain stage.

2008-2018 $200 $250

Red Muck

2008-2018. Fuzz distortion.

2008-2018 $150 $200

Retro Vibe

2007-present. Vibe/vibrato.

2007-2024 $250 $300

Ripple

2007-present. Two-stage phaser.

2007-2024 $125 $175

Ripply Fall

2017-present. Chorus/vibrato/phaser.

2017-2024 $225 $300

Rooster

2007-2018. Frequency booster.

2007-2018 $175 $225

The Big Chill

2011-2023. Super tremolo with 2 speeds and chop effect.

2011-2023 $200 $250

The Chill

2007-present. Sine-wave tremolo.

2007-2024 $125 $175

Tube Dreamer 58/Tubedreamer

2007-present. Overdrive with selectable high-gain stage.

2007-2024 $125 $175

Tube Dreamer 72

2007-2018. Overdrive.

2007-2018 $150 $200

Tube Dreamer 88

2007-2018. Double overdrive.

2007-2018 $175 $225

Tube Dreamer+

2007-2017. Overdrive with footswitchable high-gain stage.

2007-2017 $150 $200

Wahcko/Wahcko+

2007-present. Wah-wah.

2007-2024 $200 $250

WaterFall

2007-present. Chorus/vibrato.

2007-2024 $175 $225

JangleBox

2004-present. Stephen Lasko and Elizabeth Lasko build their guitar effects in Springfield, Virginia and Dracut, Massachusetts.

Jan-Mar Industries

Jan-Mar was in Hillsdale, New Jersey.

The Talker

1976. 30 watts.

1976 $75 $150

The Talker Pro

1976. 75 watts.

1976 $100 $150

MODEL YEAR	FEATURES	LOW	HIGH

Jax

1960s-1970. Japanese imports made by Shin-ei.

Fuzz Master

1960s $400 $500

Fuzz Wah

1960s $200 $350

Vibrachorus

1969. Rotating-speaker simulator, with control pedal. Variant of Uni-Vibe.

1969 $800 $1,500

Wah-Wah

1960s $500 $600

Jen

Italy's Jen Elettronica company made a variety of guitar effects pedals in the 1960s and '70s for other brands such as Vox and Gretsch name. They also offered many of them, including the Cry Baby, under their own name.

Jennings

1960s. Dick Denny, of Vox fame, designed a short-lived line of effects for Jennings Electronic Developments of England.

Growler

1960s. Fuzz and wah effect with a rotary foot control.

1960s $875 $1,500

Jersey Girl

1991-present. Line of guitar effects pedals made in Japan. They also build guitars.

Jet Sounds LTD

1977. Jet was located in Jackson, Mississippi.

Hoze Talk Box

1977. Large wood box, 30 watts.

1977 $100 $150

Jetter Gear

2005-present. Brad Jeter builds his effects pedals in Marietta, Georgia.

JHD Audio

1974-1990. Hunt Dabney founded JHD in Costa Mesa, California, to provide effects that the user installed in their amp. Dabney is still involved in electronics and builds the BiasProbe tool for tubes.

SuperCube/SuperCube II

1974-late 1980s. Plug-in sustain mod for Fender amps with reverb, second version for amps after '78.

1974-1980s $50 $75

JHS Pedals

2007-present. Located in Mississippi 2007-08, Josh Scott presently builds his guitar and bass effects in Kansas City, Missouri.

Bonsai

2007-2024 $150 $200

Colour Box V2

2007-2024 $275 $350

JAM Pedals Ripply Fall

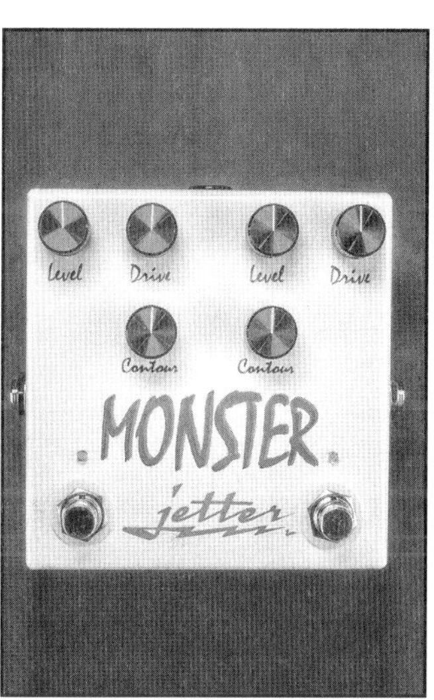

Jetter Monster

JHS Pedals Bonsai

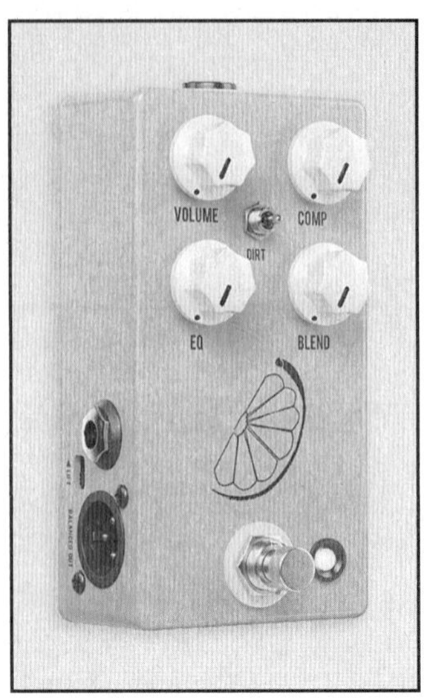

JHS Pedals Pulp 'N' Peel

JHS Superbolt
Rivington Guitars

Jordan Boss Tone Fuzz

MODEL YEAR	FEATURES	LOW	HIGH
Emperor			
2007-2022		$110	$175
Feedback Looper			
2007-2022		$100	$130
Haunting Mids			
2007-2024		$80	$125
HoneyComb			
2007-2022		$110	$200
Lime AID			
2007-2022		$130	$250
Morning Glory			
2007-2024		$130	$250
Prestige			
2007-2024		$60	$100
Pulp 'N' Peel			
2007-2023		$130	$200
Spring Tank Reverb			
2007-2023		$90	$130
SuperBolt			
2007-2023		$100	$150

Jimi Hendrix

See the listing under Dunlop.

John Hornby Skewes & Co.

Mid-1960s-present. Large English distributor of musical products, which has also self-branded products from others, over the years. The early Zonk Machines, Shatterbox and pre-amp boosts were designed and built by engineer Charlie Ramskirr of Wilsic Electronics, until his death in '68. Later effects were brought in from manufacturers in Italy and East Asia.

MODEL YEAR	FEATURES	LOW	HIGH
Bass Boost BB1			
1966-1968. Pre-amp.			
1966-1968		$1,000	$1,375
Fuzz FZIII			
1970s. Fuzz pedal, 2 control knobs, 1 footswitch.			
1970s		$225	$400
Phaser PZ111			
1970s. Phaser pedal made in Italy, 2 control knobs, 1 footswitch.			
1970s		$225	$400
Selectatone TB2			
1966-1968. Pre-amp combining treble and bass boost.			
1966-1968		$1,000	$1,375
Treble Boost TB1			
1966-1968. Pre-amp.			
1966-1968		$1,000	$1,375
Zonk Machine I			
1965-1968. Fuzz pedal, gray-blue housing, 2 control knobs, 1 footswitch, 3 germanium transistors.			
1965-1968		$3,000	$4,000
Zonk Machine II			
1966-1968. Fuzz pedal, gray-blue housing, 2 control knobs, 1 footswitch, 3 silicon transistors.			
1966-1968		$2,500	$3,500
Zonk Machine Reissue			
2000s. Reissued by JMI starting in 2013, reissues also made by the British Pedal Company, 2 control knobs, 1 footswitch.			
2000s		$150	$200
Zonk Shatterbox			
1966-1968. Combined the Zonk Machine II fuzz circuit with the Treble Boost, 2 control knobs, gold housing, 2 foot switches.			
1966-1968		$3,000	$4,000
Zonk Shatterbox Reissue			
2000s. Reissues made by the British Pedal Company, gold housing, 2 foot switches.			
2000s		$150	$200
Zoom Spring Reverb Unit			
1967-1968		$550	$750

Johnson

Mid-1990s-present. Budget line of effects imported by Music Link, Brisbane, California. Johnson also offers guitars, amps, mandolins and basses.

Johnson Amplification

Modeling amps and effects designed by John Johnson, of Sandy, Utah, starting in 1997. The company is part of Harman International. In '02, they quit building amps, but continued the effects line.

Jordan

1966-early 1970s. Jordan Electronics - originally of Alhambra, California, later in Pasadena - built a range of electronics, including, starting around 1966, solid state guitar amps and effects. Sho-Bud of Nashville, Tennessee, licensed the Boss Tone and sold it as the Sho-Sound Boss Tone. Mahoney later reissued the Boss Tone as the Buzz Tone.

MODEL YEAR	FEATURES	LOW	HIGH
Boss Tone Fuzz			
1967-1970s. Tiny effect plugged into guitar's output jack, 2 control knobs, black plastic housing, extremely delicate wiring.			
1967-70s		$200	$350
Compressor J-700			
1967-1970s. Sustain and Level control knobs.			
1967-70s		$150	$300
Creator Volume Sustainer Model 600			
1967-1970s. Volume pedal and sustainer, side controls for Sustain and Tone.			
1967-70s		$500	$600
Gig Wa-Wa Volume Pedal			
1967-1970s.			
1967-70s		$150	$300
Phaser			
1967-1970s. Black case, yellow knobs.			
1967-70s	Black case	$150	$300
Vibrasonic			
1967-70s		$150	$300

Kay

1931-present. Kay was once one of the largest instrument producers in the world, offering just about everything for the guitarist, including effects.

MODEL YEAR	FEATURES	LOW	HIGH
Effects Pedals			
1970s. Various models, includes the Graphic Equalizer GE-5000 and Rhythme.			
1970s		$55	$75

EFFECTS

MODEL YEAR	FEATURES	LOW	HIGH
Fuzz Tone F-1			
1970s		$300	$700
Tremolo T-1			
1970s		$200	$300
Wah			
1970s		$100	$200

Kazan

1970s-1980s. Effects made in Kazan, Tatarstan Republic.

Booster

1970s. Fuzz pedal with foot control.

1970s		$300	$350

Kvaker

1970s. Wah pedal.

1970s		$300	$350

Keeley

2001-present. Line of guitar effects designed and built by Robert Keeley in Edmond, Oklahoma. Keeley Electronics also offers a range of custom modifications for other effects.

Java Boost			
2001-2022		$225	$300
Katana			
2001-2024		$150	$250

Keio

1970s. Keio Electronic Laboratories of Japan would later become Korg in the '80s.

Synthesizer Traveler F-1

1970s. Multi-effects unit with foot pedal.

1970s		$500	$1,000

Kendrick

1989-2024. Texas' Kendrick offers guitars, amps, and effects.

ABC Amp Switcher			
1990s		$130	$170
Buffalo Pfuz			
1990s		$200	$250

Model 1000 Reverb

1991-2003. Vintage style, 3 knobs: dwell, tone, and mix, brown cover, wheat grille with art deco shape.

1991-2003		$800	$1,000

Powerglide Attenuator

1998-2024. Allows you to cut the output before it hits the amp's speakers, rack mount, metal cab.

1998-2024		$200	$250

Kent

1961-1969. This import guitar brand also offered a few effects.

Kern Engineering

Located in Kenosha, Wisconsin, Kern offers pre-amps and wah pedals.

Kinsman

2012-present. Guitar effects pedals built in China and distributed by John Hornby Skewes & Co. Ltd.

Klon

Originally located in Brookline, then in Cambridge, Massachusetts, Klon was started by Bill Finnegan, in 1994, after working with two circuit design partners on the Centaur Professional Overdrive.

Centaur

2010. Smaller overdrive unit with burnished silver case.

2010		$850	$1,500

Centaur Professional Overdrive

1994-2009. Standard size with gold case. A smaller unit was introduced in '10.

1994-1997	Gold, horse logo	$6,000	$8,000
1997-2008	Gold, no horse logo	$4,000	$5,000
1995-2009	Silver, no horse logo	$3,000	$4,000

KTR

2010. Smaller overdrive unit with red case.

2010		$500	$700

KMD (Kaman)

1986-ca. 1990. Distributed by Kaman (Ovation, Hamer, etc.) in the late '80s.

Effects Pedals			
1986-1990	Analog Delay	$120	$150
1986-1990	Overdrive	$80	$125
1987-1990	Distortion	$100	$135
1987-1990	Flanger	$80	$120
1987-1990	Phaser	$80	$120
1987-1990	Stereo Chorus	$80	$120

Knight

1967-1972. Effects kits sold via mail-order by Chicago's Allied Radio Company.

Fuzz Box KG-389			
1967-1972		$300	$400

Korg

Formed from Keio Electronic Laboratories of Japan. Most Korg effects listed below are modular effects. The PME-40X Professional Modular Effects System holds four of them and allows the user to select several variations of effects. The modular effects cannot be used alone. This system was sold for a few years starting in 1983. Korg currently offers the Toneworks line of effects.

PEQ-1 Parametric EQ

1980s. Dial-in equalizer with gain knob, band-width knob, and frequency knob, black case.

1980s		$60	$160
PME-40X Modular Effects			
1983-1986	KAD-301 Delay	$90	$100
1983-1986	KCH-301 Chorus	$40	$50
1983-1986	KCO-101 Compressor	$70	$80
1983-1986	KDI-101 Distortion	$70	$80
1983-1986	KDL-301 Echo	$135	$150
1983-1986	KFL-401 Flanger	$60	$70
1983-1986	KGE-201 Graphic EQ	$40	$50
1983-1986	KNG-101 Noise Gate	$40	$50
1983-1986	KOD-101 Over Drive	$70	$80
1983-1986	KPH-401 Phaser	$70	$80
1983-1986	OCT-1 Octaver	$100	$125

Keeley Hooke Reverb

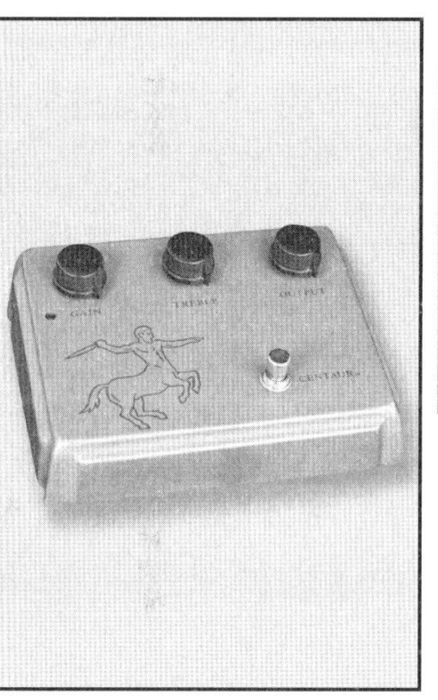
1997 Klon Centaur Overdrive
Folkway Music

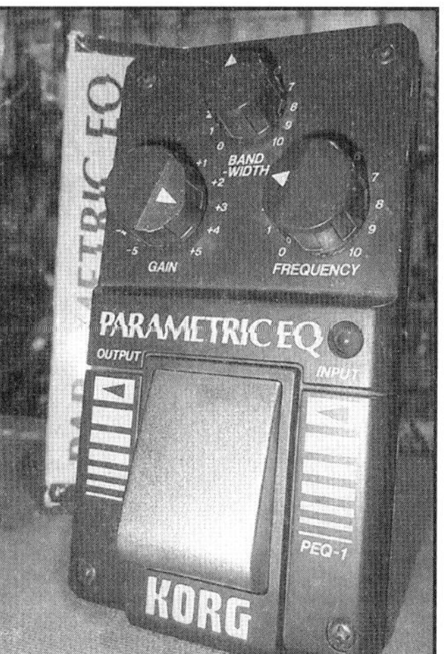

1989 Korg PEQ-1 Parametric EQ
Rivington Guitars

EFFECTS

KR Musical Mega Vibe
Keith Myers

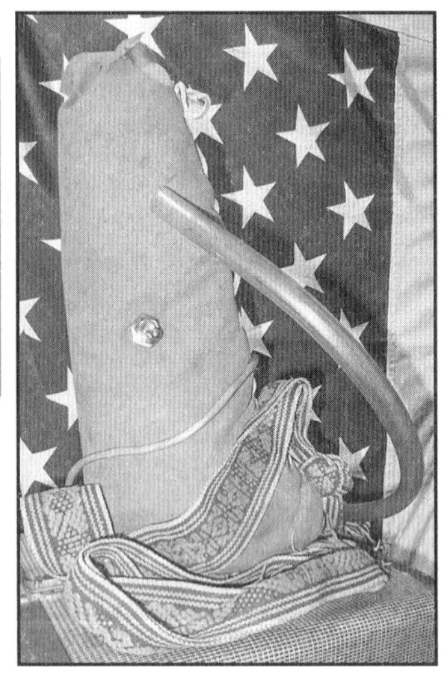

1969 Kustom The Bag
Rivington Guitars

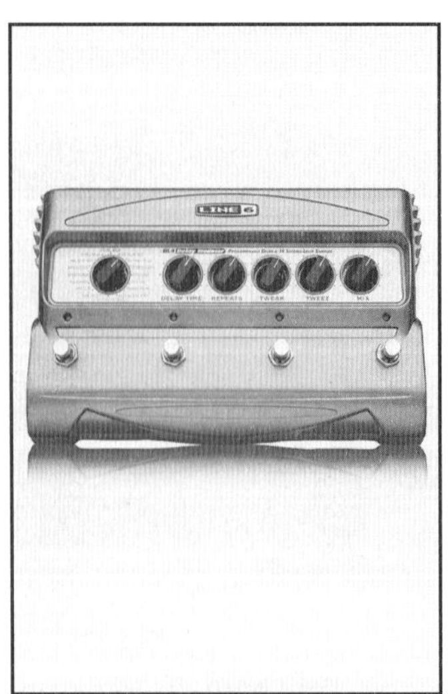

Line 6 DL-4 Delay Modeler

MODEL YEAR	FEATURES	LOW	HIGH

PME-40X Professional Modular Effects System

1983-ca.1986. Board holds up to 4 of the modular effects listed below.

1983-1986		$150	$200

SSD 3000 Digital Delay

1980s. Rack mount, SDD-3000 logo on top of unit.

1980s		$500	$650

KR Musical Products

2003-2022. Kevin Randall presently builds his vintage style, guitar effects in White Marsh, Virginia.

Krank

1996-2013, 2015-2020. Tempe, Arizona, amp builder Tony Krank also built effects pedals.

Kustom

1965-present. Founded in '64 by Charles "Bud" Ross in his Chanute, Kansas, garage to build amps for his band. While Fender, Rickenbacker, and others tried and failed with solid-state amps, Ross' Kustom creations were a big hit. Kustom likely only ever made one foray into effects, producing The Bag, designed by Doug Forbes.

The Bag

1969-1971. Pioneering "talk box" effect housed in a "bota" wineskin-type bag worn over the player's shoulder. Covered in multiple styles of mod fabrics.

1969-1971		$2,000	$2,500

Lafayette Radio Electronics

1960s-1970s. Effects that claimed to be made in the U.S. but were most likely built by Shin-ei of Japan.

Deluxe AC Super Fuzz

1969-1970s. Made by Shin-ei, AC power.

1969-70s		$400	$500

Echo Verb/Echo Verb II

1970s. Solid-state echo/reverb. Likely made by Shin-ei.

1970s	2 instrument inputs	$200	$350
1970s	Instrument & mic inputs	$100	$300

Fuzz Sound

1970s. Likely made by Shin-ei.

1970s		$200	$350

Roto-Vibe

1969-1970s. Rotating-speaker simulator, with control pedal. Variant of Uni-Vibe made by Shin-ei.

1969-70s		$600	$850

Super Fuzz

1969-1970s. Made by Shin-ei.

1969-70s		$400	$500
1969-70s	Battery power	$400	$500

Laney

1968-present. Founded by Lyndon Laney and Bob Thomas in Birmingham, U.K., this amp builder also offered a reverb unit.

Reverberation Unit

1968-1969. Sleek reverb unit, plexi-style front panel, black vinyl cover.

1968-1969		$300	$400

Larry Alan Guitars

2003-present. Luthier Larry Alan Daft offers effects pedals built in Lansing, Michigan. He also builds guitars and basses.

Lectronx

1990s. Founded by Edwin C. Clothier in North Hollywood, California.

Shark

1990s. Stereo filter pedal designed to use with 2 amps.

1990s		$200	$350

Lehle

2001-present. Loop switches from Burkhard Georg Lehle of Lehle Gitarrentechnik in Voerde, Germany.

D.Loop Signal Router

2004		$150	$180

Lenahan

Amp builder James Lenahan also offered a line of guitar pedals, built in Fort Smith, Arkansas.

Leslie

1966-1970s. In 1941, Donald Leslie began building speakers for Hammond organs to emulate pipe-organ sounds. Using a rotating baffle in front of a stationary speaker, he replicated the tremolo sound. He sold his company to CBS in 1965, and Fender launched its Vibratone based on Leslie technology in 1967. Leslie also offered its Model 16 and 18 speakers for guitarists. The Leslie 16/18 were also sold by Selmer as the Selmer-Leslie.

Model 16

1966-1970s. Rotating-speaker emulator, single fixed 4-ohm 10-inch speaker fronted by a rotating drum. Designed to be powered by an external amp. Black covering, cast Leslie badge in upper left corner.

1966-70s		$1,000	$1,500

Model 18

1966-1970s. Rotating-speaker emulator, single fixed 4-ohm 12-inch speaker fronted by a rotating drum. Designed to be powered by an external amp. Black covering, cast Leslie badge in upper left corner.

1966-70s		$850	$1,000

Line 6

1996-present. Founded by Marcus Ryle and Michel Doidic. Purchased by Yamaha in 2014. They also produce amps and guitars. All prices include Line 6 power pack if applicable.

AM-4 Amp Modeler

1996-2002. Red case.

1996-2002		$70	$120

MODEL YEAR	FEATURES	LOW	HIGH

DL-4 Delay Modeler

1999-present. Green case.

1999-2024		$95	$175

DM-4 Distortion Modeler

1999-2018. Yellow case.

1999-2018		$90	$165

FM-4 Filter Modeler

2001-2018. Purple case.

2001-2018		$170	$270

MM-4 Modulation Modeler

1999-2018. Aqua blue case.

1999-2018		$100	$200

POD 2.0

2001-2014. Updated version of the original Amp Modeler.

2001-2014		$60	$120

Little Lanilei

1997-present. Effects made by Mahaffay Amplifiers (formerly Songworks Systems & Products) of Aliso Viejo, California. They also build amps.

Lizard Leg Effects

2007-2016. Steve Miller built a line of effects pedals in Gonzales, Louisiana.

Lock & Rock

Line of floor pedal guitar and microphone effects produced by Brannon Electronics, Inc. of Houston, Texas starting in 2003.

Loco Box

1982-1983. Loco Box was a brand of effects distributed by Aria Pro II for a short period starting in '82. It appears that Aria switched the effects to their own brand in '83.

Effects

1982-1983	Analog Delay AD-01	$100	$250
1982-1983	Chorus CH-01	$100	$250
1982-1983	Compressor CM-01	$100	$250
1982-1983	Distortion DS-01	$100	$250
1982-1983	Flanger FL-01	$100	$250
1982-1983	Graphic Equalizer GE-01	$100	$250
1982-1983	Overdrive OD-01	$100	$250
1982-1983	Phaser PH-01	$100	$250

Lotus Pedal Designs

2009-ca. 2018. Guitar effects pedals built in Duluth, Minnesota by Sean Erspamer.

Loud Button Electronics

Founded in 2009 by Shawn Schoenberger in Minneapolis, Minnesota.

Morphine Dream

2010s. Analog phase shifter and distortion, based on Roland AP-7 Jet Phaser.

2010s		$300	$450

Lovepedal

2000-present. Sean Michael builds his preamps and guitar stomp boxes in Detroit, Michigan.

Lovetone

Hand-made analog effects from Oxfordshire, U.K. starting in 1995.

Ludwig

For some reason, drum builder Ludwig offered a guitar synth in the 1970s.

Phase II Guitar Synth

1970-1971. Oversized synth, mushroom-shaped footswitches, vertical silver case.

1970-1971		$1,500	$2,000

M.B. Electronics

Made in San Francisco, California.

Ultra-Metal UM-10

1985. Distortion.

1985		$100	$125

Mad Professor

2002-present. Guitar effects pedals built by Bjorn Juhl and Jukka Monkkonen in Tampere, Finland. In '24 the company was sold to Mikko Karikko and Jusa Palve. They also build amps.

Maestro

1950s-1970s, 2001-2012, 2022-present. Maestro was a Gibson subsidiary; the name appeared on 1950s accordion amplifiers. The first Maestro effects were the Echoplex tape echo and the FZ-1 Fuzz-Tone, introduced in the early-'60s. Maestro products were manufactured by various entities such as Market Electronics, All-Test Devices, Lowrey and Moog Electronics. In the late-'60s and early-'70s, they unleashed a plethora of pedals; some were beautiful, others had great personality. The last Maestro effects were the Silver and Black MFZ series of the late-'70s. In 2001, Gibson revived the name for a line of effects, banjos and mandolins, adding guitars and amps in '09. By '12 the brand was no longer listed but was reintroduced on a line of Gibson effects in '22.

Bass Brassmaster BB-1

1971-ca.1974. Added brass to your bass.

1971-1974		$2,000	$2,500

Boomerang

Ca.1969-ca.1972. Wah pedal made by All-Test Devices.

1969-1972		$200	$400

Boomerang BG-2

1972-ca.1976. Wah pedal made by All-Test Devices.

1972-1976		$250	$350

Echoplex EM-1 Groupmaster

Ca.1970-ca.1977. Two input Echoplex, solidstate.

1970-1977	Without stand	$1,750	$3,000

Echoplex EP-1

1959-mid-1960s. Original model, smaller green box, tube-driven tape echo, separate controls for echo volume and instrument volume, made by Market Electronics. Though not labeled as such, it is often referred to as the EP-1 by collectors.

1959-60s	Earlier small box	$1,500	$2,500

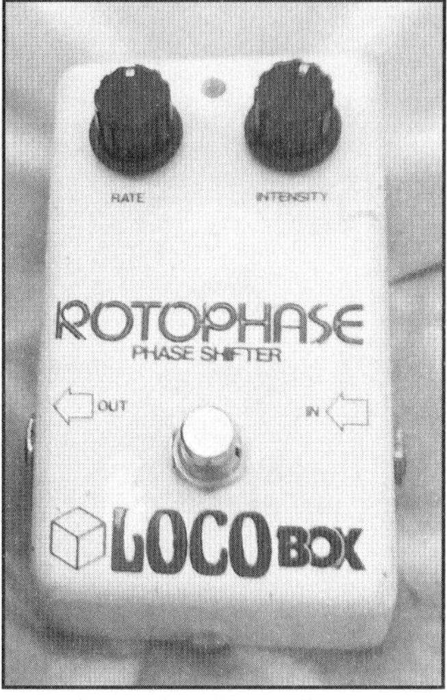

Loco Box Rotophase Phase Shifter

Jeff Jordan

Lovepedal Amp Eleven

1972 Maestro Bass Brassmaster BB-1

John Krylow

EFFECTS

Maestro Fuzz-Tone FZ-1B
Mike Lakis

1968 Maestro Octave Box
Rivington Guitars

1976 Maestro Phaser MP-1
Donald Kuntze

MODEL YEAR	FEATURES	LOW	HIGH

Echoplex EP-2

Mid-1960s-ca.1970. Larger gray or green box than original, tube-driven tape echo, single echo/instrument volume control, made by Market Electronics. Around '70, the EP-2 added a Sound-On-Sound feature. Limited-edition EP6T reissue made by Market in 1980s (see Market Electronics listing).

1960s Larger box $1,250 $2,000

Echoplex EP-3

Ca.1970-1977. Solidstate, made by Market Electronics, black box.

1970-1977 $950 $1,500

Echoplex EP-4 (IV)

1977-1978. Solidstate, the last version introduced by Maestro. See Market Electronics and Echoplex brands for later models.

1977-1978 $1,000 $1,500

Echoplex Groupmaster EM-1

1970s. Large, multi-channel echo unit.

1970s $1,500 $2,500

Echoplex Sireko ES-1

Ca.1971-mid-1970s. A budget solidstate version of the Echoplex, made by Market.

1971-1975 $350 $500

Envelope Modifier ME-1

1971-ca.1976. Tape reverse/string simulator, made by All-Test.

1971-1976 $200 $350

Filter Sample and Hold FSH-1

1975-ca.1976.

1975-1976 $775 $1,500

Full Range Boost FRB-1

1971-ca.1975. Frequency boost with fuzz, made by All-Test.

1971-1975 $250 $450

Fuzz MFZ-1

1976-1979. Made by Moog.

1976-1979 $350 $600

Fuzz Phazzer FP-1

1971-1974 $300 $600

Fuzztain MFZT-1

1976-1978. Fuzz, sustain, made by Moog.

1976-1978 $300 $600

Fuzz-Tone FZ-1

1962-1963. Brown housing, uses 2 AA batteries.

1962-1963 $500 $700

Fuzz-Tone FZ-1A

1965-1967, 2001-2009. Brown housing, uses 1 AA battery. Early model "Kalamazoo, Michigan" on front, later "Nashville, Tennessee".

1965-1967 Kalamazoo $400 $600
2001-2009 Nashville $250 $350

Fuzz-Tone FZ-1B

Late-1960s-early-1970s. Black housing, uses 9-volt battery.

1970s $400 $600

Mini-Phase Shifter MPS-2

1976. Volume, speed, slow and fast controls.

1976 $350 $500

Octave Box OB-1

1971-ca.1975. Made by All-Test Devices.

1971-1975 $300 $500

Parametric Filter MPF-1

1976-1978. Made by Moog.

1976-1978 $700 $1,000

Phase Shifter PS-1

1971-1975. With or without 3-button footswitch, made by Oberheim.

1971-1975 With footswitch $350 $800
1971-1975 Without footswitch $300 $700

Phase Shifter PS-1A

1976 $350 $800

Phase Shifter PS-1B

1970s $350 $800

Phaser MP-1

1976-1978. Made by Moog.

1976-1978 $300 $500

Repeat Pedal RP-1

1970s $300 $500

Rhythm King MRK-2

1971-ca.1974. Early drum machine.

1971-1974 $800 $1,000

Rhythm 'n Sound G-2

Ca.1969-1970s. Multi-effect unit.

1969-1975 $1,875 $2,500

Rhythm Queen MRQ-1

Early 1970s. Early rhythm machine.

1970s $300 $500

Ring Modulator RM-1

1971-1975 No control pedal $650 $1,500
1971-1975 With MP-1 pedal $750 $1,875

Rover Rotating Speaker

1971-ca.1973. Rotating Leslie effect that mounted on a large tripod.

1971-1973 RO-1 model $1,500 $2,000

Sound System for Woodwinds W-1

1960s-1970s. Designed for clarinet or saxophone input, gives a variety of synthesizer-type sounds with voices for various woodwinds, uses Barrel Joint and integrated microphone.

1960-1970s $750 $900

Stage Phaser MPP-1

1976-1978. Has slow, fast and variable settings, made by Moog.

1976-1978 $300 $500

Super Fuzz-Tone FZ-1S

1971-1975 $400 $750

Sustainer SS-2

1971-ca.1975. Made by All-Test Devices.

1971-1975 $300 $500

Theramin TH-1

1971-mid-1970s. Device with 2 antennae, made horror film sound effects. A reissue Theremin is available from Theremaniacs in Milwaukee, Wisconsin.

1971-1975 $1,500 $2,500

Wha-Wha/Volume WW-1

1970s. Wah-Wah Volume logo on end of pedal, green foot pad.

1971-1975 $300 $500

Magnatone

Ca.1937-1971, 2013-present. Magnatone built very competitive amps from '57 to '66. In the

MODEL YEAR	FEATURES	LOW	HIGH

early-'60s, they offered the RVB-1 Reverb Unit. The majority of Magnatone amps pre-'66 did not have on-board reverb.

Model RVB-1 Reverb Unit

1961-1966. Typical brown leatherette cover, square box-type cabinet. From '64-'66, battery operated, solidstate version of RVB-1, low flat cabinet.

1961-1963		$275	$400
1964-1966	Battery & solidstate	$200	$300

Mahoney

2000s. Reissues of the Jordan Boss Tone.

Buzz Tone

2000s. Similar black-plastic housing to the original Boss Tone. 2 Control knobs.

2000s		$75	$100

Manny's

Effects issued by New York-based retailer Manny's Music.

Fuzz

1960s. Same unit as the Orpheum Fuzz and Clark Fuzz.

1960s		$950	$1,250

Market Electronics

Market, from Ohio, made the famous Echoplex line. See Echoplex and Maestro sections for earlier models.

Echoplex EP-6T

1980-ca.1988. Limited-edition all-tube reissue of the Echoplex EP-2.

1980-1988		$550	$650

Marshall

1962-present. The fuzz and wah boom of the '60s led many established manufacturers, like Marshall, to introduce variations on the theme. They got back into stomp boxes in '89 with the Gov'nor distortion, and currently produce several distortion/overdrive units.

Blues Breaker

1992-1999, 2024-present. Replaced by Blues Breaker II in 2000-'23. Back to Blues Breaker in '24.

1992-1999		$300	$400

Blues Breaker II BB-2

2000-2023. Overdrive pedal, 4 knobs.

2000-2023		$50	$100

Drive Master

1992-1999, 2024-present. Overdrive pedal, 5 knobs. Reissued '24.

1992-1999		$150	$300

Guv'nor

1989-1991, 2024-present. Distortion, Guv'nor Plus introduced in '99. Reissued '24.

1989-1991		$200	$300

Jackhammer JH-1

1999-2023. Distortion pedal.

1999-2023		$50	$100

Power Brake PB-100

1993-1995. Speaker attenuator for tube amps.

1993-1995		$350	$450

MODEL YEAR	FEATURES	LOW	HIGH

Shred Master

1992-1999, 2024-present. High-gain pedal, 5 knobs. Reissued '24.

1992-1999		$200	$350

Supa Fuzz

Late-1960s. Made by Sola Sound (Colorsound).

1967		$1,250	$1,500

Supa Wah

Late-1960s. Made by Sola Sound (Colorsound).

1969		$400	$800

Vibratrem VT-1

1999-2023. Vibrato and tremolo.

1999-2023		$50	$100

Matchless

1989-1999, 2001-present. Matchless amplifiers offered effects in the '90s.

AB Box

1990s. Split box for C-30 series amps (DC 30, SC 30, etc.).

1990s		$400	$600

Coolbox

1997-1999. Tube preamp pedal.

1997-1999		$400	$600

Dirtbox

1997-1999. Tube-driven overdrive pedal.

1997-1999		$950	$1,200

Echo Box

1997-1999. Limited production because of malfunctioning design which included cassette tape. Black case, 8 white chicken head control knobs.

1990s	Original unreliable	$500	$800
1990s	Updated reliable	$800	$1,000

Hotbox/Hotbox II

1995-1999. Higher-end tube-driven preamp pedal.

1995-1999		$400	$600

Mix Box

1997-1999. 4-input tube mixer pedal.

1997-1999		$400	$600

Reverb RV-1

1993-1999. 5 controls, tube-driven spring-reverb tank, various colors.

1993-1999		$1,750	$2,250

Reverb RV-2

2000s. 5 controls, tube-driven spring-reverb tank, various colors.

2000s		$1,250	$1,500

Split Box

1990s. Tube AB box.

1997	Standard AB	$400	$600

Tremolo/Vibrato TV-1

1993-1995. Tube unit.

1993-1995		$400	$600

Maxon

1970s-2024. Maxon was the original manufacturer of the Ibanez line of effects. Until '24, they offered retro '70s era stomp boxes distributed in the U.S. by Godlyke.

AD-9/AD-9 Pro Analog Delay

2001-2021. Purple case.

2001-2021		$150	$250

Maestro Rover RO-1
Kyle Stevens.

Maestro Wha-Wha/ Volume WW-1
Robbie Keene

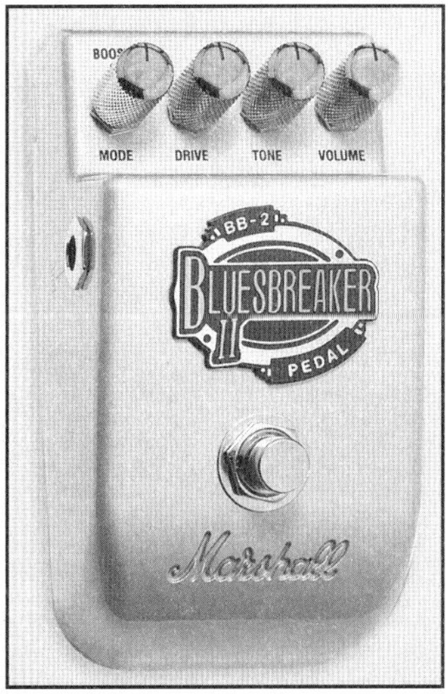

Marshall Blues Breaker II BB-2

EFFECTS

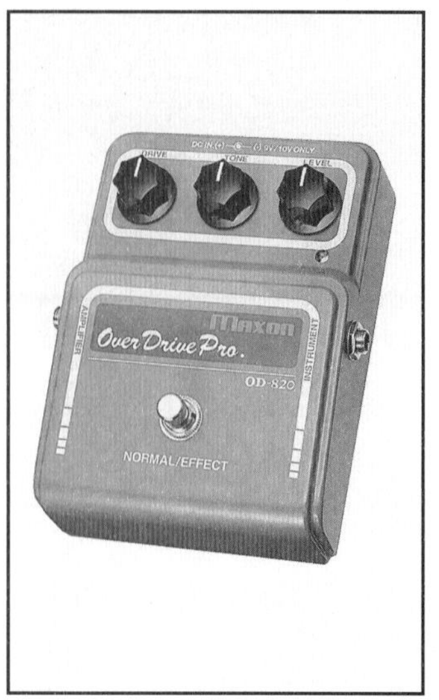

Maxon OD-820 Over Drive Pro

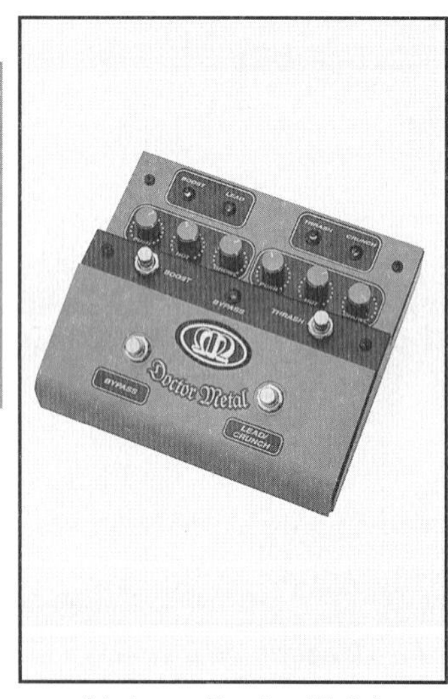

Meteoro Doctor Metal

Mica Wau Wau Fuzz
Marco Antonio Rebolledo Ferrari.

MODEL YEAR	FEATURES	LOW	HIGH

CS-550 Stereo Chorus
2001-2017. Light blue case.

2001-2017		$115	$175

DS-830 Distortion Master
2001-2021. Light blue-green case.

2001-2021		$115	$175

OD-820 Over Drive Pro
2001-2021. Green case.

2001-2021		$150	$200

PH-350 Rotary Phaser
2001-2021. Orange case.

2001-2021		$400	$750

McQuackin FX Co.

Rich McCracken II began building his analog guitar effects in 1997, first in Nashville, Tennessee, then Augusta, Georgia.

Mesa-Boogie

1971-present. Mesa added pre-amps in the mid '90s, then pedals in 2013. Mesa was acquired by Gibson in early 2021.

V-Twin Bottle Rocket

2000-2004		$100	$180

V-Twin Preamp Pedal
Dec. 1993-2004. Serial number series: V011-. 100 watts, all tube preamp, floor unit, silver case.

1993-1999		$250	$425
2000-2004	Updated tone adj	$250	$425

Metal Pedals

2006-present. Brothers Dave and Mike Pantaleone build their guitar effects in New Jersey.

Meteoro

1986-present. Guitar effects built in Brazil. They also build guitar and bass amps.

MG

Guitar effects built by Marcelo Giangrande, starting in 2004, in São Paulo, Brazil. He also built amps.

Mica

Early 1970s. These Japanese-made effects were also sold under the Bruno and Marlboro brand names.

Tone Fuzz
1970s. Silver case, black knobs.

1970s		$350	$550

Tone Surf Wah Siren
1970s. Wah pedal.

1970s		$250	$350

Wailer Fuzz

1970		$250	$350

Wau Wau Fuzz
1970s. Wau Wau Fuzz logo on end of pedal, black.

1970s		$250	$350

Mooer

2012-present. A line of guitar pedals built by Mooer Audio in China.

MODEL YEAR	FEATURES	LOW	HIGH

Moog/Moogerfooger

1964-present. Robert Moog, of synth fame, introduced his line of Moogerfooger analog effects in 1998. They also offer guitars.

Misc. Effects
2004-present.

2004-2015	MF-105 MuRF	$750	$1,500
2004-2024	Theremin	$400	$700

Moonrock

Fuzz/distortion unit built by Glenn Wyllie and distributed by Tonefrenzy starting in 2002.

Morley

Late-1960s-present. Founded by brothers Raymond and Marvin Lubow, Morley has produced a wide variety of pedals and effects over the years, changing with the trends. In '89, the brothers sold the company to Accutronics (later changed to Sound Enhancements, Inc.) of Cary, Illinois.

ABY Switch Box
1981-ca.1985. Box no pedal.

1981-1985		$40	$80

Auto Wah PWA
1976-ca.1985.

1976-1985		$40	$80

Bad Horsie Steve Vai Signature Wah
1997-present.

1997-2024		$70	$85

Black Gold Stereo Volume BSV

1985-1991		$40	$80

Black Gold Stereo Volume Pan BSP

1985-1989		$40	$80

Black Gold Volume BVO

1985-1991		$40	$80

Black Gold Wah BWA

1985-1991		$40	$80

Black Gold Wah Volume BWV

1985-1989		$40	$80

Chrystal Chorus CCB
1996-1999. Stereo output.

1996-1999		$40	$80

Deluxe Distortion DDB
1981-1991. Box, no pedal.

1981-1991		$40	$80

Deluxe Flanger FLB
1981-1991. Box, no pedal.

1981-1991		$40	$80

Deluxe Phaser DFB
1981-1991. Box, no pedal.

1981-1991		$40	$80

Distortion One DIB
1981-1991. Box, no pedal.

1981-1991		$40	$80

Echo Chorus Vibrato ECV
1982-ca.1985.

1982-1985		$200	$400

Echo/Volume EVO-1
1974-ca.1982.

1974-1982		$200	$400

EFFECTS

MODEL YEAR	FEATURES	LOW	HIGH
Electro-Pik-a-Wah PKW			
1979-ca.1982.			
1979-1982		$40	$80
Emerald Echo EEB			
1996-1999. 300 ms delay.			
1996-1999	Green case	$40	$80
Jerry Donahue JD-10			
1995-1997. Multi-effect, distortion, overdrive.			
1995-1997		$100	$150
Power Wah PWA/PWA II			
1992-2006. Wah with boost. Changed to II in '98.			
1992-2006		$40	$80
Power Wah PWO			
Ca.1969-1984, 2006-present. Reissued in '06 as 20/20 Power Wah.			
1969-1984		$60	$150
Power Wah/Boost PWB			
Introduced in 1973, doubles as a volume pedal.			
1970s		$100	$150
Power Wah/Fuzz PWF			
Ca.1969-ca.1984.			
1969-1984		$300	$450
Pro Compressor PCB			
1978-1984. Stomp box without pedal, compress-sustain knob and output knob.			
1978-1984		$40	$80
Pro Fla nger PFL			
1978-1984		$200	$300
Pro Phaser PFA			
1975-1984		$200	$300
Rotating Sound Power Wah Model RWV			
1971-1982		$200	$300
Select-Effect Pedal SEL			
1980s. Controls up to 5 other pedals.			
1980s		$100	$150
Slimline Echo Volume 600			
1983-1985. 20 to 600 ms delay.			
1983-1985		$100	$150
Slimline Echo Volume SLEV			
1983-1985. 20 to 300 ms delay.			
1983-1985		$100	$150
Slimline Variable Taper Stereo Volume SLSV			
1982-1986		$100	$150
Slimline Variable Taper Volume SLVO			
1982-1986		$100	$150
Slimline Wah SLWA			
1982-1986. Battery operated electro-optical.			
1982-1986		$100	$150
Slimline Wah Volume SLWV			
1982-ca.1986. Battery operated electro-optical.			
1982-1986		$100	$150
Stereo Chorus Flanger CFL			
1980-ca. 1986. Box, no pedal.			
1980-1986		$100	$150
Stereo Chorus Vibrato SCV			
1980-1991. Box, no pedal.			
1980-1991		$100	$150
Stereo Volume CSV			
1980-ca. 1986. Box, no pedal.			
1980-1986		$100	$150
Volume Compressor VCO			
1979-1984		$100	$150
Volume Phaser PFV			
1977-1984 With volume pedal			
1977-1984		$150	$200
Volume VOL			
1975-ca.1984.			
1975-1979		$100	$150
1980-1984		$100	$150
Volume XVO			
1985-1988		$40	$80
Volume/Boost VBO			
1974-1984		$100	$150
Wah Volume CWV			
1987-1991. Box, no pedal.			
1987-1991		$100	$150
Wah Volume XWV			
1985-ca.1989.			
1985-1989		$100	$150
Wah/Volume WVO			
1977-ca.1984.			
1977-1984		$100	$150

Morpheus

Guitar effects pedals manufactured in Salt Lake City, Utah by the same builders of the Bolt brand amps.

Mosferatu

Line of guitar effects pedals built by Hermida Audio Technology.

Mosrite

Semie Moseley's Mosrite company dipped into effects in the 1960s.

MODEL YEAR	FEATURES	LOW	HIGH
Fuzzrite			
1960s-1970s, 1999. Silver housing as well as some painted housings, 2 front-mounted control knobs. Sanner reissued in '99.			
1960s-70s	Mosrite logo	$500	$1,000
1999	Reissue, Sanner logo	$125	$225

Mu-FX

See Beigel Sound Lab.

Multivox

New York-based Multivox offered a variety of effects in the 1970s and '80s.

MODEL YEAR	FEATURES	LOW	HIGH
Big Jam Effects			
Multivox offered the Big Jam line of effects from 1980 to ca. '83.			
1980-1983	Analog Echo/Reverb	$250	$350
1980-1983	Bi-Phase 2, Flanger, Jazz Flanger	$150	$200
1980-1983	Chorus	$115	$150
1980-1983	Compressor, Phaser, 6-Band EQ, Spit-Wah	$100	$130
1980-1983	Distortion	$175	$225
1980-1983	Octave Box	$100	$130
1981-1983	Noise Gate, Parametric EQ	$85	$110

Mooer Baby Water

Morley Bad Horsie Steve Vai

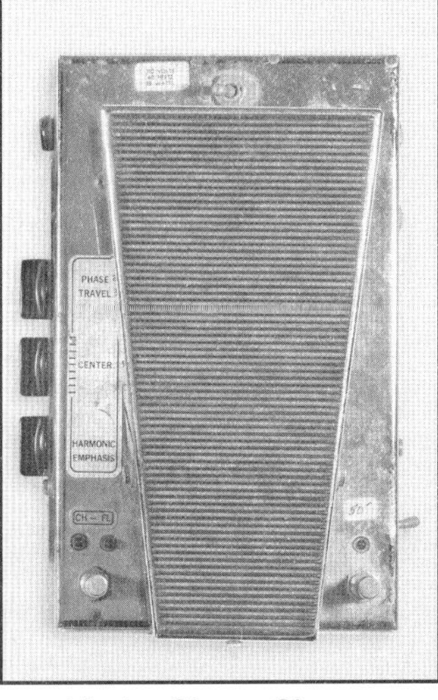
Morley Stereo Chorus Flanger CFL

1970s Multivox Full Rotor MX-2

Keith Myers

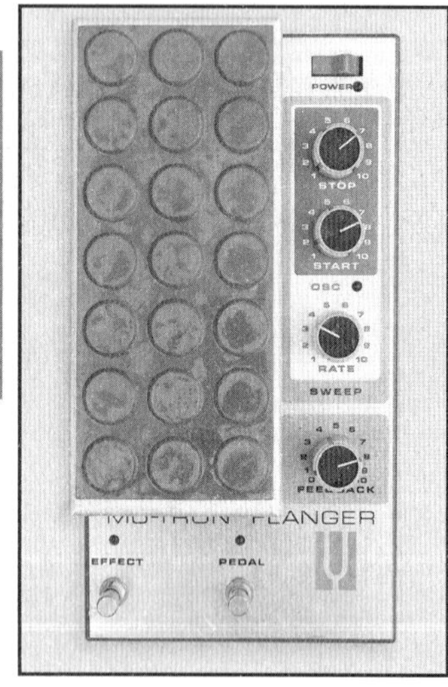

Mu-Tron Flanger

Marco Antonio Rebolledo Ferrari

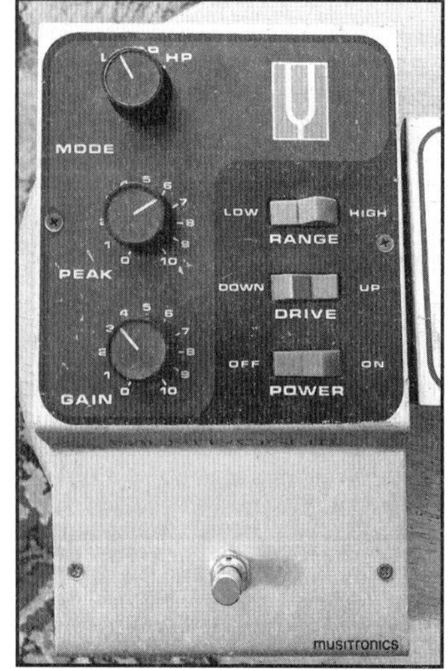

Mu-Tron III Envelope Filter

MODEL YEAR	FEATURES	LOW	HIGH
1981-1983	Space Driver, Delay	$150	$200
1982-1983	Volume Pedal	$75	$100

Full Rotor MX-2

1978-ca.1982. Leslie effect.

1978-1982		$450	$550

Little David LD-2

1970s. Rotary sound effector in mini Leslie-type case.

1970s	With pedal	$500	$650
1970s	Without pedal	$500	$650

Multi Echo MX-201

1970s. Tape echo unit, reverb.

1970s		$500	$650

Multi Echo MX-312

1970s. Tape echo unit, reverb.

1970s		$500	$650

Rhythm Ace FR6M

1970s. 27 basic rhythms.

1970s		$300	$400

Mu-Tron

1972-ca.1980. Made by Musitronics, founded by Mike Beigel and Aaron Newman in Rosemont, New Jersey, these rugged and unique-sounding effects were a high point of the '70s. The Mu-Tron III appeared in '72, and more products followed, about 10 in all. Musitronics also made the U.S. models of the Dan Armstrong effects. In '78 ARP synthesizers bought Musitronics and sold Mutron products to around '80. In '78, Musitronics also joined with Lol Creme and Kevin Godley of 10cc to attempt production of the Gizmotron, which quickly failed (see listing under Godley Crème). A reissue of the Mu-Tron III was made available in '95 by NYC Music Products and distributed by Matthews and Ryan Musical Products. As of 2013, Mike Beigel's Beigel Sound Lab has started making a hot-rodded Tru-Tron III.

Bi-Phase

1975-ca.1980. Add $50-$75 for Opti-Pot pedal.

1971-1980	Optical pedal option	$2,000	$3,000
1975-1980	2-button footswitch	$2,000	$3,000

C-100 OptiPot Control Pedal

1975-1980	Blue case	$600	$900

C-200 Volume-Wah

1970s		$500	$650

Flanger

1977-ca.1980.

1977-1980		$2,000	$2,500

III Envelope Filter

1972-ca.1980. Envelope Filter.

1972-1980		$1,250	$1,500

Micro V

Ca.1975-ca.1977. Envelope Filter.

1970s		$350	$750

Octave Divider

1977-ca.1980.

1977-1980		$500	$800

Phasor

Ca.1974-ca.1976. Two knobs.

1974-1976		$350	$400

Phasor II

1976-ca.1980. Three knobs.

1976-1980		$400	$450

Muza

Digital guitar effects made in China, starting in 2006, by Hong Kong's Medeli Electronics Co., Ltd. They also build digital drums.

MWFX

2008-present. Effects pedals built by Matt Warren in Somerset, England.

Glitch

2000s	Wooden case	$250	$400

MXR

1972-present. MXR Innovations launched its line of pedals in '72. Around '77, the Rochester, New York, company changed lettering on the effects from script to block and added new models. MXR survived into the mid-'80s. In '87, production was picked up by Jim Dunlop. Reissues of block logo boxes can be differentiated from originals as they have an LED above the switch and the finish is slightly rough; the originals are smooth.

Six Band EQ

1975-1982. Equalizer.

1975-1979		$150	$200
1980-1982		$150	$200

Six Band EQ M109 (Reissue)

1987-present. Reissued by Jim Dunlop.

1987-2024		$40	$50

Ten Band EQ M108

1975-1981, 2004-present. Graphic equalizer, with AC power cord.

1975-1981		$100	$150

Analog Delay

1975-1981. Green case, power cord.

1975-1979	Earlier 2-jack model	$350	$450
1980-1981	Later 3-jack model	$200	$300

Blue Box

1972-ca.1978. Octave pedal, M-103.

1970s	Earlier script logo	$250	$350
1970s	Later block logo	$225	$325

Blue Box M103 (Reissue)

1995-present. Reissued by Jim Dunlop, blue case. Produces 1 octave above or 2 octaves below.

1995-2024		$50	$100

Carbon Copy M169

1987-present. Analog delay. 3 Control knobs. 1 Toggle switch. Green housing.

1987-2024		$75	$250

Commande Effects

1981-1983. The Commande series featured plastic housings and electronic switching.

1981-1983	Overdrive	$60	$90
1981-1983	Phaser	$160	$250
1981-1983	Preamp	$60	$90

MODEL YEAR	FEATURES	LOW	HIGH
1981-1983	Stereo Chorus	$100	$150
1981-1983	Sustain	$100	$150
1981-1983	Time Delay	$120	$200
1982-1983	Stereo Flanger	$120	$200

Distortion +

1972-1982.

1970s	Earlier script logo	$250	$300
1970s	Later block logo	$150	$350
1980s	Block logo	$85	$125

Distortion + (Series 2000)

1983-1985		$130	$175

Distortion + M104 (Reissue)

1987-present. Reissued by Jim Dunlop, yellow case.

1987-1990		$65	$85
1991-2024		$55	$75

Distortion II

1981-1983	With AC power cord	$175	$350

Distortion III M115

1987-present. 3 Control knobs. Red housing.

1987-2024		$50	$65

Double Shot Distortion M151

2003-2005. 2 channels.

2003-2005		$55	$90

Dyna Comp

1972-1982. Compressor.

1970s	Block logo, battery	$125	$250
1970s	Script logo, battery	$250	$300
1980s	Block logo, battery	$85	$125

Dyna Comp (Series 2000)

1982-1985		$110	$130

Dyna Comp M102 (Reissue)

1987-present. Reissued by Jim Dunlop, red case.

1987-2024		$55	$70

Envelope Filter

1976-1983		$250	$300

Flanger

1976-1983, 1997-present. Analog, reissued by Dunlop in '97.

1976-1979	AC power cord, 2 inputs	$250	$350
1980-1983	AC power cord	$200	$375
1997-2024	M-117R reissue	$65	$85

Flanger/Doubler

1979	Rack mount	$500	$650

Fullbore Metal M116

1987-present. 6 Control knobs. Bare metal housing.

1987-2024		$55	$100

Limiter

1980-1982. AC, 4 knobs.

1980-1982	AC power cord	$225	$300

Loop Selector

1980-1982. A/B switch for 2 effects loops.

1980-1982		$85	$115

Micro Amp

1978-1983, 1995-present. Variable booster, creme case, reissued in '95.

1978-1983		$150	$200
1995-2024	M-133 reissue	$50	$65

Micro Chorus

1980-1983. Yellow case.

1980-1983		$150	$300

MODEL YEAR	FEATURES	LOW	HIGH

Micro Flanger

1981-1982		$175	$300

Noise Gate Line Driver

1974-1983.

1970s	Script logo	$85	$165
1980s	Block logo	$85	$125

Omni

1980s. Rack unit with floor controller, compressor, 3-band EQ, distortion, delay, chorus/flanger.

1980s		$350	$500

Phase 45

Ca.1976-1982. Battery, earlier script logo, later block.

1970s	Script logo	$250	$350
1980s	Block logo	$175	$225

Phase 90

1972-1982.

1970s	Earlier script logo	$350	$450
1970s	Later block logo	$250	$350
1980s	Block logo	$150	$200

Phase 90 M101 (Reissue)

1987-present. Reissued by Jim Dunlop, orange case.

1987-1989	Block logo	$100	$150
1990-2024	Block or script logo	$65	$85

Phase 100

1974-1982.

1970s	Earlier script logo	$300	$400
1970s	Later block logo, battery	$200	$300

Phaser (Series 2000)

1982-1985. Series 2000 introduced cost cutting die-cast cases.

1982-1985		$65	$85

Pitch Transposer

1980s		$600	$900

Power Converter

1980s		$55	$75

Smart Gate M135

2002-present. Noise-gate, single control, battery powered, gray case.

2002-2024		$65	$85

Stereo Chorus

1978-1985. With AC power cord.

1978-1979		$200	$350
1980-1985		$200	$250

Stereo Chorus (Series 2000)

1983-1985.

1983-1985		$65	$85

Stereo Flanger (Series 2000)

1983-1985.

1983-1985		$65	$85

Super Comp M132

2002-present. 3 knobs, black case.

2002-2024		$45	$60

Wylde Overdrive ZW44

2000s. Zakk Wylde signature pedal.

2000s		$75	$100

Nobels

Early 1990s-present. Effects pedals from Nobels Electronics of Hamburg, Germany. They also make amps.

1979 MXR Analog Delay
Keith Myers

MXR Fullbore Metal M116
Keith Myers

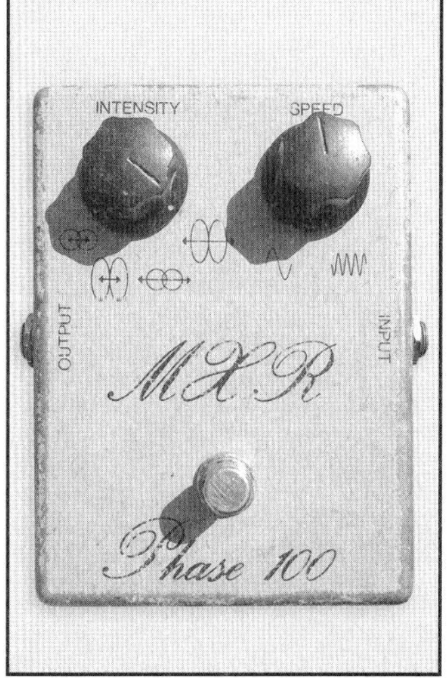

MXR Phase 100
Marco Antonio Rebolledo Ferrari

EFFECTS

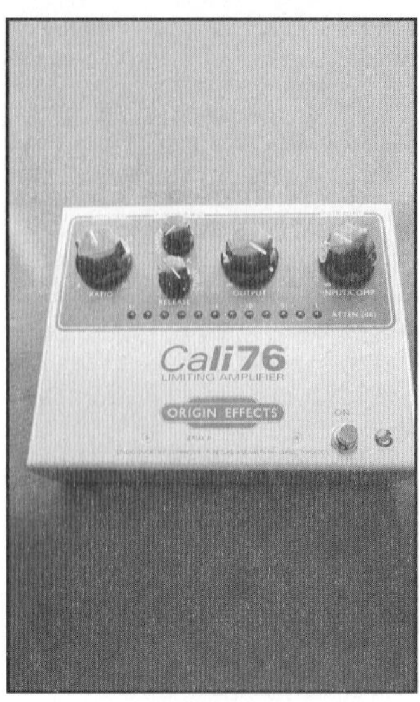

Origin Effects Cali 76

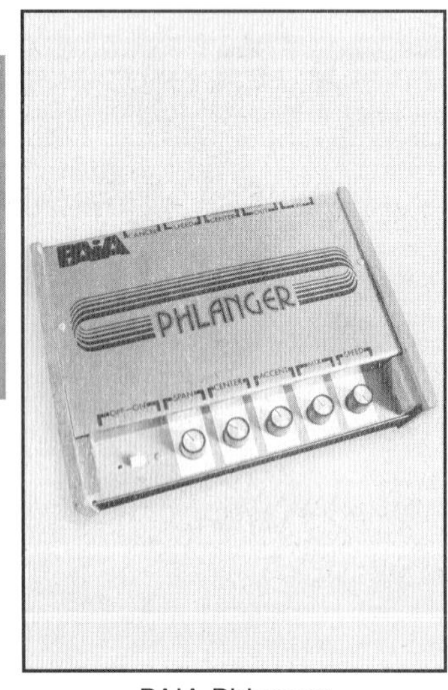

PAIA Phlanger
Jim Schreck

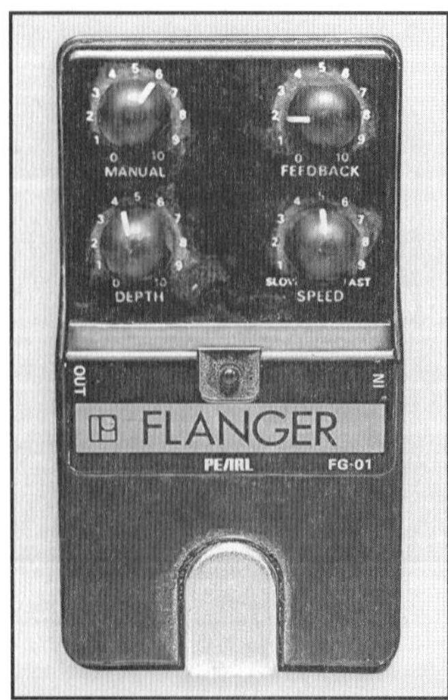

Pearl Flanger FG-01

MODEL YEAR	FEATURES	LOW	HIGH

ODR-1 Natural Overdrive

1990s-present. Classic overdrive, green case.

1990s	Early original version	$650	$1,000
1997-2024		$75	$150

TR-X Vintage Tremolo

1997-2017. Tremolo effect using modern technology, purple case.

1997-2017		$75	$150

Nomad

1960s. Effects that claimed to be made in the U.S., but most likely built by Shin-ei of Japan. Models include the Verberola and the Fuzz wah, both of which were sold under other brands such as Applied, Jax USA, and Companion.

Fuzz Wah

1960s. Fuzz wah pedal similar to Morley pedals of the era with depth and volume controls and fuzz switch, silver and black.

1960s		$150	$200

Oberheim Electronics Inc.

1970s. Electronics company based in Santa Monica, California, which offered effects under its own name as well as building effects for Gibson/Maestro.

Voltage Controlled Filter VCF-200

1970s. Voltage-controlled filter, envelope follower and sample-and-hold circuit.

1970s		$700	$900

Oddfellow Effects

Jon Meleika, began in 2013, builds guitar effects pedals in Riverside, California.

Olson

Olson Electronics was based in Akron, Ohio.

Reverberation Amplifier RA-844

1967. Solidstate, battery-operated, reverb unit, depth and volume controls, made in Japan.

1967		$100	$150

Ooh La La Manufacturing

2007-2014. Hand-made guitar effects built in St. Louis Park, Minnesota, including the models formerly offered under the Blackbox brand.

Option 5

2002-present. Jay Woods builds his guitar effects pedals in Mishwaka, Indiana.

Origin Effects

2012-present. Custom-built and production guitar effects made in Oxfordshire, U.K. by Simon Keats.

Ovation

Ovation ventured into the solidstate amp and effects market in the early '70s.

K-6001 Guitar Preamp

1970s. Preamp with reverb, boost, tremolo, fuzz, and a tuner, looks something like a Maestro effect from the '70s, reliability may be an issue.

1970s		$200	$300

PAIA

1967-present. Founded by John Paia Simonton in Edmond, Oklahama, specializing in synthesizer and effects kits. PAIA did make a few complete products but they are better known for the various electronic kit projects they sold. Values on kit projects are difficult as it depends on the skills of the person who built it.

Roctave Divider 5760

1970s. Kit to build analog octave divider.

1970s		$150	$250

Pan*Damn*ic

2007-2012. Guitar effects pedals made by PLH Professional Audio in West Chester, Pennsylvania.

Park

1965-1982, 1992-2000. Sola/Colorsound made a couple of effects for Marshall and their sister brand, Park. In the '90s, Marshall revived the name for use on small solidstate amps.

Pax

1970s. Imported Maestro copies.

Fuzz Tone Copy

1970s		$200	$300

Octave Box Copy

1970s. Dual pushbuttons (normal and octave), 2 knobs (octave volume and sensitivity), green and black case.

1970s		$200	$300

Pearl

Pearl, located in Nashville, Tennessee, and better known for drums, offered a line of guitar effects in the 1980s.

Analog Delay AD-08

1983-1985. Four knobs.

1983-1985		$150	$200

Analog Delay AD-33

1982-1984. Six knobs.

1982-1984		$175	$250

Chorus CH-02

1981-1984. Four knobs.

1981-1984		$150	$200

Chorus Ensemble CE-22

1982-1984. Stereo chorus with toggling between chorus and vibrato, 6 knobs.

1982-1984		$150	$200

Compressor CO-04

1981-1984		$150	$200

Distortion DS-06

1982-1986		$100	$180

Flanger FG-01

1981-1986. Clock pulse generator, ultra-low frequency oscillator.

1981-1986		$150	$200

MODEL YEAR	FEATURES	LOW	HIGH

Graphic EQ GE-09

1983-1985		$100	$180

Octaver OC-07

1982-1986		$150	$300

Overdrive OD-05

1981-1986		$100	$200

Parametric EQ PE-10

1983-1984		$100	$200

Phaser PH-03

1981-1984. Four knobs.

1981-1984		$100	$200

Phaser PH-44

1982-1984. Six knobs.

1982-1984		$200	$300

Stereo Chorus CH-22

1982-1984. Blue case.

1982-1984		$100	$200

Thriller TH-20

1984-1986. Exciter, 4 knobs, black case.

1984-1986		$100	$200

Peavey

1965-present. Peavey made stomp boxes from '87 to around '90. They offered rack mount gear after that.

Effects

1980s	Accelerator Overdrive AOD-2	$100	$125
1980s	Biampable Bass Chorus BAC-2	$100	$125
1980s	Companded Chorus CMC-1	$100	$125
1980s	Compressor/ Sustaioner CSR-2	$100	$125
1980s	Digital Delay DDL-3	$100	$125
1980s	Digital Stereo Reverb SRP-16	$100	$125
1980s	Dual Clock Stereo Chorus DSC-4	$100	$125
1980s	Hotfoot Distortion HFD-2	$100	$125

PedalDoctor FX

1996-present. Tim Creek builds his production and custom guitar effects in Nashville, Tennessee.

Pedalworx

Bob McBroom and George Blekas began building guitar effects in 2001, in Manorville, New York and Huntsville, Alabama. They also make modifications to wahs.

Pharaoh Amplifiers

1998-2010. Builder Matt Farrow builds his effects in Raleigh, North Carolina.

Pignose

1972-present. Guitar stomp boxes offered by the amp builder in Las Vegas, Nevada. They also offer guitars.

MODEL YEAR	FEATURES	LOW	HIGH

Pigtronix

2003-present. Dave Koltai builds his custom guitar effects originally in Brooklyn, and currently in Yonkers, New York and offers models built in China.

Plum Crazy FX

Guitar effects built by Kaare Festovog in Apple Valley, Minnesota starting in 2005.

Premier

Ca.1938-ca.1975, 1990-2010. Premier offered a reverb unit in the '60s.

Reverb Unit

1961-late-1960s. Tube, footswitch, 2-tone brown.

1960s		$400	$550

Prescription Electronics

Located in Portland, Oregon, Jack Brossart began offering a variety of hand-made effects in 1994.

Dual-Tone

1998-2009. Overdrive and distortion.

1998-2009		$200	$250

Throb

1996-2014. Tremolo.

1996-2014		$200	$250

Yardbox

1994-2014. Patterned after the original Sola Sound Tonebender.

1994-2014		$200	$250

Pro Tone Pedals

2004-present. Guitar effects pedals built by Dennis Mollan in Dallas, Texas until early-2011, and presently in Summerville, South Carolina.

ProCo

1974-present. Located in Kalamazoo, Michigan and founded by Charlie Wicks, ProCo produces effects, cables and audio products.

Rat

1978-1987. Fuzztone, large box until '84. The second version was 1/3 smaller than the original box. The small box version became the Rat 2. The current Vintage Rat is a reissue of the original large box.

1978	Fringe Logo	$3,000	$4,000
1979-1984	Large box	$500	$1,500
1984-1987	Compact box	$300	$500

Rat 2

1987-present. Classic distortion.

1987-1999		$150	$300
2000-2024		$55	$75

Turbo Rat

1989-present. Fuzztone with higher output gain, slope-front case.

1989-2024		$100	$150

Vintage Rat

1992-2005. Reissue of early-'80s Rat.

1992-2005		$150	$250

Prescription Electronics Yardbox

Rivington Guitars

ProCo Rat 2

Radial Tonebone Texas Dual Overdrive

Red Witch Synthotron

Rodger Reed

Rocktron Hush The Pedal

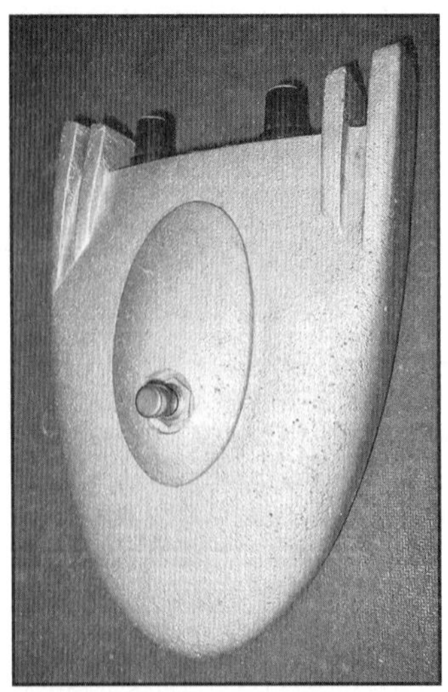

Roger Mayer Classic Fuzz

MODEL YEAR	FEATURES	LOW	HIGH

Pro-Sound

The effects listed here date from 1987, and were, most likely, around for a short time.

Chorus CR-1

1980s $50 $75

Delay DL-1

1980s. Analog.

1980s $60 $75

Distortion DS-1

1980s $50 $75

Octaver OT-1

1980s $50 $75

Power and Master Switch PMS-1

1980s $45 $60

Super Overdrive SD-1

1980s $45 $60

Providence

1996-present. Guitar effects pedals built in Japan for Pacifix Ltd. and distributed in the U.S. by Godlyke Distributing, Inc.

Radial Engineering

1994-present. Radial makes a variety of products in Port Coquitlam, British Columbia, including direct boxes, snakes, cables, splitters, and, since '99, the Tonebone line of guitar effects.

Rands

1960s. Japanese music company.

Resly Machine RM-29

1960s. Copy of Maestro PS-1 Phase Shifter built by Shin-ei.

1960s $350 $500

Rapco

The Jackson, Missouri based cable company offers a line of switch, connection, and D.I. Boxes.

The Connection AB-100

1988-2017. A/B box.

1988-2017 $45 $55

Rastop Designs

2002-present. Alexander Rastopchin builds his effects in Long Island City, New York. He also builds amps.

Ray Butts Music Co.

1950s. Ray Butts ran a music store in Cairo, Illinois, where he built his famous EchoSonic amp. He experimented with building a pioneering fuzz box that never went into production and offered his NovaMatch buffer in limited production.

NovaMatch

Late-1950s. Buffer with 1Db of gain in a lipstick-tube-like unit that plugged into guitar jacks.

1950s $350 $550

Real McCoy Custom

1993-present. Wahs and effects by Geoffrey Teese. His first wah was advertised as the Real McCoy, by Teese. He now offers his custom wah pedals under the Real McCoy Custom brand. He also used the Teese brand on a line of stomp boxes, starting in '96. The Teese stomp boxes are no longer being made. In '08 he moved to Coos Bay, Oregon.

Recycled Sound

2009-present. Greg Perrine designs attenuators in Conway, Arkansas, which are then built in China.

Red Panda

2010s-present. Based in Pittsburgh, Pennsylvania.

Bitmap

2016 $145 $200

Raster

2015 $165 $250

Red Witch

2003-present. Analog guitar effects, designed by Ben Fulton, and made in Paekakariki, New Zealand.

Reinhardt

2004-2012. Amp builder Bob Reinhardt of Lynchburg, Virginia also offers a line of effects pedals.

Retro FX Pedals

2006-ca. 2010. Guitar effects pedals built by John Jones in St. Louis, Missouri.

Retroman

2002-present. Joe Wolf builds his retro effects pedals in Janesville, Wisconsin.

Retro-Sonic

2002-present. Tim Larwill builds effects in Ottawa, Ontario.

Reverend

1996-present. Reverend offered its Drivetrain effects from '00 to '04. They also build guitars.

RGW Electronics

Guitar effects built by Robbie Wallace, starting in 2003, in Lubbock, Texas.

Rivera

1985-present. Amp builder Paul Rivera also offers a line of guitar pedals built in California.

Rocco

Introduced in 1937, the Rocco Tonexpressor was a volume pedal designed by New York City steel-guitarist Anthony Rocco and built and distributed by Epiphone. Generally credited with being the first guitar effect pedal.

Rockman

See listings under Scholz Research and Dunlop.

MODEL YEAR	FEATURES	LOW	HIGH

Rocktek

1986-2009. Imports formerly distributed by Matthews and Ryan of Brooklyn, New York; and later by D'Andrea USA.

Effects

1986-2009 Various models $50 $100

Rocktron

1980s-present. Rocktron is a division of GHS Strings and offers a line of amps, controllers, stomp boxes, and preamps.

Austin Gold Overdrive

1997-2011. Light overdrive.

1997-2011 $65 $85

Banshee Talk Box

1997-present. Includes power supply.

1997-2024 $100 $150

Hush Rack Mount

1980s-present.

2000-2024 $85 $125

Hush The Pedal

1996-present. Pedal version of rackmount Hush.

1996-2024 $55 $100

Rampage Distortion

1996-2013. Sustain, high-gain and distortion.

1996-2013 $85 $125

Surf Tremolo

1997-2000 $60 $80

Tsunami Chorus

1996-2009. Battery or optional AC adapter.

1996-2009 Battery power $60 $80

1996-2009 With power supply $65 $85

Vertigo Vibe

2003-2006. Rotating Leslie speaker effect.

2003-2006 Battery power $60 $80

2003-2006 With power supply $60 $80

XDC

1980s. Rack mount stereo preamp, distortion.

1980s $100 $150

Roger Linn Design

2001-present. Effects built in Berkeley, California by Roger Linn.

Roger Mayer Electronics

1964-present. Roger Mayer started making guitar effects in the U.K. in '64 for guitarists like Jimmy Page and Jeff Beck. He moved to the U.S. in '69 to start a company making studio gear and effects. Until about 1980, the effects were built one at a time in small numbers and not available to the public. In the '80s he started producing larger quantities of pedals, introducing his rocket-shaped enclosure. He returned to the U.K. in '89.

Axis Fuzz

1987-present.

1987-2024 $350 $450

Classic Fuzz

1987-present. The Fuzz Face.

1987-2024 $350 $450

Metal Fuzz

Early 1980s-1994.

1987-1994 $350 $450

Mongoose Fuzz

1987-2017.

1987-2017 $350 $450

Octavia

1981-present. Famous rocket-shaped box.

1981-2024 $400 $550

Voodoo-1

Ca.1990-present.

1990-2024 $350 $450

Rogue

2001-present. Budget imported guitar effects. They also offer guitars, basses, lap steels, mandolins, banjos, ukuleles, and amps.

Roland

Japan's Roland Corporation first launched effect pedals in 1974; a year or two later the subsidiary company, Boss, debuted its own line. They were marketed concurrently at first, but gradually Boss became reserved for compact effects while the Roland name was used on amplifiers, keyboards, synths, and larger processors.

Analog Synth SPV

1970s. Multi-effect synth, rack mount.

1970s $750 $1,500

Bee Baa AF-100

1975-ca.1980. Fuzz and treble boost.

1975-1980 $325 $550

Bee Gee AF-60

1975-ca.1980. Sustain, distortion.

1975-1980 $300 $500

Double Beat AD-50

1975-ca.1980. Fuzz wah.

1975-1980 $250 $450

Expression Pedal EV-5

1970s $55 $75

Expression Pedal EV-5 Reissue

2000. Black pedal, blue foot pad.

2000 $30 $40

Guitar Synth Pedal GR-33 and Pickup GK-2A

2000-2005. Requires optional GK-2A pickup, blue case.

2000-2005 $300 $500

Human Rhythm Composer R-8

1980s. Drum machine, keypad entry.

1980s $250 $450

Human Rhythm Composer R-8 MK II

2000s. Black case.

2000s $450 $1,000

Jet Phaser AP-7

1975-ca.1978. Phase and distortion.

1975-1978 $300 $650

Phase Five AP-5

1975-ca.1978.

1975-1978 $350 $550

Roger Mayer Voodoo Axe

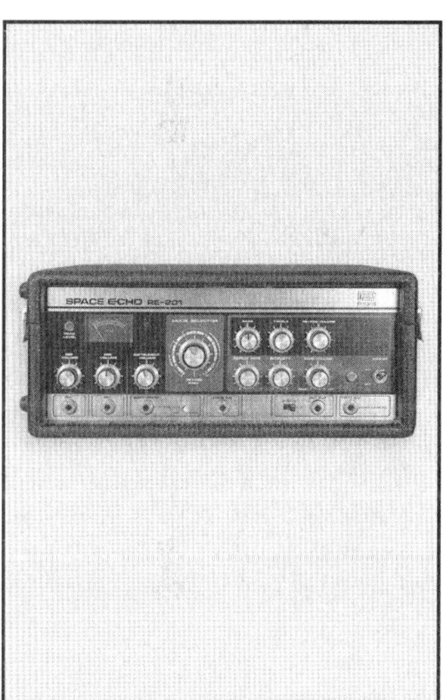

Roland Space Echo

1979 Roland Phase Five AP-5

Rivington Guitars

1978 Ross Compressor

Sam Ash Fuzzz Boxx

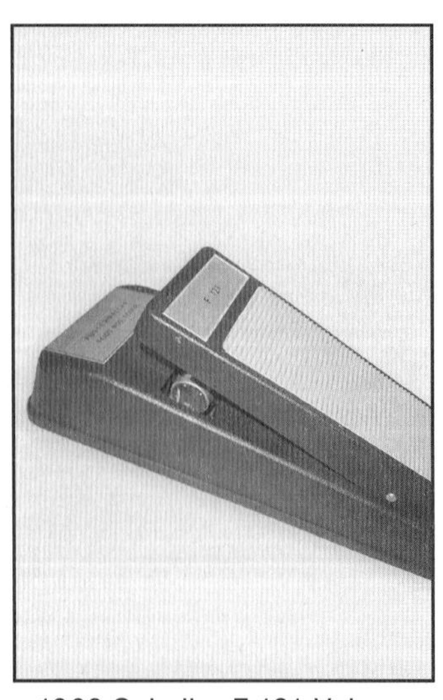
1968 Schaller F-121 Volume
Rivington Guitars

EFFECTS

MODEL YEAR	FEATURES	LOW	HIGH

Phase II AP-2

1975-ca.1980. Brown case.

1975-1980		$150	$350

Space Echo Unit

1974-ca. 1980. Tape echo and reverb, various models.

1970s	RE-101	$750	$1,000
1970s	RE-150	$750	$1,000
1970s	RE-200	$1,000	$1,500
1970s	RE-201	$2,000	$2,500
1970s	RE-301	$1,500	$2,000
1970s	RE-501	$1,500	$2,000
1970s	SRE-555 Chorus Echo	$1,500	$2,000

Vocoder SVC-350

Late-1970s-1980s. Vocal synthesis (vocoder) for voice or guitar, rack mount version of VP-330.

1980		$1,000	$2,500

Vocoder VP-330 Plus

Late-1970s-1980s. Analog vocal synthesis (vocoder) for voice or guitar, includes 2 1/2 octaves keyboard.

1978-1982		$2,000	$2,500

Wah Beat AW-10

1975-ca.1980.

1975-1980		$150	$250

Rosac Electronics

1969-1970s. Founded by Ralph Scaffidi and former Mosrite engineer Ed Sanner with backing from Morris Rosenberg and Ben Sacco in Bakersfield, California. Made the Nu-Fuzz which was a clone of Mosrite's Fuzzrite and the Nu-Wah. Closed in mid- to late- '70s and Scaffidi went on to co-found Osborne Sound Laboratories.

Ross

Founded by Bud Ross, who also established Kustom, in Chanute, Kansas, in the 1970s. Ross produced primarily amplifiers. In about '78, they introduced a line of U.S.-made effects. Later production switched to Asia.

10 Band Graphic Equalizer

1970s		$50	$120

Compressor

1970s. Gray or black case.

1970s		$700	$800

Distortion

1978-ca.1980. Brown.

1979-1980		$150	$250

Flanger

1977-ca.1980. Red.

1977-1980		$150	$300

Phase Distortion R1

1979. Purple.

1979		$150	$200

Phaser

1978-ca.1980. Orange.

1978-1980		$150	$200

Stereo Delay

1978-ca.1980.

1978-1980		$200	$300

Rotosound

1960s. English musical company.

Fuzz Box

1967-1968. Fuzz built by Sola Sound.

1967-1968		$500	$750

Rotovibe

See the listing under Dunlop.

Royal

1960s. Japanese effects company with product built by other makers, including the Thunder Electronic Co. Ltd. Of Tokyo.

Double Effect Machine RFC-1

1960s. Built by Shin-ei.

1960s		$300	$600

Fuzz Box RF-1

1960s. Expanded version of Univox Super-Fuzz with tone effects foot switch.

1960s		$300	$600

S. Hawk Ltd.

1970s. Various effect pedals, no model names on case, only company name and logo.

Hawk I Fuzz

1970s. Linear pre-amp, fuzz, headphone amp, 1 slider.

1970s		$600	$700

SAM

1970s-1980s. Effects made by the SAM Electromechanical Plant in Moscow, Russia.

Effekt-1 Fuzz-Wah-Vibrato

1970s. Fuzz pedal with foot control.

1970s		$150	$250

Sam Ash

1960s-1970s, 2013-present. Sam Ash (nee Askynase) founded Sam Ash Music, in '24, in Brooklyn, and by '66, there were about four Ash stores. During this time, Ash Music private branded their own amps and effects. In 2013, Sam Ash reissued the Fuzzz Boxx.

Fuzzola

1960s. Rebranded version of the Shin-ei Uni-Fuzz. There is also a Fuzzola II.

1960s		$300	$400

Fuzzz Boxx

1966-1967, 2013-2019. Red, made by Astro/Universal Amplifier Company, same as Astro Amp Astrotone fuzz. Reissued in '13.

1966-1967		$450	$850
2013-2019	Reissue	$150	$175

Volume Wah

1970s. Italian-made.

1970s		$250	$325

Sangil

1960s. Ed Sanner - designer of the Mosrite Fuzzrite - also built and sold effects through his own company, Sangil.

MODEL YEAR	FEATURES	LOW	HIGH

Iron Butterfly

1960s. Fuzz wah pedal.

1960s		$300	$400

Sanner

1999. Reissue from Ed Sanner, who was the engineer behind the 1960s Mosrite Fuzzrite, using identical circuitry as the original. Issued as a limited edition.

Sano

1944-ca. 1970. Sano was a New Jersey-based accordion company that built their own amps and a reverb unit. They also imported guitars for a few years, starting in '66.

Satellite Amplifiers

2004-present. Analog effects pedals made in San Diego, California by amp builder Adam Grimm.

Schaffer-Vega

1975-1982. After Mick Jagger's wireless system for the 1975 Rolling Stones Tour of the Americas began broadcasting police calls and lottery numbers, New York recording engineer Ken Schaffer invented his Schaffer-Vega Diversity System (SVDS) as a better wireless system – although it also could be used to affect guitar tones, offering overdrive as used by AC/DC's Angus Young. SoloDallas began offering Schaffer replicas in 2015.

Diversity System

1975-1982. Wireless mic and guitar transmitter and receiver.

1975-1982		$1,500	$2,500

Schaller

The German guitar accessories company, which began in 1945, offered guitar effects off and on since the '60s and currently has reissue versions of its volume pedal and tremolo.

Scholz Research

1982-1995. Started by Tom Scholz of the band Boston. In '95, Jim Dunlop picked up the Rockman line (see Dunlop).

Equalizer

1980s		$300	$350

Power Soak

1980s		$175	$275

Rockadapter

1980s		$95	$125

Rockman

1980s		$400	$500

Rockman X100

1980s. Professional studio processor.

1980s		$650	$700

Rockman XPR

1989-1991. Multi-effects unit, analog guitar preamp.

1989-1991		$3,000	$4,000

Soloist

1980s. Personal guitar processor.

1980s		$400	$500

MODEL YEAR	FEATURES	LOW	HIGH

Stereo Chorus

1980s		$250	$500

Stereo Chorus Delay

1980s		$400	$500

Stereo Echo

1980s		$1,000	$1,500

Sustainer 200

1980s		$700	$900

Wah Volume

1980s		$200	$350

Seamoon

1973-1977, 1997-2002. Seamoon made effects until '77, when Dave Tarnowski bought up the remaining inventory and started Analog Digital Associates (ADA). He reissued the brand in '97.

Fresh Fuzz

1975-1977. Recently reissued by ADA.

1975-1977		$500	$750

Funk Machine

1974-1977. Envelope filter. Recently reissued by ADA.

1974-1977		$300	$400

Studio Phase

1975-1977. Phase shifter.

1975-1977		$500	$650

Sears, Roebuck & Co.

1970s. Department-store and mail-order giant Sears sold inexpensive effects likely made in Japan by Guyatone.

Fuzz & Wa & Volume Control Pedal

1970s		$150	$200

Fuzz-Tone Control

1970s. Dallas-Arbiter Fuzz Face/Guyatone Crazy-Face copy.

1970s		$250	$350

Sekova

Mid-1960s-mid-1970s. Entry level instruments imported by the U.S. Musical Merchandise Corporation of New York.

Big Muff SE-2015

1972-1973. "Triangle" Big Muff Pi copy built by Shin-ei.

1972-1973		$650	$1,000

Fuzz

1960s		$300	$450

Selmer

1960s. English music company based in London.

Buzz-Tone

1960s		$1,000	$1,500

Seymour Duncan

In late 2003, pickup maker Seymour Duncan, located in Santa Barbara, California, added a line of stomp box guitar effects.

Shin-ei

1969-1970s. When the Honey company went bankrupt in March, '69, it was reborn as Shin-ei

Seamoon Funk Machine

Seymour Duncan Dirty Deed

Seymour Duncan Fooz

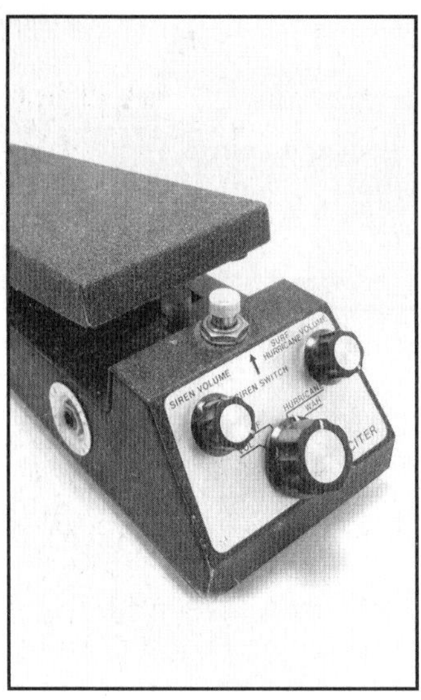

1960s Shin-ei Fuzz Wah
Keith Meyers

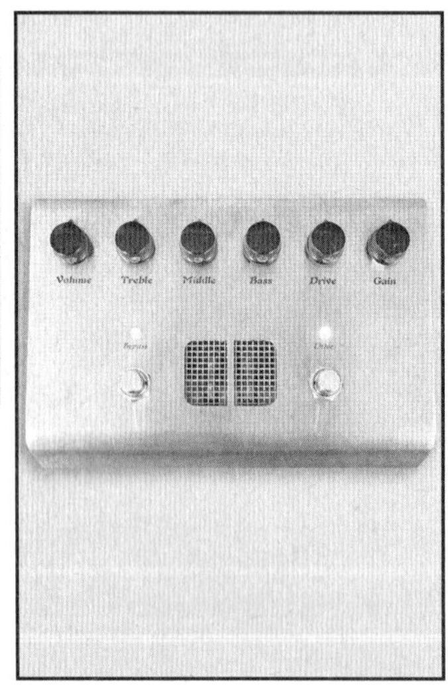

Siegmund DoubleDrive

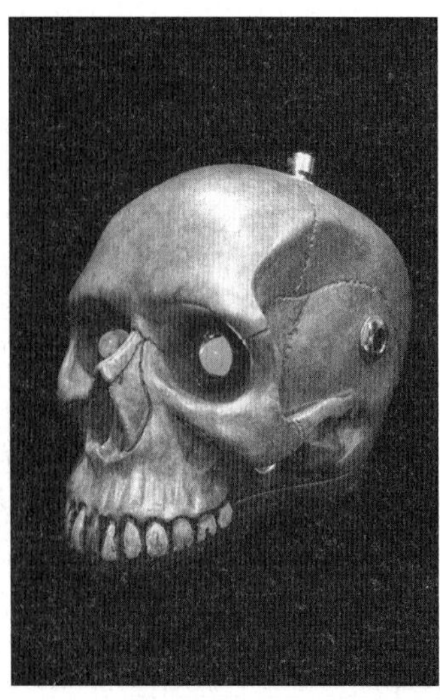
Skull Crusher

MODEL YEAR	FEATURES	LOW	HIGH

and many Honey designs continued in production in various forms. Their chief engineer was Fumio Mieda who later did design work for Korg. Shin-ei also made effects for Univox (including the Uni-Fuzz, Super-Fuzz and Uni-Vibe), Companion, Applied, Apollo, Jax, Nomad, Shaftsbury, Pax, Crown, Royal, Mica, Kent, Marlboro, Memphis, Bruno, Boomer, Alex, Ace Tone, Aria, Goya, Kimbara, Lord, National, Northland, Tele Star, Tempo, and probably others.

Fuzz Wah

1970s	$300	$500

FY-2 Fuzz Box

1969-1970s. 2 transistors.

1969-1970s	$300	$500

FY-6 Super Fuzz

1969-1970s. Built from fuzz circuitry of Psychedelic Machine, 6 transistors.

1969-1970s	$500	$600

Mica Tone Fuzz Wah

1970s	$300	$500

Octave Box OB-28

1970s. Version of the Gibson Maestro OB-1 Octave Box.

1970s	$300	$500

Phase Tone PT-18

1970s. Tremolo, vibrato and phase effects.

1970s	$500	$1,000

Psychedelic Machine

1969. Amp head-sized effect with numerous controls.

1969	$2,000	$3,000

Resly (Repeat Time) Machine

1970s. Black case, 3 speeds.

1970s	$2,000	$2,500

Sho-Bud

1956-1980. This pedal steel company offered volume pedals as well.

Sho-Sound Boss Tone

1970s-1980. Licensed version of the Jordan Boss Tone, 2 control knobs, similar black plastic housing.

1970s-80	$200	$250

Volume Pedal

1965	$150	$200

SIB

Effects pedals from Rick Hamel, who helped design SMF amps.

Siegmund Guitars & Amplifiers

Los Angeles, California amp and guitar builder Chris Siegmund added effects to his product line in '99.

Sitori Sonics

Emanual Ellinas began building his guitar effects in Birmingham, Alabama, in 2006.

Skrydstrup R&D

1997-present. Effects pedals built by Steen Skrydstrup in Denmark. He also builds amps.

Skull Crusher

2009-2015. Partners John Kasha and Shawn Crosby of Tone Box Effects built their guitar effects in Simi Valley, California.

Snarling Dogs

Started by Charlie Stringer of Stringer Industries, Warren, New Jersey in 1997. Stringer died in May '99. The brand is now carried by D'Andrea USA.

Sobbat

1995-present. Line of effects from Kinko Music Company of Kyoto, Japan.

Solasound/Colorsound

1962-2010. Sola was founded by London's Macari's Musical Exchange in '62, which was launched by former Vox associate Larry Macari and his brother Joe. The first product was the Tone-Bender fuzz box, designed by Gary Stewart Hurst and modeled in part on the Maestro Fuzz-Tone FZ-1. The first readily available fuzz in Britain was an instant success. Sola soon began making effects for Vox, Marshall, Park, and B & M and later under their own Colorsound brand. Refer to Colorsound for further listings and more company info.

Tone Bender Mk1.5

1966-1969	$2,000	$2,500

Tone Bender MkI

1965-1966	$2,500	$4,000

Tone Bender MkIII

1968-1970s	$2,500	$4,000

Tone Bender Professional MkII

1960s	$1,250	$1,800

Soldano

1987-present. Seattle, Washington amp builder Soldano also built a reverb unit.

Sho-Space Box

1987-2018. Tube-driven spring reverb.

1987-2018	$1,000	$1,500

SoloDallas

2015-present. Started by Filippo "SoloDallas" Olivieri to build replicas of the Schaffer-Vega Diversity System. Based in San Diego, California.

Schaffer Boost Solo-X

2015-2022	$100	$150

Schaffer Replica Classic

2015-2023. Stompbox replicating the SVDS guitar effect.

2015-2023	$175	$225

Schaffer Replica Storm

2015-present. Stompbox replicating the SVDS guitar effect.

2015-2024	$125	$175

Schaffer Replica Tower

2015-present. Replica of the original SVDS made by SoloDallas.

2015-2024	$800	$1,250

MODEL YEAR	FEATURES	LOW	HIGH

Songbird

See listing for Dytronics.

Sonic Edge

Guitar and bass effects pedals built by Ben Fargen in Sacramento, California starting in 2010. He also builds the Fargen amps.

Sonuus

2009-present. Guitar effects built in China and imported by owners James Clark and John McAuliffe in the U.K.

Sovtek (New Sensor Corporation)

1990s. Started by Mike Matthews, of Electro-Harmonix fame, to build EHX effects in Russia. See also Electro-Harmonix.

Bass Balls

1990s		$100	$150

Big Muff

1990s		$400	$600

Electric Mistress

1990s	Only 5 made	$2,000	$5,000

Red Army Overdrive

1990s		$2,000	$2,500

Small Stone

1990s		$200	$300

Speedster

1995-2000, 2003-2007. Amp builder Speedster added guitar effects pedals to their product line in '04, built in Gig Harbor, Washington.

Spektr

1970s-1980s. Effects made in Novosibirsk, Russia.

Spektr-1

1970s. Analog multi-effects pedal with foot control.

1970s		$200	$250

Spektr-2

1970s. Fuzz wah.

1970s		$200	$250

Spektr-3

1970s. Volume pedal with boost, fuzz, wah and auto-wah.

1970s		$300	$375

Spektr-4

1970s		$350	$450

StarTouch

Tony Chostner began in 2001, builds production/custom, effects pedals in Salem, Oregon.

Stephenson

1997-present. Amp builder Mark Stephenson in Parksville, British Columbia also offers a line of guitar pedals.

MODEL YEAR	FEATURES	LOW	HIGH

Stinger

Stinger effects were distributed by the Martin Guitar Company from 1989 to '90.

Effects

1989-1990	CH-70 Stereo Chorus	$50	$65
1989-1990	CO-20 Compressor	$60	$75
1989-1990	DD-90 Digital Delay	$80	$100
1989-1990	DE-80 Analog Delay	$95	$125
1989-1990	DI-10 Distortion	$75	$95
1989-1990	FL-60 Flanger	$75	$95
1989-1990	OD-30 Overdrive	$75	$95
1989-1990	TS-5 Tube Stack	$80	$100

Strymon

2009-present. Founded in 2004 as Damage Control, the company began offering effects pedals under the Strymon name in 2009. Owners Gregg Stock, Pete Celi, and Dave Fruehling build their line of guitar pedals in Chatsworth, California.

Big Sky

2013-present. Reverberator pedal.

2013-2024		$375	$475

BlueSky

2010-present. Digital reverb pedal.

2010-2024		$225	$300

Brigadier

2010-present. dBucket delay.

2010-2024		$225	$300

Deco

2014-present. Tape saturation and doubletracker pedal.

2014-2024		$250	$325

DIG

2015-present. Dual digital delay.

2015-2024		$225	$300

El Capistan

2010-present. Tape echo.

2010-2024		$225	$300

Flint

2012-present. Tremolo and reverb.

2012-2024		$225	$300

Lex

2011-present. Rotary effects pedal.

2011-2024		$225	$300

Mobius

2012-present. Modulation pedal.

2012-2024		$375	$475

OB.1

2009-2020. Optical compressor and clean boost.

2009-2020		$125	$175

Ojai

2016-present. High current DC power supply.

2016-2024		$125	$175

Ola

2010-present. dBucket chorus and vibrato.

2010-2024		$225	$300

Orbit

2010-present. dBucket flanger.

2010-2024		$225	$300

Riverside

2016-present. Multistage drive.

2016-2024		$225	$300

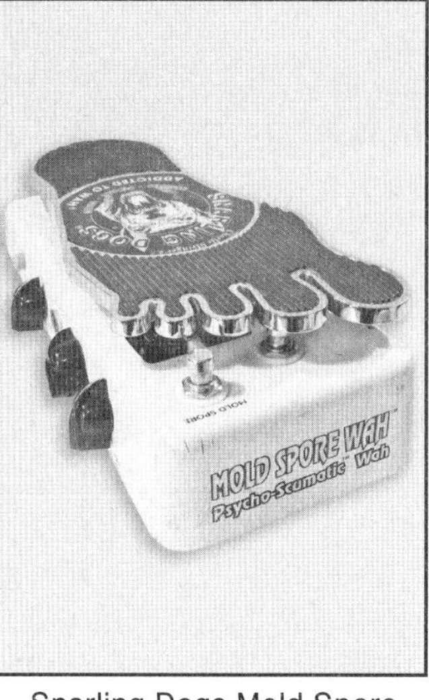

Snarling Dogs Mold Spore Psycho-Scumatic

Garrett Tung

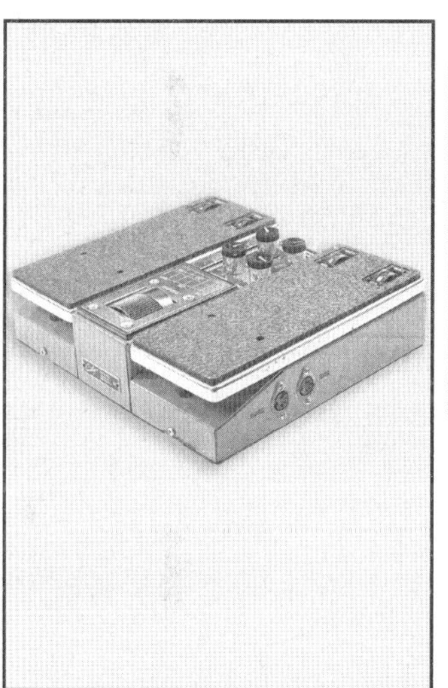

Spektr-3 Fuzz Wah

Ilya Shlepako

StarTouch AB Stereo

EFFECTS

Strymon TimeLine

Swart FuzzyBoost

TC Electronic HOF Mini
Keith Myers

MODEL YEAR	FEATURES	LOW	HIGH

Sunset

2017-present. Dual overdrive pedal.

2017-2024		$225	$300

TimeLine

2011-present. Delay pedal.

2011-2024		$325	$425

Zuma

2016-present. High current DC power supply.

2016-2024		$225	$300

Studio Electronics

1989-present. Synth and midi developer Greg St. Regis' Studio Electronics added guitar pedal effects to their line in '03.

Subdecay Studios

2003-present. Brian Marshall builds guitar effects originally in Woodinville, Washington and currently in Dundee, Oregon.

Supersound

1952-1974. Founded by England's Alan Wootton, Supersound built echo units in the 1960s. They also built amps, guitars, and basses.

Supro

1935-1968, 2004-present. Supro offered a few reverb units in the '60s. The brand name was revived in '04.

500 R Standard Reverb Unit

1962-1963. Outboard reverb unit.

1962-1963		$300	$500

600 Reverb Power Unit

1961. Independent reverb unit amp combination to be used with Supro Model 1600R amp or other amps, 3 tubes, 1x8" speaker.

1961		$400	$700

Swart Amplifier

2003-present. Effects pedals built by Michael J. Swart in Wilmington, North Carolina. He also builds amps.

Sweet Sound

Line of effects from Bob Sweet beginning in 1994, originally made in Trenton, Michigan, and then in Coral Springs, Florida. Bob died in 2008. Currently built by his brother Gerald.

Swell Pedal Company

1997-2012. Mike Olienechak builds his line of tube pedals for guitar and bass in Nashville, Tennessee.

SynapticGroove

Benjamin Harrison and Chrystal Gilles build their guitar effects in Edmond, Oklahoma, starting in 2013.

MODEL YEAR	FEATURES	LOW	HIGH

Systech (Systems & Technology in Music, Inc)

1975-1979. Started by Greg Hockman, Systech was in Kalamazoo, Michigan.

Envelope & Repeater

1975-1979		$250	$350

Envelope Follower

1975-1979. Decay and drive controls.

1975-1979		$300	$400

Flanger

1975-1979. Sweep rate, depth, and gain controls.

1975-1979		$300	$400

Harmonic Energizer

1975-1979. Filter/distortion with bandwidth, center frequency and gain controls. Silver body early, black body later.

1975-1979		$1,000	$1,500

Overdrive

1975-1979. EQ, distortion, and gain controls. Silver body early, black body later.

1975-1979		$350	$750

Phase Shifter

1975-1979. Dual sweep rate controls plus emphasis control.

1975-1979		$350	$500

T.C. Jauernig Electronics

Tim Jauernig, of Rothschild, Wisconsin, built effects for several years before launching his T.C. Jauernig brand in 2004.

TC Electronic

1976-present. Brothers Kim and John Rishøj founded TC Electronic in Risskov, Denmark, and made guitar effects pedals for several years before moving into rack-mounted gear. Currently they offer a wide range of pro audio gear and rack and floor guitar effects.

Booster + Distortion

1980s		$300	$400

Dual Parametric Equalizer

1980s		$200	$375

Stereo Chorus/Flanger SCF

Introduced in 1982 and reissued in '91.

1980s		$250	$350

Sustain + Equalizer

1980s		$200	$350

Tech 21

1989-present. Tech 21 builds their SansAmp and other effects in New York City. They also build amps.

Sansamp

1989-present. Offers a variety of tube amp tones.

1989	1st year	$350	$500
1990-2024		$150	$200

XXL Pedal

1995-2000, 2005-2012. Distortion, fuzz.

1995-2012		$75	$100

MODEL YEAR	FEATURES	LOW	HIGH

Teese

Geoffrey Teese's first wah was advertised as the Real McCoy, by Teese. He now offers his custom wah pedals under the Real McCoy Custom brand. The Teese brand was used on his line of stomp boxes, starting in '96. The Teese stomp boxes are no longer being made.

Ten

2013-present. Guitar effects built in Spokane, Washington by Ryan Dunn and Doug Harrison. From 2001-'13 they used the ToadWorks brand.

The Original Geek

Jeff Rubin began building guitar effects pedals in Los Angeles, California under the Geek MacDaddy brand in 2004. After a breakup with his business partner in '09 he began using The Original Geek brand.

Theremaniacs

2010s-present. Started by Chuck Collins, builder of Theremins, based in Big Bend, Wisconsin.

Harmonic Percolator

2010s-present. Replica of '70s InterFax Harmonic Percolator.

2010s-2024		$350	$450

Thomas Organ

The Thomas Organ Company was heavily involved with Vox from 1964 to '72, importing their instruments into the U.S. and designing and assembling products, including the wah-wah pedal. Both Thomas Organ and JMI, Vox's European distributor, wanted to offer the new effect. The problem was solved by labeling the Thomas Organ wah the Crybaby. Dunlop now offers the Crybaby. Refer to Vox listing for Crybaby Stereo Fuzz Wah, Crybaby Wah, and Wah Wah.

ThroBak Electronics

2004-present. Jonathan Gundry builds his guitar effects in Grand Rapids, Michigan. He also builds guitar amps and pickups.

ToadWorks

See listing for Ten.

TomasZewicZ or TZZ

2008-present. Guitar effects pedals built by John Tomaszewicz in Coral Springs, Florida, which he labels TZZ. He also builds amps.

Tone Box Effects

See listing for Skull Crusher.

Tonebone

See Radial Engineering listing.

ToneCandy

2007-present. Mike Marino builds his guitar effects pedals in Santa Rosa, California.

MODEL YEAR	FEATURES	LOW	HIGH

Top Gear

1960s-1970s. Top Gear was a London music store. Their effects were made by other manufacturers.

Rotator

1970s	Leslie effect	$350	$750

Top Hat Amplification

1994-present. Brian Gerhard builds his amps and effects in Fuquay-Varina, North Carolina. He previously built them in La Habra, California and Apex, North Carolina.

Traynor

1963-present. Amp and PA builder Traynor also built two spring reverb units, one tube and one solidstate, in Canada from 1966-'72 and a 7-band EQ from '73-'78.

Tremolo

See the listing under Dunlop.

T-Rex

2003-present. Made in Denmark and imported by European Musical Imports.

TSVG

Mike Klein started building his guitar effects in his shop located in Philadelphia, Pennsylvania in 2011.

Tube Works

1987-2004. Founded by B.K. Butler (see Audio Matrix) in Denver, Colorado, Tube Works became a division of Genz Benz Enclosures of Scottsdale, Arizona in 1997 which dropped the brand in 2004. They also offered tube/solidstate amps, cabinets, and DI boxes.

Blue Tube

1989-2004. Overdrive bass driver with 12AX7A tube.

1989-2004		$125	$200

Real Tube

Ca.1987-2004. Overdrive with 12AX7A tube.

1987-1999		$125	$200

Tube Driver

1987-2004. With tube.

1987-2004		$200	$250

TWA (Totally Wycked Audio)

2009-present. Boutique analog effect pedals made in the U.S. and offered by Godlyke, Inc.

Tycobrahe

The Tycobrahe story was over almost before it began. Doing business in 1976-1977, they produced only three pedals and a direct box, one the fabled Octavia. The company, located in Hermosa Beach, California, made high-quality, original devices, but they didn't catch on. Now, they are very collectible. Reissues were made by Chicago Iron.

1999 Tech 21 XXL Distortion

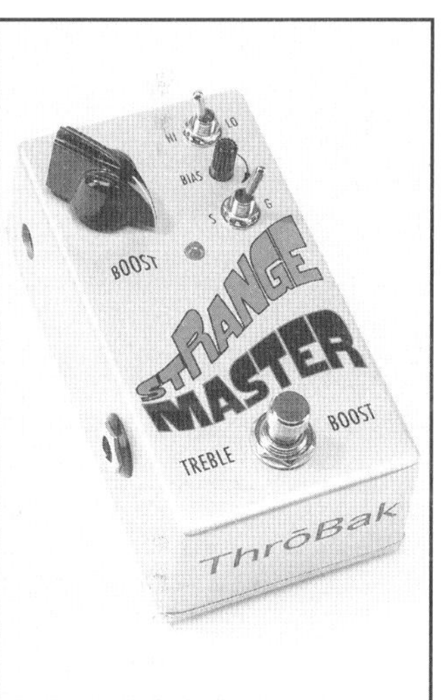

ThroBak Electronics Strange Master

TWA Little Dipper LD-01

EFFECTS

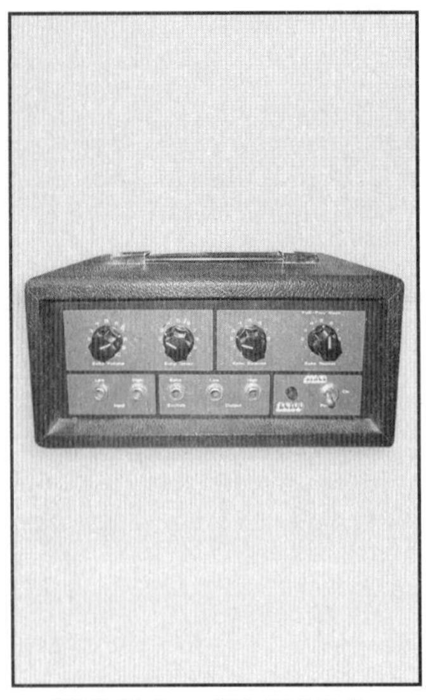
1975 Univox EC-100 Echo
Rivington Guitars

Univox Super-Fuzz
Daron Wittmayer

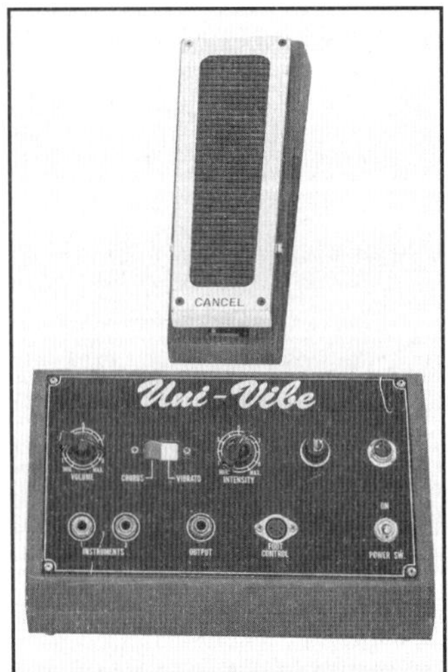

1969 Univox Uni-Vibe
Imaged by Heritage Auctions, HA.com

MODEL YEAR	FEATURES	LOW	HIGH

Octavia

1976-1977, 2000s. Octave doubler.

1976-1977		$3,500	$5,000
2000s	Octavia & Octavian reissue	$350	$500

Parapedal

1976-1977, 2000s. Wah.

1976-1977		$800	$1,250
2000s	Reissue, light blue	$350	$500

Pedalflanger

1976-1977. Blue pedal-controlled flanger.

1976-1977		$1,000	$1,500

UMI (United Musical Industries)

1960s. UMI was based in Farmingdale, New York.

Tone Booster

1960s. Primitive EQ unit with treble and bass boost controls.

1960s		$250	$350

Uni-Vibe

See listings under Univox and Dunlop.

Univox

Univox was a brand owned by Merson (later Unicord), of Westbury, New York. It marketed guitars and amps and added effects in the late-'60s. Most Univox effects were made by Shin-ei, of Japan. They vanished in about '81.

Drum Machine SR-55

1970s		$300	$400

EC-80 A Echo

Early-1970s-ca.1977. Tape echo, sometimes shown as The Brat Echo Chamber.

1970s		$450	$600

EC-100 Echo

1970s. Tape, sound-on-sound.

1970s		$350	$500

Echo-Tech EM-200

1970s. Disc recording echo unit.

1970s		$500	$750

Fuzz FY-2

1970s		$500	$650

Micro 41 FCM41 4 channel mixer

1970s		$50	$75

Micro Fazer

1970s. Phase shifter.

1970s		$125	$200

Noise-Clamp EX110

1970s		$100	$200

Phaser PHZ1

1970s. AC powered.

1970s		$200	$350

Pro-Verb UR-3

1970s. Reverb (spring) unit, black tolex, slider controls for 2 inputs, 1 output plus remote output.

1970s		$150	$250

Square Wave SQ150

Introduced in 1976. Distortion, orange case.

1970s		$300	$500

Super-Fuzz

1968-1973. Made by Shin-ei and similar to the FY-6 Super Fuzz, built from fuzz circuitry of Honey/Shin-ei Psychedelic Machine, 6 transistors, battery powered.

1968-1973	Gray box, normal bypass switch	$700	$900
1968-1973	Orange and blue	$800	$1,000

Surf Siren

1970s. Wah pedal.

1970s		$200	$300

Uni-Comp

1970s. Compression limiter.

1970s		$150	$250

Uni-Drive

1970s		$1,000	$1,250

Uni-Fuzz

1969-1973. Fuzz tone in blue case, 2 black knobs and slider switch. Made by Shin-ei, AC-powered version of Super-Fuzz, built from fuzz circuitry of Honey/Shin-ei Psychedelic Machine.

1969-1973		$600	$1,000

Uni-Tron 5

1975. A.k.a. Funky Filter, envelope filter.

1975		$500	$700

Uni-Vibe

1968-1973. Rotating-speaker simulator, with control pedal. Made by Shin-ei, built from circuitry of Honey/Shin-ei Psychedelic Machine.

1968-1973		$3,500	$5,000

Uni-Wah Wah/Volume

1970s		$175	$250

VanAmps

Amp builder Tim Van Tassel of Golden Valley, Minnesota, also offers a line of reverb effects pedals.

Vesta Fire

Ca.1981-ca.1988. Brand of Japan's Shiino Musical Instrument Corp.

Chorus/Flange FLCH

1981-1988		$100	$150

Distortion DST

1981-1988		$100	$150

Flanger

1981-1988		$100	$150

Noise Gate

1981-1988		$50	$65

Stereo Chorus SCH

1981-1988		$100	$150

Vintage Tone Project

Line of guitar effects made by Robert Rush and company in Delmar, New York, starting in 2003. They also built reissues of Dan Armstrong's '70s effects from '03 to '06.

VintageFX

2003-present. Effects based on vintage pedals from the '60s and '70s built by Dave Archer in Grand Island, New York.

MODEL YEAR	FEATURES	LOW	HIGH

Visual Sound

1995-2015. Effects pedals designed by Bob Weil and R.G. Keen in Spring Hill, Tennessee and built in China. They changed name to Truetone in '15.

VooDoo Lab

1994-present. Line of effects made by Digital Music Corp. in California.

Analog Chorus

1997-2012. Based on '76 CE-1.

1997-2012		$125	$175

Bosstone

1994-1999. Based on '60s Jordan Electronics Fuzz.

1994-1999		$100	$175

Micro Vibe

1996-2022. Uni-Vibe rotating-speaker simulator.

1996-2022		$100	$175

Overdrive

1994-2002. Based on '70s overdrive.

1994-2002		$100	$150

Proctavia

1990s. Based on '70s classic fuzz/octave.

1990s		$100	$150

Superfuzz

1999-present. Vintage fuzz.

1999-2024		$100	$150

Tremolo

1995-2022. Vintage tube amp trem tone.

1995-2022		$75	$125

Vox

1954-present. The first Vox product was a volume pedal. Ca. '66, they released the Tone Bender, one of the classic fuzzboxes of all time. A year or so later, they delivered their greatest contribution to the effects world, the first wah-wah pedal. The American arm of Vox (then under Thomas Organ) succumbed in '72. In the U.K., the company was on-again/off-again.

Clyde McCoy Wah-Wah Pedal

Introduced in 1967, reissued in 2001-2008. Clyde's picture on bottom cover.

1967	Clyde's picture	$2,000	$3,000
1968	No picture	$1,250	$1,750
2001-2008	Model V-848	$200	$300

Crybaby Wah

Introduced in 1968. The Thomas Organ Company was heavily involved with Vox from '64 to '72, importing their instruments into the U.S. and designing and assembling products. One product developed in conjunction with Vox was the wah-wah pedal. Both Thomas Organ and JMI, Vox's European distributor, wanted to offer the new effect. The problem was solved by labeling the Thomas Organ wah the Crybaby. The original wahs were built by Jen in Italy, but Thomas later made them in their Chicago, Illinois and Sepulveda, California plants. Thomas Organ retained the marketing rights to Vox until '79 but was not very active with the brand after '72. Dunlop now offers the Crybaby brand.

1960s	Jen-made	$300	$400
1970	Sepulveda-made	$200	$300

Double Sound

1970s. Jen-made, Double Sound model name on bottom of pedal, double sound derived from fuzz and wah ability.

1970s		$300	$400

Flanger

1970s		$300	$400

King Wah

1970s. Chrome top, Italian-made.

1970s		$200	$300

Repeat Percussion

Late-1960s. Plug-in module with on-off switch and rate adjustment.

1968		$200	$250

Stereo Fuzz Wah

1970s		$200	$250

Tone Bender V-828

1966-1970s. Fuzz box, reissued as the V-829 in '93.

1966-1968	Mark I, gray case	$1,250	$1,875
1969	Mark II, black case	$1,000	$1,500
1970s	Mark III	$1,000	$1,500

ToneLab Valvetronix

2003-2019. Multi-effect modeling processor (ToneLab EX or ToneLab ST), 12AX7 tube preamp.

2003-2019		$150	$250

V-807 Echo-Reverb Unit

1967. Solidstate, disc echo.

1967		$300	$400

V-837 Echo Deluxe Tape Echo

1967. Solidstate, multiple heads.

1967		$400	$500

V-846 Wah

1969-1970s. Chrome top, Italian-made.

1969	Made in Italy	$800	$1,250
1970s	Sepulveda-made	$300	$400

V-847 Wah-Wah

1992-present. Reissue of the original V-846 Wah.

1992-2024		$75	$100

Volume Pedal

1954-late 1960s. Reissued as the V850.

1960s		$50	$75

Wampler Pedals

2004-present. Brian Wampler began building effects under the brand Indy Guitarist in 2004 and changed the name to Wampler Pedals in 2007. They are built in Greenwood, Indiana.

Warmenfat

2004-present. Pre-amps and guitar effects built in Sacramento, California, by Rainbow Electronics.

Wasabi

2003-2008. Line of guitar effect pedals from Danelectro.

Washburn

Washburn offered a line of effects from around 1983 to ca. '89.

Visual Sound Visual VLM 10th Anniversary

1967 Vox Tone Bender
Dean Nissen

Wampler Clarksdale

EFFECTS

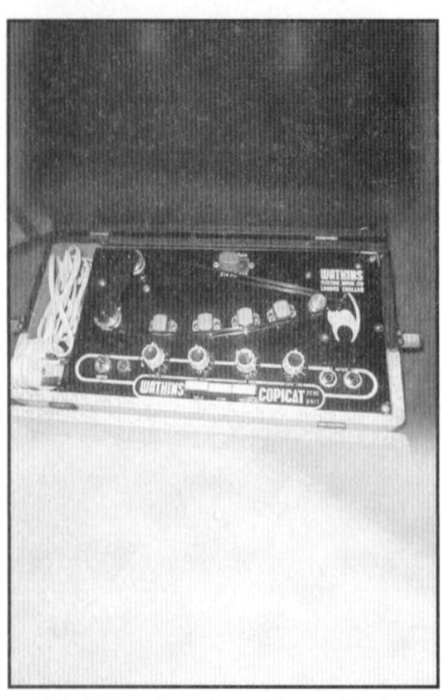

Watkins Copicat Tape Echo
Rivington Guitars

Whirlwind OC-Bass Optical Compressor

Xotic SL Drive

MODEL YEAR	FEATURES	LOW	HIGH

Effects

1980s	Analog Delay AX:9	$50	$65
1980s	Flanger FX:4	$55	$75
1980s	Phaser PX:8	$65	$85
1980s	Stack in a Box SX:3	$50	$65

Watkins/WEM

1957-present. Charlie Watkins founded Watkins Electric Music (WEM). Their first commercial product was the Watkins Dominator amp in '57, followed by the Copicat Echo in '58.

Copicat Tape Echo

1958-1970s, 1985-present. The Copicat went through several detail changes, subsequently known as the Marks I, II, III, and IV versions. It has been reissued in various forms by Watkins.

1958-1970s	Solidstate	$750	$1,500
1958-1970s	Tube	$1,250	$1,750

Way Huge Electronics

1995-1998, 2008-present Way Huge offered a variety of stomp boxes, made in Sherman Oaks, California. Jim Dunlop revived the brand in '08.

Foot Pig Fuzz

1990s		$800	$1,000

Green Rhino Overdrive II

1990s		$400	$1,000

Piercing Moose Octafuzz

1990s		$650	$850

Swollen Pickle Jumbo Fuzz

1990s		$400	$650

WD Music

Since 1978, WD Music has offered a wide line of aftermarket products for guitar players. From '91 to '02, they offered a line of effects that were copies of the original Dan Armstrong color series (refer to Dan Armstrong listing).

Blue Clipper

1991-2002. Fuzz.

1991-2002		$60	$80

Orange Squeezer

1991-2002. Signal compressor.

1991-2002	Light Orange case	$60	$80

Purple Peaker

1991-2002. Mini EQ.

1991-2002		$60	$80

Westbury

1978-ca.1983. Brand imported by Unicord.

Tube Overdrive

1978-1983. 12AX7.

1978-1983		$200	$300

Whirlwind

1976-present. Effects from Michael Laiacona, who helped found MXR, originally made in Rochester, New York. Currently the company offers guitar effects, DI boxes and other music devices built in Greece, New York.

MODEL YEAR	FEATURES	LOW	HIGH

Commander

1980s. Boost and effects loop selector.

1980s		$75	$100

Wilsic

1970s. Enginer Charlie Ramskirr designed effects for Hornby Skewes, but also offered DIY mail-order kits under the brand Wilsic.

Sound Vibration

1970s		$75	$100

Wilson Effects

2007-present. Guitar effects built by Kevin Wilson in Guilford, Indiana.

WMD (William Mathewson Devices)

2008-present. William Mathewson builds his instrument effects in Denver, Colorado.

Wurlitzer

Wurlitzer offered the Fuzzer Buzzer in the 1960s, which was the same as the Clark Fuzz.

Xotic Effects

2001-present. The roots of Xotic go back to a small garage in the San Fernando Valley of Southern California in 1996, producing and designing bass guitars and bass preamps, soon expanding to build boutique pedals.

AC Booster

2002-2020. Light overdrive with 20db+ of boost and 2-band EQ.

2002-2020		$100	$130

AC Plus

2007-2018. Stackable 2-channel light overdrive with 3-band EQ and compression.

2007-2018		$130	$175

AC-COMP

2010-2018. Custom Shop light overdrive with 3 compression modes. Internal DIP switches control level of compression, tonal character, and treble/presence levels.

2010-2018		$160	$200

Bass BB Preamp

2006-present. Bass overdrive with 2 overlapping EQs and ±15dB boost/cut.

2006-2024		$175	$225

Bass RC Booster

2006-present. Bass boost with 2-band active EQ and ±15dB boost/cut.

2006-2024		$65	$85

BB Plus

2008-2020. Stackable 2-channel overdrive with 3-band EQ and compression.

2008-2020		$150	$200

BB Preamp

2005-2020. Overdrive with 30dB+ boost and 2-band EQ.

2005-2020		$100	$130

EFFECTS

MODEL YEAR	FEATURES	LOW	HIGH

BBP-COMP

2011-2018. Custom Shop overdrive with 3 compression modes and 2-band EQ.

2011-2018		$175	$225

BBP-MB

2009-2018. Custom Shop overdrive with 12dB+ mid-treble boost and 2-band EQ.

2009-2018		$150	$200

EP Booster

2009-present. Mini boost pedal with 20db+ of boost. Internal DIP switches control boost frequencies and EQ.

2009-2024		$100	$130

RC Booster

2002-2017. Clean boost with 20dB+ of transparent boost and 2-band EQ.

2002-2017		$65	$85

RC Booster V2

2016-present. Clean boost with 20dB+ transparent boost and 2-band EQ. Added gain channel with gain 2 control knob.

2016-2024		$100	$130

Robotalk

1998-2009. Envelope filter, random arpeggiator and low-pass filter. Ultra-boutique pedal, made from scratch, in limited quantities.

1998-2009		$250	$325

Robotalk 2

2009-2022. Envelope filter with 2 separate envelope filter channels that can be combined or used individually. Internal input pad controls passive/active signals. Internal DIP switches control frequency settings.

2009-2022		$150	$200

Robotalk-RI

2011-2018. Custom Shop envelope filter with an enhanced arpeggiator for more wonderfully strange and mesmerizing sounds.

2011-2018		$175	$225

SL Drive

2013-present. Mini overdrive pedal produces tones from legendary amplifiers, the Super Lead and Super Bass. Internal DIP switches control boost frequencies and EQ settings.

2013-2024		$85	$110

Soul Driven

2017-present. Boost/overdrive with mid-boost and tone knobs. Internal bass boost DIP switches control up to 6dB+ of boost.

2017-2024		$175	$225

SP Compressor

2012 present. Mini compressor featuring a wide variety of compressor tones from vintage to subtle to modern, and more. Internal DIP switches control attack.

2012-2024		$110	$150

Stereo X-Blender

2011-2017. Custom Shop effects looper with 3 parallel effects loops equipped with a transparent buffer amplifier allowing feeding and mixing of effects without signal deterioration.

2011-2017		$175	$225

X-Blender

2006-present. Series and parallel effects looper with boost switch for 6dB+ volume boost, treble and bass EQ and phase inverter switch. Dry/Wet knob in parallel mode.

2006-2024		$110	$150

Xotic Wah

2014-present. Wah pedal that features a 20% smaller size, bias, wah-Q, treble, and bass controls, plus internal DIP switches for even more tonal possibilities.

2014-2024		$225	$300

Yack

1960s. Japanese effects company.

Fuzz Box YF-2

1960s		$150	$400

Yamaha

1946-present. Yamaha has offered effects since at least the early '80s. They also build guitars, basses, amps, and other musical instruments.

Analog Delay E1005

1980s. Free-standing, double-space rack mount-sized, short to long range delays, gray case.

1980s		$175	$325

Yubro

Yubro, of Bellaire, Texas, offered a line of nine effects in the mid- to late-'80s.

Analog Delay AD-800

1980s	300 ms	$75	$125

Stereo Chorus CH-600

1980s		$55	$75

Zinky

Amp builder Bruce Zinky added guitar effects in late 2003, in Flagstaff, Arizona. He also builds amps and has revived the Supro brand on a guitar and amp.

Zoom

Effects line from Samson Technologies Corp. of Syosset, New York.

503 Amp Simulator

1998-2000		$40	$55

504 Acoustic Pedal

1997-2000. Compact multi-effects pedal, 24 effects, tuner, replaced by II version.

1997-2000		$40	$55

505 Guitar Pedal

1996-2000. Compact multi-effects pedal, 24 effects, tuner, replaced by II version.

1996-2000		$45	$60

506 Bass Pedal

1997-2000. Compact multi-effects bass pedal, 24 effects, tuner, black box, orange panel. Replaced by II version.

1997-2000		$55	$75

507 Reverb

1997-2000		$40	$55

Xotic Effects Soul Driven

Xotic Effects X-Blender

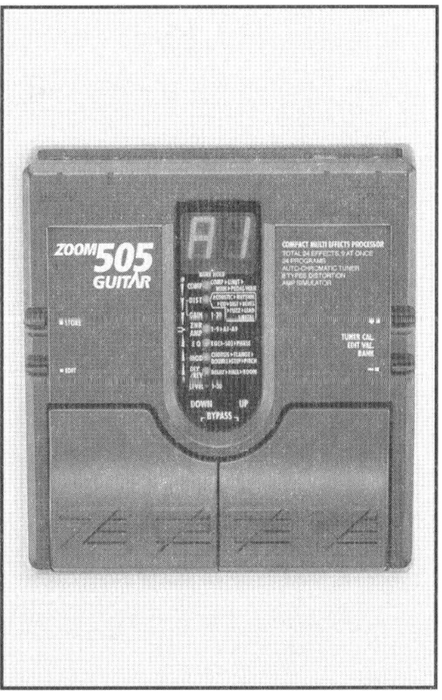

Zoom 505

EFFECTS

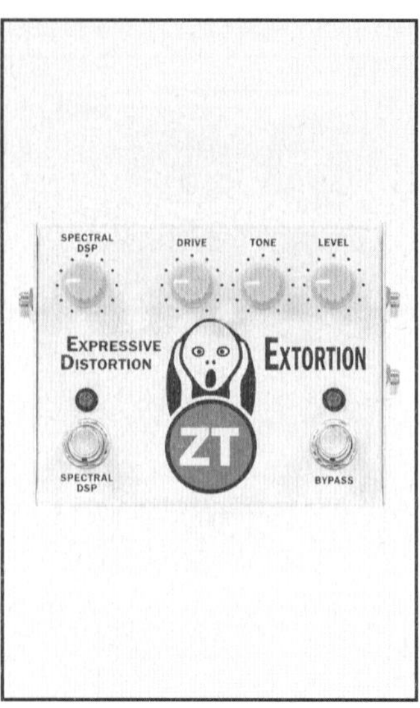

ZT Amplifiers Extortion

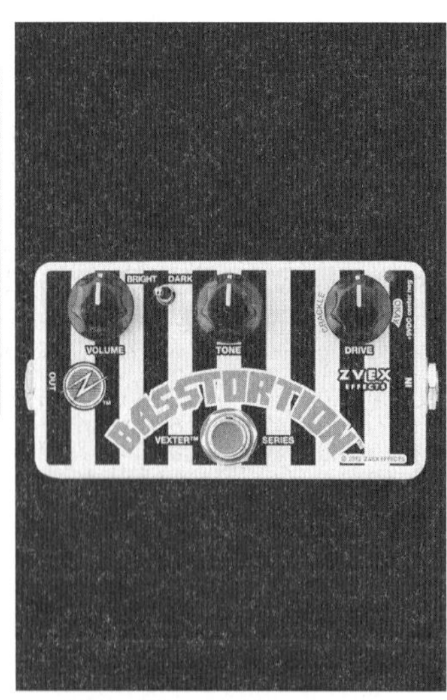

ZVex Effects Basstortion

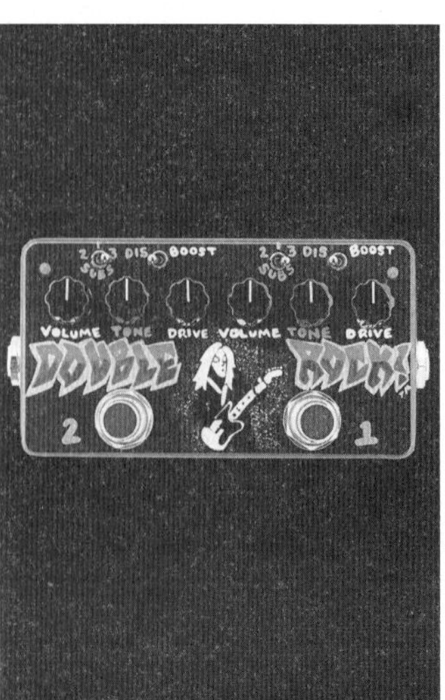

ZVex Effects Double Rock

MODEL YEAR	FEATURES	LOW	HIGH

1010 Player

1996-1999. Compact multi-effects pedal board, 16 distortions, 25 effects.

1996-1999		$60	$75

ZT Amplifiers

2009-present. Effects pedals built in China and offered by Ken Kantor in Berkeley, California. He also imports amps.

ZVex Effects

1995-present. Zachary Vex builds his effects in Minneapolis, Minnesota, with some subassembly work done in Michigan. Painters on staff create stock and custom versions of many pedals, which often bring higher prices. Vexter pedals are silkscreened pedals made in Taiwan. U.S. Vexters are manufactured in Taiwan but engraved in Minnesota. California Mini models are manufactured in California. In 2000-'02, Vex built the solidbody Drip Guitar with an onboard Wah. In '02, Vex also began building amps.

Basstortion

2011-present. Bass distortion, bright/dark switch.

2011-2024		$95	$130

Box of Metal

2007-2024. High-gain distortion, switchable noise gate.

2007-2024		$120	$150

Box of Rock

2005-present. 2-in-1 pedal. Tube amp-type distortion pedal and clean post-gain boost.

2005-2024		$100	$150

Channel 2

2014-2023. Mini boost pedal, master volume.

2014-2023		$70	$90

MODEL YEAR	FEATURES	LOW	HIGH

Distortion

2009-2020. Tube amp-style distortion, sub contour and gain switches.

2009-2020		$60	$75

Double Rock

2012-present. Dual switchable distortion/boost pedal.

2012-2024		$175	$200

Fat Fuzz Factory

2011-present. Fuzz Factory with additional 3-position mini toggle to select frequency range.

2011-2024		$175	$200

Fuzz Factory

1995-2024. Powerful, tweaky, and unique germanium fuzz pedal, with idiosyncratic hand-painted housings. Also available as Vexter and US Vexter models.

1995-2014		$120	$145
1995-2024	Hand-painted	$140	$200

Fuzz Factory 7

2013-present. Limited edition Fuzz Factory with foot-switchable EQ and 9-position rotary frequency selector.

2013-2024		$300	$375

Fuzz Probe

2000-present. Theremin-controlled Fuzz Factory.

2000-2024		$100	$175

Fuzzolo

2014-present. Mini footprint 2-knob silicon fuzz for guitar and bass.

2014-2024		$80	$100

Instant Lo-Fi Junky

2011-2024. Filter, compression, and wave shapeable vibrato and blend for chorus effect.

2011-2024		$150	$175

Inventobox

2010-2021. Dual pedal chassis for DIY builders or for use with Z.Vex modules.

2010-2021		$150	$200

MODEL YEAR	FEATURES	LOW	HIGH

Jonny Octave

2005-present. Octave pedal.

2005-2024 $140 $185

Lo-Fi Loop Junky

2002-2024. Sampler, single 20-second sample with vibrato.

2002-2024 $150 $200

Loop Gate

2012-present. Audio looping mixer with foot switchable noise gate.

2012-2024 $100 $130

Machine

1996-present. Crossover distortion generator.

1996-2024 $150 $200

Mastrotron

2009-present. Silicon fuzz with mini toggle sub contour.

2009-2024 $70 $95

Octane I, II, and III

1995-2023. Ring modulator fuzz.

1995-2023 $85 $125

Ooh Wah I and II

2003-2013. 8-step sequencer using wah filters with random sequencing.

2003-2013 $90 $115

Ringtone and Ringtone TT

2006-2013. 8-step sequencer using ring modulator.

2006-2013 $175 $190

Seek Trem I and II

2006-2013. 8-step sequencer using volume.

1999-2013 $135 $175

Seek Wah I and II

2006-2013. 8-step sequencer using wah filters.

2006-2013 $140 $180

Sonar Tremolo and Stutter

2012-present. Tremolo with wave shaping, distortion circuit, tap tempo, and auto tempo ramping.

2012-2024 $175 $190

MODEL YEAR	FEATURES	LOW	HIGH

Super Duper 2-in-1

2001-present. Dual boost with master volume on 2nd channel.

2001-2024 $120 $170

Super Hard On

1996-present. Sparkly clean boost.

1996-2024 $110 $170

Super Ringtone

2013-2025. 16-step sequencer using ring modulator with MIDI sync, tap tempo, tap tempo sync, and glissando.

2013-2024 $150 $225

Super Seek Trem

2013-present. 16-step sequencer using volume with MIDI sync, tap tempo, tap tempo sync, and glissando.

2013-2024 $150 $195

Super Seek Wah

2013-present. 16-step sequencer using wah filters with MIDI sync, tap tempo, tap tempo sync, and glissando.

2013-2024 $150 $195

Tremolo Probe

2000-2023. Theremin-controlled volume.

2000-2023 $100 $175

Tremorama

2004-2013. 8-step sequencer using volume with random sequencing.

2004-2013 $195 $230

Volume Probe

2000-2002. Theremin-controlled volume using coiled cable for antenna.

2000-2002 $100 $175

Wah Probe

2000-2023. Theremin-controlled wah.

2000-2023 $100 $175

Woolly Mammoth

1999-present. Silicon fuzz for guitar and bass.

1999-2024 $200 $290

ZVex Instant Lo-Fi Junky

ZVex Super Hard On

ZVex Super Seek Trem

STEELS & LAP STEELS

1957 Oahu Hawaiian lap steel and matching amp: Steve Siculan.

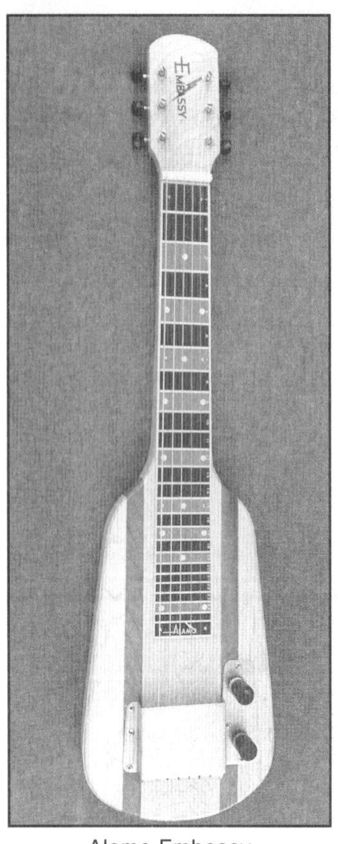

Alamo Embassy

Bronson Melody King
Jeff Thompson

STEELS & LAPS

MODEL YEAR	FEATURES	EXC. COND. LOW	HIGH

Airline

Ca. 1958-1968. Name used by Montgomery Ward for instruments built by Kay, Harmony and Valco.

Lap Steel

1960s	Res-O-Glas/plastic	$600	$800
1960s	Wood	$400	$500

Rocket 6-String Steel

1960s. Black and white, 3 legs, Valco-made.

1960s		$500	$800

Student 6 Steel

1950s	Black	$300	$375

Alamo

1947-1982. The first musical instruments built by Alamo, of San Antonio, Texas, were lap steel and amp combos with early models sold with small birch amps.

Hawaiian Lap Steels

1947-ca. 1967. Models include the '50s Challenger and Futuramic Dual Eight, the '50s and early-'60s Embassy (pear-shape) and Jet (triangular), the early-'60s Futuramic Eight and Futuramic Six, and the late-'60s Embassy (triangular Jet).

1950s		$300	$450

Alkire

1939-1950s. Founded by musician and teacher Eddie Alkire, with instruments like his E-Harp Steel built by Epiphone and maybe others (see Epiphone for values).

Aloha

1935-1960s. Private branded by Aloha Publishing and Musical Instruments Company, Chicago, Illinois. Made by others. There was also the Aloha Manufacturing Company of Honolulu which made musical instruments from around 1911 to the late '20s.

Alvarez

1965-present. Imported by St. Louis Music from mid-'60s. They also offered guitars, banjos and mandolins.

Model 5010 Koa D Steel-String

1960s		$500	$650

Aria/Aria Pro II

1956-present. Aria offered Japanese-made steels and lap steels in the '60s.

Lap Steel

1960s		$300	$375

Asher

1982-present. Intermediate, professional and premium grade, production/custom, solidbody, semi-hollow body and acoustic lap steels built by luthier Bill Asher in Venice, California. He also builds guitars.

Audiovox

Ca. 1935-ca. 1950. Paul Tutmarc's Audiovox Manufacturing, of Seattle, Washington, was a pioneer in electric lap steels, basses, guitars and amps.

MODEL YEAR	FEATURES	EXC. COND. LOW	HIGH

Lap Steel

1940s		$1,000	$1,500

Bel-Tone

1950s. Private branded by Magnatone, Bel-Tone oval logo on headstock.

Lap Steel

1950s	Pearloid cover	$400	$500

Bigsby

1947-1965, 2002-present. All handmade by Paul Arthur Bigsby, in Downey, California. Bigsby was a pioneer in developing pedal steels and they were generally special order or custom-made and not mass produced. The original instruments were made until '65 and should be valued on a case-by-case basis. Models include the Single Neck pedal steel, Double 8 pedal steel, 8/10 Doubleneck pedal steel, Triple 8 pedal steel (all ca. '47-'65), and the '57-'58 Magnatone G-70 lap steel. A solidbody guitar and a pedal steel based upon the original Paul Bigsby designs were introduced January 2002.

Triple 8-String Neck Steel

1947-1965. Bigsby steels were generally special order or custom-made and not mass produced. Instruments should be valued on a case-by-case basis.

1947-1959	Natural	$10,000	$15,000

Bronson

Ca. 1934-early 1960s. George Bronson was a steel guitar instructor in the Detroit area from the 1930s to the early '60s and sold instruments under his own brand. Most instruments and amps were made by Rickenbacker, Dickerson or Valco.

Leilani Lap Steel and Amp Set

1940s. Pearloid lap steel and small matching amp.

1940s		$450	$600

Melody King Model 52 Lap Steel

1950s. Brown bakelite body with 5 gold cavity covers on the top, made by Rickenbacker.

1950s		$800	$1,000

Model B Style

1948-1952. Rickenbacker-made.

1948-1952		$900	$1,250

Singing Electric

1950s. Round body, Valco-made.

1950s		$450	$600

Streamliner Lap Steel

1950s. Guitar-shaped body, 1 pickup, 1 knob, red-orange pearloid cover.

1950s		$500	$650

Carvin

1946-present. Founded by Lowell C. Kiesel who produced lapsteels under the Kiesel brand for 1947-'50. In late '49, he renamed the instrument line Carvin after sons Carson and Galvin. Until '77, they offered lap, console, and pedal steels with up to 4 necks.

Double 6

1960s		$750	$975

MODEL YEAR	FEATURES	EXC. COND. LOW	HIGH

Double 8

1960s	Sunburst	$775	$1,000

Electric Hawaiian Lap Steel

1950s		$250	$325

Single 8 With Legs

1960s. Large block position markers, 1 pickup, 2 knobs, blond finish.

1960s		$550	$725

Coppock

1930s-1959. Lap and console steels built by luthier John Lee Coppock in the Los Angeles area and in Peshastin, Washington. Coppock played Hawaiian music professionally in the 1920s and '30s and had a music studio where he started building his brand of steels around 1932. He moved to Washington in '44.

Cromwell

1935-1939. Budget model brand built by Gibson and distributed by various mail-order businesses.

Lap Steel

1939. Charlie Christian bar pickup.

1939	Sunburst	$450	$575

Danelectro

Known mainly for guitars and amps, Danelectro did offer a few lap steels in the mid-'50s.

Hawaiian Guitar

1958-1961. Three-tiered poplar solidbody lap steel, 1 lipstick tube pickup.

1958-1961		$1,000	$1,250

Dekley

1970s-early 1980s. Single- and double-neck pedal steels built by Bob Dekam and Jim Gurley in Bloomfield, Connecticut. They also sold volume pedals and strings.

Denley

1960s. Pedal steels built by Nigel Dennis and Gordon Huntley in England. They also made steels for Jim Burns' Ormston brand in the '60s.

Dickerson

1937-1948. Founded by the Dickerson brothers in '37, primarily for electric lap steels and small amps. Besides their own brand, Dickerson made instruments for Cleveland's Oahu Company, Varsity, Southern California Music, Bronson, Roland Ball, and Gourley. The lap steels were often sold with matching amps, both covered in pearloid mother-of-toilet-seat (MOTS). By '48, the company changed ownership and was renamed Magna Electronics (Magnatone).

Lap Steel

1940s. Dickerson appears to have offered 3 Hawaiian guitars. The Student was pear-shaped with a volume control; the Standard with had a volume and tone; both have decal 'boards and gray pearloid. The De Luxe is rare and came in tan pearloid and had sparkle plastic inlays and trim. Pre-War Dickersons have a heavier cast tailpiece; Post-War models have a metal rod and thru-body grommets. These were usually sold with a matching amp.

1940	Student or Standard	$300	$400

Dobro

1929-1942, ca.1954-2019. Dobro offered lap steels from '33 to '42. Gibson now owns the brand and recently offered a lap steel.

E-45 Lap Steel

Late 1970s-1986. Reproduction of '37-'41 wood body Hawaiian lap steel, offered as 6-, 7-, 8-, or 10-string.

1980s	6- or 8-string	$650	$850

Hawaiian Lap Steel

1933-1942. Bell-shaped wood body Hawaiian.

1933-1942		$650	$800

Lap Steel Guitar and Amp Set

1930s-1940s. Typical pearloid covered student 6-string lap steel and small matching amp (with 3 tubes and 1 control knob).

1933-1942		$750	$975

Metal Body Lap Steel

1936. All metal body, Dobro logo on body.

1936		$1,000	$2,000

Dwight

1950s. Private branded instruments made by National-Supro. Epiphone made a Dwight brand guitar in the '60s which was not related to the lap-steels.

Lap Steel

1950s. Pearloid, 6 strings.

1950s		$350	$450

Electro

1964-1975. The Electro line was manufactured by Electro String Instruments and distributed by Radio-Tel. The Electro logo appeared on the headstock rather than Rickenbacker. Refer to the Rickenbacker section for models.

Electromuse

1940s-1950s. Mainly offered lap steel and tube amp packages but they also offered acoustic and electric hollowbody guitars.

Lap Steel

1940s		$450	$575

Emmons

1970s-present. Professional and premium grade, production/custom, pedal steels built by Lashley, Inc. of Burlington, North Carolina.

Double 10 Steel

1970-1982. Push/pull pedal steel.

1970-1982		$3,500	$4,500

Lashley LeGrande III Steel

2001-2023. Double-neck, 8 pedals, 4 knee levers, 25th Anniversary.

2001-2023		$3,500	$4,500

S-10 Pedal Steel

1970-1982. Single 10-string neck pedal steel.

1970-1982		$2,500	$3,250

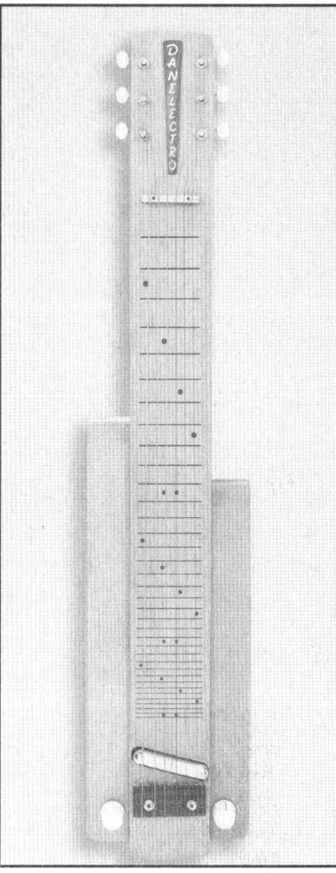

1957 Danelectro Hawaiian

Imaged by Heritage Auctions, HA.com

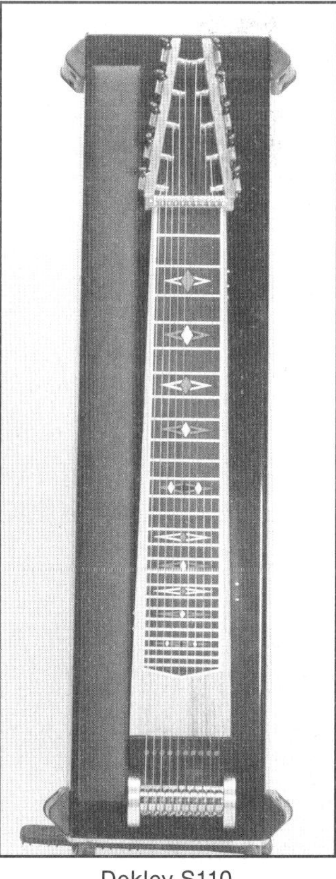

Dekley S110

Bernunzio Uptown Music

STEELS & LAPS

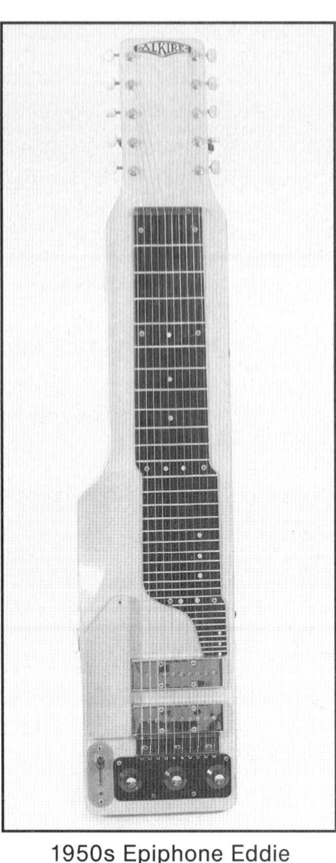
1950s Epiphone Eddie Alkire E-Harp
Jim Mathis

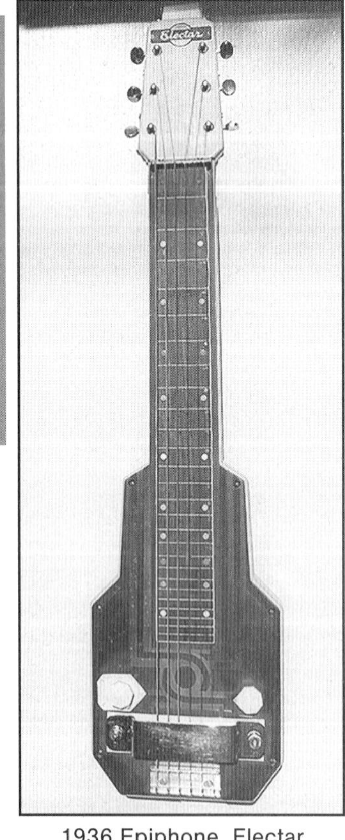

1936 Epiphone Electar
Dennis Clark

STEELS & LAPS

MODEL YEAR	FEATURES	EXC. COND. LOW	HIGH

Student, 3-Pedal Steel

1970s. Single neck.

1970s		$850	$1,125

English Electronics

1960s. Norman English had a teaching studio in Lansing, Michigan, where he gave guitar and steel lessons. He had his own private-branded instruments made by Valco in Chicago.

Tonemaster Lap Steel

1960s. Cream pearloid, 6 strings, 3 legs, Valco-made.

1960s		$425	$550
1960s	Stringtone pitch changer	$550	$700

Epiphone

1928-present. The then-Epiphone Banjo Company was established in '28. Best known for its guitars, the company offered steels from '35 to '58, when Gibson purchased the brand.

Century Lap Steel

1939-1957. Rocket-shaped maple body, 1 pickup, metal 'board, 6, 7 or 8 strings, black finish.

1939-1957		$525	$675

Eddie Alkire E-Harp

1939-1950s. 10-string, similar to Epiphone lap steel with Epi-style logo, offered in lap steel or console.

1939-1950s		$850	$1,125

Electar Hawaiian Lap Steel

1935-1937. Wood teardrop-shaped body, bakelite top, black, horseshoe pickup, 6 string.

1935-1937		$850	$1,125

Electar Model M Hawaiian Lap Steel

1936-1939. Metal top, stair-step body, art deco, black ('36-'37) or gray ('38-'39), 6, 7 or 8 strings.

1936-1939		$850	$1,125

Kent Hawaiian Lap Steel

1949-1953. Guitar-shaped maple body, 6 strings, lower-end of Epiphone Hawaiian line, Electar script logo below bottom of fretboard.

1949-1953		$350	$450

Solo Console Steel

1939-1954. Maple with white mahogany laminated body, black binding, black metal 'board, 6, 7 or 8 strings.

1939-1954		$700	$875

Triple-Neck Console Steel

1954-1957. neck version of Solo, sunburst or natural finish.

1954-1957		$1,500	$2,000

Zephyr Hawaiian Lap Steel

1939-1957. Maple stair-step body, metal 'board, 6, 7 or 8 strings.

1939-1949	Black	$850	$1,125
1950-1957	Sunburst	$850	$1,125

Ernie Ball

Best known for their strings and Music Man guitars, Ernie Ball offered a steel guitar under their own name for 1974-1979, building a very small quantity.

MODEL YEAR	FEATURES	EXC. COND. LOW	HIGH

S-10 Pedal Steel

1974-1979. 3 pedals, 3 levers.

1974-1979		$950	$1,250

Fender

1946-present. Fender offered lap and pedal steels from '46 to '80. In 2005 they introduced a new lap steel model under their Folk Music series, which lasted until 2009.

400 Pedal Steel

1958-1976. One 8-string neck with 4 to 10 pedals.

1958-1976		$800	$1,000

800 Pedal Steel

1964-1976. One 10-string neck, 6 to 10 pedals.

1964-1976		$1,000	$1,500

1000 Pedal Steel

1957-1976. Two 8-string necks, 8 or 10 pedals, sunburst or natural.

1957-1976		$950	$1,250

2000 Pedal Steel

1964-1976. Two 10-string necks, 10 or 11 pedals, sunburst.

1964-1976		$1,250	$1,750

Artist Dual 10 Pedal Steel

1976-1981. Two 10-string necks, 8 pedals, 4 knee levers, black or mahogany.

1976-1981		$1,125	$1,500

Champ Lap Steel

1955-1980. Replaced Champion Lap Steel, tan.

1955-1980		$1,500	$2,000

Champion Lap Steel

1949-1955. Covered in what collectors call mother-of-toilet-seat (MOTS) finish, also known as pearloid. Replaced by Champ Lap Steel.

1949-1955		$1,000	$1,500

Deluxe 6/Stringmaster Single Steel

1950-1981. Renamed from the Deluxe, 6 strings, 3 legs.

1950-1969	Blond or walnut	$850	$1,250
1970-1981	Black or white	$850	$1,250

Deluxe 8/Stringmaster Single Steel

1950-1981. Renamed from the Deluxe, 8 strings, 3 legs.

1950-1969	Blond or walnut	$850	$1,250
1970-1981	Black or white	$850	$1,250

Deluxe Steel

1949-1950. Strings-thru-pickup, Roman numeral markers, became the Deluxe 6 or Deluxe 8 Lap Steel in '50.

1946	Wax	$1,500	$2,000
1947-1950	Blond or walnut	$1,500	$2,000

Dual 6 Professional Steel

1952-1981. Two 6-string necks, 3 legs optional, blond or walnut.

1952-1981	Blond or walnut	$1,250	$1,500

Dual 8 Professional Steel

1946-1957. Two 8-string necks, 3 legs optional, blond or walnut.

1946-1957	Blond or walnut	$1,250	$1,500

FS-52 Lap Steel

2008-2009. Two-piece ash body, 22.5" scale, chrome hardware, white blonde gloss finish.

2008-2009		$350	$450

MODEL YEAR	FEATURES	EXC. COND. LOW	HIGH

K & F Steel

1945-1946. Made by Doc Kauffman and Leo Fender, strings-thru-pickup.

1945-1946		$3,000	$4,000

Organ Button Steel

1946-1947. Strings-thru-pickup, Roman numerals, red pushbutton for organ effect, most have a wax-like, non-lacquered finish.

1946-1947		$1,500	$2,000

Princeton Steel

1946-1948. Strings-thru-pickup, Roman numeral markers.

1946-1948		$1,500	$2,000

Stringmaster Steel (Two-Neck)

1953-1981. The Stringmaster came in 3 versions, having 2, 3 or 4 8-string necks (6-string necks optional).

1953-1954	Blond, 26" scale	$1,750	$2,250
1953-1954	Walnut, 26" scale	$1,500	$2,000
1955-1959	Blond, 24.5" scale	$1,600	$2,250
1955-1959	Walnut, 24.5" scale	$1,500	$2,000
1960-1969	Blond	$1,500	$2,000
1960-1969	Walnut	$1,250	$1,750
1970-1981	Blond or walnut	$1,250	$1,750

Stringmaster Steel (Three-Neck)

1953-1981.

1953-1954	Blond, 26" scale	$2,000	$2,750
1953-1954	Walnut, 26" scale	$1,750	$2,500
1955-1959	Blond, 24.5" scale	$2,000	$2,750
1955-1959	Walnut, 24.5" scale	$1,750	$2,500
1960-1969	Blond	$1,750	$2,500
1960-1969	Walnut	$1,600	$2,250
1970-1981	Blond or walnut	$1,600	$2,250

Stringmaster Steel (Four-Neck)

1953-1968.

1953-1954	Blond, 26" scale	$2,000	$2,750
1953-1954	Walnut, 26" scale	$1,750	$2,500
1955-1959	Blond, 24.5" scale	$2,000	$2,750
1955-1959	Walnut, 24.5" scale	$1,750	$2,500
1960-1968	Blond or walnut	$1,700	$2,250

Studio Deluxe Lap Steel

1956-1981. One pickup, 3 legs.

1956-1981	Blond	$1,250	$1,750

Framus

1946-1977, 1996-present. Imported into the U.S. by Philadelphia Music Company in the '60s. The brand was revived in '96 by Hans Peter Wilfer, the president of Warwick.

Deluxe Table Steel 0/7

1970s	White	$400	$500

Student Hawaiian Model 0/4

1970s	Red	$250	$350

G.L. Stiles

1960-1994. Gilbert Lee Stiles made a variety of instruments, mainly in the Miami, Florida area.

Doubleneck Pedal Steel

1970s		$1,000	$1,500

GFI

1989-present. Professional and premium grade, production/custom, pedal steel guitars built by luthier Gene Fields, in Arlington, Texas from '89-2008 and since in Marshfield, Missouri.

Ultra Pedal Steel

1990s	10-String	$2,000	$2,500

Gibson

1890s (1902)-present. Gibson offered steels from '35-'68.

BR-3 Lap Steel

1946-1947. Guitar-shaped, 1 P-90, 2 knobs, sunburst, mahogany. Replaced by BR-4 in '47.

1946-1947		$750	$1,000

BR-4 Lap Steel

1947. Guitar-shaped of solid mahogany, round neck, 1 pickup, varied binding, sunburst.

1947		$825	$1,125

BR-6 Lap Steel

1947-1960. Guitar-shaped solid mahogany body, square neck (round by '48).

1947-1960		$850	$1,250

BR-9 Lap Steel

1947-1959. Solidbody, 1 pickup, tan.

1947-1959		$500	$600

Century Lap Steel

1947-1968. Solid maple body, 6 or 10 ('48-'55) strings, 1 pickup, silver 'board.

1947-1968		$1,500	$2,000

Console Grand Steel

1938-1942, 1948-1967. Hollowbody, 2 necks, triple-bound body, standard 7- and 8-string combination until '42, double 8-string necks standard for '48 and after, by '61 becomes CG-620.

1938	String-mute	$1,500	$2,000
1939-1942		$1,500	$2,000
1948-1954		$1,500	$2,000
1955-1967	CG-520	$1,500	$2,000
1961-1967	CG-530	$1,500	$2,000

Console Grand Triple Neck (CGT)

1951-1956. Three 8-string necks, sunburst or natural, 4 legs.

1951-1956		$1,750	$2,250

Console Steel (C-530)

1957-1966. Replaced Consolette during '56-'57, double 8-string necks, 4 legs optional.

1957-1966	With legs	$1,250	$1,750

Consolette Table Steel

1952-1957. Rectangular korina body, 2 8-string necks, 4 legs, replaced by maple-body Console in '57.

1952-1955	P-90	$1,000	$1,500
1955-1957	Humbucking	$1,000	$1,500

EH-100 Lap Steel

1936-1949. Hollow guitar-shaped body, bound top, 6 or 7 strings.

1936-1949		$1000	$1,500

EH-125 Lap Steel

1939-1942. Hollow guitar-shaped mahogany body, single-bound body, metal 'board, sunburst.

1939-1942		$775	$1,000

1948 Fender Princeton Steel

Eric Reinertson

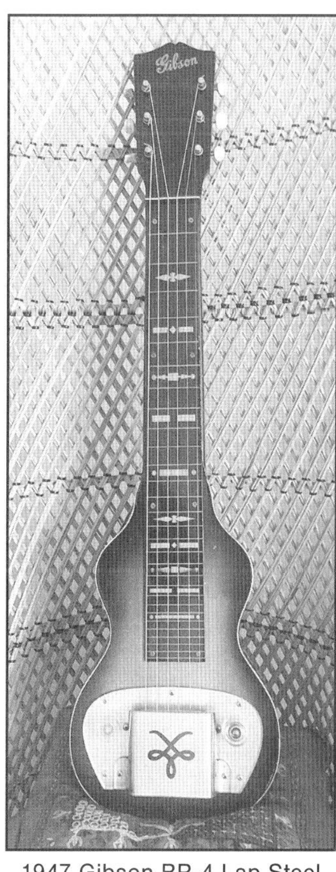

1947 Gibson BR-4 Lap Steel

Jean Claude Ferre

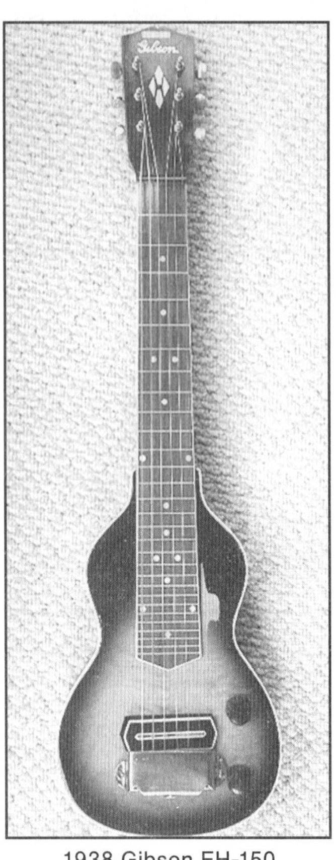
1938 Gibson EH-150
David Stone

1942 Gibson EH-185
Barney Roach

MODEL YEAR	FEATURES	EXC. COND. LOW	HIGH

EH-150 Doubleneck Electric Hawaiian Steel

1937-1939. Doubleneck EH-150 with 7- and 8-string necks.

1937-1939		$2,500	$3,500

EH-150/E-150 Lap Steel

1936-1943. Hollow guitar-shaped body, 6 to 10 strings available, bound body, first run in '36 was named E-150.

1936	1st run, metal body	$5,000	$6,000
1937-1943	Sunburst	$1,500	$2,500

EH-185 Lap Steel

1939-1942. Hollow guitar-shaped curly maple body, triple-bound body, 6, 7, 8 or 10 strings, sunburst.

1939-1942		$1,750	$2,250

EH-500 Skylark Deluxe Lap Steel

1958-1959. Like Skylark, but with dot markers.

1958-1959		$1,250	$1,750

EH-500 Skylark Lap Steel

1956-1968. Solid korina body, 8-string available by '58, block markers with numbers.

1956-1968		$1,000	$1,500

EH-610 Lap Steel

1957-1966. Six strings, 4 pedals.

1957-1966		$1,000	$1,500

EH-620 Lap Steel

1955-1967. Eight strings, 6 pedals, natural.

1955-1967		$1,000	$1,500

EH-630 Electraharp Steel

1941-1967. Eight strings, 8 pedals (4 in '49-'67). Called just EH-630 from '56-'67.

1941-1967		$1,000	$1,500

EH-820 Lap Steel

1960-1966. Two necks, 8 pedals, Vari-Tone selector, cherry.

1960-1966		$1,000	$1,500

Multiharp Steel

1956-1965. Three necks, 6 pedals, humbuckers.

1956-1965		$1,000	$1,500

Royaltone Lap Steel

1950-1952, 1956-1957. Volume and tone knobs on treble side of pickup, Gibson silk-screen logo, brown pickup bridge cover.

1950-1952	Symmetrical body	$1,000	$1,500
1956-1957	Guitar-shaped body	$1,000	$1,500

Ultratone Lap Steel

1948-1959. Solid maple body, plastic 'board, 6 strings.

1948-1959		$1,500	$2,000

Golden Hawaiian

1920s-1930s. Private branded lap guitar most likely made by one of the many Chicago makers for a small retailer, publisher, cataloger, or teaching studio.

Hawaiian Lap Acoustic

1930s. Small body, acoustic flat-top for Hawaiian lap-style playing, Golden Hawaiian logo on headstock.

1930s		$400	$550

Gourley

See Dickerson listing.

Gretsch

1883-present. Gretsch offered a variety of steels from 1940-'63. Gretsch actually only made 1 model; the rest were built by Valco. Currently they offer lap steel models.

Electromatic (5700/5715) Lap Steel

2005-present. Made in China, designed like the original Jet Mainliner (6147) steel, tobacco sunburst (5700) or black sparkle (5715).

2005-2020		$300	$500

Electromatic Console (6158) Twin Neck Steel

1949-1955. Two 6-string necks with six-on-a-side tuners, Electromatic script logo on end cover plates, 3 knobs, metal control panels and knobs, pearloid covered.

1949-1955		$950	$1,250

Electromatic Hawaiian Lap Steel

1940-1942. Guitar shaped mahogany body, wooden pickup cover.

1940-1942		$450	$575

Electromatic Standard (6156) Lap Steel

1949-1955. Brown pearloid.

1949-1955		$450	$575

Electromatic Student (6152) Lap Steel

1949-1955. Square bottom, brown pearloid, pearloid cover.

1949-1955		$400	$550

Jet Mainliner (6147) Steel

1955-1963. Single-neck version of Jet Twin.

1955-1963		$550	$700

Jet Twin Console (6148) Steel

1955-1963. Valco-made, 2 6-string necks, six-on-a-side tuners, Jet Black.

1955-1963		$1,000	$1,500

Guyatone

1933-present. Large Japanese maker. Brands also include Marco Polo, Winston, Kingston, Kent, LaFayette and Bradford. They offered lap steels under various brands from the '30s to the '60s.

Lap Steels

1960s		$300	$500

Table Steels

1960s. Three legs, 2 pickups.

1960s		$500	$950

Hanburt

1940-ca. 1950. Harvey M. Hansen built his electric Hawaiian guitars in Seattle, Washington that were sold through his wife's music instruction studio. His designs were influenced by Seattle's Audiovox guitars. He also built amps and at least one mandolin.

Harlin Brothers

1930s-1960s. Harlin Brothers, of Indianapolis, Indiana, were one of the early designers of pedal steel applications. Prices can vary because some instruments have a reputation for being hard to keep in tune.

MODEL YEAR	FEATURES	EXC. COND. LOW	HIGH

Multi-Kord Pedal Steel

1950s	Single neck	$650	$975

Harmony

1982-1976, late 1970s-present. Founded by Wilhelm Schultz and purchased by Sears in 1916. The company evolved into the largest producer of stringed instruments in the U.S. in the '30s. They offered electric lap steels by '36.

Consolectric Steel

1953. Combo unit that combines steel guitar neck and built-in amp, 3 legs, Harmony Consolectric script logo on end of case, luggage tweed cover.

1953		$750	$975

Lap Steels

1936-1960s	Various models	$400	$550

Hilo

1920s-1930s. Weissenborn-style guitars most likely made by New Jersey's Oscar Schmitt Company, Hilo orange label inside back.

Hawaiian Steel Guitar

1930s. Guitar shaped body, round sound hole, acoustic steel.

1930s		$1,500	$2,000

Höfner

1887-present. Höfner offered lap steels from the '30s into the '90s. They also built models for the Selmer brand.

Model 111 Lap Steel

1953-1992. Brazilian rosewood 'board, white body binding, 25 frets, volume and tone controls, sunburst. Same as Selmer Standard.

1953-1960		$400	$550

Jackson-Guldan

1920s-1960s. The Jackson-Guldan Violin Company, of Columbus, Ohio, offered lap steels and small tube amps early on. They also built acoustic guitars.

K & F (Kaufman & Fender)

See listing under Fender.

Kalamazoo

1933-1942, 1946-1947, 1965-1970. Budget brand produced by Gibson in Kalamazoo, Michigan. They offered lap steels in the '30s and '40s.

Lap Steel

1938-1942, 1946-1947.

1938-1947		$500	$650

Kamico

Late-1940s. Private branded by Kay for student lap steel market, Kamico logo on lap steels and amplifiers. They also made guitars.

Lap Steel and Amp Set

1948. Symmetrical 6-string lap steel with small, single-knob 1x8" amp, both with matching sunburst finish.

1948		$500	$650

Kay

Ca. 1931-present. Huge Chicago manufacturer Kay offered steels from '36 to '60 under their own brand and others.

Lap Steel

1940s-60s		$350	$750

Lap Steel With Matching Amp

1940s	Dark mahogany	$675	$875
1950s	Green	$675	$875

Kiesel

1946-1949, 2015-present. Founded by Lowell Kiesel as L.C. Kiesel Co., Los Angeles, California, but renamed Carvin in '49. Kiesel logo on the headstock. Kiesel brand name revived by Carvin in '15 for use on their guitars.

Bakelite Lap Steel

1946. Small guitar-shaped bakelite body, 1 pickup, 2 knobs, diamond markers.

1946		$450	$650

Knutson Luthiery

1981-present. Professional grade, custom, electric lap steels built by luthier John Knutson in Forestville, California. He also builds guitars, basses, and mandolins.

Lapdancer

2001-present. Intermediate and professional grade, custom/production, lap steels built by luthier Loni Specter in West Hills, California.

Lockola

1950s. Private brand lap and amp sets made by Valco for Lockola of Salt Lake City, Utah.

Lap Steel

1950s	Pearloid	$300	$375

Maestro

A budget brand made by Gibson.

Lap Steel

1940s-1950s. Pearloid, 1 pickup, 6 strings.

1940s-50s		$250	$350

Magnatone

Ca.1937-1971, 2013-present. Magnatone offered lap steels from '37 to '58. Besides their own brand, they also produced models under the Dickerson, Oahu, Gourley, and Natural Music Guild brands.

Lyric Doubleneck Lap Steel

Ca.1951-1958. Model G-1745-D-W, 8 strings per neck, hardwood body, 3 legs included.

1951-1958		$950	$1,250

Maestro Tripleneck Steel

Ca.1951-1958. Model G-2495-W-W, maple and walnut, 8 strings per neck, legs.

1951-1958		$950	$1,250

Pearloid (MOTS) Lap Steel

1950s. These were often sold with a matching amp; price here is for lap steel only.

1950s	Common	$300	$400
1950s	Less common	$475	$650

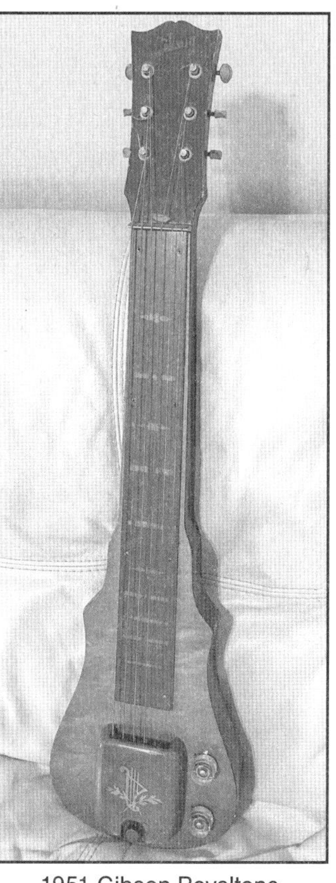

1951 Gibson Royaltone

James Seldin

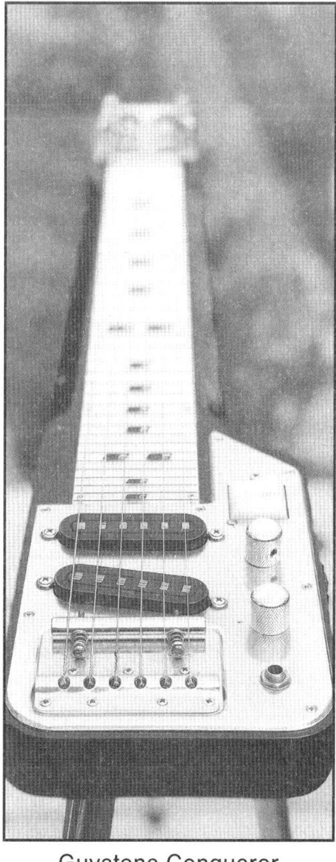

Guyatone Conqueror

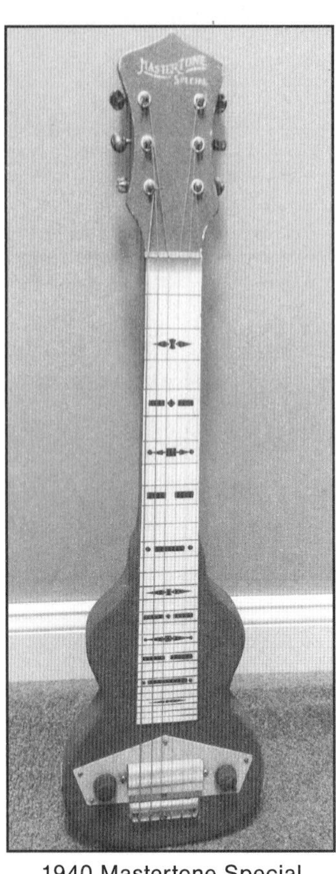

1940 Mastertone Special
Kirk Naylor

1960s Melobar
James Seldin

MODEL YEAR | FEATURES | EXC. COND. LOW | HIGH

Pearloid Steel Guitar

1950s. Six-string non-pedal steel, 3 legs, 2 knobs, 8 push buttons, star position markers, pearloid cover, Magnatone script logo at lower end of fretboard.

1950s $625 $850

Troubadour Lap Steel

1955. Wood body, 2 knobs, single metal pickup, Magnatone script logo on headstock and body.

1955 $550 $725

Marvel

1950-mid 1960s. Budget brand marketed by the Peter Sorkin Company of New York.

Electric Hawaiian Lap Steel

1950s $150 $250

Mastertone

Late 1920s-early 1940s. Mastertone was a budget brand made by Gibson and was used on lap steel, Hawaiian and archtop guitars.

Special Lap Steel

1920s-40s Brown crinkle $350 $550

May Bell

See the listing under Slingerland.

McKinney

1950s. Private branded for McKinney Guitars by Supro, blue McKinney Guitar logo on headstock.

Lap Steel

1950s. Similar to Supro Comet, white pearloid.

1950s $350 $450

Melobar

1967-2006. Designed by Walt Smith, of Smith Family Music, Melobar instruments feature a guitar body with a tilted neck, allowing the guitarist to play lap steel standing up. The instrument was developed and first made in Ed and Rudy Dopyera's Dobro factory. Most were available in 6-, 8-, or 10-string versions. Ted Smith took over operations from his father. Ted retired in late 2002. Production ceased in '06.

Electric Steel or Power-Slide Guitar

1970s-2006. Various 6-, 8-, and 10-string models.

1970s-2006 Various options $350 $1,250

MSA

1963-1983, 2001-present. Professional and premium grade, production/custom, pedal and lap steel guitars built in Dallas, Texas by Maurice Anderson. The company was dissolved in '83 and reorganized in '01.

S-12 Pedal Steel

1980s. 12-string.

1980s $1,500 $1,875

Sidekick 3/1 Steel

1970s-1980s. 10-string, 3 pedals, one lever.

1970s-80s $1,000 $1,250

MODEL YEAR | FEATURES | EXC. COND. LOW | HIGH

National

Ca. 1927-present. Founded in Los Angeles as the National String Instrument Corporation in '27, the brand has gone through many ownership changes over the years. National offered lap steels from '35 to '68.

Chicagoan Lap Steel

1948-1960. Gray pearloid, metal hand rest.

1948-1960 $400 $550

Clipper Model 1026 Lap Steel

1952-1955. Guitar-shaped wood body, celluloid bound, 1 pickup, volume, tone, 'visual octaves' position markers on neck, shaded brown finish.

1952-1955 $550 $700

Console (Dual 8) Steel

1939-1942. Two 8-string necks, parallelogram markers, black top with white sides.

1939-1941 $700 $950

Dynamic Lap Steel

1941-1968. New Yorker-style body, 6 strings, 3 detachable screw-in legs added by '56.

1941-1968 $750 $1,250

Electric Hawaiian Lap Steel

1935-1937. Round cast aluminum body, 1 pickup, square neck, 6 or 7 strings.

1935-1937 $725 $950

Grand Console Steel

1947-1967. Double (1050) or triple (1052) 8-string necks, Totem Pole 'board markers, came with or without legs, black and white finish, National's answer to Fender Stringmaster Series.

1947-1959 1052, 3 necks $1,500 $3,000

1947-1967 1050, 2 necks $1,250 $2,500

New Yorker Lap Steel

1939-1967. Introduced as Electric Hawaiian model in '35, square end body with stair-step sides, 7 or 8 strings, black and white finish.

1939-1949 $1,000 $1,500

1950-1967 $750 $1,000

Princess Lap Steel

1941-1947. Strings-thru-pickup, parallelogram markers, white pearloid.

1941-1947 $450 $575

Rocket One Ten Lap Steel

1956-1957. Rocket-shaped, black and white finish.

1956-1957 $500 $650

Studio 76 N476 Lap Steel

1964. Half and half stair-step inlay design, 3-on-a-side tuners with open-book shaped headstock, 1 pickup, 2 knobs, onyx black pearloid, soft shoulders.

1964 $300 $400

Trailblazer Steel

1948-1949. Square end, numbered markers, black.

1948-1949 $300 $400

Triplex 1088 Chord Changer Lap Steel

1944-1958. Maple and walnut body, 2 knobs, natural.

1944-1958 $725 $950

MODEL YEAR	FEATURES	EXC. COND. LOW	HIGH

Nioma

1932-1952. NIOMA was a music and arts school founded in Seattle. By '35 they added guitar instruction, offering their own branded lap steels (with matching amps), made by Dickerson. They also offered guitars.

Lap Steel

1930s	Pearloid	$250	$350

Oahu

1926-1985. The Oahu Publishing Company and Honolulu Conservatory, based in Cleveland, published a very popular guitar study course. They sold instruments to go with the lessons, starting with acoustic Hawaiian and Spanish guitars, selling large quantities in the '30s. As electric models became popular, Oahu responded with guitar-amp sets. Lap steel and matching amp sets were generally the same color; for example, yellow guitar and yellow amp, or white pearloid guitar and white amp. These sets were originally sold to students who would take private or group lessons. The instruments were made by Oahu, Valco, Harmony, Dickerson, and Rickenbacker and were offered into the '50s and '60s.

Dianna Lap Steel

1950s. Oahu and Diana logos on headstock, Oahu logo on fretboard, fancy bridge, pleasant, unusual sunburst finish.

1950s		$750	$1,250

Hawaiian Lap Steel

1930s	Sunburst, student-grade	$325	$500
1930s	Tonemaster with decal art	$450	$800
1930s-40s	Rare style, higher-end	$500	$900
1930s-40s	Rare style, student-grade	$450	$800
1940s	Pearloid, Supro-made	$450	$800
1950s	Pearloid or painted	$450	$800
1950s	Tonemaster	$450	$800

Iolana

1941-1951, Late-1950s. Gold hardware, 2 6-string necks. Early model is lap steel, later version a console.

1941-1951	Lap	$725	$950
1950s	Console	$950	$1,250

K-71 Acoustic Lap Steel

1930s. Flat-top, round sound hole, decals on lower bouts.

1930s		$425	$550

Triplex 1088 Chord Changer Lap Steel

1940s. National-built 6-string lap steel with 'tuning change mechanism'.

1940s		$850	$1,250

Ormston

1966-1968. Pedal steels built in England by Denley and marketed by James Ormston Burns between his stints with Burns London, which was bought by America's Baldwin Company in '65, and the Dallas Arbiter Hayman brand.

MODEL YEAR	FEATURES	EXC. COND. LOW	HIGH

Recording King

Ca. 1930-1943. Brand used by Montgomery Ward for instruments made by Gibson, Regal, Kay, and Gretsch.

Electric Hawaiian Lap Steel

1930s		$450	$575

Roy Smeck Model AB104 Steel

1930s-1940s. Pear-shaped body, 1 pickup.

1930s-40s		$650	$850

Regal

Ca. 1895-1966, 1987-present. Regal offered their own brand and made instruments for distributors and mass-merchandisers. The company sold out to Harmony in '54. See guitars for more company info.

Electric Hawaiian Lap Steel

1940s		$450	$650
1940s	With matching amp	$850	$1,250

Reso-phonic Steel

1930s. Dobro-style resonator and spider assembly, round neck, adjustable nut.

1930s		$750	$975

Rickenbacker

1931-present. Rickenbacker produced steels from '32 to '70.

Academy Lap Steel

1946-1947. Bakelite student model, horseshoe pickup, replaced by the Ace.

1946-1947		$550	$750

Ace Lap Steel

1948-1953. Bakelite body, 1 pickup.

1948-1953		$550	$750

Console 208 Steel

1955-1970. Two 8-string necks.

1955-1970		$950	$1,250

Console 518 Triple Neck Steel

1955-1970. 22.5" scale, 3 8-string necks.

1955-1970		$1,250	$1,750

Console 758 Triple Neck Steel

1957-1970. 25" scale, 3 8-string necks.

1957-1970		$1,250	$1,750

CW Steel

1957-1970. Single neck on wood body, several neck options, 3 attachable legs.

1957-1970		$1,250	$1,500

DC-16 Steel

1950-1952. Metal, double 8-string necks.

1950-1952		$900	$1,250

Electro Lap Steel

1940s, 1960s. Large Rickenbacker logo and smaller Electro logo on headstock ('40s), then on side ('60s).

1940s	Headstock logo	$700	$950
1960s	Side logo	$475	$650

Electro Doubleneck Steel

1940-1953. Two bakelite 8-string necks.

1940-1953		$1,250	$1,750

Electro Tripleneck Steel

1940-1953. Three bakelite 8-string necks.

1940-1953		$1,500	$2,000

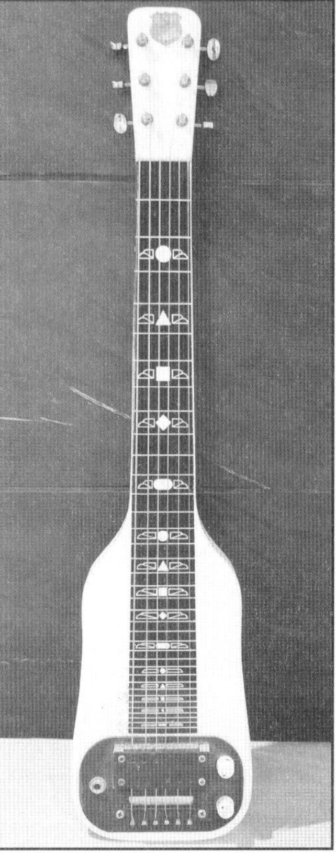

1960 National Chicagoan

Greg Narbey

1945 Rickenbacker Electro

Rivington Guitars

Mid-'70s Sho-Bud Maverick
Marco Parmiggiani

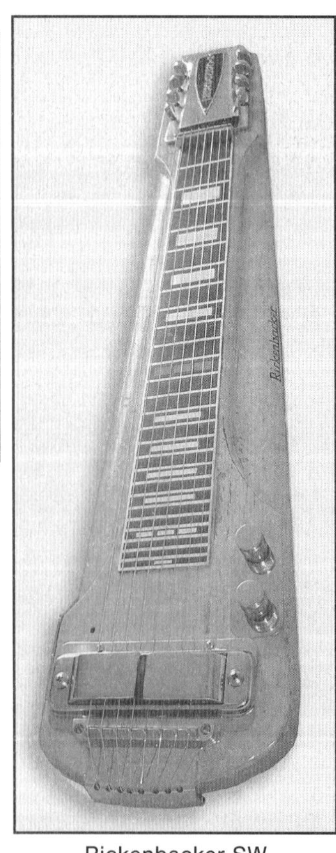

Rickenbacker SW
Mesnier Pascal

MODEL YEAR	FEATURES	EXC. COND. LOW	HIGH

Electro EH-3 Lap Steel

1970s. 6-string neck, legs.

1971		$350	$450

JB (Jerry Byrd) Model Steel

1961-1970. Single neck on large wood body, 6-, 7-, 8-, or 10-string neck, 3 attachable legs, Jerry Byrd Model logo on top plate.

1961-1970		$1,500	$2,000

Model 59 Lap Steel

1937-1943. Sheet steel body, baked-enamel light-colored crinkle finish, 1 pickup.

1937-1943		$650	$850

Model 100 Lap Steel

1956-1970. Wood body, 6 strings, block markers, light or silver gray finish.

1956-1970		$750	$950

Model 102 Lap Steel

1960s. Wood body, 6 strings, slot head, block markers, natural finish.

1960		$750	$950

Model A-22 "Frying Pan" Steel

1934-1936. Originally called A-25 with 25" scale, small round body lap steel, 22.5" scale, offered as 6- or 7-string.

1934-1936		$4,500	$6,000

Model A-25 "Frying Pan" Steel

1932-1933. Originally called the Electro-Hawaiian Guitar, small round body lap steel, 25" scale, offered as 6- or 7-string. Name changed to Model A-22 in '34.

1932-1933		$7,500	$8,500

Model B Steel

1935-1955. Bakelite body and neck, 1 pickup, strings-thru-body, decorative metal plates, 6 or 8 strings, black.

1935-1955	6- or 8-string	$2,500	$3,500

Model B-10 Steel

1935-1955. Model B with slot head and 12 strings.

1935-1955		$3,000	$3,500

Model BD Steel

1949-1970. Bakelite body, 6 strings, deluxe version of Model B, black.

1949-1960		$1,000	$1,250

Model CW-6 Steel

1957-1961. Wood body, grille cloth on front, 6 strings, 3 legs, walnut finish, renamed JB (Jerry Byrd) model in '61.

1957-1961		$850	$1,250

Model DW Steel

1955-1961. Wood body, double 6- or 8-string necks, optional 3 legs.

1955-1961		$850	$1,250

Model G Lap Steel

Ca.1948-1957. Chrome-plated ornate version of Silver Hawaiian, gold hardware and trim, 6 or 8 strings.

1948-1957		$850	$1,250

Model S/NS (New Style) Steel

1946-early-1950s. Sheet steel body, 1 pickup, gray, gray sparkle or grayburst, also available as a doubleneck.

1946-1949		$800	$1,000

Model SD Steel

1949-1953. Deluxe NS, sheet steel body, 6, 7 or 8 strings, Copper Crinkle finish.

1949-1953		$850	$1,250

Model SW

1956-1962. Straight body style, 6 or 8 strings, block markers, dark or blond finish.

1956-1962	8-string	$1,000	$1,500
1956-1962	8-string with legs	$1,000	$1,500

Silver Hawaiian Lap Steel

1937-1943. Chrome-plated sheet steel body, 1 horseshoe pickup, 6 strings.

1937-1943		$1,500	$2,500

Roland Ball

See Dickerson listing.

Scantic River Guitar Co.

Luthiers Thomas Ford, Steve Collin and Dennis Moore build their premium grade, custom, lap steel guitars in Durham, Maine. They started in 2008.

Serenader

Built by the Bud-Electro Manufacturing Company which was founded in Seattle, Washington in the late 1940s by Paul "Bud" Tutmarc, Jr., whose father built Audiovox instruments. He built mainly lap steels but also offered a solidbody bass.

Sherwood

Late 1940s-early 1950s. Lap steel guitars made for Montgomery Ward by Chicago manufacturers such as Kay. They also had archtop guitars and amps under that brand.

Deluxe Lap Steel

1950s. Symmetrical body, bar pickup, volume and tone controls, wood body, sunburst, relatively ornate headstock with script Sherwood logo, vertical Deluxe logo, and lightning bolt art.

1950s		$350	$450

Sho-Bud

1956-1981. Founded by Shot Jackson in Nashville. Distributed by Gretsch. They also had guitar models. Baldwin bought the company and closed the factory in '81.

Crossover Twin Neck Steel

1967-1971. Sho-Bud Baldwin double neck, Sho-Bud logo.

1967-1971		$3,000	$4,000

Maverick Pedal Steel

Ca. 1970-1981. Beginner model, burl elm cover, 3 pedals.

1970-1981		$1,250	$1,500

Pro I

1970-1981. Three pedals, natural.

1970-1975	Round front	$2,250	$3,000
1976-1981	Square front	$2,500	$3,500

MODEL YEAR	FEATURES	EXC. COND. LOW	HIGH

Pro II

1973-1981. Birdseye maple, double 10-string necks, natural.

1973-1975	Round front	$2,500	$3,500
1976-1981	Square front	$2,750	$3,750

Pro III

1975-1981. Metal necks.

1975	Round front	$2,750	$3,500
1976-1981	Square front	$3,000	$4,000

Super Pro

1977-1980. Doubleneck 10 strings, 8 floor pedals, 6 knee levers, Jet Black.

1977-1980		$3,500	$4,500

Sierra

1960-present. Originally designed and built by Chuck Wright in California and Oregon until '74, then by Don Christensen in Oregon. In 2003, Ed W. Littlefield Jr. took ownership, with professional and premium grade, production, lap and pedal steel guitars built by luthiers Tom Baker and Rob Girdis in Molalla, Oregon. Girdis died in '09. There is an unrelated Sierra brand of guitars.

Silvertone

1940-1970, present. Brand name for instruments sold by Sears.

Amp-In-Case Lap Steel

Early 1940s. Lap steel and amp set, amp cabinet doubles as lap case with the lap stored above the amp, amp is in a long vertical cabinet with brown tweed covering, manufacturer appears to be the same as used by Gibson in the late '30s, low to mid power, 1x10" speaker.

1941-1942		$650	$850

Six-String Lap Steel

1940s-1960s. Includes Valco-made, standard or pearloid finish.

1940s-60s	Various models	$275	$575

Slingerland

Ca. 1914-present. Offered by Slingerland Banjos and Drums. They also sold the May Bell brand. Instruments were also made by others and sold by Slingerland in the '30s and '40s.

May Bell Lap Steel

1930s. Guitar-shaped lap steel with May Bell logo. This brand also had '30s Hawaiian and Spanish guitars.

1930s		$250	$325

Songster Lap Steel

1930s. Slingerland logo headstock, Songster logo near nut, guitar-shaped body, sunburst maple top, some with figured maple back, 1 pickup, 2 bakelite brown knobs, dot markers.

1930s		$600	$775

SPG

2006-2009. Intermediate grade, custom, solidbody lapsteels originally built by luthier Rick Welch in Farmingdale, Maine and Hanson, Massachusetts, more recently by luthier Eric C. Brown in Farmingdale, Maine.

Stella

Ca. 1899-1974, 2000s. Stella was a brand of the Oscar Schmidt Company. Harmony acquired the brand in '39. The Stella brand was reintroduced in the 2000s by MBT International.

Electric Hawaiian Lap Steel

1937		$450	$575

Supertone

1914-1941. Brand name for Sears which was replaced by Silvertone. Instruments made by Harmony and others.

Electric Hawaiian Lap Steel

1930s	Various models	$350	$500

Supro

1935-1968, 2004-present. Budget brand of the National Dobro Company. The brand name was revived in '04.

Airline

1952-1962. Asymmetrical body with straight left side and contoured right (treble) side, black pearloid with small white pearloid on right (treble) side, 2 knobs, available with optional set of 3 legs, later versions available with 6 or 8 strings, described in catalog as "Supro's finest". Renamed Jet Airliner in '64.

1952-1962	6- or 8-string	$350	$500
1952-1962	With optional legs	$550	$700

Clipper Lap Steel

1941-1943. One pickup, bound rosewood 'board, dot inlay, brown pearloid.

1941-1943		$450	$600

Comet Lap Steel

1947-1966. One pickup, attached cord, painted-on 'board, pearloid.

1947-1949	Gray pearloid	$450	$575
1950-1966	White pearloid	$450	$575

Comet Steel (With Legs)

1950s-1960s. Three-leg 6-string steel version of the lap steel, 2 knobs, Supro logo on cover plate, 1 pickup.

1960s	Black & white	$575	$750

Console 8 Steel

1958-1960. Eight strings, 3 legs, black and white.

1958-1960		$700	$950

Irene Lap Steel

1940s. Complete ivory pearloid cover including headstock, fretboard and body, Roman numeral markers, 1 pickup, 2 control knobs, hard-wired output cord.

1940s		$400	$550

Jet Airliner Steel

1964-1968. Renamed from Airline, described in catalog as "Supro's finest", 1 pickup, totem pole markings, 6 or 8 strings, pearloid, National-made.

1964-1968	6- or 8-string	$600	$775
1964-1968	With optional legs	$725	$950

Professional Steel

1950s. Light brown pearloid.

1950s		$400	$550

1950s Silvertone

Peter Thomas

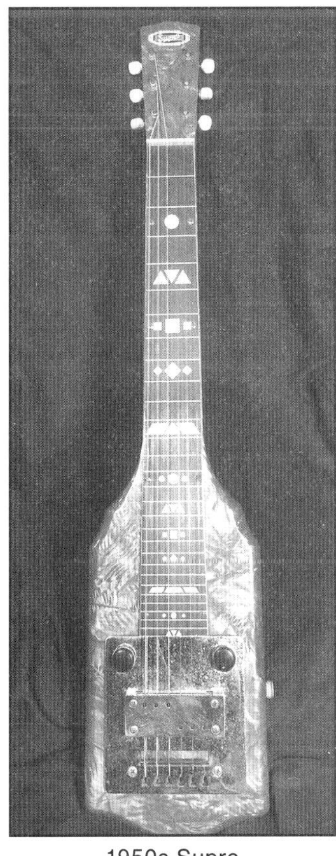

1950s Supro

James Clements, - Player Built Guitars

STEELS & LAPS

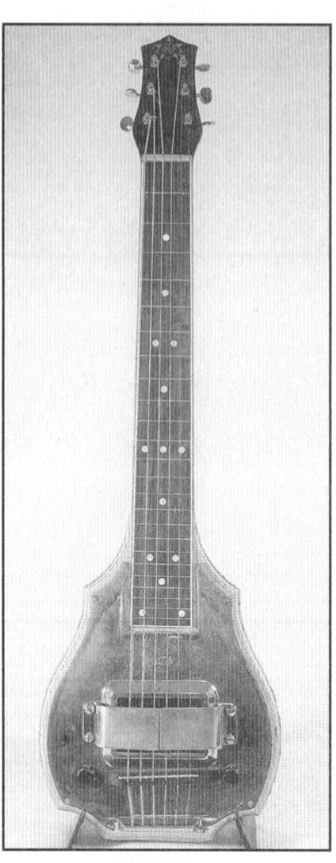

1938 Vega
Dan Bishop

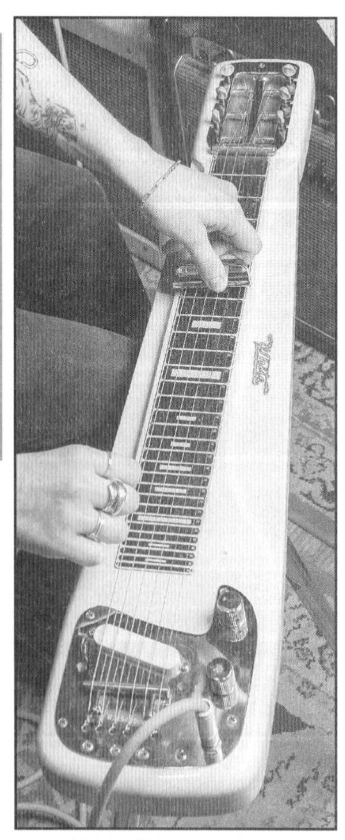

1956 White Lap Steel
Chicago Music Exchange

MODEL YEAR	FEATURES	EXC. COND. LOW	HIGH

Special Steel

1955-1962. Pearloid lap steel, student model, large script Special logo near pickup on early models, red until '57, white after.

1955-1957	Red pearloid	$400	$550
1957-1962	White pearloid	$400	$550

Spectator Steel

1952-1954. Wood body, 1 pickup, painted-on 'board, natural.

1952-1954		$400	$550

Student De Luxe Lap Steel

1952-1955. One pickup, pearloid, large script Student De Luxe logo located near pickup, replaced by Special in '55.

1952-1955	Black-white, or red pearloid	$400	$550
1952-1955	Natural or white paint	$400	$550

Studio

1955-1964. Symmetrical body, 2 knobs, priced in original catalog below the Comet, but above the Special, issued in '55 with blue plastic covered body.

1955-1964		$400	$550

Supreme Lap Steel

1947-1960. One pickup, painted-on 'board, brown pearloid until ca.'55, then red until ca.'58, Tulip Yellow after that.

1947-1960		$475	$650

Supro 60 Lap Steel and Amp-in-Case

Late 1930s-early '40s. Supro 60 logo near the single volume knob, long horizontal guitar case which houses a small tube amp and speaker, the case cover folds out to allow ventilation for the tubes, white pearloid, black amp case, the amp was made by National Dobro of Chicago.

1939-1941		$900	$1,250

Twin Lap Steel

1948-1955. Two 6-string necks, pearloid covering, renamed Console Steel in '55.

1948-1955		$700	$950

Teisco

1946-1974. The Japanese guitar-maker offered many steel models from '55 to around '67. Models offered '55-'61: EG-7L, -K, -R, -NT, -Z, -A, -S, -P, -8L, -NW, and -M. During '61-'67: EG-TW, -O, -U, -L, -6N, -8N, -DB, -DB2, -DT, H-39, H-905, TRH-1, Harp-8 and H-850.

Hawaiian Lap Steel

1955-1967		$400	$550

MODEL YEAR	FEATURES	EXC. COND. LOW	HIGH

True Tone

1960s. Brand name sold by Western Auto (hey, everybody was in the guitar biz back then). Probably made by Kay or Harmony.

Lap Steel

1960s. Guitar-shaped, single-cut, 1 pickup.

1960s		$400	$550

Varsity

See Dickerson listing.

Vega

1889-present. The original Boston-based company was purchased by C.F. Martin in '70. In '80, the Vega trademark was sold to a Korean company. The company was one of the first to enter the electric market by offering products in '36 and offered lap steels into the early '60s. The Deering Banjo Company acquired the brand in '89 and uses it on a line of banjos.

DG-DB Steel

1950s. Two necks, 8 strings.

1950s		$950	$1,250

Odell Lap Steel

1950s. White pearloid.

1950s		$400	$550

Other Lap Steels

1930s-40s	Common models	$350	$450
1930s-40s	Rare models	$850	$1,500
1940s	Art deco-style	$750	$1,500

Wabash

1950s. Lap steels distributed by the David Wexler company and made by others. They also offered guitars and amps.

Lap Steel (Hawaiian Scene Tailpiece)

1950s. Natural, 12 frets.

1950s		$300	$400

White

1955-1960. The White brand, named after plant manager Forrest White, was established by Fender to provide steel and small amp sets to teaching studios that were not Fender-authorized dealers. A standard guitar was planned, but never produced.

6-String Steel

1955-1956. White finish, block markers, 2 knobs, 3 legs. The 6 String Steel was usually sold with the matching white amp Model 80. Possibly only 1 batch of these was made by Fender in October/November '55.

1955-1956		$1,500	$2,000
1955	With matching amp	$5,500	$6,000

1930 Manuel Nunes Taro Patch Fiddle: Randy Klimpert/ VG Archive.

1920s Ditson

Imaged by Heritage Auctions, HA.com

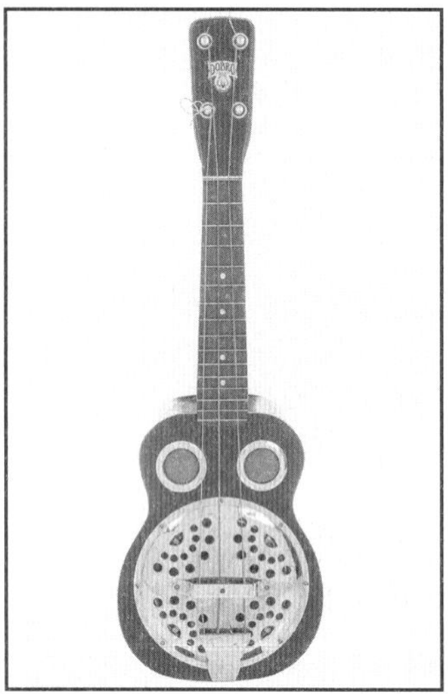

Ca. 1940s Dobro Resonator

Imaged by Heritage Auctions, HA.com

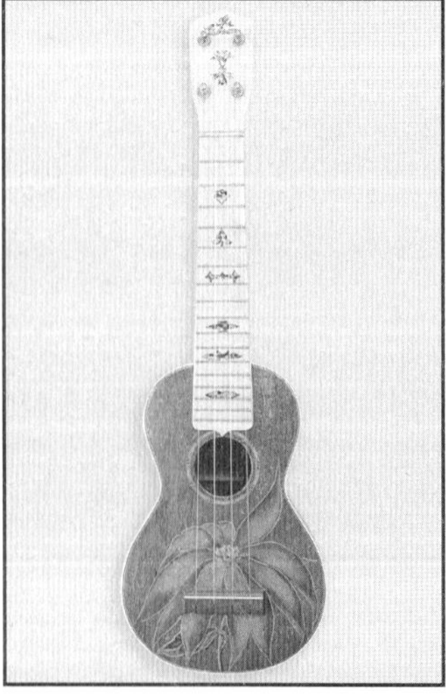

Gibson Poinsettia

Randy Klimpert

Aero Uke

1920s. Never branded, but almost certainly produced by Chicago's Stromberg-Voisenet Company, the precursor of Kay, the Aero Uke is an instrument quite unlike any other. With its spruce-capped body resembling an old-timey airplane wing and a neck and headstock that approximate a plane's fuselage, this clever '20s offering cashed in on the Lindbergh craze (like the Harmony Johnny Marvin model with its airplane-shaped bridge) and must have been a big hit at parties.

Ukulele

Airplane body.

MODEL YEAR	FEATURES	LOW	HIGH
1927	Black deco on wing	$3,200	$3,600
1927	Gold deco on wing	$3,500	$3,800

Aloha

1935-1960s. The Aloha brand turns up on numerous vastly different ukes. In fact, the variety of features exhibited by Aloha ukuleles leads the modern observer to believe that the ukes that bear this headstock decal were made by as many as a dozen different manufacturers, each with access to the same logo. Many were undoubtedly Island-made, with all Koa bodies and some with fancy rope binding; others bear unmistakable mainland traits. Some of these have a more traditional look and are stamped Akai inside the sound hole, while still others, strongly resembling mainland C.F. Martins in design, typically sport a decal of the Sam F. Chang curio shop on the reverse of the headstock.

Akai Soprano

Koa body, plain.

MODEL YEAR	FEATURES	LOW	HIGH
1930s		$500	$600

Soprano

Koa body, plain.

MODEL YEAR	FEATURES	LOW	HIGH
1950s		$600	$800

Bruno

This New York distributor certainly subcontracted all its ukulele production to other manufacturers, and as a result you'd be hard pressed to find two identical Bruno ukes.

Soprano

MODEL YEAR	FEATURES	LOW	HIGH
1920s	Koa, rope sound hole	$250	$350
1930s	Koa, rope bound body	$350	$450

Del Vecchio Dimonaco

With a design patterned after the pioneering work of Dobro and National, this Brazilian company produced a full line of resonator instruments, all constructed of native Brazilian rosewood, from the 1950s onward.

Resonator

MODEL YEAR	FEATURES	LOW	HIGH
1950s	Brazilian rosewood	$700	$800

Ditson

1915-1926. Don't be fooled. While some of the ukes that were commissioned by this East Coast music publisher and chain store were manufactured by C.F. Martin, Martin was by no means the sole supplier. The Martin-made instruments often bear a Martin brand as well as a Ditson one, or, barring that, at least demonstrate an overall similarity to the rest of the ukes in the regular Martin line, both inside and out. The most telling and desirable feature of these Martin-made Ditsons is a dreadnaught-style wide waisted body design.

Dreadnaught Soprano

MODEL YEAR	FEATURES	LOW	HIGH
1916	as Martin Style 1	$2,000	$2,500
1919	as Martin 1M	$1,600	$1,800
1921	as Martin 1K	$2,700	$3,000
1922	as Martin O	$1,500	$1,700
1923	as Martin 2M	$2,000	$2,500
1923	as Martin 5K	$12,000	$15,000
1926	as Martin 3M	$4,000	$5,000

Dreadnaught Taropatch

MODEL YEAR	FEATURES	LOW	HIGH
1916	as Martin 1	$2,200	$2,500
1916	as Martin 2	$2,500	$2,800
1916	as Martin 3	$3,500	$4,000

Standard Soprano

MODEL YEAR	FEATURES	LOW	HIGH
1917	as Martin 1M	$1,000	$1,200
1922	as Martin 2M	$1,000	$1,200
1922	as Martin O	$1,000	$1,200
1925	as Martin 3M	$2,000	$2,500

Dobro

1929-1942, ca. 1954-2019. The ukulele version of the popular amplifying resonator instruments first produced in California, the Dobro uke was offered in 2 sizes (soprano and tenor), 2 styles (f-holes and screen holes), and 2 colors (brown and black). Models with Dobro headstock decals are often outwardly indistinguishable from others bearing either a Regal badge or no logo at all, but a peek inside often reveals the presence of a sound well in the belly of the former, making them the more desirable of the two.

Resonator

Wood body.

MODEL YEAR	FEATURES	LOW	HIGH
1930s	F-holes, Regal-made	$1,000	$1,200
1930s	Screen holes	$1,200	$1,600
1935	Tenor, cyclops screen	$1,700	$2,000

Favilla

1890-1973. The small New York City family-owned factory that produced primarily guitars also managed to offer some surprisingly high quality ukes, the best of which rival Martin and Gibson for craftsmanship and tone. As a result, Favilla ukuleles are real value for the money.

Baritone

MODEL YEAR	FEATURES	LOW	HIGH
1950	Plain mahogany	$400	$500

Soprano

MODEL YEAR	FEATURES	LOW	HIGH
1925	Wimbrola, unbound teardrop, flat sides	$700	$900
1950s	Mahogany, triple bound	$650	$750
1950s	Plain mahogany	$500	$700

MODEL YEAR	FEATURES	LOW	HIGH
1950s	Teardrop-shaped, birch	$300	$500
1950s	Teardrop-shaped, stained blue	$300	$500

Fin-der

1950s. The pitch of this short-lived plastic ukulele was apparently the ease of learning, since the included instructional brochure helped you to "find" your chords with the added help of rainbow color-coded nylon strings.

Diamond Head

Styrene plastic, in original box.

1950s		$100	$150

Flamingo

1950s. If swanky designs hot-foil stamped into the surface of these '50s swirly injection molded polystyrene ukes didn't grab you, certainly the built-in functional pitch pipe across the top of the headstock would. And I ask you, who can resist a ukulele with a built-in tuner?

Soprano

1955	Brown top, white 'board	$100	$150
1955	White top, brown 'board	$100	$150

Giannini

1900-present. Ukuleles built in Salto, SP, Brazil near Sao Paolo. They also build guitars, violas, cavaquinhoes and mandolins.

Baritone

Mahogany body, rosewood fingerboard and bridge.

1972		$250	$300

Gibson

1890s (1902)-present. A relative late comer to the uke market, Gibson didn't get a line off the ground until 1927, fully nine years after Martin had already been in production. Even then they only produced three soprano styles and one tenor version. Worse still, they never made any ukes in Koa, sticking to the easier-to-obtain mahogany.

Nonetheless, Gibson ukuleles exhibit more unintentional variety than any other major maker, with enough construction, inlay, binding, and cosmetic variations to keep collectors buzzing for many a year to come. In general, the earliest examples feature a Gibson logo in script, later shortened to just Gibson. Post-war examples adopted the more square-ish logo of the rest of the Gibson line, and, at some point in the late '50s, began sporting ink-stamped serial numbers on the back of the headstock like their guitar and mandolin brethren.

DUSI

Tenor, like TU-1 but no Gibson logo, all Koa.

1950		$2,000	$2,500

ETU-1

Electric tenor, unbound body, square black pickup, 88 made.

1949		$7,000	$9,000

ETU-3

Electric tenor, triple bound body, rectangle pickup, rare.

1953		$10,000	$12,000

Poinsettia

Fancy inlays and 'board, painted body.

1930		$12,000	$25,000

TU-1

Tenor, mahogany body.

1930	Sunburst finish	$1,200	$1,500
1960	Red SG guitar-like finish	$1,000	$1,200

TU-3

Tenor, like TU-1 with fancy binding.

1935		$1,700	$1,900

Uke-1

Soprano, plain mahogany body.

1927		$500	$750
1966	Red SG guitar-like finish	$500	$750

Uke-2

Soprano, mahogany body.

1934	Triple bound	$900	$1,100
1939	Bound, X-braced	$900	$1,100

Uke-3

Soprano, dark finish.

1933	Diamonds & squares inlay	$1,500	$1,700
1935	Diamond inlay, short 'board	$1,200	$1,500
1935	Rare curved designs inlay	$2,500	$3,000

Graziano

1969-present. Luthier Tony Graziano has been building ukuleles almost exclusively since '95 in his Santa Cruz shop. Like many, he sees the uke as the instrument of the new millennium, and his entirely handmade, custom orders can be had in a variety of shapes, sizes, and woods.

Gretsch

1883-present. The first (and most desirable) ukuleles by this New York manufacturer were stamped with the name Gretsch American or with interior brass nameplates. Subsequent pieces, largely inexpensive laminate-bodied catalog offerings, are distinguished by small round Gretsch headstock decals, and a lack of any kerfed linings inside the bodies. They stopped making ukes in the late '50s, then in 2012 began offering them again.

Plain Soprano

Natural mahogany body, no binding.

1950s		$100	$150

Round

Round body, blue to green sunburst.

1940		$100	$150

Gibson Uke-2
Randy Klimpert

Gretsch Soprano

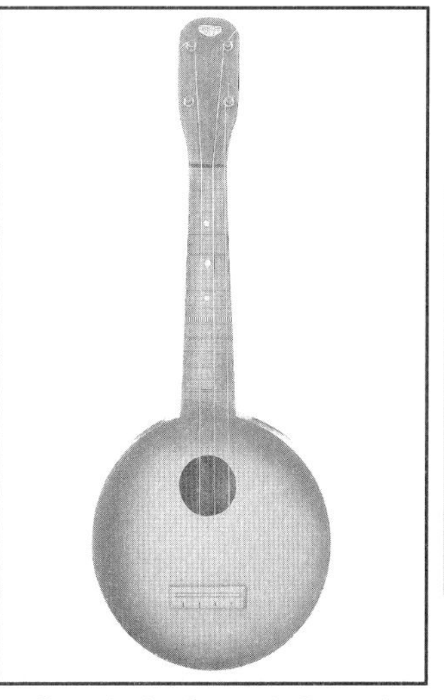

Ca. 1940s Gretsch Round
Imaged by Heritage Auctions, HA.com

UKULELES

1967 Guild B-11 Baritone
James Seldin

1955 Harmony Roy Smeck
Imaged by Heritage Auctions, HA.com

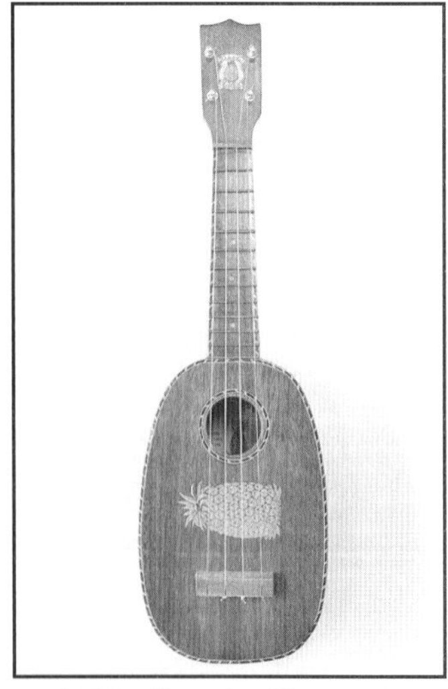
1960s Kamaka Pineapple
Randy Klimpert

MODEL YEAR	FEATURES	LOW	HIGH

Soprano

1935	Bound Koa, 'board as Martin 5K	$2,000	$2,200
1940s	Koa, fancy 'board inlay	$1,000	$1,200
1940s	Mahogany, fancy 'board inlay	$800	$900
1940s	Unbound, engraved rose peghead	$1,000	$1,200
1950s	Darker finish, dark binding border	$300	$500

Guild

1952-present. By rights this fine East Coast shop should have produced a full line of ukes to complement its impressive flat and carved-top guitar offerings. Alas, a lone baritone model was all that they could manage. And it's a darned shame, too.

B-11 Baritone

1963-1976. Mahogany body, rosewood 'board.

1960s		$800	$1,000

Harmony

1892-1976, late 1970s-present. This manufacturer surely produced more ukuleles than all other makers put together. Their extensive line ran the gamut from artist endorsed models and ukes in unusual shapes and materials, to inexpensive but flashy creations adorned with eye-catching decals and silk screening. The earliest examples have a small paper label on the back of the headstock, and a branded logo inside the body. This was replaced by a succession of logo decals applied to the front of the headstock, first gold and black, later green, white, and black. By the '60s Harmony had become so synonymous with ukulele production that they were known around their Chicago locale as simply "the ukulele factory," as in, "Ma couldn't come to the bar-b-que on-a-counta she got a job at the ukulele factory."

Baritone

Bound mahogany body.

1960s		$100	$150

Concert

Mahogany body, bound, concert size.

1935		$200	$300

Harold Teen

Carl Ed cartoon decals on front.

1930	Gray, Green	$500	$700
1930	Red, Yellow	$500	$700
1930	Blue	$650	$800

Johnny Marvin Tenor

Sports an airplane bridge.

1930s	Flamed Koa	$1,000	$1,200
1930s	Sunburst mahogany	$400	$600

Roy Smeck Concert

Concert-sized, sunburst spruce top.

1935		$400	$600

Roy Smeck

Mahogany body.

1955	Plastic 'board	$100	$150
1955	Wood 'board	$250	$300

MODEL YEAR	FEATURES	LOW	HIGH

Roy Smeck Vita

Pear-shaped body, seal-shaped f-holes.

1926		$700	$900

Tiple

Multicolored binding, 10 steel strings.

1935		$300	$500

Ukulele

1930	Koa, unbound	$200	$300
1935	Plain mahogany, unbound	$150	$250

Hilo Bay Ukuleles

2003-2017. Intermediate grade, production, tenor ukuleles made in Cebu City, Philippines for Mahalo Ken, owner of Hilo Guitars and Ukuleles in Hilo, Hawaii. He closed in April 2017 due to illness.

Kaai

Hawaiian Earnest Kaai was many things (teacher, songbook publisher, importer/exporter) during the early part of the 20th century, but ukulele manufacturer was certainly one job that he couldn't add to his resume. Still, scads of ukes proudly bear his name, in a variety of different styles and variations. Even more puzzling is the fact that while some appear to have been island-made, an equal number bear the telltale signs of mainland manufacture. It's also known that Kaai had an arrangement with Milwaukee instrument distributor William Stahl, and together they offered Kaai ukes. A very few examples - some with rope binding and some abalone inlaid presentation models, with ornate banjo-style headstocks - have surfaced which were certainly manufactured by the Larson Brothers of Chicago. These are the most highly prized of the Kaai ukes.

Soprano

Koa body.

1916	Koa, abalone inlaid	$7,000	$8,500
1916	Koa, rope bound	$1,000	$1,300
1925	No binding, decal on headstock	$400	$600
1930	No binding, rope inlaid sound hole	$400	$600
1935	Rope binding top & back	$900	$1,000
1935	White binding, abalone sound hole	$600	$800

Kala

2005-present. Mike Upton's Petaluma, California company offers budget and intermediate grade, production, ukuleles.

Kamaka

Part of the second wave of ukulele builders on the Hawaiian Islands (after Nunes, Dias, and Santos), Kamaka distinguished itself first with ukes of extremely high quality, subsequently with the most enduring non-guitar-derived designs, the Pineapple Uke, patented in 1928. Kamaka is the only maker which has been in continuous production for nearly

UKULELES

MODEL YEAR	FEATURES	LOW	HIGH

a hundred years, offering Hawaiian-made products from native woods in virtually every size and ornamentation. In the early '70s, Kamaka began rubber stamping the full date of manufacture on the end of the neck block of each uke, visible right through the sound hole. Now don't you wish that every manufacturer did that?

Concert

Koa body, extended rosewood 'board.

1975		$750	$900

Lili'u

Concert-sized Koa body.

1965	8 strings	$1,200	$1,400
1985	6 strings	$1,200	$1,400

Pineapple

1928	Abalone top & 'board	$4,000	$5,000
1928	Pineapple decal top or back	$2,000	$2,500
1930	Monkeypod wood, plain, unbound	$1,300	$1,600
1930	Rope bound top only, Koa	$1,700	$2,000
1935	Rope bound sound hole only	$1,500	$1,750
1960	Koa, unbound, KK logo	$700	$900
1970	Koa, extended rosewood 'board	$750	$900

Soprano

Traditional uke shape, plain Koa body.

1920		$600	$850

Tenor

Koa body, extended rosewood 'board.

1955		$1,200	$1,400

Kanile'a Ukulele

1998-present. Joseph and Kristen Souza build their intermediate, professional and premium grade, production/custom, ukuleles in Kaneohe, Hawaii.

Kent

1961-1969. Large, student quality ukes of laminated construction were offered by this Japanese concern throughout the '60s.

Baritone

Mahogany body, bound top, bound back.

1960s		$50	$100

Knutsen

1890s-1920s. While Christopher Knutsen was the inventor of flat-topped harp instruments featuring an integral sound chamber on the bass side of the body, he almost certainly left the manufacturing to others. Striking in both concept and design, Knutsen products nonetheless suffer from compromised construction techniques.

Harp

Koa body, large horn chamber.

1915	Bound	$2,500	$2,800
1915	Unbound	$2,000	$2,500

Harp Taro Patch

Tenor size, Koa body, 8 strings.

1915	Rope bound	$3,300	$4,300
1915	Unbound	$3,000	$4,000

Kumalae

Along with Kamaka, Kumalae was also of the second wave of Hawaiian uke makers. Jonah Kumalae's company quickly snagged the prestigious Gold Award at the Pan Pacific Exhibition in 1915, and the headstock decals and paper labels aren't about to let you forget it, either. Many assume that these all date from exactly that year, when in fact Kumalaes were offered right up through the late 1930s.

Soprano

Figured Koa body.

1919	Bound top/back/'board	$800	$1,000
1920	Rope bound top/back	$700	$900
1927	As 1919 but with fiddle-shaped peghead	$1,200	$1,500
1930	Unbound body	$600	$800
1933	Rope bound sound hole only	$800	$1,000

Tenor

Koa body, unbound top and back.

1930s		$1,500	$1,600

Laka

2010-present. Budget and intermediate grade, production ukuleles built in the Far East and distributed worldwide by John Hornby Skewes & Co. Ltd. from the United Kingdom.

Lanikai

2000-present. Line of budget and intermediate grade, production, Koa or nato wood, acoustic and acoustic/electric, ukuleles distributed by Hohner.

Le Domino

This line of striking ukuleles turned the popularity of domino playing into a clever visual motif, displaying not only tumbling dominos on their soundboards and around their sound holes, but 'board markers represented in decal domino denominations (3, 5, 7, 10, 12, etc.). The ukuleles were, in fact, produced by at least two different companies - Stewart and Regal - but you can scarcely tell them apart.

Concert

Concert size, black-finish, white bound, dominos.

1932		$800	$1,000

Soprano

Domino decals.

1930	Black finish, white bound	$400	$500
1940	Natural finish, unbound	$100	$150

Kamaka Tenor

Kanile'a K-1 Tenor

Lanikai CMTU-S Curly Mango Soprano Tuna

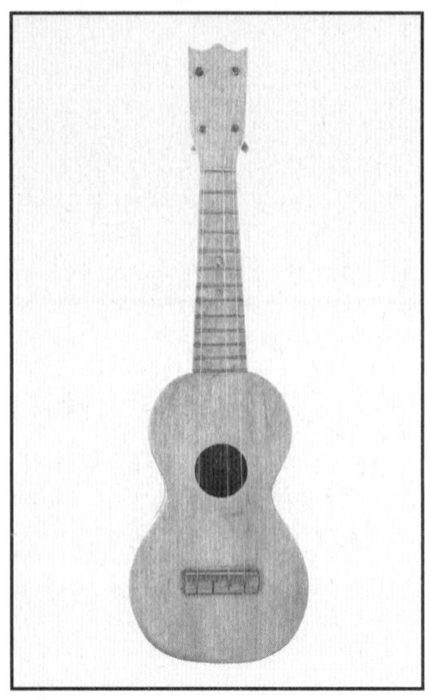
Leonardo Nunes Soprano
Imaged by Heritage Auctions, HA.com

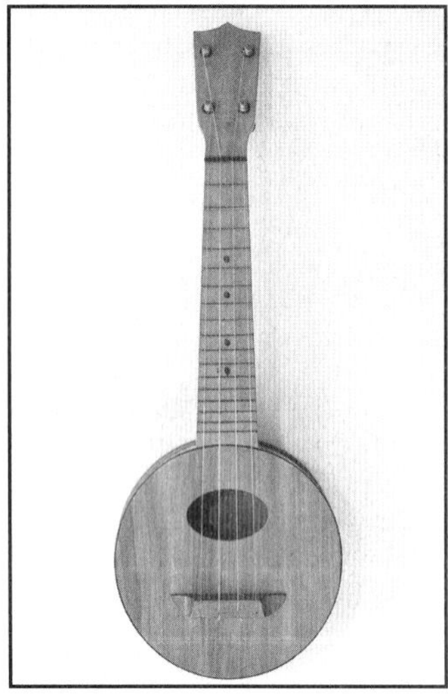
1935 Lyon And Healy Camp
Randy klimpert

1960 Maccaferri Maestro Baritone Electric
Randy Klimpert

MODEL YEAR	FEATURES	LOW	HIGH

Leonardo Nunes

Leonardo was the son of Manuel, the self-professed inventor of the ukulele. Whether actually the originator or not, Dad was certainly on the ship that brought the inventor to the islands in 1879. Leonardo, instead of joining up and making it Manuel & Son, set out on his own to produce ukes that are virtually indistinguishable from Pop's. All constructed entirely of Koa, some exhibit considerable figure and rope binding finery, making them as highly desirable to collectors as Manuel's.

Radio Tenor

Koa body, bound top, back and neck.

1935		$2,000	$2,500

Soprano

Figured Koa body.

1919	Bound top/back/'board	$800	$1,000
1920	Rope bound top/back	$700	$1,000
1927	Bound body/'board/head	$1,000	$1,200
1930	Unbound	$500	$700
1933	Rope bound sound hole only	$700	$900

Taro Patch Fiddle

Koa body, unbound top and back.

1930		$1,200	$1,500

Tenor

Koa body, unbound top and back.

1930		$1,000	$1,200

Lyon & Healy

1880s-ca.1949. During different time periods several different makers constructed ukes bearing this stamp - often with an additional Washburn tag as well. After initial production by Lyon & Healy, instrument manufacture then apparently bounced between Regal, Stewart, and Tonk Brothers all within a span of only a few short years. Adding to the confusion, ukes surface from time to time bearing no maker's mark that can be reasonably attributed to Lyon & Healy. Suffice it to say that the best of these ukes, those displaying the highest degrees of quality and ornamentation, rival Gibson and Martin for collectability and tone and beauty.

Bell-Shaped

Mahogany body.

1927		$2,000	$2,500

Camp

Round nissa wood body, black binding.

1935		$150	$200

Concert

Mahogany body, bound top and back.

1930		$1,200	$1,500

Shrine

Triangular body.

1927	Koa, green binding	$3,000	$3,500
1930	Mahogany, green binding	$2,000	$3,000
1933	Koa, abalone binding	$3,000	$3,500

Soprano (Koa)

1927	Bound top, pearl rosette	$3,500	$4,000
1934	Bound top/back	$1,000	$1,200
1935	Pearl bound top/back	$8,000	$10,000

Soprano (Mahogany)

1930	Unbound	$400	$500
1932	Bound top/back	$500	$600

Tenor (Koa)

1935	Pearl bound top/back	$7,000	$10,000

Tenor (Mahogany)

1933	Bound top/back	$1,500	$2,000

Maccaferri

1923-1990. Between the time he designed the Selmer guitar that became instantly synonymous with Django's gypsy jazz and his invention of the plastic clothespin, guitar design genius and manufacturing impresario Mario Maccaferri created a line of stringed instruments revolutionary for their complete plastic construction. The ukuleles were by far the greatest success, and most bore the tiny Maccaferri coat of arms on their tiny headstock. Mario was extremely proud of his innovations, so whether branded Islander, Maestro, TV Pal, or something else, the presence of PATENTED, PATENTS PEND, or one or more patent numbers on the headstock is your tell that it's a Maccaferri-designed uke.

Islander

Polystyrene plastic body, crest in peghead.

1953		$150	$200

Islander Baritone

Large polystyrene cutaway body.

1959		$250	$300

Maestro Baritone Electric

Large polystyrene cutaway body, pickup.

1960		$800	$1,000

Playtune

Polystyrene body.

1956		$100	$150

TV Pal

Polystyrene plastic body.

1955		$100	$150

TV Pal Deluxe

Extended 'board.

1960		$100	$150

Magic Fluke Company

1999-present. Budget grade, production, ukuleles made in New Hartford, Connecticut. With a clever design, exceptional quality, dozens of catchy finishes, and surprisingly affordable prices, it's little wonder that these little wonders have caught on. Riding - if not almost single-handedly driving - the coming third wave of uke popularity (the '20s and '50s were the first and second), Dale and Phyllis Webb of the Magic Fluke, along with Phyllis'

UKULELES

brother, author Jumpin' Jim Beloff, are downright ukulele evangelists. The Fluke is the first new uke that you're not afraid to let the kids monkey with.

Mainland Ukes

2008-present. Mike Hater imports parts built in China to set-up his budget and intermediate grade, production/custom, solid wood ukes and banjo-ukes in Nashville, Indiana.

Manuel Nunes

The self-professed father of the ukulele was at least one of the first makers to produce them in any quantity. Beginning after 1879, when he and the first boat load of Portuguese settlers landed in Hawaii, until at least the 1930s, Manuel and his son Leonardo (see Leonardo Nunes section) produced some of the most beautiful and superbly crafted ukes offered by any Island maker.

MODEL YEAR	FEATURES	LOW	HIGH
Soprano			
Koa body.			
1919	Figured Koa, bound top/back/'board	$1,000	$1,200
1920	Rope bound top/back	$900	$1,100
1927	Bound body/ 'board/head	$1,200	$2,000
1930	Unbound	$700	$900
1933	Rope bound sound hole only	$800	$1,000
Taro Patch Fiddle			
Koa body.			
1930	Rope bound top/back	$1,500	$2,000
1930	Unbound top/back	$1,300	$1,500
Tenor			
Koa body, unbound top and back.			
1930		$1,200	$1,500

Martin

1833-present. The C.F. Martin Company knew they wanted in on the uke craze and toyed with some prototypes as early as 1907 or so but didn't get around to actually getting serious until '16. The first of these were characterized by rather more primitive craftsmanship (by stringent Martin standards), bar frets, and an impressed logo in the back of the headstock. By '20, Koa became available as a pricey option, and by the early '30s, regular frets and the familiar Martin headstock decal had prevailed. Martin single-handedly created the archetype of the mainland uke and the standard by which all competitors are measured.

Martin has recently re-entered the ukulele market with its budget Mexican-made model S-0, the Backpacker Uke, as well as a limited edition of the ornate, and pricey, 5K, 5M and 3K ukes.

MODEL YEAR	FEATURES	LOW	HIGH
Style 0			
Unbound mahogany body.			
1920	Wood pegs	$600	$800
1953	Patent pegs	$600	$800
Style 0-C Concert			
Mahogany body, bound top.			
1931		$1,200	$1,500
Style 1			
Mahogany body.			
1916	Plain fingerboard, no dots	$1,200	$1,400
1920	Bound top only	$1,000	$1,200
1950	Tortoise bound top only	$700	$900
1967	Tortoise bound top only	$700	$900
Style 1-C Concert			
Mahogany body, bound top.			
1947		$1,200	$1,500
Style 1-C K Concert			
Koa body, bound top.			
1928		$2,500	$3,000
Style 1-K			
Koa body, rosewood bound top.			
1928	Wood pegs	$1,000	$1,200
1939	Patent pegs	$800	$1,000
Style 1-T Tenor			
Mahogany body, bound top only.			
1940		$1,200	$1,400
Style 1 Taro Patch			
Mahogany body, 8 strings, rosewood bound.			
1917		$1,000	$1,200
Style 1-K Taro Patch			
Style 1 with Koa body.			
1922		$1,200	$1,500
Style 2			
Mahogany body, ivoroid bound top and back.			
1917	No inlays, white binding	$1,200	$1,400
1922		$1,000	$1,200
1935		$800	$1,000
1961		$700	$900
Style 2-K			
Figured Koa body, bound top and back.			
1923		$1,500	$2,000
1939	Patent pegs	$1,500	$2,000
Style 2-C K Concert			
Same specs as 2-K, but in concert size.			
1927		$5,000	$6,000
Style 2 Taro Patch			
Mahogany body, 8 strings, ivoroid bound.			
1925		$1,500	$2,000
Style 2-K Taro Patch			
Style 2 with Koa body.			
1924		$2,200	$2,500
Style 3			
Mahogany body.			
1925	Kite inlay in headstock	$2,000	$2,300
1937	B/W lines in ebony 'board	$1,800	$2,200
1950	Extended 'board, dots	$1,500	$2,000

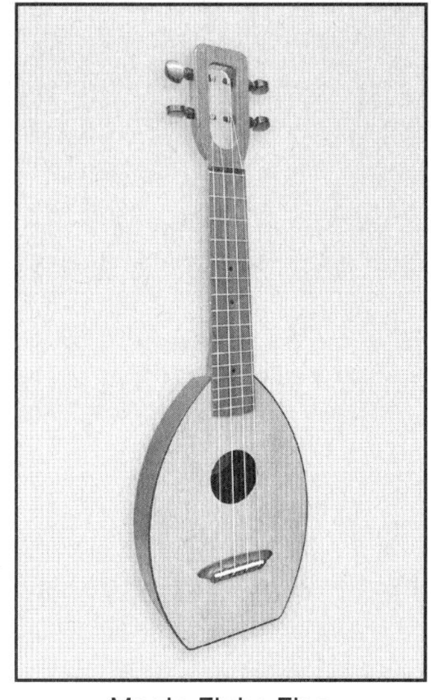

Magic Fluke Flea
Premium Tonewood

1930 Manuel Nunes
Taro Patch Fiddle
Randy Klimpert

1950 Martin Style 1
Imaged by Heritage Auctions, HA.com

UKULELES

Martin Style 5K

1925 Martin T-18
Randy Klimpert

1947 Martin T-28
Randy Klimpert

MODEL YEAR	FEATURES	LOW	HIGH
Style 3-K			
Figured Koa body.			
1920	Bowtie 'board inlay	$3,000	$3,500
1931	B/W lines, diamonds, squares	$2,500	$3,000
1939	B/W lines and dot inlay	$2,500	$3,000
Style 3-C K Concert			
Same specs as 3-K, but in concert size.			
1928		$10,000	$15,000
Style 3 Taro Patch			
Mahogany body, 8 strings, multiple bound.			
1923		$2,000	$2,500
Style 3-K Taro Patch			
Style 3 with Koa body.			
1929		$2,500	$3,000
Style 5			
Highly flamed mahogany body, all pearl trimmed, extremely rare.			
1941		$25,000	$30,000
Style 5-K			
Highly figured Koa body, all pearl trimmed.			
1926		$7,500	$9,000
Style 5-C K Concert			
Same specs as 5-K, but in concert size.			
1926		$12,000	$15,000
Style 5-T K Tenor			
Same specs as 5-K, but in tenor size.			
1929		$15,000	$17,000
Style 51 Baritone			
Mahogany body, bound top and back.			
1966		$1,000	$1,200
Style T-15 Tiple			
Mahogany body, 10 metal strings, unbound.			
1971		$800	$1,000
Style T-17 Tiple			
Mahogany body, 10 strings, unbound top and back.			
1940		$900	$1,100
Style T-18 Tiple			
Mahogany body, 10 strings, spruce top.			
1925		$1,100	$1,300
Style T-28 Tiple			
Rosewood body, 10 strings, bound top and back.			
1947		$2,200	$2,700

Maurer

The Larson brothers of Maurer & Co., Chicago, built a few ukes and at least one taro patch under this brand from 1915 into the 1930s. Their small tops and backs are built-under-tension in the Larson tradition. A few of them have surfaced with the Hawaiian teacher/player's Earnest Kaai label and were probably sold through Stahl's Milwaukee store.

Miami

Apparently endorsed by the not-so-famous "Ukulele Hughes" - whose smiling mug graces the inside labels - these ukes' actual origins are unknown, but were distributed by the Stadlmair company of New York, also the east coast distributor of Weissenborn instruments during the 1920s.

MODEL YEAR	FEATURES	LOW	HIGH
Miami "Baby"			
Smaller mahogany body, unbound.			
1925		$500	$600
Soprano			
Plain mahogany body, unbound.			
1925		$400	$500

National

Ca. 1927-present. To capitalize on the success of their amplifying guitars, the Dopyera brothers introduced metal-bodied ukuleles and mandolins as well. Large, heavy, and ungainly by today's standards, these early offerings nonetheless have their charms. Their subsequent switch to a smaller body shape produced an elegant and sweet-sounding resonator uke that soon became much sought after.

MODEL YEAR	FEATURES	LOW	HIGH
Style O			
Metal body, soprano size, sandblasted scenes.			
1931		$2,500	$3,000
Style 1			
Nickel body.			
1928	Tenor	$2,500	$2,700
1933	Soprano	$2,500	$2,700
Style 2			
Nickel body, engraved roses.			
1928	Tenor	$4,000	$4,500
1931	Soprano	$5,000	$7,000
Style 3			
Nickel body, lilies-of-the-valley.			
1929	Tenor	$7,500	$9,500
1933	Soprano	$8,000	$10,000
Triolian			
1928	Tenor, sunburst	$1,500	$2,000
1930	Soprano, sunburst	$1,500	$2,000
1934	Soprano, wood-grained metal	$1,500	$2,000

New Moon Ukulele

1978-present. Professional and premium grade, custom, acoustic ukuleles built in Greensboro, North Carolina by luthier Robert Rigaud. He also builds guitars under the Rigaud brand.

Oscar Schmidt

1879-1938, 1979-present. The same New Jersey outfit responsible for Leadbelly's 12-string guitar offered ukes as well during the same period. Many of these were odd amalgams of materials, often combining Koa, mahogany, and spruce in the same instrument. Since 1979, when the name was acquired by the U.S. Music Corp. (Washburn, Randall, etc.), they have offered a line of budget grade, production, Asian-made ukes. They also offer guitars, basses, mandolins, and banjos.

MODEL YEAR	FEATURES	LOW	HIGH
Soprano			
Spruce top, bound mahogany body.			
1930		$250	$350

Polk-a-lay-lee

1960s. These inexplicably shaped oddities were produced by Petersen Products of Chicago ca. the

UKULELES

MODEL YEAR	FEATURES	LOW	HIGH

mid-'60s, and anecdotal Midwestern lore has it that their intent was to be offered as giveaways for the Polk Brothers, a local appliance chain. This may be how they ended up, although the gargantuan original packaging makes no reference to any such promotion. The box does call out what the optional colors were.

Many have noted the striking resemblance to the similarly named wares of the Swaggerty company (see Swaggerty) of California, who also offered brightly colored plywood-bodied ukes in comically oversized incarnations, but who was copying whom has yet to be determined.

Ukulele

Long "boat oar" body, uke scale, brown, natural, red, black or fruitwood.

1965	Brown or natural	$250	$350
1965	Fruitwood	$600	$800
1965	Red or black	$400	$500

Regal

Ca. 1895-1966, 1987-present. Like the other large 1930s Chicago makers, Harmony and Lyon & Healy, the good ukes are very, very good, and the cheap ukes are very, very cheap. Unlike its pals, however, Regal seems to have produced more ukuleles in imaginative themes, striking color schemes, and in more degrees of fancy trim, making them the quintessential wall-hangers. And luckily for you, there's a vintage Regal uke to suit every décor.

Carson Robison

Top sports painted signature, cowboy scene.

1935		$500	$800

Jungle

Birch body, covered in leopard skin fabric.

1950		$500	$800

Resonator

Black body, f-holes, see Dobro uke.

1934		$200	$400

Soprano (Birch)

Birch body.

1931	Brown sunburst	$100	$200
1931	Nautical themes, various colors	$100	$200
1945	Painted body, panda theme	$600	$800
1945	Painted body, victory themes	$600	$800

Soprano (Koa)

Koa body, multicolored rope bound top.

1930		$300	$500

Soprano (Mahogany)

Mahogany body.

1930	Multiple bound top	$500	$800
1935	Spruce top, inlays	$300	$500
1940	Extended 'board	$200	$300

Tiple

1930	Birch body stained dark, black binding	$300	$400
1935	Spruce top, mahogany, fancy binding	$400	$600

Wendall Hall Red Head

Koa body, celebrity decal on headstock.

1935		$400	$600

Ricard

Alexander Ricard and son Jorge were primarily violin makers but also made mandolins and some lovely ukuleles out of their small shop in Springfield, Massachusetts from the teens to the 1920s. Though their labels only mention concert ukes, most of those that turn up today are soprano, and were probably made from leftover violin wood and parts.

Soprano

Spruce top, ebony 'board.

1920	Curly maple body	$400	$600
1925	Round concert body	$200	$300

S. S. Stewart

Not much is known about the ukuleles of this Philadelphia firm, except that they were most certainly sub-contracted from another maker or makers.

Soprano

Mahogany body, bound top and back.

1927		$200	$300

Sam F. Chang

A disciple of Kamaka, Sam F. Chang made ukuleles, guitars, and curios (according to his decal) during the 1930s for his own Honolulu shop as well as under other brand names. High quality and always Koa, the designs and ornamentation of Chang ukes are less reminiscent of Kamaka and other island makers; they are ironically more C.F. Martin inspired. (Also see Aloha.)

Soprano

All Koa, plain body.

1925	Celluloid sound hole	$600	$700
1930	Celluloid binding	$600	$800

Sammo

Flashy internal paper labels trumpet that these ukes (mandolins and guitars, too) were products of the Osborne Mfg. Co. Masonic Temple, Chicago-Illinois and what the heck any of that means is still open to modern speculation. Your guess is as good as mine. Still, the high quality and often opulent degree of ornamentation that the instruments exhibit, coupled with even the vaguest implication that they were made by guys wearing fezzes and/or men who ride around in tiny cars at parades is all the reason we need to buy every one we see.

Soprano

1925	Bound Koa, fancy headstock shape	$600	$800
1925	Figured maple, 5-ply top, back binding	$300	$500
1925	Unbound Koa, fancy headstock shape	$300	$500

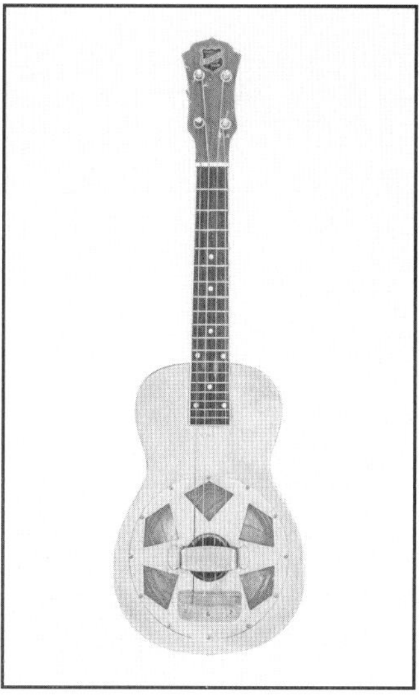

National Style 1
Imaged by Heritage Auctions, HA.com

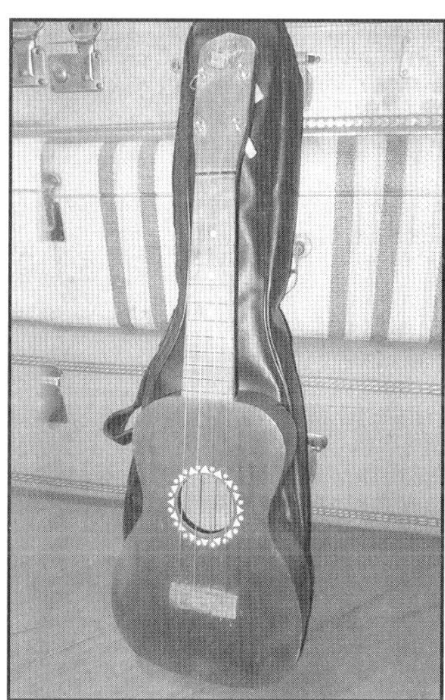

1949 Regal Soprano
Rivington Guitars

Sam Chang Ukulele
Randy Klimpert

UKULELES

Sterling

Supertone
Randy Klimpert

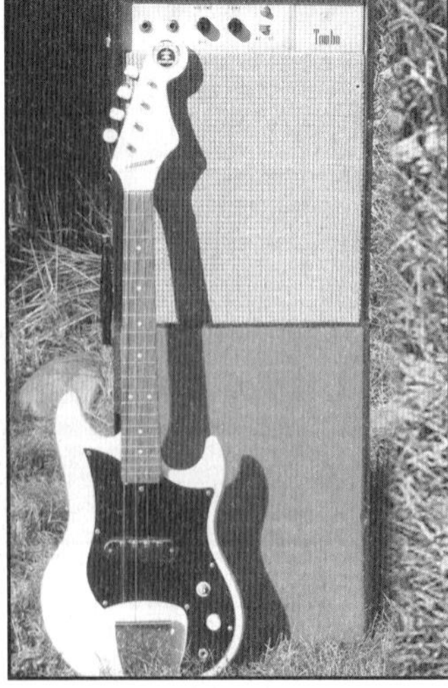

Tombo Ukulet

MODEL YEAR	FEATURES	LOW	HIGH

Silvertone

1941-ca. 1970, present. Silvertone was the house brand of Sears & Roebuck and most (if not all) of its ukes were manufactured for them by Harmony.

Soprano

Mahogany body, Harmony-made.

1950	Sunburst	$150	$200
1950	Unbound	$150	$200
1955	Bound	$150	$200
1960	Green	$150	$200

Slingerland

Slingerland started marketing ukes around 1916. Banjo ukuleles bearing this brand (see Slingerland Banjo uke section below) were certainly made by the popular drum company (banjos being little more than drums with necks, after all). Slingerland standard ukuleles, on the other hand, bear an uncanny resemblance to the work of the Oscar Schmidt company.

Soprano

Koa body, rope bound top and sound hole.

1920		$200	$300

Sterling

The miniscule reference buried deep within the headstock decal to a T.B. Co. can only mean that the Sterling ukulele somehow fits into the mind-numbing Tonk Bros./Lyon & Healy/Regal/S.S. Stewart manufacturing puzzle. Nonetheless, the brand must have been reserved for the cream of the crop, since the Sterling ukes that surface tend to be of the drop-dead-gorgeous variety.

Soprano

Flamed Koa, multiple fancy binding all over.

1935		$2,000	$2,200

Stetson

A popular misconception - to say nothing of wishful thinking and greed - has it that all instruments labeled with the Stetson brand were the work of the Larson Brothers of Chicago. While a few Stetson guitars and a very few mandolins may be genuine Larson products, the ukuleles surely were made elsewhere.

Soprano

Mahogany body, single bound top and back.

1930		$150	$200

Supertone

1914-1940s. For whatever reason, Supertone was the name attached to Sears' musical instruments before the line became Silvertone (see above). These, too, were all Harmony-made.

Soprano (Birch)

Birch body, Harmony-made, various decorations.

1930		$150	$200

Soprano (Flamed Mahogany)

Flamed mahogany body, ebony bridge.

1925		$400	$700

Soprano (Koa)

Koa body, Harmony-made.

1927	Rope bound, fancy headstock	$400	$600
1933	Rope bound body/'board	$400	$600
1935	Rope bound	$300	$500
1939	Unbound	$300	$500

Soprano (Mahogany)

Mahogany body, Harmony-made.

1930	Unbound	$150	$200
1940	Bound	$150	$200

Swaggerty

Not enough is known of this West Coast company, except that their product line of unusually shaped 4-stringed novelty instruments oddly mirrors those made by Petersen Products in Chicago at the same time (see Polk-a-lay-lee). The two companies even seem to have shared plastic parts, such as 'boards and tuners. Go figure.

Kook-a-Lay-Lee

Green plywood body, twin necks.

1965		$300	$500

Singing Treholipee

Orange plywood body, long horn.

1965		$300	$500

Surf-a-Lay-Lee

Plywood body, long horn, green, yellow, or orange.

1965		$300	$500

Tabu

The Tabu brand on either the back of a ukulele's headstock or inside its sound hole was never an indication of its original maker. Rather, it was intended to assure the purchaser that the uke was, indeed of bona fide Hawaiian origin. So rampant was the practice of mainland makers claiming Island manufacture of their wares that in the late 'teens Hawaii launched a campaign to set the record straight, and - lucky for you - a nifty little brand was the result. The Tabu mark actually was used to mark the ukes of several different makers.

Soprano

Figured Koa body.

1915	Rope bound	$600	$800
1915	Unbound	$400	$600

Tombo

This venerable Japanese harmonica manufacturer jumped on two bandwagons at once with its mid-'60s introduction of a solidbody electric ukulele. The Tombo Ukulet shares a tenor scale length and single-coil pickup with Gibson's ETU electric tenor ukes, but the Tombo's thin, solidbody design is decidedly more Fender than jumping flea. Completing the imitation-is-the-sincerest-form-of-flattery theme is a snazzy Silvertone-esque case with onboard amplifier.

Ukulet

Solid body, amp-in-case, red sunburst, white or blue finish.

1967	Sunburst	$700	$800
1968	Blue	$1,000	$1,200
1968	White	$800	$1,000

Tonk Brothers

The Tonk Brothers Company was a huge Chicago-

MODEL YEAR	FEATURES	LOW	HIGH

based distributor of musical merchandise, founded in 1893. They carried many of the popular brands of the day and also offered a line of ukuleles under their own brand name.

Soprano

Plain mahogany body, celluloid bound.

1930		$250	$400

Turturro

Unlike manufacturers like Regal and Harmony who were content to produce novelty ukes by merely spray painting or applying decals with eye-catching motifs, New York manufacturer Nicola Turturro issued novelty ukuleles from his own patented designs. The most well-known is the Turnover Uke, a playable two-sided contraption strung as a 4-string uke on one side, and an 8-string mandolin on the other.

Concert

Concert size, plain mahogany body.

1930		$400	$500

Miami

Soprano size, plain mahogany body.

1925		$300	$400

Peanut

Ribbed peanut shaped body.

1928		$800	$1,000

Turnover

Two-sided instrument, uke and mandolin.

1926		$1,000	$1,200
1926	Spruce topped mandolin side	$1,200	$1,500

Vega

Famous for their banjos, the Vega name was applied to a sole baritone uke, tied with the endorsement of 1950s TV crooner Arthur Godfrey.

Arthur Godfrey Baritone

Mahogany body, unbound.

1955		$300	$400

Washburn

See Lyon & Healy.

Weissenborn

1910s-1937, present. The mainland maker famous for their hollow-necked Hawaiian guitars was responsible for several uke offerings over the course of its 20-or-so-year run. Like their 6-stringed big brothers, they were the closest thing to Island design and detail to come from the mainland. The Weissenborn brand has been revived on a line of reissue style guitars.

Soprano

Figured Koa body.

1920	Rope bound	$2,000	$2,300
1920	Unbound	$1,200	$1,500

Weymann

Renowned for fine tenor banjos, Weyman affixed their name to a full line of soprano ukes of varying degrees of decoration, quite certainly none of which were made under the same roof as the banjos. Most were C.F. Martin knock-offs.

Soprano

1925	Mahogany, unbound	$700	$1,000
1930	Koa, fancy pearl vine 'board inlay	$1,500	$1,700

Wm. Smith Co.

1920s. Like Ditson, the Wm. Smith Co. was a company for which C.F. Martin moonlighted without getting much outward credit. The South American cousin of the uke, the tiple, with its 10 metal strings and tenor uke sized body, was first produced exclusively for Smith by Martin starting around 1920, before being assumed into the regular Martin line with appropriate Martin branding.

U-Ka-Lu-A Tiple

Mahogany body, spruce top, ebony bridge.

1920		$2,000	$2,200

Wurlitzer

Like Ditson, Wurlitzer was a retail chain for which C.F. Martin made some - though by no means all - ukuleles. Martin-made Wurlitzer ukes often bear a Martin brand as well as a Wurlitzer, or barring that, at least demonstrate overall similarities to the rest of the ukes in the regular Martin line, both in construction and decoration.

Soprano 835

1922	As Martin O	$600	$900

Soprano 836

1923	As Martin 1	$700	$1,000

Soprano 837

1925	As Martin 1K	$1,000	$1,400

Soprano 838

1923	As Martin 2K	$1,700	$2,000

Soprano 839

1922	As Martin 3K/5K	$3,500	$4,000

Soprano 841

1924	As Martin 2K Taro	$2,200	$2,800

Soprano 844

1923	As Martin 3K Taro	$3,000	$3,500

Banjo Ukuleles

Bacon

This legendary Connecticut banjo maker just couldn't resist the temptation to extend their line with uke versions of their popular banjos. As with Gibson, Ludwig, Slingerland, and Weyman, the banjo ukuleles tended to mimic the already proven construction techniques and decorative motifs of their regular banjo counterparts. In materials, finish, and hardware, most banjo ukes share many more similarities with full sized banjos than differences. The banjo ukes were simply included as smaller, plainer, variations of banjos, much as concert, tenor, and baritone options fleshed out standard ukulele lines.

Banjo #1 Uke

Walnut rim.

1927	Fancy 'board, resonator	$1,200	$1,500

Turturro Soprano

Turturro

1950s Vega Arthur Godfrey Baritone

Imaged by Heritage Auctions, HA.com

UKULELES

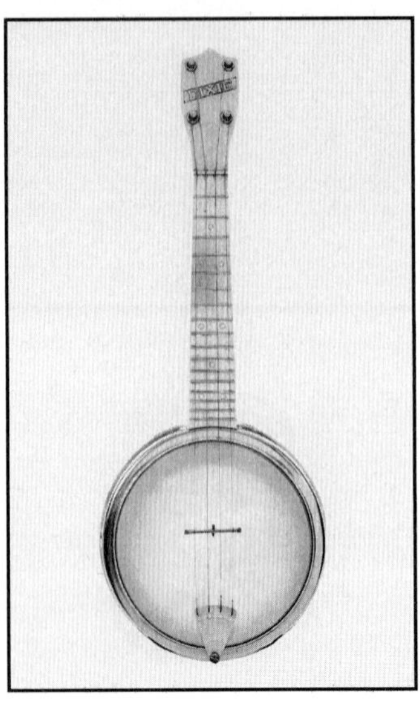
Dixie Silver Banjo Uke
Imaged by Heritage Auctions, HA.com

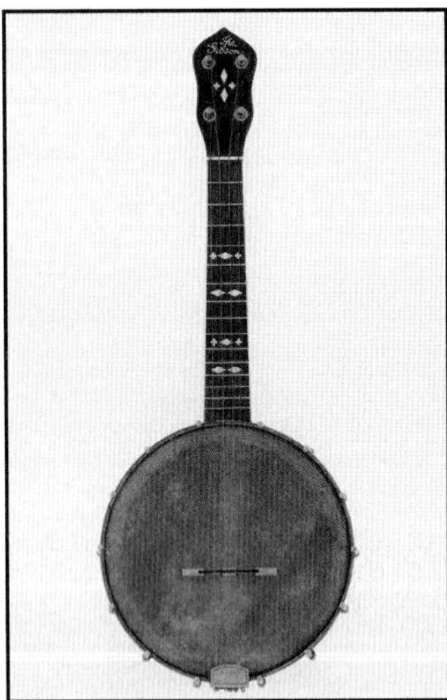
1930 Gibson UB-3

Slingerland May Bell Banjo
Richard Memmel

MODEL YEAR	FEATURES	LOW	HIGH
1927	Plain 'board, no resonator	$700	$1,000

Banjo #2 Uke

Walnut rim.

1927	Fancy 'board, resonator	$1,500	$2,000

Silver Bell Banjo Uke

Engraved pearloid 'board and headstock.

1927		$2,000	$2,500

Dixie

With chrome plated all-metal design, there's only one word for these banjo ukes - shiny. Their bodies, necks, and frets are die cast together in zinc (think Hot Wheels cars and screen door handles), the Dixie must have made the perfect indestructible instrument for Junior's birthday back in the 1960s. Similar to one made by Werko.

Banjo Uke

One-piece, all-metal construction.

1960		$200	$300

Gibson

UB Banjo Uke

"Trap Door" back design.

1925		$500	$700

UB-1 Banjo Uke

Small 6" head, flat panel resonator.

1928		$500	$700

UB-2 Banjo Uke

8" head, dot inlay.

1930		$1,000	$1,200

UB-2 Deluxe Banjo Uke

8" head, diamond and square inlay.

1930		$1,200	$1,500

UB-3 Banjo Uke

8" head, fleur de lis pearl logo inlay.

1935		$1,700	$2,000

UB-4 Banjo Uke

8" head, resonator and flange.

1932		$2,300	$2,500

UB-5 Banjo Uke

8" head, resonator and flange, gold parts.

1937		$3,500	$4,000

Le Domino

Banjo Uke

Resonator, decorated as Le Domino uke.

1933		$400	$600

Ludwig

The Ludwig was then, and is today, the Cadillac of banjo ukes. British banjo uke icon George Formby's preference for Ludwig continues assuring their desirability, while the fact that they were available in only a couple of models, for a few short years, and in relatively small production numbers only adds to the mystique.

Banjo Uke

Flange with crown holes.

1927	Gold-plated parts	$4,500	$5,000
1928	Nickel-plated parts	$3,000	$4,000
1928	Silver-plated parts	$4,500	$5,000

MODEL YEAR	FEATURES	LOW	HIGH
1930	Ivoroid headstock, rare model	$5,000	$6,000

Wendell Hall Professional Banjo Uke

Walnut resonator, flange with oval holes.

1927		$1,500	$2,000

Lyon & Healy

Banjo Uke

Walnut neck and resonator, fancy pearl inlay.

1935		$800	$1,000

Maxitone

Banjo Uke

Plain, painted various metallic colors.

1935		$150	$300

Paramount

1920s-1942, Late 1940s. The William L. Lange Company began selling Paramount banjos, guitar banjos and mandolin banjos in the early 1920s. Gretsch picked up the Paramount name and used it on guitars for a time in the late '40s.

Banner Blue Banjo Uke

Brass hearts 'board inlay, walnut neck.

1933		$900	$1,100

Regal

Banjo Uke

Mahogany rim, resonator, fancy rope bound.

1933		$250	$300

Richter

Allegedly, this Chicago company bought theguitars, ukes, and mandolins made by other manufacturers, painted and decorated them to their liking, and resold them. True or not, they certainly were cranked out in a bevy of swanky colors.

Banjo Uke

Chrome-plated body, 2 f-holes in back.

1930		$150	$250
1930	Entire body/ neck painted	$150	$250

Slingerland

May Bell Banjo Uke

Walnut resonator with multicolored rope.

1935		$150	$250

Werko

These Chicago-made banjo ukuleles had construction similar to the Dixie brand, and except for the addition of a swank layer of blue sparkle drum binding on the rim, you would be hard pressed to tell them apart.

Banjo Uke

Chrome-plated metal body and neck.

1960		$300	$400

Weymann

Banjo Uke

Maple rim, open back, ebony 'board.

1926		$1,200	$1,500

UKULELES

DEALER DIRECTORY

A GEOGRAPHICAL GUIDE

Canada

Twelfth Fret
Shane Mulchrone
2132 Danforth Avenue
Toronto, Ontario M4C 1J9
416-423-2132
416-423-1554 (Repairs)
sales@12fret.com
www.12fret.com

Folkway Music
22 Dupont Street East
Waterloo, Ontario N2J-2G9
(855) 772-0424 (toll free)
info@folkwaymusic.com
www.folkwaymusic.com

Japan

H I Guitars
7-59-103 Higashi OmiyaSaitama-Shi
Saitama, 330-0021
011-81-3-3257-7117
higuitars@aol.com
www.hi-guitars.com

United States of America

California

Guitars West
Gary Hernandez
41110 Sandalwood Cir STE 113
Murrieta, CA 92562
619-988-9777
Gary@guitarswest.net
www.guitarswest.net

Bleu-Goat Guitars
Gary Hernandez
41110 Sandalwood Cir STE 113
Murrieta, CA 92562
619-988-9777
BigHern@BleuGoatguitars.com
bleugoatguitars.com

Bay Area Vintage Guitars
Rik Walters
Danville, CA
bayareavintageguitars@gmail.com
www.bayareavintageguitars.com

California World Guitar Shows
Larry Briggs
918-288-2222
www.CalShows.TV

Drew Berlin's Vintage Guitars
Drew Berlin
213-400-4244
Drew@DrewBerlin.com
www.DrewBerlin.com

Gryphon Strings
Richard Johnston
211 Lambert Ave
Palo Alto, CA 94306
650-493-2131
info@gryphonstrings.com
www.gryphonstrings.com

Neal's Music
Neal Shelton
Huntington Beach, CA
714-330-9428
nealmuzic@aol.com
www.nealsmusic.com

Players Vintage Instruments
Lowell Levinger
Iverness, CA
415-669-1107
info@vintageinstruments.com
www.vintageinstruments.com

Schoenberg Guitars
Eric Schoenberg
106 Main Street
Tiburon, CA 94920
415-789-0846
eric@om28.com
www.om28.com

Union Grove Music
Richard Gellis
PO Box 2635
Aptos, CA 95001
(831) 427-0670
www.uniongrovemusic.com/

Delaware

Dana Sound Research
Dana Sutcliffe, Master Luthier & Ryan Lockard
By appointment only
Wilmington, DE 19810
302-439-3677
danasoundresearchinc@gmail.com
www.danamusic.com

Florida

Replay Guitar Exchange
Jim Brady
3944 Britton Plaza
Tampa, FL 33611
813-254-8800
info@replayguitar.com
www.replayguitar.com

Guitar Broker
Craig & Dustin Brody
816 NW 6th Ave
Ft. Lauderdale, FL 33311
954-646-8819
vintage@guitarbroker.com
www.guitarbroker.com

Kummer's Vintage
Timm Kummer
954-752-6063
prewar99@aol.com
www.kummersvintage.com

Illinois

Chicago Guitar Show
Ruth Brinkmann
817.312.7659
ruthmbrinkmann@gmail.com
www.wacovintageinstruments.com

Chicago Music Exchange
Daniel Escaruiza
3316 N Lincoln Ave
Chicago, IL 60657
773-525-7773
info@chicagomusicexchange.com
www.CME6.com

SS Vintage
George Coutretsis
4422 N Clark St
Chicago, IL 60640
773-472-3333
george@ssvintage.com
www.ssvintage.com

Maryland
Garrett Park Guitars
Rick Hogue
7 Old Solomans Island Rd
Annapolis, MD, 21401
410-571-9660
info@gpguitars.com
www.gpguitars.com

Massachusetts
Mill River Music and Guitars
Jon Aronstein
135 King St.
Northampton, MA 01060
413-505-0129
info@millrivermusic.com
www.millrivermusic.com

Michigan
Elderly Instruments
Stan Werbin
100 North Washington
Lansing, MI 48906
800-473-5810
elderly@elderly.com
www.elderly.com

Minnesota
Vintage Guitars & Parts Guitarville' by Eddie Vegas
Ed Matthews
Cloquet, MN 55720
218-879-3796
Ed@eddievegas.com
www.eddievegas.com

Willies American Guitars
1382 Eustis St
St. Paul, MN 55108
651-699-1913
info@williesguitars.com
williesguitars.com

Missouri
Killer Vintage
Dave Hinson
PO Box 190561
St. Louis, MO 63119
314-647-7795
info@killervintage.com
www.killervintagespecialtyguitars.com/

Fly by Night Music
Dave Crocker
204 N College
Neosho, MO 64850
417-850-4751
crocker@joplin.com
www.amigoguitarshows.com

New Hampshire
Retromusic
Jeff Firestone
38 Washington Street
Keene, NH 03431
603-357-9732
retromusicnh@gmail.com
www.retroguitar.com

New Jersey
Kebo's Bassworks
Kevin 'KeBo" Borden and Dr. Ben Sopranzetti
info@kebosbassworks.com
www.kebosbassworks.com

Lark Street Music
Buzz Levine
479 Cedar Ln
Teaneck, NJ 7666
(201) 287-1959
larkstreet@gmail.com
www.larkstreetmusic.com

New Mexico
GuitarVista
Stanley Burg & Eli Burgione
201 Dartmouth SE
Albuquerque, NM 87106
505-268-1133
gitmaven@yahoo.com
www.guitarvistanm.com

New York
Well Strung Guitars
David Davidson / Paige Davidson
330 Conklin St Unit 4
Farmingdale, NY 11735
516-221-0563
Info@WellstrungGuitars.Com
www.wellstrungguitars.com

Bernunzio Uptown Music
122 East Ave
Rochester, NY 14604
585-473-6140
info@bernunzio.com
www.bernunzio.com

Laurence Wexer, LTD
Larry Wexer
By appointment only
New York, NY 10016
917-848-2399
lwexer@gmail.com
www.wexerguitars.com

Rivington Guitars
Howie Statland
73 E 4th St
New York, NY 10003
212-505-5313
rivingtoninfo@gmail.com
www.rivingtonguitars.com

We Buy Guitars
Richie Friedman
PO Box 60736
Staten Island, NY 10306
516-221-0563
Webuyguitars@aol.com

North Carolina
Coleman Music
Chip Coleman
1021 S Main St
China Grove, NC 28023-2335
704-857-5705
OR120@aol.com
www.colemanmusic.com

Midwood Guitar Studio
Douglas Armstrong
1517 Central Ave
Charlotte, NC 28205-5013
980-265-1976
sales@midwoodguitarstudio.com
www.midwoodguitarstudio.com

Ohio
Gary's Classic Guitars
Gary Dick
Cincinnati, OH
513-891-9444
garysclssc@aol.com
www.garysguitars.com

Oklahoma
Strings West
Larry Briggs
PO Box 999 - 109 N Cincinnati Ave

Sperry, OK 74073
918-288-2222
larryb@stringswest.com
www.stringswest.com

Oregon
McKenzie River Music
Artie Leider
455 West 11th
Eugene, OR 97401
541-343-9482
artie@mrmgtr.com
www.mckenzierivermusic.com

Pennsylvania
Heritage Insurance
Ed Pokrywka
826 Bustleton Pike Ste 203
Feasterville, PA 19053
800-289-8837
edp@his-pa.com
www.musicins.com

Pennsylvania
Jim's Guitars
Jim Singleton
651 Lombard Rd #119
Red Lion, PA 17356
717-417-5655
sunburst549@aol.com
www.jimsguitars.com

Vintage Instruments
Fred Oster
507 South Broad Street
Philadelphia, PA 19147
215-545-1000
vintagephiladelphia@gmail.com
www.vintage-instruments.com

Tennesee
Gruhn Guitars
George Gruhn
2120 8th Ave S
Nashville, TN 37204
615-256-2033
gruhn@gruhn.com
www.gruhn.com

Rumble Seat Music
Eliot Michael
1805 8th Ave S
Nashville, TN 37203
615-915-2510
sales@rumbleseatmusic.com
www.rumbleseatmusic.com

Blues Vintage Guitars
Gabriel Hernandez
212-A McGavock Pike
Nashville, TN 37214
615-613-1389
info@bluesvintageguitars.com
www.bluesvintageguitars.com

Carter Vintage Guitars
606 8th Ave S #201
Nashville, TN 37203
(615) 915 1851
info@cartervintage.com
cartervintage.com

Texas
The Guitar Sanctuary
Brian Meader
6633 Virginia Parkway
McKinney, TX 75071
972-540-6420
brian@guitarsanctuary.com
GuitarSanctuary.com

Dallas International Guitar Festival
Jimmy Wallace
PO Box 4997186
Garland, TX 75049
972-240-2206
info@guitarshow.com
www.guitarshow.com

Heritage Auctions
Aaron Piscopo
2801 W Airport Fwy
Dallas, TX 75261
214-409-1183
AaronP@HA.com
www.HA.com

Killer Vintage Specialty Guitars of Texas
Dave Hinson
3738 Haggar Way Ste 108
Dallas, TX 75209
972-707-0409
killervintagedallas@gmail.com
www.killervintagespecialtyguitars.com/

Texas Amigos Guitar Shows
Ruth Brinkmann
800-473-6059
www.amigoguitarshows.com

Van Hoose Vintage
Thomas VanHoose
2722 Raintree Drive
Carrollton, TX 75006
972-998-8176
tv0109@yahoo.com
www.vanhoosevintage.com

Boingosaurus Music LLC
Garrett Tung
Austin, TX
boingosaurusmusic@gmail.com
www.boingosaurus.com

Utah
Intermountain Guitar and Banjo
Bountiful Utah
By appointment only
UT, 84102
801-322-4682/801-450-7608
guitarandbanjo@earthlink.net
www.guitarandbanjo.com

Virginia
Vintage Sound
Bill Holter
PO Box 11711
Alexandria, VA 22312
703-300-2529
bhvsound@vintagesound.com
www.vintagesound.com

Authentic Guitars
Michael Hansen
4809-1 Courthouse Street
Williamsburg, VA 23188
(757) 715-7777
Authenticguitars@hotmail.com
www.authenticguitars.com

Action Music
Matt Baker
111 Park Ave
Falls Church, VA 22046
703-534-4801
action.music@comcast.net

Wisconsin
Dave's Guitar Shop
Dave Rogers
1227 South 3rd St
LaCrosse, WI 54601
608-785-7704
info@davesguitar.com
www.davesguitar.com

Dave's Guitar Shop
Dave Rogers
914 S 5th St
Milwaukee, WI 53204

608-790-9816
info@davesguitar.com
www.davesguitar.com

Dave's Guitar Shop
Dave Rogers
200 South Central Ave
Marshfield, WI 54449
715-207-0525
info@davesguitar.com
www.davesguitar.com

Dave's Guitar Shop
Dave Rogers
110 Market St.
Sun Prairie, WI 53590
608-405-8770
info@davesguitar.com
www.davesguitar.com

Cream City Music
John Majdalani
12505 W Bluemound Rd
Brookfield, WI 53005-8026
262-860-1800
johnm@creamcitymusic.com
www.creamcitymusic.com

Brian Goff's Bizarre Guitars
Brain Goff
Madison, WI
608-235-3561
Bdgoff@sbcglobal.net
www.bizarreguitars.net

MANUFACTURER DIRECTORY

California
Dumble Amps
Drew Berlin
213-400-4244
Drew@DrewBerlin.com
www.Dumble.com

Other
Lindy Fralin Pickups
www.fralinpickups.com

Bill Tuli
Ramtuli.com

TECH/REPAIR

California
National Reso-Phonic Guitars, Inc.
871 Via Esteban Suite C
San Luis Obispo, CA 93401
805-546-8442
Repairs@nationalguitars.com
www.nationalguitars.com

Delaware
Dana Sound Research
Dana Sutcliffe, Master
Luthier & Ryan Lockard
By appointment only
Wilmington, DE 19810
302-439-3677
danasoundresearchinc@gmail.com
www.danamusic.com

Tennessee
Carter Vintage Guitars
606 8th Ave S #201
Nashville, TN 37203
(615) 915 1851
info@cartervintage.com
cartervintage.com

Texas
The Guitar Sanctuary
Brian Meader
6633 Virginia Parkway
McKinney, TX 75071
972-540-6420
brian@guitarsanctuary.com
GuitarSanctuary.com

Virginia
Authentic Guitars
Michael Hansen
4809-1 Courthouse Street
Williamsburg, VA 23188
(757) 715-7777
Authenticguitars@hotmail.com
www.authenticguitars.com

Notes

Notes

Notes

Notes

Notes

Notes

Notes

Notes

Notes

Notes